The Complete Works of
WASHINGTON
IRVING

Richard Dilworth Rust
General Editor

LETTERS

Volume IV

Washington Irving
c. 1850

WASHINGTON IRVING

LETTERS

Volume IV, 1846-1859

Edited by

Ralph M. Aderman, Herbert L. Kleinfield
and Jenifer S. Banks

Twayne Publishers

Boston

1982

Published by Twayne Publishers

A Division of G. K. Hall & Co.

Copyright © 1982 by

G. K. Hall & Co.

The Complete Works of Washington Irving
Volume XXVI

*The preparation and publication of this volume
were made possible (in part) by grants from the
National Endowment for the Humanities,
an independent federal agency.*

CENTER FOR EDITIONS OF
AMERICAN AUTHORS

AN APPROVED TEXT

MODERN LANGUAGE
ASSOCIATION OF AMERICA

®

Library of Congress Cataloging in Publication Data
Irving, Washington, 1783–1859.
Letters.

(His The complete works of Washington Irving ;
v. 23–26)
Includes indexes.
CONTENTS: v. 1. 1802–1823.–[etc.]–v. 3. 1839–1845.–
v. 4. 1846–1859.
1. Irving, Washington, 1783–1859–Correspondence.
2. Authors, American–19th century–Correspondence.
I. Aderman, Ralph M. II. Kleinfield, H. L.
III. Banks, Jenifer S.
PS2081.A4   1978   818.209 [B]   82–10907
ISBN 0–8057–8525–6 (v. 4)

Manufactured in the United States of America

CONTENTS

APPENDIX I
Newly Located Letters

APPENDIX II

APPENDIX III

APPENDIX IV

APPENDIX V

APPENDIX VI

ILLUSTRATION

FRONTISPIECE

Photograph of Washington Irving, usually described as "by Matthew Brady," and ascribed to various dates in the 1850's. This reproduction is made from a copy in the Library of Sleepy Hollow Restorations, made in turn from a negative in the possession of the New-York Historical Society.

Courtesy of Sleepy Hollow Restorations.

EDITORIAL PLAN
TO LETTERS

Although Irving's letters are scattered over the eastern United States and Western Europe, several institutions have brought together a large number of them. The New York Public Library, with its Seligman, Hellman, and Berg collections, is especially rich; and these, together with other holdings, form the largest body of Irving correspondence held by a single repository. Another valuable group is to be found in the Clifton Waller Barrett Collection of the Alderman Library of the University of Virginia. At Tarrytown, Sleepy Hollow Restorations has assembled an important collection of letters along with photocopies of items held elsewhere. Other noteworthy concentrations of Irving's letters repose in the libraries at Yale, Harvard, and Columbia Universities, in the Historical Society of Pennsylvania, and in the archives of John Murray, Irving's chief British publisher. The National Archives in Washington contain Irving's official diplomatic communications, as well as letterbook copies of his despatches and letters written as minister to Spain. A few letters remain in the hands of private collectors but the bulk of those extant are preserved in institutional libraries. Others are widely scattered, as may be observed by consulting the notes that identify the location or source of each letter printed, or, if the information is sought in summary form, by referring to the cumulative calendars appended to the final volume of this collection of Irving's letters.

This edition, arranged in chronological order, is the first comprehensive collection in print of all letters of Washington Irving presently known and available, both published and hitherto unpublished. But a considerable number of letters have escaped detection, although they have been identified through a systematic search of dealers' and auctioneers' catalogs, as well as by evidence found in journals and other letters, or from other sources. They are enumerated, along with the ones printed in these volumes, in an appendix to the final volume in order to supply the broadest possible record of Irving's letter-writing available at the time of this publication. It is hoped that this checklist will eventually lead to the discovery of additional holograph material. Letters that came to the editors' attention too late to be presented in their proper place in these volumes are printed in an appendix at the end of the final volume, in a chronological ordering of their own.

Since the present edition is not designed to include surviving letters written to Irving, no exhaustive effort was made to locate or list all of them. Many of them are not directly related to Irving's letters, and the contents of many may be inferred from what Irving wrote. Those having a special bearing on Irving's letters to these correspondents are quoted or summarized in appropriate notes, and all of them are listed, with location when known, in a separate calendar at the end of the final volume in the hope that the utility of the collection may be enhanced.

The great bulk, at least eighty-five percent, of the letters here presented has been taken from the original manuscripts. Although transcriptions of holographs are derived from photocopies, they are checked for accuracy by four or more readers, and all transcriptions were read (often twice) against the holographs. In the absence of holographs, letters derived from a printed source were collated against any other existing printed versions and explanatory notes added wherever warranted.[1] This is not to claim absolute authenticity for resulting text, but represents the best that can be done with the evidence at hand. Equally difficult are the cases where the only available text is a copy made by someone other than Irving (known or unknown), presumably from a holograph no longer extant.[2] Here again the editors can only reproduce what is before them, while noting whatever facts they have regarding the transmission of the text, and hoping that the original letter may yet come to light.

Fragments of letters, whether derived from manuscript or printed sources, are incorporated in sequence, unless they are mere scraps of little meaning or significance, in which case they are relegated to an

1. A comparison of Pierre M. Irving's four-volume *Life and Letters of Washington Irving* (1862–1864) with the three-volume edition (copyrighted 1869) reveals numerous instances of the biographer's effort to refine his earlier work. The second edition omits many letters of the first edition (or extracts them), and further bowdlerizes those remaining. The two editions of George S. Hellman's *Letters of Washington Irving to Henry Brevoort* (1915 and 1918), on the other hand, reveal few alterations. In both cases, first and later printings were collated for variants, editorial decisions were made in accord with Irving's known practice or other available evidence, and explanatory notes were added wherever indicated. These are the only two bodies of Irving letters in book form that went into second editions or settings. Other letters lacking holographs that are not in these two collections but that exist in printed forms differing from each other (some of them appearing in periodicals) are similarly treated.

2. For example, the letterbook copies of Irving's diplomatic correspondence for which holographs are not available.

appendix at the end of this volume, where they appear in sequence with notations on whatever information may be available and desirable regarding their authenticity, for many of these scraplike fragments are derived from biographical and other secondary works, some from catalogs of book dealers or autograph dealers, as well as from auction catalogs.

The circumstances under which Irving wrote determine the varying conditions of the existing holograph letters, as much as the writing materials at his disposal or the conditions under which they were stored during the long lapse of years since they were written. During his first trip to Europe in 1804 to 1806, Irving drew upon entries in his journals and frequently copied them precisely into letters to his friends and relatives in New York.[3] During periods of protracted residence in one place—whether in New York, London, Paris, Madrid, at Sunnyside, or elsewhere—he often wrote leisurely and carefully, but there is sometimes a marked falling-off in precision as a letter stretched out under his hand. Generally his business letters and official diplomatic or consular despatches were written with greater care than personal letters. At other times, especially between stints of travel, or when pressed for time, he wrote in a careless, almost illegible scrawl, with whatever pen, ink, or grade of paper came to hand. Often he used a thin or low grade of paper and a blunt pen which caused the ink to bleed through the paper. On a few occasions when he resorted to writing with pencil, the result made the work of the twentieth-century editor doubly difficult. Letters may be presumed to have been written in ink except where there is a note to the contrary. Variations in the inks used are often no longer precisely distinguishable and are not recorded unless an unusual circumstance makes a description desirable, in which case a notation is made in the notes. Similarly, the paper used covers a great variety of grades, from good to bad, laid and wove, white and tinted, lined and unlined, with and without watermarks, and of various shapes and sizes; in short, he appears to have used whatever was available. Description of kinds of paper is not attempted except in a few exceptional cases where it has textual significance.

While the editors have made every effort to record what Irving wrote, the condition of some manuscript pages and the anomalous readings occasioned by Irving's erratic handwriting produced so many problems which the eye cannot resolve that recourse was had to a

---

3. This parallelism between the journals and letters has been indicated in Nathalia Wright's edition of *Journals and Notebooks*, Vol. I, of the present edition. Parallel passages of this kind will be noted in successive volumes of the journals and letters as they appear.

set of ground rules, the chief of which is that when a word, character, spacing, construction, or mark of punctuation is in doubt, presenting equally defensible alternatives, the reading is rendered in conformity with the contextual requirement (if ascertainable), insofar as it accords with Irving's practice (if known) or with accepted usage in his day. In short, the aim has been to produce a reliable text, short of an absolutely literal transcription, which is manifestly impossible, as the sequel will demonstrate.

It does not follow that Irving's errors and inconsistencies are eliminated. Indeed, the aim of the editors, which is to present Irving as faithfully as possible, precludes this possibility. To correct his miscues and normalize his idiosyncrasies would destroy the distinctive texture of his writing. So it is that the two primary objectives of the editors—fidelity to Irving's text and utility for the reader—are constant but not always compatible aims, causing the editors to tread a very narrow line between what is ideally desirable and what is practically possible or permissible.

Despite the variety of difficulties, the editors have made a conscientious and considered effort to render faithfully the text as Irving wrote it—his oversights, inconsistencies, and often his errors included. No effort was made to correct or "improve" the holograph version, unless the error or flaw is clearly unintentional, and failure to emend would lead to misreading or misconstruction of Irving's meaning. In all such cases, editorial alterations made are signaled by square brackets or explained in the notes. No alteration is made silently. Hence any odd or erroneous idiom or phraseology, error in punctuation or spelling, or omission or transposition of letters or words in the text are to be presumed to be Irving's.

This policy of reproducing the holograph as accurately as possible perpetuates various inconsistencies, sometimes on the same page, even in the same paragraph, occasionally in the same sentence. Thus the same sentence may spell out a numeral and subsequently use the arabic form, or it may use "and" as well as the ampersand for both "and" and "*et cetera,*" in the latter case usually "&c" without a period. Words normally written as one are often separated ("every thing"), and others commonly separated or hyphenated are joined ("forgetmenots"). Irving's contractions follow no recognizable pattern, but do not often lead to obscurity or misinterpretation; when they do, missing elements are added in brackets or clarified in the notes. Similarly, his misuse or neglect of the apostrophe is not corrected unless it leads to misconstruction, in which case editorial emendations are bracketed and noted. His superscripts are uniformly brought down to the line. Often he omitted the period following a superscript but signalized the contraction or abbreviation by adding one or more dots under the superscript, by underscoring it, or by adding a dash after it. These signals are all rendered as a period, thus honoring his intention while ridding the page of eccentric mannerisms very difficult to reproduce on the printed page.

Irving's erratic terminal punctuation presents special problems. Often he used a dash, rather than a period, at the end of the sentence. This sometimes seems to have happened inadvertently because he failed to lift his pen cleanly from the paper and so elongated an intended period to look like a dash; at other times he clearly meant to write a dash. In all cases his dashes at the ends of sentences are respected as deliberate terminal punctuation. His sentence beginnings and endings are rendered as he wrote them, with or without period (or dash) if the succeeding sentence in the same paragraph begins with a capital letter, except in cases where the next sentence begins with "I" or a proper noun, in which case a bracketed period is added as a necessary signal for the reader. When the following sentence begins with a small letter, preceded by a period (or dash), it is so rendered. Only when it begins with a small letter and Irving failed to supply a period (or dash) is a bracketed period (sometimes a semicolon) added. No missing period is added at the end of the paragraph.

Similarly, his internal punctuation is respected; any necessary marks of punctuation added or changed for clarity are bracketed or footnoted (usually the former). When doubt exists among his uses internally of commas, colons, semicolons, or dashes, the questionable marks are rendered in accord with the demands of the context, compatible with Irving's general practice or the usage common in his time. His occasional use of the colon instead of a period to denote an abbreviation (usually in connection with titles of books) is respected. If, as is true in a few instances, he used what seems to be a period for a comma, or what seems to be a comma for a period, and the error is corrected, it is so noted. Commas, parentheses, dashes, and quotation marks missing from intended pairs are added in square brackets. Missing sets of quotation marks are added (in brackets) when their omission would result in misreading. Quotation marks when used by Irving at the beginning of successive lines of a quoted passage (verse or prose) are omitted.

Carets, which Irving sometimes used to indicate inserted matter, are transcribed as arrows in accordance with the system of editorial symbols explained in the table below. His abbreviations stand as he left them unless clarity demands amplifications or corrections, which are then bracketed or noted, normally the former. His occasional use of the long form of "s," "ſ" usually when the letter is doubled, is not reproduced.

Irving often wrote participial forms normally ending in *ed* without the penultimate *e*, and without an apostrophe indicating an elision or a period designating an abbreviation. These are rendered as he wrote them: i.e., "servd" rather than "serv'd" or "serv^d" or "serv[e]d." In a very few cases where the elision involves more than the *e* or some other single letter, and misreading is likely to result, missing elements in brackets are added.

Certain misspellings occur so frequently as to become routine and not worth noting or correcting, unless they convey false information, in which case a note is added. Names of passing acquaintances, even of friends and long-term associates, may vary from page to page. In the interest of unencumbered text these are allowed to stand, but where the proper form is ascertainable, the correct form is given in a note keyed to the first occurrence, and also in the index.

Loosely associated with the problem of handling proper names is the problem of distinguishing between capital and lowercase forms of initial letters of his words—not only of nouns but of all parts of speech. Often the formation of a letter is not sufficiently distinctive nor its size in relation to adjacent letters sufficiently marked to indicate clearly which Irving intended. He commonly wrote the initial letter of a word beginning with a consonant with an upward sweep which often raises it higher than the letters which follow it. This upward flourish is especially noticeable when the initial letter *y* appears at the beginning of a new line. When conformation of the letter in question is not sufficiently distinctive and the context indicates a lowercase form, the letter is rendered lowercase. Conversely, if the context calls for a capital, and the letter rises only slightly above adjacent high-rise lowercase letters, it is capitalized; it need not reach the height of high-rise letters which follow it. A more objective procedure, based on a mechanical measurement of differences in height, introduces a new body of inconsistencies and a maze of contradictions and indefensible readings or renditions, and invariably increases the incidence of error. Throughout, the editors have followed the principle that where Irving seems to use capital letters for lowercase words, the transcriptions of those letters have been rendered to accord with knowledge of his customary practice and the customary orthographical practice of his time, by transcribing as capitals only those letters which are clearly so—all intermediate forms being rendered in lowercase.

The height of initial letters in Irving's complimentary closings is also often troublesome. They can vary from an apparent "yrs Truly," "yours Very truly," "Very truly Yrs," or almost any other combination of initial lowercase or capital letters. These and other such doubtful cases are rendered as "Yrs truly," "Yours very truly," or "Very truly yrs," only the initial letter in the first word in the closing capitalized in accord with Irving's usual practice and the common usage of his time. Less formal closings such as "ever your devoted friend," are transcribed in conformity to the demands of the text, as ascertained. When doubt rises between what the eye measures and what knowledge of Irving, his handwriting and habits of expression suggest, then Irving is given the benefit of that doubt.

Another problem which occasionally presents itself is that of Irving's ending a paragraph at the bottom of a page with a short line containing very few words. He would then on the following page begin a new paragraph on a new subject with little or no ascertainable indentation of the first line of that paragraph. Rather than submit to a policy of strict measurement, the editors in such instances have honored Irving's intention by indenting the first line of the new paragraph.

Occasionally Irving would so crowd what he had to say on the last page of a letter that he left little space for a complimentary closing and signature, writing, for example, "Truly your friend Washington Irving" on, or so nearly on, the last line of the text that it is, often impossible to determine whether he intended a new line or new lines. In such instances, the complimentary close and the signature have been given each a line to itself in accordance with his customary practice.

In short, though mindful of Irving's request to his brother Peter, in a long letter of July 7–25, 1804, that "If you find anything . . . in the letters I may write that you thing[k] proper to publish, I beg that you will arrange and finish it *handsomely*," the editors have avoided complete compliance with that request, thinking it useful and instructive to present as exactly as possible what Irving wrote, sometimes in informal haste without care for niceties of spelling or punctuation, or even consistent capitalization of proper nouns, and sometimes in handwriting filled with orthographic peculiarities which are rendered in his favor when consistent with the guidelines already mentioned. The editors will try to present him as handsomely as modern textual principles allow.

In those letters where a covering sheet has been preserved, postal markings and other information which it contains have been recorded. Lines or elements of postal markings are separated one from the other with a horizontal line; when two or more discrete postal markings appear, each is separated from the other by a double horizontal line.

Lacunae in the manuscript and torn places in a page that remove a word or passage are explained in the notes. If the missing element can be conjectured, it is supplied in brackets and noted if necessary. Doubtful or alternate readings are indicated by the appropriate editorial symbol and needed explanation is supplied in the notes. Erasures and cancellations in the holographs, when recoverable, are inclosed in angle brackets. Unrecovered cancellations are marked "⟨[*unrecovered*]⟩." Some

cancellations have obviously been made by persons other than Irving—
some of them almost certainly by Pierre M. Irving, in the interest of
what the nephew-biographer considered propriety. When one or more
letters are canceled or written over (i.e., traced over), the substitution
appears immediately after the canceled matter, without intervening
space; for example "the⟨ir⟩re" and "3⟨7⟩8." Cancellations which are identical with the substitution, canceled fragments of characters which
are illegible, obvious slips of the pen, and meaningless false starts (which
often occur at the ends of lines and indicate merely that Irving ran
out of space and elected to begin the word anew on the next line but
neglected to strike the false start made at the end of the preceding
line) are not reproduced. There are many instances of this kind, even
in the letters which he seems to have written with more than usual
leisure or care.

Most of the marks in the margins and at the beginning and end of
passages (usually in pencil)—crosses, x's, checks, arrows, vertical and
horizontal lines, encirclings, parentheses, and slashes—are the work of
earlier owners or editors of the manuscripts including Pierre M. Irving,
while preparing his uncle's biography. Only those demonstrably Irving's
are reproduced. Irving's catchwords, placed at the bottom of a page
and repeated as the first word of the next page, are not reproduced.
On rare occasions Irving numbered the pages of his letters; but since
the significance of these numbers is slight, having no relevance to the
present edition, they are not reproduced.

No effort is made to reproduce Irving's irregular spacings between
characters, words, sentences, or paragraphs—unless the space has a special significance, e.g., to indicate a change of subject matter or to begin
a new sequence.

Quotations, allusions, and literary, historical, or biographical references are identified wherever possible. Such identifications are made
at their first occurrence only. Quotations of poetry in the text are
printed in reduced type size when they are known to be from other
authors. Quotations are to be presumed Irving's unless otherwise indicated, and accordingly are printed in the same type as the text.

Irving's infrequent notes, usually at the bottom of the manuscript
page or along the side, or reproduced in the notes and labeled as his.

Many of the foregoing forms and procedures in preparing the text
of Irving's letters stem from peculiarities of his handwriting, and consequently do not differ materially from those adopted for the editing
of his journals and notebooks and therefore are not dealt with in the
same detail with which they are explained by Nathalia Wright in
Volume I of the present edition, where they can be consulted on

pp. xix–xxvi. But the inherent differences in genre between journals and letters accentuate certain aspects of form and procedure sufficiently unique or peculiar to the letters as to require special treatment by the editors, and consequently need particularization and explanation.

Basic to these procedures is the numbering of the letters in simple chronological order throughout the four volumes, which correspond roughly to periods in Irving's life. A single introductory essay discussing the relation of the letters to his literary career has been adopted as the most suitable way for the reader to see them in context; there is no introductory note for successive volumes after the first, but a chronological table of Irving's activities corresponding to the period covered in each volume is provided for the reader's orientation. Each volume also has a table of editorial symbols, abbreviations, and short-title forms used, as well as a self-contained index, the final volume having the cumulative index instead.

Each letter is assigned an arabic number in accord with its position in the entire sequence. This numeral printed flush to the left margin, is followed by the name of the addressee, printed in its accepted spelling, unless the notation " To ————" appears in its place. This entire line is set in italics to serve as a caption and provide ready identification.

The transcription itself begins, in accord with Irving's normal practice, with the local or street address (if given), name of the city or place, and date on the first line. The year (or other element of the date), if not given, is added in brackets, whenever ascertainable. These elements, in whatever order, are reproduced as Irving wrote them, punctuation included, except that their location on the page (which in the holograph may appear anywhere, left to right) ends flush with the right margin, with slashes added if they occupy more than one line in the original. If Irving wrote the date at the end of the letter, it is so printed, but it is also added in brackets in the usual place at the head of the letter, so that this necessary index for cross-referencing can be found readily.

In cases of misdating, the correction is made in brackets immediately following the erroneous date, and the letter is placed in its proper chronological order. Incomplete or missing dates are supplied in brackets if they can be ascertained from postmarks, internal evidence, biographical information, perpetual calendar, or other sources. The evidence for dates supplied by the editors is explained in the notes. A letter that is dated ["Fall, 1823,"] and for which no closer dating can be made, appears at the end of November, 1823; one simply dated "1812" appears at the close of that year. Letters that cannot be dated conjecturally appear in alphabetical order according to the recipient's name at the end of the final volume immediately following the appendix which contains letters received too late to be incorporated in the regular chronological sequence. Following the undated letters are printed those for which both date and addressee are unknown.

The inside address, in whatever manner Irving wrote it, follows his text except that it is printed flush left, with slashes if separate lines need to be indicated. Immediately following is the salutation, again flush left. Following the body of the letter, the complimentary close, usually occupying several lines in the holograph, is printed in one line, flush right, with slashes if lineation needs to be indicated. The signature follows, also flush right. If, instead of placing the inside address at the beginning of the letter, Irving wrote it at the bottom of the first page or at the end of the letter, it is positioned at the end, on one line, flush left, with slashes, if needed; and if the date appears at the end, instead of the beginning, it is so placed, again flush left. The recording of postmarkings has been explained above. See vol. I, p. xlvi.

The introductory and concluding elements appear in the originals in so confusing a variety of forms and locations that they defy exact reproduction on the printed page. Hence a degree of regularization is adopted as a simple, sensible means to bring order and uniformity into Irving's calligraphic vagaries, without doing violence to his general ordering of these parts or to his intended meaning. Included in this category is the regularization of salutations for letters derived from secondary sources, such as George S. Hellman's edition of the Irving-Brevoort correspondence and Pierre M. Irving's biography of Irving, where capital letters throughout or a combination of large and small capitals are used. These are all rendered uniformly in capital and lowercase letters in accord with Irving's own practice, thus: "My dear Brother," not "MY DEAR BROTHER" or "MY DEAR BROTHER."

The first unnumbered note presents significant information on the address leaf or envelope, if available, in the following order: name of addressee, address, postmark or docketing, followed by any other details, such as the name of the ship or carrier, regular mail, ambassador's pouch, or whatever the means of conveyance, as well as endorsements and postmarkings including date on which letters were received or answered, etc. These details vary widely from letter to letter, and any omissions are to be understood as indicating that they are missing from the original. However, the numbers indicating the cost of postage or carriage are not reproduced, nor are extraneous words or symbols added by owners or readers of the letter.

The second unnumbered paragraph gives the ownership and location of the manuscript or text from which the transcription was made, and details about previous publication, transmission and provenance of the text, and other pertinent data. For letters transcribed from a printed version, only the copy-text (usually the first printed) version is cited, unless unusual circumstances obtain (e.g., variations in two or more printed forms), in which case a description or explanatory note is added.

A third unnumbered note gives biographical details about the recipient. This biographical note, usually more detailed than notes identifying persons merely mentioned in the letters, is attached to the first letter addressed to him by Irving. Earlier or later casual mentions of the addressee are cross-referenced to this main biographical notation. Biographical notes of this kind can be located through the index, where they are starred.

Numbered notes following each letter identify persons, places, events, allusions, quotations, or circumstances necessary for an understanding of the letter.

A list of abbreviations and of short titles for books cited three or more times as sources of information in the notes is supplied at the end of each volume, and a list of editorial symbols appears at the beginning of each volume.

Cross-references are made by recipient and date, rather than by letter number, and should be understood to include both text and relevant notes.

CHRONOLOGICAL TABLE
1846–1859

1846 January, visited London and Birmingham, participated in discussions on the Oregon treaty; March 6, returned to Madrid to await the arrival of his replacement; early August, left Madrid for final visits to Paris and Birmingham; October 18, arrived in Boston; fall, began expansion and extensive remodeling of Sunnyside.

1847 Resumed work on the life of George Washington; bothered with inflammation of ankles.

1848 Became one of the executors of the estate of John Jacob Astor; arranged with G. P. Putnam for publication of a collected edition of his writings and began revisions of his books.

1849 Continued revisions of earlier writings for inclusion in Putnam's Author's Revised Edition; April 15, brought out *A Book of the Hudson*.

1850 Completed *Mahomet and His Successors*; supported John Murray in the struggle over the British copyrights of his writings.

1851 Further recognition through public testimonials, election to various literary societies, and books dedicated to him; September–December, participated in memorial activities for James Fenimore Cooper.

1852 Collected material for *Life of George Washington*; July–August, renewed acquaintance with John Pendleton Kennedy at Saratoga Springs.

1853 January–March, visited Kennedy in Washington and did research in the archives of the State Department; attended the inauguration of President Franklin Pierce; June–July and October, visited Kennedy in Baltimore and western Virginia; August, vacationed with Kennedy at Saratoga Springs.

1854 Work on biography of Washington.

1855 January, attended wedding of Mary Kennedy in Virginia; February, *Wolfert's Roost* published; May, first volume of *Life of George Washington* published; December, second volume of *Washington* published.

1856 July, third volume of *Washington* published.

1857 May, fourth volume of *Washington* published.

1858 Work on last volume of biography interrupted by periods of ill health.

1859 Illness and physical distress; April, last volume of *Washington* published; November 28, died as he was preparing for bed.

EDITORIAL SYMBOLS AND ABBREVIATIONS

EDITORIAL SYMBOLS

[roman]　　　　　Editorial additions.
[*italic*]　　　　　Editorial explanations.
〈　　　〉　　　　Restorations of canceled matter.
? ? or [?]　　　Doubtful or alternate readings. The former are used within angle brackets. The latter is used for a single doubtful word, and appears immediately after the word or character in question, with no intervening space.
[*unrecovered*]　Unrecovered word. When more than one word is involved, the fact is indicated (*"three unrecovered words"* or *"two unrecovered lines"*).
↑↓　　　　　　　Interlinear insertions, above or below the line.

Editorial situations not covered by these symbols are explained in the notes.

ABBREVIATIONS AND SHORT TITLES

Bohner, *J. P. Kennedy*: Charles H. Bohner, *John Pendleton Kennedy: Gentleman from Baltimore.* Baltimore, 1961.

Bowers, *Spanish Adventures of WI*: Claude H. Bowers, *The Spanish Adventures of Washington Irving.* Boston, 1940.

Bulletin NYPL: *Bulletin of the New York Public Library*

Callahan, *Officers of the Navy*: Edward W. Callahan, *List of Officers of the Navy of the United States and of the Marine Corps from 1775 to 1900.* New York, 1969.

Columbia: Columbia University Library.

Diary 1828–1829: *Washington Irving Diary Spain 1828–1829.* Edited by Clara L. Penney. New York, 1926.

Harvard: Harvard University Library.

Haswell, *Reminiscences of an Octogenarian*: Charles H. Haswell, *Reminiscences of an Octogenarian of the City of New York: 1816–1869.* New York, 1896.

HSA: Hispanic Society of America.

HSP: Historical Society of Pennsylvania.

Huntington: Henry E. Huntington Library and Art Gallery.

Irvingiana: *Irvingiana: A Memorial of Washington Irving*. New York, 1860.

J&N, I: Washington Irving, *Journals and Notebooks*, Volume I, 1803–1806. Edited by Nathalia Wright. Madison, Wisc., 1969.

J&N, III: Washington Irving, *Journals and Notebooks*, Volume III, 1819–1827. Edited by Walter A. Reichart. Madison, Wisc., 1970.

Journal 1827–1828: "Washington Irving's Madrid Journal 1827–1828 and Related Letters," ed. Andrew B. Myers, *Bulletin NYPL* 62 (May, 1958), 217–27; (June, 1958), 300–311; (August, 1958), 407–19; (September, 1958), 463–71.

Journal 1828: Washington Irving, *Journal of 1828, and Miscellaneous Notes on Moorish Legend and History*. Edited by Stanley T. Williams. New York, 1937.

Journals of WI: The Journals of Washington Irving. Edited by William P. Trent and George S. Hellman. New York, 1970.

Langfeld & Blackburn, *WI Bibliography*: William R. Langfeld and Philip C. Blackburn, *Washington Irving, A Bibliography*. New York, 1933.

LBI: *The Letters of Henry Brevoort to Washington Irving*. Edited by George S. Hellman. 2 vols. New York, 1916.

LC: Library of Congress.

Leslie, *Autobiographical Recollections*: *Autobiographical Recollections by the Late Charles Robert Leslie, R. A.* Edited by Tom Taylor. Boston, 1860.

Letters of J. K. Paulding: The Letters of James Kirke Paulding. Edited by Ralph M. Aderman. Madison, Wisc., 1962.

LIB: *The Letters of Washington Irving to Henry Brevoort*. Edited by George S. Hellman. 2 vols. New York, 1915.

MHS: Massachusetts Historical Society.

NA: National Archives.

NYEP: New York *Evening Post*.

NYHS: New-York Historical Society.

NYPL: New York Public Library.

NYSL: New York State Library.

Odell, *NY Stage*: G. C. D. Odell, *Annals of the New York Stage*. 15 vols. New York, 1927–1949.

PMI: Pierre M. Irving; and Pierre M. Irving, *Life and Letters of Washington Irving*. 4 vols. New York, 1862–1864.

Scharf, *Westchester County*: J. T. Scharf, *History of Westchester County, New York*. 2 vols. Philadelphia, 1886.

Scoville, *Old Merchants of NYC*: J. A. Scoville (used pseudonym of

Walter Barrett), *The Old Merchants of New York*. 5 vols. New York, 1855.

SHR: Sleepy Hollow Restorations.

Stewart, *Hawthorne*: Randall Stewart, *Nathaniel Hawthorne, A Biography*. New Haven, 1948.

Strong, *Diary*: *The Diary of George Templeton Strong*. Edited by Allan Nevins and M. H. Thomas. 4 vols. New York, 1952.

STW: Stanley T. Williams, *The Life of Washington Irving*. 2 vols. New York, 1935.

Tuckerman, *Life of J. P. Kennedy*: Henry T. Tuckerman, *The Life of John Pendleton Kennedy*. New York, 1871.

Va.–Barrett: Clifton Waller Barrett Collection of American Literature, University of Virginia.

Waldron, *WI & Cotemporaries*: William Watson Waldron, *Washington Irving and His Cotemporaries*. New York, 1867.

WI: Washington Irving.

WIHM: Ben Harris McClary, *Washington Irving and the House of Murray*. Knoxville, 1969.

Wilson, *NY, Old and New*: Rufus Rockwell Wilson, *New York: Old and New*. 2 vols. London, 1903.

Yale: Yale University Library.

LETTERS, 1846–1859

Volume IV

1921. To Sabina O'Shea

[January 3, 1846]

My dear Mrs O'Shea

I send you by Lorenzo[1] the little box and the handkerchief—I hope you will carry out your intention of visiting Mrs de Wolff (no 28 Rue de la Paix) She will be delighted to make your acquaintance, for you have made a most favorable impression upon her, and you will find her a lovely character.

Yours ever very truly
Washington Irving

Saturday Evg. / Jan 3d. [1846]

ADDRESSED: Madame / Madame O'Shea / Hotel de Bristol   DOCKETED: 30th. November
MANUSCRIPT: HSA.   PUBLISHED: Penney, *Bulletin NYPL*, 62 (December, 1958), 621.

Mrs. O'Shea, wife of WI's banker, was one of his intimates in Madrid at this time. Probably the wrong envelope has been included with this letter. If not, Mrs. O'Shea erred in her docket.

1. WI's valet.

1922. To Sarah Storrow

Havre. Jany 5th. 1846

My dear Sarah,

My journey by rail road was very comfortable notwithstanding the coldness of the weather. I had all the coupé to myself, and stretched myself in the cushioned Seat and lolled as on a Sofa. The country was quite inundated by the late rains and the overflowing of the river; and in many places the rail road passed across what appeared to be a lake. Before reaching Rouen it began to snow; and continued to snow during most of the route between Rouen and Havre: this caused such a delay that instead of arriving at Havre by half past 8, I did not get there until half past twelve. Having passed rather a sleepless night, however, at Paris I was enabled to sleep for a great part of the journey which prevented its being so tedious as it might otherwise have been.

On arriving at the Diligence office at Havre I found the good Beasley[1] waiting there in his carriage; where he had been waiting since half past 8. I was really shocked to find him there at such a time of night;

3

⟨b⟩ and had fully calculated at putting up at an Inn. However I was wheeled away to Juste Milieu: where I found a comfortable fire and a Snug supper provided for me; both very acceptable to one who had been travelling upwards of twelve hours in wintry weather; and who had had merely a mouthful of bread in the course of the day.

This morning is Sunny and tranquil; it is now past mid day; the sea is calm as a lake and there is every prospect of a prosperous voyage. The Steamer sets off at 4 Oclock in the afternoon and will arrive at South-ampton about 5 Oclock tomorrow morning.

Let me hear from you soon and tell me all about your whereabouts. direct your letters care of John Miller Esqr²—Henrietta Street Covent Garden London—and they will be sure to reach me wherever I may be.

Give my affectionate remembrances to Mrs O'Shea when you see her and to my precious little friend Mrs. de Wolff. whose kind sensibility at parting I shall not easily forget Kiss me dear Kate and Tutie³ for me and believe me ever my dearest Sarah

Your affectionate uncle
Washington Irving

MANUSCRIPT: Yale.

1. Reuben Beasley (d. 1847), American consul at Le Havre from 1817 to 1847.

2. Miller, who had published the first volume of *The Sketch Book* in 1820, was now U. S. despatch agent in London.

3. WI's names for Catharine Paris Storrow (1842–1917) and Susan Van Wart Storrow (1844–1863), the children of Sarah Storrow.

1923. To Sarah Storrow

Paris¹ Jany 7th. 184⟨5⟩6

My dear Sarah

I had a remarkably fine passage from Havre to Southampton. The sea was as quiet as in Summer time. I walked the deck by moonlight until a late hour, in a most fanciful mood; humming snatches of old ditties and conjuring up recent scenes in Paris with the images of those whom I loved and those whom I admired; and I dreamt of them when I turned in for the night. The next day was murky and misty and rainy. I had a dull journey to town by rail road through a most uninteresting country; and London looked smoky and smutty and dismal. a Sad contrast to Paris.

I drove to Harley Street, but to my disappointment both Mr & Mrs M'Lane² were out of town on a visit at Lord Ashburtons.³ I ⟨found⟩ was welcomed however by Miss Kitty and Mary and Master James;⁴ whom I found taking their lunch very comfortably. They told me my room was ready for me; that their Papa would return to town in a couple of days; if not before; as Mary would write to him that I was here, and he would be glad of a pretext to shorten his visit.

I accordingly took up my quarters in the house; dined with the young folks and drove with them in the evenings to Leslies[5]; but found Mr. & Mrs Leslie and the children on the point of setting off to pass the evening (twelfth night) at Dickens[6]! So we returned home, promising to pass this evening with Leslie.

I am quite charmed with my young housemates. Kitty is somewhat staid and reserved; but quite a little lady; Mary is my delight. Full of animation & intelligence, with a beaming countenance and beautiful expressive eyes. James is home for the holydays and does the honors of the house in very hospitable style. He has put me quite at my ease; and reminds me a little of what his brother Robert[7] was at his age. He and his sister Mary have somewhat of a contest occasionally for Supremacy.

I am very well pleased with Mr Melville[8] whom I find intelligent and apparently amiable. ⟨He⟩ I breakfasted with him this morning at his lodgings where I met with John Murray the Son[9] and successor of my worthy publisher. We had a cordial meeting and the breakfast was very pleasant.

I am scrawling this in great haste to let you know of my safe arrival in London. I will write again in the course of a day or two.

Tell my charming friend Mrs de Wolff to stay where she is and not to venture into this damp, dingy, foggy city in the Winter time. It will be enough to give her the blues, if it does not put her back in her health.

Kiss my dear little Kate & Tutie

Your affectionate Uncle
Washington Irving

ADDRESSED: Madame / Madame Storrow / No 4 Rue de la Victoire / a Paris
    POSTMARKED: K / L / JA / 8 / 1846
MANUSCRIPT: Yale.

1. As the context suggests, WI should have written "London."

2. Louis McLane (1786–1857), American minister to Great Britain, and his wife, Catherine Mary Milligan (1790–1849).

3. Alexander Baring, first Baron Ashburton (1774–1848), head of Baring Brothers & Co., had close ties with the United States through his marriage and his business interests. The chief British negotiator in the treaty which settled the Maine boundary question, he was interested in promoting cordial relations with the United States.

4. Catherine Mary (b. May 12, 1829), Mary Elizabeth (b. November 1832), and James Latimer (b. September 2, 1843) were the three youngest McLane children. See Munroe, *Louis McLane*, pp. 261, 334, 430.

5. Charles Robert Leslie (1794–1857), and American-born artist and an intimate of WI's from the 1820's, had attracted attention with his painting of Queen Victoria's coronation.

6. Charles Dickens (1812–1870), the popular English novelist.

7. Robert Milligan McLane (b. October 2, 1813), McLane's third child and oldest son. See Munroe, *Louis McLane*, p. 44.

8. Gansevoort Melville (1816–1846), the older brother of Herman Melville and secretary of the U.S. legation, was acting as literary agent for his brother. WI visited him on January 6. After the breakfast which WI mentions, Gansevoort read him "various parts of the first 10 chapters of Herman's forthcoming book [*Typee*]. He was very much pleased—declared portions to be 'exquisite,' s[ai]d the style was very 'graphic' & prophesied its success—" See "Gansevoort Melville's 1846 London Journal," ed. Hershel Parker, *Bulletin NYPL*, 69 (December, 1965), 646–47.

9. John Murray III (1808–1892) had assumed control of the publishing firm upon the death of his father in 1843.

1924. To Sarah Storrow

London Jany. 15th. 1846

My dear Sarah,

I wrote to you shortly after my arrival in this city and am daily hoping to receive a reply. I had your letter[1] giving me an account of your visit to the "lively lady" and some notices of the ladies who had figured at the presentation; but above all of the concern expressed by my dear precious little Kate at my absence. Dear, blessed little being. how I could fold her to my heart for it.

I have not yet been to Birmingham having got engrossed by occupations which keep me not merely in town but in the house. I fear it will yet be some days before I can break away from them. I have seen scarce any body, excepting one or two of my old intimates, especially Leslie. I have dined out but once, at Mr Bates',[2] and am in fact quite shut up. It is delightful however to be ⟨in the⟩ under the roof of my invaluable friends the M Lanes, who make me feel that I am at home, and in a happy home.

We have had Mr Rogers[3] to ⟨dine with⟩ breakfast with us. He speaks of you in the Kindest and warmest terms; not merely to me, but to every body. Mrs M'Lane tells me of the eulogium he passed on you to her at Lord Ashburtons table and how warmly he recalled the pleasure he had experienced in his morning visits and breakfastings in the Rue de la Victoire

Mrs M Lane tells me that she hears nothing but praises of you from all the Americans who have been at Paris. So you see my dear if "lively ladies" are not as intimate with you as you could wish you are not unappreciated by your friends.

Juliette M Lane[3] writes that she will probably return about the 20th. and that Mrs de Wolff will accompany her. Neither her father nor mother are desirous that she should hasten her return provided she continues to find Paris agreeable and that her continuance there is not inconvenient to others. I think both she and Mrs de Wolff will experience a sad change in returning to this dingy capital; which ever since I have been in it this time has been envelloped in Murk and gloom and coal smoke We have not a ray of sunshine; and scarce any thing that you would call day light at Paris. Farewell my dear Sarah. Kiss my darling little Kate and Tutie for me and believe me ever

Your affectionate uncle
Washington Irving

DOCKETED: Jany 15. 1846
MANUSCRIPT: Yale.
Sarah Paris Storrow (1813–1885), WI's favorite niece, had married Thomas Wentworth Storrow, Jr. (1805–1861) on March 31, 1841.

1. This letter has not been located.
2. Joshua Bates (1788–1864) was an American partner of the Baring Brothers financial firm.
3. Samuel Rogers (1763–1855), the English poet and banker whom WI had known since 1822.
4. Juliette McLane (b. December 21, 1824) was the tenth child of Louis and Catherine McLane. See Munroe, Louis McLane, p. 166.

1925. To Sarah Storrow

London Jany 17th. 184⟨5⟩6

My dear Sarah,

Just after I had sent off my last letter I received yours of the 13th. which I need not say was most welcome.

Yesterday brought the letters of the Steamer of the 1st. I had but one; and that was from your uncle dated from Sunnyside.[1]

The last accounts he had from your mother she was rather better, having better sleep at night. This is really good ⟨kn⟩ news, for with better sleep her whole health will improve.

I am still fixed in town sadly hampered by my occupations which I have been unable to leave. I hope, however, to break away on monday next. I am quite worried at being detained so long from visiting Birmingham.

You will see by the last accounts from the United States that there is quite a War panic[2] there: I think, however, we shall eventually get out of all this quarrel without coming to blows.

Mrs M'Lane is looking for Juliette in the course of next week, and with her Mrs de Wolff, whom she intends to receive under her roof until she can suit herself with an apartment. I could not help smiling at the covert innuendo in your observation that you should almost regret Mrs de Wolff remaining in Paris lest she *might* become a fashionable woman —but you believe she possesses ["]too elevated a nature to be easily spoiled by the world"

Ah Sarah! Sarah! have you not yet got over your pique against the "lively Lady?"

I have not time to write more today. I am fagged; my head is weary and my heart is faint. I wish I had the two ⟨th⟩ little Poseys to have a good romp with them. They were always my best restoratives.

Give my affectionate remembrances to my amiable friend Mrs O'Shea when you see her and tell her I will write to her when I have a little leisure. Tell Mrs de Wolff I am looking forward with great anticipation to the pleasure of meeting with her in London.

Kiss my darling little Poseys for me

Your affectionate Uncle
Washington Irving

MANUSCRIPT: Yale.

1. The letters mentioned in the first two paragraphs have not been located.
2. This feeling was probably caused by the news that President Polk refused to resubmit his offer to accept the 49th parallel as the boundary for Oregon. For other details see WI to Pierre M. Irving, December 29, 1845.

1926. *To Sarah Storrow*

London, Feb 2d. 1846

My dear Sarah,

I thank you for your most pleasant cheerful letter[1] giving me an account of the ball at Mrs Moultons; and I thank you for mentioning as the thing which pleased you the most at the ball the Sight of Mrs Moultons father and mother honored and cherished by their daughter, and enjoying the advantages and elegancies by which she is surrounded. Th⟨is⟩e mentioning of this circumstance speaks your own good kind heart my dear Sarah; and at the same time impresses me most favorably with respect to Mrs Moulton.

I have returned within three days from a ten days visit to Birmingham. I found your Aunt[2] restored to a state of health and a capacity for social enjoyment quite beyond my most sanguine hopes. In fact with her present measure of health she may enjoy many years of easy and pleasurable existence. Henry Van Wart[3] is looking very well though rather thin. His health is much improved. Abby[4] is as usual a little darling

I was happy to find my worthy friend George[5] launched in the wine business, under the most favorable auspices. He has excellent vaults at his fathers warehouse and a snug counting house there, quite distinct from the main establishment. His business has commenced most prosperously, and bids fair the very first year to yield him a very snug income. My visit was a very cheery one, finding every body so well, and so well off.

On returning to town I found Juliette here and our charming ⟨f⟩ little friend Mrs de Wolff, in whom I delight more and more. I have been laboring since my arrival in England ⟨at⟩ on the subject I proposed before leaving Paris. I have prepared an article which I intended to publish in a pamphlet form; but I have lost heart and got out of conceit of it, and believe I shall suffer it to sleep in my portfolio.

My visit to London has I believe been of service to Mr M'Lane in facilitating some of his diplomatic affairs;[6] at least he said he thought my coming quite a god send. He has disappointed me a little in the aid I was led, ⟨fr⟩ by his letters, to expect from him, ↑in regard to the article I proposed to prepare↓ ⟨but I ought to have known⟩ but I am accustomed to be disappointed by him, when the business in hand did not exactly meet his views or serve his purposes.

The London Times is full of insulting and belligerent articles on the subject of the Oregon Question;[7] and the last arrivals from America bring more war speeches, so that the flame of war stands a chance of being blown up by the blusterers on both sides whatever diplomacy can do to prevent it.

I think it probable I shall set out on my return to Paris at the end of this week or the beginning of the next. I shall not derange your establishment for the short sojourn I shall make in Paris but will go to a Hotel. Kiss my dear little Kate and Tutie for me and tell them I will see them again soon. Give my kind regards to Mr Storrow and believe me ever

Your affectionate Uncle
Washington Irving

ADDRESSED: Madame / Madame Storrow / No 4 Rue de la Victoire / à Paris
    POSTMARKED: FEB / [unrecovered]
MANUSCRIPT: Yale.   PUBLISHED: STW, II, 192 (in part).

1. This letter has not been located.

2. Sarah Irving Van Wart (1780–1849), WI's sister who had lived in Birmingham for nearly forty years, had suffered a stroke in 1843.

3. Henry Van Wart (1783–1873), WI's brother-in-law.

4. Abbey Irving (1822–1906) was married to Henry Van Wart, Jr. (1806–1878), her first cousin.

5. George Van Wart (b. 1820), son of Henry and Sarah Van Wart.

6. WI's role is assessed by McLane's biographer: "A literary champion of the American position more to McLane's taste was Washington Irving, who was put to work on a pamphlet when he appeared in London in the middle of the controversy. The pamphlet was never completed, but Irving's very presence aided the American cause, since the high reputation he enjoyed in English literary circles helped dissipate the hostility toward things American at the time of his arrival." See Munroe, *Louis McLane*, p. 529.

7. WI probably refers to the extended articles appearing on January 30 and February 2, 1846, which stress the weak American claims and the strong possibility of war between the United States and Great Britain.

1927.   To Pierre M. Irving

London, February 3, 1846

My dear Pierre:

I have now been about a month in England, part of the time at Birmingham, and part in London. I came here under an invitation from Mr. McLane, and in the idea that I might be of more public service here, at this particular juncture, than I would be at Madrid. I think I have been of service through old habits of intimacy with people connected with the Government, and through the confidence they have in me, in inspiring more correct notions of the disposition and intentions of our Government, and in facilitating the diplomatic intercourse of Mr. McLane.

I have been closely occupied, during the greater part of my sojourn in England, in studying the Oregon question, and in preparing an article for publication, in the hope of placing our rights and our conduct in a proper light before the British public. I have not finished the article to my satisfaction, and circumstances have concurred to make it very doubtful whether I shall give it to the press.

A close and conscientious study of the case has convinced me of the superiority of our title to the whole of the territory, and of the fairness of the offers we have made for the sake of peace, and in consideration of the interests which have grown up in the country during the long period of the joint occupancy. British diplomatists have greatly erred in not closing with our proposition of the 49th parallel, with some additional items of accommodation. They should never have published so pertinaciously for the three additional degrees on the Pacific and the north bank of the Columbia. This was merely to protect the interests of the Hudson's Bay Company; but they might have been protected by some other arrangement involving no point of pride. The full possession of the Columbia River is a matter of importance in our eyes, as being one of the great outlets of our empire. By neglecting to close with our offer, and to negotiate upon the basis of the 49th parallel, the British diplomatists have left the question at the mercy of after influences, through the malignancy of the British press and the blustering of our candidates for popularity, to get up prejudice and passion on both sides, and to make diplomatic negotiation almost hopeless.

As I doubt whether I can do any further good here at present, I propose setting off for Paris in the course of a few days, thence to continue on to Madrid, where I shall await the arrival of my successor. I long to throw off diplomacy, and to return to my independent literary pursuits. My health is now excellent.

PUBLISHED: PMI, III, 381–82.

Pierre M. Irving (1802–1876) acted as his uncle's business agent while WI was abroad.

1928.   To Catharine Paris

London, Feb 3d. 1846.

My dear Sister,

I returned to London a few days since from a Visit of ten days to Birmingham. My visit, though made in the depth of winter and in very gloomy weather was a cheerful and gratifying one. I found our dear sister restored to a degree of health and a capacity for social enjoyment beyond any thing my fondest wishes had led me to anticipate. Though she has not entirely recovered the use of her limbs on one side, nor is it likely she ever will, she yet moves about the house much more freely than formerly; is able to help herself as usual; and appears to be in a uniformly cheerful state of mind; enjoying conversation and the society of her family and friends. We may therefore confidently trust that she has yet years in store for her of comfortable and pleasurable existence. Henry[2] and Abby returned to Birmingham while I was there, from a visit to Leamington. Henry is looking better than I had expected. Abby is as much a favorite with her connexions in England as she was with those in America. She is a darling little being; but it is difficult to look at her and to reconcile ones self to the idea that she is actually a staid married dame. Still less can I fancy her brother George[1] as a married man, who, when I left the United States, had scarce attained to the dignity of a long tailed coat.

One of the most agreeable circumstances attending my visit to Birmingham was the finding our Nephew George Van Wart successfully launched in business. He has set up as a wine merchant; has excellent vaults under his fathers ware house, constructed for a wine establishment in days of yore; has a snug counting room adjoining the ware house yet quite distinct from it, and thus immediately under his fathers eye and his fathers wing. The extensive dealings of Mr Van Wart with the principal manufacturers has enabled him to secure for George an immediate number of valuable customers; and the few months experience he has already had promises him a smooth and profitable career. It has been quite an event in the family circle at Birmingham, of which Georges amiable and excellent character makes him a most important member; and I was truly delighted to find him thus planted happily and prosperously at home.

Mr Van Wart is in good health and good spirits. The day before I came away from Birmingham Henry and George and William[3] dined at home; Mr Van Wart was as young in spirits as any of his sons, and appeared ↑among them,↓ more like a brother than a father. ⟨whom⟩

William Van Wart has a fine family of children; his boys are noble little fellows; with warm hearts beaming out of honest, sunshiny countenances.

I am staying in London with my friends the M'Lanes and shall remain here a few days longer. I came to England in the hope of being of some service during this critical time of our affairs with Great Britain; Such passion and prejudice is excited on both sides, however, by the slanders of the press and the speeches of demagogues that I fear at times all the efforts of diplomacy will be unavailing to prevent a war. I have studied the question assiduously and have thoroughly convinced myself of the superiority of our title to the whole of the territory in dispute: but by repeated negotiations and offers we have made it a question of Compromise; and as such it might easily have been settled; if the British negotiators had managed the matter wisely, and had not pushed for terms on which our national pride was committed; such for instance as the fore navigation of the Columbia River,—one of the great outlets of our ⟨territory⟩ Empire. Still I hope the question may in some way or other be re opened, and an honorable adjustment accomplished; but extraneous influences are daily rendering it more and more difficult.

I think it probable I shall leave London in the course of four or five days for Paris where I shall make but a very brief sojourn and then continue on to Madrid there to await the arrival of my successor.

I am in excellent health and in good travelling condition. Give my affectionate remembrances to Mr Paris[4] and to all the family—

Your affectionate brother
Washington Irving

MANUSCRIPT: Va.–Barrett.
Catharine Irving Paris (1774–1849) was WI's sister.

1. George Irving (1824–1908), the youngest son of John Treat Irving, Sr., was married on December 9, 1845, to Robertine Blackwell (d. March 3, 1858).
2. Henry Van Wart, Jr. (1806–1878).
3. William Van Wart (d. 1868).
4. Daniel Paris (1772–1851), WI's brother-in-law.

1929. To Flora Foster Dawson

38 Harley Street / London Feb. 5th. 1846

My dear Mrs Dawson,
Your letter[1] (which I did not receive until after my return to town) has indeed called up delightful reccollections of past times, of "moving accidents by flood and field"[2] and of those valued friends who shared them with me. I would at once accept your kind invitation and come to Flitwick to talk over old times, but at present I am not my own master. I have come unexpectedly to England to transact some business with the American minister at this court, and as soon as I can despatch it, which I trust will be in the course of three or four days, I have to hasten back to the continent. I expect, however, to visit England again in the course of the Spring or Summer when I will be more at leisure and will then avail myself of your invitation.

I have long been desirous of having intelligence of you all. I received a letter a few years since from one of your brothers resident in Jamaica, introducing a friend, and in my reply made enquiries about the family. As he never answered my letter I fear he did not receive it. It is a hazardous thing to make enquiries about friends after such a lapse of years, but I wish you would give me such particulars of family news as would be pleasant to give and to receive.

As to myself on my return to America I built me a pretty little cottage on the banks of the Hudson in a beautiful country, and not far from my old haunts of Sleepy Hollow. Here I passed several years most happily; my cottage well stocked with nieces and enlivened by visits from friends and connexions, having generally what in Scotland is called a house full, that is to say a little more than it will hold. This state of things was too happy to last. I was unexpectedly called from it by being appointed Minister to Madrid. It was a hard struggle for me to part from my cottage and my nieces but I put all under charge of my brother and promised to return at the end of three years. I have overstaid my time. Nearly four years have elapsed; I understand my cottage is nearly buried among the trees I set out, and over run with roses and honeysuckle and ivy from Melrose Abbey, and my nieces implore me to come back and save them from being buried alive in foliage. I have accordingly sent in my resignation to government and am now going back to Madrid to await the arrival of my successor. When relieved from the duties and restraints of office I shall make farewell visits to my friends in England and elsewhere, then ⟨hasten back to⟩ ↑ship myself for↓ America, and hasten back to my cottage where every thing is ready for my reception and where I have but to walk in, hang up my hat, kiss my nieces, and take my seat in my elbow chair for the remainder of my life.

I have thus my dear Mrs Dawson given you my own history, as they do in story books, ⟨to⟩ in the expectation that you will give me your own in return. In the mean time believe me with the kindest and warmest sentiments of regard

Most truly your friend
Washington Irving

MANUSCRIPT: Brown University Library.   PUBLISHED: PMI, IV, 406–8.

Flora Foster Dawson (1806–1876) was an acquaintance made during WI's residence in Dresden in the winter of 1822–1823. At this time while he was a social intimate of Mrs. John Foster and her two daughters, Emily (1800–1885) and Flora, he fell in love with Emily and proposed marriage, only to have his suit rejected. For a discussion of this relationship, see Walter A. Reichart, *Washington Irving and Germany* (Ann Arbor, 1957); and STW, I, 232–54.

1. This letter has not been located.
2. See *Othello*, I, iii, 135.

1930.   *To Sabina O'Shea*

London Feb 5th. 1846

My dear Mrs O'Shea

I am sadly behind hand in my correspondence with you; for which I ought to be ashamed, after receiving so kind a letter as yours of the 20th. January;[1] but I am sure you will pardon me when you know that business not pleasure has caused my apparent inattention. In fact I have been closely occupied ever since my arrival in England; so as sometimes to remain ⟨in the⟩ without going out of doors for two days at a time. I have visited very few of my London friends and have been at no parties of pleasure; unless two or three dinner parties, which I could not avoid, might be termed such. I have found London uncommonly murky and gloomy, and have looked back with regret to ⟨the⟩ Paris, which with all its rains and clouds has no coal smoke, and has occasional bright days of Sunshine. And I have had nothing to make up for the sweet drives in the Bois de Bologne with a certain person who shall be nameless and with my worthy and esteemed friend Papa Quique.[2]

I hope to arrange matters so as to leave London for Paris about the beginning of the week; where I shall stop but for three or four days and then continue on to Madrid. I sent in my resignation by the Steamer which left Liverpool on the fourth of January, and trust it has been received by Government and a successor nominated before this time. I doubt, however, whether he will reach Madrid before late in the Spring or early in the Summer, so that I may be detained there longer than I could wish.

Tell Mr O'Shea[3] I have nothing worth communicating relative to the Oregon question. No negotiation is going on here at present, nor was there any going on at Washington by the last advices. It is expected that the Steamer which was to leave the United States the first of February may bring something definitive ⟨we?⟩ as to the action of Congress in the matter; and then some further steps may be taken in diplomacy— The question has been rendered a delicate and difficult one by extraneous influences; especially by the mischevious meddlings of the press. It is a question of compromise; of mere give and take; where the honor of neither party ought to be implicated in the quantity, more or less, of land, ceded. The press, however, has roused the pride and passions of both parties, and may blow up the flame of war whatever diplomacy may do to prevent it. Still I have a strong hope that the question may ultimately be adjusted in a peaceable way and without discredit to either party. Should I be able to learn any thing positive before I leave London I will let Mr OShea know it.

While writing this letter I have received one from my niece Mrs Storrow who tells me that she had met with you at the Italian Opera and that you continued to improve in health. I expect to find you quite bright and blooming on my return.

Give my kind remembrances to Mr O'Shea and my thanks for his good news about the insurance stock. Remember me also to Willy[4] if he has returned to Paris and present my most respectful duties to Papa Quique.

> Yours ever very truly
> Washington Irving

P.S. I must not omit to tell you that I have been introduced a day or two since to Lady Ashley[5]—one of the most beautiful women on earth!

ADDRESSED: Madame / Madame O'Shea / Hotel Bristol / Place Vendome / à Paris
  POSTMARKED: [*unrecovered*] // UK / 6 FE 6 / 1846   DOCKETED: Feby 5th.
  1846
MANUSCRIPT: HSA.   PUBLISHED: Penney, *Bulletin NYPL*, 62 (December, 1958),
  621–22.

1. This letter has not been located.
2. Henry O'Shea, Jr. (1838–1905).
3. Henry O'Shea, Sr., WI's banker in Madrid.
4. William O'Shea, son of Henry O'Shea, Sr.
5. Probably Lady Emily Caroline Frances (d. 1872), daughter of Earl Cowper.
Her husband, Lord Ashley (1801–1885), was to become the 7th earl of Shaftesbury upon the death of his father in 1851.

1931. To Georgiana Bonnet

> London Feb 10th. 1846

Madam,

I did not receive the little parcel of books which you were so kind as to send me until after my return to town; I now beg you to accept my sincere thanks for them, and for the flattering expressions of esteem and good will by which they are accompanied.

I regret that I did not receive your note sooner, as I should have profited by the intimation concerning Mr Hollins[1] to pay a visit to his Studio. That, however, I hope to do when next I visit Birmingham

With great respect, I remain

> Very sincerely your obliged
> Washington Irving

Mrs Georgiana Bonnet.

MANUSCRIPT: Va.–Barrett.

1. Peter Hollins (1800–1886) was a Birmingham sculptor who produced statues of Sir Robert Peel and Rowland Hill and worked on the Priory Church at Malvern, the Lichfield Cathedral, and the church at Weston.

1932. To Rosa Van Wart

London Feb 10h. 1846

My dear Rosa,

I have spoken to Mr Putnam who is disposed to render every service in his power in promoting the success of your sisters writings;[1] and as he is acquainted with publishers in various lines, I think he may be able to render effective service Send the MSS to him and communicate freely with him on the subject. I shall leave a note with him expressive of my opinions and wishes in the matter, which note he may shew to the publishers

Mr Murray, also, has again spoken on the subject of his own accord, expressing his disposition to be of service. I fear I shall not be able to see him again before I leave town, which will be this afternoon, but I will write to him and mention the possibility of future works on the history of Greece & Rome. I think it would be well to let Mr Murray see specimens of your sisters pictorial sketches illustrative of history. He ⟨might⟩ seemed to lay some stress upon that part of any undertaking of the Kind, and ⟨indeed on his various⟩ ↑perhaps↓ might be induced, if the sketches pleased him, to give some employment for your sisters pencil.

I am scrawling this in excessive haste having all my preparations to make and many matters to attend to before four OClock this afternoon

With love to the household

Your affectionate uncle
Washington Irving

MANUSCRIPT: John Rylands Library.

Rosalinda Bond was the first wife of William Van Wart, WI's nephew, and mother of his eight children.

1. Probably WI is referring to Anne Lydia Bond, who published a *History of England for Youth* in 1847.

1933. To Henry O'Shea, Jr.

London, Feb. 10th. 1846

My dear Papa Quique,

I have just received a letter[1] from your Mamma. Such a letter! Such a passion as she is in! Such a scolding as she has given me for not writing to her! Hombre! if I had known she was such a woman I would have written to her every day in the week[.] I am frightened out of my wits. I have packed up my trunk on the spot, taken passage for Paris and shall follow this letter as fast as possible But I shall be affraid to shew my face unless you, my dear Papa Quique, speak a kind word for me and mollify her passion—

> Yours very dutifully
> Washington Irving

ADDRESSED: Henry O'Shea *Junr.* Esqr / Hotel de Bristol / Place Vendome / à Paris
   POSTMARKED: [*unrecovered*] / 12 / [*unrecovered*] / BOULOGNE // UN / 10
   FE 10 / 1846   DOCKETED: Feby 10th. 1846.
MANUSCRIPT: HSA.   PUBLISHED: Penney, *Bulletin NYPL*, 62 (December, 1958),
   622–23.

   1. This letter has not been located.

1934.   To Sarah Storrow

Bordeaux, March 3d. 1846

My dear Sarah,

   I arrived here about five Oclock yesterday afternoon after a very comfortable journey the tediousness of which I beguiled by one of Frederikas[1] pleasant novels, with which you had the kindness to provide me.

   I found on my arrival our Consul Mr Grigsby,[2] had secured places for me in the Malle poste which sets off at two oclock today for Bayonne and arrives there early tomorrow morning; he had also written to Bayonne to have the Coupè of the Malle poste for Madrid Secured for me tomorrow if vacant; in that case I shall reach Madrid before Midnight on Friday next.[3]

   The weather is delightful for travelling; vegitation is putting out rapidly and many of the trees and shrubs are in blossom. I am in excellent travelling condition; I had a capital nights rest last night, and feel this morning like a "rose of May" as little Kate says

   Lorenzo desires me to say that he regrets very much he did not see you to bid you farewell. He seems to bring away a heart full of kindness to all your household.

   Give my kind remembrances to your husband and many kisses to my little darlings Kate and Tutie; whom I think I love ⟨bett⟩ more than ever, if possible. Little Tutie was particularly sweet upon me the last day I was in Paris, as if she knew we were about to part.

God bless you my dear, dear Sarah

Your affectionate Uncle
Washington Irving

MANUSCRIPT: Yale.

1. Probably WI is referring to Frederika Bremer (1801–1865), whose novels *The Neighbours, The Home, The President's Daughters, Strife and Peace, The Bondmaid, The H_____ Family*, and *Nina* had been translated into English by this time.

2. John Warren Grigsby of Virginia was nominated on February 23, 1841 as U.S. consul for Bordeaux, a post he held until 1850. See Hasse, *Index to U.S. Documents*, III, 1720.

3. On March 6.

1935. To Sarah Storrow

Bayonne March 4th. 1846

My dear Sarah,

I arrived here about seven oclock [in the] [*MS torn*] morning, took a warm bath, and found myself in first rate order to undertake the remainder of my journey. The Coupé of the Malle Poste for Madrid was secured in advance for me so that at twelve oclock I set off again and shall be in Madrid the day after tomorrow (in the evening[)];[1] so that I shall make the journey from Paris to Madrid in Six day[s] [*MS torn*] The weather continues fine the roads a[re] [*MS torn*] in capital order and free from dis [*MS torn*] I am quite free from any irritat[ion] [*MS torn*] I have now put my ⟨?bea?⟩ constitution to the trial lately; first while in England by close literary occupation and mental excitement and now by travelling and I cannot express to you the satisfaction I feel in believing myself completely out of the clutches of my long harrassing malady.

Give my kind regards to your husband
⟨[*unrecovered*]⟩ Many kisses to little Betsy & Jenny Posey and believe me ever

Your affectionate uncle
Washington Irving

ADDRESSED: [M]adame [*MS torn*] / [M]adame [*MS torn*] Storrow / rue de la Victoire No 4 / à Paris   POSTMARKED: BAYONNE / 4 mars / 43
MANUSCRIPT: Yale.

1. WI omitted the bracketed parenthesis.

1936. To Sabina O'Shea

Madrid March 7th. 1846

My dear Mrs O'Shea,

As I have no idea of incurring another scolding I sieze my pen at an early hour to inform you that I arrived here at nine Oclock last evening after a very rapid, yet very comfortable journey of six days from Paris. I was most cordially received by the Albuquerques.[1] Madame Albuquerque excused me in the kindest and sweetest manner for not having written to her oftener; knowing, as it was natural a considerate woman should know, that I was too much overwhelmed by the multiplicity of business at Paris and London to be punctual in my correspondence, unless it be my correspondence with government. It is pleasant to have such an amiable indulgent correspondent as Madame Albuquerque that does not keep ones pen under whip and spur, as some folks do. I shan't be affraid another time to neglect her as much as I please.

I am quietly installed in the snug apartment which was occupied by Mr Livingston.[2] I had apprised him of the day I ⟨sh⟩ expected to be here; he therefore cleared out the very day and set off for Pau in the Malle poste, leaving the business of the Legation in perfect order.

I found my handmaid Juana still quartered in her old room in the establishment which Madame Albuquerque had kindly permitted her to retain until my return, as she had many of my things under her charge. She is to be married next week to her cousin the young Medico, and they then go into an apartment of their own.

According to Madame Albuquerques account there have been gay times in Madrid this winter: Dinners, balls, soirees, concerts &c &c without number. My old Saloons have been brilliant with beauty and fashion. The de Weisweillers gave a grand ball to all the world. Madame de Weisweiller is at the height of fashion. By the bye The Albuquerques dine with the de Weisweillers on sunday next. This is all the information I have been able as yet to collect about the de Weisweillers; in whom I know you take such a great interest.

Of course I have as yet seen nobody; but I mean to make a visit or two in the course of the day. My first shall be to Narvaez,[3] because I have always admired him as a man of energy, independence and spirit, and because he is a fallen man. I hear he has lost hugely in the funds. I hope not. He was so generous and magnificent when he had wealth at his command that I should be sorry to see him poor. I had no idea at one time that I should ever be brought to sympathise in the misfortunes of Narvaez.

I trust this letter will do for the present. I will write again when I have seen the world and have more to say. Give my kind remembrances to Mr O'Shea, Willy and my venerable friend Papa Quique and believe me ever

Very truly yours
Washington Irving

ADDRESSED: Madame / Madame O'Shea /Hotel de Bristol / Place Vendome / à Paris / *pr petite post*   POSTMARKED: 2me Dist / 15 / 46 // mars / 22 / 1846 // Levéeque / [*unrecovered*]
MANUSCRIPT: HSA.   PUBLISHED: Penney, *Bulletin NYPL*, 62 (December, 1958), 623–24.

1. José Francisco de Paula Cavalcanti de Albuquerque, minister of Brazil, and his wife, the former Miss Oakey of New York.
2. Jasper Livingston, who served as secretary of the American Legation in Madrid in 1844 and 1845.
3. General Ramón María Narváez (1800–1868), who had been prime minister until February 13, 1846.

1937. *To Sarah Storrow*

Madrid, March 7th. 1846

My dear Sarah,

I arrived here about nine O'clock last evening after a journey comfortable beyond my hopes. I am this morning up, between six and seven O'clock in fine health and my first occupation is to scrawl a line to you. I found every thing ready for my reception at the Albuquerques and was welcomed by them most affectionately. Mr Livingston anticipating my arrival had departed for Pau in the Malle poste that very day; so as to leave his apartment vacant for me. He left the affairs of the Legation in perfect order, with a letter explanatory of the business in hand; so that his departure causes no inconvenience. I presume he is anxious to get to Pau to be with his brothers family and to drive his newly arrived American horses. I had told him he should have carte blanche to go where he pleased the moment I arrived.

Juana is still lingering in the establishment; being kindly permitted by Madame Albuquerque to continue in the occupation of the room she had ⟨under⟩ ↑during↓ my reign. She received me with an overflowing heart; and had arranged my room and every thing against my arrival. She has sold for me some of the things I left in her charge, and has rendered me the rest in good order She is to be married next week to her cousin the young physician, and they have already taken an apartment which will be furnished in a great measure from the presents of furniture made to her by the various young gentlemen who have been in my Legation; who, on departing have generally bequeathed to Juana a part of the furniture of their rooms. I am glad the poor girl is likely to be so comfortably settled. She is in good looks, good condition and good spirits.

I have not yet seen the little folks. They were in bed when I arrived and are not up yet. I am told they were quite rejoiced to hear that "Uncle was about coming home again."

I am happy to tell you that though I have been in bed but one night between Paris and Madrid the journey has produced no irritation of the system nor any symptom of a return of my old malady. I feel convinced that I am now entirely cured of it.

I must write to Mrs OShea by this opportunity to keep her in good humor. She is such a terrible woman I am in continual fear of her.

Give my kind remembrances to Mr Storrow and many kisses to the two little Poseys

> Your affectionate Uncle
> Washington Irving

P.S. I have had the little folks about me for nearly an hour—Their first demand was for the old history of Hempen House.

MANUSCRIPT: Yale.

1938. To the Marques de Miraflores

Madrid 11 March 1846

His Excellency / The Marques de Miraflores / &c &c &c

Sir

Being desirous of paying my respects to Her Majesty on my return from an absence of some months and there appearing to be no public occasion at hand, I would solicit of Your Excellency to signify my wish to Her Majesty; and the honor I should esteem it if Her Majesty would grant me a special audience for the purpose

It would greatly add to my gratification if on the same occasion I could have an opportunity of paying my respects to Her Majesty the Queen Mother.

I have the honor to be, with sentiments of the highest esteem and regard

Your Excellencys Obdt. Servant
Washington Irving

MANUSCRIPT: NA, RG 84 (letterbook copy).

This copy is in WI's handwriting.

Manuel Pando Fernández de Pinedo, marqués de Miraflores (1792–1872), a prolific writer on historical, political, and legal topics and a moderate in politics, was prime minister from February 13 to March 16, 1846, when he resigned because he was unable to work with Cortes. See Christiansen, *Military Power*, p. 170; and H. Butler Clarke, *Modern Spain*, p. 203.

1939.   To Sabina O'Shea

Madrid 14 March 1846

My dear Mrs O'Shea

As I have now been a week in Madrid I suppose you will expect from me all the news of the place and the gossip of the Saloons; but I am not in the gossipping vein and nothing but the constant dread I have of you ever since that memorable scolding, induces me to take pen in hand and scribble mortally against the grain

I told you in my last that I was on the point of making visits and that the first should be to Narvaez, because he was out of the cabinet. I kept my resolution, but did not find him at home. He has since visited me and I had a long conversation with him, or rather he held forth for a long time, letting off steam like a loco motive engine, which has just been detached from the train. In fact he is the loco motive engine of this government, and it is the very furnace heat of his fiery nature which carries on the whole incongruous machinery at the risk of an occasional explosion. Much as they fear him they cannot do without him; and I have no doubt he will soon be steaming away again at the head of the government.[1] As to getting on with Miraflores for a leader, they might as well attempt to stem the Mississippi with a low pressure engine. Great preparations are making in Narvaez hotel for the reception of his wife; and many good natured conjectures are made as to what kind of a life they will lead there. A lady observed to me the other day, she did not think Narvaez and his wife would ever agree together, he was so passionate. "Why Madame" I replied "he seems to agree wonderfully well with all his neighbors wives, I do not see why he should not with his own." The lady had not another word to say on the subject.

I have dined with the Bressons and have played cards there two or three times; but as you were not present to tempt me I came away early without losing my money. They have their nightly reunions as usual but the Albuquerques go very seldom, the distance being so great and they keeping no carriage.

A day or two since I dined with your friends the de Weisweilers. It was a very pleasant dinner chiefly of persons with whom I am sociable. Perhaps what rendered the dinner particularly pleasant to me was my being seated beside Madame de Weisweiller who was very amiable, as you know she always is.

To day I am to have a special audience from the Queen, and the Queen Mother, to pay my respects to them after my long absence. I asked for it, as there appeared to be no besa manos nor other public occasion at hand.

Your silver coffee pot has been delivered into the hands of Don Tom? As you gave me no key with the case in which it was contained the Custom House worthies forced the lock in defiance of the remonstrances of Lorenzo; not taking my word for the nature of the contents.

I have promised La Saussaye[2] to go with him to ⟨see the house he is bu⟩ your new house or rather the old house which is refitting under his direction. When I have seen it I will write you an account of it. Madrid is being rapidly pulled to pieces and rebuilt; it is a pity they could not renovate and rebuild some of the old families which are going sadly to decay; and add a little to the height of some of the grandees as they do to their houses.

Give my kind remembrances to the three Mr. O'Sheas and believe me ever

Very faithfully yours
Washington Irving

ADDRESSED: Madame / Madame O'Shea / Hotel de Bristol / Place Vendome / en Paris / pr petite poste   POSTMARKED: [unrecovered] / 15 / [unrecovered] // [unrecovered] / 10½ dum / F // Mars / 14 / 1846   DOCKETED: 14th. March, 1846.
MANUSCRIPT: HSA.   PUBLISHED: Penney, Bulletin NYPL, 62 (December, 1958), 624–25.

1. WI was correct in his observation. Narváez returned as premier, but his tenure was brief (March 16–April 3, 1846).

2. Richard de la Saussaye, a member of the British Legion in Spain and a long-time friend of WI's.

1940. To Sarah Storrow

Madrid, March 14th. 1846

My dear Sarah,

I have your letter,[1] without particular date, giving me the news of your home and your little circle of intimates. You insinuate that my little friends the Albuquerques will soon take the place of Kate and Tutie. Far from it; they are charming children it is true; and most affectionate in their manners, and are great pets with me; but Kate and Tutie have got complete possession of my heart. I think of them continually and miss them sadly. They are darling little beings of themselves, and then they are your children, my dear Sarah, and you have no idea how that endears them to me.

I have paid all my visits of ceremony and friendship. The cordial manner in which I was received by my diplomatic associates was most gratifying. Indeed for the first few days after my arrival it really seemed as if I had returned to a home. I find my quarters very pleasant also in one end of my old establishment and am quite like a member of the Albuquerque family. By no one have I been more warmly welcomed than by Count Bresson[2] the French Ambassador. I dined at his house a day or two after my arrival and dine there again the day after tomorrow. Indeed I have dined out almost every day since I arrived.

Having been absent for so long a time, and there being no public Court ceremony at hand where I might have an opportunity of paying my respects to the Queen and the Queen Mother I applied for ⟨a private⟩ an especial audience for the purpose, and am to have it at four O'clock this afternoon; when I shall tread the vast halls and Saloons of the royal palace alone. I have no great relish for the ceremonial but then it will furnish me with a subject for a letter to your mother; who has been rather scantily supplied with court news of late.

I received letters from home a day or two Since. One from our dear Kate dated early in February. She had just heard of my having really sent in my resignation to Government, and now felt persuaded that I intended soon to return home. She gave me until the month of June, though the rest calculated upon an earlier date. For my own part I begin to feel impatient on the subject. I see by the American papers that no successor had been nominated up to the 12th. of February; and fear I shall be detained her[e][3] much longer than I could wish; as whoever is appointed will probably take Paris in the way and linger there as I did on my way to my post. I shall look with intense interest for the news by the Steamer of the 1st. March, which will probably let me know who is to succeed me and when he is to embark &c—Now that I am half dismounted I long to have done with diplomacy.

I write by this opportunity to my kind and excellent friend Mrs O'Shea; whom I miss extremely from the social circle of Madrid. I hope you keep up your visits to her. She speaks of you most kindly in her letters to Madame Albuquerque. and makes good report of your bright little *Soirée dansante* and of the pretty American ladies and the pretty toilettes she saw there.

Let me know if you hear any thing of our charming friend Mrs de Wolff. I doubt much her coming to Paris before your departure

When Kate writes again to me I beg you will forward her letters; and endeavor to get Tutie to add a post script. Kiss the dear little women for me.

Your affectionate Uncle
Washington Irving

ADDRESSED: for petit poste / Madame / Madame Storrow / Rue de la Victoire No 4 / a Paris
MANUSCRIPT: Yale.

1. This and the other letters mentioned later have not been located.
2. Count Charles-Joseph de Bresson (1798–1847).
3. WI omitted the bracketed letter.

1941.   To Catharine Paris

Madrid March 16th. 1846

My dear Sister,

I intended to write to you before my departure from Paris; but was not able to do so; being much hurried, and quite out of the mood for letter writing. Sarah had a very delightful evening party the evening before my departure at which were assembled the choicest part of the American society in Paris. It was really a beautiful scene, and I was gratified to see on all sides proofs of the cordial esteem in which Sarah and her husband are held by their country folks.

I had a sad parting with Sarah and her dear little children, from the uncertainty when we may meet again; as they are soon to set off for the United States, while ⟨my⟩ the time of my return depends upon the arrival of my successor; who was not nominated at the ⟨same⟩ date of the last accounts from home.

I made a rapid journey day & night to Madrid, where I arrived in six days. I experienced the most cordial reception from all my associates of the diplomatic ⟨reception⟩ circle, and am still eating my way through a round of dinner parties given to me in ⟨my⟩ welcome of my return. I have taken up my quarters in one end of my old establishment, and am quite domesticated with my amiable friends the Albuquerques. The children shewed great joy on "Uncles" return and seem to consider me quite as a relative. Lorenzo has entered upon his duties as Major Domo; but still has me under his particular care.

Having been so long absent from the Court, and there being no public occasion at hand where I might have an opportunity of paying my respects to the Queen, I solicited a private audience for the purpose. Four O'clock on Saturday afternoon was appointed for my reception. I accordingly arrayed myself in diplomatic uniform and drove to the palace where I found the Royal carriages at the portal and the guards drawn up in front to attend the Queen on her afternoons drive. It was a splendid Sun shiny day and never did the Royal palace look more magnificent. I passed up the vast Splendid Stair case between rows of bowing lackeys, past halbardiers, who stand like Statues and strike the butt of their halberds upon the ground in token of respect as you pass; and so on through the immense halls and gorgeous saloons of the palace, in each being received and passed on by some appropriate official. It is a very different thing to go singly through all this state and ceremonial; from what it is to go in company with others on the crowded days of public levees. ⟨The Queen being⟩ I felt peculiar interest in this visit from the idea that I should soon cease to tread these halls forever. As the prime minister was ⟨with⟩ in conference with the Queen I had to remain for some time in one of the saloons to await his departure. The lofty windows were open to admit the soft warm air of Spring. They looked down ⟨into⟩ upon the great Square before the palace where the guards were drawn up in glittering array. A band of Military Music was performing favorite passages from operas, and the music sounded delightfully through these vast silken saloons. After a while an officer of the court announced that the Queen was ready to receive me, and I was ushered into her presence by the "Introducer of Ambassadors[.]" I found the Queen standing in a small cabinet; with one lady in attendance. I was quite struck with the change in her appearance since last I saw her; which was previous to her departure for Barcelona in the month of June last. She had grown much; her tour of last year and the baths she had taken had evidently benefited her health. She had quite a womanly air; Her complexion was improved; there was a ⟨delig⟩ healthful bloom on her cheeks and she looked quite handsome, or at least, the benignant expression of her countenance persuaded me to think so. As my ⟨visit⟩ ↑audience↓ was one of mere ceremony and respect it was brief. The Queen is still unskilled in turning phrazes with strangers and is glad to get through these ceremonials. Her manner, however, was amiable and graceful, and she is evidently acquiring something of the winning graces of her mother.

I had calculated on an audience also from the Queen Mother, but she was engaged in a conference with the prime minister in another chamber. I regretted this as I always find her very affable, and I had received several kind messages from her, through Madame Albuquerque, during my absence.

March 23d. This letter has been lying by me for several days, during which I have been too much occupied to continue it. There have been several changes of late in the Cabinet here which have caused great agitation in the political circles. Narvaez, who had been in eclipse for a ↑short↓ time, is restored to power and is again at the head of the government, with a cabinet completely under his dictation.[1] The sessions of the Cortes are suspended; ⟨the⟩ a Royal decree has completely gagged the press and there is every appearance of absolute rule.[2] Many apprehend that an attempt will be made by the Narvaez cabinet to force on the marriage of the Young Queen with Count Trapani[3] (her mothers brother!) a marriage which the Queen Mother has set her heart upon, but which is odious in the eyes of the nation. Should this be persisted in it may produce public troubles and commotions. It is doubted, however, by the friends of Narvaez that he will push this matter to extremities. They think that ⟨he will⟩ if he finds it is likely to produce disturbances he will prevail upon the Queen Mother to abandon it; if not, that he will endeavor to oblige her once more to leave the Kingdom. The question of the marriage of the Young Queen becomes more and more embarrassing; until it is settled the affairs of Spain will always be in a precarious state; and the Kingdom liable to convulsions.

I had letters[4] from home a few days since—one from the cottage from my dear Kate dated in February last. She had just heard of my having sent my resignation to government and now felt persuaded that I would soon return. She gives me until the Month of June. I had hoped to be home before that time but now I see no likelihood of it. My successor was not appointed at the middle of February—When appointed it will take him some time to prepare for embarkation; then he will probably come by the way of England and France and loiter by the way; especially at Paris; which is a kind of fitting out place, ⟨where⟩ to buy furniture &c &c. I watch the American papers anxiously for some notice on the subject. Tomorrow I shall have news by the Steamer of the 1t. March, and I hope it will bring me something definitive on the subject. Now that I am in a manner half dismounted from my post I am anxious to have done entirely with diplomatic business and to be on my way home. If I am detained here for any length of time I shall get quite homesick. Sarahs intended visit to the United States, also, makes me anxious to be there.

What a gratification it would have been with me to accompany her and her dear little children on their ⟨intended⟩ voyage out. It is a satisfaction however to think they will be under the care of our worthy little captain;[5] he who brought our dear brother Peter home to us. He is quite a benefactor of the family.

I am happy to tell you that I continue in excellent health; quite the kind of health I used to enjoy when nothing ailed me from one end of the year to the other. I hope and trust it will continue, and that I may return home in a state of health and spirits fitted to enjoy a meeting with my [family][6] and to contribute to the cheerfulness of those around me.

God bless you my dear Sister. Give my affectionate remembrances to your husband and to Irving and believe me ever most affectionately

Your brother
Washington Irving

MANUSCRIPT: Va.–Barrett. PUBLISHED: PMI, III, 383–84 (in part).

1. Narváez formed a cabinet which included himself as minister of foreign affairs, Pedro Egaña (1804–1885) as minister of grace and justice, Francisco Javier de Burgos (1778–1849) as minister of the interior, Juan de la Pezuela y Ceballos (1809–1906) as minister of marine, Manuel de Mazarredo (1807–1857) as minister of war, and a Señor Orlando as minister of finance. See *La Gaceta*, March 17, 1846; London *Times*, March 23, 24, 30, 1846. For WI's official assessment of the new cabinet, see his despatch to James Buchanan, March 19, 1846.

2. See *La Gaceta*, March 19, 1846.

3. Count Francisco de Trapani (1827–1892).

4. These letters have not been located.

5. Probably Captain Funck.

6. WI omitted the bracketed word.

1942.   To James Buchanan

Legation of the United States / Madrid March 19th. 1846

No 76. / The Hon. James Buchanan / Secretary of State. Washington.

Sir

The Miraflores cabinet has come to an untimely end.[1] It never, in fact, had a vigorous existence, but was rather permitted to live during an interval of jarring interests among certain political leaders and while intrigues were going on in the palace and elsewhere, for the formation of a government likely to be tractable to the wishes of what is termed "the occult power" The discordant parties being at length brought into some degree of unison, and their plans arranged, the Miraflores cabinet was suddenly despatched by a kind of coup d'etat, and Narvaez once more placed at the head of affairs; with a cabinet already prepared, of his own composition and likely to be obedient to his dictation.

The first measures of his government are significative. The sessions of the Cortes are suspended indefinitely. A manifesto has been published by the cabinet[2] Ministers from which it appears that they intend for the present to carry on the government by decrees, thus giving as they say a "rapid impulse" to those public measures which have been impeded for years by the stormy discussions of the legislative chambers. Should they, however, "occasionally transgress the limits of their constitutional faculties" they will ultimately give an account of the same to the cortes and trust for their exoneration to the exigency of circumstances and the benefits of results. Order, morality, economy, the prompt protection of all legitimate interests, but above all *vigorous action* are to form the basis of their conduct. Anarchy will be vigorously and unremittingly assailed wherever it rears its head; nor, in repressing it, will they shrink from adopting any salutary measure however hard it may appear, and distressingly it may act in peculiar cases. No attempt at public disturbance will be suffered to be made with impunity and any public functionaries who may impede the execution of their measures by mistaken lenity towards delinquents will be instantly removed from office and should the case require it, severely punished.

The Manifesto concludes by intimating that Ministers ↑depend↓ for the effectual accomplishment of their policy, upon a numerous, well disciplined and loyal army: upon the probity, good sense and prudence of the nation and upon "the energy inspired by a generous enterprize, as exciting in its causes as it is holy in its ends"

The Manifesto is followed by a royal decree effectually gagging the press.[3]

This sudden re elevation of Narvaez to the head of affairs clothed with almost dictatorial powers has struck a degree of awe into the community. The opposition papers have generally suspended their publication. Politicians gather together in the Puerta del Sol, the political gossiping place of Madrid, and there whisper their surmises and forebodings. Some anticipate an attempt to force the Trapani marriage upon the nation; others, the most profligate schemes of finance to retrieve the immense losses which Narvaez and the Duke of Rianzares[4] are said to have sustained in recent gamblings in the funds—Many predict that the present elevation of Narvaez is but a prelude to a more complete fall.[5] He has lost much of his prestige, say they, both with the army and the State. He has multiplied his enemies both civil and military. He has become odious to a large part of the Moderado party, who will cooperate with the progresistas in effecting his downfall, as they did in effecting that of Espartero.

The very Trapani marriage will be the stumbling block over which he will fall.

The friends of Narvaez hold a different language. They give him credit for patriotic intentions and say that he really meditates important measures of public utility, but he is ambitious of doing them ↑promptly and↓ in his own way. He considers Spain as yet behind the age and behind the Spirit of her institutions; faction and corruption avail themselves of the Cortes and the press to impede the salutary march of government. He is for having a clear field of action. He will not destroy the Constitution but he will act independent of it in cases of extremity. "Give me,["]⁶ he says, "a few months to carry my plans into effect, ↑unembarrassed by the cortes and the press,↓ and I will engage to clear away some of the most important evils which are pressing upon my country. I will then report what I have done to the Cortes and will say, if I have done wrong punish me. Order me to the Scaffold if you think fit—I will go there!"⁷

All this may be honestly said and sincerely felt; but, with the best intentions, how dangerous is absolute power in such hands. How dangerous, to the very person who exercises it. I have heretofore noticed some of the characteristics of Narvaez. He is ambitious of making a figure in the eyes of the world; but in something of the ostentatious magnificent style of the old Spanish school. He is passionate in the extreme; his temper is overbearing and explosive, yet he is prone to generous impulses and capable of magnanimous actions. The very fire of his nature gives him that energy in action which has enabled him to force on the clogged and encumbered machinery of the Spanish government for the last two years; but it is at the constant risk of explosion.

It is doubted by those, who profess to know something of the real policy of Narvaez, whether he will prove as devoted to the views of the Queen Mother as she could wish. They have at different times been at variance, and nothing but their mutual interests have brought them again into co operation. Narvaez is sensible of the degree of odium the Queen Mother has brought upon herself by endeavoring to effect the Trapani marriage in defiance of the openly expressed disgust of the nation; should she persist in her endeavors and, should Narvaez discover symptoms of distaste to it in the army; it is thought he may take the popular side of the question; and that the Queen Mother may find it expedient once more to leave the country.

I am Sir, / Very respectfully / Your Obt Servt
Washington Irving

DOCKETED: Mr. Markoe
MANUSCRIPT: NA, RG 59.   PUBLISHED: STW, II, 194 (in part).

This despatch is entirely in WI's handwriting.

1. The Miraflores ministry was replaced on March 16. See *La Gaceta*, March 17, 1846.

2. For the text, see *La Gaceta* and *El Heraldo*, March 19, 1846.

3. See *La Gaceta*, March 19, 1846.

4. The husband of Queen Mother María Christina.

5. WI's perceptive assessment was accurate. The Narváez cabinet was removed on April 3, 1846.

6. WI omitted the bracketed quotation mark.

7. See *La Gaceta*, March 19, 1846.

1943. *To Ramón María Narváez*

Legation of the United States / Madrid March 19th. 1846

His Excellency the Duke of Valencia / President of the Council of Ministers / and First Secretary of State ad interim

Sir

I have the honor to acknowledge the receipt of your Excellencys note informing me that her Majesty the Queen has been pleased to nominate you President of the Council of Ministers and first Secretary of State ad interim.[1]

While I congratulate your Excellency most sincerely on this new and distinguished mark of Royal esteem and confidence I beg to assure you of the great pleasure it will give me to enter into official relations with a person for whom I entertain so high a respect and whom I have ever found so courteous, prompt and intelligent in the despatch of business

I avail myself of the present occasion to reiterate the assurance of the distinguished consideration with which I have the honor to remain

Your Excellencys obdt Servt
Washington Irving

MANUSCRIPT: NA, RG 84 (letterbook copy).

This copy is in WI's handwriting.
At this time Narváez was addressed by his title, the duke of Valencia.

1. Narváez succeeded the marques of Miraflores, whose ministry fell on March 16, 1846.

1944. To Ramón María Narváez

Legation of the United States / Madrid March 27th. 1846

His Excellency / The Duke of Valencia / &c &c &c

Sir

I beg leave most respectfully yet earnestly to represent to Your Excellency certain cases in which I concieve I have a right to complain of the inattention which the correspondence of this Legation has experienced from Her Majestys government.

On the 12th. of August last I addressed a note to Mr Martinez de la Rosa, at that time Minister of State, on the Subject of a claim of a Mr Michael Drawsin Harang an American Citizen; stating as forcibly as I could the delays which had occurred in the adjustment of the claim; and the apparent disregard with which my own representations of the case had been treated. I had trusted that the sensitiveness evinced by me, to ⟨the⟩ previous neglect would in the present instance ensure a prompt reply. I regret to say that upwards of Seven months have since elapsed without any notice being taken of that note.

In the early part of last year I urged a claim on the part of Messrs Fitch Brothers & Co American merchants resident in Marseilles, for indemnity for losses sustained in consequence of the detention by one of her Majestys guarda costas, of the Dutch Galleot Vrouw Johanna on board of which they had merchandize. At the suggestion of Mr Martinez de la Rosa I procured certain documents necessary to the Substantiation of the claim, properly verified before the Spanish Consul at Marseilles. These documents I enclosed in a note to Mr Martinez de la Rosa on the 12th June last. Nearly two months elapsed without any notice being taken of my note. On the 4th. of August I again wrote to him complaining in Strong terms of this silence and neglect. This note has likewise remained unnoticed.

To these instances of inattention I may add a third. On the 13th. June last I made a written representation to Mr Martinez de la Rosa of the loses sustained by American merchants in consequence of the Sudden and unnotified nullification, by her Majestys Government of a decree of the authorities of Cuba admitting for a certain time, lumber and provisions duty free. This note also has never been noticed; neither has any attention been paid to a Subsequent one, on the same subject, addressed to Mr Alexander Mon, at that time Minister of Finance.

This signal and repeated neglect of my most formal and earnest communications seemed so incompatible with the friendship and respect professed for the government I had the honor to represent, and so subversive of all the ends of diplomatic intercourse, that it left me at a loss how to proceed. I had thoughts of representing the whole matter to my government and soliciting instructions in the premises, when the advent of Your Excellency to the department of State inspired me with new hopes. The Courtesy I had ever experienced for Your Excellency convinced me that any communication addressed to you would not be permitted to lie unanswered and unregarded; and, from the promptness and energy manifested by you in the despatch of the multifarious business which comes under your cognizance I was satisfied that a frank appeal, such as I now make to you, would be sufficient to procure a proper attention to the matters herein pointed out, and such speedy action in the respective cases as is required by the interests and dignity of both governments,

I avail myself of this occasion to renew to your Excellency the assurance of the high consideration with which I have the honor to remain

Your Excellencys Obedient Servant
Washington Irving

MANUSCRIPT: NA, RG 84 (letterbook copy).

This copy is in WI's handwriting.

1945.   To Sabina O'Shea

Madrid March 28. 1846

My dear Mrs O'Shea

After looking in vain week after week for a letter from you I made up my mind that you had lost all thought of me as soon as I was out of sight; I abused you to all my friends as one of the most forgetful and neglectful of your sex; I determined fifty times a day to think no more about you; I vowed never to write to you again—never—never—never! When, in the midst of my ravings a letter[1] was brought me superscribed with your own well known scrawl, at the very sight of which my heart melted within me and I felt you had just as much sway over me as ever. I beg, however, that you will not put me to such another trial, for if you do I will take to admiring Madame Weisw—r with a vehemence that knows no bounds.

Here we are once more under the potent sway of Don Ramon.[2] He is playing the part of St Patrick who drove all noxious vermin out of Ireland; for one of his first measures has been to drive Buschenthal[3] out of the Country. I am told all the other scamps of his kidney are making up their pacquets and preparing to clear out. If Don Ramon pursues this course he will indeed be a benefactor to Spain, but he will have to use a large broom if he would sweep the country clean.

I have not been to the Embassy for a week past; it is so far off, and I have no inclination to play cards now you are not at hand to set me on. We are to have a grand diplomatic dinner there however on Tuesday next, at which all the new cabinet ministers will be present, as well as the new Portuguese minister,[4] whose name I forget—I have not made his acquaintance yet; but he is well spoken of as being very gentleman like and agreeable; fond of society and disposed to keep a hospitable house; having a private fortune to bear him out. He will reside in your part ⟨neighborhood⟩ of Madrid, and will be quite an addition to your society.

I have not yet been in your new house, but merely in the court yard. It was in complete confusion and had a ruinous look; de la Saussaye would not let me go inside until the alterations and repairs were in a sufficient state of progress. He gave me an idea of the plan upon which the reformations are to be made, and I am inclined to think it will turn out a very respectable looking and a very commodious habitation. I will tell you more about it when I have seen it in its improved condition.

You tell me the Montufa was to arrive in a few days; following close on the heels of her diplomatic and poetic swain. Do you know they have a Story here that she surprised him lately paying his devoirs to a young rival, and ⟨in her⟩ gave him such a handling that he fancied he had a chime of bells in each ear?

I am glad you have had such a pleasant visit from Mrs Ellis,[5] and that you found her so charming. I thought she would suit you; she is so frank and cordial and lady like. As to what you say about her blushing when you talked of Lord Howden,[6] that is all a fancy of your own, if not a wicked invention—at any rate it does not make me as unhappy as you apprehend—Though I can't say I am sorry to hear that Lord Howden has gone to England.

I went with Madame Albuquerque a few mornings since to Madrazos[7] to see your picture. We remained a long time before it, talking about you, until I thought I saw a blush kindling up on its cheek, but I rather think it was all a fancy, like yours about Mrs Ellis. Had you been there, however, instead of your picture I think your ears would have tingled. Though to be sure, in such case, I would not have ventured to speak my mind so freely. Madame Albuquerque thinks, with me, that Madrazo has made an excellent picture and an admirable likeness.

I see by your letter that Mr O'Shea is "very busy going backwards and forwards to the Rue St George." Poor dear man! What between his banks in France and his banks in Spain, he will be like the old woman who had hid her money in a dozen holes and corners, so that, after her death, her ghost had so many places to haunt, ⟨that⟩ it was the most troubled spirit in the country.

Fare well. Give my kind remembrances to your husband; to Willy and to my worthy and venerable friend Papa Quique and believe me ever your devoted friend

and attentive correspondent
Washington Irving

ADDRESSED: Madame / Madame O'Shea / Hotel de Bristol / Place Vendome
    DOCKETED: 28th. March 184⟨4⟩6
MANUSCRIPT: HSA.   PUBLISHED: Penney, *Bulletin NYPL*, 62 (December, 1958),
    625–26.

The cancellation and addition in the docket has been made in different ink.

1. This letter has not been located.
2. Ramón María Narváez, the duke of Valencia.
3. José Buschenthal, who was of French origin, became a naturalized Brazilian in 1828. He was a stock manipulator who married the reputed daughter of Emperor Pedro of Brazil. See Penney, *Bulletin NYPL*, 62 (December, 1958), 631. The London *Times*, for April 2, 1846, cites a report from Madrid on March 25 that "M. Buchenthal left Madrid in the morning for Bayonne. The cause assigned for his banishment was that, when last in London, he paid a visit to General Espartero." Probably Narváez exiled him because he held Buschenthal responsible for his own losses in stock speculation.
4. Probably Antonio da Costa Cabral, first marquis of Thomar (1803–1889).
5. The niece of William King, American minister to Paris. She served as his hostess.
6. Sir John Hobart Caradoc, second Lord Howden (1799–1873) had served with the forces fighting for María Christina from 1834 to 1839. In 1847 he was named British minister to Brazil, where he remained until 1850, when he was appointed minister to Spain.
7. Federico de Madrazo y Kuntz (1815–1894) was a fashionable portrait painter and son of José de Madrazo (1781–1859), director of the picture gallery at the court of Ferdinand VII. Among his portraits are those of Leocadia Zamora and Cecile Böhl (1796–1877) (Fernán Caballero). Later he became director of the Prado Museum and court painter for Isabella II.

1946. To James Buchanan

Legation of the United States / Madrid, April 1t. 1846

No 77. / The Hon / James Buchanan / Secretary of State. Washington

Sir,

I have the honor to enclose the accounts and vouchers of this Legation for the first quarter of 1846. Shewing a balance against the United States of $93.36. which will be carried to their debit in their next account.

Very respectfully / Your obt Servt.
Washington Irving

DOCKETED: Recd. 7 May / Mr Markoe
MANUSCRIPT: NA, RG 59.

This letter is in WI's handwriting.

1947.   To Xavier de Istúriz

Legation of the United States / Madrid April 4th. 1846

His Excellency / Don Xavier Isturiz / &c &c &c

Sir

I beg leave to ask the favorable intervention of your Excellency in the case of Mr Benjamin Wright,[1] a citizen of the United States, who has been employed for several years past, in the Island of Cuba, as civil engineer and as contractor of the Nuevitas and Puerto Principe rail road.

In the course of his enterprises he has become involved in several law suits by which, though they have not been determined against him, he has been subjected to heavy costs and has suffered serious detriment in his affairs. He is desirous, therefore, of bringing his causes to a hearing before the Supreme tribunal of Madrid, where they would be less subject to local influences.

What he wishes, at present, is an order from the Supreme tribunal of Madrid, or any other competent authority, to the Audiencia of Puerto Principe, directing it to furnish him with authenticated copies of all the "Autos" in the suits brought before it, and to which he has been a party; more especially a suit brought against him by Don Melchior Aguero. Having been much impoverished by the expenses he has already incurred, he prays that the documents in question may be furnished to him without further cost than that incurred in copying them.

As the applicant is a very meritorious person, and engaged in enterprises of great benefit to the Island of Cuba in which he has had to struggle with great difficulties; and as he is, moreover, a stranger in the land and therefore entitled to hospitable protection, I am sure your Excellency will take an interest in his case, and will do whatever is fitting to facilitate his obtaining redress for any loss or injury he may wrongfully have sustained.

I avail myself of this occasion to renew to your Excellency the assurance of the high consideration with which I have the honor to remain

Your Excellencys most Obt St.
W Irving

MANUSCRIPT: NA, RG 84 (letterbook copy).

This copy is in WI's handwriting.
Xavier Istúriz was serving as prime minister of Spain at this time.

1. Probably Benjamin H. Wright (1801–1881), a civil engineer and graduate of West Point in 1822 who had worked with his father, Benjamin Wright (1770–1842), on canal-building projects.

1948. *To Henry G. Hubbard*

Madrid April 5th. 1846

Henry G Hubbard Esq / (Consul at S. John Porto Rico)

Sir,
I have this morning received your letter of Jany 22d.[1] on the subject of your Exequatur. A regular application for that instrument was made to the Spanish government by this Legation on the 8th. November last.[2] Some time may yet elapse however before you receive it; as it is the practise of this government where a colonial consulship is in question, to send out previously to the colony for information as to the fitness and acceptability of the candidate. This of course involves a delay equal to two voyages across the Atlantic: I have attempted repeatedly and urgently to obtain the abolishment or at least a modification of his most inconvenient regulation but all my efforts have been fruitless. As soon as your Exequatur is issued it will be forwarded to you.

Very respectfully /Your Obt Sert
Washington Irving

MANUSCRIPT: NA, RG 84 (letterbook copy).

This copy is in WI's handwriting.
Henry G. Hubbard of New York was nominated as U.S. consul for St. John's, Porto Rico on December 18, 1845, and was consented to on February 24, 1846. See Hasse, *Index to U.S. Documents*, III, 1748.

1. In this letter Hubbard stated that he had been appointed U.S. consul in September, 1845, but the official documents do not support his statement (NA, RG 84).
2. This application was made by Jasper Livingston during WI's absence in Paris.

1949. To Sabina O'Shea

Madrid April 5t. 1846

Fairest & best of women!

I have received your delightful little double letter scrawled in blue ink and am now in the best of humors with you. I perceive it is better for us both to be now and then a little remiss in correspondence as it leads to a little pouting, and then a little scolding, and then we make up and are better friends than ever. As Madame Albuquerque has eloped from her husband and myself and will arrive almost as soon as this letter I shall refer you to her for all the news and gossip of this muy heroica city.

I am glad Willy was at Mrs Corbins *soiree dansante*. I have no doubt it was very pretty and very pleasant. They have a beautiful apartment, entertain in good style and I understand it was quite a young party, like that at my nieces; where Willy would meet with a number of pretty American "children." I hope you will become acquainted with Mrs Corbin. I think you will like one another. She is one of the most pleasing and ladylike of my country women in Paris.

I was amused with your account of the visit of Madame Grabation and of your return visit in which I suppose you were dismayed by the halbardiers and the files of domestics by which you had to pass. You should have gone in state with Quique in his allameda dress as a page and Willy in his highland costume as a body guard, and then you might have carried a bold front in presence of the princess. I hope you hinted to her about Lord Howdens flirtations with a certain diplomatic lady who shall be nameless. I am pretty sure you did, for now and then you have a most lady like propensity to be mischievous.

Tell Madame Albuquerque the house yesterday was quite triste without her. Poor Don Jose shook his head and sighed heavily. We dined tête a tête and he abused the dinner though I thought it a very good one. He missed the exquisite seasoning of his ladys society. In the evening I went in despair to the Embassy, where I found quite a reunion. All the Carinis—all the de Weisweillers (Madame W looked charmingly) all the Dal-Borgos; all the de la Saussayes, all the Ossunas[1] all the St Iagos &c &c &c &c. I staid there until past twelve oclock and only lost one dollar and was so pleased with my good luck that I promised the Ambassador to dine with him today.

Tell Madame Albuquerque further more, that I trust the house affairs will go on admirably as I have constituted Lilly and Aveta house keeper alternately and they are to try who can keep the most orderly house.

I forgot to tell you that the New Portuguese Minister[2] was at the Embassy last night. The Count de Bresson invited him to join the ecarte table telling him that ecarte was the standing order of the day here. He did not take the hint; but stood about the corners of the room gravely talking with different gentlemen—and soon disappeared. He is somewhat stiff, solid and serious and might figure in the old story of the Convidado de Piedra,[3] but it is probable he will become more flexible and genial as he becomes better acquainted. The Spaniards are already trumpeting forth in the news papers all the fetes and entertainments he intends to give; all which they are disposed to accept with their accustomed hospitality.

Tomorrow I take a sociable family dinner with Don Tom, at which I expect to enjoy myself; as it is the kind of dinner I like and I like the people of the house. I shall feel at home there. I have got quite in the habit of going every day about mid day to Don Toms office to gossip and to pick up the news of the day. You have no idea how cosily Mr O'Sheas part of the office is fitted up. Such capital cushioned chairs, such *lujo*! He'll make money ten times as easily there as formerly.

Farewell my dear Mrs O'Shea. Remember me kindly to Mr OShea & Willy and give my dutiful reverence to Papa Quique who, by his ghostly councils, will, I trust, accomplish the conversion of yourself and Madame Albuquerque.

Yours ever very truly
Washington Irving

Mrs Henry O'Shea

ADDRESSED: Madame / Madame O'Shea / Hotel de Bristol / Place Vendome / à Paris DOCKETED: 5th. April, 1846.
MANUSCRIPT: HSA.   PUBLISHED: Penney, *Bulletin NYPL*, 62 (December, 1958), 626–27.

1. WI probably refers to Mariano Francisco de Borja Justo Téllez-Girón y Beaufort, 12th duke of Osuna (1814–1882) and his wife. The duke, a soldier who had fought in many engagements in the Carlist wars of the 1830's, succeeded to his title on August 29, 1844, after the death of his brother, Pedro de Alcantára, 11th duke of Osuna (1810–1844). On August 24, 1845, Isabella II made him a senator for life.

2. Simon de Silva Ferraz de Lima y Castro, count de Rendufe, a well-known orator, served as Portuguese ambassador to Berlin from 1841 to 1845, to Madrid in 1845 and 1846, and later to Rio de Janeiro.

3. WI alludes to Tirso de Molina's *El burlador de Sevilla y convidado de piedra* (*The Jokester of Seville and the Guest of Stone*), a comedy which introduced the Don Juan figure into literature. See Gerald Brenan, *The Literature of the Spanish People* (Cambridge, 1951), pp. 214–18.

1950. To Sarah Storrow

Madrid April 5th. 1846

My dear Sarah,

Madame Albuquerque has suddenly undertaken another expedition to Paris to see the all attractive Mr Brewster,[1] and will probably reach there almost as soon as this letter. She has promised to call on you during her very brief sojourn in Paris—She intends to put up at the Same hotel with Mrs O'shea if she can procure accommodations there. She left us the night before last ↑in the Malle poste↓; and yesterday the house appeared quite desolate without her. Only think what energy and resolution she has to undertake such a journey a second time with no companion but a female servant.

Your party at Mrs Corbins must have been a very pleasant one; the ⟨house⟩ ↑apartment↓ is so elegant; the host and hostess so amiable, and there must have been such an assemblage of young american beauties; such as I saw at your own party. Mrs O'Shea writes me that Willy was quite delighted. He says he has enjoyed himself no where so much as at the American parties. Mrs O'Shea seems gratified by this mark of attention ↑to Willy↓ on the part of Mrs Corbin and says she intends to call upon that Lady: I hope they may become acquainted. I think they would be pleased with each other.

I see by your letter[2] the lively lady ⟨is disposed⟩ threatens to write me a letter about my friend Mrs Brigstocke. I wish she would put her threat in execution. I should be delighted to get a letter from her on any condition, even though it were quizzing me. I want to see if she can be as agreeable with her pen as she is in conversation. I will promise to reply. As to Mrs B. I did receive a letter, as you foretold, by the Courier. It was one she had promised me, relating to some circumstances in her own life, ⟨on⟩ ↑about↓ which we had once spoken incidentally. It was a sad letter ⟨shewing me⟩ ↑that made me conscious↓ how mistaken I had been in the idea I formed on first seeing her, that her smooth clear brow and her well conserved beauty where time had left no mark, betokened a happy life and a mind unclouded by care. She has had her trials, and trials of the severest kind. Her trials of the heart, not sentimental sorrows, but deep domestic afflictions. The afflictions of a wife and mother. I will shew you her letter at some future day. It has raised her much in my opinion and I cannot but feel flattered that she should think me worthy of receiving such a letter. You tell me that Mrs Brigstocke has expressed a wish to become acquainted with you, but that "as I said nothing about your making her acquaintance while I was in Paris you do not See any object in it now." I trust you understand and appreciate my motives for not seeking to launch you into a wider sphere of Society than that in which I found you. They were the result of experience and mature reflexion. ⟨M⟩ I should have been delighted to make you acquainted with Mrs B and with three or four other ladies whose acquaintance I made during my last sojourn in Paris; but they each moved in Seperate circles, and to become partially acquainted with them without mingling in the little world of their intimacy would have been as unsatisfactory to you as was your intercourse with Mrs Ellis after she had become launched in the vortex of diplomatic life. Besides, an extended and fashionable intercourse would lift you out of your present quiet, respectable domestic life and ⟨to suf?⟩ subject you to expenses beyond your means, or to repinings at not being able to cope with those around you who had ample fortunes to warrant their expenditures. When Mr Storrow has built up his fortune and you have an income independent of the vicissitudes of business and sufficient to warrant your living a life of liesure and devoting yourselves to society it will be time to extend and diversify the circle of your acquaintance. Until then ⟨you are⟩ ↑it is↓ best to live as you do, in a style of quiet yet elegant simplicity, and in a circle composed of the elite of your own country.

The court goes ⟨this⟩ about the middle of this month to Aranjuez, to pass part of the Spring there,[3] after which it will probably go down to Andalusia, to give the young queen an opportunity of seeing the Southern part of her Kingdom and of shewing herself to her subjects. If I find I am not likely to be relieved soon from my post I ⟨th⟩ believe I shall follow the court, by way of whiling away the time, which begins to hang heavy in my hands; ⟨and will⟩ Indeed if I linger here at Madrid after you have sailed for the United States I shall become completely home sick.

Farewell, my dear Sarah; kiss my darling little Kate and Tutie and keep them in mind of me when the "salt seas" roll between us.

your affectionate uncle
Washington Irving

MANUSCRIPT: Yale.

1. Brewster was a dentist in Paris.
2. This letter has not been located.
3. See *El Heraldo*, March 31, 1846.

1951.   To Xavier de Istúriz

Legation of the United States / Madrid, April 6. 1846

Mr Xavier de Isturiz / President of the Council / &c &c &c

The Undersigned, Envoy Extraordinary and Minister Plenipotentiary of the United States has the honor to acknowledge the receipt of the note of his Excellency Mr Xavier de Isturiz informing him of his having been appointed by Her Majesty President of the Council of Ministers and Minister of State[1]

The Undersigned congratulates his Excellency on this distinguished mark of royal esteem and confidence and assures him that it will give him the highest satisfaction to enter with His Excellency into the relations of business and to vie with him in cultivating the cordial understanding which so happily exists between the two nations

The Undersigned avails himself of this occasion to offer to his Excellency the assurance of his most distinguished consideration

Washington Irving

MANUSCRIPT: NA, RG 84 (letterbook copy).

This copy is in WI's handwriting.

1. Istúriz succeeded Narváez, who had held the premiership only since March 16, 1846.

1952.   To Junius Boyle

Legation of the United States / Madrid April 7th. 1846.

Junius Boyle Esq / Consul of the U States. Mahon / ad interim.

Sir,

I have just received your letter of the 26th. March, with the accompanying documents. By these it appears that a privilige formerly allowed to us of depositing coal free of duty at Port Mahon for the use of our Squadron was ⟨allo⟩ annulled by royal decree in 1843, but has continued to be enjoyed by us through the indulgence or remissness of the local authorities. That this remissness has excited the royal displeasure and produced orders for the rigorous enforcement of the existing laws; and that in consequence of these orders you are notified to re embark, as soon as possible, the coal you hold in deposit.

All this is perfectly regular; and, as the exemption from duties enjoyed for some time past ↑was in opposition to the laws,↓ I see no alternative but to pay those duties or re embark the coal. Perhaps you may obtain some indulgence as to time in the probability of the speedy arrival of some of our ships, but this can only be asked as an indulgence not as a right.

I am Sir / Very respectfully / Your ob St.
W Irving.

P. S. It may be well to keep an eye upon the French deposit for coal in the port. If any privilege is granted in that quarter we have then grounds to claim a similar privilege from the Spanish government.

MANUSCRIPT: NA, RG 84 (letterbook copy).

This copy is in WI's handwriting.

Junius J. Boyle (1802–1870), a Navy officer in the Mediterranean for ten years, temporarily assumed consular responsibilities at Port Mahon after the resignation of Obadiah Rich. See WI to Francisco Martínez de la Rosa, April 9, 1845.

1953. To Sarah Storrow

Madrid April 7th. 1846

My dear Sarah,

This will be the last letter I can send in time to find you on this side of the Atlantic. I cannot tell you how sad—sad—sad I feel at the thoughts that we are soon to have the ocean between us. I have just received a letter from Pierre M Irving dated the 27t February.[1] It appears that Mr Saunders[2] was nominated as Minister to Spain on the 25th. and confirmed by the Senate on the 26th. Pierre adds "as he has been so long an assured expectant of the post I presume his preparations are already made and that he will not long delay his departure." I trust so too and shall look out for news by the next arrival as to the time he will be likely to embark. It is quite a relief to my mind to learn that a successor is actually appointed and to think that by this time he may possibly be on his way. I was appointed in February and embarked on the 10th. ↑april↓ and my appointment had been totally unlooked for.

Pierre writes "I stopped in to see Aunt Paris this morning and find that she has already despatched a letter to you with all the family news. I asked her if she told you she was *well*. She shook her head and said she told you she was *better*. This was a good deal for her to admit. The fact is her health is wonderfully better within the last three weeks. Her sleep has become quiet and regular and though she still complains of feeling exceedingly nervous during the day it is manifest to all that she is gradually casting off the last lingerings of her most trying and capricious malady"

Before you get this letter, however, you will doubtless be in the receipt of later letters from New York which will give you family news until the latter part of March. ⟨I have⟩ I trust by the time you arrive in The United States your Mother will be quite restored to her usual state of health. The prospect of soon seeing you is acting upon her like a perfect cordial.

I told you in my last that I thought it possible I might follow the Court to Aranjuez and perhaps to Andalusia, should there not be a prospect of my being speedily relieved from my post. I find however that the movements of the Royal family are quite uncertain and that there is no probability of the Queen going to Andalusia. In fact political affairs here are in a very critical state and I should not be surprised if there are new commotions in Spain before long. You will learn by the time that this reaches you that General Narvaez has suddenly fallen from his political eminence, and been sent out of the country at less than a days warning![3] ⟨It seems th⟩ I refer you, however, ⟨for the a⟩ to the newspapers for the actual state of affairs here; we are in the midst of one of the acts of a Melodrama and looking each moment for extravagant tricks and transitions.

I presume you will receive this letter just as you are about setting off for Havre. Write to me from that place and let me know how you all are after the journey; how you will be arranged on board of the Oneida, and what preparations Kate is making for her voyage.

Give my kind remembrances to Mr Storrow Kiss the little darlings for me and remember me kindly to my excellent friend Beasley

Your affectionate uncle
Washington Irving

MANUSCRIPT: Yale.

1. This letter has not been located.

2. Romulus M. Saunders (1791–1867), a North Carolina lawyer who held public office on the state or national level almost continuously from 1815 to 1845, was a political confidant of James K. Polk. His qualifications for the Spanish post were undistinguished. Of him John Quincy Adams observed, "There is not a more cankered or venomous reptile in the country."

3. The ministerial crisis had been rumored in the newspapers several days before the resignation of Narváez. See *El Heraldo*, April 2–6, 1846.

1954. To James Buchanan

Legation of the United States. / Madrid, April 8t. 1846

No 78. / The Hon James Buchanan / Secretary of State. Washington

Sir,

The prediction cited in my Despatch of March 29th. that the actual elevation of Narvaez was but "a prelude to a more complete fall" has been speedily verified; and he is now a banished man. I have reason to believe that his fall had for some time been meditated in the secret councils of the palace. He had made himself acceptable it is true to the young queen by his chivalrous devotion to her; but he was often at variance with the Queen Mother and a kind of rivalship for influence had existed between them. All this had been tolerated by the Queen Mother so long as he essentially agreed with her in policy; for she considered his influence with the army all important to the support of government. Of late their views had begun to diverge. Queen christina, more and more under the influence of the priesthood, inclined towards absolutism. Narvaez however, absolute might be his measures under supposed circumstances of expediency, proclaimed his fixed determination ultimately to uphold the constitution. On recently resuming the reins of power he marked out a line of policy for himself which varied from that ⟨of s⟩ of the Queen mother, and signified his resolution to make every thing and every body bend to it. His intentions may have been patriotic, but he over rated his means of carrying them into effect; or rather he under rated the ⟨counter⟩ influence exercised against him. He was too confident in himself and in that fiery spirit which had borne him on to power. An intimation made by him in one of his ↑first↓ cabinet councils was fatal to him. In discussing the Trapani marriage he intimated his conviction that the army would be opposed to it. This was considered significative of his own intended course with respect to it. A schism forthwith occurred in his cabinet; but it took place on another question. A law had been framed in the preceding Cabinet regulating the Stock exchange and prohibiting bargains on time. It was expected that one of the first measures of Narvaez would be to rescind this law, as he was known to have met with heavy losses by gambling in the funds and to stand in need of further speculations to redeem them. This law, therefore was artfully chosen to be ↑made↓ his stumbling block; and its immediate and rigorous enforcement was urged by the Ministers of Justice, and of the Marine;[1] men devoted to the interests of Queen christina. The consequence was violent altercations, in which Narzaez gave way to his stormy temper and, at times, lost all guard over his language. Some of these took place in the presence of the young queen, who it is said, conducted herself on those occasions with a dignity and discretion beyond her years. Changes in the Cabinet became inevitable; but Narvaez found, to his surprise and mortification, that the countenance of the young queen was changed with respect to him, and that, though she might consent to remove certain of the Ministers, yet she objected to every person proposed by him in their place. When urged to state the ground of her objections to certain candidates, she alleged that they were enemies to her mother. Annoyed at being repeatedly thwarted in his measures by the influence of the Queen Mother, Narvaez, in an unguarded moment, hinted to the young Queen the expediency of inducing her to absent herself from the Court and sojourn for a time in the provinces. The young Queen understood the whole drift of the suggestion but clung, as was natural, to her mother, and from that moment the continuance of Narvaez at the head of affairs became impossible. He offered his resignation and it was accepted. The rudiments of a new Cabinet were hastily formed by Isturiz,[2] consisting of himself and two other ministers; loyal adherents to Queen Christina.

In the recent stormy disputes of the Cabinet, Narvaez had spoken of his consciousness of plots against him in the palace, but had vaunted his power over the army, and thrown out menaces of the lengths to which he might be provoked should attempts be made to crush him. All these were probably the empty threats of a passionate man. Narvaez was an Andalusian; the Gascon of Spain, and prone to Gasconade. His vaunts and threats, however, were now remembered, and fears were entertained that he might put them into execution. While military measures were immediately taken to ensure the tranquility of the Capital; the mission to Naples was offered to Narvaez, as a means of pacifying him and getting him out of the way, and to make the offer more tempting he was assured that the mission should be elevated to an Embassy. The offer was promptly declined. This added to the uneasiness at the palace. The ever ready gossips which infest a court now brought rumors of mutinous symptoms among the military, and of an intention among some of the chiefs to repair in a body to the palace and demand the departure of the Queen Mother. A Court panic ensued, and a royal command was issued for Narvaez to leave Madrid the very next day and repair to Naples, there to await further orders.[3] This harsh mandate, equally pusillanimous and impolitic at once gave Narvaez the character of a political martyr and elevated him into transient ⟨[pop?]⟩ and unwonted popularity. On the following day his house was crowded by persons of all parties some of whom had been his open enemies. Some came actuated, no doubt by a generous sympathy; others by the idea that his disgrace might be but temporary and that he might again return to power; and many came out of sheer hostility

to the court and the Queen Mother. These last were loud in their exclamations against the royal ingratitude toward so loyal a subject, who
had rendered such invaluable services to the throne.

Narvaez conducted himself throughout with a great shew of magnanimity, professing, to the last, his ardent and loyal devotion to the
queen. In the mean time the panic in the palace had subsided and there
was a disposition on the part of the Crown to qualify its harsh and hasty
proceeding. Just as Narvaez was about to enter his travelling carriage a
Cabinet minister arrived, bearing the royal document nominating him
ambassador to Naples.[4] Narvaez wrote a proud but respectful reply sig-
nifying that, his presence in Spain being considered an obstacle to the
march of public affairs, he had not hesitated a moment in abandoning
his country; but he entreated the queen to permit him to decline serving
a government which regarded him as an encumbrance. He then entered
his carriage and set out on the road for France.

Such is the catastrophe of the Narvaez domination, nor is it likely to
produce any great shock in the community. With all his temporary importance Narvaez had no party. He had been too individual in the exercise of authority and had neglected to form a base for his own power.
He ↑had↓ courted and conciliated no particular creed nor interest. He
was not absolute enough for the Moderados, nor liberal enough for the
progresistas. He was an object of envy and jealousy to many of his former military competitors; and offended the old nobility ↑by his osten-
tation and↓ by what they considered his arrogant assumptions. The clergy
had found him cold in his devotion to the Court of Rome, and he ↑of
late had↓ heedlessly or wilfully cast off the important support of the
French Ambassador. He had thus isolated himself in the state; without
percieving how really hazardous and fallacious was his position. After
all, his elevation ↑depended↓ upon mere favoritism. The royal favor
once lost, his fall was complete, for he had nothing to rally upon. Even
the army would shrink from supporting a man no longer in power; and,
for him to appeal from his sovreign to the army, would be to constitute
himself a traitor.

The loss of Narvaez will be felt, however, by the government, to which
he has been an arm of strength; the terror of his name & the vigor and
promptness of his measures have daunted opposition and[?] kept down
insurrection, and contributed to carry on a discordant government for
nearly three years. In this respect I see no one within the prescincts of
the court likely to supply his place. His absence from power may give
new spirits to the liberal party and precipitate the downfall of the Moderados.

Very respectfully / Your obedient Servant
Washington Irving

DOCKETED: Recd. 23 May. / Mr. Markoe
MANUSCRIPT: NA, RG 59.   PUBLISHED: STW, II, 194 (in part).

This despatch is in WI's handwriting.

1. Pedro Egana and Juan de la Pezuela y Ceballos, respectively.
2. The new cabinet formed by Francisco Xavier Istúriz included the following ministers: foreign affairs, Istúriz; war and marine, General Armero; finance, Orlando; interior, Pidal; grace and justice, Joaquín Diaz Caneja (1777–1851). See *La Gaceta*, April 5, 1846; London *Times*, April 11, 16, 20, 21, 1846.
3. See *El Heraldo*, April 6, 1846.
4. See *El Heraldo*, April 7, 1846.

1955.   To Messrs. Baring Brothers & Co.

Legation of the United States / Madrid April 16th. 1846

Messrs. Baring Brothers & Co / London.

Gentlemen.

Please pay Mr John Miller on order Six pounds Seven Shillings and Seven pence half penny and charge the same to the government of the United States for the Contingent expenses of this Legation

Washington Irving

£6.7.7½

MANUSCRIPT: SHR.

The word "Duplicate" in another hand is written to the right of the inside address.

1956.   To James Buchanan

[Madrid], April 18, 1846

While dissension has been prevalent at headquarters, an insurrection has broken out in Gallicia.[1] Symptoms of this appeared during the last period of Narvaez' administration, and apprehensions were entertained that the Prince Don Enrique,[2] who was at Corunna, would be induced to head it. Narvaez proceeded in the matter with his usual promptness. Military measures were taken to suppress the insurrection, and a royal command was issued to the Prince to leave the kingdom instantly, and choose some place in France for his residence, there to await royal orders, with the understanding that, should he absent himself from the place chosen, he would be stripped of all the honors and consideration of a royal prince of Spain; and, should he return to Spain contrary to the royal command, he would subject himself to prosecution before any tribunal in the kingdom. The Prince obeyed the royal command implicitly, and chose Bayonne as his place of exile. Scarce had he been there a few days, when Narvaez himself arrived there—a banished man! The public papers state that Narvaez, soon after his arrival, paid the Prince a visit of respect, arrayed in full uniform.[3] The interview must have been a curious one. As has been well observed, there is so much of the comic in these sudden and violent changes and transitions in Spanish politics, that we should be disposed to laugh at them, only that they occur so rapidly we have not time to laugh. Accustomed as I have become to all kinds of contradictory moves, I should not be surprised to see Narvaez back here again before long, at the head of affairs. The Government, in its perplexed condition, with differences of opinion in the Cabinet, with an active and confident opposition gaining strength in the capital, and rumors of conspiracies in the provinces, begins to feel the want of Narvaez' energy, activity, and spirit of control. This is especially the case since it is found that, in Gallicia, some of the army have joined the insurgents. Every one of the leading personages in power attempts to shift off the odium of his precipitate banishment, and to hint a wish for his return. In the mean time, the arbitrary measures instituted under his ministry continue in force; and an attempt has been made to imitate his military rigor, by issuing a circular to the *Gefes Politicos,* or heads of municipalities throughout the kingdom, authorizing them to declare martial law in their respective jurisdictions on any appearance of popular disturbance.[4] These rigorous measures, however, are considered as proofs of distrust and alarm on the part of Government, rather than of confidence and decision. A general uneasiness prevails throughout the community, and fearful forebodings of an approaching convulsion.

Published: PMI, III, 386–88.

1. Liberal elements had planned simultaneous uprisings in Madrid and Málaga as well, but these miscarried. General Concha easily suppressed the disturbance in Galicia. See *La Gaceta,* April 9–18, 1846; Clarke, *Modern Spain,* p. 204.

2. Enrique (1823–1870) was Isabella's cousin and a younger brother of Prince Francisco de Asís (1822–1902), whom she was to marry on October 10, 1846. See Aronson, *Royal Vendetta,* pp. 39–40, 57.

3. See *El Heraldo,* April 14, 1846.

4. This decree was signed on April 16. See *La Gaceta,* April 17, 1846.

1957. To Sabina O'Shea

Madrid, April 18th. 1846

My dear Mrs OShea,

I have barely time to scrawl you a line in reply to your kind letter by the last courier. I have had to write long despatches to government lately and as I have no secretary at hand to copy my despatches I have to do it myself which makes double trouble. However, upon the whole, I would rather be my own secretary.

I am glad that you have seen something more of my niece before her departure; and that she has seen something of Madame Albuquerque. She is a kind of link of amity between us; for I am disposed to love all whom she loves and who love her and Ill assure you have quite won her heart. She continually speaks of you as "your sweet friend Mrs O'Shea". Her heart is well worth winning. a kinder and warmer and purer does not beat. I have been grieviously disappointed in receiving no letter from her this week. I suppose she was too much occupied by preparations for her departure; but the approach of that departure made me the more anxious to hear from her. She and her dear little ones are now on the wide ocean and god knows when I shall ever see them again. It is a sad, sad weight on my heart.

We are here in the midst of agitation and rumors, every body prophesying changes and troubles. Those who sent off Narvaez in a moment of absurd panic are now ashamed of their cowardly and ungenerous act and attempt to shift ⟨off⟩ the blame from one to the other. No body did it; every body was against it, yet it was done—And now they begin to talk of getting him back again!

According to Madame Albuquerques letters to her husband we may expect her in Madrid again in little more than a week[.] I shall be most happy to see her for I miss her sadly. When she and you are absent from Madrid I am perfectly at a loss. I go occasionally to Don Toms and have dined there the two last Sundays, and been very much pleased. Don Tom is an excellent fine tempered fellow and I like his little wife; but in general every body talks spanish there, and though I understand it very well, I find it ⟨is?⟩ rather a toil to converse in it; and I hate conversation when it costs me an effort.

I have given your message to De la Saussaye who was much gratified by it. He will not let me visit the house yet, lest I should receive an unfavorable impression from seeing it while filled with rubbish. The more I see and know of De La Saussaye the more I value him. He is a perfect jewel among the false and glittering trash one meets with in Madrid.

Tell your husband that when he is done with making large fortunes for himself he ought to make a small fortune for poor La Saussaye. He merits it at his hands.

I hope you may be able to read this letter; ⟨as?⟩ you complain of not being able to decypher some of my last ones. The fact is I have so many to write and have to scribble them off so fast that I have not time to make them very legible. However, the longer you have to keep spelling over them the longer your thoughts will be occupied by me, and that is some consideration.

Give my kind regards to Mr O'Shea and the two juveniles and believe me ever

Very truly yours
Washington Irving

ADDRESSED: Madame / Madame O'Shea / Hotel de Bristol / Place Vendome / a Paris   DOCKETED: April 18th. 1846.
MANUSCRIPT: HSA.   PUBLISHED: Penney, *Bulletin NYPL*, 62 (December, 1958), 627–28.

1958.   To John W. Holding

Legation of the United States / Madrid, April 21t. 1846

John W Holding Esqr / Consul of the U States, Santiago de Cuba

Sir,

I herewith forward to you your Exequatur,[1] received this day from the Department of Foreign Affairs, together with the original commission Signed by the president of the United States

Very respectfully / Your obt Servt
W Irving

MANUSCRIPT: NA, RG 84 (letterbook copy).

This copy is in WI's handwriting.

1. WI had applied for this exequatur on July 24, 1845. See his letter to Martínez de la Rosa, July 24, 1845.

1959. To Catharine Paris

Madrid, April 25th. 1846

My dear Sister

I received a day or two since Your letter of the 27th. & 30 March[1] which gave me the gratifying intelligence of your improved health. Before this reaches you you will most probably have been rejoiced by the arrival of our dear Sarah and her children; and that I trust will give You new life and spirits. I am looking daily for a farewell letter from her from Havre. The idea that she and her little ones are now on the high seas and that we are every day wider and wider asunder is most painful to me, and renders me more impatient at my detention in Madrid. I had hoped that Mr Saunders would have embarked in the Steamer of the first of April, but now begin to fear it will be a considerable time before he arrives to relieve me from my post, and that, as you say, I shall not reach home before late in the Summer.

I am very comfortably accommodated in a part of my old establishment, and find my situation in the family of my kind and amiable friends the Albuquerques every thing that I could wish. Madame Albuquerque is absent at Paris, but will return in the course of a few days. She is the life of the house when at home and we miss her sadly. Lorenzo is major domo, but still finds time to attend upon me as usual   Juana has married her cousin a young Doctor just admitted to practise. They have a small apartment in my neighborhood and she visits me occasionally, to see that all my things are in order. She appears to be very happy in her new condition, and is always remarkably neat and even genteel in her appearance. For my old Coachman Pedro I have got an excellent place with my old Diplomatic friend M. DalBorgo[2] the Danish Charge d'affairs. So that all my old domestics are well off. They always manifest the utmost devotion to me; and indeed we always lived very happily together.

My health continues to be *perfect*, and I shall endeavor to keep it so. I rise early and walk for an hour and half before breakfast in the Retiro, or some other pleasant promenade; and take other exercise in the course of the day and evening.

I had a letter from our relatives in England lately by which I find sister Sarah is about to go to Brighton to pass some weeks there[.] I hope I may get away from Madrid in time to join her there; though upon the whole I would prefer visiting her at the Shrubbery; which is a little domestic world of itself and has the great charm of retirement.

The day after tomorrow we have a grand Besamanos on the birth day of the Queen Mother.[3] It will be the first grand court ceremony since my return from Paris. You will have heard of the late events in the Spanish Court; the downfall and banishment of Narvaez. It was considered a harsh and ungrateful act on the part of the Sovreigns and has added to the unpopularity of the Queen Mother. The changes and sudden transitions in the Spanish court are something like those in ⟨Eastern⟩ the Courts of the East. It only wants the bow string to make the resemblance complete. I am getting tired of courts, however, altogether, and shall be right glad to throw off my diplomatic Coat for the last time.

Give my love to all the house holds; and to my dear Sarah, if she is with you when this arrives. I shall be anxious to hear of your meeting.

Your affectionate brother
Washington Irving

Manuscript: Yale.   Published: PMI, III, 384 (in part).

1. This and the letter from the Van Warts have not been located.
2. Olinto dal Borgo di Primo (1775–1856) was chargé d'affaires for Denmark in Madrid.
3. See *El Heraldo*, April 27, 1846.

1960.   To Sabina O'Shea

Madrid April 25. 1846

My dear Mrs OShea,

If I may judge from your letter of the 17th[1] you and Madame Albuquerque have been carrying on at a fine rate in Paris. Such a couple of flirts! I expect you have quite turned the head of that ⟨grey⟩ gay deceiver, he "of the Rose"[2] with your attentions[.] I had a great mind to shew the worthy Don José[3] what you said in your letter about his wifes flirtations, but I hate to make mischief in families. These poor husbands! What a taken in class of beings they are. I think it high time Madame Albuquerque was back at Madrid at her theological studies again, though I presume when she does come back she will expect every one to be at her feet and to address her in poetry. What chance has a poor plain spoken man like myself who can only talk in prose.

The Opera is all the rage at present. Persiani, Ronconi and Salvi[4] are enchanting all the world. The prices are doubled yet the house is crowded every night. The Ambassador has set on foot a subscription to make Salamanca[5] a grand present in token of the public gratitude and old Dalbergo is running about town with it and perspiring at every pore. What has excited the Ambassador to this pitch of enthusiasm I cannot imagine, unless there is some prospect of Salamancas coming into the

Cabinet. As to Dalbergo he is moved by his general propensity to honor merit, and ⟨then⟩ by his gratitude for past favors in affairs of the Bourse. I do not know what the intended present is to be. Some say a Sword—but what has that to do with Music. Others say a Cremona fiddle. It may be so, but then it must be a first rate one; for Salamanca is not disposed to play second fiddle to any body.

To morrow we have a grand dinner at the de Weisweillers at which I expect to enjoy myself greatly, especially if I should be so fortunate as to be seated beside the fair hostess. She and the princess continue to be as inseparable as two roses on one stock—and as fair to look upon—There is a poetical flight worthy of your beau M. de la Rosa—about whom you make such a fuss!

On Monday we shall have a Besa manos, at which I shall go with less good will than usual as I am quite out of humor with the folks at the Palace for their treatment of Narvaez. But that Palace is a perfidious pile. Its very construction is characteristic. So much undermining. What meets the eye is nothing to the *Underground work.*

On Friday next we have a state banquet at the Ambassadors to celebrate the fête of Luis Phelipe—if his life should be spared so long. What wonderful escapes the King has had. He is certainly under the protection of a special providence. Indeed where ⟨th⟩ is there a life more deserving of it, or more important to the general good. I feel extremely for the poor Queen; this horrible attempt will renew all her anxieties; and in the present instan[ce][6] she partook of the danger.

Beauvallon[7] of *triste* celebrity; whose duel and trial have driven him from Paris is now here figuring on the Prado in company with Cordoba and other Spanish Cavalliers. Marnix was scandalized at seeing him received into such intimacy and exclaimed against the want of moral sense in Madrid. ⟨He ought to⟩ I was surprised that Marnix was so ignorant of the *ton* here; where the lighter ones character is the better he floats in society.—

Give my kind remembrances to Mr O'Shea and Willy; and my dutiful respects to Papa Quique. I am glad to hear he had such *fun* at the theater.

Yours ever
Washington Irving

ADDRESSED: Madame / Madame O'Shea / Hotel de Bristol / Place Vendome / à
     Paris   DOCKETED: 25th. April, 1846.
MANUSCRIPT: HSA.   PUBLISHED: Penney, *Bulletin NYPL*, 63 (January, 1959),
     23–24.

1. This letter has not been located.
2. Francisco Martínez de la Rosa, former premier and now Spanish minister to France.

3. Albuquerque.

4. Fanny Persiani (1812–1867), Giorgio (1810–1890), or Sebastiano Ronconi (1810–1900), and Lorenzo Salvi (b. 1812) were popular interpreters of Italian opera. For details, see *El Heraldo*, April 10, 16, 18, 21, 24, 1846.

5. José de Salamanca y Mayol, marquis of Salamanca (1811–1883), was a financier, lawyer, and associate of Buschenthal in the Madrid Bourse. In 1847 as a member of the Moderate party, he was appointed minister of Finance.

6. WI ran off the page.

7. Beauvallon had fought in the bullfight of June 10, 1845, in which Jasper Livingston had also killed a bull. See Penney, *Bulletin NYPL*, 63 (January, 1959), 38.

1961. *To George Read*

Legation of the United States / Madrid, April 26th. 1846

George Read Esqr / Consul of the United States, Malaga

Sir

Mr Isturiz, the Minister of State, has communicated to me a letter which he had received from the Authorities at Alicant, complaining of the conduct of Mr Arthur McCulloch, Vice Consul of the United States at that port; who is represented as taking an unwarrantable part in political affairs; as exercising against the government a considerable influence which he has acquired among the lower classes, and as having even gone so far, in a case of popular insurrection as to point a cannon against the Queens troops.

Information, which I have received from another quarter; from a person of high credibility, and who has no political nor personal hostility to Mr McCulloch, concurs in representing him as very excitable on matters of politics and prone to intermeddle in popular movements.

I need not tell you how completely this is opposite to the policy of our government⟨s⟩, and to that strict neutrality, enjoined by it upon its agents, as to the political affairs of the country in which they may be stationed. If Mr McCulloch be really chargeable with the conduct imputed to him he is certainly unfit for the office he occupies.

I am not aware whether Mr McCulloch was appointed by you;[1] but as he is within your Consulate, I beg you will inform yourself carefully in the premises, and take such measures as are necessary for the politic and decorous discharge of the Consular duties in the port of Alicant

I am Sir / Very respectfully / Your Ob St
Washington Irving

MANUSCRIPT: NA, RG 84 (original and letterbook copy).

Both the original and the copy are in WI's handwriting.
The original letter is written on official stationery imprinted "Legacion / de los / Estados Unidos / en España."
At the end of the letter is written "Mr. MacCulloch is not a / nomination from the Consulate of Malaga. / G. R."

1. In his reply of May 1, 1846, Read observed, "Neither any predecessor nor myself have ever considered the jurisdiction of this Consulate as extending beyond the Kingdoms of Granada and Jaen, because the nominations of the Government at Washington have placed the last two occupants in their situations at Alicante. . . . During the last insurrection at Alicante and Carthagena it was openly stated in the public prints, that Mr. McCulloch (who is a british subject) had been engaged most actively in favoring the party opposed to the Government of Her Majesty & you may suppose that had I considered my jurisdiction as extending over that district, such conduct would not then have been passed over unnoticed by me. I presume the complaints of Mr. Isturiz must refer to that period. But under whatever circumstances Mr. McCulloch may have been delinquent, his appointment if originating from the President, cannot be cancelled by me" (NA, RG 84).

1962. *To Nicholas B. Boyle*

Legation of the United States / Madrid, April 30th. 1846

Nicholas B Boyle Esqr / Consul of the U States, Mahon

Sir,
I herewith send you your Exequatur received this day from the Department of State, and also the original commission signed by the President of the United States.

I am Sir, respectfully, / Your Obt Servt
Washington Irving

MANUSCRIPT: NA, RG 84 (letterbook copy).

This copy is in WI's handwriting.

1963.   To James Buchanan

Legation of the United States / Madrid, ↑Qu May—?↓ April 2d. 1846
[May 2, 1846]

No 80. / The Hon James Buchanan / Secretary of State Washington

Sir

The insurrection in Gallicia is completely put down. The heart of it was broken at Santiago, where the rebel General Solis[1] made a desperate stand with about two thousand men against General Concha at the head of a much superior force. The insurgents manifested great bravery. After an irregular action of several hours continuance Concha got possession of the town and obliged the insurgents, who had taken refuge in a convent, to surrender at discretion Many were killed in the action. Solis and about a dozen of his officers have since been shot. Nearly 1400 prisoners among whom are many officers are yet to be disposed of. It is thought most of them will be pardoned, or subjected to some minor punishment. Concha has been elevated to the rank of Lieutenant general.[2]

This event has relieved the government from much anxiety and may prolong the existence of the present ministry. It lessens the probability of Narvaez being recalled to Madrid; on which his friends had been calculating. It is said the embassy to Naples will be again offered to him, and, under present circumstances, it is not likely he will refuse it. The signal failure of this insurrection, at a time when there was a ministerial crisis, must dishearten the agents of revolution and may be followed by a calm of some continuance. It is thought government may relax its rigor; that the severe restrictions on the press may be modified and that other measures may be taken to conciliate the people

Under all the adverse circumstances of the times enterprize is more and more awakening in the country; joint stock companies are forming in which ↑the↓ capital which has long lain dormant in the hands of individuals is getting embarked; and it is evident that nothing is wanting but a few years of tranquility to place the kingdom in a state of comparative prosperity.

I am Sir / Respectfully / Your Obt Servt
Washington Irving

DOCKETED: Mr. Markoe
MANUSCRIPT: NA, RG 59 (letterbook copy).

This despatch is in WI's handwriting.
WI misdated this letter. It should be May 2, 1846.

1. Miguel Solís (1816–1846), who had briefly controlled Santiago and other towns in the northwestern province of Galicia, was soon defeated and executed by General José Concha. See Christiansen, *Military Power*, pp. 133–34.

2. For details, see *El Heraldo*, April 27, 28, May 1, 1846.

1964. To Messrs. Fitch Brothers & Co.

Legation of the United States / Madrid May 5th. 1846

Messrs. Fitch, brothers & Co / Marseilles.

Gentlemen,

I have this day received from the Spanish government Eleven thousand four hundred reals de Vellon, in payment of your claim for indemnification for losses sustained by the capture of the Dutch Vessel Vrouw Johanna. The above sum is in the hands of my bankers Messrs. Henry O'Shea & Co. Madrid, subject to your orders.

I am gentlemen / Very respectfully / Your friend & Servt
W Irving

MANUSCRIPT: NA, RG 84 (letterbook copy).

This copy is in WI's handwriting.

1965. To Xavier Istúriz

Legation of the United States / Madrid, May 12th. 1846

His Excellency / Don Javier Isturiz / President of the Council / Minister of State &c &c

Sir,

I have the honor to submit to your Excellency the claim of the heirs of Don Juan Ventura Morales, deceased, formerly Intendant of Louisiana when it belonged to Spain, and subsequently of Florida and of the Island of Porto Rico.

It appears that, at the time of the death of the said Juan Ventura Morales, the Spanish government was indebted to him to the amount of Twenty three thousand five hundred and seventeen Dollars for salary and other matters, as set forth and substantiated in documents which I have the honor to annex. This debt was inherited by his daughter and sole heir, Anna Matilda Morales, born in Louisiana and married to

Bernard de Marigny a citizen of the United States.

For many years the political troubles and embarrassments of Spain and its colonies discouraged Mr Marigny and his wife from urging the payment of this debt. Perhaps the opulence of their own circumstances may have rendered them in some degree negligent in the case. Those circumstances, however, are altered; a series of losses and misfortunes have reduced them from the state of affluence in which they were once enabled to live, and have rendered the liquidation of this debt of vital importance to them.

I will not detain your Excellency by any observations in support of a claim so direct and simple in its nature, being for arrears of pay faithfully earned in the service of the Spanish government by one of its loyal functionaries, and now addressed to its justice and gratitude by the child and heir of that functionary, to prevent her falling into indigence.

I am informed that, in the liquidation of claims like the one here presented, a royal order, dated in 1834 or 1835, provides that they shall bear an interest of 5 per cent per annum until paid. I trust this equitable provision will be borne in mind in the adjustment of the present claim.

I have the honor to remain, with assurances of the highest consideration,

> Your Excellencys most Obt Servt
> Washington Irving

MANUSCRIPT: NA, RG 84 (letterbook copy).

This copy is in WI's handwriting.

1966.   To Arthur MacCulloch

Legation of the United States / Madrid May 12th. 1846

Arthur M'Culloch Esqr / Consular Agent of the U S. Alicant.

Sir,

Mr Isturiz the Minister of State communicated to me about a fortnight since a letter which he had received from the Authorities of Alicant, complaining of your Conduct in taking an unwarrantable part in political affairs during times of public agitation, and in exerting your influence with the lower classes in promoting a factious opposition to the government.

Information which I have received from other sources[1] tend to corroborate this information.

As conduct of this kind is entirely at variance with the strict neutrality enjoined by our government upon its agents as to the political affairs of any country in which they may be resident, and as it is detrimental to those cordial relations which it is anxious always to maintain with Spain, I must warn you that, should you by such misconduct involve yourself in difficulties with the Spanish authorities, you may render it out of the power of this legation to be of efficient service to you, however it might feel personally inclined, and may induce the government of the United States to withdraw that trust which it at present confides to you.

> I am Sir / Very respectfully / Your ob St.
> W Irving.

MANUSCRIPT: NA, RG 84 (letterbook copy).

This copy is in WI's handwriting.

1. See George Read to WI, May 1, 1846 (NA, RG 84).

1967. *To Benjamin H. Wright*

Legation of the United States / Madrid. May 15th. 1846

Benjamin H Wright Esq / Puerto Principe. Cuba.

Sir,

Your letter and statement reached me at a time when I was absent from my post. Since my return I have stated your case both verbally and by writing to the Minister of Foreign affairs and signified your wish that an order might be issued from the Supreme tribunal of Madrid or any other competent authority, to the Audiencia of Puerto Principe; directing it to furnish you with authenticated copies of all the "Autos" in the suits brought before it and to which you had been a party; and more especially a suit brought against you by Don Melchior Aguero. I added that, being much impoverished by the expenses you had already incurred, you prayed that the documents in question might be furnished to you without further cost than that incurred in copying them. The following is a copy of the reply just received from Mr Isturiz the Minister of State and of Foreign affairs.

Palacio 11 de Mayo de 1846

Muy Señor Mio: He recibido la nota que VS se ha servido dirigirme recomendando el que se dieren ordenes a la Audiencia de Puerto Principe para que se permitiese á Mr Wright sacar copias legalizadas de todos los

Autos que ha seguido con diferentes motivos y sin otro coste que el de escribir estos documentos.

Muy sensible me es verme en la necesidad de decir a VS que la recomendacion de cualquiera Ministerio seria de todo punto ineficaz para con el tribunal Supremo de Justicia, porque con arreglo á las leyes de España no es posible sacar un juicio de la jurisdicion competente, sino por medio de los recursos que las mismas leyes concedan á las partes litigantes. Si los pleitos que Mr Wright desea que se fallen por el Tribunal Supremo de Justicia, estan en estado de venir á este tribunal la sola apelacion del interesado bastará para que sea llamada la causa original sin necesidad de sacar copias de los autos; pero si no estan en este estado quanto se haga es inútil, puesto que la ley de procedimiento tiene que seguir su curso sin que sea dado al gobierno alterar ninguno de sus tramites.

En cuanto al mal estado en que se encuentran los intereses de Mr Wright debo tranquilizar á VS. asugurandole que por los leyes de España sin permite á los pobres litigar sin pagar derechos, con tal que justifiquen su pobreza, y este recurso se facilitara á Mr Wright de la misma manera que a cualquira español.

Me lisongio de que VS. conocerá la fuerza de mi razones y el sentimiento que me cabe en no poderle complacer, haciendo justicia á mis buenos deseos en obsequio de esa Legacion y de su digño gefe.[1]

&c   &c   &c

As I expect to be relieved from my post shortly by the arrival of Mr Romulus Saunders, recently appointed to succeed me, I would reccommend to you to address to that gentleman any further communications you may have to make to this legation.

> I am Sir / Very respectfully / Your Obt St.
> Washington Irving

MANUSCRIPT: LC; NA, RG 84 (letterbook copy).

Both the original letter and the copy are in WI's handwriting.

1. Translation:

"I have received the note which your lordship has kindly sent me recommending that orders be given to the tribunal of Puerto Principe so that Mr. Wright be allowed to make legalized copies of all the proceedings that he has followed for different reasons, and without any cost other than that of writing these documents.

"It is very unfortunate for me to find myself in the necessity of saying to your lordship that the recommendation of any minister would be utterly inefficacious for the Supreme Tribunal of Justice, because in accordance with the laws of Spain it is not possible to obtain a judgment from the competent jurisdiction except by the means that these very laws may concede to the litigating parties. If the suits on which Mr. Wright wishes the Supreme Tribunal to give a verdict are in the state of being able to come to this tribunal the mere appeal of the interested party should be sufficient for the original to be called up without the necessity of making copies of the proceedings; but, if they are not in this state, whatever is done is useless, since the law of procedure must follow its course without its being possible for the government to alter any of its procedures.

"As for the bad state in which the interests of Mr. Wright find themselves, I must calm your lordship by assuring you that by the laws of Spain the poor are allowed to litigate without paying fees, provided they justify their poverty, and this recourse will be facilitated to Mr. Wright in the same manner as to any Spaniard.

"I feel certain that your lordship will recognize the strength of my arguments and the regret I feel in not being able to please you by doing justice to my good wishes in deference to that Legation and its worthy chief."

1968. To Sabina O'Shea

Madrid, June 4th. 1846

My dear Mrs OShea,

Here is your little letter of May 2d.[1] lying before me and looking as blue as blue ink and my own conscience can make it; accusing me of the long time I have suffered to elapse without writing a reply. I can only allege in excuse that for some time past I have been under the influence of one of those fits of mental torpor to which I am occasionally subject, which render all exercise of the pen distasteful and almost impossible to me; and during which all my correspondence, and every other literary occupation lies neglected. I had such a spell upon me last year about this time accompanied by lethargic tendencies which rendered me uneasy. Our good friend La Saussaye recommended a simple course of regimen and self treatment which effectually relieved me. I have recently adopted the same course, and the first symptom of its being efficacious is the attempting of this letter.

Madame Albuquerque and myself have been extremely desirous to hear of or from you since your arrival at Biaritz; to know how you are and how you have stood the journey. The letters from Mr O'Shea to the members of his house say nothing on the subject; from which we presume that you are not the worse for your travels. I feel great hope that the air and quiet and sea bathing of Biaritz will have a favorable effect.

I was all over your new house the other day in company with La Saussaye. It was in a rough, half finished state, and encumbered with scaffolding and rubbish; yet I could ⟨see⟩ ↑distinguish↓ enough of the plan and arrangements to see that La Saussaye, out of a huge rambling Spanish mansion, had carved you a very genteel commodious abode, which will abound with conveniencies. You will have noble saloons for company; and a capital, lofty dining room, with a nice apartment for every day reception, and very comfortable bed rooms. I cannot tell you with what interest I looked round upon those scenes which are to be your quiet abiding places; and to form that home, that domestic sphere, where those who best know you, know you are most loveable. I could not but feel sad at the idea that in this home I was never to see you. I have endeavored however to leave a memento of me in the house. At ⟨the⟩ one end of the "every day" saloon are two columns, one of which crowded a small door in a corner, leading into your bed room. I entreated that the column might be moved somewhat nearer to the ⟨s⟩ other, so as to give you more room for your entries and exits. De la Saussaye promised it should be done; so I beg you to bear this in mind as one improvement I have had made with a view to your comfort. And now God bless the house, and give you many, many happy days in it.

We have nothing new in Madrid; or rather if there is, I know nothing of it; as I go no wheres excepting to the Italian Opera and once in a while to the French Ambassadors. The Opera is excellent. Persiani is enchanting the public and Ronconi is in full force. The house is constantly crowded notwithstanding the high prices. The card parties at the Embassy are not as fully attended as they used to be; and of late the Princess Carini[2] has set up Loo parties in opposition; I have not heard with what success; though it is likely she may draw off some of the younger card players.

Madame de Weisweiller set off some time since with her child, under protection of her brother for England. By the last accounts she was among her friends at Paris. I believe part of her plan is to pass a little time at Biaritz on her way back, in which case you will probably meet with her. I heard her husband lately making some enquiries concerning you and expressing himself very respectfully concerning you. I have no doubt they would be very well pleased to be once more on good terms with you; and I think it would be well for you to become reconciled, for though I have no idea you would ever take much interest in an intimacy with Madame Weisweiller, still it must be an inconvenience to you to keep up a pique with one you must meet so often in the circle of your daily intercourse: and occasionally it is an inconvenience to the other members of that circle. I say this out of no particular regard for Madame Weisweiller; for though I have joked about her occasionally in my letters I have really visited her but three or four times since my return to Madrid, and then it was in consequence of invitations to dinner.

I speak on your own account: to put you in harmony with your neighbors.

I am awaiting anxiously to be relieved from my post; but my successor seems in no hurry to arrive. Indeed I have not as yet heard of his embarking to cross the Atlantic In the mean time I find we have actually declared war against Mexico.[3] I am heartily sorry for it as I fear it is but the beginning of troubles that may shake the peace of the world. Mexico it appears to me, has had sad advisers of late. She should have received our Minister, Mr Slidell[4] and have entered into negotiations with our government, which, whatever may be said to the contrary, was disposed to settle all matters between us in an amicable manner, and on terms much more advantageous than any she will gain by the course she has adopted.

I hope you will write to me soon and let me know how you are and what are your plans for the Summer. I doubt, from what I hear, that Mr. OShea will come on here before autumn. Tell him he is keeping out of fortunes way. Every body in Madrid is growing rich in a new way. The "Bolsa" is out of fashion. Joint Stock companies are all the vogue. Happy is he who can get shares. DalBorgo is busy as a certain personage in a gale of wind. He gives financial dinners to all the directors of new companies and is inflated to such a degree with new speculations that I expect he will go up like a balloon, unless he should previously burst.

Give my kind remembrances to the three OSheas and believe me ever

Your sincere friend
Washington Irving

ADDRESSED: Madame / Madame O'Shea   DOCKETED: 4th. June, 1846.
MANUSCRIPT: HSA.   PUBLISHED: Penney, *Bulletin NYPL*, 63 (January, 1959), 24–25.

1. This letter has not been located.
2. Wife of the minister from the Kingdom of Naples.
3. President Polk delivered his war message to Congress on May 11, 1846, and war was declared on May 12.
4. John Slidell (1793–1871), a lawyer and congressman from Louisiana (1843–1845), was appointed U.S. minister to Mexico in 1845. However the Mexican government refused to establish diplomatic contact through Slidell.

1969.   To Dion Acebal

Legation of the United States / Madrid June 6th. 1846

Dion Acebal, Vice Consul, U S. / Jijon (Asturias)

Sir,

I regret that I cannot comply with your request to provide you with a seal of office, a flag and the arms of the United States, the Legation not being instructed nor empowered to furnish consuls and commercial agents with any of the insignia or impliments of office.

I am Sir, respectfully / Your obt Servt
W. I.

MANUSCRIPT: NA, RG 84 (letterbook copy).

This copy is in WI's handwriting.

1970. To Bernard de Marigny

Legation of the United States / Madrid June 18th. 1846

Bernard de Marigny Esq

Sir,

Your letter of Octr. 17th. and that of Mrs Marigny of the same date, with the accompanying documents reached me at a time when I was absent from Madrid. On my return to the Capital I addressed a note to the Minister of Foreign affairs[1] stating the nature and merits of your claim and I subsequently supported it in private conversations. It was referred to the Minister of Finance, as coming within his department and it was not until yesterday that I recieved a note from the Minister of Foreign affairs communicating the decision of the Minister of Finance, which I regret to find is unfavorable to your chaim. I subjoin a copy of the note. The documents you sent me, which I percieve are copies of originals in your possession, remain in the archives of this legation subject to your orders.

I remain Sir / Very respectfully / Your Ot St
W. I.

MANUSCRIPT: NA, RG 84 (letterbook copy).

This copy is in WI's handwriting.

1. See WI to Xavier Istúriz, May 12, 1846.

1971. To Sarah Storrow

Madrid, June 23d—1846

My dear Sarah,

Your letter of the 28th.[1] reached me yesterday, giving the gratifying intelligence of your safe arrival after a pleasant and comfortable ⟨sp⟩ voyage. I shall like the worthy little Captain more than ever for his kind attention to you and your little folks[.] I am glad to see that you are all such excellent sailors. I did not suppose you would have much trouble with your children on board ship. Nice children are always favorites with passengers, to whom they furnish amusement; and in fine weather, ⟨the Ship is⟩ they have the cabins and deck to play about, with enough persons to keep an eye upon them so that they are as safe as in the nursery.

It seems strange to receive a letter from you written from the little drawing room of Sunnyside, and to think that Kate and Tutie are gambolling about the paths and green banks of that dear little domain; but it gives me a sad twinge of home sickness to think that I should be so far away. I have been kept in my tantalizing uncertainty about the Movements of my successor. It was asserted ⟨some⟩ in a recent number of Galignani's that he was actually in Paris on his way to Madrid; and the Madrid papers affirmed that he would be here in the course of a few days. Supposing that he had actually come out in some Havre ship, and was pushing on for his post, I made preparations to depart as soon after his arrival as possible, and my trunks were nearly packed when I received yesterday the letters and papers by the Steamer of the first of June, by which I found he was a passenger in that vessel, to Liverpool, and might not arrive here until Autumn. I now give up all idea of getting home before late in the year, and my mind has become reconciled to the disappointment. I am fortunate in having the kind and amiable family of the Albuquerques around me who appear more like relatives than mere friends, and who make something of a home to me even at Madrid.

Mr Storrow sent me a letter from Mrs de Wolff to you, which did not come to hand until after your departure. At his request I wrote to her explaining the circumstance and have received a charming letter in reply. She says "I am sorry my letter did not reach Mrs Storrow previous to her departure from Paris. She is indeed one whom I most truly love, and should months and even long years elapse before we meet, I feel I shall never forget her—never love her less. If I knew her address in the States I would write her now but I hope you will do it for me, saying every thing that you know a sincere affection dictates." In a post script she adds "Tell your dear niece she must write to me occasionally. She has only to address me thus in Spanish Señora Emila Renshaw de Wolff—Caracas. Venezuela for it to reach me in all Safety."

You have been kindly mentioned repeatedly in letters from my most amiable friend Mrs O'Shea, who is at present at Biaritz at the little country retreat which Mr O'Shea has built for the benefit of co[a]st[2] air and Sea bathing in the Summer months, when Madrid is an oven. ⟨I wish I were with them⟩ I have promised to pay them a visit there on my way homeward. I wish I were there at present for the Summer heats have commenced unusually early this year and are quite ennervating.

I shall look for a letter from you by the Steamer which was to leave New York about the 7th. of June: though it is very possible in the hurry of engagements and occupations you may not find leisure and mood to write: but you are now surrounded by every thing and every body most interesting to me, and your letters will be more acceptable than ever. I want to know all about those little travellers Kate and Tutie and how they make out among their American relatives.

Let me know what articles are in most want at the cottage, that I may supply the wants at Paris or London, where I can get the articles cheap. ⟨and⟩ Of course I cannot afford to go to much expense, but a few things well chosen may serve to set off the little establishment to advantage. I am affraid it must begin to grow threadbare after so many years of constant use.

I fear I shall not be able to write to your mother by this opportunity. Give my love to her and my hearty congratulations. I hope Kate still remembers Unty—as to Tutie she must long since, have forgotten me—

Your affecnt uncle
W I.

ADDRESSED: Mrs Sarah Storrow / care of E Irving Esqr / New York.
MANUSCRIPT: Yale.

1. This and the other letters mentioned herein have not been located.
2. WI omitted the bracketed letter.

1972. To Pierre M. Irving

Madrid, June 24, 1846

I regret exceedingly that we have got engaged in a war with Mexico. That power has been badly advised; she should have received Mr. Slidell, and the matters between us might have been amicably arranged.

She has been induced to believe that certain foreign powers would back her, very probably; if so, she will find that, after all their tampering, they will leave her in the lurch. The situation in which our little army under General Taylor[1] was placed, apparently cut off from his supplies, and surrounded by a superior force, gave me great uneasiness. I feared some humiliating blow, and saw that the English press was preparing to trumpet it forth to Europe with the customary insults and exaggerations. I feared, also, that a blow of the kind would tend to prolong the war, as we could not think of peace until we had completely obliterated the disgrace. When I read, therefore, the account of the gallant manner in which Taylor and his little army had acquitted themselves, and the generous manner in which they had treated their vanquished enemies, the tears absolutely started into my eyes, and a load was taken from my heart. I sincerely hope this brilliant victory will be followed up by magnanimous feeling on the part of our Government, and that the war may be brought to a speedy close on fair and honorable terms.

PUBLISHED: PMI, III, 388–89.

1. Zachary Taylor (1784–1850), who spent forty years in the U.S. Army, was commander of the Army of Occupation on the Mexican border in 1845–1846. After he had established Fort Texas on the bank of the Rio Grande River opposite Matamoros, the Mexican general, Mariano Arista, notified him that the Mexicans regarded hostilities as already started. On April 24, 1846, a Mexican force crossed the river and attacked an American scouting party, killing eleven, wounding five, and capturing forty-seven. On May 8 Taylor with 2,300 men defeated 6,000 Mexican troops at Palo Alto, and the next day routed the Mexican army at Resaca de la Palma and drove it back across the Rio Grande.

1973. To Xavier Istúriz

Legation of the United States / Madrid, June 24th. 1846

His Excellency / Don Xavier Isturiz / &c &c &c

Sir,

On the 27th. of May 1844 I had the honor to address a note to his Excellency Don Alexander Mon, at that time Minister of State, ad interim, representing the case of Mr James Wood, an American merchant residing at Canary; who having imported merchandize into the said island on the faith of paying duties in conformity to the privileged or exclusive tariff granted to the Canaries; found his merchandize on its arrival, subjected to duties comfortably to the Spanish peninsular Tariff, without due notice having been given of this change of the Custom House regulations The consequence was a loss to him of upwards of one thousand dollars, for which he claimed indemnification

I am happy to say that the justice of his claim being made apparent to Her Majestys government, orders were issued by the Minister of Finance, for the relief required.

By letters just received from Mr James Cullen[1] Consul of the United States for the Canary islands, I find that other American houses, resident in those islands are exactly in the same category with Mr Wood, having been subject to the same e⟨x⟩rroneous exaction of duties. I subjoin documents illustrative of the case, by which your Excellency will percieve that the Intendent of the Canary islands, though profoundly convinced of the propriety of extending the relief granted to Mr Wood, to all others who should be in like manner aggrieved, yet did not feel himself authorised to do so without express instructions from Superior authority.

Confiding, therefore, in the well known justice and equity of Her Majestys government I most respectfully reccommend the case to your Excellencys attention, and, as the principle ↑involved in it,↓ has already been admitted and acted upon in the case of Mr Wood, I trust the matter will, in the present instance meet with prompt despatch.

I have the honor to renew to your Excellency the assurance of the high consideration with which I have the honor to remain

Your Excellencys Obedt. Servt
W. I.

MANUSCRIPT: NA, RG 84 (letterbook copy).

This copy is in WI's handwriting.

1. In a letter of May 5, 1846, from Tenerife, Cullen outlined the points which WI presents in his letter. WI mistakenly called him "James" instead of "Joseph."

1974. To Sabina O'Shea

Madrid, June 24th. 1846.

My dear Mrs O'Shea,

Your letter of the 9th. inst.[1] reached me safely after being about twelve days on the journey. The mail must travel rapidly in the neighborhood of Biaritz. I am glad to find you are doing so well on the sea coast and congratulate you on not being in Madrid where the summer heats have set in with such violence that we are all baking and broiling, and some are already done brown.

After I wrote you last we had a gay banquet in Mr Bulwers garden, under an arbour over run with clambering vines There were several ladies present, including Madame de Bresson and Madame Albuquerque. The whole was got up of a sudden, but was done in good style and went off charmingly. A band of music was stationed among the trees at a distance and played a variety of pieces from popular operas. Bulwer was all gallantry and softness, and put me in mind of Solomon in his song: "I am come into my garden.—↑my sister, my spouse.↓ I have gathered my myrrh with my spice. I have eaten my honey comb with my honey. Eat, o friends; drink, yea drink abundantly o beloved."[2] Upon the whole it was one of the nicest little impromptu parties I have ever seen in Madrid.

Last evening, or rather last night, being the Eve of St John we kept the verbena[3] at Mr Arcos; where some of the elite of the Madrid society assembled toward midnight and danced in defiance of hot weather. I accompanied the Albuquerques there, but did not remain much above half an hour. The ladies all looked very well, their complexions being in a glow with the fervor of the season. Madame Albuquerque intends to write you an account of the party ⟨and⟩ I will, therefore, refer you to her for particulars[.] I left her talking with the Campoalange[4] who was arrayed in all her virgin charms

I have just learnt that my Successor Mr Saunders, arrived by the last Steamer and is actually in London. I have written to him to know when it is likely he will arrive in Madrid. I apprehend however, it will be late in the Season, as he will probably linger in Paris and else where, on the road.

I have also letters from my niece Mrs Storrow who was safely arrived in the United States and enjoying herself in my cottage with her children frolicking about the paths and green banks. It is a sad disappointment to me that I should be absent at the time of her visit there. She had a most comfortable and pleasant voyage and a joyful meeting with her mother and all her connexions.

You spoke to me in a former letter about engaging Lorenzo, in case he should not enter into the service of Madame Albuquerque: I had to give him up to her on my arrival, though he still continues to serve me as effectually as ever. Madame Albuquerque finds him all that I had represented him and would be sorry indeed to part with him. I would advise you, however, to secure him whenever the Albuquerques go away.

I paid another visit to your new house sometime since, and was gratified to find that my suggestions had been adopted in arranging the two columns at the end of the Saloon. I beg you to hint to Mr. O'Shea that as these two columns are set up at the entrance to his Harem it would be well for him to inscribe the old motto between them, *Ne plus ultra!*

With kind remembrances to all the O'Sheas; and my particular duties to Papa Quique

Your affectionate friend
Washington Irving

ADDRESSED: Madame / Madame O'Shea   DOCKETED: Washington Irving [*right edge of top of envelope*] / 24th. June 1846. [*verso*]
MANUSCRIPT: HSA.   PUBLISHED: Penney, *Bulletin NYPL*, 63 (January, 1959), 26.

1. This and other letters mentioned herein have not been located.
2. See Song of Solomon 5:1.
3. A special observance on the eve of a saint's day.
4. María Manuela de Negrete y Cepeda Adorno de la Torre, countess of Campo de Alange (d. 1883), whose husband was a firm supporter of Isabella II. See Penney, *Bulletin NYPL*, 63 (January, 1959), 38.

1975.   *To Xavier Istúriz*

Legation of the United States / Madrid June 26th. 1846

His Excellency / Don Xavier Isturiz / President of the Council / Minister of State of / Foreign Affairs &c

Sir

I beg leave most respectfully yet earnestly to solicit from your Excellency a definite reply in the case of Mr Michael Drawsin Harang, a citizen of the United States, claiming indemnification for exhorbitant duties wrongfully levied on the estate of his deceased father by the Intendente of Porto Rico.

This claim, of many years standing has ↑been↓ too often and too fully stated in notes from this Legation[1] to need any further specification at present. It has long since been referred from the department of State to the department of finance, and I was led, as far back as July 1844, to expect the immediate decision of the Minister of ⟨T⟩ the latter department in the matter

As it is evident, therefore, that her Majestys government has had more than ample time fully to possess itself of all the merits of the case, I trust I shall not be considered importunate in once more asking that decisive answer, which I have so long been entitled to expect

I avail myself of this occasion to renew to your Excellency the assurance of the high consideration and respect with which I have the honor to remain

Your Excellencys most Obt St.
Washington Irving

MANUSCRIPT: NA, RG 84 (letterbook copy).

This copy is in WI's handwriting.

1. See WI to Count Almodóvar, September 24, 1842; and to the marquis de Viluma, June 16, 1844.

1976. To Xavier Istúriz

Legation of the United States / Madrid, June 28th. 1846

His Excellency / Don Javier Isturiz / &c &c &c

Sir

Having received information that my Successor, Mr Romulus M. Saunders, appointed Envoy Extraordinary and Minister Plenipotentiary of the United States at this court, is actually on his way to Madrid and will be here in the course of a few days, I will be much obliged to your Excellency if you will cause, with as little delay as convenient, the necessary orders to be issued to the Custom house at Irun for the admission of his baggage and effects duty free.

I have the honor to subscribe myself

with high consideration / Your Excellencys most Ob St.
Washington Irving

MANUSCRIPT: NA, RG 84 (letterbook copy).

This copy is in WI's handwriting.

1977. To ——

[Madrid, June?, 1846]

I have some Scotch blood in my veins, and a little of the feeling, with respect to my cottage, that a poor devil of a laird has for the stronghold that has sheltered his family. Nay, I believe it is the having such an object to work for, which spurs me on to combat and conquer difficulties; and if I succeed in weathering a series of hard times without striking my flag, I shall be largely indebted to my darling little Sunnyside for furnishing me the necessary stimulus. So no more talk of abandoning the cottage. In the words of Thomas the Rhymer[1]—

> "Betide, betide, whate'er betide,
> Haig shall be Haig of Bemerside."

PUBLISHED: PMI, III, 394.

1. Thomas of Erceldoune (1220?–1297?), called "the Rhymer," is associated in Scottish folklore with prophecies concerned with the future of Scotland. Walter Scott included "Thomas the Rhymer" in his *Minstrelsy of the Scottish Border*, of which one section was his original composition. The lines which WI quotes have not been located.

1978. *To James Buchanan*

Legation of the United States / Madrid July 2d. 1846

No. 81. / The Hon / James Buchanan / Secretary of State. Washington

Sir,

I have the honor to enclose the accounts and vouchers of this Legation for the Second quarter of 1846 shewing a balance against the United States of $2.26 which will be carried to their debit in my next account.

I am Sir / Very respectfully / Your Obt Servt.
Washington Irving

DOCKETED: Recd 11 Aug./Mr. Markoe
MANUSCRIPT: NA, RG 59.

1979. *To Henry G. Hubbard*

Legation of the United States / Madrid, July 2d. 1846

Henry G Hubbard Esqr / Consul of the United States / St Johns. Porto Rico.

Sir,

I have the honor to forward herewith your Exequatur, received this day from the Minister of State, also the original commission signed by the President of the United States

Very respectfully / Your Obt St.
—W. I.

MANUSCRIPT: NA, RG 84 (letterbook copy).

This copy is in WI's handwriting.

1980. *To Xavier Istúriz*

Legation of the United States / Madrid July 3d. 1846

His Excellency / Don Javier Isturiz / &c &c &c

Sir,
I will be much obliged to Your Excellency if, in addition to the orders issued to the Custom House at Irun, for the free admission of the baggage and effects of my successor, Mr Romulus M Saunders, you will cause similar orders to be issued to the Custom House at Cadiz, for which port, I understand, he has caused his most important effects to be shipped

I have the honor to remain

with high consideration / Your Excellencys Obt St
W. I.

MANUSCRIPT: NA, RG 84 (letterbook copy).

This copy is in WI's handwriting.

1981. *To Xavier Istúriz*

Legation of the United States / Madrid, July 6th. 1846

His Excellency / Don Xavier Isturiz / &c &c &c

Sir,
Being on the point of sending a few packages of my effects to Malaga, to be shipped to the United States; I will thank Your Excellency to cause the necessary orders to be given that any examination of them which may be customary, may take place in Madrid before the packages are closed; in order that, being forwarded under seal, they may be exempted from further search at the place of Shipment

I make this request in consequence of finding that, for want of such precaution, the effects of my predecessor Mr Vail, were subjected to very vexatious examination and derangement at the Malaga Custom House

I avail myself of this occasion to renew to Your Excellency the assurance of the high consideration with which I have the honor to remain

Your Excellencys obt St
WI.

MANUSCRIPT: Archivo de Ministerio de Asuntes Exteriores (Madrid); NA, RG 84 (letterbook copy).
Both the original and the copy are in WI's handwriting.

1982.   To Alexander Burton

Madrid July 10th. 1846

Alexander Burton Esq / Consul of the United States, Cadiz

Dear Sir,

Having understood that my Successor Genl Romulus M Saunders had caused his heavy luggage to be shipped to Cadiz to your address, I applied to the Minister of State to have the necessary orders issued for their free admission. In reply he writes under the date of the 8th. inst. "Tengo la honra de manifestar a V.S. que por el Ministerio de Hacienda se han comunicado a las Aduanas las ordenes convenientes para que los equipajes de Mr Saunders gocen a su entrada en el Reino de todas las franquicias á que tiene derecho por su calidad de Representate de los Estados Unidos"[1]

I am, Dear Sir / Very respectfully yours
W. I.

MANUSCRIPT: NA, RG 84 (letterbook copy).

This copy is in WI's handwriting.

1. Translation: "I have the honor of expressing to your lordship that the secretary of the treasury has communicated to the Customs the pertinent orders so that the baggage of Mr. Saunders will have upon its entry into the Kingdom all the exemptions to which he is entitled by virtue of being a representative of the United States."

1983. To Thomas W. Storrow, Jr.

Madrid July 12th. 1846

My dear Storrow,

I duly received your letter of June 20,[1] and have had others from Sarah, giving me the gratifying intelligence of the prosperous voyage and safe arrival of herself and her little ones. They appear to be enjoying themselves greatly among their friends and relatives; and I am thinking they will have made a lucky escape from the extreme heat prevailing and threatening to prevail this Summer in Europe. I regret extremely that I shall not be able to see you before your departure. I at one time hoped we might make the ⟨y⟩ voyage together; but the delay of Mr Saunders prevents all chance. By a letter recently received from him I am given to expect his arrival here about the 20th. and I shall take my departure as soon afterwards as official arrangements will permit; making the best of my way to England to pay a visit to the Shrubbery.

I left a trunk of clothes &c at the house in Rue de la Victoire. I will thank you to have it placed where I can get at it should I come to Paris; or can have it Shipped to New York, should I send orders to that effect.

I congratulate you on the fair and honorable settlement of the Oregon question; ⟨which⟩ and the decisive victory we have obtained on the Rio Grande. They are two events calculated to elevate the national name in Europe; and I trust will both have a beneficial effect on the national prosperity.

Very affectionately yours
Washington Irving

Thomas W Storrow Jr Esqr

MANUSCRIPT: Yale.

1. This and other letters mentioned herein have not been located.

1984. To Xavier Istúriz

Legation of the United States / Madrid July 17th. 1846

His Excellency / Don Xavier Isturiz / &c &c &c

Sir

In compliance with your Excellencys request I now repeat in writing the purport of the communication I had the honor verbally to make to you yesterday morning.

On the evening ⟨of the⟩ preceding I had received despatches from my government dated the 14th. may giving me the important intelligence that on the preceding day the President of the United States had issued a proclamation declaring the existence of a state of war between the United States and Mexico; and announcing that a strict blockade of the ports of Mexico both on the Atlantic and the Pacific was about to be established. These facts I was instructed immediately to communicate to Her Majestys government. By some unaccountable delay the despatches were upwards of two months in reaching me, instead of about twenty four days. This will account to your Excellency for the apparent tardiness with which this important intelligence contained in them has been officially announced to Her Majestys government.

I was furthermore instructed to accompany this intelligence with some explanation of the policy and feelings of the government of the United States in regard to this war. The long interval which has elapsed, however, since the date of my despatches, and the various documents published in the interim by our government, render any lengthened exposition of the kind superfluous: I shall content myself therefore with a brief summary of facts.

Whatever may be said of the ambitious designs and the aggressive policy of the United States with regard to Mexico, I feel authorized to assure your Excellency that we have engaged in this war with extreme reluctance. It is our interest, and it has ever been our inclination that Mexico should be an independent and powerful republic, and that our relations with her should be of the most friendly character The Successive revolutions by which she has been afflicted and the avaricious and unprincipled men who have placed themselves at the head of her government have brought her to the brink of ruin. We feel deeply interested that she should establish a stable government, sufficiently powerful and pacific to prevent and punish aggressions upon her neighbors. We have conducted ourselves to her accordingly; but our friendly dispositions and manifestations have met with no return. On the contrary, our intercourse for many years has been marked on her part by a series of wrongs and

insults. These she pledged her public faith, in solemn treaties, to redress; but the treaties have been disregarded and the wrongs complained
of have been reiterated. Our commerce with her has been almost anni-
hilated by the outrages and extortions practised by her authorities upon
our merchants, while all attempts to obtain indemnity have been fruitless. For some years we have incurred much of the expense and suffered
many of the inconveniencies of war, while nominally at peace. Still we
have endured all this with a patience and forbearance which we should
never have exercised toward a more formidable power. Ultimately the
Mexican government chose to consider the annexation of Texas to the
United States as a violation of her rights, though that republic was an
independent power, owing no allegiance to Mexico, constituting no part
of her territory or rightful jurisdiction, and although its independence had
been acknowledged by the most powerful and enlightened nations of
Europe. She accordingly broke off all diplomatic relations with us, avow-
ing an intention to make war upon us either by open declaration or an
invasion of the annexed territory. As a matter of self preservation we
prepared to repel the threatened aggression. Still we persisted in our efforts for recconciliation and endeavored to ascertain whether Mexico
notwithstanding all her menaces and warlike demonstrations, might not
be disposed to settle all our differences in an amicable manner. Having
received informal assurances from the Mexican government that it was
willing to renew diplomatic intercourse and would accredit a Minister
from the United States, we waived all ceremony as to the manner of
reviving our relations, assum⟨ed⟩ing the initiative and sending an Envoy
Extraordinary and Minister plenipotentiary to Mexico, clothed with full
powers to adjust and definitively settle all pending difficulties between
the two countries including those of boundary between Mexico and the
State of Texas. Our envoy was courteously received at Vera Cruz but
before he had time to enter upon his mission a Military revolution took
place in Mexico and General Paredes[1] took possession of the government
by force of arms. Under his administration the form of government was
changed as well as the high functionaries by whom it was administered
Our Envoy was refused reception and credence notwithstanding that he
came under the plighted faith of the Mexican government. No attempt
was made to ascertain what propositions he was empowered to offer;
no propositions were suggested on the part of Mexico. His passports were
given him and the door of peace was in a manner shut in his face.

Nothing now was heard from Mexico but threats of immediate invasion
for the recovery of Texas which she persisted in claiming as her rightful
territory. Troops were embodied and marched by her in that direction;
while the troops of the United States were ordered to advance to the
frontier but to abstain from all aggressive acts towards Mexico or Mexi-

can citizens, and to regard the relations between that republic and the United States as peaceful, unless she should declare war or commit acts ↑of hostility↓ indicative of a state of war. The public papers have informed your Excellency of the result. After the armies had remained encamped on the opposite banks of the Rio del Norte which we claim as the boundary of Texas, the Mexican troops crossed the river, surprised and killed some of our soldiers and took others prisoner. When these facts were made known to the Congress of the United States all party distinctions vanished before the necessity of asserting the national rights and vindicating the National honor, and the President was authorized, by a vote of unprecedented unanimity, to declare the existence of war between the United States and Mexico. There were but fourteen dissenting voices in the House of Assembly and two in the Senate.

Such is a summary of the circumstances which have led to this war; it has in a manner been forced upon us by the conduct of Mexico; who has either mistaken our forbearance for pusillanimity or has been edged on by evil councils to take advantage of a crisis when we appeared to be on the point of hostilities with England on the Oregon question.

I am instructed to say that we go to war with Mexico solely for the purpose of conquering an honorable and permanent peace. Whilst we intend to prosecute the war with vigor both by land and sea, we shall bear the olive branch in one hand and the sword in the other and whenever she will accept the former the latter will be sheathed

The events which have occurred since the opening of this war are in accordance with the temper and principles above expressed. It has been commenced with vigor and success; but success in the field has been followed up by humanity, moderation and by a scrupulous respect for private property and personal rights.

The Blockade heretofore mentioned has now been some time in existence. The object is to deprive Mexico of the revenues derived from customs, in the hope of speedily compelling her to offer or accept reasonable terms, and to induce foreign nations, who now enjoy the monopoly of her commerce, to exert their influence with her government in effecting a fair and honorable peace. The liberal mode in which this blockade has hitherto been conducted by the officers of our Navy, has been acknowledged in the English journals.

There is one circumstance to which I am especially instructed to draw the attention of your Excellency. Apprehensions were entertained by the government of the United States, at the date of my despatches, that two Mexican Steamers which had recently been transferred to Havana, were sent there for the purpose of privateering against the commerce of the United States; and that an attempt might be made to fit out privateers with the like object, in the ports of Cuba and Porto Rico, bearing letters of marque and reprisal from the Mexican government. I was instructed, therefore, to desire that your Excellency would transmit instructions to the authorities of Cuba and Porto Rico to be vigilant in executing the 14th. article of the Treaty of the United States with Spain, in 1795, and in preventing the equipment and departure of all vessels fitted for privateering. It would be a circumstance lamentable in itself and full of danger to the friendly relations we are so anxious to preserve and cherish with Spain, should the ports of Cuba and Porto Rico become stations whence privateers might depredate upon our commerce.

I feel confident that the good faith manifested towards us on all other occasions by the Spanish government will continue throughout the present conflict in which we are unwillingly involved, and that it will discountenance every thing calculated to add to the evils of a war which it is the desire of the United States to conduct and terminate with as little injury as possible to the general interests of the civilized world.

I have the honor to subscribe myself, with the highest consideration,

Your Excellencys obt Sert
W.I.

MANUSCRIPT: NA, RG 84 (letterbook copy); NA, RG 59 (copy); Va.–Barrett (draft copy). PUBLISHED: Manning, *Diplomatic Correspondence*, 354–57; STW, II, 195–96 (in part).

All copies are in WI's handwriting.

1. Mariano Paredes y Arrillaga (1797–1849), a Mexican general and politician who had entered Mexico City on January 2, 1846, and set up a military dictatorship with himself as president, refused to recognize or meet with John Slidell, the U.S. envoy. See R. S. Ripley, *The War with Mexico*, 2 vols. (New York, 1970), I, 69.

1985.   To James Buchanan

Legation of the United States / Madrid July 18th. 1846

No 83. / The Hon. James Buchanan / Secretary of State. Washington

Sir,

Your despatches No 52 and 53 though dated the 14th of May last, did not reach me until three evenings since. (the 15th. inst.) Their arrival relieved me from a somewhat irksome position. The existence of a state of war between the United States and Mexico and of our blockade of the Mexican ports had been known throughout Europe for several weeks, and officially announced by our diplomatic agents at other courts, yet I had not received a line from government on the subject, nor was authorized to make any official communication to this cabinet about matters so closely affecting the interests and sympathies of Spain.

I felt the embarrassment of the circumstances in the interviews I have had of late with Mr Isturiz the prime minister, in the course of which he has more than once incidentally spoken of the war and manifested some solicitude concerning it; but I had to confess myself without official instructions on the matter, and could only give my private opinions as to the causes which led to it, and the temper and spirit with which it would probably be carried on. I am happy to find those opinions borne out by my present instructions.

I mention these circumstances to account for some little sensitiveness I may have evinced in my last despatch, on the subject of correspondence, and from which I have been happily relieved by the receipt of the despatches in question.

On the morning after their receipt I had a long conversation with Mr Isturiz on the subject of their contents, and subsequently at his request, passed him a note, to the same purport, a copy of which I enclose. He expressed much regret at the war; said it was the ardent desire of Her Majestys government that an honorable peace might speedily be effected but assured me that Spain would observe throughout the strictest neutrality. He also said that he would issue orders by the first opportunity, to the authorities of Cuba and Porto Rico, to exert their utmost vigilance in preventing any attempts to fit out privateers against us in those islands.

In the course of this conversation I took occasion again to disclaim the grasping and unprincipled avidity of empire charged upon us by the British press and which I feared had gained some credence in Spain. Fortunately Great Britain had recently furnished a signal refutation of her own calumnies; for, after charging us with the most flagitious grasping after our neighbors territory in the Oregon question, she had just settled that question on terms which we had repeatedly offered her and which are now declared, in her parliament, to be fair and honorable to both nations.

In fact the manner in which we have passed through the great ordeal of the Oregon question, and the firm and fearless way in which we have maintained our rights, to the very verge of a war with the most powerful nation in the world, will have a salutary effect on all our foreign relations. I already feel the benefit of it in my own sphere; and rejoice in seeing the national name breaking with fresh lustre through a cloud of prejudice which had artfully of late years been cast over it in Europe.

The opening of this Mexican war has also been propitious: should it be carried on in the same spirit and temper in which it has commenced, and brought to a speedy triumphant and magnanimous close, the present year will add a page to our national history of which every American patriot may well be proud.

I am Sir / Very respectfully / Your Obt Sert
Washington Irving

P S. Despatch No 51. has not yet come to hand. I presume it will be brought by Genl. Saunders whose arrival in Madrid is daily expected.

DOCKETED: Mr. Markoe [*upper left corner of page 1*] / No. 83. W. Irving. Madrid. 18 July 1846
MANUSCRIPT: NA, RG 59. PUBLISHED: Manning, *Diplomatic Correspondence*, 357–58; STW, II, 386 (in part).

This despatch is in WI's handwriting.

1986. *To Reuben G. Beasley*

Legation of the United States / Madrid, July 20th. 1846

Reuben G Beasley Esq / Consul of the United States. Havre

Sir,
I enclose a bill of Henry O'Shea & Co of Madrid on Messrs. Gil Kennedy & Co of Paris for One hundred and seventeen francs, twenty five centimes, being the amount of your postage account against this legation from April 9th. 1845 to June 30th. 1846 inclusive

Very respectfully / Your obt St.
Washington Irving

MANUSCRIPT: NA, RG 84 (letterbook copy).

This copy is in WI's handwriting.

1987. *To Xavier Istúriz*

Legation of the United States / Madrid, July 22d. 1846

His Excellency / Dn Xavier Isturiz / &c &c &

Sir
Mr Romulus M Saunders, appointed by the President of the United States to succeed me as Envoy Extraordinary and Minister Plenipotentiary

at Her Majestys Court, has arrived in this City and is desirous that your
Excellency would name a day and hour when it would be convenient for
you to receive from him in person a copy of his letter of credence.

I shall, at the same time, have the honor of presenting to your Excellency a copy of the letter of the President to Her Majesty, announcing
my recall, and beg your Excellency will have the kindness to ascertain in
what manner it will be most agreeable to Her Majesty to receive the
original

I have the honor to remain with the highest consideration

> Your Excellencys Obt Servt
> **W. I.**

MANUSCRIPT: Archivo de Ministerio de Asuntes Exteriores (Madrid); NA, RG 84
(letterbook copy).

Both the letter and the copy are in WI's handwriting.

1988. *To Pierre M. Irving*

[Madrid], July 25, 1846

I, of course, am busy preparing to pass the legation into his [General
Romulus Saunders, WI's successor] hands as soon as he has been accredited, which will probably be two or three days hence. I shall then
take my departure almost immediately, having made all my travelling
preparations.

PUBLISHED: PMI, III, 390–91.

1989. *To Catharine Paris*

Madrid July 25th, 1846

My dear Sister,

I received a day or two since your letter of June 28th.[1] as likewise one
from my dear Sarah. The accounts they give of your happy meetings
with your children are of the most heartfelt and gratifying interest to me;
the only drawback is that I should not be present to Share your happiness.

It has been most unlucky for me that Sarahs visit to the U States should
have been in this year; or rather that I should have been detained so
much longer than I had anticipated, at my post, we might otherwise have

been together in the united states. I now fear I shall hardly have time to see her before she re embarks for Europe. Genl Saunders, my successor arrived here three or four days since. I am very well pleased with him. He is highly respectable in appearance and manners and I have no doubt will represent us very creditably at this Court. I am ⟨well⟩ happy to leave the mission in such respectable hands.

I am very busy as you may suppose, in winding up the affairs of the legation and preparing for my departure. In the course of two or three days I shall have an audience from the Queen to deliver the letter of the President to her, announcing my recall, and to take my leave. Genl Saunders will then have his audience, to deliver his letter of credence and to be accredited. My functions then cease, and I have nothing to do but pay leave taking visits of Ceremony and friendship, and set off on my homeward route. I shall make my way to England with as little delay as possible and repair to the Shrubbery. What time I shall embark for New York is yet uncertain.

I shall have a sad parting with my friends the Albuquerques; in whose family I have felt myself completely as if among relatives

Farewell my dear Sister, this is a very brief and hasty letter but I have no time to write a better or longer one If I do not write to Sarah tell her ⟨it⟩ the reason and give her my best love.

Your affectionate brother
W. I.

MANUSCRIPT: Yale.

1. This and other letters mentioned herein have not been located.

1990. To Pierre M. Irving

[Madrid, Late July, 1846]

The settlement of the Oregon question is a vast event for our national credit and national prosperity. The war with Mexico will in all probability be wound up before long, and then our commercial affairs will have no external dangers to apprehend for a long series of years.

I have reason to congratulate myself that, in a quiet way, I was enabled, while in England, to facilitate the frank and confiding intercourse of Mr. McLane and Lord Aberdeen, which has proved so beneficial to the settlement of this question; so that, though I did not publish the pamphlet I had prepared, my visit to England was not without its utility.

PUBLISHED: PMI, III, 390.

This letter may be a part of the one dated July 25, 1846. Without the holograph letter it is not possible to ascertain with absolute certainty.

1991.   To W. H. L. E. Bulwer?

[Madrid, July?, 1846]

Bulwer, I should deplore exceedingly a war with England, for depend upon it, if we must come to blows, it will be serious work for both. You might break our head at first, but by Heaven! we would break your back in the end.

PUBLISHED: PMI, III, 390.

1992.   To Pierre M. Irving?

[Madrid, June–July? 1846]

A rancorous prejudice against us has been diligently inculcated of late years by the British press, and it is daily producing its fruits of bitterness.

PUBLISHED: PMI, III, 390.

1993.   To James Buchanan

Legation of the United States / Madrid August 1st. 1846.

No 84. / The Hon James Buchanan / Secretary of State, Washington

Sir,

Since I had last the honor of addressing you I have received despatch No. 50—by the hands of General Romulus M Saunders, informing me of the appointment of that gentleman to succeed me in the mission to this court.

On the evening of the 29th. ulto. I had an audience of the Queen to receive the letter from the president announcing my recall, when I made her the following address in Spanish.

Madam, I have the honor to deliver into the hands of your Majesty a letter from the President of the United States announcing my recall from the post of Envoy Extraordinary and Minister Plenipotentiary in this court.

I am charged by the President to express, on delivering this letter to Your Majesty, his constant and earnest desire to maintain the amicable relations which so happily exist between the two countries.

For my own part, I can assure Your Majesty that I shall carry into private life the same ardent desire for the wellfare of Spain, and the same deep interest in the fortunes and happiness of its youthful sovreign which have actuated me in my official carreer; and I now take leave of Your Majesty wishing you, from the bottom of my heart, a long and happy life and a reign which may form a glorious epoch in the history of this country

The following was the Queen's reply.

Con mucho sentimiento mio recibo el anuncio de vuestra llamamiento del puesto de Enviado Extraordinario y Ministro plenipotentiario circa de mi persona

Muy gratos me son los votos que expresais por la felicidad de los Españoles; en alla fondo la que desenes a mi persona y la gloria de mi reinado.

Podeis llevas á la vida privada el intimo convencimiento de que vuestra leal y franco proceder ha contribuido á estrechar las amistosas relaciones que existen entre la America del Norte y la Nacion Española y que vuestras distinguidas prendas personales han gañado en mi corazon el aprecio que por mas de un titulo mereceis.[1]

On last evening (31st July) General Saunders had his audience wherein he delivered his letters of credence and was duly accredited. I have therefore, this morning, delivered the archives and properties of the Legation into his hands, together with an inventory of them, as received by me from Mr Vail, and as augmented during my mission. The archives and properties having been found on examination, to agree with the inventory, I have received from Genl Saunders a receipt for the same.

I have the honor to enclose a statement of my account with the government up to the present day.

I am Sir / Very respectfully / Your Obt St.
Washington Irving

DOCKETED: Mr. Markoe. [*upper left corner, page 1*] / No 84. W. Irving. Madrid 1 Aug. 1846
MANUSCRIPT: NA, RG 59; NYPL—Berg Collection (draft copy).   PUBLISHED: STW, II, 196 (in part).

This despatch is in WI's handwriting.

1. WI has given a translation of the queen's speech in his letter to Catharine Paris, [Early August, 1846].

1994. To Catharine Paris

[Madrid, Early August, 1846]

A few evenings since,[1] I had my audience of the Queen, to deliver the letter of the President announcing my recall. Ten o'clock was the hour appointed. Though sated with court ceremonies, I could not but feel a little sensitive on visiting the royal palace for the last time, and passing through its vast apartments but partially lighted up. I found the Queen in an inner cabinet, attended by the Minister of State and several ladies and gentlemen in waiting. I had prepared my speech in Spanish, which was to the following effect:

"Madam:

"I have the honor to deliver into the hands of your Majesty a letter from the President of the United States, announcing my recall from the post of Envoy Extraordinary and Minister Plenipotentiary in this Court.

"I am charged by the President to express, on delivering this letter to your Majesty, his constant and earnest desire to maintain the amicable relations which so happily exist between the two countries.

"For my own part, I can assure your Majesty that I shall carry with me into private life the same ardent desire for the welfare of Spain, and the same deep interest in the fortunes and happiness of its youthful sovereign, which have actuated me during my official career; and I now take leave of your Majesty, wishing you, from the bottom of my heart, a long and happy life, and a reign which may form a glorious epoch in the history of this country."

The following is as close a translation as I can make of the Queen's reply:

"It is with much regret that I receive the announcement of your recall from the post of Envoy Extraordinary and Minister Plenipotentiary of the United States near my person.

"Very gratifying to me are the wishes you express for the happiness of Spain. On that, I found the happiness which you desire for me personally, and the glory of my reign.

"You may take with you into private life the intimate conviction that your frank and loyal conduct has contributed to draw closer the amicable relations which exist between North America and the Spanish nation, and that your distinguished personal merits have gained in my heart the appreciation which you merit by more than one title."

This little speech reads stiff in translation, but it is very graceful and gracious in the original, and I have been congratulated repeatedly on receiving one so much out of the cold, commonplace style of diplomacy. In fact, my farewell interview with the whole of the royal family was extremely satisfactory. * * *

The Minister of State (Mr. Isturiz) has likewise been uncommonly cordial in his expressions of regret at my departure. In a word, from the different members of the Cabinet, and from my colleagues of the diplomatic corps, I have met with nothing but the most gratifying testimonials of esteem and good will in my parting interviews.

Thus closes my public career. At six o'clock this evening I set off from Madrid, in company with Mr. Weismuller, a connection of the Rothschilds, stationed at this capital, to post for France in a private carriage. My saddest parting will be with the Albuquerques, who seem to me more like relatives than friends. * * *

My intention is to push for England almost without stopping, so as to be ready to embark in one of the August steamers, should certain public business with which I may be intrusted by the Spanish Government render it necessary.

I regret that the late arrival of General Saunders at Madrid, and various concurring circumstances, should oblige me to give up all the farewell visits I had promised to pay to certain of my European friends, and should render my stay with our dear sister so brief as it must now be. I have promised them and myself, however, a supplementary visit to Europe after I have been home some time, and have got all my American affairs in order; when I will pass a few months in revisiting persons and places endeared to me by past pleasures and kindnesses.

PUBLISHED: PMI, III, 391–93.

1. On July 29. See WI to James Buchanan, August 1, 1846.

1995. To James Bandinel

Paris, Aug 12th. 1846

My dear Bandinel,

Permit me to introduce to your acquaintance my friend Mr George Sumner of Boston, New England, but of late years a citizen of the world, having travelled more and to more purpose than most of my countrymen, and whose conversation, if it gives you half the pleasure and information that it has given me, will amply repay you for any civilities you may find it convenient to bestow upon him, and which will be considered by me in the light of personal favors.

Ever my dear Bandinel / Very faithfully yours
Washington Irving

James Bandinel Esq / &c &c &c

MANUSCRIPT: Duke University Library.

1996.   *To James Buchanan*

London August 15th. 1846

The Hon James Buchanan / Secretary of State. Washington

Sir,

A few mornings before my departure from Madrid, after I had had my audience of leave, General Saunders called upon me and had some conversation with me about the state of our affairs with Mexico. He expressed his conviction of the desire of the government to bring the war to a close as speedily as possible, and thought that an offer of mediation on the part of Spain would be well received by our Government and might facilitate the return of peace. He enquired, therefore, whether I did not think I could, in my present position, advantageously and without any official responsibility, suggest such a measure to the Spanish government.

As I considered General Saunders in the confidence of the President and the Cabinet and fully possessed of their policy, and as I viewed the measure itself in a favorable light I immediately sought an interview with Mr Isturiz and made him the proposed suggestion; I let him know, however, that it was entirely unofficial, and unauthorized by any instructions from government, but made on my individual responsibility, in consequence of my general conviction of the wishes and views of the American Cabinet, and of conversations with General Saunders who was recently from Washington in the confidence of the executive[.] Mr Isturiz was evidently surprised and gratified by the suggestion, but ⟨expressed a⟩ enquired whether an offer of mediation would be accepted by our government. To this I could only reply that I was sure it would be more readily accepted from Spain than from any other government; that circumstances induced me to believe it would be favorably entertained, and that, even if it were declined, it would be in such terms as to testify our high respect and consideration for the

Spanish government and our friendship for the Spanish nation. That such an offer would come with peculiar grace from Spain and would contribute to strengthen her amicable relations with her ancient colonies &c. Mr Isturiz wanted to know my idea as to the terms on which they should mediate. I replied that Spain should act not as an arbiter, but a mutual friend; listening to the claims of both parties and suggesting such modifications and compliances as would be fair and expedient under all the circumstances of the case. Mr Isturiz said it would be necessary to have a cabinet council on the Subject and intimated a wish that, should the measure be adopted I would be the bearer of the proposition to my government. I replied that the measure to be effective ought to be as prompt as possible. That I was on the point of departure from Madrid, and, should it be deemed expedient I should be the bearer of the offer, ⟨I⟩ and it were confided to me forthwith, I should endeavor to arrive in England in time to depart in the Steamer of the 19th. August.

I had a Subsequent conversation with Mr Isturiz in which he again expressed doubts of the offer being accepted by our government. I could only repeat what I had before said on the subject, adding that I made the suggestion the more confidently ⟨the⟩ from the sincere good will I entertained for Spain and my conviction that the proposition, whether accepted or declined, would be treated in such a manner that it could not but redound to the dignity and advantage of the Spanish government.

Mr Isturiz then suggested the idea of sending instructions to their Minister at Washington to sound our government whether a proposition of the kind would be accepted if made, and to act accordingly. I agreed that such appeared to me the most judicious plan, but again urged that the instructions should be sent in time for the Steamer of the 19th August as promptness was all important in the matter. He told me there was to be a cabinet council on the following day when the matter would be considered, and, if the measure were determined upon he would endeavor to send off the necessary despatches to the Minister at Washington by the time I designated. He afterwards, on the same day, had a conversation with Genl Saunders on the subject, a statement of which, I believe, the General sends to Government by the same Steamer which takes this letter.[1] To that statement I refer you for more particular details; these hasty lines being written merely to explain to you how I came to make the foregoing suggestion to the Spanish Government, lest you should attribute to officious intermeddling what was done in compliance with the intimations of General Saunders founded, as I supposed, upon the policy of our Cabinet.

I am Sir / Very respectfuly / Your Obt. Servt
Washington Irving

DOCKETED: Mr. Markoe [*upper left corner, page 1*] / W. Irving. London. 15 Aug. 1846 – // Mr. Irving. (Min: to Spn) / *London, Aug. 15. 46*
MANUSCRIPT: NA, RG 59; Yale (draft copy).

Both of these texts are in WI's handwriting.

1. For the results of WI's suggestion, see his letter to Buchanan, October 8, 1846.

1997.   To Sarah Storrow

Birmingham, Aug 18th. 1846

My dear Sarah,

I have just received your letter of July 29th.[1] giving me information of the recovery of dear little Kate and Susie from an alarming illness. I had been congratulating myself that you had by your visit to the United States escaped the excessive heat which has prevailed throughout Europe this summer; and which has produced so much sickness among children; but I find you have encountered the same evil on the other side of the Atlantic. Thank God the darling little beings have recovered—I trust the fine sea breezes of Rhode Island will restore them to their usual health and spirits.

I have come on here post haste from Madrid under the idea that I might embark in the Steamer of the 19th. (tomorrow) but Circumstances have put it out of my power. I have sent down to Liverpool to have a State room secured for me in the Great Britain; so that I hope to arrive at New York a week or so after the receipt of this letter[2] and I need not tell you that one of the most joyful circumstances of my arrival will be ⟨to⟩ the meeting with you and your dear little folks. Till then God bless you.

Your affectionate Uncle
Washington Irving

MANUSCRIPT: Yale.

1. This letter has not been located.
2. WI was able to book passage on the *Cambria*, which arrived in Boston on September 18. See PMI, III, 393.

1998. To —— Wright

Birmingham, Aug 20th. 1846

My dear Sir,

I feel very much obliged to you for the trouble you have taken in securing a berth for me on board the Steamer The delay in the departure of the G Britain obliges me to give up the berth secured in her.

I have the option of a berth ↑(No 46)↓ in the after cabin of the Cambria but I have to take it ⟨wi⟩ ↑in↓ companionship with another passenger. This I will do, unless I can have a state room to myself on the usual terms (the price of a passage and a half) and am willing to take a stateroom in the fore Cabin if none preferable can be had

Will you have the kindness to attend to the matter for me and let me know the result.

With kind remembrances to Mrs Wright & many pleasant reccollections of old times believe me very truly

Your obliged friend
Washington Irving

P. S. Mr Boyd[1] (our Secretary of Legation) has written to Mr Wilding at the U States Consulate, on the same subject; but he may be out of the way, and I wish to make sure of the matter.

MANUSCRIPT: Princeton.

The addressee is probably a Birmingham acquaintance with whom WI had socialized in June, 1824.

1. James McHenry Boyd of Maryland was secretary of the U.S. legation at London in 1846. See Hasse, *Index to U.S. Documents*, I, 132.

1999. To William C. Bouck

Tarrytown, Sept 26th. 1846.

Sir,

My nephew Mr Pierre M Irving has for four years past performed the duties of Pension Agent of the United States under Mr John A Stevens[1] President of the Bank of Commerce How well he has discharged those duties may be ascertained by a reference to that gentleman. Understanding that the payment of pensions in this District will henceforth devolve upon you in your capacity of assistant Treasurer, I take the liberty of reccommending my nephew to your favorable attention should you find any occasion for assistance in the department in which he has officiated. As I might be Suspected of the partiality of a relative were I to dwell upon the character of my nephew for general intelligence, practical experience, close attention to business and scrupulous integrity, I must refer you for his merits in these respects to those who best know him.

Should it meet with your views to continue him in the trust he at present occupies I can only say it would be a matter of great gratification to me. Trusting you will excuse the liberty I take in thus addressing[2] you which arises from the favorable opinion I have concieved of you from general report I remain Sir

Very respectfully / Your Obedient Servt
Washington Irving

The Hon. / William C. Bouck / &c &c &c

MANUSCRIPT: Va.–Barrett.

William C. Bouck (1786–1859), New York canal commissioner from 1821 to 1840, had assumed the position of federal assistant treasurer of New York City after completing his term as Democratic governor of New York.

1. John A. Stevens (1795–1874), well known and highly respected in New York financial circles, was president of the Bank of Commerce from 1839 to 1866.
2. Although WI wrote "addresses," the sense requires "addressing."

2000. To James Buchanan

New York, Octr. 8th. 1846.

The Hon James Buchanan / &c &c &c

Sir,

I had the honor to address a letter to you from London in August last[1] in which I stated the probability that the Spanish government would send instructions by the Steamer of Aug 19th to their Minister at Washington,[2] authorizing him, with certain provisos, to make an offer of mediation on the part of that government, in our war with Mexico. These instructions, however, being sent via Havre, did not reach Mr Calderon until a very few days since. Yesterday he communicated them to me confidentially, having long been in habits of intimacy with me and having been authorized by his government to consult me on the matter. I found that his instructions restricted him from taking any step, great or small, in the affair, unless it should appear to be desired by one or other of the con-

flicting parties; nor was he to make any offer of mediation to our government unless with the certainty that it would not be refused, and would
not give offence to those powers[3] with which her Spanish Majesty desires to maintain close relations of friendship.

Mr Calderon seemed at a loss how to proceed, nor did I pretend to
advise him. The face of affairs had changed considerably since the time
I made the suggestion to the Spanish govt. and the very delay[4] in forwarding the despatch to Mr Calderon was calculated to defeat the proposed measure.

Mr Calderon expressed an intention of writing to his official correspondents in Mexico[5] on the subject; and ⟨said he⟩ of so wording his communications to our government as to leave an opening for an encouraging
intimation on our part that might lead up to our offer of mediation,
should it be within the scope of our present policy to accept one.

I have thought it advisable to state these matters for your government,
should Mr Calderon really make any communication, direct or indirect,
on the subject.

I am Sir / Respectfully / Your Obt Servt
Washington Irving

P. S. Before leaving Europe I drew for what appeared to be the balance
of my account with the government, as there may have been some in-
accuracies in my accounts I would be much obliged to you if you ⟨ha⟩
would have a correct statement sent to me from the Treasury, that I
may make a final adjustment. My address is Tarry Town, N York—

DOCKETED: Mr. Markoe / Make Extract & / send to Mr. Stubbs / R. [top of MS
page 1]
MANUSCRIPT: NA, RG 59.

1. See WI to Buchanan, August 15, 1846.
2. Don Angel Calderón de la Barca (1790–1861), who served in the post from
August 5, 1844, to August 2, 1853. See Hasse, Index to U.S. Documents, I, 176–77.
3. Great Britain and France.
4. In his letter of August 15, 1846, WI had urged promptness in sending
despatches.
5. Probably Bermudez de Castro, the Spanish ambassador to Mexico. See Almanach de Gotha pour l'Année 1846 (Gotha, 1846), p. 467.

2001.   To Catharine Paris

[October 9, 1846?]

My dear Sister,
   I will thank you to let the bearer have my likeness for an engraving
to be made from it

Yours affectionately
Washington Irving

N York, Octr. 9th. [1846?]

MANUSCRIPT: Va.–Barrett.

   The date is conjectured as 1846. On November 21, 1846, WI wrote to Mrs.
Paris, authorizing her to give the bearer the portrait of WI by Gilbert Stuart Newton. It is possible that an earlier attempt to procure the portrait for the engraver
had failed. WI wrote to Rufus W. Griswold about the portrait on January 14,
1847, mentioning that his sister had been unwilling to hand it over to the engraver in rainy weather without adequate protection.

2002.   To George Harvey

Sunnyside Octr 16th 1846

My dear Mr Harvey,
   We are all very much pleased with the addition, which certainly harmonizes admirably with the main building. Would it admit of being enlarged to about 18 feet Square, heightening it in proportion? This would
give better sized rooms. I am disposed to place the store room in the north
west corner of the wash room, so as to give the latter the full benefit
of the south window; which is important both in Summer and winter.
I find there is no need of an oven in the wash room; I find there is one in
the kitchen range. Nothing is necessary but an ordinary cooking Stove;
one of which is used in the present wash house. A flue or pipe can be
carried into the flue of the Kitchen chimney across the space occupied
at present by the Kitchen stairs.
   I am interrupted and must send this off leaving further particulars to
a future letter. My present one is mainly to know whether the addition
admits of the enlargement I mention without injuring the effect

Yours very truly
Washington Irving

   I have Stone enough quarried out—I presume the stone work is not to
be more than 3 feet below & 3 feet above the ground—Six feet in all

MANUSCRIPT: SHR.

George Harvey was the architect who remodeled WI's original cottage into Sunnyside. For WI's suggestions and instructions to Harvey, see his letters of November 23, 1835, and November 14, 1836. WI again consulted Harvey concerning the extensive changes made in 1846 and 1847.

2003. To Sarah Storrow

Sunnyside Octr 18h. 1846

My dear Sarah,

Since your departure[1] we have had a severe gale[2] from the south west which has done much damage both on Sea and land. I console myself however, with the idea that you had probably gained upwards of two hundred miles casting before the gale occurred; and may therefore have escaped it altogether; at any rate you had good sea room. Still I feel an anxiety while you and your dear little folk are on the ocean which I never felt on my own account; and I shall most heartily rejoice when I receive tidings of your being safely landed at Havre.

I have not seen your mother since the gale. I saw her twice, before, and was gratified to find her composed and even cheerful. She talked of nothing but you and your children of course; but then I was glad to observe that she was full of pleasant reccollections; dwelling upon the sayings and doings of dear little Kate and Tutie.[3] In fact your visit has been invaluable to her; storing her mind with agreeable reccollections and associations.

The day after your departure I dined at Treats where I met Mr Schermerhorn and Ann,[4] with General Jones[5] at dinner—and Kate and Liney and Bruce[6] came in, in the evening. It was quite a cordial, pleasant meeting. Mrs Schermerhorn was not present; being occupied in attending upon poor Cortlandt[7] who is not expected to recover. I returned on Saturday to Sunnyside, where I have been ever since, and where I shall be likely to remain for some time to come, as I am making preparations to commence, in the course of a day or two, the addition to the Cottage. In fact I have already quarried the Stone necessary for the foundation &c out of the side of the hill between the Coal house & the barn; where, ↑had I thought of it at the time,↓ I might have quarried out Stone enough for the whole cottage. I have a plan from Mr Harvey which harmonizes with the rest of the building and will not be expensive enough to ruin me. When the whole is completed you shall have a sketch of the addition; that you may ⟨carry⟩ ↑have↓ a complete idea of the Cottage in your minds eye. I find this occupation necessary to call my thoughts home and fix them there. I feel at times a little flagging of the spirits in coming upon the Scene of my old cares and anxieties, and finding the shadow of them now and then falling upon me; but occupation drives off every thing of the kind: and when I get once more employed with my pen I shall give all my cares to the wind. I have been looking over my manuscripts within the last few days and feel the *animas* reviving within me. That will make sunshine around me.

I saw Mr Astor, the day after your departure. He is very much bowed down and almost helpless, being obliged to be aided by two men whenever he moves about the house. He speaks so low that it is difficult to hear him; yet he is in full possession of his intellect and may live for some time yet.[8] He expressed great satisfaction in seeing me and pressed me to pass the winter with him in town. I had to promise to make him a visit as formerly. I shall be perplexed with a variety of homes in the city: Julia Grinnell, Helen Treat, your Aunt Abby and Mr Astor all claiming me as a guest, beside my comfortable quarters at Oscars. I think, if I get fairly occupied with my pen, I shall pass the principal part of the winter at the Cottage. My mind is more tranquil and composed there than in the city; where there is too much hurry excitement and distraction. Indeed if I had a chosen few of my relatives and friends in the Cottage and its vicinity I think I could pass the rest of my days there more happily than any where else. I am glad I had your dear little children there with me; they have given new associations to the place; I never look up to the window of your mothers room without fancying the bright faces of Kate and Tutie beaming out upon me from among the honeysuckles.

Much anxiety begins to be felt about the Great Britain,[9] which was to have sailed on the 22d. of last month, and has not yet arrived It is hoped she may have been detained for further repairs, or may have put back after the gale, which the Great Western experienced, and which the Great Britain must have encountered when about two or three days out. I feel particular solicitude on the subject from Mr King[10] & Mrs Ellis being on board.

Oct 19th. I understand poor Courtland Schermerhorn died on Friday last. His death, after so much painful lingering, will almost be a relief to his family; especially to his poor Mother who has Sacraficed herself in attendance upon him.

Last evening (Sunday) while seated in the little drawing room with the girls around me, we were roused by the arrival of Mrs Hamilton (*Mere*) and Alexander,[11] who had come on foot by the line of the aqueduct. It was as you may suppose a most welcome agreeable visit. Mrs Hamilton was cordial and animated as usual. She told us that Alexander had promised to come up on Saturday afternoons throughout the winter, and they were to have little family gatherings on Saturday evenings, with Whist and Supper, ⟨to⟩ ↑at↓ which we were invited to attend. This will be a cheerful arrangement for the winter months, and I shall take care to Reciprocate. I think we may get up some social, informal merry makings.

A day or two since I drove with your uncle and two of the girls to make my visit to the McKenzies Perrys and Creightons.[12] McKenzie has improved his farm greatly, and has rendered the house much more respectable in appearance than I had supposed it capable of being. He is likely to have a poor mans fortune, a house full of children. He has four already; two boys and two girls. I saw the two boys,[13] who are fine healthy manly little fellows[.] McKenzie was absent on business, being in active employment at present on confidential matters connected with the Mexican war. I am glad he has the confidence and countenance of Government, which he well merits.

I saw Mrs Perry (still handsome) and one of her daughters.[14] Anna[15] (Pierre's daughter) and a sister of Mrs McKenzie,[16] are on a visit to the two establishments. The situation of Perrys house commands splendid prospects of the river; but it is lonely and ⟨tedious an⟩ of tedious and difficult approach.

I am very much pleased with Pierres daughter Anna. She has a sweet interesting countenance and very prepossessing manners, and every one speaks well of her.

I presume you have been to Dr Creightons place[17] ⟨some⟩ during your recent visit. His new entrance is a great improvement. The Doctor himself is not improved in appearance ⟨since I⟩ during my absence. He has grown very full in his habit; dangerously so I apprehend. Only he and his sister were at home; who received us very cordially and pressed us to stay to dinner, which of course we declined. I have now got through my *Salutation* visits to my neighbors.

19   I must conclude this letter as I am just about setting off for town to Consult Mr Harvey about some points in the plan of my addition to the Cottage. Your Mother I learn went to town a few days since and is comfortably quartered in the same house with your brother and with Uncle Nat.[18]

Kiss the dear little women for me and keep them in mind of their uncle with kind remembrances to Mr Storrow

Your affectionate Uncle
Washington Irving

MANUSCRIPT: Yale.   PUBLISHED: PMI, III, 395 (in part).

1. Thomas and Sarah Storrow, their two children, and a servant left New York on October 8, 1846, on the packet ship *La Duchesse d'Orleans* for Le Havre. See NYEP, October 10, 1846.

2. A violent storm occurred in New York on October 13. See NYEP, October 14, 1846.

3. A nickname for Susán Van Wart Storrow, the Storrows' younger child.

4. John Treat Irving, Jr. was married to Helen Schermerhorn, daughter of Abraham and sister of Anna.

5. Roger Jones (1789–1852) was adjutant-general of the U.S. Army from 1820 until his death.

6. Kate, Liney, and Bruce are Catharine (1828–1858), Caroline (1830–1908), and Archibald Bruce (1814–1862), the children of Abraham Schermerhorn. See Richard Schermerhorn, *Schermerhorn Genealogy and Family Chronicles*, p. 166.

7. Augustus Van Cortlandt Schermerhorn (1812–1846), who married Ellen Bayard on December 10, 1844. See *Schermerhorn Genealogy*, p. 166.

8. Although in poor health, as WI suggests, Astor lived until March 29, 1848.

9. Launched in 1843, the *Great Britain* was the largest steamship in the world at that time—322 feet long and built entirely of iron and propelled by screw instead of paddle wheel. At 11:00 A.M. on September 22 it left Liverpool for New York and ran ashore in the Bay of Dundrum nine and one-half hours later. It was carrying 180 passengers, all of whom reached shore safely. See Captain Christopher Claxton, *History and Description of the Steamship Great Britain* (New York, 1845), pp. 3, 21; London *Times*, September 25, 1846.

10. William Rufus Devane King, U.S. minister to France, who had been recalled at his own request. WI had first met King in Liverpool in 1817. See WI to Sarah Storrow, May 24, 1844.

11. Mrs. James Hamilton and Alexander Hamilton, Jr. (1816–1889).

12. These were Tarrytown neighbors of WI's—Alexander Slidell Mackenzie, Matthew C. Perry, and William Creighton.

13. Ronald Slidell Mackenzie (1840–1889), and Alexander Slidell Mackenzie, Jr. (1842–1863).

14. Mrs. Matthew C. Perry was the former Jane Slidell (1797–1879), a sister of Alexander Slidell Mackenzie. Her daughter, to whom WI refers, was either Caroline Slidell Mackenzie Perry (1829–1892) or Isabella Bolton Perry (1834–1912). See Samuel Eliot Morison, *"Old Bruin," Commodore Matthew C. Perry, 1794–1858* (Boston, 1967), pp. 447–48.

15. Anna Duer Irving (1830–1884), daughter of Pierre Paris Irving.

16. Miss Robinson.

17. The Reverend Dr. William Creighton (1793–1865), who was the rector of Christ Church, Tarrytown, lived over the Mt. Pleasant borderline in Ossining. He was married to Jane Schermerhorn (1792–1866) and had a daughter Catherine. See J. T. Scharf, *History of Westchester County*, II, 252, 312; *Schermerhorn Genealogy*, pp. 158–59.

18. Nathaniel Paulding (1776–1858), James K. Paulding's older brother and a wine merchant on Vesey Street.

2004. To Madame Albuquerque

Sunnyside, Octr. 19th. 1846

My dear Madame Albuquerque,

It is about a month since I returned once more to my sweet little rural home, and I have ever since been so much occupied with domestic concerns and the greetings and treatings of my family and friends that I have not had liesure nor quiet of mind for letter writing. My return to little Sunnyside, as you may suppose, has been quite a jubilee to ⟨the⟩ ↑its↓ inmates, and it is with real heartfelt delight I find myself once more surrounded by them. I have found my little nest almost buried among trees and over run with clambering vines. My first move has been cut down and clear away so as to make openings for prospects and a free circulation of air, my next to commence building an addition, so that I have my hands full of occupation.

When in town I saw and had a long conversation with your brother William[1] who enquired about you with the greatest interest. He says he intends to write to you regularly every month; and thinks some of his letters written to you heretofore must have miscarried. I charged him to be punctual in his correspondence and told him how much you had been distressed at times by the long silence of your family. He has grown somewhat grey since I saw him, but still maintains his good looks; and reminds me very much of you. I have not been able to visit at his house (our interview was at his office) but shall do so when I go to town to make any stay, hitherto my visits to the city have been extremely brief. Just as I was coming out of your brother Williams I met your younger brother[2] going in. I had but a moment to speak to him. He is well bearded and mustached and looks almost too gay a horse for harness; but I fancy has good stuff in him. When I have time to see more of your family I will write more about them.

I arrived at home in time to see something of my niece Mrs Storrow and her children before their departure. They sailed for Havre about ten days since and I have felt the parting with them severely. A separation by land seems nothing so painful as a separation by water. The Sea is a terrible divider of friends. This having ones attachments scattered about the world, too widely to be ever brought together, is one of the sad drawbacks upon this active and extending intercourse which is promoting the friendship of nations. I am scarce at home here before I find my heart yearning after friends on the other side of the Atlantic. I would give any thing, just now, to have a long mornings cosey chat with you and dear Mrs O'Shea in her *palacio* in which I presume she is at present installed. I trust you will give me a full account of her and of it; and recollect that you can never write enough about her and yourself. God bless you both! what Sweeteners you were to my otherwise insipid existence in Madrid.

I am anxious to have a little court gossip about the young Queen and her Marriage; one never gets the cream and marrow of these matters from the public papers. I hope she may get a husband[3] she can be happy with and one who will be acceptable to her subjects.

I have slipped so completely back into my old occupations, old scenes and old habits that I can hardly realize I have been away so long from my cottage; and that not three months have elapsed since I, who am now trimming my trees and regulating my poultry yard, was figuring a minister at the court of Spain. I have very pleasant meetings occasionally with Alexander Hamilton; when we talk over scenes in Madrid and amuse ourselves by turning diplomacy inside out, and shewing up the ragged lining that so often lurks under the gold lace. The Hamiltons you know are my country neighbors; scarce a mile distant. Alexander and his little wife[4] live in town; but he is to come up to the family homestead every saturday throughout the winter and saturday evenings there is to be whist and a Supper, at which I have engaged to attend.

And now I must conclude with many warm reccollections to my friends Jerningham,[5] La Saussaye, Marnix ⟨and⟩ the great and good Dalborgo and such others as were in the narrow circle of our intimacy. I shall endeavor to write to Mrs OShea and La Saussaye by the same steamer which takes this; if not, by the next one.

Give my love to the princesses and to Don Jose the younger and my affectionate regards to the commander.

Yours ever
Washington Irving

Tell Count de Bresson that I delivered his letters and the parcel to Mr John R Livingston.[6] The latter informed me that he had just written to M de Bresson in full upon the subject about which we conversed prior to my departure from Madrid.

Remember me to my faithful Lorenzo. I received a letter from him just before leaving England, and will write to him when ⟨ev⟩ I find leisure.[7]

ADDRESSED: Madame Cavalcanti de Albuquerque / Legation du Brasil / à Madrid
    POSTMARKED: [*unrecovered*] / OC / [*unrecovered*] // PAID [*unrecovered*] /
    1846 // [*three postmarks unrecovered*] // CC / 6 NO 6 / 1846   DOCKETED:
    Sunnyside / October 19th. 1846.
MANUSCRIPT: HSA.   PUBLISHED: Penney, *Bulletin NYPL*, 63 (January, 1959),
    27–28.

1. William Forbes Oakey was a New York merchant with a business at 35 Beaver Street and a residence at 27 Bond Street. See *New York City Directory for 1846–47*, p. 295.

2. Probably Daniel Oakey, Jr. (d. 1888), who was in business at 33 Beaver Street. He lived at 4 Bond Street. He visited WI in Madrid in February of 1843. See *New York City Directory for 1846–47*, p. 295; and WI to Catharine Paris, February 6, 1843.

3. Queen Isabella II (1830–1904) was married to her cousin, Ferdinand de Asís, on October 16, 1846.

4. Hamilton had married Angelica Livingston in 1845. See WI to Sarah Storrow, March 27, 1845.

5. Henry V. Jerningham was the secretary of the British legation in Madrid. See *Almanach de Gotha pour l'Année 1846*, p. 355.

6. Probably John R. Livingston (1755–1851), the brother of Chancellor Robert R. Livingston.

7. The last two paragraphs are written vertically along the left margin of page 1 over the first part of WI's letter.

2005.   To Rufus W. Griswold

Sunnyside Octr. 21—1846

Sir,

I have repeatedly of late declined to sit for my portrait; partly from a great dislike to the operation itself, and partly because I think there are already portraits sufficient of me before the public. I could not comply with your request, therefore, without the risk of displeasing those, whose requests I have heretofore ⟨rejecte⟩ refused. I hope however, you may find one or other of the portraits by Leslie[1] and Newton[2] sufficient for your purpose. There is one in the possession of my sister[3] in New York, taken by Newton shortly before we parted, some years since, in England. It is an excellent painting and was thought at the time a good likeness. It has never had justice done to it by the engraver—I enclose you a copy of an engraving of it published Some time Since in this country. It misses the character and expression of the original and is in face and person out of drawing. The original can at any time be placed in the hand of your engraver, if in New York; but I doubt whether my Sister would trust it to a distance.

I am Sir

Very respectfully / Your obt Sert
Washington Irving

MANUSCRIPT: SHR.   PUBLISHED: *Passages from the Correspondence . . . of Rufus W. Griswold* (Cambridge, Mass., 1898), p. 212 (in part).

Rufus W. Griswold (1815–1857), an anthologist and editor, brought out in 1842 *The Poets and Poetry of America*, the first of a series of popular collections of American writing. He is remembered for his slanderous attacks upon Edgar Allan Poe after that writer's death.

1. Charles Robert Leslie had painted WI in England in 1820. This painting was engraved by M. I. Danforth in 1831. See STW, I, 202.

2. Gilbert Stuart Newton (1797–1835) painted two portraits of WI, one in 1820 and one in 1831. See STW, I, frontispiece; and WI to Catharine Paris, October 14, 1831.

3. Catharine Paris.

2006.   To John. P. Kennedy

Sunnyside Nov 8t. 1846

My dear Kennedy,

My nephew Lewis G. Irving[1] visits your city with the view to solicit an agency at New York of one of the Baltimore Insurance companies. He has thorough knowledge of the business, having acted as secretary to two companies. He bears testimonials to his fitness for the charge and ⟨for⟩ to his general merits from many of the best houses in our city. To these I can add my own assurances of his sound judgement, great discretion, thorough business habits and scrupulous integrity. As I have his success greatly at heart I shall esteem it a great favor to myself if you will exert your influence in his favor

I had thought to have been at Baltimore before this, on my way to Washington, but I feel so thoroughly delighted at finding myself once more in my little nest on the Hudson, that I cannot bear to budge from it even for a day. Beside, I have no immediate business to call me to Washington, so I defer my visit there to a future day; when I shall stop to see my Baltimore friends, and hope to find you and Mrs Kennedy[2] as well and happy as your hearts can wish. Present Mrs Kennedy my kindest remembrances, and believe me ever, my dear Kennedy

Most truly and cordially yours
Washington Irving

J. P. Kennedy Esq / &c &c &c

ADDRESSED: John P Kennedy Esq / &c &c &c / Baltimore   DOCKETED: 1846 / Washington Irving

MANUSCRIPT: Peabody Library.   PUBLISHED: *Sewanee Review*, 25 (January, 1917), 5.

John Pendleton Kennedy (1795–1870), a Baltimore lawyer, author, and Congressman. WI became intimate with his family in the 1850's.

1. Lewis Graham Irving (1795–1879) was the oldest child of William and Julia Paulding Irving.

2. Elizabeth Gray (1809?–1889), whom Kennedy married on February 5, 1829.

2007. To Sabina O'Shea

Sunnyside, Nov 8t. 1846

My dear Mrs O'Shea,

By this time I trust you are comfortably fixed in your new house at Madrid enjoying an occasional gossip with Madame Albuquerque; at which I grieve I cannot be present. I in the mean time am once more seated in my elbow chair in snug little Sunnyside, which I find a more delightful little nook than ever. Indeed I am so bewitched with the sweet quiet of this little rural nest that I have scarcely been able to leave it for a day at a time since my return, and, though within twenty four miles of New York, where reside most of my friends and relatives, I have as yet paid it but one or two flying visits, deferring, until winter has set in, to make my sojourn in the city and renew my intercourse with the circle of my intimates. In fact I have so completely slipped back into my old rural habits and occupations, that I can scarcely realize, as I go dawdling about trimming and planting and transplanting trees and inspecting the poultry yard, that so short a time has elapsed since I was playing the Courtier and treading the saloons of Royal palaces. I rather think I am more at home as well as happier in my present condition, and am delighted to play the Monarch in my little domain of twenty Acres. My five nieces are all at home and we form a very happy household. I doubt whether ever monarch was received with heartier congratulations on his return to his dominions.

The Hamiltons are my near neighbors and have féted me on my arrival; and Alexander Hamilton and his pretty and very ladylike little wife visit me occasionally. She promises soon to make him a father, with which he is not a little tickled.

My niece Mrs Storrow sailed for France about three weeks after my return. It is a sad trial to be separated from her and her lovely children, who have taken such fast hold on my heart. I hope when you go to Paris you will keep up your acquaintance with her; she values your friendship, and she is truly worthy of it.

I am anxious for news from Madrid. I want news both public and private. We have uncertain accounts of royal marriages &c but nothing that can be depended upon; and a delay in the arrival of the Steamer keeps us in a tantalizing state of Suspense. But I chiefly want to know the gossip of the court and the capital: that kind of news which never appears in news papers. I want, to have personal anecdotes about those who manage public concerns, and about the circle of our intimates. I want to know how Narvaez fares, and whether he is likely soon to be reinstated in favor and authority. But above all I want to know the domestic affairs of the palace and all that concerns the young queen and her sister; whose fortunes to me have a romantic interest

Now that I am away from Spain my heart yearns towards it, and I find that long habitude and residence have ⟨given me⟩ fixed deep and immoveably that strong interest in its welfare which I concieved when I only Knew it through the medium of history and romance. Were I a young man I think I should have an irresistible hankering to return to it. I had no idea that this feeling would return upon me so soon and so strongly.

I am longing to hear from Madame Albuquerque; who I expect, will give me the first news of your return to Madrid; and of your induction into your new establishment. In fact I have been so much secluded in my little country retreat since my return, and have seen so little of the gay or busy world in my own country of late, that I have scarce any new impressions to efface those made by scenes and associates at Madrid.

——————————

While writing this letter I have received one from dear Madame Albuquerque dated the 25th. September[1] at which time it appears you had not yet arrived in Madrid; but were to do so at the end of the month; so you are long before this tolerably settled in your palacio.

I am glad to find that the marriage question is completely set at rest, by both the young Queen and her sister being married.[2] I hope and trust it will tend to the quieting of Spain. What gay times you will have in Madrid! De Bressons house I presume will be in a continual revel. I look to seeing de Bresson laden with the favors of Louis Philippe. He well merits them for he has had a most arduous and unpleasant mission and has acquitted himself in it apparently with great energy and ability.

I suspect, however, it was DalBorgo who principally brought about the royal matches, and this accounts for his incessant restlessness and ubiquity for the last year or two; and his daily attendance at the French Embassy.

Madame Albuquerque writes me that she is to have her carriage, against the Royal ceremonies. This will enable her to be with you oftener than she could otherwise have been; and I expect her carriage will be as often at your door as mine used to be, for I really believe she loves you almost as much as I do.

I presume both Mr O'Sheas daughters will be at Madrid by the time you receive this letter—if so, I beg you to remember me to them most kindly.

Tell Madame Albuquerque to send me now and then, through the American Legation, a Madrid paper, giving accounts of any public fétes and political events in these eventful times.

I hope you are well pleased with your house, and that you have expressed yourself so to La Saussaye. Should any of his arrangements not suit you, do not find fault ⟨with⟩ to him; for he has taken a great deal of pains and had a great deal of trouble, and displayed great taste and management in conquering the difficulties of the old mansion and rendering it habitable and commodious. Indeed had it not been for him the job would never have been accomplished.

I must ask of Mr O'Shea and yourself kind feelings and social attentions to my successor General Saunders; or Genl Saunder*son* if that pleases you better. He is a most respectable amiable and worthy man; and I think you will like him when you know him.

Give my affectionate regards to all the OSheas father, sons and nephew, and also to Don Tom and his spouse, and believe me ever your devotedly attached friend

Washington Irving

MANUSCRIPT: HSA.   PUBLISHED: Penney, *Bulletin NYPL*, 63 (January, 1959), 28–30.

1. This letter has not been located.

2. Luisa Fernanda (1832–1897) married the duke of Montpensier (1824–1890), the fourth son of Louis Philippe on October 16, 1846, in a double ceremony with her sister. See Theo Aronson, *Royal Vendetta*, p. 57.

2008.   *To Catharine Paris*

Sunnyside, Nov. 21. 1846

My dear Sister,

I will thank you to let the bearer[1] have my portrait by Newton; it will be detained but Six or eight days in the hands of the Engraver

Affectionately Yours,
Washington Irving

ADDRESSED: Mrs. Daniel Paris / at Mrs Stanton's / Murray St / near Greenwich St. / New York.
MANUSCRIPT: Washington University Library, St. Louis.

1. Probably Rufus W. Griswold or his agent. Griswold had requested WI to sit for a portrait a month earlier, but WI, in declining, had suggested that an engraving might be made from the painting by Newton in the possession of Mrs. Paris. See WI to Griswold, October 21, 1846.

2009. To the Reverend Robert Bolton

Sunnyside Decr 24th. 1846

My dear Sir,

I thank you most heartily for your kind letter of greeting.[1] I should have driven over to see you long before this; but soon after my return I took to building an addition to my house,[2] and have been closely occupied ever since; urging on the country workmen; so as to accomplish the job in defiance of wind and weather. This you must be sensible was an arduous undertaking during the late very inclement season: but I have succeeded in it even beyond my hopes. I had a very agreeable and interesting visit from your son[3] lately—who I find is deep in researches as to the local history of Westchester County.[4] It will give me great pleasure to contribute any thing in my power to the promotion of his task.

I am gratified to hear the most satisfactory accounts of the prosperity of your establishment[5] but I always thought it had peculiar elements of success. I look forward with great interest to the paying of it another visit.

I am expecting my brother in law Mr Van Wart today: to pass Christmas with me. He is quite recovered from the bruises and exhaustion of his ship wreck. His account of the horrors of the scene is truly appalling

I cannot express to you how happy I am to find myself once more in my sweet quiet little home. Indeed I am so wedded to it that I have found it difficult to leave it even for a day; and have ⟨be⟩ made very few and very brief visits to town since my return

Give my kindest remembrances to Mrs Bolton and the younger members of your family[6] and believe me ever, with the highest esteem and most cordial regard

Yours faithfully
Washington Irving

MANUSCRIPT: SHR.

Robert Bolton, Sr. (1788–1857) was an Episcopal clergyman at Pelham Priory, Westchester County.

1. This letter has not been located.
2. For other details, see WI to George Harvey, October 16, 1846; and to Sarah Storrow, October 18, 1846.
3. Robert Bolton (1814–1877), who was born and educated in England, came to the United States in 1836. He prepared *The Guide to New Rochelle* in 1842, then went to Tarrytown, where he became principal of the Irving Institute. See J. T. Scharf, *History of Westchester County*, I, 607.

4. Bolton's *History of Westchester County* was published in two volumes in 1848. A set of this edition is in WI's library at Sunnyside.

5. Probably Bolton Priory, which was a young ladies' school under the direction of Nanetta Bolton. See Scharf, *History of Westchester County*, I, 608.

6. Which ones WI has in mind is not clear. The younger daughters included Rhoda (b. 1825), Abby (b. 1827), the twins Adelaide and Adele (b. 1830), and Frances Georgiana (b. 1831). Of Bolton's sons five became ministers; the girls distinguished themselves in teaching, literarture, or art. See Scharf, *History of Westchester County*, I, 607; and Henry C. Bolton and Reginald P. Bolton, *The Family Bolton in England and America* (New York, 1895), chart 22.

2010.   To Pierre M. Irving

[December 31, 1846]

You see, I asked higher than the sum you proposed to ask[1] [of Lea & Blanchard for publication of his works]; indeed, much higher than they could have afforded to give with advantage. I think, however, a similar arrangement for my works would be much more profitable at present than it would have been at that time.

* * * * *

I was greatly disappointed at not seeing you at Christmas. I wished much to talk to you about my literary affairs. I am growing a sad laggard in literature, and need some one to bolster me up occasionally. I am too ready to do anything else rather than write.

PUBLISHED: PMI, III, 396–97.

1. Before departing for Spain in 1842, WI had proposed the publication of a new edition of his works by Lea & Blanchard with a payment of $3,000 a year, an offer which they rejected. See PMI, III, 395–96; and WI to Lea & Blanchard, March 10, 1842. What sum WI was now suggesting has not been ascertained. Since he had overtures from other publishers, he was anxious to have a firm commitment or rejection from Lea & Blanchard; then he could make an arrangement which would provide funds to help pay for his remodeling and building projects at Sunnyside.

2011.   To Pierre M. Irving

Sunnyside, Jan. 6, 1847

My dear Pierre:

* * * I am glad to hear you are receiving such a snug little bag of money from the Screw Dock.[1] In faith, the Dock deserves its name. I fancy there must be a set of Jews at the windlasses to screw the ships so

handsomely. Tell them to screw on, and spare not! These are building times, when all the world wants money.

＊   ＊   ＊   ＊   ＊   ＊

You now know the full extent of all my "indebtedness," excepting what relates to my new building, and to domestic expenses.

I know I am "burning the candle at both ends"[2] this year, but it must be so until I get my house in order, after which expenses will return to their ordinary channel, and I trust my income will expand, as I hope to get my literary property in a productive train.

PUBLISHED: PMI, III, 397.

1. The Screw Dock Company, in which WI had invested funds, had just paid a quarterly dividend of five percent. It was located on South Street between Pike and Market. See PMI, III, 397; and *New York City Directory for 1846–7*, p. 28.

2. Alain René LeSage, *Gil Blas*, VII, xv.

2012.   To Rufus W. Griswold

New York, Jany 14th. 1847

Dear Sir,

You have been misinformed as to the disposition of my sister with regard to the loan of my portrait[1]—She was prepared to confide it to the hands on the engraver,[2] but he sent for it on a wet day, and the person who called for it was disposed to take it out of its frame, but was apparently unprovided with any means of protecting it from injury. My sister therefore expressed reluctance to letting it go out of her hands under such circumstances and the person went away with the intention as she supposed, of calling again in better weather She has been expecting him ever since—The portrait is quite at the service of the engraver.

Respectfully / Your obt Servt
Washington Irving

Rufus W. Griswold Esq

MANUSCRIPT: HSP.

1. On November 21, 1846, WI had written to Catharine Paris, asking her to allow Griswold's engraver to borrow the painting for a few days.

2. John Sartain (1808–1887) engraved the portrait painted by Gilbert Stuart Newton, and Griswold used is as the frontispiece for *The Prose Writers of America*, an anthology which appeared later in 1847. WI wrote "on" for "of."

2013. *To Messrs. Wiley & Putnam*

Sunnyside Jany 30th. 1847—

Messrs Wiley & Putnam

Gentlemen,

On returning home last evening after a fortnights absence, I found your letter of the 21st. inst.[1] I know nothing of the origin of the Newspaper paragraph you inclose, and have said and done nothing to warrant the assertion it makes ↑respecting ⟨my mode of publishing⟩ ↑the form of the proposed republication of↓ my works↓ I↑ ⟨made no plan⟩ ⟨made no plan on the subject⟩↓ have no idea of publishing with any house but yours, and as soon as I can get my literary matters in train ⟨for publication⟩ I will make a final arrangement with you ⟨and⟩ ↑in which we shall↓ determine in which form & manner the works[2] shall be put forth. I regret to say I have been very dilatory in making the necessary preparations; having been very much occupied in building an addition to my house; in ⟨visiting & receiving the[3]⟩ ↑making &↓ visit ⟨of my friends on⟩ ↑incidental to↓ my return from so long an absence ⟨&c &c⟩. but I trust I shall now be more settled and composed in mind and enabled to resume my literary habits

I am Gentlemen

With great regard and respect / Very truly yours
Washington Irving

MANUSCRIPT: NYPL—Berg Collection.

John Wiley (1808–1891) and George P. Putnam (1814–1872) were partners in a publishing and bookselling firm.

1. This letter has not been located.

2. Apparently after receiving an unfavorable response from Lea & Blanchard, with whom he had been negotiating after his return to America about republication of his writings, WI approached Wiley and Putnam. See WI to PMI, December 31, 1846.

3. WI probably did not intend to delete "receiving the," so that the passage should read "making & receiving the visits . . ."

2014. To John Y. Mason

Sunnyside Feb. 4th. 1847.

Sir,
Permit me to offer an earnest reccommendation of Mr L Howard Newman[1] of New York, for a Midshipmans warrant. He is the son of the late
William D Newman,[2] of the United States Navy, ⟨of⟩ ↑with↓ whose unfortunate unfortunate[3] end, while in Command of the U. S. Brig Bainbridge, you are probably acquainted. I knew his father from his boyhood and was instrumental, through my brother,[4] then a Member of
Congress, in procuring him a Midshipmans warrant. He served for many
years with bravery, intelligence and faithfulness and rose in the profession through his own merits, ⟨being⟩ not having a friend to back him
during my long absence in Europe. He acquitted himself with equal
merit in private life and was a model of honesty, integrity and modest
worth He fell a victim, I fear, to a too accute sensibility to professional
reputation and an anxious apprehension of incurring reproach for a circumstance in which he had really nothing to reproach himself with, and
in which he was acquitted of all blame by his superior ⟨command⟩ officer. He has left a family to be provided for—His son, I believe, inherits
his worth. He has recently finished his studies and is anxious to enter
upon the carreer of his late father. I take the same interest in his fortunes
that I did in those of his father, and should feel deeply gratified should
my reccommendation have any effect in promoting his wishes
    I am Sir

Very respectfully / Your obt Servt
Washington Irving
The Hon / John Y. Mason / &c &c &c / Washington

DOCKETED: 5213 and / N. 71 Feb. 8. Welsh / What is his age? / This is the first
application / made in his behalf / & does not state / his age.

MANUSCRIPT: Va.–Barrett; Yale (draft copy).
    John Y. Mason (1799–1859) was secretary of the navy at this time. He was con-
gressman from Virginia from 1831 to 1837, secretary of the navy in 1844 and from
1846 to 1849, attorney general in 1845 and 1846, and U.S. minister to France from
1853 to 1859.
    1. L. Howard Newman entered the Navy as a midshipman on September 24,
1847, and worked up to lieutenant-commander before his death on May 31, 1866.
See Callahan, *Officers of the Navy*, p. 405.
    2. W. D. Newman became a midshipman on February 1, 1814. He was a com-
mander when he died on October 9, 1841. See Callahan, *Officers of the Navy*,
p. 405.
    3. WI repeated "unfortunate."
    4. William Irving (1766–1821) served in Congress from 1814 to 1819.

2015. To Helen Dodge Irving

Sunnyside, Feb. 14, [1847]

My dear Helen:

Your letter[1] was like manna in the wilderness[2] to me, finding me mewed up in this little warm oven of a house, where, if I remain much longer without getting out of doors occasionally, I shall grow quite rusty and crusty. Fortunately, I was troubled for two or three days with an inflammation in my eyes, which made me fear I was about to be blind; that has passed away, and you cannot think what a cause of self-gratulation it is to me to find out that I am only lame.[3] We have all abundant reason to be thankful for the dispensations of Providence, if we only knew when and why.

Still it is some little annoyance to me that I cannot get about and find some means of spending that sum of money which you tell me Pierre has been making for me.[4] I think he takes advantage of my crippled condition, which prevents my going on with my improvements; and I fear, if I do not get in a disbursing condition soon, he will get the weather gage of me, and make me rich in spite of myself.

* * * * * * *

Your account of Mrs. ——'s reception was quite animated. I cannot expect you to abstract yourself from so much social enjoyment, and come to sober little Sunnyside while the gay season lasts; therefore I retract all that I said in my last letter to Pierre about your making me a visit just now, and will not say a word more on the subject; not but that it would be an act of common humanity—to say nothing of natural affection.

PUBLISHED: PMI, III, 398–99.

1. This letter has not been located.
2. See Deuteronomy 8:15–16.
3. Apparently WI's ailment was caused by his being outside in inclement weather as he supervised the building and remodeling at Sunnyside. See PMI, III, 398.
4. See WI to PMI, January 6, 1847, for other details.

2016. To Sabina O'Shea

Sunnyside Feb 14th. 1847

My dear Mrs O'Shea

Why have you not replied to a letter I wrote to you upwards of three months since. Has it not come to hand: or are you so taken up with gay life and your new establishment at Madrid, and such a belle that you have not time or thought to bestow upon me? I declare, I think I am wrong in writing again to you until I am satisfied on this head, as it does not do to let you women know the power you have over us. But I ⟨will persuade myself⟩ am so anxious once more to see your hand writing and to have a kind word directly from yourself that I will lay aside all dignity and pique and write a second letter before I have received a reply to the first.

I want to know what you are doing at Madrid: whether you are very gay; whether your new house pleases you; whether your health is good and whether you are able to keep the Doctors at a distance—only think what an escape you had out of their clutches at Paris, when you were beleaguered by a whole band of them. How does my venerable friend Quique and how does my gay friend Willy. Tell him I met the young lady (Miss Gibbes) at a ball at New York recently, where she was quite a belle. I mean the eldest of the three pretty sisters with whom he flirted at my nieces party ↑at Paris↓. She bears him in kind reccollection and said some very kind things about him which, however, I will not repeat lest I should make him vain.

I dont mean to make this a long letter, and will wait until I hear from you before I give free scope to my pen.

I shall write by this occasion to H O'Shea & Cy. to have the shares which they hold for me, sold, and the money remitted. I hope they have made a good bag of money for me for I am much in want of it just now, having spent all the money in my pocket in building an addition to my house; and being a little put to it to keep the Kitchen chimney smoking.

With kindest remembrances to the three Mr. O'Sheas I am ever my dear Mrs O'Shea

> Your sincerely attached friend
> Washington Irving

ADDRESSED: Madame / Madame O'Shea / Madrid   DOCKETED: Feby 14th. 1847.
MANUSCRIPT: HSA.   PUBLISHED: Penney, *Bulletin NYPL*, 63 (January, 1958), 30.

2017.   To Sarah Storrow

Sunnyside—Feb. 15. 1847.

My dear Sarah,

I know you are wondering at my long silence[1] and reproaching me with it; but for some time past I seem to have been spell bound with respect to letter writing and indeed with respect to any kind of exercise of the pen. I cannot even bring myself to the literary task of preparing my works for re-publication; much as I need an addition to my income from that source. I hope this may wear away before long; but I fear the exercise of the pen is daily becoming more and more irksome to me, and nothing but sheer necessity will ever drive me again to full literary application. Beside, I have been much out of Sorts for some time past, being harrassed by a return of my old malady, which has siezed upon one of my ankles and fetters me so that I have not been out of the house for upwards of a week. It was brought on, or rather aggravated, by stand- ing too much[2] out of doors, in cold and wet weather, superintending the building of the new part of my house. I trust with the return of mild and genial weather I shall once more get rid of this annoying malady.

By dint of great exertions I got the addition to my house in a great measure completed some time since, so that there will be but little to be done in the Spring and the whole will be in order by the ⟨open⟩ com- mencement of the visiting season. It is a most convenient addition to the house and harmonizes with the rest of the building; forming at the same time one of its most striking and picturesque features.[3]

We had a pleasant Christmas. Helen,[4] Mr Van Wart and your brother were our visitors from the city. The little Cottage as usual was dressed with evergreens; and, though we did not dance as formerly, yet we con- trived to pass the time very merrily.

I have since been in town for a fortnight. I went down to attend the wedding of one of Mr Brevoorts daughters[5] with my friend young Bristed grandson of Mr Astor; and was kept in town by unavoidable dinner and evening invitations, which I found very pleasant, but which helped to send me home to Sunnyside an invalid.

One of these dinners was given by Mr Robert Ray[6] on the opening of his new house. He has a spacious mansion, built with good taste and well furnished The dinner was quite in the European style and we were a large party of ladies and gentlemen; composed of the real Knicker- bockers: those with whom I had been accustomed to associate in my younger days. I took your friend Mary King[7] in to dinner and sat between her and Mrs Ledyard,[8] and a most entertaining time I had of it. They both spoke a great deal about you, and most kindly and affectionately as you may suppose. Some evenings afterwards I accompanied Julia Grin- nell to the same house to a grand ball, a housewarming at which we had all the elite of the city, and where I seemed to meet every body that I had ever known or cared for. Mr Grinnell had a cold and could not go, so I was Julias escort and I really felt proud of her as I took her in, she looked so well and she was so beautifully dressed in one of the dresses you sent out to her.

I think if you had passed a winter in New York you would have enjoyed it. The parties at which I was present were in better taste than any I have seen in New York. The houses are more spacious and commodious than formerly; some of them would be considered really beautiful even in the finest cities of Europe. The circle in which you would have moved is more of the old set; ⟨of⟩ who have grown very clannish and hold themselves a little aloof from the new comers. They are the most genteel & the best bred; and being well acquainted with each other, are the most cordial. I had no idea I should have enjoyed myself so much among them.

I met your friend Mrs Gibbes[9] occasionally, with her oldest daughter; who is just coming out, and looking very pretty—she was one of the bridesmaids to her cousin Miss Gibbes,[10] lately married to young John Astor[11] son of Mr William Astor—That was another wedding which took me to town previous to that at Mr Brevoorts; and which brought me among all my old acquaintances. I only regret that I am not in condition to go to town and pass a little time right socially and joyously among my old friends. I only half enjoyed the visits I made; having to lie on the sofa all day to prepare for the fatigues of the evening.

You, of course, have heard all about little Charlies engagement.[12] The little sly boots was so quiet about it—I had not an inkling of the matter until I was told of it, ⟨the morn⟩ by Julia Grinnell the morning of my last arrival in town. The youth[13] has since passed a week at the Cottage and we are all highly pleased with him. He is frank, open and cheery, and often reminds me of his uncle Mr Grinnell; of whom he is a great favorite, and who is quite delighted with the match—I am half inclined to think he had a hand in promoting it. The young couple are to be married I believe in June and are to take up their abode at Ingleside on ⟨lake⟩ Cayuga lake: which I am told is a very commodious and indeed beautiful place, with a large farm belonging to it. I think it probable Kate will accompany Charlotte on her first visit—at least such is the wish of William Grinnell; and I think the expedition would be both pleasant and beneficial to Kate.[13a]

Your Mother when I was in town was looking extremely well, and was in cheerful spirits. Indeed I think for some months past she has altogether been in a more healthful state, mental and physical, than for years previously. We have always long talks about you and the children—an inexhaustable and animating theme to her.

To jump from one thing to another—I wish you would send out to me by Captain Funck,[14] the Album presented to me by Mr Vattemare[15]—it will be quite a resource at the Cottage.

What a trick you pla⟨i⟩yd me with that Case of articles *for my family*; which was to be opened at Mr Grinnells—What an irresistible propensity you ladies have to play the Smuggler. It is well Mr. Grinnell and I knew nothing of the matter or we might have marred the game. I believe Julia is very much pleased with every thing you have sent her: she certainly may well be as to articles of dress; ↑for↓ she ⟨certainly⟩ is always one of the best dressed ladies in New York.

I shall not oppose any inclination she may ever express to go to Europe; but I believe she has too correct a judgement and too generous a self denial to seek to gratify any such inclination at present; and I should think you would understand sufficiently all the bearings of the case and the importance of her husband and herself remaining just now in the United States, ↑not↓ to seek to shake her resolution by any tempting representations of Parisian life. Both her husband and herself are now taking a position in society ↑and are forming intimacies and friendships↓ which will be of advantage hereafter to themselves and their immediate family; while they form a rallying point for our own scattered connexion which has long wanted something of the kind in New York. If Julia were not surrounded with substantial comforts and elegant enjoyments, it might be worth her while to leave her house and wander with her children abroad in quest of pleasure; but she has a happy home, and the more she centres her feelings and desires there the happier she will be.

Mr Henry Grinnell[16] and his daughter Sarah are on the point of sailing for Europe. You will no doubt see them at Paris. Sarah is a very nice girl, a great friend of Charlottes. I trust you will be attentive to her

I find you could not resist the temptation of seeing Kate figure at a childrens ball. I see you will now and then treat self denial a little. I wish I had Kate at the Cottage ↑for↓ a few years, I dread her becoming a Parisian belle—yet I confess I should have liked to see her dressed out for the ball—with her sattin boots

Feb 20th. This letter has been lying by me for a few days and I must now finish it in a hurry to send it to town by Pierre M Irving. He and Helen came up here a couple of days since.[17] Helen remains with us and I shall keep her as long as possible—She is such a delightful companion: so full of *conversation*; which, in general, is the one thing wanting in my quiet domestic fireside.

Farewell my dear Sarah. Kiss your dear children for me and, if possible, keep them in mind of their uncle. Give my kind remembrances to Mr Storrow and believe me ever most affectionately

Your uncle
Washington Irving

P. S Remember me Kindly to the Corwins—to Mr Sumner[18] &c—I hope you see a great deal of Posey Rhinelander.[19]

ADDRESSED: Madame / Madame Storrow / aux soins de Mr. T. W. Storrow // 9
    Rue du Faubg Poissonniere / à Paris / "Cambria" via Boston March 1/47
MANUSCRIPT: Yale.

1. WI's letter of October 18, 1846, is the last one which has been located.

2. At this point is a cancellation, "Sunnyside Feb 15th. 1847," written upside
down. Probably it results from WI's having started the letter with the sheet turned
in the other direction, being interrupted, and absentmindedly starting anew with
the sheet reversed.

3. The addition provided more commodious accommodations for family and
servants with "[no] material changes ... in the internal arrangement of the older part
of the building, but externally, as a whole, the alteration was very marked: the
sky-line was much enlivened by the pagoda-like roof over one portion ... and
when it was completed the house had a picturesque charm uncommon enough at
that time." See Clarence Cook, "A Glimpse of Sunnyside," *Century Illustrated
Monthly Magazine*, 34 (May, 1887), 57.

4. Probably Helen Schermerhorn Irving, the wife of John Treat Irving, Jr. WI
had mentioned to Helen Dodge Irving that he had missed not seeing her over
the holidays. See WI to Helen Dodge Irving, February 14, 1847.

5. Laura Brevoort (d. 1860) was married on January 14, 1847, to Charles
Astor Bristed (1820–1874).

6. Ray (1794–1879), a lawyer at 65 Wall Street and a member of the firm of
Prime, Ward, Daniels, and King, opened his new house in Fitz-ray Place, at the
corner of 28th Street and 9th Avenue, with a big party on January 28, 1847. Ray
was married to Cornelia Prime. See *The Diary of Philip Hone*, ed. Allan Nevins.
2 vols. (New York, 1927), II, 784–85; and William S. Pelletreau, *Historic Homes
and Family History of New York* (New York, 1907), II, 94–102.

7. Mrs. Mary Colden Rhinelander King, the wife of John Alsop King, who had
visited Sarah Storrow in Paris in 1841. See WI to Sarah Storrow, October 3, 1841;
and Walter W. Spooner, *Historic Families of America* (New York, 1907), pp. 68,
70, 77–78.

8. Mrs. Henry Ledyard, the former Matilda Frances Cass and daughter of
Lewis Cass, was married on September 19, 1839. WI had met her in Paris in
1842, when her husband was U.S. chargé d'affaires there. See WI to Sarah Storrow,
October 10, 1842.

9. Probably the former Caroline Elizabeth Guignard, who married Robert M.
Gibbes in 1827 and lived on 5th Avenue north of 11th Street. See *The Guignard
Family of South Carolina, 1795–1930*, ed. Arney R. Childs (Columbia, S.C., 1957),
p. 150.

10. Charlotte Augusta Gibbes (d. 1890), the daughter of Thomas S. Gibbes
(d. 1856), one of the founders of the Union Club, who lived in the same block
as his brother Robert. Charlotte was married on December 9, 1846. See Harvey
O'Connor, *The Astors* (New York, 1941), pp. 75–76, 131.

11. John Jacob Astor III (1822–1890), the son of William B. and Margaret
Armstrong Astor, was a lawyer who later managed the family's real estate holdings
and fostered the development of the Astor Library.

12. WI is referring to Charlotte, Ebenezer's youngest daughter.

13. William R. Grinnell (1819–1898) was the fiancé of Charlotte Van Wart
Irving. The couple was married on June 7, 1847.

13a. Catharine Ann Irving (1816–1911), seventh child of Ebenezer.

14. Captain of a packet ship operating between LeHavre and New York. See
WI to Sarah Storrow, October 3, 1841.

15. Nicholas Marie Alexandre Vattemarre (1796–1864), a Parisian ventriloquist and impersonator who made his American debut in New York in 1839, established a plan for exchanging duplicate books and art objects between libraries and museums in the United States and Europe. The album has not been identified.

16. Henry Grinnell (1800–1874), a brother of Moses H. Grinnell, was a member of the firm of Grinnell, Minturn & Co.

17. In his letter of February 14 to Helen Dodge Irving, WI had complained about his ailments and the fact that he had not seen Helen and Pierre since the previous fall. Apparently they hurried to Sunnyside to see him.

18. George Sumner (1817–1866), a political economist and author, lectured extensively on philanthropic subjects and wrote for the *North American Review* and the *Democratic Review* and for French and German periodicals. His advocacy of the system of solitary confinement in prisons led to its adoption in French penitentiaries. Sumner, who was living in Paris at this time, had met WI in Spain a few years earlier. See R. C. Waterston, *Memoir of George Sumner* (Cambridge, Mass., 1880), pp. 13, 14; and *Herringshaw's Encyclopedia of American Biography* (Chicago, 1898), p. 906.

19. Mary E. Rhinelander (b. 1826), the daughter of Frederick W. and Mary Stevens Rhinelander, was nicknamed Posey. She married Thomas H. Newbold in 1843. See B. D. Hassell, *The Rhinelander Family in America* (New York, 1896), chart.

2018. *To L. Howard Newman*

Sunnyside Feb 20t. 1847

My dear Sir,

Since the receipt of your last letter[1] I have written again to the Secretary of the Navy on the subject of your appointment.[2] As you appear sensible of the uncertainty of success in this application and disposed to try ⟨for⟩ your fortunes in the Merchants Service, I have written at large in your favor to the house of Grinnell Minturn & Co. and now enclose you a mere letter of introduction to them

In delivering it I wish you to ask for Mr Moses Grinnell or Mr Minturn,[3] as these are the two partners to whom my reccommendation has been particularly addressed.

In entering the Merchants Service you must be aware that you have to begin at the very beginning. That is to say, to begin before the mast. Should you, however, prove yourself capable and reliable, I trust I may get you put forward early.

The Service on board the fine ships in these great shipping houses, is a very advantageous one; and the captains are apt to acquire a competency much sooner than officers in the Navy

Very truly yours
Washington Irving

ADDRESSED: Mr L. Howard Newman
MANUSCRIPT: Andrew B. Myers.

1. This letter has not been located.
2. See WI to John Y. Mason, February 4, 1847.
3. Robert B. Minturn, Grinnell's brother-in-law.

2019.   To Romulus M. Saunders

Sunnyside March 7h. 1847.

My dear Sir,

This will be handed to you by our Countryman Mr Robert LeRoy[1] of New York for whom I would ask your kind civilities during his sojourn in Madrid.

Hoping you find your residence in Spain agreeable and that you continue in good health

I am, my dear Sir, / Very respectfully and / truly yours
Washington Irving

His Excellency. / Genl R. M Saunders / &c &c &c

MANUSCRIPT: SHR.

1. Robert LeRoy was a nephew of Jacob LeRoy, of the prominent New York firm of LeRoy, Bayard & Co. See Edward A. LeRoy, *Genealogical Chart and History of the LeRoy Family* (New York, 1933), chart.

2020.   To Helen Dodge Irving

Sunnyside, March 12, 1847

❋ ❋ ❋ ❋ ❋ ❋ ❋

We were in hopes, a day or two since, that we had got rid of winter. The frost was out of the ground, and the roads were beginning to settle; but cold weather has suddenly returned upon us, and everything is again frozen up. This keeps me back in the finishing of my new building, for I was on the point of putting the workmen upon it. I am impatient to complete the job. I want to get my study in order, and my books arranged. I feel rather cramped for room, now that I have resumed literary occupations, and am at the same time an invalid. Besides, the interior of my household wants some different arrangement, as you must be aware. ❋ ❋ ❋

But the fact is, I am growing a confounded old fellow; I begin to be so studious of my convenience, and to have such a craving desire to be comfortable.

Give my love to all the household, and tell Pierre to make money for me as fast as possible, as my expenses will break out anew with the blossoms of spring, and will need all his *screwing*[1] to keep pace with them.

Affectionately, your uncle,
Washington Irving

PUBLISHED: PMI, III, 399.

1. WI is alluding to the dividends from his stock in the Screw Dock Company, of which PMI had notified him two months earlier. See WI to PMI, January 6, 1847.

2021.   To Catharine Paris

Sunnyside March 12th. 1847

My dear Sister,

Helen must have told you all the very scanty news of the Cottage, so that I have not much to Communicate. Her visit was most cheering to us all; but particularly to me being so completely cut off from out of doors recreation and confined to the house by this unlucky ankle

It is true I have driven out three or four times of late, when the weather and roads permitted, and have even managed to pay visits to Dr Creighton and Mr McKenzies;[1] but I cannot stir aboard on foot, while the ground is wet or there remains any snow. I trust this teasing obstinate malady may wear away as spring advances; at any rate I shall be able by and bye to get out on the grass and lounge under the trees—But what a change from my usual active habits! My great annoyance is not to be able to go about my place and see to getting things in order, and having them done to suit me. There is nothing like the eye of a master, however active and faithful may be the servants. I am anxious also to resume operations on my new building and get it finished that I may regulate my house and household and establish myself more conveniently; feeling much the want of a bed room separate from my study and more accommodation in my study for my books and papers. Perhaps my invalid condition makes me a little more sensible to inconveniences than formerly.

We have a nice, tidy handy girl as a waiter in lieu of a boy. It was a change I suggested and which the girls gladly adopted, and are much pleased with. I own I rather like to be waited upon by the "Woman Kind", provided they are of the right kind, and I think in a little mansion like this garrisoned by young ladies a nice waiting ⟨made⟩ ↑maid↓ is much more serviceable and appropriate than a lubberly boy.

If you continue to like the people with whom you board you should secure an apartment in their house when they move up town. In fact when Julia moves away from College place[2] you would find a residence in the lower part of the city quite a separation from your friends. All the world is moving up town.

You talk of taking lodgings for the summer at Kellengers.[3] It is a good place and has the advantage of being near to Julias[4] and within a drive of the Cottage; but a much better one is likely to present. ⟨in⟩ Mr Holmes is busied in making great additions to his house for the purpose of taking boarders. He is raising it a story, making a number of bed rooms in the attic; turning the present Kitchen into a dining room and putting the Kitchen in the basement. This would be a delightful situation for you. You could pass much of your time at the Cottage, beside being in continual communication with it, when at home: and Mr Paris would have Tarry town at hand for an occasional stroll to hear the news, and break the back of a long morning.

I had a letter from Sarah[5] some time since giving me news of some of my Paris friends but referring me to you for information about the children. I wish you would inclose her letters in an envellope to me and send them by the next opportunity to the Cottage. I dont know when I shall be able to get to New York in my present crippled State.

The weather continues cold; or rather we have a return of frost; which binds up the ground and retards all operations. I begin to fear we shall have a late spring, in which case we shall be in a complete hurry and worry of work of all kinds. It was lucky that I got my new building so far done in the early part of Winter.

Give my affectionate remembrances to Mr Paris and Irving

ever your affectionate brother
Washington Irving

MANUSCRIPT: Yale.   PUBLISHED: PMI, III, 400 (in part).

1. WI's Tarrytown neighbors. See WI to Sarah Storrow, October 18, 1846.

2. Julia and Moses Grinnell lived at 6 College Place. College Place, a street extending from Barclay to a junction with West Broadway, was on the western side of the Columbia College campus. It was later eliminated. See the map in David T. Valentine, *History of the City of New-York* (New York, 1853), opp. p. 379.

3. In 1860 Sarah Kellenger, a widow, had a boarding house on South Broadway and Guion Streets, Yonkers. See *Westchester County Directory* (New York, 1860), p. 159.

4. Julia Grinnell's summer house was in Yonkers, seven miles from Sunnyside. See WI to Sarah Van Wart, August 29, 1847.

5. This letter has not been located.

2022. To George A. Ward

Sunnyside March 23d 1847

My dear Sir

I have forborne to answer your obliging letter of the 5th[1] instant until I should have read the volume which accompanied it.[2] I have done so, and I now return you my sincere thanks for the pleasure and edification which it has afforded me. It is indeed a very interesting volume in itself and impresses me deeply in favor of its author; but it is still more interesting as throwing an entirely new light upon the motives and feelings of many of that class of our Countrymen who were designated as Tories during our revolution; and who have so generally been held up to obloquy as traitors to their country; whereas it is shown that their opposition to the new order of things might be consistent with the stanchest loyalty and purest patriotism:

I shall certainly profit greatly by the new light thus given me in the prosecution of the work[3] to which you allude and which I am sorry to say has been greatly interrupted and retarded by ill health and the concurrence of various other occupations.

I am dear Sir, with great respect

Your truly obliged friend & Sert
Washington Irving.

George A. Ward Esq / &c &c &c

PUBLISHED: *Essex Institute Historical Collections*, 83 (1947), 85.

George Atkinson Ward (1793–1864), a native of Salem, Massachusetts, was a businessman in that city until 1821, when he entered the mercantile field in New York. In 1863 he returned to Salem. See letter from Mrs. Charles A. Potter, September 18, 1975.

1. This letter has not been located.

2. Probably *Journal and Letters of the Late Samuel Curwen, Judge of Admiralty, etc., an American Refugee in England, from 1775 to 1784, Comprising Remarks on Prominent Men and Measures of the Period, to Which Are Added Biographical Notices of Many American Loyalists and Other Eminent Persons* (New York, 1842). A copy of the third edition (1845) of this book is in WI's library at Sunnyside.

3. WI's biography of George Washington.

2023.   To Pierre M. Irving

[Sunnyside, Late March, 1847]

* * * I am getting on well with my delinquent ankle, and am able, now the snow is gone, to take a turn occasionally out of doors, and visit the garden and poultry yard, which is very refreshing. I hope, by the time Helen gets through her "spring arrangements,"[1] disposes of her band-box and carpet bag, and comes up here, she will find me

"once more able
To stump about my farm and stable."[2]

I expect the carpenters this morning, to resume operations on the new building, and I shall keep all hands at work until the job is finished.

PUBLISHED: PMI, III, 400.

1. Probably WI is quoting from a letter written by PMI or his wife.
2. No source has been found for this quotation. It may have been made up by WI himself.

2023a.   To ———

April 12, 1847

I am afraid, from the extract from Mr. Brown's letter, that he has formed expectations concerning my forthcoming life of Mahomet which the work will not realize. It is a work without pretension, composed some year's since for popular circulation and originally intended for Mr. Murray's family library; circumstance prevented its publication at the time; it has been revised and almost rewritten in consequence of after views taken of the subject. Its publication is now delayed merely that it may appear with a new and revised edition of my works which I am preparing for the press.

PUBLISHED: Carroll A. Wilson, *Thirteen Author Collections of the Nineteenth Century and Five Centuries of Familiar Quotations*, ed. Jean C. S. Wilson and David A. Randall, I, 169.

2024. To Pierre M. Irving

Sunnyside, April 13, 1847.

My dear Pierre:

I was just setting off for town, this morning, to meet Mr. Prescott[1] at dinner at Mr. Cary's,[2] when a few drops of rain and the prognostications of the weatherwise made me draw back. I regret it now, as I hardly know when I shall be able to get away from superintending the arrangement of my grounds, house, &c.; and I long to have a "crack" with you.

✿ ✿ ✿ ✿ ✿

I cannot afford a new saddle to my new horse. I am getting my old saddle furbished up, which must serve until I can recover from the ruin brought upon me by the improvement of my house. You see, I am growing economical, and saving my candle now that I have burnt it down to an end.

✿ ✿ ✿ ✿ ✿

I am surprised and delighted at the windfall from Milwaukie, and shall now not despair of the sky's falling and our catching larks. Toledo,[3] too, begins to crawl. There's life in a muscle! The screw,[4] however, is the boy for my money. The dividends there are like the skimmings of the pots at Camacho's wedding.[5]

PUBLISHED: PMI, III, 401.

1. William Hickling Prescott (1796–1859), the historian.
2. Henry Carey (1793–1879), the economist and author.
3. A reference to WI's real estate investments. Apparently the Milwaukee venture, along with one in Green Bay, was handled by John Jacob Astor. The Toledo purchases were made during PMI's residence there in 1836. See PMI, III, 91.
4. WI is referring to the Screw Dock Company, which had paid a dividend in January, 1847. See WI to PMI, January 6, 1847.
5. WI alludes to the unfortunate man in Don Quixote who was cheated of his bride just as he had prepared a great feast for the wedding.

2025. To Pierre M. Irving

[Sunnyside, April 14, 1847]

Don't snub me about my late literary freak.[1] I am not letting my pen be diverted in a new direction. I am, by a little agreeable exertion, turning to account a mass of matter that has been lying like lumber in my trunks for years. When I was in Madrid, in 1826-'27, just after I had finished Columbus, I commenced a series of Chronicles illustrative of the wars between the Spaniards and the Moors; to be given as the productions of a monk, Fra Antonio Agapida.[2] The Conquest of Granada[3] was the only one I finished, though I roughly sketched out parts of some others. Your uncle Peter was always anxious for me to carry out my plan, but, somehow or other, I let it grow cool. The Chronicle of the Conquest of Granada was not so immediately successful as I had anticipated, though it has held its way better than many other of my works which were more taking at first. I am apt to get out of conceit of anything I do; and I suffered the manuscript of these Chronicles to lie in my trunks like waste paper. About four or five weeks since, I was tired, one day, of muddling over my printed works, and yet wanted occupation. I don't know how the idea of one of these Chronicles came into my head. It was the Chronicle of Count Fernan Gonzalez,[4] one of the early Counts of Castile. It makes about sixty or eighty pages of my writing. I took it up, was amused with it, and found I had hit the right vein in my management of it. I went to work and rewrote it, and got so in the spirit of the thing, that I went to work, *con amore*, at two or three fragmentary Chronicles, filling up the chasms, rewriting parts. In a word, I have now complete, though not thoroughly finished off, The Chronicle of Pelayo;[5] The Chronicle of Count Fernan Gonzalez; the Chronicle of the Dynasty of the Ommiades in Spain,[6] giving the succession of those brilliant sovereigns, from the time that the Moslem empire in Spain was united under the first, and fell to pieces at the death of the last of them; also the Chronicle of Fernando the Saint,[7] with the reconquest of Seville. I may add others to the series; but if I do not, these, with additions, ilustrations, &c., will make a couple of volumes; and I feel confident that I can make the work a taking one—giving a picture of Spain at various periods of the Moorish domination, and giving illustrations of the places of noted events, from what I myself have seen in my rambles about Spain. Some parts of these Chronicles run into a quiet, drolling vein, especially in treating of miracles and miraculous events; on which occasion Fray Antonio Agapida comes to my assistance, with his zeal for the faith, and his pious hatred of the infidels. You see, all this has cost me but a very few weeks of amusing occupation, and has put me quite in heart again, as well as in literary vein. The poring over my published works[8] was rather muddling me, and making me feel as if the true literary vein was extinct. I think, therefore, you will agree with me that my time for the last five weeks has been well employed. I have secured the frame and part of the finish of an entire new work, and can now put it by to be dressed off at leisure.

PUBLISHED: PMI, IV, 14–16.

1. WI is probably referring to "The Chronicle of Count Fernan Gonzalez," mentioned later in this paragraph.

2. WI was irritated when John Murray, his publisher, included his name on the title page along with that of his persona, Fray Antonio Agapida. See WI to John Murray, May 9, 1829.

3. Published in 1829.

4. WI's biographical sketch of Gonzalez (d. 970), the most renowned of the early counts of Castile, was published posthumously in *Spanish Papers* (1866).

5. Parts of the story of Pelayo (d. 737), who had repulsed the Muslims at Covadonga in 718, had appeared in the *Knickerbocker Magazine* (January, 1840) as "Pelayo and the Merchant's Daughter." Other portions were printed in *The Spirit of the Fair* (1864).

6. WI had published another version of this biography in the *Knickerbocker Magazine* in May, 1840. Abderahman was the first of the Ommiades, the dynasty of caliphs who ruled in Spain from 661 to 750 A.D. See Stanley Lane-Poole, *The Story of the Moors in Spain* (New York, 1888), pp. 59–60.

7. WI's account of Fernando III (1197–1252), king of Castile and Leon, remained unpublished until it appeared in *Spanish Papers* (1866).

8. WI had been reexamining his writings with the idea of bringing out a revised edition.

2026.   To Catharine Paris

Sunnyside, April 14th. 1847

My dear Sister,

I send you a part of one of Sarah's letters to you, which I overlooked when I returned the others to you. I also send you one which I received from her[1] some time since. It relates chiefly, however, to some of my Parisian acquaintances[2] whom she met at a party.

I was stepping into the Waggon to drive to the Steam boat yesterday, having a dinner invitation in town to meet Mr Prescott,[3] when it began to rain, and threatened to be a rainy day; so I gave up the jaunt and now I hardly know when I shall make it; the various concerns of the *farm* and house pressing upon me as the spring advances. I find the advantage of taking time by the forelock and "going ahead" In consequence of commencing last autumn and taking advantage of every tolerable day in the early part of the winter I have my house and grounds ready for the opening of Spring; so that every thing will grow into order with the growth of the grass and the unfolding of the leaves.

I am glad to learn that you have comfortable quarters at the Franklin House[4] until Mr. Holmes' house is ready. I think you will be pleased with both of the houses. The one at Tarry town is well spoken of; the people who keep it are said to be very respectable and obliging.

My ankle is so well that I am on my legs and about the place all the time that I am not at my table writing[.] I am glad to find moreover that it has not been the worse for pretty close literary application for some few weeks past.

I am scribbling this while the girls are getting ready to drive to the Steam boat, and must conclude in all haste

Your affectionate brother
Washington Irving

MANUSCRIPT: Yale.

1. These letters of Sarah Storrow have not been located.

2. In his letter of February 15, 1847, WI asked Mrs. Storrow to greet the Corwins, George Sumner, and Percy Rhinelander for him.

3. During a visit to New York in April of 1847 William H. Prescott went out to Sunnyside to see WI. See C. Harvey Gardiner, *William Hickling Prescott: A Biography* (Austin, 1969), pp. 259–60.

4. In Tarrytown the Franklin House (James West, Jr., proprietor) at Broadway and Franklin Streets was "well located for families desiring a healthy and beautiful residence during the summer season...." See advertisement in *Westchester County Directory*, p. xx.

2027.   To Pierre M. Irving

Sunnyside, April 15, 1847.

My dear Pierre:

I am glad I did not receive your note of this morning[1] before my new work was beyond the danger of being chilled by a damper. You can know nothing of the work, excepting what you may recollect of an extract of one of the Chronicles which I once published in the Knickerbocker[2] The whole may be mere "skimmings,"[3] but they pleased me in the preparation; they were written when I was in the vein, and that is the only guide I go by in my writings, or which has led me to success. Besides, I write for pleasure as well as profit; and the pleasure I have recently enjoyed in the recurrence, after so long an interval, of my old literary vein, has been so great, that I am content to forego any loss of profit it may occasion me by a slight postponement of the republication of my old works.

These old Morisco Spanish subjects have a charm that makes me content to write about them at half price. They have so much that is highminded and chivalrous and quaint and picturesque and adventurous, and at times half comic about them.

However, I'll say no more on the subject, but another time will ride my hobby privately, without saying a word about it to anybody. I have generally found that the best way. I am too easily dismounted, if any one jostles against me.

PUBLISHED: PMI, IV, 17.

1. This letter has not been located, but in it PMI, according to his later testimony, suggested that WI defer publication of his Moorish chronicles until the contemplated revised edition of his works had appeared. See PMI, IV, 16.

2. This was "Pelayo and the Merchant's Daughter," which was published in *Knickerbocker Magazine*, 15 (January, 1840), 65–70.

3. Apparently a phrase which PMI had used in his letter.

2028.   To Pierre M. Irving

Sunnyside, April 26, 1847.

My dear Pierre:

* * * The horse purchased by Mr. Van Wart[1] is a very fine animal, and very gentle, but he does not suit me. I had ridden him once, and find him, as I apprehended, awkward and uncomfortable on the trot, which is the gait I most like. He is rather skittish also, and has laid my coachman in the dust by one of his pirouettes. This, however, might be the effect of being shut up in the stable of late,[2] and without sufficient exercise; but he is quite a different horse from the easy, steady, quiet "parson's" nag that I wanted. I shall give him one more good trial, but rather apprehend I shall have to send him to town, to be sold for what he will fetch.

PUBLISHED: PMI, IV. 20.

1. Earlier in the year WI had asked his brother-in-law, Henry Van Wart, to purchase a saddle horse for him. See PMI, IV, 20.

2. The horse had been confined for several weeks in New York, where Van Wart and his son had used and trained him. See PMI, IV, 20.

2029.   To Pierre M. Irving

April 28, 1847

In my letter,[1] the other day, I spoke rather disparagingly of my new horse. Justice to an injured animal induces me to leave the enclosed letter open for your perusal, after which you will hand it to I. V. W.[2]

PUBLISHED: PMI, IV, 20.

1. See WI to PMI, April 26, 1847.

2. See WI to Irving Van Wart, April 28, 1847.

2030. To Irving Van Wart

Sunnyside, April 28, 1847.

My dear Irving:

In a letter to Pierre M. Irving, the other day,[1] I gave an unfavorable opinion of the horse, as it regarded my peculiar notions and wishes. That opinion was founded on a slight trial. I yesterday took a long ride on him among the hills, and put him through all his paces, and found him fully answering the accounts given of him by your father and yourself. His trot is not what I could wish; but that will improve, or will be less disagreeable as we become accustomed to each other, and get into each other's ways. He shies a little now and then, but that is probably the result of having him kept in the stable of late, without use. Daily exercise will in a great measure cure him of it. He canters well, and walks splendidly. His temper appears to be perfect. He is lively and cheerful, without the least heat or fidgetiness, and is as docile as a lamb. I tried him also in harness in a light wagon, and found him just as gentle and tractable as under the saddle. He looks well and moves well in single harness, and a child might drive him. However, I mean to keep him entirely for the saddle. To conclude: when you write to your father, tell him I consider the horse a prize; and if he only continues to behave as well as he did yesterday, I hardly know the sum of money would tempt me to part with him.[2]

I now look forward to a great deal of pleasant and healthy exercise on horseback—a recreation I have not enjoyed for years for want of a good saddle horse. It is like having a new sense. * * *

Instead of being pinned down to one place, or forced to be trundled about on wheels, I went lounging and cantering about the country, in all holes and corners, and over the roughest roads.

PUBLISHED: PMI, IV, 21–22.

1. See WI to PMI, April 26, 1847.

2. WI changed his mind a short time later, for PMI observed that within a month Irving Van Wart took the animal back to New York and sold him at Tattersall's. See PMI, IV, 22; and WI to Sarah Storrow, June 6, 1847.

2031.   *To Helen Dodge Irving*

Sunny Side April 30t 1847

My dear Helen,

The girls say you can come up to Sunnyside as soon as you please
There is nothing in the house cleaning to prevent; the house having already got over the crisis of its yearly complaint. To day my "Women
Kind" of the Kitchen remove bag and baggages into the new *tower*[1]
which is getting its outside coat of white so that when you come up you
will find it like the trees, in full blossom

The Country is beginning to look lovely: the buds and blossoms are
just putting forth; the birds are in full song, so that unless you come up
up soon you will miss the overture of the season; the first sweet notes of
the year.

You tell me Pierre was quite distressed lest any "thoughtless word of
his should have marred my happy literary mood" ⟨It⟩ Tell him not to be
uneasy Authors are not so easily put out of conciet of their offspring. Like
the good Archbishop of Granada that model and mirror of authorship
I knew "the homily in question to be the very best I had ever composed" So like my great prototype I remained fixed in my self com-
placency, wishing Pierre "toda felicidad con un poco de mas gusto."[2]

When I once get you up to Sunnyside I shall feel sure of an occasional
Sunday visit from Pierre. I long extremely to have a sight of him, and as
there seems to be no likelihood of my getting to New York much before
next autumn I do not know how a meeting is to be brought about unless
he comes up here. I shall see him with the more ease and confidence
now, as, ⟨I⟩ my ⟨building has⟩ improvements being pretty nigh completed,
he cannot check me nor cut off the supplies.

Tell him I promise not to bore him about literary matters when he
comes up. I have as great a contempt for these things as anybody, though
I have to stoop to them occasionally for the sake of a livelihood—but I
want to have a little talk with him about stocks, and rail roads and some
mode of screwing and jewing the world out of more interest than ones
money is entitled to[3]

Washington Irving

Manuscript: NYPL.—Seligman Collection.   Published: PMI, IV, 18 10 (in part).

1. This was part of the addition to Sunnyside undertaken in the fall of 1846.
"[E]xternally, . . . the alteration was very marked: the sky line was much enlivened
by the pagoda-like roof over one portion." See Clarence Cook, "A Glimpse of
Washington Irving at Home," *Century Illustrated Magazine,* 34 (May, 1887), 57.
2. "All happiness with a little more pleasure" or "a little pleasure added."

3. The printed version in PMI concludes with "God bless you and him, prays your affectionate uncle," but this passage has been clipped from the holograph.

2032.   *To Pierre M. Irving*

[April?, 1847]

That you may not be frightened at my extravagance, and cut off supplies, I must tell you that I have lately been working up some old stuff which had lain for years lumbering like rubbish in one of my trunks, and which, I trust, will more than pay the expense of my new building.

PUBLISHED: PMI, III, 401–2.

2033.   *To John Murray III*

Sunnyside May 8. 1847.

My dear Sir,

Permit me to reccommend to your kind civilities Mr St George T Campbell,[1] who visits Europe on a tour of health. He is a gentleman of intelligence and worth and nephew to Mr Dallas the Vice President of the United States. Any attentions you may find it convenient to bestow upon him will be considered as personal favors rendered to myself.

With kind remembrances to your family

Yours ever very faithfully
Washington Irving

John Murray Esqr / &c &c &c

ADDRESSED: John Murray Esq / Albemarle Street / London
MANUSCRIPT: John Murray.   PUBLISHED: WIHM, p. 185.

John Murray III (1808–1892) became head of the Murray publishing firm in London upon the death of his father in 1843.

1. St. George T. Campbell was the son of Maria Charlotte Dallas and Alexander Campbell of Norfolk, Virginia. He married a daughter of Thomas Mason of Culross, Virginia and left a large family. See James Dallas, *The History of the Family of Dallas* (Edinburgh, 1921), p. 515.

2034. To Sarah Storrow

Sunnyside June 6th. 1847

My dear Sarah,

Your letter of May 15th.[1] received last evening made my conscience
fly in my face ⟨with⟩ at the idea of the long time I had suffered to elapse
without writing to you.[2] ⟨I am howe⟩ I have however been a sad delinquent of late to all my correspondents; part of the time being absorbed
in literary occupations; part busied in finishing and arranging my house
and grounds and part sunk into listless depression after the excitement
of these occupations was over. I now sieze the pen, though by no means
⟨,⟩ in the writing mood, with the determination not to ⟨let another⟩ remain delinquent for another day.

My last letter gave you an account of a visit which I made to town in
January last. I have not been there since a partial return of my old malady in one of my ankles rendered it advisable for me to keep within
doors during the wintry weather, and by degrees the "stay at home"
habit got quite the mastery of me. Besides as spring opened, and I began
to have workmen about me, I did not dare to go from home, lest they
should make blunders, as the[y][3] worked according to my plans and under my supervision.

By dint of working in season and out of season and in defiance of wind
and weather I have got my house completely finished and inhabited and
all my grounds in order by the time Spring opened; so that I have not
lost a single day of ↑the↓ enjoyable season; and my place looks as if it
had never been disturbed. The additions and alterations have turned out
beyond my hopes, both as to ⟨looks⟩ ↑appearance↓ and convenience, and
meet with universal approbation. I have an excellent laundry; kitchen
pantry, coal cellar Servants rooms, a little store room and laboratory for
the girls with which they are delighted, and in which they seem to pass
half their time, and very snug closets. A communication being cut through
the wall, in one of the closets of the upper hall, the appartment over the
Kitchen is united to the main building. A partition at the head of the
Kitchen stairs shuts off the heat; while a door permits the use of that
Stair case for the Service of the upper part of the house; which is a great
convenience. The smallest of the two rooms ↑formerly↓ occupied by the
Servants is now old Mammys[4] asylum. The largest is very prettily arranged, and is occupied by Kate & Sarah; and the old store room affords
an excellent closet for the girls. We have thus a gain of two bed rooms
in the family part of the house; and I have taken possession of the north
one; where I have had a neat closet put up behind the door, to hang
up clothes &c—⟨you have ↑add[.]↓ shelv⟩ The north end of my study has

been shelved like the other parts; the books which were so long were exiled to the garret have been brought down and arranged; and my library now makes a very respectable appearance.

You have now an idea of the internal additions and improvements—of the external you shall judge whenever I can have a sketch made. As to my grounds, I have cut down and transplanted enough trees to furnish two ordinary places and still there are, if any thing, too many. but I have opened beautiful views, and have given room for the air to circulate. The ⟨place is now Sup⟩ season is now in all its beauty; the trees in full leaf, but the leaves fresh and tender; the honey suckles are in flower, and I think I never saw the place look so well. I only wish you were here to enjoy it with me.

The girls are in the midst of preparations for Charlottes wedding,[5] which takes place the day after tomorrow (Tuesday, June 8th). in the morning, as yours did. I have left the whole arrangement, invitations &c &c to the girls; not presuming to say any thing in the matter lest I should thwart or constrain any of their plans or wishes. I do not know even who all are to be here, but trust the little mansion will be able to hold them all as you know it is almost magical in its capability ⟨of⟩ in that respect. After the wedding the young couple make an excursion and then return here to take their departure for their home;[6] where our dear Kate will accompany them. I trust this will be a happy marriage. Grinnell appears to be an amiable worthy young man and likely to make a Kind affectionate husband. Their mode of life will be suited to ⟨both of them⟩ the tastes and habits of both of them; and is in itself a mode of life free from many of the cares and collisions and heart burnings of the world. I think it will be good for the girls to have a Sister married and settled at a distance; as visits to and fro will diversify the somewhat monotonous life of the domestic circle. The idea of Separation however is a very sore one to them all and has to be very tenderly touched upon, they are all so attached to one another.

I am grieviously disappointed at your mothers choosing Kellengers instead of Mr Holmes, for her Summer residence. I trusted to have seen her almost every day and to have had her a great part of the time at the Cottage; now it is a days operation to make her a visit, and ⟨in⟩ the heat of summer; the interruptions of visitors and the frequent demand of the horses for "the landings," conspire to make it impossible to see her often. ⟨Beside⟩, Your father I believe would have preferred Mr Holmes; which in fact is in almost every respect far superior to Kellengers; but your mother preferred the latter in the hope that Irving would be able to board there during the Summer months. She appears to be well pleased there; and is, as she has been ever since my return from Europe, in better health and spirits than I have known her to be for years past.

As soon as my household is thinned out I shall endeavor to get her here for a good long visit; but she ought to have taken board at Mr Holmes. Eliza and Helen[7] have taken rooms for a few weeks at the Franklin House[8] ↑(Tarry town)↓ where likewise is Sanders and his wife[8a]; so that it is quite a Colony. The House is said to be very well kept; the furniture is new; the people ↑are↓ extremely civil, and everything ↑is↓ bright and clean. The sojourn of such a portion of the family in the neighborhood will be quite enlivening—but your Mother ought to have gone to Mr Holmes—

You are pleased to hear that I have a saddle horse[9]—Unfortunately I have him no longer. Your Uncle Van Wart purchased one for me which appeared to be all that I could wish—handsome, young, gentle and of excellent movement. I rode him two or three times and was delighted with him; when one day the lurking fault came out. As I was taking a sauntering ride over to the Saw Mill river, and had gone a couple of miles he all at once stopped and declined to go any further. I tried all manner of means but in vain; he would do nothing but return home. ⟨I⟩ on my way homeward I tried him by different roads but all to no purpose; home he would go. He was not restive, but calmly stubborn; and when I endeavored to force him round would quietly back against the fence or get on two legs—So as I did not care to waste time and temper on a sullen beast, home I did go—got off of his back, and never mounted him again. He baulked twice in like manner, but not so bad, with my coachman; so I gave him over to Irving Van Wart to be sold at auction; and was glad to get rid of him ⟨at the⟩ with the loss of twenty or thirty dollars.[10] I shall not indulge in another Saddle horse at present; as my extra expenses are too heavy this year to permit of such a luxury. It is a great disappointment, however, for I cannot tell you how much I enjoyed my first rides; it seemed like having a new sense. Instead of being pinned down to one place, or forced to be trundled about ⟨a⟩ ↑on↓ wheels, ⟨carriages⟩ I went lounging and cantering about the Country, in all holes and corners and over the roughest roads. ⟨Ind⟩ My first ride was over the hills toward the nest of old Mrs Martling.[11] It was a soft spring day; when the trees were just budding forth and the birds beginning to sing. ⟨I do not know when ↑where↓ I have⟩ It was the first time I had been along that road since my return—I believe the first time since your departure from the Cottage. Every ⟨aspect⟩ feature of the landscape every turn of the road brought you to my mind; and the rambles we had so often taken together there, at this very season. I felt continually my heart in my throat, and the tears in my eyes; yet my feelings though half sad were delicious. Ah my dear Sarah how continually you are brought to my mind, in the Cottage and throughout the neighborhood; where you are associated with every thing pleasant to the eye, and where my happiest days have been made happy by your company. *If* I only had you and your children here with me!—but what an *if*!

When you see Mlle. d'Houen tell her I was in Paris only from twelve Oclock one day until day break the next day; ⟨du⟩ about eighteen hours, during which I had to transact both public and private business, beside endeavoring to get a little sleep after several days and nights of travel. I saw nobody except on business and had to hurry forward, under diplomatic high pressure—otherwise I should undoubtedly have called upon her—I will endeavor to get her an autograph of Franklin,[12] ⟨but⟩ as soon as I get once more in the current of society. I do not wonder you are delighted with her—She is one of the most *enlivening* persons I met with during my last visit to Europe.

You talk about my coming out to pay you a visit, as if I had money in both pockets. *I cannot afford it.* I am now living at the rate of twice my income; and until I can get my literary property into productive operation I must continue from day to day to grow gradually poorer; and that I can only make productive by remaining quiet—nursing my literary moods, which grow more and more capricious, and working whenever the spirit of work is upon me. For the last few weeks I have been idle and inert; and when so I feel as if I can afford nothing. I hope, however, before long, to get again in the vein and to be able to prepare my old works for ⟨a⟩ new lau[n]ch—When I have effected that I shall feel comparatively at ease.

I shall be quite proud of the handkerchief worked by my dear precious little Kate. and should be glad of one from Tutu, even though it should be ⟨worked⟩ sewn with a bodkin. I have always long talks with your mother about the two little women when we meet; indeed you and your children form our constant and inexhaustable topic. God bless you my dear Sarah; give my kind remembrances to your husband and Kiss dear little Betsy Posey and Jenny Posey[13] for me

Your affectionate uncle
Washington Irving

Manuscript: Yale.

1. This letter has not been located.

2. Apparently WI last wrote on February 15, 1847.

3. WI omitted the *y*.

4. Apparently one of WI's servants.

5. Charlotte, the daughter of Ebenezer, married William R. Grinnell (1819–1888).

6. They established themselves on a farm near Auburn, New York. See STW, II, 382.

7. WI's nieces, daughters of Ann Sarah and Richard Dodge.

8. This, the principal hotel in Tarrytown and a favorite of summer visitors, was owned by H. Wilson. See Robert Bolton, Jr., *A Brief History of Westchester County,* 2 vols. (New York, 1848), I, 199.

8a. Sanders Irving (1813–1884), son of Ebenezer, and Julia Granger (1822–1897), whom he had married on September 15, 1840.

9. Other details about the horse are to be found in WI to PMI, April 26, 1847.

10. Henry Van Wart had purchased the horse about March 5, 1847 for $110. See PMI, IV, 20.

11. Probably Mary Martling, who owned a house on Water Street in Tarrytown next door to William Paulding. See WI to Sarah Paris, December 10, 1846.

12. Presumably Benjamin Franklin (1706–1790).

13. WI's playful names for Sarah Storrow's children.

2035. To Harvey Baldwin

Sunnyside, July 3d. 1847

My dear Sir,

I enclose letters of introduction to persons in Paris whose acquaintance I trust may be of service to you. Mr. Green[1] of the house of Green & Co is an old and valued friend of mine and has a very amiable family. I would advise you to bank with his house should you not be otherwise engaged in that respect.

I know no person in Germany to whom to give a letter. It is upwards of twenty five years since I was in that country;[2] I have kept up no corespondence with any one there, and all ⟨my⟩ the acquaintanceships I formed during my visit are far beyond the Statute of limitation, or have died a natural death.

With Affectionate remembrances to your wife and best wishes that you may make a pleasant tour, I am with great regard

Yours ever very cordially
Washington Irving

H Baldwin Esq

ADDRESSED: H. Baldwin Esq / Syracuse / N. Y.
MANUSCRIPT: NYPL—Berg Collection.

Harvey Baldwin (1797–1863) was a wealthy Syracuse lawyer involved in the real estate business. He was the first mayor of Syracuse and was one of the originators of the common school system. He was married to WI's niece, Ann Sarah Dodge (1816–1886). See Charles C. Baldwin, *The Baldwin Genealogy* (Cleveland, 1881), pp. 665–66; and *Daily Journal City Register and Directory* (Syracuse, 1851), p. 85.

1. WI was on intimate social terms with the Greens in Paris in August and September of 1825, but they have not been otherwise identified, except by WI's allusions in this letter. See *J&N*, III, 383, 385, 386, 387, 393.

2. WI had traveled in Germany, Austria, Bohemia, and Saxony from August, 1822, to July, 1823.

2035a.   To Robert Walsh

Sunnyside July 3d. 1847

My dear Sir,

Permit me to reccommend to your kind Civilities my friend and relative Mr H Baldwin, of the State of New York. He visits Europe for the first time. Any attentions you may find it convenient to bestow upon him during his sojourn in Paris will be considered as personal favors to myself

With kind remembrances to Mrs. Walsh and the Young ladies[1] I am my dear Sir

Ever very faithfully yours
Washington Irving

Robert Walsh Esqr
&c   &c   &c

MANUSCRIPT: Daniel I. Larkin.

Robert Walsh (1784–1859), a journalist, editor, and literary nationalist who edited the *American Quarterly Review* from 1827 to 1837, served as American consul in Paris from 1844 to 1851. While minister to Spain, WI had met him on visits to Paris.

1. Mrs. Walsh was the former Anna Maria Moylan. It is not possible to ascertain which of the six Walsh daughters WI is referring to. See J. C. Walsh, "Robert Walsh," *Journal of the Irish American Historical Society*, XXVI (1927), 223–224.

2036.   To Gouverneur Kemble

Sunnyside July 8th. 1847

My dear Kemble,

I have long been looking out for your promised visit; but now your letter[1] throws it quite into uncertainty. I should have come to you before this for I long to take you once more by the hand, but I have been detained at home by building and repairing, and by the necessity of fighting off, by baths and prescriptions, the return of a malady which beset me in Spain,[2] and which endeavors to keep possession of one of my ankles. However, I trust to finish all my buildings and improvements and to conquer my malady before long; and then I shall endeavor to look in upon you at Cold Spring.

In fact I have not been in town for the whole winter, excepting to attend the wedding of a daughter of Brevoort,[3] who by the way, is marrying his children[4] to all the fortunes in the Country. I was recently in town two or three times on business, for a few hours each time; and the effect of these visits has been almost to lame me.

As to the pagoda[5] about which you speak it is one of the most useful additions that ever was made to a house; beside being so ornamental. It gives me laundry; store rooms; pantrys; servants rooms cold cellar &c. &c. &c. converting what was once rather a make shift little Mansion into one of the most complete snuggeries in the country; as you will confess when you come to see and inspect it. The only part of it that is not adapted to some valuable purpose is the Cupola, which has no bell in it and is about as serviceable as the feather in ones cap. Though, by the way, it has its purpose, for it supports a weather cock brought from Holland by Gill Davis[6] (the King of Coney island) who says he got it from a Windmill which they were demolishing at the gate of Rotterdam; which windmill had been mentioned in Knickerbocker. I hope, therefore, I may be permitted to wear my feather unmolested.

Ever my dear Kemble / Affectionately yours
Washington Irving

Gouvr Kemble Esqr.

Addressed: Gouverneur Kemble Esqr / Cold Spring / Putnam County   Docketed: 1847
Manuscript: Va.–Barrett.   Published: PMI, III, 402–3 (in part).

Gouverneur Kemble (1786–1875), a life-long friend of WI's, operated the West Point Foundry and manufactured guns for the American armed forces.

1. This letter has not been located.

2. In February of 1843 WI had a "herpetic attack" similar to the one which sent him to the spas of southern Germany in 1822. As a result, he had inflammation and pain in his legs and ankles which bothered him from time to time during the rest of his stay in Spain and prevented him from working on his literary projects. See WI to Sarah Storrow, February 24, 1843.

3. Laura Brevoort, who married Charles Astor Bristed on January 14, 1847. See WI to Sarah Storrow, February 15, 1847.

4. Brevoort's other married children at this time were James Carson, who married Elizabeth Dorothea Lefferts in 1845; Henry, who married Jane Stewart in 1838; and a third son, possibly Samuel, who married Eliza Bell in 1842. See *The Story of the Brevoort Family* (Brooklyn, 1964), pp. 13, 14.

5. Kemble, who had noticed the new addition to Sunnyside from a steamboat en route up the Hudson, had called it a pagoda, probably because of the appear-

ance of the roof line. See PMI, III, 402. In a letter of July 21, 1847, James K. Paulding reported to Martin Van Buren that WI had "built a Tower with a tall Spire and a weathercock on the Top, which came from an Old Dutch Church at Antwerp which was pulled down recently. Gill Davis got hold of it and gave it to him." See *Letters of J. K. Paulding*, p. 463.

6. Gilbert Davis (1786–1868), a wine merchant with stores at 45 Pine Street and 53 William Street, lived at 37 Bond Street. In 1835 he became known as the "Governor of Coney Island" because of a burlesque map of Coney Island and an enticing prospectus detailing the possibility of great profits from speculation in the sandy land of the island. Although he was sued by speculators, the case was thrown out of court. Thereafter Davis was facetiously called the "Governor of Coney Island," an epithet which WI changes to "King." See New York *Times*, July 11, 1882, p. 8.

2037. To Lewis G. Clark

[Sunnyside, July 28, 1847]

My dear Mr. Clark:

I have been intending every day for some time past to drive down and make you a visit; but every day something or other has prevented. Do not, however, stand upon ceremony, but come to Sunnyside whenever you feel in the notion. It is but a pleasant walk by a foot-path along the Aqueduct. We dine at three o'clock, and shall always be happy to have you as a guest; but come at any time in the fresh of the morning, and lounge away the day under the trees. I can furnish you with books and leave you to yourself.

I am still busy with building and improving, and shall be at home for some time to come, excepting perhaps Saturday, Sunday, and part of Monday next. So come when you please, without further invitation.

I am much obliged to you for the loan of the periodicals, which I shall return to you in good order.

Very truly yours,
Washington Irving

Sunnyside, July 28th, 1847.

Published: *Knickerbocker Magazine*, 55 (January, 1860), 115.

Lewis Gaylord Clark (1808–1873) was editor of the *Knickerbocker Magazine* from 1834 to 1861.

In paragraph 2 the second and third lines in the printed version were transposed by the printer. They have been properly arranged in the present text.

2038. *To Charlotte Grinnell*

August 13, 1847

* * * For a month past I have been busy and bothered in an un-
exampled manner, in the improvement of my farmyard, building of
outhouses, &c., which has been altogether the most fatiguing and irksome job I have had in the whole course of my additions and improvements. I have now nearly got through, but it has almost made me fit to
lie by again on the sofa. However, this job finished, I shall have my
place in tolerable order, and will have little more to do than to see that
my men keep it so.

PUBLISHED: PMI, IV, 23–24.

2039. *To Sarah Storrow*

[August 23, 1847]

My dear Sara[h] [*MS torn*]
     I am on a three [days visit?] [*MS torn*] at Mr Grinnells where I re-
ceived the day before yesterday the unexpected news of another addition
to your family.[1] I rejoice to hear that you and the new comer are doing
so well and that you expect soon to be in condition to remove for the
summer to Versailles. I long to know what little Betsey Posey and Jenny
Posey[2] say to their new sister. Really my dear Sarah you have quite a
boquet of poseys. I paid your mother a long visit yesterday morning; she
was in excellent spirits and seemed quite animated with the news—She
continues to be remarkably well for her; evincing all that ⟨characteristic⟩
↑mental↓ elasticity and that excitability of temperament which characterize her. Indeed ⟨ever⟩ since my return from Europe I have seen none
of that morbid state of feelings which formerly afflicted her; and, though
her [*MS torn*] paired her mind [*MS torn*] healthful state than I have
known it for years. Your visit, and the acquaintanceship she formed with
your dear children have acted upon her as a restorative, and have
furnished her with constant themes of delightful reccollection. In our
long conversations you and your children furnish us with inexhaustible
topics of which neither of us are every weary.
     You have had from Julia[3] and others accounts of Charlies wedding;[4]
which went off very cheerily in presence of a numerous gathering of
family connexions. our excellent friend Dr Creighton officiated, and his
daughter and niece, the latter of whom was a particular friend of Char-

lottes were present. Charlotte was beautifully dressed, under the pre-
siding taste of her cousin Julia; who presented her with her wedding
dress. She was a perfect model of a bride; I never saw any thing more
truly lovely and loveable; but though the match was every way satisfactory, yet when we came to the ceremony that took her from my
⟨domestic⟩ Side and severed her from my household I felt completely
overcome. It brought to my mind my former bereavement, and though
Charlotte was not like you, to be separated from me by the Ocean, I
felt it was a sad separation.

   She has now been upwards of two months settled at her new house
at Ingleside, and all accounts represent it as a very beautiful and a very
happy home Our dear Kate is with her and is enjoying herself to a
degree that she has not done for years. Mr Grinnell and Julia who have
just returned from a visit there, give the most gratifying accounts of the
whole establishment; the order and system with which it is carried on;
the charming manner in which charlie acquits herself in her new situation; the constant hilarity which reigns in the household and the glow
of health and flow of spirits which seem to have given freshness and
life and buoyancy to poor Kate and to have made her ten years younger.
Dr Creighton and his daughter have likewise visited Ingleside in the
course of a summers tour, and as you may suppose were most joyfully
received. The Doctor I am told went all over the farm, ⟨and⟩ inspected
it thoroughly with a learned eye and gave it his unqualified approbation.
In fact William Grinnell is an admirable manager and takes pride and
interest in ⟨his⟩ agricultural pursuits. With all this he is of a happy disposition; never fretting, and never daunted or worried by difficulties;
possessing much of the genial temperament of his uncle.[5] Kate is thoroughly delighted with him: and he and she are great friends and have
quite[6] romps together. The house is beautifully situated on the border
of the lake; so that there is good bathing at any hour of the day; and good
boating also; charlie and Kate having a little row boat which they manage
of themselves ⟨and pride⟩ ↑priding↓ themselves upon being capital
oarsmen.

   I intend as soon as the Summer heats are over and I have completed
the improvements of my place to set out on a short visit to Ingleside;
stopping at Governeur Kembles by the way. Indeed I need an excursion
of the kind, for I find as long as I am at home I task myself too much,
and keep my system in a state of irritation. This has been a toilful year
to me for after I had completed the additions to my house I proceeded to
bring my place into complete order; to inclose a Kitchen yard; to enclose the stable and make a large farm yard, poultry yard, out houses
&c and as I had to do this in an economical way; working as much as

possible with my own people and planning and superintending every thing myself it has kept me continually on my legs; in the heat of the summer ⟨and⟩ fagged me excessively and kept up and encreased the inflammation of my unlucky ankles. I have now got through with all the essential improvements and shall be able to give myself repose: and this visit to Julias, is the first excursion of pleasure and relaxation that I have made this year. I have the satisfaction to have brought my place into order and to have placed it in a condition to be comfortably and conveniently managed hereafter. It is a snug establishment both within doors and without.

I have had two of Pierre P Irvings daughters staying with me for some time past, Lilly and Hatty.[7] I requested the girls to invite them, as I wish to become familiarly acquainted with the younger branches of the family and Pierres children are intelligent and interesting. I have been much pleased with them and hope to have them frequently at the Cottage. I intend to have others of his children with me in the Autumn after my return from Ingleside. I must keep up my supply of nieces at the Cottage.

I have seen very little of our neighbors this summer; and indeed have been so much occupied and at times so much shackled by the irritation of my ankles that I have kept very much at home—I now shall begin to go about a little. Mrs Constant was at the Cottage not long since. She is somewhat ⟨pl⟩ pale and thin, and I believe her health is by no means confirmed; but she appears to me as lovely as ever. Mrs Sheldon has lost both her father and mother lately, and does not go out. Her daughters intended[8] is on a visit to their house. I find he is a son of my old friend and fellow traveller Mr Ritchie[9] with whom I once made a tour in lower Normandy. His mother[10] too, a daughter of Harrison Gray Otis,[11] is an old acquaintance with whom I was always delighted. The young gentleman is handsome, genteel, well bred, and I make no doubt intelligent. The young couple are often driving and riding out together, and are very prepossesing in their appearance.

We have another pair of young lovers in our neighborhood Helen Jones and young Langdon.[12] They also are driving and riding together about the country, but with rather more style and pretension than the others, ⟨tho⟩ but to my mind, not with better effect. Young Langdon however is a very amiable gentlemanlike young man and quite distinguished in his appearance. The match seems to have put Mrs Colford[13] in a little state of effervescence, as she has resumed her liveries and gold lace which she had laid aside; and drives about the country in a style which astonishes the Westchester yeomanry. The family makes but brief sojourns at their country retreat, however; the trees having so embowered

it that the heat at times is stifling and they have to make excursions to
Rockaway &c to get fresh air.

I must now break off to attend to the children. Lilly and Hatty have
come down in the boat with Sarah[14] this morning to pass the day at Julias
and return with me in the boat this afternoon. I hear high Jinks going on
under the trees and must be there to assist. Julias children[15] continue to
be every thing that Mothers heart could wish. How I wish yours could
be here to grow up with them. I shall never forget that day when they
were all together here and formed such lovely groupes and were so
full of frolic happiness.

Sunnyside. Aug 27th. I have kept this letter open my dear Sarah, but
have nothing of moment to add. I returned here after a very pleasant
visit to Julia's, and resumed my toils in completing my improvements.
I find I cannot keep quiet while at home, so am determined to set out
in the course of a few days on my visit to Cold Spring and Ingleside;
though not altogether in condition for travelling and visiting. Your
brother Irving made his appearance here the evening before last, much
to our gratification. I shall keep him as long as I can—for I know he
enjoys the country, and he is a most welcome visitor; full of agreeable
intelligent conversation. The country is fresh and green this summer;
and ⟨never was so beautiful⟩ in this neighborhood is daily growing more
and more beautiful, from the improved taste in building, in decorating
grounds, in setting out trees &c. The roads instead of being naked in
⟨many⟩ most parts as formerly are now bordered with trees which are
continually becoming more umbrageous and are softening and enriching
the whole landscape. My own place has never been so beautiful as at
present. I have made more openings by pruning and cutting down trees,
so that from the piazza I have several charming views of the ⟨river⟩
↑Tappan Zee[16]—and the ⟨opp⟩ hills beyond;↓ all set as it were in verdant
frames, and I am never tired of sitting there in my old Voltaire chair,
of a long summer morning, with a book in my hand, sometimes reading,
sometimes musing on the landscape, and sometimes dozing and mixing
all up in a pleasant dream.

I drove up the day before yesterday ↑with the girls↓ to Dr Creightons,
and made a delightful visit. The Doctors place is looking beautiful. He
has ⟨made⟩ dammed up a stream and made quite a large lake embosomed
in woods with pretty islands. It is quite his hobby at present. He made
very kind enquiries after you and begged me to remember. him to you
when I wrote. His daughter Catherine and his niece are coming here this
morning to pass the day.

I have just recieved a long and charming letter from my excellent
friend Mrs O'Shea,[17] who is at Biaritz—Should she visit Paris she will

be sure to call upon you as she always speaks of you with the greatest regard.

Fare well my dear Sarah. Let me hear from you soon. Give my kind remembrances to your husband

Your affectionate Uncle
Washington Irving

When you see Mr Sumner remember me to him most cordially. Tell him his letter to La Martine[18] does him great credit. It is admirable

MANUSCRIPT: Yale.   PUBLISHED: PMI, IV, 24–25 (in part).

1. The new baby, Julia Grinnell Storrow (d. July 12, 1920), later made a name for herself as a novelist in the 1890's, writing under the name of Julien Gorden. She married Colonel Stephen Van Rensslaer Cruger (1844–1898), a wealthy real estate broker, on April 21, 1868, and had homes in Manhattan and Oyster Bay. In 1908 she married Wade Chance (b. 1838) and was divorced from him in 1915. See New York *Times*, July 13, 1920.

2. WI's playful names for Catharine and Susan Storrow.

3. Julia Grinnell, with whom WI was staying.

4. WI is referring to Charlotte Irving with this nickname. She had married William R. Grinnell on June 7, 1847. WI had used the same epithet for her in his letter of February 15, 1847, to Sarah Storrow.

5. Probably Moses Hicks Grinnell.

6. WI apparently omitted a word inadvertently here.

7. Elizabeth (1834–1906) and Harriet Robinson Irving (1835–1906).

8. Mary Sheldon (d. 1913) married Harrison Ritchie (1825–1894) on May 3, 1849. He was admitted to the bar in 1848, was twice a member of the general court from Boston, and served on the staff of Governor Andrew of Massachusetts in the Civil War. In 1868 he removed permanently with his family to Paris. See Samuel Eliot Morison. *Harrison Gray Otis, 1765–1848, The Urbane Federalist* (Boston, 1969), p. 519; and William A. Otis, *A Genealogical and Historical Memoir of the Otis Family in America* (Chicago, 1924), pp. 141–44, 202.

9. Andrew Ritchie (1786–1862), with whom WI left Paris on November 8, 1820, for Rouen. Their trip together was brief, as Ritchie remained behind in Louvriers the next day to visit a factory. See *Journals of WI*, I, 29–31.

10. Sophia Harrison Otis (1798–1874) married Andrew Ritchie in December, 1823. See Morison, *Harrison Gray Otis*, p. 519.

11. Otis (1765–1848) was a staunch Federalist who served in both houses of the U.S. Congress and as mayor of Boston.

12. Helen Colford Jones married Woodbury Langdon (1824–1892) on November 9, 1847. Langdon was the grandson of John Jacob Astor. See Strong, *Diary*, I, 306; and O'Connor, *The Astors*, p. 465.

13. Mrs. Rebecca Mason Colford Jones, the mother of Helen Jones.

14. Sarah Irving, Ebenezer's daughter, who was living at Sunnyside.

15. The children of Julia and Moses Grinnell were Julia (1837–1915), Irving (1839–1921), and Fanny (1842–1887).

16. The name given to a widening of the Hudson River near Tarrytown and Tappan which Sunnyside overlooked.

17. Mrs. Henry O'Shea, the wife of an English banker in Madrid, with whom WI was on friendly terms when he was minister to Spain.

18. George Sumner published a letter to Lamartine, pointing out certain factual errors in Lamartine's *The History of the Girondists* which reflected discredit on America. Lamartine not only corrected his misstatements but included the letter in the appendix to his next edition. See Waterson, *Memoir of George Sumner*, p. 14.

2040.   To Catharine Storrow

Sunnyside, August 27, 1847

My dear Kate:

I thank you very much for the beautiful handkerchief which you have sent me. I am very proud of it, and show it to everybody, to let them see how capitally my dear little Kate can sew. I hope you will teach Tutu[1] to handle her needle as well as you do, and then you and she will be able to do all your mamma's sewing, which will be a great saving to her, and a great help to Henriette.[2]

I am happy to hear that you have a nice little new sister. I trust, as you are a big girl now, you will take great care of her; and, above all things, set her a good example, by being a very good girl yourself, and very obedient to your mamma. As soon as she is old enough, you must take her with you and Tutu to the garden of the Tuileries, and show her to the little fish that used to give good little Betsey Posy a silver dish, and tell him that this is the new little sister of Betsey Posy and Jenny Posy, and that her name is Julie Posy, and then perhaps he will give her a silver dish also.

Give my love to Tutu, and remember me kindly to Nanna and Aya.[3]

Your affectionate uncle,
Washington Irving

PUBLISHED: PMI, IV, 26–27.

1. Susan Storrow, Kate's sister.
2. The Storrows' nursemaid. See WI to Catharine Storrow, July 15, 1852.
3. Probably the children's names for their mother and father.

2041. To Sarah Van Wart

Sunnyside Aug 29th. 1847

My dear Sister,

I am delighted to receive from various sources the most favorable accounts of your health and spirits. When I last saw you you had recovered beyond my most sanguine hopes; ⟨I⟩ yet I learn that you have gone on improving and are every day more and more capable of entering into the enjoyments of social life and of contributing to the happiness of the domestic circle. You seem to have something of ⟨the⟩ Sister Catharines constitutional elasticity and faculty of renovation; who, after all her ailments and repeated prostrations of health, is now enjoying a more healthful state of body and mind than I have witnessed in her for many years past

Your husbands return,[1] after so long an absence, must of itself [have][2] been sufficient to give you a new lease of life and good spirits. It is most gratifying to hear of his reception not merely by his family and intimates, by whom he has always been idolized, but by the public at large. He has left a large circle of warm friends on this side of the Atlantic who always speak of him with unqualified regard; while he has grappled the hearts of all his connexions to him more strongly than ever. Indeed I have been glad that he remained long enough in the Country to gather up all the links of our ⟨con?⟩ now wide family connexion and to make himself well known to all the members of it.

You have now also Irving with you, with his excellent little wife and his two noble boys.[3] I regret that Irving did not come up to Sunnyside before his departure[.] I had been expecting him up, and should have gone to town to see him had I known he was going to sail so promptly. Indeed I had been projecting an excursion with him to ⟨the⟩ Craigville and other parts of the Country and was shaping all my occupations for the purpose— I should not however have been able to carry the project into effect; having a return of my old malady, which very much shackles me and confines me to my home. I have had rather a toilful life since my return home, having been occupied in alterations and additions to my house, in building out houses, making enclosures, and bringing the whole place into order. This, as I have to be economical and superintend every thing myself, keeps me incessantly occupied, and by obliging me to be continually on my legs; ⟨prevents my⟩ keeps up the inflammation in my ankles. How often do I wish that I had your son William at my elbow to lend a hand in my rural labors. He would be just the one to put my place into first rate order, and it would be a little paradise to him; for really it is one of the sweetest little domains I ever saw.

I have not seen Abby and her little one since their arrival. They are on Long Island.[4] I have seen Henry twice, in town at the Counting House; but in the Summer time we are all ⟨so⟩ scattered; ⟨about⟩ and are only brought together again by the return of cold weather, which assembles the main part of the family in town. For my part, I am so fettered by my malady that I cannot go about much, and have to remain at home and depend upon my friends to make me visits. I have now three or four ⟨of the⟩ members of the different branches of the family on a visit to me; and indeed my little mansion is generally well filled. On Sundays we have quite a family gathering; and are pretty sure of a visit from Julia Grinnell and her husband, who have a country retreat about seven miles distant

I often think what a strange world you would find yourself in, if you could revisit your native place and mingle among your relatives[.] New York as you knew it, was a mere corner of the present huge city and that corner is all changed, pulled to pieces, burnt down and rebuilt—all but our little native nest in William Street, which still retains some of its old features; though those are daily altering. I can hardly realize that within my term of life, this great crowded metropolis, so full of life bustle, noise, shew and splendor, was a quiet little City of some fifty or sixty thousand inhabitants. It is really now one of the most rucketing cities in the world and reminds me of one of the great European cities (Frankfort for instance) in the time of an annual fair—Here it is a Fair almost all the year round. For my part I dread the noise and turmoil of it, and visit it but now and then, preferring the quiet of my country retreat; which shews that the bustling time of life is over with me and that I am settling down into a sober, quiet good for nothing old gentleman.

Your old resort of Tarry town is as much changed as the metropolis. It is now quite an extensive village with several churches; fine buildings; two hotels; and the country around beautified by tasteful cultivation and dotted with country seats.

As to our family connexion you would find yourself among ↑grand↓ nephews and nieces whose parents perhaps were not born when You were last here; and it would be a perfect study to find out the various ramifications of relationship that have spread out in every direction

I am scribbling this letter while the family are all at church—I hear the carriage at a distance and shall soon have all hands at home. Oh my dear Sister, what would I give if you and yours could this day be with us and join the family gathering round my board. Every day I regret more and more this severance of the different branches of the family, which casts us so widely asunder, with an ocean between us

Sept: 2d. This letter has been lying by me for several days, but I have not been able to add to it as I could wish. Letter writing seems every day to be growing a more difficult task to me, while unfortunately, the calls upon me from all quarters are continually augmenting. I think my mind is losing its promptness and pliancy and refuses to lend itself to the easy exercise of the pen; and, while I am waiting for a favorable mood, which is so slow in coming, my table gets loaded with unanswered letters and I look with despair at the accumulating debt. Give my love to Marianne and Matilda and Rosa[5] and tell them I will endeavor before long to answer their affectionate letters, but they must not think hard of my long silence. I really cannot help it. Remember me most affectionately to Irving and his wife. I wish he could find time to scribble me a letter and tell me how he finds all things and "all bodies" on his return to England. His visit must be most interesting to him. I should like to see his two brave boys gambolling about the shrubbery; or to witness their meeting with Williams children.

Ever my dear Sister

Your affectionate brother
Washington Irving

MANUSCRIPT: Va.–Barrett.   PUBLISHED: PMI, IV, 25–26 (in part).

1. Henry Van Wart had spent several months early in 1847 in New York attending to business affairs.

2. WI omitted this word.

3. Irving Van Wart, the son of Henry and Sarah Van Wart, was married to Sarah Ames. Their sons were twins, Ames and Irving, born on January 20, 1841.

4. Abigail Irving (1822–1906), daughter of John Treat Irving, had married her first cousin, Henry Van Wart, Jr., on September 23, 1845. Their child, Sarah Irving Van Wart, had been born earlier in 1847.

5. Marianne and Matilda were the daughters of Henry and Sarah Van Wart, Sr., and Rosalinda Bond was their daughter-in-law, the wife of their son William.

2042. *To Catharine Paris*

Sunnyside Sept 9th. 1847.

My dear Sister,

When do you intend to pay me your promised visit? I hope you will come ⟨f⟩ before the Autumn advances too far and the nights grow cold.

I am too much fettered by my malady to make any excursions at present; and begin to fear I shall not be in condition to make any this autumn. This will be quite a disappointment to me as I had set my heart on visiting Charlotte in her new home.

The recurrence and aggravation of my malady are very disheartening as well as extremely embarrassing, disabling me from bustling about my place and giving it the attention and supervision which it requires.

I have, however, just finished my last job, making a new ice pond in a colder and deeper place in the glen just opposite our ⟨↑old ice pond↓⟩ entrance gate: and now I would not undertake another job, even so much as to build a wren coop; for the slightest job seems to swell into a toilsome and expensive operation

I presume you have heard from Sarah by the late arrivals. I long to see her hand writing again; and to have from herself a history of her dear little household. I wrote a long letter to her[1] when I was down at Julias; and enclosed another to Kate, thanking her for her handkerchief.

We had a delightful visit from Julia, two or three days since. I wish she lived a little nearer, for what with occupation, lameness, hot weather and busy horses I have seen but little of her this summer

I hope Irving is in good trim again. He was a little out of order while he was with us. I was sorry that I could not detain him with us longer.

With affectionate remembrances to Mr Paris.

Your affectionate brother
Washington Irving

MANUSCRIPT: Va.–Barrett.   PUBLISHED: PMI, IV, 26 (in part).

1. See WI to Sarah Storrow, August 23, 1847.

2043.   *To Sabina O'Shea*

Sunnyside Sept. 18. 1847

My dear Mrs O'Shea,

I have just received your letter dated from Biarits in July, which you commence by asking whether I had ever received your letter from Madrid dated February. The question startled me. Could I indeed have been guilty of such delinquency as to suffer a letter from *you* to remain so long unanswered! I looked to my file of letters. It was too true. There was a letter dated the 23d. January last,[1] to which I had never written a reply. My dear friend I am shocked at my own negligence and forgetfulness, and am made the more sensible of your superior faith and excellence in friendship in continuing to write to me notwithstanding such apparent neglect. But you are one of the truest and kindest hearted of women and it is no wonder that all who know you love you.

Let me however say a word in palliation of this seeming neglect. At any rate it is not particular, but general, and extends to my whole correspondence. A spell seems to have fallen upon my faculties, in this respect, ever since my return home. It is but within a few days that I have written, ⟨to m⟩ for the first time, to my Sister in England since I parted with her upwards of a year since. Months have elapsed between my letters to my darling niece Mrs Storrow, to whom, while I was in Madrid, I used to write every week—and so with all my correspondents.

The fact is on my return home my whole thoughts and exertions were suddenly turned into a new channel which has almost ever since engrossed them. I found my place very much out of order, my house in need of additions and repairs and the whole establishment in want of completion. I set to work immediately, and kept on at all times and seasons, in defiance of heat and cold, wind and weather and as I was pretty much my own architect; projector and landscape gardener, and had but rough hands to work under me, I have been kept busy out of doors from morning until night and from months end to months end until within a week or two past, when I brought my labors to a close, or rather relinquished them, finding I had spent all ⟨my⟩ the money in my pocket and fagged myself into an irritation of the system which has rendered me almost as lame as I used to be in Madrid. I have now returned to my books and my study, and taken up my long neglected pen; and hope once more to go on according to my old habitudes.

You cannot think, however, what an altered being I am in all my habits and pursuits, from what I was at Madrid. I am a complete rustic. Live almost entirely at home; have not slept but twice from under my own roof for eight months past; and, though within five and twenty miles of New York, with rail road and steam boat conveyances, have suffered between four and five months to elapse without visiting it. I am surrounded, however, by my family of nieces, who are like daughters and most affectionate daughters to me, and my little mansion is generally well filled with relatives and friends on visits, so that it is always cheerful.

Your letters as well as the glimpses I have now and then of Spanish affairs in the public papers, give me a shocking idea of the state of affairs in Madrid. The instability of every thing there, however, the whirl of events and the rapid and topsy turvy changes in the positions and fortunes of individuals,[2] distract and confuse the mind and ⟨mak⟩ give real history the appearance of an incoherent and feverish dream. It was ⟨ha⟩ difficult enough for me to follow the course of events while I was a spectator of them in Madrid; but at this distance it is impossible. The dramatis personae change places as suddenly and strangely as in a pantomime; and now you have Salamanca[3] to play Harlequin, and with one slap of his wooden sword to produce the most wonderful and farcical transitions. By

the bye I still look forward to seeing him one day or other on the Boule-
vards at Paris with his hand organ and dancing dogs. The height of his
present position is but a prelude in Spain to as deep a fall; and beside,
the organ and dancing dogs form but a natural declension from the brazen
trumpets and dancing strump-ts over which he presided so worthily in
his opera house.

From an intimation in a London paper I am led to suppose that Salamancas *fides Achates* Buschenthall, with his immaculate spouse, are
among the intimates at the palace. Is this so? If it is, the queen is in a
fair way of becoming as knowing as Queen Sheba was, after her visit to
King Solomon.

The newspapers reported the death of Madame Sta Cruz; but by your
letters she only appears to have had an attack of apoplexy from which
she had recovered. How is her health now, and what is her position?
How does our friend the Introductor de los Embajadores fare during all
these vicisitudes? I hope he still retains his place. You will all miss the de
Bressons and the rallying place their house afforded—though to be sure
it was apt to be a little expensive

I want to know how my worthy successor Genl. Saunders makes out,
now that *Madame* has joined him. I hope he will get good quarters for
his family and that they will be pleased with Madrid; though I think
their american notions will be a little startled at first at some of its ways.
However, after a while one[s][4] virtue and morality get to be thick skinned
at Madrid as ones face does by being exposed to hard weather. I regret
very much that I did not See Mrs Saunders previous to her embarkation. I might have given her some preparatory hints and suggestions for
↑her↓ ⟨Mad⟩ launch on Madrid. I hope you will find her an agreeable
acquaintance and if so I am sure you will contribute greatly to render
her residence pleasant. When you see General Saunders remember me
most kindly to him. I received some time since a very obliging letter from
his Secretary of Legation[5] who informed me he had forwarded me some
Madrid newspapers. They never came to hand; which I regret, as the
English and American papers give me very scanty information concerning Spanish politics.

I have not heard from Madame Albuquerque for a long time. I believe
the fault lies with me in not answering her last letter. If so I shall soon
amend it, now that I have once more taken pen in hand. ⟨A⟩ Information
received some time since from Count de Bresson through the American
Consul at New York gave very bad accounts of her health; and from your
letter I find she was at Biaritz for the benefit of Sea bathing. I hope and
trust it will have a reviving effect upon her. Indeed I have no serious
apprehensions about her health. She is naturally thin and apparently delicate; but I rather think her constitution is a tenacious one, and I do not

believe she has any tendency to pulmonic complaints. I have a sister as thin and apparently fragile as she is; who from her girlhood had to be as much taken care of as a piece of cracked china. She has been a delicate looking being all her life time, but has gone through severe trials and afflictions in the loss of children; has outlived the robuster members of the family and is now, in her seventy fourth year, more healthy in mind and body than she was many years since, and is as bright in the eye and as animated in spirit as in the days of her youth—She is the mother of Mrs Storrow, and has taken out a new lease of life in consequence of the visit paid her last year by her daughter and her grand children. I trust Madame ⟨Storrow⟩ ↑Albuquerque↓ will prove just as much of an evergreen, however fragile as she may appear at present.

By the way my niece Mrs Storrow has recently presented her husband with a *third* daughter;[6] and is now with her children at Versailles. She will be most happy to see you whenever you revisit Paris; for she has quite an affectionate regard for you.

How is my worthy friend La Saussaye. I am shamefully in debt to him also, in letter writing: but will pay him off before long. I hope ⟨in at⟩ he has been able to turn some of his various projects to account, though I am a little apprehensive that the wheel of fortune has been turning the wrong way of late for our friends in Spain. Let me know whether he is still in Madrid, and how he is making out, and remember me to him most cordially.

How do you and the Wieswiellers agree together. I trust I succeeded in restoring harmony between you. It is very inconvenient to be on jarring terms, or in a false position with those whom we have to meet often in the circle of our intimacy. I found Mr. Wieswieller very obliging and accommodating on our journey together to Paris, and, our journey was quite a pleasant one.

I have never answered Mr O'Sheas letter of business. Tell him I am very much obliged to him for the care he took of my interests in the sale of my stocks; and I hope all his investments on his own account may prove as satisfactory. I see there is great havoc and desolation among the companies; a catastrophe which I anticipated. The three per cents have also gone down ⟨to⟩ at a headlong rate. I presume the new carriages which sprang up suddenly like mushrooms on the Prado have most of them changed owners, and that many of those who lolled for a brief period so sumptuously in their carriages are now mounted on the coach box in front or the foot board behind. *Sic tempora mutantur et trumpery mutantur etiam.*

I am delighted to hear such good accounts of my friend Quique, and that he is becoming so erudite. Encourage as much as you can his love for reading. It is the cheapest, purest and most enduring of pleasures;

beside being the most varied and substantial aliment of the mind. You talk of sending him one day or other to pay me a visit and to take up his abode with me for a time. I feel the full force of this testimonial of your friendly confidence in me; but I doubt whether my simple country retreat and the simple and almost rustic mode of living there, would be to his taste: our rural habitudes are so different from all that he has been accustomed to. However; I should always recieve him with a hearty welcome; and as a child of yours I should take him to my heart. As to the notion for a sailors life which he has taken up from reading Marryats works;[7] it is very common to boys of his age when they hear or read of nautical adventures. When I was a boy the adventures of Robinson Crusoe; and the voyages of the discoverers of America, made me crazy for going to sea; and I had actually at one time a notion of running away from home and turning sailor. When I grew to more knowing years this boyish propensity became modified; and I have since gratified the roving ⟨f⟩ inclination, thus early awakened, in a more regular way. So with Quique, when he grows older he will find it is pleasanter to make voyages as a cabin passenger than as a sailor; and that it is better to be able to keep below in a warm berth in foul weather than to be obliged to climb to the mast head. He will always have the means I trust to work off his roving and adventurous humors in a gentlemanlike way. Tell him from me, who have made many voyages in ships of war as well as merchant ships, that a sailors life is the life of a dog; very pleasant to read about; but very hard to undergo.

I observe by your letter that Don Tom and his family are at Biaritz. I hope the little girl grows in grace and continues to be the joy and pride of ⟨its⟩ ↑her↓ parents. Give them my kind remembrances and best wishes.

And now my dear friend I will conclude for the present; hoping that I may draw from you another of your long and most interesting letters. Remember me most cordially to Mr O'Shea, to my dear Willy and my most respectable friend papa Quiqui and believe me ever affectionately your friend

Washington Irving

P.S. my place is not called Van Tassel House. It is a name put on the engraving by the publisher. Address your letters to me simply New York & they will be sure to find me

ADDRESSED: Madame / Madame O'Shea / Aux Soins de Messrs. Henry O'Shea & Co / Madrid / per U. S. Mail Steamer / Washington / for Bremen POSTMARKED: [two postmarks unrecovered] // OUTRE-MER / OCT / [unrecovered] // LIGNE-DU-Havre 1 / 11 / OCT / 47 DOCKETED: Sunnyside / Septer. 1847 MANUSCRIPT: HSA. PUBLISHED: Penney, Bulletin NYPL, 63 (January, 1959), 31–34.

1. This and the letter mentioned in the first sentence have not been located.

2. In the interval since WI's departure from Spain the ministry of Istúriz was replaced by that of the count of Sotomayor on January 28, 1847; this cabinet was replaced on March 28, 1847, by that of Joaquín Francisco Pacheco (1808–1865), who was rather puritanical in his social views. When Pacheco incurred the displeasure of María Christina, he was supplanted on September 1, 1847, by Florencio García Goyena (1783–1855), who lasted until October 4, 1847, when Narváez returned as premier. See H. Butler Clarke, *Modern Spain* (Cambridge, 1906), pp. 207–9; and E. Christiansen, *The Origins of Military Power in Spain, 1800–1854* (Oxford, 1967), p. 170.

3. José Salamanca (1811–1883), who had been involved with Buschenthal in the management of the Madrid Bourse, was named minister of finance in 1846.

4. WI omitted the bracketed letter.

5. Thomas C. Reynolds of South Carolina served as Saunders's secretary of legation. See Adelaide R. Hasse, *Index to United States Documents Relating to Foreign Affairs 1828–1861*, 3 vols. (Washington, D.C., 1914–1921), III, 1834.

6. Julia Grinnell Storrow. The exact date of her birth has not been ascertained.

7. Frederick Marryat (1792–1848), a British naval officer, wrote numerous novels dealing with the sea. Among the most popular were *Frank Mildmay* (1829), *Peter Simple* (1834), *Jacob Faithful* (1834), and *Mr. Midshipman Easy* (1836).

2044.   To Pierre M. Irving

[Late September, 1847]

I am so much occupied, mind and pen, just now, on the History of Washington,[1] that I have not time to turn these matters[2] over in my mind.

PUBLISHED: PMI, IV, 31.

1. Apparently WI had just started working steadily on his long-delayed biography of George Washington.

2. According to PMI, WI had received proposals from several publishers concerning the republication of his writings.

2045.   To George R. Graham

Sunnyside, Oct. 15, 1847

. . . The limited portion of time which considerations of health permit me at present to devote to literary occupations is so fully engrossed by talks on which I have for some time been engaged that I am obliged to forego all desultory exercise of my pen.

PUBLISHED: *The Collector*, no. 831 (1973), 12.

George R. Graham (1813–1894), a lawyer turned journalist, launched *Graham's Magazine* in 1839. In the 1840's his monthly was one of the most widely read of American popular magazines.

The context of this excerpt suggests that Graham had solicited WI to become a contributor to his magazine.

2046.   To Charles Lanman

Sunnyside Octr. 15 1847

My dear Sir

I would not reply to your very obliging letter of Sept 10th.[1] until I had time to read the volumes[2] which accompanied it. This, from the pressure of various engagements, I have but just been able to do; and I now return you thanks for the delightful entertainment which your summer rambles have afforded me. I do not see that I have any "literary advice" to give you excepting to keep on as you have begun. You seem to have the happy enjoyable humor of old Isaak Walton[.][3] I anticipate great success therefore in your works on our American fishes, and on Angling which I trust will give us still further scenes and Adventures on our great internal waters;[4] depicted with the freshness and graphic skill of your present volumes. In fact the adventurous life of the Angler amidst our wild scenery on our vast lakes and Rivers must furnish a striking contrast to the quiet loiterings of the English Angler along the Trent or Dove; with country milk maids to sing madrigals to him and a snug decent country Inn at night where he may sleep in sheets that have been laid in lavender. With best wishes for your success I am my dear Sir

Very truly / Your obliged
Washington Irving

Charles Lanman Esqr

MANUSCRIPT: Harvard.   PUBLISHED: PMI, IV, 30–31; Charles Lanman, *Adventures in the Wilds of the United States and British American Provinces*, 2 vols. (Philadelphia, 1856), I, iv.

Charles Lanman (1819–1895), who was born in Monroe, Michigan, worked for ten years as a merchant's clerk in New York, after which he traveled around the Great Lakes and turned to newspaper editing (Monroe *Gazette* and Cincinnati *Chronicle*) and literary pursuits.

1. This letter has not been located.
2. Apparently Lanman had sent WI copies of *Essays for Summer Hours*, 2d ed. (Boston, 1842) and *A Summer in the Wilderness* (New York, 1847). Although

a number of Lanman's books, including *Letters from the Alleghany Mountains* (New York, 1849), and *Adventures in the Wilds of the United States*, 2 vols. (Philadelphia, 1856), are to be found in WI's library at Sunnyside, the earlier editions were not preserved.

3. Izaak Walton (1593–1683) described his fishing experiences along the Trent and Dove Rivers in *The Complete Angler* (1653).

4. In 1848 Lanman brought out *A Tour to the River Saguenay, in Lower Canada*, which fulfilled some of WI's expectations.

2047. To George Bancroft

Sunnyside, Nov 3d. 1847

My dear Sir.

This will be handed to you[1] by my friend the Rev Edward N Mead[2] of New York who with his family is about to set off for a Tour of Europe. Any attentions you may find it convenient to bestow upon them during their sojourn in London will be esteemed personal favors by

Yours ever very truly
Washington Irving

His Excellency / George Bancroft / &c &c &c

MANUSCRIPT: LC.

In another hand below WI's signature is written "6 Conduit St."

1. At this time Bancroft (1800–1889) was U.S. minister to Great Britain.

2. Edward Nathaniel Mead (1803–1877) was minister of St. Paul's Episcopal Church in Sing Sing from 1834 to 1839. He married Jane Creighton, daughter of the Reverend William C. Creighton of Tarrytown, whom WI knew well. At the time of this letter Mead was living at 152 Waverley Place. See Spencer P. Mead, *History and Genealogy of the Mead Family* (New York, 1901), p. 371; Robert Bolton, Jr., *A Brief History of Westchester County*, I, 497; and *New York City Directory for 1846–47*, p. 269.

2048. To Richard Rush

Sunny Side Novr. 3d. 1847.

My dear Sir,

Permit me to present to you[1] my friend the Rev Edwd. N. Mead of New York, who with his family will visit Paris in the course of a tour of Europe. Any civilities you may find it convenient to bestow upon them will be esteemed favors shewn to myself.

With high respect & esteem / My dear Sir / I remain yours faithfully
Washington Irving

His Excellency / Richard Rush / &c &c &c

ADDRESSED: His Excellency / Richard Rush / &c &c &c / Paris   DOCKETED: Washington Irving. / Nov: 3. 1847 / Introducing the / Revd Mr Meade / & family.
MANUSCRIPT: Princeton University Library.

1. At this time Rush (1780–1859) was the U.S. minister to France.

2048a.   To J. S. Lyon

Sunnyside, Novr 27h. 1847

Dear Sir,

I feel very much obliged to you for the pamphlet which you have had the kindness to send me.

I trust this note will serve for the Autograph which you request, and am

dear Sir / Very respectfully / Your Ob servt
Washington Irving

J. S. Lyon Esqr

MANUSCRIPT: NYPL.

2049.   To Catharine Irving

[New York, December 20, 1847]

My dear Kate,

I had expected to return home before this, but am so entangled in engagements that I shall not be able to return before Christmas eve (Friday next). I expect Pierre and Helen will accompany me, and I intend to invite Miss Ulshoeffer[1] & of course Irving Paris to pass Christmas with us. Sanders and Julia[2] and Ogden[3] will of course take their christmas with us. I trust you will have the rooms decorated with greens as usual.

I shall have to return to town again for my New Years dinner and to pass a few days with Mr Astor, after which I hope to settle down again to quiet life at home.

I have been very busy and very dissipated ⟨since⟩ ↑during↓ my sojourn in town; at work all the mornings in the libraries and frolicking in the evenings. I have attended every opera. The house is beautiful the troupe very fair and the audience very fashionable. Such beautiful young ladies! but the town is full of them—almost as beautiful as the young lady I saw in my dream at the Cottage.

Julia is slowly getting her house in order; but the upper part and the basement are arranged and we are most comfortably accommodated. The house is the perfection of comfort and convenience—almost equal to the Cottage.

I would write more fully but *"the carriage is at the* door" so I postpone all news and gossip until I come home—

Give my love to all bodies

Your affectionate Uncle
Washington Irving

New York. Decr 20–1847

Manuscript: SHR.   Published: PMI, IV, 32 (in part).

1. Nancy Gracie Ulshoeffer (1823–1884) was the fiancée of Irving Paris. The couple was married on November 1, 1848.

2. WI is referring to Sanders and Julia Graham Irving.

3. Possibly Henry Ogden Irving (1807–1869), son of William Irving.

2050.   To ——

[1847?]

Kate,[1] who was my idol when I was in Paris, and used to take such possession of me, and oblige me to *put away my spectacles,* and give up my book, and entertain her for the hundredth time with the story of little Miss Muss and Hempen House.

Published: PMI, IV, 26.

1. Catharine Paris Storrow, the daughter of Sarah and Thomas W. Storrow, Jr.

2051.   To J. Hedges

[January 22, 1848]

The frequent applications to me for "Sentiments" &c for albums oblige me generally to decline furnishing anything of the kind. I trust this note however, will suffice for the autograph you desire.

PUBLISHED: *Sale of the Collection of the Late William F. Gable* (New York, 1923), part 3, item 435.

2052. To Sarah Storrow

New York, Feb. 27th. 1848

My dear Sarah,

I have again suffered a long long time to elapse without writing to you, but have been so engrossed by literary occupations and fashionable dissipation that I have never seemed to have liesure enough to undertake a letter—I now mean to write one peace meal, or by instalments, at such intervals as I can command.

For five months past I have been hard at work at the life of Washington,[1] and make it a daily task. This of course monopolizes my time and scarce ⟨leaves⟩ ↑permits↓ me to attend to ⟨the⟩ my correspondence, which falls quite behind hand After eleven months seclusion in the country during which I made but three or four visits of business to town going down and returning the same day in the boat, I came down on a visit early in the winter, having recovered sufficiently from my old malady to go again into society. The cordial and I may say affectionate reception I met with every wh[ere] [*MS torn*] and the delight I felt on mingling once more among old friends had such an enlivening ⟨and⟩ an effect upon me that I soon repeated my visit and have ended by passing almost the whole of the winter in town. I think it has had a good effect upon me in every way. It has rejuvenated me, and given such a healthful tone to my mind and spirits that I have worked with greater alacrity and success. I have my books and papers with me and generally confine myself to the house and to my pen all the long morning, and then give up the evening to society and amusement.

One great charm of New York at present is a beautiful opera house[2] and a very good troupe; we have ⟨one⟩ a prima donna, named Truffi[3] who delights me as much as Grisi[4] did, and in the same line of characters, though I will not say she is equal to her excepting in occasional Scenes. She is an admirable actress and an excellent singer. We have an excellent tenor also ⟨who, when⟩ a young man,[5] who when he gets more cultivaion and training will be worthy of the Paris stage. The theatre is well arranged, and so fashionable in every part that there is no jealousy about places, as in the old opera house[6] here—Ladies are seated every where; and ⟨make⟩ with their gay dresses make what is the parterre in other theatres look like a bed of flowers. It is filled every night; every body is well dressed, and it is altogether one of the gayest, prettiest and most

polite looking theatres I have ever seen. Mr Grinnell has a double box
with the Hamiltons and Schuylers. He is a subscriber for five years; for
all the performances, which are three times in a week. I have not missed
a single performance since I have been in town. When I tell you that the
accommodations of the house throughout are both elegant and convenient, and the admission but one dollar a ticket, you will not think
it ↑an↓ extravagant amusement as at Paris.

Your little friend Mrs Henderson has a box where I see her every
opera evening. She is getting on very well here and is much liked. At my
request the Jones's called on her and she has been at their parties. I
also got the Schermerhorns to call on her on the eve of a ball which
they gave, and they have taken quite a fancy to her. She has, beside,
a very good and growing circle of acquaintances but I only mention
these as being procured for her by myself.

Feb 28. Julia's new house[7] is spacious well built and both elegant and
convenient. She has furnished it with great taste and is very much
pleased with the articles sent to her by Mr Storrow, which are universally
admired. I was at a large dinner party there on Saturday Twenty two
sat down to table, ladies and gentlemen. It was an excellent dinner,
well served, the company appeared to great advantage and the whole
went off gaily. The drawing rooms lighted up brilliantly. Altogether it
was the pleasantest dinner I have been at this season

The Gibbes's whom you knew in Paris, have opened a very beautiful
house this winter in the neighborhood of Julia's[8] and gave a brilliant
ball. I am to dine there today. I have made Julia acquainted with them
since their ball. Their eldest daughter is in society this winter and is
quite a belle.

New York is wonderfully improved in late Years. A complete new
region has been built, and well built. The houses are beautiful and are
furnished with great luxury. The tone of Society also is greatly improved
and the opera house which is the fashionable assembling place this
winter, is giving quite an air of refinement to the city. Altogether it is
becoming a most agreeable place of residence.

You want to know whether there are not better accommodations to be
had than at boarding houses. At present there are establishments whose
apartments are to be had on the European plan; where you may have ⟨s⟩
meals in your apartment, and only pay for what you order. Others are
erecting on a large scale. All these are in the upper ↑and most fashion-
able↓ part of the city, near Union Square. The pleasantest and most
fashionable part. I agree with you that a winter visit to the United States
would be preferable to a summer one, both on account of health and
convenience. By coming here in the autumn and returning late in the
Spring you would have comfortable voyages and be enabled to pass

several months delightfully among your friends. You would then be able to see what New York really is at present; of which you have ⟨a⟩ very probably a false and unfavorable idea.

Your Mother has great comfort in the visits of her future daughter in law Miss Ulshoeffer,[9] with whom I am very much pleased. She is very attentive in making frequent visits and her manners are very endearing. I wanted to have her at the cottage at christmas, but she had recently been in a delicate state of health and her father did not like her to risk a winter visit in the Country. I hope to see her up there when the country is in its spring dress.

I have not sent you a sketch of the Cottage because there has been no one at hand to make one. Mr. Harvey went to England before the additions were finished. I shall endeavor to have it sketched this year when ⟨the it is in⟩ the trees are in foliage. By the way I have made great havoc among the trees, cutting down some and transplanting others, so as to open views, admit a free circulation of air and *unbury* the house.

Feb. 29 t. The dinner at Mr Gibbes yesterday was a very handsome one; twenty persons at table; every thing in French style. Mrs Gibbes is becoming quite at home in New York and expresses herself as greatly pleased with it. Her daughters are delighted of course; ⟨as⟩ finding themselves so much more at liberty than when in Paris. Her second daughter will not come into Society until next winter.

From Mr Gibbes, I went to the Opera where we had Verdi's Ernani extremely well performed. Truffi played admirably. She is just the kind of performer you would like, very exciteable and impulsive, and full of energy and feeling. One meets all ones acquaintances at the opera, and there is much visiting from box to box and pleasant conversation between the acts. The Opera house in fact is the great feature in polite society in New York; and I believe [it] is the great attraction that keeps me in town. Music is to me ⟨the⟩ a great sweetener of existence, and I never enjoyed it more abundantly than at present.

March 8. Here this letter has been lying in a corner of a drawer for days and days; in the mean time a Steamer has gone without it. I am now about setting off for the Cottage to be gone a couple of days, but am determined to leave this with your mother, to be forwarded, as it is, intending to commence another letter on my return. Your Mother tells me she has referred you to me for an account of a Fancy Ball recently given at the opera house,[10] of which I, sorely against my will, was made one of the managers. I have not time however, to give particulars; nor have I the knack of it; the whole being a confused medley in my mind— It was very beautiful, however, and presented one of the gayest and brightest scenes of the kind I have ever witnessed. There were a great many very rich and very beautiful dresses, some of them very accurate costumes. Julia Grinnell made her mind up at the eleventh hour to go, and arrayed herself in an elegant Greek costume which I believe you sent out to her a few years since. She looked admirably in it, but did not feel altogether at her ease; being in pantalettes, or rather trousers, which, however, ↑being very large and full↓ were as unobjectionable as skirts would have been. I was amused to see her shrinking sensitiveness when launched upon the grand saloon. Mary and Julia were with her— Dresses had been hastily got up for them, the former as a Scotch lassie the latter as a flower girl. The dresses being arranged under Julia Grinnells eye were of course in perfect good taste and looked very pretty.

On thursday next there is to be another large dinner party at Mr Grinnells at which your friend Mrs Henderson is to be a guest She is a darling little woman. Mr Henderson has recently purchased a house on Lafayette place, so that they are fairly fixed in New York.

I ought to have mentioned that one of the most fanciful and piquante costumes at the fancy ball was worn by the eldest of Mrs Gibbes daughter; who appeared as a female *Mousquetaire*—a dress fashionable in France a century and half since, a Scarlet military coat, fitting close to the body; the hair plaited clubbed and powdered and a small three cornered hat, set knowingly on one side of the head. I saw nothing at the ball that pleased me more.

And now I'll conclude—sending many loves and kisses to the dear little women. I am quite delighted to hear that Tutu is so zealous in pursuit of knowledge, exacting rigidly her ten minutes portion of the school hour—

With kind remembrances to Mr Storrow. Your affectionate uncle
Washington Irving

ADDRESSED: Madame / Madame Storrow / 17. Rue de Faubg Poissonniere / à Paris
MANUSCRIPT: Yale.   PUBLISHED: PMI, IV, 33–35 (in part).

1. WI had mentioned his occupation with the biography of George Washington in late September of 1847. See PMI, IV, 31.

2. The Astor Place Opera House with seating for 1,800 opened on November 22, 1847. Its presentations of Italian operas included *Ernani, Beatrice di Tenda, La Sonnambula, Lucia di Lammermoor, I Puritani, Lucrezia Borgia, Capuleti e Montecchi*, and *Il Giuramento*. See Odell, *NY Stage*, V, 381–83. Philip Hone's comment after attending a performance on January 21, 1848, is the reaction of a cultivated New Yorker: "This was my first visit to this beautiful edifice, so advantageously situated and admirably adapted to contribute to the enjoyment of our citizens.... This opera of ours is a refined amusement, creditable to the taste of its proprietors and patrons; a beautiful parterre in which our young ladies, the flowers of New York society, are planted to expand in a congenial soil, under the sunshine of admiration; and here also our young men may be initiated into the habits and forms of elegant social intercourse, and learn to acquire a taste for a science of the most refined and elegant nature...." See *The Diary of Philip Hone*, ed. Allan Nevins, II, 836.

3. WI probably heard Teresa Truffi sing in *Lucrezia Borgia* and in *Il Giura-mento*. Her singing in the role of Elvira in Verdi's *Ernani* was enthusiastically acclaimed. See NYEP, February 1 and 15, 1848; and J. W. Ireland, *Records of the New York Stage* (New York, 1966), II, 515.

4. WI had seen and heard Giulia Grisi (1811–1869) in Paris in 1843. See WI to Sarah Storrow, November 26, 1843.

5. Probably Sesto Benedetti, whose temperamental refusal to sing in *Norma* with Madame Laborde caused the audience subsequently to hiss and boo him. He married Teresa Truffi in Boston in May of 1850. See T. Allston Brown, *History of the American Stage* (New York, 1870), p. 29.

6. Palmo's Opera House at 39 & 41 Chambers Street had opened on February 3, 1844, for the purpose of presenting Italian opera. The first performance was Bellini's *I Puritani*. See Odell, *NY Stage*, V, 49–50; and Ireland, *Records of the New York Stage*, II, 423–25.

7. The new house of Julia and Moses Grinnell was located at 1 East 14th Street.

8. The Gibbeses lived at Fifth Avenue north of 11th Street.

9. For other details about Nancy Gracie Ulshoeffer, see WI to Catharine Irving, December 20, 1847.

10. The ball at the Opera House, with the food catered by Delmonico's, was held on Monday, March 6 and was attended by 1,200 persons, plus spectators in the amphitheater. The gala affair was in celebration of the Carnival marking the beginning of Lent on March 8. According to one newspaper account, "The whole affair was dreadfully *genteel*" and was marked by "feverish excitement among the fashionables." See *The Spirit of the Times*, March 11, 1848.

2053.   To the Irving Literary Society

New York, March 1st, 1848

Gentlemen—An awkward circumstance has prevented my replying at an earlier date to your kind letter of the 24th of February.[1] That letter arrived in a moment of hurry, was mislaid and has cost me much embarrassment and chagrin, for I had forgotten the college and place whence it was dated and knew not where to address a reply. I have made repeated searches for it during the past month, but it was only this morning that, in making a scrupulous rummage of the chaos of papers by which I am apt to be surrounded, I found it between the leaves of a manuscript which had been repeatedly in my hand.

I make this explanation that you may not think me capable of treating with neglect or indifference such a testimonial of good opinion and good-will as that with which you have honored me.

I beg you will communicate this explanation to your society, with the assurance of my deep and grateful savor of the honor they have done me in electing me a member and still more in thinking my name worthy of being chosen for their designation.

You ask for a device and motto for your banner and badge.

If you wish them to have any connection with my name you have thus honored, I would observe that the device of the Scottish family of Irving, from which I claim descent, is the holly leaf, the motto, "sub sole, sub umbra virens."[2]

These were the armorial bearings of Robert Bruce[3] when a fugitive and in disguise in Scotland and were probably intended to signify his confidence that his fortunes, like the evergreen he had adopted as an emblem, would survive every vicissitude. In a moment of his great adversity he was harbored in the house of Irving, who gave him his son as a standard bearer. He afterwards bestowed these arms upon the family in token of the loyalty to him when in misfortune. At the risk of being tedious, I will give the Scottish tradition of the circumstances as related to me by Sir Walter Scott.

Robert Bruce, when a fugitive, took refuge in the house of a poor man of the name of Irving, who, having no other means of entertaining his royal guest, killed his only cow, serving up the flesh at the table and making a bed of the hide.

Bruce, at parting, told his host to repair to him should he ever hear of his coming to the throne. Irving did so, but appearing in humble garb, was denied admission to the palace. He sent in a message to the King to know whether His Majesty slept more sweetly on his royal couch than on the hide of a brindle cow.

The King understood the message and instantly sent for his poor but loyal adherent and bestowed on him lands and the armorial bearings, already mentioned. It is this old story, however it may be tainted with fable, which has given the device and motto their chief value in my eyes.

I am, gentlemen, respectfully your obliged and humble servant,

Washington Irving

PUBLISHED: Clipping of an unidentified newspaper, a reprint from the Baltimore *American* (in SHR).

The Irving Society was organized by the Right Reverend John B. Kerfoot, headmaster of the College of St. James near Hagerstown, Maryland. At the time of their publication in the *American* this letter and three others (December 11, 1848, and two dated May 15, 1851) were framed and hanging on the walls of the "chapter room" at the college.

1. This letter has not been located.
2. In a letter of January 13, 1841, to D. Henderson, WI had described the coat of arms and the motto of the Irving family.
3. Robert Bruce (1247–1329) was a Scottish soldier who fought against the English in the struggle for the independence of Scotland.

2054.   *To Charles A. Bristed*

[March 6, 1848?]

My dear Charles

I have not answered your note[1] sooner because I was uncertain as to my movements. If it will be convenient to you I will dine with you on thursday next.

Yours very truly / Washington Irving

Monday, March 6th. [1848?] / Charles A Bristed Esqr

MANUSCRIPT: University of Chicago Library.

The date 1848 has been assigned to this letter because WI was in New York City at this time. Charles Astor Bristed was probably attending his grandfather, John Jacob Astor, in his last illness.

1. This letter has not been located.

2055.   *To John F. Watson*

New York, April 6th. 1848

Dear Sir,

I have duly received your letter of April 1st.[1] offering yourself as secretary, cashier &c to the Executors of the Will of the late John J. Astor.[2] As yet the will remains in the Surrogates office to be proved and none of the executors[3] have qualified. When the board of executors shall be formed it will give me pleasure to communicate to it the purport of your letter; though, as I shall be but one among six executors, all more practised men of business than myself, I cannot expect to have much influence among them in matters of this kind. I would observe, too, that it is not likely any situation will present worthy of your acceptance The affairs of the late Mr Astor have always been conducted with great system and regularity by tried, competent and confidential persons in every department, who will, in all probability be continued in employ by the Executors.

Should any thing occur to your advantage I will not fail to let you know; in the mean time, I remain with great respect and esteem

Your sincere well wisher
Washington Irving

John F Watson Esqr.

MANUSCRIPT: HSP.

John Fanning Watson (1779–1860) was a bookseller in the early years of the nineteenth century and the publisher of *Select Reviews of Literature, and Spirit of Foreign Magazines* from 1811 to 1813. He organized the Bank of Germantown in 1814 and helped to establish the Historical Society of Pennsylvania in 1824. An historian and antiquarian, he wrote several books on the history of Pennsylvania and New York in his later years.

1. This letter has not been located.
2. Astor had died on March 29, 1848, at the age of eighty-four.
3. Besides WI, the executors of Astor's estate were his son William B. Astor, his grandson John Jacob Astor, James G. King, James Gallatin, and Daniel Lord. See Kenneth W. Porter, *John Jacob Astor, Business Man*, 2 vols. (New York, 1966), II, 1271, 1278, 1291.

2056. To Aaron Ward

New York, April 7th. 1848

My dear Sir

Mr Kemble informs me that you are to draw out the papers[1] requisite to my arrangement with the Rail Road Commissioners and wishes me to let you know whether there are any incumbrances on any part of the property. There are none. If any other information is wanting I will thank you to drop a line to me at No 90 Eighth Street N York

Very truly yours
Washington Irving

ADDRESSED: Aaron Ward Esqr / Sing Sing / Westchester   POSTMARKED: NEW-YORK / 7 / APR / 1848   DOCKETED: Washington Irving
MANUSCRIPT: SHR.

Aaron Ward (1790–1867) served in the War of 1812 with distinction and afterward rose to the rank of major general in the New York State Militia by 1830. After serving six terms in the U.S. Congress, beginning in 1825, he practiced law at Sing Sing.
1. WI is referring to the legal documents concerning the building of the Hudson River Railroad, which ran through his property along the east bank of the Hudson River.

2057.   *To Catharine Irving*

New York, April 10th. 1848

My dear Kate

I have this moment received your very welcome letter[1] and sit down in Pierre's law shop to scribble a reply. I am glad to find all things are going on so well, and that the cottage stands its ground notwithstanding my long absence. I have been intending for some time past to come up, but one thing or another prevents me. I have settled with the Rail Road Company who have paid me $2500 in cash and $1000 in stock at par— which draws Seven per cent interest. So I think I have done as well as my neighbors who have been more litigious.

I am now negotiating an arrangement with Mr Putnam for the republication of my works,[2] which promises to be a very satisfactory one—and I am attending preliminary meetings of the board of Executors of Mr Astors estate. All these things detain me in town, and may oblige me hereafter to visit town frequently,—but they all contribute to encrease my pecuniary means, and of course to advance the well being of the Cottage and its inmates; so I trust you will not scold me for being such a truant.

I am glad to find the new house maid gives so much satisfaction, though I must say I am sorry that slow Willy Mowbray is likely to be displaced. There was something in the girls appearance and demeanour that pleased me, and you know I have rather a soft feeling toward the sex; especially when young and good looking. However, in matters of house wifery handsome is that handsome does. So if Slow Willy Mowbray cannot be quicker, let her march.

I trust the men are widening and cleaning out the foot walks ⟨as⟩ I shall send or bring up some seed or young plants, of running vines ⟨to⟩ for the porch & the front of the house. Yearly plants: to serve while the roses are growing.

The Mr Skeely[3] who you say is treating for Mrs Jones' house is an importing dry good merchant, and lives in Clinton place. I know nothing of him but Pierre Munro says he has been once or twice in his office on business and is pleasing and gentlemanly in his appearance of that you have had an opportunity of judging. I should like to have a quiet agreeable neighbor there, one not violently bent on being fashionable. Mrs Colford Jones tells me that Mr Boreel[4] (Mr Astors Son in law) has thought somewhat of taking Mr George Jones house for the summer.

Give my love to all at home and to my dear Julia at Tarrytown

Your affectionate uncle
Washington Irving

MANUSCRIPT: SHR. PUBLISHED: PMI, IV, 39 (in part).

1. This letter has not been located.

2. On July 26, 1848, WI entered into a contract with Putnam for the republication of his writings and the issuance of several new works. See STW, II, 215–16.

3. WI probably erred in setting down this name as "Skeely." Rufus R. Skeel, a partner in the dry goods firm of Skeel, Hurlbut, and Sweetser at 54 Maiden Lane and 29 Liberty Street, lived at 6 Clinton Place. See *New York City Directory for 1847–48*, p. 373.

4. Baron Robert Boreel, who married Sarah Shelburne Langdon, daughter of Dorothea Astor Langdon, in Paris on May 2, 1834, was actually John Jacob Astor's grandson-in-law. See O'Connor, *The Astors*, p. 465; Lucy Kavaler, *The Astors* (New York, 1966), p. xii; and Walter W. Spooner, *Historic Families of America*, 3 vols. (New York 1907), III, 242.

2058. To Pierre M. Irving?

[April 10, 1848]

Why, I am harder on them than the wagoner was on Giles Gingerbread;[1] for he let him walk all the way to London alongside of his wagon without charging him anything, while I make them pay for only passing my door.

PUBLISHED: PMI, IV, 38.

The recipient of this comment was probably PMI himself, who in the same context quotes two passages from WI's letter of April 10, 1848, to Catharine Irving as if all three were from the same letter. In preparing his text, PMI sometimes combined passages on the same topic from WI's letters to different people at about the same time.

1. WI alludes to *The Renowned History of Giles Gingerbread: A Little Boy Who Lived upon Learning* (1765), the authorship of which is attributed variously to John Newbery, Oliver Goldsmith, Giles Jones, and Griffith Jones. See S. Roscoe, *John Newbery and His Successors, 1740–1814, A Bibliography* (Wormley, Herts., 1973), p. 11.

2059. To James Boorman

New York, April 17th. 1848

Dear Sir,

I enclose a letter[1] which I hope may serve your purpose, and which you are at liberty to publish.

I made a request some time since to the company[2] to have the space between the river bank and the rail road in the north part of my premises filled up, so as to exclude the influx of the tide. This Mr Jervis[3] gave me reason to hope would be done, and indeed the construction of the road was commenced to that effect. Recently, however, and since the conclusion of my arrangement with the company, I learn that ↑a↓ contrary course has been pursued, and a wet ditch is to be left open along my whole premises. As you know the position of my house and the nature of my grounds, you can easily imagine how destructive to comfort and pleasure, if not to health, such a hideous deformity must be. The trouble and expense of the modification I ask would not be much to the company, having the means, materials and facilities at hand; I earnestly entreat therefore the considerate attention of the company to this matter; which is of vital importance to my family.

I am my dear Sir, / Very truly yours
Washington Irving

J Boreman Esqr

MANUSCRIPT: SHR.

WI misspelled the name of James Boorman (1783–1866), a Scotch-born merchant and a partner in the importing firm of Boorman, Johnston, Ayres, and Company who founded and became vice-president of the Hudson River Railroad in 1847 and in 1849 succeeded Azariah C. Flagg as president. Boorman held that post until 1851, when the railroad reached East Albany. See Thomas C. Cochrane, *Railroad Leaders, 1845–1890: The Business Mind in Action* (Cambridge, Mass., 1953), pp. 23, 266; and Bonner, *New York, The World's Metropolis*, p. 709.

1. This letter has not been located.

2. The Hudson River Railroad. For details about the development of the line, see Cochrane, *Railroad Leaders*, p. 23; and Scharf, *Westchester County*, I, 479–80.

3. John B. Jervis (1795–1885), an engineer with extensive experience in canal and railroad building, was chief engineer for the Hudson River Railroad. He directed its construction to Poughkeepsie.

2060.   To James H. Hackett

New York, April 17, 1848

My dear Sir:

I have detained your manuscript notes[1] an unconscionable time, but I could not help it. I wished to read them attentively, for they are remarkably suggestive, and not to be read in a hurry; but for the last two or three months, spent among my friends and relatives in my native city after an absence of several years, I have been kept in such a round of engagements, and such constant excitement, that I have only now and then been able to command a little leisure and quiet for reading and reflexions. At such moments I have perused your manuscripts by piece meal, and now return you my hearty thanks for the great pleasure they have afforded me. I will not pretend to enter at present into any discussion of the topics they embrace, for I have not sufficient faith in my critical acumen to commit my thoughts to paper; but when I have the pleasure of meeting with you personally, we will talk over these matters as largely as you please. I have seen all the leading characters of Shakespeare played by the best actors in America and England during the present century; some of them, too, admirably performed in Germany. I have heard ↑some of↓ them chaunted in the Italian opera, and I have seen the ballet of "Hamlet" gravely danced at Vienna.[2] Yet, with all this experience, I feel that I am an amateur rather than a connoisseur; prone to receive great pleasure without easily analyzing the source, and sometimes apt to clap my hands where grave critics shake their heads.

Excuse this scrawl, written in a hurried moment, and believe me, with great respect and regard

Your obliged friend and servt.

Washington Irving

James H Hackett Esq

MANUSCRIPT: Boston Public Library.   PUBLISHED: PMI, IV, 39–40.

James Henry Hackett (1800–1871), an actor who was acclaimed for his comic portrayals of Yankees and Westerners and of Falstaff, was the first American to star on the English stage. One of his outstanding roles was Colonel Nimrod Wildfire in James K. Paulding's *The Lion of the West*. He was very much interested in problems of dramatic production and acting.

1. Probably WI is referring to some of the materials which were incorporated in Hackett's *Notes and Comments on Certain Plays and Actors of Shakespeare*, (1863).

2. WI had seen *King Lear* in Prague on November 23, 1822, and May 30, 1823; *Hamlet* in Dresden on February 9 and 13, 1823, and in Prague on June 4, 1823; and *The Merchant of Venice* in Dresden on April 21, 1823. See *J&N*, III, 81, 125, 126, 141, 169, 171. He did not record in his journal his attendance at the ballet in Vienna in 1822.

2061. To Sarah Storrow

New York, April 18th. 1848

My dear Sarah

Like yourself I have deferred writing to you until the last moment and now must scrawl a line in a hurry. We have all been and are still extremely anxious about yourself and your dear little family in these

tumultuous times;[1] not that I apprehend any personal danger; but I fear
a great interruption of your domestic quiet and serenity. You are in the
midst of stirring scenes, such as a young man would delight in, and such
as even I should enjoy; but they are not the kind of Scenes for a female
with a family of little ones to feel at ease in. I think it more than probable this letter will find you in England, awaiting the subsiding of the
troubled waters. I shall direct it accordingly. I beg you not to say any
thing more in your letters about my coming out to Europe. You ought
to know that in my circumstances such a move is out of the question. I
have not above half income enough to meet my actual expenses and
you want me to encrease them by travel. I am now occupied with my
pen, and am making new arrangements for the republication of my
works. I have just entered also upon the executorship of Mr Astors estate: all these may encrease my means and put me at ease as to income;
but they all chain me down to home. I have no prospect of seeing you,
therefore, until you and your family again cross the Atlantic and I would
to God you could do it soon, and cast your lot in your native country
and among your friends and relatives before a too long residence abroad
has confirmed you in foreign tastes and habitudes and weakened the
home feeling; and before your little ones grow up foreigners rather than
americans.

I have been passing a long time in New York; almost ever since the
middle of December—having all my books and papers about me here,
and being detained in town by business occupations. My time, however,
has passed very pleasantly, and I continue to think New York a city in
which one can live very agreeably. I have been staying for some time
past at Treats, where I am fixed much to my taste. The more I know of
Helen the more I like her. She is quietly affectionate, with calm good
sense and a perfect temper. She and Treat live most happily together.
I do not think there has ever been a cloud between them. Their household is a very cheerful one.

Your mother is in her usual health and spirits, though at times a little
anxious about you. Your letters, however, are written in a tone that encourages her. She will be at Mr Holmes' this summer, so that I will have
her at hand, to let her have the use of the Carriage and to have her
often at the Cottage. Henry Van Wart and Abby are to pass the summer at Mr Archers; so that we shall be all in each others neighborhood.

We are looking with anxiety for the arrival of a Steamer. Every arrival from Europe now is of the utmost interest; each giving a new
chapter of the thrilling story that is going on there. God bless you and
your dear little ones my beloved Sarah, and keep you from all harm.
Would to God you were all once more safe at home with us.

With kind remembrances to Mr Storrow and many kisses to the dear little folks

Your affectionate uncle
Washington Irving

MANUSCRIPT: Yale.

1. WI is referring to the overthrow of the French monarchy in late February of 1848.

2062.   To the Reverend I. Prince

New York April 24. 1848

Dear Sir,

Absence from home has prevented the receipt of your letter of the 17th. instant[1] in time for an earlier reply.

Although I hold the copy right of the biography of Margaret Miller Davidson yet I had it published entirely for the benefit of her mother the late Mrs Davidson retaining merely the privilege of including it in any collective edition I might publish of my works.

I do not reccollect the terms I made on behalf of Mrs Davidson with the publishers, Messrs Lea and Blanchard of Philadelphia,[2] but these gentlemen might feel aggrieved should I grant permission for the publication of a condensed sketch or an abbreviation, ⟨which⟩ calculated as they might suppose to interfere with the sale of the original work.

I am Sir / Very respectfully / Your Obt Servt.
Washington Irving

The Rev I. Prince

MANUSCRIPT: Va.–Barrett.   PUBLISHED: Carroll A. Wilson, *Thirteen Author Collections of the Nineteenth Century*, 2 vols. (New York, 1950), I, 168.

1. This letter has not been located.
2. WI had suggested to Lea & Blanchard that a suitable payment for the *Biography and Poetical Remains of the Late Margaret Miller Davidson* would be thirty cents per volume, the amount he received for each of the numbers of *The Crayon Miscellany*. See WI to Lea & Blanchard, February 25, 1841.

2063.   To Sarah Storrow

New York, May 5th. 1848

My dear Sarah,

According to your request I scrawl you a few lines in a moment snatched from a multitude of occupations, though I have nothing particular to write about, for, in fact, every thing here fades into insignificance in comparison with the startling events of Europe. Your letter of the 12th.[1] is satisfactory as shewing that your mind is tranquil and your domestic quiet undisturbed, though in the midst of the turmoils of Paris. I feel anxious for the course of affairs there on your account, as the interruption of business and the embarrassment of the financial world, must affect all your comforts and arrangements. I wrote to you some short time since and directed my letter to the Care of Mr Van Wart at Birmingham, for I thought it probable you would have put your plan in execution of visiting England and being there during the Paris elections. I trust that letter has been forwarded to you. I am still passing the greater part of my time in New York (at present at Julia Grinnells) being detained here by arrangements for the republication of my works and by the duties of the Executorship to Mr Astors estate—I made a visit of two days to the Cottage last week, and found every thing ⟨t⟩ coming out beautifully, under the soft breath of Spring. I have made great clearings away, about the Cottage and it is all the better for them—We have now fine quiet slopes of green lawn, and beautiful openings upon the river. We are to have Mr Boreel and his family for neighbors this Summer in Mrs Colford Jones house. He is the Young gentleman (from Holland) who married the eldest Miss Langdon—a very pretty and very amiable woman with a beautiful family of children—I think we shall find them very pleasant neighbors. Your Mother ⟨he⟩ will be quartered for the summer at Mr Holmes's as will Sanders & Julia Irving. Henry Van Wart and Abby have taken rooms at Mr Archers: So that we shall have Several of the family within an agreeable drive.

I am anxious for the time for your mother to get into the country—She has had an attack of influenza for some days past which, as usual, has made her very weak; but it has taken a favorable turn and her elastic constitution is beginning to react. Rose is her faithful nurse and comforter and she could not have a better one. She is a perfect Godsend to her. A daughter could not be more kind and considerate and attentive.

You are mistaken in your idea that "one cannot form a *quiet* but *elegant* little establishment in New York as one can in Paris." There are many such in this city in which families live very pleasantly, keep the best Society and yet bring their expenses within a very moderate compass. It

is not necessary to keep expensive equipages and give expensive entertainments to be respectable and even fashionable—Those who wish to
be leaders of fashion, or to make a decided figure in the gay world, do
so, but they are not always the most respected and most esteemed. Our
city is now so large and has so many circles of Society that people live
more independently than they did formerly and may be very happy
and *decidedly genteel* on a very moderate income: and now it is getting
more and more the custom to live in furnished apartments, ⟨with⟩ as in
Europe, large establishments for the purpose having been recently
formed and others being in progress of construction.

I say all this to let you see that it is not absolutely necessary to make
a large fortune before you can return and live happily at home. Fortune cannot repay the loss of home ties ⟨and⟩ home feelings and home
habitudes; and a family can never take so sure and deep a root as in the
native soil.

I observe with much concern, among the failures in Paris that of the
house of Mr Thurnhuysen.[2] I had learned to take an interest in his
family from the character you gave of them and from the regard they
evinced for you. I hope the failure may not be a bad one and that the
house may be able to resume business. How is it with the Greenes? I
fear badly. Madame Lavalette[3] I apprehend has also been a loser in these
times; but I presume she was only interested in the banking house to a
limited amount.

I believe all that you say of your little Julie who I make no doubt is
the ⟨very⟩ most beautiful little fairy in the world. I am satisfied also that
Tutu is a miracle of cleverness, and now that you have two such para-
gons to be proud of, I wish I had your third one, Kate, to take command
of my cottage, and live with me for the rest of my days. She is quite
beautiful enough and good enough for me.

Kiss all the little folks for me. Give my kind remembrances to your
husband and my best wishes that he may have a quiet pillow during
these anxious times.

Ever my dear Sarah / Your affectionate uncle
Washington Irving

MANUSCRIPT: SHR.

1. This letter has not been located.
2. Mr. Thurnhuysen is perhaps the "Mr. Thurneyston" whom WI mentioned in
his letter of November 30, 1844.
3. Probably either Madame la Marquise de Lavalette, Rue St. Dominique-St.
Germaine 70, or Madame la Comtesse de Lavalette, Rue Matignon 10. See
Almanach des 2500 Adresses (1840), p. 371.

2064.   To Catharine Irving

N York, May 30. 1848

My dear Kate,

I have engaged a young man to take Patricks place. He has but one eye, but the other appears to be a very good one and I trust will be sufficient for him to guide the horses by. He has been accustomed to live in the country and do farm work as well as to drive horses. He has been but a few months in this country and has no wife young or old, for which I trust he is humbly thankful. Finally, his name is Barney Aspen and he is brother of Mary the little hand maid who has lived so long at Edgar's and whom I have so often coveted as a waiter. Appearances are much in his favor ⟨(⟩ excepting the want of an eye; so, that, though half blind I flatter myself with the hope he will not prove a blind bargain.

He will come up on Monday next; so Patrick may make ready quietly to transfer ↑to him↓ the reins of government (of the horses) by that time.

I have just had an unexpected windfall of Seventy five dollars from the Harpers on account of my abridgement of Columbus, so if you want to spend any more money now is your time!

With respects to the Governor and love to all the rest of the household

Your affectionate Uncle
Washington Irving

Manuscript: SHR.

2065.   To William C. Bryant

New York June 24th 1848

My dear Sir,

Permit me to present you my nephew Theodore Irving recently professor of Political Economy and Moral Philosophy in Geneva College[1] He is desirous of obtaining your countenance to an application he is making for a professor ship in the Free Academy.[2] If you find it convenient to meet his wishes you will much oblige

Yours, with the highest respect and esteem
Washington Irving

Wm C. Bryant Esqr

Addressed: William C. Bryant Esq / New York
Manuscript: NYPL–Bryant-Goodwin Collection.

Bryant (1794–1878), whose poems WI had seen through the press in London in 1832, was editor of the New York *Evening Post*.

1. Theodore Irving (1809–1880), third son of Ebenezer Irving, taught at Geneva College in upstate New York from 1836 to 1848.

2. The Free Academy, which was established in 1848 and became the College of the City of New York in 1866, was strongly endorsed by William Cullen Bryant, the editor of the NYEP. Theodore Irving was professor of history and belles lettres during the first four years of the Academy. In 1852 he resigned to become pastor of a church on Staten Island. See Willis Reedy, *The College of the City of New York: A History* (New York, 1949), pp. 18, 56.

2066. To Sarah Storrow

Sunnyside July 17th. 1848

My dear Sarah,

Your husband has just gone to town after passing Sunday at the Cottage where we were all delighted to have him. By the way I must tell you that I have never seen him look so well as he does at present. I had expected, after the perilous scenes and vicissitudes through which he had passed, to see him haggard and care worn; but the moment I laid eyes on him on his arrival in New York, his bright beaming countenance told me he had passed through the ordeal without serious injury. It is a general remark that he is younger and handsomer in looks than he was years since; gayer in spirits and easier and more engaging in manners. But what I most admire in him is the ⟨admirable⟩ self possession he has displayed throughout those troubles and alarms which overcame others with panic—The calmness and circumspection with which he made all his business arrangements and the tender care yet prudent forecast with which he provided for the security of yourself and your helpless little ones. Such are the rare occasions which thoroughly try the *man,* and in these he has proved himself *first rate.* I cannot express to you how much his conduct in these trying times has raised him in my estimation.

I find he has strong doubts about the policy of taking you all back to Paris; and he talks some thing about bringing you all out to this country: in which case he might like to have a retreat in the country, to pass part of the year. I have not presumed to give advice on such a subject to one who has proved himself so perfectly competent to manage his own concerns and take care of the happiness of his family; but I have shewn him about my place and told him ⟨if⟩ he might build a little rural retreat on any part of it and I would give the land in fee simple. ⟨You w⟩ It would be a cheaper place than he could find elsewhere; as one garden would serve for both families, and many other things might be in com-

mon ↑(Kate says she would furnish you with vegetables and milk!)↓
⟨which⟩. You would then be once more at your own home; surrounded by
those who would take care of you and your children when your husband
might be away. You could make winter visits to town taking furnished
⟨lodgings,⟩ apartments; which are now to be had in good style. Thus you
might live very pleasantly, very genteelly and very economically. Until
your Cottage were built you might hire George Jones or Mrs Colford
Jones' house—You see I have made quite a plan for you and as I think
a very pleasant one.

I see you still have hankerings after Paris. My own opinion is that even
if Paris had remained unchanged, it would not have been advantageous to
your ultimate happiness or to the well being of your family to have
remained there much longer. You would have become unfitted for a contented residence in your native country; ⟨you would⟩ your children
would have become parisiens in habits, notions and inclinations—and
would in fact have had no real home of the affections—As it is, to return
with your family to a city which has so repeatedly been the scene of
popular tumults and bloody conflicts and so near being the scene of universal pillage and rapine would be to imitate the conduct of the country people about the foot of a volcano; who rebuild their cottages on the
lava as soon as it has grown cold.

I am occupied at present in bringing out a revised edition of my works
—the first volume, comprising the Sketch Book is to appear in September—The others to follow monthly. I trust through my arrangements with
my bookseller and further exercise of my pen in completing works now
nearly finished, I shall make my income adequate to my support. The
executorship to Mr Astors estate is by no means so lucrative a post as you
seem to have heard; but must yield some ↑tolerable↓ profit, and with me
every little tells—My health is excellent, my spirits are good, and while
these do not fail me, I can make my way stoutly through the world.

I wish you and your dear[1] little folk were with me at the Cottage
just now, The place never looked more lovely and the weather is heav-
enly. However, I hope to see you all here before long and to have your
little folks frolicking about the paths and gambolling on the grass. By
the bye they must have fine times at present in the Shrubbery;[2] which is
quite a little green world of itself. It is a great satisfaction to think
that in your present situation, while you and your little flock are in such
perfect security, you are living in ⟨the⟩ constant communion with a branch
of the family and your children becoming ⟨acquainted⟩ playmates of
new batches of cousins. I am delighted that you have had an opportunity
of being almost domesticated with your aunt Van Wart, It must be a
great gratification to her, as well as to yourself. You of course have been

to William Van Warts pleasant little country mansion and seen his fine family of children. ⟨Ros⟩ I do not know whether you saw Rosa when you were in England before. She is a woman of very superior character and endowments. I should have taken delight in making excursions with you in the neighborhood of Birmingham; or rather about Warwickshire—It is a part of the country abounding with places of interest, and endeared to me by agreeable reccollections.

Your mother appears to be well pleased with her situation at Mr Holmes. She is indeed very well placed there; the house is finely situated & respectably conducted and the boarders ↑are↓ the proper kind of people. Kellingers was to me somewhat of a horror.

Give my love to your Aunt, your Uncle Van Wart and to all your Cousins[.] I owe letters to some of them, but I have too much fagging of the pen at present to write letters and doubt whether I should have written this one to you had I not felt particularly interested about your domestic affairs and desirous of showing you that you had a home to come to on this side of the Atlantic.

Kiss Kate and Tutu for me; I hope they have not quite forgotten their uncle. You may Kiss Julie, also, though I have never been introduced to her.

Your affectionate uncle
Washington Irving

MANUSCRIPT: SHR.

1. WI wrote "deal."
2. The name of Henry Van Wart's residence in Birmingham.

2067. *To George Sumner*

New York, Aug 2d. 1848

My dear Sumner,

This will be handed to you by our young countryman Mr William H Powell,[1] who has already distinguished himself by the productions of his pencil and who is engaged to furnish one of the paintings for the Rotunda at Washington He goes to Paris to execute the work. Any assistance you can give him in the prosecution of his design such as access to libraries, collections—artists &c will be considered as personal favors rendered to myself. You are living in the midst of extraordinary scenes. I have read some of your accounts of them with great interest and hope you intend to give us, one day or other, in full Your experience in insurrections and Revolutions; which has been extensive in France, Spain & elsewhere

Yours very truly and cordially
Washington Irving

George Sumner Esqr

MANUSCRIPT: NYPL.—Seligman Collection.
George Sumner (1817–1863) was an American writer and traveler whom WI knew in Madrid in 1843 and 1844.

1. William Henry Powell (1823–1879), of Cincinnati, was an historical and portrait painter who had studied with Henry Inman. In 1847 he won the commission to paint "The Discovery of the Mississippi by DeSoto" for the Rotunda of the U.S. Capitol. Powell worked on the eighteen by twelve canvas in Paris for five years.

2068.   To George P. Putnam

[August 3, 1848]

My dear Sir,
As Mr Pierre M Irving and myself will be both out of town I will thank you to send me the proof of the introduction to the Sketch Book[1] by mail addressed to me at Tarry Town West Chester Cy. You need not send the copy with the proof.

Yours very truly
Washington Irving

Aug 3d. 1848. / Geo. P Putnam Esqr

MANUSCRIPT: Va.–Barrett.

1. *The Sketch Book* appeared a few weeks later as volume 2 of the Author's Revised Edition.

2069.   To Thomas L. Dunnell

Sunnyside Aug 5th 1848

Dear Sir,
I feel properly sensible of the honor done me by the invitation to deliver a lecture next winter before the intelligent community of Providence. An insuperable repugnance, however, to appearing before the public in

this manner obliges me, most respectfully, to excuse myself from what would otherwise be a source of great pride and satisfaction

I remain / Dear Sir / Very respectfully / Your obliged & hbl **Servt**
Washington Irving

T. L. Dunnall Esqr.

DOCKETED: Washington Irving / Aug 5. 1848
MANUSCRIPT: Va.–Barrett.

Thomas L. Dunnell (1816–1895) was a Pawtuckett calico printer whose mill employed 450 workers. He was president of the Franklin Lyceum in Providence, at which Ralph Waldo Emerson lectured for its first series in 1840. Probably Dunnell had invited WI to lecture at the Lyceum. See Welcome A. Greene, *The Providence Plantations* (Providence, 1886), p. 215; *Alphabetical Index of Births, Marriages, and Deaths, Recorded in Providence* (Providence, 1908), XII, 239.

2070.   To Henry Carey

Sunnyside Aug 11t. 1848

My dear Sir,

My account with the house of Messr. Lea & Blanchard remains unadjusted. At the close of our term of contract in May 1842, which they declined to renew,[1] a large number of copies of my different works remained in their hands unsold. I was absent in Spain at the time and no arrangement was made with respect to those copies—and partly through negligence and partly through other occupations on my part the matter has ever since remained at loose ends. In the mean time ⟨the⟩ Messr Lea and Blanchard have continued to sell off the residue copies, and I presume have sold the whole or the greater part, as for some time past they have generally been pronounced out of print. I consider myself of course entitled to a share of the profits and have written to Messr Lea & Blanchard to have the matter adjusted on fair and equitable terms; but as we may possibly differ in opinion as to those terms and as I wish every thing to be done in the most friendly manner, I have proposed to them to request you to look into the matter and to judge between us. As it was my original dealings with you that first produced my business relations with them I feel as if there is a propriety in applying to you for the amicable adjustment of any question that may arise between us.

Ever, my dear Sir, with great regard

Yours very truly
Washington Irving

Henry Carey Esqr

MANUSCRIPT: HSP.

1. WI had tried to negotiate a new contract with them before he left for Spain in 1842. See WI to Lea & Blanchard, February 26 and March 10, 1842; to PMI, September 5, 1842; and to Ebenezer Irving, September 8, 1842.

2071. To George P. Putnam

Sunnyside, Sept 24th. 1848

My dear Sir,

I have not received a proof sheet[1] since I left New York on thursday although[2] I have sent every day to the post office. The pacquets containing them, if really put into the post office in N York must be thrown aside there, by the clerks. Whoever takes them to the post office should see them mailed. My nephew Mr Henry Van Wart who takes this note will return to the country by the Steamer of tomorrow (Monday) afternoon. I will thank you to send by him all the proofs that have been struck off since the one I last corrected when in town—and I beg that no plates may be cast until I have made my corrections.

Very truly yours
Washington Irving

P S   I shall be in town on Wednesday

MANUSCRIPT: SHR.

1. WI is probably referring to the proof sheets for the revised edition of *The Sketch Book*, which was published in October, 1848.
2. WI wrote "athough."

2072. To George P. Putnam

[October 7, 1848]

My dear Sir

I observe a trivial error in the Sketch Book which I will thank you to have corrected. Page 231. Line 2d. for *slats* read *stalls*.

Yours truly
W I.

Sunnyside. Octr 7th. [1848] / Washington Irving.

MANUSCRIPT: Va.–Barrett.

2073. *To Matthew Clarkson*

Sunnyside Oct. 10th. 1848

Dear Sir,

I regret that it is not in my power to furnish you with any information as to the emigration from Holland to this country of the family of the Van Hornes.[1] The name is one of the most ancient and respectable both in Holland and Belgium. There have been Stadtholders of the name in Gueldres and Princes in Brabant, and various branches of the old stock have been interwoven by marriage with Aristocratic families of various parts of Europe. From some branch or other of these old races no doubt have come the offshoots which sought their fortunes in this new world.

In the autumn of 1833 I made a tour with Mr Van Buren through the Dutch villages along the Hudson, in the course of which we visited the village of Communipaw.[2] Here we found a primitive family of Van Hornes living in patriarchial style in the largest and best house of the place. The old people spoke Dutch, as did several of the family; indeed it seemed to be the household language. Old Mr Van Horne shewed us his title deeds executed in the early times of the province.[3] There were articles of furniture in the house which had come from Holland; as well as several Dutch books. The old gentleman remembered seeing from his house the conflagration of New York during the revolution. The family appeared to be well off and living most respectably and comfortably. If the old homestead is still kept up ⟨it⟩ you might find some information there on the subject of your researches

I am Sir, / Very respectfully / your obt Servt
Washington Irving

Matthew Clarkson Esqr

MANUSCRIPT: Va.–Barrett.

Matthew Clarkson (1822–1913) was the son of David and Elizabeth Van Horne Clarkson. There were other intermarriages between the Clarksons and Van Hornes. See Spooner, *Historic Families of America*, III, 281, 285–86.

1. WI draws upon the historical background of this family in his sketch, "The Count Van Horne," which appeared in *Knickerbocker Magazine* for March, 1840, and later collected in *Wolfert's Roost*.

2. WI mentions this trip in a letter to Peter Irving, October 28, 1833, and re-counts the early history of the village in "Communipaw," published in *Knickerbocker Magazine* for September, 1839, and later in book form in *A Book of the Hudson* and in *Spanish Papers and Other Miscellanies*.

3. Rutger Van Horne (1667–1741) bought land in Communipaw in 1711, and the property passed through his family. WI probably met his grandson, John Van

Horne (b. 1742). See Charles S. Williams, *Joris Janzen Van Horne and His Descendants* (New York, 1911), pp. 6, 11.

2074. To Charles R. Leslie

New-York, Octr 19th. 1848

My dear Leslie,

Mr Putnam of this city is publishing a revised edition of my works, which meets with success beyond my expectations[1] Next Spring he will put forth ⟨a? revised⟩ an illustrated edition of Knickerbocker[.] I wish you would give me a pen or pencil sketch of Diedrich for a frontispiece[.][2] I think you could hit off my idea of the little Dutch Historian better than any one else. There is a vile caricature of him which was published with an American edition while I was in Europe, and which is copied on all the Knickerbocker Omnibuses Steam boats &c &c. I wish a genuine likeness of him to supplant it

I scrawl this in great haste just as Mr Putnam is on the point of embarking

With kind remembrances to Mrs Leslie and your family

Yours ever my dear Leslie / Most affectionately
Washington Irving

ADDRESSED: Charles R. Leslie Esqr. / London
MANUSCRIPT: Va.–Barrett.

This letter is written on the business stationery of Geo. P. Putnam. Below the address is written: "This letter was given to me by my friend Saml Stone / C. R Leslie's Brother in law—Decr. 20. 1848. / Henry *Bicknell*"

1. *Knickerbocker's History of New York*, which appeared about September 1, 1848 as the first volume in the Author's Revised Edition, required a second printing by the time WI was writing this letter. See Jacob Blanck, *Bibliography of American Literature* (New Haven, 1969), V, 48.

2. On November 22, 1848, Leslie acknowledged receipt of WI's letter and indicated that he had sent Putnam "a pen sketch of 'Diedrich,' the slightness of which you must excuse me, as I am much engaged, and am obliged to spare my eyes all I can, for they are failing me. I am entirely out of practice in little things of this kind, and have no doubt you will be able to have something done much more to your mind in America. If so, pray throw it away without scruple." See *Autobiographical Recollections by the Late Charles Robert Leslie, R. A.*, ed. Tom Taylor (Boston, 1860), p. 341. When Putnam's new edition appeared in 1848, it did not contain this or any other illustration of Diedrich Knickerbocker. See Blanck, *Bibliography of American Literature*, V, 52.

2075. To James Wynne

New York, Oct. 23, 1848.

Dear Sir,

The pressure of various engagements,[1] which cut up my time at present, and keep me divided between town and country, must plead my excuse for not sooner answering your letter.[2]

I am sorry to say I have little faith in the efficiency of any association among literary men for their mutual protection and profits in the publication of their works. I have thought a great deal on the subject, have known various plans to be discussed and even commenced, among which was one in London, patronized, if I recollect right, by Thomas Campbell,[3] the poet. They all, however, came to nothing. I have not time at present to go into the various considerations which have convinced me of the impracticability of any attempt by a combination of authors to regulate and control the course of the "trade." I can only say that the conclusion I have come to on this subject is the result of much reflection and inquiry.[4]

The main thing wanting at present for the protection of our native literature is an international law of copyright. This once obtained, all authors of merit would be able to take care of their own wants, and original works worthy of publication would readily find a profitable market.

I am, very respectfully, your obedient servant,

Washington Irving

PUBLISHED: *Harper's Magazine*, 24 (February, 1862), 351.

James Wynne (1814–1871), a physician and journalist, had written to WI at the request of Sir Henry Lytton Bulwer, the British minister to the United States, for his opinion about an authors' association to protect literary property. Wynne wrote *Lives of Eminent Literary and Scientific Men of America* (1850) and *The Private Libraries of New York* (1863).

1. WI was involved in revising his writings for Putnam's new edition.
2. This letter has not been located.
3. WI is probably alluding to Campbell's establishing in London in 1829 a club, "The Literary Union, the object of which is to bring the literary men of the Metropolis into habits of more social and friendly intercourse. . . ." See William Beattie, *Life and Letters of Thomas Campbell*, 3 vols. (New York, 1973), II, 334; III, 55. It is not known if WI, who was secretary of the American legation at the time, was a participant in the activities of the group.
4. WI had expressed his views on the international copyright in *Knickerbocker Magazine*, 15 (January, 1840), 78–79, and in a letter to William H. Prescott, January 21, 1840. For other details about copyright agitation at this time, see

Andrew J. Eaton, "The American Movement for International Copyright, 1837–1860," *The Library Journal*, 15 (April, 1945), 95–122.

2076. To the Irving Literary Society

New York, December 11, 1848

Gentlemen—Absence from home has prevented my receiving and answering your letter of November 23d[1] in due season. I feel duly sensible of the honor done me by your society in writing me to be present and to deliver an address at the approaching celebration of its anniversary. I regret, however, to say that I have an insuperable repugnance to public speaking, which obliges me to decline all invitations of the kind. My engagements in New York[2] will not allow my absence from that city for some time to come.

I am, gentlemen, with great respect, your humble and obliged servant,

Washington Irving

PUBLISHED: Baltimore *American* (undated clipping at SHR).

1. This letter has not been located.
2. WI was revising his writings for the edition being published by Putnam.

2077. To Maunsell B. Field

Fifth Avenue. Decr 19th. 1848

My dear Sir,

I must apologize to you for not having sooner acknowledged the receipt of the moulding from the Alhambra which you were so very kind as to send me; but in truth I have been so much engrossed and hurried of late by a variety of occupations and engagements and recently so discomposed by family intelligence of an afflicting nature, that I have found it impossible to attend to my correspondence with that promptness and regularity that I could wish, and must trust to the indulgence of my friends to excuse my tardiness

I am my dear Sir, / With great respect / Your truly obliged

Washington Irving

Maunsell B Field Esqr

DOCKETED: Washington Irving / Decr. 19 1848 — / New York —
MANUSCRIPT: University of Wisconsin—Milwaukee Library.

Maunsell B. Field (1822–1875), who had graduated from Yale with highest honors in 1841, left in the spring of 1843 on an extensive tour of Europe, Asia Minor, and Egypt. He probably picked up the molding from the Alhambra during this trip. Later after being admitted to the bar, he held various posts in the Treasury Department.

2078. To [Joel T. Headley]

New York—Decr 19th. 1848

Dear Sir,

I am sorry to say that it is not in my power to render any service to your friend in the way she solicits. I have no work relative to the peculiar subject on which she is occupied; nor does any one occur to me at this moment excepting Clemencins noble eulogium on Queen Isabella,[1] which she no doubt possesses. The true source whence to draw her materials should be the old Spanish Chronicles; excellent editions of the best of which have been published in modern times and must be in every tolerably furnished Spanish library. These, if not to be found in this City might easily be procured from Cuba; if not directly from Spain.

I am dear Sir— / Very respectfully / Yours
Washington Irving

MANUSCRIPT: Harvard.

At the bottom of MS page 4 written upside down in another hand is "To J. T. Headley." Joel Tyler Headley (1813–1897), a prolific popularizer of history, geography, and biography, was associate editor of the New York *Tribune*.

1. Diego Clemencín (1765–1834) was the author of *Elógio de la Reina Catolica Doña Isabel* (Madrid, 1834).

2079. To John A. Dix

New York 30th Decr 1848

Hon John A Dix / U S. Senate—Washington

Sir:

There being a vacancy in the Board of Trustees of the "Astor Library" occasioned by the Death of Mr. Henry Brevoort,[1] and it being the wish of the Board to have the benefit of your counsel & Cooperation in the discharge of its important Trusts I am requested to inform you that your consent to fill that vacany will give the Board great pleasure.[2]

I transmit herewith a copy of the will founding the Library and am with great respect

Your obedient Servant
Washington Irving / President pro tem

P.S. You will oblige me by sending your reply under an envelope addressed to the care of W B Astor.

ADDRESSED: Hon John. A. Dix / U S. Senate / Washington / D C.   DOCKETED: Washington Irving / of the "Astor Library," / 30 *Dec. 1848.*
MANUSCRIPT: Columbia.

John Adams Dix (1798–1879), who had served as secretary of state of New York from 1833 to 1839, was U.S. senator from 1845 to 1849. He later held posts as secretary of the treasury (1861), U.S. minister to France (1866–1869), and governor of New York (1872–1874).

Only the signature and WI's title are in WI's handwriting.

1. WI was one of the pallbearers for Henry Brevoort (b. 1782). See *The Diary of Philip Hone,* II, 852.

2. The trustees for the library named in Astor's will were WI, William B. Astor, Daniel Lord, Jr., James G. King, Joseph G. Cogswell, Fitz-Greene Halleck, Henry Brevoort, Samuel B. Ruggles, Samuel Ward, Jr., and the mayor of New York and the chancellor of the State of New York, ex-officio. See Harry M. Lydenberg, *History of the New York Public Library* (New York, 1923), pp. 6, 10. Dix accepted the offer to serve on the board. See WI to Dix, January 10, 1849.

2080.   To John A. Dix

New York 10th Jany 1849

Hon John A. Dix / U S. Senate Washington

Dear Sir

It gave me great pleasure to receive your esteemed lines of the 2d Int[1] informing me that you would consent to become a Trustee of the Astor Library Association—

I lost no time in laying your Communication before the Board[2] who have accordingly elected you Trustee at their meeting of this day and instructed me to notify you accordingly.

With great respect

I remain / Your obedient Sert / Washington Irving
Pres: pro Tem

ADDRESSED: Hon John A Dix / U S. Senate / Washington / D C.   POSTMARKED:
   NEW-YORK / JAN 11   DOCKETED: Washington Irving. / Jany. 10 1849. /
   Trustee, Astor Library.
MANUSCRIPT: Columbia.

Only the signature of this letter and WI's title are in WI's handwriting.

1. This letter has not been located.
2. For membership of the board of the Astor Library Association, see WI to
Dix, December 30, 1848.

2081.   To Lewis Irving

New York, Feb—9th. 1849

My dear Nephew,
   In the course of your adventurous expedition to California the enclosed
letter[1] may be of service to you—I have been so much of a cosmopolite
that I have acquaintances scattered all over the world, but I do not
know who of them may be in California. Th⟨is⟩e enclosed is to serve as a
general passport to their good will.
   With best wishes for your wellfare

Your affectionate uncle
Washington Irving

Dr Lewis Irving

ADDRESSED: <L> Dr. Lewis Irving / New York.
MANUSCRIPT: Helen Irving Horton.

Lewis Irving (1795–1879) was the eldest son of William and Julia Paulding Irving.

1. WI's general letter of introduction was apparently retained by Lewis Irving.
It is printed immediately following this one.

2082.   To ——

New York. Feb 9th. 1849

The bearer of this, my nephew Dr Lewis Irving I reccommend to the kind
attentions and good offices of any person who may be a friend of mine,
or who may place confidence in my reccommendations. He is a young
gentleman of high principles, correct conduct and sound judgement, and
I believe ↑him↓ to be extremely well instructed in his profession. As I

take a deep interest in his welfare I shall consider any attentions shewn to him in consequence of this letter as favors conferred on myself.

Washington Irving

ADDRESSED: Mrs. Lewis G. Irving / Sing Sing
MANUSCRIPT: Helen Irving Horton.

This letter of introduction was enclosed with WI's letter of February 9, 1849, to Lewis Irving.

2083.   To Ephraim G. Squier

New York. March 6th. 1849.

Dear Sir,

Mr Everett[1] has so fully and cogently expressed my own opinions and wishes in regard to the object of your researches, that I have nothing to add, but heartily to concur with him in the hope that in extending those researches into Central America you may receive such aid and countenance from Government, either by official station, or otherwise, as may enable you to carry them into full effect.

I remain—Dear Sir / Yours very respectfully
Washington Irving

E Geo. Squier Esqr

MANUSCRIPT: NA, RG 59.

Below WI's signature and the inside address is the start of a letter,, apparently Squier's reply: "Philadelphia March 13(?) / Dear Sir, / I have great pleasure in."

Ephraim George Squier (1821–1888) was appointed chargé d'affaires to Latin America in April, 1849. As a result of his diplomatic experience in Latin America, Squier published a number of books about the region, including *Nicaragua; Its People, Scenery, Monuments, and the Proposed Interoceanic Canal* (1852); *The States of Central America* (1858); and *Peru: Incidents of Travel and Exploration in the Land of the Incas* (1877). Prior to this time Squier had published *Ancient Monuments of the Mississippi Valley* (1847).

1. Edward Everett (1794–1865), congressman from 1825 to 1835, governor of Massachusetts from 1836 to 1839, U.S. minister to Great Britain from 1841 to 1845, served as president of Harvard College from 1846 to 1849.

2084.   To John M. Clayton

New York. April 4t. 1849

Sir,

Understanding that my friend Mr John Howard Payne,[1] late Consul at Tunis, is desirous of obtaining some public situation or employment I take the liberty of stating that I have known him intimately in early life and at different times during his residence in Europe and since his return to this country His life has been one of vicissitudes but I have had opportunities of witnessing his upright and honorable conduct in the midst of difficulties and perplexities. He appeared to me capable and industrious in the despatch of business. His residence abroad has made him well acquainted with foreign languages, and, in his own language he has ever commanded one of the most graceful flowing and perspicuous styles that I am acquainted with.

Of the ability with which he acquitted himself in his consulship the archives of the State department must furnish the most reliable evidence; all that I ever heard of him in that respect was satisfactory. I should have great satisfaction in hearing of his receiving some employment under government suited to his talents and capacity.

I am Sir / Very respectfully / Your Obt Servt
Washington Irving

The Hon. John M Clayton / &c &c &c

MANUSCRIPT: NA, RG 59.

John M. Clayton (1796–1856), a farmer and lawyer from Delaware, was elected to the U.S. Senate in 1828, resigned in 1836 to become chief justice of the Supreme Court of Delaware, returned to the Senate in 1845, and then served as President Taylor's secretary of state. Upon Taylor's death he left the post and was reelected to the Senate in 1852.

1. Payne (1791–1852), who began his career as actor and dramatist, served as U.S. consul in Tunis from 1842 to 1845 and from 1851 until his death.

2085.   To Lewis G. Clark

[April 27, 1849]

My dear Mr Clark:

I will thank you to send me the two numbers of the Knickerbocker which contain the story of Mountjoy.[1]

You once spoke to me about some work in print or manuscript in the possession of your Oriental correspondent, relative to the History of Persia; which might be of service to me in writing the life of Mahomet. Can you procure me a sight of it.

I send you a plan of a rural cemetery projected by some of the worthies of Tarrytown on the woody hills adjacent to the Sleepy Hollow Church. I have no pecuniary interest in it, but I hope it may succeed as it will keep that beautiful and umbrageous neighborhood sacred from the anti-poetical and all levelling axe. Beside, I trust I shall lay my bones there. The projectors are plain matter of fact men ⟨and⟩ but are already aware of the blunder they have committed in naming it the *Tarrytown* instead of the *Sleepy Hollow* Cemetery.[2] The latter name would have been enough of itself to secure the patronage of all desirous of sleeping quietly in their graves. I beg you to correct this oversight should you, as I trust you will, think proper to notice this sepulchral enterprise.

I hope as the spring opens you will accompany me in one of my brief visits to Sunnyside—when we will make a visit to Sleepy Hollow and ↑(thunder and lightning permitting)↓ have a colloquy among the tombs.

Yours very truly
Washington Irving

N York. April 27th. 1849 / No 46. East Twenty first St.

ADDRESSED: L Gaylord Clark Esqr   DOCKETED: Irving
MANUSCRIPT: SHR.   PUBLISHED: *Knickerbocker Magazine*, 55 (January, 1860), 118; *Sleeepy Hollow Cemetery at Tarrytown-on-Hudson* (New York, 1891), p. [2]; Alvah P. French, ed., *History of Westchester County, New York* (New York, 1925), II, 735 (in part).

On page 3, following WI's letter, Clarke wrote in pencil: "I rode through the Hollow with him in a little wagon in the almightiest storm I ever encountered; and that is what he alludes to."

1. "Mountjoy" appeared in *Knickerbocker Magazine*, 14 (November–December, 1839), 402–12, 522–38.
2. The cemetery, which was developed under the name of Sleepy Hollow, was WI's final resting place. In the *Knickerbocker*, 33 (June, 1849), 548–49, Clark, perhaps as a result of WI's reference to the burial ground, described Sleepy Hollow Cemetery and recommended it as a beautiful and convenient place.

2085a.   To John E. Warren.

New York. May 8.–1849

My dear Sir,

I beg you to accept my thanks for the copy of Mr Streets poem[1] which you have had the kindness to send me. I am happy to hear that it has been favorably noticed by transatlantic critics; which will have a good effect in calling attention to it on its republication in this country.[2] I hope and trust it will meet with a cordial reception from the American public.

I percieve by your letter you intend to try for the Secretaryship of the Brasil Legation[3] that of Madrid being pledged by the president to a candidate from Kentucky.[4] I would again observe that though the post of Secretary is in the gift of government it is always customary to consult the wishes of the Minister in making the appointment. Genl Jackson used to say he would as soon think of appointing the Aid de Camp to a general as the Secretary to a Minister. When I was nominated for Spain Mr Tyler was extremely anxious to give the Secretary ship to a person for whom he had a friendship, but deferred to my wishes, and during my mission three several appointments to the post were made conformably to my request. It is all important to the advantageous discharge of the duties of a legation that there should be harmony and good will between the Minister & the Secretary.

I would advise you therefore to ascertain who is likely to receive the appointment of Minister, and secure a good footing in that quarter

In great haste / I am my dear Sir

Yours very truly
Washington Irving

John E[*unrecovered*] Warren Esqr

MANUSCRIPT: NYPL.

John E. Warren of Minnesota was commissioned secretary of American legation in Central America on April 6, 1853, but he declined the appointment. Apparently he was unsuccessful in his earlier attempts at a secretaryship. See Hasse, *Index to U. S. Documents*, III, 1791, 1806, 1816, 1830, 1910.

1. Alfred B. Street's *Frontenac: or the Atotarko of the Iroquois,* a metrical romance of 7000 lines, had recently been published by Richard Bentley in London.

2. Baker and Scribner of New York republished Bentley's edition.

3. T. I. Morgan of Ohio, who had been commissioned secretary of the American legation in Brazil on June 9, 1847, remained in that post until his death on March 30, 1850. See Hasse, *Index to U. S. Documents*, III, 1780.

4. Actually H. J. Perry of New Hampshire was commissioned secretary of the Madrid legation on July 5, 1849. See Hasse, *Index to U. S. Documents*, III, 1835.

2086.   *To William C. Macready*

New-York, Wednesday, May 9, 1849.

William C. Macready, Esq.

Dear Sir:

The undersigned, having heard that the outrage at the Astor Place Opera House,[1] on Monday evening, is likely to have the effect of preventing you from continuing your performances, and from concluding your intended farewell engagement on the American stage, take this public method of requesting you to reconsider your decision, and of assuring you that the good sense and respect for order prevailing in this community, will sustain you on the subsequent nights of your performances.[2]

Ambrose L. Jordan,
Edward Sandford,
Willis Hall,
James Foster, Jr.,
Duncan C. Pell,
Ogden Hoffman,
Howard Henderson,
Saml B. Ruggles,
James Collis,
Edward S. Gould,
William Kent,
John W. Francis,
Wessell S. Smith,
W. M. Pritchard,
Benj. D. Silliman,
David Austin,
M. M. Noah,
F. R. Tilou,
Henry J. Raymond,
Charles A. Davis,
Pierre M. Irving,
Moses H. Grinnell,
Henry A. Stone,
George Bruce,

Washington Irving,
Francis B. Cutting,
Joseph L. White,
Matthew Morgan,
David C. Colden,
Ogden P. Edwards,
John R. Bartlett,
Rich'd Grant White,
Evert A. Duyckinck,
J. Prescott Hall,
Robert J. Dillon,
Ralph Lockwood,
Wm. C. Barrett,
David Graham,
Edward Curtis,
James Brooks,
J. E. Dekay,
Jacob Little,
H. W. Field,
J. Beekman Finley,
Denning Duer,
Simeon Draper,
Herman Melville,
Cornelius Mathews.

PUBLISHED: NYEP, May 9, 1849; James Grant Wilson, *The Memorial History of the City of New York* (New York, 1893), III, 432.

William Charles Macready (1793–1873), an English actor acclaimed for his Shakespearean roles, was associated with the Drury Lane Theatre for many years.

1. The "outrage" was a disturbance provoked by the supporters of Edwin Forrest when Macready appeared on the same night in another theater (the Opera House in Astor Place) in the same play (*Macbeth*) in which Forrest was performing. The crowd, a mixture of working men agitated by Forrest's partisans and well-dressed gentlemen, swarmed into the theater and disrupted the performance with their noisy, boisterous behavior. As a result, Macready threatened to cancel the rest of his engagement. See NYEP, May 8 and 9, 1849; Wilson, *Memorial History of . . . New York*, III, 432–33.

2. When Macready agreed to reopen on Thursday, May 10, the mob supporting Forrest determined to prevent it, by violence if necessary. A fight between the crowd and the police and its reinforcements from the Seventh Regiment followed, with the killing of thirty-four of the rioters and the wounding of many and with injuries to 141 soldiers and policemen. Macready completed the performance, went into hiding, and left two days later for Boston and his return to England. See NYEP, May 10, 11, 12, 14, 15, and 16, 1849; Wilson, *Memorial History of . . . New York*, III, 434–35.

2087. To Dorothea A. Langdon

New York May 25th. 1849

Madam

We acknowledge the receipt of your letter of 22d of this month.[1]

In that letter as in your previous letters you inform us that by consultation with the best legal advisers you are satisfied that any act or direction short of a duly executed codicil or revocation has no effect upon your rights; and you have never intimated that any other proofs of your fathers intentions would govern your action. It therefore would have been useless for us to spread before you, what we might consider plain evidence of such intentions, if ↑they were↓ not contained in a codicil or revocation legally executed. We therefore forbore from doing so, as of no avail to prevent a litigation to which you are advised "by the best legal advisers" and as tending to increase rather than lessen the useless discussion.

Without intending to deviate from this course, we nevertheless place a single fact before you, which will shew with what consideration we speak of evidence without the will.

After our letter of 3 of this month, there was found among your fathers papers the draft of the codicil of January 9. 1839 which he had kept, on executing the codicil, for his own reference. On the margin of this draft at the close of the Item and opposite to the clause giving 100000 Water Loan to your six children we find in your father's hand writing in pencil the following words:

"The stock here alluded to has been transferred to Mrs L. & her children say 100000 Life Insurance and 100000 Water Stock." And on the back of the same draft, is endorsed in ink in your father's own hand as follows: "The stock herein given is the same which W. B. Astor holds in Trust for Mrs Langdon & children.

J. J. Astor 1 Oct. '40"

and in pencil, in your fathers hand writing

"gave 14 St H. & L
do Grand 9 lots
do 100000 5 per cent stock
do 100000 Life certificates

200000 J. J. A."

We present this however merely to justify the statement in our last letter and not with a view of going fully into this subject in a correspondence. This is now in such a position that we cannot suppose that your letters are not written under the advice of counsel: and we respectfully request that any further communications on your claims may be made by your council directly; and an interview may be had with them by Mr Lord, between whom all suggestions on the subject of your claims may be considered, without the delay or liability to misunderstanding ↑to↓ which written communications have seemed to give rise.

We are very respectfully / Your obedt servants

Washington Irving / Jas. Gallatin / Daniel Lord / James G. King

Mrs Langdon

MANUSCRIPT: ROSENBACH FOUNDATION.

Dorothea Astor (1795–1853) had eloped with Colonel Walter Langdon (d. 1847) in 1812. Displeased by the action, her father, John Jacob Astor, for many years, would have nothing to do with the couple.

The other signers, along with WI, were trustees of the Astor estate. The letter is not in WI's handwriting.

1. This and the letter mentioned in the fourth paragraph have not been located.

2088.   To Lewis G. Clark

[June 5, 1849]

My Dear Mr Clarke

Dont trouble yourself any more about the Oriental work in question—"I have fought my battle without it."[1]

I send you a few scraps which are all I have by me. There are two or three from Lilly[2] the father of the school of the euphuests.

Yours truly
W. I.

Tuesday June 5th [1849]

MANUSCRIPT: Robert K. Black.

The year is determined by the perpetual calendar and by WI's reference to the Oriental work which he had mentioned in his letter to Clark on April 27, 1849.

1. Possibly a variation of John Dryden, "Alexander's Feast," line 67.
2. John Lyly (1554–1606), author of *Euphues, the Anatomy of Wit* (1579) and *Euphues and His England* (1580), used a literary style employing excessive balance, antithesis, and alliteration.

2089.   *To Thomas Picton*

Sunnyside, June 10th. 1849

Dear Sir,

I must apologize to you for this long delay in answering your note. It was received at a hurried moment, with several other letters and mislaid. I have searched for it repeatedly among my papers in town but in vain. It was not until this morning that I found it by mere chance in the pocket of a coat which I had left behind when last in the country. And now to answer your inquiry. No person by the name of Beate[?] was ever a contributor to the Salmagundi. The only contributors were Mr James K. Paulding and myself with occasionally some poetical sketches and some suggestions for essays by my brother William

Very respectfully / Your obt Servt
Washington Irving

Thomas Picton Esqr / &c &c &c

MANUSCRIPT: Va.–Barrett.

Thomas Picton (1822–1891), soldier of fortune and journalist who was born Thomas Picton Milner, graduated from college in 1840, went to France, and served in Louis Philippe's army before returning to New York in 1848. As a journalist he later wrote for the *Era*, the *Sachem*, the *True American*, the *True National Democrat*, the *Sunday Dispatch*, and the *Sunday Mercury*, frequently under pseudonym of Paul Preston. The reason for his query about *Salmagundi* has not been ascertained.

2090.   *To Sarah Storrow*

Sunnyside July 5t. 1849

My dear Sarah

I am rejoiced to learn by your letters to your mother that you are really coming out with your dear little family in one of the August steamers: I cannot express to you how much the news has gratified me, for I had begun to ⟨fear you would⟩ give up the hope of seeing you here again, or perhaps any where else; as I do not expect ever again, to cross the Atlantic, and you appeared likely to linger in Europe from year to year, until those who most love you here, were dead and gone—I was endeavoring to accustom and recconcile myself to the idea, but I confess it ⟨is⟩was the most painful one that has ever haunted my thoughts. However, we will not dwell on so irksome a subject.

The immediate object of this letter is to beg that on your arrival you will come up immediately to the Cottage. It will be in the month of September when the city is hot and uncomfortable and the country delightful. The addition I have built to my little establishment gives me much more house room than formerly, and enables me to offer you better accomodations for your little flock than you can find any where else in the country. Kate[1] who is most anxious to have you once more at home, promises to do every thing in her power [to][2] make you all comfortable. Your Mother,[3] is at Mr Holmes's[4] so that you will be quite near her and can see each other every day. Do not therefore stop in the city even to get all your luggage on shore if there should be likely to be any delay, but come up immediately: Mr Storrow can return to town to attend to it. Do not disappoint me in this matter. If you knew how delightful the idea is to me of seeing you once more beneath my roof you could not disappoint me in it.

For upwards of a year past I have been very much from home, obliged to be for the most of the time in the city, superintending the publication of a new and revised edition of my works;[5] making researches for other works on which I am employed,[6] and attending to the settlement of Mr Astor's estate[7] and the organization of the Astor library. Altogether I have had more toil of head and fagging of the pen for the last eighteen months than in any other period of my life and have been once or twice fearful my health might become deranged, but it has held out marvelously; and now I hope to be able to ease off in my toils and to pass my time at home as usual. The result of all this labor is to put me more at ease in my circumstances, for, though I have not made all the money you seem, by some of your letters, to suppose, ⟨still I am now able to cope with⟩ nor have the means to launch out in extra indulgences, still I am able to cope with ⟨my⟩ current expenses, ⟨which⟩ without devouring my little capital, which I assure you is quite an era with me in house keeping.

Mr Grinnell,[8] as I suppose you know, has taken for the Summer, a house built ⟨to⟩ by Colonel Webb[9] a year or two since, in ⟨I⟩ a part of Beekmans woods, just on the bank of the River. It is a spacious stone house with every convenience, and surrounded by noble forest trees. It is an easy drive from here, so that the establishments can keep up a frequent intercourse. I hope to see your little flock[10] and Julias,[11] mingling together and sporting about both places.

Julias children will make delightful companions for yours—I well recollect the happy afternoon and evening they passed together at her country retreat near Yonkers, and I then thought what a pity it was such a lovely groupe of little relatives and playmates should be severed. God bless us and bring us all happily together again.

With kind remembrances to your husband and kisses to the young folk—

Your affectionate uncle
Washington Irving

ADDRESSED: Madame / Madame Storrow. / aux soins de Mr T W. Storrow / 19. Rue dr Faubg Poissonniere / a Paris
MANUSCRIPT: Yale.   PUBLISHED: PMI, IV, 52 (in part).

1. Catharine Ann, Ebenezer Irving's daughter, who was in charge of the household at Sunnyside.

2. WI omitted the bracketed word.

3. Catharine Paris, WI's sister.

4. Operator of a boarding house in Tarrytown.

5. Between mid-1848 and early 1850 George P. Putnam brought out a fifteen-volume "Author's Revised Edition" of WI's writings.

6. These included *A Book of the Hudson*, published in April, 1849, and *Mahomet and His Successors*, published early in 1850.

7. For his efforts as executor of the estate of John Jacob Astor WI received $10,592.66. See PMI, IV, 52–53.

8. Moses Hicks Grinnell, a New York merchant and husband of Julia Irving.

9. James Watson Webb (1802–1884) was editor of the influential Whig newspaper, the New York *Courier and Enquirer*, until 1861.

10. Sarah's children included Catharine (1842–1917), Susan (1844–1863), and Julia (1847–1920).

11. Julia Grinnell's children were Julia (1837–1915), Irving (1839–1921), and Fanny (1842–1887).

2091.   To George P. Putnam

[July 12, 1849]

My dear Sir,

Take care that the Dutch motto is not omitted on the title page.[1] I think upon the whole I would omit the dedication to the Hist Society, as it might be taken by some of the members in a wrong sense.

The title page should specify that this is the Authors revised edition.

Yours very truly
W Irving

Thursday—July 12th [1849]

ADDRESSED: Geo Putnam Esqr / Bookseller / Broadway   POSTMARKED: [*unre-covered*]
MANUSCRIPT: Wellesley College.

The year has been determined by the perpetual calendar.

Some printings of the "Author's Revised Edition" included only the general title page. Apparently WI, after seeing one of these copies of *Knickerbocker's History of New York*, wrote the following letter to Putnam with his specific directions. See Blanck, *Bibliography of American Literature*, V, 47–48.

1. The motto was "De waarheid die in duister lag, / Die komt met klaarheid aan den dag."

2092.   To Charles Dexter

New York July 14th. 1849

Dear Sir

Through an error in the transmission of my letters during a late excursion to the Western part of the state your letter of the 12th June[1] has been loitering in Country post offices and has but just reached me. I presume the yacht of the Sophomore boat club has before this recieved a name; at least I hope so, as my memory is not so stored with "soft musical and appropriate Indian names" as you seem to think it. A few only occur to me at present, such as Mekaia[,] Flavona, Oondata, Aramilya, Winona[,] Sagateya; but I doubt whether any of these will suit you. I have not time to rummage my brain or my books for any more, for I am impatient to reply to your letter and to put an end to a silence in my part which may have been attributed to slight or indifference—

With many thanks to the Sophomore Boat club for the compliment paid me in seeking a name at my hands; and wishing them many pleasant cruises on their yacht. I remain Sir,

Very respectfully / Your Obt Servt
Washington Irving

Charles Dexter Esqr

MANUSCRIPT: Cincinnati Historical Society.

Charles Dexter (1830–1893), who received a B.A. in 1851 and an M.A. in 1857 from Harvard, entered his father's wholesale grocery and liquor business in Cincinnati after graduation. He was the author of *Versions and Verses* (1865) and *In Memoriam, Versions and Idle Measures* (1891). See Harvard University, *Quinquennial Catalog of Officers and Graduates, 1636–1930* (Cambridge, Mass., 1930), p. 250; and William Coyle, ed., *Ohio Authors and Their Books* (Cleveland, 1962), p. 168.

1. This letter has not been located.

2093.   To George P. Putnam

Sunnyside Aug. 25t 1849

My dear Sir,

I note a few errors ⟨in⟩ of the press in Goldsmith.[1] Page 280. line 12 for 1722 read 1772. Page 282. for idem velle atque idem *volle*—read idem velle atque idem *nolle*—P. 360 third line from the bottom for "made *wrong*" read "made *weary*" P 379. for familiar *features* of life read "familiar *pictures* of life" P 318 line 20 for "thought *or*" read "thought *of*" P 285. line 7. for "Augustales" read "Augustalis" P 278 line 9 "the love *of* all who knew him" *of* is wanting. Preface 2 P—line 15 circumstantial[2] P 162 line 6 for most ludicrous read *almost* ludicrous
P 184. Note at the bottom of the page Forster for Foster

I am glad to see by the advertisement at the end of the volume that you intend to publish a complete edition of Goldsmiths works.[3] I intended to suggest it to you, when I should next see you. I think it cannot fail to be profitable to you.

Very truly Yours
Washington Irving

ADDRESSED: George P. Putnam Esq / 155 — Broad Way / New York   DOCKETED: Washington Irving
MANUSCRIPT: SHR.

1. WI had probably examined one of the early bound copies of the book. His preface to it is dated August 1, 1849.

2. This note and the two following are written along the upper two-thirds of the left margin of the page.

3. This notice appeared on page [383]. Putnam did not publish a complete edition of Goldsmith's writings until 1908.

2094.   To Pierre M. Irving

September 21, 1849

I am getting on very well, but am not yet in a mood to take up my pen; so Mr. Putnam must stay his stomach with Goldsmith a little longer. I suppose, because I knocked off that work in such an offhand manner, he thinks it a very easy matter with me "to blow up a dog."[1]

PUBLISHED: PMI, IV, 59.

1. WI alludes to a passage in the preface to Cervantes, *Don Quixote,* part 2: "Once upon a time there was a madman in Seville that hit upon one of the prettiest out-of-the-way whims that ever madman in this world was possessed withal.

"He gets him a hollow cane, small at one end, and catching hold of a dog in the street, or anywhere else, he clapped his foot on one of the cur's legs, and holding his hind-legs in his hand, he fitted his cane to the dog's back-side, and blew him up as round as a ball; then giving him a thump or two on the guts, and turning to the bye-standers, who are always a great many upon such occasions: 'Well, gentlemen,' said he, 'what do you think, is it such an easy matter to blow up a dog?' And what think you, sir, is it such an easy matter to write a book?..." (Miguel de Cervantes Saavedra, *Don Quixote of La Mancha,* trans. P. A. Motteux, 4 vols. [New York, 1920], III, 3–4).

2095.   To ———

[October 22, 1849]

My dear Sir

It is with the greatest regret I have to give up the pleasure of dining with you today. I was thrown from my waggon on Saturday evening and so battered and bruised that, with all my exertions, I have not been able to get myself in trim for a dinner party. I have tried to the last moment to persuade myself that I could come, but I find it impossible.

Yours very truly
Washington Irving

Monday, Octr–22d. [1849]

MANUSCRIPT: Fales Collection, New York University Library.

The date is determined by the perpetual calendar. Below WI's signature and the date, "1849" is written in another hand.

2096. To Gouverneur Kemble

New York, Feb. 7, 1850

My dear Kemble:

I have called with ——— to see Durand's picture,[1] and we were both delighted with it. It is beautiful—beautiful. Such truth of detail with such breadth; such atmosphere, such harmony, such repose, such coloring. The group of trees in the foreground is admirable; the characters of the trees so diversified and accurate; the texture and coloring of their barks; the peculiarities of their foliage. The whole picture had the effect upon me of a delightful piece of music. I think it would be a charming addition to the *Kemble gallery.*

✻   ✻   ✻   ✻   ✻   ✻

I shall avail myself of the railroad,[2] one of these days, to pay you the visit you suggest; but I must first get out of the clutches of the printers.

PUBLISHED: PMI, IV, 66–67.

1. Asher B. Durand (1796–1886) painted *Early Morning at Cold Spring*, a canvas measuring 59 by 47½ inches, for Gouverneur Kemble. It was exhibited at the National Academy of Design in 1850, and WI may have seen it there. For other details about the painting and a color reproduction of it, see *A. B. Durand, 1796–1886* (Montclair, N. J., 1971), pp. 9, [37], 61.

2. WI is referring to the Hudson River Railroad, which ran through Sunnyside along the shore of the river and continued on to Albany.

2097. To Charles A. Davis

Sunnyside, February 11, 1850

I thank you for your very entertaining letter,[1] and the kind solicitude which you manifest in regard to a recent attack upon me in the Herald. This charge of not having rendered justice to Navarette is an old calumny long since refuted.[2] Navarrete's work was not history but a mere collection of documents, which formed a part only of my materials, and for which I gave him ample credit in my preface, and in notes at the bottom of the pages throughout my work . . . which is a sufficient answer to all cavils on this head. As you may not have seen it, I will requote it for you, though at the expense of my modesty [*then follows a lengthy description in Spanish*]. . . . You need not fear my being drawn into a scuffle with the rough and tumble fellows of the press. If my literary reputation is not old enough to go alone and take care of itself, it is not worth fighting about. If it cannot stand by itself at this time of day, I am not going to prop it up.

PUBLISHED: *Catalogue of the George P. Upton Collection* (American Art Association–American Art Galleries, April 23, 1914), item 168.

Charles Augustus Davis (1795–1867), who wrote a series of letters by "Major Jack Downing" for the New York *Daily Advertiser*, had been WI's friend since the early 1830's.

1. This letter has not been located.
2. For an earlier reaction to the same charge, see WI to PMI, November 12, 1842.

2098. To Henry Panton

Sunnyside, Feb. 15, 1850

. . . The house in which I was born was No. 131 William-street, about half-way between John and Fulton streets. Within a very few weeks after my birth the family moved into a house nearly opposite, which my father had recently purchased; it was No. 128, and has recently been pulled down and a large edifice built on its site. It had been occupied by a British commissary during the war; the *broad arrow* was on the street door, and the garden was full of choice fruit-trees, apricots, green-gages, nectarines, &c. It is the first home of which I have any recollection, and there I passed my infancy and boyhood.

PUBLISHED: *Irvingiana*, p. v.

Henry Panton was an amateur artist who exhibited in the National Academy of Design shows between 1851 and 1860 and was an honorary member of the Academy between 1854 and 1860. See *National Academy of Design Exhibition Record*, 2 vols. (New York, 1943), II, 63.

2099. To George Ticknor

Sunnyside, Feb. 15th. 1850

My dear Ticknor,

I ought long since to have thanked you for the Copy of your work which you had the kindness to send me but I thought it best to read it first. This the pressure of various affairs have permitted me to do only at intervals so that I have not yet got further than the threshold of the third volume; but I will delay an acknowledgement no longer. I have read enough to enable me to praise it heartily and honestly. It is capital—capital It takes me back into dear old Spain, into its libraries; its theatres; among its chronicles, its plays; among all those scenes, and characters and customs that for years were my study and delight. No one that has not been in Spain can feel half the merit of your work; but to those who have it is a perpetual banquet. I am glad you have brought it out during my life time for it will be a vade mecum for the rest of my days. When I have once read it through I will keep it by me like a Stilton Cheese to give a dig into whenever I want a relishing morsel. I began to fear it would never see the light in my day, or that it might fare with you as with that good lady, who went thirteen years with child and then brought forth a little old man, who died in the course of a month of extreme old age; but you have produced three strapping volumes full of life and freshness and vigour, and ⟨which⟩ ↑that↓ will live forever. You have laid the foundations of your work so deep that nothing can shake it; you have built it up with a care that renders it reliable in all its parts and you have finished it off with a grace and beauty that leave nothing to be desired. It is well worth a life time to achieve such a work.

By the way, as you appear to have an extensive collection of the old Spanish plays, there is one which Captain Medwin[1] mentioned to me, the story of which had made a great impression on Lord Byron. It was called El Embozado de Cordoba—(or perhaps Encapotado) I have sought for it in vain in all the libraries and collections in Spain. If you should have a copy of it let me know; though I apprehend Captain Medwin has given me a wrong name as I could find none of the dramatic antiquarys that knew any thing about it.

I regret that you did not fall into the hands of my worthy publisher Mr Putnam; who is altogether, the most satisfactory man in his line that I have ever had dealings with; but I trust you have made a good arrangement with the Harpers, who command a vast circulation.

When you see Prescott give him my cordial remembrances. You two are shelved together for immortality.

Ever my dear Ticknor / Yours very faithfully
Washington Irving

George Ticknor Esq

MANUSCRIPT: Dartmouth College.   PUBLISHED: George Ticknor, *Letters to Pascual de Gayangos*, ed. Clara Louisa Penney (New York, 1927), pp. 549–50.

George Ticknor (1791–1871) had recently completed a three-volume history of

Spanish literature which was published by Harper and Brothers in 1849. WI refers
to it in the opening paragraph of his letter.

1. Captain Thomas Medwin (1788–1869), friend and biographer of Shelley and
Byron, had met WI in Paris in 1824 and 1825 and told him about Byron's interest
in Calderon's *El Embozado.* In his notebook WI set down Medwin's details about
the plot of the play and sketched scenes for his own dramatic version. Later he
wrote an essay, "An Unwritten Drama of Lord Byron," for *The Gift. A Christmas
and New Year's Present for 1836,* ed. Eliza Leslie (Philadelphia, 1835), pp. 166–71.
See *J&N,* III, 267, 278–80, 289–90, 292, 324, 326, 465–66, 468, 519–21, 710–12;
and STW, I, 466–67.

2100.   To Sabina O'Shea

Sunnyside Feb 2⟨8⟩4th. 1850

My dear Mrs OShea,

I have suffered a long time to elapse without writing to you, but you
must not be out of patience with me. You have no idea what a drudge I
have been with the pen for a long time past revising and correcting my
old works for the press and writing new ones; and how little time I
have had for friendly letter writing. I dont think in the whole course of
my literary career I have been such a slave to the pen as for the last
eighteen months, and have been so much behind hand in all my correspondence.

I had very good accounts of you from the Saunders family as they
passed through New York on their return from Spain. They appeared to
have been well pleased with their residence in Madrid, especially the
young lady who is very pretty and I think must have been admired, on
that account, if on no other. The old general[1] will no doubt be much
more at home in his own country than in the Spanish court circle. Of
our present Minister at Madrid[2] I know nothing ⟨favorably⟩ ↑personally↓
having never seen him. In fact I know nothing about him excepting that
he bears a very fair public character. I hope he may prove an agreeable
and popular addition to ⟨the⟩ ↑your↓ diplomatic circle, which I find
has enlarged considerably since I was one of it.

I often look back with kind reccollections to ↑my↓ residence in Madrid
where many of my happiest hours were passed under your hospitable
roof; and I often wish I could be taking a stroll with you and my worthy
friend *Papa Quique* along the promenade beyond the Prado[.] I am
glad to hear that Henrique (I will *not* call him *Quique* which sounds too
much like a nick name) continues to be fond of his book. One of the

greatest safeguards to a young man is a steady habit of reading. It furnishes him with domestic occupation and amusement, while, if his reading
be properly directed, it stores his mind with knowledge, ⟨and⟩ improves
his taste and strengthens and confirms his principles. There is scarce any
thing which makes a man so independent of the world for his enjoyments
⟨and so⟩ as a fondness for reading; or which puts him so much above the
vicissitudes of fortune. It has been my standby throughout a life which
at times has been chequered by vicissitudes.

My niece Mrs Storrow whom you knew in Paris, is at present in New
York with her family (three lovely little girls) She and her husband
passed over into England during the tumults which followed Louis
Philipes down fall.[3] After residing some months in England they returned
to Paris, and thence came out here ⟨last⟩ early last Autumn. They resume their residence in Paris early next summer, where I presume Mr
Storrow will remain until he has amassed sufficient fortune, which I
hope and trust ⟨will be⟩ he will be able to do in the course of two or
three years more as his circumstances continue to be very prosperous. I
trust when you revisit Paris you will find Sarah out; you will always be
able to learn her residence at the American Legation or Consulate. She
will be delighted to see you, for I assure you you quite won her heart It
will be a sad trial for me to part with her again. Since her return home
she has had the affliction of losing her mother (my sister) who died after
an illness of three or four weeks.[4] It was a severe blow to us all; though
her delicate constitution and advanced age prepared us for such an
event. To Sarah it was a great consolation that she had returned home
⟨to pass⟩ in time to pass some time with her mother before her last illness, and to be by her bed side during her mortal struggle. It was a great
happiness to my sister also; to have her only daughter and her grand
children with her in the last few months of her existence.

I am living very quietly and comfortably in my little nest on the
banks of the Hudson; which I have improved considerably since my return, and which, to my taste, is one of the pleasantest little nookeries
in the world. Much of its cosyness, however, is no doubt owing to my
having a number of nieces to take care of it, and to take care of me; who
take care of both in first rate style. I dont think there is any old bachelor
going who is better off in that respect than myself.

How does Willy come on with his Spanish bride[5]—I presume he will
now take rank among the Spanish noblesse. I hope she will prove a good
wife to him, and that their union will be a happy one.

Give my kind remembrances to Mr O'Shea who I trust goes on his way
prosperously through all the shiftings and changes of affairs in Madrid—

remember me cordially also to William and Henrique and believe me ever, my dear Mrs OShea

Your sincerely and strongly attached friend
Washington Irving

Mrs Henry O'Shea.

Addressed: Mrs Sabina O'Shea / care of Henry O'Shea Esq / Madrid   Docketed: Washington Irving / 1850. // Feby 24th. 1850
Manuscript: HSA.   Published: Penney, *Bulletin NYPL*, 63 (January, 1959), 34–35.

1. Romulus M. Saunders (1791–1867) succeeded WI as U.S. minister to Spain in July, 1846.

2. Daniel M. Barringer (1806–1873), a North Carolina lawyer who had served in Congress from 1843 to 1849, was U.S. minister to Spain from June 18, 1849, to September 4, 1853.

3. Louis Philippe abdicated his throne on February 24, 1848, following demonstrations by reformers and defections from the National Guard.

4. Catharine Paris (b. January 1, 1776) died on December 23, 1849.

5. Willy O'Shea married Cristina Osorio de Moscoso y Carvajal, duchess of San Lúcar la Mayor. See Penney, *Bulletin NYPL*, 62 (December, 1958), 629.

2101. To Robert Balmanno

Sunnyside April 15. 1850

My dear Sir,

I thank you for your account of the visit to Dame Honeyball[1] which I have read with great zest and only regret that it is so short. It has all the flavor of Old *London proper* about it. The accidental touch about the tower calls up the reccollection of a place which used to be one of my antiquarian haunts. Many a time have I loitered the greater part of a day about it exploring every part from the Beauchamp tower, now the mess room of gay young ⟨tower⟩ officers to the venerable "Stone Kitchen" the resort of the Beefeaters.[2]

I think from this specimen, your rambles during the brief escapes from the Desk in old London Street might furnish some racy papers. The Idlings of a busy man about "famous London Town"

Yours my dear Sir / Very faithfully
Washington Irving

Robert Balmanno Esqr

Addressed: Robert Balmanno Esqr / New York.
Manuscript: Huntington.

Robert Balmanno (1780–1861) published *The Adventures of a Night on the Banks of the Devon; A Reminiscence of Early Life* (1846) and *Stoke Church and Park, the Scene of Gray's Elegy, and the Residence of the Penns of Pennsylvania* (1848), but apparently the work he sent to WI was never published.

1. WI described a Dame Honeyball in "Boar's Head Tavern, Eastcheap" in *The Sketch Book*.

2. In "Little Britain" in *The Sketch Book* WI alluded to the Tower of London and to the Beefeaters protecting the lord mayor in it.

2102. To John C. Peters

[May 6, 1850]

My dear Doctor,

My particular friend Madame Cavalcanti, wife of the Brazilian minister just arrived is suffering with a cold, and one of her daughters[1] with a severe sore throat. As the latter is a charming singer, her indisposition is a calamity to all her friends. I will take it as a particular favor if you will call upon them IN THE COURSE OF THE DAY and make them both well, as I told them you would do immediately. They are at Madame Cavalcantis mothers. No 43. Twenty fourth Street West.

Yours truly
Washington Irving

Monday. May. 6t. [1850]

ADDRESSED: Dr Peters
MANUSCRIPT: NYPL—Berg Collection.

John C. Peters (1819–1893), who received his medical training in Berlin, Vienna, and Leipzig and was licensed to practice in New York in 1842, was an active supporter of homeopathy in the 1850's. He attended WI throughout the last decade of his life, including his final illness.

The date was determined by the perpetual calendar.

1. Emilia Cavalcanti was the daughter of José Francisco de Paula Cavalcanti de Albuquerque, who had been Brazilian minister to Spain at the time WI was American minister. Madame Albuquerque was the former Miss Oakey of New York City. In 1850 Cavalcanti was councillor of state extraordinary; he had previously held the posts of minister of marines and minister of finance in the Brazilian cabinet. See Joaquim Manuel de Maceda, *Brazilian Biographical Annual* (Rio de Janeiro, 1876), II, 497–503; Carlos Xavier Paes Barreto, "A Familia Cavalcanti No Brasil," *Revista Genealogica Latina*, 4 (1952), 91–92; and Bowers, *Spanish Adventures of WI*, pp. 138–39.

2103.   To John V. Hall

Sunnyside May 19th. 1850

Dear Sir,

A uniform edition of my works is in course of publication and nearly complete. The publisher is George P Putnam 155 Broad way New York; but I presume the edition is to be had from any of the principal booksellers throughout the union.

Respectfully / Your ob Servt
Washington Irving

John V. Hall Esqr

DOCKETED: Washington Irving / May 19./50
MANUSCRIPT: SHR (copy of letter formerly in the Charles E. Feinberg Collection).

2104.   To David Thomas

Sunnyside June 4th 1850.

My dear Sir.

I have to thank you for the choice variety of rose plants which you had the kindness to send me last autumn. I am happy to say they ⟨have⟩ are all flourishing and promise to deck my little homestead with some of the beauties which I admired so much in your garden. I fear however I am very deficient in the tact and knowledge as a florist which makes every thing of the kind thrive 'so much with you. Still I trust whenever you may favor Sunnyside with a visit you will find you have contributed largely to its embellishment. With respectful remembrances to Mrs Thomas I remain my dear Sir,

Your truly obliged friend
Washington Irving

Mr David Thomas.

MANUSCRIPT: SHR.

2105. To ——

New York. June. 7th. 1850

Dear Sir,

I have delayed answering your note in consequence of a little perplexity. For some time past I have been resisting or evading the applications of Mr Putnam and also of Messrs Goupel & Vibart, ⟨th⟩ for a portrait having a great repugnance to sitting for one. Your note brings me
to a stand. I have agreed to sit to Elliott[1] for Mr Putnam with the understanding that the portrait should be at the service of yourself &
Messrs Goupel & Vibart should either of you deem an engraving from it
worthy of a place in your collections.

I have to apologize to you for not returning the volume concerning
Columbus which you had the kindness to lend to me some time since. It
is up in the country and has been mislaid until very recently—On my return home I will send it down to you. In the meantime let me thank you
most sincerely for the kindness of the loan.

Very respectfully / Your obliged friend & servt
Washington Irving

Manuscript: University of Pennsylvania Library.

1. Charles Loring Elliott (1812–1868) was an itinerant portrait painter in central
New York state until 1840, after which he worked primarily in New York City.
He was elected to the National Academy of Design in 1846. There is no record
of his painting a portrait of WI.

2106.   To Sarah Storrow

Sunnyside July 18th. 1850

My dear Sarah,

Your letter could not have arrived at a more welcome moment, for it
has found me in a state of languor and debility, and somewhat depressed
in spirits, the effects of an intermittent fever from which I am but imperfectly recovered. I find I do not rally from any an attack of the kind so
Speedily as I used to do, and this one has pulled me down so much that
I think I shall make an excursion for change of air. I would be inclined
to pay my promised visit to Mrs Henderson at Staten Island, but do not
feel in trim for such a gay quarter, and rather think that I shall set off
in a day or two with Helen Pierre[1] for Mr Ames'[2] country residence in
Orange County, where I shall find Sarah Van Wart[3] and her children,[4]

and be at home among relatives. I have been almost entirely at home since you left us, visiting the city but two or three times and never passing a night there. Helen has been passing several weeks at the cottage and Pierre comes up every evening. ⟨so it is⟩ I shall endeavor to keep her with us as long as possible. Your father[5] has paid us two visits, coming up on Saturday and remaining until Monday and has promised to come frequently. We have had a similar visit from Mr Storrow[6] who I likewise hope will often repeat it. Such ⟨are⟩ is one of the advantages of the rail road. Mr Storrow has since been on a visit to the Grinnells[7] and drove down to the Cottage with the whole family. The Grinnell country mansion is in a state of ↑slow↓ progress, the site having been digged out and various arrangements made in the grounds. It will be a beautiful place when finished, the situation of the house commanding fine air and a splendid prospect and the natural disposition of the grounds being favorable to picturesque arrangement. Julias health at present appears to be very good; she looks extremely well. The children are in fine health and spirits. Owing to indisposition I have not been able to get up this season to their residence at Colonel Webbs place.

Just as I had got out of the clutches of my fever we had a visit from Mr James,[8] the novelist and his family. He had arrived in New York several days previous, but I had been too unwell to go down to visit him. As soon as I could crawl out I went to N York & called upon him. I found he had intended seeking me out the next day. I kept him to the intention and returned home to put the household on the alert; carrying up a Salmon by way of a Stand by. The next morning by one of the early trains he came up with his wife,[9] his daughter[10] a very pretty and intelligent girl about Sixteen years of age and his two sons,[11] one of seventeen the other of fourteen years of age. They passed the day with us, the weather was delightful and the visit went off charmingly. James is a worthy, amiable fellow, full of conversation and most liberal in his feelings. We were much pleased with his wife, who is quiet intelligent and lady like; his daughter is very pleasing in looks and manners and his sons are fine lads. ⟨He is s⟩ They returned to town in the Six Oclock train, expressing themselves much gratified by their visit. They are now on a visit to the Hamiltons,[12] and I dined there yesterday in company with them; but was so out of sorts from the lingerings of my indisposition that I was in no mood for company. Mr James proposes visiting the Springs and making excursions about the country for a time and then going to Canada, where he has an idea of fixing his sons, if not of taking up his own abode there.

I was very glad to hear that your voyage was a comfortable one. I feared you would find it very tedious; as we saw it was likely to prove a long one. I can easily imagine your satisfaction at finding yourself so delightfully fixed for the Summer at Versailles; with its noble gardens at hand and its charming drives. How I should like to be passing the Summer there with you, and rambling with the children about the shady alleys and the tapis Vert. I am glad you have a good teacher for them and that Kate has commenced music. You want however a governess who could ⟨?se?⟩ pass most of her time with them to get them into habits of order and self restraint. That I presume you will be able to effect when you return to Paris. What they want is *regulation*. and that can only be produced by a person who is systematic herself and has a quiet and persevering method of ⟨producing⟩ ↑commanding↓ attention, and obedience

How I should like to hear ⟨J⟩ little Julie exercise her tongue now that it has at length broke loose. I presume she talks a kind of poplimento[?] language; something like that Kate used to talk and which always needed an interpreter. Her great friend Kate (Irving) is at Ingleside where she went with Charlotte[13] when she returned home. I miss her very much and hope she will not remain away long from the cottage. Charlottes health has greatly improved since her return home.

We have all been shocked and distressed by the death of our good old president General Taylor[14] after a very brief illness.

It is a great loss to the country, especially in our present perplexed state of affairs. He has left a name behind him that will remain one of the most popular ever in american history. He was really a good and an honest man. ⟨with singular⟩ uniting the bravery of the Soldier with the simplicity and benevolence of the quiet citizen. He had not been long enough in political life to have straightforward honesty and frankness falsified; nor his quick sense of right and wrong rendered obtuse. I deeply regret not to have seen him. I had always looked forward with confidence to taking him by the hand either in New York or Washington—Report speaks well of his successor Mr Fillmore,[15] but I am entirely unacquainted with him, and of course feel nothing of the personal interest that I felt for the good old General.

And now I must break off, my dear Sarah, I have written a longer letter than I thought I should be able to ⟨do⟩ ↑write↓ when I undertook it, I wish it were a more amusing or interesting one; but you must take the will for the deed; Ill write a better one when I feel better. Give my love to the dear little folk and keep them in mind of me. Gaga however, will soon forget the poor uncle she used to shoot so often. Kate I presume is pretty nigh learned up in fairy lore and will have to come down soon to sober reality in her reading, having exhausted the whole range of fairy literature. In such case she must make over her library to Susy who is rather slower in her inroads into fairy land.

God bless you my dear Sarah, it is a sad grievance to me to be thus completely severed from you and yours, and I never feel it more sensibly than in moments like the present when ⟨the⟩ Strength and Spirit seem to be failing me. Give my affectionate remembrances to your husband and believe me ever with tenderest affection—

Yours most truly—

Washington Irving

MANUSCRIPT: Yale.   PUBLISHED: PMI, IV, 72–74 (in part).

1. WI's designation for Helen Dodge Irving, used to distinguish her from "Helen Treat," or Helen Schermerhorn, the wife of John Treat Irving, Jr.

2. Barrett Ames, the father of Sarah Ames, who had married Irving Van Wart in 1832.

3. The wife of Irving Van Wart, mentioned in note 2.

4. These included Ames and Irving, twins born on January 20, 1841.

5. Daniel Paris (1772–1851), now a widower following the death of his wife Catharine on December 23, 1849.

6. Thomas Wentworth Storrow, Sr. (1779–1862), a friend of WI's since the 1820's. The two families were drawn more closely together by the marriage of Sarah Paris to Thomas Storrow, Jr.

7. Moses Hicks Grinnell (1803–1877) and his wife Julia Irving (1803–1872).

8. George Payne Rainsford James (1799–1860), a prolific writer of popular romances, arrived in New York on July 4, 1850, and soon removed to Hell Gate, where he lived in John Jacob Astor's former house, rented from Charles Astor Bristed, Astor's grandson. Later in his American residence James lived in Massachusetts and Virginia. See S. M. Ellis, *The Solitary Horseman, or The Life and Adventures of G. P. R. James* (Kensington, 1927), pp. 122–23, 141, 168, 211.

9. Frances Thomas (1800–1891), who married James in 1828 and died in Eau Claire, Wisconsin. See Ellis, *The Solitary Horseman*, pp. 50, 252.

10. Florence (1835–1894), who married John Williams and lived in Australia before settling in the United States. See Ellis, *The Solitary Horseman*, p. 59.

11. George Walter (1832–1887), who settled in Eau Claire, Wisconsin and died there. The other son, Courtenay Hunter (1836–1864), was a twin whose brother died as a child. Courtenay was killed at the Battle of Winchester in the Civil War. See Ellis, *The Solitary Horseman*, pp. 59, 70.

12. James Hamilton (1788–1878), son of Alexander Hamilton and a neighbor of WI's, resided at Nevis, a home he built in 1835.

13. Charlotte Van Wart Irving (1824–1911), Ebenezer's daughter and Kate's sister, was married to William R. Grinnell and lived in upstate New York.

14. Zachary Taylor (b. 1784), who defeated Santa Anna in the Mexican War in 1847, was the Whig winner in the presidential election of 1848.

15. Millard Fillmore (1800–1874), a New York lawyer and congressman who succeeded Taylor as president, signed the Clay Compromise of 1850 and tried to enforce the Fugitive Slave Act. The resulting unpopularity caused him to lose the Whig nomination in 1852.

2107. To Gouverneur Kemble

Sunnyside, Aug. 7, 1850

My dear Kemble:

Excuse my not answering sooner your kind letter. It found me in a terrible state of shattered nerves; having been startled out of my first sleep at midnight, on Saturday night last, by the infernal alarum of your railroad steam trumpet. It left me in a deplorable state of nervous agitation for upward of an hour. I remained sleepless until daybreak, and miserable all the following day. It seemed to me almost as if done on purpose, for the trains had ceased for several days to make their diabolical blasts opposite my house. They have not molested me in this way since, and have clearly shown, by the cautious and tempered management of their whistle, that these unearthly yells and howls and screams, indulged in for a mile on a stretch, and destructive to the quiet of whole neighborhoods, are carried to an unnecessary and unwarrantable excess. They form one of the greatest nuisances attending railroads, and I am surprised that, in the present state of mechanical art, some signal less coarse and brutal could not be devised.

You will laugh at all this; but to have one's family disturbed all day, and startled from sleep at night by such horrific sounds, amounts to a constant calamity. I feel obliged to the company for the attention that has been paid to the complaints made in this instance, and I trust to their continuing to protect my homestead from the recurrence of such an evil.

It would give me great pleasure, my dear Kemble, to come at once to you; but I am advised, as soon as I have sufficient strength to leave home, to go where I may have the benefit of a complete change of air. I intend, therefore, to pay a visit to my niece, Mrs. Gabriel Irving,[1] at her place at Oyster Bay, where I shall have the benefit of salt air and sea breezes. My visit to you I shall defer until I feel in more companionable trim.

Ever, my dear Kemble, yours, affectionately,

Washington Irving

PUBLISHED: PMI, IV, 67–68; Scharf, *Westchester County*, II, 237.

1. The former Eliza Eckford (1813–1866), widow of Gabriel Irving (1807–1845).

2108. To John Murray III

Sunnyside Aug. 8th 1850.

The work entitled the Companions of Columbus was purchased of me by the late Mr John Murray of Albemarle Street London, and I am ready when called on to make a formal assignment of the same to his heirs.

Washington Irving

MANUSCRIPT: John Murray.　PUBLISHED: WIHM, p. 193.

This note was enclosed with the longer historical statement written by WI on the same day.

2109. To John Murray III

Sunnyside Aug 8th. 1850

My dear Sir

I am grieved to find you so much cut up on the publication of my works by the cheap editions with which the market appears to be glutted.[1] Any aid I can give in remedying the evil you may thoroughly command.

In reply to your enquiry about ⟨the⟩ which of my works were written in England—The Sketch Book was written in England—Bracebridge Hall partly in France partly in England. Tales of a Traveller, partly in France partly in England Companions of Columbus, partly in Spain partly in England. Alhambra—the same. Mahomet partly in England partly in the United States Successors of Mahomet—the same. Abbotsford and Newstead Abbey—the same.

For the registers of the births of my parents you will have to search the opposite ends of the earth. My father William Irving, Son of Magnus Irving and Catharine Williamson was born in Shapinsha in the Orkneys Aug 31st. 1731. (Old Style)

My mother Sarah Sanders, daughter of John Sanders and Anna Kent, was born in Falmouth April 14th. 1738 (Old Style) My parents were married in Falmouth May 18th. 1761 and left England for the United States May 21.st. 1763.[2]

I shall be ready to sign the deed of assignment of which you make mention, as soon as it arrives.

With kindest remembrances to your family I remain my dear Sir,

Yours with great regard
Washington Irving

Docketed: W. Irving Esq / 8 Augt 50 / as to plans / when Books / written &c
Manuscript: John Murray.   Published: WIHM, p. 193.

1. The success of the new American editions of WI's writings had renewed
the interest of British publishers, especially the pirates, in him. Murray's immediate
concern was caused by Henry Bohn's cheap reprints of WI's books. See WIHM,
pp. 190–92.

2. WI supplied details about the composition of his books and about his parents
to help Murray prepare his legal case against Bohn and other pirates.

2110.   To William A. Graham

Sunnyside Aug 10th. 1850

Sir,

I trust you will excuse the liberty I take in soliciting the situation of
Midshipman for William B. Newman,[1] of Brooklyn in this state. He is the
son of the late ↑Lieutenant↓ William D Newman[2] of our Navy. I was instrumental in obtaining a Midshipmans warrant for his father during our
last war with Great Britain. He gradually rose in the service, without
patronage or influence, merely by his own merit and good conduct—an
excellent officer, whose whole pride was in his profession, and who fell
a victim to that pride, having drowned himself at Monte Video, when in
command of the Brig Bainbridge, in a fit of morbid depression from the
idea that he had incurred censure as an officer in a transaction in which
his conduct was ultimately cleared of all blame. It is for one of his
sons that I now make this application He is in his sixteenth year; a most
engaging promising youth, who has been carefully educated by his widowed mother. In a note to me she says, "He can produce ample testimonials from his teachers and others as to his character and good conduct. He has always proved himself a good boy and *seems desirous of aid-
ing me in supporting my somewhat large family*"—In this last trait he
resembles his father, who while yet a boy aided in supporting and edu-
cating an orphan sister out of his midshipmans pay.

Excuse this long letter which is forced out of me by the deep interest
I take in his application

With great respect / Your obedient Servt
Washington Irving

Hon William A. Graham. / Secretary of the Navy.

Docketed: Wm. B. Newman / 824 / his brother L Howard Newman / was appd
a Midn. on the / recommendation of Mr / Irving on the same grounds / that
are set forth in this letter / in behalf of Wm. B Newman / Ansd
Manuscript: Va.–Barrett.

William A. Graham (1804–1875), a North Carolina lawyer and politician who served as governor and U.S. senator, was appointed secretary of the navy by Millard Fillmore.

1. Apparently William B. Newman did not join the Navy until October 12, 1861, when he was enrolled as a mate. He advanced through the ranks and retired as a commander in 1896. See Callahan, *Officers of the Navy*, p. 405.

2. William D. Newman was appointed midshipman on February 1, 1841. He died on October 9, 1844. See Callahan, *Officers of the Navy*, p. 405.

2111. To John Murray III

Sunnyside, Aug. 19th. 1850

My dear Sir,

By the ship which takes this letter you will recieve the Assignment of copy rights duly executed.[1] The power of attorney[2] which you suggest shall be sent by another opportunity. In a former letter I gave you the information you request concerning the birthplaces &c of my parents—I now however repeat the same

My father William Irving son of Magnus Irving and ↑his wife↓ Catharine Williamson was born in Shapinsha in the Orkneys Aug 31. 1731. old style Married in Falmouth to Sarah Sanders May 18t. 1861[3]

Sarah Sanders daughter of John Sanders and his wife ⟨Sarah⟩ Anna Kent born in Falmouth April 14th 1738 (old style)

My parents left England for America May 21st 1763[.] I was born in the city of New York 3d. of April 1783.

I presume it will be necessary to search for the register of my fathers birth at Kirkwall (in the Island of Pomona) which is the county town.

With kindest regards to your family, I remain

My dear Sir Yours ever very truly
Washington Irving

P. S. The witnesses to the Assignment are nephews of mine, both are well known—Pierre M Irving is United States Pension Agent, and Notary of the N York Bank of Commerce. Sanders Irving is Secretary of the Hudson River Rail road Company.

John Murray Esqr.

DOCKETED: W. Irving Esq / 19 Augt 50 / as to Parents
MANUSCRIPT: John Murray.   PUBLISHED: WIHM, pp. 194–95.

1. This document, now in the John Murray Archives, states that John Murray II had purchased the copyrights of WI's books published by the firm.

2. Dated August 21, 1850, and preserved in the Murray Archives, this document was designed to enable Murray to develop his lawsuit against H. G. Bohn, who had pirated WI's books copyrighted by Murray. In a statement which Murray had sent to WI Bohn contended that WI was an alien whose writings were not protected by copyright in England. WI repeated his genealogy, as given in his letter of August 8, 1850, to provide Murray with details to counter Bohn's arguments. Murray also planned to emphasize the fact that WI wrote many of the books in question while he was living abroad. See WIHM, pp. 191–95, 216.

3. WI intended to write "1761."

2112. To Gouverneur Kemble

Sunnyside, Aug 22d. 1850

My dear Kemble,

I returned home on Saturday last[1] from a weeks visit to Oyster Bay[2] where the salt air and sea breezes quite set me up. Since my return however I have had another attack, though a slight one and am in hopes that I shall be able to stave it off with quinine. As soon as I feel in proper flight I shall pay you a visit. You spoke some time since of having two rooms at my service; have you them still vacant as I may feel inclined to bring a couple of nieces with me.

Yours ever
Washington Irving

MANUSCRIPT: Cornell University Library.

1. August 17.
2. In his letter of August 7, 1850, to Kemble WI had stated his intention of visiting Mrs. Gabriel Irving at Oyster Bay.

2113. To Joseph G. Cogswell

Sunnyside Aug 27th. 1850

My dear Cogswell,

I will attend the meeting[1] tomorrow but I shall have to leave it before six oclock, so as to get to the rail road station in time for the last train, as I have to be at home the same evening.

I have been prevented from attending the last two meetings by illness; and at present am but on the recovery.

Yours very truly
Washington Irving

2114. To George Harvey

Sunnyside, Aug 1850

My dear Sir

You complain of my long silence It is a complaint which several of my dearest relatives and friends may echo whose letters lie by me unanswered *I cannot—cannot help it*[.] I never was a punctual and regular correspondent when I had youth health and leisure on my Side. Now that I am at a time of life when I ought to throw by the pen forever, when my health is occasionally injured by the exercise of it, I am engrossed by a daily task and harrassed by interruptions of all kinds. My friends must bear with me and not attribute tardiness in correspondence to intentional neglect. I wilfully neglect no one.

I return you the letter of Mr Field[1] and shall be curious to see the pamphlet which you informed me some time since Mr Browne of Alston St Boston intended to publish on the Subject of the birthplace of Washington. I presume it will soon appear unless he has abandoned the idea.

I send you back your pamphlet[2] respecting the illustrations, with ⟨such⟩ ↑pencilled↓ corrections & suggestions, ⟨in⟩ which may be of service to you should the pamphlet go to another edition. I would only observe that I do not wish my name to appear as having had any thing to do with the work

I scrawl this with some difficulty; being very languid from the heat of the weather and the lingerings of an indisposition from which I am just recovering

Yours very truly
Washington Irving

George Harvey Esq

MANUSCRIPT: Princeton University Library.

1. This letter has not been located, nor has Mr. Field been identified.

2. This pamphlet was probably an earlier version of *Harvey's Scenes in the Primitive Forests of America, at the Four Seasons of the Year, Spring, Summer, Autumn & Winter, Engraved from His Original Paintings, Accompanied with Descriptive Letter-press* (London, 1841). Harvey visited London in 1838 with a

plan to have forty of his landscapes engraved and sold by subscription and to have WI edit the accompanying text. See *The Britannica Encyclopedia of American Art* (Chicago, 1973), pp. 271–72.

2115. To Benson J. Lossing

Sunnyside, Sept. 17th. 1850

Dear Sir

You are perfectly welcome to make the use you propose of the illustration, from my Life & Voyages of Columbus, of his letter to the treasurer of the King of Spain[1]

Yours very truly
Washington Irving

Benson J Lossing Esqr

P. S. Absence from home has prevented my replying more promptly.

MANUSCRIPT: SHR.

Benson J. Lossing (1813–1891), wood-engraver, author, and editor, was preparing *The Pictorial Field-Book of the Revolution*, 2 vols. (1850).

1. This illustration was not included in Lossing's book, apparently because of WI's delayed response.

2116. To George H. Throop

Sunnyside, Sept. 17th, 1850.

My dear Sir—

Though I received in due time your letter dated August 11th,[1] your book[2] did not reach me until within a week past. I thank you most heartily for the pleasure afforded me by the perusal. You have depicted scenes, characters, and manners which were in many respects new to me, and full of interest and peculiarity. I allude more especially to the views of Southern life.[3] We do not know sufficiently of the South; which appears to me to abound with materials for a rich, original and varied literature.

I hope the success of this first production will be such as to encourage you to follow out the vein you have opened, and to give us a new series of scenes of American life both by sea and land.

With best wishes for your success,

I remain, very truly / Your obliged friend and servant
Washington Irving.

PUBLISHED: Captain Gregory Seaworthy, *Bertie; or, Life in the Old Field* (Philadelphia, 1851), pp. vii–viii; *North Carolina Historical Review,* 33 (January,
1956), 13–14.

George Higby Throop (1818–1896), who used the pseudonym Gregory Seaworthy, was a New Yorker who as an itinerant school teacher taught in North
Carolina, Pennsylvania, and Georgia before settling in West Virginia. For a discussion of Throop's life, see Richard Walser, "The Mysterious Case of George
Higby Throop (1818–1896); or, the Search for the Author of the Novels *Nag's
Head, Bertie,* and *Lynde Weiss,*" *North Carolina Historical Review,* 33 (January,
1956), 12–44, esp. 35–44.

1. This letter has not been located.
2. *Nag's Head; or, Two Months among the Bankers,* which is attributed to the
author on the title page of *Bertie.*
3. *Nag's Head* dealt with life in eastern North Carolina. See Walser, "The
Mysterious Case of George Higby Throop," pp. 17–20.

2117.   To John Murray III

Sunnyside Sept. 22d. 1850

John Murray Esq

My dear Sir,
    The following memoranda are partly in reply to enquiries contained in
a letter from your house dated the 9th. of August last[1]—and are partly
intended to correct errors in the statement of Mr Bohn. They are for
your private use and I trust no undue publicity will be given to them.
It will not be in my power to come to England to give testimony in this
matter, as has been suggested by your lawyer; but I am ready to send
you all the testimony ⟨within my power⟩ ↑that I can command.↓ I am
not disposed to enter into litigation on my own account and wish no
legal measures to be taken on my behalf—above all I have no idea of compromising my character as a native born and thoroughly loyal American
citizen in Seeking to promote my pecuniary interests, though I am willing to take all proper steps to protect yours.

———————

Memoranda[2]

My father embarked at Falmouth to Settle in America 25 May 1763 and
arrived in New York 18th. July following He resided in New York until
his death, with the exception of two years sojourn in a country town,
during the war of the revolution. He was strongly devoted to the American cause throughout the war, and of course, on the return of peace took
every step necessary to establish his character as an American citizen. He
had been engaged in mercantile business for twenty years before my birth

(April 3d 1783) and continued in it until 1802 when he retired with a competency. He died Octr 25th. 1807. I was brought up and educated at his expense and not at that of my two elder brothers as has erroneously been asserted in the statement of Mr Bohn[.] I was destined for the bar; but, before I had completed my studies was sent to Europe for the benefit of my health. I embarked for Bordeaux on the 19th. May 1804, remained ⟨about⟩ ↑nearly↓ two years abroad, visiting Italy Sicily, Switzerland France, Belgium, Holland, & England, and returned home in March 1806

Resuming the study of the law I was admitted to the bar Nov 21. 1806 but never practiced, having imbibed a taste for literary pursuits. In the indulgence of this I wrote some of the papers on Salmagundi and produced Knickerbockers Hist N York, which first appeared 6 Decr 1809. To enable me more completely to follow out my literary vein, two of my brothers in 1810 gave me a share in a mercantile concern which they were establishing in New York and Liverpool, requiring no attention to business on my part. I continued therefore, my literary avocations

The Military Service of which Mr Bohn makes mention took place during our last war with Great Britain, when the destruction of the Capitol at Washington in 1814 roused every one to take some active part in the war. I then joined the Military Staff of the Governor of the State of New York as aid de Camp, and continued as such until the return of peace

On the 25th May 1815, I embarked for Liverpool on a second visit to Europe. The sudden and great reverses in business which took place on the return of peace overwhelmed the house in which my brothers had so kindly given me an interest, and involved me in its ruin

I then determined to try my pen as a means of support and began the papers of the Sketch Book. While thus occupied I resided in London in furnished apartments, from July 1818 to August 1820. The ↑MS. for the↓ Sketch book was transmitted piece meal to the United States to be published in numbers in New York. After several numbers had thus appeared I was induced to publish the work collectively in London. The first volume was published in Feb. 1820. The Second volume (partly printed from Manuscript) was published by Mr Murray 15th. July. The Seventh number of the American edition, comprising Westminster Abbey, Stratford on Avon Little Britain and the Angler was not published in New York until Sept. 13th. 1820 nearly two months after the publication of the Sketch book in two volumes in London—The Sketch book, therefore, as a whole was first published in London The Copy right for the 7th numbe[r]³ was taken out here 12th August 1820.

In Aug 1820 I removed to Paris where I remained until July 1821, when I returned to England with the rough manuscript of Brace bridge

Hall; which was not completed for publication until the following year. It was then published both in London and New York. The London edition appeared 23d. May 1822. The American May 21st.

I observe that Mr Bohn alleges the New York edition to have been published by Mr Van Winkle on the 5th April of the above year This is a mistake. I find by my correspondence with my brother that the MS. of the 1st volume was sent from London Jany 29. 1822 and of the 2d vol not until Feby 25th. The volumes were not published seperately in New York and the second volume could not certainly have been received in time ⟨for⟩ to publish it at the alleged date—five weeks from the time it was sent.

In 1822 I crossed to Holland and passed the Summer, ⟨and⟩ winter and following spring in Germany returning to Paris Aug 3d. 1823. There I sketched out the Tales of a Traveller, but crossed to England in May 1824 before they were finished. The introduction to these tales is dated from the Hotel de Darmstadt—Mayence, where I was actually detained by indisposition; but the tales in reality were written partly in Paris and partly in England They were published collectively in London ⟨25⟩ in two volumes August 25th. 1824 but appeared in New York in four parts.

```
1st part published Aug 24th 1824
2d.    "       "      Sept 7.    "
3      "       "        "  25.   "
4th ⟨October⟩         Octr. 9    "
```

These parts, therefore were published subsequent to the London publication. I returned to Paris early in the Autumn ⟨in⟩ and in October made an excursion into Touraine; for though Paris was my head quarters in France I made occasional excursions to various parts of the country; especially into Normandy.

The Autumn of 1825 was passed among the vineyards of Medoc and the subsequent winter in Bordeaux, until the latter part of February (1826) when I set out for Madrid; where I took up my residence for two years, during which time I wrote the Life of Columbus and transmitted it in MS. to London and New York. It was published in London Feb. 8th. 1828 and in New York March 15th. of the same year—

In March 1828 I set out on a tour to the South of Spain, visiting the scenes and localities of the campaigns for the Conquest of Granada, having made a rough draught of a chronicle of that war—At Seville I prepared the chronicle for the press and transmitted it to London and New York for publication. It appeared in New York 20th. April 1829 and in London 23d. May of the same year.

Part of the summer of 1828 I passed at a country house in the neighborhood of Port St Mary's opposite Cadiz, where I sketched out some of the voyages of the Companions of Columbus, from Notes ⟨t⟩ and Memoranda taken in Madrid and Seville. ⟨In the Autumn I⟩ The following winter was passed in Seville.

In the Spring of 1829. I made a second visit to Granada; where I passed three months in the Alhambra, during which time I collected materials for a work since published under that name.

In July I set out for England being appointed Secretary to the American Legation in London. I remained ⟨th⟩ in that city until the Spring of 1832 during which time I completed and published the Voyages of the Companions of Columbus (published in London 31st. Decr. 1830. In New York March 7th. 1831).

In the Spring of 1832 I returned to the United States where I arrived about the last of May.

Dates of Publication in U S. of my subsequent works—

Alhambra June 11. 1832

Crayon Miscellany No 1. containing Tour on the Prairies April 14 / 35

    ″   ″   No 2. Abbotsford &c. June 1   ″

    ″   ″   No 3. Legends of Spain Oct 10   ″

Astoria. Oct. 26. 1836

Bonnevilles adv. in Rocky Mountains. June 20. 1837.

The foregoing memoranda are crudely thrown together and some of them are probably superfluous.

Yours my dear Sir very truly
Washington Irving

ADDRESSED: John Murray Esq / Albemarle St / London
MANUSCRIPT: John Murray.   PUBLISHED: WIHM, pp. 195–200; *Harper's Weekly* [*Supplement*], May 27, 1871, pp. 492–93 (in part).

1. This letter has not been located. With it was sent a copy of H. G. Bohn's statement alleging that WI's writings were not protected by English copyright.

2. These notes greatly expand the brief details WI had included in his letter of August 19, 1850.

3. WI omitted the bracketed letter.

2118.   To Andrew J. Downing

Sunnyside Sept 28t. 1850

My dear Sir,

I have to return you many thanks for your care and trouble in getting safely to my hands the choice plants sent me by my fair but unknown friend in England—And more thanks still for the kind words spoken about me and my little country retreat; to which I especially attribute this testimonial of cordial good will on the part of Miss Rivers. I shall not fail promptly to write to her a grateful acknowledgement of of[1] the receipt of this very tasteful and flattering present; and shall cherish and prize the plants she has sent me, at least as much for her sake as for their own.

With great regard / My dear Sir / Yours ever very truly

Washington Irving

A. J. Downing Esq

MANUSCRIPT: Dr. Noel Cortes, Philadelphia.

Andrew Jackson Downing (1815–1852), an architect and horticulturist, was recognized as an authority on "rural art" following the publication of *A Treatise on the Theory and Practice of Landscape Gardening, Adapted to North America* in 1851. In 1850 he visited England and France and formed a partnership with Calbert Vaux, an English architect. The team designed the grounds for many estates on Long Island and along the Hudson River. Downing was engaged in 1851 to plan the landscaping for the Capitol, the White House, and the Smithsonian Institution in Washington.

1. WI repeated "of."

2119.   To the Reverend Frederick G. Clark

Sunnyside. Octr. 4th. 1850

My dear Sir,

One of the effects of my long indisposition has been to put me behind-hand in all my correspondence; which I must plead as an excuse for suffering your note of August 27th.[1] to remain so long unanswered.

As you express a desire for an Autograph I send you a note from Heeren,[2] which I intended for my work on the Successors of Mahomet, but never used.

Very respectfully / My dear Sir / Your friend & Servt.

Washington Irving

The Rev Fredk G. Clark.

MANUSCRIPT: Andrew B. Myers.

1. This note has not been located.
2. WI's note, on a separate sheet, follows:

Babylon.

In the earliest records of the human race, says the learned Heeren, the name of

Babylon appears as the primeval seat of political society and the cradle of civili-
zation, and this name endured great and renowned for a long succession of ages.
At last when Babylon declined—just at the time when, according to the projects
of the Macedonian conqueror it was destined to form the capital of ↑all↓ Asia
and the central point of his new monarchy. Seleucia sprung up and flourished
near it on the Tigris; ere this city fell it was eclipsed by Ctesiphon the capital
of the Parthian empire; when both these were destroyed by the conquering Arabs,
the royal cities of Bagdad and Ormus arose in their place; and the last glimmer,
as it were of the ancient splendor of Babylon seems still to hover over the half
ruined Bassora.

Note from Heeren.

2120. *To Sarah Storrow*

Sunnyside Octr 31st. 1850

My dear Sarah,

    I presume you are by this time completely settled and at home in your
new apartment, in the place Vendome. How fortunate you are to get
fixed in that most desirable locality; where you have ↑every↓ thing that
is most agreeable in Paris, within reach. Your apartment, in itself also,
from what I have heard, is peculiarly convenient. I am desirous of knowing in what part of the place it is situated[.] I have an idea it must be
about where Mr & Mrs Ray had their apartment. You will now have
almost the advantages of the country, while residing in the heart of
the city. I presume the children will almost live in the Garden of the
Tuilleries. I want to know if you still have the Servants who accompanied you to the United States, the faithful Henriette and the good,
kind hearted Canterel. I hope and trust they are still with you; for I
have a great regard for them.

    I have had a "trying time" of it this last Summer; two severe attacks of
bilious intermittent fever; the second one almost broke me down; and I
thought at one time it would leave me a complete wreck. I came out of
it more of a Scare crow in appearance than after my severe illness at
Madrid. However, I have rallied surprizingly and begin to think my constitution will carry me on comfortably for some little time longer. I need
not tell you how carefully I was nursed and tenderly I was treated during
my illness. I dont think any parent could experience more devoted affection from his children than I have done from my good little nieces. Certainly I am one of the most favored and fortunate of old bachelors.

    As soon as I was well enough to leave home, I set off for Eliza
Gabriels[1] at Oyster Bay accompanied by my faithful little family Doctor
Sarah. Our visit was a delightful one[.] I gathered strength, appetite
and good spirits on the shores of the Sound; the Sea air was invigorating;

the country around was beautiful and we drove out daily, through the locust woods and round the little inlets which indent the coast. Eliza has refitted her house and made it a very cheerful residence; and she has the enviable talent of diffusing happiness around her.

After returning home and remaining quiet for a week or so, I set out on a long promised visit to Gouverneur Kemble. I took with me Mary Irving and Anna,[2] Pierre P.s daughter who was ⟨st⟩ on a visit to the Cottage. We passed a week at Kembles bachelors nest, and the Girls enjoyed it greatly. They were over at West Point to see the breaking up of the Summer encampment of the cadets; a time of great gaiety at the point. They found very pleasant companions in William Kembles daughters.[3] Gouverneur & William Paulding[4] also, who were quartered at Cold Spring were very attentive to them. In fact they thought themselves in fairy land. Mrs Parrot (Mary Kemble)[5] unfortunately left Cold Spring the day after our arrival on a visit with Mr Parrot to his family, so that we missed the pleasure of her society, but the girls experienced the utmost hospitality from Mrs William Kemble.

How often I thought of you my dear Sarah while in this romantic neighborhood where we have made such pleasant excursions. In one of our drives we past the place where I left you ⟨with⟩ ↑seated on the road beside↓ the wreck of our waggon, in our Second break down, while I went to Uncle Sam (Governeurs) for aid. I presume you reccollect that circumstance of our haphazard tour up one side of the river and down the other through the beautiful valley of the Ramapo.

During my visit to Kemble, I set off with him one day by Rail road for James Pauldings country residence,[6] where I had never ↑been.↓ We went by Rail road to Poughkeepsie and then took a carriage to Pauldings. He has a lovely situation, commanding one of the most beautiful prospects of Hudson Scenery with the Kats Kill mountains in the distance His grounds are naturally beautiful and have been laid out with good taste, under his own supervision assisted by the Council and Cooperation of Kem and uncle Nat.[7] We had a very pleasant dinner there and got back to Cold Spring in the evening. This rail road makes every place accessable on the easiest terms.

Kemble Still lives on in the old hospitable way, though I think his establishment seems to want the advantage of careful womans eye. It is not kept in such order as it was while Mary Kemble presided there. He has pleasant dinners on Saturday; on which day, summer and winter, the professors from West Point dine with him as a matter of course— They look forward to it through the week as their rallying point for social festivity. They are ⟨a⟩ very intelligent agreeable men and harmonize with each other like brothers. I have promised Kemble to be a ⟨[unrecovered]⟩ ↑guest↓ with him occasionally in these Saturday dinners.

Indeed the Rail road brings us quite into each others neighborhood. One hours drive places me at his door.

My last excursion from home was with Mr & Mrs George Schuyler and ⟨the⟩ Mary and Angelica Hamilton.[8] We set off in open waggons for a tour about the upper part of West Chester County. Our first days drive took us through a beautiful country a ⟨great⟩ part of which you have seen; lying along the Bedford road. We ⟨arrived in the afternoon⟩ lunched in the woods no[t][9] far from the place where you and Kate and I once made a pic-nic repast. In the afternoon we arrived at the village of Somers where we put up at the Elephant, a spacious stone house, more like a private dwelling than a hotel. Here we found a dinner ready for us; the landlord having been written to. This house we made our head quarters and soon found ourselves quite at home there. The next day we drove through a succession of lovely scenes in Westchester and Put-nam Counties—mountain and valley, lakes and forests and bright running streams.—We lunched on the borders of a little wild lake and got back to the Elephant by five Oclock in the afternoon. The third day we re-turned home by the way of Bedford, driving about forty miles through the same kind of beautiful scenery and arrived home after dark; having made one of the pleasantest excursions I ever enjoyed. Having had fine weather, lovely scenery and most agreeable company. The Hamiltons are first rate companions for the country. I have had several very pleasant rides with them on horseback about the nieghborhood this autumn. They enjoy every thing with fresh feeling and with the discrimination of intelligent and cultivated minds.

The day before yesterday I was surprized by a visit from David Dav-idson,[9a] as I did not know he was in the country, though he had arrived nearly a fortnight previously. I had not seen him since before my de-parture for Spain, and in the interim he had grown from a mere Stripling to a very manly looking man. He has come out to this country to reside; intending to do business as an Agent for the London Booksellers, and has very fair prospects—He remained with us until the evening train, dining and taking tea with us. I was extremely pleased with him. He acquitted himself in a very well bred gentlemanlike manner and conversed with intelligence and vivacity on a variety of subjects; giving us many amusing anecdotes of his travels on the Continent. It was evident he felt a little nervous and embarrassed for a time, but grew more and more at his ease the longer he remained with us, for we endeavored to make ⟨him-self f⟩ him feel really at home with us. There was nothing awkward, how-ever, in his diffidence, his whole deportment was most pleasing and satis-factory. I hope often to see him under my roof for I feel a kind of pater-nal regard for him; and am delighted to See how admirably he has con-ducted himself in every situation in which he has been placed. I write thus much about him, because I trust you take a strong interest in his favor as you will reccollect that he was your protegé; ⟨as your⟩ and it was your being pleased with his physiognomy and manner that first brought him under our roof. He has proved you a good physiognomist.

You will see by the papers that the world has all been Music mad here on the arrival of Jenny Lind.[10] With all my love of music I have not yet heard nor seen her; but expect to do so next week. I do not like ⟨to⟩ any more to cope with crowds; and have become a little distrustful of these public paroxysms. Beside I am not over fond of concerts and would prefer somewhat inferior talent when aided by the action and scenic effect of the theatre—I anticipate more pleasure therefore from Parodi[11] as prima Donna of the opera; than from the passionless performances of Jenny Lind as a singer at a concert.

Novr 2d. We have just had a visit from Eliza Gabriel and Abby (Van Wart)[12] They came up in the Cars yesterday and went down this morning. These are the pleasant san façon visits that we gain by the Rail Road. Next week we are to have Sarah Clark and Henrietta Irving[13] with us. Eliza Gabriel has quite recovered her good spirits and good looks and is indeed a most agreeable visitor. I hope to see her often at the Cottage now it is so easy to Get here ⟨and le⟩ by the Rail road

⟨This letter⟩ By the time you receive this letter Mr Storrow (Pere) will no doubt be with you and I congratulate you on having such an inmate of your household. I can imagine how much pleasure he will have with the children and how much delight they will have with him. I am glad for all your sakes that you have prevailed on him to sojourn for a time with you in Paris—He will have infinite enjoyment in revisiting old scenes in the metropolis and he will be enabled to enjoy its various mental resources much more than formerly; having his mind free from commercial cares and concerns and turned into channel[s][14] more suited to his ⟨cultivate⟩ natural and cultivated tastes. He is one of the most amiable and estimable men I have ever known; and one peculiarly fitted for domestic life. He will bring sunshine into your family circle—

Tell Mr Storrow (you[r][15] husband) that I am much obliged to him for the Galignanis which he has had the kindness to send me occasionally—and a parcel of which I have just recieved. They are extremely welcome and give me a panoramic view of affairs in Europe. I think it one of the very best papers in the world and quite a god send to one living like myself in the retirement of the country.

Grinnells country seat is growing in magnitude and will soon be roofed. It will be finished in time for the family to move in next June; and then we shall have a little rural world of our own. The ⟨plans⟩ grounds will be laid out by a German landscape gardener, and ⟨made⟩ the walks will connect with mine so as to make the two places like one.

Julia has become a bold equestrian and has been almost daily on horseback this season. I anticipate many pleasant rides with her next year.
She removed to town yesterday.

Farewell my dear Sarah. Let me hear from you occasionally and tell
me all about yourself and your children—You cannot write about topics
more interesting to me, while I have none of equal interest to write
about in return. Tell me all about your establishment—your plans—how
you manage as to the education of your children—what they are studying and acquiring, how they look &c &c. God knows if I shall ever see
them again, but I shall ever keep them in mind as I last saw them. and
should almost be sorry to find them changed.

Give my affectionate remembrances to your husband and believe me
ever

Your affectionate Uncle
Washington Irving

PS. Nov: 4th. Monday morning. As this letter is still open I will add
that your father[16] came up to the Cottage on Saturday, passed Sunday
with us and goes to town this morning. He is in good health and seems
to have enjoyed his visit. He finds himself well situated in ⟨thi⟩ town in
the quarters lately occupied by Mr Storrow. He will take this letter to
town with him—

ADDRESSED: Madame / Madame Storrow / aux Soins de Mr T. W. Storrow / Rue
    de Faubg Poissonniere / à Paris
MANUSCRIPT: Yale.   PUBLISHED: PMI, IV, 74–75 (in part).

1. Here, as elsewhere, WI combines the first names of wife and husband in
order to distinguish the wife from another relative with the same first name. WI
is referring to Eliza, the widow of Gabriel Irving.

2. Mary Elizabeth Irving (1820–1868) was the eleventh child of Ebenezer
Irving, and Anna Duer Irving (1830–1884) was her niece and the second child of
her brother Pierre Paris Irving (1806–1878).

3. Probably Ellen (1827–1905) and Mary (d. 1901), the younger daughters of
William Kemble (1795–1881) and his wife, Margaret Chatham Seth (d. 1865).

4. Gouverneur (1829–1913) and William Irving (1825–1890) were sons of
James Kirke Paulding.

5. Mary Kemble (1804–1877), sister of William Kemble and Mrs. James K.
Paulding, had married Robert Parker Parrott (1804–1877) in 1839.

6. Paulding's home, Placentia, was located north of Hyde Park. For a description of it, see Paulding to Martin Van Buren, October 22, 1845, in *Letters of J. K.
Paulding*, p. 409.

7. Kemble (1819–1900) and Nathaniel, Paulding's son and brother, respectively.

8. George Lee Schuyler (1811–1890), who was married to Eliza Hamilton
(d. 1863), the daughter of James Alexander Hamilton, WI's neighbor. Mary and
Angelica were Hamilton's daughters.

9. WI omitted the bracketed letter.

9a. Davidson (d. 1863), for whom WI had written recommendations in 1841.

10. Jenny Lind (1820–1887), a Swedish soprano who toured the United States under the management of P. T. Barnum, made her American debut at Castle Garden in New York on September 11, 1850. By September 24 she had given six concerts, after which she went to Boston. Upon her return to New York on October 24 she appeared at Tripler Hall. See Odell, *NY Stage*, VI, 83–90.

11. Teresa Parodi (b. 1827), an Italian soprano who was encouraged by Giuditta Pasta, came to the United States as a rival of Jenny Lind. Her first American performance was in Bellini's *Norma* at the Astor Place Opera House in New York on November 4, 1850.

12. Abigail Irving (1822–1906), daughter of John Treat Irving, had married Henry Van Wart, Jr., her first cousin, on September 23, 1845.

13. Henrietta Irving (d. 1921) was the daughter of Gabriel and Eliza Irving.

14. WI omitted the bracketed letter.

15. WI omitted the bracketed letter.

16. Daniel Paris.

2121. *To James Fenimore Cooper*

Putnams Desk. N Y. Nov 11th. 1850

My dear Sir,

I had hoped to send you by this time Mr Crisps book,[1] as Mr Putnam had undertaken to write ⟨the⟩ to Messrs Ballard Lee & Co on the subject. He forgot his promise, however, until reminded of it this morning. He has just written a letter in my presence, and I trust the books will arrive in due season; when I will see that they are forwarded to their respective destinations

Permit me to congratulate you on the great and well merited success of your daughters delightful work.[2] I hope it will encourage her to the further exercise of her pen.

Yours very respectfully
Washington Irving

J. Fennimore Cooper Esqr.

MANUSCRIPT: Yale. PUBLISHED: *Correspondence of James Fenimore Cooper* (New Haven, 1922), II, 690.

James Fenimore Cooper (1789–1851) was an American novelist and social critic who gained fame as the creator of Leatherstocking and as a writer of historical tales.

1. No title published by a Crisp at this time is listed in the *National Union Catalog*.

2. Susan Cooper (1813–1894) kept a journal from 1848 to 1850 which served as the basis for her most important work, *Rural Hours* (1850).

2122. To Mary M. Hamilton

Sunnyside Nov 12th. 1850

My dear Miss Hamilton,

The address of Sarah Storrow is to the care of Mr Thomas W Storrow Rue du Faubg Poissonniere, a Paris.

You wish to know what I think of the "Priestess of Nature"[.][1] I have seen and heard her but once, but have at once enrolled myself among her admirers. I cannot say, however, how much of my admiration goes to her singing; how much to herself. As a singer she appears to me of the very first order; as a specimen of Woman kind—a little more. She is enough, of herself, to counterbalance all the evil that the world is threatened by the great convention of Women. So God save Jenny Lind!

Parodi's Norma[2] is the best I have seen ⟨since⟩ ↑except↓ Grisi's, but Grisi's in some respects is much superior. Parodi has much dramatic talent a good voice a commanding person and a countenance very expressive *in spite of her teeth*, which are a little on the "Carker" order.[3] I doubt however, with all her tragic fire I shall like her as much in Lucrezia Borgia[4] as the fair Truffi;[5] for whom I still cherish a certain degree of *tendresse*. But I do not pretend to be critical; having had all conceit of that kind killed by Ford[6] the gatherer in Spain, who in one of his papers in the Quarterly Review denominated me "the easily pleased Washington Irving"[.] I presume our social rides are all over for the season, and that you and Angelica will abandon the rocks and wood lands and other scrambles on horseback for Broadway and the opera. I took a ride on Dick this morning but he seemed to miss his companions Ned and Dandy and to have lost all spirit. As we have a kind of intermittent Indian Summer, which incessantly returns after very brief intervals—I still hope to have some more rides among the hills before winter sets in **and** should be rejoiced to take them with the female chivalry of Tillietudlem—

Yours very truly
Washington Irving

Docketed: Washington Irving / Novr. 12th. / 1850 / upon Jenny Lind
Manuscript: SHR.   Published: PMI, IV, 75–76.

1. This epithet was given to Jenny Lind.

2. Teresa Parodi had sung in *Norma* at the Astor Place Opera House on November 4, 1850. See Odell, *NY Stage*, VI, 63. WI had heard Giulia Grisi (1811–1869) in Paris in October, 1843. See WI to PMI, October 13, 1843.

3. In Dickens's *Dombey and Son* James Carker, Dombey's office manager, had "two unbroken rows of glistening teeth, whose regularity and whiteness were

quite distressing. . . . He showed them whenever he spoke. . . ." See Charles Dickens, *Dombey and Son* (London, 1950), p. 171.

4. Parodi sang Lucrezia on November 11, 13, and 15, 1850. See NYEP, November 11–15, 1850.

5. WI had heard Teresa Truffi sing in *Lucrezia Borgia* in January or February of 1848. See Odell, *NY Stage*, V, 382.

6. Richard Ford (1796-1858), English author and critic, contributed to the *Quarterly, Westminster,* and *Edinburgh Reviews.* In 1845 he brought out *A Hand-Book of Travellers in Spain and Readers at Home,* 3 vols. (London, 1845), based in part on his residence in Spain from 1830 to 1834. His phrase describing WI has not been located in his *Quarterly* articles.

2123. To Helen Dodge Irving?

Sunnyside, Nov. 17, 1850

My dear Helen:

I am sorry to find my hegira from town caused you so much regret and uneasiness. It was a sudden move, on finding that the party for the concert would be complete without me,[1] and that, if I stayed, I should have to look about for quarters, and put others to inconvenience. Besides, I find myself growing more and more indisposed to cope with the bustle and confusion of the town, and more and more in love with the quiet of the country. While tossing about, therefore, on the troubled sea of the city, without a port at hand, I bethought myself of the snug, quiet little port I had left, and determined to " 'bout ship" and run back to it.

You seem to have pictured my move as a desperate one, and my evening as solitary and forlorn; but you are mistaken. I took a snug dinner at Frederick's, where I met A—— H——. He was bound to Staatsburg, to rejoin his wife. We went up in the four o'clock train together. I endeavored to persuade him to stop and pass the night at the cottage, when we would break open the storeroom and cellar, rummage out everything that the girls had locked up, and have "high jinks" together. He was strongly inclined to yield to my temptation, but the thought of his wife overawed him. He is evidently under petticoat government, like other married men, and dare not indulge in a spree, like we free and independent bachelders.

When I arrived at the cottage, all was dark. Toby barked at me as if I were a housebreaker. I rang at the front door. There was a stir and commotion within. A light gleamed through the fanlight. The door was cautiously opened by Bernard; behind him was Sophia, and behind her Hannah, while Peter and the cook stood ready as a *corps de reserve* in the kitchen passage. I believe, for a moment, they doubted whether it was myself or my ghost.

My arrival caused no little perplexity, everything being locked up. However, by furbishing up the kitchen plate and china, the tea table was set out after a fashion by Sophia, and I made a very cosy though somewhat queer repast.

My evening passed very serenely, dozing over a book, and dreaming that the girls, as usual, were all silently sewing around me. I passed a comfortable night; had a cosy bachelor breakfast the next morning, took a ride on gentleman Dick, and, in fact, led a life of single blessedness, until my womankind returned, about two o'clock, to put an end to my dream of sovereignty.

PUBLISHED: PMI, IV, 77–78.

1. WI and his nieces had gone to New York on Friday, November 15 to attend a concert, but WI found "that another lady had been added to the party, which would make up the number without him, and being withal a little out of mood, he suddenly decamped for home, to the great surprise of his nieces...." (PMI, IV, 77).

2124.   To Henry Lee, Jr.

Sunnyside Decr. 18th 1850

My dear

I ought to apologize for not replying sooner to your very welcome and agreeable letter;[1] but in fact I am always far astern of my correspondence and toiling ineffectually to overtake it. Your letter brings up pleasant reccollections of our wayfaring together by sea and land; though ⟨eight⟩ the lapse of eight years has disposed of some of the personages you allude to. Our worthy Captain *Holdridge*,[2] (whose name in spite of your vaunted memory you write *Holden*) has "broken his last biscuit" He died some few years since. I trust his storm hat, which you bear in mind, was carried to the grave on his coffin. Of that Gil Blas of the seas Whitfield,[3] who used to beguile the watches of the night with his long yarns, I have heard nothing since; but hope that he soon attained to the nautical dignity to which he aspired of being *first* mate. I should not be surprised however, to hear of him some day figuring on the Coast of California or dealing again in niggers and black pepper. The pretty girl of Sulgrave, whom we discovered in the course of our Washingtonian researches, and who seems to have a tender place in your memory, is I trust by this time the honest mother of a numerous progeny; peradventure the mistress of the little ale house where we encountered her. The quaint and excellent Bandinel[4] sleeps with his fathers, and I hope has a quiet grave somewhere about his favorite haunts in Westminster Abbey. He was dislodged from his curious nest in the little cloisters a year or two after we partook there of his hosp[i]tality.[5] On revisiting London I found him established in quarters almost as peculiar, at the corner of Berkeley Square; whither he had transferred all his reliques and curiosities, himself among the number and where he kept bachelors hall in the same quaint and genial style—He was a humorist of the rarest kind, and withal one of the very worthiest beings that I ever was entitled to call my friend. Hector[6] the young Telemachus to whom you was so kind as to enact Mentor, is still a wanderer. After a short diplomatic apprenticeship with me he gave up the thought of qualifying himself to be an Ambassador and returned home. His father then thought of making him a merchant and sent him to Mobile for the purpose; but he returned as little of a merchant as a diplomat. He then entered the law office of his quondam associate in diplomacy, Alexander Hamilton,[7] once my Secretary of Legation, but now a rising lawyer at the New York bar. Having qualified himself as an attorney the youthful Hector again looked round for some new career. His father advised him to return to Europe ⟨and⟩ make a complete tour and then return to settle down for life; but our young Telemac[h]us[8] took a course of his own and set off for California. There he remains; he has dabbled a little in mining I believe, also a little in law and a little in land speculation but as yet has not made a fortune; sending no gold dust home to his father, but now and then drawing on him for a little spending money. His principles are proof against all the trials of that pandemonium, I only wish his constitution was as staunch. I look to see him home again before long and then I would advise his father to yield to the wish he has uniformly expressed and buy a snug place for him in the country where he might devote himself to agricultural pursuits. I think he would make an excellent country squire and might rise to be president of an agricultural society or perhaps a country justice of the peace

The account you give of your own fortunes is most gratifying; prosperous in business and happy in your home, with a wife and children to share and encrease your happiness. You seem to have turned up nothing but trumps in the game of life, and yet like all mortal beings you are not content Toujours pardrix! You want a change. You dislike business and begin to long for a life of leisure Have a care! A life of leisure, especially to one who has been a busy man, is one of the most soul wearying, self teasing, temper souring lives in the world. I tried it once for a few years in my younger days, when I had "horse to ride and weapon to wear"[9] and "all the world on a string" In a little while having nothing to care for I cared for nothing, became a prey to ennui tired of everything and particularly tired of myself Fortunately I was ruined be-

fore I was spoiled, and being driven to my pen and obliged to fag with
it for a living I have been too busy ever since to give way to the meg-
rims.

You talk of setting up a rural residence at Brookline and remaining
there all the winter. Do so and cultivate rural habits and tastes and
occupations, ⟨in⟩ ↑with↓ which to diversify you[r][10] commercial pursuits;
⟨and which will⟩ You will then have rural employments to retire upon
instead of a life of leisure. A rural retreat when it is a mans own, and of
his own formation produces a new set of pleasures and interests and am-
bitions, and every tree he plants awakens a new hope and attaches him
to the spot which he has improved. I speak from experience having
never been happier than in my present little country nest, where the
house is of my own building, the trees of my own planting the garden of
my own cultivating and where my continual blunders give me continual
occupation in rectifying them. If then an old bachelor like myself can take
such delight in a rural home what must you take who have a wife to sit
at your board, and children to sport under your trees and to love and
cherish them for your sake when you are gone. I do not mean to repine
at my single state, however; for I am one of the most fortunate old
bachelors living. I am in fact a father of a family; for I have a family of
nieces who are like daughters to me—and affectionate daughters and who
make my home a very happy one; so that I am better off than Monkbarns[11] in regard to my Women Kind. Beside these I have lots of relatives
coming and going so that I have generally what is called a Scotch housefull, that is to say a little more than it will hold. Here since my return
from Spain I have settled down, living almost entirely at home—in a
simple half rustic way, for I have not money enough to be luxurious; but
among scenes beautiful in themselves, and dear to me from boyish reccollections and my great delight is to ⟨[unrecovered]⟩ amble quietly on
horseback through all the wild ⟨scenes th⟩ nooks and corners that I have
scrambled about when a boy. Here I hope to pass the handful of years
I can yet count upon winding up my varied and precarious life by a
healthful and cheerful old age. It is not often that one who has been so
much of a wanderer and at times been so buffeted by fortune, reaches
such a quiet haven at last—and I am tempted like Gil Blas to inscribe
over my door,

Invini portum, spes et fortuna valete.[12]

I think after all this talk about myself you will not think it necessary
to apologize again for any egotism on your own part—

I thank you for the books you have been so kind as to send me. The
"Scarlet Letter"[13] I already possessed and had read it with infinite in-

terest and delight. It is one of the very best works ever produced in American literature. Whipples lectures[14] I had not read, but am now reading them. They are admirable. I again thank you for sending me those books

And now as it is wearing into the small hours of the night I must conclude my letter and betake myself to my bed. So with a blessing on you, your wife and those fine children you boast of, I remain very truly and cordially

Your friend
Washington Irving

MANUSCRIPT: Va.–Barrett.

The recipient of this letter is Henry Lee, Jr., (1817–1898) of Boston, with whom WI had traveled to England in April, 1842. For details, see WI to Catharine Paris, May 7, 1842.
The surname has been expunged from the salutation.

1. This letter has not been located.
2. Captain of the *Independence*, the ship on which WI sailed to England.
3. Probably an officer or sailor on the *Independence*.
4. James Bandinel (1783–1849), who had served as a clerk in the British Foreign Office. For other details, see WI to James Bandinel, May 28, 1830, and to Sarah Storrow, June 21, 1841.
5. WI omitted the bracketed letter.
6. Hector Ames, who was a member of WI's legation staff.
7. Alexander Hamilton, Jr. (1816–1889), the son of WI's neighbor, James Alexander Hamilton, had served as secretary of the U.S. legation in Madrid until May, 1844.
8. WI omitted the bracketed letter.
9. *King Lear*, III, iv, 137.
10. WI omitted the bracketed letter.
11. Jonathan Oldbuck, the Laird of Monkbarns in Scott's *The Antiquary*, was an irascible, sarcastic misogynist who was interested in ancient lore, particularly coins and medals.
12. WI quotes from *Gil Blas*, bk. 9, chap. 10 (last lines): "We shall soon be settled in our country retreat; and there will I write these two Latin verses over the door of my farmhouse in gold, for the pious edification of my neighbors: Inveni portum. Spes et fortuna, valete. / Sat me lusistis; ludite nunc alios" ("I have reached the gate. Farewell, Hope and Fortune. You have hoaxed me sufficiently; now play tricks on others").
13. Hawthorne's novel had been published on March 16, 1850. See Randall Stewart, *Nathaniel Hawthorne* (New Haven, 1948), p. 95.
14. *Lectures on Subjects Connected With Literature and Life* by Edwin Percy Whipple (1819–1886) was published earlier in 1850. He was a popular lecturer on the Lyceum circuit.

2125. To Mr. Betts

[December 24, 1850]

Mr Washington Irving regrets that engagements in the country prevent his having the pleasure of accepting Mr Betts polite invitation for Thursday evening

Sunnyside. Decr 24th. [1850]

MANUSCRIPT: Yale.

A notation "A. D. 1850." in another hand appears at the bottom of the page.

2126. To Benson J. Lossing

[January 17, 1851]

Dear Sir,

Owing to my absence from home I did not receive your note[1] until last evening. There is no engraved portrait of me later or better than the very miserable one to which you allude: but I am at present sitting to Mr Martin[2] for a sketch of my likness[3] in chalk, If when it is done it proves satisfactory it shall be at the service of the Messrs. Harpers to have an engraving made from it.

Yours very respectfully
Washington Irving

N York. Jan 17th 1851 / Benson J Lossing Esqr

MANUSCRIPT: MHS.

1. This note has not been located.
2. Charles Martin (1820–1906) was a portrait and landscape painter. The portrait to which WI alludes was engraved by Frederick W. Halpin (1805–1880), a portrait engraver and book illustrator. An idealized rendering, this likeness was WI's favorite in his later years. See George C. Groce and David H. Wallace, *Dictionary of Artists in America, 1564–1860* (New Haven, 1957), pp. 286, 425; and Andrew B. Myers, *The Worlds of Washington Irving* (New York, 1974), p. 115.
3. WI omitted the first "e."

2127.   To Robert F. Adair

Sunnyside, Feby. 6th. 1851.

Robert F Adair Esq / Corresponding Secretary &c

Dear Sir,

I have to acknowledge the receipt of your letter of the 22d. ultimo[1] informing me of my being unanimously elected an honorary member of the Prescott Literary Society.

I beg you to communicate to the society my grateful sense of the honor they have conferred upon me and of the very kind and flattering expressions with which they have instructed you to accompany its announcement.

While I appreciate highly the pure, intellectual objects for which the society is formed I augur well of its discernment and discriminating taste from its having chosen for its designation the name of an author who has achieved such classic honors for our literature; and whom I esteem it a happiness to be able to consider among my dearest friends.

I am, dear Sir, / very respectfully / Your obedient Servant
Washington Irving

Manuscript: NYPL—Seligman Collection.

1. This letter has not been located.

2128.   To ———

Sunnyside, Feb. 8, 1851

Dear Madam:

While I sincerely sympathize with you in the affliction caused by your great bereavement, and have no doubt your brother was worthy of the praise bestowed on his memory, I must most respectfully excuse myself from the very delicate and responsible task of giving an opinion of his poems. I have no confidence in the coolness and correctness of my own judgment in matters of the kind, and have repeatedly found the exercise of it, in compliance with solicitations like the present, so productive of dissatisfaction to others, and poignant regret to myself, that I have long since been driven to the necessity of declining it altogether.

Trusting you will receive this apology in the frank and friendly spirit in which it is made, I remain, with great respect, your obedient servant,

Washington Irving

PUBLISHED: PMI, IV, 79–80.

PMI (IV, 79) indicates that the recipient was "a young lady, who proposed to come to [WI] and ask his counsel about the publication of some poems of a brother who had graduated with distinction, and been cut off in the bloom of his youth." However, PMI does not identify the lady.

2129. To Jesse Merwin

Sunnyside Feb 12th. 1851

You must excuse me, my good friend Merwin, for suffering your letter to remain so long unanswered; you can have no idea how many letters I have to answer, beside fagging with my pen at my own literary tasks, so that it is impossible for me to avoid being behind hand in my correspondence. Your letter was indeed most welcome, calling up as it did reccollections of pleasant scenes and pleasant days passed together in times long since at Judge Van Nesses[1] at Kinderhook. Your mention of the death of good old Dominie Van Ness[2] recalls the apostolic zeal with which he took our little sinful community in hands, when he put up for a day or two at the judges; and the wholesome castigation he gave us all one Sunday, beginning with the two Country belles who came fluttering into the school house during the sermon, decked out in their city finery, and ending with the judge himself, in the strong hold of his own mansion. How soundly he gave it to us! how he peeled off every rag of self righteousness with which we tried to cover ourselves, and laid the rod on the bare backs of our consciences! The good plain spoken, honest old man! How I honored him for his simple, straight forward earnestness; his homely sincerity. ⟨with which he⟩ ↑He certainly↓ handled us without mittens, but I trust we were all the better for it. How different he was ⟨by⟩ from the brisk, dapper selfsufficient apostle who cantered up to the Judges door a day or two after; who was so full of himself that he had no thought to bestow on our religious delinquencies; who did nothing but boast of his public trials of skill in argument with rival preachers of other denominations, and how he had driven them off the field and crowed over them—You must remember the bustling self confident little man with a tin trumpet in the handle of his riding whip, with which I presume he blew the trumpet in Zion!

Do you remember our fishing expedition in company with congress man

Van Allen[3] to the little lake a few miles from Kinderhook; and John Moore the vagabond admiral of the lake who sat crouched in a heap in the middle of his canoe in the centre of the lake, with fishing rods stretching out in every direction like the long legs of a spider. And do you remember our piratical prank, when we made up ⟨by⟩ for our own bad luck in fishing by plundering his canoe of its fish when we found it adrift. and do you remember how John Moore came splashing along the marsh on the opposite border of the lake, roaring at us, and how we finished our frolick by driving off and leaving the congress man to John Moores mercy; tickling ourselves with the idea of his being scalped at least. ah well aday, friend Merwin; these were the days of our youth and folly, I trust we have grown wiser and better since then; we certainly have grown older. I dont think we would rob John Moores fishing canoe now. By the way that same John Moore ↑and the anecdotes you told of him,↓ gave me the idea of a vagabond character, Dirk Schuyler, in my Knickerbocker history of New York, which I was then writing.

You tell me the old school house is torn down and a nice one built in its place. I am sorry for it. I should have liked to see the old school house once more; where ⟨I used⟩ after my mornings literary task was over, I used to come and wait for you occasionally until school was dismissed: and you used to promise to keep back the punishment of some little tough broad bottomed dutch boy until I should come, for my amusement—but never kept your promise. I dont think I should look with a friendly eye at the new school house, however nice it might be.

Since I saw you in New York I have had severe attacks of bilious intermittent fever which shook me terribly; but they cleared out my system, and I have ever since been in my usual excellent health; able to mount my horse and gallop about the country almost as briskly as when I was a youngster. Wishing you the enjoyment of the same inestimable blessing and begging you to remember me to your daughter who penned your letter and to your son whom out of old kindness and companionship, you have named after me

                I remain ever, my good friend, / Yours very truly and cordially
                                                                Washington Irving

Jesse Merwin Esqr.

MANUSCRIPT: Yale; NYHS and LC (facsimiles).   PUBLISHED: NYEP, March 1, 1851; *National Anti-Slavery Standard*, March 20, 1851; *Irvingiana*, p. lx; PMI, IV, 81–83; *The Guardian: A Family Magazine*, 2 (May–June, 1851), 51–52.

Jesse Merwin (1778–1852), the schoolmaster at Kinderhook whom WI had met in 1809, served as the model for Ichabod Crane.

1. William P. Van Ness (1778–1826), who lived at Kinderhook, had been a

close friend of Aaron Burr and had served as his second in his duel with Alexander Hamilton.

2. WI wrote "Nest." William Van Ness, Sr., uncle of W. P. Van Ness, was a deacon in the Dutch Reformed Church of Claverack. For other details, see WI to William P. Van Ness, June 24, 1809.

3. James Isaac Van Alen (1776–1870), the half brother of Martin Van Buren, had served in the U.S. Congress from 1807 to 1809.

2130. To Lewis G. Irving

[February 20, 1851]

To L. G. Irving / Secretary of the Niagara Insurance Company

Please pay to my Attorney, Pierre M Irving, the dividend now due me, & any future dividends—Feb 20. 1851

Washington Irving

DOCKETED: Order from Washington / Irving for the payment / of dividend Feb 20th 1851
MANUSCRIPT: Helen Irving Horton.

2131. To Pliny Miles

Sunnyside Feb 21. 1851

Dear Sir

I thank you sincerely for the kind tenor and expressions of your letter of Jany 31.[1] As to your forth coming work[2] I am perfectly willing it should be dedicated to me, if you think it would be of any service; or if it would render you any gratification; I only stipulate that the dedication should be of the simplest kind; and free from Compliment

very respectfully / Your friend & Servt
Washington Irving

Pliny Miles Esqr.

ADDRESSED: Pliny Miles Esq.   DOCKETED: Washington Irving / Sunnyside / Feb. 21. 1851.
MANUSCRIPT: Princeton University Library.

Pliny Miles (1818–1865) was a writer and lecturer who traveled extensively in the United States and Europe. He was greatly interested in improving the U.S. postal system.

1. This letter has not been located.

2. The work in question has not been identified. No new publication by Miles appeared until 1854.

2132.   To William H. Bogart

Sunnyside Feb 23d. 1851

Dear Sir,

I have the honor to acknowledge the receipt of your letter of the 27th.[1] ultimo accompanying copies of a resolution of the Senate and of its Journal for the Session of 1850.

On referring to the appendix to that journal I am made sensible of the signal compliment intended me by the Senate in directing the transmission of this document.[2]

To be deemed by that honorable and enlightened body worthy to have my name in any degree associated with that of the illustrious discoverer whose achievements I have attempted to relate is indeed a reward beyond the ordinary lot of Authors.

I am unacquainted with the forms of the Senate but I beg you will communicate, in a suitable way, to that honorable body, my deep and grateful sense of this very flattering mark of their consideration.

I have the honor to be

Very respectfully / Your Obt Servt
Washington Irving

William H. Bogart Esq / &c &c &c

DOCKETED: Mrs Morgan Grinnell / Washington Irving / Sunnyside / Feby 23 / 1851
MANUSCRIPT: LC.   PUBLISHED: *Journal of the Senate of the State of New-York* (Albany, 1851), p. 237.

A comment by Bogart is written below the docket: "A portrait, said to be of Columbus, given to the Senate by Mrs Farmer, a descendant of Jacob Leisler of New York Colonial history was *restored* during my clerkship—My report was published in the Senate Journal, and a copy of the Journal directed by vote of the Senate to be transmitted to Mr Irving—This I did, and this letter is his answer—"

William H. Bogart (1810–1888), a lawyer who was elected to the New York legislature in 1840, served as clerk of the Senate for several sessions. He wrote numerous articles on historical subjects for the New York *Courier and Enquirer* and the New York *World*.

1. This letter has not been located.

2. The *Senate Journal* for 1851 records that the Senate resolved that "the Clerk of the Senate transmit to Washington Irving, a copy of the Senate journal of 1850, containing proceedings had by the Senate relative to the preservation of the portrait of Columbus, now in the Senate chamber" (*Journal of the Senate*, p. 68). In the appendix of the *Senate Journal* for 1850 is a report by the clerk of the

Senate, dated April 9, 1850, on the restoration of a portrait of Columbus which had hung in the Senate anteroom. It was to be cleaned and hung in the Senate chamber. The report traces the history of the portrait (donated to the Senate by Mrs. Maria Farmer in 1784) and in the last sentence states that "one of our own native citizens has so intertwined his fame with that of the Great Discoverer, that there will henceforth be an enduring association between the names of Columbus and Irving" (*Journal of the Senate* [1850], app., pp. 789–92).

2133. To Caleb Lyon

Sunnyside, Feby. 28th 1851.

My dear Sir,

Accept my sincere and cordial thanks for the kind expressions of your letter,[1] and still more for the public testimonial of your good opinion and good will in voting for me as a Senator of the United States. I confess it was a matter of vast surprise to me, who am so totally removed from politics and public life, to see my name suddenly coupled with such an office. My surprise has ceased since I have read the speech which accompanied your letter. Your briliant and generous defense of poetry against those who would scout and sneer it out of the legislative chamber, shews you to be something more than a mere politician and I feel it indeed a compliment to recieve the vote of one evidently of such cultivated tastes and extended views, and capable of such noble and elevated sentiments.

With great respect / My dear Sir / Yours very faithfully
Washington Irving

Hon Caleb Lyon / &c &c &c

MANUSCRIPT: NYHS.

Caleb Lyon (1822–1875), traveler, lecturer, poet, and writer, was elected to the New York State Assembly in 1850, to the State Senate in 1851, and to the U.S. Congress in 1853. He was appointed first governor of the Territory of Idaho in 1864.

1. This letter has not been located.

2134. To ———

Sunnyside March 31st 1851

Dear Sir

I understand you have in your possession several letters of General Washington addressed to Mr Wm B Pearce[1] at Mount Vernon. I would esteem it a great favor if you would grant me the loan of them for a short time and promise you they shall be taken great care of and faithfully returned to ⟨them⟩ ↑you↓. My publisher Mr Putnam 155 Broadway would take charge of them and forward them to me

Very respectfully / Your obt Servt
Washington Irving

MANUSCRIPT: Va.–Barrett.

1. William B. Pearce was George Washington's plantation manager from 1794 to 1796, when he resigned because of ill health. Washington wrote him weekly letters with lengthy instructions about the management of Mount Vernon. See John A. Carroll and Mary W. Ashworth, *George Washington* (New York, 1957), VII, 125, 128, 387, 423.

2135.   To Pierre M. Irving

[April 12, 1851]

My dear Pierre

Forces Am: Archive[s][1] are not in the Astor library; but Brodhead[2] Writes me that he has a set of them at my service. You can have the use of them of course by applying to him—I am glad you have written about the Washington Mss.

Yours affly
Washington Irving

Saturday Apl 12t. [1851]

MANUSCRIPT: NYPL—Seligman Collection.

The date was determined by the perpetual calendar.

1. Peter Force (1790–1868) was a New York printer who began work in 1837 on *American Archives*, a collection of documents on the history of the North American colonies. Only the fifth and sixth series, covering the period from March 7, 1774, to December 31, 1776, were published when the project was discontinued in 1853. WI omitted the bracketed letter.

2. John Romeyn Brodhead (1814–1873) had spent three years searching in European archives for documents relating to the early history of New York. These materials were translated and edited by E. B. O'Callaghan and published as *Documents Relating to the Colonial History of the State of New York*, 11 vols. (1856–1886). In 1851 Brodhead was working on a history of New York. For other details, see WI to William H. Seward, July 11, 1842.

2136.   To William W. Waldron

Sunnyside, April 15th 1851

Dear Sir:

The documents concerning General Washington came safely to hand, and were, some of them quite new to me. For your kindness in sending them accept my sincere thanks, and believe me to be,

Very respectfully, / Your obliged and obedient servant,
Washington Irving

William W. Waldron, Esq.

PUBLISHED: Waldron, *WI & Cotemporaries*, pp. 144, 243–44.

Waldron was a writer and editor whom WI first met in 1853, when he invited him to Sunnyside after the publication of "Chieftain and Child," a poem describing the meeting of Washington and WI. See Waldron, *WI & Cotemporaries*, pp. xii–xvi.

2137.   To ——

[April 25, 1851]

My dear Sir,

I regret extremely that my engagements for this evening will not permit me to avail myself of your kind invitation to the club.

Very truly yours
Washington Irving

Friday. April 25th. [1851]

DOCKETED: Washington Irving
MANUSCRIPT: Va.–Barrett.

The year was determined by the perpetual calendar. The club has not been identified.

2138.   To ——

Sunnyside April 26th 1851

Dear Sir

The Irving Institute, after having ceased to exist for a year or more, has recently been revived by one of the brothers, Mr William P Lyons[.][1]

I am unable, however to give you any further information concerning it than that furnished in its own advertisements. I gave my name as a referee to the original establishment; I see it in the advertisements, but I have not had leisure or opportunity to make myself acquainted with its internal concerns since its revival

Respectfully / Your obt Servt
Washington Irving

MANUSCRIPT: SHR.

1. William P. and John Lyon established the Irving Institute, a private boarding school for boys, in 1838. For other details, see WI to William and John Lyon, February 24, 1841.

2139. To John P. Kennedy

Sunnyside April 27th. 1851

My dear Kennedy

The recent death of a Brother in law[1] must plead my apology for declining the invitation of the ⟨Balti⟩ Maryland Historical Society;[2] but to tell you the truth I have a nervous horror of all public dinners, and other occurrences of the kind where I may be called on for a speech or a toast, or in any way to play the part of a notoriety; and I avoid them as much as possible.

It would give me great delight to meet you and a friend or two in a social way and I hope to do so some time or other on my way to ⟨an⟩ or from Washington where I shall have to go some time or other to make researches in the archives of the Department of State but when that will be I cannot say. I have been kept from Washington by the rancorous discussions and disputes about this detestable slave question.

I wish to heavens nature would restore to the poor negroes their tails and settle them in their proper place in the scale of creation. It would be a great relief to both them and the abolitionists, and I see no other way of settling this question effectually.

Give my kind remembrances to Mrs Kennedy, and believe me ever

Yours very truly
Washington Irving

MANUSCRIPT: Peabody Library.   PUBLISHED: Sewanee Review, 25 (January, 1917), 6.

1. Daniel Paris, the widowed husband of WI's sister Catharine, had died on April 4, 1851.

2. In a letter of April 25, 1851, Kennedy had asked WI to attend the dinner of the Maryland Historical Society. Others invited included Rufus W. Griswold, William Gilmore Simms, Sir Henry Bulwer, Martin F. Tupper, and President Millard Fillmore. See *Sewanee Review*, 25 (January, 1917), 6.

2140. To Henry R. Schoolcraft

Sunnyside May 5th. 1851

My dear Sir,

I beg you to accept my most grateful thanks for the splendid copy of your historical work on the Indian Tribes[1] which you have had the kindness to send me. I am reading it with deep interest and great satisfaction—; it enlightens me on so many points about which I was ignorant and about which I was extremely desirous of information.

I rejoice to see the character customs and habits of our Indian Tribes as well as their Archeology rescued from a thousand misapprehensions and misrepresentations and placed clearly and truthfully before the public eye. I[n][2] this respect your work will remain an historical monument; when the people of whom it treats may possibly have passed away, circumstances, as well as natural qualifications, have peculiarly fitted you for your interesting task; and you have undertaken it at the critical moment, while it was yet time, but when it was on the eve of being too late. I am happy that Government has enabled you to prosecute your researches so thoroughly and to illustrate them in so satisfactory a manner

With best wishes for your continued success in the intelligent and patriotic career in which you are so honorably embarked, I remain

My dear Sir / with the highest respect and regard / Your obliged friend
Washington Irving

Henry R Schoolcraft Esqr / &c &c &c

MANUSCRIPT: NYPL—Emmett Collection.

Henry Rowe Schoolcraft (1793–1864), who lived at Michilimackinac for nearly twenty years, published numerous studies of frontier exploration and of Indian customs and conditions.

1. Probably volume 1 of *Historical and Statistical Information Respecting the History, Condition and Prospects of the Indian Tribes of the United States*. WI's library at Sunnyside contains volumes 1, 2, and 4 inscribed by Schoolcraft and volume 3 presented by "L. Lea. Comr. Ind. Affrs.", plus volumes 1–3 of an 1853 printing presented to WI by the author.
2. WI omitted the bracketed letter.

2141. To Sarah Storrow

Sunnyside, May ⟨5⟩6th. 185⟨0⟩ ↑1851↓

My dear Sarah,

Your most delightful letter of March 5th.[1] has remained too long un-answered, but it found me crowded with occupation getting out a revised edition of the Alhambra,[2] in which I was making many alterations and additions with the press close at my heels.

Since then we have been visited by a sudden bereavement in the short illness and death of your father.[3] I do not know any thing that ever took me more by surprise. He was to have come up to the Cottage on Satur-day, to remain over Sunday with us. I was in town on Friday when I first heard of his illness. I hastened to his lodgings but arrived too late. You have the consolation my dear Sarah, of knowing that during his brief illness he received the kindest and most unremitting attention from various members of the family beside Irving and Nancy.[4] Helen and Eliza[5] were continually there. Indeed since your mothers death every attention has been paid to prevent him as much as possible from feeling lonely. He used to pass his evenings occasionally at Judge Ulshoeffers;[6] Pierre & Helens—Oscars &c take his hand at whist in talk over old times, and appeared always to be cheerful. Pierre says he never knew him to be more animated and entertaining than one evening about three months since when he sat there for several hours giving anecdotes of early times during and just after the Revolutionary War; all which he related ⟨th⟩ with that accuracy and freshness of memory for which he was remarkable.

When I consider the ripe age to which he had arrived, in the enjoy-ment of excellent health; and the use of all his faculties; the brief term of his illness and the little pain that attended it, I cannot but consider his end an enviable one. He lived, without the burthen of infirmity, to the full measure of his term; and then departed in peace, without lingering to wear out a suffering remnant of existence. Such I hope may be my lo⟨s⟩t, when the time⟨,⟩ (which cannot be far distant) arrives for me to follow him.

I am delighted with the accounts you give me of your lovely children. Oh! how happy I should be to see them all once more. I see Kate is be-coming quite a belle. You know, according to her own account, she *entered into Society* before leaving New York. Susies face will be a pass-port for her through the world and, with her loving nature, will win all hearts. As to little Julie is[7] she is any thing more beautiful than she was in New York she must be indeed a paragon. How I recall the little creature with her high tragedy gesticulations when she would put on grand airs, and the style in which she would shoot me dead. What a delight it would be to have the children here this summer; when the Grinnell house will be finished; and the ⟨Grin⟩ two places forming one great play ground for the little folks. The House will be completed in the course of four or five weeks and the family will move in in June, on returning from a Weeks visit to New Bedford in which I am to accompany them.

Pierre & Helen are to pass this summer with the Grinnells. Eliza & Oscar are staying at the Cottage at present but in the course of a few days take up their quarters until late in the autumn at Mr Holms's. I trust we shall have Julia Sanders with us a great part of the time, so that there will be quite a family gathering in the neighborhood. I have just bought a very pretty Barouche for the girls to open the summer campaign with, as the close carriage was rather heavy for afternoon drives; So they are anticipating a very pleasant Season. The residence of Julia in our immediate neighborhood will alter our whole plan of life——

I have been very little in town this winter. Indeed I may say that I have lived almost exclusively in the country since your departure. My time has been very much occupied with my pen, preparing & printing my revised editions &c and it will continue to be so occupied until I finish the life of Washington on which I am now busy. I am always happiest when I have a considerable part of my time thus employed, and feel reason to be thankful that my intellectual powers continue capable of being so tasked. I shall endeavor however not to overta⟨k⟩sk myself; shall mount my horse often and break off occasionally to make an excursion, like that to New Bedford.

You have never told me which side of the place Vendome you live— whether on the left or right side as you go toward the Rue de Rivoli. Let me know as nearly as you can the exact locality. You can easily make a diagram in a letter and mark the exact spot. I put you, in my mind, somewhere about the place where the Rays used to live.

I received a few days since several numbers of Galignani[8] for which I presume I am indebted to your good husband. If so I beg you will thank him for me, and tell him they were very acceptable.

How agreeable it must be to you all to have Grandpere Storrow with you—What a time he and the children must have together. I rejoice to hear of his varnished boots and white cravat, notwithstanding they make him miserable. Its a sign that he still keeps in the current of Society for which he is so well fitted, and which I think is very ⟨service?⟩ bene-ficial in keeping a mans philosophy from ⟨growing⟩ overgrowing his good humor. I think his situation in Paris must be very much to his taste; having a domestic circle around him and the libraries and other resources of the great city at his command. Remember me to him most cordially and tell him I trust he is amusing himself with the historical research he had cut out for himself before leaving America.

You speak in one of your letters to the family, of the pleasure you have had in reading the "Reveries of a Bachelor." It is indeed a very beautiful work. The author[9] was kind enough to send me a copy, and to call on me. I am much pleased with him He is quiet and gentlemanlike in manners and appearance and I shall be very glad to cultivate his acquaintance. I understand he is engaged to be married; I hope to ⟨the worthy⟩ one worthy of being the subject of one of his reveries.

There are two very clever works which have made their appearance within a year or so, one quite recently—The *Scarlet letter* and *The house with the Seven Gables*.[10] They are by Hawthorn—and two of the best works of fiction that ha⟨s⟩ve issued from the American press.

Remember me affectionately to your husband and kiss the dear little women for me

ever my dear Sarah / Your affectionate uncle
Washington Irving

P.S. The girls send abundance of love to you as does also Eliza Oscar. The[y][11] desire me to inform you of the marriage of Beulah Livingston to a Mr Atterbury of Trenton New Jersey. He is a gentleman of good appearance and good property, about forty years old, a widower with two or three children. Beulah is his third wife. Mary Livingston is to be married in June next, to Mr Rogers, son of Dr Rogers of the old Rogers family of New York. The engagement was formed last summer when the Rogers's boarded at Mr Holmes.

MANUSCRIPT: Yale. PUBLISHED: PMI, IV, 84–86 (in part).

1. This letter has not been located.

2. Putnam published the Author's Revised Edition of *The Alhambra* in early May, 1851.

3. Daniel **Paris.**

4. Irving Paris (1816–1879), Daniel's son, was married to Nancy Ulshoeffer (1825 or 1826–1884).

5. Mrs. Pierre M. Irving and Mrs. Gabriel Irving.

6. Michael Ulshoeffer (1793–1881), who was admitted to the bar in 1813 and was a New York City attorney in the 1820's, was appointed judge of the Court of Common Pleas in 1834 and 1843. See *History of the Bench and Bar of New York* (New York, 1897), I, 504.

7. WI probably intended to write "if."

8. *Galignani's Messenger*, the English language paper published in Paris.

9. Donald Grant Mitchell (1822–1908) (pseudonym "Ik Marvel"), a Yale graduate who traveled extensively in the United States and abroad, wrote *Fresh Gleanings* (1847), about his European travels, and *The Battle Summer* (1850),

about the French revolution of 1848. *Reveries of a Bachelor* and *Dream Life* appeared in 1850 and 1851, respectively. He married Mary Frances Pringle of South Carolina on May 31, 1853, and went to Venice as U.S. consul, a post he held until February, 1854.

10. *The Scarlet Letter* appeared on March 16, 1850, and *The House of the Seven Gables* in April, 1851. See Randall Stewart, *Nathaniel Hawthorne*, pp. 95, 113.

11. WI omitted the bracketed letter.

2142. *To the Irving Literary Society*

Sunnyside, May 15, 1851

Gentlemen—It gives me great regret that I cannot accept your very obliging invitation to your second anniversary celebration, as I have engagements which will take me to the western part of this state about the time it is to be held.

Very respectfully, gentlemen, your obliged and humble servant,

Washington Irving

PUBLISHED: Baltimore *American* (undated clipping at SHR).

2143. *To the Irving Literary Society*

Sunnyside, May 15, 1851

Gentlemen—I appreciate most deeply and sensibly the very kind dealings of respect and good-will which must have dictated the request contained in your letter of the 5th instant.[1] Mr. Brady[2] has already taken one or two daguerrotypes from an excellent portrait recently taken of me by Mr. Merton,[3] which portrait is now in the hands of a first-rate engraver. I have directed that the portrait be submitted to Mr. Brady to take a daguerrotype for your society. I have a great repugnance to having a daguerrotype taken from me personally. The process is irksome in the extreme and the likenesses, when taken, are apt to be harsh and contracted. I hope the mode I have adopted will meet your wishes.

I remain, gentlemen, yours very faithfully,

Washington Irving

PUBLISHED: Baltimore *American* (undated clipping at SHR).

1. This letter has not been located.
2. Matthew Brady (ca. 1823–1896), who was already well known as a daguerreotypist, gained fame as a Civil War photographer.

3. A mistranscription of Martin. For other details about Charles Martin's portrait and Frederick Halpin's engraving, see WI to Benson J. Lossing, January 17, 1851.

2144.   To George P. Putnam

Sunnyside, May 15th / 51.

My dear Sir

I have a letter from a Committee of the Irving Society of the College of St James, Baltimore, requesting me to sit to Mr Brady for a daguerriotype, they having made arrangements with him to take one and forward it to them. As I have a horror of the process I wish you would let Mr Brady take another daguerriotype of Martins portrait of me. I am sure it ⟨is a⟩ would be more satisfactory than any he could take from me personally—

When do you sail for England and when will you want the article for the book of landscapes.[1] I have made a rough sketch of one, relating to the Hudson River ⟨with⟩ in which the Cats Kill mountains are introduced. This I trust will answer your purpose and I can dress it up against the time it may be wanted.

I will thank you to send me any thing readable; for I have read through all the current literature on my table. I like Mayo's Romance Dust,[2] as I do every thing he has written— I did not object to the title as being affected; he has no affectation; but it appeared rather far sought.

Yours very truly
Washington Irving

Geo P Putnam Esqr

Docketed: W. Irving / May 15 / 51
Manuscript: Va.–Barrett.

1. In 1852 Putnam published *The Home Book of the Picturesque; or, American Scenery, Art, and Literature, Comprising a Series of Essays by Washington Irving, W. C. Bryant, Fenimore Cooper ... etc.* WI's essay, "The Catskill Mountains," was printed on pages 71–78.
2. Earlier in 1851 William Starbuck Mayo (1812–1895) had brought out *Romance Dust from the Historic Placer,* a collection of tales suggested by events in the California gold fields. His earlier works, *Kaloolah, or Journeyings to the Djebel Kumri* (1849) and *The Berber; or the Mountaineer of the Atlas* (1850), were drawn from his travels in Africa.

2145.   To Moses H. Grinnell

Sunnyside May 20th. / 51.

My dear Grinnell,
I must beg you to excuse me from dining with you tomorrow. Sunny-side is possessed by seven devils and I have to be continually on the watch to keep all from going to ruin. First we have a legion of Women Kind, cleaning and scouring the house from top to bottom; so that we are all reduced to eat and drink and have our being in my little library. In the midst of this our water is cut off. An Irishman from your establishment undertook to shut up my spring as he had yours, within brick walls; the spring shewed proper spirit and broke bounds and all the waterpipes ran dry in consequence. In the dearth of painters I have employed a couple of country carpenters to paint my roofs and it requires all my vigilance to keep them from painting them like Josephs coat of divers colours. Your little man Westerfield is to plaster my chimneys tomorrow and your plumbers and bell hangers to attack the vitals of the house. I have a new coachman to be inducted into all the mysteries of the stable and coach house, so all that part of the establishment is in ⟨a⟩ what is called a halla baloo. In a word I never knew of such a tempest in a teapot as is just now going on in little Sunnyside [.] I trust, therefore, you will excuse me for staying at home to sink or swim with the concern.

Yours affectionately
Washington Irving

M H Grinnell Esqr

P. S.   Lee has not yet commenced the long promised filling up, which was certainly to be begun yesterday. I begin more fully to understand what is meant by *lee-way.*

ADDRESSED: M H Grinnell Esqr / *or Lady* / No 1. Fourteenth St. East.
MANUSCRIPT: Julia Bowdoin Key.   PUBLISHED: PMI, IV, 86–87.

2146.   To James W. Beekman

Sunnyside, June 25, 1851

Dear Sir:
Several months since, I received from Messrs. G. & C. Mer[r]iam[1] a copy of their quarto edition of Webster's Dictionary. In acknowledging

the receipt of it, I expressly informed them that I did not make it my standard of orthography, and gave them my reasons for not doing so, and for considering it an unsafe standard for American writers to adopt. At the same time I observed the work had so much merit in many respects *that I made it quite a vade mecum.*

They had the disingenuousness to extract merely that part of my opinion which I have underlined, and to insert it among their puffs and advertisements as if I had given a general and unqualified approbation of the work. I have hitherto suffered this bookseller's trick to pass unnoticed, but your letter obl[i]ges[2] me to point it out, and to express my decided opinion that Webster's Dictionary is not a work advisable to be introduced "by authority" into our schools as a standard of orthography.

I am sir, with great respect,

Your obedient servant,
Washington Irving.

To Hon. James W. Beekman, Chairman / of the Senate
Committee of Literature

PUBLISHED: *National Anti-Slavery Standard,* 12 (July 24, 1851), 36.

James W. Beekman (1815–1877), who was a graduate of Columbia College in 1834, was elected a state senator for New York in 1850 and served two terms. He was active in New York hospital affairs and in the New-York Historical Society.

1. G. & C. Merriam was a printing house established in 1831 in Springfield, Massachusetts by brothers George (1803–1880) and Charles (1806–1887) Merriam. Upon the death of Noah Webster in 1843 it acquired the unsold copies of his *American Dictionary of the English Language* and the rights to its publication. In 1847 the firm issued a revised one-volume edition which had extensive sales. The bracketed letter was omitted from the printed version of the letter.

2. The printed version omitted the bracketed letter.

2147. To Sir Robert Harry Inglis

Sunnyside June 29th. 1851

My dear Sir Robert,

Permit me to introduce to your acquaintance the Rev. Charles D. Cooper, who visits London in the course of an European Tour. He is a gentleman of much worth and of amiable manners, and a kind of connexion of mine by marriage.

Any attentions you may find it convenient to bestow upon him during his sojourn in London will add to the many claims you already possess upon the gratitude and affection of

> Your Sincere and devoted friend
> Washington Irving

Present my kindest remembrances to Lady Inglis.[1]

Sir. Robert Harry Inglis. Bart / &c &c &c

MANUSCRIPT: SHR.

Sir Robert Harry Inglis (1786–1855) was a Tory politician and a member of Parliament from 1824 to 1854. He was president of the Literary Club, a fellow of the Society of Antiquaries and of the Royal Society, and in 1850 was elected antiquary of the Royal Academy.

1. The former Mary Brisco, whom Inglis married in 1807.

2148. To John Murray III

> Sunnyside June 29th. 1851

My dear Mr Murray,

This letter will be handed to you by the Rev. Charles D Cooper a gentleman of much worth and most amiable manner and a kind of connexion of mine by marriage. Any attention you may find it convenient to pay him during his sojourn in London will be considered favors bestowed on myself.

I hope and trust the late decision in the matter of copyright will prove efficient in protecting you against the pirates of the press

> Yours ever very faithfully
> Washington Irving

John Murray Esqr / &c &c &c

MANUSCRIPT: John Murray.

2149. To Richard Bentley

> Sunnyside, July 7th 1851

Dear Sir

I have received your two letters dated June 3 & 4th. informing me of your intention to proceed against certain booksellers for an infringement of the copy rights of the Alhambra[,] Astoria[,] and Bonneville; and, inasmuch as you had no formal deed of assignment from me, requesting me to authorize your solicitor, Frederick Nicholls Devey Esq to institute proceedings in my name.

As the whole proceeding is for your account and benefit, and at your expense I cannot refuse to delegate this authority to the gentleman named; but I confess I give my consent most reluctantly to a measure by which I am made to appear as a litigant and though only nominally so yet at the great hazard of misconception.

If your Solicitor could prepare an assignment or other instrument which might have a retroactive operation and enable you to sue in your own name I would greatly prefer it. If this be impracticable, then you may take this letter as a warrant to your Solicitor to appear for me, with full power and authority to represent me in any suit you may deem necessary in regard to the before mentioned works, and before any court. I wish it to be publicly understood, however, in this contingency that you have recourse to my name on your own behalf and only from a technical necessity; and that I have no personal interest in the event of the proceeding.

Yours very truly,
Washington Irving

Richard Bentley Esq

MANUSCRIPT: NYPL—Berg Collection.   PUBLISHED: PMI, IV, 88.

Richard Bentley (1794–1871) was a successful London publisher and proprietor of *Bentley's Miscellany*.

2150.   To Charles A. Davis

Sunnyside 12th Sept 1851

My dear Major

Your letter[1] was as welcome as the flowers in spring, finding me just getting over a casual visit of chills and fever to which I have occasionally been subject ever since I undertook to "look a gift horse in the mouth" in other words to drain a piece of ground which the H R. Railroad Cy.[2] gratuitously filled up at my request.

I read and enjoyed your ballad in the height of my indisposition and have reread and enjoyed it still more since I have been told the quarter whence it came. It is well done—and it is served up just at the nick of time—which you know doubles the zest of a dish.

As to the *gammon* on which you pride yourself, it may do for the *Marines* but I am to old a salt to be taken in by such yarns. I consider it, however, as clever as any other part of the article Altogether you have made a capital hit; the better for being so good natured a one—but such yours always are.

As to Lopez[3] he has been rightly served—and as to those who followed him, they have experienced nothing but what they were forewarned would be their lot. I think it a pity their cowardly instigators,[4] who remained here after launching them forth, could not share their fate

The prompt crushing of this unprincipled enterprize has prevented a vast deal of trouble and perplexity in which we might have been involved with foreign nations—however we have a spirit of mischief working within us which I presume will find some other vent.

I am glad you have moved up town though I wonder when once under way you did not keep on to the house you built near Gramercy park.[5] I am scrawling this letter in a state of great lassitude and profuse perspiration the effects of the weather and my recent fever; as soon as I get strength enough I shall be off to the highlands to visit my friend Gouv Kemble and benefit by a change of air.

Give my kind remembrances to Mrs Davis and your daughter and believe me my dear Major ever yours very cordially

Washington Irving

Chas A Davis Esqr

MANUSCRIPT: Va.–Barrett.

Charles Augustus Davis (1795–1867), a New York merchant and journalist, imitated Seba Smith's creation, Major Jack Downing, in *Letters Written During the President's Tour, "Down East," by Myself, Major Jack Downing, of Downingville* (1833). Davis was WI's close friend in his later years.

1. This letter has not been located.
2. The Hudson River Railroad pushed its right of way along the east bank of the Hudson River at the edge of WI's property at Sunnyside. WI found the noise from the trains distracting and in April, 1848, was given a settlement of $3,500. See PMI, IV, 38.
3. Marcisco Lopez (1799–1851), a Venezuelan soldier who also fought for Cuba and Spain, tried to foment insurrection among Cubans in the spring of 1850. After failing to secure Cuban support, he returned to the United States, where he was arrested. Upon his release he launched a filibustering expedition into Cuba in August, 1851, but was caught in the jungle and killed. See Strong, *Diary*, I, 64; and NYEP, September 8, 9, 1851.
4. These included Moses Y. Beach, owner of the New York *Sun*, and John A. Quitman, a soldier in the Mexican War and a former governor of Mississippi. See Strong, *Diary*, I, 65.
5. Gramercy Park was situated between 20th and 21st Streets and Third and Fourth Avenues. Created by Samuel B. Ruggles, a real estate developer, Gramercy

Park was reclaimed from a marsh and enclosed by an eight-foot iron fence. Owners and tenants of the sixty-six lots were given keys to open the iron gates. See *New York City Guide* (New York, 1939), pp. 191–95.

2151. To Rufus W. Griswold

Sunnyside, Thursday, Sept. 18, 1851.

My dear Sir:

The death of Fenimore Cooper,[1] though anticipated, is an event of deep and public concern, and calls for the highest expression of public sensibility. To me it comes with something of a shock: for it seems but the other day that I saw him at our common literary resort at Putnam's, in full vigor of mind and body, a very "castle of a man," and apparently destined to outlive me, who am several years his senior. He has left a space in our literature which will not easily be supplied.

I shall not fail to attend the proposed meeting on Wednesday next.

You have not specified the hour of meeting, but I shall readily learn it at Mr. Putnam's. I would observe that, on Wednesday next, I have to attend monthly meetings of the Executors of the Astor estate, and the Trustees of the Astor Library. These generally occupy the time from eleven o'clock in the morning until one.

Very respectfully, your friend and servant,
Washington Irving

Rev. Rufus W. Griswold, D. D.

PUBLISHED: New York *Times*, September 25, 1851; and *Memorial of James Fenimore Cooper* (New York, 1852), [p. 7] (in part).

Rufus W. Griswold (1815–1857) was a New York journalist, editor, and anthologist.

1. Cooper had died on September 14, 1851.

2152. To Henry R. Schoolcraft

Sunnyside Sept 20t 1851

My dear Sir

The debility and languor consequent to an attack of chills and fever have prevented an earlier reply to your letter of the 10th inst.[1] With regard to the Convention of Authors which you suggest, I do not clearly see the scope and object of it and therefore cannot give an opinion as to its utility. At any rate I am not the person to originate or take a prominent part in any thing of the kind, being a silent, diffident inefficient man in all public assemblies unfitted by my retired and somewhat shy habits for the bustle of affairs, and daily growing more and more unwilling to engage in any thing that ⟨draws⟩ ↑may draw↓ me from my home and my study.

Excuse me therefore if I do not meet your idea with the ready and warm concurrence you could wish. I should probably do so were I a younger man and entirely beyond the effects of chills and fever.

Very truly yours
Washington Irving

Henry R Schoolcraft Esqr

DOCKETED: Washington Irving Cy / 20 Sep 51 / Ackd. 4th Oct.
MANUSCRIPT: Huntington.

1. This letter has not been located.

2153. *To Lewis G. Clark*

Sunnyside, Oct. 6th, 1851.

My dear Mr. Clark:

I am sorry to say that it is not in my power to act upon your suggestions, being incompetent at present to do justice to such a theme. In the course of a long ride last week through Sleepy Hollow and parts adjacent, my horse came down with me and gave me a fall that sent me home in some such bruised and battered plight as the hero of La Mancha after one of his forays. The same evening I had an attack of intermittent fever, which has hung about me ever since. Between the fall and the fever I am at present good for nothing. I am anxious to know what the Cooper Committee, of which I believe you are one, is doing and when the general meeting is to take place. It ought not to be deferred much longer.[1]

Whatever tribute to his memory may be determined upon, I trust it will be met by the public with the spirit which animated them in the days of his ripe renown. It has been suggested by some, that of late years he has done much to awaken the hostility of the press; but I trust there is too much magnanimity in the gentlemen of the press to carry their resentment against such a man beyond the grave. With the nation his name will remain a treasured property. His works form an invaluable part of our literature, and from the nature of their subjects are in some measure identified with our political and social history. His "Leather-

Stocking Tales" and his "Tales of the Sea," those eminent inventions of his genius, have opened regions of romance which he has made his own. Whoever ventures into them hereafter will be accused of treading in his foot-prints. While an author is living, he is apt to be judged by his last works, and those written by Cooper in recent years have been somewhat cavilled at. When an author is dead, he is judged by his best works, and those of Cooper excited enthusiasm at home and applause throughout the world. When his countrymen would do honor to his memory, let them think of these works.

Yours truly,
Washington Irving

PUBLISHED: *Knickerbocker Magazine*, 55 (February, 1860), 230.

1. The public meeting which honored Cooper did not take place until February 25, 1852 at the Metropolitan Hall, with William Cullen Bryant delivering the major eulogy. See PMI, IV, 103–4.

2154. To Edward B. Turney?

Sunnyside Oct 8th 1851

Dear Sir

I have to apologize to you for the delay in answering your letter of the 30th September[1] enclosing a card of invitation to attend a meeting of the Irving Association. It arrived at a time when I was much indisposed; my horse having fallen with me; and the bruizes thereby recieved having brought on a recurrence of intermittent fever; the letter therefore was put by ↑unread↓ with other letters and papers, and it is but now in looking over them that I become aware of its purport. I beg you will communicate these circumstances to the association and at the same time assure them of the high and grateful sense I entertain of the proof they have given me of their esteem

I am Sir / very respectfully / Your obliged & humble Servt
Washington Irving

Edward B. Turney[?] Esq.

MANUSCRIPT: NYPL–Seligman Collection.

1. This letter has not been located.

2155. To Rufus W. Griswold

Sunnyside, Oct. 15th, 1851.

My dear Sir:—

My occupations in the country prevent my attendance in town at the meetings of the committee, but I am anxious to know what is doing. I signified at our first meeting what I thought the best monument to the memory of Mr. Cooper—a statue. It is the simplest, purest, and most satisfactory—perpetuating the likeness of the person. I understand there is an excellent bust of Mr. Cooper extant, made when he was in Italy.[1] He was there in his prime; and it might furnish the model for a noble statue. Judge Duer[2] suggested that his monument should be placed at Washington, perhaps in the Smithsonian Institute. I would rather for New York, as he belonged to this state, and the scenes of several of his best works were laid in it. Besides, the seat of government may be changed, and then Washington would lose its importance; whereas New York must always be a great and growing metropolis—the place of arrival and departure for this part of the world—the great resort of strangers from abroad, and of our own people from all parts of the Union. One of our beautiful squares would be a fine situation for a statue. However, I am perhaps a little too local in my notions on this matter. Cooper emphatically belongs to the nation, and his monument should be placed where it would be most in public view. Judge Duer's idea therefore may be the best. There will be a question of what material the statue (if a statue is determined on) should be made. White marble is the most beautiful, but how would it stand our climate in the open air? Bronze stands all weathers and all climates, but does not give so clearly the expression of the countenance, when regarded from a little distance.

These are all suggestions scrawled in haste, which I should have made if able to attend the meeting of the committee. I wish you would drop me a line to let me know what is done or doing.

Yours, very truly,
Washington Irving

Rev. Rufus Griswold.

PUBLISHED: *Memorial of James Fenimore Cooper*, p. 12.

1. Cooper sat for a portrait bust by Horatio Greenough while he was in Florence early in 1829. See Nathalia Wright, *Horatio Greenough, The First American Sculptor* (Philadelphia, 1963), p. 67.

2. John Duer (1782–1858), who studied in the law office of Alexander Hamilton, had a distinguished legal career climaxed by his election to the Superior Court of New York City in 1849.

2156.   To Chester P. Dewey

Sunnyside Octr 16th. 1851

Dear Sir

I cannot but feel highly sensible of the complement paid me by the Lecture committee of the Rochester Athanaeum[1] in inviting me to deliver a lecture before the institution[.] I regret to say, however, that a nervous repugnance to appearing in this manner before any public body, which amounts almost to a disability, obliges me to decline all invitations of the kind.

I beg you will communicate this my excuse to the Committee and accept at the same time my thanks for the very kind and flattering expressions with which you have accompanied the invitation

I am, Dear Sir

Very respectfully / Your obliged & hbl Servt
Washington Irving

Chester P Dewey Esq / Chairman of the / Lecture Committee &c

MANUSCRIPT: SHR.

Chester P. Dewey (1784–1867), who was professor of mathematics and natural philosophy at Williams College from 1810 to 1827, was principal of the Collegiate Institute at Rochester from 1836 to 1850. With the founding of the University of Rochester in 1851, he became professor of chemistry and natural sciences, a post he held until his retirement in 1861.

1. The Rochester Athenaeum was founded in 1821. Dewey arranged the lecture programs and supervised its library. See Blake McKelvey, *Rochester, the Water-Power City, 1812–1854* (Cambridge, 1945), pp. 194, 275.

2157.   To Henry R. Schoolcraft

Sunnyside Oct 20th. 1851

My dear Sir,

Your letter of the 4th. inst.[1] having, through mistake at the post office, been forwarded to Syracuse instead of Sunnyside, has been some time in reaching me.

The treatment of which you complain in having the titles of your works altered and misapplied by certain book jobbers is undoubtedly a flagrant wrong. Even where a man has purchased the copy right of a work I do not consider that he has any right to alter that work without the privity and consent of the author. The reputation of an author depends upon his writings and may be injured, if not destroyed, by their mutilation and perversion. In parting with a copy right, therefore, it is with the implied condition that the work transferred remain, as to its literary organization, intact, as it came from the hand of the publisher; unless he grant a license to the contrary.

You must be aware, however, that the rights of authors in this country are very imperfectly protected, and awaken little interest in legislative bodies or sympathy on the part of the public. It is to be hoped, however, that a better time is coming; when the property of an author in the creations of his brain will be perfectly recognized and thoroughly secured; by legal enactments and universal usage; and that not for a sordid term of years, but *forever*; not for his own life, but *throughout all generations*; not partially and conditionally but absolutely and entirely; there is no property under heaven in which a man has a more natural and indefeasable right—

Ever my dear Sir / Yours very faithfully
Washington Irving

Henry R. Schoolcraft Esqr

MANUSCRIPT: Huntington.
PUBLISHED: *The Literary World*, 9 (November 15, 1851), 389.

1. This letter has not been located.

2158. To Sarah Storrow

N York Oct 21t 1851

My dear Sarah

I have just recd. your letter of the 29th Septr.[1] which makes me consider that your two preceding letters remain unanswered. The truth is I have been ⟨trying to⟩ deferring writing to you until I should find time for a long letter—and so have written none. I now will scrawl a mere line by way of avoiding further postponement.

And first let me reply to your repeated and affectionately urgent invitations for me to come out to you ⟨this wint⟩ this autumn. It would give me great delight to do so; but I cannot without too great sacrfices.

I am now fully engaged on the life of Washington. A task which was commenced nine years ago ·but which has been repeatedly interrupted and laid aside. At my time of life, and with the liability to attacks of ill health, I cannot afford to risk any more interruptions. I am now in good working trim and ⟨b⟩ if I keep on as I am doing at present I shall achieve the work in the course of the coming winter. If I suffer myself to be interrupted by a change of scene, change of country and all the excitements of Paris life I may never achieve it. When this work is done, if life and health continue, I may be able to 'spare myself from home; though even then other objections may arise Your uncle E. I. has been in very precarious health. Last winter severe rheumatic attacks rendered him almost helpless and at one time I ⟨dou⟩ feared he would scarcely survive the spring. He is now freer from pain and his general health is again good: but the coming winter may bring on a return of his acute maladie's. I could not go away from home while his health was in a critical situation.

I still entertain the hope of seeing you once more settled in your own country and among your relatives and friends, before my capacity for enjoying such a happiness is entirely gone. Mr Storrow talks very much of coming out here to fix himself and has seriously examined the piece of ground which I offer him for a site for a cottage on the other side of the lane. You can have no idea how our domestic enjoyments are encreased since Mr Grinnell has finished his house and we have his family in our neighborhood—when you [are]² fixed on the other side of us we should make one of the happiest little neighborhoods that the heart could desire.

Mr Storrow will tell you how we all get on together. Our grounds are all in a manner in common. The children range over the whole sometimes on foot sometimes with their ponys and there is a constant interchange of visiting and gossipping between the two houses—Do come out to us before your children are too old to make childish associations and let them grow up in heart and mind and body among their relatives and in the land of their parents—

Paris is a sad artificial hot house for the rearing of children.

I scrawl this in great haste at the desk of my publisher, merely that I may not let another day elapse without writing to you—

Give my love to the dear little folks
ever my dear dear Sarah

> Most affectionately /Your uncle
> Washington Irving

ADDRESSED: Madame / Madame Storrow / aux soins de Mr T. w Storrow / Rue de
   Faubg Poissonniere / a Paris
MANUSCRIPT: Yale.

1. This letter has not been located.
2. WI omitted the bracketed word.

2159. To Thomas W. Storrow, Sr.

Sunnyside. Octr. 27th. 1851

My dear Storrow,

The circumstances you relate concerning the portrait possessed by Mr Geo Field[1] supposed to be of the Mother of Washington, and the traditions therewith connected, had already been furnished me by Mr George Harvey.[2]

As I concur very much with Mr Custis[3] and Mr Sparks[4] in my estimation of these historical documents and discoveries I have ⟨not⟩ given them but a passing attention and doubt whether I shall deem it worth while to make them matter of discussion. I return you the printed extracts with many thanks for your kind attention in sending them to me.

Thomas has gone off without my being able to get down to New York and wish him farewell For about a week past I have been tripped up with one of my feverish attacks—the fifth I have had this summer—and am just getting about again. I wish I could take your advice, get on board a Steamer and be off to Paris: a change of air would be of Service to me beside the delight of being with my dear Sarah and her little ones, but this is out of the question for the present—

I think Tom begins to think more seriously of coming out to America; and I have ↑again↓ endeavored to tempt him by the offer of a snug site for a country retreat on a part of my little domain. The addition to our rural domestic circle by the establishment of the Grinnells close by has made it a delightful one and seemed to make him think his little family could be very happy here. I wish you could come on and pay us a visit, and before the Grinnells return to town. You can't think how cosily we get on together. Remember, whenever you choose to come we have always quarters ready for you and you shall be master of yourself and your time

Give my affectionate remembrances to Charles and his family and believe me ever

Yours truly
Washington Irving

Thos W Storrow Esqr

MANUSCRIPT: Harvard.

1. George Field (1777–1854), an English chemist known for his discoveries in the manufacture of pigments and dyes, was an avid collector of art. He wrote treatises on painting and color, including *Chromatography* (1835) and *Rudiments of the Painter's Art* (1850).

2. George Harvey (ca. 1800–1878) was a painter and architect who prepared the designs for remodeling Sunnyside.

3. George Washington Parke Custis (1781–1857), the son of John P. Custis, George Washington's stepson, grew up at Mount Vernon under the tutelage of Washington. Custis's *Recollections of Washington*, which appeared originally in the *National Intelligencer*, was published in book form in 1860.

4. Jared Sparks (1789–1866), a dedicated student of early American history and a collector of manuscripts and documents relating to the Revolutionary War and the Founding Fathers, had edited *The Writings of George Washington*, 12 vols. (1834–1838).

2160.   To Joseph E. Bloomfield

Sunnyside Oct 28th. 1851

Dear Sir

There is no portrait extant of Columbus on which thorough reliance can be placed.[1] Most of the portaits given as his, are either too young or have dark hair, whereas his was white by the time he was thirty years of age, or have the ruff, a flemish fashion which did not come into vogue in the south of Europe until after the death of Columbus. I think in the time of Charles V.[2]

In one of my editions of Columbus I published an engraving of a head copied from an old Italian biographical work.[3] The head was considered by Navarrete[4] and the Duke of Veraguas[5] ⟨the⟩ more likely than any other to be authentic. I did not consider it so, as in the text of the Italian work describing the portrait the hair was said to be black.

In my second revised edition I have published a copy of an engraving taken from a portrait which recently came under the observation of the Librarian of the Royal library at Paris.[6] The portrait was ancient and bore in one corner the name of Christopher Columbus. This portrait however, has the ruff—The Librarian thinks the portrait may have been a ⟨copy of an older⟩ a[7] copy made after the death of Columbus, from an older picture painted during his life time, and that the Ruff may have been added in compliance with the fashion of the day when the copy was made. The portrait is a very intellectual dignified one, and answers ⟨very⟩ ↑tolerably↓ well to the very precise description given by Fernando Columbus,[8] of his fathers countenance, but a doubt hangs about it as about all other alleged portraits of the discoverer.

I am Sir / Very respectfully / Your ob Servt
Washington Irving

Jos. E. Bloomfield Esqr

Manuscript: Huntington.

Joseph E. Bloomfield was, in 1848, a vestryman of the Grace Episcopal Church of Mexico, New York, a town three miles from Lake Ontario in Oswego County. Bloomfield had lived in the south of Spain for several years. See Elizabeth M. Simpson, *Mexico, Mother of Towns* (Buffalo, 1949), p. 42.

1. WI had carefully investigated the surviving portraits of Columbus and copies of them when he was writing his biography. For a discussion of his findings, see WI to Lady Granard, May 7, 1827.

2. Charles V (1500–1558) became joint ruler of Spain with his mother in 1517. Three years later he was crowned Holy Roman Emperor.

3. In the abridgment of Columbus published by John Murray in 1850 WI included the portrait which had first appeared in *Ritratti de cento capitani illustri, intagliati da Aliprando Capriole* (Rome, 1596). See John Boyd Thacher, *Christopher Columbus, His Life, His Work, His Remains*, 3 vols. (New York, 1967), III, 68–70.

4. Martín Fernández de Navarrete (1756–1844) was the Spanish historian who collected the documents in Spanish archives relating to the life and discoveries of Columbus.

5. Pedro María Gorgonio Colón de Larreátegui y Remirez de Baquedano Jeménez de Embrún y Quiñones (1801–1866), 13th duke of Veragua and a lineal descendant of Columbus.

6. Edmond François Jomard (1777–1862), a geographer, engraver, and archeologist, was named librarian of the Royal Library in 1839. In 1844 in a gallery in Vicenza Jomard discovered a portrait of Columbus which was believed to have been painted by Titian or Domenico Campagnola between 1530 and 1540. Although an idealized portrait, it was acclaimed by Jomard as the "best and most life-like image" of Columbus. See Thacher, *Columbus*, III, 62. In November of 1845 Jomard presented WI with an engraving of this portrait. See WI to Catherine Ellis, November 6, 1845.

7. WI repeated the "a."

8. Fernando Columbus (1488–1539) was an illegitimate son who accompanied his father on the fourth voyage to America (1502–1504).

2161. To John Barney

Sunnyside, Oct. 30th 1851.

My dear Mr. Barney:

Your letter of the 25th[1] has acted upon me like a charm, calling up such pleasant scenes in times long past, when we were both gay young fellows, that I cannot go to bed before answering it.

What you mention of kind reccollections of me that were cherished by your sister, flatters my old bachelor heart even now; for she was one of my early admirations, and her image dwells in my memory as she appeared to me at the time, so amiable, graceful, and ladylike.[2] I well remember seeing her also at Baltimore, after her marriage, with her first child, a fine boy and though a mere infant, remarkably sensible to music being easily moved by it either to tears or transports. I believe I have since met[3] him a man grown. You talk of children and grandchildren, I have nothing but literary bantlings to boast of. I trust your progeny will out live mine and increase and multiply and continue your name from generation to generation; which is more than can be expected from the progeny of the Muse, however prolific she may be.

Wishing you many pleasant and prosperous days, I will now bid you good night and will endeavour to continue in my sleep the agreeable dreams you have awakened—

Yours ever very truly
Washington Irving

John Barney Esq

MANUSCRIPT: SHR (copy).
PUBLISHED: PMI, IV, 90–91.

John Barney (1784–1856), a congressman from Maryland from 1825 to 1829, was engaged in literary pursuits in Washington, D.C. At his death he left uncompleted his *Personal Recollections of Men and Things.*

1. This letter has not been located.
2. The manuscript copy does not contain the preceding four words.
3. The manuscript copy has "met with him."

2162.   *To William C. Bryant*

Sunnyside. Nov 1. 1851.

My dear Sir,

The letter to Mr Bloomfield[1] was written in too great haste to be very satisfactory. I spoke of the Librarian of the Royal Library at Paris; I ought to have mentioned his name M Jomard; too important a one in the learned world to be omitted. I enclose a reply to Mr Bloomfields last letter transmitted through you. If you really think the purport of this correspondence worth laying before the public, and will send the whole of it back to me I will endeavor to throw it into a more readable shape.[2]

Very truly Yours
Washington Irving

P. S. I am happy to learn that you have consented to deliver the discourse on the character & writings of Fenimore Cooper.

ADDRESSED: William C. Bryant Esq / office of the Evg Post / New York
MANUSCRIPT: SHR.

1. See WI to Joseph E. Bloomfield, October 28, 1851.

2. The letter was returned to WI, who revised and expanded it. It was then printed in NYEP, December 26, 1851.

2163.   To Pierre M. Irving

[Nov. 4, 1851]

My dear Pierre,

Julia Sanders[1] tells me you or Helen[2] were expecting me in town to morrow to attend a meeting in the evening of the Cooper Committee. I have received no notification of such a meeting, and, having no *zite* in town, ⟨do not⟩ and not feeling in the most robust health just now do not feel disposed to come to town on an uncertainty. I wish you would make this apology for me in case there really should be a meeting

Yours affectionately
Washington Irving

Sunny side, Tuesday Evening, Nov 4th. [1851]

MANUSCRIPT: SHR.

In another hand in the lower left corner is written "1857." The correct year is determined by the perpetual calendar and the references to the Cooper Committee.

1. Julia A. Granger, the wife of Sanders Irving, the son of Ebenezer.
2. Mrs. Pierre M. Irving.

2164.   To William H. Seal

Sunnyside Nov. 6th. 1851

Dear Sir:

The committee in New York have in contemplation a public testimonial of respect to the memory of the late J Fenimore Cooper. In connexion with it Mr Bryant ↑I understand↓ is to deliver a public discourse on the character and writings of the deceased. Though chairman of the committee indisposition has prevented my attending its recent meetings, and I am not able to give particulars of the proceedings. The result will of course be made public in due season.

Respectfully / Your Obt Servt
Washington Irving

Wm H Seal Esq

MANUSCRIPT: Pierpont Morgan Library.

2164a.   To David Davidson

Sunnyside Nov 10th. 1851

My dear David

My address for the future is DEARMAN *West Chester Cy* where a post office has just been established. Have the Literary World sent there.

I thank you for the extra numbers which you had the kindness to send me lately. The notice of the Alhambra by Mr Duyckinck[1] is written in his own happy and gentlemanlike vein.

Yours very truly
Washington Irving

David Davidson Esq

ADDRESSED: David Davidson Esqr / office of the Literary World / New York
MANUSCRIPT: Ralph M. Aderman.

In the lower left corner of the envelope, in pencil, is written "109 Nassau."

1. Two and one-half columns of *The Literary World* for October 18, 1851 (pp. 307–308) were given over to this notice, mostly a reprinting of "The Story of the Enchanted Soldier."

2165.   To Evert A. and George L. Duyckinck

[November 10, 1851]

To the Editors of the Literary World. / ⟨To the⟩

Gentlemen,

A quotation from Mr Schoolcrafts work in your last number[1] has drawn from me the following note to that gentleman, which I will thank you to insert in your next

Yours very truly
Washington Irving

Novr. 10th. 1851.

MANUSCRIPT: MHS.   PUBLISHED: *The Literary World*, 9 (November 22, 1851), 408; NYEP, November 26, 1851; and *Irvingiana*, p. xvi.

Evert A. Duyckinck (1816–1878) and George L. Duyckinck (1823–1863) were editors of *The Literary World* from 1848 to 1853. They compiled and edited the material for the *Cyclopaedia of American Literature* (1855).

1. See the review of Schoolcraft's *Personal Memoirs of a Residence of Thirty Years With the Indian Tribes on the American Frontiers* in *The Literary World*, 9 (November 8, 1851), 361–62.

2166. To Henry R. Schoolcraft

Sunnyside, Nov. 10, 1851.

Dear Sir—

In your "Personal Memoirs,"[1] recently published, you give a conversation with the late Albert Gallatin, Esq.,[2] in the course of which he made to you the following statement:

"Several years ago John Jacob Astor put into my hands the journal of his traders on the Columbia, desiring me to use it. I put it into the hands of Malte Brun,[3] at Paris, who employed the geographical facts in his work, but paid but little respect to Mr. Astor, whom he regarded merely as a merchant seeking his own profit, and not a discoverer. He had not even sent a man to observe the facts in the natural history. Astor did not like it. He was restive several years, and then gave Washington Irving $5000 to take up the MSS. This is the History of 'Astoria.' "[4]

Now, sir, I beg leave to inform you that this is *not* the History of Astoria. Mr. Gallatin was misinformed as to the part he has assigned me in it. The work was undertaken by me through a real relish of the subject. In the course of visits in early life to Canada, I had seen much of the magnates of the North West Company, and of the hardy trappers and fur-traders in their employ, and had been excited by their stories of adventurous expeditions into the "Indian country." I was sure, therefore, that a narrative, treating of them and their doings, could not fail to be full of stirring interest, and to lay open regions and races of our country as yet but little known. I never asked nor received of Mr. Astor a farthing on account of the work. He paid my nephew, who was then absent practising law in Illinois, for coming on, examining and collating manuscript journals, accounts and other documents, and preparing what lawyers would call a brief, for me. Mr. Fitzgreene Halleck[5] who was with Mr. Astor at the time, determined what the compensation of my nephew ought to be. When the brief was finished, I paid my nephew an additional consideration on my own account, and out of my own purse. It was the compensation paid by Mr. Astor to my nephew which Mr. Gallatin may have heard of, and supposed it was paid to myself; but even in that case the amount, as reported to him, was greatly exaggerated.

Mr. Astor signified a wish to have the work brought out in a superior style, supposing that it was to be done at his expense. I replied that it must be produced in the style of my other works, and at my expense and risk; and that whatever profit I was to derive from it must be from its sale and my bargain with the publishers. This is the true History of "Astoria," as far as I was concerned in it.

During my long intimacy with Mr. Astor, commencing when I was a young man, and ending only with his death, I never came under a pecuniary obligation to him of any kind. At a time of public pressure when, having invested a part of my very moderate means in wild lands, I was straitened and obliged to seek accommodations from monied institutions, he repeatedly urged me to accept loans from him, but I always declined. He was too proverbially rich a man for me to permit the shadow of a pecuniary favor to rest on our intercourse.

The only monied transaction between us was my purchase of a share in a town he was founding at Green Bay;[6] for that I paid cash, though he wished the amount to stand on mortgage. The land fell in value, and some years afterwards, when I was in Spain, Mr. Astor, of his own free will, took back the share from my agent, and repaid the original purchase money. This, I repeat, was the only monied transaction that ever took place between us; and by this I lost four or five years' interest of my investment.

My intimacy with Mr. A. was perfectly independent and disinterested. It was sought originally on his part, and grew up, on mine, out of the friendship he spontaneously manifested for me, and the confidence he seemed to repose in me. It was drawn closer when, in the prosecution of my literary task, I became acquainted from his papers and his confidential conversations, with the scope and power of his mind, and the grandeur of his enterprises. His noble project of the Astor Library, conceived about the same time, and which I was solicitous he should carry into execution during his lifetime, was a still stronger link of intimacy between us.

He was altogether one of the most remarkable men I have ever known: of penetrating sagacity, massive intellect, and possessing elements of greatness of which the busy world around him was little aware: who, like Malte Brun, regarded him "merely as a merchant seeking his own profit."

Very respectfully, / Your friend and servant,
Washington Irving.

PUBLISHED: *The Literary World*, 9 (November 22, 1851), 408; NYEP, November 26, 1851; *Irvingiana*, pp. xvi–xvii; and PMI, III, 87 (in part).

1. Schoolcraft's *Personal Memoirs of a Residence of Thirty Years With the Indian Tribes on the American Frontiers* had recently been published in Philadelphia.

2. Albert Gallatin (1761–1849), who was secretary of the treasury from 1801 to 1814, later served as a diplomat to Russia, Great Britain, and France. Upon his

return to the United States he was president of the National Bank of New York from 1831 to 1839.

3. Conrad Malte-Brun (1775–1826) wrote *Précis de la Géographie Universelle; ou, Description de Toutes les Parties du Monde sur un Plan Nouveau*, 5 vols. (Paris, 1810–1817).

4. This paragraph was quoted in *The Literary World*, 9 (November 8, 1851), 362.

5. Fitz-Greene Halleck (1790–1867), known for his Croaker satires on New York celebrities in 1819, had served as John Jacob Astor's private secretary until the latter's death in 1848.

6. WI had invested $4,000 in land in Green Bay, Wisconsin Territory in 1836. See WI to Peter Irving, February 16, 1836.

2167.   To [Henry Grinnell?]

[New York, November 14?, 1851]

At a meeting of Friends of the late J. Fenimore Cooper, (formed for the purpose of creating to his memory a monument, in the City of New York), held at the Astor House, on Thursday evening, November 13, 1851, on motion of Mr. Gulian C. Verplanck,[1] seconded by Mr George Bancroft,[2] it was

Resolved, That Mr Henry Grinnell be requested to act as Treasurer of the Funds to be raised by this committee; and that the President and Secretary of this committee communicate this resolution to Mr Grinnell.

Washington Irving   President

Rufus W. Griswold / Secretary

MANUSCRIPT: Pforzheimer Library.

Only the signature is in WI's handwriting.

Henry Grinnell (1799–1874), a partner in the shipping firm of Grinnell, Minturn & Co. from 1825 to 1849, was interested in exploration and geography. He outfitted two vessels in 1853 to search for the missing arctic explorer, Sir John Franklin.

1. Gulian C. Verplanck (1786–1870) was a well-known lawyer, politician, orator, and writer of New York City.

2. George Bancroft (1800–1891) was a historian and diplomat who wrote a ten-volume *History of the United States* between 1834 and 1874.

2168.   *To the Editors of New York Tribune*

[Sunnyside, November 16, 1851]

Editors of the Tribune

Gentlemen,

Please address your paper to me in future at DEARMAN *West Chester Cy.* where a post office has just been established

Respectfully / Your Obt Servt
Washington Irving

Sunnyside ⟨Dec⟩ Nov 16t. 1851

MANUSCRIPT: Va.–Barrett.

Horace Greeley (1811–1872) and Charles A. Dana (1819–1897) were editors of the New York *Tribune* at this time. See Frank Luther Mott, *American Journalism*, 3d ed. (New York, 1962), pp. 267–70.

2169.   *To Sir Robert Harry Inglis*

New York, Nov 20th 1851

My dear Sir Robert,

Permit me to recommend to your civilities my intelligent and estimable friend Thurlow Weed Esqr.[1] who will make a short visit to your metropolis in the course of a brief tour of curiosity in Europe. Any attentions and facilities you may find it convenient to bestow upon him will add to the many favors and kindnesses for which I am your debtor,

With kindest remembrances to Lady Inglis

I remain my dear Sir Robert / Ever most truly & affectionately yours
Washington Irving

Sir Robert Harry Inglis Bart / &c &c &c

MANUSCRIPT: Va.–Barrett.

1. Thurlow Weed (1797–1882), a Whig politician and close friend and adviser of William H. Seward, was a New York newspaper editor.

2170.   To John Murray III

New York Novr 20th 1851

My dear Sir

This will be handed to you by my worthy and intelligent friend Thurlow Weed Esqr. who makes a short visit of curiosity to Europe. He of course is desirous of seeing something of the literary world of London and if you can contribute in any Way towards gratifying this desire you will confer on me an especial favor. If Lockhart[1] is in town I wish you would make him acquainted with him.

With kindest remembrances to your family

Yours ever very faithfully
Washington Irving

John Murray Esqr.

MANUSCRIPT: NYPL–Seligman Collection.

1. John G. Lockhart (1794–1854), a well-known British journalist and editor, was the biographer of Sir Walter Scott.

2171.   To Donald G. Mitchell

Sunnyside Nov 15.th 1851

My dear Sir,

Though I have a great disinclination in general to be the object of literary oblations and compliments, yet in the present instance I have enjoyed your writings with such peculiar relish and been so drawn toward the author by the qualities of head and heart evinced in them, that I confess I feel gratified by a dedication, overflattering as I may deem it, which may serve as an outward sign that we are cordially linked together in sympathies and friendship.

I would only suggest that in your dedication you would omit the LL. D.,[1] a learned dignity urged upon me very much "against the stomach of my sense," and to which I have never laid claim.

Ever, my dear Sir, / Yours, very truly,
Washington Irving

Donald G. Mitchell Esq.

MANUSCRIPT: Va.–Barrett (copy).
PUBLISHED: Donald G. Mitchell, *Dream Life*, in *The Works of Donald G. Mitchell*, Edgewood Edition, vol. 2 (New York, 1907), ix–x; PMI, II, 431–32 (in part).

Donald Grant Mitchell (1822–1908), who used the pen name "Ik Marvel," gained popularity as the author of *Reveries of a Bachelor* (1850) and *Dream Life* (1851). WI's letter is in response to his request to dedicate *Dream Life* to him. The precise date is given in PMI, II, 431.

1. WI had received this honorary degree from Oxford University on June 15, 1830. See PMI, II, 430–31.

2172. To Mary Irving

[December 5, 1851]

My dear Mary.

Send me two shirts three white pocket Hkfs and two or three collars as I may be detained in town over Monday. Bubb[1] will bring them down; but take care he does not forget to call at the Cottage for them

Your affectionate Uncle
Washington Irving

⟨Satur⟩ / Friday Evg. Decr. 5th. [1851]

P. S. Pierre tells me in his letter[2] that Helen was to write to you that morning; so I trust your indignation at her silence has been appeased.

I am glad to hear Angeline is home again and hope she brought no cold with her. See that she takes care of herself this cold spell of weather and that she does not go about in the snow.

MANUSCRIPT: SHR.

The year is determined by the perpetual calendar.

1. The nickname of Irving Grinnell (1839–1921), son of Moses Hicks Grinnell and Julia Irving.
2. This letter has not been located.

2173. To Edward Everett

New York Dec 6th. 1851

My dear Sir

Your presence is earnestly desired at the meeting to be held at Trip-ler Hall[1] in this city on the evening of the 24th Decr (christmas eve) to testify respect to the Memory of the late J Fenimore Cooper. Mr Webster I understand has promised to preside[2] and hopes to meet his Boston friends there [.] Mr Bryant will deliver a discourse on the character & writings of the deceased and other addresses of gentlemen of note are promised. I hope and trust you will find it convenient to attend. If you ⟨can⟩ ↑could↓ be of the number ⟨who⟩ to speak on the occasion you would add infinitely to the interest of the evening

Very truly yours
Washington Irving

Hon Edward Everett / &c &c &c

DOCKETED: Washington Irving / Rec'd 10 Dec. 1851 / Ans. do —— / wrote again 20th. MANUSCRIPT: MHS.

1. Tripler Hall, located at 667 Broadway, was a leading concert hall. After it burned early in 1854, a new structure housing the New York Theater and the Metropolitan Opera House was opened on September 18, 1854. See William T. Bonner, *New York: The World's Metropolis* (New York, 1924), p. 191.

2. Because Webster was unable to attend on December 24, the meeting was postponed until February 25, 1852. See *Memorial of James Fenimore Cooper*, p. 13.

2174. To George Ticknor

New York Dec 6th. 1851

My dear Ticknor

You are probably aware of the meeting that is to be held at Tripler Hall in this city on the evening of Decr 24th. of the friends & admirers of the late J Fenimore Cooper; to testify their respect for his memory. Mr Webster I understand is to preside. Bryant is to discourse on the character and writings of the deceased. Others have promised also to speak, though briefly. We want your presence among the distinguished cotemporaries of the deceased. I am desired to urge you to come on, and I am sure I need no prompting to urge you to ⟨any⟩ ↑a↓ meeting where I shall have the great pleasure of taking you by the hand.

Ever yours very truly
Washington Irving

George Ticknor Esqr / &c &c &c

MANUSCRIPT: Dartmouth College Library.

2175. To Daniel Webster

New York Decr. 13th. 1851

My dear Sir,

I am requested to inform you that the meeting at Tripler Hall to pay a tribute of respect to the memory of the late J. Fenimore Cooper, and at which I understand you have kindly promised to preside, will take place on the evening of the twenty fourth of this month (Christmas Eve)

I remain my dear Sir / with high respect and / cordial regard / Yours very truly Washington Irving

The Hon. Daniel Webster / &c &c &c

Manuscript: Yale.

2176. To Rufus W. Griswold

Sunnyside, Dec. 15th 1851

My dear Sir,

I enclose a letter just received from Mr. Webster. A letter[1] from another person says that Mr. Kossuth[2] is in the way of Mr Websters coming on "since it is not well known on what day if on any, he may arrive at Washington and the president desires the presence of Mr Webster in that event. In two or three days Mr Webster can give a *definite* answer."

Yours very truly Washington Irving

The Rev Rufus W Griswold

Manuscript: St. Nicholas Society, New York.

1. This and the letter mentioned in the preceding sentence have not been located.
2. Lajos Kossuth (1802–1894), a leader in the Hungarian revolt against Austria in 1848, served briefly in the independent government. When Austria regained control, he went into exile in Turkey until 1851. During his American visit he urged U.S. support of Hungarian independence.

2177. To William C. Bryant

Sunnyside Decr 20th 1851

My dear Sir,

I must apologize to you for the long delay in furnishing the accompanying article;[1] but really I have been so much occupied, as well as interrupted, of late that I have not had time to attend to it. Beside I knew it was not a subject of the day that pressed. I now send it to you, to do what you please with. There are so many subjects of moment just now crowding upon you that you may find the article too long for present insertion; publish it when you find it convenient or omit it entirely if you think proper. I have done it merely in compliance with the wish you seemed to express, and only regret that I have not at hand some authorities to consult by which I could make it more worthy of publication.

Yours ever very truly
Washington Irving

William C. Bryant Esqr

MANUSCRIPT: NYPL—Goddard-Roslyn Collection.

1. This was an open letter to Bryant which he published in NYEP on December 26, 1851.

2178. To William C. Bryant

[December 20?, 1851]

William C Bryant Esq

My dear Sir,

I[n][1] consequence of the interest expressed by you as to a recent correspondence with Mr Joseph E. Bloomfield of Mexico, N Y.[2] on some points relative to Columbus, I have thrown the purport of my replies to that gentleman into some thing of a connected form.

Mr Bloomfield was desirous of my opinion of a portrait of Columbus existing in the Lonja or Royal Exchange at Seville[3] and which he says was the only one acknowledged in Spain as a true likeness. In reply I have stated that I know of no portrait extant which is positively known to be authentic. The one in question according to his account of it is full length and that of a person from thirty to thirty five years of age, armed in mail and wearing a full white ruff. Now Columbus by the time ⟨of⟩

his discoveries had made him a subject for such a painting was quite advanced in years The ruff, too, was not an article of dress in Spain until after his death. It was a Flemish fashion, brought I believe from Flanders to Spain in the time of Charles V, who did not arrive in the Peninsula until 1516: ten years after the death of Columbus. The portrait may have been one of Diego Columbus,[4] the heir and successor of the discoverer and who, like him, was denominated 'the Admiral.'

Various portraits of Columbus have appeared from time to time in Italy not one resembling the others, and all differing essentially from the description given by Fernando of his father. Theodore de Bry in his AMERICA[5] published in the sixteenth century gave an engraving of one in his possession which he pretended had been stolen from a saloon of the council of the Indias and sold in the Netherlands, where it fell into his hands. The same has been copied in an Eulogium of Columbus by the Marquis of Durazzo, printed by Bodoni[6] and in a life of the discoverer published in Milan by the Chevalier Bossi.[7] This pretended portrait also differs entirely from the graphic description given by Fernando Columbus of his father ⟨s countenance⟩ according to this, ⟨it was⟩ his ⟨fac⟩ visage was long and neither full nor meagre; the cheek bones rather high, his nose aquiline, his eyes light gray, his complexion fair and high colored (acceso di vivo colore) In his youth his hair was blond; but by the time he was thirty years of age it was *quite white*"[8] This minute description I consider the touch stone by which all the pretended portraits of him should be tried. It agrees with accounts given of him by Las Casas[9] and other contemporaries

[Peschiera,[10] a sculptor, employed in Genoa to make a bust of him for a monument erected][11] to his memory in that city in 1821, discarded all existing portraits as either spurious or doubtful and guided himself by the descriptions I have cited.

While I was in Madrid in 1826 Don Martin Fernandez de Navarrete, president of the Royal Academy of History published a lithograph copy of an engraved portrait of Columbus which he found in an old Italian work containing likenesses of distinguished persons.[12] He and the Duke of Veraguas (the descendant of Columbus) placed confidence in ⟨the portrait⟩ ↑it↓ because other portraits in the same work were known to be correct. I doubted its authenticity. It did not agree sufficiently with the description before mentioned, and the hair especially, in the notice which accompanied it in the Italian work, was said to be *black*. Still, I published a copy of the engraving some years since in an abridged edition of my life of the discoverer.

While I was in Paris in 1845 Mons. Jomard, the learned principal of the Royal (now National) Library, had the kindness to send me a lithograph copy of a portrait in oil, recently discovered ⟨,⟩ .[13] ⟨he⟩ The original bore in one corner of the canvas the inscription CHRISTOPORUS COLUM-BUS.[14] The countenance was venerable and dignified and agreed more than any I had seen with the description given by Fernando Columbus. Around the neck, however, was the Flemish Ruff which I pointed out as an anachronism. Mr Jomard endeavored to account for it by supposing the portrait to have been made up toward the year 1530 by some scholar of Titian, from some design or sketch taken during the life time of Columbus, and that the Artist may have decked it out in the costume in vogue at the time he painted it. This is very possible. Such a custom of vamping up new portraits from old ones seems to have been in-dulged in the time of Charles V, when there [were][15] painters of merit about the court.

In 1519 Juan de Borgoña[16] a Spanish artist, executed a whole series of portraits of the primates of Spain for the chapter room of the Cathedral of Toledo; some of them from the life; some from rude originals and some purely imaginary. Some degree of licence of the kind may have been indulged in producing this alleged portrait of Columbus. As it is evidently a work of merit and bears the stamp of his character I have published an engraving of it in one of the editions of his biography.

Painting had not attained much eminence in Spain during the life time of Columbus, though it was improving under the auspices of Ferdinand and Isabella. There were as yet no Italian painters ⟨in Spain⟩ ↑in the peninsula↓; and the only Spanish painter of ⟨eminence⟩ ↑note↓ was Antonio Rincon;[17] who is said to have been the first who "left the stiff Gothic style and attempted to give to his figures some thing of the graces and proportions of nature." He executed portraits of Fer-dinand and Isabella, who made him their painter-in-ordinary.

The originals have disappeared in the war of the French intrusion; but copies of two of his full length portraits of the Sovreigns exist in one of the lower corridors of the Royal gallery of Madrid. It is very probable that he painted a portrait of Columbus at the time when he was at the court, the object of universal attention on account of his dis-coveries, but if so it likewise has disappeared, or may exist anonymously in some corner of Spain or in the collection of some picture hunter.

So much for the portraits of Columbus. Another subject of enquiry with Mr Bloomfield was the name of the discoverer; he asks why we should not call him by the name he signed to all his letters now in the Royal Exchange of Seville, *Christoval Colon*; and he wishes to know "how did or could *Colon* be changed to *Columbus*."[18] So also in a royal cedula of May 12th 1489 signed by the sovereigns, the public functionaries through-out the kingdom are ordered to furnish accommodations and facilities to Cristóbal *Colomo*.

And the Duke of Medina Celi,[19] his first patron in Spain, in a letter to the Grand Cardinal dated 19 March 1493, says, "I do not know whether your Lordship knows that I had for much time in my house Cristóbal *Colomo*; who came from Portugal" &c.

In the capitulations entered into between him and the Sovreigns 17th. April 1492, by which he was constituted Admiral, Viceroy and Governor of any lands he might discover, we find him for the first time recorded as Don Cristóbal *Colon*.[20] In adopting this appellation he may have recurred to what his son Fernando intimates was the original patrician name of the family ⟨at⟩ in old times at Rome, *Colonus*, and may have abbreviated it to Colón, to adapt it to the Spanish tongue.

Columbus was a latin version of his family name adopted occasionally by himself and his brother Bartholomew[21] according to the pedantic usage of the day. His son Fernando says (chap XI) that his father before he was declared Admiral used to sign himself 'Columbus de Terra rubra,' that is to say Columbus of Terra rossa a village or hamlet near Genoa. So also his brother Bartholomew, on a map of the world which he presented to Henry VII dated London 13 Feb. 1488 inscribed on it some latin verses of which the following gave the name and country of the author: Janua cui patria est; nomen cui Bartolomaeus Columbus de Terra rubia opus adidit istud.

By this latin version of his family name he has always been known in English literature. If we change it we ought to go back to the original Italian, Cristoforo Colombo. Long usage, however, like long occupancy constitutes a kind of right, that cannot be disturbed without great inconvenience

Yours my dear Sir, very truly
Washington Irving

MANUSCRIPT: NYSL. PUBLISHED: NYEP, December 26, 1851; *Literary World*, 10 (January 24, 1852), 73–74; and PMI, IV, 93–98.

1. WI omitted the *n*.

2. See WI to Bloomfield, October 28, 1851, and to William C. Bryant, November 1, 1851.

3. This portrait was painted in 1839 by M. Lassalle, using properties supplied by M. Barthelet in Seville. See John Boyd Thacher, *Christopher Columbus, His Life, His Work, His Remains*, III, 78.

4. Diego Columbus (ca. 1480–1526), the only legitimate son of Columbus, won his father's hereditary rights and honors only after a long legal contest with King Ferdinand.

5. This portrait by an unidentified painter was first published in *Collectiones Peregrinationum in Indiam Occidentalem* (1595) by Theodore De Bry (1528–1598), a Flemish engraver. See Thacher, *Columbus*, III, 42.

6. Giacomo, Marquis of Durazzo (1718–1795) brought out *Elogi Storici* in 1781. Giambattista Bodoni (1740–1813) was an Italian painter. See Thacher, *Columbus*, III, 511.

7. Luigi Bossi (1758–1853) was the author of *Vita de Cristoforo Columbo* (1818). See Thacher, *Columbus,* I, 246.

8. WI did not indicate the opening quotation mark.

9. Bartolomé de Las Casas (1474–1566) was a Dominican priest, son of one of the companions of Columbus, and author of a history of the Indies which was not published until 1875–1876.

10. Ignazio Peschiera (1777–1839) carved a bust of Columbus for the municipal building of Genoa.

11. The bracketed passage, which is missing from the manuscript, is taken from the version printed in *Literary World,* 10 (January 24, 1852), 73, and of which WI read proof. See his letter to David Davidson, January 10, 1852.

12. This was the Aliprando Capriolo portrait which WI had mentioned in his letter to Joseph E. Bloomfield, October 28, 1851.

13. WI alluded to this engraved portrait in a note to Catherine Ellis, November 6, 1845.

14. Following this passage, which ends about one third of the way down the holograph sheet, WI's narrative resumes on the lower third of the sheet and fills it with two and one-half sentences, as far as "toward the." The text then continues in the middle third of the sheet to the end of the paragraph. The versions printed in the *Literary World* and in PMI follow this sequence.

15. WI omitted the bracketed word.

16. Juan de Borgoña (d. 1533 or 1534) was one of the painters who restored the Toledo Cathedral.

17. Antonio del Rincón (b. 1466), known for his paintings of religious subjects and of fantastic themes, purportedly painted Columbus from life after his return from the second voyage. The portrait is very similar to the Capriolo engraving and may in fact have been copied from it. See Thacher, *Columbus,* III, 29–31.

18. At this point in the printed version is inserted the following paragraph: "In regard to the name, there is some petty mystery. That of the family in Genoa was *Colombo,* and his original Italian designation was Cristoforo Columbo. When he first came into Spain from Portugal, he seems to have retained his Italian family name, with a slight variation, for in the records of Francisco Gonzalez, of Seville, the royal treasurer, there are still extant three [error for "there"?] several entries of money paid, in 1487 and 1488, by the order of the Catholic sovereigns, to him, by the name of Cristóbal *Colomo.*"

19. Luis de la Cerda, Count of Medina Celi (d. 1501) provided a residence for Columbus from the summer of 1486 until early in 1487. See Thacher, *Columbus,* I, 413.

20. In the text printed in the *Literary World* WI adds the following passage at this point: "[Since the publication of the foregoing article in the *Evening Post* I find, by a document which I had overlooked, that I was mistaken in giving the above as the first time he appears on record by the name of Colon. In a letter written to him by the King of Portugal, dated 20th March, 1488, giving him safe admission into that kingdom, he is addressed as *Cristóbal Colon,* while the super-scription is in Portuguese—'a Cristovam Colon noso especial amigo en Sevilha' (To Cristovam Colon, our especial friend in Seville). This letter is among the historical documents published by Navarrete. The original is in the archives of the Duke of Veraguas. It adds to the perplexity in accounting for this change or modification of the name of the discoverer.]"

21. Bartolomé Columbus (1437–1514 or 1515).

2179. *To Donald G. Mitchell*

Sunnyside Decr 31st 1851

My dear Sir,

Accept my warmest thanks for the copy of the Dream of life which you have had the kindness to send me.[1] I had already procured and read it and it was passing from hand to hand of my domestic circle. Could you witness the effects of the perusal of it upon us all, you would feel satisfied of your success in touching the true chords.

Be assured your little work will remain one of the cherished favorites of our literature, making its way into every American home and securing a niche for its author in every American heart—

Yours ever my dear Sir / very truly
Washington Irving

PUBLISHED: Donald Grant Mitchell, *American Land and Letters*, in *The Works of Donald G. Mitchell*, Edgewood Edition, vol. 14, pp. 233–34 (facsimile reproduction of holograph letter).

1. On November 25, 1851, WI had granted Mitchell permission to dedicate *Dream Life* to him.

2180. *To* ———

Sunnyside, 1851

I really cannot inform you where you would be likely to find a copy of the first edition of Knickerbocker's New York. It has been long out of print.

PUBLISHED: *The Collector*, 15 (October, 1902), 143.

At this point WI was probably more interested in promoting the 1848 revision of *Knickerbocker's History of New York* which was included in his collected works published by Putnam than he was in the 1809 edition.

2181.   To ——

[1851?]

Dear Sir:

I would be happy to furnish you with the "original thought" you require; but it is a coinage of the brain not always at my command, and
certainly not at present. So I hope you will be content with my sincere
thanks in return for the kind and complimentary expressions of your
letter.

PUBLISHED: PMI, IV, 80.

PMI (IV, 80) states that WI wrote this note as "a reply to a modest application from an unknown admirer to 'pen (him) just *one* original *thought.*'"

2182.   To ——

Sunnyside Jany 4t. 1852

My dear Sir,

I return you thanks in advance for the copy of your work which you
offer me, and which I shall value for your sake, as well as for its own
merits. I have provided myself with the numbers as they appeared and
have them constantly by me for perusal and reference. While I have been
delighted by the freshness, freedom and spirit of your narrative and the
graphic ⟨truth⟩ effect of your discriptions I have been gratified at finding how scrupulously attentive you have been to accuracy as to facts,
which is so essential in writings of an historical nature. As I observed on
a former occasion there is a genial spirit throughout your whole work that
wins for you the good will of the reader.

I am surprised to find in how short a time you you[1] have accomplished
your undertaking, considering you have had to travel from Dan to Beer-
sheba; to collect facts and anecdotes, sketch, engrave, write, print and
correct the press—And with all this to have accomplished it in so satisfactory a manner.

I hope you have made a good bargain with your publishers—and that
you retain the copy right, or a permanent interest in the publication,
for I think it a work calculated to make its way into every american
family, high and low, and to be kept at hand for constant thumbing by
old and young.

Believe me my dear Sir / With cordial regard / Yours very truly
Washington Irving

P. S. My address is Dearman, West Chester Cy.

MANUSCRIPT: NYPL—Berg Collection.

1. WI repeated "you."

2183.   To David Davidson

[January 10, 1852]

My dear David,

I am much obliged to Mr Duyckinck for furnishing me a proof of my article on the portrait &c of Columbus. For want of a proof from the Evening Post two or three errors occurred in the printing of it which I have corrected.[1]

We all reciprocate your wishes for a happy New Year and thank you for your kind present of filberts, which I presume are at the Rail road station at Dearman.

Yours very truly
Washington Irving

Sunnyside Jany. 10th. 1852

MANUSCRIPT: Colorado College Library.
The surname of the recipient has been identified from the references to Duyckinck and WI's article on Columbus. See also WI to David Davidson, November 10, 1851.

1. WI's revised essay on the portraits of Columbus (originally a letter published in NYEP, December 26, 1851) was printed in *The Literary World*, 10 (January 24, 1852), 73–74. For details about WI's changes in the text, see WI to W. C. Bryant, December 20, 1851.

2184.   To Sarah Storrow

Sunnyside Jany 13th. 1852.

My dear Sarah,

We have all been quite electrified by the Coup d Etat of our friend Louis Napoleon.[1] It is one of the most complete things of the kind I have ever heard or read of and quite Napoleonic. His uncle[2] could not have done the thing better, in his most vigorous day. Who would have thought "when his gracious majesty took his *disjeune* with us at Tillieludlem" he had so much in him. You are in a fair way of becoming experienced in warfare and seasoned to alarms by your residence in a capital where every political change is a military convulsion. At present you are likely to have a great deal of the pomp and parade of arms, without any more of the ⟨wa⟩ raggamuffin warfare of the barricades, for I trust Louis Napoleon will keep up such a military force in the capital as to ⟨repress⟩ ↑render↓ insurrection hopeless[.] I should not be surprised if there were a long spell of tranquility in Paris under his absolute sway Had his *coup d Etat* been imperfectly effected or his election been but moderately successful France might have been thrown into a terrible turmoil; but now he will hold her down with a strong hand until she has kicked out the last spasm and convulsion of French liberty and is quiet. You will then most probably have all the splendors of the imperial court, with the spectacles and public improvements by which Napoleon used to dazzle ⟨his⟩ the Capital and keep the Parisians in good humor. All this I presume will be more to the taste of temporary residents like yourself than the stern simplicity of republicanism, and a long interval of quiet would be a prosperous interval for the commercial world; so both you and Storrow may find yourselves comfortable under the absolute sway of Napoleon the Second.

It is a pity Van Wart had returned to England before this event took place he lost an opportunity of seeing that grand spectacle Paris in a tumult and under arms; though perhaps he might have had a propensity to go about and see every thing, as I should have done in like case, and have paid for the spectacle by being shot down at a barricade. I never could keep at home when Madrid was in a state of siege and under arms and the troops bivouaking in every street and square, and I had always a strong hankering to get near the gates where the fighting was going on.

We have had a great turmoil and excitement though of a peaceful kind here on the arrival of Kossuth the Hungarian patriot. New York you know is always ready ⟨to⟩ for a paroxysm of enthusiasm on the advent of any great novelty whether a great singer a great dancer, a great novelist or a great patriot, and it is not often ⟨she⟩ ↑it↓ has so worthy an object to run mad about. I have heard and seen Kossuth both in public and private and he is really a noble fellow quite the beau ideal of a poetic hero. There seems to be no base alloy in his nature. All is elevated, generous, intellectual and refined and with his manly and daring spirit there is mingled a tenderness and sensibility of the gentlest kind. He is a kind of man that you would idolize. Yet poor fellow, he has come here under a great mistake and is doomed to be disappointed in the high wrought expectations he had formed of co operation on the part of our Government in the affairs of his unhappy country. Admiration and sympathy he has on abundance from individuals; but there is no romance in councils of state or deliberative assemblies. There cool judgement and cautious policy must restrain and regulate the warm impulses of feeling. I trust we are never to be carried away by the fascinating eloquence of this second Peter the Hermit[3] into schemes of foreign interference that would rival the wild enterprizes of the Crusades.

I scarcely know what news of a domestic nature to give you. We are so severed that it is difficult to carry on the thread of domestic events or to know what of them would amuse or interest you. Scenes and persons fade from the mind ⟨inst⟩ and grow colourless and indistinct with time and distance; especially when one is surrounded, as you are, with the stir and splendor of a brilliant capital. What is poor little Sunnyside when you look back upon it through the glare of Paris!

Yet we have our own share of enjoyments here, and the past year has been a very happy one from the rural home which the Grinnells have established in our vicinity. You can have no idea how it has multiplied our domestic and social pleasures—Our grounds are contiguous; there are no fences no barriers between us; the walks run into each other The consequence is there is a constant outpouring of one house into the other; the children are sporting about our walks and lawns, sometimes with their pet poney and a troop of pet dogs, Helen and Pierre passed the Summer at the Grinnells, we as usual had a house full, so that there was a perpetual jubilee. I never saw any man ride a new ⟨hopp⟩ hobby with such delight as Grinnell does his new country establishment. He never before had a country retreat that belonged to him and was built and laid out by himself, and the difference of interest between such a one and a hired one can scarcely be imagined. It has opened a new source of occupation and enjoyment to him. He is incessantly busy setting out trees, laying out walks or amusing himself on land or water with his children, and he carries perfect sunshine with him wherever he goes. He remained up in the country until the very verge of winter and then went to town with extreme reluctance. He and the children have been up repeatedly since, and the whole family stole away from town and passed New Years day in the country. Mr Minturn[4] has purchased Mr Constants place so that we shall have him and his family for permanent neighbors. It will be a great source of happiness to the children who are very much attached to each other and continually together. Indeed Julias children have a charming circle of little intimates, who I trust will grow up with them in love and kindness and form their circle of friendship throughout life.

I can give you but little of New York news indeed I have not been much there ever since you were last here. I draw more and more into the little world of my country home as the silver cord which binds me to life is gradually loosening; and indeed I am so surrounded here by kind and affectionate hearts and have such frequent visits from one or other of the family that I feel no need and but little inclination to look beyond for enjoyment. Even the opera does not draw me to town so often as formerly although we have had a very excellent one, and New York in ↑fact↓ is inundated with musical talent. When I was last in town I sat next to Mr[s][5] General Jones (Elizabeth Schermerhorn)[6] at a dinner party. She is looking uncommonly well; was in fine spirits and gave me very gratifying accounts of you, your children and your establishment. She seems glad to be at home again though she says she has been very much pleased and gratified by her ⟨las⟩ visit to Europe; I do not think she took as much delight in Paris as most American ladies do. She did not think it on the whole a very desirable residence. Mr Grinnell and Julia were at the dinner party (which was at Mrs Edward Jones the elders)[.] Julia looked uncommonly well and was richly and beautifully dressed in a ↑blue↓ dress I fancy you sent her from Paris though I cannot describe it. Julia is growing much fuller in person than formerly but retains her good looks surprisingly. I wish you could see what a lovely girl her daughter Julia[7] is growing, lovely in character as well as person. She is quite tall of her age Little Fan[8] is a perfect little sprite; full of whim, of talent and fun; she is very inventive and continually devising something to enliven the house. We had repeatedly fancy balls in the country last summer got up impromptu by her and her play mates, when they would come down stairs of an evening rigged out in all kinds of fantastic finery from the rummage of her Mothers ward robe, and would dance to the music of the piano—But how I am rambling from one thing to another—it is time for me to wind up. It is now half past twelve at night and I am sitting here scribbling in my study long after all the family are abed and asleep; a habit I have fallen much into of late. Indeed I never fagged more steadily with my pen than I do at present. I have a long task in hand which I am anxious to finish, that I may have a little liesure in the brief remnant of life that is left to me. However I have a strong presentiment that I shall die in harness, and I am content to do so provided I have the cheerful exercise of intellect to the last

Your brother Irving[9] is asleep up stairs. He came up from town this evening on a visit of business to General Paulding[10] whose law agent he is. He tells me Nancy[11] and the little girl[12] are well. He is well himself, and doing well in a worldly sense; though I do not approve of a pair of mustaches which he has recently cultivated and which make him look rather snuffy about the nose. I shall send this letter to town by him in the morning. And now good night and farewell my dear Sarah. Give my love to the dear little girls of whom I have charming accounts from every

body who sees them Remember me affectionately to Mr Storrow, and
believe me ever—

Most affectionately your uncle
Washington Irving

MANUSCRIPT: Yale.   PUBLISHED: PMI, IV, 99–102 (in part).

1. Charles Louis Napoleon (1808–1873), nephew of Napoleon Bonaparte, had
been elected president of the French Republic in December, 1848. After a struggle
with the Assembly he placed his men in key positions in the government and on
December 2, 1851, seized political power.

2. Napoleon Bonaparte.

3. Peter the Hermit (ca. 1050–ca. 1115) was a French monk who preached in
support of the First Crusade.

4. Robert B. Minturn (1805–1866) was a partner of Moses H. Grinnell in their
shipping firm.

5. WI omitted the bracketed letter.

6. Elizabeth Schermerhorn (1816–1875), daughter of Abraham Schermerhorn,
had married James I. Jones on August 30, 1838. See Robert Schermerhorn, Jr.,
Schermerhorn Genealogy and Family Chronicles (New York, 1914), p. 166.

7. Julia Irving Grinnell (1837–1915) was the oldest child of Moses and Julia
Grinnell.

8. Fanny Leslie (1842–1887) was the third and youngest child of the Grinnells.

9. Irving Paris (1816–1879).

10. William Paulding (1770–1854), a brother of James K. Paulding, lived near
WI in the Tarrytown area.

11. Nancy Gracie Ulshoeffer (1825–1884) had married Irving Paris on November
1, 1848.

12. Mary Ulshoeffer Paris, who was born on August 17, 1849.

2185.   To Frederick Saunders

Sunnyside Jany 14th. 1852

My dear Sir

You ought to have received before this my hearty thanks for the beautiful little volume[1] which you have had the kindness to send me, but it
has just come to hand having been lying for some time in my nephew
Pierre M Irvings office. I have looked through it with mingled melancholy and delight for it brings dear old London before me and all those
familiar haunts in which I have passed so many pleasant hours with
friends now passed away or parted from me by distance perhaps forever.

Your little work is a complete handbook for the literary traveller; and those who like myself are curious about every thing appertaining to old lore old characters and old customs in the venerable metropolis of our literature and language.

Wishing you all possible success in your literary enterprizes I remain very truly

Your obliged friend & Sevt
Washington Irving

P.S. I find newspapers &c still come for me from Mr Putnam addressed to me at the Tarrytown

MANUSCRIPT: NYPL—WI Papers.   PUBLISHED: *Bulletin NYPL*, 36 (April, 1932), 218.

Frederick Saunders (1807–1902), an English-born journalist who worked for a time on NYEP and an advocate of an international copyright, joined the staff of the Astor Library in 1859 and became librarian in 1876.

1. *Memories of the Great Metropolis or London from the Tower to the Crystal Palace* (1852).

2186. To Charles Lanman

Sunnyside Jan 23d. 1852

My dear Sir

I am glad to learn that you intend to publish your narrative and descriptive writings in a collective form.[1] I have read parts of them as they were published separately and the great pleasure derived from the perusal makes me desirous of having the whole in my possession. They carry us into the fastnesses of our mountains the depths of our forests, the ⟨[unrecovered]⟩ watery wilderness of our lakes and rivers giving us pictures of savage life and savage tribes Indian legends, fishing and hunting anecdotes, the adventures of trappers and back wood men; ⟨the⟩ ↑our↓ whole arcanum in short of indigenous poetry and romance; to use a ↑favorite↓ phrase of the old discoverers "they lay open the secrets of the country to us."

I cannot but believe your work will be well received and meet with the wide circulation which it assuredly merits

With best wishes for your success I remain my dear Sir

Yours very truly
Washington Irving

Charles Lanman Esqr

MANUSCRIPT: NYPL—WI Papers.   PUBLISHED: Charles Lanman, *Adventures in the Wilds of the United States and British American Provinces*, 2 vols. (Philadelphia, 1856), I, v.

Charles Lanman (1819–1895), who was born in Monroe, Michigan, traveled extensively in the Great Lakes area and recorded his impressions and observations in a series of books including *A Summer in the Wilderness* (1847), *Letters from the Alleghany Mountains* (1849), and *Haw-ho-noo; or, Records of a Tourist* (1850).

1. Lanman originally published separate essays in journals and periodicals, especially the *National Intelligencer*, and then collected them into book form. WI's statement should not be construed as meaning that Lanman was planning a uniform collected edition of his writings. See Lanman, *Adventures in the Wilds*, I, [iii].

2187.   To Nathaniel Hawthorne

Sunnyside Jany 29th. 1852.

My dear Sir

Accept my most cordial thanks for the little volume[1] you have had the kindness to send me. I prize it as the right hand of fellowship extended to me by one whose friendship I am proud and happy to make; and whose writings I have regarded with admiration as among the very best that have ever issued from the American press.

Hoping that we may have many occasions hereafter of cultivating the friendly intercourse which you have so frankly commenced

I remain with great regard / Your truly obliged
Washington Irving

MANUSCRIPT: Huntington.   PUBLISHED: Julian Hawthorne, *Hawthorne and His Wife*, 2 vols. (Boston & New York, 1891), I, 440; and *Hawthorne at Auction*, ed. C. E. Frazer Clark, Jr. (Detroit, 1972), p. 137 (in part), (*letter misdated as July 29, 1852*).

Nathaniel Hawthorne (1804–1864), who had written many stories and sketches which were collected as *Twice-Told Tales* (1837, 1842) and *Mosses from an Old Manse* (1846), was well into his career as a novelist with the appearance of *The Scarlet Letter* (1850) and *The House of the Seven Gables* (1851).

1. Julian Hawthorne indicates that the book sent to WI was *The House of the Seven Gables*. See *Hawthorne and His Wife*, I, 440. However, Hawthorne, in a letter to WI on July 16, 1852 (Yale), indicates that he had sent *The Wonder Book*.

2188. To James Nack

Sunnyside Jany 29th. 1852

My dear Sir,

I cannot but feel sensible of the peculiar proof you have given me of cordial regard in introducing my name to your family fireside and giving it to the little stranger in the cradle.

When I was a child General Washington laid his hand upon my head and gave me his blessing. That blessing I now transmit to my little name sake and hope it may prove to him, as I sometimes think it has proved to me, a protection through life

ever my dear Sir / Yours very truly
Washington Irving

James Nack Esqr.

MANUSCRIPT: Vassar College Library.

James Nack (1809–1879), who lost his sight and speech in a childhood accident, was a local poet and assistant to the city and county clerk of New York. In 1839 he had sent WI a copy of a collection of his poems. See WI to Nack, August 22, 1839.

2189. To James L. Whitney

Sunnyside Feby. 2d. 1852

James L Whitney Esqr / Corresponding Secretary / of the Irving Literary / Institute.

Dear Sir,

I have the honor to acknowledge the receipt of your letter informing me of my being elected an honora[r]y[1] member of your Institute. I beg you will communicate to the institute my very grateful sense of this mark of consideration and good will.

Yours very respectfully
Washington Irving

MANUSCRIPT: HSP.

James L. Whitney (1835–1910), who was later associated with the Boston Public Library for thirty-five years, was a student at Northampton Collegiate Institute. He entered Yale later in 1852.

1. WI omitted the bracketed letter.

2190. *To Gouverneur Kemble*

Sunnyside Feb 5t. 1852

My dear Kemble,

I have received with much satisfaction the intelligence of a further remittance from the enchanted purse of Godfrey[1] and have drawn upon William[2] for my share.

You talk of having made a jovial tour among the gastronomes of Philadelphia, Baltimore & Washington so it is. Some men may steal a horse with impunity while others are hanged for only looking over a hedge. I did but venture to town about two weeks since to eat a dinner or two when I returned home with an attack of bile and have been confined to the house ever since. I this afternoon, for the first time, ventured out in my sleigh to breathe a little fresh air.

I have not been able to get over to Brooklyn to see your bust; I had intended going when last in town but my indisposition prevented me. I hope the artist has succeeded to your satisfaction.

Address your letters to me at Dearman, where at present there is a post office. I only casually send to the post office at Tarrytown Any time that you will stop on your way to ⟨f⟩ or from town I shall be happy to see you and to give you the best my humble house affords⟨;⟩—not pretending to rival the luxurious aristocrats with whom you have been jollifying

Yours ever my dear Kemble
Washington Irving

Gouvr Kemble Esqr

MANUSCRIPT: HSP.

1. David Godfrey had served as an agent for WI and Kemble to buy Michigan land in 1838. See WI to Kemble, July 28, 1838.
2. Possibly William Irving (1811–1854), WI's nephew.

2191. *To ——*

Sunnyside Feby 5th. 1852

Dear Sir

I feel very much obliged to you for your proposition to submit to me your collection of facts and views connected with the history of the City of New York. I regret to say, however, that the very limited time I can now, through considerations of health, devote to literary occupations, prevent my turning my attention to any other than those on which I am already engaged

very respectfully / Your obliged & hbl Servt
Washington Irving

MANUSCRIPT: Va.–Barrett.

2192.   *To Mary Hamilton*

Sunnyside–Saturday [February 14, 1852]

My dear Miss Hamilton,

I have most reluctantly to give up the pleasure of dining with you today. The state of the weather and the state of my health admonish me to stay at home.

I do not know whether ⟨you⟩ the Servant told you that I called at Nevis on Monday last. I had heard that you came up on saturday, and trusted to find you at home: but I was told I was too late by half an hour The ladies had set off for town on the one oclock train

Yours very truly
Washington Irving

DOCKETED: W. Irving / Feby. 14th. / 1852 / Nevis
MANUSCRIPT: Va.–Barrett.

2193.   *To Joseph G. Cogswell*

Sunnyside Feb 15th. 1852

My dear Cogswell,

You will r[ece]ive [*MS torn*] tomorrow by express a box containing the books which you had the kindness to procure for me from Ticknor and Prescott. Also Piedrahita[1] which I present to the Astor Library.

I wish the two volumes on the Mohammedan Dynasties in Spain to be handsomely bound before they are returned to Mr Prescott. I could not think of sending them back to him in their present condition

I was sorry not to be able to attend the last meeting of Trustees. I hope you had a quorum and that there was an election of a new member of the board in place of Mr Ward and that it was Carson Brevoort.

I trust I sh[all] [*MS torn*] be able to attend the next meeting: though

I have been very much out of order and almost entirely confined to the house for the last three weeks.

Yours very truly
Washington Irving

Jos. G. Cogswell Esq / &c &c &c

Manuscript: Boston Public Library.

1. Probably Lucas Fernández de Piedrahita (1624–1688), *Historia general de las conqvistas de Nvevo Reyno de Granada* (Amberes, [1688]).

2194. To M. D. Phillips

Sunnyside Feb 17th. 1852.

Dear Sir,

I certainly do *not* make Websters Dictionary my Standard of Orthography[1] though I regret to say I often find myself inadvertently falling into ↑some of↓ the vitiations which the industrious circulation of his work has made so prevalent in our country. From the same cause also I find it almost impossible to have a work printed in this country free from some of his ↑arbitrary↓ modifications; which are pronounced provincialisms by all foreign scholars critical in the English language

Respectfully / Your Obt Serv
Washington Irving

Manuscript: NYPL—Berg Collection.

A Dr. Phillips from Henrietta, Monroe County, New York had served in the War of 1812. He was probably related to Daniel Phillips, a Revolutionary War soldier and one of the earliest settlers of Monroe County. See *Landmarks of Monroe County, New York* (Boston, 1895), p. 292.

1. WI had expressed his dislike for Noah Webster's dictionary in a letter to James W. Beekman, June 25, 1851.

2195. To Pierre M. Irving

[Sunnyside, Feb. 19, 1852]

We had a very pleasant dinner. I was much pleased with Leutze.[1] * * * I shall come to town in the beginning of next week—on Monday, if Webster's address to the Historical Society[2] is on that night, though I rather think it is on Tuesday. The Cooper celebration[3] is advertised for Wednesday.

PUBLISHED: PMI, IV, 103.

1. Emanuel Leutze (1816–1868), a German-born historical and portrait painter, gained fame for his *Washington Crossing the Delaware.*

2. Webster spoke to the New-York Historical Society on "The Dignity and Importance of History" on February 23, 1852. For the text of his address see *The Writings and Speeches of Daniel Webster,* 18 vols. (Boston, 1903), XIII, 463–97.

3. The memorial meeting for James Fenimore Cooper, postponed from December 24, 1851, was held on February 25, 1852, in Metropolitan Hall. Daniel Webster presided at the meeting, and William C. Bryant delivered an address on the life, character, and genius of Cooper. See NYEP, February 26, 1852.

2195a.   To David Davidson

Sunnyside March 4th. 1852

My dear David,

I enclose a general letter of reccomendation of the kind you intimate and hope it may answer your purpose. I am glad to hear that you are making your way quietly and surely; which, though at first it may be slowly, is more likely to prove prosperous in the end, than an apparently flourishing business suddenly run⟨s?⟩ up on credit and speculation.

And now we are talking of business I must give you a hint, out of pure interest for your welfare. If you wish to get credit at banks and with sober solid men reform your costume. The last time we met you were so bearded and be hatted that I could scarcely recognize you. Discard all personal excentricity of the kind; it will injure you with the truly considerate and respectable. conform to the fashions prevalent among quiet unassuming people and do not aim at singularity in any thing—*not even in your hand writing.*

With best wishes for your welfare and happiness.

Yours very truly
Washington Irving

MANUSCRIPT: Ralph M. Aderman.

2195b.   To ———

[Sunnyside, March 4, 1852]

A long and intimate acquaintance with Mr David Davidson, commencing in his boyhood and kept up since, has given me an opportunity of knowing his character and conduct; which have always been fair and irreproachable. He is a person in whose integrity and conscientiousness I have always had implicit confidence. He has had many years experience in the kind of business in which he is at present engaged and I believe him to be very capable of conducting it

Washington Irving
Sunnyside, March 4th. 1852

DOCKETED: Recvd. from / Washington Irving Esqr
MANUSCRIPT: Ralph M. Aderman.

This letter, enclosed with WI's letter of March 4, 1852, was apparently retained by Davidson.

2196.   To George L. Duyckinck

Sunnyside, March 15t 1852

My dear Sir

A note from Mr Panton[1] makes me sensible of the unconscionable time I have detained your copy of the Arabian Nights Entertainment. I was on the point of sending it home some time since but was induced to retain it a little longer by being occupied on an Oriental theme. I now return it to you with many thanks for the use of it.

Very truly / Your obliged
Washington Irving

Geo L Duyckinck Esqr.

MANUSCRIPT: NYPL—Duyckinck Papers.

1. Probably Henry Panton, the brother of Mrs. Evert Duyckinck.

2197. To George Bancroft

Sunnyside March 23d 1852

My dear Bancroft,

I have just read your fourth volume[1] with intense interest and the highest satisfaction. To me it surpasses all the others. Your work rises as it proceeds, gaining in unity of subject and in moral grandeur as it approaches the great national theme.

I scrawl this brief and hasty line merely to congratulate you on the successful manner in which you are accomplishing your noble and arduous undertaking. You are securing for yourself what Milton looked forward to achieve by lofty aspirations, meditative thought and patient labor—"an immortality of fame."

Yours ever very truly
Washington Irving

The Hon George Bancroft.

DOCKETED: W. Irving

MANUSCRIPT: MHS.

1. *The History of the United States,* volume 4, had been published a short time before.

2198. To Lewis G. Clark

Sunnyside, April 10th, 1852.

My dear Clark:

Perhaps the following title for your work may pass muster among "Wine and Walnuts," "Pippins and Cheese," and other such after-dinner notions:

KNICK-KNACKS
FROM AN EDITOR'S TABLE.
By L. Gaylord Clark.

It is probable something much better may suggest itself to you, or be suggested by some friend: in which case have no hesitation in discarding the above.

Yours truly,
Washington Irving.

P. S.: Young D. Willard F——,[1] whom you have so kindly noticed in your last, has been passing the winter at the University of Upsala, attending lectures, etc. His intelligence, assiduity in pursuit of knowledge under all kinds of difficulties, and his surprising acquirements for his years, have gained him great favor among the professors and other learned men. He goes to Denmark in May, and embarks at Copenhagen for Iceland, where he intends to pass the summer. His immediate object is to make himself well acquainted with the languages, literature, history, and traditions of the northern nations, their sagas, etc.; and he is in a fair way of accomplishing it.

I cannot but contrast the conduct of this poor youth, bravely struggling forward to intellectual eminence, in defiance of poverty and privation, with that of the host of young Americans, spendthrift sons of wealthy fathers, who are wasting time and opportunity, degrading themselves and disgracing their country, amid the enervating and licentious pleasures of Paris. Which of these may be considered a real specimen of "*Young America?*"

PUBLISHED: *Knickerbocker Magazine*, 55 (February, 1860), 231; and Horatio S. White, *Willard Fiske, Life and Correspondence* (New York, 1925), p. 18 (in part).

1. Daniel Willard Fiske (1831–1904), who studied in Copenhagen and Uppsala from 1850 to 1852, worked for the Astor Library for seven years and eventually went to Cornell, where he served as librarian and taught Northern European languages from 1868 to 1883. He had visited WI at Sunnyside in early June, 1850. See White, *Willard Fiske*, p. 346.

2199. To Robert Balmanno

Sunnyside, Wednesday Evg / April 21t. 1852

My dear Sir,

I have just received your note of the 19th. inst.[1] inviting me to your proposed dinner on Shakespeares birth day.[2] I regret to say that I am not in mood and trim for such a convivial meeting. I returned home yesterday from a weeks visit to New York, and from present symptoms, fear I have provoked the recurrence of the bilious attacks which have dogged me for a year past. I dare not venture on further indulgence for the present.

As to the Presidency of the projected Shakespeare Society; it is an honor for which I must decline being a candidate[.] I have neither tact nor taste for posts of the kind.

I am glad to hear from you so excellent a character of Mr Burton[3] in private life. As an actor I have been greatly pleased with him and have formed a high opinion of his judgement and good taste ⟨in⟩ ↑from↓ the manner in which he conducts his theatre and selects his plays and performers. In the course of my recent visit to town I had quite a treat in attending the performance at his theatre of Shakespeares Twelfth Night.[4] His Sir Toby Belch made me think he might make an excellent Falstaff.[5] I do not know whether he has ever attempted the character; but he seems to possess the shrewd discriminating good sense and the rich, mellow and varied play of humor required for the part. It is a part easily buffooned but difficult to be hit off with truth; as all Shakespeares masterpieces are. The actor who plays Falstaff ought to be a *gentleman*—though a jovial one; and in this respect I should suppose Mr Burton to be well qualified for it.

By the way, I saw at his theatre that evening a very pretty and promising young actress in the part of Viola[6] who acquitted herself with much grace and spirit.

Yours my dear Sir / Very truly
Washington Irving

Robert Balmanno Esqr

DOCKETED: Washington Irving / Sunnyside 21 April 1852
MANUSCRIPT: Va.–Barrett.

1. This note has not been located.
2. Shakespeare was born on April 26, 1564.
3. William Evans Burton (1804–1860), an English actor who first appeared on the American stage in 1834, became manager of a theater on Chambers Street in 1848. He remained there until 1854.
4. *Twelfth Night* opened at Burton's theater on March 29, 1852, and ran for twelve successive nights, plus several other performances later in the season. See Odell, *NY Stage*, VI, 128.
5. Burton first played Falstaff in *The Merry Wives of Windsor* in January, 1858. See Odell, *NY Stage*, VII, 12.
6. Lizzie Weston (Mrs. A. H. Davenport) played the role of Viola. See Odell, *NY Stage*, VI, 129.

2200.   *To Franklin B. Hough*

Sunnyside April 21t 1852

Dear Sir

My reccollections of the tour in the northern counties of New York,[1] to which you allude are too indistinct to furnish the data for your work[2] which you require. Neither can I recall any "incidents or facts" of my journey worthy of record. I regret to add that considerations of health oblige me at present to be as sparing as possible in the exercise of my pen; already overtasked by literary occupations in which I am engaged.

Wishing you all possible success in your meritorious enterprize I remain

Very respectfully / Your Obt Servt
Washington Irving

Franklin B Hough Esqr A. M.

Manuscript: SHR.

Franklin B. Hough (1822–1885), a physician living in Somerville, New York, was interested in local history and in collecting and editing documents of the Revolutionary and Indian wars.

1. WI made this tour in the summer of 1803. For details see *J&N*, I, 3–30.
2. At this time Hough was preparing a *History of St. Lawrence and Franklin Counties, New York,* which was published in 1853.

2201. *To William W. Waldron*

Sunnyside, April 22d, 1852

Dear Sir:

It will give me pleasure to see you at Sunnyside, at any time it may be your convenience to favor me with a call.

Yours very respectfully,
Washington Irving

William W. Waldron, Esq.

Published: Waldron, *WI & Cotemporaries,* p. 244.

2202. *To Lewis G. Clark*

[April, 1852]

My dear Clark

I am glad the title I sent suits you.

You are welcome to make what ⟨y⟩ use you please of that part of my note which relates to Young Fiske[.] I observe what you have already inserted in your Magazine respecting him has given great satisfaction to his friends in Syracuse and been republished in the ↑"Syracuse↓ Journal." By that paper it appears that his visit to Iceland the coming summer is for the purpose of studying the ancient and original language of the people of that island. It forms a part of his general enterprize which appears to me a very noble, spirited and comprehensive one.

Yours truly
Washington Irving

L Gaylord Clark Esqr

MANUSCRIPT: NYHS.

The date has been determined from WI's reference to the title, which is probably the one he suggested in his letter to Clark on April 10, 1852. WI's mention of Fiske suggests that it is the omitted surname in the April 10 letter.

2203. *To Thomas W. Storrow, Sr.*

Sunnyside Thursday [May 13?, 1852]

My dear Storrow,

I have barely had time to read through your Manuscript[1] having had to go to town yesterday & return this morning. Had I had more time I should have taken the liberty ⟨of shaking out⟩ occasionally ↑of shaking↓ some superfluous words out of the sentences, which weaken them. I have been much interested by it; Some of the facts in it are quite new to me; especially that part of his heroic undertaking among the Savage tribes in the neighborhood of Guatemala.

I think it will be appreciated by the public. Your idea of the character of Las Casas is, I think, just, and is well discriminated. I scrawl this in haste having to go to a vestry meeting

Yours truly
Washington Irving

P S. I wish when you have a literary project in hand, or are in any way inclined for a literary lounge, you would come and take up your quarters with me. We would all make you quite at home and be delighted to have you; And you could have any books you want sent up to you from New York. Think of it—and *do it*. My girls consider you a kind of uncle and feel towards you as if you were one—and I know no one who would more completely suit me for an inmate

ADDRESSED: T W Storrow Esqr   DOCKETED: Ansd May 19 [*in pencil*] / May / '52
MANUSCRIPT: Harvard.

1. From WI's comments later in the letter it would seem that Storrow's essay relates to Bartolomé de Las Casas, a planter and missionary in the New World in the early sixteenth century.

2204. To Henry R. Schoolcraft

Sunnyside May 27th. 1852.

My dear Sir,

Accept my most grateful thanks for the second volume of your splendid and valuable work on the Indian Tribes.[1] It is indeed a most fortunate and gratifying circumstance that Government has enabled you to prosecute and illustrate your researches and disquisitions in so thorough a manner. Your work will absolutely be a national monument.

I took the liberty sometime since of addressing you through the public papers[2] in regard to an erroneous statement you had made, on the authority of Mr Gallatin, of the terms on which I had undertaken to write the account of Mr Astors Oregon Enterprize You may have thought I ought to have addressed this letter to you privately; but in fact I was glad to avail myself of the opportunity which the statement gave me of setting the public right as to ↑the↓ circumstances and conditions under which that work was undertaken and published and as to the whole of my intercourse with Mr Astor; about which I found there had been much misapprehension. I, therefore, consider that the error in which both Mr Gallatin and yourself were betrayed in the matter, was eventually a real service to me.

With best wishes, my dear Sir, for continued success in your distinguished and meritorious career I remain, very faithfully

Your obliged friend & Servt
Washington Irving

Henry R Schoolcraft L L D / &c &c &c

MANUSCRIPT: LC.

1. *Information Respecting the History, Condition and Prospects of the Indian Tribes of the United States*, 6 vols. (1851–1857).

2. See WI's letter of November 10, 1851, which appeared in *The Literary World*, 9 (November 22, 1851), 408, and in NYEP, November 26, 1851.

2205. *To Sarah Storrow*

Sunnyside. May 29t. 1852

My dear Sarah,

Your husbands recent arrival came near being a surprise[1] to me, as I had only heard a day or two previously that he had the intention of coming. It is always somewhat of a disappointment to see him come out alone; yet we cannot expect he should bring his whole family with him each time he crosses the ocean. In fact, I am endeavoring to recconcile myself to the separation which I percieve is inevitable,—but it is one of the sorest I have ever experienced.

We have had Mr Storrow *pere* passing a day or two with us lately to our great delight. I have urged him to come to the Cottage whenever he has an inclination for literary research or a literary lounge—& he shall have all the books at his command that my little library and the libraries of New York can furnish; perfect quiet and ⟨self command⟩ the disposal of himself and his time according to his humors, and a household that will rejoice to have him as an inmate. I hope to coax him out of a longer visit another time. I know of no one who more completely suits me as a household companion. I am glad to find he ⟨f⟩ occupies himself so much among books and with his pen. He does it, also, in so agreeable a manner both to others and to himself. He has written various articles for the periodicals full of good sense and often with a pleasant vein of humor. In many respects he reminds me of my dear brother Peter; he has his happy art of extracting amusement from passing scenes and objects and the same disposition to look on every thing with an indulgent and good natured eye He is a great favorite at the Cottage. The girls all look on him as a Kind of uncle and are disposed to act toward him like nieces. I wish New York was his fixed residence—I should then see a great deal of him.

Charlotte is on a visit to us with her husband and her two children; who are really two fine little fellows; very good looking and very good natured. The youngest is yet a babe in arms—but a bright, pleasant faced, happy little being[.] Charlotte herself, is thin, and a very small mother for two chubby children.

Mary has been in delicate health for some time past, but is improving. I think I shall take her to the sea side this Summer and try the effect of sea breezes and sea bathing. The Grinnells are projecting an excursion in July to Lake George Lake Champlain and Canada, down to Quebec; and I have promised to accompany them. It is probable Pierre. M. and Helen will be of the party—we shall be absent about twelve days. I wish to visit some of the scenes noted in our Revolutionary history.

My life of Washington lags and drags latterly. I have repeatedly been interrupted by turns of ill health—bilious attacks—Which have dogged me for the last two or three years, and obliged me occasionally to throw by the pen and take to horse back. This spring I have been almost entirely idle; from my mind's absolutely refusing to be put in harness. I no longer dare task it as I used to do. When a man is in his seventieth year it is time to be cautious. I ⟨hav⟩ thought I should have been through this special undertaking by this time; but an ⟨unlo⟩ unexpected turn of bilious fever in Mid winter put me all aback—and now I have renounced all further pressing myself in the matter.

I received the ⟨two letters⟩ ↑letter &c↓ written to yourself which you enclosed to me—and which I was for a long time at a loss to assign to the right author—the signature being an illegible scrawl. I at length made out that it must be General Stuart of Baltimore,[2] & as I reccollected you had mentioned your being acquainted with him. The General is a very good fellow and a little of the queer fish; as I suppose you have found out. Full of nods and hints and suggestions and whisperings in the ear; and deeply concerned in matters of state and military operations. I trust he has made himself acceptable at the Court of Louis Napoleon.

By the way I am glad to find the Prince President is getting on so quietly and that the 10th of May has passed off without explosion. I hope Paris may be spared for a time all further paroxysms either imperial or republican, and that the schemes set on foot for its improvement and embellishment may be carried out before every thing is again thrown into chaos; not that I expect ever to enjoy the result of them; but it is a city associated with too many happy scenes of my life not to be endeared to me; and, though I may never see it again, I carry so familiar a picture ⟨of⟩ in my mind of all its localities, that I can fancy to myself every new modification that I read of. If Louis Napoleon continues in power he will make Paris the centre of every thing splendid and delightful and will treat its féte loving inhabitants to continual spectacle and pageant. He seems to understand the tastes and humors of the Parisians.

The Grinnell family moved up to the country bag and baggage last week and happy are they all to get out of the dust and turmoil of the city into this beautiful region. Within the last two or three weeks the spring, after being so long retarded, has broke forth in all its beauty[.] I never saw a more lovely season; or one that promised greater abundance. You know perhaps that Mr Grinnell bought some additional ground and built a very handsome house a little to the north of his own, for the Holdredges.[3] The two places, with the grounds belonging to them are already brought into order; a great many trees and shrubs set out; with carriage roads, foot paths &c and as their walks communicate with ours the whole three establishments make an extensive and beautiful domain; and afford fine rambles and continual intervisiting.

Julia Grinnell shewed me a letter which you had written to her. I was glad you had done so, for she had complained to me that you had not replied to two letters you must have received from her. Dont be so remiss again—and when you do write—do not leave it to the last moment and then hurry off a letter as if you were despatching an irksome task—but take time to write as if you felt an interest in what you were doing—This is not meant to refer to the letter just mentioned—but to other letters which you now and then squib off *at the last moment*—a very bad moment for letter writing.

Your letter to Julia gives good accounts of your young folks. I am glad to hear that my dear little Kate is such a great reader and that Susan shews such a talent for drawing and Music as to little Gaga she of course will "beat all creation."

Your husband came up with Mr Grinnell this afternoon, (Saturday) to stay until Monday. He has been passing the evening with us. He is looking uncommonly well and is in excellent spirits, having accomplished his business arrangements to his satisfaction He read me a part of a letter just received from you, giving an account of your going with the children and Henriette,[4] to see Louis Napoleon pass by with his splendid cortege on his way to the grand review. It must have been a brilliant pageant, and the Arab part of it must have given it great novelty and interest. We have had a long delightful chat about Paris, Louis Napoleon, yourself and your children[.] I should have liked to have been with Kate on her first visit to the opera. You know I used to *assist* at the first musical entertainments she enjoyed—when the man played the hand organ under the windows on Sunday mornings and she used to throw coppers to him—But it is getting late and I must to bed—so good night and farewell with love to all the young folk.

Your affectionate Uncle
Washington Irving

ADDRESSED: Madame / Madame Storrow /chez Mons T. W. Storrow / Rue du Faubg Poissonniere / à Paris.
MANUSCRIPT: Yale.   PUBLISHED: PMI, IV, 105–6.

1. WI wrote "sarprise."
2. General Stuart of Baltimore has not been identified.
3. Probably the family of Henry Holdredge, whose home was located north of the mansion of Moses Grinnell. Mrs. Holdredge was Grinnell's niece. See Scharf, *Westchester County*, II, 240, 242.
4. The nurse of the Storrow children.

2206. To Henry Ogden

· Sunnyside June 16t. 1852

My dear Ogden

I enclose a letter which I will thank you to forward to your brother.[1] I have really become very much interested by the perusal of his manuscript. Some of the scenes it presents are very singular and novel—such for instance as that of the Indian causing himself to be buried alive! All the scenes and anecdotes bear the stamp of truth, and as such would be highly valued, especially by those given to ethnological studies, which are very much the vogue at present. What the writings want are style and handling—such as are given by a practised hand.

If I had had these scenes and anecdotes at my command at a former day when I was executing works, on frontier and savage life I should have considered them invaluable.

I think your brother had better try the plan I propose; publish an article from time to time in some periodical work. If his articles are well received he can then bring them out collectively with additions &c.

I will take an early opportunity of returning the Manuscript to you; or rather of sending it to the offices of my nephew Pierre M Irving, Bank of Commerce, where you will find it—

Your ever very truly
Washington Irving

Henry Ogden Esqr

P. S. I shall send the MS. to my nephews at the same time that I send this letter to town.

ADDRESSED: Henry Ogden Esqr
MANUSCRIPT: Va.–Barrett.

Henry Ogden was an old friend of WI and one of the "Lads of Kilkenny," known as "Supercargo." See STW, I, 398.

1. Peter Skene Ogden (1794–1854) was the chief factor of the Hudson's Bay Company in British Columbia and Washington from 1835 to 1854. He wrote *Traits of American-Indian Life and Character*, which was published anonymously in London in 1853. See William Wheeler Ogden, *The Ogden Family in America* (Philadelphia, 1907), pp. 102–3.

2207.   To [William J. Lewis]

[July 5, 1852]

Dear Sir,

The Quod Correspondence was written by my nephew, Mr John Treat Irving.[1] I had no part in it.

Respectfully Your Ob Servt
Washington Irving

Sunnyside July 5th. 1852

MANUSCRIPT: SHR.

William J. Lewis is listed as the addressee in the SHR catalog.

1. John Treat Irving, Jr. (1812–1906) brought out *The Quod Correspondence; or, The Attorney* in 1842 under the pseudonym of John Quod. The book was published in two volumes by Otis, Broaders and Company of Boston.

2208.   To Thomas W. Storrow, Sr.

Sunnyside July 7th. 1852

My dear Storrow

I ought long before this to have acknowledged the pleasure I received from the perusal of your papers upon the history and character of the cat.[1] They are written in a delightful vein of quiet humor and serio comic philosophy and successfully vindicate the cause of a "down trodden" people for whom I have always entertained great kindness. If the cats have a proper feeling of gratitude they ought to give you a nightly Serenade—You are fully as deserving of ⟨it⟩ ↑one↓ as Jenny Lind or the great Kossuth himself—

My womenkind are all well and will be happy to welcome you to Sunnyside whenever you are di[s]posed[2] to pay it a visit.

About a week hence I set off on an excursion with the Grinnells to be absent eight or ten days, after which I shall remain quietly at home where I shall be always rejoiced to see you

Yours ever very truly
Washington Irving

DOCKETED: July 8
MANUSCRIPT: Harvard.

1. A series of five articles entitled "The Birth and Parentage of the Cat" by Felinus appeared in *To-Day*, 1 (March 6, 13, 20, 27, April 10, 1852), 146–47, 164–66, 180–82, 206–8, 235–39.

2. WI omitted the bracketed letter.

2209. To William C. Preston

Sunnyside, July 13th. 1852

My dear Preston,

Your letter of March 31st.[1] has remained a shameful time unanswered, but I am an incorrigible laggard in letter writing, or rather the claims on my pen are so incessant that I find it impossible to avoid falling behind hand on my correspondence. In the present instance I was less pressed to reply inasmuch as my publisher Mr Putnam informed me he had received a letter from you on the same subject, enquiring after the most correct edition of my works, and had attended to it.

Your letter adverts to the early times of our intimacy and in so doing calls up a thousand delightful reccollections Our ramble, for instance, about the borders of Wales in company with my my[2] worthy brother. Do you remember our loiterings about the valley of Llangollen and how much we made ourselves at home in the ample farm house of old "Jones of the Brin."[3] Calling for his best cheese and ale; mounting his horses to ride to Chirk Castle and back, with his man to attend upon us; all in the firm persuasion that we were in a kind of inn, and were to pay roundly for our entertainment—and how we were astonished ↑on parting↓ when the fine old fellow said he should feel offended if we spoke of such a thing.

Do you reccollect also our rambles in Scotland,[4] our adventures on Loch Katrine where you swam across from the ladys island in emulation of the feat of James Fitz James; our tramp with the young Campbells across to Loch Lomond in the course of which they were continually sounding their bugle; our climbing Ben Lomond with them, and our hunting a Macgregor (our guide) down the mountain, to the tune of "the Campbells are coming"

Do you reccollect our pilgrimage to Burns cottage and the Banks of Bonnie Doune; and Kirk Alloway, where we found a man at work on the old church who had known Tam O'Shanter.

Do you reccollect our pleasant scenes at Mrs Craigs in Forth Street where you had poor Lagaré[5] for a house mate, who used to play snake at his window ogling and 'charming' a bevy of sewing girls in an opposite house?

And do you reccollect when you billetted your limbs about a box in one of the minor theatres and came near throwing a Cockney into the pit because he presumed to move one of your legs without asking your consent?

These are all very foolish questions for an old gentleman like myself to ask one of your gravity and standing—but I cannot help it, they crowd upon me as I write, and if I do not stop I shall fill pages with these whimsical reccollections.

You say you have always hoped to see from my pen some account of our old friend Ogilvie,[6] that philosophical oratorical Quixote. I did once begin a tale in which he was to bear a prominent part, and wrote several chapters, but laid it aside and never continued it. I presume you know the tragical end of the poor fellow, who committed suicide at Perth, at a time when an ample legacy had put him at perfect ease in pecuniary matters; and enabled him to indulge the benevolent impulses of his nature.

I am grieved to find your retirement to the country is on account of bad health; but hope that rural quiet and rural occupations may have the same salutary effect upon you that they have upon me. I reccollect meeting you at New York, when I was busy erecting my little country retreat and you warned me to take care that I did not outbuild my means, as poor Scott did at Abbotsford. I never did a more fortunate thing in my life. It completely anchored me and secured for me a delightful home where I have passed one of the tranquillest and happiest portions of my life and where I hope quietly to pass the little that can now remain to me. When I look back upon my past wanderings and and[7] round upon my tranquil little nestling place I am reminded of the verses which Gil Blas thought of putting over the door of his house.

> Inveni portum! Spes et fortuna valete!
> Sat me lusistis, ludite munc alios.[8]

Ever my dear Preston / Yours very truly
Washington Irving

Wm C. Preston Esqr

Docketed: W Irvine—

Manuscript: South Caroliniana Library, University of South Carolina.   Published: *American Literature*, 19 (November, 1947), 256–59.

William C. Preston (1794–1860) of South Carolina was WI's traveling companion in Great Britain in 1817. He served in the U.S. Senate from 1833 to 1842 and became president of South Carolina College in 1845.

1. This letter has not been located.
2. WI repeated "my."

3. Preston also had vivid memories of Jones and the excursion into Wales. See Minnie C. Yarborough, "Rambles with WI: Quotations from an Unpublished Autobiography of William C. Preston," *South Atlantic Quarterly,* 29 (November, 1930), 430–32.

4. WI and Preston began their tour of the Scottish Highlands on September 6, 1817. On part of their trip they traced the route in Scott's *The Lady of the Lake,* and Preston, like James Fitz-James and Malcolm Graeme, swam to the island. In his memoirs Preston describes other incidents from the tour. See "Rambles with WI," pp. 436–37.

5. Hugh S. Legaré, who had served as secretary of state when WI was minister to Spain, had died in 1843. The incidents at Mrs. Craig's took place in 1818, nearly a year after their visit to Scotland. See "Biographical Notice" in *Writings of Hugh Swinton Legaré,* ed. [Mrs. Mary Swinton Legaré Bullen] (Charleston, 1846), I, xxxix–l.

6. James Ogilvie (1774–1820), an English teacher of rhetoric and oratory whom WI first met at Aaron Burr's trial in Richmond in 1807. Since WI had met Ogilvie in London shortly before departing for Scotland in August, 1817, he probably remembered him in connection with Preston and the tour of Scotland. See WI to Henry Brevoort, May 11, 1809, and August 28, 1817.

7. WI inadvertently repeated "and" at the beginning of a new line.

8. "I have arrived at the gate. Farewell, hope and fortune– You have deceived me enough. Now deceive others." See Alain René LeSage, *Histoire de Gil Blas de Santillane* (Geneva, 1970), II, 148.

2210. To Edward Everett

Sunnyside July 14th 1852

My dear Sir

I should have thanked you before this for the number of "To day" containing your historical notice of the line in Goldsmiths Traveller;[1] but you had piqued my curiosity so much in the matter that I wished first to ascertain whether a copy of the Respublica Hungarica,[2] or of the Geographie Curieuse[3] were in the Astor Library; or Nicolas Isthvanfios History of Hungary,[4] from which Moveri draws his facts. I had not time, however, to make the research when I was in town, and I am now on the point of setting off on an excursion elsewhere; so I must defer it. I am satisfied however you have set the matter in a right light; and that Goldsmith has placed the Iron Crown on a wrong head, and his commentators have given a wrong name to the Dosa family.[5]

You observe that in my life of Goldsmith I have adopted Boswell's statement as to the name of the individual crowned.[6] I think you will find you are mistaken and that I have not alluded to the subject in my biography. That work, however, was written so ⟨s⟩ rapidly, with the printers devil at my heels that I should not be surprised if many errors were detected in it. I had no time to refer to authorities that were not immediately at hand.

Ever my dear Sir / With great regard / Yours very truly
Washington Irving

Edward Everett Esqr / &c &c &c

DOCKETED: Washington Irving / Rec'd 17 July 1852.
MANUSCRIPT: MHS.

1. See *To-Day, A Boston Literary Journal*, 1 (May 29, 1852), 361, where Everett explains that Samuel Johnson actually furnished the lines, "How small, of all that human hearts endure, / The part that laws or kings can cause or cure," for Oliver Goldsmith's *The Traveller*. For Boswell's discussion of Johnson's contribution to the poem, see *Boswell's Life of Johnson*, ed. G. B. Hill, 6 vols. (Oxford, 1934), II, 5–7.

2. *Respublica et Status Regni Hungariae. Ex Officina Elzeviriana* (1634), the source which Boswell used. See *Boswell's Life of Johnson*, II, 7.

3. A source mentioned in Granger's *Biographical History*, which, in turn, is cited by John Forster in *The Life and Times of Oliver Goldsmith*, 2 vols. (London, 1854), I, 395. WI consulted Forster when he revised his biography of Goldsmith.

4. Nicolas Isthvanfi, *Historiarum de rebus Ungaricis libri XXXIV* (1622).

5. For a discussion of this confusion, see *Boswell's Life of Johnson*, II, 7.

6. See *Boswell's Life of Johnson*, II, 7.

2211. *To Catharine Storrow*

Sunnyside, July 15, 1852

My dear Kate:

I thank you for your charming little letter.[1] It is very well expressed and very nicely written, and, what pleases me most of all, it is written to me. You must have had a pleasant time at Compiegne with such an agreeable party. I recollect the place well,[2] and the beautiful palace, with the pretty boudoir which you all liked so much because there was a glass there in which you saw yourselves four times. I did not notice that glass, and therefore was not so much struck with the boudoir. I recollect Pierrefond[3] also, and was all over the ruins and the surrounding forest, which put me in mind of what I had read about old castles in fairy tales. If I could only have seen you driving through the forest in your open carriage with four white horses, I should have thought you one of the enchanted princesses. You should take care how you venture out of your carriage in such a place to gather lilies of the valley and other wild flowers. Don't you know what happened once to a young lady (I think her name was Proserpine), who was carried off by a wicked king in sight of her mamma, as she was gathering flowers in the same way you were? Your mamma will tell you the story, if you have not heard it.

You say you would like to live at Compiegne always, it is so pretty, and you passed your time so pleasantly in the park, "sitting on the grass, making beautiful wreaths of buttercups and daisies." I think one might pass one's life very pleasantly and profitably in that manner. I recollect trying my hand at buttercups and daisies once, and finding it very agreeable, though I have got out of the way of it of late years, excepting that Dick, my horse, now and then cuts daisies with me when I am on his back; but that's to please himself, not me.

To-morrow I am going to set out on a journey with a large party, including your cousins Julia, Fanny, and Irving Grinnell. We shall see no castles, but will voyage on great lakes and rivers, and through wild forests. I wish you were going with us, but I suppose I must wish in vain; that must be for some future day. And now, my dear Kate, give my love to Susie and Julie, and my kind remembrances to Henriette.

Your affectionate uncle,
Washington Irving

Published: PMI, IV, 27–29.

1. This letter has not been located.
2. WI had visited Compiègne, about fifty miles northeast of Paris, with the Storrows, Peter Irving, and Gilbert Stuart Newton on September 2–4, 1825. See J&N, III, 514–15.
3. In the village of Pierrefonds, about ten miles from Compiègne, are the ruins of a fourteenth-century castle. See J&N, III, 514–15.

2212. To Sarah Storrow

Sunnyside, July 15th 1852

My dear Sarah,

I write a hasty line in the midst of preparations for an excursion. Tomorrow, Mr Grinnell, Julia and the young folks, with Susan Grinnell, Pierre M. Irving and Helen set off on a tour to Canada, and some of them to the White mountains. I shall accompany them to Saratoga, Lake George and Lake Champlain but think it probable I shall then return to the Springs and take the Saratoga waters. It is a hot time of the season for such an excursion and, therefore, I am dubious of following it out; but Mr Grinnell could not conveniently time it better. I do not feel the same disposition to travel as I did in younger days; the quiet of home is becoming more and more delightful to me and I find it difficult to tear myself away from it, even for a short absence. But I am sensible even too much quietude is to be resisted; a man as he grows old must take care not to grow rusty or fusty or crusty—an old bachelor especially. And for that reason it is good for him now and then to dislodge ↑himself↓ from the chimney corner. In this hot summer weather, however how delicious it is to loll in the shade of the trees I have planted and feel the sweet southern breeze stealing up the green banks, and look out with half dreaming eye on the beautiful scenery of the Hudson and build castles in the ⟨air⟩ clouds, as I used to do, hereabouts, in my boyhood.

"Oh. bless'd retirement! friend to life's decline"[1]

how fortunate has been my lot in being able so completely to enjoy it, so completely to realize what was once the mere picturing of my fancy— I wish you could see little Sunnyside this season, I think it more beautiful than ever. The trees and shrubs and clambering vines are uncommonly luxuriant. We never had so many singing birds about the place and the humming birds are about the windows continually after the flowers of the honey suckles and trumpet creepers which overhang them.

You speak of your excursion to Compiegne and the old Chateau of Pierrefonds. I made a delightful excursion there once, in company with Mr & Mrs Storrow, Susan, ⟨Minnie⟩ ↑Louisa.↓ and Sam, and your dear Uncle Peter. I had been told by an English lady of the beauty of the forest scenery and of the fine old ruin of Pierrefonds. ⟨and suggested the expedition⟩ It was one of the sweetest excursions I ever made. of all our happy party, some of them so young too, Mr Storrow and myself are the only survivors!

I received a letter some short time since from our amiable and half Spanish friend Mrs de Wolff—whom you must reccollect, having an appartment in the Rue de la Paix, when Juliet McLane[2] was in Paris, and afterwards making a visit to the M[c]Lanes in London. She informed me that she was about to embark at NYork, on a visit to the South of Europe for her health; and was desirous to see me before she sailed, and to know whether you were with me. I met her by appointment in New York and found her as amiable and interesting as ever. One of her brothers, about twenty two years of age travels with her—She has also her little son about five years of age and the same faithful old black nurse who was with her in Paris and who has been with her since her childhood. She sails this day in the Steamer for Liverpool. I have given her your address in Paris and told her to let you know of her arrival. I went twice to town to see her; which is a great stretch of gallantry for an old gentleman of seventy—and in the dog days!

I have not seen the Newbolds and Rhinelanders since their return— In fact I scarcely see any one out of the family, as I rarely go to town except on business and then but to remain a part of a day. I shall endeavor to see them however after my return from my excursion.

I must now conclude, as I have but little time to spare and wish to reply to my dear Kates letter,[3] which has perfectly delighted me. You must reccollect Mr Westons schoolboys who attend church at Tarrytown —and always look like little gentleman. One of them strikes us all as resembling Kate—I need not say he is a nice looking little fellow and one who finds great favor in our eyes. I mean to cultivate his acquaintance.

And now farewell my dear Sarah give my kind remembrances to your husband

> Your affectionate uncle
> Washington Irving

P.S. Your letter addressed to me simply at New York, would come safe to hand.

MANUSCRIPT: Yale.   PUBLISHED: PMI, IV, 106–7.

1. Oliver Goldsmith, "The Deserted Village," line 97.
2. Juliette McLane (b. December 21, 1824) was the eighth child of Louis and Catherine McLane.
3. This letter has not been located.

2213.   *To Catharine Irving*

Saratoga Springs July 17th. 1852

My dear **Kate**,

We had glorious hurry scurry drive along the rail road: left Steam boats behind as if they had been at anchor A flight of wild pigeons tried to keep up with us, but gave up in despair. We arrived here between eleven and twelve. The weather was pleasant, and there was but little dust. We all enjoyed the journey excepting Julia Grinnell, who having fatigued herself the day before by packing—and the night before by not sleeping—had to keep her room on ar[r]iving[1] with a severe headache— She is her self again, however, this morning.

I have found some old friends here—Mr & Mrs Kennedy[2] of Baltimore— Mr Stevens[3]—presdt of the Bank of Commerce, and his family—Our neighbor Mr Bartlett; but without his pleasant little wife—who remains at home castle building—by the bye they do not expect to get into their castle before October—if then.

We were all at a little *Hop*, as they call it, last evening, in one of the Saloons of the Hotel. It was not very brilliant, but gratified the small folks; who however could not summon up resolution to dance. At least little Julie could not—and Fan could not dance unless she did, of course.

The Springs appear to be quiet and sociable without any attempt at dashing and flashing—and therefore suit me better than they would at a gayer season. I should like very well to pass some days here and take the waters; but we have marching orders for 11 Oclock for Lake George. I find it so easy to get here and in such brief ⟨them⟩ ↑time↓ that I shall be apt to pay the Springs another visit. I have no idea of remaining mew'd up at home until I grow to be an old fogy. Tell Mary there are a number of most beautiful young ladies here—one of whom has paid me some small attentions; but I have not given her much encouragement.

One must not let oneself be too easily won. Farewell my dear Kate. Give my love to all the household—*and dont let any one see this letter.*

Your affectionate Uncle
Washington Irving

P S. I forgot to tell you that Mr Kennedy ⟨S⟩ asked after you all particularly about the little lady who carrys the Key's—which I presume is Sarah Mrs Kennedy is almost as handsome as ever—which is a great blessing

MANUSCRIPT: SHR.   PUBLISHED: PMI, IV, 107–8.

After the postscript "1852" is written by another hand.

1. WI omitted the bracketed letter.
2. John Pendleton Kennedy (1795–1870) had married Elizabeth Gray (d. 1889) of Ellicott's Mills, Maryland on February 5, 1829. See Bohner, *J. P. Kennedy*, p. 59.
3. John Austin Stevens (1795–1874), who became president of the Bank of Commerce in New York City in 1839, had married Abby Weld in 1824. One son was John Austin Stevens (1827–1910), a financier and author.

2214. *To Mary Irving*

Saratoga Springs July 21t 1852

My dear Mary,

Having written to Kate and Sarah (who have my permission to shew you my letters, though in great confidence) I now write a hasty line to you in turn. A letter which I forwarded from Helen to Eliza has no doubt given you all an idea of our voyage across Lake George and our visit to Ticonderoga in all which we were favored with delightful weather, bright yet temperate, and enjoyed to perfection the interesting and beautiful scenery. ⟨At Sar⟩ At Ticonderoga I made up my mind to give up the visit to Canada and return here and take the waters. The party went off in splendid style yesterday morning at 11 oclock in a fine steamer down the lake. At two oclock I embarked on board of another one for Whitehall and after a fine run through lovely scenery, ⟨arrived⟩ got into the rail road cars at the latter place and arrived here about 6 oclock in the Evening

Here to my great joy I found Mr Gouverneur Kemble, and **Mr Davis** (Major Jack Downing) So that I am well provided with Cronies. My friend Mr Kennedy however leave[s][1] here tomorrow for Washington being appointed Secretary of the Navy.[2] His wife however and her father and sister[3] remain here and I have promised Kennedy to pay some small attention to Mrs Kennedy during his absence, taking his seat beside her at table. I have therefore a little domestic party to attach myself to in place of the Grinnell party—but I see I shall be at no loss for acquaintances here. I began this morning to take the waters regularly and mean to give them a fair trial

This morning after breakfast I set off in a carriage with Mr Kemble and Mr Stevens (presdt of the Bank of Commerce[)];[4] to visit the scene of the battle of Saratoga; about twelve miles off we had a fine drive through beautiful scenery—crossing Saratoga lake in a Scow. The day was very warm, but there was a pleasant breeze which tempered it After passing an hour or two on the battle ground and acquainting ourself with all its localities, we returned to a hotel on the banks of the lake where we had an excellent dinner of black bass, lake trout and game and enjoyed ourselves in what little Fan would call tip top style. A pleasant drive home completed one of the most charming days I have had in the course of my charming tour.

I wish one or other of you would write me a line addressed to me at this place letting me know how you all are and what events have taken place at Sunnyside since my departure—

Give my love to all bodies

Your affectionate uncle
Washington Irving

Miss Mary Irving

MANUSCRIPT: SHR.   PUBLISHED: PMI, IV, 108–9.

Below "Miss Mary Irving" is written "My."

1. WI omitted the bracketed letter.

2. Kennedy was formally appointed secretary of the navy on July 22 and began his duties on July 26, 1852. See *Biographical Dictionary of the American Congress* (Washington, 1928), p. 16.

3. Edward Gray (1776–1856), the owner of a cotton-spinning factory on the Patapsco River eight miles west of Baltimore. He and his daughter Martha lived with the Kennedys in Baltimore. See Bohner, *J. P. Kennedy*, p. 63.

4. WI omitted the bracketed parenthesis.

2215.   To Catharine Irving

Saratoga, July 24th. 1852

My dear Kate,

I really dont know when I shall get home, for either the waters or the Company agree so well with me in this place that I find myself in first rate health and spirits and very much tempted to prolong my sojourn. It is really delightful to me to have this social out break after my long course of quiet life. I have found some old friends and have made new acquaintances here, all very cordial and agreeable There is no ceremonious restraint, nor pretensious shew, but every one seems disposed for social enjoyment. We have fine music sometimes professional, sometimes by amateurs—and all of an excellent quality

This morning we had splendid performances on the piano, ⟨by⟩ in the Saloon, by M Iael[1] (or some such name) I believe a Norwegian, and one of the best performers on that instrument I have ever heard. Afterward we had charming singing by Miss Lucretia Stevens[2] who has cultivated her fine voice in a high degree since I heard her two or three years since.

This afternoon I am going to a childrens ball at the country seat of Mr Finlay[3] in the vicinity of the Springs—He has laid down an immense platform on the grass under the trees and has invited all the little people at the Hotels—It will be a complete fairy scene.

Mr Mitchell (Ik Marvell) is here and we are very much together. He was at the Franklin house at Tarrytown recently and was down at the Cottage the day after my departure but finding me gone, did not enter the house but contented himself with strolling about the place. I told him he would have found a cordial welcome, even though I was absent.

Gouvr Kemble return[e]d yesterday to his old bachelors nest in the Highlands. I did all I could to keep him here but in vain—I wonder he should be so anxious to get home when he has no women kind to welcome him, as I have, yet even I, you see, can keep away.

There are some very agreeable talking ladies her[e],[4] and a great number of very pretty ↑looking↓ ones; two or three with dark Spanish eyes, that I sit and talk to, and look under their dark eye lashes, and think of dear old Spain.

Mr Frank Granger[5] is here, and has joined the Kennedy set with which I am in a manner domesticated. I am strong in the belief that Mr Granger will ⟨receive⟩ have the situation of Post Master offered to him and that he will accept of it;[6] though he shakes his head whenever it is mentioned. I regret extremely that Adele[7] is not with him—She is on a visit to a friend at Niagara

It is dinner time and I must travel down stairs from my room which is near the roof. Give my love to all the household.

Your affectionate Uncle
Washington Irving

Miss Kate Irving

MANUSCRIPT: SHR.   PUBLISHED: PMI, IV, 110–11.

1. Alfred Jaell (1832–1882), who was born in Trieste, had first performed at Tripler Hall on November 5, 1851. On November 22, 1851, he accompanied Adelina Patti, aged seven, in a vocal recital; and on May 20, 1852, he assisted Ole Bull, the Norwegian violinist, in a concert at Metropolitan Hall. See Odell, *NY Stage*, VI, 181–82, 186.

2. Probably the daughter of John Austin Stevens, who was visiting Saratoga Springs at this time. See WI to Catharine Irving, July 17, 1852.

3. John Beekman Finlay (1810–1869) was president of a bank in Saratoga Springs. See *Boyd's Saratoga Springs Directory for 1868–9* (Saratoga Springs, 1868), p. 62; and *Our Country and Its People* (Boston, 1899), p. 190.

4. WI omitted the bracketed letter.

5. Frank (or Francis) Granger (1792–1892), a former Whig congressman and postmaster general in the Tyler administration, was the uncle of Julia Ann Granger (1822–1897), wife of Sanders Irving (1813–1884), Ebenezer's fifth son. See James N. Granger, *Launcelot Granger of Newbury, Massachusetts and Suffolk, Connecticut: A Genealogical History* (Hartford, 1893), pp. 301–6.

6. Granger was not appointed. Instead, Samuel D. Hubbard (1779–1855) held the postmaster generalship from August 3, 1852, to March 7, 1853. See *Biographical Dictionary of the American Congress*, pp. 16, 1124.

7. Cornelia Adelaide (1819–1892) was the daughter of Frank Granger and Cornelia Van Rensselaer. See Granger, *Launcelot Granger*, pp. 301–6.

2216.   *To Catharine Irving*

Saratoga Springs July 25t. 1852

My dear Kate

I have just received your letter of yesterday[1] which gives me intelligence of the great event at Sunnyside—the departure of Sarah and Mary for the Sea side. I am rejoiced to hear it, and feel very much obliged to Henry Van Wart for inviting and persuading them to make the visit to his cottage. I am convinced the change of scene, with Sea air and seabathing will have a most beneficial effect on the the health of both, and would advise them to remain there as long as possible. ⟨Their⟩ The absence of us all must make your situation rather lonely; but you shall have your turn my dear Kate, by and bye.

In my letter of yesterday I told you that I was going to a childrens party at a gentlemans country seat in the neighborhood. It was at the house of a Mr Finlay, son of an old friend who married into the Beekman family of New York, but also is now dead. The present Mr Finlay inherits much of the property of that family, especially of his uncle John K Beekman[2] ⟨late⟩ deceased, an old bachelor and once an intimate of your uncle Peter & myself. The house was of stone spacious and solid; built in the skirts of what had once been a forest; but which was now thinned out into ⟨clumps⟩ groves and clumps, and green lawns until it had the air of ⟨a⟩ British park scenery A platform had been laid beneath some spreading trees and here the little fairy people danced while the grown up people sat around in groupes. It was one of the most charming little fêtes of the kind that I have ever seen. There were beautiful children very beautifully dressed; from the age of two and three years upwards. I felt like a patriarch among them; for among the spectators was Mrs James. an aunt of Mr Finlay, whom I had danced with in my younger days when she was a Miss Beekman, but who was now a venerable grand mother—and there was a maiden lady Miss Betsy Lawrence, whom I had likewise danced with ⟨below?⟩ nearly fifty years since, who now looked near eighty. I sat by them and talked of old times and looked on the dancing groupes, in which we recognized the descendants (some two or three generations off) of some of our early cotemporaries. To strike a balance, however, I paid some small attentions to two or three little belles, from six to ten years of age, and was received with smiles that might have made me vain had I been fifty or sixty years younger.

Among the leading personages at the Springs is Mrs Rush[3] of Philadelphia, a great notoriety, with whom I became slightly acquainted in Europe; where she made quite a distinguished figure; being very tall, very rich, very clever, and speaking several languages fluently. We have now become extremely intimate and I find her uncommonly agreeable from her ⟨great sens⟩ ↑originality↓ of mind; her independent frankness and her great conversational powers. Tomorrow Mr Mitchell (Ik Marvel[)],[4] and myself are to accompany her in her carriage on a drive into the country on search of the picturesque; as she is acquainted with all the fine points of view in the neighborhood.

I think it is the excitement of this cheerful society in which I am mingling, even more than the water; which has had an effect of lifting me into a more elastic buoyancy of frame and spirits than I have experienced for a long time; and I am convinced that if I had come up here for a few days, when I felt so heavy and bilious several weeks since, I should have swept all the clouds out of my system immediately

Give my love to your father and to such of the family as you have with you.

Your affectionate Uncle
W I.

MANUSCRIPT: SHR.   PUBLISHED: PMI, IV, 111–12.

Upside down above the complimentary close on page 4 of the manuscript is "Sunnyside" partially smeared. WI had apparently begun a letter on the wrong side of the sheet.

1. This letter has not been located.
2. John K. Beekman (1777–1842) was "a crusty old bachelor, who lived the last years of his secluded life near Saratoga Springs." See *The Diary of Philip Hone*, ed. Allan Nevins, II, 755.
3. Probably Phoebe Ann (1797–1857), the wife of Dr. James Rush, a Philadelphia physician and author. She was well known for her brilliant conversations and for her elaborate, luxurious entertainments for the fashionable society of Philadelphia.
4. WI omitted the bracketed parenthesis.

2217.   To Catharine Irving

Saratoga July 28th. 1852

My dear Kate,

I received in due course your letter of the 25th[1] and should have replied to it sooner, but that I expected before this to have seen you, face to face. Here however I linger, as it were, with one foot in the stirrup, and as I may continue to linger indefinitely I have thought proper to scrawl you another line. The truth is I am passing my time so agreeably, and find my sojourn here operating so admirably on health and spirits, that I am continually tempted to prolong it. I am linking up so many old friendships that had almost run out, and meeting, on the easiest of terms, so many pleasant and interesting people from all parts of the union, that every day brings some new gratification and excitement. ⟨This⟩ One sees society here without the trouble, formality, late hours and crowded rooms of New York. Th⟨is⟩e Hotel in which I am quartered (the United States) is a little world of itself with its spacious saloons long galleries, broad piazzas, and shady walks; where there is a constant succession of polite society circulating, and you may throw yourself in the current or remain aloof and look on just as you please— I think I have never seen a watering place on either sid[e]² of the Atlantic, where things were on a better footing and better arranged than in this—especially at the particular hotel in which I reside.

I take the waters every morning and think they have a great effect ⟨i⟩on my system—I have entirely got rid of all bilious symptoms; and find my mental faculties refreshed, invigorated and brightened up. I have no doubt I derive some benefit from gossipping away part of the day in very agreeable female society ⟨who⟩ in which I experience such favorable treatment as inclines me to think old gentlemen are coming into fashion —they wont allow me for a moment to enrol myself in the respectable order of old fogies. My worthy co-executor and co-trustee Mr Lord, is here, with his wife and daughter³ and I am to take my afternoons drive with them—Yesterday I had a beautiful drive among the hills with Mrs Rush and a party in her carriage and saw a succession of lovely landscapes such as I had no idea were to be found in the neighborhood of Saratoga.

Tomorrow morning I attend the wedding of Chancellor Walworths son, and step daughter,⁴ in the Catholic chapel and in the evening a grand reception at the Chancellors in the evening;⁵ I doubt whether I get home before the beginning of next week; so that you may drop me a line on the receipt of this; letting me know how all are at home and what news you have from Mary and Sarah. With love to all bodies

Your affectionate Uncle
W I.

P S. Ik Marvel is still here—We are very much together. The more I see of him the more I like him. Our neighbor Mr Bartlett is also here having made a visit home and returned here during my sojourn.

Mr Aspinwall and his daughter⁶ are here—h⟨is⟩e looks emaciated and I fear is in a critical state of health.

If Julia Sanders is with you tell her her uncle Mr Frank Granger is in the Kennedy party at table so that we are together at every meal beside being together a dozen time[s]⁷ a day in the saloons. piazzas &c. He is capital company ⟨[blot] we [unrecovered]⟩ We sit each side of Mrs Kennedy a[t]⁸ table and have rare times.

MANUSCRIPT: SHR.   PUBLISHED: PMI, IV, 112–13.

1. This letter has not been located.
2. WI omitted the bracketed letter.

3. Daniel Lord (1795-1868), John Jacob Astor's attorney and first president of the Astor Library, founded the law firm of Lord, Day & Lord. He married Susan de Forest (1799–1879) in 1818 and had two daughters: Phoebe (b. 1823), who married Henry Day and had two children by 1852, and Sarah (b. 1829), who married Henry C. Howells. Probably Sarah is the daughter to whom WI refers. See Kenneth Lord, *Genealogy of the Descendants of Thomas Lord* (New York, 1946), pp. 166–68.

4. Reuben Hyde Walworth (1788–1866), a Plattsburg lawyer, served as chancellor of New York State from 1828 to 1848. After the death of his first wife he married Sarah Ellen Smith, who had two sons and a daughter by a previous marriage. The daughter, Ellen Hardin, married her step-brother, Tracy Walworth, a novelist. See William L. Stone, *Reminiscences of Saratoga and Ballston* (New York, 1855), pp. 333–38; and George Waller, *Saratoga, Saga of an Imperious Era* (Englewood Cliffs, 1966), p. 72.

5. WI repeated "in the evening."

6. Thomas Aspinwall (1786–1876), who was U.S. consul in London from 1815 to 1852, served as WI's literary agent in London for many years. Eliza King (1816–1899) was the only Aspinwall daughter alive in 1852. See Algernon A. Aspinwall, *The Aspinwall Genealogy* (Rutland, Vt., 1901), p. 81; and Charles C. Smith, "Memoir of Col. Thomas Aspinwall," *Massachusetts Historical Society Proceedings*, 2d ser. 8 (November, 1891), 32–38.

7. WI omitted the bracketed letter.

8. WI omitted the bracketed letter.

2218. To Catharine Irving

Saratoga, July 31t 1852

My dear Kate

My present idea is that I shall leave Saratoga on Monday next so as to be home in the train which arrives at Dearman about 8 OClock in the evening. Have a waggon therefore at the station at that hour.

Judge Ulshoeffer arrived here last evening with Nancy; who found the air at Sharon Springs[1] too keen for her She looks very pale and emaciated The rest of the party will come here as soon as the Judge can secure rooms for them at the United States Hotel.

I presume you have heard that Theodore[2] has been elected or appointed Professor at Union College, Schenectady. I think it probable his arrangement with Mr Abbot will be preferred by him to the appointment; though under other circumstances it would be a very desirable one

I write in haste as the dinner bell is ringing.

Your affectionate Uncle
Washington Irving

MANUSCRIPT: SHR.

1. Sharon Springs is in Schoharie County, about 130 miles southwest of Saratoga Springs.
2. Theodore Irving (1809–1880), who had published a study of DeSoto's conquest of Florida in 1835, had become a professor at Geneva College in 1836. See WI to Joseph C. Cabell, May 8, 1841; and PMI, III, 69.

2219. To Catharine Irving

Saratoga Springs. Aug. 1st 1852

My dear Kate,
I wrote a hasty line yesterday requesting you to send ⟨the⟩ ↑a↓ carriage to the station for the 8 Oclock train on Monday evening. I still request it; but you must not be disappointed if I do not come on. I may be tempted to prolong my stay here a little as Alboni[1] has arrived, and there is a talk of a concert. Should one be advertised for Monday or Tuesday Evening I shall remain to attend it, as I should hear her to more advantage here than at New York.
I continue to enjoy my sojourn here Yesterday an old friend arrived whom I have not seen for upwards of thirty years, and who had his wife with him (a Charlestown lady) with several of her relatives and friends, so that I found myself launched in a new and very pleasant circle. This is a wonderful rallying point for agreeable people from all parts of the Union
Judge Ulshoeffer expects the rest of his party on Tuesday. I find Henrietta[2] is with them. They come on in company with Mrs Suydam (Anne Schermerhorn) and her mother.[3]
I continue to take the waters; which I trust will clear me of all bilious tendencies for the rest of the year.
I am glad to find Oscar and Eliza are with you. I feel easy, therefore, as you will have cheerful company: the house keeping will be attended to and my horses will have exercise.
What an awful affair this is of the Henry Clay.[4] It is well it did not occur in our neighborhood. I grieve to think of the sad affliction into which poor Mrs Downing[5] is plunged; whom lately I met at the Hamiltons, so full of gaiety and happiness. Give my love to your father, to Eliza Oscar and all enquiring friends

Your affectionate uncle
Washington Irving

Miss Kate Irving

MANUSCRIPT: SHR.

1. Marietta Alboni (1826–1894), a contralto who was the protégé of Rossini, was in the United States for a concert tour.

2. Henrietta Ulshoeffer was the daughter of Judge Michael Ulshoeffer and the sister of Nancy, the wife of Irving Paris.

3. Anne White Schermerhorn (1818–1886), who married Charles Suydam in 1849, was the daughter of Mrs. Abraham Schermerhorn (née Helen White, 1792–1881) and the sister of Mrs. John Treat Irving, Jr. See Richard Schermerhorn, Jr., *Schermerhorn Genealogy and Family Chronicles*, p. 166.

4. During a race down the Hudson River from Albany with the *Armenia* the *Henry Clay* caught fire in its boiler room. Having no fire extinguishers or life boats, it ran ashore two and one-half miles south of Yonkers in an effort to discharge passengers. Nearly one hundred persons perished when rescue efforts failed. Among the dead was Maria Louisa, the sister of Nathaniel Hawthorne. See New York *Times*, July 30, 31, 1852.

5. The wife of Andrew Jackson Downing, a horticulturist and landscape gardener who was on his way to Washington, D.C. from Newburgh to lay out the public grounds near the Capitol. See New York *Times*, July 31, 1852.

2220. To Catharine Irving

Saratoga Springs / Aug 5th. 1852

My dear Kate,

I have lingered at the Springs to hear Albon⟨y⟩i, who sings tonight. I propose to set off tomorrow for home and expect to arrive at the Dearman station about 8 OClock You will have a vehicle there accordingly.

Judge Ulshoeffer is here with all his party; the girls are enjoying themselves greatly—Nancy is improving in health—

I received a letter from Helen Pierre[1] a day or two since. I presume she will be with you by the time this reaches you

love to all / Your affectionate Uncle
Washington Irving

Miss Kate Irving

MANUSCRIPT: SHR.

1. This letter has not been located.

2221. To Richard C. McCormick

Sunnyside, Aug. 9, 1852

My dear Sir:

Three weeks' absence from home has prevented an earlier reply to your letter of the 21st of July, and to the letter from your Society which accompanied it.[1] I now thank you heartily for the kind expressions of your letter, and assure you that I appreciate most deeply the esteem and goodwill manifested by yourself and your associates in adopting my name as a designation for your literary union.

To inspire such sentiments in the bosoms of the young and ingenuous, is one of the purest and dearest rewards that an author can receive; and as my long and desultory career is drawing to a close, I regard such demonstrations on the part of my youthful countrymen as a soothing assurance that, with all my shortcomings, and however imperfectly I may have performed my part, I have not lived entirely in vain.

With great respect, your obliged and humble servant,

Washington Irving

PUBLISHED: PMI, IV, 117–18.

Richard C. McCormick (1832–1901), who was working on Wall Street at this time, was a member of a literary club called the Irving Literary Union. He later served as correspondent in the Crimean and American Civil Wars and as a congressional delegate from the Territory of Arizona from 1869 to 1875.

1. These letters have not been located.

2222. To George Sumner

Sunnyside Aug 9th. 1852

My dear Sumner,

On returning from Saratoga the evening before last, your letter of the 24th of July[1] was put into my hands; by which I found you must have passed through New York while I was absent at the Springs

I hope when you next visit New York you will find your way up here. The rail road cars stop at Dearman Station, within just ten minutes walk of my house. Putnam will tell the hours of departure. I want very much to have a long talk with you about old times and foreign scenes.

I was glad to hear such good accounts of my charming friend Mrs. Ellis[2] and to receive so kind a message from her. Should I visit Washington it would give me the greatest pleasure to find her and her uncle[3] there.

With great regard / My dear Sumner / Yours very truly

Washington Irving

George Sumner Esqr

MANUSCRIPT: Dr. Noel Cortes.

George Sumner (1817–1863) was an American author and traveler whom WI had known in Paris and Madrid while he was minister to Spain.

1. This letter has not been located.
2. Catherine Ellis was the niece of William R. King, the U.S. minister to France from 1844 to 1846. She served as the official hostess at the Paris legation.
3. William R. King (1786–1853).

2223. *To Charles A. Davis*

Sunnyside Aug 10t. 1852

My dear Davis.

Your letter[1] found me lolling under the trees and ruminating, like one of my own cows, over the past pleasures of Saratoga. It was most welcome, smacking as it did of that eminently social resort, and bringing back the flavor of the happy hours passed there. It will take me some time however to get over the excitement of gay scenes, gay company and the continual stimulus of varied and animated conversation and bring myself down to the mute quiet of country life and the sober equanimity of Sunnyside. You who are always enjoying your chirping glass of society have no idea what an effect such a long draught has upon one of my abstemious habits. I really think that for a part of the time I was in a state of mental intoxication[.] I trust however it will be beneficial in the end; as I have heard it said by old fashioned doctors in the days of hard drinking, that it is good for a mans health now and then to get tipsy. Still it will not do for me to repeat the revel very soon; so I am not to be tempted by your suggestion of another ⟨outbreak at⟩ ↑visit to↓ Saratoga during the present season. That must be for next summers outbreak.

I envy you the long quiet conversation with alboni about her art. I delight in conversations of the kind with eminent artists; whom I have always found very communicative and interesting when properly drawn out. So I have found Talma, Pasta, Mrs Siddons, and Cooke[2] who were the greatest in their respective lines that I ever was acquainted with.

I should have liked to had a talk with Alboni when there were none by to criticise my bad French or Spanish, but I cannot bear to stumble among the dark mountains of a foreign language, ⟨when⟩ in the company of Americans or English to witness my blunders. So I was tongue tied when I met her in presence of Mrs Rush and others of her coterie, though I had no unkind criticism to apprehend on their part. I was content to let them draw her out which they did sometimes very effectually. She appears to be of a frank happy joyous nature, and I think it is ⟨the⟩ ↑her↓ rich mellow genial temperament which pours itself forth in her voice like liquid amber.

I thank you, my dear Major, for saying a kind word for me to such of my intimate[s]³ at the Springs as I came away without seeing. I made several delightful acquaintances there, whom it is probable, considering my time of life, and my retired habits, ⟨it is probable⟩ I may never see again. Yet I shall always retain them in choice reccollection. Really such an easy, social intercourse with the intelligent the matured, the young, the gay and the beautiful, rallys ⟨me⟩ ↑one↓ back from the growing apathy of age and ⟨opens⟩ ↑reopens↓ ones heart to the genial sunshine of society.

Farewell my dear Major, give my kind remembrances to your wife and that discreet Princess your daughter and tell Mrs Rush I shall ever remember her as one of the most striking and interesting features of my visit to Saratoga

Yours very faithfully
Washington Irving

MANUSCRIPT: NYPL—Seligman Collection.   PUBLISHED: PMI, IV, 116–17 (in part).

1. This letter has not been located.

2. François Joseph Talma (1763–1826) was a French actor whom WI had met on April 25, 1821, through the agency of John Howard Payne. (See J&N, III, 234.) Giuditta Pasta (1798–1865) was an Italian opera singer whom WI had heard in Paris as early as October 7, 1823. He met her on February 14, 1825. (See J&N, III, 229, 455.) Sarah Siddons was a famous English actress whom WI had met in 1822. (See WI to Henry Brevoort, June 11, 1823.) George Frederick Cooke (1756–1811) was an English Shakespearean actor whom WI had seen in London in 1805. (See WI to William Irving, October 26, 1805.)

3. WI omitted the bracketed letter.

2224. To Catharine Irving

N York, Sept 14th. 1852

My dear Kate,

I am in snug quarters at Mrs Lowes having Helen & Pierres appart-ment.[1] It is true Broadway is a little like an unremitting rail road, and I have been beset by an army of musquitoes, but I begin to be accustomed to the first and I have made terrible slaughter among the second.

A[l]boni's[2] concert[3] went off admirably. She sang deliciously and looked handsomer and handsomer every song, until I thought her down-right beautiful

I presume you got the basket of grapes which Mr Kemble left at Dear-man Station. I have promised Mr Kemble that I would make him a visit with some of my women Kind next week. So get ready to go up with me on Monday next, and if you think Mary will stand the jaunt she had bet-ter accompany us. Helen ta[l]ked of making a vis[i]t[4] at the same time to Mrs Parrot[5]—which would add to the felicity of the expedition. I shall return home next Saturday afternoon; perhaps by the two Oclock train—

Be ready to start on Monday as I have to carve out my time in por-tions for the next two or three weeks, *having numerous engagements.*

Your affectionate uncle
Washington Irving

PS. I send some Spinach seed by Pierre; which you will give to Robert[6]

MANUSCRIPT: SHR.

1. Helena Lowe kept a boarding house at 706 Broadway between Fourth Street and Washington Place. See *New York City Directory for 1851–52.*
2. WI omitted the bracketed letter.
3. Marietta Alboni sang seven concerts during September at Metropolitan Hall. WI heard her on either September 7 or 10. See Odell, *NY Stage*, VI, 263–64.
4. WI omitted the bracketed letters in two words in this sentence.
5. Mrs. Robert Parrott was the sister of Gouverneur Kemble, who also lived in Cold Spring.
6. Robert McLinden (d. December 1, 1891) was WI's Irish-born gardener who began working at Sunnyside in 1849.

2225. To Mary Hamilton

[September 20, 1852]

My dear Miss Hamilton,

When I engaged to join your party on the 28th. I was not aware that the following day was the last Wednesday in the month; when I have to attend the stated meetings of the Executors to the Astor Estate and the Trustees of the Astor library. I cannot be absent on this occasion as it is the last meeting of the library board previous to Mr Cogswells departure for Europe.

Should you set off on Tuesday I can join your party at any designated place on Thursday.

I set off this morning for Mr Kembles in the Highlands to be absent until the last of the week

How the breakfast went off at Mr Kings at Highwood; and how the Sontag[1] looked and moved and conducted herself, and how I admired but did not talk with her; and how I returned to town with the Stanards[2] in their carriage; and how I went with Mrs Stanard to Niblos theatre; and how Mr Stanard was to join us there, and how he did not join us there, but left me to be her cavalier for the whole evening; and how I wondered that he should trust such a charming wife with such a gay young fellow; all this, and more also, I will recount unto you when next we meet   until when farewell

Yours truly
Washington Irving

Sunnyside, Monday Morng / Sept. 20th. [1852]

DOCKETED: Mr Irving / Sepr. 20th. / 1852
MANUSCRIPT: Va.–Barrett.   PUBLISHED: PMI, IV, 118–19.

1. Henrietta Sontag (1806–1854) was a German opera singer who made a concert tour in 1852.
2. Tarrytown neighbors of WI.

2226. To Philip J. Forbes

Sunnyside, Oct 25th 1852

My dear Sir,

I hope you will excuse me for having so long delayed to thank you for the volume of the World Displayed[1] which you have had the kindness to send me. It is indeed a most acceptable relique from the happy days of my boyhood. It was your good father[2] that first put this series of little volumes in my hand finding I had a great relish for accounts of voyages and discoveries and I dont think I was ever more fascinated by any course of reading. I used to take the little volumes to school with me and read them slyly to the great neglect of my lessons. The early volumes treated of the voyages of Columbus and the conquests of Mexico and Peru. They were more delightful to me than a fairy tale and the plates by which they were illustrated are indelibly stamped on my reccollection[.] I dont know any thing that would give me greater delight than to recover these identical volumes.

Believe me my dear Sir

With great regard / Your truly obliged
Washington Irving

Philip J Forbes Esqr

MANUSCRIPT: NYHS.

Philip J. Forbes was the librarian of the New York Society Library, a position he had held since he succeeded his father. He lived on Staten Island. See *New York City Directory for 1851–52*.

1. *The World Displayed; or, A Curious Collection of Voyages and Travels, Selected from the Writers of All Nations*, in twenty volumes. Volume 17 (Dublin, 1779), which is preserved among the books in WI's library at Sunnyside, is probably the one which WI is acknowledging in this letter.

2. John Forbes served as librarian of the New York Society Library from 1794 to 1824. See Evert A. & George L. Duyckinck, *The Cyclopaedia of American Literature*, 2 vols. (Philadelphia, 1881), I, 404.

2227. (*deleted*)

2228.   *To Sarah Storrow*

Sunnyside Nov 10th 1852

My dear Sarah,

I was glad, a day or two since, to recieve your letter dated some time in October.[1] I wrote to both you and Kate last July when I was about to depart for Saratoga; but received nothing in return excepting a few numbers of Galignani last month, which I presume were to 'stay my stomach' until you had time to indite an epistle. However I dont complain. I know it is inevitable for correspondence to decline during a long separation; but let us ⟨in some degree to⟩ endeavor in some degree to keep it alive; being perhaps the only link of communion that now remains between us.

It has given me great satisfaction to find that you renewed your intimacy with Mrs De Wolff during her sojourn in Paris. I was delighted to see her last summer, with he[r][2] faithful old Negro attendant, who came down in the parlor to see me with her mistresses little son in her hand. Mrs De Wolff is still the same, gentle, amiable, and ladylike, with that dark Spanish style of beauty which is very much to my fancy.

We have had Irving Van Wart, his excellent little wife and his two fine sturdy boys[3] up at the Cottage all in fine spirits[.] Irving is looking well and was extremely agreeable entertaining us with anecdotes of his visit to Europe; giving us an account of yourself and your household and telling us of his visits to his old haunts when a schoolboy at Paris.

George Sumner has also been twice up here once on a visit to us and another time at the Hamiltons. He was as usual full of floating history about the men and the events of the day; having mingled in the most striking scenes and among the most striking people of the countrys in in which he has travelled and sojourned. I really was heartily glad to meet him again for he is altogether one of the most curiously instructed American⟨s⟩ ⟨that⟩ travellers that I have ever met with. The girls thought him one of the very pleasantest gentleman visitors I had ever had. Mr Mitchell (Ik Marvell author of Reveries of a bachelor, Dream life &c) ⟨was pass⟩ came up from town and passed a day with us while Sumner was making his visit. I had become very intimate with Mitchell at the Springs last summer. He is a very gentleman like amiable little fellow and I have taken a great liking to him both as an author and a man.

As to Sumner I should not be surprised if under the new administration he should get some situation abroad, if desirous of one. I do not know whether he has taken any side on politics since his return, but presume he is of the predominant one. His brother belongs to it I believe, and he is a member of the Senate and may have influence ⟨i⟩ at Washington

You will see that Mr King (*Mon Ami*) is to be our Vice President. I wish he were to have the higher office since we are to have a president from that party. He is an upright honorable man; a gentleman in spirit and deportment. I have not seen Mrs Ellis since my return from Europe. She has been to the North (at Newport) this last summer looking I am told even better and younger than when in Paris; having gained a little in flesh without losing in spirit. I shall probably see her in Washington the coming winter as I have promised my friend Kennedy (at present Secretary of the Navy) to pay him and Mrs Kennedy a visit there; having occasion to rummage the public archives for historical information.

I meet with Constant occasionally, and his son Willie, who far out tops his father. Constant talks of remaining this winter in New York, finding Mrs Constant can console herself for his absence among the Gaieties of Paris. Perhaps, now that his party is uppermost, he may again be hankering after some diplomatic situation abroad. What a home-less dislocated family they have become. How different from what they were in their beautiful rural home, where they lived so respectably and apparently happily; surrounded by friends who loved and neighbors who honored them. Is Mrs Constant happier for this wandering heartless kind of life?

I have not seen your brother since his return. he has not been at home when I called at his father in law's,[4] and he has been too much occu-pied with bring[ing][5] up his affairs, as yet, to make a visit to the Cot-tage. I am told he is in fine health and spirits. Delighted with all that he has seen and delighted to be home again. Nancy is in rather delicate health, but I believe only wants a little care and caution to do well. Her little girl grows very pretty and much more engaging than she used to be. We have become great friends

Farewell my dear Sarah. Remember me affectionately to your hus-band and give my love to the three young princesses.

Your affectionate uncle
Washington Irving

MANUSCRIPT: Yale.   PUBLISHED: PMI, IV, 119–20 (in part).

1. This letter has not been located.
2. WI omitted the bracketed letter.
3. Irving Van Wart (b. 1807) and Sarah Ames had twin sons, Irving and Henry, born on January 20, 1841.
4. Judge Michael Ulshoeffer was the father-in-law of Irving Paris.
5. WI omitted the bracketed letters.

2229. *To Miss Falford*

[Sunnyside, November 15, 1852]

Rogers[1] the poet, one of the men most sought after in high society gave me an amusing instance of the sincerity of dinner invitations.

He was invited by Lady J——— to dine with her on a certain day. He en-deavored to excuse himself as he was about to leave town on a country excursion. She would take no excuse—he must come—She would be glad to have him on any terms—would take her chance of his return &c &c. He accordingly promised to come if he should return from the country in time

He was asked by Lady. B——— P——— to dine with her on the same day. He made the same excuse. She would not listen to it—he had disap-pointed her so often—he must come—She would expect him &c &c

The Duchess of —— told him that when he returned to town he must come and dine with her—She was always at home and would always be glad to see him &c &c

He returned to town on the day designated in the invitations, ⟨Lady B—— P——⟩ and made a morning call on Lady J——

Rogers had now his dernier resort, the Duchess of —— who was always at home, and was always glad to see him—and would always take it as a favor if he would come *Sans ceremonie*—He accordingly called on her, but she never said a word about his coming to dinner. In fine the man of many invitations ate his dinner alone at a chop house and spent a dull evening at a theatre.

Written for Miss Falford / ⟨Sunnysi⟩ / by
Washington Irving

Sunnyside Novr. 15th. 1852.

MANUSCRIPT: SHR.

1. Samuel Rogers (1763–1855), the banker and poet whom WI knew intimately during the years of his residence in England.

2230. *To Henry Ogden*

Sunnyside Novr. 23d. 1852

My dear Ogden

I duly received your letter written eight or ten days since[1] and intended to answer it immediately; but I was closely occupied at the time, and your letter was crowded aside by the number that succeeded it. In fact, with all my efforts I find it impossible to keep up with my correspondence

Dedications should always be simple; and modified according to the relative situations of the parties and the degree of intimacy or familiarity that exists between them

I give you on the next leaf[2] something that may serve; or at any rate that will furnish an idea on which your brother[3] may build, according to feelings and circumstances

Yours ever my dear Ogden / cordially as in days of old
Washington Irving

MANUSCRIPT: Va.–Barrett.

Henry Ogden was a friend of WI's youth and a member of the "Lads of Kilkenny."

1. This letter has not been located.
2. This sheet has not been preserved with the letter.
3. Possibly Francis Barber Ogden (1783–1857).

2231. To Charles A. Davis

Wednesday 8 Decr 1852

Worthy and dear friend

Lest you shd make another philological *"tour"* at the tail of Burns' plough, I send you a colation from Dr. Jamieson's Scotish Dictionary (Edinburgh Edition MDCCCXLI):[1] *stour-stoure-stourr-sture*—dust in a state of motion, pronounced *stoor*,

> "Yestreen I met you on the moor
> Ye spak na, but gaed by like stoure
> Burns IV. 286.["]²

This term is also used, but improperly, with resp. to dust that is laid,

> "My books like useless lumber ly
> Thick cover'd owre wi *stour*, man
> A. Douglas. Poems. page 41["]³

Hoping the above may suffice to put the plough in the right furrow, I remain

As ever thine
Dryasdust

MANUSCRIPT: NYPL—Berg Collection.   PUBLISHED: *Studies in Scottish Literature,* 10 (January, 1973), 189.

WI's letter is a copy made by Charles A. Davis and enclosed in a letter to PMI, dated June, 1863. It is impossible to ascertain whether or not the variations in spelling are WI's or Davis's.

A passage from Davis's letter sets WI's note in its proper context: "Among my rambling recollections of our lamented friend, I recall a little incident which may illustrate a leading feature of his character: his readiness to listen to any thing that interested or amused him, his avoidance of immediate controversy but his quiet industry to seek the truth. It happened to me that in conversation with an intelligent Scotch gardener in my employ (in planting trees and shrubs in Gramercy Square) I found he came from *Ayrshire* and was quite familiar with the writings and character of *Robert Burns*; and in the course of quoting and reciting what he conceived to be among the best specimens of Burns' poetry, he recited '*The Mountain Dasiy*'. And I noticed that instead of using the words '*the stour*' in the third line he substituted 'this tour'—insisting that 'stour' was a misprint, that he knew the very field where Burns was 'plouin,' and being *hilly* he could only *plou* in *tours*—round and round; otherwise the furroughs would be channels for water and become gullies, or in other places, *dams*, to hold the water in 'puddles.' He seem'd so earnest and pertinacious, and his reading so natural, and noting after all the difference of a misprint was simply changing an 'e' to an 'i,' I yielded to him for the sake of hearing a *true Scot* read with the real Scotch pronunciation a poem of rare beauty from the pen of *Robert Burns*: 'Wee—modest—*crimson tipped*—flower' (enunciating each adjective separately, slowly and distinctly).

"Meeting Mr. Irving a few evenings afterward, I narrated to him this little incident which, coupled with the mode of 'plouin' as graphically sketched by the honest old *Scotch gardener*, interested him exceedingly. He was of course familiar with every thing from Burns' pen, but this was a *new reading* to him. 'If *authorities* are not against the old gardener,' said he, 'I'll do my best to couple his name with 'The Mountain Daisy' and he shall have all the credit of this new reading.' It was quite midnight before he left us that evening, and at eight o'clock next morning I found on my breakfast table a letter bearing a carefully written superscription and a big *seal in wax*—showing pretty clearly that it had been written near a lamp or taper, and if so after midnight and before morning:"

After quoting WI's letter, Davis continues: "I note this little incident as an illustration of his courtesy and industry. He no doubt knew *authorities* were against the honest and enthusiastic Gardener, but he would not mar a harmless and agreeable confab by controversy at the time. He seem'd to enjoy it as others did, and as soon after as he could (under sanction of authority) blew me and my Scotch gardener to the winds."

1. John Jamieson, *An Etymological Dictionary of the Scottish Language*, 2d ed., 2 vols. (Edinburgh, 1840–41).

2. From "Tibbie, I Hae Seen the Day," in *The Works of Robert Burns*, ed. J. Currie (Liverpool, 1800), IV, 286.

3. From "To a Friend on the Hard Times," in *Poems, Chiefly in the Scottish Dialect; by Alexander Douglas, Strathmiglio* (Cupar-Fife, 1806), p. 41.

2232. *To John Murray III*

Sunnyside Decr. 8t. 1852

My dear Sir,

This will be handed to you by my friend Mr Henry T. Tuckerman[1] who is probably already known to you by his writings, full of amenity and grace, which have stamped him one of our best critics and most classic essayists.

Reccommending him as a gentleman worthy from his personal character and amiable manners of your kind civilities I remain

Yours ever very truly
Washington Irving

John Murray Esqr.

MANUSCRIPT: John Murray.

1. Henry T. Tuckerman (1813–1871) was an essayist, poet, and journalist whose writings were greatly admired by American readers. Among his books are *The Italian Sketch Book* (1835), *Rambles and Reveries* (1841), *Thoughts on the Poets* (1846), *The Optimist, A Collection of Essays* (1850), *Poems* (1851), and *Essays, Biographical and Critical, or Studies of Character* (1857).

2233.   *To Henry T. Tuckerman*

Sunnyside, Dec. 8, 1852

My dear Sir:

I send you three letters of introduction,[1] which I hope may be of service to you. My poor friend Rogers,[2] I fear, is growing too infirm to render those attentions he was formerly so prompt to show to Americans of worth. Sir Robert Harry Inglis is a man of the most genial character, full of intelligence, and in communion with the most intellectual society of England. He is a man *I love and honor.*

John Murray has succeeded to his father in the literary realm of Albemarle street, which I used to find a favorite haunt of notorieties.

Permit me to make my acknowledgments for the very kind and flattering notice you have taken of me and my little rural nest, in Putnam's late publication.[3] I wish I could feel myself worthy of half that you have said of me.

Yours ever, very truly.
Washington Irving

PUBLISHED: PMI, IV, 92.

1. WI's letters to Rogers and Inglis have not been located.

2. Samuel Rogers (1763–1855), the English banker-poet whom WI had first met in 1822.

3. In a review of *The Homes of American Authors* Tuckerman had observed that "the old age of Irving is made glad by more than competence, worthily won by his pen." In summary Tuckerman had noted that "Irving tells quaint stories of the Western hunters, or of Spanish Dons, or of old English cheer, as we sit beneath the fantastic gables of Wolfert's Roost." See *Putnam's Magazine,* 1 (January, 1853), 25, 30.

2234.   *To* ———

Sunnyside Decr 11t. 1852

Dear Sir

I have the honor to acknowledge the receipt of your letter on the subject of contributions in this country towards erecting a monument in
England to the memory of Wordsworth

While I honor the liberal feelings which have actuated you in this
matter I would observe, that, before we pay homage to the memory of
foreign authors, we have some duties of the kind to perform at home.
A proposition has been for some time before the public for a subscription towards erecting a monument in honor of the late Fenimore Cooper.
I have had to officiate as chairman at meetings held on the subject Persons have been nominated to whom subscriptions might be forwarded.
A ⟨chairma⟩ treasurer has been appointed to take charge of the funds so
raised. Now, though months have elapsed since the matter was made
public through the press, I am not aware that any subscriptions have been
received excepting from Mr Prescott and myself.

It appears to me therefore that we may lay ourselves open to reproach
if we carry our sympathies abroad on behalf of foreign authors, while
we evince such apathy at home ⟨towards⟩ ↑respecting↓ a native author
of Mr Coopers genius.

I remain Dear Sir / Very respectfully / Your obt Servt
Washington Irving

MANUSCRIPT: Scripps College Library.

2235.   *To Thomas W. Storrow, Sr.*

Sunnyside Decr 14th 1852

My dear Storrow,

You will think me very dilatory in acknowledging the receipt of the
numbers of To Day which you were so kind as to send me, but I can
only plead in excuse the constant fag of the pen to which I have for
some time past been subjected, and the correspondence from all quarters
which multiplies upon me and defies all my efforts to cope with it.

I have read your rambling notes on Paris and its ⟨grand⟩ notorieties[1]
with great satisfaction and reccommend to you to follow out the vein
you have opened. Paris is becoming more and more the point of interest
and curiosity in Europe to Americans; they are getting as many literary

sympathies with it as they used to have with London. Your long residence there and your familiar knowledge of its inhabitants enables you to furnish ⟨s⟩ anecdotes, descriptions and speculations which, though they might appear *vieilleries* to you would be novelties to your American readers. I have heard you give amusing accounts of the habitudes of old Frenchmen ⟨f⟩ residents of Paris, their mode of passing their time of economising their means so as to allow their eau sucré their tasse de café and their ticket to the theatre. You have a capital vein of quiet humor which gives a great zest to any picturings of the kind and which every now and then lurks in your semi philosophical speculations; such for instance as you indulged in the historical treatise upon cats.[2] At any rate keep your pen going, it is a healthful exercise of your mind and occupation of your leisure; and a source of entertainment to your friends.

I wish you would come on and pay us a visit at Sunnyside. You would find yourself quite at home with my little household and would be master of your time and yourself—I have as you know, a little library of odds and ends at home, and the Astor library in town to draw on. I have in a manner taken charge of the latter since Cogswells departure; and sleep there when in town: so that I can literally bury you among among[3] books. Think of it, and come—We have warm winter quarters.

Yours ever affectionately
Washington Irving

MANUSCRIPT: Harvard.

1. Storrow's articles entitled "Rambling Notes, Taken While in Paris During the Winter of 1850-51" and written under the pseudonym of Mathew Markwell, appeared in *To-Day*, 2 (August 7, 28, September 4, 25, October 16, 1852), 84–87, 139–41, 158–60, 202–5, 252–55.

2. For details, see WI to Storrow, July 7, 1852.

3. WI repeated "among."

2236.   *To Alfred Clarke*

Sunnyside Decr. 21t 1852

Sir

I have not sooner replied to your letter of Nov 11t.[1] because I had nothing definite to say on the subject. At the request of Several of the friends and admirers of the late Fenimore Cooper in New York, I presided at meetings on the subject of erecting a monument to his memory. I am sorry to say the matter has not been followed ⟨out⟩ up with the zeal I had anticipated. Some funds were collected by the sale of tickets to hear an address and Eulogium on the character and writings of the deceased by Mr Bryant: and persons were nominated to receive subscriptions and a treasurer appointed to take charge of the amount so raised. Since then nothing has been done, and as far as I am aware, but one or two subscriptions have been recieved.

The matter however is again to be agitated and will then I trust be carried out more effectually Whenever a meeting takes place I shall not fail to lay your letter before it.

Respectfully / Your Obt Sevt
Washington Irving

Alfred Clarke

ADDRESSED: Alfred Clarke Esq / Springfield / Otsego / N. Y. / Care of Henry Scott Esqr / Otsego County Bank DOCKETED: Dearman, N. Y. Washn Irving / December 22d
MANUSCRIPT: Va.–Barrett.

Alfred Cooper Clarke (b. 1813) was the son of Ann Low, who had married Richard Cooper (1775–1813), James Fenimore Cooper's older brother. Shortly after Richard's death she married George Clarke, and Alfred was born later in 1813. Never certain of his paternity, he later used the name of Alfred Cooper Clarke. WI had corresponded with Mrs. Clarke in 1834. See WI to Ann Clarke, May 2 and June 26, 1834.

1. This letter has not been located.

2237. To Charles Lanman

Sunnyside Decr 22d. 1852

My dear Sir

I have delayed answering your letter,[1] until I could acknowledge the receipt of the work[2] which was to have accompanied it; and which has but just come to hand; having been lying in the office of my nephew in New York.

I have been reading it with great interest and satisfaction. The familiar pictures which it gives of Mr Webster in domestic life and at his rural home, are extremely endearing and calculated to enhance the admiration caused by his great talents and eminent services in his public career.

Accept my sincere thanks for the work and for the kind expressions of your letter and believe me

Very respectfully / Your obliged friend & servt
Washington Irving

Charles Lanman Esqr.

MANUSCRIPT: Pierpont Morgan Library; NYPL–Hellman Collection (copy).

1. This letter has not been located.

2. *Private Life of Daniel Webster,* which drew upon Lanman's close association as private secretary to the statesman, who had died on October 24, 1852.

2238. To George P. Putnam

Sunnyside, Decr 27th. 1852

My dear **Sir,**

Your parcel of books reached me on Christmas morning; your letter not being addressed to Dearman went to Tarrytown and did not come to hand until today.[1]

My nieces join with me in thanking you for the beautiful books you have sent us, and to you and Mrs Putnam[2] your wishes for a Merry Christmas and a happy New Year.

For my own especial part let me say how sensibly I appreciate the kind tone and expressions of your letter; but as to your talk of obligations to me I am conscious of none that have not been fully counterbalanced on your part; and I take pleasure in expressing the great satisfaction I have derived, throughout all our intercourse, from your amiable, obliging and honorable conduct. Indeed I never had dealings with any man, whether in the way of business or friendship more perfectly free from any alloy.

That these dealings have been profitable is mainly owing to your own sagacity and enterprise. You had confidence in the continued vitality of my writings when [my former publishers][3] . . . . had almost persuaded me they were defunct You called them again into active existence and gave them a circulation that I believe has surprised even yourself. In rejoicing at their success my satisfaction is doubly enhanced by the idea that you share in the benefits derived from it.[4]

Wishing you that continual prosperity in business, which your upright, enterprising, tasteful and liberal mode of conducting it merits, and is calculated to ensure; and again invoking ⟨for⟩ ↑on↓ you and yours a happy New Year

I remain very truly & heartily yours,
Washington Irving

Geo. P. Putnam Esq

MANUSCRIPT: See note below. PUBLISHED: LIB, I, v (in part); J. C. Derby, *Fifty Years Among Authors, Books and Publishers* (New York, 1884), p. 308 (in part).

The original holograph has not been located. Facsimiles of this letter are found in such collections as LC, Harvard, Va.–Barrett, National Library of Scotland, New York State Library, Huntington Library, and Rosenberg Library of Galveston, Texas. Apparently these realistic copies were distributed by Putnam as promotional pieces.

1. This letter has not been located.

2. Mrs. Putnam was the former Victorine Haven, whom Putnam had married on March 13, 1841, when she was sixteen years old.

3. An ellipsis of two and one-half lines occurs on the facsimile. The bracketed words are printed in Derby, *Fifty Years Among Authors, Books and Publishers* (p. 308) and may constitute the omitted passage.

4. WI refers to the arrangement with Putnam for the publication of the Author's Revised Edition in fifteen volumes between 1848 and 1850, from which WI reportedly received about $80,000. See PMI, IV, 237–38.

2239. *To* ——

[December 27, 1852]

Dear Sir

I am sorry to say it is not in my power to furnish you with the autograph you require of Sir Walter Scott.

Respectfully / Your obt Servt
Washington Irving

Sunnyside Decr 27h. 1852

MANUSCRIPT: Va.–Barrett.

2240. *To John P. Kennedy*

New York Decr 31st 1852

My dear Kennedy

My engagements in these parts extend to the 12th of January, within a day or two after which I shall shape my course to Washington to take possession of that "very comfortable room" which you say Mrs Kennedy has kindly prepared for me. I shall not fail to stop on the way to see Mr & Miss Gray, and will apprise you in time of the day of my departure.

With kindest remembrances to Mrs Kennedy

Yours my dear Kennedy / Very truly
Washington Irving

P. S.—My address is Dearman Westchester Co Your letter[1] lingered at Dobbs Ferry with which I have no dealings

MANUSCRIPT: Peabody Library.   PUBLISHED: *Sewanee Review*, 25 (January, 1917),
6–7.

This manuscript is a copy, probably made by Kennedy.

1. This letter has not been located.

2241. *To George P. Morris*

Sunnyside Jany 3d. 1853

My dear General,

As I have already signified in conversation to Dr Griswold, if I can get any thing ready in time for the Miscellaneous volume[1] proposed, I will gladly furnish it. At present however, I am an overtasked man.[2] I am continually obliged to forego literary occupation from the derangement it causes to my system, and am actually under a course of medical treatment on that account. Whatever time I can venture to devote to the exercise of the pen is completely engrossed. Under all these circumstances I can make no positive promise but only repeat that which I have made to Dr Griswold

Wishing you a happy New Year and many happier ones to follow it I remain

My dear General / Yours very truly
Washington Irving

ADDRESSED: Gen. *Geo. P. Morris* / 107 Fulton St / New York
MANUSCRIPT: Yale.

George Pope Morris (1802–1864) founded the *New-York Mirror* (1823), which published many writings by members of the Knickerbocker School. An officer of the New York State Militia, Morris was well known for his verses and song lyrics, including "Woodman, Spare That Tree."

1. This book was *The Knickerbocker Gallery*, a miscellany compiled by Morris and Griswold from selections written by regular contributors to the *Knickerbocker Magazine*. WI's essay, "Conversations with Talma," based on notes he had made in 1821, was the first selection in the volume. Profits from the sale of the book were used to buy a house for Lewis Gaylord Clark, the editor of the *Knickerbocker Magazine*.

2. In consequence of his work on the *Life of Washington*.

2242. *To George P. Morris*

Sunnyside Jan 6 1853

My dear General

My former note[1] was written in perfect sincerity and truth and if properly credited should have prevented the clark committee[2] from, as you say, *'leaning upon me as upon a rock'* If they do so they will assuredly be disappointed. If I am able to render any aid at all it must be very trivial. My general health is good, but symptematic intimations have obliged me repeatedly to throw by my pen and travel, within the last eighteen months[3] and I am conscious that I am now exercising it at a constant risk. No one, therefore who has a regard for my well being, would impose an additional task, however light, upon me. So I beg that no promises may be made to the public in my name. I can make none *even to myself.*

Yours my dear General / very truly
Washington Irving

ADDRESSED: Genl Geo. P Morris / Office of the Home Journal / New York   POST-MARKED: Dearman N. Y. / Jan 7th
MANUSCRIPT: Yale.

1. See WI to Morris, January 3, 1853.
2. This committee was trying to raise funds to assist Lewis Gaylord Clark, editor of the *Knickerbocker Magazine.*
3. WI's travels included a visit to William Swain at New Bedford in late April or early May of 1851 (see PMI, IV, 84), to Saratoga Springs in July and early August of 1852 (see PMI, IV, 106–13), and to Gouverneur Kemble in the Highlands in September, 1852 (see PMI, IV, 119).

2243. *To William W. Waldron*

Sunnyside, January 10th, 1853

Dear Sir:

My time and attention having been much taken up by various occupations and engagements, I have failed to comply with the request in your letter of October last[1] to furnish you with a walking staff from the Sunnyside premises;[2] and I am now on the point of departing for Washington[3] to be absent three or four weeks, when your request is called to mind. I shall be careful to comply with it on my return, until when I hope you will tolerate the delay.

                                                    Yours with much respect,
                                                        Washington Irving

William W. Waldron, Esq.

PUBLISHED: Waldron, *WI & Cotemporaries*, p. 245.

1. This letter has not been located.
2. Waldron was not the only person to request a souvenir from WI's estate. One aspiring young writer "craved merely a scrap of the master's blotting paper." See STW, II, 204.
3. WI was planning to gather information for his *Life of Washington* in the official archives in Washington, D.C. See PMI, IV, 122.

2244.   To ———

                                        [New York, January 10, 1853]

Understanding that the Industrial Association of New York intend to send an Agent to Europe to promote the interests of the Exhibition[1] by securing the favorable attention of foreign governments procuring rare contributions &c &c I take the liberty of reccommending Mr George Sumner as one peculiarly fitted for that purpose. I do this from personal knowledge of his standing in Europe; his extensive acquaintance among the most valuable men there in Science & literature and his information respecting the state of the arts in different country.[2] I make this reccommendation without his knowledge and without the solicitation of any person.

                                                        Washington Irving

N York Jany 10th 1853

DOCKETED: Washington Irving.
MANUSCRIPT: Va.–Barrett.

1. The exhibition was a world's fair for the exhibition of industry of all nations and was housed in "The Crystal Palace," a building of glass and iron in the shape of a Greek cross erected on what became Bryant Park. The exhibition, which lasted from May until the autumn of 1853, was a national attraction and was regarded as proof of the progress in art, science, and industry in New York and the United States. See Wilson, *NY, Old and New*, I, 355–56. A long account of the opening of the exhibition filled most of the first three pages of the New York *Times* for July 15, 1853.
2. WI probably intended to write "countries."

2245. To Sarah Irving

New York, Jany 13th 1853

My dear Sarah,

Being weatherbound by that storm which you have been so long predicting "I set down to write you these few lines", to make up for that letter which you did not receive last Summer. The day of my arrival in town I tried to get a ticket to hear S⟨a⟩ontag, but finding there was trickery in disposing of seats, I went off in a huff to the other house, and saw Alboni in the Somnambula which she performed to admiration.[1] After the opera I went to the Ulshoeffers,[2] and found myself among the early ones. I think it one of the pleasantest balls I have been at for a long time, inasmuch as I sat all the evening on a Sopha beside Nancy,[3] in the front room up stairs, where they received their guests, so as to leave the rooms down stairs free for the dancers. In this way I saw a great part of the company in the course of the evening without fatigue and without going into the ball rooms, to be crowded and cramped and kicked into a corner. Beside the dances that are the fashion put me out of countenance and are not such as a gentleman of my years ought to witness. It was a very gay party and I am told there were a great many very beautiful dresses there; I can answer for it there were a great many very pretty young ladies.

Tuesday I dined with Helen (—Pierre dined with Mr Grinnel) we had a very cosy dinner, though Helen is not very well having been troubled for a week past with a return of the complaint in her head. In the evening feeling in want of City Amusement I went to Wallacks[4] and saw the old play of the Road to Ruin[5] played in excellent style.

Yesterday I packed my trunk to be ready for a start, but it began to Snow, and by six Oclock when I went to dine at Mr Astors[6] it was a perfect Storm. However we had a very pleasant dinner. It was given to young Lord[7] and his bride and we had all the Lord family there with whom you know I am on the most sociable terms; our friend West[8] the painter also was there; and Mr Brodhead.[9] In a word it was a right down friendly pleasant party. This morning finding the storm continuing and the snow deep I gave up all idea of setting out on my journey—and shall not set out until the storm is over.

Sarah Van Wart[10] is on a visit to Julia Grinnels and talks of coming up to the cottage sometime next week. Julia G has been indisposed with a cold but is now well, and Fanny has had an attack of influenza.

I presume the snow is deep in the country and you will have good sleighing. I hope you will take advantage of it and drive out; though I should not be surprised if this storm ends with rain

I have scolded Helen and Eliza for not writing oftener to the Cottage and trust they will reform They have promised to pay you visits during my absence.

You have read, no doubt, all about Ericksons[11] ship with the new motive power—It is a great event and must produce almost a revolution in marine affairs. I trust the invention will be equally applicable to locomotives on rail roads. Give my love to all the family—

I hope Angeline[12] has returned from her holyday visit to the city

Your affectionate uncle
Washington Irving

MANUSCRIPT: Yale.

1. WI, who arrived in New York on January 10, 1853, was irritated when he discovered that Niblo's Theater had raised the price of tickets for Donizetti's *La Figlia del Reggimento*, with Henrietta Sontag as Maria, to two and one dollars. Opening the same night at the Broadway Theater was Marietta Alboni as Amina in Bellini's *La Sonnambula*. See Odell, *NY Stage*, VI, 201, 241.

2. WI is referring to Michael Ulshoeffer, a former judge of the New York Common Pleas Court.

3. Ulshoeffer's daughter, who had married Irving Paris on November 1, 1848.

4. James W. Wallack (1795–1864) established a theater which opened on September 8, 1852, and was, for thirty years, to be the most distinguished theatrical establishment in New York City. See Odell, *NY Stage*, VI, 213.

5. Thomas Holcroft's play, *The Road to Ruin*, was presented on January 5, 1853, with a cast which included Laura Keene, Lester Wallack, Charles Walcot, Charles Hale, Mr. and Mrs. William R. Blake, and Mrs. Ann Stephens. See Odell, *NY Stage*, VI, 218; and NYEP, January 5, 1853.

6. William Backhouse Astor, the son of John Jacob Astor.

7. Probably James C. Lord (1825–1869), the son of Daniel Lord, who was, along with WI, an executor of the Astor estate.

8. William Edward West (1788–1857), an American painter famed for his portraits of Lord Byron and Countess Guiccioli, had illustrated WI's "The Pride of the Village" and "Annette Delarbre." See *J&N*, III, 439ff.

9. John Romeyn Brodhead, who was writing the *History of the State of New York*, published later in 1853. For other details, see WI to PMI, April 12, 1851.

10. Sarah Van Wart (1847–1919), the daughter of Henry and Abigail Van Wart.

11. John Ericsson (1803–1889), a Swedish-born engineer and inventor who had come to America in 1839, had designed a ship propelled by a "caloric" or hot-air engine. The vessel was not a commercial success because the engines were too large and inefficient and because the speed was not up to commercial requirements.

12. One of the housemaids at Sunnyside.

2246. To Catharine Irving

Baltimore Jany 17 1853

My dear Kate

In a letter to Sarah (which I suppose as usual she shewed to all the family) I gave an account of my where abouts and what abouts while in New York last week, where I was detained beyond my intended time by a snow storm. I was rather in a hum drum mood during my sojourn and, although I had big dinners, gay balls, Italian operas and Banvards Georama[1] to entertain me, I would willingly have stolen back to my "native plains" and given up the "gay world" and all terrestrial joys. The last evening of my detention however the weather and my dull humor cleared up; the latter doubtless under the influence of Sontags charms; who in the 'Daughter of the Regiment' looked, played and sang divinely.

The next morning proving bright and fair I broke up my encampment and got down to the foot of Courtland Street in time for the ferry boat which took over passengers for the Express train. I looked forward to a dull wintry journey and laid in a stock of newspapers to while away time but in the gentlemans cabin of the ferry boat whom should I see but Thackery.[2] We greeted each other cordially. He was on his way to philadelphia to deliver a course of lectures.[3] We took seats beside each other in the cars and the morning passed off delightfully. He seems still to enjoy his visit to the U States exceedingly, and enters into our social life with great relish. He had made a pleasant visit to Boston;[4] seen much of Prescott (whom he speaks highly of) Ticknor, Longfellow &c.—Said the Bostonians had ⟨wr?⟩ published a *smashing* criticism on him ⟨;⟩— which however ⟨did⟩ ↑does↓ not seem to have ruffled his temper, as I understand he cut it out of the newspaper and enclosed it in a letter to a female friend in New York.[5] He had been at a ball ⟨a night or two be⟩ at Mr Kernochans[6] where he saw some of my family—a niece (Sarah Clarke)[7] who was engaged to be married—he admired her—gave her his blessing, and was pleased with the young man her intended. One of my nieces (I presume Henrietta)[8] was overcome by the heat of the room and fainted.—

I parted with Thackery at Philadelphia after which I should have felt rather lonely but I was consoled by the sight of an uncommonly handsome ↑and genteel↓ young couple, who were travelling in company with others, but seemed to be especially devoted to each other and happy in each others society. I set them down for lovers and hope it will be a match; for they seemed especially suited to each other. I took considerable interest also in another young couple; brother and sister; who from the names on their trunks, I found to be Gambles of Virginia[.] I set them down for children or grand children of a young fellow of Rich-mond, whom I knew in Paris ⟨about⟩ nearly fifty years since,[9] and ⟨whom⟩ with whom I had many joyous scenes. The young lady[10] was very hand-some with large dark eyes, and arched eyebrows, but appeared to be in delicate health having a sad cough. I hope it was only from a transient cold. Just before our departure from New York I had seen her hanging on the arm of a tall elegant young man, who had apparently come to the ferry to see her off—I hope it is some love affair that may bring her back to New York. I should like to see her dark pensive eyes again and to find her recovered from her cough.

By the aid of noticing these young couples and weaving little his-toriettes about them I managed to while away time through out the rest of the journey; until I arrived after dark in Baltimore.

I had to enquire my way to Mr Kennedys; or rather Mr Grays, as Mr K. shares the house of his father in law in Baltimore. The door was opened by Mr Grays old factotum and Valley de Sham, Phil[11]—an old negro who formed a great friendship with me at Saratoga last summer[12] and, I am told, rather values himself on our intimacy. The moment he recognized me he seized me by the hand with such exclamations of joy that he brought out old Mr Gray and then Miss Gray into the hall, and then a scene took place; worthy of ⟨being⟩ forming a companion piece to the return of the prodigal son.[13] In a moment I felt myself in my pa-ternal home; and have ever since been a favored child of the house. To be sure there was no fatted calf killed but there was a glorious tea table spread with broiled oysters and other substantial accessories worthy of a travellers appetite.

Here then I am delightfully fixed, in this most hospitable spacious, comfortable mansion—with Kennedys library and study at my command where I am scribbling this letter—and with my friend Phil ever at hand to take care of me and attend to all my wants and wishes.

How long I shall tarry in Baltimore I cannot say. ↑Probably↓ not above a day or two. My charming friend Mrs Stanard[14] of Richmond, who has been on a visit to Mrs Kennedy, will be in Baltimore tomorrow, to consult her Physician,[15] being out of health. I look forward with pleasure to meet-ing her and should be delighted to have her for a fellow traveller in the rail road cars to Washington. Give my love to all bodies and let me have the news of the Cottage

Your affectionate uncle
Washington Irving

(Write to me care of the Hon. J P Kennedy) / Washington[?]

MANUSCRIPT: Sally Grinnell Metzger.   PUBLISHED: PMI, IV, 123–25 (in part);
    Tuckerman, *Life of J. P. Kennedy*, pp. 252–53 (in part); James G. Wilson,

Thackeray in the United States, 1852–3, 1855–6 (New York, 1904), p. 157 (in part).

1. John Banvard (1815–1891) was a painter and writer who had constructed a "georama" or panoramic painting of the Holy Land and Jerusalem and placed it on exhibition in a building adjoining the Metropolitan Hotel and near Niblo's Theater. See Odell, *NY Stage*, VI, 263; and NYEP, January 3, 1853.

2. William Makepeace Thackeray (1811–1863), who had attracted considerable attention with *Vanity Fair* and more recently with *Henry Esmond*, was lecturing in the United States on "English Humorists of the Eighteenth Century."

3. Thackeray lectured at the Music Fund Hall in Philadelphia. See Wilson, *Thackeray in the United States*, p. 108.

4. Thackeray had spoken at the Melodeon, the music hall in Boston, on December 21, 24, 28, 31, 1852, and January 4, 7, 1853. See *The Letters and Private Papers of William Makepeace Thackeray*, ed. Gordon N. Ray (Cambridge, Mass., 1946), III, 150–51.

5. Probably Mrs. George Baxter or her daughter Sally, with whom Thackeray was quite intimate during his stay in New York in December, 1852. See Gordon N. Ray, *Thackeray: The Age of Wisdom, 1849–1863* (New York, 1958), pp. 207–10. In a note on January 17, 1853, to Harriet, his daughter, Thackeray observed that "Some of the Boston papers were very savage and abused me daily. . . ." For this letter and details of the Boston *Courier's* attack on January 8 and its retraction on January 10, see *Letters and Private Papers*, III, 174.

6. Possibly John Murray Carnochan (1817–1887), a prominent New York surgeon with an international reputation.

7. Sarah Clark (b. 1833) was the daughter of Edwin Clark (1802–1878) and Sarah Sanders Irving (1811–1836), the youngest daughter of John Treat Irving. Miss Clark married James Kent in April of 1853. See WI to Elizabeth Kennedy, April 24, 1853.

8. Henrietta Eckford Irving, daughter of Gabriel and Eliza Eckford Irving.

9. WI's journals and surviving letters of 1805 do not mention Gamble. He was Richard Gamble of Richmond, Virginia and later of Tallahassee, Florida. See Mary Selden Kennedy, *Seldens of Virginia* (New York, 1911), I, 96.

10. Letitia Gamble, who married Lewis P. Holliday and later Charles H. Latrobe. See Kennedy, *Seldens of Virginia*, I, 96–97. In a letter to Sarah Irving on January 22, 1853, WI calls her "Kate"; on February 16, 1853, in another letter to Sarah, WI calls her "Letty."

11. WI talks about Phil in letters to Elizabeth Kennedy, November 11, 1853; and to John P. Kennedy, December 20, 1853.

12. See PMI, IV, 106–13.

13. See Luke 15:11–32.

14. Mrs. Stanard may be related to Jane Stith Stanard, whom Edgar Allan Poe celebrated in "To Helen."

15. Mrs. Stanard may have consulted Dr. Thomas Hepburn Buckler (1812–1901), a prominent Baltimore practitioner and a family friend of the Kennedys. See Tuckerman, *Life of J. P. Kennedy*, p. 140.

2247. *To Mary Irving*

Baltimore, Jany 18t 1853

My dear Mary,

My letter to Kate[1] will have informed you all of my travels to this city where I am enjoying myself extremely. I came near being carried off to Washington yesterday by my charming little friend Mrs Stanard; who with her husband paid Baltimore a visit on the morning train; but I resisted the temptation being involved in engagements for two days, but consoled myself with the idea that I should see a great deal of Mrs S in Washington, where she is passing the winter.

I drove out in the morning with the Stanards and Miss Gray to see Mrs Tiffany[2] (little Sally McLane in bygone days) whom I found living in a superb house in the centre of a little park at a short distance from the city. The house is finished and furnished in excellent taste, and in a truly noble style. I think I have seen nothing better in this country. It is situated on a rising ground and commands an extensive prospect. Mrs Tiffany told me she she[3] had written to me, inviting me to pay her a visit; which letter must have reached Sunnyside after my departure.[4] I had to make her a half promise to pay her a visit for a day or two on my way home.

Yesterday I dined at Mr Meredith's;[5] where I met two of Mr Gardiner Howlands[6] daughters one of them a young and lovely widow, Mrs Brown,[7] whose husband you may reccollect was unfortunately killed a year or two since on a fourth of July, by the discharge of a toy cannon. As the widow is young and lovely and rich, I doubt of her remaining a widow long; and hope she may meet with a husband worthy of her—which is not an easy matter considering her own merits, and the degeneracy of the "opposite Sex."

Her unmarried sister[8] I am told is engaged, and I dont wonder at it, for she is a perfect love—besides being an heiress. Their mother Mrs Howland[9] did not appear at table. Tell Julia Sanders, if she is with you, that Miss Meredith made very kind enquiries after her, and spoke of her with great friendship—The Merediths live immediately opposite Mr Greys and the families are extremely intimate.

This day we have a family gathering at Mr Greys, at dinner, and music in the evening, the old gentleman being a great amateur. Tomorrow morning I take my departure in the nine oclock train for Washington; where the cars take me in less than two hours. I shall leave Baltimore with regret for they have made me completely at home here and I have passed my time very much to my taste; having a capital library to retire to when I wish to be alone or to ⟨oc⟩ exercise my pen, and my old friend

Phil, to hover about me like a guardian spirit—though rather a black one.

Mr Grey is a capital specimen of the old Irish gentleman—warm hearted—benevolent—well informed and, like myself, very fond of music and pretty faces, so that our humors jump together completely. I believe it was our sympathies on these two last matters, which linked us together so cordially last summer and made him exact a promise from me to visit him this winter

10 OClock at night—I have left this letter open and now must close it and go to bed.

We had a very pleasant dinner; a small party but a very lively and social one. In the evening we had some excellent music by two professional artists on the piano and the violin; who gave us some choice pieces from Mozarts operas. Mr Grey has them once a week, with occasionally amateurs to perform with them—In the evening came in a Miss Delaney[10] a very beautiful girl, one of old Mr Greys pets, who I am pleased to find, goes to Washington the day after tomorrow on a visit to Mrs Kennedy— She is to be accompanied by a Miss Andrews,[11] who I am told is an excellent musician; so we shall have a gay household.

I set off tomorrow morning in the nine OClock train; unless I should again be embargoed by a Snow storm, as it has begun to snow this evening.

I hope the cold weather of the last few days has enabled the men to get some ice into the ice house.

Good night my dear little good for nuffin—give my love to all the household, take care of yourself and follow all the doctors directions that when I return home I may find you good for sutthing—

Your affectionate uncle
Washington Irving

MANUSCRIPT: SHR.   PUBLISHED: PMI, IV, 125 (in part); Tuckerman, *Life of J. P. Kennedy*, p. 252 (in part); Bohner, *J. P. Kennedy*, p. 66 (in part).

1. January 17, 1853.
2. Sally McLane (b. September, 1820) was the daughter of WI's old friend, Louis McLane, who was minister to Great Britain from 1829 to 1831. Sally had married Henry Tiffany (1811–1877) in June, 1840.
3. WI inadvertently repeated "she."
4. This letter has not been located.
5. Jonathan Meredith, a noted Baltimore lawyer, who lived at 29 North Calvert Street, was a neighbor of Edward Gray, who lived at 26 North Calvert Street.
6. Gardiner Greene Howland (1787–1851) was a partner in the New York merchandising firm of G. G. and S. Howland and a strong backer of the Hudson River Railroad. See Scoville, *Old Merchants of NYC*, I, 309.
7. Louisa Howland had married James Brown of the firm of Brown Brothers and Company. She was widowed when, as WI notes, Brown was shot on the piazza

of his father-in-law's home in Flushing, New York. See Scoville, *Old Merchants of NYC*, I, 309–10.

8. Probably either Anabella, who married Rufus Leavitt, a New York dry goods merchant, or Abbey, who married a son of Judge Frederick Wolcott of Litchfield, Connecticut. See Scoville, *Old Merchants of NYC*, I, 309.

9. The former Louisa Meredith, daughter of Jonathan Meredith, who had married Howland in 1829 as his second wife. See Scoville, *Old Merchants of NYC*, I, 310.

10. Mary Grafton Dulaney (1835–1897), daughter of Grafton Lloyd Dulaney, a Baltimore lawyer. She married Gardiner Greene Howland, Jr. (1834–1905) in 1856. See King A. Hagey and William A. Hagey, *The Hagey Families in America and the Dulaney Family* (Bristol, Tenn., 1951), pp. 581, 609.

11. Louisa Andrews, along with Mary Dulaney, was a frequent guest in Edward Gray's home. WI refers to her frequently in his letters.

2248. To Sarah Irving

Washington Jany 22d. 1853

My dear Sarah,

I arrived here safely this morning between eleven & twelve and found Mr Kennedy waiting for me at the Station, where he put into my hands your nice long letter and also one from Pierre Munroe.[1]

I presumed you would be nearly snowed under in the late storm, which was deep in the city and is always deeper in the country. It is probable you will have some days of good sleighing, and I trust you will all take advantage of it. I am glad to learn that Robert was about to attack the ice; we cannot be choosers this year, but must take what we can get; solid or not. The continuance of very cold weather may enable the men to get a second cutting of clear solid ice to put on top.

⟨I am⟩ The geese were well sold; whoever bought them will have the worth of their money in chewing. Tell Robert to furnish you with more of the poultry; there must be two or three dozen more than we want for stock and they won't grow better by keeping[.] I wish him in the course of the winter to put the fence between our ground and Dr McVickars[2] in sufficient repair to keep the cattle from breaking through. There is no need of bestowing pains upon the looks of the job as I trust to making an arrangement with the Doctor to put up an entirely new fence in the course of the year.

The derangement of Mr Grinnells health does not surprise me, I have for some time expected it. I hope the counsel of his doctor has made sufficient impression on him to induce him to be more cautious in his mode of living. He is all the while pushing forward on the high pressure system at the risk of an explosion.

I am most comfortably fixed at Mr Kennedys with a capital room and every thing snug about me for writing or reading or lounging. Mrs Kennedy recieved me in her own frank kind manner—She could not treat me better *even if she were a niece.* I understand my friend Major Jack Downing is in Washington with his family; also Alexander Hamilton— who is here pleading a cause before the Supreme Court. I found my darling little friend Mrs Stanard on a morning visit ⟨at⟩ to Mrs Kennedy on my arrival, so that I see I shall meet with lots of agreeable company. I wish, however, to keep out of the whirl as long as I can; that I may get among the archives of the State department, before I am carried off my feet by engagements. On friday evening is the presidents[3] levee where I shall attend—and then I shall be launched—As yet I have not looked about me—merely passing from the parlour to my room where I have been unpacking my trunk, arranging my things and scribbling this letter. I shall ⟨pa⟩ keep it open, in case I may have any thing more to say this evening

½ *past 10.* We had a pleasant informal dinner. Mr Corwin[4] the Secretary of the Treasury Commodore Shubrick[5] and a Captain Dupont[6] of the Navy dined with us. The conversation was very interesting and varied and occasionally very amusing[.] I felt, however, rather below par and found it difficult to bear my share in the conversation. For several nights past I have slept very little indeed ⟨my⟩ it was the case before I left home, but has been still worse of late; though I have taken no sleep in the day time. It has an exhausting effect ⟨upon me⟩ upon my mind and spirits. I attribute it to derangement of the stomach causing acidity or heart burn, and have put myself on regimen as well as I can, not having you at hand to advise and take care of me. I hope to sleep well to night. With love to all the family

Your affectionate uncle
Washington Irving

Jany. 23d. I had enclosed the foregoing for the post office when I recieved your letter dated the 30th but mailed the 21st,[7] to which I will reply in post script. And first—I am glad to hear that the ice house is filled; it is the all important operation of the winter, after the accomplishment of which, the elements may act as they please. I am glad to learn also that the fences have been painted; which I gather from the circumstance of Tony being bedaubed with coal tar, doubtless from his assisting in the job. I am glad to hear that the little dogs[8] guard the house well, and would suggest that Robert provide a sentry box ↑lined↓ with ⟨some⟩ ↑an↓ old buffalo skin, for them to nestle in at night when on duty. It might be put under one of the iron seats in the porch.

You wish to be kept informed of all the beautiful ladies I meet with—so I will begin by the three belles of our household. One of them, Miss Mary Kennedy[9] is a niece of Mr Kennedy, she is about your own size; light and graceful in her movements, of a very pleasing prepossessing countenance, a frank, truthful demeanour, with perfect tact and self possession. She is Mrs Kennedys right hand in every thing, and has quite the gift of society, with ⟨the⟩ excellent qualifications for domestic life. She acts as my secretary to answer all notes of invitation &c taking somewhat of a mischievous pleasure in baulking my fair correspondents of my autograph.

Another, Miss Dulaney, is really a beautiful girl, young, fresh, plump and dimpling, with beautiful black eyes, small mouth fine teeth and the sweetest smile imaginable. She is ⟨a good⟩ unspoiled as yet, by admiration, ⟨very⟩ with great simplicity and naturalness of manner, and with none of the insolence of beauty, ⟨that sometimes⟩ for which young belles are sometimes noted in the hey day of their charms. I ⟨tak⟩ took her into the presidents levee the other evening with the conviction that I was conducting the belle of the assembly—I soon lost her however among five hundred admiring young gentlemen.

The third, Miss Andrews, is a very pretty genteel young lady who reminds me continually of my little good for nuffin Mary. She is about her size, and like her ⟨very⟩ is never to be seen, from morning till night, with a hair out of place or the least derangement of her toilette. She is a perfect little lady and fit to be put under a glass case, and set on the mantle piece.

Of these three girls, were I a young man, I should be at a loss which to prefer—but rather think I should fall in love with all three—As an old gentleman I feel a serene pleasure in noticing their little ways and graces, and listening to their discussions about dresses parties, beaux &c—They have the freshness and gayety of youth, but with that thorough good breeding which tempers its buoyancy. As yet, we have been so much taken up with engagements and visitors that I have had but little opportunity of ⟨hearing⟩ enjoying Miss Andrews talent for music, which from a small specimen, appears to be of a high order.

I forgot to mention, in speaking of the presidents levee, that I caught sight in the grand saloon, of the ⟨bea⟩ Virginia beauty with large dark eyes, whom I studied in the rail road cars between N York and Philadelphia. She is Miss Kate Gamble, formerly of Virginia, at present I believe of Florida, and I have no doubt she is daughter of my friend Gamble with whom I frolicked in Paris in my young days. I had but a glimpse of her at a distance. I was in a crowd; with Mrs Stanard on my arm and people shaking hands with me on right and left—The crowd closed between me and the dark eyed beauty and I saw no more of her[.]

I shall doubtless meet with her again in my perambulations about Washington, and if so, you shall hear more about her.

In one corner of the Presidents saloon I was accosted by a Naval officer, who had met me on board of Chaunceys Squadron[10] at anchor off Sackets harbor, during the last war with G Britain. He was then a Midshipman on board. I was up there as aid de Camp of Gov Tompkins[11] to consult with the army & naval commanders and order out Militia. He introduced me to his wife; who claimed a right to my acquaintance having often heard her mother talk about me. Her mother had a copy of verses which I once wrote about her!—It turned out that she was the daughter of a Virginia belle whom I had admired and berhymed about half a century since at Richmond—So ones youthful sins rise in judgment against one. She beckoned to a very pretty little girl (her daughter) who was at a distance—before the latter came up she began to telegraph with her fingers telling her mother she knew me by my likeness—She was deaf and dumb!

P S. None of the Washington belles wear caps[12]—

MANUSCRIPT: SHR.   PUBLISHED: PMI, IV, 126 (in part).

1. These letters have not been located.

2. Dr. William McVickar (1827–1877) was the rector at St. Barnabas Church in Irvington.

3. Millard Fillmore (1800–1874), who became president upon the death of Zachary Taylor on July 9, 1850, did not receive the Whig presidential nomination in 1852. He was then nearing the end of his term.

4. Thomas Corwin (1794–1865), a lawyer, congressman (1831–1840), and a U.S. senator (1845–1850) from Ohio, was secretary of the treasury under Fillmore and later U.S. minister to Mexico (1861–1864).

5. William B. Shubrick (1790–1874), a longtime friend of James Fenimore Cooper, had served as head of the Philadelphia Navy Yard and was now chairman of the lighthouse board.

6. Samuel F. DuPont (1803–1865), who had become a midshipman in 1815 and a commander in 1843, was a member of a commission to set up a curriculum for the Naval Academy. Subsequent promotions brought him to the rank of rear admiral during the Civil War.

7. This letter has not been located.

8. WI mentioned "Taffy and Tony, two pet dogs of a dandy race, kept more for show than use . . . [and a] little terrier slut Ginger" in a letter to Elizabeth Kennedy, March 11, 1853.

9. Mary E. Kennedy was the daughter of Andrew and Mary Riddle Kennedy. She married Henry Pendleton Cooke on January 1, 1855. WI was to write to her frequently later in 1853.

10. Isaac Chauncey (1792–1840), who organized and commanded the U.S. naval forces on Lakes Ontario and Erie during the War of 1812, later held important administrative posts in the navy.

11. Daniel D. Tompkins (1774–1825), as governor of New York, served as

commander of the New York State Militia during the War of 1812. He was later vice-president of the United States from 1817 to 1825.

12. The ladies' caps at this time were rather shapeless beribboned doilylike affairs worn on the back of the head. See Carl Köhler, A History of Costume (New York, 1963), pp. 449–53.

2249. To Catharine Irving

Washington, Jany 23d. 1853.

My dear Kate

I am in the midst of terrible dissipation and in great danger of being carried away by it in spite of all my efforts at sober life. I have three young belles in the house with me on a visit to Mrs. Kennedy, they are very pretty very amiable very ladylike and one of them very musical and I could make myself very happy at home with them if Tom, Dick and Harry out of doors would leave me alone, but I am assailed with invitations of all kinds which I find it impossible entirely to fight off.

Yesterday I made a delightful excursion, with some of our household and some of the ⟨P⟩ young folks of the Presidents family,[1] down the Potomac in a steamer to Mount Vernon. We began by a very pleasant breakfast at the Presidents where we met Mr Augustine Washington[2] the proprietor of Mount Vernon who accompanied us on the excursion. The day was superb. It was like one of those Indian summer days we had just before I left home. On board the steamer we were joined by Mrs. Davis (Mrs Jack Downing) and two very agreeable ladies from Boston. Everything conspired to render our visit to Mount Vernon a very interesting and delightful one and we returned in the steamer by four Oclock in the afternoon

In the evening I was at the President's levee. It was very crowded. I met with many interesting people there and saw many beauties from all parts of the Union; but I had no chance of enjoying conversation with any of them; for in a little while the same scene began that took place here eleven years ago[3] ⟨when⟩ on my last visit. I had to shake hands with man woman and child who beset me on all sides, until I felt as if it was becoming rather absurd, and struggled out of the throng. From the levee I was whirled away to a ball where I found my friend Madame Calderon[4] the Spanish Ministers lady and was getting ⟨as⟩ a world of ⟨news⟩ chat about Madrid and our acquaintances there, when the system of hand shaking began again and I retreated and came home

It is certainly very gratifying to meet with such testimonials of esteem and cordial good will but at the same time it is extremely embarrassing

The day before yesterday I came by surprise upon Sarah ⟨[*unrecovered*]⟩ and her husband; strolling quietly along Pennsylvania Avenue. I had no idea they were in Washington; and was sorry to find they were on the point of departure. Sarah was as happy and handsome as ever. I sat chatting with her and ⟨[*unrecovered*]⟩ for some time at the hotel; where I find she was a ⟨grate⟩ ↑great↓ favorite among the lady inmates.

This morning I have taken my seat ⟨at⟩ as an honorary member at a meeting of the Smithsonian Institute.[5] It is a noble institution and is beginning to make itself known through out the world. The edifice is a very imposing one, of brown stone in the Norman style of architecture, built by Renwick,[6] the interior excepting part of the wings, yet unfinished.

Today there is a dinner party at Mr Kennedys—members of the Senate and house of Representatives—I fear it will be a dull one, especially to me who am unacquainted with most of the guests—however I am doomed to ⟨these⟩ this kind of trials and inflictions

I have been repeatedly interrupted in writing this letter, which must apologize for its dullness. I find it impossible as yet to have any time to myself in this city of engagements, interruptions and distractions.

I have been much pleased with what I have seen of the President and his family and have been most kindly received by them. Indeed I should have a heart like a pebble stone if I was insensible to the very cordial treatment I experience wherever I go—The only fault I find is that I am likely to be killed by kindness[7]

With my best love to all at my dear little home

Your affectionate uncle
W I.

Manuscript: NYPL—Seligman Collection. Published: PMI, IV, 126–28; Tuckerman, *Life of J. P. Kennedy*, p. 233 (in part).

1. These included Mary Abigail Fillmore (1832–1854) and Millard Powers Fillmore (1827–1889). See Robert J. Rayback, *Millard Fillmore: Biography of a President* (New York, 1959), pp. 46–47.

2. John Augustine Washington (1821–1861), great-great grandson of George Washington's brother John Augustine, inherited Mount Vernon but later sold it to an association which maintained it as an historical property.

3. WI was in Washington in March, 1842, prior to his departure for Spain. See PMI, III, 185–87.

4. Frances Erskine Inglis (1804–1882), of Scottish origin, had married Angel Calderón de la Barca in 1838. WI had known her in Madrid in late 1843 and early 1844 before her husband was sent to Washington as Spanish minister.

5. WI's honorary membership in the Smithsonian Institution had been conferred on August 1, 1849. Since it rarely bestowed such memberships, WI's election was considered an unusual honor. See STW, II, 392.

6. James Renwick (1818–1895), son of WI's old friend of the same name, was an engineer and self-trained architect who worked in Gothic and Romanesque

styles. He designed Grace Church and St. Patrick's Cathedral in New York City.

7. WI may be alluding to Thomas Heywood's *A Woman Killed With Kindness* (1603).

2250.   (deleted)

2251.   To Sarah Irving

Washington Jany 25th. 1853

My dear Sarah,

I received this morning your letter dated the 24th.[1] but which I think must have been written on Sunday the 23d and even in that case it has reached me promptly. I thank you for your prescription, but have no further need of it, having got rid of the heart burn and being now in prime order.

The pictorial field book of the Revolution had been promised me by Mr Los[s]ing in a letter received previous to my departure from home[2]— It is a capital family book—a grand work of reference concerning our revolutionary history

As to the letters which have come for me read them and send on such ⁊s you think I would like to recieve. If you should occasionally come across a billet doux, dont let the other girls see it for the world Consider yourself my confidant

I devote my mornings to researches in the archives of the State Department, which are kindly put at my disposal by my friend Mr Everett the Secretary of State. I find enough there to occupy me for some time, and am rejoiced to find what I came in quest of and to have such free access to it.

Though I have endeavored to decline engagements I find myself committed for several dinners. Evening parties, however I steer clear of as much as possible; though I shall have to go tomorrow evening to the Soiree of my friend Madame Calderon wife of the Spanish Minister This I do for the sake of Spain and "auld lang Syne" The experience I had at the Presidents levee makes me rather shy in getting into another gay crowd to be fussed about.

27th. I was interrupted when writing the foregoing—and it has remained unfinished. Yesterday I was rather good for nothing; having passed a somewhat sleepless night Still I worked all the morning in the Archives of State and had to play my part at a large dinner party at home; but in the evening I gave up Madame Calderons Soiree; heard Some good music from Miss Andrews on the piano; went to bed at a reasonable hour, slept well and this day am myself again. I have to dine however at Mr Everetts with a large party and have two invitations for balls in the evening; but think I shall not go to either of the latter. I cannot keep my spirits up to these continual claims on them Besides, I wish to keep my mind as quiet as possible for my morning researches in the Archives.

I have begun this letter on the inside of the sheet through inadvertence. It is now time to dress for dinner, so I cannot fill it up. To make amends however I enclose you a scrap of a Baltimore paper[3] sent me in an envelope by John Barney[4] of that city but now in Washington. I presume it was written by him, as he was at my elbow in the crowd at the Presidents levee; ⟨and⟩ playing the part of gentleman usher and introducing man woman and child to me[.] I shall take care not to give him another chance

I recieved a letter from Helen[5] yesterday which I will answer when more in writing mood at present I am *extinct*. Playing the lion has killed me. I should like to repose for a few days in my den at Sunnyside.

Have you seen any thing of the Hamiltons lately. Mrs Stanard tells me she hears they are coming on to Washington. I fear it will be after I am gone.

Give my love to all at home—I suppose You have my dear Julia Sanders with you by this time and it is a matter of great regret to me to be absent during her visit

Your affectionate uncle
Washington Irving

MANUSCRIPT: Florence Forbes Locke.   PUBLISHED: PMI, IV, 128 (in part).

1. This letter has not been located.

2. Benson J. Lossing's *The Pictorial Field Book of the Revolution* appeared in two volumes in 1850 and 1852. WI omitted the bracketed letter. Lossing's letter has not been located.

3. The text of the clipping, attached to the sheet below WI's signature: "Among the most brilliant soirees of the season, was one of Friday last given by our young friend Mr. C. [William Corcoran; see WI to Sarah Irving, February 16, 1853], one of the highly respectable and prosperous firm of the bankers of that name. It was attended by the President's family, every member of the Cabinet except the Secretary of State, who does not mingle in the gaieties of Washington, foreign Ministers, and all the celebrities of this attractive metropolis, including Washington Irving, the lion of the literary world, who every where receives most marked attention. Naturally reserved and shrinking from notoriety, the attraction of social intercourse is distasteful to him, but that benevolence of feeling which illumines his countenance and is the prominent characteristic of his soul, induces him to acquiesce in the univer[s]al desire to enjoy a presentation to one who has contributed so much to the pleasure[?] [*paper torn*] as well as instruction and improvement [*unrecovered—paper torn*] He certainly is the best read man in our country, and deservedly the most esteemed. The happiness of having pressed

his hand will be among the cherished recollections of the hundreds who clustered around him at the President's reception and the agreeable soiree alluded to."

4. Barney had been a Maryland congressman. For other details, see WI to Barney, October 30, 1851.

5. This letter has not been located.

2252.   To Henry R. Schoolcraft

[January 28, 1853]

My dear Sir,

I have this morning received a note from you dated Friday Jany 21st inviting me to Supper. Either there is a mistake in the date, or the note has been long in reaching me. If the invitation is really for this evening I am sorry to say that previous engagements prevent my having the pleasure of accepting it.

I regret to hear of your lameness and shall take an early occasion to call on you sociably[.] I should have done so before this had I known your address

with great regard / Yours very truly
Washington Irving

[*Unrecovered*] Street / Friday. Jany 28 [1853]

Manuscript: LC.

The date is ascertained by the perpetual calendar and by the fact of WI's being in Washington, where Schoolcraft lived, at that time.

2253.   To Daniel Lord

Washington Feb 3d. 1853

Worthy friend & co executor,

The invitation of your good lady[1] received the very day of her fête, found me irrevocably engaged half a life time ahead for all kinds of festivities and whether I shall have half a ⟨f⟩ life left when I get through with them is a matter somewhat dubious

You talk of my going about like a "roaring lion." My good sir theres not a roar left in me; not even one of Nick Bottoms roar of a sucking dove.[2] I am the tamest most broken down lion that ever was shewn in a menagerie—not even to be stirred up with a long pole. A course of heavy dinners and hot crowded evening parties have done my business completely. I now dont roar even when feeding but am the dumbest of guests going and at evening parties I can no longer muster up a fine speech to a fine lady though she were as fair as queen Sheba[.] I have no doubt I am set down for a take-in and a humbug, and begin to have my own suspicions in the matter. I certainly cannot cope with society at the rate it goes on here and shall soon have to eat and run lest I should be killed with kindness

I gave your remembrances to Mr and Mrs Kennedy, who received them with sensation and spoke of you in a manner that you would be glad to hear, but which I shall not repeat.

They are both very popular here and their house very happy and well frequented one. It has been enlivened during my visit by a groupe of Baltimore belles; with all of whom, had I been a young man, I should indubitably have fallen in love; but being now a quiet hearted old gentleman, I have amused myself with noticing how they manage affairs in their little realm of beauty; and discovering (now that I am behind the scenes) those little strategys of the sex that bothered me sadly in my juvenile and amatory days—However, Ill say no more on this subject lest this letter should fall into your daughters hands.

I am sorry to see you have not yet digested the charge of the Judge in the Jones trial. I had supposed you had by this time the stomach of an ostrich in matters of the kind. You are like the giant in Rabelais who had been accustomed all his life to swallow mill stones, but was at last choked by a roll of butter which he found at the mouth of an oven—I wonder Mrs Lords consolations have not subdued you to patience in this matter.

With kind remembrances to the ladies

Yours very faithfully
Washington Irving

MANUSCRIPT: Va.–Barrett.

Through the salutation and the allusions to Mrs. Lord at the end of the letter the addressee is identified as Daniel Lord, who, like WI, was an executor of the estate of John Jacob Astor.

1. This invitation from Susan de Forest Lord has not been located.
2. See *Midsummer Night's Dream*, I, ii, 83–84.

2254.   To Catharine, Sarah, and Mary Irving

Washington Feb 4t. 1853

My dear Girls,

I am in debt for several letters from home[1] so this must do for you all. I have in fact been so much taken up by hard work at the State department, when I can manage to get there, and by the incessant demands of society in all kinds of shapes, that I have niether leisure nor mood to write. I have at times been nearly done up, and would have broken away and hurried home but for the mine I have to dig at in the Archives.

I foresee I shall be detained here some time longer; having such a world of documents to examine and being so often interrupted in my labors. You must not think I am staying here for pleasures sake—for pleasure just now I would gladly dispense with if I could. I do manage to keep clear of most of the evening parties; but the long dinners are inevitable; and the necessity of returning visits cuts up my time deplorably.

Had I nothing to do but amuse myself I should find Washington really delightful, for I meet pleasant and interesting people at every turn; but I have no time to follow up ↑new↓ acquaintances, and am only tantalized by proffered friendships which I cannot cultivate.

Mrs Kennedy had one of her soirees a few Evening[s][2] since; when all Washington poured in upon us and I had to go through some such a scene of hand shaking as took place at the presidents. On this occasion an officer of the Navy delivered to me a small paper box containing a minature anchor. It was made from the bolt to which Columbus was chained in the prison at St Domingo. A purser of the Navy[3] had gouged the bolt out of the wall and sent part of it to the National institute of this city the other part he designed for me. The poor fellow was taken ill and died of the yellow fever; but his sister had executed his wishes in having a little anchor wrought out of the relique and had forwarded with a letter to me. Both the letter and the anchor have been between six and seven years in reaching me: having lain in the hands of a naval officer at Washington

I shall treasure them up in the archives of Sunnyside.[4]

Two of the young belles who have been the pride and delight of our house, Miss Dulaney and Miss Andrews have returned to Baltimore to figure at a grand assembly there. I kissed them both at parting, as piously as if they had been my own nieces, and I felt all the regret of an uncle at losing them. Mr & Mrs Kennedy have likewise gone for a couple of days at Baltimore and Miss Mary Kennedy and myself are left to keep house together. Yesterday was reception day, when we recieved morning calls, fortunately a great part of the gay world had gone to Baltimore to the fete, so that we got through the ceremony without a crowd.

Captain Hiram Paulding[5] arrived here within a day or two to take command of the Navy Yard. You may reccollect he was quite sore at being disappointed of the Navy Yard at New York and put in the Japan Expedition; and thought Mr Kennedy had not treated him well. Every thing has been explained to his satisfaction—He has a post more advantageous than that of New York, and he has met with so many favors and accommodations from Kennedy that the Secretary has quite won his heart.

If this letter should find Julia Sanders still with you give my love to her and tell her I will write to her when I have a little more liesure.

I now and then meet persons here who reccollect her and speak of her affectionately, as all do who know her. I have met with a Mrs Walton[6] also who knew Helen and Eliza at Oswego and speaks of them on the kindest terms—She sat next me at a great dinner party the other day, and by her agreeable conversation made it a very pleasant one. Two other of Helens admirers are Mrs Eames[7] and her sister Miss Campbell (the latter we met at Mr Kembles in the Highlands last summer)[8] They seem to think they cannot speak highly enough of Helen—I have promised to take tea with them next Sunday evening—

We have very soft foggy weather—and if the same prevails in your neighborhood it will take the frost out of the ground and make the roads deep—However—we have our ice house filled and are secure—Give my love to your father, who I hope, is free from rheumatism

Your affectionate uncle
Washington Irving

MANUSCRIPT: HSA.
PUBLISHED: PMI, IV, 128–29.

1. These letters have not been located.

2. WI omitted the bracketed letter.

3. Robert S. Moore of Newbern, South Carolina served as a purser from 1841 until his death in 1845. See PMI, IV, 129; and Callahan, *Officers of the Navy*, p. 389.

4. According to Joseph T. Butler, present curator of Sunnyside, the locations of the miniature anchor and Moore's letter are not known.

5. Hiram Paulding (1797–1878), who became a midshipman in 1811, had served in the U.S. Navy all over the world with distinction before becoming commander of the Washington Navy Yard. He later promoted the use of ironclad vessels during the Civil War.

6. Possibly the wife or a relative of H. N. Walton, who was a member of the board of health in Oswego in 1832. See Crisfield Johnson, *History of Oswego County, New York* (Philadelphia, 1877), p. 149.

7. Fanny Campbell married Charles Eames (1811–1867) in 1845. Eames was

the editor of the Washington *Union* from 1849 to 1854, and his home was a gathering place for celebrities in society, politics, and the arts.

8. WI had visited Gouverneur Kemble from September 20 to 25, 1852. See WI to Mary Hamilton, September 20, 1852.

2255. To Pierre M. Irving

Washington Sunday Feb—6th 1853.

My dear Pierre

I am making a longer sojourn in Washington than I had intended, but it takes time to make the necessary researches in the Archives of State, especially as I am continually interrupted by the claims of society, which in Washington are overwhelming. I cannot say that I find much that is new among the MSS of Washington, Sparks[1] having published the most interesting; but it is important to get facts from the fountain head, not at second hand, through his publications. I have made one visit to Mount Vernon since I have been here, and shall probably make another; having been invited by the proprietor, Mr Augustine Washington to make one of a day or two. I mean also to visit old Mr Custis at Arlington who has many personal recollections of Washington which he is fond of relating.

If I had nothing to do but amuse myself, I should find Washington a most agreeable place, abounding as it does with interesting personages, and intellectual resorts but at present I am anxious to achieve the purpose of my visit, and return home, and am continually struggling against the current of dissipation; but struggling in vain. The evening parties I contrive in a great measure to keep clear of,—but there is no escaping the huge dinner parties; and I stand engaged for a succession of them for more than a week a head.

I have met with two friends of Helen, Mrs Eames and her sister Miss Campbell, who are most enthusiastic in their praises of her; and have so won my heart thereby that I have promised to attend Mrs Eames Soiree this evening—and shall keep my promise, if the weather, which is now raining Cats and dogs, will permit me; or if I am not prevented by a cold which I have taken in this soft, damp ⟨w⟩ thawing season and which has kept me coughing and sneezing for the last day or two.

Hiram Paulding arrived here a few days since to take command of the Navy Yard at this place. It is an excellent command, and will prove a more advantageous one to him than that at New York, of which he was desirous

I am to dine in company with him on Friday next at Mr Purser Stockton,[2] with whom he is a guest. He appears to be much pleased with his appointment, and I know that Mr Kennedy is disposed to do every thing in his power to render the station agreeable to him

The worthy captain has just set up his carriage and pressed me to make use of it, intimating that it was rather a stylish one; but as I had the use of my friend Kennedys carriage beside any quantity of *Omnibi* I declined his offer. I was glad, however, to see the good fellow setting up his Ebenezer[3] so cheerily.

I hope Helen will go up soon to the cottage—It is a continual draw back on my enjoyment here to be so long absent from home, in this dull season of the year; but it will not do for me to hurry away and leave unfinished the task I have undertaken. I depend upon Helen and Eliza to brighten the little household at Sunnyside by occasional sojourns of a few days at a time and on my return home I will kill a fatted pig and have a grand barbecue.

With love to Helen / Your affectionate Uncle
Washington Irving

Manuscript: SHR.   Published: PMI, IV, 130 (in part).

1. Jared Sparks collected and published *The Writings of George Washington* between 1834 and 1837 in twelve volumes. At times Sparks changed Washington's grammar and phrasing to conform to his own standard of correctness.

2. Francis B. Stockton (d. January 15, 1858) was appointed purser in the U.S. Navy on March 11, 1829. See Callahan, *Officers of the Navy*, p. 523.

3. "To set up one's Ebenezer" is to make up one's mind firmly. See *Dictionary of Americanisms*, ed. Mitford M. Mathews (Chicago, 1951), p. 543.

2256.   To Sarah Irving

Washington Feb 6h. 1853.

My dear Sarah

I have this morning (Sunday) received a letter from Kate,[1] which, among other things tells me that Angeline has taken a heavy cold and has been ill for a week[.] I beg you to have her taken care of in the best manner—Let the physician attend upon her frequently—She must not expose herself to the weather, by going to and from her mothers in this uncertain season of the year. Do not let her sleep in the attic of the tower, while she is indisposed, but have her near you where you can have an eye upon her. Though she appears to have been gaining strength within the last year or two her constitution is too fragile to stand any severe shock

I wrote to you all the day before yesterday and have nothing new to relate. Yesterday we had a large diplomatic dinner at home; at which some of the foreign Ministers and their ladies were present and some members of the Senate—Mr James Hamilton was likewise a guest, having arrived at Washington the evening before. I find from him that Dr M Vickar had had some difficulty with the ⟨bui⟩ architects of the new church from deficiency of funds; but that the matter had at length been arranged, probably with the assistance of Trinity church. I think that is doomed to be a "church militant" fighting against all kinds of difficulties

I see by the papers that Mr Dakin[2] has died suddenly. This of course puts an end to the huge chateau which he had commenced to build. I hope it will not prove disasterous to the architects and workmen employed. I never had any confidence in the stability of his fortune. He seemed to be a speculative builder of air castles.

I am sorry to hear from Mr Hamilton that Angelica[3] has been unwell with a severe cold. I had hoped to have seen her by this time in Washington. This soft thawing weather is very treacherous—I am myself suffering from a cold which keeps me coughing half the night, but I have a tough constitution that withstands every thing of the kind—

You must not get out of patience with my prolonged absence. I find so much here to consult, in the Archives, and so little liesure to devote to it, that, were I to cut short my sojourn I should have to make another visit to Washington, and that, at a time when I would not have the peculiar advantages which I enjoy at present.

Give my love to all the family

Your affectionate uncle
Washington Irving

P. S. I wish Thomas or Robert, or both, to paint the hen houses—also the farm waggon

MANUSCRIPT: SHR.

1. This letter has not been located.
2. Samuel Dana Dakin (b. 1803), a graduate of Hamilton College and a practicing lawyer in Utica, New York, had died on January 27, 1853. See Albert H. Dakin, *Descendants of Thomas Dakin of Concord, Mass.* (Rutland, Vt., 1948), p. 88; and New York *Times*, January 29, 1853.
3. The daughter of James Hamilton.

2257. *To Helen Dodge Irving*

Washington Feb. 10th. 1853

My dear Helen

If you knew how hard it was to find liesure and quiet to write letters in this distracted place you would not twit me ⟨f⟩ with want of condescension in not noticing your and Pierres epistles.[1] Of late I have fallen off cour[s]e in my correspondence with the cottage, though I feel duty bound to make up with my pen for the prolonged absence of my person from the domestic circle.

I have met with two or three ladies here who claim acquaintance with you and are loud in your praises. One was a Mrs Walton, who knew you and Eliza at Oswego. I sat beside her at a large dinner party of which I had stood in awe, being rather ⟨under⟩ out of mood for company, but she by her lively conversation and agreeable manners rendered it a very pleasant one. Then there is a Mrs Eames with her sister Miss Campbell, ⟨dau⟩ the latter we saw in the highlands last summer staying with the Kembles. They are daughters of my early friend the late Judge Campbell of New York,[2] and very intelligent women. I was to have passed last Sunday evening with them—but it stormed and I had caught a cold (from which I am not yet quite recovered) so I did not go—but have promised to visit them promiscuously.

I had hoped Lent which put a stop to the balls would likewise put a stop to the dinner parties—but the latter continue and I stand committed for several. The last one for which I am engaged is at the Presidents—on Saturday week. It is to be a small social party his huge dinners being rather unwieldy and somewhat promiscuous. I shall accept no invitations after that; hoping then to turn my face homewards: tarrying a day or two at Baltimore on the way.

The day before yesterday I set off to make a visit of two or three days at Mount Vernon in company with Miss Mary Kennedy; having notified the family of our coming. To our mortification we arrived at the place of embarkation too late for the steam boat, which plies between Washington and Mount Vernon three times a week. ⟨so⟩ It was quite a disappointment. However I hope we may be able to make the visit before I set off homewards. I wanted very much to see a little of the country round Mount Vernon, and to ⟨examine som⟩ rummage some old papers still in the archives of the house and which Mr Augustine Washington had promised to place at my disposal.

Thackeray has delivered one of his lectures here and delivers another tomorrow evening.[3] I attended the first and shall attend the next. He is well recieved here, both in public and private, and is going the round of dinner parties &c. I find him a very pleasant companion

I see you are in the midst of hocus pocus with moving tables &c. I was at a party last evening where the grand experiment was made ⟨f⟩ on a large table round which were seated upwards of a dozen young folks of both sexes. The table was for a long time obdurate. At length a very pretty bright eyed girl—who in England would have passed for a Lancashire witch, gave the word—tip table!—whereupon the table gradually raised on two legs until the surface was at an angle of 45 Degrees and was not easily to be put down until she gave the word—down table. It afterwards rose and sank to a tune—performed gyrations about the room &c—All which appeared very mysterious and diabolic—unfortunately two or three of us tried an after experiment and found that we could tip table —and make it move about the room without any very apparent exertion of our hands. So we remain among the unconverted—quite behind the age.

I am rejoiced to learn—at the conclusion of your letter, that Mr Grinnell is so much recovered as to give up the southern excursion. I trust he will be cautious for the future—This is not so long a letter as you deserve but it is the best and longest I can write at present. With love to Pierre

Your afft uncle
Washington Irving

MANUSCRIPT: NYPL–WI Papers.   PUBLISHED: PMI, IV, 130–31 (in part); James G. Wilson, *Thackeray in the United States, 1852–3, 1855–6*, pp. 107–8 (in part).

1. These letters have not been located.
2. Probably Henry J. Campbell, who had been a county judge in New York prior to 1826.
3. In Washington, Thackeray lectured at Carusi's Saloon on February 9, 12, 16, 19, 23, and 26. See *The Letters and Private Papers of William Makepeace Thackeray,* ed. Gordon N. Ray, III, 195.

2258. *To Sarah Irving*

Washington Feb. 16t. 1853

My dear Sarah,

I began a letter to you three days since, in reply to yours of the 10th.,[1] but was interrupted and had to throw it aside; and have been too much hurried and worried by society to resume it until now. I was glad to find by your letter that Angeline was better, but sorry to learn that she was not at the cottage; where she would be much more comfortable than at her mothers. Get her there as soon as possible and take care of her until the Spring is advanced and the weather settled and pleasant; but I know I need not counsel you in any matter of kindness your own nature inclining you to everything that is kind and considerate.

I have nearly got rid of the cold which ↑has↓ hung about me for eight or ten days and which at one time was rather troublesome. I have avoided evening parties as much as possible, though occasionally I have to dip into them, the dinner parties, however, are of almost daily occurrence and are sometimes very tedious being so large that there is no general conversation. I however have generally been fortunately placed between agreeable neighbors. Some of the dinners have been very elegant; especially two at Mr Corcorans and Mr Riggs[2]—wealthy bankers. I have three dinners to eat through, this week—the last at the Presidents—after which I mean to decline further invitations. I wish, before I set my face homeward, to make another visit to Mount Vernon, having an invitation from Mr Augustine Washington to ⟨come⟩ pass a day or two there. I set off for the purpose last week, accompanied by Miss Mary Kennedy, who is an intimate friend of Mrs Washington; but by a mistake in the hour, we were too late for the Steam boat.

Tell Kate I have become acquainted with the darkeyed belle whom I saw in the railroad car, as I came on to Washington She turns out to be the daughter of Colonel Gamble formerly of ⟨Florida⟩ Virginia now of Florida; whom I knew in Paris in my youthful days, when we were both about twenty two years of age. Her name is Miss Letty Gamble;[3] and she is one of the most elegant girls I have seen at Washington and appears to be extremely amiable. I am happy to add that she has no longer the cough which when I first saw her made me think her in a critical state of health She appears to stand the dissipation of Washington admirably, and to be in the full career of conquest.

Tell your father that I have seen William[4] and his little family repeatedly. I am happy to find that he has acquitted himself with great ability in the Census department and has a staunch friend in the Mr Kennedy[5] who has charge of that department. (who is not related to the Mr Kennedy with whom I am staying) It will be some months before the business of the department can be wound up; during which time Williams services cannot be dispensed with. Mr Kennedy promises to use all his influence to promote his interests either in that or some other department. The more I see of Williams wife[6] the more I am pleased with her. She appears to have good sense ⟨and⟩ kind feelings and an excellent disposition and wins general favor wherever she is known—William has nice children.[7] His little daughter Kate is quite a beauty, with remarkably fine eyes, and I am told is a very intelligent child apt and quick at learning. The children are quite engaging in their manners.

You are all very good in not getting out of patience at my prolonged absence. I sometimes get out of patience with it myself and now and then yearn after dear little Sunnyside—but I must ⟨f⟩ accomplish the object of my visit before I set out for home—and when I do set out I shall have to stop a day or two at Baltimore where I find Mrs Tiffany (Sally McLane) insists on my paying her a visit.

I presume this letter will find Helen Pierre with you. Tell her she must make a good long visit—By Mr Joseph Grinnell[8] who has just arrived in Washington I am sorry to learn that Mr M Grinnels health is not fully restored but that he is still troubled with remains of the Vertigo. He tells me that the excursion to the south is fully determined on. The sooner he sets off on it the better.

None of your letters of late have spoken of Marys health; from which I infer that she is doing well. I hope the doctor pays frequent visits

With love to all bodies

Your affectionate Uncle
Washington Irving

Manuscript: SHR.

1. This letter has not been located.

2. William W. Corcoran (1798–1885) and George Washington Riggs (1813–1881) were partners in a banking firm from 1840 to 1848. At that time Riggs resigned. In 1854, when Corcoran retired, Riggs bought his interest and operated the firm as Riggs and Company until his death.

3. For other details about Miss Gamble, see WI to Catharine Irving, January 17, 1853, and to Sarah Irving, January 22, 1853.

4. William Irving (1811–1854), Ebenezer's fourth son.

5. Joseph Camp Griffith Kennedy (1813–1887) of Meadville, Pennsylvania came to Washington in 1849 to serve as secretary of a board to plan the seventh and subsequent censuses. He was appointed superintending clerk of the censuses of 1850 and 1860 and continued in the position until 1865. He was instrumental in convening the first International Statistical Congress in Brussells in 1853.

6. Sarah Mann of Boston, whom William married in 1844.

7. Katherine (b. 1845), William, and Francis.

8. Joseph Grinnell (1788–1885), who was in partnership with his brothers Henry and Moses in the 1820's, returned to New Bedford and became president of the Marine Bank there. From 1843 to 1851 he was congressman from Massachusetts.

2259. To Catharine Irving

Washington Feb 21t 1853

My dear Kate

It is time that I should write a letter to you all at home; though I am in the very worst mood in the world for letter writing. For two or three days past I have been utterly good for nothing. Incapable of work and in no mood for play. Thank fortune I have nearly eaten through all my dinners; being only engaged to one more tomorrow ↑(Tuesday)↓ at the Secretary of Wars,[1] which I accepted to complete my set of Cabinet dinners. On Wednesday I hope to be able to make my visit to Mount Vernon; on my return from which I shall endeavor to wind up affairs at Washington and prepare to shape my course homewards.

Sarah Baldwin and her husband[2] are again here and will remain here until after the inauguration.[3] I met Sarah at a very brilliant Soiree last week, looking as usual, fresh, fair and happy; one of the greatest or at least largest belles of the evening. She certainly enjoys life

Your news of the engagement of Caroline Schermerhorn[4] to William Astor[5] is very satisfactory to me. As executor to the will of the late Mr Astor I am anxious to see all his descendants well provided for, and Caroline will bring the youth a very snug fortune; beside being a very nice girl.

I am pleased to hear that the wedding of Sarah Clark and the young chancellor comes off in April.[6] It is upon the whole one of the best matched matches of the year

Helen writes me that the engagement of Mr Curtis[7] (the Howadji) and Miss Winthrop is off—How is this. Are not his last writings to the young ladies taste. Young Ik Marvel[8] is engaged to a very amiable ⟨loveable⟩ lovely girl at the South: whom I saw at Saratoga last summer and with whom I was very much pleased. Indeed I pointed her out to Mitchell as one of the most estimable of all the young belles who were figuring there. She is a Miss Pringle of Charleston. One of twelve children, and her mother, who much resembles her, might pass for an elder sister.

Helen writes that Mr Sheldon[9] has sold his house and eighteen acres for thirty five thousand dollars—a round Sum—I am sorry the purchaser is in the shoe and boot line—but hope it is on the grand scale. I presume Sheldon will now fulfil the wish of his heart and build a *stone* mansion, on the south lot. I dont think he has ever been perfectly happy in his wooden house

Mrs Kennedy has been in Baltimore for a week past; with her father who has been dangerously ill. Mr Kennedy too has been down there occasionally; so that Miss Mary and I have been left to keep house together, which we do very cosily. She begins to seem very much like a niece to me, and I wish she was one—She would add very much to my assortment.

I am glad to learn that Mr Grinnell and Julia have sailed for the South, and hope they will not return until he has completely recovered from those vertigoes which are so alarming. Helen tells me that the physicians give Mr Minturn the assurance that his malady is not of the heart. I trust therefore, he may recover from it completely

Give my love to all the home circle. I hope to be with you soon, but cannot fix the time.

Your affectionate Uncle
Washington Irving

MANUSCRIPT: SHR.

1. Charles M. Conrad (1804–1878), a New Orleans attorney who had served in the state legislature and in the U.S. Senate and House of Representatives, became Fillmore's secretary of war in 1850.

2. Ann Sarah Dodge (1816–1886) was the granddaughter of WI's sister Ann Sarah and the daughter of Patience Aikin (1793–1879) and William Irving Dodge (1790–1873). She married Harvey Baldwin (1797–1863) on February 12, 1833.

3. Franklin Pierce (1804–1869) was inaugurated fourteenth president of the United States on March 4, 1853.

4. Caroline Schermerhorn (1830–1908) was the daughter of Abraham Schermerhorn. See Richard Schermerhorn, *Schermerhorn Genealogy and Family Chronicle*, p. 166.

5. William Astor (1829–1892), the son of William B. Astor and grandson of John Jacob Astor, married Miss Schermerhorn on September 23, 1853.

6. For other details about the engagement of Sarah Clark and James Kent, see WI to Catharine Irving, January 17, 1853.

7. George William Curtis (1824–1892) was a popular traveler, writer and lecturer. For other details, see WI to Curtis, November 20, 1856.

8. Donald Grant Mitchell, who used the pen name "Ik Marvel," was married to Mary Frances Pringle of Charleston, South Carolina on May 31, 1853.

9. Henry Sheldon, a silk merchant living in Tarrytown, sold his house and property to A. H. Benedict. See Scharf, *Westchester County*, II, 245.

2260. To Sarah Irving

Washington, Feb. 25, 1853.

My dear Sarah:

I have just received your letter, dated 24th,[1] by which I am happy to find all is going on well at home.

I went down, yesterday, in the steamer Vixen,[2] with a large party, to visit the caloric ship Ericsson.[3] In our party were the two Presidents

(Fillmore and Pierce), all the Cabinet,[4] and many other official characters. The Ericsson appeared to justify all that has been said in her praise,
and promises to produce a great change in navigation.

After inspecting the machinery, and visiting all parts of the ship, which
is a noble vessel, and beautifully fitted up, we partook of a plentiful col-
lation, and returned, well pleased, to the capital.

This morning I went down to Mount Vernon, in company with Miss
Mary K——.[5] We were joined at the steamboat by Mr. B——[6] and Sarah,
and found Mr. Augustine Washington on board. Our visit to Mount
Vernon was but for two or three hours, returning in the afternoon. I went
merely for the purpose of taking one more view of the place and its vicinity, though pressed by Mr. Washington to make a longer visit.

This evening I have been at the last reception of President Fillmore.
It was an immense crowd, for the public seemed eager to give him a
demonstration, at parting, of their hearty goodwill.

I see you are all conjuring, and setting the tables waltzing.[7] It is really
high time for me to come home. I beg you won't set the table in my study
capering. If that gets bewitched, I am undone.

PUBLISHED: PMI, IV, 131–32.

1. This letter has not been located.
2. For John P. Kennedy's account of the event, see Tuckerman, *Life of J. P.
Kennedy*, pp. 223–24.
3. For other details about this vessel, see WI to Sarah Irving, January 13, 1853.
4. Fillmore's Cabinet consisted of Edward Everett, secretary of state; John P.
Kennedy, secretary of the navy; Charles M. Conrad, secretary of war; Samuel D.
Hubbard (1799–1855), postmaster general; John J. Crittenden (1783–1863),
attorney general; Thomas Corwin, secretary of the treasury; and Alexander H. H.
Stuart (1807–1891), secretary of the interior.
5. Mary Kennedy. PMI omitted the surname in his printed version of the letter.
6. Harvey Baldwin.
7. WI's nieces, who were interested in the occult, held amateur seances at
Sunnyside. See STW, II, 233.

2261.   To Helen Dodge Irving

Washington Feb 2⟨7⟩8th. 1853

My dear Helen

I have been thinking of setting off homeward for the last week yet here
am I still lingering, and I begin to question whethe[r] I shall not make
good your surmise, that I would stay until after the inauguration. I really
am yearning for home but my friends the Kennedys will not hear of my

going off until they break up their camp which will probably be at the end of the week.

I have become acquainted with the President elect and am much pleased with him. He is a quiet gentlemanlike man in appearance and manner—and I have concieved a good will for him from finding in the course of our conversation, that he has it at heart to take care of Haw-thorne who ⟨is⟩ ↑was↓ his early fellow student.[1]

I have made my visit to Mount Vernon with Miss Mary Kennedy, though we had to cut it down to a single day. Sarah Baldwin & her husband visited Mount Vernon on the same day and we had a very pleasant time together.

I have a letter from Sarah Storrow,[2] ⟨whic⟩ giving an account of the grand spectacle of the Emperor and Empress going to Notre Dame with all their wedding retinue.[3] It must have been a magnificent pageant.

I believe I have told you that I knew the grandfather of the Empress. Old Mr Kirkpatrick,[4] who had been American Consul at Malaga. I past an evening at his house in 1827, near Adra on the coast of the Mediter-ranean. A week or two after I was at the house of his son in law the Count Téba,[5] at Granada. A gallant, intelligent gentleman much cut up in the wars having lost an eye and been maimed in a leg and hand. His wife the daughter of Mr Kirkpatrick was absent, but he had a family of little girls, mere children about him. The youngest of these must have been the present empress. Several years afterwards, when I had recently taken up my abode in Madrid; I was invited to a grand ball at the house of the Countess Montijo one of the leaders of the ton. On making my bow to her I was surprised ⟨to⟩ ↑at↓ being recieved by her with the warmth and eagerness of an old friend.[6] She claimed me as the friend of her late husband, the Count Teba (subsequently Marquis Montijo) who she said had often spoken of me with the greatest regard She took me into another room and showed me a miniature of the Count, such as I had known him, with a black patch over one eye. She subsequently introduced me to the little girls I had known at ⟨Madrid⟩ ↑Granada↓ now fashionable belles at Madrid—

After this I was frequently at her house which was one of the gayest in the Capital. The Countess and her daughters all spoke english. The Eldest daughter was married while I was in Madrid to the Duke of Alba, & Berwick[7]—the lineal successor to the pretender to the British Crown— The other now sits on the throne of France!

Pierre in a late letter[8] gave me a flourishing report of the state of my finances upon which I immediately drew upon him for forty dollars—I am in constant dread of growing rich in spite of myself—and have now and then twinges of meanness worthy of a millionair. My only mode of counteracting them is to draw instantly on Pierre.

With kind remembrance to that worthy gentleman

Your affectionate uncle
Washington Irving

MANUSCRIPT: NYPL—WI Papers.   PUBLISHED: PMI, IV, 132–34 (in part).

1. Pierce and Hawthorne had been classmates at Bowdoin College. Because Hawthorne had written a biography of Pierce for the 1852 presidential campaign, Pierce wanted to reward his friend with a lucrative appointment and did so with the consulship at Liverpool. See Randall Stewart, *Nathaniel Hawthorne*, p. 140.

2. This letter has not been located.

3. The marriage of Louis Napoleon (1808–1873) and Eugenia Maria de Montijo de Gúzman (1826–1920) occurred on January 29, 1853.

4. William Kirkpatrick was a Scottish-born American citizen who was appointed U.S. consul at Málaga in 1791. See Bowers, *Spanish Adventures of WI*, p. 123.

5. Cipriano Gúzman Palafox (1786?–1839), later count of Teba and marques of Montijo, married Maria Manuela Kirkpatrick (1794–1879) in 1817. WI related the same details in a letter to Sarah Storrow on January 15, 1843. See also Harold Kurtz, *The Empress Eugénie, 1826–1920* (Boston, 1964), pp. 5, 6, 316; and Philip W. Sergeant, *The Last Empress of the French* (Philadelphia, n.d.), pp. 4, 7, 10.

6. See WI to Sarah Storrow, January 15, 1843.

7. Francesca (or Paca) (1825–1860) married James Luis Stuart Fitz-James, duke of Alba and Berwick, early in 1844.

8. This letter has not been located.

2262. To Mary Abigail Fillmore

[Washington, March 7, 1853]

My dear Miss Fillmore

Understanding you do me the honor to desire my autograph I here send it, with best wishes that you may have a pleasant tour[1] and a happy return home

With great regard / Yours very truly
Washington Irving
Washington (D C) / March 7th. 1853 / Miss M. A. Fillmore.

MANUSCRIPT: Free Library of Philadelphia.

Mary Abigail Fillmore (1832–1854), the only daughter of Millard and Abigail Fillmore, often served as hostess at the White House when her mother was ill. See Robert J. Rayback, *Millard Fillmore*, pp. 47, 160, 171, 254, 394.

1. The tour was canceled because of the death of Mrs. Fillmore on March 30, 1853. For details about its effect upon John P. Kennedy, see WI to Elizabeth Kennedy, April 2, 1853; and Tuckerman, *Life of J. P. Kennedy*, p. 241.

2263. To John P. Kennedy

Washington. March 7th. 1853

My dear Sir,

Being on the eve of my departure homeward I take the liberty of speaking a word in behalf of my nephew William Irving,[1] at present a clerk in the census office. Of the ability with which he has descharged the duties of that office of which for some time he had the principal management, I have the most satisfactory assurances from those competent to judge.

Washington Irving—

MANUSCRIPT: Peabody Library.   PUBLISHED: *Sewanee Review*, 25 (January, 1917), 7.

1. For other details about William Irving, see WI to Sarah Irving, February 16, 1853.

2264. To Charles Lanman

Washington March 7h. 1853

My dear Mr Lanman,

I see an appropriation has been made for the Augmentation of the Library in the Executive Mansion. As I understand that all the books already there were purchased by you at the suggestion of Mr Webster to President Fillmore I think you ought to endeavor to have the task of completing the library.[1] It would be a pleasant and a creditable labor to you, for which your past experience and your acquaintance with the American and British booksellers[2] peculiarly fit you. Should the task require a visit to Europe I could procure you the best advice and the most essential letters from Mr Cogswell the Superintendent of the Astor library, who has been repeatedly to Europe and is now there making extensive purchases for our library.

As you are at the head of the Copy right bureau in the State department[3] you might undertake this new duty without *extra compensation—* I should think it would be a labor of love to you. ⟨Should⟩ Mr Cogswell could give you advice as to the ⟨kind of⟩ books most suitable for the library in question

In great haste / Yours very truly
Washington Irving

Charles Lanman Esq

MANUSCRIPT: SHR.

1. The library in the White House had been established because of Abigail Fillmore's love of reading. In 1851 President Fillmore had asked Congress to appropriate funds for a reading room on the second floor of the White House and upon receiving them requested Lanman to procure suitable books.

2. Lanman's own books had been published on both sides of the Atlantic.

3. Lanman was appointed librarian of copyrights in the Department of State in 1851.

2265. *To Elizabeth Kennedy*

Sunnyside March 11t. 1853.

My dear Mrs Kennedy

I was really sad at heart on parting with you and Mary Kennedy at Washington. Indeed, had not your establishment fallen to pieces around me I hardly know when I should have gotten away. I could almost have clung to the wreck so long as there was a three legged stool and a horn spoon to make shift with You see what danger there is in domesticating me. I am sadly prone to take root where I find myself happy. It was some consolation to me in parting that I had Mrs Hare and the Gentle Horse Shoe[1] for fellow travellers. Without their company I should have been completely down hearted. The former was bright, intelligent and amiable as usual—and as to "John," you know ⟨tha⟩ he is a sympathizing soul. He saw I needed soothing—So he cracked some of his best jokes—and I was comforted.

I was rejoiced to find your father down stairs, and seemingly almost if not quite as well as when I left him. My reception by him and your sister made me feel that I was in another home; or rather in another part of the family circle in which, for some time past, I had been flourishing so happily. I arrived too late ↑by half an hour↓ to see Mary Dulaney who had just left your fathers to go home and dress for an evening party; the same party ⟨kept me⟩ prevented my seeing Louisa Andrews; who was engaged there. It was a double disappointment; for I had pleased myself with the hope of once more seeing them both as I know your fathers house was one of their favorite resorts. He abounds, however, in pets, and summoned another who gave us some delightful music and enlivened the evening by her sprightliness and naiveté. Upon the whole my visit was a very, cheerful gratifying one; I had no idea of finding your father in such an enjoyable condition of mind and body, and I took leave of him in the morning in the confident hope that we shall again pass pleasant days together in future meetings.

I arrived in New York too late for the Hudson River rail road cars, so I had to remain in the city until morning. Yesterday I alighted at the Station within ten minutes walk of home. The walk was along the rail road in full sight of the house. I saw female forms in the porch and I knew the Spy glass was in hand. In a moment there was a waving of handkerchiefs and a hurrying hither and thither. Never did old bachelor come to such a loving home; so gladdened by blessed woman kind. In fact I doubt whether many married men recieve such a heart felt welcome—My friend Horse Shoe and one or two others of my acquaintance may; but there are not many as well off in domestic life as I—however, let me be humbly thankful and repress all vain glory.

After all the kissing and crying and laughing and rejoicing were over I sallied forth to ⟨over⟩ inspect my domains, welcomed home by my prime minister Robert, and my master of the horse Thomas and my keeper of the poultry yard William. Every thing was in good order—all had been faithful in the discharge of their duties; my fields had been manured my trees trimmed; the fences repaired and painted—I really believe more had been done in my absence than would have been done had I been home. My horses were in good condition. Dandy and Billy, the coach horses, were as sleek as seals, gentleman Dick, my saddle horse shewed manifest pleasure at seeing me—put his cheek against mine—laid his head on my shoulder and would have nibbled at my ear had I permitted it. One of my chinese Geese was setting on eggs; the rest were sailing like frigates in the pond, with a whole fleet of white top knot ducks. The hens were vying with each other which could bring out the earliest brood of chickens. Taffy and Tony; two pet dogs of a dandy race, kept more for shew than use, received me with well bred though rather cool civility while my little terrier slut Ginger, bounded about me almost crazy with delight, having five little Gingers toddling at her heels, with which she had enriched me during my absence.

I forbear to say any thing about my cows, my Durham heifer, or my pigeons, having gone as far into these rural matters as may be agreeable. Suffice it to say everything was just as heart could wish; so having visited every part of my empire, I settled down for the evening in my elbow chair, and entertained the family circle with all the wonders I had seen at Washington

To day I have dropped back into all my old habits—after sitting some time after breakfast petting my little invalid Niece Mary who I am sorry to say is still in delicate health, I have resumed my seat at the table in the Study where I am scribbling this letter while an unseasonable Snow storm is prevailing out of doors.

This letter will no doubt find you once more at your happy home in Baltimore—⟨an end to all⟩ all fussing and bustling at an end—with time to nurse yourself and get rid of that cold which has been hanging about you for so many days.

And now let me express how much I feel obliged to you and Kennedy for drawing me forth out of my little country nest and setting me once more in circulation. This has grown out of our fortunate meeting and sojourn together at Saratoga last summer—and I count these occurrences as among the most pleasant events of my life. They have brought me into domestic communion with yourselves your family connexions and dearest intimacies, and have opened to me a little world of friend ship and Kindness in which I have enjoyed myself with a full heart.

God bless you all and make you as happy as you delight to make others.

Ever yours most truly
Washington Irving

Mrs J. P Kennedy.

Manuscript: Peabody Library. Published: PMI, IV, 135–37 (in part); and Tuckerman, *Life of J. P. Kennedy*, p. 234 (in part).

1. WI often used this name for John P. Kennedy. It was taken from Kennedy's novel, *Horse-Shoe Robinson* (1835).

2266. To Mary E. Kennedy

Sunnyside March 19th 1853

My dear Miss Kennedy

Whether you were in earnest or not in asking me to send you my likeness[1] I take you at your word; for I wish to be remembered by you.

The one I send according to your aunt's opinion is at least a score of years too young—and I believe she is right. No matter—I certainly have been as young in my time. To help it out, however, I send with it a copy of my works.[2] When you read them fancy I am talking with you, and may they prove more entertaining than I am apt to be in conversation. Let them recall the pleasant days we passed together in Washington— pleasant they were to me at least and most pleasant they are in recollection.

You see I am once more in my quiet little country home which my nieces are trying to make me contented with. One is exercising her music to make me forget the music I have enjoyed. Another undertakes to pare apples for me of an evening and insists she can do it as well as it was done for me in Washington—and I endeavor to think so.

Farewell my dear Miss Kennedy think of me now and then in kindness. It is true we have known each other but for a short time, but long enough for me to discover in you a host of estimable and attaching qualities—and not long enough to find out any faults.

With kindest remembrances to your father[3]

Your sincerely attached friend
Washington Irving

PUBLISHED: *American Literature*, 6 (March, 1934), 45.

1. Possibly Charles Martin's portrait, later used as the frontispiece to PMI, volume 4.

2. WI may have sent her a set of the Author's Revised Edition of his *Works*, published by Putnam between 1848 and 1851.

3. Andrew Kennedy (1797–1858), Mary's father, was a lawyer and farmer who lived at "Cassilis," Charlestown, Jefferson County, Virginia.

2267. To Sarah Storrow

Sunnyside, March 28t. 1853

My dear Sarah,

A letter recieved ⟨by me⟩ from you[1] while I was at Washington gave an account of the Marriage procession of Louis Napoleon and his bride to the Church of Notre Dame, which you saw from a window near the Hotel de Ville.[2] One of your recent letters, I am told, speaks of your having been presented to the Empress. I shall see it when I go to town[.] Louis Napoleon and Eugenia Montigo Emperor and Empress of France! One of whom I have had a guest at my Cottage on the Hudson—the other whom when a child I have had on my knee at Granada! It seems to cap the climax of the strange dramas of which Paris has been the theatre during my life time. I have repeatedly thought that each grand *coupe de Theatre* would be the last that would occur in my time—but each has been succeeded by another equally striking—and what will be the next—who can conjecture!

The last I saw of Eugenia Montigo she was one of the reigning belles of Madrid and she and her giddy circle had swept away my charming young friend the beautiful and accomplished Leocadia Zamora,[3] into their career of fashionable dissipation—Now Eugenia is upon a throne and Leocadia a voluntary recluse in a convent of ↑one of↓ the most rigorous orders! Poor Leocadia!—perhaps however her fate may ultimately be the happiest of the two—"The Storm" with her, "is oer," and ["]she's at rest"[4] but the other is launched from a returnless shore on a dangerous sea infamous for its tremendous shipwrecks—am I to live to see the catastrophe of her career and the end of this suddenly conjured up Empire, ⟨?⟩ which seems to be of such stuff "as dreams are made of?"[5] I confess my personal acquaintance with the individuals who figure in this historical romance gives me uncommon interest in it; but I consider it stamped with danger and instability and as liable to extravagant vicissitudes as one of Dumas novels. You do right to witness the grand features of this passing pageant—you are probably reading one of the most peculiar and eventful pages of history, and may live to look back upon it as a romantic tale.

I have passed part of the Winter at Washington delightfully situated in the house of my friend Kennedy, who was Secretary of the Navy. I do not know whether you were ever acquainted with him and his wife; he a genial fellow, full of talent and of a most happy humor; she one of the most loveable little women in the world. Their house was a very gay one but the company which frequented it choice—I found the dissipation of Washington, however, at time[s][6] almost too much for me—I was anxious to prosecute some researches among the Archives of the State department; but found myself continually carried off my legs by a tide of engagements of all kinds. Washington is the great gathering place of talent and beauty from all parts of the union as well as from abroad. The cordial attentions I met on all sides ⟨was⟩ were certainly deeply gratifying, but occasionally were overpowering and I now and then felt myself casting back a longing eye to the quiet of little Sunnyside.

I was present at the going out of one Administration and the coming in of another; was acquainted with both presidents and most of the members of both cabinets and witnessed the inauguration of General Pierce. It was admirable to see the quiet and courtesy with which this great transition of power and rule from one party to another took place. I was at festive meetings where the members of the opposite parties mingled socially together and have seen the two presidents arm in arm as if the sway of an immense empire was not passing from one to the other.

I was much pleased with what I saw of the new president. His appearance and manner were quiet and gentlemanlike; and I was gratified by the determination which he expressed to me in private of taking care of Hawthorne the author, who had been his early friend & fellow student. Hawthorne has accordingly recieved the appointment of Consul at Liverpool,—a lucrative post. I ⟨f⟩ believe you have read Hawthornes admirable novels and essays—Some of the best productions in our literature.

The letters of your brother and Nancy[7] of course keep you acquainted with the main topics of family news. The death of poor Jane,[8] which leaves Theodore a widower with five young children.[9] The latter are at present at their grand mothers at Geneva. Theodore will break up house keeping. I have invited him to come up here for the present.

Mr Grinnell has in a great measure recovered from his very serious malady; Still it will take time for him to regain his Mental strength and activity—His head is easily fatigued by the bustle of business and he has to avoid the city and all perplexing cares. He and Julia are about to set out on a weeks visit to Charlotte[10] at cayuga lake and I have prevailed on our Sarah to accompany them. I think it probable that this illness will make a complete change in Mr Grinnells mode of life; that he will give up many of the varied engagements and occupations of a public nature with which he was crowded; that he will ease off in business as much as possible and pass the chief part of his time in the country, ⟨of⟩ ↑in↓ which he takes great delight and finds abundance of healthful occupation.

At the last of this week I expect some of the family up here to birth day the 3d of april when I come of age—of full age—70 Years! I never could have hoped at such an advanced period of life to be in such full health, ⟨and⟩ such activity of mind and body and such capacity for enjoyment as I find myself at present. But I have reached the allotted limit of existence—all beyond is especial indulgence. So long as I can retain my present health and spirits I am happy to live, for I think my life is important to the happiness of others—but as soon as my life becomes useless to others and joyless to myself, I hope I may be relieved from the burthen and I shall lay it down with heartfelt thanks to that almighty power which has guided my incautious steps through so many uncertain and dangerous ways and enabled me to close my career in serenity and peace, surrounded by my family and friends, in the little home I have formed for myself, among the scenes of my boyhood

With affectionate remembrances to Mr Storrow and love to the dear little folks

Your affectionate Uncle
Washington Irving

MANUSCRIPT: Va.–Barrett.   PUBLISHED: PMI, IV, 138–40 (in part).

1. This letter has not been located.

2. For other reactions to this marriage by WI, see WI to Helen Irving, February 28, 1853.

3. Leocadia Zamora was a beautiful Cuban singer who was a friend of the countess of Montijo. WI saw much of her in 1844. For other details, see Bowers, *Spanish Adventures of WI*, pp. 248–52.

4. WI omitted the opening quotation mark. The quotation has not been located.

5. *The Tempest*, IV, i, 156. WI omitted the opening quotation mark.

6. WI omitted the bracketed letter.

7. The letters of Irving and Nancy Paris have not been located.

8. Jane Sutherland, who had married Theodore Irving on August 28, 1838, died on March 28, 1853.

9. The five children of Theodore Irving were Fanny, Elizabeth, Mary, Cornelia, and Sutherland.

10. Charlotte (1824–1911), the youngest child of Ebenezer, had married William R. Grinnell (1819–1898) on June 7, 1847.

2268. To Elizabeth Kennedy

Sunnyside April 2d. 1853

My dear Mrs. Kennedy,

I have been extremely shocked by the death of our amiable and excellent friend, Mrs Fillmore; especially as I am inclined to think she in a manner recieved the death blow when standing by my side on the marble terrace of the Capital, in snow and cold listening to the inaugural speech of her husbands successor. What sad domestic bereavements have visited the two presidents, one just before entering upon office;[1] the other just after leaving it. I feel deeply for the affliction of the amiable Fillmore family, the loss of such a member—so gentle, so good, so kind in all her ways. This melancholy event of course puts an end to the southern tour and leaves your husband to the quiet of his library; which must be most grateful to him after his late hurried and somewhat harrassed life—though I believe he is of a constitution of mind not easily harrassed. As you tell me I must write to you instead of him, you must be the medium of my reply to his letters. Tell him I recieved his two printed addresses[2] which he sent to me, and suffered them to lie for a long time on my table unread—I had so many things to attend to on my return that I had not liesure—and to tell the truth I had not inclination—Somehow or other I did not expect much enjoyment from them, not being a great amateur of addresses. At length I took them one night to my chamber and read them in bed. Never was I more agreeably disappointed. The address about Baltimore interested me in the early part by the anecdotes of the early history and wonderful growth of the city; told too with pleasant dashes of humor—and it warmed and delighted me by the noble manner in which it wound up; but the little story of the poor poet weaver Thom—his ⟨st⟩ sore struggles with penury and the strange mixture of poetical excitement with utter wretchedness completely took me by surprise. I do not know anything of the kind that ever excited me more. I had to stop repeatedly to wipe away the tears that blinded me. Never has Kennedy written anything with better tact and better feeling—It made my heart throb toward him.[3] My nieces are now crying over the story and learning to love the writer of it.

I have just recieved a very kind and friendly letter from Mr Winthrop[4] announcing a volume of his writings[5] which he has sent me, but which has not yet arrived. He appears to look back, like myself, with very pleasant reccollections on the time we sojourned together under your roof at Washington and first became acquainted with each other, and it is one of the many agreeable circumstances connected with my visit that it has linked me in friendship with a gentleman of his talent, cultivation, and refinement.—But in fact, now that I have sunk back again into my quiet elbow chair at Sunnyside, that whole visit begins to appear to me an agreeable dream, and I sit and muse and try to call up one fleeting reccollection after another, and bring back the images of worth and beauty that passed before me in constant succession in the phantasmagoria of Washington. The charm of all was the happy home in which I was placed, where the feelings might rally back to domestic life from the whirl of dissipation. I could never have stood the tumult and excitement of Washington if quartered in one of its tower of Babel hotels, but your house was like a gleam of my own home and I could almost fancy you and Mary Kennedy two of my nieces. By the way, I have sent Mary a set of my works to accompany my lithographed likeness which she asked.[6] I hope they arrived safe. I ⟨gave⟩ told my publisher to direct them to her fathers at Charlestown, in Jefferson county.

Farewell my dear Mrs Kennedy. Give my most heartfelt remembrances to your worthy father your sister and Kennedy; I hope, now that the latter has given up his tour, you may all keep together and so make each other happy

affectionately your friend
Washington Irving

MANUSCRIPT: Peabody Library.   PUBLISHED: *Sewanee Review*, 25 (January, 1917), 8–9.

1. Pierce's eleven-year-old son Benjamin was killed in a railroad accident in January of 1853 while his parents watched helplessly. See Roy F. Nichols, *Franklin Pierce: Young Hickory of the Granite Hills* (Philadelphia, 1958), p. 224.

2. "Address Before the Maryland Historical Society on the Life and Character of George Calvert" (1845) and "Lecture on Thom" (1846). See Tuckerman, *Life of J. P. Kennedy*, p. 274.

3. WI's "delight in these products of Kennedy's 'gentlemanlike exercises of the pen' tells eloquently the story of his degeneration." See STW, II, 209.

4. An excerpt from Winthrop's letter is printed in PMI, IV, 141. Robert C. Winthrop (1809–1894), who studied law with Daniel Webster, served as congressman from Massachusetts from 1840 to 1850 and was appointed U.S. senator upon the resignation of Webster in 1850.

5. Winthrop's *Addresses and Speeches* (1852) is among the books in WI's library at Sunnyside.

6. See WI to Mary Kennedy, March 19, 1853.

2269. To Robert C. Winthrop

Sunnyside April 4th. 1853

My dear Mr. Winthrop.

I have deferred replying to your very kind and acceptable letter[1] until I could acknowledge the receipt of the volume it announced. It has now come to hand and I shall prize it not only for its own merit but as a memorial of the very pleasant time we passed together under the hospitable roof of Kennedy at Washington and I assure you I esteem it one of the most gratifying circumstances attending my delightful sojourn there that it brought me into domestic companionship with you.

I regret to learn that, you like Kennedy, have been a sufferer in health since we parted; though I trust you are both fully recovered. You have no doubt been shocked, like myself, at the sad bereavement which has afflicted the worthy Filmore family

I almost think poor Mrs Filmore must have recieved her death warrant while standing by my side on the marble terrace of the Capital exposed to chilly wind and snow listening to the inaugural speech of her husbands successor. This sad event, as you percieve, has put an end to the southern tour, which did not seem to meet your approbation; and has left Kennedy to the quiet of his home and his library which I should think he would relish after the turmoil of Washington.

As to myself, to echo your own words I am "safely at Sunnyside and in the best of health" The shadows of departed years, however, are gathering over me, for yesterday I celebrated my seventieth birth day. Seventy years of age! I can scarcely realize that I have indeed arrived at the allotted verge of existence, beyond which all is special grace and indulgence. I used to think that a man at seventy must have survived every thing worth living for. That with him the silver cord must be loosed—the wheel broken at the cistern—That all desire must fail and the grasshopper become a burden[2] Yet here I find myself unconscious of the withering influences of age—still strong and active—my sensibilities alive and my social affections in full vigor.

> "Strange that a harp of thousand strings
> Should keep in tune so long!"[3]

While it does keep in tune—while I have still a little music in my soul to be called out by any touch of sympathy—while I can enjoy the society of those dear to me, and contribute, as they tell I can, to their enjoyment I am content and happy to live on. But I have it ever present to my mind that the measure of my days is full and running over—and I feel ready at any moment to lay down this remnant of existence with a thankful heart that my erratic and precarious career has been brought to so serene a close among the scenes of my youth and surrounded by those I love.

The sketch of me by Wilkie[4] which you tell me you have in one of his published volumes cannot be an attempt at a likeness[.] I reccollect the composition—the scene I think was at Seville. I was seated in a dusky chamber at a table looking over a folio volume which a monk who was standing by my side had just handed down to me. Wilkie thought the whole had a Rembrandt effect, which he aimed at producing—but if I reccollect right my face could not be seen distinctly

Farewell my dear Winthrop and believe me with no common regard

> Your friend,
> Washington Irving

Hon Robert Winthrop

MANUSCRIPT: MHS.   PUBLISHED: PMI, IV, 141–43.

1. PMI (IV, 141) prints the following portion of Winthrop's letter: "Do you remember my telling you that I had a sketch of you, by Wilkie, in one of his published volumes? I have found it, since my return, in a volume which I purchased in London, and which was just out when I was there, in 1847. The sketch is entitled 'Washington Irving consulting the Archives of Cordova,' and is dated 25 April, 1828. It forms the frontispiece to a large volume dedicated to Lord Lansdowne. The original of the sketch of you is said to be in the possession of Sir William Knighton, Bart."

2. WI is paraphrasing Ecclesiastes 12:5–7.

3. Quoted from Hymn 19, book 2, in Isaac Watts's *Hymns and Spiritual Songs*, in three books (London, 1707).

4. Sir David Wilkie (1785–1841) was the English painter with whom WI was intimate in Madrid and Seville in 1827 and 1828. See Bowers, *Spanish Adventures of WI*, pp. 39–48, 67–72. A reproduction of a drawing of WI made by Wilkie in Seville on April 23, 1828, is to be found in STW, I, opposite 334. This is a different pose from the one WI describes here.

2270.   To Francis C. Wemyss

New York, April 8th. 1853

Francis F Wemyss Esq

Dear Sir

I regret to say that circumstances put it out of my power to avail myself of the invitation with which the President Trustees and Directors of
the Dramatic Fund Association have honored me for the Dinner on the
11th. instant. I inclose an order for twenty dollars ($20) which I beg leave
to contribute to the Dramatic Fund.

Very respectfully / Your Obdt Sevt
Washington Irving

MANUSCRIPT: University of California at Los Angeles Library.

Francis C. Wemyss (1797–1859), an English actor and theatrical manager who
came to the United States in 1821, was active in New York, Philadelphia, Pittsburgh, and Baltimore. From 1841 he was associated with several New York
theaters, and he helped found and administer the theatrical fund for needy actors.
WI erroneously uses "F." for his middle initial.

2271.   To Mary E. Kennedy

Sunnyside April 10th. 1853

My dear Miss Kennedy

It was quite a relief to me to learn from your letter[1] that the books and
blunder in the transportation of them. The kind welcome you have given
them is most gratifying; you have recieved them in the same spirit in
which they were sent. I trust they will help to keep up our acquaintance
with each other, however widely we may be separated.

Your letter called up delightful recollections of our little home circle at
Washington—our council fires of an evening to talk over our campaigns,
—our quiet rainy days, (to me full of sunshine), sweetened occasionally
by the music of your fair friend Juliet or enlightened by the gambols
of your little "sweetheart" Bob, desperately bothered between love and
ennui. I always honored that magnanimous little man for being capable
in his boyish heart of entertaining such a full grown passion. And then
Lady Marys[2] *levees* to which you allude—what pleasure I had in con-
templating those levees from my retired corner of Sleepy Hollow. To see

her preside over her little circle of admirers with such a frank spirit so free from coquetry, apparently so unconscious of her own merits and attractions.

But it was not in this sphere of her triumphs that Lady Mary appeared to most advantage in my eyes,—nor yet when figuring at balls and receptions, even though arrayed in that marvellous white dress of woven cob-web with rose coloured ribbons in which she once broke upon my sight like a wonder. Neither was it when she mingled in every day life, so bright, so cheerful so considerate of others, so little mindful of herself—there was something beyond all that. It was that unpretending but strict conscientiousness with which she adhered to a sober path of duty marked out for herself amid the bewildering mazes of gaiety and fashion.

It was this sweet rectitude of mind which seemed to keep her unspotted by the world, drawing round her a robe of light and shedding a grace about her steps of which she was unconscious. I declare to you that the sound of her light step on the stairs going forth to her early devotions while I was yet lingering in my bed has sent a rebuke to my conscience at my own short comings—There are[3] a daily beauty and purity in her life that read homilies to me—I hope I may profit by them.

And now my dear Miss Mary if to the pure regard and perfect esteem thus inspired you add a little of that sentiment of devotion to the sex which may be permitted to linger about the heart of an old bachelor of seventy, you have an idea of that friendship which it is a happiness for me to entertain for you—for it is by such friendships the heart is softened and purified and made better. I think I profited greatly in this respect by my intercourse with you and your aunt last winter. God bless you both for it.

You give me reason to hope I shall one day recieve the likeness we talked about. You may judge from what I have said whether I shall not prize it—yet I forebore to recur to it in my former letter, lest it might be mistaken for a mere piece of antiquated gallantry. I shall value it from higher motives.

Farewell my dear Miss Kennedy—I shall keep in mind your invitation to the mountains if ever I should revisit your uncle at Baltimore; in the meantime should you or your father come to the banks of the Hudson, Sunnyside will be happy to recieve you, and my nieces will take a delight in manifesting their gratitude for the kind attentions bestowed upon their uncle.

With best remembrances to your father

> Yours ever very truly
> Washington Irving

PUBLISHED: *American Literature*, 6 (March, 1934), 46–48.

1. Mary E. Kennedy's letter of April 4, 1853, is printed in *American Literature*, 6 (March, 1934), 45–46.

2. WI referred to Miss Kennedy as "Lady Mary."

3. Probably this word should be "is."

2272. *To Thomas W. Storrow, Sr.*

Sunnyside April 17th. 1853

My dear Storrow,

Some how or other I have left a shameful time elapse without answering your letter;[1] but I have so many claims and interruptions to distract my attention that I am continually behind hand in my correspondence

I am very much concerned to learn that you have been so much of an invalid but trust the return of Spring and genial weather will set you right again. My brother[2] was almost a martyr to acute rheumatism a year or two since, but has almost completely recovered from it and is now in his usual health. I hope it will be the same with you. I wish as the Spring opens You would pay a visit to my little nest where we should put you as much at your ease and make you as comfortable as possible. I was not at Washington for the purpose of pushing forward the Copy right law as You suppose; but to pay a promised visit to my friend Kennedy, then Secretary of the Navy; and a very pleasant sojourn I had for several weeks under his hospitable roof. I cannot say that I am very sanguine about the Copy right law, or treaty; there are too many ↑active and↓ sordid interests at work to defeat it and too many mean and despicable ⟨moti⟩ feelings to be wrought upon for it to be successful. We are not sufficiently enlightened and high-minded as yet to legislate properly on the true interests of literature.

I spoke to Putnam about your Las Casas.[3] He would be well disposed to publish any paper of the Kind that would be suitable to his magazine; and he pays, liberally I believe, but I do not know, at what rate. I do not reccollect the composition of your historical essay, ⟨to⟩ sufficiently to judge how it would tell in a magazine—whether it would not be too long for one article—and whether it would cut up into sufficiently striking and piquant parts. Magazine articles you know, must be of such a nature as to tell. I could judge if I had the article by me; and might then, if I thought it advisable, submit it to Mr Putnam and his elbow critics. Such articles as you contributed to To Day[4] I should think would be very acceptable.

I read the Cloister Life of Charles V[5] some time since.—the author having sent me a copy—I was very much pleased with it. A week or two since I had some of the family up here to celebrate my seventieth birth day; so as a friend says I have spent my capital of life and must now live on my earnings. I am happy to say however tha⟨n⟩t I never enjoyed better health than I have for some time past and I think my visits to Saratoga last summer and to Washington last winter have had a fine effect upon health, spirits and bodily vigor.

Your nieces all desire to be affectionately remembered to you

Ever my dear Storrow / Yours very truly
Washington Irving

Thos W Storrow Esqr

MANUSCRIPT: Harvard.

1. This letter has not been located.
2. Ebenezer Irving.
3. Storrow's article on Bartolomé de las Casas (1474–1564), a Spanish missionary who wrote an account of Columbus's voyages, never appeared in *Putnam's Magazine*.
4. For Storrow's contributions to *To-Day*, see WI to Storrow, July 7 and December 14, 1852.
5. Sir William Stirling-Maxwell (1818–1878), a British historian of Spain, wrote *The Cloister Life of the Emperor Charles the Fifth* in 1852. An American edition appeared in 1853. A copy of the 1852 London edition is among the books in WI's library at Sunnyside.

2273. To Donald G. Mitchell

New York. April 21t. 1853.

My dear Mr Mitchell

I enclose a letter to the President[1] which I hope may serve your purpose, in case you make ⟨the⟩ ↑an↓ application for the office you talk of.[2] I am not sanguine that a reccommendation from me will be of much value. I am not a politician and not of the Presidents party. Some civilities passed between us just before I left Washington, and I was much pleased with his appearance and manners and have been generally pleased with his conduct since in office.

There will be some difficulty in your Way from the number of offices already given to New York which I am told begins to cause remark and jealousy.

I have been much gratified to hear of your engagement to Miss Pringle.[3] I considered her one of the loveliest and most amiable of the young belles that we saw at Saratoga last Summer; with such an air of frankness and sincerity. In her mother you may see what you have to calculate on in future years. ⟨She has⟩ Age had produced no withering effects. She looked like an elder sister to her daughter. May all happiness attend you both. If you have time to spare I should like to have another visit ⟨to your?⟩ from you at Sunnyside

Yours ever most truly
Washington Irving

Donald G Mitchell Esq

ADDRESSED: Donald G. Mitchell Esq
MANUSCRIPT: Yale.

1. See WI to Franklin Pierce, April 21, 1853.

2. As WI suggests in his letter to Pierce, Mitchell wished to obtain a consulship in the Mediterranean area. Pierce appointed him U.S. consul at Venice, a post he held from June, 1853, to February, 1854.

3. Mitchell and Mary Frances Pringle of Charleston, South Carolina were married on May 31, 1853. For other details, see WI to Catharine Irving, February 21, 1853.

2274.   *To Franklin Pierce*

New York April 21st 1853

My dear Sir,

My friend Mr Donald G. Mitchell author of several works of great and deserved popularity, is meditating a historical work on an Italian subject. As the necessary researches will call him to Italy, he is desirous as a means of furthering his object to obtain the appointment of Consul to some port in the Mediterranean[1]

Should he make application for such a post, I take the liberty of recommending him in the strongest manner as a gentleman of high worth and integrity, amiable character and manners, and one calculated to acquit himself in matters of business with intelligence and punctuality. His literary merits are too well known and universally acknowledged to need any eulogium at my hands

With great respect / Your Obt Servt
Washington Irving

His Excellency / Franklin Pierce / &c &c &c &c

DOCKETED: April—'53 / *Mitchell D. G.* / recommended for / a Consulate at "Some port / in the Mediterranean," / by / Washington Irving / EWT
MANUSCRIPT: NA, RG 59.

1. Pierce appointed Mitchell to the consulship at Venice.

2275. To Edward Gray

Sunnyside, April 24th. 1853

My dear Mr Gray,

The hams which you have had the kindness to send me came safe to hand. One of them was served up today at dinner. All my family partook of it with uncommon relish. Never did a ham achieve such sudden popularity. In a word it covered itself with glory! I must get your receipt for curing hams; but there must be much in the breed of the animal, as well as in the treatment and feeding. I never attempt any thing but a few green hams in which I succeed very well; but hams so rich, high flavored and thoroughly cured as those you have sent me are quite beyond my art. I thank you most heartily for this specimen of what Maryland can furnish in this line. If I had the ordering of things I should have all our pigs sent to Maryland to be *cured,* as they send patients to southern climates.

I am happy to learn from Mrs Kennedy that your health is restored to its usual state, and anticipate the pleasure of again meeting you in the ensuing summer.[1] Since we parted I have celebrated my seventieth birthday and passed that boundary beyond which a man lives by special privilege Your example shews me, however, that a man may live on beyond that term[2] and retain his sensibilities alive to every thing noble and good and pleasurable and beautiful—and enjoy the society of his friends and spread happiness around him. On such conditions, old age is loveable. I shall endeavor to follow your example.

Ever affectionately / Your friend
Washington Irving

Edward Gray Esqr.

MANUSCRIPT: Peabody Library.   PUBLISHED: PMI, IV, 143–44; and Tuckerman, *Life of J. P. Kennedy,* p. 253 (in part).

1. WI was to visit Gray in June, 1853, and again in July upon his return from Cassilis and Bath (Berkeley Springs). See PMI, IV, 149, 154.

2. Gray was born in 1776. See Tuckerman, *Life of J. P. Kennedy,* p. 246.

2276. To Elizabeth Kennedy

Sunnyside April 24t. 1853

My dear Mrs Kennedy,

I am truly concerned to learn that Kennedy still continues unwell. He has overtasked himself and has led a life of too much excitement for some months past and is now in a state of collapse. He must give his mind perfect repose for a time. Do as they do with the horses, when they take off their shoes and turn them out to grass. His study is no place for him just now. I think the idea a good one to make an excursion; try change of scene and a course of agreeable society. I think Mrs Stanard a capital prescription for his present case and the sooner you pay her your proposed visit the better. I should indeed like to be of your party for I am bewitched with the South and Virginia has always been a poetical region with me. But I begin to doubt whether these high seasoned regales of society that I have had of late at Saratoga and Washington, do not unsettle me a little, and make it hard for me to content myself with the sober every day fare of Sunnyside. I have now to work hard to make up for past dissipation and to earn any future holyday. By the bye, two nieces of mine have just gone on an excursion to the South. One, a bride,[1] with her husband a son of Judge Kent, the other, Henrietta Irving, her cousin and bridesmaid. It is probable you will see or hear of them in the course of your excursion; though they travel very quietly. It is in every way a well suited match and promises to be a happy one.

I have just been writing to your father to thank him for the hams, which have arrived in prime order, and to give him an account of the brilliant manner in which one of them acquitted itself at dinner today. I strike my flag to him completely, and confess that for hams we cannot pretend to cope with old Maryland (always saving and excepting certain *green* hams peculiar to Sunnyside) It gives me sincere pleasure to learn that your father continues in his usual health. I trust he has his musical evenings and his pet minstrels to play and sing for ⟨the⟩ him. There will never be any wrinkles in his mind as long as he can enjoy sweet music and have youth and beauty to administer it to him.

I am writing late at night and it is high time to go to bed. So give my kindest remembrances to your sister and your husband and believe me ever

Your affectionate friend
Washington Irving

Mrs J. P. Kennedy.

P S When you see Mary Dulaney and Louisa Andrews give my love to them

MANUSCRIPT: Peabody Library.   PUBLISHED: PMI, IV, 144–45 (in part); and Tuckerman, *Life of J. P. Kennedy,* p. 253 (in part).

1. Sarah Clark, who married James Kent. For other details, see WI to Catharine Irving, January 17 and February 21, 1853.

2277. *To W. W. Follett Syne*

Sunnyside, April 26, 1853

You have my best wishes for a happy voyage to dear old England. I hope Mrs. Syne may find it as kind and as lovable a country as it has ever proved to me.

PUBLISHED: *The Collector,* 63 (January, 1950), 20, item D192.

2278. *To William W. Waldron*

Sunnyside, April 29th 1853

My Dear Sir:

I thank you for the copy of verses[1] you have had the kindness to send me, in which you have, with so much tact and talent, illustrated a little incident of my childhood.[2] I shall be most happy to receive the visit you promise me in the first week in May. I am almost always at home, and know not of any engagement that will call me away in that week. I dine about half past three, and hope you will partake of a family dinner without ceremony.[3]

Yours truly,
Washington Irving

William W. Waldron, Esq.

PUBLISHED: Waldron, *WI & Cotemporaries,* p. xiv.

1. Waldron's verses, printed in *WI & Cotemporaries,* follow:

Chieftain and Child

The mighty chieftain placed his hand
Upon the bairn's head,
And not, as erst, he gave command,
In gentle accents said:

"Oh, may a Providential care
    Unto this child be given,
For such we're told the angels are
    Who minister in heaven."

The very contact cast a glow
    Throughout the youthful frame,
Such as none other here below
    Has e'er produced the same.

And so it ever still remains,
    Though many a rolling year
Has brought its pleasures, brought its pains,
    To vary life's career.

The words, as manna, seem to drop
    Like morning dew from heaven,
And to life's pilgrim brought a hope
    No other since have given.

How little dreamt the warrior then,
    As forth the words he poured,
That little child would wield a pen
    As potent as his sword.

This reaps its glory from the field
    Where laurels hold the sway,
And that—where richer harvests yield
    The olive and the bay.

Long since life's evening casts its grey
    Upon those tresses fair,
Still does that benediction stay
    And all its blessings bear.

And may its influence never rest
    'Till the celestial shore
Receives the blesser and the blest,
    Where parting is no more.

Well may Columbia proudly boast,
    Exultingly exclaim:
"These are the gems I value most,
    They bring undying fame."

2. WI is referring to the episode in which he was presented by his nurse to George Washington, who placed his hand on the boy's head and blessed him. In 1852 WI recounted the experience to Charles Lanman, who in turn related it to Peter Force: "Mr. Irving had himself seen General Washington. He said there was some celebration going on in New York, and the General was there to participate in the ceremony. 'My nurse,' continued Mr. Irving, 'a good old Scotchwoman,

was very anxious for me to see him, and held me up in her arms as he rode past. This, however, did not satisfy her; so the next day, when walking with me in Broadway, she espied him in a shop; she seized my hand, and darting in exclaimed in her bland Scotch: "Please, your excellency, here's a bairn that's called after ye!" Gen. Washington then turned his benevolent face full upon me, smiled, laid his hand upon my head, and gave me his blessing, which,' added Mr. Irving earnestly, 'I have reason to believe has attended me through life. I was but five years old, yet I can feel that hand upon my head even now.'" See Charles Lanman to Peter Force, February 20, 1853, printed in *National Intelligencer*, March 23, 1857.

3. Waldron accepted the invitation and enjoyed the hospitality of WI and his nieces. See Waldron, *WI & Cotemporaries*, pp. xii–xiii.

2279. To Frederick S. Cozzens

Sunnyside May 5th. 1853.

My dear Sir,

Excuse my delay in answering your note[1] and acknowledging the receipt of the volume[2] you were so kind as to send me. I find it impossible to avoid falling behind hand in correspondence.

I have read your little volume through with great pleasure and am charmed with the variety of talent displayed in it, and the good feeling and good taste that prevail throughout.

I cherish an agreeable reccollection of Your visit last summer[3] and hope now that the beautiful season is opening you will be tempted to repeat it.

Yours very truly
Washington Irving

Fredk S Cozzens Esq

MANUSCRIPT: SHR.

Frederick S. Cozzens (1818–1869), a New York wine merchant and humorist who contributed articles and poems to *Yankee Doodle* and *Knickerbocker Magazine*, collected his *Knickerbocker* sketches in 1853 under the title *Prismatics*, using the pen-name of Richard Haywarde.

1. This note has not been located.

2. *Prismatics*, recently published by D. Appleton and Company.

3. Actually Cozzens, accompanied by William Makepeace Thackeray, had visited Sunnyside in November, 1852. See James G. Wilson, *Thackeray in the United States*, p. 42.

2280. To Robert C. Winthrop

Sunnyside, May 23d. 1853

My dear Mr. Winthrop

I thank you and Mr Prescott for your kind remembrances of me; it is very gratifying to be so remembered by such men. I have heretofore consulted Frothinghams History of the Siege of Boston,[1] about which you speak. It merits the character you give it as being "the best thing written about the Bunkerhill period." I am also much obliged to you for the clippings which you send me from newspapers, giving familiar anecdotes of Washington. It is surprising how few anecdotes there are of him in his familiar life—but he was essentially a public character and so regulated in conduct by square and rule as [to][2] furnish very little of the amusing and picturesque anecdote that we find in the lives of more irregular men

I doubt whether the world will ever get a more full and correct idea of Washington than is furnished by Sparks collection of his ↑letters with the accompanying↓ notes and illustrations; and the preliminary biography.[3] I cannot join in the severe censures that have been passed upon Sparks for the verbal corrections and alterations he has permitted himself to make in some of Washingtons letters. They have been spoken of too harshly. From the examination I have given to the Correspondence of Washington in the archives of the State Department, it appears to me that Sparks has executed his task of selection, arrangement and copious illustration with great judgement & discrimination and with consummate fidelity to the essential purposes of history. His intelligent and indefatigable labors in this and other fields of American history are of national and incalculable importance. Posterity will do justice to them and him.

I am glad to learn that you are supervising a lithographic portrait of our friend Kennedy, ironing out "the wrinkles and crows feet" and fitting it to figure to advantage in the shop windows. It will rejoice the heart of his good little wife, who thinks he has never had justice done him in that line; and was half piqued at a lithographic effigy of myself, where the painter and engraver had represented me as flourishing in "immortal youth"[4]

⟨These⟩ ↑Such↓ likenesses "corrected and amended" will do well to go with the homes of American Authors recently published, to give Europeans a favorable idea of literary men and literary life in this country. In commenting on that publication a London critic observes, "The American authors seem to court the muse to some purpose;" he did not know that most of those so well housed had courted a rich wife into the bargain.

Ever my dear Mr Winthrop

Yours with great regard
Washington Irving

Robert C Winthrop Esqr / &c &c &c

MANUSCRIPT: MHS.   PUBLISHED: PMI, IV, 146–47; and *Proceedings of the Massa-chusetts Historical Society*, 9 (1866–1867), 160 (in part); 10 (1867–1869), 269 (in part).

1. Richard Frothingham (1812–1880), editor of the Boston *Post* and a local historian, had written the *History of the Siege of Boston* in 1848.
2. WI omitted the bracketed word.
3. Jared Sparks had issued *The Writings of George Washington* in twelve volumes (1834–1837).
4. "Probably the likeness prefixed to Mr. H. T. Tuckerman's article on Sunnyside and its Proprietor, in the Homes of American Authors" (PMI's footnote, IV, 147). See *Homes of American Authors* (New York, 1854), p. 34. The portrait, done by Charles Martin and engraved by F. Halpin, was dated January, 1851.

2281.   To Henry Hallam

Sunnyside May 26th. 1853.

My dear Mr Hallam,

Permit me to reccommend to your civilities my friend Mr Alexander Hamilton Jr grandson of *the* Alexander Hamilton so celebrated in our History as the friend and associate of Washington and one of the founders of our Revolution. I am not certain whether you have not heretofore, been acquainted with Mr Hamilton. He accompanied me to Spain as Secretary of Legation, and at that time visited London—He is a gentleman of whose amiable character and intellectual worth I cannot speak too highly—

Ever my dear Mr Hallam / Yours very truly
Washington Irving

MANUSCRIPT: Christ Church Library, Oxford.

Henry Hallam (1777–1859) was an English historian of the Middle Ages whom WI had first met in John Murray's drawing room in 1820. See WI to James K. Paulding, May 27, 1820.

2282. *To Julia Irving*

Sunnyside, May 26th. 1853

My dear Julia;

Your long delightful letter[1] giving account of your expedition to Lexington has lain by me upwards of a month unanswered. But you know how much I am fagged by literary tasking and that it is as difficult for me to exercise my pen in the way of friendly and agreeable correspondence as ⟨for⟩ it is for a postillion to mount his horse and gallop out for an airing after he has been floundering all day through mud and mire.

If I had written at an earlier date I might have given you some account of my visit to Washington, but that is now as old an affair as a last years News paper. I met some persons there who spoke very kindly of you, among the number Mrs Hamilton Fish,[2] who once boarded in the same house with you. I found ⟨he⟩ her very agreeable and lady like—a kind of person by whom I should think you would like to be reccollected[.] Washington is the best place in the Union for varied and intelligent society. It draws together intellect and beauty from all parts of the union. It is like a great watering place where one is as much at home as another; where there is no local gossip, where conversation turns on general topics and topics of general interest, and where every one is excited by novelty. I found, however, the incessant excitement and dissipation rather overpowering, and now and then longed for the quiet of my "native plains" and ⟨my⟩ the untasked indulgence of my elbow chair at Sunnyside.

Helen or some other of your family correspondents have no doubt kept you posted up in the affairs of the family circle. The most important event was the wedding of Sarah Clark. It brought together the ten tribes[3] of the family connexion; even some of the "lost tribes" made their appearance. I allude especially to your Aunt Abbys son ⟨whom⟩ who is called after me,[4] and whom I had not seen for years, as he lives out of sight, somewhere on Long Island, like an owl in a hollow tree. I was surprised to find him so little the worse for his rustication, and that he could bear day light so well. I wish he would not lead such a strange life and keep himself so much aloof, for he is really an amiable worthy fellow and might render himself very acceptable company.

The young couple have made a longer sojourn in the South than they had intended, Sarah having been indisposed for several days—they will return shortly.

You of course know of the engagement of *your niece* Anna Irving to young Routh.[5] We had a gathering at Sunnyside a few days since of her intended—three of his sisters, two of her sisters[6] and one of her cousins, a daughter of William Duer[7] Unfortunately Anna herself was prevented from attending by an inflamed eye. I was very much pleased with the young gentleman, and with his sisters and think it will be a happy match and an agreeable connexion. The day passed off pleasantly The weather was fine and the country in its fresh spring dress. Kate did the "handsome thing" in showing the company about the grounds—while Sarah (who you know is the model house wife) did the hospitable thing in attending to the dinner arrangements—Each was great in her particular way.

Since this festivity Sunnyside has been possessed by a legion of—womankind, and given up to the annual torment of a thorough cleaning. ⟨Tr?⟩ Mrs Odell and Mrs Cunningham took the lead; then there was Matilda the cook and Bridget the housemaid, and Susan the hand maid, and Angeline the ornamental maid, with occasionally Maria, the *ex* cook, now wife to Robert the gardener. You may think what a time we have had of it. Poor Mrs Odell gave out in the middle of the job and had to stay at home with Angeline to nurse her.

Next Maria the ex cook was lacking. Robert appeared one morning with an embarrassed look—"Please Sir—may I stay home this morning with Maria?["]8—"Is she unwell?"—"Oh—no sir. Nothing particular—She'll soon be about again"—I saw by his looks there *was* some thing particular & surmised the fact—"What is it Robert—a *boy* or a *girl?*"—"*Both* sir,["] replied Robert snatching his head. So there's a match for the news you sent me while at Washington about the prolific Ginger.

Helen and Pierre are coming up tomorrow or next day to pass some days with us. I was in town yesterday and found Helen preparing for her annual hegira to the country. The Hall outside of her door full of large black trunks containing all her earthly effects, which I believe are to be stored for the summer in Pierres office. A family is waiting to take possession of her apartment as soon as she & Pierre move out of it. Mrs Lowe has all her rooms engaged for the summer at great rents, and is making a rapid fortune. I expect by the time you have made yours and return to New York you will find her living on the fifth avenue and driving out in her own carriage.

New York, as usual at this season, is all pulled to pieces, the streets full of rubbish and the hotels full of strangers. Hippedromes,[9] and operas[10] and Chinese theatres[11] and *crischal* palaces[12] and all kinds of sights and shows—I have seen none of them. I have only been in town once for a month past and that was yesterday to attend to the affairs of the library and the orphan, and I returned home before nightfall[.] I am growing much steadier than I used to be. I came of age last third day of April when I had some of the family up here to celebrate my seventieth birth day. Since then I have given up many of my wild courses—the girls wish me to give Dick up also and I did think of it once—but could not find any other saddle horse to suit me—so I mount him as usual and think he has given up some of his capers as well as his master.

Farewell my dear Julia—give my love to Sanders and believe me

Your affectionate Uncle
Washington Irving

ADDRESSED: Mrs Sanders Irving / Cincinnati   POSTMARKED: Dearman N. Y— / May 27th
MANUSCRIPT: John Granlund.

1. This letter has not been located.

2. Julia Kean had married Hamilton Fish, a New York lawyer who was serving as U.S. senator, on December 15, 1836. Noted for her graciousness and tact, she made her home in Washington a center of social activity.

3. An allusion to the ten tribes of ancient Israel which were taken into captivity in 722 B.C. by Sargon. See 2 Kings 17.

4. Washington Irving, Jr. (1814–1894) was the fifth child of John Treat and Abigail Irving.

5. Anna Duer Irving (1830–1884), daughter of Pierre Paris Irving and grand-daughter of Ebenezer, married Frederick R. Routh (b. 1830) on June 7, 1854.

6. Anna Duer Irving's sisters living in 1853 were Elizabeth (1834–1906), Harriet (1835–1906), and Ellen (1840–1895).

7. William Duer (1780–1858) was a jurist and a contributor to Peter Irving's *The Corrector* and *Morning Chronicle*.

8. WI omitted the bracketed quotation marks here and elsewhere in this passage.

9. Franconi's Imperial Hippodrome on Fifth Avenue opened on May 2, 1853, with an elaborate program involving a chariot race, a "Grand Tournament of the Field of the Cloth of Gold" with two hundred horses and performers, and a steeplechase. The circuslike spectacle continued until November. See Odell, *NY Stage*, VI, 259–60.

10. Marietta Alboni, Lorenzo Salvi, Francesco Beneventano, and Ignazio Marini performed at Niblo's Theater in April and May in such operas as *Don Pasquale*, *La Sonnambula*, *La Gazza Ladra*, *Lucrezia Borgia*, *La Figlia di Reggimento*, and *Don Giovanni*. See Odell, *NY Stage*, VI, 241–42.

11. The Great Tung, Hook, Tong Chinese Company opened at Niblo's on May 21 for a brief run. See Odell, *NY Stage*, VI, 242.

12. The Crystal Palace, modeled on the London original, opened on July 14, 1853, at Sixth Avenue and 42nd Street, now the site of Bryant Park. Although primarily a merchandise display, it frequently presented Dodworth's Band, Noll's Military Band, a large chorus, and a great organ for musical entertainment. See Odell, *NY Stage*, VI, 260–61.

2283. *To Mary E. Kennedy*

Sunnyside May 27th. 1853

My dear Miss Kennedy

I thank you for your most welcome letter[1] giving me such pleasant accounts of the happy life you have been leading with your "Richmond cousins" your "dearest friend" and a gallant knight to accompany you in "delightful rides" about your "beautiful valley." Your letter is full of youth and springtime and bespeaks the sunshine of the heart, which makes everything bright and beautiful about you.

You say I cannot imagine how lovely the country is now. Indeed I *can*—though I have not your young eyes and young feelings with which to regard it. I don't know when I have been more conscious of the sweetness of the spring than this season. It has opened with uncommon freshness and is surrounding me with its delights. The grass is growing up to my very door,—the roses and honeysuckles are clambering about my windows, the acacias and liburnums are in full flower, singing birds have built in the ivy against the wall and I have concerts at daybreak almost equal to the serenades you used to have at Washington. This is the very revel of our year. The last half of May and the first half of June forms one of the most perfect months in this latitude. Nature is in full dress, of brightest green. The young and tender leaf is as yet without a blemish. The air is fragrant and balmy, the temperature genial; everything is full of present enjoyment and sweet promise for the future. Such is the country in my neighborhood. I am aware that you live in a more genial climate, that spring is earlier with you than with us and vegetation more luxuriant. I have a romantic idea of your mountains and valleys, though my experience of them has not been favorable. I once scaled the Blue Ridge[2] in quest of the picturesque but a storm gathered up just as I crossed it; the valleys were drenched with rain all the time I was in them, and I was entangled among streams so much swollen as [to][3] be unfordable. I saw enough however to convince me how grand and beautiful the scenery must be in fine weather.

Your invitation, therefore, to pay your part of the country a visit is a most tempting one and indeed your uncle John when I was in Washington talked something of our making an excursion together among the Virginia mountains[4] of which he spoke in the highest terms for their beauty and salubrity. I fear however his indisposition has changed all his plans; and before he returns from Richmond the weather will be too warm for an excursion to the south. As soon as the summer heat commences my activity is at an end and then my greatest luxury is to sit in the shade and enjoy the southern breeze as it steals up the Hudson. I have some capital trees for the purpose just on the river bank and there I pass a great part of my time in summer weather.

I feel very much concerned at the state of your uncles health. He over-tasked himself at Washington; the toils of office and the constant excite-ment of society kept his intellect and spirits continually on the stretch and I presume a collapse has been the consequence. He should now give himself a long spell of relaxation.

I long to be with him. I have need of relaxation myself, for too much sedentary occupation has produced symptoms of late which oblige me to suspend literary occupation and may exile me for a time from my study.

In sober sadness I believe it is high time I should throw by the pen altogether, but writing has become a kind of habitude with me; and un-less I have some task in hand to occupy a great part of my time I am at a loss what to do. After being accustomed to literary research, mere desultory reading ceases to be an occupation. There is as much differ-ence between them in point of interest as between taking an airing on horseback and galloping after the hounds. It is pretty hard for an old huntsman to give up the chase.

By the bye your mention of Mr Washington Lewis[5] and his trunk full of Washington letters and diarys has started some game which I should like to run down. I enclose a letter to Mr Lewis[6] making an inquiry on the subject. As I do not know his exact address I will thank you to add it to the superscription.

Do you not occasionally consult the news papers for the whereabouts of the naval enterprises launched under your uncles auspices—Ringolds[7] especially? I shall never forget the gallant assemblage of naval officers that thronged your uncles rooms a day or two before we left Washington and how the kind heart of your aunt was near overflowing at her eyes on parting with them, and how you gave a parting smile to them from the window as they in a manner passed in review before you. How soon will those fine fellows be scattered to the ends of the earth—careering over every sea, on enterprises of difficulty and danger. I shall feel addi-tional interest in watching the course of those enterprises from knowing something personally of the brave spirits engaged in them.

It often strikes me how many scenes and characters and incidents of an especial kind were crowded into that little space of time which passed with us like a dream at Washington. Every thing that passes before ones eyes, in every day life, in a place like that, the seat of government of a great empire, is a portion of history, and those with whom we converse familiarly may be destined, perhaps, to figure conspicuously in its pages.

Farewell my dear Miss Kennedy. Do not think it necessary to apolo-gize to me should you leave my letters long unanswered. It is a pleasure with me to write to you, and a still greater pleasure to hear from you;

but I know that letter writing is an irksome task to most people and I would not impose a task of any kind on your bright and happy spirit. So if days and weeks elapse without a line from "Lady Mary" I shall console myself with the idea that she is better employed, that she has another influx of cousins from Richmond, that she is rejoicing with the friends of her youth, or that she is taking 'delightful rides' through the 'beautiful valley' with some 'chosen knight' to attend upon her. So wishing that all her ways may continue to be ways of pleasantness and all her paths be peace,

I remain her sincerely attached friend

Washington Irving

PUBLISHED: *American Literature*, 6 (March, 1934), 48–51; PMI, IV, 147–48 (in part).

1. This letter has not been located.

2. WI visited the Blue Ridge Mountains during the spring of 1833. See PMI, III, 51–52.

3. WI omitted the bracketed word.

4. WI and John P. Kennedy traveled in Virginia and Maryland from June 20 to July 11, 1853. See STW, II, 209, 391.

5. Washington Lewis was the grandson of Lawrence Lewis, to whom George Washington had written letters in 1797 and 1798. When WI visited Lewis's plantation, he examined the letters. See Tuckerman, *Life of J. P. Kennedy*, pp. 358–59; and Rose M. MacDonald, *Clarke County, A Daughter of Frederick* (Berryville, Va., 1943), pp. 44–46.

6. This letter has not been located.

7. Cadwalader Ringgold (1802–1867) commanded a surveying expedition which left Norfolk in June, 1853, charted numerous Pacific shoals and islands, and reached China in 1854. For John P. Kennedy's connection with the expedition, see Tuckerman, *Life of J. P. Kennedy*, p. 223.

2284. To Robert Balmanno

Sunnyside May 29th. 1853

My dear Sir,

I feel properly sensible of the honor and kindness done me by the Shakespeare Society in electing me an honorary member; and will take occasion, as you suggest, to attend and inscribe my name on the Record Book.

I must forewarn you, however, that I am likely to prove a very delinquent member, as I am growing more and more recluse in my habits and slow to respond to the claims of Society. All kinds of public and society dinners I avoid. I am no longer *clubable*. Quiet life in the country has been the ruin of me!

With this premonition I subscribe myself

With great regard / Yours faithfully
Washington Irving

Robert Balmanno Esqr.

ADDRESSED: Robert Balmanno Esqr. / South Brooklyn.   POSTMARKED: Dearman,
    N. Y— / May 31t   DOCKETED: Washington Irving / Sunnyside 29 May 1853 /
    ackg his Election as an Honorary Member
MANUSCRIPT: Folger Shakespeare Library.

Robert Balmanno (b. 1780) was a Scotsman who lived in New York many years and contributed articles to *Knickerbocker Magazine*, *Graham's Magazine*, and the New York *Evening Post*. For other details, see WI to Balmanno, April 15, 1850.

2285. *To Mary E. Kennedy*

Sunnyside June 10th. 1853

My dear Miss Kennedy,

Your last letter[1] has set me manuscript hunting. Mr Washington Lewis[2] writes that he cannot let the Mss go out of his possession but if I will visit him at Audley they will be submitted to my inspection.

As I am ordered to throw by my pen and abstain from head work of all kinds for a time I have determined to make the excursion to the mountains you suggest, before the intense heats of summer commence. I shall set off for Baltimore therefore on Monday next, and have written to your uncle John hoping he will accompany me to Cassilis, whence I presume I can ride over to Mr Lewis', and examine the manuscripts.

I write in haste to be in time for the mail. With kind remembrances to your father believe me my dear Miss Kennedy

Yours ever very truly
Washington Irving

PUBLISHED: *American Literature*, 6 (March, 1934), 51.

1. This letter has not been located.
2. In his letter of May 27, 1853, WI had asked Miss Kennedy to forward a letter to Washington Lewis in which WI inquired about the manuscripts relating to George Washington. Lewis's letter to WI has not been located.

2286.   To William W. Waldron

Sunnysid[e]. June 10t. 1853

My dear Sir,

Accept my thanks for the beautiful little dog[1] which you have had the kindness to send me as a specimen of the porcelain manufacture of Mr Charles Cartlidge.[2] It does great credit to his factory.

You say it is intended to guard bank notes; If it can keep mine from vanishing it will prove a more effective guard than any I have as yet set upon them

Yours very truly
Washington Irving

William W Waldron Esqr

MANUSCRIPT: NYPL—Seligman Collection.   PUBLISHED: Waldron, *WI & Cotemporaries*, p. 246.

1. The porcelain dog now sits on the desk in WI's study at Sunnyside.
2. Charles Cartlidge, a Staffordshire native, began making porcelain doorknobs and buttons in the United States about midcentury. In 1853 he exhibited his ware at the Crystal Palace and won a prize for high quality. See Marvin D. Schwartz and Richard Wolfe, *A History of American Art Porcelain* (New York, 1967), p. 29.

2287.   To Pierre M. Irving

[Philadelphia], June 13, 1853

Inform my beloved family of my well-being, as well as of my extraordinary prudence and self-restraint in not continuing on in the night train with Mr. P——, to which I confess I felt sorely tempted. But I gain in prudence with years, and, I trust, will in time be all that my friends could wish.

PUBLISHED: PMI, IV, 148.

2288.   To Helen Dodge Irving

Ellicotts Mills June 15t. 1853

My dear Helen,

I arrived at Baltimore yesterday between one and two Oclock, after a pretty warm and dusty ride from Philadelphia. However as I sat by a window on the shady side of the cars I did not suffer much from the heat.

I found Kennedy on the look out for me. He had expected me the evening before. The family were all out of town at old Mr Grays country establishment where I am now writing. We dined at Kennedys brother Anthonys,[1] in Baltimore and had a very gay family dinner, after which we came out in the evening train and had a beautiful drive along the lovely valley of the Patapsco ⟨on which⟩ ↑on↓ the banks of which stream the country residence is situated. You may have an idea of the house from an engraving in Putnams Homes of Authors.[2] We found the family all assembled round the tea table; and a bright happy gathering it was, there being a matter of five young ladies guests in the house. Among the number I was delighted to meet with one of the three young belles with whom I was domesticated at Washington—Louisa Andrews—the one who plays so admirably on the Piano. There was great greeting on all sides and most especially by my warm hearted old friend Mr Gray The evening passed delightfully—We had music from Miss Andrews, we sat out in the Moon light on the piazza, and strolled along the banks of the Patapsco after which I went to bed had a sweet nights sleep and dreamt I was in Mahomets paradise.

I have given myself entirely into Kennedys hands; who has planned our whereabouts. I am to remain here until Monday next when Kennedy sets off with me for his brother *Andrews* near Harpe[r]s[3] Ferry (I told Pierre *Anthonys* by mistake)[.] I shall then be in the neighborhood of Mr Washington Lewis', who has the Mss. and will be within a short distance of some places noted in Washington history. After our sojourn there we go to Berkeley county[4] among the mountains—visiting among some of Kennedys friends who live in hospitable Virginia style—so now you know about as much of our plans as I do myself. I think they promise well. I am scribbling this before breakfast because I do not know whether I shall have time afterwards as I may be on horseback among some of the beautiful wild mountain scenery by which we are surrounded.

Give my love to all the good folks at both houses. I shall write again soon.

Letters to me should be addressed—care of Edward Gray Esqr. Ellicotts Mills Maryland.

Your affectionate Uncle
Washington Irving

Mrs Pierre M Irving

12 Oclock—Before closing my letter I must tell you that I have been enjoying a great treat my beautiful young friend Louisa Andrews playing all the airs in Don Govanni[5] for me—⟨and⟩ ↑together with↓ several other

Master pieces—playing and singing and looking *divinely*. Dont you envy me?

MANUSCRIPT: Yale.   PUBLISHED: PMI, IV, 149 (in part); Tuckerman, *Life of J. P. Kennedy*, p. 145 (in part).

1. Anthony Kennedy (1810–1892) was an agriculturist and Whig politician who was elected to the U.S. Senate in 1854 on the "Know-Nothing" ticket.

2. For the engraving of the house, see *Homes of American Authors*, p. 341.

3. WI omitted the bracketed letter.

4. Berkeley County is in the extreme northeastern tip of what is now West Virginia.

5. Mozart's opera written in 1787. WI misspelled the title.

2289.   *To Catharine Irving*

Ellicotts Mills June 19th. 1853

My dear Kate,

Hitherto my excursion has been every thing that heart could wish. I am getting on delightfully at the hospitable mansion of my worthy old friend Mr Gray, on the banks of the beautiful Patapsco, in the midst of a happy circle; ⟨for⟩ The house is always full for the old gentleman has the knack of surrounding himself with agreeable people and putting them all at their ease. ⟨Dur⟩ We have had some hot days, but I have weathered them very pleasantly, by keeping within doors until evening, reading or gossiping with the ladies or listening to the music of our little pet prima donna Miss Andrews, who plays mornings and evenings for us and is an excellent musician. I have had some delightful rides and drives about the neighborhood, along the banks of the Patapsco and through ⟨the⟩ woods and romantic ravines. This is a capital country for horseback exercise and I have been well mounted upon Mrs Kennedys favorite horse Douce Davie, who well deserves his name, a quieter pleasanter horse I never rode—I wish I could transfer him to the banks of the Hudson.

Tell Mr Grinnell that I have paid a visit to the country seat of Mr Lorman which he talks about so often. He has only seen it in the Winter time. He should see it at this season when the vast magnificent prospect which it commands is in all its beauty. Mrs Lorman is a superb looking woman—worthy to preside over such an establishment.

Tomorrow morning I set off at nine Oclock ↑With Mr John Kennedy↓ on the train for his brother Andrews, near Harpers Ferry—nearly a hundred miles from this. ⟨There I shall see my[?]⟩ ↑Thence I shall visit↓ Mr Washington Lewis; and afterwards make excursions among the mountains visiting some of the old Virginia families[.] I anticipate a very interesting and delightful excursion having such a capital travelling companion.

I am scrawling this in great haste just to keep you acquainted with my whereabouts. Direct to me care of Edward Gray Esqr Ellicotts Mills Maryland. Give my love to your father and all the household at both houses.

Your affectionate Uncle
Washington Irving

Miss Catharine A. Irving

MANUSCRIPT: SHR.

2290. To Sarah Irving

Cassilis, June 22d. 1853.

My dear Sarah,

I write merely to keep you informed of my movements, for I am in no mood for pen exercise this warm weather, and the letter I scrawled to Kate a day or two since gave me a weariness of the brain.

Mr John Kennedy and myself left Ellicotts Mills yesterday (Monday) morning, in the train which passed at nine Oclock. I left ⟨that⟩ the hospitable nest of Mr Gray with great reluctance, having passed a most delightful time there; but I left it with the consolation that I should return there after my excursion among the mountains. We had an extremely hot drive of about a hundred miles, but through lovely scenery. The rail road[1] follows up the course of the Patapsco to its head springs—and a romantic stream it is throughout. The road then crosses some fine open fertile country on the summit of Elk ridge[2] and ⟨then down⟩ descends along the course of Reynolds Creek and the Monocasy[3] to the Potomac all beautiful; At Harpers Ferry we changed cars and pushed on to Charleston,[4] where we found Mr Andrew Kennedy waiting for us with his carriage—A drive of about a mile and half brought us to his Seat whence this letter is dated. Here I am in the centre of the Magnificent Valley of the Shenandoah—the great valley of Virginia. and a glorious Valley it is—equal to the promised land for fertility; far superior to it for beauty and inhabited by infinitely superior people—*choice* though not chosen.[5] Mr Kennedy inhabits a fine spacious stone mansion, standing on a rising ground among noble forest trees and commanding extensive prospects over the wide varied region comprised in this valley. Here I am made completely at home, as I am every where—in this family connexion. Mr Kennedy was with us for a time last Winter at Washington, so that I met him as an old acquaintance. His daughter Mary Kennedy, who supplied the place of a niece to me at Washington was at home, and I find her still more amiable and charming in her own home than she was when gracing her uncles establishment at the Capitol. The weather is excessively hot—but we manage to get on pleasantly by keeping within doors until evening. And as there is good company, cheerful and intelligent conversation—and occasionally a little music time slips away ⟨with⟩ delightfully. Tomorrow I expect to go in company with the two Mr Kennedys on a visit to Mr G Washington Lewis, who has a noble estate about twelve miles off, where we shall remain until the next day. ⟨Mr Lewis has some⟩

I have several places to visit in this vicinity connected with the history of Washington, after which we shall push on to the mountains where we shall find a cooler temperature. Notwithstanding the heat of the weather my excursion hitherto has been one of constant enjoyment; how could it be otherwise surrounded as I continually am by hospitable and most agreeable people and in the midst of glorious scenery.

Give my love to all bodies

Your affectionate Uncle
Washington Irving

Miss Sarah Irving

This is a sad scrawl but I cannot write a better one—I find my head will not bear work of this kind.

Manuscript: SHR. Published: PMI, IV, 150.

1. The Baltimore and Ohio Railroad.
2. Elk Ridge is about eight miles southwest of Baltimore.
3. Monocasy Junction is about forty miles west of Baltimore.
4. Charles Town, the county seat of Jefferson County, was laid out by George Washington's brother Charles in 1786.
5. For the promised land and the chosen people, see Deuteronomy 32:48–52.

2291. To Pierre M. Irving

Cassilis, June 25, 1853

My dear Pierre:

Your letter of the 19th,[1] received two or three days since, has put me quite in spirits. From your opinion of my manuscripts,[2] I begin to hope that my labor has not been thrown away. Do not make a toil of reading the manuscripts, but take it leisurely, so as to keep yourself fresh in the perusal, and to judge quietly and coolly of its merits and defects.

I have paid my visit to Mr. George Washington Lewis, to inspect the manuscripts in his possession. His seat (Audley) is about twelve or fourteen miles from this. Andrew and John Kennedy accompanied me. We went on Wednesday, and returned on Thursday. The visit was a most agreeable one.[3] We were hospitably entertained by Mr. Lewis, who is a young man of engaging appearance and manners. * * * His mother,[4] however, is the real custodian of the Washington reliques and papers, which she laid before me with great satisfaction. I did not find much among the manuscripts requiring note. In less than an hour I had made all the memoranda necessary. * * *

Yesterday I drove out with the Kennedys, to visit two other establishments of the Washington family in this neighborhood, the proprietors of which had called to see me during my absence at Audley. These visits are all full of interest; but I will tell you all about them when we meet. * * *

To-day we are to visit some other places of note in the neighborhood. On Monday, the day after to-morrow, I set off with Mr. John Kennedy and his bachelor brother, Pendleton Kennedy,[5] for the mountains.

I must again apologize for my wretched scrawl; but it seems hard work for me to extract any ideas out of my weary brain, which is as dry as "a remainder biscuit."

I hope you will continue to mount guard at Sunnyside during my absence.

With love to all, your affectionate uncle,
Washington Irving

PUBLISHED: PMI, IV, 151–52.

1. This letter has not been located.

2. WI's biography of George Washington.

3. See Tuckerman, *Life of J. P. Kennedy*, pp. 358–60, for J. P. Kennedy's account of the trip to Audley, located in Clark County. Built by Warner Washington (not of George Washington's family), it was later sold to Lorenzo Lewis.

4. Mrs. Lewis, now a widow, was the former Miss Cox of Philadelphia. See Tuckerman, *Life of J. P. Kennedy*, p. 358.

5. Philip Pendleton Kennedy (1802–1864), the youngest brother of John P. Kennedy, wrote a woodland adventure, *The Blackwater Chronicle* (1853). An erratic genius, he was troubled with alcoholism in later life. See Bohner, *J. P. Kennedy*, pp. 13, 189–90.

2292. *To Helen Dodge Irving*

Cassilis. June 26t. 1853

My dear Helen,

Many thanks for your letter of the 22d.[1] Which gave me some account of your affairs at Sunnyside during the late roasting weather. I trust you are participating in this delightful change which has taken place for the last two days and has braced us all up again Tomorrow I set off with John and Pendleton Kennedy for Bath, a kind of watering place among the mountains. I shall leave the hospitable mansion of Mr Andrew Kennedy with extreme regret. I have been treated like one of the family and have made a most delightful visit. Nothing reconciles me to parting with them but the thoughts that I shall visit them again at some more temperate season admitting of exercise on horseback for⟨th⟩ which this is the very country. I was at church this morning and was struck with the number of persons in the congregation of the name of Washington. It is a common name in this county: as some of General Washingtons finest lands were in this neighborhood and are portioned out among members of the family[2]

Your letter, like Pierres, has given me great satisfaction speaking so encouragingly of my MS. I never shall be ⟨of⟩ able I fear to give it the toning up ⟨with⟩ which a painter gives to his picture before finishing it. I am affraid my head will not bear much more work of the kind. It gives me hints even when I am scrawling letters.—

We shall pass three or four days at Bath,[3] for the advantage of bathing then perhaps make a dash for a day as far as Cumberland and then turn our faces homeward—However. I find plans are apt to be altered by circumstances; so shall not pretend to mark out one precisely—

I hope you and Pierre find the sojourn at the Cottage pleasant enough to indemnify you for being kept from Staten Island. Tell the girls I charge them to let you have your own way in every thing

I am scrawling this merely to keep you all advised of my movements so with love to all bodies I conclude

Your affectionate Uncle
WI.

Mr[s] Pierre M Irving

MANUSCRIPT: NYPL—WI Papers.   PUBLISHED: PMI, IV, 152 (in part).

1. This letter has not been located.

2. One of the letters which WI examined at Audley, the estate of George Washington Lewis, mentioned a bequest of two thousand acres from General Washington to Lewis, his nephew. See Tuckerman, *Life of J. P. Kennedy,* p. 359.

3. Later called Berkeley Springs, Bath was a popular watering place in northwestern Virginia before the Civil War. Its waters were fresh and sweet, without the medicinal taste usually found in mineral springs. For sketches of the springs, see Perceval Reniers, *The Springs of Virginia: Life, Love, and Death at the Waters* (Chapel Hill, 1941), pp. 33–41; and *West Virginia, A Guide of the Mountain State,* American Guide Series, (New York, 1941), pp. 169–72.

2293. To Catharine Irving

Berkeley Springs (Bath) July 1t 1853

My dear Kate

I received ↑yesterday↓ your letter of Sunday and Monday last,[1] and rejoice to find you have all survived the late intense weather. I have been for four or five days in this watering place, which is in a small valley among the Mountains, and, as far as my experience goes, one of the hottest places in the known world. You will be surprised to learn however that my greatest amusement, during the heat of the day, is at the ten pin alley, and that I am getting quite expert at bowling—The perspiration it produces is awful—and only to be allayed by the cool baths for which this place is famous. Tomorrow I trust to emerge from this oven and to return with Mr Andrew Kennedy to ⟨his⟩ Cassilis, where I shall be once more within the reach of cooling breezes. Mr. John Kennedy rejoins us there on Monday, and then in the course of a day or two I shall return with the latter to Ellicotts Mills—and thence—(in the fullness of time) homewards.

Tell Robert I charge him not to work in the sun during the hottest hours of the day—should this intense warm weather continue. He injured himself by it last summer—and I would not have any thing happen to him for all the hay in the country.

I am sorry to hear that Mrs Coits fete champetre[2] proved such a failure—although I am no friend to these attempts to bring city show and extravagance into the country. The[y][3] put an end to all our rural jollifications of former days. Our neighborhood is gradually growing too fine for real rural life. I prefer the joyous, informal rurality that I find in Virginia.

I am glad to find that Julia has at length cast loose from Ingleside[4] and in[5] on her way home to the Cottage—I trust you will have a fatted chicken killed ⟨for her sake⟩ on the occasion Farewell—The weather is so hot that I cannot write—nor do any thing else but play at bowls and fan myself—

With love to all / Your affectionate Uncle
W. I.

MANUSCRIPT: SHR.   PUBLISHED: PMI, IV, 152–53 (in part).

1. This letter has not been located.
2. Mrs. Coit, apparently a Tarrytown neighbor, had held a garden party.
3. WI omitted the bracketed letter.
4. Julia Irving, Ebenezer's daughter, had been visiting her sister Charlotte Grinnell in upstate New York.
5. WI probably intended to write "is."

2294.   To Pierre M. Irving

Ellicotts Mills July 8th. 1853

My dear Pierre,

I have just recieved your letter of the 6th.[1] which I need not tell you has been most gratifying and enspiriting to me. I thank you for writing it; for I was looking most anxiously and dubiously for your verdict[2] after reading the narrative of the war in which the interest ⟨is⟩ I feared might suffer from diffusion, and from the difficulty of binding up a variety of enterprises and ⟨ba⟩ campaigns into one harmonious whole. I now feel my mind prodigiously relieved; and begin to think I have not labored in vain.

I left Bath shortly after I wrote to Kate. We had intended a tour among the All[e]ghanies, but the intense heat of the weather discouraged us and we determined to postpone that part of our plan to another season

Returning to Cassilis we passed a few days more under the hospitable roof of Mr Andrew Kennedy; where I saw something of a harvest home in the noble valley of the Shenandoah and experienced a repetition of those kind attentions which made me feel almost as if I were a member of the family.

Leaving Cassilis on Wednesday ⟨evening⟩ ↑morning↓ we arrived here before sunset. It was my intention to proceed home almost immediately, but I found it impossible to resist the kind entreaties of the family to remain here until next Monday, when I shall set off early in the morning for Baltimore to take the train for New York where I expect to arrive on Tuesday and then to push for the Cottage.

Tell Sarah I ⟨recie⟩ have recieved her letter of the 1st July—but cannot answer it at present. To tell the truth though my excursion has put me in capital health and spirits—I find I cannot handle the pen even in these miserable scrawls without feeling a sensation in the head that admonishes me to refrain. Think then how gratifying it must be to me to learn from your letter that I may dispense from any severe task work in completing my historical task. ⟨I shall never⟩

I feel that my working days are over; and rejoice that I have arrived at a good stopping place.

Give my love to Helen and to all at the Cottage

Your affectionate Uncle
Washington Irving

Pierre M Irving Esq

MANUSCRIPT: NYPL–Seligman Collection.   PUBLISHED: PMI, IV, 154.

1. This and Sarah's letter mentioned later have not been located.

2. Pierre had appraised WI's efforts as follows: "Familiar as I am with the story, I have been equally surprised and gratified to perceive what new interest it gains in your hands. I doubt not the work will be equally entertaining to young and old." See PMI, IV, 153.

2295.   *To Mary E. Kennedy*

Sunnyside July 19th. 1853

My dear Miss Kennedy,

On our way to Ellicotts Mills your uncle John and myself made a pleasant halt at Harpers Ferry, taking a lunch, or rather an early dinner, with your friends on the hill; whom we found very hospitable and agreeable, and who spoke of you as you deserve to be spoken of; which put me so much the more in good humor with them.

The prospects from the hill merit all that you have said of them. That looking toward the Potomac where the mountains approach each other put me in mind of a view from West Point looking up the Hudson between the promontories of the Highlands. The view up the shining course of the **Shenandoah** is lovely—as is every thing connected with that beautiful river; which I trust your uncle John and I will prove when we come to write our joint romance about the lilly that flourishes on its borders.

Having brought my "historical researches" to a close before leaving Cassilis I had intended to push homeward directly; but was brought to a stand at Ellicotts Mills, and prevailed on to stay there until Monday. There was no company there; but I did not feel the want of any. I drove out with your aunt to visit Mr McTavish and his bride at the beautiful Hall built by my old friend the late Mr John McTavish[1]—and afterwards to visit the Carroll manor house.[2] McTavish and his bride were just in the first quarter of their honeymoon and in a place that might have been a paradise for a pair of lovers, yet the bride finds it rather lonely and talked of setting off soon for the watering places—with a hint of a tour in Europe—Domestic bliss is rather a travelling enjoyment nowadays.

I had two or three more delightful rides on horseback with your uncle about the romantic scenery of the Patapsco. On Monday morning after an early breakfast your uncle and aunt drove in to Baltimore with me in the carriage and took leave of me at the station. I was swept away in a railroad car as in the car of an enchanter—and—hey presto! found myself in the evening quietly seated in Castle Garden at New York listening to Sontag in an Italian opera![3] Surely modern reality outstrips ancient illusion—and fairy tale is no longer a fable.

And here I am once more at little Sunnyside seated at my study table, with trumpet creepers flaunting their flowers about the windows and humming birds humming almost in my ear; but my mind is still teeming with delightful recollections of scenes in Maryland and Virginia; noble mountains, spacious forests and romantic streams—above all the lovely valley of the Shenandoah—a region equal to the promised land of yore, and fortunately not occupied by the *chosen people.* I rejoice that I visited it during the time of harvest; when I saw it in all its glory— a veritable land of abundance. I shall never forget that fourth of July evening when we took tea in rural style on the front porch, with the noble Englishlooking landscape spread out before us and the harvest scene going on in the broad wheat field beyond the grove of oaks. And our visit to the field when your brotherinlaw[4] came forth from among the harvestmen to welcome us and little Lizzy[5] threw her arms round his neck and patted his manly sunburnt cheek with her tiny hands. What a glorious sunset we had—and what a play of lightening among the clouds that lay piled along the horizon—and how charmingly the evening was closed by music, that sweetness of home—without which no home is complete. By the way I was glad that on the last evening of my sojourn I set your fathers flute going and awoke the host of delightful old familiar tunes that seemed to have been sleeping in it.

A letter from your uncle John[6] has just been handed to me telling me that he and his party will be in New York tomorrow. I shall go down to town to meet them; though I do not feel ready or inclined to go on to Saratoga immediately. In fact I would much rather be with them among the delightful home scenes in which I have seen them recently.

Farewell—I hope when you find time and mood to write to me you will give me all the domestic news of Cassilis. Recollect I have been among you and been made, for a time, like one of the household. I now know you all, and feel an interest in you all, and am more or less acquainted with all the neighborhood. They say a woman is never truly known until you see her in her own home. I have seen you there, and have only found more reason to esteem and value you. Give my kindest remembrances to your father mother and sisters. I am glad your sister Sarah[7] returned home in time for me to become acquainted with her. I met your brother[8] at Charlestown as we were on the way to the cars— he was just from Shepherdstown—but had no Shepherdess on his arms. I hope his Pastora is not cruel. Keep my dear little Lizzy in mind of me. How I should be delighted to have her little soft hands patting my cheek again—or see her parading the piazza with drum and trumpet and your father playing the grand military air of bambanani.

Ever my dear Miss Kennedy

Yours with affectionate regard
Washington Irving

PUBLISHED: *American Literature*, 6 (March, 1934), 51–54.

1. John MacTavish (ca. 1787–1852) was associated with the Northwest Fur Company in Montreal, where WI had met him in 1808. See STW, I, 99; and WI to Sarah Storrow, March 12, 1845. WI had just visited his old friend's son, who had married the granddaughter of Charles Carroll of Carrollton. See *Maryland, A History, 1632–1974*, ed. Richard Walsh and William Lloyd Fox (Baltimore, 1974), p. 521.

2. Doughoregan, a Gothic-Revival style mansion built in about 1727, is three hundred feet long with two ells, in one of which was a Roman Catholic chapel. George Washington was a frequent guest there. See Thomas A. Glenn, *Some Colonial Mansions and Those Who Lived in Them* (Philadelphia, 1899), pp. 335–63.

3. Henriette Sontag and Balbina Steffanone took the leading roles in Jacob Meyerbeer's *Robert le Diable* at Castle Garden on July 18. See NYEP, July 18, 1853.

4. John Selden married Anne Rebecca Kennedy (1825–1854) in 1845. They had four children—Andrew, Wilson, Mary, and Elizabeth.

5. The youngest child of Anne and John Selden.

6. This letter has not been located.

7. Sarah P. Kennedy (b. 1834).

8. Mary had two brothers—Andrew (1824–1900) and Edmund (1831–1881). Both were unmarried at this time.

2296. To John C. Peters

[July 22, 1853]

My dear Dr Peters

My friend the Hon J. P. Kennedy wishes to consult you on a complaint similar to the one from which you relieved me. He is at the New York Hotel[.][1] I wish you would make it convenient to call on him at ½ past ten tomorrow morning

Yours truly
Washington Irving

Friday morning

MANUSCRIPT: NYPL—Berg Collection.

Since Kennedy and WI met in New York City on Thursday, July 21, WI probably wrote this note to Dr. Peters on Friday, July 22. See STW, II, 391, n. 417.

This copy is not in WI's handwriting.

1. The New York Hotel was located at 721 Broadway between Washington and Waverly Places. See Haswell, *Reminiscences of an Octogenarian*, p. 417.

2297. *To Sarah Storrow*

Sunnyside July 29th. 1853

My dear Sarah,

I have suffered a long time to elapse without answering your last letter, or the charming one from my dear little Kate which accompanied it.[1] The fact is for some time past I have had to lay aside the pen almost entirely, ⟨and to⟩ having overtasked myself, and produced a weariness of the brain, that renders it an irksome effort even to scrawl an ordinary letter. Being obliged to abandon my study I have made an excursion into Maryland and Virginia and passed some time very pleasantly with the Kennedys and their connexions. I was in some of the ⟨d⟩ most beautiful parts of Virginia and saw harvest home in perfection in the noble Valley of the Shenandoah; a veritable region of abundance. I have always been partial to Virginia and the Virginians and my excursion has contributed to encrease that partiality. I returned from the south between two and three weeks since in excellent general health; but still unable to resume my literary occupations; which I doubt whether I shall be able to resume until the bracing weather of Autumn.

I am now on the point of setting off for Saratoga. The waters were of great service to me last year, and may be this—though I believe all that I require is a good spell of *literary abstinence.*

I see you are quite enthusiastic about the Empress,[2] and I do not wonder at it. There is much in her appearance and character to captivate, ⟨you⟩ and her situation is deeply interesting. I sincerely hope her career may be prosperous and happy; but I fear for her—she is surrounded by awful perils.

I am sorry you have to give up your appartments in the Place Vendome—one of the very choicest situations in Paris but hope you may be able to find others near to the garden of the Tuilleries—that healthful and delightful resort for the children.

Farewell my dear Sarah. This is a mere apology for a letter, but it is the best I can furnish at this "present writing." When I am more in force and mood to wield the pen I will write more at length and I trust in better vein; and then I will reply to the letter of my dear Kate. I forgot to mention that Mr Storrow[3] has been passing a couple of days with us on his return from Sharon. We wished to detain him for a longer visit but in vain.

With love to all bodies / Your affectionate uncle
Washington Irving

Should Mr Dix[4] become Minister to France I can reccommend him to you as a very intelligent worthy and amiable man. He is one of the trustees of the Astor Library which has brought us often together. I am unacquainted with his family.[5]

ADDRESSED: à Madame / Madame Storrow / aux soins de Mon. T. W Storrow. / Rue du Faubg. Poissonniere / à Paris
MANUSCRIPT: Yale.   PUBLISHED: PMI, IV, 156 (in part).

1. These letters have not been located.

2. WI had recounted his own acquaintance with Eugenia Montijo, who married Louis Napoleon and became empress of France, in a 'letter to Sarah Storrow, March 28, 1853.

3. Sarah's father-in-law, Thomas Wentworth Storrow, Sr.

4. John A. Dix, who was then serving as assistant treasurer of the United States at New York City, was not appointed minister to France by President Pierce. He later held that post from 1866 to 1869.

5. This postscript is written vertically along the left margin of the first page of the manuscript.

2298.   To Sarah Irving

Saratoga Aug 2d. 1853.

My dear Sarah,

I arrived here safe about eight oclock last evening, after what would have been an astonishingly ⟨qu⟩ rapid journey in former times; but which I found rather tedious from interruptions and delays, waiting at certain places on the single track for down trains to arrive and pass and above all, being detained between three and four mortal hours in Troy; one of the most noisy, racket-y places in the whole world; especially in front of the hotel where I stopped and where all the rail road trains and omnibusses in the world seemed to have a rendezvous—and all the porters, hack men, loafers, and rowdies conspired to make a clamor; the only thing that quieted them for a time was a storm of rain that came on of a sudden and threatened to produce a second deluge—It lasted until late in the evening and at intervals in the night—but has ended by allaying the sultry heat and producing bright temperate weather.

At Tarrytown I found young Mr McVickar[1] about to take a seat in the cars on his way to the mountains and lakes of Hamilton County.[2] He was equipped as an angler, and was to be joined at Saratoga by Robert Minturn.[3] We kept together all day, and I found him a most agreeable companion. No one could be more kind, obliging and attentive; more thoroughly the amiable gentleman. This morning as I sallied out to take the waters at the Spring I found him, Robert Minturn and Willy Constant[4] just about setting off on their excursion, all equipped in angler style, with their potent rods neatly bound up to the dimensions of walking staffs. Three nicer or better suited companions I have never seen; I gave them my parting wishes for plenty of sport and a pleasant excursion. The latter they are sure to have, from the stock of good spirits and right feelings that they carry with them.

I found an excellent room ready for me, which Mr Frank Granger[5] had vacated in the morning—though I deeply regretted his departure, having calculated much on his society. I was recieved with a hearty welcome by the Kennedys, and by several of my acquaintances of last year. ⟨and⟩ Old Mr Gray is in full force; his little favorite Louisa Andrews is here, and he has had a piano brought up from Albany that she may perform at the cottage which he and the Kennedys occupy. So we shall have a relish of the life we led at Ellicotts Mills; and some what of the same set gathered together.

Last night I slept soundly and sweetly after the days journey. This morning I have commenced taking the waters—And feel that the change of scene—and the meeting with friends have already had an enspiriting effect upon me—

My paper is full—I have barely room to send love to all the families at the two houses

> Your affectionate uncle,
> W. I.

P. S. See that Mr Grinnell gets the half barrel of fish passed through the custom house.[6]

MANUSCRIPT: SHR.

1. This may be William McVickar (1827–1877), who later became the rector of St. Barnabas Church at Irvington.

2. Hamilton County is a large forested area in the Adirondack Mountains north of Gloversville and Johnstown.

3. Possibly the son of Robert B. Minturn, a New York businessman who was associated with the Grinnells in shipping and banking activities.

4. Possibly the son of Anthony Constant, who lived in Hastings in Westchester County. See Scharf, *Westchester County*, II, 182–83.

5. WI had associated with Francis Granger, a lawyer and former Whig congressman, at Saratoga Springs the preceding summer. See WI to Catharine Irving, July 24, 1852.

6. The postscript is written vertically along the edge of page four of the manuscript.

2299. To Sarah Irving

Saratoga Aug 6t. 1853

My dear Sarah,

I thank you for your long letter[1] giving me such a budget of domestic news. That about Angelines[2] engagement is particularly interesting: I hardly know whether to be glad or sorry about it. I hope in her new condition she will not be obliged to work hard for she is not fitted for it. With us she would always have been taken care of, and her health and strength consulted, but we could hardly expect that she would remain with us long—she is too pretty and amiable in her appearance not to attract attention and have admirers, and she might have made some unfortunate match. If the man she has chosen is steady and industrious and can support her comfortably all may go well with her. If he had been a thriving carpenter I should have been well pleased; but he may do well as a carman, I am ignorant of the profits of the calling. Mr. Grinnell may be able to ⟨throw bus⟩ give him employment. I feel quite attached to the poor little girl and shall miss her from our household. Tell her I shall endeavor to be present at the wedding—in the mean time put a hundred dollars at her command as a wedding present from me.

I am sorry Mr Grinnell has deferred coming to the Springs for some days yet—as I doubt whether I shall remain here after their arrival. I feel a little fatigued with the bustle of the place and with the very[3] attentions I recieve begin to be a task upon my spirits. ⟨However⟩ I begin to doubt whether the water of the Springs is beneficial to me, and whether it is not apt to act unfavorably upon the head—I have ceased to drink it.

Where are Pierre and Helen and what are to be their movements. I should like to fall in with them.

I am glad to hear that your brother Williams little Kate[4] is to pay a visit to the Cottage. I beg you all to make a pet of her and keep her with you until I return.

I am writing on half sheets of paper for my stock is out. Writing still is a labor to me so you must excuse my scrawl—

With love to all

Your affectionate uncle
Washington Irving

MANUSCRIPT: SHR.   PUBLISHED: PMI, IV, 156–57 (in part).

1. This letter has not been located.

2. Angeline was the "ornamental maid" in WI's household. See WI to Julia Irving, May 26, 1853.

3. WI omitted a word or words in the holograph at this point.

4. Catherine Irving (b. April 20, 1845) was the eldest child of William and Sarah Mann Irving and the granddaughter of Ebenezer.

2300. To Sarah Irving

Saratoga Aug 9th. 1853

My dear Sarah

I write merely to say that I shall leave Saratoga tomorrow morning in company with Mr Kennedy. We take the rail road for White Hall, then the steamer on Lake Champlain for Plattsburg or Rouses Point— Then the rail road to Ogdensburg—then a steamer for Oswego where we part; Kennedy continuing, on to Buffalo, and I proceeding to Syracuse where I shall pass a day or so with the Baldwins—Then visit Charley for a day or two and then steer homeward.

My time has passed very pleasantly at Saratoga; ⟨though⟩ I dined a day or two since at Mr John Hamiltons,[1] with a very ⟨pl⟩ agreeable party and had the pleasure of sitting next to Marys friend Miss Danforth[2] who looked very pretty although she wore no cap.

I have been hoping to recieve a letter from home given me an account of the state of affairs after the heavy rain of Saturday, which appears to have done so much damage in various places.

I shall leave orders to have any letters that may arrive for me, returned to Dearman

With love to all bodies

Your affectionate Uncle
Washington Irving

MANUSCRIPT: SHR.

1. John C. Hamilton (1792–1882), an eminent New York lawyer, was the son of Alexander Hamilton. He was married to Susan Van Heuvel. See Scoville, *Old Merchants of NYC*, IV, 195; V, 41.

2. The Danforths were close neighbors of WI's in the Tarrytown area. See Scharf, *Westchester County*, II, 281.

2301. To Sarah Irving

Niagara Aug 12th. 1853

My dear Sarah,

Mr Kennedy & myself made a delightful voyage along Lake Champlain on Wednesday last, while all the world was broiling on shore,—at Plattsburg we took the rail road for Ogdensburg—where we arrived between twelve and one at night. ⟨The⟩ Part of the next day I spent about the site of the old French Fort,[1] ⟨which among⟩ in the ruined barracks of which I was quartered on my visits there fifty years since,[2] with the Hoffmans and Ogdens. The whole surrounding country was then a wilderness—now it is covered with towns and villages. ⟨and we⟩ There was a grand congregation of Firemen companies at Ogdensburg—And Mr Kennedy & myself were invited to dine with them, but declined and embarked at 2 O'Clock on board of the Steamer Bay State for Lake Ontario It was my intention to land at Oswego & take the rail road for Syracuse but I found the steamer did not land there—So I continued on all night & landed this morning ⟨f⟩ at Lewistown[3]—where Mr Kennedy & myself took a carriage for the falls.

I have passed the morning on Goat Island[4]—seen the falls at every point of view and shall set off this afternoon on the rail road for Cayuga bridge where I shall take the steam boat tomorrow morning on Cayuga lake and stop at Charleys—

Mr Kennedy goes this evening to Buffalo to visit Mr Fillmore.

The weather is insufferably hot and I shall be glad to get at rest at Charleys where I can keep cool. I shall, however, stay there but a day or two for I am anxious to get home.

With love to all

Your affectionate uncle
W I.

MANUSCRIPT: SHR.

1. The fort, located at the mouth of the Oswegatchie, was constructed as Fort La Presentation by Abbé François Picquet as part of a Sulpitian mission in 1749; it was subsequently held by the British from 1760 to 1796. See J&N, I, 27, n. 103.

2. WI visited the region in July, 1803, with Josiah Ogden Hoffman and Thomas Ludlow Ogden and their families. See J&N, I, 3–30; and STW, I, 28–34.

3. Lewiston is located about five miles north of Niagara Falls.

4. Goat Island, along with Luna Island, serves to divide the Niagara River into three falls.

2302. *To Sarah Irving*

Ingleside, Aug 15t. 1853

My dear Sarah,

After broiling through a deadly hot day at Niagara falls I set off in the rail road train at 5 O Clock in the afternoon for Cayuga A terrible hot dusty ride I had of it in cars crowded with somewhat rowdy company. Arrived at Cayuga bridge at eleven at night—My carpet bag missing—had been ⟨left⟩ ↑put out↓ by mistake at Canandaigua—the baggage master sent back for it and assured me it would be forwarded by the morning train—slept in an oven of a room with a stranger for room mate—detained in the morning waiting for my bag which did not arrive until half past eleven—passed the morning looking for shady places and endeavoring to keep cool, but broiling and stewing notwithstanding—About 2 Oclock embarked on board the steam boat—had the bell rung as ⟨it⟩ ↑we↓ passed Charlies—Nobody on shore noticed it—Landed and had a terriffic walk from the landing to the house under a red hot sky and along a sunburnt road that felt to my feet like a brick kiln—On reaching the house sat down for a time on the piazza to recover myself before I entered—Then I was found by the family one of the most way worn beaten out travellers that had passed that way for a long time. It took me a day to get over the fatigue of my dog day journey—but the weather is now changed and we have a breathing spell—

I ⟨f⟩ was glad to find Theodore and his children[1] here—He returns with them to Auburn this morning—

Tomorrow (Tuesday) I shall set off for home, by the Mohawk rail road and shall endeavor to get the Conductor to set me down at Dearman as he did Theodore—If not I think it not unlikely I shall get on the 11 O Clock train at N Y—and push for home. So do not be surprised if I apply for admittance after midnight—I am anxious to get home for I am tired out with travelling in hot weather.

I think, after all, this knocking about, though very trying at the time will be of service to me

I see by your letter to Charlie you are likely to have Sarah and her children[2] with you about this time—I hope to find them at the Cottage when I ar[r]ive.

With love to all

Your affectionate uncle
W I

MANUSCRIPT: SHR.

1. For further details about the widowed Theodore Irving and his five children, see WI to Sarah Storrow, March 28, 1853.

2. Probably Sarah Mann Irving, wife of Ebenezer's son William, and her three children, Katherine, William, and Francis.

2303. *To John P. Kennedy*

Sunnyside, Aug. 24th 1853.

My dear Kennedy,

After much weary travelling by land and water by night and day, through dust and heat and 'fell morass' I reached home on Wednesday last, and almost immediately broke down. Whatever it was of evil that had been lurking in my system for some time past took vent in a spell of chills, fever, and delirium, which hung over me for several days and has almost torn me to rags. I avail myself of a tolerably sane fragment of myself, which is left, to scrawl these lines.

You will now percieve, my dear Horse shoe, that when I was a little techy under your bantering at Niagara, it was not the fault of your jokes, which were excellent as usual; but because I was too miserably out of tune to be played upon, be the musician ever so skillful.

I trust this outbreak of malady when I get through with it, will carry off with it all the evils that have been haunting my system for some time past, and that when next we meet I shall relish your jokes with my usual hearty zest, even though, by singular chance, they should happen to be bad ones.

I fear however I shall not be strong enough to go sight seeing with you in New York; and indeed have seen so much of the Christal Palace in my delirium that I am affraid the very sight of it would bring on a paroxysm.

I look forward however to a visit from you all at my "small contentment," where however I may be, my nieces will be happy to entertain you in their own modest way, on our rural fare—"a couple of short legged hens, a joint of mutton, with any pretty little tiny kickshaws,"[1] or peradventure with a juicy ham sent to me from the banks of the Patapsco, ⟨f⟩ by a much valued and somewhat musical friend who flourishes in that quarter. To that excellent friend and his two inestimable daughters[2] give my most affectionate remembrances.

"Thine evermore, my dear Horseshoe, while this machine is to him["]"[3]

Geoffrey—

John P Kennedy Esqr

MANUSCRIPT: Peabody Library.   PUBLISHED: PMI, IV, 159–60; and Tuckerman,
   Life of J. P. Kennedy, p. 378 (in part).

1. See *Henry IV*, Part II, 5, i, 27–28.
2. WI refers to Edward Gray, Mrs. Elizabeth Kennedy, and Miss Martha Gray.
3. WI omitted the bracketed quotation mark.

2304. To Joseph G. Cogswell

Sunnyside Aug 28th. 1853

My dear Cogswell

I wish you would be particular in your summary for the next meeting
so as to ensure a quorum without me for I think it extremely improbable
that I shall be able to attend.

I have had an attack of bilious fever which has reduced me extremely,
and I am still struggling with the remains of it. I trust Carson Brevoort[1]
will be more faithful to his post than he was the last time, when I put
off a journey and came down in bad weather; and all in vain in consequence of his absence

Yours very truly
Washington Irving

MANUSCRIPT: British Library.

1. J. Carson Brevoort (1818–1887), son of WI's early friend Henry Brevoort, had
accompanied WI to Spain in 1842 as his secretary. From 1852 to 1854 Brevoort
served as a trustee of the Astor Library.

2305. To John P. Kennedy

Sunnyside, Aug. 28th 1853

My dear Kennedy

I find, by your most welcome letter, that you must be now in New York,
to remain there part of this week. I am too weak to come down; for
though the fever has been cast forth, by the aid of a high German doctor,
it has left my unfortunate stomach in such a state, that I have scarce
tasted food for nine days past, and I am reduced almost to poetical dimensions. Still I am gradually regaining strength, and shall be able to recieve you cheerily if you and my dear Mrs Kennedy will pay me that visit
of which you give me hopes. The sight of you both would be a real restorative. I only regret that the state of Mr Grays health will not permit

him and Miss Gray to accompany you. Why cannot you both come up on Tuesday? A train leaves the Chamber[s][1] Street Station at 10 Oclock which will land you at Dearman between 11 & 12, where my carriage will be waiting for you. We dine at 3 Oclock, and a train starts from Dearman at 6 Oclock which will take you down. I trust we can make your time pass pleasantly while you are up here, and you cannot imagine what pleasure your visit will give us all. Let me know, by my nephew Mr Pierre M. Irving, who will take this, whether we are to expect you

I am very sorry to learn that Mr Gray has had a touch of asthma while in the country; but hope he will be well enough to enjoy his visit to the city. I need not say how truly delighted I should be should he be able to venture up here with you[2]

With affectionate regards to all your party

Yours ever my dear Kennedy,
Washington Irving

John P. Kennedy, Esq

MANUSCRIPT: Peabody Library.   PUBLISHED: *Sewanee Review*, 25 (January, 1917), 10–11.

1. WI omitted the bracketed *s* here.
2. Edward Gray and his daughter Martha did accompany the Kennedys to Sunnyside. See WI to Mary E. Kennedy, September 8, 1853.

2306. To Mary E. Kennedy

Sunnyside Sept. 8th. 1853

My dear Miss Kennedy,

Indisposition has prevented me from replying earlier to your welcome letter of the 4th. August,[1] which I received about three weeks since on my return from Saratoga.

I passed some days very pleasantly at the latter place. It is true I found the hot weather and the crowd of company rather oppressive, but I had the parlour of your uncle John's cottage for a retreat. Old Mr Gray had provided a piano there and we had some good amateur music almost daily. Louisa Andrews was prime performer for a time until a Miss Kelleran arrived, who had received letters in Paris from the best masters and played in superior and a rare precision and delicacy of touch. Poor little Louisa immediately went into eclipse, and could not be prevailed on to touch the piano after she had heard the other. Nothing however could have been more charming and lady-like than her behaviour on the occasion. She attended upon Miss K., turned the music for her, and manifested sincere admiration of her talents and execution. All this was done in a quiet unofficious way. In a word she behaved so sweetly that I was more delighted with her than I should have been had she played like a St Cecilia.[2] She set off shortly afterward on a tour to Canada and the White Mountains with a party of which Miss Kelleran was one. I trust they had frequent opportunities of practising together.

The hot weather was as intolerable at Saratoga as I had found it at Berkeley Springs. So after passing about ten days there I set off on a tour with your uncle John who wished to visit the Fillmores at Buffalo. We went by the way of the Lakes and had a magnificent *sail* (if I may use the word) down Lake Champlain in a steamer to Plattsburg, whence we made a night journey by rail road to Ogdensburg. Here we passed part of a day, a very interesting one to me. Fifty years had elapsed since I had visited the place, in company with a party of gentlemen proprietors, with some ladies of their families. It was then a wilderness, and we were quartered in the remains of an old French fort at the confluence of the Oswegatchie and the St Lawrence. It was all a scene of romance to me for I was then a mere stripling and everything was strange and full of poetry. The country was covered with forest; the Indians still inhabited some islands in the river and prowled about in their canoes. There were two young ladies of the party to sympathize in my romantic feelings and we passed some happy days there, exploring the forests or gliding in canoes on the rivers.

In my present visit I found with difficulty the site of the old French Fort, but all traces of it were gone. I looked round on the surrounding country and river. All was changed. A populous city occupied both sides of the Oswegatchie; great steamers plowed the St Lawrence and the opposite Canada shore was studded with towns and villages. I sat down on the river bank where we used to embark in our canoes, and thought on the two lovely girls who used to navigate it with me and the joyous party who used to cheer us from the shore—all had passed away—all were dead!—I was the sole survivor of that happy party, and here I had returned after a lapse of fifty years to sit down and meditate on the mutability of all things and to wonder that I was still alive!

From Ogdensburg we made a voyage up the St Lawrence, through the Archipelago of the Thousand Islands, and across Lake Ontario to Lewistown on the Niagara river, where we took a carriage to the Falls. There we passed an insufferably hot day, and parted in the evening, your uncle to go to Buffalo to visit the Fillmores—I to Cayuga Lake to visit one of my nieces;[3] whence I went to Syracuse to visit Mrs Baldwin and then hastened homeward. All this tour was made during a spell of intensely hot weather that deranged my whole system. The consequence was that the day after my return home I was taken down with a violent fever and delirium, which confined me several days to my bed. Just as I had got rid of the fever and was beginning to recover, I had a delightful visit from your uncle and aunt and Mr and Miss Gray who passed the day at Sunnyside. Their visit acted for the time as a perfect restorative. I do not know when I enjoyed a day more thoroughly. I only wish you had been here to make the party complete. A day of excitement, however, was followed by two days of excessive languor. A recurrence of extremely hot weather conspired to keep me in a state of debility. It is only today that a cool breeze from the north has braced me up a little and enabled me to take pen once more in hand.

I presume before this you have made your visit to Berkeley Springs. Since my experience of hot weather at Saratoga I acquit Berkeley Springs of all peculiar delinquency in that respect and am ready whenever I meet Judge Pendleton[4] to recant all I may have said in disparagement of a place of which he is in a manner the tutelar genius. I can easily concieve it must be a delightful gathering place for the people of Virginia and Maryland who are well acquainted with each other.

I am grieved to hear that my dear little friend *Miss* Lizzy has been ill, but trust the pure air of Capon[5] has restored her to health and good spirits. I should like to see her transmitting to her doll the hereditary air of bambanini.

You do well to keep up your early morning rides. I think I can see you in your green riding dress cantering through the oak grove. I know the alertness of your spirit when any duty is to be performed; or any kind of service to be rendered to others. I hope you will not flag when merely your own gratification or benefit is in question. According to your own account you are likely to have your brother Andrew at home soon. He I believe was your early companion in horsemanship, when you undertook to break colts while you were mere colts yourselves. His company will enspirit you to keep up your equestrian exercises.

You speak of my promised visit to Cassilis in October. I bear it ever present in mind and am endeavoring to shape things so as to effect it. This fit of illness has put me back in my plans. I have this day commenced the building of a house for my gardener and shall hurry it forward, so that it may not stand in my way. I assure you there is nothing I look forward to with more delightful anticipations than another visit to the lovely valley of the Shenandoah and the kind inmates of Cassilis.[6]

With kindest remembrances to your father and mother and all the two households great and small, believe me ever with affectionate regard

Yours very truly
Washington Irving

PUBLISHED: *American Literature*, 6 (March, 1934), 54–57; and PMI, IV, 157–58, 160 (in part).

1. This letter has not been located.

2. St. Cecilia was a second or third century Roman virgin martyr known as a patroness of music.

3. Charlotte Grinnell.

4. Philip Clayton Pendleton, the eccentric brother of John P. Kennedy's mother Nancy Pendleton Kennedy, was a Virginia lawyer interested in politics. See Bohner, *J. P. Kennedy*, pp. 8–9.

5. Capon Springs is located on the southern tip of Hampshire County, now in West Virginia.

6. WI was to visit Cassilis again in mid-October, 1853. See PMI, IV, 163–67.

2307. To Frederick Saunders

Sunnyside Sept 8th. 1853

My dear Sir

Indisposition has prevented me from acknowledging at an earlier date the receipt of the copy of your new work[1] which you had the kindness to send to me while I was at Saratoga.

I now give you my hearty thanks for a Salad which is peculiarly to my taste and which I have relished with somewhat of the curious palate of a literary epicure.

I am happy to see that the work meets with general acceptation and applause. I trust its success will encourage you to pursue a line of authorship full of enjoyment in itself, and fertile of innocent delight to others. Works of the kind while they call up pleasant reccollections to old stagers like myself, are full of suggestions to young minds and stimulate them to explore the literary regions of which such tempting glimpses are given them.

Ever my dear Sir / with great regard / Yours truly
Washington Irving

MANUSCRIPT: NYPL—WI Papers. PUBLISHED: *Bulletin NYPL*, 36 (April, 1932), 219.

1. Saunder's *Salad for the Solitary* had recently been published.

2308.   To Sarah Storrow

Sunnyside, Sept 19th. 1853

My dear Sarah,

I received your last letter[1] just after my return from a visit to Saratoga and a tour by the lakes to Niagara, and I should have answered it before this, but that I was taken down with a bilious fever, the result of extensive travelling by land and water during an uncommonly hot spell of weather. I am now myself again, and I feel as if this fit of illness has carried off some clouds that have been hanging about my system for some months past.

One of the most interesting circumstances of my tour was the sojourn of a day at Ogdensburg, at the mouth of the Oswagatchie river where it empties into the St Lawrence[.] I had not been there since I visited it fifty years since, in 1803, when I was but twenty years of age; when I made an expedition through the Black River country to Canada in company with Mr & Mrs Hoffman and Anne Hoffman Mr & Mrs Ludlow Ogden and Miss Eliza Ogden. Mr Hoffman & Mr Ogden were visiting their wild lands on the St Lawrence. All the country then was a wilderness; we floated down the black river in a scow, we toiled through forests in waggons drawn by Oxen—We slept in hunters cabins and were once four and twenty hours without food—but all was romance to me. arrived on the banks of the St Lawrence we put up at Mr Ogdens agent who was quartered in some rude buildings, belonging to a ruined French fort at the mouth of the Oswegatchie.

What happy days I passed there; rambling about the woods with the young ladies; or paddling with them in ⟨Ca⟩ Indian Canoes on the limpid waters of the St Lawrence; or fishing about the rapids and visiting the Indians who still lived on Islands in the river. Every thing was so grand and silent and solitary. I dont think any scene in life made a more delightful impression upon me.

Well—here I was again after a lapse of fifty years. I found a populous city occupying both banks of the Oswegatchie, connected by bridges. It was the Ogdensburg of which a village plot had been planned at the time of our visit. I sought the old French fort where we had been quartered—not a trace of it was left. I sat under a tree on the Site and looked round upon what ⟨had be⟩ I had known as a wilderness. Now teeming with life—crowded with habitations, The Oswegatchie River dammed up and encumbered by vast stone mills—The broad St Lawrence plowed by immense steamers.

I walked to the point where with the two girls I used to launch forth in the canoe, while the rest of the party would wave handkerchiefs and cheer us from shore: it was now a bustling landing place for steamers. There were still some rocks where I used to sit of an evening and accompany with my flute one of the ladies who sung—I sat for a long time on the rocks ⟨and end⟩ summoning Reccollections of byegone days and of the happy beings by whom I was then surrounded—All had passed away —all were dead and gone; of that young and joyous party I was the sole survivor—they had all lived quietly at home out of the reach of mischance —yet had gone down to their graves—while I, who had been wandering about the world, exposed to all hazards by sea and land—was yet alive. It seemed almost marvellous. ⟨I dont then think any thing has ever⟩ I have often, in my shifting about the world, come upon the traces of former existence; but I do not think any thing has made a stronger impression on me than this second visit to the banks of the Oswegatchie

Sept. 29th. I was interrupted when writing the foregoing, and the letter has lain in my table drawer ever since, having been rather crowded of late by occupations and engagements. I forgot to mention to you that at Saratoga I met with a very agreeable young lady a Miss Kelleran who had seen a good deal of you in Paris and spoke of you in the warmest terms. I found her to be very well instructed in music and was delighted with her performances on the Pianoforte.

I have just recieved a letter from Mrs de Wolff[2] (dated in June from Spa) introducing a Miss Alderson of Caracas. The latter lady forwarded her letter from New York where she is passing a few days, and I called upon her there, but she was not at home. I shall now have to post pone seeing her until she returns to New York (from Mobile) in the spring as I am on the point of setting off on a visit to my friends the Kennedys in Maryland, having engaged to accompany Mr & Mrs Kennedy on their annual visit to their Relatives in Virginia. This will take us again to the beautiful valley of the Shenandoah, which I will see in all its autumnal splendor. We shall then make an excursion into the Mountains; which we were prevented from making last July by the excessive heat. Kennedy sends up his carriage and a couple of saddle horses, that we may travel as we please among the mountains.

I trust this tour will completely brace me up so that when I return I may be able to resume the exercise of my pen without any further derangement of my system. One way or other I have been repeatedly interrupted in my literary task which often lies for months neglected

I have had one solemn and sacred duty to perform ⟨this⟩ of late; which was to remove ↑⟨from New York⟩↓ ⟨the of Such of the family⟩ from New York the remains of such of the family as were interred in the vault in front of the Brick church in Beekman Street.[3] That street was to be widened,[4] and of course the church yard invaded. I have always apprehended some such event and am glad that it has taken place while

I am here to protect the ashes of those I loved from desecration[.] I accordingly purchased a piece of ground in a public cemetery established within a few years on the high ground adjacent to the old Dutch church at Beekmans Mill pond, commonly called the Sleepy Hollow church[5] The Cemetery, which is secured by an act of the legislature, takes in a part of The Beekman woods, and commands one of the most beautiful views of the Hudson. The spot I have purchased is on the southern slope, just on the edge of the old church yard; which is included in the cemetery. I have had it inclosed with an iron railing and shall have evergreens set out round it. It is shaded by a grove of young oaks.

There I have seen the remains of the family gathered together and interred where they cannot be again disturbed; and a vast satisfaction it was to have rescued them from that restless city where nothing is sacred.

As I was selecting this place of sepulture I thought of Byrons lines—

> "Then look around
> And choose thy ground
> And take thy rest.'[6]

I have marked out my resting place by my mothers side, and a space is left for me there.

This may seem to you rather a melancholy theme for letter writing— yet I write ⟨it⟩ without melancholy—or rather without gloom. I feel deeply satisfied at having been able to perform this duty and I look forward with serene satisfaction to being gathered at last to a family gathering place, where ⟨wh⟩ my dust may mingle with the dust of those most dear to me.

God bless you my dear Sarah. I owe my dear little Kate a letter but have not time at present to answer it. Give my love to her and the other young princesses and my affectionate remembrances to Mr Storrow.

Your affectionate Uncle
Washington Irving

P S—I set off on my expedition this afternoon and expect to be absent nearly all October

MANUSCRIPT: Yale.   PUBLISHED: PMI, I, 60–61; IV, 160–62 (in part).

1. This letter has not been located.

2. Mrs. de Wolff was WI's "half Spanish friend" and a friend of the Louis McLanes. She had an apartment in Paris. See WI to Sarah Storrow, July 15, 1852. Her letter and that of Miss Alderson have not been located.

3. The Brick Church at Beekman Street, which was an offshoot of the Presby-

terian Church on Wall Street, conducted services from 1767 to 1856. The Potter
Building later covered the site of hundreds of graves there. See Wilson, *NY, Old
and New*, II, 116–17. For a picture of the church, see Haswell, *Reminiscenses of
an Octogenarian*, p. 93.

4. In 1853 Beekman Street was widened from Nassau to Pearl Street. See Haswell,
Reminiscences, p. 485.

5. The Old Dutch Church was erected in the late seventeenth century by
Frederick Philipse in what is now North Tarrytown. See Scharf, *Westchester County*,
I, 173, 518; II, 237.

6. The concluding lines of Lord Byron's "On This Day I Complete My Thirty-Sixth
Year" (January 24, 1825). WI used a single closing quotation mark.

2309. To John P. Kennedy

Sunnyside Sept 28th. 1853

My dear Kennedy

I have just time to write a line to say that I propose to leave New
York on Saturday morning and hope to reach Ellicotts Mills at the
hour you mention. With loving remembrances to all bodies

Yours ever very truly
Washington Irving

MANUSCRIPT: Va.–Barrett.

2310. To Sarah Irving

Irving House / Friday Evg Sep 29th. [1853]

My dear Sarah,

I hasten to inform you of my well being as I know you will be anxious.
I arrived in town safe and proceeded to the Irving House,[1] where I
asked for a room. What party had I with me?—None. Had I not my
lady with me?— No—I was alone. I saw my chance was I[2] bad one and
I feared to be put in a dungeon as I was on a former occasion. I bethought my self of your advice and when the book (press) was presented wrote my name at full length—from Sunnyside—My dear Sarah,
I was ushered into an apartment on the first floor (second story) furnished with rose wood, yellow damask, pier glasses & a sumptuous
bed room with a bed large enough for an alderman and his wife; a
bath room adjoining—In a word I am accommodated completely *en
prince* The nigger waiters all call me by name and vie with each other

in waiting on me. The chambermaid has been at uncommon pains to put my rooms in first rate order and if she had been pretty I absolutely should have kissed her— but as she was not, I shall reward her in sordid coin. Henceforth I abjure all ⟨diffidence⟩ ↑modesty↓ with hotel Keepers and will get as much for my name as it will fetch. Kennedy calls it travelling on ones capital.

I am at a loss where to go this evening—the Christal Palace—Julians,³ or the Opera⁴—I shall let you know before I go to bed my decision in the matter

My dear Sarah, I have just returned; it is near 12 Oclock, they have made such a fire in my sitting room that it is roasting to sit there, and I am sleepy so I must be brief.

I determined to go to the opera; but on the way, as it was early, I strolled into the St Nicholas Hotel,⁵ to take a look at it. It beats every thing of the Hotel kind I have ever seen. I wandered up stairs and down stairs and into the ladies ⟨chamber⟩ saloon—such splendor—such extent: such long corridors and vast saloons and such crowds of well dressed people—and beautiful ladies. In the course of my rambles I came upon Mr Baldwin, who is boarding there. He took [me]⁶ all about to see the wonders of the house and among other places took me into the bridal chamber about which so much has been said. It is very magnificent: but I am told has never been occupied excepting by a Californian Prince and his bride.

In passing along one of the corridors; full of gay company whom should I meet but Miss Gamble the young lady with the beautiful eyes; who interested me so much in the cars when I was going on to Washington last winter and who I found out afterwards to be a daughter of one of my Paris intimates in my youthful days. She was surrounded by beaux; but greeted me most cordially and told me her father was staying in the Hotel and would be delighted to see me—I ⟨was⟩ ↑am↓ really sorry that my departure will prevent our meeting, but hope they may linger in New York until after my return. Mr Baldwin accompanied me to the Opera. It was La Favorita⁷—rather a heavy Opera. Steffanone was the heroine and I was much pleased with her[.] Salvi was the hero— but he is too old to play the young lovers—and I never fancied him much when I saw him in Madrid and he was eight or ten years younger.

On returning to the Hotel I found the landlord waiting up to make my acquaintance—You are aware ⟨th⟩ I presume that Mr Howard is no longer the proprietor of the Irving; he has made a fortune and gone to Europe. The present proprietor is a very good looking well mannered man; and was extremely civil. He tells me the 8 Oclock train is a kind of accommodation train to Philadelphia. If I ⟨take⟩ took it I should have to wait in Philadelphia an hour. Whereas the 9 Oclock train is an Express and goes directly through. So I shall go by it. Had I known this I might have come on in the 6 Oclock train from Dearman in the morning and been in time. However I have passed my evening pleasantly and am in excellent quarters for the night—

Love to all bodies—I am going to take a shower bath and then to bed

Your affectionate uncle
Washington Irving

Morning—After a good nights rest a bath and a breakfast I went to pay my bill when mine host insisted on my being his guest for this time at least—After some demur I at length consented on condition it should be only for this time—otherwise I should not be willing to come again to the house—on these terms we ⟨parted⟩ agreed.

MANUSCRIPT: SHR.   PUBLISHED: PMI, IV, 162–63 (in part); and Tuckerman, *Life of J. P. Kennedy,* p. 379 (in part).

1. The Irving House was a fashionable hotel at the corner of Broadway and Chambers Street. See Wilson, *NY, Old and New,* II, 114.

2. WI probably intended to write "a."

3. Louis Jullien's orchestra had begun a second month's series at Metropolitan Hall on September 26. The program for September 29 was billed as a "Grand Beethoven Night" which included symphonies no. 5 and no. 6, the *Lenore Overture,* and other selections. See NYEP, September 29, 1853.

4. Max Maretzek (1821–1897) had moved his operatic company from the Astor Place Opera House to Niblo's and was offering Italian opera with members of the Havana Company, including Balbina Steffanone, Lorenzo Salvi, Francesco Beneventano, and Ignazio Marini. See Odell, *NY Stage,* VI, 314.

5. The St. Nicholas was a one-million-dollar luxury hotel built in the early 1850's at Broadway and Broome Street. See Maxwell M. Marcuse, *This Was New York* (New York, 1965), pp. 160–61.

6. WI omitted "me."

7. Gaetano Donizetti's *La Favorita,* first performed in Paris in 1840, was one in the series of Italian operas performed at Niblo's in the fall of 1853.

2311.   *To Catharine Irving*

Ellicotts Mills—Oct 3d. 1853

My dear Kate,

My letter to Sarah[1] gave the history of my adventures until my departure from New York. The journey to Baltimore was rather a lonely one, though I was continually among crowds—I did not see a single person that I knew or felt a disposition to know, and none about whom I could weave an imaginary story. The latter part of the journey was made in the rain and by the time we arrived in Baltimore the evening had set in murky and dismal. As ill luck would have it my trunk and bag were so far inside of the baggage car that by the time they were extricated it was too late to get to the Cumberland Cars by which I was to be transported to Ellicotts Mills; ⟨so I had⟩ Nor was there any hackney coach at hand to take me to a hotel; so I had a tramp through rain and muck and mire of a mile and half to Barnums Hotel;[2] having subsidised two boys to carry my luggage. At Barnums, having written out my name in full, according to Sarahs knowing advice, I was accommodated with an excellent room: passed a comfortable night, and the next morning (Sunday) set off in the cars about 8 Oclock— before 9 I was at Ellicotts Mills, and then ten minutes walk took me to Mr Grays, where I was most cordially welcomed by the whole house- hold—They had sent the carriage to the station for me the preceding evening—but as I did not come—they supposed the weather had pre- vented me—not knowing that when once under way, I allow nothing to stop me or turn me aside

I arrived in time to drive to church with Mrs Kennedy and Miss Gray. and afterwards passed the rest of the day very cheerily with the family.

This morning (Monday) I have taken a beautiful ride on horseback with Mrs. Kennedy; through fine forest scenery, and along wild brooks and dells. The weather is perfect and the country looking magnificent, with the first light touch of Autumnal frost. This afternoon Miss Andrews is coming out to pass a few days at Mr Grays and perhaps Mary Dulaney so that we shall have a lively household

Mr Gray and the Kennedys has made the kindest enquiries after you all and have repeatedly expressed the pleasure they had on their visit to Sunnyside.

We shall not probably set off for Virginia for several days, as most of Mr Andrew Kennedys family ⟨to⟩ ↑with↓ whom we shall make our first halt, are absent at a wedding

I am well content to remain a little time at Ellicotts Mills under the hospitable roof of my worthy friend Mr Gray. It is a happy establishment and surrounded by a beautiful country.

I expect frequent letters from the household. You must take turns— letting me know all that is going on—and ⟨how the⟩ ↑all about the↓ new house.

Give my love to all bodies not forgetting little Kate and Nancy Ann—

Your affectionate Uncle
Washington Irving

MANUSCRIPT: SHR.

1. Of September 29, 1853.

2. Barnum's City Hotel was built in Baltimore about 1826 on the southwest corner of Calvert and Fayette Streets. See Raphael Semmes, *Baltimore As Seen By Visitors: 1783–1860* (Baltimore, 1953), p. 73, and opp. p. 85.

2312. *To Sarah Irving*

Sunnyside Oct 6th. 1853

My dear Sarah,

I have just recieved your most welcome letter of the 4th.[1] giving me the Sunnyside news. I trust you will continue to keep me posted up on the events of that interesting region; as, notwithstanding thier importance, I can never get any intelligence concerning them in the public papers[.] I am glad the new house pleases you as the finishing proceeds. Keep an eye on it, and make any suggestions that your judgement and taste may suggest. I hope the painter will hit the right tone of Colour— The roof should be reddish—about the tone of the roof of the Cottage. I am sorry to be absent while this little building is in progress; but trust all will turn out to my satisfaction.

I am convinced demure quiet fellow William Fallon[2] is poaching among my womankind: and that Bridget will soon be led to the 'halter' like her sister. I begin to tremble for the safety of Susan—She is too comely not to attract admirers—If she is carried off by matrimony I shall be driven to give up all comely women as household stock.

I am passing my time very pleasantly. The weather is delightful and I am every day on horseback for several hours taking rides with Mr or Mrs Kennedy about the beautiful woodland country, by which we are surrounded.

The day after my arrival my charming young friends Mary Dulaney and Louisa Andrews came out to pass a few days here. Their presence has added to the brightness and gaiety of the house. They are lovely in character as well as in person; Miss Andrews you know is an accomplished musician, and ever ready to take her seat at the piano. Mary Dulaney returned to Baltimore last evening, to prepare for a visit to New York, where she goes next week for the first time. She is full of anticipation having heard so much of the Chrystal Palace. Broad way— the Opera &c &c I can easily ↑imagine↓ ⟨what would be⟩ what a first visit to New York must be to a young girl of eighteen. I only regret that I should not be in New York at the time—as I certainly should have her up on a visit to Sunnyside.

Perhaps you may meet her at the christal palace. You will know her by her being the most beautiful creature there.

We shall set off for Virginia sometime in the early part of next week.

I suppose our visit there will occupy about a fortnight—after which I shall push for home as fast as possible—though I foresee there will be some attempt to hold me by the skirts.

With love to all in both houses

Your affectionate Uncle
Washington Irving

MANUSCRIPT: SHR.

In another hand "Sunnyside" in the dateline is underscored and encircled, with the notation: "Ellicotts Mills, Md. / a mistake—"

1. This letter has not been located.
2. William Fallon was one of WI's hired men, ostensibly in charge of the poultry. See WI to Elizabeth Kennedy, March 11, 1853.

2313. *To Helen Dodge Irving*

Ellicotts Mills, Oct–11th. 1853

My dear Helen

I recieved a day or two since your welcome letter of the 6th. inst.[1] and should have answered it yesterday but that I accompanied a part of the family to Baltimore to escort hence our little musical pet Louisa ⟨Mathews⟩ Andrews, who has been the delight of the house for a week past. I am sorry to hear that the weather has been so cold and blustering on the banks of the Hudson. With us it has been glorious. I have been every day on horse back for several hours riding about this finely wooded country and along the romantic banks of the Patapsco. The forests have their ⟨au⟩ first autumnal tinge and are perfectly splendid. On thursday (the day after tomorrow) Mr & Mrs Kennedy and myself set off for Mr Andrew Kennedys in the valley of the Shenandoah. We have been prevented from going earlier by the absence of part of Mr Andrew Kennedys family to attend a wedding and to his house being crowded with visitors. This alters our plans and obliges us ⟨to⟩ again to ⟨f⟩ give up that part of our excursion which extended to the glades of the Alleghanys; the weather would be too sharp there for the state of Mr Kennedys health. Beside the cholera has prevailed in part of the region we were to visit, and Mrs Kennedy has great dread of it having once suffered from it severely. We shall spend ten or twelve days therefore in the beautiful valley of the Shenandoah, under the hospitable roof of Mr A Kennedy; visiting some historical points which I was prevented from visiting during my last sojourn by the intolerable heat of the weather. Now I shall see all that magnificent country in its autumnal glory. My intention is to regulate my movements so as to be in New York on the 26th. of the month, to attend the meeting of the Executors of the Astor estate & the trustees of the library. The death of Mr James G King,[2] one of the most efficient members of both boards, renders my presence there of more than usual importance. The news of his death was quite a shock to me He was with us at our last meeting, just before my departure for the south; and appeared to be in excellent health; having thoroughly recovered as he said, from his illness of last spring. His last words were to advise me not to go south until the black frosts had set in. He was a most valuable worthy man a sterling character in public life and endeared by his social qualities to a wide circle of friends and relatives. His loss will be sever[e]ly[3] felt at the two boards at which I have been in the habit of meeting him.

Present my congratulations to Irving and Nancy Paris on the addition to their family. I approve of the name ⟨of⟩ they have given to their infant daughter[4] though I should not have been surprised had they called her Nancy Ann as that has been introduced into the family.

with remembrances to Pierre / Your afft un[c]le
W I.

P. S. I have just recieved Kates letter of the 9th.[5] which I have not time to answer today. Tell her to have the ground in front of the new house sloped instead of terraced if she and a jury of the womenkind think it will be preferable.[6]

Manuscript: NYPL—Seligman Collection.

1. This letter has not been located.
2. James Gore King (b. 1791), a financier associated with the New York banking firm of Prime, Ward, and King, was instrumental in securing the British loan of specie for relief in the panic of 1837. He had died on October 3, 1853.
3. WI omitted the bracketed letter.
4. Catharine Irving Paris was born on September 26, 1853.
5. This letter has not been located.
6. This postscript is written vertically along the left margin of the first page of the manuscript.

2314.   To Catharine Irving

Ellicotts Mills. Oct. 12th. 1853

My dear Kate

I thank you for your letter of the 9th.[1] which, though you thought it hardly worth sending, gave me a budget of domestic intelligence. I shall be glad to have particulars of your patriarchal visit to the Crystal palace with your father at the head of the ten tribes of Irvings and little Kate and Nancy Ann at the tail. You would miss the sight of the *Koh-i-noor*[2] —the great diamond of the Exhibition, Mary Dulaney, as she and her party set off for New York this morning

In a letter which I wrote yesterday to Helen, and which I presume you have seen, I gave an idea of our movements. We set off tomorrow morning by rail road for Mr Andrew Kennedys where we shall pass eight or ten days, in the midst of the beautiful scenery of the Shenandoah Valley. I intend to be in New York on the 26th. to attend the meetings of the Executors & Trustees, and I presume shall be at home that evening.

If you "all think it would be prettier to slope down the ground before the new building than to terrace it," let it be done so. I intended to regulate it according as it should please my eye, and had no fixed ⟨pre⟩ idea in the matter. I am sorry to be absent at the time of finishing off the house, but presume I shall be home before Robert and Maria move into it, as I ⟨sca⟩ think it will scarcely be dry enough before the 26th. I should like to see it before it is occupied in case I see any alterations to be made.

I presume you have taken care to have the door of the porch room shifted while the carpenters and plasterers are at hand to do the needful. The books can be put aside any where for the present.

I am glad Julia and Fanny have made acquaintance with the little Kneelands.[3] I have an idea that they will find them both agreeable and profitable acquaintances—They appear to me to be very intelligent, well bred, lovely little girls.

We have a continuance of lovely Autumnal weather. The country is looking magnificent and I anticipate a delightful time in the Shenandoah Valley

I wish you all to make a visit of civility to our new neighbors the Olmsteads;[4] who had moved into their house (late Mr Lents)[5] three or four weeks before I left home. Also to the Duncans,[6] where I shall call on my return. These little attentions ↑to new comers↓ are important ⟨at⟩ to good neighborhoods, and need not be followed up by any particular intimacy, if not desirable.

Having now said out my say I conclude with love to all,

Your affectionate Uncle
Washington Irving

Miss Kate Irving

MANUSCRIPT: SHR.

1. This letter has not been located.

2. Koh-i-noor diamond from India, which was associated for centuries with bad luck, became part of the British crown jewels in 1849.

3. Possibly members of the family of Henry Kneeland, a cotton merchant at 49 William Street, New York City. See Scoville, *Old Merchants of NYC*, II, 38.

4. Possibly Silas Olmstead, a grocer who is buried in the Sleepy Hollow Cemetery. See Scharf, *Westchester County*, II, 297.

5. Possibly George W. Lent, who is also buried in the Sleepy Hollow Cemetery. See Scharf, *Westchester County*, II, 297.

6. WI again mentions the Duncans in a letter to Helen Irving, January 14, 1855.

2315. *To Sarah Irving*

Cassilis Oct. 16th. 1853

My dear Sarah,

I am quite disappointed in recieving no letter from any of you for the last four days. When absent I like to hear frequently from home, if it be but a line at a time. When you have nothing to tell, say so, for that is a sign that all is going on well; whereas when you are silent I may imagine that something is wrong. I have been here (Mr Andrew Kennedys) since thursday last: in a hospitable cheerful house where I am made to feel perfectly at home. I have been every day on horseback riding about this beautiful country in splendid weather and enjoying myself greatly. To-morrow I set off with Mr Andrew and John Kennedy for Winchester whence we shall extend our excursion to Greenway Court;[1] once the residence of old Lord Fairfax,[2] the early patron of Washington, and an occasional resort of the latter in his youthful days. Our excursion will occupy us for two and perhaps three days, and will take us to some interesting historical points and among noble scenery. After our return to Cassilis, we shall remain here until Saturday, when we set off for Ellicotts Mills; whence I shall take my departure for New York in time to be there on Wednesday the 26th. Continue to write to me until I am on the way homeward.

I have been very much surprised and grieved to hear of the failure of Mr Draper.[3] I hope it may be but a temporary suspension of payments. I see the Herald is endeavoring to get up a panic on the occasion. It is, in fact, time to expect a reverse in the monied and commercial world; there has been such expansion, such speculation and extravagance of all kinds.

Having no letter from home to answer and none to expect until after my return from Winchester I shall conclude by love to all and a hope for more frequent correspondence in future

Your affectionate Uncle
Washington Irving

MANUSCRIPT: SHR.

1. Greenway Court was owned by a Mr. Kennerly and is located about ten miles south of Winchester. For John P. Kennedy's account of the trip, see Tuckerman, *Life of J. P. Kennedy,* pp. 237–40.

2. Thomas Fairfax (1693–1781), the sixth Lord Fairfax of Cameron, was the proprietor of the "Northern Neck" of Virginia. In 1752 he came to America to protect his property from the Virginia Assembly and settled in the Shenandoah Valley. An early friend of George Washington, he was accorded the privileges of a Virginia citizen and was not molested during the American Revolution, though he was a resident peer of England.

3. Simeon Draper (1804–1866), a Whig politician, businessman, and friend of William H. Seward, defaulted on his payments for stocks and bonds when a bank refused to honor his checks and he was not supported by other brokers. The reactions of the *Herald* were alarmist: "The suspension of Simeon Draper has created a great deal of excitement in Wall Street, and in the minds of those familiar with the rise, progress, and result of the speculative mania previous to 1837 has produced apprehension of the most alarming character. We see in the future events of the most startling nature, and those who are prepared for the approaching crisis may be thankful that they are so fortunate." See New York *Herald,* October 13, 1853.

2316.   To Sarah Irving

Cassilis Oct 21 1853

My dear Sarah,

I returned from Winchester the day before yesterday, when I found your letter of the 14th.[1] waiting for me.

The expedition to Winchester and Greenway Court, in company with Messrs. John and Andrew Kennedy, was very pleasant—We went to Winchester by rail road, and then hired a carriage and an old Negro coachman to take us to Greenway Court (once the residence of old Lord Fairfax and a resort of Washington in his younger days[)].[2] We set off from Winchester in the afternoon. The distance to Greenway Court was said to be about 12 miles but the roads so bad that it would be impossible to return to Winchester the same evening. What was to be done? Greenway Court was no longer habitable—There was no good country Inn near at hand— Mr ⟨K⟩ Andrew Kennedy determined to seek quarters at the house of a Mr Nelson,[3] who resided about three miles from the Court, and with whom he was acquainted. We hoped to reach his house before sunset; so as to seek quarters elsewhere, should we fail to find them there. We had a delightful afternoons drive through a fine country diversified by noble forests in all the glory of their Autumnal hues. I saw some of the noblest specimens of Oaks I have ever seen in this country. The roads in many places were very bad; we travelled slowly. The sun went down in great

splendor and the landscape soon began to darken. Our black John knew
nothing of the situation either of Greenway Court or of Mr Nelson. We
made enquiries along the roads, but ⟨[*unrecovered*]⟩ received replies
which rather perplexed us. It grew quite dark before we reached a gate
which we were told ⟨led⟩ ↑opened↓ into Mr Nelsons grounds. We drove
across two or three broad fields—opend as many common country gates—
⟨so⟩ nothing had the appearance of the approach to a gentlemans seat.
I began to feel dubious—It seemed very much of an intrusion for three
persons to drive up to a gentlemans house after dark and ask quarters for
the night. The Kennedys laughed at my scruples. It was ⟨Virginia⟩ the
custom in Virginia—Mr Nelson would be glad to recieve us—Perhaps said
I he may not have room—Oh Yes—he has lately enlarged his house—He
has been in Europe and knows how to live—You will find yourself in
Clover—We drove on—no signs of a house—We might have mistaken the
road—At length we saw a light twinkling at a distance. It appeared to be
from a small house—More consultation—this might not be Mr Nelsons—
or he might not have enlarged his house—For my part I was so fatigued
that I declared myself resigned to quarters in a barn provided Mr Nelson
would allow me a little ⟨qu⟩ clean straw. The road gradually wound up
to the house; as we approached, the Moon rising above a skirt of forest
trees lit up the scene and we saw a noble mansion crowning a rising
ground; with grand portico & columns. and wings surmounted with battle-
ments—we drove up to the door. A Negro boy came ⟨out⟩ forth, like a
dwarf from an enchanted castle—Mr & Mrs Nelson were both from home!
What was to be done—it was too late to go wandering about the country
in quest of other quarters. Would Mr & Mrs Nelson be home soon? Oh
yes—they had gone to make a visit in the neighborhood and would be
back to tea—Mr Nelsons mother in law was in the house—that would do—
We alighted—entered a spacious hall upwards of twenty feet wide with
a beautiful circular stair case—⟨being?⟩ thence into a noble dining room,
where the tea table was set out, but no body present—After a time the
old lady made her appearance. Mr John Kennedy ⟨[*unrecovered*]⟩ was
slightly acquainted with her and introduced us. She was very civil and
by no means disposed to set the dogs on us—I began to have hopes of
something better than the barn. After a time Mr & Mrs Nelson came
home. They accosted us in true Virginian style. Mr Nelson claimed some
acquaintance with me. He reminded me of his having introduced himself
to me three years before, at the Revere House in Boston[4] when I was
in there with the Grinnels—and said he had a prior acquaintance ⟨being⟩
↑having been↓ one of a committee of the students of the University at
Charlottesville, who about twenty year's since, waited on me at the hotel
to invite me to accept a ⟨↑fine?↓ dinner⟩ public dinner[5]—

In a word—we were made at once to feel ourselves at home—invited to pass several days there—Mr Nelson would take us all about the country and make us acquainted with all his neighbors—⟨We We promised to ↑remain↓ pass the next day for dinner but had to r We could⟩ We had glorious quarters that night—My room was hung with ⟨pa⟩ French paper —displaying all the Parisian palaces—The next day Mr Nelson took us to Greenway Court; had a large party of the neighboring gentlemen to meet us at dinner—As it was with great difficulty we got away in time to return in the evening to Winchester. Mr Nelson repeatedly urged me to make him a visit on some future occasion when he would shew me all the country and accompany me into the lower part of Virginia, to visit his friends in that quarter—

So much for my expedition to Greenway Court.

I have no time to tell of my further movements since my return to Cassilis.

To morrow I set off with Mr & Mrs Kennedy on our return to Ellicotts Mills and in the beginning of next week shall take my departure for New York: to be at my post at the Astor library on Wednesday

I am scrawling this in extreme haste With love to all bodies

Your affectionate uncle
W. I.

Miss Sarah Irving

Manuscript: SHR.   Published: PMI, IV, 164 (in part).

1. This letter has not been located.

2. WI omitted the bracketed parenthesis.

3. Hugh Mortimer Nelson bought "Long Branch" in 1836. He was married to Adelaide Holker of "Springsbury." See Rose M. MacDonald, *Clarke County, A Daughter of Frederick*, p. 50; and H. T. Tuckerman, *Life of J. P. Kennedy*, p. 238.

4. The Revere House was a hotel designed by William Washburn and built in Bowdoin Square in 1847. See Edwin M. Bacon, ed., *Boston Illustrated* (Boston, 1893), p. 83.

5. The invitation was issued late in May, 1833. See PMI, III, 51–52.

2317.   To Henry R. Schoolcraft

Sunnyside Oct 27th 1853

My dear Sir

I cannot but feel deeply sensible of the friendship and esteem which you have manifested towards me on various occasions and more especially at present in proposing to dedicate to me a volume of your Indian work.[1]

As I consider that work entitled and destined to take a high rank in our literature and to remain a lasting monument of the aboriginal races of which it treats I feel that you are doing me a signal honor in thinking me worthy of such a dedication.

I am happy to learn that your health ⟨remains⟩ continues good and your "spirits and hopes serene," and that you entertain strong hopes of being able to survive the counter blasts of criticism. Go on, my dear Sir, complete the noble work you have commenced and be assured your name will remain among the loved and honored names of our country. You have secured for yourself a lasting reputation that will outlive the temporary clouds of criticism.

With kind remembrances to Mrs Schoolcraft[2] believe me ever

> Yours very truly
> Washington Irving

Henry R. Schoolcraft Esqr

Manuscript: LC.

1. Schoolcraft dedicated volume 2 of his *Information Respecting the History, Condition and Prospects of the Indian Tribes of the United States* to WI. For WI's reaction to the dedication, see his letter to Schoolcraft, February 21, 1854.

2. Mary Howard of Beaufort, South Carolina had married Schoolcraft in 1847. Since he suffered from a partial paralysis in his hand, she served as his amanuensis.

2318. To Alexander R. Boteler

> Sunnyside Novr. 11th. 1853

My dear Sir,

From the tenor of a letter recently recieved from my friend Mr Andrew Kennedy,[1] I am fearful I have failed to acknowledge by letter your kindness last summer in sending me some Revolutionary documents, and in offering to submit the papers of the late Governor Stockton[2] to my inspection.

If I have been guilty of such remissness I beg you will attribute it to the true cause, a confusion of mind and a relaxation of all habits of mental application which troubled me throughout the summer and obliged me to seek a relief in change of Scene and climate; but which were encreased by the extreme heat of the weather.

I now offer you my sincere thanks for your Courtesy and Kindness, and hope to offer them in person, should I be able to make another visit to Virginia; when it would give me great satisfaction to have a sight of the historical materials which you have in your possession.

With great respect / My dear Sir / Your obliged & hbl Servt
Washington Irving

Alexander R Boleter Esqre

MANUSCRIPT: Yale.

Alexander R. Boteler (1815–1892), a Princeton graduate who devoted himself to agricultural and literary pursuits, was living at "Fountain Park," his father's estate near Shepherdstown, Jefferson County, Virginia. From 1859 to 1861 he served in the U.S. Congress; during the Civil War he served in the Confederate Congress.

1. This letter has not been located.
2. Thomas Stockton (1781–1846), son of a Revolutionary army officer and a soldier in the War of 1812, became governor of Delaware in 1845.

2319. To Elizabeth Kennedy

Sunnyside, Nov. 11th. 1853

My dear Mrs Kennedy

I am shocked at what you tell me[1]—that old Phil has cut ⟨off⟩ his master ↑off↓ with a shilling! I think it would not have happened had I been in Baltimore. I flatter myself that Phil has a kindness for me, and think I could have prevailed on him to forgive your father on condition of his never enquiring again into the state of the larder—As to your sisters ⟨intimation⟩ ↑insinuation↓ that Phils burst of noble ire "is all owing to his young wife," it is just of a piece with her persecution of that virtuous couple. Her whole conduct in regard to this little African love story has been barbarous and might furnish a supplementary chapter to Uncle Toms Cabin when it goes to a fiftieth edition. The winding up of the chapter, however, would be a triumph to Mrs Stowe and on recording Phils lofty discharge of his old master she might exclaim with Zanga—"Afric thou art revenged!"[2]

How comes on the "House that Jack built"—or is to build. I envy Kennedy the job of building that tower,[3] if he has half the relish that I have for castle building—air castles or any other[.] I should like nothing better than to have plenty of money to squander on stone and mortar, and to build chateaus along the beautiful Patapsco with the noble stone which abounds there but I would first ⟨pull down⟩ blow up all the cotton mills (your fathers among the number)[4] and make picturesque ruins of them—

and I would utterly destroy the railroad—and all the cotton lords should live in baronial castles on the cliffs and the cotton spinners should be virtuous peasantry of both sexes; in silk skirts and small clothes and straw hats with long ribbands and should do nothing but sing songs and chorus's and dance on the margin of the river.

Of late I have gratified my building propensity in a small way by putting up a cottage for my gardener and his handsome wife and have indulged in other unprofitable improvements incident to a gentleman cultivator. A pretty country retreat is like a pretty wife—one is always throwing away money on decorating it. Fortunately I have ⟨Sunnyside Novr⟩[5] but one of those ↑two↓ drains on the purse and so do not repine.

I see you are again throwing out lures to tempt be[6] back to Baltimore and sending me messages from Mary Dulaney and dear little Lu.[7] And I have a letter[8] from Mr Andrew Kennedy inviting me to ↑come to↓ Cassilis and the Shenandoah when I am tired of the Hudson. Ah me! I am but mortal man and but too easily tempted—and I begin to think you have been giving me love powder among you—I feel such a hankering toward the south: But be firm my heart! I have four blessed nieces at home[9] hanging about my neck and several others visiting me and holding me by the skirts—How can I tear myself from them? Domestic affection forbids it!

And so with kindest remembrances to your father, sister and husband and lots of love to Mary Dulaney and "Lu"

Yours affectionately
Washington Irving

MANUSCRIPT: Peabody Library.   PUBLISHED: *Sewanee Review*, 25 (January, 1917), 11; PMI, IV, 167–68 (in part); and Tuckerman, *Life of J. P. Kennedy*, pp. 144–45 (in part).

1. Elizabeth Kennedy's letter has not been located.

2. At the conclusion of Edward Young's play, *The Revenge* (1721), Alonzo, a Spanish general, stabs himself and then remarks to the captive Moor, "*Afric*, thou art reveng'd."

3. To Edward Gray's house on the Patapsco, Kennedy added a large library with a room above it. The design included a campanile tower. See Bohner, *J. P. Kennedy*, p. 212.

4. WI's wishes were partly fulfilled in July, 1868, when a flood caused extensive damage to the mill. See Tuckerman, *Life of J. P. Kennedy*, pp. 143–44.

5. WI had apparently started a letter on this sheet, abandoned it, and then used the paper for this letter.

6. WI probably intended to write "me."

7. Louisa Andrews was a young lady whom, along with Mary Dulaney, WI had met at Edward Gray's home.

8. This letter has not been located.

9. Mary, Catharine, Sarah, and Julia Irving were residing at Sunnyside in 1853.

2320.   To Henry S. Randall

Sunnyside Nov 26th. 1853.

Dear Sir,

I have the honor to acknowledge the receipt of your obliging letter[1] proposing to send me the 3d & 4th volumes of the Quarto Edition of the documentary history of this state.[2] I shall be very happy to recieve them. I recieved some time since the first and second volumes and, I believe, acknowledged the receipt of them. If I have not done so it must have been an oversight which I hope will be excused. I have been rather irregular in correspondence for some time past, in consequence of indisposition and related absences from home.

The volumes in question may be sent by Express directed Dearman, Westchester County which is a station on the Hudson River rail road as as well as a post office.

With sincere thanks for your kindness I remain my dear Sir

Very truly Your obliged & hbl Servt.
Washington Irving

Henry S. Randall Esq / Secy of State of the State N Y. / &c &c &c

DOCKETED: Washn. Irving
MANUSCRIPT: HSP.

Henry S. Randall (1811–1876), who wrote numerous books and articles on agricultural subjects, served as New York secretary of state from 1841 to 1853.

1. This letter has not been located.
2. *The Documentary History of the State of New York*, ed. E. B. O'Callaghan, was issued in four volumes between 1849 and 1851. These books are in WI's library at Sunnyside.

2321.   To Benjamin Silliman

Sunnyside Decr 13th 1853.

My dear Sir

I beg you to accept my warmest thanks for the copy of your Tour in Europe[1] which you have had the kindness to send me, and still more for the expressions of esteem and good will in the letter[2] which accompanied it. I had read your work before the receipt of this copy, and while interested and instructed by the new and scientific lights occasionally thrown on old and familiar scenes and objects I was particularly charmed by the freshness and almost youthfulness of feeling which pervades the narrative; giving evidence of your possessing two of the greatest blessings that can attend upon Age, a cheerful spirit and an unwithered heart. It is these that shed a golden sunshine on the decline of life and render it one of its serenest and most genial seasons

I regret extremely that I was from home at the time of your visit to my neighborhood, but hope you were ⟨suf⟩ sufficiently pleased with this part of the country to repeat your visit; ⟨I⟩ in which case I shall be most happy to welcome you to my little rural retreat. Should I happen ever to be in New Haven I shall not fail to seek you out and reciprocate in person those assurances of regard and esteem with which you have honored me In the mean time believe me

Your truly obliged friend
Washington Irving

Professor Benjamin Silliman / &c &c &c

ADDRESSED: Professor Benjamin Silliman / Yale College / N Haven
MANUSCRIPT: Yale.

Benjamin Silliman (1779–1864) was a chemist, geologist, and naturalist who taught chemistry and natural history at Yale from 1802 to 1853. He was one of the leaders in science education in the United States during the first half of the nineteenth century.

1. *A Visit to Europe in 1851* (2 vols., 1853) was an account of Silliman's second trip to Europe. It is among the books in WI's library at Sunnyside.
2. This letter has not been located.

2322.   *To Mary E. Kennedy*

Sunnyside Dec. 17th. 1853

My dear Miss Kennedy,

I received a letter above a month since from your father,[1] jogging my memory about replying to a very kind offer of Revolutionary documents made me by Mr Boteler. I hope my answer to your father and the one enclosed for Mr B. proved satisfactory.

I could have wished your father, while he had pen in hand, could have given me a little of family gossip and the chronicles of Cassilis. It is really tantalizing, after having been for a time domesticated among you, and in the current of your every day concerns, to come away and hear nothing further about you. It is like getting interested in the story of a work, and not being able to get the second volume.

I really long to know how all goes on in the household. Whether your sister Sarah is getting the better of that cruel neuralgia which tormented her. Whether you continue to be awakened by the sound of the steam whistle from all quarters as if you were at the junction of half a dozen railroads. Whether Andrew still thinks that beautiful young lady that *did not come in to dinner*, the most charming girl in the neighborhood and whether he and the Doctor[2] keep office together and practise 'Love Law and Physic' for the benefit of Charlestown and the country round. Whether Edmund[3] is likely to get an advantageous situation in Baltimore under the auspices of Mr Gray; who I know entertains a very favorable opinion of him.

I hope all things are going on as cheerily as usual at the Cane Farm;[4] and that your sister may have health to enjoy her happy home. Remember me I beg of you most cordially to her and her worthy husband. I want, above all things, to hear something about darling little Lizzy and her dolls; and any new winning ways she may have learned, and whether she still gives that odd shake of the head and forbids her grandpa to sing 'rock a by baby.'

My mind is full of pleasant recollections of the home scenes I have witnessed and enjoyed among you all, and especially during my last visit, when I had become more familiar with the ways of the family, and when there was such a gathering of its various members at Cassilis. What an animated household it made. What life about the house; what pleasant excursions about the neighborhood. What a pity is it that families could not always remain young and united. That the cares and concerns of the world must scatter them asunder, just as they are fitted to be most happy together. But you have a great deal of frank, intimate cordial life in Virginia. I am delighted with every thing I have seen in your state; and as to the Valley of the Shenandoah, it has become a perfect 'dream land' to me. How much I am indebted to you for having drawn me thither.

I presume you have read your uncle Pen's book.[5] It is very spirited, graphic and amusing and has been well received by the public. I trust its success will prompt him to the further exercise of his pen; occupation of this kind could not fail to contribute greatly to his happiness. Your uncle John I understand is occupying himself very much with rail roads.[6] I wish he would put his mind on a better track and leave such every day concerns to every day people.

Farewell my dear Miss Kennedy, give my kindest remembrances to every body about you, for I have an affectionate regard for you all. I hope your excellent mother may escape her rheumatism this winter and be able to go about with her usual alacrity doing good and taking care of everybody.

> Yours ever my dear Miss Kennedy / very truly
> Washington Irving

PUBLISHED: *American Literature*, 6 (March, 1934), 57–59.

1. This letter has not been located.

2. Dr. Henry Pendleton Cooke, the son of John Rogers Cooke, who later married Mary Kennedy.

3. Edmund and Andrew, mentioned in the preceding sentence, were Mary Kennedy's brothers.

4. John Selden, husband of Anne Kennedy, operated Cane Farm.

5. Philip Pendleton Kennedy's book, *The Blackwater Chronicle*. For other details, see WI to Pierre M. Irving, June 25, 1853.

6. John P. Kennedy was a member of the boards of directors of three railroads which he helped to consolidate into the North Central Railroad Company. See Bohner, *J. P. Kennedy*, p. 215.

2323.   *To Frederick S. Cozzens*

N York. Dec 20t. 1853.

My dear Sir

The hero of the Andre[1] capture was not named Pawling but Paul*ding*[2] —ding that into your memory.

The verse of the ballad[3] which I cited to you is

> Then up stepped John Paul*ding*
> And unto him did cry
> If that I draw this glittering sword
> One of us two must die!

Nota bene. The word Sword was always given with the full sound of the W; which gave me the idea always that it must have been a broad S*w*ord.

Yours very truly
Washington Irving

Fred S. Cozzens Esqr.

MANUSCRIPT: Va.–Barrett.

1. Major John André, an adjutant of the British army during the American Revolution, was entrusted with the correspondence between Sir Henry Clinton and the traitor Benedict Arnold.

2. John Paulding (1758–1818), along with Isaac Van Wart and David Williams, stopped Major André on September 23, 1780, discovered the incriminating papers on him, and turned him over to the American army.

3. WI is referring to an anonymous thirteen-stanza ballad entitled "Brave Paulding and the Spy." For the full text, see *Poems of American History*, ed. Burton E. Stevenson (Boston, 1908), pp. 237–38.

2324. *To John P. Kennedy*

Sunnyside, Decr. 20t. 1853

My dear Kennedy,

It would give me the greatest delight to attend the anniversary dinner of your Historical Society,[1] having, as you know, a sneaking kindness for all gastronomical solemnities of the kind; but all great dinners are strictly forbidden me by a homeopathic physician,[2] who has my head in his hands, and is poisoning me into a healthy state of the brain by drachms and scruples. As to oratorical display which you hold out as a bait to me I believe it is my bane.[3] I don't believe I have yet got over my last attempt of the kind; it was at the meeting in which Bryant read his eulogium on Fenimore Cooper. I had to announce from the stage that Mr Webster was to preside for the evening. I made a speech of nearly a minute, with but one break down, but the pangs of delivery were awful.[4]

I beg you will make an apology for me to the Society in your best manner. Say something handsome about my great respect for the institution; my veneration for Maryland in general, my love for Baltimore in particular, and if you can introduce something spicy about the siege, and the various achievements of the Baltimore volunteers (yourself among the number)[5] so much the better.

You do not tell me whether ⟨old Phil⟩ the rupture between Mr Gray and old Phil still continues, and whether, like that between the Czar and the Turk it is almost beyond the healing powers of diplomacy.

I rather think I shall have to come on and negotiate, and if I can only prevail upon old Phil to take Mr Gray again into favor we will kill a fatted calf on the occasion.

With affectionate remembrances to Mr Gray and the two ladies I remain as ever my dear Kennedy

Yours truly
Washington Irving

J. P Kennedy, Esqr

DOCKETED: 1853 / Washington Irving

MANUSCRIPT: Peabody Library.   PUBLISHED: *Sewanee Review*, 25 (January, 1917), 12.

1. John P. Kennedy was a member of the Maryland Historical Society. See Tuckerman, *Life of J. P. Kennedy*, p. 395.

2. Dr. John C. Peters.

3. WI, who lacked confidence in his own powers of oral extemporizing, disliked speaking in public. See STW, II, 32–35.

4. WI's performance took place at Metropolitan Hall on February 25, 1852. See STW, II, 210.

5. WI is alluding to the siege of Baltimore during the War of 1812 and to Kennedy's part in the defense of the city. See Tuckerman, *Life of J. P. Kennedy*, pp. 64–80.

2325. To Henry S. Randall

Sunnyside, Jany 3d. 1854.

My dear Sir,

You have again laid me under great obligations by your kindness in sending me a volume of the Colonial History,[1] which has come safely to hand; and in promising to place my name on the list for the subsequent volumes. I assure you I feel deeply sensible of these kind attentions on your part. As to the other sets of the Documentary History[2] which you offer to place at my service, I have no need of them at present; but should circumstances render it desirable for me to furnish them to any person or institution to whom they would be of importance I shall not fail to avail myself of your frank and liberal offer

With high respect / Your obliged friend & servt
Washington Irving

Hon Henry S. Randall.

MANUSCRIPT: NYHS.

1. Probably this is *Documents Relative to the Colonial History of the State of New York*, ed. E. B. O'Callaghan (Albany, 1853), a volume still preserved in WI's library at Sunnyside.

2. Fifteen volumes of the *Documentary History of the State of New York* are to be found among WI's books at Sunnyside.

2326. To James Narine, Daniel Northrup, and John W. Forbes

Sunnyside Jany 16t. 185⟨3⟩4

Messrs. James Narine ⎫
   Daniel Northrup ⎬ Committee
  & John W Forbes ⎭

Gentlemen,

It will give me great pleasure to attend the Printers Banquet[1] to which you have done me the honor to invite me, provided the state of my health, which is somewhat deranged, will permit me to come to town.

Your note[2] being sent to Tarrytown instead of Dearman post office[3] did not reach me in time for an earlier reply.

Very respectfully / Your obliged & hbl Servt
Washington Irving

MANUSCRIPT: Va.–Barrett.

James Narine, a printer with a shop at 7 Broadway, resided in Jersey City. John W. Forbes lived at 22 N. Moore. See *Trow's New York City Directory for 1853–54.*

1. The New York Typographical Society celebrated the 148th anniversary of Benjamin Franklin's birth on January 17, 1854, at the Assembly Rooms. The banquet began at 10:00 P.M., and the festivities extended into the early morning hours. See New York *Times,* January 18, 1854. It has not been determined whether or not WI attended.

2. This invitation has not been located.

3. In April, 1854, the residents of Dearman changed the name of their town to Irvington. See PMI, IV, 173.

2327. To Henry Fox

Sunnyside / Jany. 17. 1854

Sir

I have no knowledge of any printed copy or translation of the Manuscript[1] to which you allude nor do I believe there is any—it is much to be desired that there should be one—there is another document in the Columbian Library at Seville a volume containing the Imago Mundi of Pedro de Aliasco & other of his works. it[2] is full of marginal notes by Columbus & his brother Bartholemew[3] referring to passages which bore upon his theories & was *his vade mecum* before his great discovery. an[4] edition of this work with *fac similes* of the marginal notes would be a worthy present to the New World by some learned or Historical Society—

(Signed) Washington Irving

Henry Fox Esqr

MANUSCRIPT: Columbia (copy).

1. From WI's reference it is impossible to ascertain which manuscript by Columbus is meant. A list of letters and documents in the handwriting of Columbus is found in John Boyd Thacher, *Christopher Columbus, His Life, His Work, His Remains* (New York, 1967), III, 84–85.

2. The copyist did not capitalize "it."

3. For a reproduction and transcription of a page from this volume and a discussion of Columbus's notes, see Thacher, *Christopher Columbus*, III, 475–87.

4. The copyist did not capitalize "an."

2328. *To Sarah Storrow*

Sunnyside Jany. 25th. 1854

My dear Sarah,

To relieve your mind in respect to Mr Vesey and the Beasley portrait[1] I inform you that I write again to him by the ship which takes this letter, though I certainly wrote to him some months since on the subject, and sent the letter by Theodore Irving to New York, to be put in the letter bag; and rather think I had written to him previously.

Your solicitude on the subject has had one good effect; it has drawn a letter from you after a long interval; which serves as the Indians say to "brighten the chain of friendship." You say you have nothing new or interesting to write about—and then you go on to give a budget of pleasant and interesting information. Are you not living in the very centre of the worlds intelligence political, scientific, literary, artistical and fashionable. Are you not continually seeing persons of our own country, known to us both, passing as it were in review before you. If you in the whirl of Paris can find nothing to write about, what can I, "wearing out lifes evening gray"[2] in my little study at Sunnyside. I am glad Gouverneur Kemble saw so much of you and your family; as he will be able to give me ⟨[*unrecovered*]⟩ particulars about you all. I have not seen him since his return. I had hoped to have had a visit from him; but have been disappointed; ⟨I shall⟩ and I have been so much shut up at home that I have had no chance of meeting him in New York. I trust I shall do so before long as I purpose passing a few days in New York the coming week.

I was surprised when you spoke of Sally McLane (Mrs Tiffany) being in Paris.[3] I supposed her in Baltimore; where she has a beautiful residence; and where I was to have paid her a visit last spring, on my way back from Washington, but circumstances prevented it. She has refined from a very charming child into a very lovely woman, as I have no doubt you have found on further acquaintance with her.

I am not acquainted with our new minister to the Court of France;[4] but I hear him spoken of as a man likely to be hospitable and of social qualifications. He is a Virginian and in general I like the Virginians. They are frank generous hearted people.

I am pleased with the spirit of the Empress[5] in regard to Cuba. She speaks like a true Spanish woman on the subject. It is almost the last Colonial jewel in the Crown of poor old Spain, and I do not wonder after having been stripped of a great part of two continents, with all their treasures and mines of wealth she should cling to this relique of past magnificence.

Our Minister Mr Soule[6] has been making himself sadly conspicuous at Madrid; and I fear will find his situation there very dreary and inefficient He is a man of talents, but wanting in judgement and discretion. I foresaw he was preparing embarrassment for himself, by the way in which he talked and acted in New York and Paris, while on the way to his diplomatic station.

Our Christmas holidays passed off with quiet enjoyment There was as usual a gathering of part of the family at the Cottage that is to say, as many as it could hold and a little more. The little mansion as usual was decked with Christmas greens, and when the party broke up and returned to town they all professed to have passed a very Merry christmas.

Our neighborhood has filled up very much of late. Villas are springing up in all directions, and some of them very tasteful and picturesque. Some of our new neighbors are very agreeable people, and live through the whole year in the country. We have had several public lectures this winter, not a mile ⟨off⟩ distant from Sunnyside, which have been very interesting and very well attended. So you see this part of the country is quite looking up.

Our household for some months past has been greatly enlivened by a bright little inmate, another Kate Irving[7] ↑about nine years old↓. She is a daughter of William Irving, and of course a niece of the girls. I met with her at Washington last winter, where William had a situation in ⟨one of⟩ the Census office, and I was so much pleased with her, that I got her parents to let her make a visit at the Cottage. She came here in august or September and has been here ever since and I shall be very unwilling to give her up. She is pretty, graceful, quick intelligent and full of life and enjoyment. Her aunts attend to her education and she is quite a pet among us all.

Theodore ⟨st?⟩ was with us a part of the Autumn; he is now with the Sutherlands at Geneva.[8] He has no situation at present but I expect he will have a professorship before long. in the mean time he is preparing himself for the Ministry; and will probably take orders towards the end of the year.[9]

I must conclude for it is late at night and I must ⟨finish⟩ to bed. Give my love to the young folks. I am glad to hear that my dear Kate is fond of her book; cultivate in all of them a habit of reading. It is a main source of enjoyment that lasts throughout life

With kind regards to Mr Storrow

ever my dear Sarah / Your affectionate Uncle
Washington Irving

Mrs Thos Storrow

MANUSCRIPT: Yale.

1. Probably a portrait of Reuben Beasley, who was U.S. consul at Le Havre from 1817 to 1847 and a longtime friend of WI's. Vesey has not been identified.

2. Samuel Johnson, "Parody of Thomas Warton," in *Works of Samuel Johnson*, ed. E. L. McAdam and George Milne (New Haven, 1964), VI, 294, line 2.

3. For other details about Mrs. Tiffany, see WI to Mary Irving, January 18, 1853.

4. John Y. Mason (1799–1859), a congressman and federal judge from Virginia, served as American minister to France from 1853 until his death.

5. The empress of France was Eugenia de Montijo (1826–1920), whom WI had known in Spain. She married Napoleon III on January 29, 1853.

6. Pierre Soulé (1801–1870), a French-born lawyer who had been involved in politics in New Orleans and Washington, was appointed U.S. minister to Spain in 1853. He actively supported Franklin Pierce's plan to annex Cuba and worked out the details of the Ostend Manifesto, which proposed the annexation of Cuba through either purchase or forcible seizure. Because of adverse public reaction to the proposal, Soulé resigned his post in December, 1854.

7. Earlier impressions of Ebenezer's granddaughter are to be found in WI to Sarah Irving, February 16, 1853, and August 6, 1853.

8. The Sutherlands were the parents of Jane, the wife of Theodore Irving.

9. He was ordained as a priest in the Protestant Episcopal Church later in 1854 and served in parishes on Long Island and Staten Island for the next twenty years.

2329.   *To* ―――

Sunnyside Feb 6th. 1854.

Gentlemen,

It will give me great pleasure to to[1] be present at your meeting on the twenty second ⟨of Feby⟩—Mr Paulding[2] is with me, do him the honor if you please;

Very respectfully yours,
Washington Irving

MANUSCRIPT: NYPL—Berg Collection (copy).

1. WI repeated "to."

2. Probably James Kirke Paulding, WI's collaborator on *Salmagundi*.

2330.   To William W. Waldron

Sunnyside, February 13th 1854

My Dear Sir:

On arriving in town a day or two since, the little painting which you have had the kindness to send me, was put into my hands, having been, for some time, in possession of my nephew, Pierre M. Irving. This will account to you for my not having, at an earlier date, expressed how much I feel obliged to you for this additional testimonial of your good will. I trust that the young gentleman[1] who has illustrated so ingeniously the subject of your little poem, will cultivate the talent evinced in this picture, and make himself eminent in one of the most popular and delightful of the elegant arts.

Very respectfully, / Your obliged friend and servant,
Washington Irving

PUBLISHED: Waldron, *WI & Cotemporaries,* pp. xvi–xvii.

Waldron explained the circumstances relating to WI's letter: "Lieutenant G. B. Butler, then about fourteen, illustrated, at my request, the same subject [as Waldron's poem, 'The Chieftain and the Child,' dealing with George Washington's placing his hand on WI's head] in a very interesting picture, a copy of which I sent to Mr. Irving; on receipt of which he expressed his thanks in the following letter." See Waldron, *WI & Cotemporaries,* p. xvi.

1. George Bernard Butler (1838–1907), who studied with Thomas Hicks, went on to distinguish himself in the areas of portraits, still life, animals, and genre painting. Although he lost his right arm in the Civil War, he continued to paint with his left hand. He was elected to the National Academy in 1873.

2331.   To Elizabeth Kennedy

Sunnyside Feb. 21st. 1854

My dear Mrs Kennedy,

I am grieved to recieve such bad accounts of your fathers health;[1] and of the cloud his illness casts over your cheerful household. However, as you say, spring is coming, and I trust its genial influence will revive his health and spirits as it did last year. In the mean time he has dear little Louisa Andrews at hand to cheer him with her music and Mary Dulaney to look in upon him with her beaming countenance[.] I think two such comforters would have beguiled Job himself of his misery

I met Mr Meredith in town on Saturday last, and he told me that Kennedy had been unwell. If it is that affection of the head of which he complained last year, tell him I have found, in my own case, great relief from Homeopathy,[2] to which I had recourse almost accidentally; for I am rather slow at adopting new theories. I can now apply myself to literary occupation day after day for several hours at a time without any recurrence of the symptoms that troubled me. In fact my head seems to be as hard as ever it was—though perhaps somewhat heavier

You tell me Kennedy is about to set off with Mr Fillmore on his southern tour and would like to have me for a companion. Heaven preserve me from any tour of the kin⟨g⟩d! To have to cope at every turn with the host of bores of all kinds that beset the paths of political notorieties. To have to listen to the speeches that would be made at dinners and other occasions to Mr Fillmore and himself; and to the speeches that Mr Fillmore and ⟨himself⟩ ↑he↓ would make ⟨and⟩ ↑in↓ return. Has he not found out by this time how very bore-able I am? Has he not seen me skulk from bar rooms and other gathering places where he was making political capital among the million? Has he forgotten how last summer a crew of blatant beasts of firemen, whose brass trumpets gave him so much delight, absolutely drove me into the wilderness? No—No—I am ready ⟨to⟩ at any time to clatter off on Douce Davie[3] into the woods, with the gentle Horse Shoe;[4] or to scale the Allghanies with him (barring watering places) but as to a political tour I would as leave go campaigning with Hudibras or Don Quixote[5] You ask me how I have passed my time this winter. Very much at home. Dipping into town occasionally to pass a few hours at the Astor library but returning home in the evening. I have been but once or twice at the Opera and to none of Julliens concerts.[6] Still my time has passed pleasantly in constant occupation; though I begin to think that I often toil to very little purpose excepting to keep off ennui and give a zest to relaxation.

I had a very agreeable letter from Mary Kennedy lately giving me a budget of family news. I am glad to find that your father has placed her brother Edmund advantageously in Baltimore. He appeared to me to be a very promising lad and I liked him because he looked so much like Mary[.] I hope and trust he will prove worthy of the interest your father has so kindly taken in his welfare. [end of MS]

MANUSCRIPT: Peabody Library.   PUBLISHED: PMI, IV, 170–71 (in part); and Tuckerman, *Life of J. P. Kennedy*, p. 319 (in part).

1. Edward Gray suffered frequently from asthma. See Tuckerman, *Life of J. P. Kennedy*, pp. 251–52.

2. A method of treating illness with minute doses of drugs which in a healthy person would produce symptoms like those of the disease. For mention of WI's own "affection of the head," see WI to PMI, July 8, 1853; and to J. P. Kennedy, August 31, 1854.

3. Mrs. Kennedy's saddle horse which WI rode when he visited the Kennedys. See PMI, IV, 169–70.

4. WI's epithet for J. P. Kennedy. See PMI, IV, 134.

5. Both Samuel Butler's poem *Hudibras* (1663–1668) and Cervantes's picaresque satire (1605–1615) were accounts of extensive travels on horseback.

6. Beginning on August 29, 1853, Louis Jullien (1812–1860) conducted an orchestra of about 100 musicians in several series of popular concerts at Castle Garden and Metropolitan Hall. See Odell, *NY Stage*, VI, 332–33.

2332.   To Mary E. Kennedy

Sunnyside Feb. 21st. 1854

My dear Miss Kennedy,

Your letter of Jany 12th.[1] is lying beside me on my table and reproaching me for the long time I have suffered to elapse without sending a reply. So pleasantly written a letter too—in the true vein—easy, natural and unambitious—giving me lively anecdotes of home; and those who abide there, and those who have "launched forth on the tide of the world's caprice." Happiness and good fortune attend them! I shall be glad to hear that Sarah's[2] *debut* in gay life has been propitious. Richmond, as I recollect it in my young days, was a charming place full of cordiality, and though in the many years that have passed since, great alterations must have taken place, we will hope they are all for the better, and that the generous old Virginia spirit still remains in all its flavour and richness. I hope her gaiety has not been thwarted in any degree by that neuralgia which harrassed her at Cassilis last autumn.

And so my brave little friend Edmund[3] has an excellent situation at Baltimore and is "determined to make a man of himself." I shall be much mistaken and much disappointed if he don't succeed. He seemed to me to have the elements of a manly character, and everything I heard of his domestic conduct was in his favour. I feel additional good will to Mr Gray for carrying his good intentions toward Edmund into such prompt effect. But I was sure Edmund had a strong friend in the old gentleman.

I trust before this your sister 'Annie'[4] has regained her usual health, as you said the doctor pronounced her in a fair way of recovery. Is there any thing in the locality of the Cane farm unfavorable to her constitution? It seemed to me one of the most bland and healthful of situations. The landscape as it appeared on that golden afternoon when we dined there remains in my mind as a picture.

My dear little Lizzie[5]—"patting her doll that was *crying for its head*" —how delightfully you bring her before me; with her peculiar and winning ways. With what motherly concern and tenderness she used to run to her 'crying baby' and fondle and kiss it, when it was made to utter those spasmodic sounds as if in pain. She is a most loving and loveable little being. I never knew a more attaching child.

I have recieved a letter from your aunt[6] within a day or two by which I learn that the usual cheerfulness of their home has been checked this winter by the illness of Mr Gray, who has been suffering from a severe attack of asthma. I am in hopes however that the return of spring will have the same favorable effect upon him that it had last year. Your uncle John is about to set out on the southern tour with Mr Fillmore that was to have taken place last spring, but was prevented by the melancholy death of Mrs Fillmore.[7] He intimates a wish that I would accompany them; but I have no inclination to travel with political notorieties, to be smothered by the clouds of party dust whirled up by their chariot wheels, and beset by the speechmakers, and little great men, and bores of every community, who might consider Mr Fillmore a candidate for another presidential term.

I feel very sensibly the kind expressions in that part of your letter where you look back upon the year that is past and speak of the formation of our friendship as one of its most pleasing events. It belongs to the excellent considerateness of your nature to extend your regards beyond the gay circle of your youthful associates to one who is in the "sear the yellow leaf"[8] of existence; but for me to value your friendship is nothing more than for one among the gathering chills of winter to value anything that brings back a gleam of the verdure and sweetness of springtime.

And now my dear Miss Kennedy, with many kind remembrances to your father and mother and all the households of both houses believe me ever

Yours very truly
Washington Irving

PUBLISHED: *American Literature*, 6 (March, 1934), 59–61; PMI, IV, 169 (in part).

1. This letter has not been located.
2. Mary Kennedy's twenty-year-old sister.
3. Mary's brother, who was eighteen years old.
4. Anne Rebecca, Mary's oldest sister, who died on July 14, 1854.
5. Elizabeth Gray, Anne's youngest daughter.
6. Elizabeth Kennedy's letter has not been located.
7. See WI to Elizabeth Kennedy, April 2, 1853.
8. See *Macbeth*, V, iii, 22.

2333. To Henry R. Schoolcraft

Sunnyside, Feb 21st. 1854

My dear Sir,

I may have appeared slow in acknowledging the receipt of the copy of your work[1] which you have had the kindness to send to me, but through some delay in the hands of Mr Putnam and some blundering in the office of the rail road it has been long in reaching me. I now return you my warmest thanks for this testimonial of your continued esteem and good will, and especially for the very cordial and complimentary letter addressed to me at the commencement of your second volume.[2] I trust I have no undue craving for popular applause; but I confess the friendship and approbation of Men like yourself are inexpressibly dear to me and I am happy to have a memorial of them thus recorded by you in a work which is destined to endure, one of the literary monuments of our country.

With kind remembrances to Mrs Schoolcraft I remain my dear Sir

Your truly obliged friend
Washington Irving

Henry R Schoolcraft Esq / &c &c &c

Manuscript: Huntington.

1. This copy of the second volume of *Information Respecting the History, Condition and Prospects of the Indian Tribes of the United States,* inscribed by Schoolcraft, is among the books still at Sunnyside.

2. For details concerning this dedication, see WI to Schoolcraft, October 27, 1853.

2334. To Catharine Storrow

Sunnyside, Feb. 21 1854

My dear Kate:

I have just received the slippers which you have been so very good as to work for me, and which have been a long time in the shoemaker's hands. Having put them on, I sit down to tell you how well they fit me; how much I admire the colors you have chosen; how much I am astonished and delighted with the needlework; and how very sensibly I feel this proof of affectionate remembrance. I assure you I take great pride in exhibiting this specimen of the taste and skill of my Parisian niece, and, if I were in Paris, should be very much tempted to go to Court in them, even at the risk of causing a question of costume.

I dined, a few days since, in company with your father's partner, Mr. B. * * * He told me that it was very possible you might all pay a visit to America this year. That, however, I put about as much faith in as in the return of the fairies. I hope, however, you still keep up a recollection of your home on this side of the water, and of your young cousins who were your playmates. They and their intimates make a very happy circle, and it grieves me much that you and your sisters are not with them, all growing up together in delightful companionship. If you remain much longer separated, you will all forget each other. * * *

Farewell, my dear Kate. Give my love to my dear little nieces Tutu and Gaga[1] (who I fancy have completely forgotten me), and to your mother, to whom I wrote recently. Tell your father we should all give him a hearty welcome if he should really come out this summer; and a still heartier one should he bring you all with him.

Your affectionate uncle,
Washington Irving

PUBLISHED: PMI, IV, 29–30.

1. The nicknames for Kate's sisters Susan and Julia.

2335. To Anna Irving

New York March 6t. 1854

My dear Anna,

As I understand you are making preparations for an approaching event in which all your friends take cordial interest, I enclose a cheque which may be of some assistance. I have made it payable to the order of your father, who will put the proceeds at your disposal

With best wishes for your happiness I am—my dear Anna

Your affectionate uncle
Washington Irving

Miss Anna Irving

MANUSCRIPT: Va.–Barrett.

Anna Duer Irving (1830–1884), daughter of Pierre Paris, married Frederick R. Routh on June 7, 1854.

2336.   To Lyman C. Draper

Sunnyside March 17th. 1854

Lyman C. Draper Esq / Corresponding Secretary &c.

Sir

I have the honor to acknowledge the receipt of your letter informing me of my being elected an honorary member of the State Historical Society of Wisconsin.[1]

I beg to assure the Society that I most deeply and gratefully appreciate this this[2] mark of their favorable consideration

I remain, Sir

Very respectfully / Your Obt Servt
Washington Irving

MANUSCRIPT: State Historical Society of Wisconsin.

Lyman C. Draper (1815–1891), a collector of American historical manuscripts and documents, was secretary of the State Historical Society of Wisconsin from 1854 to 1886.

1. In 1854, at Draper's suggestion, certificates of membership in the State Historical Society of Wisconsin were sent to 600 prominent figures in literature and other fields. Draper hoped that the honorary members would contribute copies of their writings to the collection being formed at the Society. See William B. Hesseltine, *Pioneer's Mission: The Story of Lyman Copeland Draper* (Madison, 1954), pp. 124–25.

2. WI inadvertently repeated "this."

2337.   To Osmond Tiffany

Sunnyside March 19th. 1854

My dear Sir,

I must apologize to you for having delayed so long in answering your letter,[1] but in fact I have been so ⟨much⟩ unsettled for the last few weeks, shifting my residence backward & forward between town and country that all my correspondence is behind hand.

With [respect][2] to the poet Camoens there is a memoir of his life and writings in two volumes octavo by ———[3] Adamson of New Castle England: it was published in London in 1820.[4] There is also in Italian an Elogio Storico de Luigi Camoens, by Filippo Mordani published in Bologna 1844.[5]

I am happy to find that further contemplation of Miss Mary Dulaney's countenance has made you a convert to my opinion of its merits. When you become as old an observer as I and have seen as much of womankind, you will be aware how rare such beauty is.

Hoping that it may always abound in your path and cheer you with its smiles I remain, Dear Sir,

Yours very truly
Washington Irving

Osmond Tiffany Esq

MANUSCRIPT: SHR.

Osmond Tiffany (1823–1895), who attended Harvard from 1840 to 1842, was engaged in mercantile and literary activities in Baltimore at this time. He contributed to such periodicals as the *North American Review*, *Knickerbocker Magazine*, and *Atlantic Monthly* and wrote two books, *The Canton Chinese, or the American's Sojourn in the Celestial Empire* (Boston, 1849) and *Brandon, A Tale of the American Colonies* (New York, 1858). WI probably met him during one of his visits to the Kennedys in Baltimore.

1. This letter has not been located.
2. WI omitted the bracketed word.
3. WI's dash.
4. John Adamson, *Memoirs of the Life and Writings of Luis de Camoens* (London, 1820).
5. This work has not been located in the printed catalogs of various national libraries.

2338.   *To Julia G. Irving*

Sunnyside, April 3d. 1854

My dear Julia,

Sarah has engaged that I shall write a post script to her letter, but I am in a sad state of incompetency to do it. My faculties seem[1] benumbd probably from the long spell of dismal wintry weather we have *enjoyed* for the last fortnight. It is quite tantalizing to read your account of your roses and rhododendrons and the budding and blossoming of spring in the "sweet south country" through which you have been pilgrimaging. I should have liked to be with you in your voyage up the Tennessee. I begin to long for a wild unhackneyed river unimproved by ⟨American⟩ cultivation and unburthened by Commerce.

Today is my seventy first birth day, and opens with a serene, sunny, beautiful morning. Oscar and Eliza were to have come up to keep it with me; but the ⟨we⟩ foggy, rainy weather on Saturday deterred them; so we shall celebrate it without company and with a reduced household; as Mary is still in town ↑and Kate goes down this morning to join her.↓ I have wished a thousand times, my dear Julia, ⟨that yo⟩ since your departure that you were with me; making your home under my roof as you do in my heart, and I never wished it more strongly than at this moment. I feel very much this long separation; and grieve that it is likely to be so much prolonged, and that you are moving to further and further distances from me. I wish Sanders could have some employment near at hand so that you could take ⟨yo⟩ up your abode with me entirely—and that we all wish—and how we would cherish you! But let him go on enlightening the world ⟨and⟩ and making money as fast as possible—And when he has secured a small bag full then come home without waiting to make a fortune.

By your ⟨last⟩ letter[2] I find you have heard of Pierre and Helens hejira to North Carolina[.][3] Helen has been at the height of human grandeur and felicity; passing several days at the Capital visiting presidents, dining with Senators and dancing at Brazilian Ministers balls. The last heard of her, she was at the Brazilian Ministers fete at one OClock on Friday morning and was to set off for Richmond at 5 Oclock in the morning in the steam boat—How was she to pack up her trunk in the interim!—Pierre did not intend to go to bed—Had I been there I should have advised him to pack up Helen in the trunk in her ball dress: it would have saved a world of time and trouble and arrangement and derangement of toilette. It might however have damaged a stupendous dress cap with which she took the field; and in which she *had* figured to great advantage at a dinner party at Julia Grinnells before her departure. It surpassed, for glory of ribbands, any cap in her wardrobe, and was of unquestionable taste—Frinch my dear! Dear, good, excitable Helen. I am glad they managed to sojourn a few days at Washington, for I am sure she would enjoy it; and she is calculated to win friends wherever she sojourns. Her delightful gaiety of heart and play of humor ⟨g⟩ mingled with such genuine sensibility and kindness ⟨mak⟩ fit her to become the delight of society. I know no one who is more truly fitted for social life and who at the same time possesses more endearing qualities for the domestic circle.

I am in hopes the slate quarry is going to prove a real gold mine—and then—between slate and gas, we shall have two branches of the family in fortunes way, and enabled to rally once more to the home stead. The only danger is that if Pierre becomes a Millionaire Helen will not be content with a *flat*, the present height of her ambition; but will wing her flight to Europe, figure at the Tuilleries and pay a visit to the pyramids—

I shall be very happy to recieve a visit from General Barrows whenever he comes to New York—And I shall give Mrs Stewarts book of "Western Travels" an attentive and friendly perusal whenever I recieve it. By the bye the 'women Kind' at Sunnyside have been very much puzzled and amused, by a daguerrotype likeness of a lady; enclosed in a Morocco case, ⟨which and directed to me⟩, which was made up in a parcel directed to me and left at the Tarry town station of the Hudson River Railroad. No letter came with it; but in a paper envellope was written *Mrs. Maria L Norvell, Claiborne, Ala. for Washington Irving Esq.* Fortunately there is no room for scandal nor vanity in the case as the lady is long past her teens and of mature aspect. From a book which she holds in her hands I judge her to be literary—she may be an Authoress like Mrs Stewart and the book intended for my inspection; but in the picture it remains closed. Should you see or hear any thing of such a personage in your travels, give me some inkling who and what she is—if it is only to relieve the curiosity of my women Kind. In the mean time, do not repeat this anecdote to any one, lest it might be misunderstood, and I be thought to make a jest of what may be intended as a mark of respect on the part of this 'unbeknown princess.'

I suppose you know that I have another Kate Irving at Sunnyside—daughter of William Irving, a fine bright eyed little creature that I met at Washington above a year since. She has been on a visit to us since august or September last, and I shall not be willing to give her back to her parents, for she has quite got hold of my heart. She is really a fine, quick witted intelligent child and a little lady in form and manners. The girls attend to her education and she makes herself the life of the house. Indeed it was time for me to look out for a fresh supply of nieces, so many were wandring away from me.

And now I think I have written long enough for a post script. When I began I doubted whether I should be able to fill a single page and here have I scribbled nearly two sheets full. So, with a thousand good wishes and kind remembrances to Sanders I remain my dear Julia

Your affectionate Uncle
[*Signature cut out*]

Mrs. Julia G. Irving

Wednesday. 12th. As I found Sarah was writing to you on Sunday, I with held my letter that it might reach you on a different day, and so be the more welcome. I have nothing more to add, excepting that Kate and I took advantage of the last of the sleighing the day before yesterday to visit some of our new neighbors. Our first visit was to Castle Stebbins. This is a great and solid Stone castle built on the summit of a hill on the east of the Post road and adjoining the "Paulding Manor" so called although there is neither Manor no manners there. As the Snow on this mountain was very much melted we had ⟨a h⟩ or rather our horses had a hard pull up a steep, winding gravelly carriage road; but were repaid by an extensive and magnificent prospect. We found the lord of the castle at home and likewise the lady;—met with a kind reception, and was very well pleased with both. The lord of the castle (Stebbins[4] by name, so called no doubt after his domain) has still extensive dealings in New York and visits the City daily.

Our next visit was to Castle Cunningham.[5] This noble castle was formerly owned by Count Coffin[6] but he parted with it, having undertaken to build another castle which is now nearly completed on the mountain ⟨near nea⟩ opposite the school house in the upper part of our lane[.] Castle Cunningham is now in possession of a nobleman of that name who has recently acquired an immense fortune in California (By the way why not Sanders turn his enterprising thoughts in that direction instead of Alabama) ⟨The own⟩ The lord of Castle Cunningham was not at home but we were graciously received by ⟨his⟩ lady ↑Cunningham.↓ She appeared to be very amiable, but complained of being very lonely. Her eldest daughter had married recently, and left her, her younger daughter was at school in New York, and her son was at the other end of the world engineering so that there was no one to occupy the castle but herself and her husband.—and he I dare say was taken up the greater part of his time counting over his money and piling up his bags of gold. Upon the whole we returned from our visits well pleased with our neighbors but more pleased with our cottage at the foot of the hill than these Great Castles on the *Mountings*

So remember me kindly to Sanders and believe me your affectionate and home contented uncle

Washington Irving

MANUSCRIPT: NYPL—Berg Collection.   PUBLISHED: PMI, IV, 171–72 (in part).

WI's letter was written in response to one from Julia Irving in Montgomery, Alabama. See PMI, IV, 171.

1. WI wrote "seen."

2. This letter has not been located.

3. PMI and his wife spent the first week of April, 1854, in North Carolina. See PMI, IV, 172.

4. Probably David M. Stebbins, who operated a mercantile establishment at 43 and 45 Barclay Street in New York City. He resided at Tarrytown. See *Trow's New York City Directory for 1853–54*, p. 658.

5. J. Cunningham lived east of the Boston Post Road, directly east of Sunnyside. See 1857 map in *Portraits of a Village. Wolfert's Roost: Irvington-on-Hudson* (Irvington-on-Hudson, 1971), p. 49.

6. E. Coffin owned several properties in Irvington, a short distance north of Cunningham's and also south of Sunnyside, west of the Post Road. See 1857 map in *Portraits of a Village*, p. 49.

2339. *To Helen Dodge Irving*

April 6, 1854

Another of my dissipations was an evening at the dancing school, where I was very much pleased and amused. I met your friend Mrs. M——[1] there, whom I found very agreeable, and who made me acquainted with her bright little daughter. The scene brought my old dancing-school days back again, and I felt very much like cutting a pigeon wing,[2] and showing the young folks how we all footed it in days of yore, about the time that David danced before the ark.[3]

The next morning, where should I breakfast, but at Judge Duer's![4] It was to meet Mr. Lawrence,[5] the English portrait painter, who has come out with letters from Thackeray, and I don't know who all, and is painting all the head people (some of whom have no heads) in town. It was a very agreeable breakfast party, three or four gentlemen besides Mr. Lawrence and myself; but what made it especially agreeable was the presence of two of the Miss ——— ———. My dear H——,[6] I was delighted with them—so bright, so easy, so ladylike, so intelligent! H—— has one of the finest, most spiritual faces I have seen for a long time. Why, in heaven's name, have I not seen more of these women? We have very few like them in New York. However, I see you are beginning to laugh, so I will say no more on the subject.

PUBLISHED: PMI, IV, 172–73.

1. This and other dashes in proper names were probably inserted by PMI.
2. A fancy dance step in which one jumps and touches the feet together. WI had taken dancing lessons around 1798. See PMI, I, 37.
3. See 1 Chronicles 13:8.
4. Probably John Duer, a New York state judge. For other details about him, see WI to Rufus W. Griswold, October 15, 1851.
5. Samuel Laurence (1812–1884), who painted portraits of Carlyle, Browning, and Thackeray, also sketched Lowell and other American writers during his visit to the United States.
6. Probably Helen Irving.

2340. To ——

Sunnyside, April 8t. 1854

Dear Sir,

It would give me great pleasure to deliver a lecture before the "Young mens Association" of Po'keepsie[1] were I skilled or practised in that kind of intellectual exercise. As the very reverse is the case I am obliged most respectfully to decline all such invitations as that with which you have honored me.

Your obliged & humble Servt
Washington Irving

MANUSCRIPT: Rush Rhees Library, University of Rochester.

1. Probably the Poughkeepsie Lyceum of Literature, Science, and the Mechanic Arts, which was incorporated in 1838. The Poughkeepsie Young Men's Christian Union was founded in 1856; the YMCA, in 1863. See Edmund Platt, *The Eagle's History of Poughkeepsie* (Poughkeepsie, 1905), pp. 146, 157, 188.

2341. *To William W. Waldron*

Sunnyside, April 13th, 1854

My Dear Sir:

The little poem to which you allude,[1] in your last, belongs to yourself, and you have a right to do with it what you please, and having already published it, I do not see that you need my permission to publish it in any other form. I never interfere in any way or matter which may be considered complimentary to myself. I am sorry that I cannot promise to revise the poems which you tell me you are preparing for the press. I distrust my poetical tact too much to exercise it in that manner, and two or three mortifying experiences have deterred me from playing the part of chamber critic.

When you have your volume ready for publication, I shall have no objection to introduce it to Mr. Putnam, leaving him to judge of its marketable qualities. I would observe, however, that he has recently made a complete change in his establishment, sold off almost all his old books and adopted a different method of doing business, abandoning, in a great measure, the publishing line. I suppose you have seen an account of the great sale of his stock and the advertisement of his future course. He may not, hereafter, be as ready, as heretofore, to undertake the publication of new works.

I remain, my dear sir,

Yours truly,
Washington Irving

William W. Waldron Esq.

PUBLISHED: Waldron, *WI & Cotemporaries,* pp. 242–43.

1. "The Chieftain and the Child," which dealt with the meeting of WI and George Washington. For other details, see WI to Waldron, February 13, 1854.

2342.   To Edward Everett

Sunnyside April 22d. 1854

My dear Sir

Permit me to introduce to you my friend Mr Charles T H Barton[1] a young gentleman connected with my excellent friends the Bartons and Guestiers of Bordeaux[2] but who has recieved his education at Harrow, in England and now visits this country on a tour of improvement. Any attentions you may bestow on him during his sojourn in Washington will be considered as personal favors by

Yours my dear Sir / ever very truly
Washington Irving

The Hon Edward Everett / &c & c &c

DOCKETED: Washington Irving / 22 Sept. 1854.
MANUSCRIPT: MHS.

1. Probably the son of Nathaniel Barton and the grandson of Hugh Barton (1766–1854), who was associated with Daniel Guestier (1755–1847) in the well-known Bordeaux wine firm.
2. Whenever WI passed through Bordeaux, he always visited the Bartons and Guestiers. He last saw them on July 16–18, 1842. See WI to Catharine Paris, July 20, 1842.

2343. To Hamilton Fish

Sunnyside April 22d. 1854

My dear Sir,
I take the liberty of introducing to you my amiable young friend
Charles T H Barton Esq a young gentleman of excellent connexions
in England and France and related to some very dear friends of mine
at Bordeaux. He visits our country on a tour of liberal curiosity and
improvement. Any civilities You may find it convenient to bestow on
him during his Sojourn in Washington will be very gratefully considered
by, My dear Sir

Yours ever very truly
Washington Irving

The Hon. Hamilton Fish / &c &c &c

MANUSCRIPT: SHR.

2344. To Robert C. Winthrop

Sunnyside, April 23d. 1854

My dear Mr Winthrop,
I am in a poor mood for letter writing being just on the recovery from
a fit of indisposition brought on I believe by the late unseasonable and
intolerable snow storm; yet I cannot defer thanking you for the Copy
of your lecture before the Boston Mercantile Library Association which
you have had the kindness to send me.[1] I do not know whether I have
not been ↑even↓ more delighted by the perusal of it than I was with
that "Introductory to a course on the application of science to art:"[2]
though that particularly interested me by its admirable Collocation of
Archimedes with Franklin—and by its allusions to Syracuse—a place
which I visited in the days of my youth and among the ruins of which
I recollect searching with some young officers of our navy for sites
for some of the anecdotes concerning Archimedes.[3]
The beautiful and well wrought out tribute to the memory of Algernon
Sydney in your last lecture, however, comes home to both head and
heart; and is full of suggestion and instruction to our young countrymen.
It is a noble plan you have adopted thus to single out and hold up
⟨high⟩ historical characters as illustrative high principles, and useful
and honorable conduct. Our people want *toning up*—and this is one

of the best modes of giving it. I hope you will be tempted to add many more to your gallery of historical portraits for their edification

You see expresident Fillmore and Kennedy have nearly accomplished their projected tour;[4] and apparently with all the success they could have anticipated. What is the object I do not pretend to know; Something, I presume, beyond the honor of being feted with public dinners and bored with complimentary speeches; two of the glorifications of this world which (to use Miss Bremers[5] words) may well be put in the litany. I wish Kennedy would give up the wear and tear of political life resume his pen and devote himself to some literary tasks which he has projected and which would give him both present popularity and lasting fame.

With kindest remembrances to Mrs Winthrop and your family[6]

I am ever my dear Mr Winthrop / Yours very faithfully
Washington Irving

DOCKETED: Washington Irving
MANUSCRIPT: MHS

1. Winthrop's lecture, *Algernon Sidney: A Lecture, Delivered Before the Boston Mercantile Library Association, Dec. 21, 1853,* was published as a pamphlet in Boston in 1854. Sidney (1622?–1683) was an English politician who was beheaded for high treason on December 7, 1683.

2. Winthrop's *Archimedes and Franklin: A Lecture, Introductory to a Course in the Application of Science to Art Delivered Before the Massachusetts Charitable Mechanic Association, November 29, 1853* was published in Boston in 1853. Duyckinck notes that the lecture was so popular that it "gave the suggestion and impulse to the erection of a statue of Franklin in Boston." See *Cyclopaedia of American Literature,* II, 348–49.

3. WI visited Syracuse in Sicily in February of 1805, but he does not refer specifically to Archimedes in his journal. See *J&N,* I, 179.

4. Fillmore and Kennedy toured the Southern states in March, April, and May, 1854, to test the political support for the ex-president in preparation for his unsuccessful attempt to regain the presidency in the 1856 election. See WI to Mrs. Kennedy, February 21, 1854.

5. In 1849 WI had met Fredrika Bremer (1801–1865) at a dinner at the home of his neighbor James Alexander Hamilton. Subsequently she visited Sunnyside. See Fredrika Bremer, *Homes of the New World* (London, 1853), I, 59–63.

6. Winthrop married his first wife, Eliza Blanchard of Boston, in 1832, and she died in 1842, leaving him with three sons and a daughter. On October 15, 1849, he married Laura Derby Welles (d. 1861). See Lawrence S. Mayo, *The Winthrop Family in America* (Boston, 1948), pp. 343–44.

2345. *To Sabina O'Shea*

Sunnyside, May. 4th. 1854.

I cannot express to you my dear Mrs O'Shea how much I was rejoiced when on opening the envellope of your letter I recognized your well known handwriting.[1] So long a time had elapsed without hearing from you that I feared you had quite given me up. Do not, I entreat you suffer yourself to relapse again into such a long silence. The happiness I derived from your kind friendship while in Madrid, and the many pleasant hours we passed together at Paris are dear to my reccollection and will ever keep you present to my mind. It was truly a delight to me to recieve a letter from England from your son Henry while he was at school there; dear Papa Kiki[2]—do you reccollect what good care he used to take of us when we went lion hunting and theatre visiting to-gether at Paris? His letter was indeed a charming one: full of good sense and good feeling, but what I valued most was the proof it gave of a steadfast character, faithful in its attachments and true to old friendships. It is not often that we find a youth of his age so considerate as to volunteer a letter to a man in years, out of a regard to former intimacy. It is an excellent sign, and augurs well of both head and heart. I trust my dear Mrs OShea he will always be a source of pride and happiness to you

I am glad to have such good accounts of Mr OSheas health. You tell me he never has gout or any other ailment—excepting when it is brought on by imprudence. As he must now be pretty nigh past his imprudent years, I trust he will give the gout less frequent provocation—however if a man will dance now and then he must not think it hard if called on to pay the piper.

You ask me how I am?—Whether I am looking *young*—whether I enjoy society—and whether I am spending my time happy at Sunnyside?—There's a string of home questions for an old bachelor to answer.

First as to my health. In general it is excellent; better than it was in Madrid In fact I am never out of order excepting when I keep too close in my study among my books and papers; and then I have only to throw them by; mount my horse and take plenty of exercise in the open air and all is right again.

As to whether I look young or no—some of my friends say that I have not changed in looks since I returned from Spain, excepting that I look healthier—but this I presume is by way of compliment. I certainly however look as young as any man has a right to do who has just passed his seventy first birthday. It is hardly respectable for a man to look young at such a time of life.

As to society I enjoy it as much as ever I did in a social way; with a few choice friends, but I soon grow tired of great crowds and brilliant parties.

As to my mode of life at Sunnyside—I have an affectionate family of nieces around me, who take all household care from off my mind and take care of me into the bargain. My house is a kind of family gathering place continually enlivened by the visits of relatives. I live in an agreeable neighborhood on the best of terms with every one far and near. Upon the whole I am journeying pleasantly along in the evening of life; with some of its lingering sunshine and nothing of its gloom— much better off than most old bachelors, and infinitely better off (I say it in strict confidence) than any of the order deserve to be.

I am sorry to find that our minister Mr Soulé is so out of favor at Madrid[.] I hope it may not prove any detriment to him in his transactions with the government. I am but very slightly acquainted with him, having met him but once or twice in public at the seat of government. He is a man of talents; very eloquent as a parliamentary speaker and one who, the ladies say, can make himself very agreeable in society. In Madrid he appears to be entirely in a false position as regards society and must appear to a disadvantage. How completely the diplomatic circle has changed since I was in Madrid. I believe there is none of the old set there except the *Baron del Asilo*[3]—bless his title! I hope he has made a fortune on the three per cents to match it. Give him my kind remembrances and best wishes—May he live a thousand years—since he is so proud of his eighty years and a half—

It must be very satisfactory to you to have your friend Lord Howdon[4] in the diplomatic circle. He is a gentleman of the true stamp, and one whom I hold in great regard. The Count Rachynski,[5] of whom you speak so highly, I have never met. I think from your account of him I should like him much. He must be quite a loss to the circle of your intimacy—but what can you expect from the shifting sands of diplomacy, where there is no abiding place.

You have no idea how interesting every anecdote is, which you give me of persons and scenes around you. It is like so much dug up from the catacombs; for in truth poor Spain is almost as dead to the rest of the world. How little one reads about her in the European papers; how little one hears of her in current conversation. Whenever there arrives a batch of news from Europe I run my eye over the columns of the papers in search of tidings from Spain; but find almost nothing. Now and then there is a chance paragraph which shews that changes have taken place in the court and cabinet; and disturbances in the country; but the thread of events is wanting—and there is no filling up.

I used to take great interest in the affairs of the palace when I was in Madrid, and in the fortunes of the Queen and her sister when they were children surrounded by difficulties and dangers. How strangely affairs have changed in that quarter since I left Madrid. The Arana family[6] I perceive are in high favor at the palace. The elder members of the family elbow counsellors to a very exalted personage; and Pepe, that stripling of promise, now grown up to be—the Lord knows what— about the royal person. So the world turns round!

Salamanca[7] I see has finished his palace on the Delicias—So I presume I am to prove a false prophet and the dancing dogs an extravagant prediction; unless some new revolution of the wheel should send him with a hand organ to the boul[e]vards[8] of Paris.

But of all the changes of this changing world think of Louis Napoleon, who once breakfasted with me at my little nest at Sunnyside and strolled with me about my grounds; now Seated on the Imperial throne of France and by his side Eugenie Montijo; whom I knew when a mere child at the house of her father Count Teba, at Granada—and afterwards as a gay young belle at her mothers house in Madrid.—Eugenie Montijo Empress of France!—and poor Leocadia Zamora a nun in a convent! Are we not getting back into the times of fairy tales?

My niece Mrs *Storrow*, of whom you speak so kindly⟨,⟩ (though you call her Mrs *Story*) is still residing in Paris; but has removed from the place Vendome to somewhere in the neighborhood of the Elysee Bourbon: Her husband has just come out on a visit to this country but without her I am sorry to say. He returns to France almost immediately and talks of travelling with her this summer in Switzerland and elsewhere and of spending next winter in Italy. It is a grievous thing for me to give up all hope (as I begin to do) of ever seeing her again; but she is too happy in Europe and her husband too much occupied in business there to come home soon. And I am getting too old; and my presence here too important to the welfare of those around me for me to uproot myself and go again voyaging across the Atlantic. So year after year will slip away without our seeing each other—and when she does come back—my chair will be vacant. I sometimes regret that I ever suffered myself to dote so much on her as I certainly did. By the way, she always speaks of you with the utmost regard—You quite won her heart, and I assure you it is a kind and good one.

And now my dear Mrs O'Shea with many kind remembrances to your husband and to my worthy friend Henry (Papa Kiki of yore) I remain most affectionately

Your friend
Washington Irving

Mrs Henry O'Shea

ADDRESSED: Mrs Henry O'Shea / Care of Henry O'Shea & Co / Madrid. POST-
MARKED: NEW-YORK / MAY 5 / 1854 / / [*Two postmarks unrecovered*]
DOCKETED: Sunnyside / May 4th. 1854.
MANUSCRIPT: HSA. PUBLISHED: Penney, *Bulletin NYPL*, 63 (January, 1959),
35–38.

1. This letter has not been located.

2. WI's knickname for Henry George O'Shea (1838–1905), who was also called
"Kicky," "Quiqui," "Papa Quiqui," and "Henrique."

3. Olinto dal Borgo di Primo, Maria Emilio de Gaspara d'Andrea Giusti, baron
del Asilo (1775–1856) was the Danish chargé d'affaires in Madrid for many years.
He and WI were quite close during WI's ministership.

4. Sir John Hobart Caradoc, second Baron Howden (1799–1873) combined
military and diplomatic careers. He was British minister in Madrid from 1850 to
1858.

5. Atanazy Raczynski (1788–1874), member of an illustrious Polish family,
represented Prussia at the Spanish court from 1848 to 1852. A collector and
historian of European art, he was the author of *Histoire de l'art moderne en
Allemagne*, 3 vols. (Paris, 1836–1841); *Les arts en Portugal* (Paris, 1846); and
Dictionnaire historico-artistique du Portugal (Paris, 1847).

6. José Ruíz de Arana, duke of Baena, was introducer of ambassadors at the
Spanish court. For other details, see WI to Joaquín de Frías, September 4, 1843.

7. José Salamanca y Mayol (1811–1883) was a Spanish financier and cabinet
officer.

8. WI omitted the bracketed letter.

2346.   To Robert C. Winthrop

Sunnyside 22d. May 1854

My dear Mr Winthrop,

I regret to say that my engagements and occupations will not permit
me to accept your kind invitation; being committed for an excursion to
the Highlands of the Hudson on a visit to an old friend.[1]

My health I am happy to say is excellent at present, being perfectly
recovered from the slight indisposition to which Mr Cogswell alluded.

With kind remembrances to Mrs Winthrop and your family I remain

My dear Mr Winthrop / Yours very faithfully
Washington Irving

The Hon. Robt C. Winthrop.

DOCKETED: Washington / Irving. — / (Irvington)
MANUSCRIPT: Princeton University Library.

1. Gouverneur Kemble of Cold Spring, where WI visited for two days at the
end of May. See WI to Mary Kennedy, May 30, 1854.

2347.   *To George P. Putnam*

Sunnyside, May 27th, 1854.

My Dear Sir:

This will be handed to you by Mr. William W. Waldron, the author of the manuscript[1] which I left with you some little time since. I recommend him to your kind civilities, and am

Yours very truly,
Washington Irving.

PUBLISHED: Waldron, *WI & Cotemporaries*, p. 245.

1. Probably a collection of Waldron's poems which WI promised to "introduce" to Putnam. See WI to Waldron, April 13, 1854.

2348.   *To William W. Waldron*

Sunnyside, May 27, 1854

My Dear Sir:

I left your manuscripts[1] with Mr. Putnam when I was last in town, which was some little time since, and told him you would probably call upon him to know his disposition with respect to it. I enclose you a note of introduction to him.[2]

In great haste,

Yours very truly,
Washington Irving

William W. Waldron, Esq.

PUBLISHED: Waldron, *WI & Cotemporaries*, p. 244.

1. The final letter is probably Waldron's addition, since WI was usually careful about agreement of pronouns and antecedents (Note: "it" at the end of the sentence). WI uses the singular form in his letter to Putnam, May 27, 1854. A check of some of the printed sources of other letters which Waldron quoted reveals that he was quite careless in his copying.
2. See WI to George P. Putnam, May 27, 1854. Either Waldron did not present this letter or else he retrieved it from Putnam, for he quotes it in his book (p. 245).

2349. *To Mary E. Kennedy*

Cold Spring, Putnam County / May 30th 1854

My dear Miss Kennedy

I recieved your last letter[1] just as I was recovering from an attack of chills and fever, brought on I believe by that same unseasonable snow storm of which you complained and which suddenly threw us back from the middle of April into the depths of winter. In fact we have had three winters this year and have since been nearly torn to pieces by torrents and inundations. However, nature after struggling through them all has at length come out fresh and verdant and in all the beauty of the young and tender leaf.

I am sorry to have such bad accounts of your domestic life during the past winter, the sickness that has visited some branches of the family and the comparative loneliness of Cassilis.[2] I trust however that all this has now passed away and you are all well and cheerful again. I find by your letter that your brother Andrew has pitched his tent at Wheeling. I should think he would have more scope for the exertions of talent there than at Charlestown, and hope he will at least remain long enough to give the place a fair trial. He has to struggle against the attractions of a happy paternal home continually calling him back; but he must stay there until a home feeling grows up around him.

I presume your Sister Sarah has returned before this from her campaign at Richmond and Washington—crowned with myrtle and roses, like a young warrior with her first laurels. Her sojourn at the capital with Miss Randall must have been delightful to her. She could not have been under more charming auspices.

I am happy to hear that my dear little Lizzie[3] still bears me in mind, and that the doll continues to be a link of remembrance between us. I can easily imagine how her illness must have increased her endearing claims upon the affections of you all. She is wonderfully endowed with what the French call sympathetic qualities.

I see your uncle John has at length got home from his long and triumphal tour with Mr Fillmore. The reception they met with every where must have been extremely gratifying. I went down to New York to see Mr Fillmore when I heard of his being in the city; but he had departed for home the same morning that I made my call. I have had no letter from Baltimore since your uncles return. I presume he requires some repose after such a long campaign of feasting and speech making.

I am on a two days visit at the old bachelor nest of my friend Mr Gouverneur Kemble in the very heart of the highlands with magnificent scenery all round me; mountains clothed with forests to their very summits, and the noble Hudson moving along quietly and majestically at their feet. The day after tomorrow I return home.

In the course of eight or ten days I shall again be called from home to be present at the wedding of a niece, or rather a grand niece.[4] After a short wedding tour the young couple are to pay me a visit and pass part of their honeymoon at Sunnyside. All this will carry me well on towards the end of June, and make it too late for my intended visit to Virginia; as my experience of last year makes me cautious of travelling in summer weather, lest it bring on another attack of bilious fever.

—By the bye—to recur to your sister Sarah. If she is still troubled by that neuralgia which tormented her so much during my visit to Cassilis, I would suggest that she should try galvanism[5] as a remedy. I have a friend and connexion who has been very subject to it for years past and finds great relief from galvanism during the severest paroxysms of his malady. He has a small apparatus for the purpose, and I have witnessed the immediate relief which it imparted. I speak of it only as a palliative— I cannot infer from his case that it would be a permanent remedy, though it might be so where the malady had not become chronic as it has with him.

Farewell my dear Miss Kennedy. Present my affectionate remembrances to all the inmates at Cassilis and the Cane farm. And believe me with the most perfect esteem and regard

Your friend
Washington Irving

PUBLISHED: *American Literature*, 6 (March, 1934), 61–63; PMI, IV, 173 (in part).

1. This letter has not been located.
2. The name of the estate of Andrew Kennedy, Mary's father, in western Virginia.
3. Mary's niece, the daughter of her sister Anne, who died on July 14, 1854.
4. Anna Duer Irving (1830–1884), daughter of Pierre Paris Irving, married Frederick R. Routh in early June.
5. The use of electrical stimulation for the treatment of disease.

2350. *To Sarah Storrow*

New York, June 22d 1854

My dear Sarah,

My friend Mrs Davis is on the point of sailing for Europe with her husband & children on a tour of health, and I have given her this letter in case she should meet you while travelling or find you in Paris.[1] She

is a lady for whom I have the highest regard—*I am sure you will like
each other* —so let this letter make you acquainted with each other

Your affectionate Uncle
Washington Irving

Mrs Thos W. Storrow

ADDRESSED: Mrs Thos. W. Storrow / Paris
MANUSCRIPT: Yale.

Mrs. Davis is called "a Southern lady" from Natchez, but her precise identity
has not been ascertained. See WI to Sarah Storrow, November 23, 1854, where he
indicates that she did not use the letter of introduction.

2351. *To John P. Kennedy*

Sunnyside June 29t. 1854

My dear Kennedy,
Your letter[1] is perfectly satisfactory as explaining Mrs Kennedys long
silence and relieving me from some apprehensions on her own account;
having heard that you had been suddenly summoned home from your
feasting and speech making ⟨tour⟩ by intelligence of her indisposition.[2]
I trust your presence has restored her to health, and your writing to
me has quieted her conscience, and that you are now enabled to
take your hat and walk out on the *Pont Neuf* whenever you please.
I am really glad that you have got home safe and well from your
Southern tour; which, from all that I have seen reported of it in the
papers, must have been very satisfactory. I went down to town to
see Mr Fillmore; but he had set off for home an hour or two before my
visit.[3]

I am very much struck with the illustration which accompanies your
letter, setting forth the new tower to the chateau on the Patapsco.[4]
It is something to inspire romance and if I were a year or two younger
and were ⟨[unrecovered]⟩ not troubled with chills and fever and a
villainous catarrh, I should be tempted to take your hint and attempt
a serenade in the gondola, especially if your wife and Miss Gray would
promise to appear at the hanging balcony.

This has been rather an unfortunate season with me, having had
two returns of my old complaint of chills and fever, the last just as I
was on the way to attend a wedding of a grand niece, at which all the
ten tribes of the family were assembled. However I have had the young
couple to pass part of their honeymoon at Sunnyside and that has
consoled me.

I cannot promise you any visit to the patapsco during hot weather. The state of my system, and the experience of last year has determined me to keep quiet at home until the sultry season is over; yet my heart yearns to be with you all again and to make another visit to the Shenandoah Valley.[5] However, ⟨that I⟩ all that I keep in perspective as a boy keeps ⟨the⟩ Christmas holydays or the fourth of July.

My nephew Pierre M Irving and his wife came home perfectly delighted with a visit they had paid your family on their way to the South during your absence.[6] Pierre was especially pleased with a long conversation he had with Mr Grey, who has quite won his heart. I am glad they were able to look in on the family during their brief sojourn in Baltimore. I like that good people should know one another, especially good people in whom I take especial interest.

I write this letter with a head confused and almost stupified with a catarrh, which must apologize for its insufficiency. Give my most affectionate remembrances to all the family and believe me ever my dear Kennedy

Yours very truly,
Washington Irving

John P Kennedy Esqr

MANUSCRIPT: Peabody Library.   PUBLISHED: *Sewanee Review*, 25 (January, 1917), 12–13; PMI, IV, 174 (in part).

1. This letter has not been located.

2. Kennedy had been traveling in the South with ex-president Fillmore. See WI to Mrs. Kennedy, February 21, 1854.

3. For another account of WI's attempt to see Fillmore, see WI to Mary Kennedy, May 30, 1854.

4. WI first alluded to Kennedy's building and remodeling in his letter to Mrs. Kennedy, November 11, 1853.

5. WI had visited western Virginia in the summer and early fall of 1853.

6. Pierre and Helen Irving had toured the South and visited relatives in Washington in the spring of 1854. See WI to Julia Irving, April 3, 1854.

2352.   *To James Boardman*

Sunnyside, June 30, 1854

...But indeed my health has been so often deranged for a year past, accompanied at times by an affection of the head, produced by over talking, that I have repeatedly been obliged for long intervals to throw by the pen altogether—and in consequence my correspondence as well as all my literary tasks have fallen in arrears.

I now return you my sincere thanks for the literary relique which you have sent me, and which I shall treasure up among my momentoes of the eminent men whom it has been my good fortune to see in the course of my sojourns in Europe.

PUBLISHED: Maggs Bros., Catalog 360, Autumn, 1917, item 1903.

According to a note accompanying the quotation of this passage in the autograph catalog, WI had received a gift of a paper knife made from wood of the Roscoe tulip tree. WI had known William Roscoe (1753–1831) in Liverpool during his second stay in Europe. After Roscoe had read a paper before the Linnean Society of London on the Scitminean order of plants, he was honored by having the genus of Roscoea plants named after him. See George Chandler, *William Roscoe of Liverpool* (London, 1953), p. xviii. WI had celebrated him in the "Roscoe" section in *The Sketch Book*.

2353.   *To William Creighton*

Sunnyside July 18th 1854

My dear Dr Creighton,

I do not think the attack on our friend Webb in the public paper to which you have called my attention is likely to prove of any detriment to him in the prosecution of the business which takes him again to England.[1] At least it does him no harm here among those who know him and I trust will not do him injury abroad. His public position exposes him to these "paper pellets" and I believe he has done enough to provoke them from the party in question.[2]

I am glad to hear that professor Buckman[3] makes so favorable a report of the Guyandotte estate; which, after all, is what the parties in England will be most solicitous about. I make no doubt, therefore, that the arrangement in England will be completed to the advantage and satisfaction of all parties and I shall be glad to see Webb return to our neighborhood[4] crowned by that success due to his energy and enterprize; and which his generous and hospitable spirit fit him so creditably to enjoy.

ever my dear Dr Creighton / Yours most truly
Washington Irving

The Rev. William Creighton, D. D. / &c &c &c

P. S. I trust in the day of his success the General *will not forget the Church.*

MANUSCRIPT: SHR.

1. James Watson Webb went to London three times in 1853 and 1854 to promote the sale of stock in the Guyandotte Land, Coal, and Iron Company of western Virginia. While in England, he engaged in a spirited dispute with John T. Delane, the editor of the London *Times,* over the issue of privateering. See London *Times,* October 3, 1853; March 9, 1854.

2. Probably a reference to Webb's opposition to the Kansas-Nebraska Bill which was expressed in the New York *Courier and Enquirer,* which he edited. See James L. Crouthamel, *James Watson Webb: A Biography* (Middletown, Conn., 1969), p. 126.

3. James Buckman (1816–1884), an English botanist and geologist who taught at the Royal Agricultural College in Cirencester. Webb had probably sought him out to endorse his stock promotion venture.

4. Webb lived in a stone mansion about a mile north of Sunnyside. See WI to George D. Morgan, July 4, 1856.

2354. To John P. Kennedy

Sunnyside, July 25t. 1854

My dear Kennedy,

The "Schuyler affair" has no doubt made a great noise in your community as it has every[where][1] else. To me it has been a severe shock from my intimacy with George Schuyler[2] and his connexions the Hamiltons. From all that I know of George I have acquitted him, from the first, of any participation in his brothers delinquency,[3] and such I am happy to find is the verdict of some of our most able and experienced men of business who have investigated the matter; and who intend, I am told, at the proper time to testify publicly their conviction of his integrity.

The circumstance that may operate most against George until explained is that ↑while↓ he was President of the Harlem rail road Similar over issues of stock took place with those on the New Haven rail road. The facts of the case are these. The laws of Connecticut obliged Robert Schuyler to resign the presidency of the Harlem road. The board of directors urged George who was one of their number, to accept it. He expressed his willingness to attend to the ordinary business of the road excepting its financial concerns, to which he felt totally incompetent. A finance committee of three was appointed to take charge of these, with Robert as chairman, of whose reputed skill in these matters the company were anxious to avail themselves[4] By that committee all the financial concerns were transacted; George taking no part in them excepting to sign his name as President. Kyle[5] the Secretary who issued the spurious certificates had been thirteen years in the employ of the company, and enjoyed its implicit confidence. It does not appear that there was any collusion between Robert Schuyler and him ↑(Kyle)↓ in regard to the over issues on this company. It was entirely an act of Kyles, on his own account; or rather a series of floundering attempts to recover a false step in stock speculations.

I do not know whether I state the matter very clearly; being but little versed in these matters. I wish, however, to shield poor George Schuyler from being inculpated in the disgrace[6] as he is involved in the ruin of his unworthy brother. His conduct since the astounding development which took him by surprise, as it did everyone else, has been open, frank and manly, winning both sympathy and respect. You would be delighted with the noble conduct of Mrs Schuyler under this overwhelming and crushing calamity.[7] It has risen her higher than ever in my estimation.

I hope my dear Kennedy that by this time you have cast forth the seven devils of architecture from your new building and are seated in your stately tower on the banks of the Patapsco; and that Mr Grey approves of what you have done. With affectionate remembrances to him and his daughters twain

Yours ever my dear Kennedy
Washington Irving

DOCKETED: 1854 / Washington Irving / ansd Aug. 8
MANUSCRIPT: Peabody Library.   PUBLISHED: *Sewanee Review*, 25 (January, 1917), 13–14.

1. WI omitted the bracketed word.

2. George Lee Schuyler (1811–1890) was married to Eliza Hamilton (d. 1863), daughter of James A. Hamilton, WI's neighbor. After Eliza's death Schuyler married her sister, Mary Morris Hamilton.

3. Robert Schuyler, a partner in the firm of George L. and Robert Schuyler, was president of several railroads in the New York City area. As WI explains in the next paragraph, Robert Schuyler was forced to resign as president of the New York and Harlem Railroad Company and was succeeded by his brother George. Then Robert Schuyler was accused of issuing about 19,000 shares of additional stock in the New Haven Railroad, worth about $2,000,000. See New York *Times*, July 6, 1854; New York *Courier and Enquirer*, July 6, 1854.

4. The finance committee assisting George Schuyler was composed of attorneys R. M. Blatchford, George R. J. Bowdoin, and Samuel L. M. Barlow. However, George Schuyler resigned as president on July 7. See New York *Courier and Enquirer*, July 7, 8, 1854.

5. Apparently Alexander Kyle, secretary of the New York and Harlem Railroad, without the knowledge or collusion of Robert Schuyler, overissued 5,000 shares of the stock of that railroad at about the same time as Schuyler's action. See New York *Times*, July 8, 1854; New York *Courier and Enquirer*, July 12, 1854.

6. Even Robert Schuyler, in his letter resigning as president of the New York and Harlem Railroad, stated that his brother George was unaware of his fraudulent transactions. See New York *Courier and Enquirer*, July 7, 1854.

7. Mrs. George Schuyler had purchased $500 worth of the stock issued by Kyle. See New York *Times*, July 22, 1854.

2355. To Mary E. Kennedy

Sunnyside July 30t. 1854

My dear Miss Kennedy,

It is with the most painful surprise and concern that I have just recieved through a newspaper sent to me by your father the sad, sad intelligence of your sisters death.[1] I will not pretend, while the shock of the
news is still agitating me, to offer any consolation, but merely to express
my deep and heartfelt sympathy What a blow is this to her manly, affectionate, kind hearted husband—but what a bereavement to you all!
Brief as has been my acquaintance with your sister, it has been long and
intimate enough to acquaint me with the excellence and loveliness of her
character Indeed one of the most delightful pictures that I brought away
from the Shenandoah valley was that of your sister as I saw her in her
happy rural home, on that bright day which I passed there surrounded
by your family. That day and scene have ever been vividly impressed on
my memory, and although the reccollection will henceforth be tinged
with melancholy, it will be so much the more endearing Much as I deplore her loss, it is a happiness to me that I have known her.

But I will not dwell upon this theme—My letter, as I have said, is
merely one of sympathy, written at the moment. Give my most affectionate remembrances to your father and mother and your sister Sarah,
and my sincere condolences to Mr Selden—

My dear darling little Lizzie[2] is, I trust, at home with you. poor child!—
but she will be drawn closer than ever to your heart, and find there a
mothers tenderness; for this heavy dispensation, my dear Miss Kennedy,
is calculated to call into action all the higher qualities of your nature, and
I have seen enough of you to know that the call will not be in vain.

ever your affectionate friend,
Washington Irving

Miss Mary E. Kennedy.

MANUSCRIPT: Peabody Library.   PUBLISHED: *Sewanee Review*, 25 (January, 1917),
14–15.

1. Anne Rebecca Kennedy, wife of John Selden, died on July 14, 1854. For other
details about her illness and death, see WI to Mary Kennedy, February 21, 1854;
and to John P. Kennedy, August 31, 1854.
2. Elizabeth Gray, daughter of Anne and John Selden.

2356. *To Sarah Storrow*

Sunnyside, Aug 7th. 1854

My dear Sarah,

Your letter[1] introducing Mr de Wolff reached me on Friday last; I was informed at the same time that he was in New York, intending to Embark for Europe on the following Wednesday. I was on the point of setting off with Pierre M Irving and Helen on a visit to Irving & Sarah Van Wart at Mr Ames in Orange County;[2] but I let them go without me and remained at home to See Mr de Wolff. He came up on Sunday with Miss Renshaw, Sister of Mrs de Wolff and her young brother. We all dined together at Mr Grinnels, after which they visited the cottage and saw all the girls. They returned to town by an evening train

We were all greatly pleased with Mr de Wolff. The excellence of his character we knew before, but we were not prepared to find him so very agreeable in manners. There is such an air of sincerity and truth about him; such quiet good sense and perfect benevolence. He is hastening back to France through anxiety ⟨on⟩ about Mrs deWolffs health, her recent letters having caused him uneasiness. I think it very probable he will bring her out to reside permanently in this country, probably in Baltimore; as the climate at Curraccos is unfavorable to her constitution.[3]

He speaks with great regard of you and your family and has given us very gratifying accounts of you all. I look forward with hopeful anticipation to his return to this country with Mrs de Wolff and should be indeed delighted if they could establish a Summer residence on the banks of the Hudson. He appeared to be very much pleased with what he saw of the river and the country which borders it; but he fears the severity of our winter's

I do not know where this letter will find you as I understand you left Paris some time in the course of last month to make a tour with Mr Storrow & the children in Switzerland and Germany and perhaps into Italy, so that it is uncertain when you will be back. I was pleased to learn from Mr Storrow his business arrangements, which relieve him from the risks and harrassments of a ⟨life⟩ Mercantile life, and give him leisure for rational and intellectual enjoyments. Your present tour is one of the first fruits of these arrangements and will be a source of present gratification and delightful remembrances.

Mr Storrow threw out some hints when here of the possibility of your all coming out here in the course of a year or two. I presume, however, only to pay a visit; though I should think it the country where you would wish to plant your family, and that, too, while your children are young enough to form those attachments and sympathies ⟨that⟩ which constitute the home feeling.

I see by the papers that one of Mr Corbens[4] daughters has made what I presume he thinks a brilliant match. I hope it may prove a happy one. I thought he would have inclined more toward an English connexion. The young ladies heart I presume decided the matter.

You will have heard no doubt of the death of poor William Irving[5] son of your Uncle E. I. It was quite sudden, from an over dose of morphine, taken to quiet his nerves during a slight indisposition. He had an excellent situation in one of the offices of the department of State, was pleased with his situation and had given great satisfaction by the manner in which he discharged the duties of it. His death was quite a shock to his family especially to his father who had begun to entertain hopes that William was at length in a prosperous Career. He has left a good name behind him in Washington and is spoken of in high terms by the papers there.

Farewell my dear Sarah. Wherever this letter may find you; may it find you and yours happy. Give my love to the young princesses who are becoming quite travelled ladies. With kind remembrances to Mr Storrow

Your affectionate Uncle
Washington Irving

MANUSCRIPT: Yale.

1. This letter has not been located.
2. Barrett Ames, the father of Sarah Ames Van Wart and a longtime friend of WI's, had a residence at Craigville in Orange County, New Jersey. See WI to Charles A. Davis, August 2, 1859.
3. Both de Wolffs died in May or June of 1855. See WI to Sarah Storrow, June 24, 1855.
4. Probably Francis P. Corbin (1801–1876) of Virginia, a cosmopolite educated in England and France. He had known Sarah Storrow in Paris as early as 1843. See WI to Sarah Storrow, May 25, 1843.
5. William Irving (b. 1811) had died on July 28, 1854. He had worked in the census office in Washington. See WI to John P. Kennedy, March 7, 1853.

2357.   *To Joseph Henry*

Sunnyside August 26, 1854

From a perusal of the accompanying letter,[1] drawn up as I understand by Buckingham Smith, Esqr.[2] late Secretary of Legation in Mexico, I am induced to believe that the documents therein specified[3] are well worthy of publication, both in their original language⟨s⟩, and in translation, by the Smithsonian Institution

Washington Irving

MANUSCRIPT: Huntington.

The attribution to Joseph Henry was made by the Huntington Library.

Joseph Henry (1797–1871), who experimented and published extensively in the fields of electricity and magnetic physics, was the first director and secretary of the Smithsonian Institution.

1. This letter has not been located.

2. Buckingham Smith (1810–1871), a lawyer and antiquarian, was secretary of the American legation in Mexico from 1850 to 1853. He was the author of *The Narrative of Alvar Nuñez Cabeça de Vaca* (1851) and *Narratives of the Career of Hernando de Soto in the Conquest of Florida* (1866).

3. Probably these include *Letter of Hernando de Soto and Memoir of Hernando de Escalante*, which appeared later in 1854 with Smith as editor.

2358. To Elizabeth Kennedy

August 31, 1854

* * * * *

You ask me whether the homeopathics still keep me quite well.[1] I really begin to have great faith in them. The complaint of the head especially, which troubled me last year, and obliged me to throw by my pen, has been completely vanquished by them, so that I have fagged with it as closely as ever. * * *

My nephew, P. M. I., is about to build a cottage in my immediate vicinity, I having given him a site for the purpose—one of my fields, which lies on the south side of the lane leading down to my dwelling.[2]

PUBLISHED: PMI, IV, 179.

1. WI, who had consulted a homeopathic physician, Dr. John Peters, for several years, had advised John P. Kennedy to see a homeopath. See WI to Mrs Kennedy, February 21, 1854.

2. This building project was apparently never undertaken. It is not mentioned by WI later, and in 1859 during WI's illness PMI commuted from Manhattan to attend his uncle.

2359. To John P. Kennedy

Sunnyside Aug 31t 1854

My dear Kennedy,

Wherever this letter finds you, whether in your Tower on the banks of the Patapsco, at your brothers in the Shenandoah Valley, or with that rare old Cavalier your uncle Pendleton, in his favorite resort the cool hollow of Berkeley Springs,[1] may it find you in the enjoyment of good health and good spirits—And yet there has been evil enough to cast a gloom of Sadness over all your domestic circle. Before I recieved the letters from yourself and Mrs Kennedy[2] I had been apprised of the death of your favorite niece Mrs Selden, by a news paper forwarded to me by her father, in which it was noticed. I was not aware, however, of the circumstance connected with her death; that it took place but a few days after giving birth to a son. This renders the event so much the more affecting. I can easily concieve how deeply afflicting it must have been to you all; for in the brief time that I had the happiness of knowing her, I saw enough of the loveliness of her character to make me sensible how well she merited the affection with which every one seemed to regard her

I am concerned to learn that Mr Grays health has been feeble of late and that he has had days of suffering and "nights of prolonged nervous distress" Your account of his firm presentiment that he was to close his earthly career on his birthday, the 16t. of last July; of his business arrangements for the event and the calm serenity with which he awaited it, is really touching and beautiful It only proved how truly worthy he is of length of days, for none is so fitted to live as he who is well prepared to die. God send him many more years, with a body as free from pain as his mind is from evil or his heart from unkindness; he has every thing that "should accompany old age,

"As honor, love, obedience troops of friends"[3]

and he is an instance how loveable old age may render itself.

I lately made a days excursion up the Hudson in company with Mr & Mrs Moses Grinnell and two or three others to visit Willis in his poetical retreat of Idle Wild.[4] It is really a beautiful place. The site well chosen, commanding noble and romantic Scenery; the house commodious and picturesque and furnished with much taste. In a word it is just such a retreat as a poet would desire. I never saw Willis to such advantage as on this occasion. He was natural, easy unaffected and gentlemanlike. I was also very much pleased with his wife;[5] of whom you and Mrs Kennedy have so often spoken well but ↑with↓ whom I had never been much acquainted[.] Willis talks and writes much about his ill health, and is really troubled with an ugly cough, but I do not think his lungs are seriously affected and I think it likely he will be like a cracked pitcher which lasts the longer for having a flaw in it; being so much the more taken care of.

I was glad to find Mr and Mrs Joseph Grinnell[6] on a visit there; as I had repeatedly counselled the former to build this house for Willis, and found him now quite proud of the place as if it had all been a creation of his own taste and fancy. I can see that Willis makes it a very enjoyable resort for him; and does it with sincere good will.

Poor Willis! Had he only started in life in the easy gentlemanlike circumstances in which he finds himself at present, what a different life it would have been with him.[7] However, I hope and trust, he [has][8] a pleasant portion of life yet before him to cultivate to advantage in Idle Wild.

By the way Mr Joseph Grinnell spoke of having seen you at Baltimore after your return from your gastronomical ⟨tour⟩ and oratorical tour with Mr Fillmore and he seemed very much haunted by the reccollection of some jocose ⟨story⟩ ↑account↓ you ⟨tol⟩ gave of various deputations of "White Waistcoats" from divers communities to welcome the Ex President and yourself But though the reccollection of the joke seemed still to shake his diaphragm, he could not do any justice to it. So I shall put you in mind of it when next we meet; that I may have a companion picture to ⟨your⟩ those of your interviews with Kossuth[9] and with Fredericka Bremer;[10] the reccollections of which I always summon up as sure pills to cure melancholy.

I have been passing the summer entirely at home; determined not to travel any more in hot weather. I have had no return of the chills ⟨th⟩ and fever that paid me a slight visit early in June; and am now in fair health for such a green old gentleman. I wish I had Douce Davie[11] here to mount occasionally for Gentleman Dick[12] is in such disgrace that my Women Kind will not hear to my mounting him any more. The last time I did so he took a start from ↑hearing↓ a young horse in a pasture gallopping along inside of the fence, and fancying it to be a challenge to a race, set off *ventre a terre*[13] and gave me a run of nearly three miles before I could bring him to a stop. Fortunately I had a fair road, every body and every thing turned aside and ⟨gave me⟩ made way for me; and Dick shewed such speed and bottom that I am thinking of entering him for the cup at the next races.

God bless you My Dear Kennedy

Yours very faithfully
Washington Irving

John P Kennedy Esqr

DOCKETED: 1854 / Washington Irving / ansd. / Sept 19
MANUSCRIPT: Peabody Library. PUBLISHED: PMI, IV, 174–76 (in part); and Tuckerman, *Life of J. P. Kennedy*, p. 381 (in part).

1. WI is repeating Kennedy's possible whereabouts as the latter had given them to him in a letter of August 8, 1854 (quoted in Tuckerman, *Life of J. P. Kennedy*, pp. 387–88). The tower on the Patapsco refers to Kennedy's country house (actually Edward Gray's) about eight miles west of Baltimore and one mile below

Ellicott's Mills on the Patapsco River. Andrew Kennedy's estate, Cassilis, was located in western Virginia, and Philip Clayton Pendleton lived near the warm spring at Berkeley Springs, northwest of Martinsburg.

2. WI had received a letter dated August 8, 1854, from Kennedy. See Tuckerman, *Life of J. P. Kennedy*, pp. 384–88.

3. See *Macbeth*, V, iii, 22.

4. Nathaniel P. Willis (1806–1867) was a poet and journalist who founded the *American Monthly Magazine* in 1829. Later he was the foreign correspondent on social affairs for the *New-York Mirror* (1832–1836) and published *Pencillings by the Way* (1835) and *Loiterings of Travel* (1840) from his reports. In 1853 he established a country residence on the plateau of the Highlands of the Hudson beyond West Point.

5. Cornelia Grinnell, Willis's second wife, whom he had married in 1846.

6. Joseph Grinnell (1788–1885) and his wife, the former Sarah Russell (d. 1862), had adopted their niece Cornelia.

7. Despite his popularity, Willis had suffered financial reversals from bad investments and the failure of his publisher.

8. WI omitted the bracketed word.

9. Louis (Lajos) Kossuth, the Hungarian revolutionary and patriot, had visited the United States in 1851–1852. See WI to _____, December 15, 1851; and to Sarah Storrow, January 13, 1852.

10. For other details about Miss Bremer, see WI to Robert C. Winthrop, April 23, 1854.

11. Mrs. Kennedy's gentle saddle horse. See WI to Mrs. Kennedy, February 21, 1854; and to Catharine Irving, June 19, 1853.

12. WI's unruly saddle horse which was finally sold. See PMI, IV, 176; and WI to John P. Kennedy, April 23, 1855.

13. "At full speed."

2360.   To Mary E. Kennedy

Sunnyside Sept 1st. 1854

My dear Miss Kennedy,

I have just recieved your most interesting and affecting letter of Aug 18th.[1] which has filled both my heart and my eyes. I wrote to you some short time since on recieving from your father a newspaper containing a notice of your sisters death; but it was not until I recieved a letter from your aunt (Mrs J P Kennedy) that I knew the touching circumstance attending her death; that it was shortly after having given birth to a son.

I can easily concieve the deep affliction you must all experience in the loss of so pure, loving and happy a member of the domestic circle; but, with you, affliction must be soothed and sanctified by a reccollection of the sweet intercourse which you say took place between you for several weeks previous to her illness, during which she expressed the firmest conviction that she had not long to live. It has been beautifully said that the love of sisters for each other is like the love of angels;—but how truely so when one is about to put on her angelic nature. In that intercourse she left her robe of light with you as the way ascending to immortality.

I regret that you have not the care of dear little Lizzie as I know her to be your darling and I feel a peculiar interest in her; but I have no doubt a mothers judgement in the matter was for the best, and that it was more important that Mary,[2] who is of an age when the character is taking its bias, should be under your guardian eye. She, of course, being older was not such a pet with me as Lizzie; but she appeared to be a child of a fine, frank nature, and coming from such stock on both sides, she cannot but be good.

And now, as to yourself, my dear Miss Kennedy. It is with the sincerest pleasure that I hear of the intended change in your condition. I had some vague idea that such might be the result of the intimacy I saw growing up between the Doctor[3] and yourself during my last visit. In fact I could not concieve how a young gentleman of his apparent decernment and susceptibility could have such a daily opportunity of becoming acquainted with your merit, without loving you. I trust my dear Miss Kennedy it will be a happy union. I was much pleased with all that I saw of the Doctor. You have the advantage of knowing each other well and of having those numerous and mutual sympathies which result from growing up together in the same domestic and social circle. Tell the Doctor that he has drawn a prize and that I wish him joy of it.

Give my affectionate remembrances to your father and mother, your sister and Mr Selden who has my sincere condolences.

With love to my dear little Lizzie

Your affectionate friend
Washington Irving

PUBLISHED: *American Literature*, 6 (March, 1934), 63–64.

1. This letter and the one from Mrs. Kennedy mentioned in the next sentence have not been located.

2. The oldest child of the Seldens.

3. Henry Pendleton Cooke, whom Mary Kennedy married on January 1, 1855. See WI to Catharine Irving, January 1, 1855.

2361.   *To Bayard Taylor*

Sunnyside, September 12, 1854

My dear Bayard Taylor,

I am quite grieved that I was from home when you visited Sunnyside last Saturday, and that you did not make yourself at home notwithstanding my absence. Why did you not take command of my little library, such as it is, or while away the sultry day under the trees? My womenkind would have been happy to give you the best entertainment the house afforded. One of my nieces hastened down-stairs to welcome you and was extremely disappointed at finding you had gone. I trust you will act better on any future occasion, and will feel assured that whoever is in the house will be happy to receive you, and should nobody be at home, that the house itself is at your service.

I feel very much obliged to you for the volume[1] you were so kind as to leave, and promise myself great pleasure in once more accompanying you in your African travels.

Yours very cordially and sincerely,
Washington Irving

PUBLISHED: *Life and Letters of Bayard Taylor,* ed. Marie Hansen-Taylor and Horace E. Scudder (Boston, 1884), I, 282.

Bayard Taylor (1825–1878) was a journalist and world traveler who served as secretary of the United States legation in Russia in 1862 and 1863 and as United States minister to Germany in 1878.

1. Probably *A Journey to Central Africa, or Life and Landscapes from Egypt to the Negro Kingdoms of the White Nile,* which had been published a few weeks earlier.

2362.   *To Lewis G. Clark*

Sunnyside, Sept. 18th, 1854.

My dear Clark:

Bayard Taylor dines with me on Wednesday: come over and join us,[1] and we will have a rummage for that "little, thin, very witty and amusing Spanish duodecimo tome with a brown leather cover," of which you speak;[2] though I doubt whether there can be such a very peculiar tome in existence.

Yours very truly,
Washington Irving

L. Gaylord Clark, Esq.

P. S.: If we find this curious work, had we not better send it to Barnum's Museum?[3]

Published: *Knickerbocker Magazine,* 55 (February, 1860), 233.

1. Because of an engagement in New York, Clark was unable to accept WI's invitation. See *Knickerbocker Magazine,* 55 (February, 1860), 233. Taylor reported his reaction to the dinner in a letter to Mary Russell Mitford, September 20, 1854: "I have just returned from Tarrytown, where I spent the afternoon with Washington Irving, who is a charming old man and a good friend of mine." See *Life and Letters of Bayard Taylor,* I, 287.

2. Clark had apparently been asked to present WI with a book and had done so before this time. In 1860 he could not recall who had asked him to do so: "Was it 'J. W. B.,' now in Washington?" See *Knickerbocker Magazine,* 55 (February, 1860), 233.

3. P. T. Barnum (1810–1891), who had promoted Jenny Lind's concert tour in 1850, was the proprietor of a museum at Broadway and Ann Street. See Wilson, *NY, Old and New,* I, 332–33.

2363. To Bayard Taylor

Sunnyside Oct 1st. 1854

My dear Bayard Taylor

Accept my sincere thanks for your offer of the dedication of your forthcoming volume of travels.[1] You have won my good opinion and good will so thoroughly by ⟨what I hav⟩ your writings and by what I have seen and known of you personally, that it will give me both pride and pleasure to recieve such a public testimonial of the friendship which exists between ⟨y⟩ us.

Yours very truly
Washington Irving

Bayard Taylor Esq.

Manuscript: Yale.

1. *The Land of the Saracens; or, Pictures of Palestine, Asia Minor, Sicily, and Spain,* which was published by G. P. Putnam later in October, contained the following dedication:

TO
WASHINGTON IRVING.

This book—the chronicle of my travels through lands once occupied by the Saracens—naturally dedicates itself to you, who, more than any other American author, have revived the traditions, restored the history, and illustrated the character of that brilliant and heroic people. Your cordial encouragement confirmed me in my design of visiting the East, and making myself familiar with Oriental life; and though I bring you now but imperfect returns, I can at least unite with you in admiration of a field as rich in romantic interest, and indulge the hope that I may one day pluck from it fruit instead of blossoms. In Spain, I came upon your track, and I should hesitate to exhibit my own gleanings where you have harvested, were it not for the belief that the rapid sketches I have given will but enhance, by the contrast, the charm of your finished picture.

BAYARD TAYLOR

2364.   To John P. Kennedy

Sunnyside Octr 5. 1854

My dear Kennedy,

Your letter has remained too long unanswered;[1] but I find it impossible to be regular and prompt in correspondence, though with the best intentions and constant efforts to that effect. I console with you sincerely on the loss of your mother,[2] for, from my own experience, it is one of the losses which sink deepest in the heart. It is upwards of thirty years since I lost mine,[3] then at an advanced age, yet I dream of her to this day and wake up with tears on my cheeks. I think the advanced age at which she died endears her memory to me and gives more tenderness and Sadness to the reccollection of her. Yet, after all a calm and painless death, closing a long and well spent life, is not a thing in itself to be lamented. And from your own account your mothers life was happy to the end, ⟨y⟩ for she was as you say "well conditioned in mind and body" and one of her last employments was to perform for her grand children on the piano.[4] I regret that I have not known her. I met with some of her music books at your brother Anthonys and Mary Kennedy used to play some of the airs she had learnt of her; the airs that were popular in my young days and were, therefore, full of delightful associations. What a blessing it is to have this feeling for music which attended your mother to the last. It is indeed a sweetner of life and a fountain of youth for old age to bathe in and refresh itself.

The intelligence of Mary Kennedys engagement I had already learnt from herself in a very sweet and sad letter[5] which she wrote not long after her sisters death. I trust it will be a happy match. I was much pleased with what I saw of her intended during our visit at Andrews. Dear Mary! she is a noble girl and deserves a fine fellow for a husband. The more I have seen of Mary the more I have seen to prize and admire in her. I am heartily glad she is to be married to a man of her choice and one with whom her family are well pleased.

In regard to Putnams failure I am not sufficient of a man of business to give you the kind of information you require. He had a meeting of his creditors; laid a statement of his affairs before them shewed that his assets exceeded considerably his liabilities but that he required time. This has been given very liberally for there appears to have been a very good feeling towards him, and an idea that with time and prudence he would work his way through. My nephew Pierre M Irving looked into the matter on my part; and found it much better than he had expected. The payments of some notes which would be falling due about this time, will take place later, but he thinks ⟨will⟩ may be relied on. In a word, I am continuing on with Putnam, and intend, as soon ⟨,⟩ as possible, to put forth another volume of my revised works;[6] consisting of miscellaneous writings that have appeared in various periodicals.

Your letter mentioned that Mr Gray was better than he had been when you parted with him to go on your visit into Virginia[.] I hope he continues well and that he has his good fairy dear little Loo Andrews[7] to enliven him with her music

Give my most affectionate remembrances to him, your wife and Miss Gray and believe me

Dear Kennedy / Yours heartily
Washington Irving

John P Kennedy Esqr.

MANUSCRIPT: Peabody Library.   PUBLISHED: PMI, IV, 179–80 (in part).

1. This letter has not been located.

2. Nancy Clayton Pendleton Kennedy (b. 1777) died at Martinsburg, Virginia in September, 1854, the victim of a cholera epidemic.

3. Sarah Sanders Irving, who was born on April 14, 1738, died on April 9, 1817, while WI was in Europe.

4. Since John P. Kennedy had no children, these were the offspring of Anthony and Andrew Kennedy.

5. Of August 18. See WI to Mary Kennedy, September 1, 1854.

6. WI is referring to *Wolfert's Roost*, which Putnam published in early February, 1855. Most of the items had appeared in *Knickerbocker Magazine*. See Langfeld & Blackburn, *WI Bibliography*, p. 44; PMI, IV, 185–89.

7. Louisa Andrews, a friend of the Grays and Kennedys whom WI had met on his visits with them. See WI to Mrs. Kennedy, February 21, 1854.

2365. To Edward Everett

Sunnyside. Octr. 18th 1854

My dear Mr Everett.

This will be handed to you by Mr Douglas Leffingwell who desires to obtain your countenance to a Literary Union or Association, the nature and object of which he will explain. As it appears to me likely to be of great public utility I have consented to let my name appear among those reccommending it to public attention

Yours very faithfully
Washington Irving

Hon Edward Everett / &c. &c &c

MANUSCRIPT: MHS.

2366.   To George H. Moore

Sunnyside Octr. 26th. 1854

Dear Sir

I must apologize for not acknowledging at an earlier date the note[1] you have forwarded to me from the Committee of the New York Historical Society, relating to their anniversary festival.[2]

I beg you to inform the Committee that I shall not fail to do myself the honor of being present on that very interesting occasion.[3]

Very respectfully / Dear Sir / Your Obedient Servt
Washington Irving

Geo. H. Moore Esqr / Secretary &c ———

DOCKETED: Recd. Oct. 30.
MANUSCRIPT: NYHS.

George H. Moore (1823–1892) was undersecretary of the New-York Historical Society from 1848 to 1891. In 1876 he was made superintendent and trustee of the Lenox Library in New York.

1. This note has not been located.
2. The New-York Historical Society celebrated its fiftieth anniversary on November 20, 1854, with an oration by George Bancroft at Niblo's Theater at 3:00 P.M. followed by a dinner at the Astor House at 6:00 P.M. Four hundred invitations were issued. See NYEP, November 20, 21, 1854.
3. Although WI heard Bancroft's speech, he did not attend the dinner. See WI to John P. Kennedy, November 22, 1854.

2367.   *To George Bancroft*

Sunnyside Oct 27t. 1854

My dear Bancroft

It will give me great pleasure to dine with you on Tuesday next.

I have just finished the reading of your last volume,[1] which has given me the most thorough satisfaction. I cannot enough admire the manner in which you have wrought your multifarious materials into your page. So so[2] clear, so graphic and at times so dramatic, yet so vigorous and concise. I never read any historical work wherein I was made more sensible that every step I took was on firm ground; for every fact rests on documentary proof, and the motives and views of every personage ⟨is⟩ are cited from their own speeches or writings.

New England and Boston in particular will owe a vast debt of gratitude to you for your glorious exposition and illustration of the rise and progress of the revolution in that quarter. Your work will be a greater glorification of Boston than ↑even↓ the Bunker Hill monument.

Yours my dear Bancroft / very truly
Washington Irving

DOCKETED: Washington Irving / Octr. 27th / 54
MANUSCRIPT: Cornell University Library.

1. Volume 6 of Bancroft's *History of the United States from the Discovery of the American Continent,* subtitled *The Crisis,* concluded his treatment of the Revolutionary War. See M. A. DeWolfe Howe, *The Life and Letters of George Bancroft* (New York, 1908), II, 102.

2. WI repeated "so" when he turned to write on a new sheet.

2368.   *To Francis P. Corbin?*

[November 3, 1854]

My dear Sir,

I have to thank you of the loan of the books and manuscripts; and likewise to make my acknowledgements to Mrs Corben for the admissions to your opera box;[1] of which my niece and myself will be happy to avail ourselves

Very faithfully yours
Washington Irving

Friday, Nov. 3d. [1854]

MANUSCRIPT: Va.–Barrett.

It is possible that WI is writing to Francis P. Corbin, to whom he had referred in his letter of August 7, 1854, to Sarah Storrow.

1. Probably WI used the tickets to see performances of *Semiramide* and *The Barber of Seville.* See WI to John P. Kennedy, November 22, 1854.

2369. To Frank W. Ballard

Sunnyside, Nov 14th. 1854

To Frank W. Ballard, Esqr

My dear Sir

I cannot but feel deeply and gratefully sensible of the honor done me by the Mercantile Library Association in soliciting a marble bust of me to be placed in their new establishment[1]

I am well aware of the talents of Mr Randolph Rogers[2] as a sculptor and should most willingly stand to him for a bust, but I have some time since come to a fixed determination to stand or sit for no more likenesses either in painting or sculpture, and have declined repeated and urgent solicitations on the subject. The last one I declined was from Mr William B. Astor, who wished it for the Astor Library.[3] I offered him however the use of a model of a bust executed some years since by Mr Ball Hughes[4] and which ↑at the time↓ was considered by my friends an excellent likeness. ⟨From⟩ ↑Of↓ this Mr Astor had a copy made ⟨wh⟩ (by I think Mr Brown of Brooklyn)[5] which is now in the Astor Library. Should the Mercantile Library Association be disposed to have a similar copy made, the model by Mr Ball Hughes which is in the possession of one of my relatives is at their disposition

In concluding I would observe that viewing the nature and circumstances of your institution and its identification with the dearest interest and sympathies of my native city I do not know any one from which an application of the kind you make would be more intensely gratifying.

Accept my dear Sir, my thanks for the kind expressions of your letter and believe me very respectfully

Your obliged & hbl Servt
Washington Irving

MANUSCRIPT: New York Mercantile Library. PUBLISHED: *Irvingiana,* pp. lxi–lxii.

Frank Wade Ballard (1827–1887) was a resident of New York and a director of the Mercantile Library Association. See Louis E. DeForest, *Ballard and Allied Families* (New York, 1924), p. 19.

1. Ballard's letter of November 2, 1854, to WI is printed in *Irvingiana*, p. xli.

2. Randolph Rogers (1825–1892), an American artist who studied in Italy from 1848 to 1853, received a commission to execute the bronze doors of the Capitol in Washington. In 1855 he returned to Italy and remained there the rest of his life. See George C. Groce and David H. Wallace, *The New-York Historical Society's Dictionary of Artists in America, 1564–1860*, p. 545.

3. WI's refusal occurred after January, 1851, when he had sat for Charles Martin. See PMI, IV, 83.

4. Robert Ball Hughes (1806–1868) sculptured a bust of WI in 1836 which was widely reproduced. See STW, II, 50.

5. Probably Henry Kirke Brown (1814–1886), who studied in Italy from 1842 to 1846. In 1850 he established a Brooklyn studio in which he produced statues of William C. Bryant and George Washington.

2370. To Henry Hallam

New York Nov 17th. 1854

My dear Sir,

I take the liberty of presenting to you Colonel Wade Hampton[1] a gentleman of talents and worth of Virginia and member of the Legislature of that state. Any attention you may find it convenient to bestow upon him will be considered an especial favor by

Yours my dear Sir, / very faithfully
Washington Irving

Henry Hallam E[s]qr / &c &c &c

MANUSCRIPT: South Caroliniana Library, University of South Carolina.

1. Wade Hampton (1818–1902) was a conservative Southern planter who distinguished himself as a Confederate cavalry officer in the Civil War. During the Reconstruction he worked for the establishment of white supremacy in South Carolina. WI erred in calling him a Virginian.

2371. To William C. Preston

New York Nov 17t. 1854

My dear Mr Preston

Your letter was delayed a few days in the hands of Mr Putnam or you would have received an earlier answer.[1]

It is now upwards of twenty two years since I mingled much in English society and almost all my old intimacies have died out so that it is not in my power to furnish many letters of introduction. I send three—one to Sir Robert Harry Inglis; long the ⟨Represent⟩ Member of Parliament for Oxford, a staunch tory and churchman, but one of the warmest hearted, noble spirited men I have ever known Another is to Henry Hallam author of a work on the Middle ages which must be known to you—The third is to John Murray, the son of my old publisher (now deceased) who keeps up the old establishment in Albemarle Street and is in constant communication with the literary men of the day

I am grieved to have such a melancholy account of the state of your health and your domestic bereavements. I dined lately, in company with your brother[2] at Mr Bancrofts. As he entered the room I at first almost thought it yourself, he looks so much like you as you was when I last saw you.

My own health at present is excellent ⟨though⟩ and I continue active as ever though I have passed the allotted term of life and am now living by special favor.

Ever my dear Mr Preston / Your attached friend
Washington Irving

William C Preston Esqr

MANUSCRIPT: South Caroliniana Library, University of South Carolina.

1. This letter has not been located.
2. John S. Preston (1809–1881), who was a South Carolina planter, lawyer, and legislator.

2372.   To John P. Kennedy

Sunnyside Novr. 22d. 1854.

My dear Kennedy,

Your last letter[1] was in cheerful contrast to those which preceded it. I had heard, in a circuitous way, of Mrs Kennedys illness and was about to write to you on the subject when I recieved from you the intelligence that she had routed the enemy, was "gathering strength with her accustomed energy of action;" walked, rode and ate with a determination to be as well as ever; and that you hope she would even be better than ever. I rejoice in your bulletin; and trust that she and her allies, the doctor and quinine, will be more prompt and complete in their triumph than the allied powers in the Crimea with whom you have compared them.

I am glad to find also that Mr Gray continues to falsify his predictions, and to grow fat and hearty in spite of himself. I trust nature will continue to make him a false prophet,[2] in this respect; she is very apt to surprise

Valetudinarians with a latent fund of longevity of which they had no conception.

I think if he were to take a jaunt to New York and hear Grisi[3] and Mario through their principal characters it would be like a dip in the fountain of youth to him. I have had some delicious treats since their arrival in New York[.] I think Grisi's singing and acting would be just to Mr Grays taste. There is a freshness and beauty about her, in voice and person that seem to bid defiance to time. I wish Mr Gray could see her in Semiramide, and in Rosina (Barber of Seville)[4] which exhibit her powers in the Grand and the Comic. I had always seen her in the former and considered her a magnificent being; it was only lately on my last visit to town that I saw her in comedy; when she played Rosina, twice, and surprised me by the truthfulness with which she could assume the girl; and the unforced whim and humor with which she could illustrate all her caprices. But to percieve her thorough excellence in this part one must be able to discern every play of her countenance and especially of her eye. Her acting, like all great achievements of art, is worthy of especial examination. It is a perfect study. Like all great achievements of art, it is delightful from its simplicity.

The Semiramide and the Barber of Seville, as now performed in New York, are worthy of a winters journey from Baltimore.

Just before I left town there was a Semicentennial Anniversary of the New York Historical Society.[5] Indeed I staid in town to be present at it; but when the time arrived my incorrigible propensity to flinch from all public ceremonials and festivals came over me. I mingled in the crowd and heard Bancrofts Erudite address from the 'Auditorium,' but kept clear of the banquet, which took place afterwards. Among the dignitaries and invited guests on the stage I saw our friend Winthrop; who, ⟨of⟩ ↑I↓ find by the papers made an eloquent speech at the banquet.[6] This I regret not to have heard. I have never heard him speak in public but have heard much of his talent for public speaking; and I think from what I have seen of him he would be apt to acquit himself well and gracefully.

I hope to hear good accounts of your visit to Virginia and that you found all well at your brother Andrews and that they are regaining their usual cheerfulness

With affectionate remembrances to Mr & Miss Gray and your (much) better half,

> Yours my dear Kennedy very truly
> Washington Irving

John P Kennedy Esq

MANUSCRIPT: Peabody Library.   PUBLISHED: PMI, IV, 180–82 (in part).

1. This letter has not been located.

2. Gray, who suffered from asthma, had been speculating about his own death. On August 8, 1854, Kennedy had written to WI that Gray had been "musing fancies of death." See Tuckerman, *Life of J. P. Kennedy,* pp. 347–48. For Gray's death, see WI to Kennedy, March 22, 1856.

3. WI had heard Giulia Grisi in Paris on October 12, 1843, and perhaps on other occasions as well. See WI to PMI, October 13, 1843. Probably he had heard Giuseppe Mario (1810–1883) at the same time.

4. Rossini's *Semiramide* was performed at the New York Academy of Music on October 30, November 1, 3, and 6; and Rossini's *Il Barbiere di Siviglia* with Grisi as Rosina and Mario as Count Almaviva was offered on November 17 and 20. See NYEP, October 30–November 22, 1854. It has not been determined which performance of *Semiramide* WI saw, but he saw both of the performances of *The Barber of Seville* which were given before he wrote to Kennedy.

5. The meeting and dinner took place on November 20. For the text of Bancroft's speech and a report on the dinner, see NYEP, November 21, 1854.

6. Robert C. Winthrop, president of the Massachusetts Historical Society, replied to the ninth toast in honor of sister historical societies with "a very long but otherwise excellent speech. It was like all speeches of the day, too much a glorification of every thing and every body American for our taste but of its kind it was very good." The news story included several long quotations from it. See NYEP, November 21, 1854.

2373.   To Henry H. Brigham, Henry Clark, and J. D. Miller

Sunnyside, Novr. 23d. 1854

Messrs. Henry H Brigham ⎫
       Henry Clark   ⎬
      & J. D. Miller   ⎭
      Committee &c

Gentlemen,

I feel highly sensible of the honor done me by the 'Young Mens Literary Society' in inviting me to deliver an address, but regret to say that a Diffidence of my talent for public speaking or lecturing has obliged me to decline every invitation of the kind.

I remain Gentlemen

very respectfully / Your obliged & hbl Servt
Washington Irving[1]

MANUSCRIPT: Historical Museum of the Darwin R. Barker Library, Fredonia, New York.

Henry H. Brigham was vice-president and Henry Clark, president of the Young

Men's Association of Fredonia Academy in 1854. See *Annual Catalogue of Fredonia Academy* (1854) and letter of Miss Louise F. Belden, September 29, 1976.

1. The signature has been clipped off; WI's name is written in another hand.

2374. To Evert A. Duyckinck

Sunnyside Nov. 23d. 1854

My dear Sir,

I have been prevented by various occupations and engagements from giving an earl[i]er reply to your letter of Oct. 20th. I now enclose a note of my intimacy with Allston.[1] Should it be too long for your purpose I will thank you to return it to me, as I should not like to have it abridged or mutilated.

Yours very truly
Washington Irving

Evert A Duyckinck Esqr.

P. S. Should you insert my article I should like to have a proof—⟨of it⟩

MANUSCRIPT: NYPL–Duyckinck Papers.

1. WI wrote a personal reminiscence of Washington Allston (1779–1843) for Duyckinck's *Cyclopaedia of American Literature* (New York, 1855), II, 14–16.

2375. To Sarah Storrow

Sunnyside Nov 23d. 1854

My dear Sarah

Your last letter[1] has taken me over many scenes of former travel and brought up delightful reccollections. Switzerland, the Rhine and the Southern parts of Germany bordering on the Tyrol, with the quaint old towns and cities Baden Baden, Stratsburg, Ulm, Augsburg, Salzburg, &c &c Did you when at Baden Baden, visit those awful chambers or dungeons under the old castle; one of the Seats of the Vehm Gericht or Secret Tribunal; that mysterious and tremendous association that once held such sway over Germany?[2] I do not know whether they are generally shewn to strangers; but having read a great deal on the subject of that secret institution I sought them out, and visited them with thrilling interest. You say you found my name written in the visitors books at Augsburg *thirty two* years since. Had there been a visitors book at Zurich of sufficiently

ancient date you might have met my name written there *forty nine* years
since, as I made a visit to it in 1805 in the course of my first European
tour and well do I reccollect how much I was charmed with it and how
willingly I would have lingered there.

You do not say whether when at Salzburg you visited the famous Salt
mine[3] and made a Subterranean excursion. I presume you did not, as you
would have found it rather *'awesome'* as the ↑Scotch↓ say; though I was
very much interested by it. Salzburg and its vicinity struck me as a very
region for legendary romance. I presume you reccollect the Untersberg
or Wunderberg a few miles from Salzburg, within which according to
popular tale the Emperor Charles sits in state with golden crown on his
head and sceptre in his hand.[4] In the interior of the same mountain are
palaces and churches and Convents and gardens; and untold treasures
guarded by dwarfs, who sometimes wander at midnight into ⟨the⟩ Salzburg, to say their prayers in the Cathedral. No doubt Kate[5] has come
across all this in the course of her German studies and was able to put you
on the track of these wonders. Before the breaking out of any war the
Emperor Charles issues out of the mountain with all his army and marches
round it with great blast and bray of trumpet, and then returns into his
subterranean palace. I wish you could have seen a procession of this kind.
It would has[6] surpassed all the state of the mongrel Emperors and Em-
peresses in whom you delight.

I agree with you that posting is the perfection of travelling. During
the year which I passed in Germany I posted up the Rhine (making lateral
excursions through the Taunus Mountains and along the Berg strasse)
through the Black forest, to Ulm⟨s⟩ to Augsburg, Munich, Salzburg,
Vienna—then through Bohemia to Dresden where I passed a winter. Then
through beautiful Silesia, across the Giant Mountains back into Bohemia,
where I made a months sojourn at Prague ↑my second visit to that romantic capital↓—Then back to Dresden ⟨wen⟩ whence I posted to Leipsick,
across the Hartz Mountain (that region of Hobgoblins) to Cassel and
along the lower Rhine to Holland.[7] It was a year crowded with incident
and full of historical, legendary and poetical associations. ⟨At a⟩ All
which I am sorry to say have very much faded away from my treacherous
memory. I shall look to having part of them revived when Kate publishes
the journal of her travels, which I understand she has kept with great
industry and exactness.

We are enjoying great treats just now in New York in the performances
of Grisi and Mario at the Splendid new Opera house. I was affraid I
should find Grisi much changed for the worse by the lapse of years but
was agreeably disappointed[.] I think I have been as much charmed by
her appearance and powers as ever I was at Paris, and have had opportunities of studying her performances much more closely. I have been

surprised too by her excellence in Comedy. I have seen her repeatedly in Rosina in the Barber of Seville, in which I had apprehended a failure; but which proved a delicious piece of comic acting. So full of whim and humor, yet so simple and true to nature. To appreciate her full merits in this part (and perhaps in any other) it is necesary to be near enough to see the play of her countenance and the expression of her eye. Her countenance while acting is a perfect study, and requires an opera glass.

Our opera troupe just now is an excellent one; the house magnificent, and we enjoy this species of amusement in perfection.

I hope you found your friend Mrs deWolff[8] in Paris on your return and that she is still with you. I have heard nothing of her return to America. If she is still there remember me to her most cordially. She is an amiable, gentle refined little being whom I hold in affectionate remembrance.

There was a Southern lady, A Mrs Davis from Natches, with whom I became acquainted at ⟨the⟩ ↑Saratoga↓ Springs and who had a little Kate a great pet of mine.[9] Mrs Davis with her husband and children set off last spring to make a brief tour in Europe and I gave her a letter to you hoping you might meet in the course of your travels. She returned recently without having seen you. I regret it, for ⟨sh⟩ I think you would have been as much charmed with her as I was; She ⟨was⟩ is about the Age of Mrs De Wolff; as delicate and lady like in person and as interesting in manners.

Give my love to the princesses, who, I understand are growing in grace as in years. You are devoting yourself to their education. Do not attempt to make remarkable women of them. Let them acquire those accomplishments which enliven and sweeten home but ⟨rather than⟩ do not seek to fit them to shine in fashionable society. Keep them as natural, simple and unpretending as possible. Cultivate in them noble and elevated sentiments and above all the feeling of *veneration*—so apt to be deadened, if not lost, in the gay, sensuous world by which they are surrounded. They live in the midst of *spectacle*, every thing around them is addressed to the senses; the society with which they mingle is all of a transient kind, travelling Americans; restless seekers after novelty and excitement. All this you must bear in mind and counteract as much as possible by nurturing home feelings and affections, habits of thought and quiet devotion and a reverence for grand and noble and solemn and sacred things.

Give my kindest remembrances to your husband and believe me my dear Sarah.

ever your affectionate Uncle
Washington Irving

Mrs Thomas W. Storrow

MANUSCRIPT: Yale.   PUBLISHED: PMI, IV, 182–84 (in part).

1. This letter has not been located.

2. For WI's travels in Switzerland in 1805 and in Germany in 1822, see *J&N*, I, 391–97; and *J&N*, III, 25–53; and WI to Elias Hicks, May 4, 1805; and to Thomas Moore, October 16, 1822.

3. For WI's visit to the salt mines of Hallein, see *J&N*, III, 46; and WI to Sarah Van Wart, October 27, 1822.

4. WI records the legend of Charles V in *J&N*, III, 51–52; and in WI to Susan Storrow, November 16, 1822.

5. Sarah Storrow's daughter.

6. WI probably intended to write "have."

7. See *J&N*, III, 3–205; and WI's letters written from July, 1822, to July, 1823.

8. For other details about the de Wolffs, see WI to Sarah Storrow, July 15, 1852 and August 7, 1854.

9. WI wrote a letter of introduction for Mrs. Davis to Sarah Storrow on June 22, 1854.

2376.   To James Lenox

Sunnyside Dec 4th. 1854

My dear Sir

I feel greatly obliged to you for a second volume of tracts relating to the early history of New York[1] which you have had the kindness to send me and which I find full of curious and interesting matter.

As you take an interest in these documents of old times I would observe that there must be some where extant a small volume of Dutch poems in manuscript[2] very neatly copied out, relating to personages and events in New Amsterdam in the early times of the settlement. Some of the poems are epithalamiums;[3] one of which was addressed to Dominie Egidius Luyck[4] rector of the Latin school upon his marriage with Judith Van Isendoorn.[5] Others were Grafschrefts (Epitaphs[)] on noted personages. One poem commemorates the conflagration of Dominie Luycks school house. The author of the poems was D. Selyn;[6] the earliest poet of the province

This volume was lent to me between forty and fifty years since by the late Dr Bruce.[7] He died during my long absence in Europe[.] I have made enquiries after it since my return but can hear nothing of it. It was too neatly bound and neatly written a volume to be wantonly destroyed and I am in hopes it is still existing, in the hands of some one or other of Dr Bruces connexions. Perhaps you may learn something concerning it in the course of your curious researches.

I am my dear Sir

Very respectfully / Your obliged
Washington Irving

James Lenox Esqr.

P S. I must apologize for not having sooner acknowledged the receipt of your volume—which in fact was detained several days in New York before it reached me

DOCKETED: Washington Irving / Verlorgh[?] — / ansd. 7. Decr.
MANUSCRIPT: NYPL—WI Papers.   PUBLISHED: *Anthology of New Netherlands,*
   ed. Henry C. Murray (New York, 1865; reprint ed., Port Washington, N.Y.,
   1969), pp. 14–15 (in part).

James Lenox (1800–1880), a lawyer who inherited a fortune from his father, was a book collector whose vast accumulation became the foundation of the Lenox Library, established in 1870 and merged into the New York Public Library in 1895.

1. This volume has not been identified. It may have been one of the collections edited by E. B. O'Callaghan.

2. This manuscript of more than two hundred birthday, marriage and congratulatory poems and epitaphs written in Dutch, Latin, and Greek was preserved by Mrs. Henry Pierrepont of Brooklyn, who made it available to Henry C. Murray. He transcribed and translated these and other poems relating to New Amsterdam and included them in his *Anthology of New Netherlands,* pp. 132–69.

3. Actually two of Selyns's poems celebrate the marriage of the couple: "Bruydts-lofs-Liedt" or "Nuptial Song," and "Bruydloft Toorts" or "Bridal Torch." See *Anthology of New Netherlands,* pp. 132–47, for the Dutch text and English translation on facing pages.

4. Aegidius Luyck was a teacher who instructed the sons of Governor Stuyvesant, and later he served as burgomaster in New Amsterdam. He returned to Holland after the English captured the Dutch province. See *Anthology of New Netherlands,* p. 171.

5. Murray discusses the scanty factual details about Judith Van Isendoorn in *Anthology of New Netherlands,* pp. 171–73.

6. Dominie Henricus Selyns (1636–1701), a Dutch clergyman who spent four years in Brooklyn (1662–1666), then returned to Holland, and emigrated to America again in 1682. He was the author of many poems in Dutch and a long Latin poem which prefaced Cotton Mather's *Magnalia Christi Americana.* See memoir of Selyns in *Anthology of New Netherlands* and James G. Wilson, *The Memorial History of the City of New York* (New York, 1893), 578–80.

7. Dr. Archibald Bruce (1777–1818), a New York physician and a lineal descendant of Nicholas Bayard, who received the manuscript from his intimate friend, Henricus Selyns. Upon the death of Dr. Bruce the poems apparently went to Peter A. Jay, the father of Mrs. Pierrepont (see note 2 above). See *Anthology of New Netherlands,* p. 15.

2377.   *To Thomas W. Storrow, Sr.*

Sunnyside Decr 9th. 1854

My dear Storrow

Before the receipt of your most welcome letter[1] I had read the article in Putnam[2] to which you allude; and which I presume has been written by one of our gastronomical Aldermen, returned from ⟨its⟩ his travels. The research displayed in it is truly astonishing. The remote antiquity to which it has carried the art of eating has excited the wonderment of all my womenkind. ⟨Sa⟩ My niece little dame Sarah, who is especially curious in all matters relating to the cuisine was ⟨a⟩ rather disappointed in that part which related to the ancient larder of the children of Israel; expecting to have a special account of the *flesh pots* of Egypt to which they looked back so longingly which she inclines to think were *pot pies*; establishing the antiquity of that most excellent though homely dish. I hope the author will clear up this matter in some future article: In the mean time his article as it is dished up is considered very savory and has met with universal acceptation.

We are all cosy and comfortable at Sunnyside notwithstanding the cold weather and have always a warm corner ready for you whenever you choose to quarter yourself here—Where your nieces[3] desire me to tell you they will be most happy to welcome you

Ever My dear Storrow

Yours very truly
Washington Irving

Thomas W Storrow Esqr.

MANUSCRIPT: Harvard.

1. This letter has not been located.
2. "The Art of Eating, from the Earliest Ages Down to the Present Time," *Putnam's Magazine*, 4 (December, 1854), 581–91.
3. WI's facetious reference to his own nieces at Sunnyside who treated the widowed Storrow like an uncle when he came to visit.

2378.   *To Evert A. Duyckinck*

[December 26, 1854]

My dear Sir:

I am just called away to the south and shall be absent about a fortnight. When I return I will call on you[.] I return the Ms:[1] but have not had time to make much addition. I shall like to have a proof when it goes to press

Yours very truly
Washington Irving

Sunnyside Dec 26 1854 / Evert A Duyckinck Esqr.

MANUSCRIPT: NYPL—Duyckinck Papers.

1. For other details about this reminiscence of WI's associations with Washington Allston, see WI to Duyckinck, November 23, 1854.

2379.   To Mary E. Kennedy

Sunnyside, Dec. 26t. 1854

My dear Miss Kennedy,

I received your kind letter of invitation[1] yesterday; and am now making preparations to accept it A sudden summons to a journey in mid winter somewhat discomposes the arrangements of an old gentleman like myself; however, I trust to be with you at Cassilis by the end of the week.

With kindest remembrances to the family, Your affectionate friend,

Washington Irving

Miss Mary E. Kennedy.

MANUSCRIPT: Peabody Library.   PUBLISHED: *Sewanee Review*, 25 (January, 1917), 15.

1. Mary Kennedy's letter inviting WI to her wedding on January 1, 1855, to Henry Pendleton Cooke has not been located.

2380.   To Helen Dodge Irving

Baltimore Decr 29t. 1854

My dear Helen

Notwithstanding the dull dismal, misty weather I had a very comfortable journey to Baltimore where I arrived between four and five oclock. I saw nobody in the cars that I knew; but liked the physiognomy of one of my fellow travellers and determined to 'take to him' at our halting places. I accordingly took my seat beside him when we stopped for dinner of[1] Philadelphia—when he let me know that he knew me and had once been introduced to me. In a word he was Mr Adams who had married one of the Smedburys. So from that time we became quite 'thick' and I found him all that his physiognomy promised. We parted at Baltimore as he continued on —being bound for Charleston.

I took up my quarters at Barnums[2] and then called at Mr Grays where I was recieved with open arms and a servant instantly despatched for my trunk, in spite of all my remonstrances; for I really did not wish to desturb the household by a flying visit. However here I am; as much at home as if I were in the cottage, and tomorrow morning (Saturday[)][3]

I set off in company with John and Anthony Kennedy for their brother Andrews.

I find Mrs Kennedy quite restored to health,[4] but looking thinner than usual. Mr Gray somewhat of an invalid, but kind and warm hearted as ever—⟨At th⟩ All the family have made kind enquiries after you and Pierre. Your visit seems to have given them great satisfaction and to have left very favorable impressions—doubtless because you did not stay long enough for them to find you out.

I scrawl this in great haste having many things to do and as Kate says 'the carriage is at the door'[.] I merely write because I promised to do so.

When you write to the cottage send this scrawl that they may know my "whereabouts" as I have not time to write to them

Your affectionate uncle
Washington Irving

Mrs Pierre M Irving

MANUSCRIPT: NYPL—WI Papers.

1. WI probably intended to write "at" or "in."

2. Zenus Barnum's City Hotel at Fayette and Calvert Streets on Monument Square, not far from the home of the Grays and Kennedys, also on Monument Square. See Francis F. Beirne, *The Amiable Baltimoreans* (New York, 1951), pp. 193–96.

3. WI omitted the closing parenthesis.

4. Ill for several months, she did not attend the wedding of her niece Mary. See WI to Mrs. Kennedy, January 1, 1855.

2381. *To Catharine Irving*

Cassilis Jany 1, 1855.

My dear Kate,

A happy New Year to you and all the family—so there I have ⟨cal⟩ caught you all.[1]

I presume Helen has transmitted to you the letter I wrote to her from Baltimore telling of my journey ⟨to⟩ from New York to that place. I remaind there until Saturday when I set off for this place in company with Mr John Kennedy and Mr & Mrs Anthony Kennedy and daughter and arrived here about two Oclock of the same day after a pleasant journey in beautiful weather. There is somewhat of a gathering here of the immediate relatives but no one out of the limits of the family excepting myself. The wedding is to be strictly private; at home, this evening. It was to have been in public at the church with a train of bridesmaids grooms men &c but the sudden death of the father of the bride groom[2] changed the whole plan.

This is a splendid morning,—the weather as bright and golden as it is with us in October. I am glad to leave the old disasterous year behind me and enter upon one which I hope and trust is to be more happy and prosperous.

I shall return with Mr John Kennedy on Wednesday to Baltimore, where I have promised to remain a few days, so that you need not expect me at home until a week or so from that time. I hope to have a letter from home at Baltimore

This is a mere scrawl of a letter but I am not in a writing vein and can furnish nothing better—So with love to all bodies I remain

Your affectionate Uncle
Washington Irving

MANUSCRIPT: SHR.

1. PMI (IV, 185) indicates that there was usually a contest to see who would be the first to wish "Happy New Year."

2. John Rogers Cooke (b. 1788), the father of Henry Pendleton Cooke, had died on December 10, 1854.

2382. *To Elizabeth Kennedy*

[Charlestown, Jefferson County, Va.] / [January 1, 1855]

My dear Mrs Kennedy

Wishing you a happy new year I hasten to inform you that John is laying close siege to a castle of a lady, seeking to regain her good graces after having forfeited them by neglecting her at a watering place.[1] I am affraid however he will retire as unsuccessful as the allies are likely to die firm before Selden castle. All this may require explanation which I will be happy to furnish when we meet. Best wishes for a thousand happy new years to Mr Gray and your sister.

Yours respectfully
Washington Irving

MANUSCRIPT: Peabody Library.   PUBLISHED: *American Notes and Queries*, 5 (March, 1967), 100.

According to William S. Osborne (*American Notes and Queries*, 5 [March, 1967], 101), WI's note was added to a letter which Kennedy wrote to his wife on January 1, 1855.

1. WI is referring to the attentions Kennedy was paying to his little grandniece, Elizabeth Selden, whose mother had died the preceding summer. In his journal on

January 1, 1855, Kennedy noted that "Little Lizzie is a great favorite of Irvings, and she has been nestling upon his breast, at every interval from play since his arrival." Quoted by Osborne, p. 101.

2383. *To Helen Dodge Irving*

Baltimore Jany 4t. 1855

My dear Helen

I have just recieved your letter of the 2d. inst. and in replying to it will also reply to one from Kate received previously,[1] so that one reply will do for you both. I have to be very sparing in my correspondence just now, the writing vein being much below par with me.

I left Baltimore early on Saturday morning for the residence of Mr Andrew Kennedy travelling in company with John P Kennedy and Mr & Mrs Anthony Kennedy and daughter. We arrived at our journeys end about two oclock The weather was beautiful so it was during the three or four days that I passed in the Shenandoah Valley: that mellow golden weather which we have in October. Mr Kennedys family are all in deep mourning for the deaths of his mother, and his eldest daughter Mrs Selden a very lovely woman, who died last spring within a few days after the birth of a son. I found my little favorite Mary rather pale and thin. She has suffered deeply from the death of her sister; and the task she imposed on herself of taking charge of the children.

The wedding was to have taken place in the church. Seven brides maids were engaged and it would have drawn together the *elite* of the surrounding country; for the family connexion is large and Mary is a universal favorite The church was to have been decorated and lighted up in compliment to her. Just before the appointed day however came tidings of the sudden death of the father of the bridegroom. This changed the whole arrangement invitations of all kinds were countermanded and it was determined that the wedding should take place at home and be strictly private; none but the immediate relatives present. The countermand to my invitation must have reached the cottage after my departure, and they all expressed much satisfaction that it did so; as it was only sent in conformity to a general rule.

⟨A⟩ Notwithstanding all countermands there were a considerable gathering, though almost entirely of near relatives. The bride had laid aside her mourning for the occasion; and looked sweetly interesting. Her father was so affected during the ceremony that he could not come forward to give her away—"I have done so already!["] said he as the tears gushed forth. His brother John P was at hand and officiated in his place[.] I can easily understand the fathers feelings. Mary has been the light of his house and though she will reside in the neighborhood not above a mile distant yet her bright countenance, her cheerful voice, her light step and her prompt considerate assiduity will be missed every hour in the day from the home she has been accustomed to gladden.

I am sorry to say I was in poor plight for wedding festivity. During the whole of my sojourn in the Shenandoah valley ⟨I was⟩ my system was completely out of order: probably from the hurry and fatigue of travelling; from having taken cold &c. I could not rally myself up to the occasion; was nervous feverish and began to fear that weddings were unwholesome for me and that I was about to have chills and fever as I had at the time of Annas[2] wedding. This hung about me until I got back last evening to Baltimore. However a good nights rest, and the quiet of Mr Grays house have put me quite in tune today and I have no doubt a day or two ⟨of⟩ passed in the tranquil repose of Kennedys well stored library will "make me my own man again."

I am glad that Mary[3] has had such opportunities of seeing Grisi and Mario. I trust these regales followed by the loss of a tooth will do her good, though it is not advisable to follow up every theatrical entertainment with such an after piece.

By Kates letter I find she was expecting a rush of visitors on New Years day. I hope the carriages of the Stebbins's and Cunninghams and Duncans[4] were not jammed on the occasion. I shall look with strong interest for her account of the days visitations

I think of leaving this for home in the beginning of next week, though old Mr Gray protests against it. I am as comfortable in this most comfortable house as heart of man could desire when away from home; but the home feeling is growing stronger and stronger with me as I grow ⟨old⟩ elderly and I think before long it will be hard to get me away from my nest even to attend a wedding.

Send this letter to Kate as soon as you have read it—and now with love to all in town and country

Your affectionate Uncle
Washington Irving

Mrs Pierre M Irving / & after her / Miss Kate Irving

P. S I was called away from my letter to recieve a visit from a lady in the parlour. Who should it be but Mrs Tiffany once my little pet Sally McLane. In fine health and looking beautiful. She saw a great deal of Sarah Storrow and her children in Paris. Little Kate was a great friend of her daughter[.] I am happy to learn from her that Kate prides herself in being an american and longs to return to this country

MANUSCRIPT: NYPL—WI Papers.

1. These letters have not been located.

2. Anna Duer Irving, who married Frederick R. Routh in early June, 1854. See WI to J. P. Kennedy, June 29, 1854.

3. The daughter of Ebenezer who lived at Sunnyside.

4. Neighbors in the Sunnyside area. See WI to Catharine Irving, October 12, 1853, and to Julia G. Irving, April 3, 1854.

2384.   To Charles G. Leland

Sunnyside Jany 10th 1855

Dear Sir

You pay me a very high compliment in attributing to my writings such influence over your mind;[1] though I hardly know whether to consider that influence beneficial; should it have contributed to seduce you into the precarious paths of literature. The papers which you have published in the Knickerbocker[2] give promise that you will tread those paths with success; that you may ⟨also⟩ ever find them "ways of pleasantness" and free from the thorns too often hidden among their flowers is the sincere and hearty wish of

Your friend
Washington Irving

Charles G Leland Esq

MANUSCRIPT: HSP.

Charles Godfrey Leland (1824–1903), who wrote under the pseudonym of Hans Breitman, was a Philadelphian who came to New York in the early 1850's to edit the *Illustrated News*. In 1855 he returned to Philadelphia to edit the *Evening Bulletin*, and in the following year his "Hans Breitman's Barty" appeared in *Graham's Magazine* and made him famous. He was highly regarded for his translations of Heinrich Heine's poetry and for his humorous dialect poems which were collected in *The Breitman Ballads* (1871).

1. Leland's letter to WI has not been located.

2. Over a period of years the *Knickerbocker Magazine* published sections of *Meister Karl*. Later in 1855 they were collected and issued in book form.

2385.   *To Sarah Irving*

New York Jany 22d. 1855.

My dear Sarah,

In the omnibus at thirty first Street on Saturday I found one of the Misses Routh ⟨and⟩ with another lady of a very sweet engaging countenance who I have since learned was her sister, Mrs Mann—a widow.[1] She does not look like any of the rest of the family being of a fair complexion with light hair. If good looks win favor it will be her own fault of[2] she continues widow very long—however—let that pass. Miss Routh informed ⟨the there was⟩ ↑me that↓ a boat left Whitehall for Brighton on Sunday mornings at 20 minutes past nine—This was confirmed by ⟨Pier⟩ your brother Pierre[3] whom I saw at his office and who wished me to go down with him on Saturday afternoon However I remained in town, and set off by times in the morning. Easterly wind—threatening a storm—It began to sprinkle before I reached the Ferry boat and I had no umbrella—However I kept on. By the time I reached New Brighton there had been a slight fall of rain, which made a glare of ice and rather slippery walking. I pushed for the church. Before I reached it I was overtaken by Theodore,[4] and had the shelter of his umbrella. I was one of the first in church but had not been there long when I found dear little Nelly[5] by my side. The others soon came in, with the rest of the congregation which, owing to the weather and the ⟨Season⟩ ↑time of the year↓, was not very numerous. It was a deeply interesting sight to me, Theodore and his brother officiating together in Pierres church. For a time I felt my heart swelling in my throat and could hardly restrain my tears. Theodore acquitted himself extremely well. His canonicals become him and he makes a good figure in the reading desk, as you will readily suppose. He read the early part of the Service rather fast, as I told him afterwards, and as Pierre likewise thought. He had some thing nasal also in his enunciation; which I trust he will amend. His delivery of the Sermon was very satisfactory; and the Sermon itself excellent. Upon the whole I was very highly gratified and make no doubt that, with a little practice, he will make himself a popular preacher; as I am sure he will an attentive and conscientious pastor.

I dined at Pierres and had a very pleasant repast. You know of course all about Theodores call to Bay Ridge.[6] By his account of the place it must be the very situation he could wish. He found himself at home there immediately, among most agreeable friends. Mr Perry the first Warden, at whose hospitable house he stayed, married a Miss Pierrepont with whom Theodore was acquainted in his younger days. Another lady, the wife of a wealthy member of the congregation, claimed him as an early acquaintance. She proved to be a Miss Prentiss (I think) one of your schoolmates who used to visit you at Bridge Street. He seems already to have caught the good will of the congregation who unanimously express a great desire that he would accept the call. If he does so a parsonage will be built for him by June. The country about Bay Ridge is pleasant. The neighborhood polite and agreeable, it is within a short distance from the city. Not far from Pierres and within the reach of all his connexions. It is very gratifying to see him so promptly fixed to his notion and advantage.

He will be up at the Cottage on Saturday to stay until Monday, and I have asked him to bring Lizzie[7] and one of the other girls with him[.] Lizzie and Nelly have holiday from school from Friday until Monday, and are well disposed to come up. The other girls are engaged in parochial duties. I think it probable your brother Pierre will pass Saturday with us, as it is your fathers birth day.[8] Dr Creighton[9] must be apprised in the course of the week, that Theodore is ready to officiate for him on Sunday next.

I returned to town in the boat that left New Brighton twenty minutes past three. The walk from Whitehall up Broadway to the cars at the foot of the park was one of the bleakest walks I have taken for a long time. In the face of a cold wet east wind; that seemed to penetrate to my very bones; notwithstanding I was protected by that 'Talma'[10] which Maria[11] has lined so comfortably. However I got home safe; and when once more in cosy comfortable quarters looked back upon the day and all its scenes and occurrences with heartfelt satisfaction.

I may be kept in town for part of the week as I have business transactions with Mr Putnam and have to make arrangements about my new publications.[12] I wish also to collect some money for that poor widow the niece of Oliver Goldsmith—However, I shall be home again as soon as possible

With love to all bodies

Your affectionate Uncle
Washington Irving

Miss Sarah Irving

Manuscript: SHR.

1. These women are probably the sisters of Frederick R. Routh, who married Anna Duer Irving in June, 1854. They had visited Sunnyside in June, 1853. See WI to Julia Irving, May 26, 1853.

2. WI probably intended to write "if."

3. Pierre Paris Irving, eldest son of Ebenezer and brother of Sarah, was secretary of the Episcopal Foreign Mission on Astor Place, as well as rector of the Episcopal Church at New Brighton on Staten Island.

4. Theodore, the brother of Pierre Paris and Sarah, had been a professor at Geneva College from 1836 to 1848 and at the Free Academy of New York from 1848 to 1852. In 1854 he was ordained a priest in the Protestant Episcopal Church.

5. Cornelia, the fourth child of Theodore Irving.

6. Theodore became rector of Christ Episcopal Church in Bay Ridge, Long Island.

7. Elizabeth, the second child of Theodore Irving.

8. Ebenezer was born on January 27, 1776.

9. William Creighton was rector of Christ Episcopal Church, Tarrytown.

10. A large cape worn by men, probably named after François-Joseph Talma, the French actor.

11. Mary Nevins McLinden, the cook and housekeeper at Sunnyside and wife of Robert the gardener. She was called "Maria" to distinguish her from Mary Irving.

12. *Wolfert's Roost* was published in February, 1855. See Langfeld & Blackburn, *WI Bibliography*, p. 44.

2386. *To Nathaniel Scarse*

Sunnyside Jany 31t 1855

My dear Sir

I have detained the letters of Washington, in my possession some days after the receipt of your note of the 15th inst.[1] wishing to make some memorandums of their contents[.] I now return them to you in the same condition I trust in which I recieved them and beg you to accept my most grateful thanks for your kindness in furnishing me with the use of them

With great respect / Your obliged friend & Servt
Washington Irving

Nathl Scarse Esqr

MANUSCRIPT: SHR.

1. This letter has not been located.

2387. *To George Lunt*

Sunnyside, Feb. 3d. 1855

Dear Sir,

Accept my sincere thanks for the copy of your work[1] which you have had the kindness to send me and for the great pleasure I have derived from the very interesting and agreeable pictures which it presents of domestic life in New England

With great respect / Your obliged friend & Servt
Washington Irving

George Lunt Esqr.

MANUSCRIPT: Morristown National Historical Park.

George Lunt (1803–1885), a lawyer from Newburyport, Massachusetts who was active in local and state politics, was editor of the Boston *Daily Courier*. He wrote numerous collections of poems and essays.

1. *Eastford; or, Household Sketches*, published under the pseudonym of Wesley Brooke in Boston in 1855.

2388. To Elizabeth Kennedy

Sunnyside Feb. 8t. 1855

My dear Mrs. Kennedy,

There are two things favorable to letter writing, one to have a great deal to write about, the other, to be in a mood to write a great deal about nothing. As neither has been the case with me of late, I have remained silent. I hope you will recieve this as an excuse for my letting a month elapse since my return home without writing to you. The life I lead in my little nest at Sunnyside is what Byron stygmatised as a "mill pond existence"[1] without events or agitations; and which he was glad to vary by matrimonial broil. My bachelor lot affords no variety of the kind; and if my womankind have any fault in their management, it is that they make things too smooth ⟨and quiet⟩ around me; so that I float quietly along without a ripple to fret or to write about

I was down to Staten Island about two weeks Since, to see my nephew Theodore officiate in his brother Pierres church, and to hear him preach one of his first sermons. It was very interesting to see the two brothers officiating together—and very strange to me, to see Theodore in the pulpit. Seventeen years passed in teaching and in studying as a professor, have made a vast change in him which I can scarcely realize—recalling him when he was a youth under my care in Spain and in the United States. He retains all his early amiability and his winning ease of manner and has always been singularly popular as a teacher. He has ⟨now⟩ accepted a call to a church situated on Long Island on the New York bay a few miles below the City; in a polite neighborhood and a beautiful part of the country; with some of his early friends for parishioners. I trust "the lines have fallen to him in pleasant places."[2]

The only other event in my domestic circle, is that I went down to New York last week to ⟨the we⟩ attend the wedding of a *great* niece; the grand daughter of my brother the Judge, and niece to Treat[3]—She was married to Smith Van Buren[4] Son of the Ex president. The wedding took place in Grace Church, which seemed half filled with relatives and connexions. I counted eighteen nieces and grand nieces great and small among those present of my kith and kin. The happy couple set off for Washington ⟨f⟩ where for aught I know they still are—passing their honey moon.

So now I think I have given you enough about family matters, which cannot be of moment to you—but you will have a letter "no matter how busy I am"—So you must take what you get.

I am sorry to hear that your father has been so unwell as to be confined a great deal to his room. I had no idea how much he suffered until my last visit to you; when I was in a part of the house where I could hear how wretchedly he passed his nights. The greater part of the winter however, is over; spring will soon be at hand and then, I trust with you, he will regain his usual state of health and his capacity for enjoyment[.] I am affraid he is not in a way to have his musical evenings this winter which were so great a resource to him. Give him my kindest and most affectionate remembrances.

I find from your letter[5] that Kennedy suffers from inflamed eyes, and at the same time is working very hard. It is a pity he could not give himself and his eyes a little holyday. A little gentleman like exercise of the pen, such as he had marked out for himself, would not be amiss; but this rail road episode[6] I abominate. I know he takes a pride in shewing the world that a literary man can be a man of business; but in my humble opinion a literary man on a locomotive is worse than a beggar on horseback—and will bring up at the same end of the journey in half the time.

What you tell me about Mr M'Lanes domestic trouble is very sad. I knew when I was in Baltimore from what he and Mrs Tiffany said, that some trouble was hanging over them, but had no idea what it was.[7] I really feel deep sympathy for poor McLane in his desolate situation and am provoked at the wrong headed and wrong hearted conduct of his daughter; ⟨and the⟩ who no doubt imagines herself a religious heroine. It is the old romantic feeling that used to lead to elopements, runaway matches and other poetical modes of breaking parents hearts—that is now operating in a different way but to the same end. A sister of mercy! forsooth!—should not mercy, like charity, begin at home?

I hope Mary Dulaney has entirely recovered from her cold and the effects of her Newport dissipation; and that the spring will find her in full bloom. And that dear little girl Louisa Andrews, who is so soon ⟨to⟩ like Mary Kennedy to "settle down into a staid married woman" what a pity it is these charming girls should not always remain young and blooming and *single*—So at least says an old bachelor admirer.

I have already sent my kind remembrances to your father—give the same to your husband and to your noble hearted sister—who is a true sister of mercy—and believe me

Affectionately your friend,
Washington Irving

Mrs John P Kennedy.

P. S. I regret sincerely that I did not see Emily Hoffman[8] when I was in Baltimore (I do not reccollect her present name and I cannot decypher it in your letter) I have know[n][9] her from her childhood and have many interesting and endearing reccollections connected with her—both when in England and in this country—Give my kindest regards to her when you see her—

MANUSCRIPT: Peabody Library.   PUBLISHED: *Sewanee Review*, 25 (January, 1917), 15–17.

1. Probably a reference to Byron's description in *Don Juan*, canto 15, stanza 41.

2. See Psalms 16:10.

3. Henrietta Eckford Irving (d. 1921), daughter of Gabriel Irving, was married on February 1, 1855, at Grace Church.

4. Smith Thompson Van Buren (1816–1876) was the third son of Martin Van Buren.

5. This letter has not been located.

6. John P. Kennedy, a director of three railroads running through the Susquehanna valley, took part in the negotiations which consolidated them into the Northern Central Railroad Company In December, 1854, he became president of the new railroad, a post which he held for two years. See Bohner, *J. P. Kennedy*, p. 215.

7. Louis McLane, with whom WI had worked in the American Legation in London in 1829, was now in poor health. Although McLane was a strong Methodist, several of his daughters became Catholics. Probably WI is alluding to the marriage of Juliette McLane (b. 1824) to Peter B. Garesché, a devout Catholic, in 1849 and to her later becoming a missionary in New Zealand. Mrs. Tiffany was Sally McLane, who was married to Henry Tiffany of Baltimore. See John A. Munroe, *Louis McLane: Federalist and Jacksonian* (New Brunswick, 1973), pp. 166, 580–81, 598.

8. Emily Hoffman was probably the daughter of the Mr. Hoffman from Baltimore with whom WI resided in London for about six weeks, beginning on December 26, 1821. See PMI, II, 70; and WI to Thomas W. Storrow, February 1, 1822.

9. WI omitted the bracketed letter.

2389.   *To Julia I. Grinnell*

Sunnyside Friday morning / Feb. 16t. 1855

My dear Julia,

I am in despair! Your Mammas invitation[1] to the party of young folks, although written several days since did not reach me until last evening, having loitered I suspect in that *dead letter office* your Papas pocket. It came too late. I had already declined an invitation from Dr Bellows[2] for this evening on the plea of engagements and occupations which would detain me in the Country until Saturday. Under the same envelope with your Mammas note was one from Mr W C Schermerhorn[3] dated Feb 12th. inviting me to his house last evening to the performance of an Amateur Comedy. It also was of course too late—oh that pocket!

Hoping that you and all our young friends will have merry times I remain your affectionate

but afflicted Uncle
Washington Irving

Miss Julia I. Grinnell

ADDRESSED: Miss Julia I Grinnell / Care of M H Grinnell Esq / Corner 14th St & 5t Avenue / N Y. / *with speed*   POSTMARKED: Irvington, N. Y. / Feb. 16 MANUSCRIPT: Cornell University Library.

Julia Irving Grinnell (1837–1915) was the daughter of Moses and Julia Irving Grinnell, who had a summer residence adjoining Sunnyside.

1. This and the other invitations mentioned in this letter have not been located.
2. Probably Henry Whitney Bellows (1814–1882), pastor at the First Unitarian Church in New York City.
3. William Colford Schermerhorn (1821–1903), a member of an old New York family who served for forty-three years as a trustee of Columbia College and for ten years as president of its board. The private theatrical which WI missed was *The Ladies' Battle*, according to George Templeton Strong. See Strong, *Diary*, II, 212, entry for February 18, 1855.

2390.   *To Charles M. Watson*

New York. March 12th 1855

Dear Sir,

Your letter of the 5th. inst.[1] is but just recieved, I being absent from home The notices of Washingtons expeditions in 1754–5. might be very serviceable to me if I could recieve them immediately. The first volume of my work is in the press and the printers are just on the part relating to those years.[2]

Could you not cut the passages in question out of the Newspapers and send them to me by return of mail. I would return them to you punctually and they might be pasted again to the news paper. Should you stop to have them copied I fear they will arrive too late. Any documents relative to Washington in subsequent years might be forwarded at your leisure and would be most thankfully recieved and carefully returned

Very respectfully / Your obliged friend & Servt
Washington Irving

P. S. You may address to me at present at the Astor Library, N York[3]

Charles M Watson Esqr

Manuscript: NYPL—Berg Collection.

1. This letter has not been located.
2. WI finished correcting proofs of volume 1 in mid-April, 1855, and the work was published shortly thereafter. See PMI, IV, 189. Washington's expeditions of 1754–1755 are described in chapters 10–19 of volume 1.
3. Located at 32 Lafayette Place. See *Trow's New York City Directory for 1854–55*, p. 167, under Jos. G. Cogswell.

2391.   *To John Murray III*

New York March 19th. 1855

My dear Sir,

I have requested my publisher Mr Putnam to forward to you the sheets as printed of the first volume of the Life of Washington, which is now going through the press. The work when complete will form three volumes. As a copy right is not to be obtained in England I can only bargain for the advantage of having the first publication. For this I ask to have ten per cent on the retail price. Should it not suit your views to undertake the publication of the work I will thank you to hold the sheets sent to you subject to the order of Mr Putnam or his agent.[1]

It is a long while since I have heard from you. I am happy to see that you are going on prosperously. With kindest remembrances to your family I remain

Very truly yours
Washington Irving

John Murray Esqr

DOCKETED: Irving, Washn. / *Mar. 1855*
MANUSCRIPT: John Murray.

1. At first Murray accepted the offer to publish *The Life of Washington* on WI's terms, but he later changed his mind and, acting as WI's agent, offered it to H. G. Bohn on "a promise of £ 50, and a hope of something more if he could keep the field to himself." See PMI, IV, 193; and WIHM, p. 205.

2392. *To Samuel C. Foster*

New York. March 23d. 1855

Dear Sir,
I shall be very much obliged to you for the copy of an autograph letter of General Washington which you are so kind as to offer me
My address is either 33 Lafayette Place New York or Irvington Westchester Cy. Your letter being addressed to the Tarrytown post office was some time in reaching me

Very respectfully / Your obliged & hble Serv
Washington Irving
S. C. Foster Esqr.

P S. It will be best, for the present, to address letters at Lafayette place, N. Y.

MANUSCRIPT: NYPL—WI Papers.

Probably the addressee is Samuel C. Foster, a physician at 24 East 21st Street, New York. See *Trow's New York City Directory for 1854–55*, p. 263.

2393. *To George P. Putnam*

[March?, 1855]

Advertisements that my life of Washington will be completed during this year. I have authorized no such statement—Neither have I authorized your previous advertisements that the second volume would be published in August and the third in October.[1] I wish you would make no promises on my behalf but such as I distinctly warrant.

DOCKETED: Wash. Irving / no date
MANUSCRIPT: Va.–Barrett.

1. WI is probably responding to the notice in *Norton's Literary Gazette and Publisher's Circular*, March 15, 1855, or one similar to it :"G. P. Putnam . . . have in press *George Washington, a Biography*, by Washington Irving, in 12mo., uniform with

Irving's other works. Also an octavo edition. . . . The work is expected to be completed in three volumes—the first volume to be ready in May; the second in August; and the third in the Autumn . . ." (quoted in Jacob Blanck, *Bibliography of American Literature*, V, 56).

2394. *To Jonathan D. Steele*

[New York, April 7, 1855]

To J D Steele Esq president Niagara /Fire Insurance Company.

Dr Sir,
My Nephew Pierre M Irving holds in his Name as Trustee for me Fifty Shares of the stock of the New York Floating Dry Dock Company,[1] certificate No 624, which he is hereby authorize[d][2] to transfer to the Niagara Fire Insurance Company

New York April 7. 1855

Washington Irving

MANUSCRIPT: Helen Irving Horton.

Only the signature is in WI's handwriting. The docket on the verso—"Order from Washington / Irving the paym / of dividends Feb 20h 1851"—does not seem to apply to this order.

Jonathan D. Steele was the second president of the Niagara Fire Insurance Company, which was incorporated on December 29, 1849, and began business on August 1, 1850, with a paid-up cash capital of $200,000. See Moses King, *King's Handbook of New York City*, 2d ed. (New York, 1893), pp. 646–47.

1. The New York Dry Dock Company, founded in 1825, was chartered with banking privileges. See *King's Handbook of New York City*, p. 715; W. T. Bonner, *New York: The World's Metropolis*, p. 410; and Haswell, *Reminiscences of an Octogenarian*, p. 151.

2. The copyist omitted the bracketed letter.

2395. *To James Watson Webb*

Sunnyside April 21t 1855

My dear General,
I thank you for your kind enquiries.[1] I am doing very well. I did not suffer as much from my accident[2] as you had been told, though rather

battered and bruised. I trust to be able to mount a *quieter* horse in the course of a few days

Yours very truly
Washington Irving

Genl J Watson Webb.

Manuscript: Yale.

1. Webb's letter has not been located.
2. On April 19, 1855, WI had fallen from his unruly horse, Gentleman Dick. For details of the accident, see PMI, IV, 189–92; WI to John P. Kennedy, April 23, 1855; and to Sarah Storrow, late May or June, 1855.

2396. To John P. Kennedy

Sunnyside April 23d. 1855

My dear Kennedy,

The telegraphic report was, as usual exaggerated. I have been thrown from my horse[1] but not as dangerously hurt as reported. Thanks to a hard head and strong chest, I have withstood a shock that would have staved in a sensitively constructed man. My head was pretty well battered and ⟨my⟩ came nigh being forced down into my chest, like the end of a telescope, and my chest is still so ⟨*[unrecovered]*⟩ wrenched and sore that I am like one suffering with the asthma. But I have left my bed and am on my legs again. Its all the doings of that rascal *Gentleman Dick*,[2] who, knowing my fondness for him has played me all kinds of tricks. This is the second time he has fairly run away with me, but at least the tenth time he has attempted it. The first time[3] I kept my seat, but this time he was determined I should not, so he ran me among trees and we both came down together.——I have cut him off with a shilling.

I have been anxious to hear about Mr Grays health; which Mrs Calvert informed me was very bad when she was in Baltimore and I observe you excused yourself from attending the Clay dinner. Do let me know how you all are and tell me whether dear little Lu[4] is married

I am scrawling this note in defiance of my little nurse Sarah—You must excuse its being scarce legible.

Give my affectionate regards to Mr Gray and the sisters twain

Yours ever my dear Kennedy
Washington Irving

John P Kennedy Eq

MANUSCRIPT: Va.–Barrett.

1. For other details about WI's fall, see PMI, IV, 189; and WI to James Watson Webb, April 21, 1855.

2. Gentleman Dick was an unruly horse which WI had owned for several years.

3. WI related this incident to Mrs. Kennedy on August 31, 1854. The horse was sold shortly after the second mishap. See PMI, IV, 192; and WI to Sarah Storrow, late May or early June, 1855.

4. A reference to Louisa Andrews, a young friend of the Kennedy and Gray families whom WI had met in 1853. Later in the year Kennedy wrote that he had just "served in the capacity of father of the family and have given away to Sam Early,— a very good fellow—our little friend Louisa. . . ." See *Sewanee Review*, 25 (January, 1917), 18.

2397. To John Murray III

Sunnyside April 27t. 1855

My dear Sir,

In conformity to your letter of the 5th. inst.[1] I have drawn upon you this day, at ten days sight, in favor of Messrs. Irving, Van Wart & Co for one hundred and five pounds.[2]

In regard to the forth coming life of Washington I accept the terms you offer Viz. "10 per cent on the retail price of all copies sold. *as soon as the original outlay is repaid.*"[3]

You will consult your own judgement in regard to any arrangement with Mr Bohn or others in the republi[c]ation of the work

You mention my excellent friend Mr Latrobe,[4] of whom I have not heard any thing for a long time. Should you see him again I beg you to assure him of my most affectionate remembrance.

I will write to you more fully on some future occasion. I find it a little inconvenient at present, having not quite recovered from the effects of a fall from my horse

With kindest regards to your family I remain my dear sir

Yours very truly
Washington Irving

DOCKETED: Irving / Washington / Apl 1855
MANUSCRIPT: John Murray.

1. This letter has not been located.

2. This sum probably came from Murray's reprinting *The Sketch Book, Bracebridge Hall,* and *Tales of a Traveller* in inexpensive editions. See WIHM, p. 200.

3. Murray later changed his mind about publishing the biography and sold it to H. G. Bohn. See WIHM, p. 205; PMI, IV, 192–93; and WI to Murray, March 19, 1855.

4. Charles J. Latrobe (1801–1875) had accompanied WI on his western trip in 1832. See STW, II, 37–39.

2398. *To Joshua Bates*

Sunnyside May 2d. 1855

My dear Sir,

This will be presented to you by my friend the Hon. Edwin B Morgan,[1] a Member of Congress from this state, who, with two or three of his colleagues, proposes to make a visit to Europe in the interval between the sessions.

Reccommending him to your kind civilities as a gentleman of great worth and of amiable manners; I remain my dear Sir, with cordial remembrances to Mrs Bates

Yours ever very truly
Washington Irving

Joshua Bates Esqr / &c &c &c

ADDRESSED: Joshua Bates Esqr / &c &c &c / Portland Place. / London / By the / Hon. E. B Morgan   FRANKED: *W Irving*
MANUSCRIPT: Wells College Library.

Since this letter is among the Morgan Papers at Wells College, it either was never presented or was retrieved at the time of presentation to Bates.

The following note is included with the letter: "Joshua Bates (1788–1864) American financier, Began business in Boston but failed during the war of 1812. Became associated with Grays, large ship owners, and went to London as their representative. In 1826 formed partnership with John Baring son of Sir Thomas Baring. Became senior partner and very influential financier. In 1853–54, impartial judgment in claims arising from War of 1812. In 1852–55 he contributed $100,000 in books & cash for a Public Library in Boston. Reading room now named Bates Hall. During Civil War his sympathies strong for Union and he prevented raising of loans for the Confederacy."

1. Edwin B. Morgan (1806–1881), a banker and merchant of Aurora, New York and a congressman from 1853 to 1859, was one of the founders and first president of the Wells-Fargo Express Company and a director of the American Express Company. He was a trustee of Cornell University and of Wells College.

2399. *To Henry Van Wart*

Sunnyside May 3d. 1855

My dear Brother

This will be handed to you by my friend the Hon Edwin B. Morgan, Member of Congress from this state; who with several of his colleagues is about to make a visit to Europe in the interval of the sessions

He is well acquainted with some branches of our family and is a man of great worth and of amiable manners. I reccommend him to your kind civilities. With love to the family

Your affectionate brother
Washington Irving

Henry Van Wart Esq

ADDRESSED: Henry Van Wart Esq / Birmingham / favd by the Hon / Edwin B. Morgan.
MANUSCRIPT: Wells College Library.

As in the case of the letter written to Joshua Bates, May 2, 1855, Morgan either did not deliver this letter or reclaimed it upon presentation.

2400. *To Evert A. Duyckinck*

Sunnyside, May 4t. 1855

My dear Sir:

I return the proof, which appears to have been very correctly printed.[1]

As to the Leslie picture of Anne Page & Master Slender I may have been mistaken in my idea that I had seen it at Mr Hones. You may correct the statement concerning it in the way you suggest.[2]

I shall be in town in the course of a few days when I will have the pleasure of calling upon you

Yours truly
Washington Irving

Evert A Duyckinck Esqr

ADDRESSED: Evert A Duyckinck Esq / 20 Clinton Place / N York   POSTMARKED: NEW-YORK / MAY / 5
MANUSCRIPT: NYPL—Duyckinck Papers.

1. This is the proof of WI's reminiscences of Washington Allston, for which WI had requested proof. See WI to Duyckinck, November 23 and December 26, 1854.

2. In his original comment on Allston WI had apparently stated that Charles R. Leslie's painting of *Anne Page and Master Shallow* from Shakespeare's *The Merry Wives of Windsor* was owned by Philip Hone, a fact corroborated in H. T. Tuckerman, *Book of the Artists* (New York, 1867), p. 181. In a footnote to the Allston article in the *Cyclopaedia of American Literature* (1855 ed., II, 16) Duyckinck pointed out that "This picture was exhibited in the 'Washington Gallery' in New York, in 1854," a statement with which WI agreed. The painting is now in the collection of the Pennsylvania Academy of Fine Arts. See Mantle Fielding, *Dictionary of American Painters, Sculptors and Engravers* (New York, 1945), p. 214.

2401. To William Irving Dodge

Sunnyside May 6t. 1855

My dear William

I thank you and my other friends and relatives at Syracuse for the kind solicitude manifested on my account. The effects of my late accident were not so serious as represented in the papers; but sufficiently grave to keep me in bed for a couple of days. I am now almost entirely recovered from them and ready to resume the saddle—but not on the same horse; having consented to part with him, though a great favorite. I was not thrown from him last year; though he took fright and gave me a hard run of about three miles,—but then I had a fair level road and tired him out. This time it was all down hill and winding; and ended by our both coming down together, among trees in the front of the house. I begin to think it is time for me to give up Spirited horses; and I shall look out for some quiet old-gentleman like nag that is past cutting capers.

Give my love to your wife, children and grand children[1] and believe me my dear William

Your affectionate Uncle
Washington Irving

W Irving Dodge Esqr.

MANUSCRIPT: NYPL—WI Papers.

William Irving Dodge (1790–1873) was the oldest child of Ann Sarah Irving and Richard Dodge.

1. William was married to Patience Akin. They had five children: Ann Sarah, married to Henry Baldwin; Julia Irving, married to James L. Humphrey; Elizabeth Russell; William James, married to Martha Humphrey; and Richard, married to Elizabeth Stouts.

2402.   To William W. Waldron

Sunnyside, May 16th, 1855

My Dear Sir:

I thank you for your inquiries in regard to the accident I met with.[1] I am perfectly recovered. You say you are about to make me the intended visit which I would be glad you would defer for a short time, as my house is at present undergoing thorough repairs, painting, &c. I am sometimes, myself, compelled to go outdoors.

Yours very truly,
Washington Irving

William W. Waldron, Esq.

PUBLISHED: Waldron, *WI & Cotemporaries,* p. 247.

1. Waldron's letter has not been located.

2403.   To Pierre M. Irving

May 20, 1855

I enclose a letter, just received from Murray,[1] which I will thank you to hand to Mr. Putnam. You will see that some negligence or omission in forwarding advance sheets to London may mar my interests in that quarter. But no matter. If my work be well received by the public, I shall be content, whatever be the pecuniary profits.

PUBLISHED: PMI, IV, 192–93.

1. PMI (IV, 193) quoted from and commented on Murray's letter: "The letter from Murray informed him [WI] that he had placed the advance sheets of 'Washington' in the hands of Bohn, on 'a promise of £50, and a hope of something more if he could keep the field to himself[']; but added that there was a risk of perfect copies coming over from America before Bohn could complete his edition, in consequence of there being some pages missing from the proof sheets sent over. 'It is quite absurd to think of sending sheets of a book otherwise than in duplicate sheets.'

"If there were demand for a large edition, he would print one himself, in conformity with the terms of his last letter; 'but I fear the publication in volume would be fatal to a large edition. The prospects of literature seen athwart the war are not encouraging, and I am disposed, consequently, to publish as little as possible.' "

2404.   To the Library Committee, New York Society Library

[Sunnyside, May 23, 1855]

To the Library Committee of the New York Society Library

Gentlemen,

Understanding that Mr Forbes[1] has resigned the post of Librarian to Your establishment I take the liberty of reccommending Mr Charles T. Evans[2] as his successor, knowing him to be a man of worth and believing him to be well qualified for the situation[3]

very respectfully /Your obt Servt
Washington Irving

Sunnyside, May 23d. 1855

MANUSCRIPT: Va.–Barrett.

1. Philip J. Forbes (1807–1877) was librarian at the New York Society Library from 1828 to 1855.

2. Charles T. Evans was a bookseller at 109 Nassau Street. See *Trow's New York City Directory for 1854–55*, p. 238.

3. Evans did not receive the appointment. John MacMullen, who succeeded Forbes, held the post from June, 1855 to May, 1857. The position was vacant until October, 1857, and then filled by Wentworth S. Butler, who held it until October, 1895. See Austin B. Keep, *History of the New York Society Library* (New York, 1908), p. 563.

2405.   To Elisha Bartlett

Sunnyside May 28t. 1855.

My dear Sir,

Accept my sincere thanks for the copy of your "Simple Sittings"[1] which you have had the kindness to send me; and which has hung up a set of "portraits and pictures" in my mind, suggestive of a host of delightful reccollections. I am sure Dickens will feel flattered to see the offspring of his imagination thus poetically portrayed: for my own part I feel myself honored by your deeming my 'bust' worthy of a niche in your gallery.[2]

I am, my dear Sir / Yours very truly
Washington Irving

E. Bartlett Esq.

MANUSCRIPT: LC.

Elisha Bartlett (1804–1855) was a professor at the College of Physicians and Surgeons in New York City and a prolific writer of medical articles and books, his chief work being his treatise on *The Fevers in the United States* (1842).

1. Bartlett's *Simple Settings, in Verse, for Six Portraits and Pictures, from Mr. Dickens' Gallery* (Boston, 1855) contained three sketches from *Nicholas Nickleby,* two from *Bleak House,* and "An Allegory. Pickwick to Hard Times." WI probably intended to use a double quotation mark.

2. Bartlett devoted one section (28 lines) of "An Allegory" to WI's settings and characters. See *Simple Settings,* pp. 56–57.

2406. To Lewis G. Clark

Sunnyside, June 14th, 1855.

My dear Mr. Clark:

I thank you for the likeness of Washington which you have had the kindness to send me. I ought to have acknowledged the receipt of it sooner, but I am hurried just now in preparing a volume for the press; in looking for a pair of horses; and in endeavoring to cope with five dozen "regular correspondents," beside a *cloud of applicants for autographs, those pestilent musquitoes of literature.*

I shall be happy to see you and Mr. L—— any day that you may feel inclined to make me a visit. My dining-hour is three o'clock, if you will take your chance for family fare. If you send me word beforehand, I will not promise you a better dinner; but that I will be home to eat it with you. With kind remembrance to Mrs. Clark from 'self and "daughters,"[1]

Yours, very truly
Washington Irving

L. Gaylord Clark, Esq.

PUBLISHED: *Knickerbocker Magazine,* 55 (February, 1860), 232.

1. Clark explained that "'self and daughters" alludes to a New York *Herald* correspondent who mistook WI's nieces at Sunnyside for his daughters. WI is playing upon the mistake in his reference. See *Knickerbocker Magazine,* 55 (February, 1860), 232–33.

2407.   To George P. Putnam

[Sunnyside, June 24, 1855]

My dear Sir

I have a letter from the Rev. Sylvanus Reed, Rector of Holy Innocents Albany:[1] who informs me that I have mispelled the name of his ancestor who fought at the battle of Bunkers Hill, mentioning him as Colonel Re*a*d instead of Reed.[2] He is anxious that it should be corrected in future impressions—I wish you would have it done both in the 8 mo & 12 mo plates. It occurs. Page 473 4th line from the bottom. P 476 line 28. P. 480 line 30.[3]

Yours very truly
Washington Irving

Sunnyside. June 24t. 1855

MANUSCRIPT: Va.–Barrett.   PUBLISHED: Carroll A. Wilson, *Thirteen Author Collections of the Nineteenth Century*, I, 170.

1. This letter has not been located. Sylvanus Reed was the first rector of the Church of Holy Innocents and served from 1850 through 1861. The cornerstone of the church was laid on June 7, 1849, and the building was consecrated on September 3, 1850. See Arthur James Weise, *The History of the City of Albany* (Albany, 1884), pp. 495–96.

2. Joseph Reed (1741–1785), a Revolutionary soldier and member of the Continental Congress, directed the prosecution of Benedict Arnold in his trial for treason.

3. These errors occur in WI's *Life of George Washington*, v. 1, chap. 41, "Battle of Bunker's Hill." In the second impression of the Putnam first edition later in 1855 "Read" is changed to "Reed" at pages 471.18, 476.28, and 480.30. WI's reference to page 473 is in error; it should be page 471.

2408.   To Sarah Storrow

Sunnyside June 27th. 1855

My dear Sarah,

The "sad accident" about which you express so much concern[1] was by no means so sad as the Newspapers represented it. To be sure I was somewhat battered and bruised and was confined to my bed for a couple of days; but I was soon as well as ever again. The worst result was that I had to sell my favorite Saddle horse 'Gentleman Dick,' or there would have been no peace in the house hold, the women kind were so clamorous against the poor Animal—Poor Dick! His character was very much misunderstood by all but myself. He was one of the gentlest finest tempered animals in the world. But a scamp of a coachman had played tricks with him and made him so timid that he was apt to get into a panic when suddenly startled, take the bit between his teeth and trust to his heels for safety. I am now looking out for a quiet sober old-gentleman-like horse if such a thing is to be met with in this very young country; where every thing is so prone *to go ahead.*

You sent me some time since one or two Galignanis;[2] containing details of the visit of the Emperor and Empress to England.[3] I must say I read them with any thing but pleasure. Much as England has deserved to be punished for the arrogance and contumely with which she is accustomed to treat other countries and especially ⟨ourselves⟩ ↑our own,↓ I could not but feel grieved to see her obliged to undergo such a humiliation Do you think that proud nation did not feel it to her hearts core? Do you think Queen Victoria did not write[4] in spirit when compelled to welcome Louis Napoleon to her court and to go through all that Mummery of conferring on him the order of the Garter.[5] For Louis Napoleon it was a greater triumph than if he had taken Sebastopol—It eclipsed the field of Waterloo—But for England what an abasement! To have to play off such an elaborate piece of toadyism to the nephew of the man whom she rejected from her shores and sent to die on the rock of St Helena!

I am sorry to hear very bad accounts of poor Constants health.[6] He had recently built a new house in New York and set off for Europe in the hope of bringing Mrs Constant back with him and again having a home in his ↑own↓ country. Poor fellow—I understand he was struck down with Malady in London, as he was on his way home—*alone.* I am told, however, that he has got back to Paris and is slowly recovering. Poor Constant! that I should ever ⟨th⟩ have thought him a man to be envied!

Your account of the last illness and death of that lovely being Mrs DeWolfe is deeply affecting. I had heard of her husbands death at Nice and that her own health was extremely precarious—but I had hoped she would reach Paris where I was sure she would experience from you a Sisters tenderness and might have ⟨cha⟩ some chance for recovery. Every thing about that fragile delicate being was calculated to enspire sympathy and affection so pure, so gentle, so refined. I know of no one, that I have seen so transiently and at such distant intervals with whom I have been so deeply interested. But as you say—she is at rest—or rather, she is in a better world, and is happy.

I am writing late at night—as I have to go to town on business in the morning. It is a beautiful moonlight night and I have been kept up late by the young folk; having two of Pierre P Irvings daughters with me, Hatty and sweet little Nelly, and they have been with the young Grinnells cruising by Moonlight on the Tappan Sea in a beautiful Yacht which

Mr Grinnell has recently bought. It puts me in ⟨th⟩ Mind of the water parties in former days in the Dream—with the Hamiltons, Bowdoins &c when the old chorus used to be chaunted—"We wont go home till morning—till day light doth appear." It is a different Yacht and a different generation, that have taken up the game and are now sailing by moonlight and singing about the Tappan Sea. So rolls the world—

I have just been putting little Sunnyside in thorough repair, plastering and painting it inside and outside, laying down a new pavement in the hall and working it all up into picture.[7] I think if you could See it this moon light night you would say that it looks better than ever. It does so at least, to me,—and I feel every day more and more content to nestle down in it.

I have just learnt that my old friend James Renwick[8]—the professor— is about to sail for Europe in company with ⟨? his?⟩ one of his sons and the wife of the latter (an Aspinwall) so that it is very probable you will see him in Paris.[9]

I must conclude—for it is high time to be in bed. Remember me affectionately to Mr Storrow Give my love to the three young princesses

Your affectionate uncle
Washington Irving

ADDRESSED: Madame / Madame Storrow / ⟨aux soins de Mr T. W. Storrow / Rue du Faubg Poissonniere / à Paris⟩ / hotel frascate / — havre —
MANUSCRIPT: Yale.   PUBLISHED: PMI, IV, 192 (in part).

1. Sarah's letter has not been located.
2. Copies of *Galignani's Messenger*, an English-language newspaper published in Paris.
3. Napoleon III and Empress Eugénie visited England from April 15 to April 21, 1855. See London *Times*, April 16–23, 1855.
4. WI probably intended to write "writhe."
5. The ceremony took place on April 18 at Windsor. For a detailed account, see London *Times*, April 24, 1855.
6. The Constants were former neighbors of WI's whom Sarah Storrow knew in Paris. See WI to Catharine Paris, March 22, 1838; and to Gouverneur Kemble, July 28, 1838.
7. For another allusion to the repairs, see WI to W. W. Waldron, May 16, 1855.
8. James Renwick (1792–1863) was a longtime friend of WI's. An engineer, he taught at Columbia College from 1820 to 1853.
9. James Renwick (1818–1875), the second son, was an architect who designed Grace Church and many other buildings in New York City. He was married to Anna Lloyd Aspinwall, daughter of the New York merchant, William H. Aspinwall.

2409.   To Alexander Jones

Sunnyside July 19t 1855

Dear Sir

Accept my thanks for the copy of your work on the Cambrian races[1] which you have had the kindness to send me. I find it very interesting and suggestive. It recalls delightful excursions in former days among the Welsh mountains[2] when I was not more struck with the magnificence and grandeur of the scenery than with the distinct and original character of the people which inhabited it.

I am surprised to learn from your work how many of the most eminent characters in British and American history are descended from the Cambrian Mounta[i]neers. They were truly a brave unconquered people and guarded among their mountains the fountain heads of ↑that↓ civil and religious liberty which is now the boast of the pseudo Anglo Saxons.

Very respectfully / Your obliged & hbl Servt.
Washington Irving

Alexander Jones Esq

MANUSCRIPT: SHR.

Alexander Jones (1802–1863), a physician and journalist who was a regular correspondent for British newspapers, was the first general agent of the New York Associated Press. In 1851 he became commercial reporter for the New York *Herald*.

1. *The Cymry of '76; or, Welshmen and Their Descendants of the American Revolution* (New York, 1855).
2. WI had traveled in Wales in the summers of 1815 and 1817. See PMI, I, 336, 368; and STW, I, 148–49.

2410.   To Henry A. Smythe

Sunnyside July 19th. 1855

My dear Sir,

I can make no promise to come down to Audubon Park[1] during this oppressively hot weather;[2] I was prevented by it the other evening, as you rightly supposed. Even the inducement of music fails to have its effect, lest there should be "melting airs" of which I have more than enough at home. Should the heat moderate—moderate I may venture; at present I am only fit to sit perfectly still, on a cake of ice with another on top of me.

With my kind regards to the ladies and my love to the "three little Kittens"; who, I hope, have found their Mittens.

I am My dear Sir / Yours truly
Washington Irving

H. A Smythe Esqr.

MANUSCRIPT: NYPL—Berg Collection.

Henry A. Smythe, a merchant with a store at 45 Broadway, resided on West 155th Street. See *Trow's New York City Directory for 1855–56*, p. 776.

1. In 1844 John James Audubon bought a forty-four acre tract fronting the Hudson River between 155th and 158th Streets. Probably the musical entertainment was held on a part of the estate. See Wilson, *NY, Old and New*, II, 326–28.

2. The temperature reached ninety degrees on July 19, 1855, according to the New York *Times* for that date, with even higher temperatures on succeeding days.

2411.   To Robert Torrey, Jr.

Sunnyside, July 20, 1855

I have the honor to acknowledge the receipt of your letter[1] informing me that it is the wish of a literary association of which you are a committee to adopt my name as a designation. I shall consider my name highly honored by being so appropriated.

PUBLISHED: *Sale of the Renowned Collection of William F. Gable* (New York, 1923), vol. 1, pt. 1, item 505.

1. This letter has not been located.

2412.   To Robert C. Winthrop

Sunnyside July 31t 1855

My dear Mr Winthrop,

I thank you for your kind letter of the 27th. inst.[1] and am very much obliged to your venerable friend for the interest he appears to take in my biographical task and for the information which he furnishes. I shall keep in mind the foot note in Davis' life of Burr[2] to which he alludes.

I am endeavoring to get my second volume ready for the press;[3] but this summer weather is very much against me and for some days past some of the "thousand strings" have been sadly out of tune. This I hope will be recieved as an excuse for the brevity of this letter.

With kind remembrances to Mrs Winthrop

Yours ever very truly
Washington Irving

Hon. R C. Winthrop

MANUSCRIPT: Bowdoin College Library.

1. This letter has not been located.
2. Matthew L. Davis (1773–1850), a close friend of Aaron Burr for forty years, wrote the *Memoirs of Aaron Burr* in two volumes (1836–1837).
3. The second volume of the *Life of George Washington* was published by Putnam in December, 1855.

2413. To George W. Childs and Robert E. Peterson

Sunnyside Aug 23d. 1855

Messrs Childs & Peterson

Gentlemen,

Accept my thanks for the Specimen You have sent me of Mr Allibones Critical Dictionary of English Literature.[1] The undertaking does honor to that gentlemans enterprise and the manner in which, from the Specimen before me, he appears to execute it does honor to his intelligence, perspicuity, wide and accurate research, impartiality and good taste. When completed the work cannot fail to be a valuable library companion and family book of reference. The beautiful manner in which the work is got up is highly creditable to American typography.

very respectfully Gentlemen / Your obliged & hbl Servt
Washington Irving

MANUSCRIPT: Huntington.

George W. Childs (1829–1894) was a Philadelphia bookseller and publisher who was married to the daughter of his partner. Their firm flourished from 1853 to 1860. Robert E. Peterson (1812–1894) was a lawyer and hardware merchant before he helped establish Childs and Peterson. After its dissolution he studied medicine at the University of Pennsylvania and was licensed in 1862.

1. On August 2, 1855, Childs and Peterson had sent WI a portion of Allibone's *Dictionary* containing the first three letters of the alphabet (letter to WI at Yale). Later they asked for the return of the "Specimen." See WI to Childs and Peterson, May 6, 1857.

2414.   *To Charles R. Terry*

Sunnyside Aug 23? 1855

Dear Sir,

I feel duly sensible of the compliment paid me by the Franklin Library Association in inviting me to deliver a lecture before them. A doubt however, of my talent for that species of intellectual exercise has induced me to decline all invitations of the kind.

Very respectfully / Your obliged & hbl Servant
Washington Irving

Charles R Terry Esq / Corr Secy &c &c

MANUSCRIPT: Andrew B. Myers.

2415.   *To Charles Lanman*

Sunnyside Aug. 24. 1855

Copy)

My dear Sir,

I am much obliged to you for your kind offer to borrow for me the newspapers containing accounts of the death and funeral of Washington, —but will not task your kindness in that respect; as I have at hand copious details of those events in the volumes of contemporary newspapers in the New York libraries.

I should be most happy to see Mrs Lanman and yourself at Sunnyside should your excursion bring you into these parts.

Yours very truly
Washington Irving

Charles Lanman Eq / Norwich Conn.

MANUSCRIPT: NYPL—Hellman Collection (copy).

2416. *To Elizabeth Kennedy*

Sunnyside Aug 24th. 1855

My dear Mrs. Kennedy,

I have suffered a shameful time to elapse without replying to your last letter,[1] ⟨sin⟩ but in fact my epistolary debts have encreased upon me so awfully of late and are so overwhelming that I am almost driven to bankruptcy and despair; especially as there is a constant fagging of the pen and tasking of the brain in preparing another volume of my biographical work for the press.

I hope quiet and country air ⟨at⟩ on the beautiful banks of the Patapsco have had a restorative effect upon your father; and that he is again able to enjoy his little circle of friends and favorites in his own kind hearted way. I trust dear little Louisa Andrews (who by your account still lingers in the land of single blessedness) is now and then at hand to cheer him with her music, and that Mary Dulaney occasionally gives him the light of her beautiful countenance.

I am glad to hear that Mary Kennedy flourishes as a busy and happy housewife, and that her honey moon had not waned in six months of matrimony. I trust her husband knows the value of the prize he has drawn.

Kennedy you tell me is studying German—I presume as a relaxation from his railroad labors. He has an aptness, I should think, for the northern languages; from the facility with which I have heard him render a conversation between Miss Bremer and one of her countrymen. I should like to rub up my own reccollections of the German in the course of a few rides with him in the woods, on the back of Douce Davie.[2] I think I could repay him in bad German for some of the metaphysics he occasionally wasted on me in the course of our woodland colloquies.

I trust your sister Martha does not intend to be jocular in speaking of Mr Fillmores 'deportment' as exhibited in the Queens drawing room.[3] By all accounts his appearance there was most impressive and successful. I hope he will be present at the meeting of Sovreigns at Paris; he will be a capital specimen of a Republican King to be exhibited among the productions of our country at the Christal Palace. Were Kennedy with him he would be regarded with interest as one of his cabinet—quite a cabinet curiosity.

Farewell my dear Mrs Kennedy; with affectionate remembrances to your father, your sister, and that self tasking man your husband, who I hope will not over task himself, I remain

ever very truly yours
Washington Irving

MANUSCRIPT: Peabody Library.   PUBLISHED: *Sewanee Review*, 25 (January, 1917), 17.

1. This letter has not been located.
2. Mrs. Kennedy's gentle saddle horse.
3. Millard Fillmore, the former president of the United States, had sailed for Liverpool on May 17, 1855. He was presented to Queen Victoria on June 12. See London *Times*, June 13, 1855.

2417. To R. Shelton Mackenzie

Sunnyside Sept 4th 1855

My dear Sir,

Your very obliging letter of the 20th of August, remained several days at the Astor Library before it was put into my hands.[1] The letter of Washington to Sir John Sinclair dated Dec 11. 1796.[2] is in the Correspondence published by Sparks,[3] which I possess. I do not know whether the Collection of Sir John Sinclairs correspondence[4] is in the Astor library or not. If it is not, I shall request Mr Cogswell to procure it. In the mean time, not having immediate necessity of referring to Washingtons correspondence with Sir John I will not avail myself of your kind offer to lend me the two volumes, lest they should be mislaid in the chaos of books and papers that is apt to gather around me.

I find I am indebted to you for a very favorable critique on my work which appeared in the Daily Times.[5] It is deeply gratifying to meet with approbation at such hands.

Yours my dear Sir / very truly
Washington Irving

R Shelton MacKenzie Esq

MANUSCRIPT: NYPL—Seligman Collection.

Robert Shelton Mackenzie (1809–1881), formerly editor of the Liverpool *Journal*, had come to America in 1852, settled in New York City, and become literary editor of the New York *Times*.

1. Mackenzie's letter has not been located. WI often used the Astor Library on Lafayette Place for mail delivery when he was in New York.
2. The letter of Sinclair (1754–1835) may be found in *The Writings of George Washington*, ed. John C. Fitzpatrick, XXXV, 324–31.

3. *The Writings of George Washington,* edited by Jared Sparks, appeared in twelve volumes between 1834 and 1837.

4. *The Correspondence of the Right Honourable Sir John Sinclair* (2 vols.) was published by Colburn and Bentley in London in 1831.

5. Mackenzie's three and one-third column review of WI's *Life of George Washington* appeared in New York *Times* on June 4, 1855.

2418. To Martin Van Buren

Sunnyside ⟨Aug⟩ Sept: 4t. 1855

My dear Sir,

It gives me great pleasure to accept your kind invitation to Lindenwald.[1] If the weather should not prevent I shall take the train on Friday next, which arrives at Stuyvesant about two Oclock

I shall apprise Kemble[2] by this mail of my intentions.

Yours very truly
Washington Irving

The Hon. Martin Van Buren.

MANUSCRIPT: NYSL.

1. Van Buren's invitation has not been located. Lindenwald was Van Buren's home in Kinderhook which he had purchased in 1841 after his defeat for re-election. WI had stayed in the house in 1809 when it was owned by John P. Van Ness and had written part of *Knickerbocker's History* there.

2. Gouverneur Kemble's home at Cold Spring lay along the route of the railroad WI would take. It is possible that Kemble accompanied him on the visit.

2419. To William A. Duer

Sunnyside Sept 6. 1855

My dear Sir,

As a *virtuous* woman I cannot say that Lady B's reputation stood very high.[1] Her Beauty, her talents, and her amiable manners drew a wide circle around her; but of gentlemen rather than ladies. I do not think her Soirees in England were frequented by those of her own sex who were fastidious as to the morals of their acquaintances; on the Continent she had a wider circulation, as a cracked reputation passes more currently there, and a gay luxurious house is sure to be popular.

Moore (anacreon)[2] who was a great friend of Lady B, and first made me acquainted with her, gave me an amusing anecdote of her in early life. She and her sister,³ who had both been belles in Ireland, were left young, ⟨desitut⟩ beautiful and destitute and were at a loss to know what to do, or what was to become of them—"*It would not do to be wicked?* Said one to the other with a shy, dubious, enquiring look. I do not know what was the reply—but ⟨I believe⟩ ↑Moore intimated that↓ they were a little wicked at the outset.

                              Yours, my dear Sir / very truly
                                        Washington Irving
William A Duer Esq.

MANUSCRIPT: NYHS.

1. Probably the Countess Marguerite Blessington (1789–1849), who was a friend of Lord Byron and prominent in London society after the death of her husband. For about fifteen years Count D'Orsay lived with her.

2. Thomas Moore (1779–1852), WI's friend whom he identifies by his translation of Anacreon made while he was a student at Trinity College, Dublin.

3. Probably Mary Anne Power, who in 1832 married the Baron de St. Marsault.

2420.   To George P. Morris

                                        Sunnyside Sept 6t. 1855

My dear General,

    I shall be very happy to recieve you and Mr Richards at Sunnyside whenever you think proper to make the proposed visit.¹ I will only intimate that I leave home tomorrow (Friday) to be absent three or four days; but you will find me at home any time after the middle of next week.

                                        Yours very truly
                                        Washington Irving
Gen. Geo P. Morris

P. S. I am sorry to say I cannot offer Mr Richards a bed as my "Spare room" is bespoke by successive visitors for some time to come. My little mansion has generally what is called a *Scotch housefull* that is to say, rather more than it will hold.

MANUSCRIPT: NYPL—Berg Collection.

1. Thomas Addison Richards (1820–1900), who emigrated from England in 1831, became known as a landscape painter and teacher. Secretary of the National Academy of Design for forty years, he was associated with the Hudson River School of painting.

2421. To John H. B. Latrobe

Lindenwald, Sept. 10th. 1855

My dear Mr Latrobe,

I have left your kind letter[1] too long unanswered, but I find it impossible, fagged as I am by daily literary labor, to keep from falling behind hand in my correspondence[.] I thank you for the copy of your address[2] which you have had the kindness to send me and which posts me up on the subject of "Mason and Dixons line" that 'House hold word' with regard to which I was rather indifferently informed; but I especially value your letter and its accompanyment as linking up the acquaintance of our former years,[3] and proving that its continuance is still desirable to you.

Believe me my dear Mr Latrobe with the highest esteem and regard

Yours very faithfully
Washington Irving

John H. B. Latrobe Esq

MANUSCRIPT: Maryland Historical Society.

John H. B. Latrobe (1803–1891), son of Benjamin Latrobe, who was architect of the United States Capitol, and cousin of Charles Joseph Latrobe, with whom WI traveled to the Indian Territory in 1832, was associated with the Baltimore and Ohio Railroad all of his life.

1. This letter has not been located.
2. *The History of Mason and Dixon's Line; Contained in an Address Delivered by John H. B. Latrobe ... before the Historical Society of Pennsylvania, November 8, 1854* ([Philadelphia], 1855).
3. WI had probably met Latrobe through his acquaintance with Louis McLane, who was associated with the Baltimore and Ohio Railroad, and John P. Kennedy, who was a resident of Baltimore.

2422. To Gustav W. Lurman

Sunnyside Sept 25t. 1855

My dear Sir,

The press of various engagements has prevented an earlier expression of the great pleasure you have given me by Your kind letter of the 8th. inst.[1] My first volume of the life of Washington was put to press with almost painful diffidence; and I have been affraid of trusting implicitly to the favorable notices of it in the public papers, which are so ⟨futh?⟩ often the result of the management of publishers and booksellers.

It is most gratifying to me therefore to recieve such a cordial note of approbation from a gentleman like yourself, given too so promptly and spontaneously on the warm impulse of the moment.

I have just given the manuscript of my second volume to the press;[2] I hope it may experience as favorable a fortune as the first.

Present my kindest respects to Mrs Lurman[3] and believe me very truly

Your obliged friend
Washington Irving

Gustav. W. Lurman Esqr

MANUSCRIPT: VA.–Barrett.

Gustav W. Lurman was a German-born Baltimore merchant and a prominent member of the Baltimore German Whig Club. He supported the Confederacy during the Civil War and lost most of his fortune. See Ellinor Stuart Heiser, *Days Gone By* (Baltimore, 1940), p. 312; and Dieter Cunz, *The Maryland Germans: A History* (Princeton, 1948), p. 267.

1. This letter has not been located.

2. The second volume of WI's *Life of George Washington,* which appeared in December, 1855, was being printed at this time. See PMI, IV, 197.

3. Mrs. Lurman was the former Frances Lyman Donnell, daughter of John Donnell, a wealthy resident of Baltimore. See Heiser, *Days Gone By,* p. 86.

2423. *To George H. Moore*

Sunnyside, Sept. 25th. 1855

My dear Sir,

I feel much honored by the request of the Special Committee on papers of the New York Historical Society that I would furnish a paper to be read at the monthly meeting in October, or a chapter in advance of the life of Washington. I regret to say however that it is impossible for me at present to find ⟨tim⟩ liesure to prepare a paper and that I do not consider any chapter of my work well calculated for effect when read detached, in the manner proposed.

I shall be happy on some future occasion, when not so much occupied and engrossed as I am just now, to meet the wishes of the committee

I remain, my dear Sir / Yours very respectfully
Washington Irving

Geo Henry Moore Esqr. / Secy of the Committee

MANUSCRIPT: NYHS.

2424. To Stephen J. W. Tabor

Sunnyside Sept 25t. 1855

My dear Sir

Columbus in his third voyage was accompanied by a monk of the order of St Jerome who made himself well acquainted with the language of the natives of Hispaniola, and their ceremonies and antiquities. At the request of Columbus he wrote down all that he knew concerning them. His manuscript was inserted, at full length, by Fernando Columbus in his History of the Life and Actions of his father. Fernando's history was originally ⟨p⟩ written and published in Italian[1]—I made us[e][2] of a Spanish translation of it. An English translation is to be found in the Second volume of Churchills Collection of Voyages.[3] ↑(third edition London 1744)↓ In this the Friars account of the Natives[4] occupies about ten and a half folio pages (double columns)[.] I am not aware nor do I think the Friars treatise has ever appeared otherwise than embodied in Fernando Columbus' History.

Roman *Pane* I apprehend to be a misnomer. It should be Fray Roman or Padre Roman—in latin Romanus.

I have not the Spanish translation from which I originally cited—In the english translation in Churchill the Friars account is headed—*The manuscript of F Roman concerning the antiquity of the Indians, which he, as being skilled in their tongues, has carefully gathered by order of the Admiral—*

It begins

I, F. Roman, a poor anchorite of the order of St Jerome, by order of the most illustrious Lord admiral, viceroy &c &c &c write what I could hear and learn of the belief and idolatry of the Indians and how they serve their gods, &c.

I should have answered your letter sooner but had not books at hand to refer to

Yours very respectfully
Washington Irving

Stephen J W Tabor M. D.

P. S. It is in Page 156 not 136 of Schlözers Briefwechsel[5] that the friar is alluded to as Roman Pane a Spanish hermit—but he ↑evidently↓ derives his knowledge from Churchills Collection.

MANUSCRIPT: Va.–Barrett.

Stephen J. W. Tabor (1815–1883) was a journalist who studied medicine and practiced in New York from 1840 to 1855. After eight years in Iowa as a newspaperman and country official, he was appointed fourth auditor of the Treasury by President Lincoln, a post which he held until a few years before his death. He possessed a fine collection of books, with many important works relating to tea, coffee, and tobacco.

1. *Historie della vita e de' fatti dell' Ammiraglio D. Christoforo Colombo* (Venice, 1571).

2. WI omitted the bracketed letter.

3. Awnsham and John Churchill compiled *A Collection of Voyages and Travels,* published in London in 1704 in four volumes.

4. Tabor may have been prompted to inquire about Friar Roman because of WI's footnote reference to him in the 1850 edition of *The Life and Voyages of Columbus.*

5. August Ludwig von Schlözer, *Briefwechsel, Meist Historischen und Politischen Inhalts* (1774–1782).

2425. To Henry Onderdonk, Jr.

Sunnyside Sept. 30t. 1855

Dear Sir

Accept my thanks for the volume of Revolutionary facts which you have had the kindness to send me, and which does credit to your research as well as to your patriotism:[1]

Accept my thanks also for the kind expressions in the note which accompanied the volume[2] and believe me my dear Sir

Your truly obliged friend & Servt
Washington Irving

Henry Onderdonk Jr. Esqr.

Manuscript: Long Island Historical Society.

Henry Onderdonk, Jr. (1804–1882), who was the principal of the Union Hall Academy on Long Island from 1832 to 1865, published several histories of Long Island, including *Documents and Letters Intended to Illustrate the Revolutionary Incidents of Queens County* (1846), *Revolutionary Incidents of Suffolk and Kings Counties* (1849), *Long Island and New York in Olden Times* (1851), and *The Annals of Hempstead* (1878).

1. Among the books in WI's library at Sunnyside is *Revolutionary Incidents of Queens County.* Onderdonk probably thought that the volume would be useful to WI in his work on Washington in the New York area during the Revolutionary War.

2. This note has not been located.

2426.   To Joseph E. Worcester

Sunnyside Oct 3d. 1855

Dear Sir

Accept my thanks for the copy of your pronouncing, Explanatory and Synonimous Dictionary which you have had the kindness to send me.[1] As far as I have had time to examine it, it gives me great satisfaction and appears to me to be well calculated to fulfil the purpose for which it professes to be intended—to supply the wants of Common Schools and to be a sufficient manual for schools of a higher order.

With best wishes for your success I remain, dear Sir

With great respect / Your obliged & hbl Servt
Washington Irving

Joseph E. Worcester L. L. D.

MANUSCRIPT: MHS.

Joseph E. Worcester (1784–1865) was a geographer and lexicographer whose first publications were *Geographical Dictionary, or Universal Gazette* (1817) and *Elements of Geography, Ancient and Modern* (1819). After some work as a lexicographer on editions of Johnson's and Webster's dictionaries he produced his *Pronouncing and Explanatory Dictionary* in 1830. This was followed in 1846 by the *Universal and Critical Dictionary*, which was revised and enlarged in 1847, 1849, and 1855.

1. WI apparently received a copy of the 1855 revision.

2427.   To Thomas S. Hastings

Sunnyside Oct 6t. 1855

Dear Sir,

I feel very much obliged to You for Your kind offer to furnish me with copies of certain original letters of Gen Washington

I should like to have copies of the letter of instructions to Col Wm DeHart dated Decr 22[1]

The letter of instructions dated Head quarters Morristown Jany. 8. 1780[2]

The letter dated from the same place Jan 14 1780 concerning Stirlings proposed attack on Staten Island and that of June 14th. concerning the rumored Evacuation of N York.[3]

I feel reluctant to task your civility in this manner but the very frank and cordial manner in which you have proffered it must be my apology.

Very respectfully dear Sir / Your obliged friend & Servt

Washington Irving

The Rev. Thomas S Hastings

MANUSCRIPT: SHR.

Thomas S. Hastings (1827–1911), a graduate of Hamilton College and Union Theological Seminary, was a minister at Mendham, New Jersey. In 1856 he became pastor of the West Presbyterian Church in New York City, where he remained for twenty-five years.

1. Probably Washington's letter of December 22, 1779, to De Hart. See *The Writings of George Washington,* ed. John C. Fitzpatrick, XVII, 301–2.

2. See *The Writings of George Washington,* XVII, 362–65. For WI's use of it, see *Life of George Washington,* IV, chap. 1.

3. See *The Writings of George Washington,* XVII, 389–98 for several letters of January 14, 1780, dealing with Stirling's attack. The letter of June 14, 1780, is not included in *The Writings of George Washington.*

2428.   To [Thomas S. Hastings?]

Sunnysid[e][1] Oct 15th. 1855

My dear Sir,

I am really very heartily obliged to you for the promptness with which you have followed up your kind offer in procuring me copies of the letters of Washington in the possession of Miss N. I. Thompson.[2] I enclose a note of thanks to that lady which you will have the goodness to deliver.

You speak of two lectures upon "Washington in Morris County" by the Rev. J. F Tuttle.[3] Should they be in print I should be glad to be put in a way of getting them, as you say they contain facts which Mr Bancroft deemes "quite valuable"

With great respect / My dear Sir / Yours truly obliged

Washington Irving

MANUSCRIPT: Huntington.

In view of the context, it is probable that the addressee is the Reverend Thomas S. Hastings, to whom WI had written on October 6, 1855.

1. WI omitted the bracketed letter.

2. Miss Thompson was probably an acquaintance or parishioner of Hasting's at Mendham, New Jersey. In the edition of Washington's writings prepared for publication in 1932, John C. Fitzpatrick acknowledged the use of photostats and

originals supplied by Julian F. Thompson, who was probably a relative of the Miss Thompson mentioned here. See *The Writings of George Washington*, XVII, 302, 362, and 394.

3. Joseph F. Tuttle (1818–1901), a graduate of Marietta College (1841) and Lane Theological Seminary of Cincinnati (1844), was pastor of the Presbyterian Church at Rockaway, New Jersey from 1847 to 1862, following which he was president of Wabash College for about thirty years. Apparently Hastings persuaded Tuttle to send WI the manuscripts of his lectures. For WI's grateful letter returning the manuscripts, see WI to Tuttle, February 2, 1856.

2429.   To Miss N. I. Thompson

Sunnyside Oct. 15th 1855

Miss Thompson will please to accept my sincere thanks for her kindness in permitting copies to be taken for me ⟨from⟩ ↑of↓ the original letters of General Washington in her possession
   With great respect I remain

> her obliged friend & servt
> Washington Irving

Miss N. I. Thompson.

Manuscript: SHR.

For background see WI to [Thomas S. Hastings?], October 15, 1855.

2430.   To Benjamin Silliman

Sunnyside Oct 18t. 1855

My dear Sir,
   I feel really very much obliged to you for the extracts from letters written during the Revolution, which you have had the kindness to send me.[1] The plot to which they allude is that formed among the Tories of New York in June 1776. to aid the British troops on their arrival. It was traced up to Governor Tryon.—Many arrests took place, among others the Mayor, David Mathews, who had disbursed money for the purchase of arms. Washingtons guards had been tampered with; and one of them, Thomas Hickey, was hanged as a traitor.[2] The general report concerning the plot was that upon the arrival of the British troops the conspirators were to murder all the staff officers, blow up the magazines and Secure the passes of the town—but the country was full of exaggerated rumors on the subject.

I thank you for your kind expressions concerning my work. The Success of the first volume relieves me from much doubt and diffidence in the matter, and encourages me to persevere in my attempt to depict revolutionary times as they were; with the medley of passions, interests virtues and vices which prevailed. Thank god the virtues were predominant.

With great respect

My dear Sir / Yours very truly
Washington Irving

B. Silliman, L.L.D.

ADDRESSED: B. Silliman L. L. D. / New Haven / Connecticut   POSTMARKED: Irvin[gton] O / N. Y
MANUSCRIPT: Yale.

1. Silliman's extracts prepared for WI have not been located, and WI does not acknowledge them as sources for his discussion of the 1776 campaign. However, in a footnote he quotes an extract from a letter about the conspiracy. See *Life of George Washington*, II, chap. 24. WI may have added it after the rest of the text was set in type.

2. The incidents involving colonial governor William Tryon (1729–1788), David Matthews, and Thomas Hickey were treated early in chapter 24.

2431.   To John W. Leslie

Sunnyside Oct 29t. [1855]

My dear Sir

I have recieved revises or plate proofs from p. 1 to 98 inclusive, excepting pages 73. 74. 75. 76. 77. 78.

Then from page 121 to 128 inclusive.

The only errors I remark are page 37 at the end of the third line *fresher* ought to be *further*—the date 1775 wanting at the head of Page 121.[1]

I shall be in town tomorrow (tuesday)

Yours truly
W I.

J. W. Leslie Esq

MANUSCRIPT: Yale.

John W. Leslie joined Putnam's as a partner in 1854. In 1855 Putnam discovered that Leslie had speculated heavily with company funds, leaving the firm in debt. Although plates and sheets had to be sold to pay the debts, Putnam did not remove

Leslie, who subsequently drowned in a boating accident in 1857. See John Tebbel, *A History of Book Publishing in the United States* (New York, 1972), I, 310.

The year has been determined by the perpetual calendar.

1. Proofreading of volume 2 of WI's *Life of George Washington* had begun as early as October 5, 1855. See PMI, IV, 197.

2432.   To George P. Putnam and Company

Sunnyside Nov 1. 1855

Messrs. Putnam & Co

Gentlemen,

The following are all the corrections to be made in a lot of revises or plate proofs sent to me yesterday.[1]

P. 144—Fifth line from the bottom *Sterling* should be spelled Stirling.[2]

P 145. third line from the bottom "*in* Long Island" should be "*on* Long Island."

P 204 The * after Washington should be after opinion, on the line above.

P 216 lines 12. & 25 Deschambeault should be Deschambault.

P. 217. line 9 The same error occurs in the same name.

These are all the errors I percieve. I will thank you to point them out to the Printer.

I left the two last sets of proofs corrected, at No 32. La Fayette Place for Mr Pierre M Irving to look over them and hand them to you. I presume he has done so

Yours very truly
Washington Irving

Manuscript: Haverford College Library.

1. These are corrections for volume 2 of WI's *Life of George Washington*.
2. WI placed a double line under the "i" in "Stirling" and "in" in the next line.

2433.   To Charles Gould

Sunnyside Nov 13th 1855

Dear Sir,

I duly received some time since your obliging note[1] inviting me to call at your house and look at a picture of Leutzes representing the embarkation of Columbus[2] and intended promptly to avail myself of it. But I have rarely been in town since, and then only on brief visits, connected with the literary task on which I am engaged, and am really so engrossed by it just now that I have not had time to make the visit I intended. I trust to find liesure shortly when I can escape from the hands of the printers

Very respectfully / Your obliged & hbl Servt
Washington Irving

Charles Gould Esqr.

MANUSCRIPT: Harvard.

Charles Gould lived at 5 Madison Square North. See *Trow's New York City Directory for 1855–56*, p. 333. According to George Templeton Strong, Gould and Prosper M. Wetmore, who organized a Union League group during the Civil War, were recognized as embodiments "of corrupt, mercenary, self-seeking sham-patriotism and as representing a dirty set of false-hearted hack stump orators and wire-pullers. . . ." See Strong, *Diary*, III, 297–98, 312, 319.

1. This note has not been located.
2. Emanuel Gottlieb Leutze (1816–1868) was a German-born historical and portrait painter chiefly remembered for his *Washington Crossing the Delaware*. He painted several pictures with Columbus as the subject, but the one mentioned here has not been identified.

2434. To [George P. Putnam]

[November 23, 1855?]

My dear Sir

I sent you two chapters (37 & 38 I believe) by yesterdays mail—I presume you have received them. There will yet be about seventy pages of my manuscript to complete the volume. You should have had them before this time had ⟨it⟩ not ⟨been⟩ my painful indisposition prevented me from giving them a last revision. I will finish them off and bring them with me to town on Monday morning.[1]

I have no corrections to make on the revises of the first hundred pages

Yours very truly
Washington Irving

Sunnyside, Nov. 23d. [1855?]

ADDRESSED: Geo. P. Putnam, Esq / 155 Broadway / N York
MANUSCRIPT: Louisville Free Public Library.

Probably the year is 1855. In November WI was completing the text and proof-reading the galleys for volume 2 of his *Life of George Washington*.

1. November 23, 1855, fell on Friday. WI would thus have the weekend to complete his revisions.

2435. To Duncan F. Curry

N York Nov. 24t. 1855

Dear Sir

It would give me great pleasure to accept the obliging invitation of the Stewarts of the St. Nicholas Society[1] to their 'tasting dinner,' but unfortunately it comes on Saturday[2] and would oblige me to be absent from home on the following Sunday, on which day I have special engagements there.

Very respectfully / Your ob Servt
Washington Irving

D. F. Curry Esqr.

MANUSCRIPT: SHR.

Duncan F. Curry, who had an office at 74 Wall Street, resided at 92 West 27th Street. See *Trow's New York City Directory for 1855–56*, p. 203.

1. The Saint Nicholas Society, of which WI was one of the founders in 1835 and one of the officers until 1841, promoted literary activities in New York City. See Haswell, *Reminiscences of an Octogenarian*, p. 295; STW, II, 53, 344; and WI to Sarah Storrow, December 1, 1841.
2. WI was in error. The dinner was scheduled for Thursday, December 6 at Delmonico's. See NYEP, December 1, 1855.

2436. (deleted)

2437. To William A. Duer

Sunnyside Decr 5th 1855

My dear Sir,

I must trust to your indulgence for my delay in answering your letter[1] but really I have been so hurried of late in ⟨propose⟩ getting a volume of my work through the press and making additions and alterations, to the last moment, that all my correspondence is behind hand and in confusion

I am very much obliged to you for your offer of the profile of Washington[2] and if you will send it to Mr Denning Duer,[3] I will get my publisher Mr Putnam to call on him for it. The forthcoming volume will have an engraving of ⟨has f⟩ Stewarts portrait of him; and a copy of Peals is likewise in preparation.[4] The profile you offer will be interesting from its associations and may be given in the third volume; with an accompanying memorandum.

I am my dear Sir / with great respect / Yours very truly

Washington Irving

W. A. Duer Esq—

MANUSCRIPT: NYHS.

1. This letter has not been located.
2. The profile of Washington appeared in WI's *Life of George Washington*, IV, chap. 31 (1857). Under the black profile is the note: "From the Original (cut with scissors) by Miss De Hart, Elizabethtown, N. J., 1783. Presented by Mrs. Washington to Mrs. Duer, Daughter of Lord Stirling."
3. Denning Duer was a banker who worked at 53 William Street. See *Trow's New York City Directory for 1855–56*, p. 247.
4. Gilbert Stuart's portrait of Washington, taken from life in 1795, served as the frontispiece for volume 3 of WI's *Life of George Washington*. Charles Willson Peale's painting of Washington as a colonel in the Virginia militia, done in 1772, was the frontispiece for volume 2. These portraits are discussed in Henry T. Tuckerman's essay, "Portraits of Washington," which appeared in the appendix of volume 5 of the *Life of George Washington*.

2438.   *To Eugene H. Munday*

Sunnyside Decr. 5t. 1855

Dear Sir

The account of "the ⟨"⟩*little White Lady*" given by me in my visit to Newstead Abbey,[1] is *strictly according to facts* furnished me by Colonel and Mrs Wildman[2] aided by inspection of that singular persons own manuscripts. There is *no "fiction nor filling up"* of my own—

The press of various occupations has prevented an earlier reply to your letter[3]

Yours very respectfully

Washington Irving

Eugene H Munday, Esqr

ADDRESSED: Eugene H. Munday Esq / Philadelphia   POSTMARKED: NEW YORK / DEC / 6
MANUSCRIPT: HSP.

Eugene H. Munday was a Philadelphia writer who brought out a series of articles on Philadelphia newspapers and magazines and *Cabinet Poems* (1879). See Frank Luther Mott, *A History of American Magazines*, IV, 683–84.

1. WI told the sentimental story of Sophia Hyatt, the "little White Lady," in *Newstead Abbey* (in *The Crayon Miscellany*, vol. 2 [Philadelphia, 1835], pp. 202–30), which was reprinted in *The Crayon Miscellany*, volume 9 of the Author's Revised Edition (1850).

2. Thomas Wildman (1787–1859), who had purchased Newstead Abbey, Lord Byron's ancestral home near Sherwood Forest, in 1818 for £95,000, welcomed WI as a house guest for several weeks in January, 1832. See WI to Charles R. Leslie, January 9, 1832; to Catharine Paris, January 20, 1832; and to Peter Irving, January 20, 1832.

3. This letter has not been located.

2439. *To Alvah Beebe*

Sunnyside Decr 7th. 1855

My dear Sir,

The hurry of various occupations has prevented an earlier acknowledgement of the receipt of the pamphlet which you have had the kindness to lend me. The letters it contains appeared originally in London and were reprinted in New York, while the city was in the hands of the British They were fabrications[1] by some unknown hand; possibly founded on family letters of Washington which had been intercepted; but interlarded with opinions and sentiments totally at variance with his character and conduct and the cause he was so zealously vindicating. The object doubtless was to inspire distrust of him and of the cause and to injure both with the public. They failed entirely. Washington did not notice them at the time, but in after years when they were insidiously revived for political purposes, he in a letter to the Secretary of ⟨Sp⟩ State pronounced them spurious and false[2]

You will find mention made of them in Sparks Life of Washington p 265. With your permission I will retain the pamphlet a little while longer but will carefully return it to you

With many thanks for your obliging civilities, I remain

Dear Sir / Yours very respectfully
Washington Irving

Alvah Beebe Esqr.

MANUSCRIPT: Va.–Barrett.

Alvah Beebee (d. 1880) was a broker in real estate, loans, and bonds at 195 Broadway. See *Trow's New York City Directory for 1855–56*, p. 64.

1. WI treats the subject of the forged letters in his *Life of George Washington,* III, chap. 29.

2. Washington's letter of March 3, 1797, setting the record straight is printed in *The Writings of George Washington,* ed. John C. Fitzpatrick, XXXV, 414–16.

2440. To Abiel S. Thurston

Sunnyside, Dec. 11th, 1855.

My dear Sir:

Accept my thanks for the curious document concerning Jacob Van Tassel, which you have had the kindness to send me.[1] I shall carefully lay them up in the archives of my little mansion; which, as you suppose, is built on the identical site, and I may add, partly with the materials, of the "stone house" once the castle of the redoubtable Jacob. I regret to say that I have not the *"Goose-Gun"* which once formed its artillery, and which, if tradition speaks true, could carry a ball across the Tappan Sea.[2] I saw it once in the possession of old Mr. Henry Brevoort,[3] of the Bowery, who promised I should have it at his death; but he is dead, and the "Goose-Gun" has gone into other hands.

I must have seen old Mr. Van Tassel about the time you became acquainted with him. I had a long conversation with him at his abode in Greenwich-street, New-York, in which I gathered some of the particulars I have since recorded. He was a type of the bel[l]igerent[4] yeomanry of Westchester County, who figured in the border feuds of Skinner and Cowboy in the time of the Revolution, and kept watch along the shores of the Tappan Sea.[5]

Very respectfully / Your obliged and humble servant,
Washington Irving

Abiel S. Thurston, Esq.

PUBLISHED: *Knickerbocker Magazine,* 55 (February, 1860), 225.

Abiel Thurston was a lawyer from Elmira, New York. He may have read *Knickerbocker's History* in the revised edition of 1854, which was a further revision of the major reworking of the material prepared for the Author's Revised Edition of 1848. See *A History of New York,* ed. Edwin T. Bowden (New Haven, 1964), "A Note on the Text," p. 19; *Knickerbocker Magazine,* 55 (February, 1860), 225.

1. The "curious document" was the original pension-certificate voucher with which Jacob Van Tassel received his Revolutionary War pension. See *Knickerbocker Magazine,* 55 (February, 1860), 225.

2. In "Wolfert's Roost," Chronicle II, which first appeared in *Knickerbocker Magazine* in April, 1839, WI describes Van Tassel's goose-gun which was used to fire upon British ships from the shore of the Hudson River during the Revolutionary

War. The farm, which Van Tassel acquired from Wolfert Acker, was purchased by WI in 1835. See *Wolfert's Roost and Other Papers, Now First Collected* (New York, 1855), pp. 15–23; and *Wolfert's Roost,* ed. Roberta Rosenberg, The Competer Works of Washington Irving, XXVII (Boston: Twayne Publishers, 1979), 3–16.

3. Henry Brevoort, Sr. (1747–1841), the father of WI's friend of the same name.
4. The printed version omitted the bracketed letter.
5. The printed version used the old Dutch spelling.

2441. To Moses Thomas

Sunnyside, Decr 14t. 1855.

My dear Thomas:

I thank you heartily for your kind and hospitable invitation[1] to your house, which I should be glad to accept did I propose attending the Godey complimentary dinner;[2] but the annoyances I suffer at dinners of the kind in having to attempt speeches, or bear compliments in silence has made me abjure them altogether. The publishers festival[3] at which I had the great pleasure of meeting you was an exception to my rule, but only made on condition that I would not be molested by extra civilities

I regret that on that occasion we were separated from each other and could not sit together and talk over old times; however, I trust we shall have a future opportunity of so doing. I wish when you visit New York you would take a run up to Sunnyside; the cars set you down within ten minutes walk of my house, where my 'women kind' will recieve you (*figuratively speaking*) with open arms; and my dogs will not dare to bark at you.

Yours ever very truly
Washington Irving

Moses Thomas Esqr

MANUSCRIPT: Va.–Barrett. PUBLISHED: PMI, IV, 199–200; *Irvingiana,* p. lxii; J. C. Derby, *Fifty Years Among Authors, Books and Publishers* (New York, 1884), p. 40.

1. This letter has not been located.
2. A dinner held in Philadelphia for Louis A. Godey (1804–1878), founder and coeditor of *Godey's Lady's Book.* See PMI, IV, 199.
3. This gathering, a compliment to authors and publishers, was held at the Crystal Palace in New York City on September 27, 1855. See PMI, IV, 196–97.

2442.   To T. Addison Richards

Sunnyside Decr. 15t. 1855

My dear Sir

The hurried degree to which I have been engrossed of late in passing a volume of my work through the press has rendered it impossible for me to be punctual in letter writing Yours of the 24th of november[1] has consequently remained with many others unanswered until now that I have time to take breath and look about me.

I am very much obliged to you for the copy of your Romance of American Landscape;[2] it lay for some time at Mr Putnams so that it is not until recently I have had it on my parlour table to the great satisfaction of my nieces by whom it is much admired—

I trust your ensuing work will be still more interesting from the Specimens I have seen of the sketches you have made for it.[3] I regret to say that I can suggest nothing for the text; but if you would submit the sketches of Sunnyside to my nephew and niece Mr & Mrs Pierre M Irving (No 262 Fou[r]th[4] Avenue) they may be able to give you some hints and incidents as they are frequent inmates of my little home

With best wishes for your success / Yours very truly
Washington Irving

T. Addison Richards Esq

MANUSCRIPT: NYPL–Berg Collection.

1. This letter has not been located.
2. This volume, published in New York by G. A. Leavitt, is among the books in WI's library at Sunnyside.
3. Richards had been sketching in the Sunnyside area in the late summer and early fall of 1855. See WI to George P. Morris, September 6, 1855. Richards's sketches appeared in "Sunnyside, The Home of Washington Irving," *Harper's Magazine*, 14 (December, 1856), 1–21.
4. WI omitted the bracketed letter.

2443.   To Osmond Tiffany

Sunnyside Decr 15t. 1855

Dear Sir

Your letter of Nov 19[1] arrived at a time when I was absent from home. It was mislaid by a servant and has just come to hand, otherwise it would have been promptly answered.

A work of fiction such as you suggest,[2] embracing scenes in the Ancient Dominion one hundred years since with the customs, manners and celebrated characters of the times and in the north, with passages of Wolfes famous expedition cannot fail if well executed of commanding general attention and being very successful.

I am distrustful of my own judgement of works of the kind and do not like to give it where it might influence authors or publishers to their detriment. but if you will send your Manuscript to my publisher Mr Geo. P. Putnam (10 Park Place N.Y.) I will get him to Submit it to one of his experienced 'Elbow Critics' whose opinion is influential with the press; and would be a surer guide to you. I do not know that Mr Putnam, himself, would in any case, undertake the publication, he having rather avoided new enterprises of late; but he would be able to favor it with other publishers.

I am so much out of town and out of the busy world at present that I have but little intercourse with the gentlemen of the trade or of the press; and indeed have no intimacy with any of them but my own publishers. Indeed for some time past I have been incessantly occupied and engrossed by my literary labors, preparing my work for the press.

With best wishes for your success I am dear Sir,

Very respectfully Yours
Washington Irving

Osmond Tiffany Esqr.

MANUSCRIPT: Va.–Barrett.

1. This letter has not been located.
2. *Brandon; or, A Hundred Years Ago. A Tale of the American Colonies.* The book was finally published in 1858 by Stanford & Delisser of New York. In the preface Tiffany noted that the book had been written three years earlier but that he had been unable to find a publisher.

2444. To Robert Forsyth

Sunnyside Decr 18th. 1855

Dear Sir

There must be some mistake about the little poem which you have sent to me. It must be a selection which you have found among your daughter['s][1] papers and which you have mistaken for one of her original effusions. You will find it with some slight verbal variations in a collection of poems published in London in 1816 and entitled "ELEGANT EXTRACTS—*poetry*" it is at page 427 and is called 'a winter piece.'[2] The collection

is extracted from various authors; the piece in question is given as anonymous.

Very respectfully / Your obt St
Washington Irving

Robert Forsyth Esqr

MANUSCRIPT: Va.–Barrett.

1. WI omitted the bracketed portion.

2. The edition WI cites has not been located; but in *Elegant Extracts: or, Useful and Entertaining Pieces of Poetry, selected for the Improvement of Young Persons* (London, 1801), p. 492, is "A Winter Piece," an anonymous piece about a young woman and her infant who are turned out into the cold and snow by her parents after, it would seem, her "lad" had forsaken her. The young mother kisses the baby's "pale lips" and then dies in the snow. *Elegant Extracts* is not among the books in WI's library at Sunnyside.

2445. To James K. Paulding

Sunnyside Decr 24t. 1855

My dear Paulding,

I enclose an autograph for the "paragon of a young lady"[1] whose beauty you extol beyond the stars. It is a good sign that your heart is yet so inflammable.

I am glad to recieve such good accounts as you give of yourself and your brother,[2] "jogging on together in good humor with each other and with the world" Happy is he who can grow smooth as an old shilling as he wears out; he has endured the rubs of life to some purpose

You hope I am "sliding smoothly down the hill;" I thank you for the hope—I am better off than most old bachelors are, or deserve to be. I have a happy home; the happier for being always well stocked with women kind, without whom an old bachelor is a forlorn dreary animal. My brother the "General"[3] is wearing out the serene evening of life with me; almost entirely deaf, but in good health and good spirits more and more immersed in the study of news papers (with which I keep him copiously supplied) and, through them, better acquainted with what is going on in the world, than I am, who mingle with it occasionally and have ears as well as eyes open His daughters take care of us both and keep the little world of home in perfect order.

I have had many vivid enjoyments in the course of my life, yet no por-
tion of it has been more equably and serenely happy than that which I have passed in my little nest in the country. I am just near enough to town to dip into it occasionally for a day or two, give my mind an airing,

keep my notions a little up to the fashion of the times, and then return to my quiet little home with redoubled relish.

I have now my house full for the Christmas holydays; which I trust you also keep up in the good old style. Wishing a Merry Christmas and a happy New Year to you and yours I remain, my dear Paulding

Yours ever very truly
Washington Irving

James K Paulding Esqr.

MANUSCRIPT: James Kirke Paulding III.   PUBLISHED: *Letters of J. K. Paulding,* pp. 558–59; PMI, IV, 201–2 (in part); *Literary Life of James K. Paulding,* ed. William I. Paulding, pp. 366–67.

1. On December 16, 1855, Paulding had requested WI's autograph for Emily Pearson (1837–1901), who married his youngest son, James Nathaniel (1833–1898), on October 10, 1860. See *Letters of J. K. Paulding,* pp. 558, [615]. On a separate sheet preserved with WI's letter is written, in WI's hand, the following: "Written at the request of James K Paulding, for 'one of the most beautiful young ladies in this or any other world'—as he says." WI's autograph above this passage has been clipped off.

2. Nathaniel Paulding (1776–1858), who lived with his brother in a country home near Hyde Park.

3. Ebenezer Irving.

2446.   To Henry A. Smythe

Sunnyside Decr. 26th. 1855

My dear Sir,

Your canvas back Ducks and Stilton cheese came in good time to figure at my Christmas dinner at which your health was drunk with acclamations; I wish you had been there to respond.

Trusting that you have had a merry christmas and wishing that you may have a Happy New Year and including your family kittens and all in that wish—I remain most cordially yours

Washington Irving

H. A. Smythe Esq

P. S. Dont fail to buy that lot of ground

ADDRESSED: H. A. Smythe Esq / 45. Broadway / N York   POSTMARKED [handwritten]: Irvington N Y / Decr 27

MANUSCRIPT: Va.–Barrett.

2447.   To William H. Prescott

Sunnyside Decr 31t. 1855

My dear Prescott,

I have just finished devouring Your two volumes[1] and cannot resist the impulse to sieze my pen and tell you how thoroughly I am delighted with them. You have outdone your former outdoings. Your work will shed a splendor on our literature and elevate the American name. It is written with the fidelity of a scholar and the generous spirit of a cavalier. So liberal, so discriminating, so truthful, so magnificent. It has already hung up a gallery of grand historical pictures in my brain, and I foresee still grander yet to come. I only hope you will bring them out soon,[2] for I am growing old and I wish to enjoy them all before I die. In the mean time I shall begin again and read your volumes a second time, quietly and calmly that I may enjoy them like a true epicure

This is a hasty scrawl—but it is merely to grasp your hand while my heart is warm from the perusal of your work, and to bid you God speed in your glorious enterprise

Ever yours most truly
Washington Irving

ADDRESSED: William H Prescott Esq / Boston / Mass.   POSTMARKED: IRVING[TON] / JA / [*unrecovered*]   DOCKETED: Irving
MANUSCRIPT: Va.–Barrett.

1. Prescott had just brought out the first two volumes of his *History of the Reign of Philip the Second.*
2. The third and last volume appeared in 1858.

2448.   To George Sumner

New York, January 4, 1856.

George Sumner, Esq.:

Dear Sir:

Your well-known and rare opportunities of acquaintance with the public men and the public life of Europe, induce us to ask of you the favor of a lecture upon her institutions,[1] as they connect themselves with American interests and prospects. We are satisfied that any part of this general subject, treated with your resources, would be highly instructive and interesting.

Allow us to hope that your leisure and inclinations will permit you to name a time and place when the wishes of our intelligent citizens may be gratified by hearing you.

Very respectfully yours, Washington Irving, / Frederic De Peyster,[2] / Henry W. Bellows, / Wm. C. Bryant, / Stephen H. Tyng,[3] / George L. Prentiss.[4]

PUBLISHED: NYEP, January 10, 1856.

1. In his reply published with the invitation Sumner agreed to speak on "the effect of education upon the material and moral destiny of certain countries of Europe" on January 16. His lecture, "Old Europe and Young America," was presented to a "large and fashionable audience" at the Mercantile Library. See NYEP, January 17, 1856.

2. Frederick De Peyster (1796–1882), a wealthy New York lawyer interested in charitable and educational projects, was president of the New-York Historical Society and a trustee of the New York Society Library.

3. Stephen H. Tyng (1800–1885) was the minister at St. George's Episcopal Church in New York.

4. George L. Prentiss (1816–1903) was the minister at Mercer Street Presbyterian Church near Washington Square. From 1858 to 1871 he was professor of theology at Union Theological Seminary.

2449. To Henry T. Tuckerman

Sunnyside Jany. 8t. 1856.

My dear Mr Tuckerman,

I thank you most heartily for your letter;[1] which I frankly assure you was very seasonable and acceptable; being the first intimation I had recieved of the fortune of the volume I had launched upon the world.[2] It was very considerate and obliging in you to seek to relieve me from the suspense of "waiting for a verdict;" which with me is apt to be a time of painful doubt and self distrust. You have discerned what I aimed at "the careful avoidance of rhetoric, the cal⟨l⟩m, patient and faithful narrative of facts" My great labor has been to arrange those facts in the most lucid order and place them in the most favorable light; ⟨and⟩ without exaggeration or embellishment; trusting to their own characteristic value for effect. Rhetoric does very well under the saddle but is not to be trusted in harness; being apt to pull facts out of place or upset them. My horse *Gentleman Dick* was very rhetorical and shewed off finely, but he was apt to run away with me and came near breaking my neck.

I have availed myself of the license of biography to step down occasionally from the elevated walk of history and relate familiar things in a familiar way; seeking to shew the prevalent passions, and feelings and humors of the day, and even to depict the heroes of seventy six as they really were, men in cocked hats, regimental coats and breeches; and not Classic Warriors in shining armor and flowing mantles with brows bound with laurel and truncheons in their hands—But enough of all this—I have committed myself to the stream and, right or wrong, must swim on or sink. The latter I will not do if I find the public sustain me.

The work as I am writing it will inevitably over run three volumes. I had supposed originally that it would not, though I did not intend that number should be specified in the title page[3] It was specified by my publishers; who will put an authors incidental surmises into print and make positive promises of them

Should I have occasion to avail myself of the papers you so kindly put at my disposition concerning Gouverneur Morris, Early American Society &c[4] I shall have no hesitation in applying to you for them; in the mean time let me repeat how very sensibly I feel the generous interest you have manifested in my literary success on the present occasion

Yours very truly
Washington Irving

Henry T. Tuckerman Esq.

MANUSCRIPT: NYPL—Berg Collection.   PUBLISHED: PMI, IV, 206–7.   DOCKETED:
    W. Irving

1. In his letter of January 5 Tuckerman expressed his "gratification derived from your second volume," adding "The spirit of your biography most happily accords with that of the subject; the careful avoidance of rhetoric, the calm, patient & faithful narrative of facts speak to the heart more eloquently than all the high-wrought pictures through which more questionable heroes are delineated; the manly & sustained simplicity, so adapted to the theme, will prove the guarantee of a standard work; & your conscientious purpose is manifested on every page & especially, in the recognition of a prevalent tory feeling in this city, at the epoch described" (MS. at Va.–Barrett).

2. The second volume of the biography of Washington had appeared in late December, 1855. See Langfeld & Blackburn, WI Bibliography, p. 42.

3. The title pages of volumes 1 and 2 carried the line "In Three Vols." See Langfeld & Blackburn, WI Bibliography, p. 42.

4. WI is repeating the phrase in Tuckerman's letter. Gouverneur Morris (1752–1816) was a member of the Continental Congress in 1778–1779 and American agent and U.S. minister in Paris from 1789 to 1794.

2450. To Lewis G. Clark

(Copy.)

Sunnyside Jan 10th. 1856

My dear Mr Clark

The manuscript purporting to be an autograph of Moores[1] was received at the same time with the sheets of Meister Karls Sketch Book,[2] but was considered an envellope and thrown aside without examination. It was by mere chance that it was not destroyed, and that on receiving your last note I was able to lay my hand on it. I doubt its being Moores hand-writing. I think it probably a copy. I enclose you a veritable autograph of the little man ↑to compare with it,↓ which you may keep or give to your friend as you think proper.

I enjoyed Meister Karls Sketch book exceedingly and keep it by me like a Stilton cheese, to recur to it now and then and take a morsel as a relish.

I ought to have written about it long since, but my pen like myself is over fagged—

Yours very truly
(signed) Washington Irving

L. Gaylord Clark Esq

MANUSCRIPT: HSP (copy).

This copy is not in WI's handwriting.

1. Thomas Moore (1779–1852), the Irish poet and biographer with whom WI was intimate in the 1820's.
2. Charles Godfrey Leland was the author of *Meister Karl's Sketch Book*, written in German dialect and published in December, 1855. For other details see WI to Leland, January 10, 1855.

2451. To Gouverneur Kemble

Sunnyside Jan 21st. 1856

My dear Kemble,

If I were as young a fellow as you I would not mind facing this bitter weather in a visit to the Highlands; but being nearly three years your Senior, I confess the very name of *Cold* Spring[1] makes my teeth chatter.

I will come and keep your seventieth birth day[2] in the time of birds and blossoms.

Yours affectionately
Washington Irving

Gouvr Kemble Esq

MANUSCRIPT: Eleutherian Mills Historical Society.

1. Kemble lived in Cold Spring, across the Hudson River from West Point.
2. Kemble's birthday was on January 26.

2452. To George Bancroft

Sunnyside Jany 30t 1856

My dear Bancroft

I thank you sincerely for your cordial and well timed note.[1] It is always an anxious time with an Author when he has just launched a volume and is waiting for a verdict, and especially with one like myself apt to be troubled with self distrust. I never was more troubled with it than in the presentation of my present task when I am occasionally venturing in a some what familiar ⟨style⟩ ↑way↓ upon themes which you will treat in such an ampler, nobler and more truly historical style

Indeed I am putting to sea at a hazardous time when you and Macaulay[2] and Prescott (with his grand Spanish Armada) are afloat; however I am ready to drop my peak whenever any of you come into the same waters.

Give my best thanks to Mrs Bancroft[3] for her favorable opinion of my volume—As Sir Fretful Plagiary[4] says, the Women are the best judges after all.

ever my dear Bancroft / Yours most heartily
Washington Irving

MANUSCRIPT: Cornell; MHS (copy).   PUBLISHED: PMI, IV, 208–9.

1. This note has not been located.
2. The third and fourth volumes of *History of England from the Accession of James II* by Thomas Babington Macaulay (1800-1859) appeared in 1855.
3. Elizabeth Davis Bliss, a widow whom Bancroft had married on August 16, 1838. Bancroft's first wife had died in 1837. See Russel B. Nye, *George Bancroft: Brahmin Rebel* (New York, 1944), p. 120.
4. A playwright in Richard Brinsley Sheridan's *The Critic*, whose dramas were filled with "stray jokes and pilfered witticisms" "glean[ed] from the refuse of obscure volumes."

2453.   To Jacob Snider, Jr.

Sunnyside Jan 30t. 1856

Dear Sir,

I feel very much obliged to You for your offer to lend me an orderly book of the American Army at Valley forge[1] and shall be most happy to avail myself of your kindness. If you will send the MS. to the care of my publishers Mess Geo P Putnam & Co New York it will come safe to hand and shall be returned to you promptly and in good order.

with great respect / Yours very truly
Washington Irving

Jacob Snider Jnr Esq.

MANUSCRIPT: American Philosophical Society.

1. This orderly book has not been identified. Since volume 3 of the *Life of George Washington*, which dealt with the Valley Forge period, was already at the printer's, WI could not have used it in his treatment.

2454.   To the Reverend Joseph F. Tuttle

Sunnyside Feb 2d. 1856

Dear Sir

I return your manuscript[1] with many thanks for your kindness in submitting it to my perusal. I have detained it much longer than I had intended, but I have been out of health of late and much hurried and confused by the daily demands of the press for Copy; my third volume being in the printers hands.[2]

I should think if your Manuscript were a little pruned of matters of mere local interest, relating to persons with whom the public are entirely unacquainted it would be worthy of publication, to use your words, "as a monograph." Every thing relating to revolutionary times and giving familiar pictures of those times, is full of interest to the American public at large.

As a subject for lectures the revolution in inexhaustable and it is a pity that you should not pursue the vein which you have so happily opened With best wishes for your success in all your undertakings I am my dear Sir,

Your truly obliged friend & Servt
Washington Irving

Rev. Jos F Tuttle.

MANUSCRIPT: Va.–Barrett.

For details about Tuttle, see WI to the Reverend Thomas W. Hastings, October 15, 1855.

1. Tuttle's manuscript consisted of two lectures on "Washington in Morris County," to which WI had referred in a letter to Hastings, October 15, 1855.

2. This volume appeared in July 1856. See Langfeld & Blackburn, *WI Bibliography*, p. 42. Following "hands." is written "(Life of Washington)" in pencil in another hand.

2455. *To George Bancroft*

Sunnyside Feb. 6th. 1856

My dear Bancroft

It will give me great pleasure to meet Mr Everett at your table on the 1t of March[1] provided I am in a sufficient state of repair by that time. I have been so much out of order lately as to be obliged to excuse myself from all invitations

Yours very truly
Washington Irving

MANUSCRIPT: Va.–Barrett.

1. Everett was to present his lecture on George Washington in New York on March 3. WI was unable to attend Bancroft's dinner party. See WI to George Bancroft, March 1, 1856.

2456. *To Edward Everett*

Sunnyside Feb. 6h 1856

My dear Mr Everett,

I am very much obliged to the young men of the Mercantile Library Association[1] for the invitation to their festival on the 22d of this month,[2] but my health is so much deranged at present that, during this ⟨p⟩ inclement season I am fit for no place but home. I hope, however, to be well enough by the first of March to meet you at the table of our friend Bancroft and to attend the lecture on Washington which I understand you are to deliver on the 3d.[3]

Yours with the highest regard
Washington Irving

Hon Edward Everett

MANUSCRIPT: MHS.   DOCKETED: Washington Irving. / Rec'd 7 Feb. 1856.

1. This invitation has not been located.

2. Everett had agreed to lecture before the Mercantile Library Association of Boston on the character of Washington to commemorate the one-hundredth anniversary of Washington's first visit to Boston. See Paul Revere Frothingham, *Edward Everett: Orator and Statesman* (New York, 1925), pp. 373–74.

3. Everett repeated his oration at the Music Hall in New York on March 3, 1856. See Frothingham, *Edward Everett,* p. 375.

2457.   To Pierre M. Irving

Sunnyside February 1⟨5⟩6t. 1856

My nephew Pierre M Irving having for some years kindly and gratuitously attended to ⟨my⟩ the management of my pecuniary affairs and being still further in need of his assistance in my literary researches, I prevailed on him last year to give up his office business and put his time at my disposal; offering to give him an equivalent, in monthly payments, to the profits of the business so given up. I now continue the arrangement, and authorise ⟨himself⟩ him to pay himself out of any funds of mine which may be in his hands at the rate of on[e][1] hundred and thirty five (135) dollars per month

Washington Irving

DOCKETED: W. I. to P. M. I. / Feb: 16. 1856
MANUSCRIPT: SHR.

1. WI omitted the bracketed letter.

2458.   To Isaac W. Stuart

Sunnyside Feb. 16th. 1856

Dear Sir

Indisposition has prevented an earlier acknowledgement of your kindness in sending me a copy of your life of Captain Nathan Hale,[1] which ⟨you⟩ ↑I↓ have read with great interest

The fact which you state in a note[2] concerning my mother is no doubt correct. I know that she was in the practice of relieving American prisoners, especially clergymen; sometimes visiting them in person at other times sending them supplies. I have often heard her relate instances of it and of the kind of surly indulgence with which she was treated by the brute Cunningham.³ On one occasion when she asked his permission to send in food and raiment to a clergyman just brought in a prisoner, "with all my heart madam" was the reply; "but I would much rather you would send him a rope." That was Cunninghams style of pleasantry when he was in a gracious mood.

very respectfully / Your obliged & hb Servt
Washington Irving
I. W. Stuart Esqr.

MANUSCRIPT: Connecticut Historical Society.

Isaac W. Stuart (1809–1861) was a local historian and orator.

1. Stuart had just brought out *The Life of Captain Nathan Hale, The Martyr-Spy of the American Revolution* (Hartford, 1856) under the pseudonym of "Scaeva."

2. In a note (pp. 123–24) Stuart referred to a "lady of distinction" who aided and encouraged the Reverend Moses Mather of Darien, Connecticut when he was mistreated by William Cunningham.

3. William Cunningham (d. 1791), who became provost-marshal of the British army soon after his arrival in the colonies in 1774, later took charge of prisons in Philadelphia and New York. During his administration 2,000 prisoners starved to death and 250 were hanged without trial. He was later executed in London for forgery.

2459. To George Bancroft

[March 1, 1856]

My dear Bancroft—
I am grieved to send you an apology at the eleventh hour, but really, after coming down to dine with you in spite of indisposition, I find myself so much out of order since my arrival in town that I must beg to be excused. It is a great disappointment to me, for I have been nursing myself up for your dinner party¹

Yours very truly
Washington Irving
No 1. East 14th St. / Saturday March 1. [1856]

MANUSCRIPT: LC.

The date is determined by the perpetual calendar and by WI's letters to Bancroft and to Edward Everett, dated February 6, 1856.

1. Bancroft was giving a dinner in honor of Edward Everett, who was lecturing on George Washington on March 3.

2460. To ———

New York, March 4h. 1856

My dear Sir,

I am sorry to learn that the scheme of your proposed institution has appeared in a pamphlet form in which my name is given as a trustee. I had no intention of committing myself, as such, in the conversation we had a few evenings since but reserved the matter for after consideration. That determined me to decline the responsibility when we should have further conversation on the subject, and I now beg you will have the kindness to omit my name in any further publicity you may give to the undertaking

I thus decline the honor you are disposed to confer upon me, not from any doubt of the merit and advantages of your proposed institution but from a consciousness of my own deficiencies and short comings which makes me avoid committing myself for any post or office which I cannot faithfully and thoroughly discharge

Very truly and respectfully / My dear Sir / Your friend & Servt
Washington Irving

Manuscript: SHR.

2461. To John Murray III

Sunnyside March 12t. 1856

My dear Sir

I have this day drawn on you at three days sight in favor of Messrs. Grinnell, Minturn & Co.[1] for fifty pounds sterling, according to Your directions.[2]

With kind remembrances to your family Yours ever, very truly

Washington Irving

John Murray Esqr

Docketed: Irving / Washington / March 1856
Manuscript: John Murray.

1. A New York banking and shipping firm, one of whose partners, Moses H. Grinnell, was married to WI's niece Julia.

2. Murray's letter with its directions has not been located. Apparently it indicated that WI was to draw £50 in payment for Bohn's edition of volume 2 of the *Life of*

George Washington, which had been published in New York in December, 1855. See Langfeld & Blackburn, *WI Bibliography,* p. 42.

2462.   To Benson J. Lossing

Sunnyside March 15t. 1856

My dear Sir,

Accept my most cordial thanks for your letter[1] and for the very very encouraging opinion you express of my life of Washington a task on which I engaged with diffidence and about which I have often had many misgivings.

I am glad you have undertaken the biography of Schuyler.[2] It is a noble theme and affords a grand scope combining so many scenes and transactions on savage and civilized life; and treating of so much of the romantic history of our own state Having had occasion to treat of Schuyler occasionally in the work on which I ⟨have⟩ am engaged I have had opportunities of judging of his merits and appreciating his high and generous character.[3] I am sure he will recieve justice at your hands. There is a genial spirit in your writings that warms with the recital of any thing gallant, and kind hearted and high minded and noble; and it will be sure to kindle in recording Schuylers generous and patriotic career.

You talk of paying me a visit at Sunnyside. My dear Sir I shall be most happy at any time to recieve you and to extend to you the right hand of fellowship as a brother of the pen

Yours ever very truly
Washington Irving

Benson J Lossing Esqr

MANUSCRIPT: Va.–Barrett.

1. This letter has not been located.

2. Lossing's biography, *The Life and Times of Philip Schuyler,* prepared from family documents, was published in 1860. A revised and enlarged edition appeared in 1873. Schuyler (1733–1804), a New York landowner who gained military experience in the French and Indian War, was one of four major generals serving under Washington during the early stages of the Revolutionary War. When his military tactics were questioned, he demanded a court-martial. After he was acquitted with honor, he resigned from the service. His daughter Elizabeth married Alexander Hamilton.

3. WI deals extensively with Schuyler in the first three volumes of his life of Washington.

2463.   To John P. Kennedy

Sunnyside March 22d. 1856

My dear Kennedy,

The sight of your letter just recieved,[1] with its black seal and edgings, gave me a severe shock, though I thought I was prepared for the event it communicated.

The death of my most dear and valued friend Mr Gray is a relief to himself and to the affectionate hearts around him who witnessed his prolonged sufferings but I who have been out of the hearing of his groans,[2] can only remember him as he was in his genial moments, the ⟨genial and⟩ generous and kind hearted centre of a loving circle dispensing happiness around him. My intimacy with him in recent years had fully opened to me the varied excellence of his character and most heartily attached me to him. My dear Kennedy my intercourse with your family connexion has been a great sweetener of the last few years of my existence, and ⟨my⟩ the only attraction that has been able to draw me repeatedly from home. And in all this I recognize the influence of the kind, cordial sympathetic character of Mr Gray. To be under his roof in Baltimore or at Ellicotts Mills was to be in a constant state of quiet enjoyment to me. Every thing that I saw in him, and in those about him, in his tastes, habits, mode of life, ⟨and⟩ in his domestic relations, and chosen intimacies, continually struck upon some happy chord in my own bosom and put me in tune with the world and with human nature. I cannot expect in my brief remnant of existence to replace such a friend and such a domestic circle rallying round him, but the remembrance will ever be most dear to me

Give my most affectionate remembrance to your wife and her noble hearted sister and believe me my dear Kennedy

ever yours most truly
Washington Irving

John P Kennedy Esq

MANUSCRIPT: Peabody Library.   PUBLISHED: PMI, IV, 210–11; Tuckerman, *Life of J. P. Kennedy*, p. 389 (in part).

1. Kennedy's letter of March 21, 1856, announcing the death of his father-in-law, Edward Gray, is preserved in NYPL–Hellman Collection.

2. Gray was a chronic sufferer from asthma. Often when his attacks were so severe that he could not lie down, he would sit in his chair and groan. See Tuckerman, *Life of J. P. Kennedy*, pp. 251–52.

2464. To Gouverneur Kemble

Sunnyside, April 23, 1856

My dear Kemble:

The roots and cuttings sent by your gardener arrived safe, and are all properly disposed of.[1] I should like to have a few more cuttings for out of doors, and a black Hamburg[2] or two, if you have any. I shall raise some of the grapes under glass, having a small hothouse which will accommodate a few. I hope your visit to Washington was pleasant and profitable, and that you will be favored with a seat in the Cabinet, or a foreign mission in this or the next Presidency.

I am happy to learn that your lawn is green. I hope it will long continue so, and yourself likewise. I shall come up, one of these days, and have a roll on it with you.

> Yours ever, my dear Kemble,
> Washington Irving

PUBLISHED: PMI, IV, 211–12.

1. On January 21, 1856, WI had asked Kemble to send "any cuttings or plants of grapes and figs" he could spare for the new hothouse WI was constructing.
2. A black, juicy grape native to Europe.

2465. To Sarah Storrow

Sunnyside April 24th 1856

My dear Sarah

Though very much fagged by my literary labors I will not postpone ↑answering↓ your letter of the 7th.[1] just recieved as I continually experience the danger of postponement in letter writing; over tasked and hurried as I am by the necessity of incessantly supplying manuscript for the press while ⟨my⟩ the publication of my work is going on

My dear Sarah I cannot express to you how happy I was again to see your hand writing in a letter to me. I have read your letter ⟨over?⟩ three or four times already, and carry it in my pocket to read again. You say it is a *long long* time since you have heard from me, yet I wrote to you in the latter part of the winter, two or three months since.[2] My letter must have miscarried, as I begin to think my letters to Europe now and then do, from being transmitted to New York by private hand, to be forwarded —However you lost nothing if that letter should come to hand for it was written at a time when I was somewhat out of health and out of spirits and nervous; having been shut up too much in my study during a hard winter in which I took no exercise and worked too hard with my pen. The spring is now opening beautifully and I feel like another being.

You say you have been pained by hearing that I complained of your remaining so long in Europe—My dear Sarah you must not mind my being a little querulous and unreasonable now and then on that subject, but place to account of the strong, heartfelt and unceasing affection which I bear for you. The separation from you has been one of the greatest bereavements I have ever experienced. You were with me so much for many years, you suited me so well and sympathized with me so much in tastes and feelings, that you had grown to be as it were a part of myself. When you left me it was as if one half of my heart was torn away—can you wonder that the other half will still be yearning after it. And then your dear little children, ⟨which⟩ ↑who↓ were such delights to me—Kate who was my idol when I was in Paris and used to take such possession of me and oblige me to *put away my spectacles* and give up my book and entertain her for the hundredth time with the story of little Miss Muss and Hempen House—now she is growing up a fine travelled journalizing young ↑lady↓ and I shall not know her when I meet her. However—I am glad to hear they are all growing up so well—and that dear Susy has recovered her health and is herself again as to Julie, I only wish I could see her again as she once was—little *Gaga*—with her grand heroic style—But I am growing garrellous—I am really rejoiced to learn that your affairs are all arranged and "the world again looks bright and cheerful[.]" God grant it may ever be so to you my dear Sarah.

And now as to your places, about which you seem to ask my opinion. By all means go to Italy—and pass the winter there. If you pass part of the coming summer in Germany why do you return to Paris ⟨f⟩ before you go south? Why should your having a leased apartment on hand shackle your movements. Why not devote as much as possible of your remaining residence in Europe to visiting its most remarkable places. I can easily understand your enjoyment in visiting old, curious and historical places. It is exactly what I used to feel in Europe—Modern places gave me little pleasure in comparison

But it is time for me to finish and go to bed; for I am writing at a late hour of the night after a hard days work. I have about two thirds of my third volume of Washington in type and shall be heartily glad when the whole volume is completed—when I will give myself repose before I commence another It is a toilsome task though a very interesting and I may say delightful one—It expands and grows more voluminous as I write; but the way it is recieved by the public cheers me on—for I put it to the press with more doubt and diffidence than any work I ever pub-

lished. The way the public keep on with me is a continual wonderment
to me, knowing my own short comings on many things, and I must say
I am sometimes surprised at my own capacity for labor at my advanced
time of life—when I used to think a man must be good for nothing

You speak of your uncle Ebenezer He has been very ill—with a severe
cold and influenza. At one time I thought he would sink under his illness. He was perfectly prostrated—and thought himself that his time was
come—but he has recovered and is himself again though still rather weak.
However we have got through the hard lingering winter and he has now
the blessed genial spring weather to cheer and strengthen him.

You tell me you have sent me a little cushion for the drawing room
sofa worked by yourself and Kate. I promise myself pleasant dreams on
it, when I take my afternoon naps after a toilful morning in my study
and shall put on the slippers which Kate worked for me,[3] when I lie my
head upon it, and then I shall be sure to dream of her.

And now good night my dear Sarah give my love to the dear young
folk and my affectionate remembrances to Mr Storrow and if ever you
hear any more of my scolding about your absence—only laugh and say
ah! poor uncle!—how much he dotes on me![4]

MANUSCRIPT: Yale.   PUBLISHED: PMI, IV, 26, 212 (in part).

1. This letter has not been located.

2. No letter to Sarah Storrow from this period has been located.

3. WI had received these slippers two years earlier. See WI to Kate Storrow,
February 21, 1854.

4. The lower third of the page containing the complimentary close and WI's signature has been clipped away.

2466.   To Washington Smith

Sunnyside April 28t. 1856

Washington Smith Esqr

Dear Sir,

I will thank you to send me eighty feet of ⟨5⟩ ↑five↓ Inch drain pipe
and two elbows, by the Hudson River Rail Road directed to me at *Irvington Westchester County.*[1]

Your obt Servt
Washington Irving

MANUSCRIPT: Boston Public Library.

"Washington Smith, pottery, 261 W. 18th, v. pres. 63 Wall & 61 Chambers & gov. almshouse, h. 241 W. 19th" is listed in *Trow's New York City Directory for 1855–56*, p. 774. He apparently operated a brick yard or tile kiln.

1. About two years earlier the residents of Dearman, a small village south of Sunnyside, changed its name to "Irvington," in honor of their illustrious neighbor. See George S. Hellman, *Washington Irving Esquire* (New York, 1925), pp. 333–34.

2467.   To John Murray III

New York May 13th. 1856

My dear Mr Murray,
This will be handed to you by my nephew the Revd. Pierre [P.][1] Irving who makes a short visit to England Any civilities you may find it convenient to bestow upon him during his sojourn in London will be considered personal favors to.

Yours ever very truly
Washington Irving

John Murray Esqr

ADDRESSED: John Murray Esqr / Albemarle St / London // By the / Revd P. P Irving
MANUSCRIPT: John Murray.   PUBLISHED: WIHM, p. 206.

1. WI wrote "M" here but "P" on the cover. Pierre Paris Irving visited England about this time. See PMI, IV, 222; and WI to Sarah Storrow, October 27, 1856.

2468.   To Commodore Matthew C. Perry

Sunnyside May 24th. 1856

My dear Commodore,
The following is the passage in your paper on the enlargement of Geographical Science[1] to which I alluded in conversation with you a few days since In speaking of the Bonin Islands[2] you observe "In respect to these islands it would be of little importance whether they were occupied by the English or Americans, whether the time honored cross of St George, or the more youthful emblem, the Stars and Stripes of our own country, floated over their barren hills; yet, let it be so arranged that the wearied and care worn sailor, of whatever nation, shall find, on entering their ports, an equally kind and generous welcome. And I cheerfully take occasion here to remark, that wherever I have found the British Flag, in

whatever part of the World, there have I always found a courteous and hospitable reception.["]³

My dear Commodore this passage does infinite honor to your head and your heart; and the last sentence is worthy of being written in letters of gold; as illustrative of that comity which should distinguish the nautical intercourse of the two kindred nations.

                              Ever my dear Commodore / Yours most truly
                                                              Washington Irving
Commodore M. C. Perry. U. S. N.

ADDRESSED: Commodore M C. Perry. U. S N. / New York.   POSTMARKED: [IRVIN]GTON N Y / [Ma]y 26 [*envelope torn*]   ENDORSED: For His Excellency / Mr Van Hale / M. C. Perry

MANUSCRIPT: Bibliotheek der Universiteit van Amsterdam.

Matthew C. Perry (1794–1858) had entered the U.S. Navy as a midshipman in 1809 and had served with distinction as commander of several squadrons before being sent to negotiate a treaty with Japan and to open its ports to American commerce, tasks which he carried out successfully. Perry had lived in the northern part of Tarrytown after 1841, and he and WI were frequently fellow passengers on the same ship to New York City.

1. On March 6, 1856, Perry's paper, "On the Encouragement of Commerce in the Pacific Islands, Particularly by a Settlement on the Bonin Islands," was read at a meeting of the American Geographical and Statistical Society at the chapel of Columbia University by the Reverend Francis L. Hawks, president of the Society. See Samuel Eliot Morison, *"Old Bruin": Commodore Matthew C. Perry 1794–1858* (Boston, 1967), pp. 427–28.

2. The Bonin Islands, with an area of about forty-one square miles, are located about 600 miles southeast of Japan.

3. WI omitted the bracketed quotation mark.

2469.   To Charles G. Leland

                                                    [Sunnyside, May 31, 1856]

. . . I trust your work¹ has met with a wide circulation, for such it merits by its raciness, its quaint erudition, its graphic delineations, its veins of genuine poetry and true Rabelais humor. To me it is a choice book to have at hand for relishing morsel occasionally, like a Stilton cheese² or a *pâté de foie gras.*

PUBLISHED: Elizabeth Robins Pennell, *Charles Godfrey Leland: A Biography*, 2 vols. (Boston, 1906), I, 330.

1. *Meister Karl's Sketch-Book*, published in December, 1855.

2. WI was apparently fond of the Stilton cheese simile, for he had used it earlier in a letter to Lewis G. Clark, January 10, 1856.

2470. To William Duane

Sunnyside June 3d. 1856

Dear Sir,

I must apologize for answering your letter[1] so tardily, but my pen has been so much overtasked of late that my correspondence is completely in arrears.

The Hessian Journals[2] about which you enquire were lent to me by Mr Cogswell Superintendent of the Astor Library to whom I returned them some time since. They belong to a gentleman[3] whose name I do ⟨nt⟩ not reccollect, but who I understand is occupied either in translating them or forming an historical memoir from them.

Those which I had in my hands would make an octavo volume of between two and three hundred pages.

Very respectfully / Your Obedient Servt
Washington Irving

William Duane Esqr

MANUSCRIPT: Yale.

In the upper left corner of the sheet is written in another hand "C C–".
William Duane (1807–1882) was a Philadelphia writer and editor interested in the Revolutionary War.

1. This letter has not been located.
2. WI drew extensively upon the journals of two Hessian lieutenants and a corporal for his details about the capture of the German mercenaries in the closing pages of the second volume of *The Life of Washington*. He refers to them as "Tagebuch eines Hessischen officiers," "Journal of Lieut. Piel," and "Tagebuch des corporals Johannes Reuber" (pp. 472, 487).
3. PMI (IV, 199) states that "At the moment of completing his second volume, he [WI] received from Mr. Charles L. Brace some manuscript Hessian journals, which had been copied for the Historical Society, and which led him to recal[l] and revise some of his proofs, and make some additions and alterations." These changes and additions probably occurred in chapters 43 and 44 of volume 2. Brace (1826–1890) was a philanthropist who worked extensively with and published much about the underprivileged of New York City. See Brace's enthusiastic letter of January 22, 1856, about the second volume of *The Life of Washington* in PMI, IV, 207–8.

2471. To Charles Boner

Sunnyside June 18th. 1856

My dear Sir

I recieved, some time since, your letter of April 4th.[1] inquiring whether a packet of books sent to me in October last, had reached its destination.

It had not—but I postponed replying to your letter until I could make inquiry in New York, where it might be detained.

I now am happy to inform you that I have just recieved it. As yet I have merely had time to glance over your volumes[2] but see at once, that they are calculated to delight me. Your Chamois Hunting especially will carry me into the Mountains of Bavaria, which I merely skirted in the course of a tour in the Autumn of 1822,[3] but which have ⟨left⟩ stamped themselves upon my memory clothed with romantic and legendary associations.

I feel deeply gratified by the tenor of your letter and the manner in which you express yourself concerning my writings. If they have indeed produced upon you the effect you mention they have attained one of the highest purposes of an author. Excuse the briefness of this letter. The object of it is merely to inform you of the receipt of your books; the uncertain fate of which had caused you some solicitude. When I have had time to read them I will write to you more fully. In the mean time believe me With great respect

Your obliged friend / & Servt
Washington Irving

Charles Boner Esqr

MANUSCRIPT: SHR.

Charles Boner (1815–1870) was an English journalist and traveler who served as tutor of the family of the prince of Thurn and Taxis from 1839 to 1860 and subsequently as the Vienna correspondent of the London *Daily News*. He also wrote for the New York *Tribune* and other newspapers.

1. This letter has not been located.
2. By this time Boner had written *Charles Boner's Book, For Those Who're Young, and Those Who Love What's Natural and Truthful* (1848), *Chamois Hunting in the Mountains of Bavaria* (1853), and *Cain* (1855), a verse drama. He had translated Hans Christian Andersen's *Danish Story Book* (1846), *The Nightingale, and Other Stories* (1846), and *Dream of Little Tuk* (1848).
3. See *J&N*, III, 28–29, 37–43.

2472.   To [Charles A.?] Davis

Washington Irving

Sunnyside / June 18t. 1856.
The pressure of various occupations has prevented an earlier compliance with Mr Davis's request.[1]

MANUSCRIPT: Fales Collection, New York University Library.

Probably this note is addressed to Charles A. Davis, an old crony with whom WI had spent time in Saratoga Springs in the summer of 1852.
The name and place are written at the top of the sheet as if to represent a letterhead.

1. The nature of Davis's request and the manner of WI's compliance have not been ascertained.

2473.   To Emily Fuller

Sunnyside, July 2d. 1856

My dear Mrs Fuller,
   You can scarcely imagine my surprise and delight on opening your letter[1] and finding by the first lines that it came from *Emily Foster*! A thousand reccollections broke at once upon my mind of Emily Foster, as I had known her at Dresden, young and fair and bright and beautiful, and I could hardly realize that so many years had elapsed since then, or form an idea of her as Mrs Emily Fuller "with four boys and one little girl" one of the boys[2] old enough to think of shouldering an axe, seeking his fortune in the New World and building a log cabin for himself in the wilderness of the 'Far West.'
   By this project of his I percieve he inherits somewhat of his mothers imaginative character and is picturing to himself a poetical life in the wilderness He has probably imbibed some heroic notions about "roughing it in the bush," and has not informed himself well of the hard and stern realities that overpower all the romance of "back wood" life. Before he embarks on any scheme that may require an outlay of funds, or interfere ⟨s⟩ with his freedom of choice and action let him visit the land of promise of his dreams, and judge for himself, how far it is likely to realize his anticipations, and how far he is fitted to cope with its difficulties and privations A tour ↑of observation↓ in the "Far West" might be made with moderate expense and would do him no harm did he determine not to settle there; but might save him from being the dupe of land

speculators in making a purchase. In all this I am giving advice at a venture—not knowing what may be his real plan, or whether he may not already have informed himself warily on the subject. I am supposing that it is merely a vague dream not yet reduced to any thing definite and practical, and I wish to render him wary.

I wish you had given me a few more particulars about yourself and those immediately connected with you, whom I have known—After so long an interval one fears to ask questions, lest they should awaken painful reccollections. By the tenor of your letter I should judge that, on the whole the world has gone smoothly with you Your children, you tell me, *"are all so good and promising as to add much to your happiness."* How much of what is most precious in life is conveyed in those ⟨words⟩ few words!

You ask me to tell you something about myself. Since my return in 1846 from my diplomatic mission to Spain, I have been leading a quiet life in a little rural retreat I had previously established on the banks of the Hudson; which in fact has been my home for twenty years past. I am in a beautiful part of the country; in an agreeable neighborhood, am on the best of terms with my neighbors and have a house full of nieces, who almost make me as happy as if I were a married man. Your letter was put into my hands just as I was getting into the carriage to drive out with some of them. I read it to them in the course of the drive, letting them know that it was from Emily Foster, the young lady of whom they had often heard me speak; who had painted the head of Herodias,[3] which hangs over the piano in the drawing room, and who I had always told them was more beautiful than the picture she painted—which they could hardly believe though it was true. You reccollect, I trust, the miniature copy of the head of Herodias, which you made in the Dresden Gallery—I treasure it as a precious memorial of those pleasant days.

My health is excellent though at times I have tried it hard by literary occupation and excitement. There are some propensities that grow upon men with age and I am a little more addicted to the pen than I was in my younger days, and much more, I am told, than is prudent for a man of my years. It is a labor however, in which I delight; and I am never so happy of an evening as when I have passed the whole morning in my study, hard at work, and have earned the evenings recreation.

Farewell my dear Mrs Fuller. If any of those of your family whom I once knew and valued are at hand, assure them that I ever retain them in cordial remembrance and believe me ever my dear "Emily Foster"

Your affectionate friend
Washington Irving

MANUSCRIPT: Va.–Barrett.   PUBLISHED: PMI, IV, 218–20.

A copy which omits WI's discussion of Mrs. Fuller's son and his plans is also to be found at Va.–Barrett. It is not in WI's handwriting.

Emily Foster (1804–1885), who had married Henry Fuller, was the object of WI's attention and affection during his residence in Dresden in the winter of 1822–1823. There is reason to believe that he proposed marriage to her and that she rejected his offer.

1. Emily Fuller's letter of May 25, 1856, is printed in PMI, IV, 217–18.

2. Henry Fuller, her oldest son. See PMI, IV, 217–18.

3. As WI suggests, Emily Foster painted the miniature from the original of Bartolommeo Veneto's half-length picture of Herodias, or Salome, with the head of John the Baptist on a platter in the Dresden Gallery. He received it in Paris on December 15, 1823. See Henner Menz, *The Dresden Gallery* (London, 1962); and *J&N*, III, 258.

2474. To George D. Morgan

Sunnyside July 4t. 1856

Worthy and dear Sir,

We live in portentous times and every thing is full of direful omen. I paid a visit yesterday to my neighbor Mr Hoge[1] and forthwith a formidable cudgel was presented to me on the silver head of which was engraved *Fort Duquesne*, being fabricated from the ruins of that strong hold of former days.[2] I came home and lo another weapon of the kind is put into my hands from your castle of Wood cliff.[3]—What does all this mean Are we preparing for the contest of the cudgel? Is club law to rule the land?—In the midst of all this a herald in hot haste has summoned me to a feast to be given by the great Sachem of Pokahoe[4]—doubtless a war feast, in honor of the hero of the Rocky Mountains—[5]

Now Sir I am a peaceable man. I have declined the Sachems invitation ↑to his War feast—↓ I accept the Cane under condition that, if club law is to be the order of the day, I be permitted to keep my cudget quiet—and, if I accompany you this morning to pay a visit to ⟨the?⟩ Colonel Fremont at the ↑Sachems↓ Wigwam I shall certainly leave my cudgel at home.

Yours truly but pacifically
Washington Irving

Geo. D. Morgan Esq.

MANUSCRIPT: SHR.   PUBLISHED: Scharf, *Westchester County*, II, 238 (in part).

George D. Morgan, a neighbor of WI's, was responsible, along with Moses H. Grinnell, for changing the name of Dearman to Irvington in 1854. See Scharf, *Westchester County*, II, 190.

1. William Hoge (d. 1875), a well-known New York banker, lived on the premises which were later owned and occupied by the New York Institution for the Instruction of the Deaf and Dumb. See Scharf, *Westchester County*, II, 238, 244.

2. Fort Duquesne, the present site of Pittsburgh, was built by the French at the junction of the Allegheny and Monongahela Rivers. In 1758 the British seized control of it and renamed it Fort Pitt.

3. George D. Morgan's residence in Irvington which he had occupied on April 29, 1853. See Scharf, *Westchester County*, II, 190, 192.

4. James Watson Webb (1802–1884), editor of the New York *Courier and Enquirer* from 1829 to 1861, lived in a stone mansion called "Pokahoe" about a mile north of the Pocantico bridge, between the Hudson River and Broadway in the Tarrytown area. See Scharf, *Westchester County*, II, 238.

5. John Charles Frémont (1813–1890), who is mentioned by name in the next paragraph, was a Western explorer elected senator from California in 1850 and nominated for the presidency by the Republicans in 1856.

2475. *To Samuel Mordecai*

Sunnyside, July 6, 1856

❅ ❅ ❅ ❅ ❅ ❅ ❅

I had especially intended to thank you for your little volume, for it was particularly acceptable to me. *Richmond in By-Gone Days*[1] was Richmond as I knew it in the days of my youth, nearly fifty years since.[2] Every page of your volume brought up some delightful recollection of scenes and characters long since passed away; for at Richmond, at the time of my visit, there was a rare assemblage of the talent and beauty of Virginia; and the impressions I received then have ever made the "Old Dominion" dear to me.

PUBLISHED: Samuel Mordecai, *Virginia, Especially Richmond, in By-Gone Days; with a Glance at the Present; Being Reminiscences and Last Words of an Old Citizen* (Richmond, 1860), p. [iii].

1. For full title see the publication note above.

2. WI spent several weeks in Richmond from May to early July, 1807, attending the trial of Aaron Burr. See STW, I, 96–98; and PMI, I, 190–97.

2476. To Benjamin Silliman

Sunnyside July 15th. 1856

My dear Sir,

I should like very much to avail myself of the manuscript diary of Colonel Jonathan Trumbull[1] which you mention[2] and will gladly defray the expense of having a copy made of it.[3]

For the kind interest you have taken in my historical task accept my most grateful thanks and believe me with high respect

Your truly obliged friend
Washington Irving

Prof. B. Silliman

ADDRESSED: Professor Benjamin Silliman / New Haven / Conn.   POSTMARKED: Irvington / July 16
MANUSCRIPT: Yale.

1. Jonathan Trumbull (1740–1809) was the first comptroller of the U.S. Treasury from November, 1778, to April, 1779, and secretary to General George Washington from 1781 to 1783, during which he kept the diary to which WI refers. Trumbull later served in the U.S. House of Representatives and Senate from 1789 to 1796, and from 1797 until his death he was governor of Connecticut.

2. Silliman's letter has not been located.

3. Silliman copied the diary himself and sent it to WI. See WI to Silliman, July 19, 1856. Since Silliman's first wife, Harriet (d. 1850), was the daughter of Jonathan Trumbull, she had probably acquired the diary among her father's effects. See John F. Fulton and Elizabeth H. Thomson, *Benjamin Silliman* (New York, 1968), pp. 78, 218.

2477. To Benjamin Silliman

Sunnyside July 19t. 1856

My dear Sir,

I have just recieved the copy of Colonel Trumbull's diary,[1] but almost grieve to find that you have taken the trouble to make it yourself. This certainly adds greatly to the obligation, but it distresses me to have unintentionally tasked your kindness to such a degree

The diary is a very interesting document; placing us in immediate companionship with Washington. What vivid reality there is in such simple jottings down of an eye witness

It will give my little household and myself great pleasure to see you and Mrs Silliman at Sunnyside in the course of your proposed visit to my worthy neighbors the Thomas's.

With great respect, my dear Sir

Your obliged friend
Washington Irving

Professor B. Silliman / &c &c &c

MANUSCRIPT: Pierpont Morgan Library.

At the bottom of the first page of the letter Silliman wrote three lines of a note and continued on the lower third of the verso: "This letter was written on the occasion of my sending a copy of the daily MS Journal written by Coln afterwards Govn Jonathan Trumbull—of the events of the seige of York Town in the revolutionary war ending with capture of Lord Cornwallis & his army.

"Col Trumbull was private secretary to Gen Washington and enjoyed his full confidence as appears by his letters written after the peace from Mt Vernon. They are highly confidential and affectionate as from a father to a son."

1. In his letter of July 15, 1856, WI accepted Silliman's offer of a copy of Trumbull's journal.

2478.   To William A. Thomas

Sunnyside, July 31t. 1856

My dear Sir

I regret to find that in citing Graydons Memoirs I have neglected to specify that it was the edition by Mr Littell.[1] The high respect I entertain for that gentleman will make me careful to have this omission corrected in any future reprint of my work

Yours very truly
Washington Irving

William A Thomas Esqr

MANUSCRIPT: Va.–Barrett.

The addressee is probably a printer at 168 Essex Street, as listed in *Trow's New York City Directory for 1855–56*, p. 815.

1. John Stockton Littell (1807–1875) edited Alexander Graydon, *Memoirs of His Own Time* (Philadelphia, 1846). WI cited the *Memoirs* of Graydon, a Revolutionary soldier, in *The Life of Washington*, II, 283 and III, 90, without noting the edition. WI's library at Sunnyside contains a copy of Graydon's *Memoirs*.

2479.   To Thomas W. Storrow, Sr.

Sunnyside Aug 6t. 1856

My dear Storrow

Your promised visit will give us all great joy at Sunnyside. My nieces anticipate great entertainment from your anecdotes of gay and fashionable life at Sharon;[1] while I shall be glad to have a philosopher under my roof with whom I can speculate on those grave and high matters which womenkind in general do not affect

Yours ever very truly
Washington Irving

Thomas W Storrow Esq

MANUSCRIPT: University of Pennsylvania Library.

1. Probably the resort town in northwest Connecticut, about twenty-five miles east of Rhinebeck, New York.

2480.   To the Reverend J. B. Wakely

Sunnyside Aug 6t 1856

My dear Sir

A temporary absence from home has prevented my replying at an earlier date to your very welcome letter.[1]

I have read the greater part of the volume you were so kind as to leave with me and have been much interested by the biographical sketches and anecdotes which it contains of the "Heroes of Methodism["][2] They are characteristic and graphic and free from false colouring and exaggeration The volume merits, and I trust will have, a wide circulation.

I wish I could write down the anecdotes you require about the Revd Barnabas Matthias[3] and my black friend "Gentleman Dick,"[4] but "I am not in the vein." My head is out of order and all exercise of the pen is at present irksome if not hurtful to me. When You favor me with another visit[5] I will give them to you again by word of mouth.

I am sorry to find your own brain has been out of order of late; but trust it is well again—We must both give our heads a little holiday occasionally

With many thanks for the kind expressions of your letter I remain

very truly your friend
Washington Irving

The rev. J B. Wakeley.

Manuscript: LC.

Joseph Burton Wakeley (1809–1875) was a Methodist clergyman and student of the history of early Methodism. An acquaintance in WI's later years, he was present at WI's funeral. See *Irvingiana*, p. xxiv.

1. This letter has not been located.

2. Wakeley's *The Heroes of Methodism* was published in New York by Carlton & Bates earlier in 1856.

3. Robert Matthews, or Matthias, a resident for a time at Ossining, was a religious fanatic who lived in 1834 and 1835 at Sparta, New York in a dwelling called Zion Hill. William L. Stone wrote an account of his activities, *Matthias and His Impostures; or, the Progress of Fanaticism* (1835). See Scharf, *Westchester County*, II, 364–65.

4. The name of WI's saddle horse. See PMI, IV, 136, 190, 192.

5. The times of Wakeley's visits have not been ascertained.

2481. To Lewis G. Clark

Sunnyside Aug. 15th. 1856

My dear Sir,

I am much obliged to Mr Van Zandt for the invitation to attend the opening of the R. C. Female Institute but regret to say that my engagements and occupations do not permit me to accept of it.

I thank you for the composite portrait of General Washington which I shall place at the discretion of Mr Putnam for the series of illustrations which he is publishing[1]

Yours very truly
Washington Irving

L. Gaylord Clark Esq

Manuscript: Va.–Barrett.

1. In 1859 Putnam published a quarto volume containing Henry T. Tuckerman's essay on Washington, together with his essay on the portraits of Washington. These were accompanied by appropriate illustrations. See Evert A. and George L. Duyckinck, *Cyclopaedia of American Literature*, II, 493. It is possible that some of the material which WI mentions here was later used in Putnam's publication. Part of it was included in an appendix to volume 5 of WI's *Life of Washington*.

2482.   To the Reverend Charles K. McHarg

Sunnyside Sept. 26t. 1856

My dear Sir,

I have deferred acknowledging the receipt of your copy of the Life of Talleyrand[1] which you have had the kindness to send me until I should have made myself acquainted with its merits[.] I have now read it nearly half through with deep and unflagging interest and only lay it down to write this note and congratulate you on the happy manner in which you have ⟨acq⟩ executed your task. You have managed your various materials with judgement, discrimination, candor and impartiality so as to command the confidence of the reader, while the pure graphic style in which the whole is delivered enchains his attention

I feel persuaded that your work will be well recieved by the public and will meet with a wide circulation and I trust its success will stimulate you to still greater enterprises in that high literary career for which you appear to be so well calculated.

With great respect and regard / Yours very faithfully
Washington Irving

The Rev. Charles K McHarg

MANUSCRIPT: A. Janier.

Charles K. McHarg (1823–1903), who was educated at Union College, held pastorates in Presbyterian Churches in Cooperstown, Syracuse, and Irvington, New York.

1. McHarg had recently completed *The Life of Prince Talleyrand, With Extracts from His Speeches and Writings.*

2483.   To [George P. Putnam?]

Sunnyside Octr. 5th. 1856

My dear Sir,

The bearer Mr W H Tudor has placed in my hands a manuscript work which he is desirous I should examine You know how I am hurried and harassed at this moment. I will thank you therefore to get some one of your critical friends to look at the manuscript, with a kind and favorable eye, and that you will put the author in a way of bringing his ⟨of?⟩ writings, if meritorious, in an advantageous way before the public

Yours very truly
Washington Irving

MANUSCRIPT: SHR.

2484.   *To Mary Kennedy Cooke*

Sunnyside Oct 9th 1856

My dear Mrs Cooke

I was rejoiced once more to see your hand writing, and to recieve from you a letter[1] written in such a cheerful, happy vein. I had recieved from your Aunt Kennedy good accounts of you and your domestic establishment and of that "blessed baby"[2] of which you and your husband, according to your own accounts, are so proud. I thought from what I saw of your husband when at Cassilis that you had made a good choice, and I am delighted to find it proves so, and that I shall have no occasion to come with that big stick to enforce domestic harmony.

I have for a long time intended to write to you, but since I saw you last I have been so engrossed by my literary labors in preparing volume after volume for the press that I have had to give up all additional exercise of the pen and my correspondence is entirely behind hand. The same engrossing task will prevent my accepting your kind invitation to come on with your Uncle and Aunt Kennedy and pay you a visit this autumn. I am hard at work endeavoring to get the fourth volume of my life of Washington ready for the press. Until that is launched, which will not be, I fear, until some time in the winter,[3] I cannot give myself holyday. In the coming year I hope to be more at liberty and then there is no place I shall be more delighted to revisit than the Valley of the Shenandoah.

I am happy to find that the "blessed baby" has not supplanted my dear little Lizzy Gray;[4] but I might have been sure that you had room enough in your heart for both. I hope little Lizzy has not quite forgotten me.

Give my kind regards to your husband, since he proves such a good one, remember me affectionately to the household at Cassilis, and believe me, my dear Mrs Cooke,

Affectionately your friend
Washington Irving

PUBLISHED: *American Literature*, 6 (March, 1934), 64–65.

1. This and the letter from Mrs. John P. Kennedy have not been located.

2. Henry Pendleton Cooke, Jr.

3. This volume appeared in May, 1857. See Langfeld & Blackburn, WI *Bibliography*, p. 42.

4. Lizzy Gray was the daughter of Mrs. Cooke's sister, Annie Kennedy Selden,

who died shortly after the birth of a son on July 14, 1854. See WI to Mary Kennedy, September 1, 1854.

2485. To ——

Sunnyside Oct. 16th. 1856

Dear Sir,

I have to acknowledge the receipt of the maps which you have had the kindness to send me and which come most opportunely. I shall be careful to return them to you when I have done with them. You mention some "curious old revolutionary documents" in your possession. I should like extremely to see them. If you could send them to my publishers, G. P Putnam & Co. 321 Broad way they would be sure to reach me safe and would add greatly to the favors you have already conferred upon me.

With great respect / Your obliged friend & servt
Washington Irving

MANUSCRIPT: Columbia.

2486. To Thomas I. McGrath

Sunnyside Oct 24t. 1856

Thomas I McGrath Esqr. / Corresponding Secretary &c

Dear Sir

I feel sensibly the honor done me by the Goethean Literary Society[1] in choosing me to deliver a biennial oration before the Literary Societies of Franklin and Marshall College; but regret to say that an unconquerable diffidence in regard to public speaking compels me to avoid every thing of the kind.

Very respectfully / Your Obliged & hbl Servt
Washington Irving

MANUSCRIPT: Franklin and Marshall College Library.

1. WI had been elected an honorary member of the Goethean Literary Society in December, 1836. See WI to George W. Welker, Daniel Miller, and Hugh Downey, January 5, 1837.

2487. To Sarah Storrow

Oct 27. 1856

My dear Sarah,

I am glad to learn by your September letter[1] that you saw my friends the Kennedys while they were in Paris.[2] They are friends that I value very highly and with whom I have been especially intimate of late years. The death of Mrs Kennedys father has been a great loss to me. I had become strongly attached to him, and was never so content from home as when I was under his roof. He was a sterling character of the old school, and his daughters inherit many of his estimable qualities. Mrs Kennedy is indeed a lovely woman. You do not mention her sister, Miss Gray. She is noble spirited, intelligent and true hearted. Her devotion to her father during several years of his precarious, health was admirable—It has undermined her own constitution; but I hope change of scene and climate and the excitement and variety of an European tour will reestablish it.

Pierre P. Irving who returned home not long since speaks in grateful terms of the hospitable attentions he recieved from yourself and Mr Storrow, and extols your children to the skies. Kate he says, was his companion and guide in some of his sight seeing in Paris and he found her an excellent one. I think she must be ⟨some such a⟩ just the kind of a one that would suit me.

After Pierres return from France to England he made an expedition to the end of the world—in other words to the Orkneys![3] It was in those islands that the branch of the Irving family from which we are descended, vegetated for centuries; once having great landed possessions; ultimately much impoverished.

Pierre found a highly intelligent circle of society existing at Kirkwall the capital of the Orkneys; principally composed of persons from Edinburgh holding official stations. He was hospitably entertained by them; in a style of elegance which he had not expected in that remote region.

At Shapinsha, the island whence my father came, Pierre was shewn the house in which he was born, and whence he emigrated about a century since. It is a house of modest pretensions and still bears its old name of Quholme (pronounced Home) In the flourishing days of our family it must have owned the greater part of Shapinsha. Mr Balfour, the present proprietor, recieved Pierre very hospitably in his noble residence of Balfour Castle, and submitted to his inspection a chest full of deeds and documents of several generations, shewing how by piece meal the landed property passed out of the hands of the Irvings and centred in those of the family which at present hold it [.] Pierre brought home one of those documents, given to him by Mr Balfour, three or four centuries old, bearing the name of one of our ancestors with the old family arms of the three holly leaves. He also brought home a genealogy of the family, which, some official gentleman, curious in antiquarian research, had digested from deeds and other documents existing in the Orkneys and in the public archives at Edinburgh. ⟨of⟩ This genealogical ↑table↓ which is officially certified, establishes the fact of our being descended from the Irving of Bonshaw, who gave shelter to Robert the Bruce[4] in the day of his adversity.

The whole story of Pierres visit to the Orkneys is interesting, and the genalogical research in question, which had been going on for several months before his arrival, is a curious instance of ⟨the⟩ Scottish antiquarianism and the national propensity to trace up pedigree.

The foregoing has been lying for some time in the drawer of my writing table; in the mean time the Kennedys have arrived and I have spent a day or two with them in New York. Mrs Kennedy gave me Kates letter,[5] as soon as I can command sufficient liesure.[6] At present I am engrossed, as far as ⟨I am⟩ incessant interruptions will permit, by the task of preparing my fourth volume of the life of Washington for the press. The Kennedys, like every body else, speak ⟨of⟩ ↑in↓ the most gratifying terms of you and your children. I regret, with you that their visit to Paris was so brief; indeed their whole visit to Europe was a hurried one, Mr Kennedy being desirous of returning home before the Presidential election[7]

I doubt whether this letter will reach you before you enter Italy. You are going to pass the winter at a City I never visited: Florence. At the time I was in Italy a cordon of troops was drawn round Tuscany on account of a malignant fever prevalent there, and I was obliged to omit the whole of it in my Italian tour.[8] I also failed to see Venice, which I have ever regretted.

In[9] your letter of last June[10] mentions your being just returnd from an excursion of four days to Touraine. It recalled a tour I once made ⟨their⟩ there with your Uncle Peter, in which, ⟨after⟩ beside visiting the places you speak of we passed a day or two in the beautiful ⟨of⟩ old Chateau of Ussy,[11] belonging to the Duke of Duras, the Duchess having given me a letter to the Concierge which put the chateau and its domains at my disposition. Our sojourn was very interesting. The chateau had a half deserted character. The duke had not fortune enough to keep it up in style and only visited it occasionally in the hunting season. There were the traces of former gaiety and splendor. A private theatre all in decay and disorder, an old chapel turned into a granary—State apartments with stately family portraits in quaint antiquated costumes; but some of them mouldering in their frames. I found afterwards ↑that↓ the Duchess had hoped I might be excited to write something about the old Chateau in the style of Bracebridge Hall, and it would indeed have been a fine subject.

The Hamiltons are all returned in good health and spirits and very much gratified by their tour.

Lest this letter should again linger I will bring it to a close. Give my kind remembrances to your husband and kiss the three princesses for me

> Your affectionate uncle
> Washington Irving

P. S. You no doubt remember Mr Stewart the chaplain in our Navy who accompanied Louis Napoleon on his visit to the Cottage.[12] He some time since wrote an article for the public papers, vindicating the character and conduct of Louis Napoleon during his residence in America. He has in consequence recieved a snuff box with[13] ⟨the⟩ ↑having on its cover↓ a miniature likeness of the emperor set in diamonds.

Sunnyside Octr. 27th. 1856. / Madame / Madame Storrow

MANUSCRIPT: Yale. PUBLISHED: PMI, IV, 222–24 (in part).

1. This letter has not been located.
2. Mr. and Mrs. John P. Kennedy were in Europe from May to October, 1856, recovering from the anxiety caused by the illness of Edward Gray, who died on March 21, 1856. See Tuckerman, *Life of J. P. Kennedy*, p. 259; and Bohner, *J. P. Kennedy*, p. 217.
3. This group of seventy islands, of which fewer than a third are inhabited, lies off the northeast coast of Scotland.
4. Robert the Bruce (1274–1329), who was king of Scotland from 1306 to 1329, was a leader in the fight for Scottish national independence.
5. This letter has not been located.
6. WI did not complete his thought.
7. Kennedy had returned to campaign for Millard Fillmore's election to the presidency. See Bohner, *J. P. Kennedy*, p. 217.
8. See WI to William Irving, Jr., April 12, 1805.
9. WI apparently forgot to cancel this word.
10. This letter has not been located.
11. WI and his brother visited this castle on October 18 and 19, 1824. See *J&N*, III, 408–9; and WI to Catharine Paris, October 24, 1824.
12. Charles Louis Napoleon Bonaparte (1803–1873) had visited WI at his cottage on the Hudson in the spring of 1837. See PMI, III, 116–17.
13. WI neglected to cancel this word.

2488.   To Townsend Ward

Sunnyside Oct 27th 1856

Townsend Ward Esqr / Secretary &c

Dear Sir,
I feel highly obliged by the invitation with which the dinner committee have honored me, to dine with the Historical Society of Pennsylvania
on the 8th. of November next; but regret to say my occupations and engagements compel me reluctantly to decline it.

Very respectfully / Your Obedient Servant
Washington Irving

MANUSCRIPT: HSP.

2489.   To Andrew P. Peabody

Sunnyside Novr. 3d. 1856

My dear Sir,
Accept my sincere thanks for the copy of a letter of Washington which
you have had the kindness to send me and believe me very respectfully

Your obliged friend & Servt
Washington Irving

A. P. Peabody Esqr.

MANUSCRIPT: Miriam Lutcher Stark Library, University of Texas.

Andrew Preston Peabody (1811–1893), a Unitarian clergyman and author, was
editor and proprietor of the *North American Review* from 1853 to 1863.

2490.   To Hiram Paulding

Sunnyside. Novr. 11th. 1856

My dear Commodore,
Your kind invitation[1] having been directed to the Tarrytown post office
has but just reached me as I only send there occasionally for letters; my
post office is Irvington, West Chester, Can you not fix another day for
the visit to your ship,[2] say Saturday next, when, if it will suit you, I will

be most happy to come on board, with Mr Grinnell and some of the ladies of our family. Let me hear from you on receipt of this and believe me

very sincerely and heartily / Yours,
Washington Irving

Commodore H Paulding

P. S. If Saturday is not convenient name any other day.
P. S. *No* 2. An answer sent to Mr Grinnells Counting House No 78 South Street will reach me promptly

DOCKETED: Washington Irving. / Nov. 11 — 1856.
MANUSCRIPT: Andrew B. Myers.

1. This letter has not been located.
2. At this time Commodore Paulding was commander of the West India, or Home, Squadron of the U.S. Navy.

2491.   To George W. Curtis

Sunnyside Nov 20t. 1856

My dear Mr Curtis
    You are at perfect liberty to put my name among those who recommend Mr Oscanyans lectures[1] as worthy of public attention. I have not read his book[2] but have seen a specimen of it which gives me a favorable opinion of it and of the author. I wish him all possible success with the public
    I hear golden opinions of you and your political Knight errantry,[3] and feel confident you will acquit yourself in your new career in a manner that will be worthy of yourself and will elevate you still higher in the estimation of your country
    You have a noble field before you and are fitted by nature and education to signalize yourself in public life. I shall ever watch your course with extreme interest

Yours ever very truly
Washington Irving

George Wm Curtis Esq

MANUSCRIPT: SHR.

    George William Curtis (1824–1892) was a popular author who had attracted attention with his travel sketches, *Nile Notes of a Howadji* (1851), *The Howadji in Syria*, and *Lotus-Eating* (both 1852), and his satiric commentary on New York society, *The Potiphar Papers* (1853). From 1863 to 1892 he was the editor of *Harper's Weekly Magazine*.

1. Hatchik (later Christopher) Oscanyan (b. 1818) was a Turkish writer and editor who lectured before popular audiences on "The Domestic Life of the Turk." He was accompanied on stage by three ladies dressed in harem pajamas. See Gordon Milne, *George William Curtis and the Genteel Tradition* (Bloomington, 1956), p. 70.

2. Oscanyan's *The Sultan and His People* carries an 1857 copyright date. A presentation copy is among the books in WI's library at Sunnyside.

3. Curtis supported the candidacy of John C. Frémont for president and campaigned for him and his antislavery position in New York, New Jersey, Pennsylvania, and New England. See Milne, *George William Curtis*, pp. 91–94.

2492. To T. Addison Richards

Sunnyside Nov 20th. 1856

My dear Sir

Accept my thanks for the copy of Harpers Magazine for December[1] which You have sent me in advance, and for the pleasant and favorable manner in which you have sketched, with pen and pencil, my little rural homestead and its occupants.[2] I shall be very lucky if the public think I merit half the kind things You say of me.

We shall all be happy to see you again at Sunnyside.

With great respect / Yours very truly
Washington Irving

T Addison Richards Esqr.

Manuscript: SHR.

1. "Sunnyside, The Home of Washington Irving," a long, comprehensive article, profusely illustrated with twenty-nine drawings and sketches, appeared in *Harper's Magazine*, 14 (December, 1856), 1–21.

2. Richards and George Pope Morris had visited Sunnyside in September, 1855, and some of Richards's sketching may have been done at that time. See WI to Morris, September 6, 1855.

2493. To George Bancroft

Sunnyside Decr. 24th. 1856

My dear Bancroft

I feel greatly obliged by your kind offer to lend me the Harrisburg volume or to show me the passages in it relating to Col John Armstrong[1] and his share in the expedition of 1758. I have done with that part of my subject, but shall be happy to avail myself of your offer for a glance at the volume when I come to town—

Wishing a Merry Christmas to you and yours

I remain, my dear Bancroft / Yours very truly
Washington Irving

DOCKETED: W. Irving / Decr. 24 / 56
MANUSCRIPT: Cornell University Library.

1. John Armstrong (1717–1795) attacked and destroyed Kittanning, an Indian town near Fort Duquesne, in 1756. WI probably intended to write "1756" instead of "1758."

2494. To Catharine Irving

[January 22, 1857]

My dear Kate

As you are probably all snowed dunder[1] I shall not attempt to come today, but, should nothing prevent, will come up tomorrow in the train which leaves New York at One Oclock

Your affectionate uncle
Washington Irving

N York. ⟨Jany Frid⟩ ↑Thursday↓

P S. Should I not come up on that train you need not expect me until Saturday.

ADDRESSED: Miss Kate Irving / Irvington / West chester Co / N Y POSTMARKED: NEW YORK / JAN / 25

MANUSCRIPT: SHR.

Written in ink below "25" in the postmark is "1875", apparently an unintended inversion of the last two digits.

A heavy snowstorm which had begun on Sunday, January 18 continued until late Monday, leaving the New York area paralyzed. See New York *Daily Times*, January 20–23, 1857. Perhaps the delayed date of cancellation of the letter is an aftereffect of the storm.

1. Probably WI's deliberate attempt at humor.

2495. To Henry T. Tuckerman

Sunnyside, Jan. 26, 1857

My dear Mr. Tuckerman:

I wrote to you, some days since,[1] on the subject of your new work,[2] when I had read but a part of it. I have just finished the perusal of it, and cannot rest until I have told you how thoroughly I have been delighted with it. I do not know when I have read any work more uniformly rich, full, and well sustained. The liberal, generous, catholic spirit in which it is written, is beyond all praise. The work is a model of its kind.

I have no doubt that it will take a high stand in England,[3] and will reflect great credit on our literature, of which it will remain a lasting ornament.

Congratulating you, with all my heart, on this crowning achievement of your literary career I remain, yours, very cordially and truly,

Washington Irving

Published: PMI, IV, 229.

1. WI's letter has not been located.

2. Tuckerman's *Essays, Biographical and Critical, or Studies of Character* had been published earlier in January by Phillips, Sampson and Company of Boston. A copy with the inscription "Presented to Washington Irving by the Author" is among the books in WI's library at Sunnyside.

3. Probably because the volume included many biographical sketches of Englishmen.

2496. To Anna K. Hiener

Sunnyside Feb. 7th. 1857

Dear Madam

I feel very sensible of the extreme kindness of the invitation[1] you make me in your mothers name to your house to inspect the papers of your ancestor General Hand.[2] I regret to say, however, that I find it impossible to leave home for the purpose. Could the papers be forwarded to my publishers Messrs. Geo P Putnam & Co New York they would reach me in safety and I would gladly pay the expense and engage to return them in good order; but I am aware that one does not like to risk the loss of such interesting documents and I do not expect that you will comply with my suggestion[3]

Be that as it may I already feel myself deeply your debtor for your hospitable invitation and remain with great respect

Your obliged friend & Servt
Washington Irving

Mrs Anna K Hiener

MANUSCRIPT: Va.–Barrett.

1. This letter has not been located.

2. Edward Hand (1744–1802), who headed a corps of Pennsylvania riflemen during the Revolutionary War, was breveted major general in 1783. He served in the Continental Congress in 1784 and 1785. His orderly book of 1778 was published in the *Pennsylvania Magazine of History and Biography*, 41 (1917), 198–223, 257–73, 458–67.

3. Since WI had already dealt with Colonel Hand in volume 2 of his *Life of Washington* and does not refer to him later, it is unlikely that the documents were forwarded.

2497. To John A. King

Sunnyside Feb. 8th. 1857

My dear Sir,

After expressing the hearty satisfaction I feel in common with all good New Yorkers, but especially with those of your early acquaintance, in having you to govern us, I take the liberty of enclosing a letter from my nephew Edgar Irving[1] who I find is an applicant for the renewal of his appointment as Notary Public. Hoping his application may be successful

I remain with great regard / Yours very faithfully
Washington Irving

His Excellency / John A. King / &c &c &c

MANUSCRIPT: SHR.

John Alsop King (1788–1867), son of Rufus King and brother of Charles and James G. King, served as Republican governor of New York from 1857 to 1859.

1. Edgar Irving (1808–1873) was the second son of Ebenezer. WI had interceded in his behalf several times two decades earlier. For example, see WI to Gouverneur Kemble, February 3 and June 2, 1838.

2498. To Charles Lanman

Sunnyside March 2d. 1857

My dear Mr. Lanman,

I am suffering a long time to elapse without acknowledging the receipt of the copy of your work[1] which you have had the kindness to send me and expressing to you the great delight I take in the perusal of it. But when I remind you that I am approaching my seventy-fourth birth day; that I am laboring to launch the fourth volume of my life of Washington, and that my table is loaded with a continually increasing multitude of unanswered letters which I vainly endeavor to cope with, I am sure you will excuse the tardiness of my correspondence.

I hope the success of your work has been equal to its merits. To me ⟨it⟩ your 'adventures in the wilds' are a continual refreshment of the spirits. I take a volume of your work to bed with me, after fagging with my pen, and then I ramble with you among the mountains and by the streams, in the boundless interior of our fresh unhackneyed Country and only regret that I can but do so in idea; and that I am not young enough to be your companion in reality.

I have ⟨foun⟩ taken great interest of late in your expeditions among the Alleghany Mountains,[2] having been campaigning *in my work* in the upper parts of the Carolinas and especially in the 'Catawba country' about which you give such graphic sketchings. Really I look upon your work as a vade mecum to the American lover of the picturesque and romantic unfolding to him the wilderness of beauties and the varieties of adventurous life to be found in our great chains of mountains and systems of lakes and rivers. You are in fact the picturesque explorer of our country.

With great regard my dear Mr Lanman

Yours ever very truly
Washington Irving

Charles Lanman Esq.

MANUSCRIPT: Alan L. Belinkoff; NYPL–Hellman Collection (copy).
PUBLISHED: PMI, IV, 225–26.

1. At this point the copyist placed an asterisk and at the bottom of the page wrote *"Adventures in the Wilds of America."* Actually the title of the volume is *Adventures in the Wilds of the United States and British American Provinces,* and it is among the books in WI's library at Sunnyside.

2. WI refers to Lanman's *Letters from the Alleghany Mountains* (New York, 1849), a copy of which is in his library.

2499. To John S. Williams

Sunnyside March 4th. 1857.

Dear Sir,

I have delayed acknowledging the receipt of the copy of your work[1] which you have had the kindness to send me until I had time to read it

I now give you my sincere thanks for calling up in so vivid a manner past times and scenes so deeply interesting, and for throwing such light upon a dubious page in our history.

No one is more competent to judge of the merit of your work than our friend John P Kennedy having mingled in the military scenes which it depicts.

I feel very sensibly the expression of esteem with which you conclude your letter[2] and remain with great regard

Your truly obliged friend
Washington Irving

Major J. S. Williams / &c & &c

MANUSCRIPT: Va.–Barrett.

John S. Williams was a brigade major and inspector of the Columbian Brigade in the War of 1812.

1. *History of the Invasion and Capture of Washington, and of the Events Which Preceded and Followed* (New York, 1857). A presentation copy is among the books in WI's library at Sunnyside.
2. Actually Williams's praise of WI occurs in the opening paragraph of his letter. See John S. Williams to WI, February, 1857 (Va.–Barrett [copy]).

2500. To William Fox

Sunnyside March 5th. 1857

William Fox Esqr. / Corresponding Secretary / &c &c &c

Dear Sir,

I feel properly sensible of the honor conferred on me by Your association in adopting my name as its designation and am highly grateful for this proof of the good will of its members.

Should I visit Schenectady it would give me great pleasure to make the call at your rooms to which you so kindly invite me, and trust I should find them in a flourishing condition present my most respectful acknowledgements to your association and believe me your truly obliged

friend and Servt
Washington Irving

MANUSCRIPT: Rush Rhees Library, University of Rochester.

2501.   *To Thomas W. Olcott et al.*

Sunnyside March 14t. 1857

Messr Thomas W Olcott ⎫
     Erastus Corning |
     Thurlow Weed |
     Edward C Delavan ⎬
     J T. Headley |
   & J. H Armsby |
     Committee &c &c   ⎭

Gentlemen
    I feel deeply grateful for the honor you have done me by your kind invitation[1] to be present on the occasion when Mr Edward Everett is to deliver before you his admirable Discourse on the character of Washington, one of the noblest of those eloquent and classic productions, wherewith he has enriched our national literature and gained for himself a lasting fame. I regret to say however, that at present I am so closely engaged and occupied in getting a volume of my work through the press[2] and am so incessantly subject to the printers call that I am unable to absent myself from home
    I remain Gentlemen

With the highest respect / Your obliged & humble Servt
Washington Irving

MANUSCRIPT: MHS.

    Thomas W. Olcott (1795–1880) was president of the Albany Bank, later named the Olcott Bank, from 1836 until his death.
    Erastus Corning (1794–1872), an Albany businessman, manufacturer, politician, and civic leader, was president of the New York Central Railroad at this time.
    Edward C. Delavan (1793–1872) was a reformer and publisher who helped to organize the New York State Temperance Society in 1829.
    James C. Armsby (1809–1875), an Albany physician, was one of the founders of the Young Men's Christian Association.

1. The invitation to attend Edward Everett's oration on Washington on March 18 has not been located. WI had heard Everett speak on the same subject on March 3, 1856.

2. The gist of WI's refusal to attend the oration was reported in the New York *Times*, March 31, 1857.

2502. To Charles King

Sunnyside March 19th. 1857

My dear King

Enclosed I send you an order on my publishers to continue to furnish the College library[1] with my works as they appear. I have already spoken to Mr Putnam on the subject.

Yours ever very truly
Washington Irving

Charles King L. L. D. / &c &c &c

MANUSCRIPT: Va.–Barrett.

Charles King (1789–1867), son of Rufus King, was editor of the New York *American* from 1823 to 1845 and president of Columbia College from 1849 to 1864.

1. Apparently WI was responding to a request from King to contribute copies of his writings to the college library.

2503. To Pierre M. Irving

Sunnyside, March 20, 1857

My dear Pierre:

Page 161 must be carefully collated with the manuscript. There are two places where I cannot supply the deficit.[1]

I have struck out some lines in page 172, so that the chapter may end on page 173,[2] and save the great blank in page 174. The printers appear to be fond of ending a chapter at the top of a page.

I have no doubt of getting the Inauguration[3] into this volume; but the printers must not make blank pages unnecessarily.

PUBLISHED: PMI, IV, 227.

1. WI, who was correcting proofs without access to the manuscript, apparently could not recall the appropriate passages printed on page 161.

2. With this deletion WI ended chapter 12 of volume 4 of his *Life of Washington* on page 173.

3. WI's account of Washington's inauguration as president of the United States occurs in chapter 37, pages 512–15.

2504. To Pierre M. Irving

Sunnyside, March 22, 1857

I send you the page which was missing. Fortunately, I had *impaled* it, as I now do all cancelled pages. * * *

PUBLISHED: PMI, IV, 227.

2505. To Pierre M. Irving

Sunnyside, Monday Evening / [March 23, 1857]

There is a passage in, I think, De Rochambeau's Memoirs,[1] about the sending in a flag, at Yorktown, to Cornwallis,[2] to obtain permission for Secretary Nelson[3] to leave the town; and about his being brought out on a litter, being old, and ill with the gout. I wish you would copy it, and send it to me with the nexts proofs, as I wish to make immediate use of it. You will find De Rochambeau's Memoirs in the American department of the Astor Library.

If it is not in De Rochambeau's Memoirs, it is in Chastellux;[4] but I think it is in the former.

PUBLISHED: PMI, IV, 227.

1. Jean Baptiste Donatien de Vimeur, comte de Rochambeau (1725–1807) was commander of a French expeditionary force in 1780 which strategically reinforced Washington's troops in Virginia and assisted in the defeat of Cornwallis and the British army at Yorktown in October, 1783. The incident to which WI refers was not recorded in Rochambeau's *Mémoires militaires, historiques et politiques*, 2 vols. (Paris, 1809).

2. Charles, first Marquis Cornwallis (1738–1805) was the commanding general of the British forces.

3. Thomas Nelson (b. 1716), who was appointed secretary of the Virginia colony in 1743, was allowed safe conduct out of Yorktown to Williamsburg on October 10, 1781. See Clyde F. Trudell, *Colonial Yorktown* (Old Greenwich, Conn., 1938), p. 108. For WI's treatment of this incident, see *Life of Washington*, IV, 372.

4. *Voyages de m. le marquis de Chastellux dans l'Amérique Septentrionale dans les années 1780, 1781, et 1782*, 2 vols. (Paris, 1786) or the English translation, *Travels in North America*, 2 vols. (New York, 1827). PMI (IV, 227) indicates that the incident was related in Chastellux, not in Rochambeau.

2506.   *To Pierre M. Irving*

Sunnyside, Tuesday Evening [March 24?, 1857]

* * * I shall send no copy for a day or two, for I am fagged and a little out of order, and need rest; and I wish to be careful about the ensuing chapters, which I have been patching, and must revise to avoid muddling. * * * I shall be heartily glad to receive the last proof sheet.

Published: PMI, IV, 227–28.

2507.   *To George W. Childs and Robert E. Peterson*

Sunnyside April 9th. 1857

Messrs Childs & Peterson,

Gentlemen,

I feel extremely sensible of your great forbearance in not being indignant at my sending no reply to your previous letters;[1] a delinquency of which I have been conscious and which has been a matter of severe self reproach. But I am continually sinning and repenting and endeavoring to reform in point of correspondence; but always remaining behind hand. The fact is my pen for some time has been overtasked, and I believe You are aware of it.

When I recieved from Dr Kane a copy of his work[2] I intended to write to him on the Subject as soon as I had read it; before that time he had sailed for Europe and then the letter became a matter of procrastination—

You ask my opinion of his work. What can I say that has not been already said by more competent critics? I do not pretend to critical acumen; being too much influenced by my feelings; Still I may give some opinion in this department of literature, having from childhood had a passion for voyages of discovery, and I know of none that ever more thoroughly interested and delighted me than this of Dr Kane. While I read the work I had the author continually in my "minds eye." I was present when he lectured in the Smithsonian Institution in 1853,[3] on the Arctic expedition which he had already made; when we all wondered that one of a physicke apparently so slight and fragile having once gone through such perils and hardships should have the daring spirit to encounter them again. I saw him after his return from that Second expedition, a broken down man, broken down in all but intellect, about to embark for Europe in the vain hope of ⟨shatt⟩ bracing up a shattered constitution.

It was this image of the author continually before me that made me read his narrative so simply, truthfully and ably written with continued wonder and admiration. His expedition, and his ⟨res⟩ narrative of it form one of the most extraordinary instances of the triumph of mental energy and enthusiasm over a frail physical organization that I have ever known. His name, like that of Henry Grinnell[4] will remain an honour to his country.

> I remain Gentlemen / Yours very truly
> Washington Irving

MANUSCRIPT: Yale.

1. These letters have not been located.

2. Elisha Kane (b. 1822), who had died in Havana on February 16, 1857, had written *Arctic Explorations: The Second Grinnell Expedition in Search of Sir John Franklin, 1853, '54, '55,* published in September, 1856.

3. Kane had lectured at the Smithsonian Institution on January 30, 1853. See George W. Corner, *Dr. Kane of the Arctic Seas* (Philadelphia, 1972), p. 117.

4. Henry Grinnell (1799–1874) was a New York merchant and philanthropist who founded the American Geographical and Statistical Society.

2508. To George W. Childs and Robert E. Peterson

> Sunnyside May 6th. 1857

Messrs Childs & Peterson

Gentlemen,

I have made diligent search among my books but cannot find the volume you mention, containing the first three letters of Mr Allibones dictionary of authors.[1] I apprehend some one of my family connexion must have taken it away. I will make enquiry and should I find it will forward it to ⟨b⟩ you by express—

> Yours very respectfully
> Washington Irving

MANUSCRIPT: Huntington.

1. On August 23, 1855, WI wrote to Childs and Peterson, acknowledging receipt of the specimen of Allibone's *Critical Dictionary of English Literature.* Listed among WI's books at Sunnyside is a volume of Allibone's work dated 1855.

2509.   To Charles C. Lee

Sunnyside May 6t. 1857

My dear Mr Lee

I feel greatly obliged to you for your two letters[1] which I will endeavor
to profit by, in future impressions of my work.

I have endeavored to be accurate ⟨but⟩ and to state nothing but what
I concieved to be founded on competent authority; but am more and
more aware how difficult it is with all ones efforts, to attain historical
accuracy.

My fourth volume ⟨has just⟩ is about to issue from the press[2] and I
am now resting from my labors; rather fatigued by the toil of furnishing
manuscript and correcting proof sheets with the imps of the press at my
heels; this I trust will serve as an apology for the brevity and hurried
nature of this scrawl.

I have consulted your brothers "Campaign of 1781"[3] just before
putting my volume to the press—and shall procure a copy of his "Observations on the writings of Jefferson"[4]

With great regard my dear Mr Lee

Your obliged friend
Washington Irving

C. C. Lee Esqr.

ADDRESSED: C. C. Lee Esqr / Windsor / Near Fire Creek Mills / Powhatan / Va.
    POSTMARKED [*handwritten*]: Irvington / NY / May 7
MANUSCRIPT: Va.–Barrett.

Charles C. Lee (1798–1871) was the second son of Henry "Light-Horse Harry"
Lee (1756–1818) and his second wife, Anne Hill Carter, and a full brother of
Robert E. Lee (1807–1870) and a half-brother of Henry Lee (1787–1837), the
author mentioned in WI's letter.

1. These letters have not been located.
2. Volume 4 of *The Life of Washington* appeared later in May, 1857. See Langfeld & Blackburn, *WI Bibliography*, p. 42.
3. Henry Lee's *The Campaign of 1781 in the Carolinas* had been published in
Philadelphia in 1824.
4. In *Observations on the Writings of Thomas Jefferson* (1832) Henry Lee again
defended his father against what he considered unwarranted attack.

2510.   To Charles Lanman

Sunnyside May 9t. 1857.

My dear Mr Lanman,

I have been too thoroughly occupied in getting a volume of my work through the press to acknowledge at an earlier date your letter of March 24th[1] respecting your letter which has found its way into the Intelligencer[.][2] I can only say that I wish you had had a worthier subject for your biographic pen, or that I had known our conversation was likely to be recorded—I should then have ⟨take⟩ tasked myself to say some wise or witty things to be given as specimens of my *off hand table talk*—One should always know when they are sitting for a portrait that they may endeavor to look handsomer than themselves and attitudinize

I am scrawling this in great haste, merely that your letter may not remain longer unacknowledged am[3] am very truly

Your friend
Washington Irving

Charles Lanman Esqr

MANUSCRIPT: Harvard; NYPL—Hellman Collection (copy).   PUBLISHED: PMI, IV, 228–29; New York *Commercial*.

The undated clipping from the New York *Commercial* is to be found in the notebook of Dr. J. C. Peters, page 9 (NPYL—Berg Collection).

1. This letter has not been located.
2. After Lanman had visited WI at Sunnyside early in March, 1853, he described his meeting in a letter to Peter Force on February 20, 1853. Probably the appearance of the fourth volume of *The Life of Washington* prompted Force to pass it along to Joseph Gales and William W. Seaton, who published it in the *National Intelligencer* on March 23, 1857.
3. WI probably intended to write "and" for the first "am."

2511.   To Frederick Saunders

Sunnyside May 9h 1857

My dear Sir,

I fear you will consider me an incorrigible delinquent in regard to letter writing having suffered so long a time to elapse without acknowledging the receipt of your favor of the 6t of April[1] and of the beautiful copy of the new Edition of Common Prayers[2] which you had the kindness to send me by the express. I can only say in excuse that for some time past I have been excessively occupied and engrossed in getting the fourth volume of my life of [Washington through the]³ press and that all my correspondence has fallen behind hand.

I now thank you most heartily and sincerely for this testimonial of your remembrance and regard and shall take occasion when I come to town to call on you, thank you in person and make myself acquainted with the new establishment⁴ ⟨to⟩ ↑with↓ which you have connected yourself

With great regard / Yours very truly

[*signature cut from sheet*]

F. Saunders Esqr.

DOCKETED: Washington Irving / to F Saunders Esq. / (Name taken away)
MANUSCRIPT: NYPL—WI Papers.

1. This letter has not been located.
2. WI's library at Sunnyside contains several copies of *The Book of Common Prayer*. One which has the title page and copyright date missing may be the volume referred to in this letter.
3. The bracketed words were removed when WI's signature was clipped from the verso of this page.
4. Probably a reference to Saunders's editorial position with the New York *Evening Post*.

2512.   *To W. Alfred Jones*

Sunnyside May 10t. 1857.

My dear Sir,

Accept my sincere thanks for the copy of your revised edition¹ which you have had the kindness to send me and for the choice reading it has furnished me in a department of literature very much to my taste, and in which you have proved yourself a master.

The sound judgement, nice discrimination, cultivated thought, kind spirit and perfect candor evinced throughout your volumes, render them worthy of being treasured as furnishing models of true criticism⟨s⟩, as well as standards of opinion on the subjects to which they relate.

This sincere appreciation of your critical acumen would of course make me value the favorable mention you have made of me in various passages of your writings; but they have been gratifying to me on another account; your worthy father² was one of the first to applaud and encourage my early attempts at authorship, and it is peculiarly grateful to my feelings to have his kind plaudits echoed as it were by his son, toward the end of my career, when I am about to retire from the stage.

With best wishes for your continued success in authorship and your welfare in every respect I remain

My dear Sir / Your obliged friend
Washington Irving

W Alfred Jones Esqr

DOCKETED: Washington Irving / 1857
MANUSCRIPT: Columbia; Va.–Barrett, Harvard, Long Island Historical Society (copies).

This letter was reproduced in facsimile, and copies are to be found in several libraries.

William Alfred Jones (1817–1900), who graduated from Columbia College in 1836, was its librarian from 1851 to 1865. He wrote critical essays which were collected in book form as *The Analyst, A Collection of Miscellaneous Papers* (1840), *Essays upon Authors and Books* (1849), and *Characters and Criticisms* (1857).

1. *Characters and Criticisms* is among the books in WI's library at Sunnyside. Jones's gift may have been in response to WI's donation of copies of his writings to the Columbia College Library. See WI to Charles King, March 19, 1857.

2. David S. Jones (1777–1848), a graduate of Columbia in 1796 who was interested in library matters, served as trustee and legal adviser to Columbia College, the Society Library, and the General Theological Seminary for many years. He was connected by marriage to the Livingston, Clinton, and LeRoy families.

2513. To W. F. Smith

Sunnyside May 12th. 1857

W. F. Smith Esqr

Dear Sir

I feel deeply and gratefully sensible of the good opinion and good will manifested toward me by the Literary Association to which you belong in adopting my name as a designation.

The value of such associations to young men preparing to enter upon the busy scenes of life is too well established to need enforcement or illustration. Your letter shews that the members are well aware of the practical course to be pursued by them; diligent study and self culture at home, and a free interchange of thought, and candid discussion of theories and points of knowledge, in the Association.

With best wishes and confident hopes of the success of your enterprise I remain

very respectfully / Your obliged & hbl Servt
Washington Irving

MANUSCRIPT: Va.–Barrett.

2514. To F. C. Yarnall

Sunnyside May 12th. 1857

Dear Sir,

I must trust to your indulgence to excuse my tardiness in replying to your obliging favor of the 15th.[1] Feb. last; ⟨but⟩ I received it at a time when I was engrossed and rather harassed by the labor of preparing a volume for the press; which rendered me inevitably remiss in my correspondence. I had already disposed of the subject[2] to which the narrative you so obligingly offered me referred; and had diligently consulted every authority I could find relating to it. I have endeavored to treat the matters as candidly and dispassionately as possible; which is not a very easy task where there is so much to touch and interest the feelings.

Thanking you for your very kind offer I remain,

Your obliged & humble Servt
Washington Irving

F. C. Yarnall Esqr.

ADDRESSED: F. C. Yarnall / 39 Market St / Phila
MANUSCRIPT: NYPL–WI Papers.

1. This letter or manuscript has not been located.
2. According to Edward Wagenknecht, Yarnall had offered to provide WI with an account of the capture of Major John André. See *Washington Irving: Moderation Displayed* (New York, 1962), p. 186.

2515. To Daniel Appleton

Sunnyside May 14t. 1857

Dear Sir

The pressure of occupation in preparing a volume of my work for the press has prevented an earlier reply to your letter of February 17th.[1] I am really gratified to find my casual notices of the specific services of the 'Amphibious Warriors' of Marblehead[2] so kindly appreciated, and yet I have scarcely done those brave fellows sufficient justice. They were eminently serviceable in two of the most critical operations in the course of the Revolution; the conveying of our troups across the sound in the Retreat from Long Island, and across the icy Delaware in the night expedition against Trenton—and how nobly did they acquit themselves on both occasions! and how providential was their *amphibious* character!

I am just resting from the labor of launching my fourth volume and my weary pen refuses to be put in harness for letter writing[.] I am obliged therefore to be brief, and again thanking you for your kind letter and the good wishes with which it concludes I remain

Very respectfully / Your obliged friend & servt
Washington Irving

Daniel Appleton Esqr

MANUSCRIPT: Va.–Barrett.

The specific Daniel Appleton to whom WI refers remains in doubt. It may be Daniel Sidney Appleton (b. April 9, 1824), who married Malvina W. Marshall of New York City. She died at Dobbs Ferry in 1873. Or it may be Daniel Fuller Appleton (b. January 31, 1826), who was born at Marblehead, married Julia Randall of Manilius, New York, and was living in New York City in 1857. Still another possibility is Daniel Appleton (b. September 29, 1825), who had been born at Marblehead and was living there in 1857. See W. S. Appleton, *A Genealogy of the Appleton Family* (Boston, 1874), pp. 49, 41, 45.

1. This letter has not been located.
2. This epithet was given to the Massachusetts regiment of Colonel John Glover. See *The Life of Washington,* II, 331, 477, where WI uses similar terms as he recounts the trips across Long Island Sound and the Delaware River by Glover's men.

2516. To George Bancroft

Sunnyside May 15th. 1857

My dear Bancroft,

I lay down your letter[1] to answer it immediately, while the effect of it is yet tingling in my veins. It is one of the best timed, kindest and most gratifying that I have ever recieved, and relieves me from a host of doubts and misgivings by which I am apt to be dogged at the conclusion of any literary task, and by which I have been continually beset throughout the task ⟨i⟩ on which I have of late been engaged.

I will confess, moreover, that I rather stood in awe of your criticism in the premises, from the great scope, yet minute accuracy, of your intellectual vision, and your thorough knowledge of the department of history into which my biographical enterprise obliged me occasionally to adventure. I felt how casual and limited were my forays, as a biographer, into that department, merely intended to illustrate the actions and character of an individual—in comparison with what will be your grand operations as a historian—For you in fact, are destined to be the real historian of our revolution in all its bearings and in all its relations with the contemporary history of the world[2] and in your hands it will form the noblest part of that stupendous fabric which you undertook with such a daring spirit, such a wide forecast, and are executing with such persevering zeal and unflinching industry.

I again thank you most heartily for your kind letter and your most indulgent criticism. You have no idea how much your letter has gratified and affected me.

With kindest remembrances to Mrs Bancroft[3] believe me my dear Bancroft

Gratefully and truly yours
Washington Irving

George Bancroft Esqr

DOCKETED: Washington Irving / May 15 / 57
MANUSCRIPT: Cornell University Library.

1. This letter has not been located.
2. The phrase "are destined . . . world" is underscored in another hand.
3. Elizabeth Davis Bliss (d. 1886), Bancroft's second wife, whom he had married in August, 1838.

2517.   To George P. Putnam

Sunnyside May 15th. 1857

My dear Sir,

I have recieved the two copies of the fourth volume which you sent to me. I will thank you to send postage paid, a copy of the fourth volume to Mrs Anna K Hiener[1] addressed to the care of Mrs S. B. Rogers Lancaster Pennsylvania.

Pierre M. Irving will specify the members of my family to whom I wish copies sent.

Yours truly
Washington Irving

MANUSCRIPT: John Rylands Library.

1. See WI to Mrs. Hiener, February 7, 1857.

2518.   To Henry C. Wetmore

Sunnyside May 20t. 1857.

Dear Sir

I must trust to your indulgence to excuse me for suffering your letter of January last[1] to remain so long unanswered Had it been in my power to furnish you the information you sought, I should have replied immediately; but I had no "facts nor correspondence" in my possession relative to President Reed[2] that had not already appeared in print. I know nothing of the 'parties' which you hint as being in feud with respect to his memory. I have spoken of him without partiality or prejudice; as fairly and dispassionately as I could, judging of him from the facts that lay before the public.

At the time I received your letter[3] I was excessively tasked in preparing a volume for the press and had to spare my pen, as much as possible, from all extra labor—my whole correspondence has consequently fallen behind hand

Wishing you the fullest success in your literary undertaking I remain very respectfully Yours &c

Washington Irving

H. C. Wetmore Esqr

MANUSCRIPT: SHR.

Henry C. Wetmore (b. 1823), a writer who contributed to *Neal's Gazette*, *International Magazine*, and *Harper's Magazine*, was the author of *Rural Life in America; or, Summer and Winter in the Country* (New York, 1854).

1. This letter has not been located.
2. Joseph Reed (1741–1785), who was the president of the Executive Council of Pennsylvania from 1778 to 1781, was accused of being unpatriotic and of engaging in treasonous correspondence with the British.
3. Probably Wetmore had sought from WI information which would help to clear Reed of the charge of treason and to refute the accusation that WI had falsified history by suppressing evidence damaging to Reed. For a review of the matter, see Horace W. Smith, *Nuts for Future Historians to Crack* (Philadelphia, 1856), pp. 4–11.

2519. To Frederick S. Cozzens

Sunnyside, May 22, 1857

My dear Mr. Cozzens:

Your letter[1] has been most acceptable and animating; for letters of the kind are not, as you presume, "common to me as blackberries." Excepting a very cordial and laudatory one from Bancroft,[2] yours is the only one, relative to my last volume, that I have yet received. Backed by these two letters, I feel strong enough to withstand that self-criticism which is apt to beset me and cuff me down at the end of a work, when the excitement of composition is over.

You speak of some misgivings which you felt in the course of my literary enterprise, whether I would be able to go through with it, and "end as happily as I had begun." I confess I had many misgivings of the kind myself,[3] as I became aware of the magnitude of the theme upon which I had adventured, and saw "wilds immeasurably spread" lengthening on every side as I proceeded. I felt that I had presumed on the indulgence of nature in undertaking such a task at my time of life, and feared I might break down in the midst of it. Whimsical as it may seem, I was haunted occasionally by one of my own early pleasantries. My mock admonition to Diedrich Knickerbocker not to idle in his historic wayfaring, rose in judgment against me: "Is not Time, relentless Time, shaking, with palsied hand, his almost exhausted hourglass before thee? Hasten, then, to pursue thy weary task, lest the last sands be run ere thou hast finished thy history of the Manhattoes."[4]

Fortunately, I had more powers of endurance in me than I gave myself credit for. I have attained to a kind of landing place in my work, and, as I now rest myself on the bank, feel that, though a little weary, I am none the worse for having so long tugged at the oar.

And now, as the winter is past, the rains are over and gone, and the flowers are appearing upon the earth, I mean to recreate myself a little, and may, one day or other, extend my travels down even to Yonkers,[5] but will always be happy to welcome you to Sunnyside.

With kindest remembrances to Mrs. Cozzens,[6] believe me, very truly, your obliged friend,

Washington Irving

PUBLISHED: PMI, IV, 230–31.

1. This letter has not been located.

2. Bancroft's letter has not been located. WI replied to it on May 15, 1857.

3. For other instances of WI's misgivings, see WI to George Bancroft, May 15, 1857, and to Henry T. Tuckerman, January 8, 1856; and STW, II, 230–31.

4. Apart from punctuation and capitalization, WI is quoting from the Author's Revised Edition of *Knickerbocker's History of New York,* bk. 6, chap. 4, p. 337.

5. Cozzens was "a resident of Yonkers, about eight miles south of Sunnyside." See PMI, IV, 230.

6. The former Susan Meyers of Philadelphia.

2520. To G. Washington Warren

Sunnyside May 29th. 1857

Dear Sir,

I feel greatly obliged to the Bunker Hill Monument Association[1] for the honor they have done me in inviting me to attend the inauguration of the Statue of General Warren[2] but regret to say that my engagements are such as to prevent my having the pleasure of being present on that interesting occasion

With great respect I have the honor to be

Your Obt Servt
Washington Irving

G. Washington Warren Esqr / President of the B. H. M. / Association.

MANUSCRIPT: Va.–Barrett.

George Washington Warren (1813–1883), who believed that he was related to General Joseph Warren, was active in the Bunker Hill Monument Association. He served as director from 1836 to 1839, as secretary from 1839 to 1847, as president from 1847 to 1875, and again as director from 1875 to 1883. He wrote *The History of the Bunker Hill Monument Association* in 1877. See *National Cyclopaedia of American Biography,* V, 90.

1. This group was formed in 1823 to raise money for a suitable monument to commemorate the battle at Bunker Hill. Among its charter members were Daniel Webster, Edward Everett, George Ticknor, and Joseph Story. See Richard Frothingham, *History of the Siege of Boston* (New York, 1970), p. 354.

2. Joseph Warren (1741–1775), a friend of John Adams, was a member of many revolutionary committees and author of the "Suffolk Resolves." On August 23, 1775, he was killed while rallying the troops during the fighting at Bunker Hill.

2521.　*To Lyman C. Draper*

Sunnyside June 1st 1857.

Lyman C. Draper Esqr. ⎫
Corresponding Secretary &c ⎰

Dear Sir,

I have the honor to acknowledge the receipt of the works[1] forwarded by you on behalf of the State Historical Society of Wisconsin. I beg you to assure the Society of my most grateful sense of this interesting proof of their favorable appreciation, and to accept on your own part assurances of my high respect and esteem

Very truly Your obliged / friend & Servt
Washington Irving

MANUSCRIPT: State Historical Society of Wisconsin.

1. The titles of these works have not been ascertained.

2522.　*To Charles A. Davis*

Sunnyside June 2d. 1857

My dear Major,

Authors, like parents, when they are waxing old, are always well pleased to be complimented on the vigor and comeliness of their last bantling; you, who are a knowing man, are aware of this, and have taken care to touch me in the tender, in pronouncing my last volume "one of the most perfect and beautiful of the family[.]"[1] I confess to you I am heartily glad to be safely delivered of it and to find that it ⟨meets⟩ ↑recieves↓ the approbation of my friends.[2] It is a most anxious task to tell over a long story which every body knows; when every body stands ready to pounce upon you if you make the least error in point of facts and when you have to be in constant guard lest your feelings and imagination carry you astray. It has been the most wearing and engrossing task that I have had in the whole course of my literary career; and, had I been aware how it would have enlarged under my hand, I should hardly have ventured at my time of life, to undertake it However, I have got safely to a resting place without once breaking down, and am now rejoicing in the sempervivent vigor of one of the patriarchs The indisposition of which Kennedy spoke was a touch of influenza caused by the late mixture of Spring and winter; but which has passed away.

It is, as you say, a long time since we have met; I have been very rarely in town for a year past, and then only to make visits of a day; chiefly errands to the library; being very much mewed up in my study. Opera troupes have come and gone without my hearing or seeing them—In a word I have dropped quite astern of the gay world and shall have hard work to pull up and get on board again

I shall soon come to town in a gentlemanlike way, to walk about with a stick under my arm, see sights and amuse myself, and then I shall present myself at No 1. University Place[3] and put myself at the feet of your fair lady and the discreet Princess.

> Yours ever very truly
> Washington Irving

Ch. Aug Davis Esqr.

MANUSCRIPT: Va.–Barrett.

1. Davis's letter, from which WI is quoting, has not been located.
2. WI acknowledged the compliments of George Bancroft and Frederick S. Cozzens. See WI to Bancroft, May 15, 1857; and to Cozzens, May 22, 1857.
3. The address of Davis's residence in New York City.

2523.   *To Francis Lieber*

Sunnyside June 10t. 1857

Dear Sir,

I will lay your application[1] before the board of trustees of the Astor library at the next meeting, which will be on the last Wednesday of the month. Dr Cogswell, the Superintendent of the library, is the person whose views are most consulted on questions of the kind. I would observe, however, that the Rules of the library are so stringent in regard to granting permission to take books thence, that I have not sought the indulgence in preparing the work on which I am engaged, but have gone to town occasionally, to make my researches and take notes, in the library, or have employed another person[2] to do so for me, when my occupations did not permit me to leave the country.

My own inclination will be to give you every possible facility that the rules of the library will permit.

With the highest respect and regard.

Yours very truly
Washington Irving

Francis Lieber L. L. D. / &c &c &c

DOCKETED: *Irving*
MANUSCRIPT: Huntington.

Francis Lieber (1800–1872), with whom WI had corresponded in the 1830's, was a German-born reformer and educator. After teaching at South Carolina College from 1835 to 1856, he was appointed professor of history and political science at Columbia College in 1857.

1. This letter has not been located.
2. PMI usually served as WI's researcher and amanuensis during the writing of *The Life of Washington*. For example, see PMI, IV, 227.

2524.   To the Reverend Lucius H. King

Sunnyside June 17th. 1857

My dear Sir

I thank you heartily for the letter[1] you have so kindly volunteered. It found me reposing from an arduous and anxious task, which had been accompanied with many doubts and misgivings. At such a time it was deeply satisfactory to recieve such a cordial expression of approbation and good will. It cheered me with the conviction that I had not labored in vain; in endeavoring to produce an acceptable work on the great national theme which I consider the palladium of our country

You urge me "to give the residue of Washingtons life with as little delay as possible"—My own feelings prompt me to do so; knowing that with me the night is fast approaching when no man can work. Be assured, my dear Sir, when I do resume my pen, your letter will have its effect in encouraging me onward.

With high respect / Your obliged friend & servt.
Washington Irving

The Rev L. H. King / &c &c &c

MANUSCRIPT: British Library.

Lucius H. King was a Methodist Episcopal clergyman living at 176 Duane Street, New York City. See *Trow's New York City Directory for 1857*, p. 452.

1. This letter has not been located.

2525.   *To George Bancroft*

Sunnyside, June 24th. 1857

My dear Bancroft,

I feel truly sensible of the kindness of your invitation to Newport, and regret that I have to decline it. It would interfere with engagements I have made to visit some of my connexions to whom I have long been in arrears. Beside—I have a dread of Newport—It is too gay and fashionable for me, who am growing more and more rusty and rustic in my retirement, and can scarcely muster spirit sufficient ⟨for an ever⟩ to figure at a Soirée in Tarry town or a fête champetre in Sleepy Hollow.

Present my kindest remembrances to Mrs Bancroft, and believe me, my dear Bancroft, with the warmest appreciation of your friendship

Yours very truly
Washington Irving

The Hon George Bancroft.

DOCKETED: Washington Irving / June 24 / 57
MANUSCRIPT: Cornell University Library.

2526.   *To S. Austin Allibone*

Sunnyside June 29t. 1857

Dear Sir

Excuse my unavoidable tardiness in acknowledging your kindness in sending me a copy of the paper read before the Historical Society of Pennsylvania by Major Charles I Biddle.[1] I have read it with great interest and entire satisfaction. It is a masterly paper; and I am happy to find myself in unison with Major Biddle in the view I have taken of the André affair in my recently published volume of the Biography of Washington;[2] especially as he has given the subject such wide and deep investigation

Yours my dear Sir very truly
Washington Irving

S. Austin Allibone Esqr

MANUSCRIPT: Biddle Family Papers.

1. Charles J. Biddle (1819–1873), son of Nicholas Biddle and a Philadelphia attorney who had served with distinction in the Mexican War, had prepared "Case

for André. Review of the Statement of It in Lord Mahon's History of England,"
which was published in *Memoirs* of the Historical Society of Pennsylvania, vol. 6
(1858) and in Biddle's *Contributions to American History* (Philadelphia, 1858),
pp. 317–411. WI must have seen Biddle's assessment in a separate pamphlet
issued soon after his address.

2. WI treats the activities of André in chapters 9–11 of volume 4 of *The Life
of George Washington,* published in May, 1857. See Langfeld & Blackburn, *WI
Bibliography,* p. 42.

2527.   To John L. Motley

Sunnyside, July 17th, 1857

My dear Sir,

Mr. Cogswell apprises me of his having received at the Astor Library
a copy of your work[1] which you have done me the honour to send to
his care for me.

A short time since on reading the first volume of your history I was
so much struck by its merit that I was on the point of writing to you
to express my admiration of this great literary achievement and my
delight at such a noble accession to our national literature; but I checked
the impulse, lest it should be deemed an intrusive assumption on my
part. You may judge therefore how sincerely and deeply I appreciate
the proof you give me of your favorable consideration. I am now on
the third volume of your History, reading it with unflagging interest
and increasing deference for its author. The minute and unwearied
research, the scrupulous fidelity and impartial justice with which you
execute your task, prove to me that you are properly sensible of the high
calling of the American press—that rising tribunal before which the
whole world is to be summoned, its history to be revised and rewritten,
and the judgment of past ages to be cancelled or confirmed. I am happy
to learn that you are about to return to the field of your labours[2]—an
ample field it is—and the three teeming volumes you have so suddenly
laid before the public show how well you know where to put in your
sickle.

With warmest wishes for your continued success, I am, my dear sir,

Most truly your obliged friend and servant,
Washington Irving

J. L. Motley, Esq.

PUBLISHED: *The Correspondence of John Lothrop Motley,* ed. G. W. Curtis (New
York, 1889), I, 202–3.

John Lothrop Motley (1814–1877), who received his doctorate from Göttingen, first attracted attention with his novels, *Morton's Hope: or, The Memoirs of a Young Provincial* (1839) and *Merry-Mount: A Romance of the Massachusetts Colony* (1849). He later wrote on historical and political subjects.

1. *The Rise of the Dutch Republic,* published in three volumes in 1856. The set is among the books preserved at Sunnyside.

2. WI is probably referring to Motley's *History of the United Netherlands,* which appeared in four volumes between 1861 and 1867.

2528. *To* ⸺⸺⸺

Sunnyside July 22d. 1857

Sir

I have to acknowledge the receipt of your letter informing me of my being elected an honorary member of the Washington National Literary Institute

I beg you to assure the Institute that I feel deeply and gratefully sensible of this testimonial of its esteem and appreciation

With many thanks for the kind expressions of your letter I remain

Very respectfully / Your obliged & hbl Servt
Washington Irving

MANUSCRIPT: Fales Collection, New York University Library.

The heading and date are written by the same hand in the same ink on a detached piece of paper which fits perfectly above the text of the letter.

2529. *To Charles C. Lee*

Sunnyside July 31t. 1857

My dear Mr Lee

A throng of occupations and engagements has prevented an earlier acknowledgement of your letter of the 24th.[1] and of your kindness in pointing out various errors in my work. They are in the way of rectification—one of my nephews, who acts as my elbow critic having undertaken to have corrections made in the Stereotyped plates.

I crave pardon for the misuse of the word *magniloquent* in speaking of your father. I ought to have ⟨applied⟩ ↑confined↓ it to the passage quoted from his work;[2] though even then *poetical* or *rhetorical* would have been better; but I was decidedly wrong in ⟨speaking⟩ ↑using↓

of[3] it as characteristic of his *'way'* or "style" which in general is excellent, and obnoxious to no such reproach.

I have been charmed with the bold and buoyant character and hardy exploits of your father in his youthful and military days. ⟨His⟩ The popular apellation of 'Light Horse Harry' by which he was known in ⟨Revolutionar⟩ the Revolution had a peculiar relish to me, and stamped him with individuality.

I shall attend to having the passage in question modified.

With respect to General Charles Lee[4] at the battle of Monmouth.—In his defence on his trial before ⟨the⟩ ↑a↓ general Court Martial after speaking of the stand he made on a height with a body of troops to check the advancing enemy, he adds, "These battalions having sustained with gallantry and returned with vigor, a very considerable fire, were at length successively forced over the bridge; the rear I brought up myself. I then addressed his Excellency in these words, "Sir, Here are my troops, how is it your pleasure I should dispose of them? Shall I form them in your front, alline them with your main body or draw them up in the rear."[5] He answered that I should arrange them in the rear of English Town.—"[6]

———

My account of the battle of Monmouth was founded on various ⟨accounts⟩ statements; but I governed myself in the use of them by the published "Proceedings of the General Court Martial"

I am writing in excessive haste and amidst incessant interruptions which must serve as an excuse for this mere scrawl—I hope to have more liesure and quiet when next I write in the mean time believe me with the most cordial regard

Yours very faithfully
Washington Irving

Charles C Lee Esqr.

ADDRESSED: Charles C Lee Esqr / Windsor near Fire Creek / Powhatan / Va.
   POSTMARKED:[*handwritten*]: Irvington / NY / Aug 3
MANUSCRIPT: Va.–Barrett.

1. This letter has not been located. See WI to Lee, May 6, 1857.

2. WI had used "magniloquent" in connection with a passage quoted from Lee's *Memoirs of the War in the Southern Department of the United States*, I, 319. See *Life of Washington*, IV, 262.

3. WI neglected to cancel "of."

4. Charles Lee (1731–1782), who had earlier served in the British forces, was a strong supporter of the patriot cause in the early days of the Revolution. Captured by the British in 1776, he was thought to have given a plan to General Howe for defeating the American forces. He was exchanged in 1778 and placed in command of troops at Valley Forge just before the Monmouth campaign. His withdrawal of

forces during the battle of Monmouth led to confusion among the American soldiers, and only quick action by Washington blunted Clinton's attack and prevented a rout of the patriots. WI had described this episode in his *Life of Washington,* III, chap. 34.

5. WI used a double quotation mark at this point.

6. WI had quoted the first sentence of Lee's statement in his *Life of Washington,* III, 431. The entire passage here is taken from *Proceedings of a General Court Martial ... for the Trial of Major General Lee, July 4, 1778,* originally printed in Philadelphia, 1778. See *The Lee Papers,* vol. 3, in *Collections of the New-York Historical Society for the Year 1873,* pp. 189–90.

2530. To Henry Van Wart, Jr.

Sunnyside July 31st. 1857

My dear Henry,

We shall be happy to recieve the visit of Mr Storrow[1] in the order you propose; as there will be spare room in the Cottage next week.

With love to the little women[2]

Your affectionate uncle
Washington Irving

Henry Van Wart Jr.

MANUSCRIPT: Va.—Barrett.

Henry Van Wart, Jr. (1806–1878) was the eldest son of Henry and Sarah Irving Van Wart. He was married first to Susan Storrow (b. 1807), who died in September, 1843. His second marriage on September 23, 1845, was to his cousin Abigail (1822–1906?), daughter of John Treat and Abigail Furman Irving.

1. Thomas W. Storrow, Sr., father of Henry Van Wart's first wife. See WI to Sarah Storrow, August 4, 1857.

2. Henry Van Wart's daughters were Sarah (1847–1919), Helen, and Marion (1854–1874). There was also a son, Henry, Jr. (1855–1867).

2531. To Sarah Storrow

Sunnyside Aug 4th. 1857

My dear Sarah,

Your letter from the Baths of Lucca recently recieved,[1] confirms what I had previously learnt from your brother,[2] that the plan of returning to the United States is postponed for another year[.] I now give up the hope of seeing much more of you in this world as my advanced age cannot afford such postponements, and I have no wish nor idea of ever making the visit to Europe which you are fond of suggesting. 1 hope your husband may realize those "brighter prospects" in the expectation of which he appears to be shaping the course of his family; but I cannot but lament that he did not return some time since to make a home and take quiet and certain root in his native soil.

Your brother no doubt keeps you informed of the main events of family history; and your long protracted absence from the domestic circle and the sphere of family gossip, renders it more and more difficult to furnish a letter from home with topics likely to prove interesting. Life glides away smoothly and serenely with me at Sunnyside; but the incidents by which it is sweetened and enlivened would appear very *fade*[3] to you amid the excitements of travel and the spectacles of Europe.

I will relate one incident, however, which I am sure will interest you. You will recollect 'little John Schell' the German boy,[4] whom I brought from on ship board when I returned from Europe in 1832; who lived with me at the homestead in Bridge Street; at Oscars near Tarrytown; who accompanied us in our tour up the Hudson and round by Connecticut River and who was a favorite with Every body.

You may remember his accompanying his father when the latter emigrated with his family to Quincy in Illinois; deluded by the promises of a land speculator who left them in the lurch on their arrival there, and how I saved them from despair by sending a little money with which the father bought a lot and set up a black smiths shop, while John got a situation in a country store. They had hard times for a while. Every thing was in a depressed state. Quincy was a raw newly built place of five hundred inhabitants, in an almost uncultivated country. John and his father were pulled down by chills and fever and quite disheartened; but I wrote to them to hope and persevere; and to take their chance of growing with the place.

⟨Thirty⟩ ↑Twenty↓ two years have since elapsed and John Schell made his appearance at Sunnyside two or three days since; the first time he had returned from the West. He was now a fine looking respectable man thirty six years of age; one of the Aldermen of Quincy which has grown to be a beautiful city of twenty thousand inhabitants. He owns houses and lands; has a manufactory of Alcohol and Camphine; is in a prosperous career of business and already worth seventy thousand dollars, he is married and has four children Every thing in short has gone well with him and he bids fair to fulfil a prediction which I made in jest, when he set out ↑in his boyhood↓ for the West, that he would one day or other be a member of congress.

He was very much affected when we met; and could scarcely speak. He was welcomed by the house hold as one of the family; he dined and passed a great part of the day with us, during which I strolled with him about the vicinity; where he was continually recalling incidents of his boyhood. His heart appeared to be full, throughout his visit, and tears were often in his eyes. He declared it was one of the happiest days he had ever passed, and his visit certainly made it a very happy one at Sunnyside So much for the fortunes of "little John Schell."

My friends the Kennedys are to be here in the course of a few days before embarking (on the 15th) for a second visit to Europe.[5] I have no doubt you will meet them in the Course of their travels as they intend to visit Italy.

Give my affectionate remembrances to the Jones's. Tell Mrs Mary Jones I feel sensibly the kindness of her invitation and should be happy to accept it could any thing induce me again to cross the Atlantic.

Give my love to the three princesses tell them I am daily looking for a visit from their Grandfather (Mr Storrow) on his way homeward from Sharon Springs; when we shall have, as usual, a great deal of talk together about them.

Ever my dear Sarah / Your affectionate Uncle
W Irving

Mrs T. W Storrow Jr.

ADDRESSED: Madame / Madame Storrow / ⟨aux Soins de Messrs. B. G. Wainwright & Co / 13 Rue de Faub. Montmartre / a Paris⟩ / Hotel de l'Europa / Ponte a Serraglio / Bagni di Lucca / Toscana. POSTMARKED: PARIS / 22 AUG 57 MANUSCRIPT: Yale.

1. This letter has not been located. These baths, in central Italy near the Tyrrhenian Sea, date from Roman times.

2. Irving Paris.

3. Insipid, dull.

4. For details about Schell, see WI to Catharine Paris, September 2 and October 9, 1832; and PMI, III, 36.

5. John P. and Elizabeth Kennedy were absent for fifteen months on this European trip. See C. H. Bohner, J. P. Kennedy, p. 218.

2532.   To William H. Prescott

Sunnyside Aug 25t. 1857

My dear Mr Prescott,

You say you dont know whether I care about remarks on my books from friends, though they be brothers of the craft.[1] I cannot pretend to be above the ordinary sensitiveness of authorship and am especially alive to the remarks of a master workman like yourself. I have never been less confident of myself and more conscious of my shortcomings than in this my last undertaking and have incessantly feared that the interest might flag beneath my pen; you may judge therefore how much I have been gratified by your assurance that the interest felt by yourself and Mrs Prescott[2] in reading the work "went on *Crescendo* from the beginning and did not reach its climax till the last pages"

I thank you therefore most heartily for your kind and acceptable letter which enables me to cheer myself with the persuasion that I have not ventured into the field once too often, and that my last production has escaped the fate of the Archbishop of Granadas homilies.

You hint a wish that I would visit your northern latitudes and partake of the good fellowship that exists there, and indeed it would give me the greatest pleasure to enjoy communionship with a few choice spirits like yourself; but I have a growing dread of the vortex of gay society into which I am apt to be drawn if I stir from home;

⟨Th⟩ In fact the habits of literary occupation, which of late ⟨years I have indulged to excess, have almost unfitted me for idle gentlemanly life. Relaxation and repose begin to be insupportable to me and I feel an unhealthy hankering after my study and a disposition to relapse into hard writing

Take warning ⟨from me⟩ ↑by my case↓ and beware of literary intemperance

                          Ever my dear Prescott / Yours very truly
                                         Washington Irving

William H Prescott Esqr

DOCKETED: From / Washington Irving / AUG 1857
MANUSCRIPT: NYPL—WI Papers.   PUBLISHED: George Ticknor, *Life of William Hickling Prescott* (Boston, 1864), p. 394.

1. WI is quoting from Prescott's letter of August 7, 1857. See PMI, IV, 232–33.
2. Prescott had married Susan Amory of Boston on May 4, 1820.

2533.   *To Hannah E. North*

                                          Sunnyside Sept 16th. 1857

My dear Madam

The letter of General Washington to which you allude is probably the same inserted by Sparks in the 7th. volume of his 'Writings of Washington' Page 32.[1] It is there addressed "to James Duane,[2] in Congress," and dated Morrestown *14*. May 1780. If it be the same I have had Sparks version of it[3] before me while preparing my work for the press. I am never-

theless extremely indebted to you for your kindness in offering to furnish
me with a copy of it, and am, dear Madam, with great respect

Your obliged friend & servt
Washington Irving

Miss Hannah E. North

MANUSCRIPT: University of Delaware Library.

A different version of this letter, probably a discarded draft, is preserved at
SHR. Also dated September 16, 1857, it covers essentially the same points: "I
am greatly obliged by your kind offer to furnish me with a copy of a letter from
General Washington to your ↑great↓ grandfather Judge Duane, dated May 1⟨4⟩3th.
1⟨8⟩780. In Sparks "Writings of Washington" vol VII. p 32 he gives a copy of a
letter 'to James Duane in Congress' dated *14* May 1780. This it is probably the
same letter to which you allude; and I have had his printed version of it before
me while preparing my work for the press."

Hannah E. North was a child of Mary Duane and William North (1755–1836),
a Revolutionary soldier and a U.S. senator.

1. In volume 4 of his *Life of Washington*, p. 36, WI refers to this letter as
appearing on page 34 of the Sparks edition.

2. James Duane (1733–1797), a New York attorney who served in the Continental
Congress from 1774–1784, was mayor of New York City from 1784 to 1789 and
a U.S. judge for the New York district from 1789 to 1794.

3. Ten volumes of the twelve-volume *Writings of George Washington* are among
the books preserved at Sunnyside.

2534.   To S. Austin Allibone

Sunnyside, Sept. 17, 1857

He [Obadiah Rich][1] was one of the most indefatigable, intelligent, and
successful bibliographers in Europe. His house at Madrid was a literary
wilderness, abounding with curious works and rare editions, in the midst
of which he lived and moved and had his being, and in the midst of which
I passed many months while employed on my work.[2] . . . He was withal
a man of great truthfulness and simplicity of character, of an amiable
and obliging disposition and strict integrity.

PUBLISHED: S. Austin Allibone, *Critical Dictionary of English Literature and
British and American Authors*, II, 1788.

1. Obadiah Rich (1783–1850) was a bibliographer and bookseller specializing
in manuscripts and early printed books relating to the settlement and early history
of America.

2. When WI first arrived in Madrid in 1826, he lived with Rich and gathered
material for his life of Columbus in Rich's library. In later years Rich gave himself

credit for suggesting the project to WI. See Obadiah Rich, *Bibliotheca Americana Nova* (London, 1846), II, 209.

2535. To Charles J. Everett

[September 19, 1857]

My dear Sir

With many thanks for the kind expressions contained in your note,[1] I send you the Autograph you request and am

Yours very respectfully
Washington Irving

Sunnyside / Sept. 19th. 1857. / Charles J Everett Esqr

MANUSCRIPT: NYPL—WI Papers.

1. This note has not been located.

2536. To Gulian C. Verplanck

New York Sept 30t 1857

My dear Mr Verplanck

Understanding that my friend Mr Henry Panton[1] is desirous of obtaining the appointment ⟨to⟩ of Librarian of the New York Society Library,[2] I take pleasure in recommending him as one well fitted by education, acquirements, literary tastes and talents and urbane and obliging manners to fill such a situation in a creditable and satisfactory manner. He is a native of New York; his connexions I have known and valued from childhood and I take a sincere interest in his success

Yours ever, very respectfully / and truly
Washington Irving

Gulian C. Verplanck Esqr.

MANUSCRIPT: William H. Scheide Library, Princeton University.

1. For details, see WI to Panton, February 15, 1850.
2. The New York Society Library, chartered in 1754, had been in existence since 1700. After the Revolution it was rechartered and moved from the City Hall to Nassau Street. John Forbes was librarian from 1794 to 1824; he was succeeded by his son, Philip J., whose replacement was being sought in 1857. For a detailed study of the Library, see Austin B. Keep, *History of the New York Society Library*.

2537. To S. Austin Allibone

Sunnyside, Nov. 2, 1857

My dear Sir:

We have in the Astor Library a copy of Owen Jones's work illustrative of the Alhambra.[1] I have lately seen a number of photographs of various parts of the Alhambra, which I believe are intended for publication. They will give a perfectly truthful idea of the old pile.

The account of my midnight rambles about the old palace[2] is literally true, yet gives but a feeble idea of my feelings and impressions, and of the singular haunts I was exploring.

Everything in the work relating to myself, and to the actual inhabitants of the Alhambra, is unexaggerated fact.

It was only in the legends that I indulged in *romancing*; and these were founded on materials picked up about the place.

With great regard, my dear sir, yours very truly,

Washington Irving

PUBLISHED: PMI, IV, 236; and S. Austin Allibone, *Critical Dictionary of English Literature and British and American Authors*, I, 943 (in part).

1. Owen Jones (1809–1874), a London architect, brought out *Illustrations of the Palace of the Alhambra* in two volumes in 1842 and 1845.

2. In his letter of October 28, 1857, Allibone had queried: "May I venture to ask, whether the thrilling sketch of your midnight 'night-walking' through the halls of the Alhambra is an account of a real ramble, or whether it is partly a fancy picture founded on fact?" See PMI, IV, 236. WI had described this walk in "The Mysterious Chamber" section of *The Alhambra*.

2538. To George Wilkes

Sunnyside Nov 4t. 1857

Dear Sir

The bearer Thomas Shehan who has been two years in my employ is desirous of obtaining medical relief at the Infirmary for a severe inflammation of the eye. He is an honest good lad, in whose welfare I take an interest and I solicit for him kind and careful treatment

I remain / Dear Sir / Yours very respectfully
Washington Irving

Dr George Wilkes / &c &c &c

Dr. George Wilkes was a New York physician residing at 28 Laight Street. He was married to Harriet King, daughter of James Gore King, a fellow trustee of the Astor Library with WI. See *Trow's New York City Directory for 1857*, p. 885; and Martha Lamb, *History of the City of New York*, II, 735.

2539.   To Samuel B. Woolworth

Sunnyside Nov 6th. 1857

S. B. Woolworth Esqr
Secretary of the Regents }
   of the University

Dear Sir,

The first volume of Documents relating to the Colonial History of New York[1] was recieved during my absence from home, which prevented its reciept being duly acknowledged.

I have no copy of the *Second* volume but two copies of the *third* and no copy of the *eighth* volume.

Very respectfully / Your Obt Servt
Washington Irving

Samuel B. Woolworth served as secretary of the Board of Regents of the University of the State of New York from December 4, 1855, to January 9, 1880. See *The Regents of the University of the State of New York*, comp. Albert B. Corey, Hugh M. Flick, and Frederick A. Morse (Albany, 1959), p. 19.

1. This collection was edited by E. B. O'Callaghan (vols. 1–11) and Berthold Fernow (vols. 12–15). WI's missing volumes can be explained by the fact that they were not published in chronological sequence. For example, volume 2 was not published until 1858, and volume 8 until 1857.

2540.   To Jesse B. Turley

Sunnyside Nov. 9th. 1857.

Sir

There is not the least foundation for the report that I intend to write the
life of Kit Carson.[1]

Very respectfully / Your Obt. Servt.
Washington Irving

Jesse B. Turley, Esq.

MANUSCRIPT: Missouri Historical Society (copy of MS. owned by Jesse B. Turley).

Jesse B. Turley (ca. 1800–1861), who grew up in Missouri and lived later in
Santa Fe and Taos, knew Kit Carson and assisted him in the preparation of his
autobiography. See *Kit Carson's Autobiography,* ed. Milo M. Quaife (Lincoln,
1935), p. xxii.

1. Christopher Carson (1809–1869), who was a trapper in the Santa Fe area and
a guide on Frémont's first exploring expedition in 1842, lived in Taos from 1853
to 1861.

2541.   To Jane Major

Sunnyside Nov 2⟨5⟩6th. 1857

My dear Miss Major,

It gives me sincere pleasure to furnish you with my autograph since you
think it worthy of a request.

With great regard for yourself and endearing recollections of the lang
syne of which you remind me I remain

very truly and respectfully / yours
Washington Irving

Miss Jane Major

MANUSCRIPT: Andrew B. Myers.

2542.   To the Reverend Robert Bolton

Sunnyside, December 11th, 1857.

My dear Sir:

It is with great concern that I receive the intelligence of the death of your father; for I cherished the hope that we should meet again on this side of the Atlantic. He was one of the gentlest, purest, worthiest beings I have ever known, and he has gone to receive the reward of his goodness; for we are told "the pure in heart shall see God."

Yours very faithfully, / My dear Mr. Bolton,
Washington Irving

Robert Bolton Esq. / Beekmantown.

PUBLISHED: Henry Carrington Bolton and Reginald Pelham Bolton, *The Family of Bolton in England and America, 1100–1894*, p. 334.

Robert Bolton (1814–1877), the eldest son of Robert Bolton, Sr., had visited WI in 1846 during his researches on the history of Westchester County. For other details, see WI's letter to his father, December 24, 1846.

2543.   To James A. Maitland

Sunnyside Dec 12th 18[57]

Dear Sir

I have repeatedly, through the press, given a general apology for a want of promptness in replying to my almost innumerable correspondents. The literary task on which I am engaged[1] engrosses all the time and mind I can devote to the pen at my advanced period of life, so that I find it impossible to cope with the correspondence which over whelms me.

I read your work[2] with interest and satisfaction. It is written in a good style [;] is graphic in its details and [gives animated and interesting pictures of scenery, manners and characters in Norway. Different members] of my family have derived both pleasure and information from the perusal of it. I think therefore that it will prove a succesful publication and that you will be encouraged to proceed in your literary enterprises

Wishing you a prosperous career I remain

Yours very respectfully
Washington Irving

James A Maitland Esqr

MANUSCRIPT: Fales Collection, New York University Library; LC, Maryland Historical Society, and Haverford College (facsimile copies).

Since the paper of the original holograph is brittle, portions of the bottom and side of the sheet have broken away and have been lost. The missing words have been supplied in brackets from the LC facsimile.

James A. Maitland, a novelist and editor of the New York *Dispatch*, was apparently trying to use WI's name and literary reputation to promote his novel *Sartaroe*, the work mentioned in the second paragraph of the letter. In a separate advertisement on the opening pages of the novel and again on its title page is printed the following letter:

Sunnyside, Irvington, Nov. 1st, 1857.

My Dear Friend:

According to promise, I have read 'Sartaroe,' and now will give you my opinion of the book in a word. It is highly creditable to your genius. It is excellent; all in all, the best novel issued from the American press for some years past. It *must certainly* meet with success. I will do my best for you. You ought to clear, at least, $4,000 or $5,000 by it. I have written to Murray, of London, my old publisher, as I told you I would, and I have advised him to reprint the book there, and have assured him that he ought to send the Author £200 sterling for the privilege of printing the work in England. You may use this when the book comes out.

With the greatest esteem / I am your Friend,
Washington Irving.

Jas. A. Maitland, N. Y.

Despite Maitland's assertion that this letter was printed with WI's permission, G. P. Putnam saw fit to publish the following disclaimer in the NYEP for March 17, 1858 and in the New York *Times* for March 18, 1858: "An advertisement of a new work, entitled, 'Sartaroe,' repeated in the journals and in the circulars, contains what purports to be a letter from Mr. Washington Irving. Will you permit me the room to state that some one connected with the book has been greatly imposed upon, for no such letter has been written by Mr. Irving? An explanation from the publishers in Philadelphia has been requested, but as Mr. Irving's name is again so conspicuously paraded in connection with a spurious letter, it is but just that this correction should be made at once. Who is responsible for this forgery, remains to be seen. / Respectfully yours, / G. P. Putnam, No. 321 Broadway[.]"

The controversy continued in the *Times* on March 20, 1858, when Putnam released copies of letters from T. B. Peterson, publisher of *Sartaroe*, and James Maitland, its author. In his letter of March 18, 1858, Maitland confessed that he forged the letter of November 1, 1857, attributed to WI. This confession was followed by the true text of WI's letter of December 12, 1857. In NYEP of March 22 (and the *Times* of March 23, 1858) Putnam issued another statement exonerating Peterson from complicity in Maitland's forgery. Maitland's confession is again printed, together with an additional statement in which he takes sole responsibility for the forgery. In an adjoining column of NYEP is an ad for *Sartaroe* and a "Card" which reproduces the letters written by the various parties. On March 24 Peterson replied with his "Card," in which he accuses Putnam of altering the text of his "Card" of March 22. This is followed by Putnam's "A Last Word to Mr. Peterson," in which Putnam vigorously denies Peterson's charges. On March 29 NYEP printed a "Card," called "Peterson's Final Reply to Putnam," which reiterates the point that Putnam altered the text to which Peterson had agreed. The notice concludes with a "perfect fac-simile" of WI's letter of December 12, 1857.

1. WI was now working on volume 5 of his *Life of Washington*.
2. *Sartaroe: A Tale of Norway*.

2544.   To Joseph G. Cogswell

Sunnyside Decr. 21st. 1857

My dear Cogswell

The bearer M Schroeder is desirous of information and advice as to some literary enterprise he has in view. Will you give him a hearing, and such advice as may put him in the way of carrying his plans into operation

Yours very truly
Washington Irving

ADDRESSED: Joseph G. Cogswell Esq / Astor Library
MANUSCRIPT: LC.

2545.   To Henry W. Muzzey, Henry A. Hildreth, and Charles L. Wheeler

Sunnyside Decr 27th. 1857

Messrs Henry W Muzzey ⎫
       Henry A Hildreth ⎬
      & Charles L Wheeler ⎭
      Committee &c

Gentlemen,

I cannot but feel deeply sensible of the honor done me by your Association in adopting my name as a designation and in electing me an honorary member. The value of all societies of the kind as a means of intellectual advancement, is too well known and has too often been publicly discussed and illustrated to need any demonstration at my hands.

Your request for a motto has somewhat perplexed me not being very apt in matters of the kind. Perhaps, as you have chosen the name of *Irving* for your designation, you may think it apposite to take with it the motto of its armorial bearings, *Sub sole sub umbra vivens*,[1] given to the family by Robert the Bruce for its fidelity in adhering to him in time of his adversities.

Very respectfully Gentlemen / Your obliged & humble Servt
Washington Irving

DOCKETED: Washington Irving. / De 27. 18[57] [*MS torn*] / His answer to a letter / of a Committee of the "Irving / Association."
MANUSCRIPT: Va.–Barrett.

1. For WI's translation of the motto—"Flourishing in the sun and in the shade"— see his letter to Catharine Paris, May 29, 1842. For other comments on the family's coat of arms and motto, see WI to D. Henderson, January 13, 1841; and to the Irving Literary Society of the College of St. James, March 1, 1848.

2546.   *To* ⸺

Sunnyside 28t. 1857[1]

Dear Sir,

I have this day sent the Valley Forge Orderly Book to your address, care of A Clark Esqr 63 Amos Street New York. According to your directions; and beg you to accept my grateful thanks for the loan of this interesting relic of the Revolution; which I have detained for a rather unreasonable time.[2]

Very respectfully / Your obliged & hbl Servt
Washington Irving

MANUSCRIPT: HSP.

1. WI neglected to write the month.
2. Probably this is the same orderly book which WI mentioned in a letter of January 30, 1856, to Jacob Snider, Jr.

2547.   *To Lydia H. Sigourney*

Sunnyside, 1857

Thanks for the volume of your poems.[1] It came most opportunely at a time when I was suffering under indisposition and much depressed in spirits, and acted quite as a restorative. . . . Your name is enough to insure a welcome anywhere.

PUBLISHED: *The Collector*, 51 (May, 1937), 81, item 1708.

Mrs. Lydia Huntley Sigourney (1791–1865), who was known as the "Sweet Singer of Hartford," achieved widespread popularity from her sentimental verses.

1. Possibly *The Western Home, and Other Poems* (Philadelphia, 1854) or *Illustrated Poems* (Philadelphia, 1853).

2548. *To* ———

[1857]

"En écrivant comme cela sur mes ouvrages, vous avez été bien aimable, monsieur, mais bien plus vous l'avez été surtout pour me l'envoyer. Si je n'étais pas à la campagne quand arriva le paquet postal, bien sûr vous receviez ma réponse plus prochaine. Très-flatté je fus à vous lire, et très-flattée doit aussi être votre pays, car vous me paraissez un des vrais critiques qui y sont. Par malheur nous le voyons bien d'ici (et de loin comme il faut pour mieux voir ou bien juger des choses de la partie morale,) en France la critique n'est plus! Après dix ans retiré dans ma retraite à Sunnyside, où vous admettre me rendrait bien flatté et chaleureux, j'ai arrangé mon affaire pour lire tous les journaux de Londres et de Paris relatifs à la littérature dont le mouvement en essor fut si magnifique depuis 1818 jusqu'à 1838, dix ans de grande commotion par la poésie et le théâtre. C'était mon goût de lire tout cela, et depuis plusieurs années tristement. Peu d'oeuvres et surtout pas *du tout de critique.* On est trop passionné, trop vindicatif, trop compromis par des coteries pour juger noblement et avec utilité pour le public, bien occupé pour tous ses intérêts de l'argent, et indécis pour savoir où est le bien, ou est le mal dans la littérature. Anarchie dans cette littérature comme dans votre art; plus d'écloe et pas de tradition, monsieur, pardonnez-moi! C'est cela qui m'a flatté dans votre critique, car c'est *critique* et pas *louange* aveugle, c'est-à-dire une chose de compaisance, sans priz pour un coeur élevé qui la lit en ne s'abusant pas sur le mérite de ses ouvrages, et qui doit terminer de plus le bien qu'on dit des parties touables, si on condamne franchement les parties reprochables. Pour cela, monsieur, je vous honore, et je suis bien flatté que vous m'avez supposé un homme à entendre la vérité.

Non, plus de critique dans votre journalisme, et rien que des passions hostiles ou des complaisances coupables. On voit clairement que toujours le critique pense à l'auteur plus qu'il ne pense à l'oeuvre, et que soit le désir de la flatter, soit l'intention de le peiner, dirige sa plume avec louanges trop chaleureuses ou dénigrement trop méprisant. Nous sommes quelquefois bien surpris et indignés des petites oeuvres que nous trouvons après que, sur les éloges des critiques, nous avons avec confiance voulu nous en régaler! Aussi bien souvent quelque chose de bon est maltraité, surtout dans les théatres, parce que là il y a beaucoup de passions et d'intérets agités plus que pour la librairie. Je citerai par example combien j'ai trouvé de scandale dans les excessifs et aveugles éloges donnés par (. . . . . . .) au sujet de (. . . . . . .,) le même critique qui, avant trois mois, avait si malicieusement et hostilement traité (. . . . . . .,) ce qui m'a indigné, ayant lu l'ouvrage, un bon ouvrage! M. * * * lui, troune que tout est bien et bon, a la Pangloss, et ne croit rien digne d'être par lui, sérieusement discuté. L'autre, M. * * * ne se plait qu'à abattre ce qu'il serait je crois impossible a lui d'élever."

PUBLISHED: *Le Monde Illustré [unlocated]*; New York *Times*, January 27, 1860; *Lippincott's Monthly Magazine*, 45 (May, 1890), 744; STW, I, 462.

The article in the New York *Times*, which serves as copy-text, was sent from Paris by its correspondent, Malakoff, who noted that "M. Jules Lecomte has just published, in the *Monde Illustré*, an autograph letter from the late Washington Irving, addressed to a literary gentleman of this city, and which is inserted verbatim and literatim, in order to show the kind of French written by the illustrious deceased. It is a rather curious specimen of French. . . . I ought to add that the letter was written 3 years ago, to a gentleman who had just published a French translation of Mr. Irving's works."

2549. *To D. Appleton & Company*

Sunnyside, Jany. 6th. 1858

Messrs. D Appleton & Co

Gentlemen

The copy of the first volume of the New American Cyclopedia[1] which you have had the kindness to send me, having remained some time in the hands of my publisher in New York has but recently reached me.

From the specimen before me it promises to be a work of great merit and utility and universal acceptance For the credit of American literature which is closely connected with such an undertaking. I am happy to see that the work will be edited by such able hands as Messrs Ripley[2] and Dana.[3]

My nephew Mr Pierre M Irving will furnish you with information for the article which you specify.

Very respectfully, Gentlemen / Your obliged & hbl Servt
Washington Irving

MANUSCRIPT: Va.–Barrett.

The publishing firm of D. Appleton and Company was established in New York by Daniel Appleton (1775–1849) in 1838 when he took his son William Henry (1814–1899) into partnership.

1. This work appeared in sixteen volumes between 1858 and 1863. Two editions of it sold more than 3,000,000 copies.

2. George Ripley (1802–1880), a Unitarian minister, charter member of the Transcendental Club, and editor of *The Dial*, was founder and manager of Brook Farm. He later went to New York City and worked on the New York *Tribune* and *Harper's New Monthly Magazine*.

3. Charles A. Dana (1819–1899), a graduate of Harvard who joined Ripley at Brook Farm and remained there for five years, later edited the New York *Tribune* and collaborated in the preparation of *The New American Cyclopaedia*.

2550. To ———

Sunnyside Jany 8–1858

Thomas Fitzharris lived with me for a great part of last year as a coach man and acquitted himself in every way to my satisfaction. He left me on account of ill health; from which I find he has perfectly recovered. I can recommend him in the fullest manner as understanding his business and discharging it faithfully

Washington Irving

Manuscript: SHR.

2551. To John E. Williams

[January 19, 1858]

An Auncient Author to whom a lyttel boys father sent a present of Sausage meat; accompanied by a written lament that his lyttel boy should grow slower than ye pigge whereof ye Sausage was made, thus pleasauntly and consolingly replyed—

> Gif ye lyttel boy doth grow
> Yn ye lyttel pigge more slow
> Still he is yn pigge more sweet
> Even though pigge be sausage meat.

It is said that this happy reply prevented the lyttel boys mother from being put out of conceit of her chylde

(Washington Irving.)[1]

Jany 19. 1858.

ADDRESSED: John E. Williams Esq / Strawberry Hill
MANUSCRIPT: Rabbi Howard A. Berman.

A separate slip of paper includes the inscription: "To. / Mr Williams / at his house on /ye. Strawberry Hill".
John E. Williams (1804–1877), cashier of the Metropolitan Bank in New York, lived in Greenburgh Township near WI. See Scharf, *Westchester County*, II, 271.

1. The signature and the date at the bottom are not in WI's hand.

2552. *To Albert L. Huntt et al.*

Sunnyside Jany 22d. [1858]

To Messrs Albert L Huntt ⎫
            Henry Fleming ⎪
            Jos. L. Serbert ⎬
            & S. M Dent ⎪
            Committee &c ⎭

Gentlemen
I have to acknowledge the receipt of your letter of the 18th inst[1] informing me of my being elected an honorary member of the Irving Literary Associatio[n.]
I beg you to assure the Society of th[e] very grateful sense I entertain of the testimonial of their favorable appreciatio[n.]

Very respectfully gentlemen / Your obliged & hble Servt.
Washington Irving

MANUSCRIPT: Va.–Barrett.

A narrow strip along the right margin of the sheet which had been folded over has broken away because of the brittleness of the paper. The numerals and letters which are missing as a result have been supplied in brackets.

1. This letter has not been located.

2553.   To Edgar Irving

Sunnyside, Jany. 28th 1858

My dear Edgar,

I requested Pierre M Irving to speak with you on the subject of your application to me for a letter to the Collector,[1] but lest he should delay to do so I send these lines.

I have no claims on the civilities of Mr Schell, never having been in company with him but once and that accidentally It would be a hard matter, therefore to ask a favor of him, but, ⟨to ask⟩ when that favor is to ask him to displace a man from the office on which he depends for his bread and give that office to a nephew of mine—it is a thing which I can never have the heart or conscience to do.

In your present line of business[2] you appear to have been making a sure, though perhaps a slow, progress before the late panic[3] put a stop to every thing—With the revival of prosperity your business, ⟨in that time⟩ would revive, and, if properly followed up would be better than any precarious place in the Custom House, provided you could get one. I had intended to distribute your cards among my commercial friends and ask their custom for you, but your expedition to the West prevented me. That I shall do against business revives[?]; provided I am sure you ⟨are to⟩ ↑will ↓ be found at your post. At present the best advice I can give you is to ⟨be⟩ hold on, be patient and look for better times

Talk fully and frankly of your affairs with Pierre M Irving; you could not have a sounder and more conscientious adviser

Your affectionate Uncle
Washington Irving

Edgar Irving Esqr

MANUSCRIPT: Dr. Noel Cortes.

1. Augustus Schell (1812–1884), a lawyer, New York politician and businessman, and associate of Cornelius Vanderbilt in the New York Central Railroad, was collector of the port of New York from 1857 to 1861. He later succeeded William M. Tweed as Grand Sachem of Tammany Hall and was twice president of the New-York Historical Society.

2. Edgar Irving was a member of the brokerage firm of Irving & Willey, established in 1854. See W. T. Bonner, *New York: The World's Metropolis*, p. 485.

3. A money crisis and numerous bank failures had occurred during the preceding fall. See New York *Times*, October and November, 1857, *passim*.

2554.   To Samuel L. Waldo

Sunnyside Feb 5t. 1858

Dear Sir

I feel much obliged to you for your kind and flattering proposition that I should sit to you for a portrait and doubt not that you ⟨cou⟩ would execute one with consummate ability and truth; but I have for some time past declined every proposition of the kind, and could not now comply without giving cause of complaint to persons whom I hold in great regard. With sincere thanks for the cordial expressions of your letter[1] believe me very truly

Your obliged friend & Servt
Washington Irving

Saml. L. Waldo Esqr

MANUSCRIPT: Yale.

Samuel L. Waldo (1788–1861) was a portrait painter who had established a business in New York City in partnership with William Jewett.

1. This letter has not been located.

2555.   To William A. Whitehead

Sunnyside Feb. 5th 1858

To W. A. Whitehead Esq / Corresponding Secretary / &c &c &c

Dear Sir

I have the honor to acknowledge the receipt of your favor notifying me of my having been elected an honorary Member of the New Jersey Historical Society

I beg you to assure the Society that I feel deeply and grateful⟨y⟩ly sensible of this very flattering testimonial of their favorable appreciation

For the kind expressions with which you accompany this notification accept my sincere thanks. With Newark, as you observe, are associated in my mind many pleasant recollections of early days, and of social meetings at an old mansion on the banks of the 'Passaic',[1] of which now I believe scarce a trace remains.[2] The literary task on which I am engaged, however, and other inevitable claims upon my pen, will, I fear leave me no liesure to put those reminiscences upon paper as you suggest

> Very respectfully / Your obliged & hble Servt
> Washington Irving

DOCKETED: Washington Irving / Feby 5 1858
MANUSCRIPT: New Jersey Historical Society.

William A. Whitehead (1810–1884), who was a founder of the New Jersey Historical Society in 1845, served as its secretary until his death. He collected and published *The Papers of Lewis Morris* (1852) and *Documents Relating to the Colonial History of the State of New Jersey* (1880–1885).

1. This house, which was owned by Gouverneur Kemble and served as a rural retreat for the Lads of Kilkenny, was featured in *Salmagundi* as "Cockloft Hall."
2. Whitehead added the following note in pencil on the opposite page: "The House referred to is not, as Mr Irving presumed, in a dilapidated condition, being now, the residence of Mr Whiting at Mount Pleasant—It was ↑from the gatherings↓ there, that ⟨the⟩ many of the papers originate[d] ↑which were issued↓ under the title of 'Salmagundi.'—WAW"

2556. To ———

Sunnyside, Feb. 5, 1858.

Dear Sir:

I can give you no other information concerning the localities of the story of Rip Van Winkle, than is to be gathered from the manuscript of Mr. Knickerbocker, published in the Sketch Book. Perhaps he left them purposely in doubt. I would advise you to defer to the opinion of the "very old gentleman" with whom you say you had an argument on the subject. I think it probable he is as accurately informed as any one on the matter.

> Respectfully, your obedient servant,
> Washington Irving

PUBLISHED: PMI, III, 54.

1. WI is responding to an inquiry from a boy at Catskill. For other details, see PMI, III, 53.

2557.   To James Watson Webb

Sunnyside Feb. 13th. 1858

My dear General,

I cannot lay my hand on the document you specify but will make a thorough search and if I find it will either send it to you or bring it with me to church to morrow

Yours very truly
Washington Irving

DOCKETED: Sunnyside Feb. 13th. 1858. / Washington Irving
MANUSCRIPT: Mercury Stamp Company, 10 East 40th Street, New York City.

2558.   To Sarah Storrow

Sunnyside, Feby 15th. 1858

My dear Sarah,

Your letter of Jany. 9th. came to me like a reproach making me feel my delinquency in not having answered your previous letter;[1] but I am unavoidably a delinquent on this score, my weary brain being overtasked by my literary undertaking, and unable to cope with the additional claims of an overwhelming correspondence. I am endeavoring to accomplish a fifth volume, ⟨to⟩ wherewith to close the Life of Washington, but I work more slowly than heretofore.[2] For two or three years past I have been troubled by an obstinate catarrh, but this winter it has been quite harassing; at times quite stupifying me. Recently I have put myself under medical treatment and begin to feel the benefit of it.

Mr. Storrow must have brought you lamentable accounts of the state of affairs in this country during the late revulsion.[3] He was here in the height of the storm when we seemed to be threatened with an almost universal shipwreck. Happily the crisis is past; things are returning to order, but it will take some time for business to regain its usual activity. I was for some time kept in anxious suspense as to my own affairs; stocks seeming to have lost their value and my publisher being in a state of insolvency. Fortunately I have experienced but a very moderate loss ↑in my investments↓ and my relations with my publisher have been placed on a different footing, which I trust will prove advantageous to us both.[4]

I have never been more struck with the energy and elasticity of the national character than in observing how spiritedly it has struggled with this overwhelming calamity; and is exerting itself, amidst the ruins of past prosperity, to build up the edifice anew. The crisis has been felt severely in my immediate neighborhood among men who were largely in business, some of whom have been completely ruined; yet they have borne their reverses manfully, and are looking forward hopefully to better times. I have a very pleasant social neighborhood and it has been more social than usual this winter; people seeming to draw closer together and seek refuge in cordial intercourse from external evils. Indeed I am so happy in my neighborhood, and the home feeling has grown so strong with me, that I go very little to town and have scarcely slept a dozen nights there within the last twelvemonths. Perhaps it is the effect of gathering years to settle more and more into the quiet of ones elbow chair.

When I was last in town I was at your Irvings,[5] for the first time since he has set up house keeping. He has a bright little establishment, is very nicely fixed and seems thoroughly delighted with having a house and home of his own. Nancy[6] makes him a capital wife[.] I dont think Jock (as you call him) was ever fixed in a way more calculated to make him happy and to bring out the sterling points of his character. His house is becoming quite a family resort and "place of call" and he and Nancy show every disposition to make it so. I hear continually of cosy social evenings passed there by members of the family casually dropping in.

You have no doubt learnt before this that the Grinnells[7] intend to set out in June next on a European tour. I can easily imagine what a delightful meeting it will be when you all come together. I wish they could bring you all back with them, and put an end to your protracted absence from your natural home which I cannot help considering a protracted error.

With kind remembrances to Mr Storrow and love to the young folks

Your aff[*remainder of complimentary close and signature clipped off*]

MANUSCRIPT: Yale.   PUBLISHED: PMI, IV, 239–41 (in part).

1. These letters have not been located.

2. On this same day WI had written the first page on Washington's biography in about a month. See PMI, IV, 239.

3. WI had alluded to the financial crisis in his letter to Edgar Irving, January 28, 1858.

4. Because Putnam needed cash, WI agreed to purchase from him the stereotype plates of all his works, to allow Putnam to act as his agent, and to rent the plates as needed. See PMI, IV, 237–38.

5. WI's manner of distinguishing Sarah Storrow's brother from Irving Van Wart and Irving Grinnell.

6. Nancy Ulshoeffer, the wife of Irving Paris.

7. Julia and Moses Grinnell were accompanied by their children, Julia, Irving, and Fanny. See PMI, IV, 259.

2559. To the Reverend Franklin Babbitt

Sunnyside March 5th 1858

My dear Sir,

I return the volumes you have been so kind as to lend me and must apologize for having kept them so long; but they have had to go the rounds of the house hold, my nieces being all desirous of reading them— We have all read them with great interest and satisfaction and feel highly obliged to you for the treat you have afforded us.

With great respect / Yours very truly
Washington Irving

The Rev Franklin Babbit

Manuscript: NYHS.

Franklin Babbitt was ordained in the Protestant Episcopal Church by Bishop Jonathan M. Wainwright on July 3, 1853. In 1857 he established a mission in Beekmantown, later known as North Tarrytown. Later, after his departure, the mission was organized as St. Mark's Episcopal Church. See George Burgess, *List of Persons Admitted to the Order of Deacons in the Protestant Episcopal Church, in the United States of America, From A. D. 1785, to A. D. 1857* (Boston, 1874), p. 41; and Scharf, *Westchester County*, II, 301.

2560. To Harriet Backus

Sunnyside March 6th 1858

Dear Madame

I regret that I cannot furnish you with the date of the birth of Washingtons mother,[1] having never met with any record of it.

I should have answered your letter sooner but it was accidentally mislaid

Very respectfully / Your obt Servt
Washington Irving

Mrs Harriet Backus.

Manuscript: NYPL–Seligman Collection.

1. Mary Ball, who married Augustine Washington on March 6, 1730, as his second wife, was born in 1708. She died in 1789.

2561. To Henry A. Smythe

Sunnyside March 30t. 1858

My dear Mr Smythe,

The wren boxes arrived all in good order and will soon be put up on the trees within piping distance of my house, so that I shall before long have a merry tenantry about me. It is true, when I ask for rent, they will be apt to fob me off with a song but even then I will not be worse off than many landlords in these hard times.

I send you a card of my my[1] nephew[2] about whom I spoke to you some time since. He is a brother of my nieces who live with me. If you can throw any business in his way it will be a great satisfaction to me, and I can assure you it will be faithfully attended to. He is well acquainted with Custom House matters, having for a number of years had the sample office under his care.

Give my kindest remembrances to Mrs Smythe and my love to the Kittens

Yours very truly
Washington Irving

H. A. Smythe Esqr

MANUSCRIPT: SHR.

1. WI repeated "my."
2. Edgar Irving. For other details, see WI to Edgar Irving, January 28, 1858.

2562. To George Jones

Sunnyside April 8th 1858

My dear Mr Jones,

I regret extremely that a severe cold obliges me to forego the pleasure I had promised myself of attending your daughters wedding this morning. Present my sincere felicitations to the young couple and accept my warmest wishes that it may prove a happy event to you all.

Yours very truly
Washington Irving

George Jones Esqr

MANUSCRIPT: NYPL—Kohns Collection.

George Jones was a neighbor of WI's. See WI to Sarah Storrow, July 17, 1848.

2563.   To George Bancroft

Sunnyside April 14t. 1858

My dear Bancroft

I thank you for the *leckerbissen*[1] from Germany which you have had the provident kindness to send me and in return will tell you that I have just read in the Tribune[2] a notice of your forthcoming volume accompanied by extracts, which I find *capital*. I reccollect your once telling me that you had not ⟨the⟩ ↑Prescotts↓ relish for writing about battles, but I think nothing could be more full of life and stir and graphic circumstance than your affairs of Lexington and Bunker hill. Every word tells—a vigorous fire runs through the language and flashes out occasionally in epithets and phrases that startle. You have an admirable talent at condensation, and at being picturesque and characteristic without being diffuse.

The character of Washington, which forms one of the extracts, is truthful and masterly, and struck as clean and concisely as with a die. In a word, I am convinced from the specimens before me, that your work is to be, what I anticipated from the preliminary volumes—*the* history of the Revolution, and *a* history for all time and all people.

With kindest regards to Mrs Bancroft

Yours my dear Bancroft / very truly
Washington Irving

DOCKETED: W. Irving / 14 April '58.
MANUSCRIPT: Cornell University Library.

1. A tidbit or fine morsel. In 1858 Bancroft's son John was studying art in Germany, and it is possible that the gift was something sent or brought home by the younger Bancroft. See Russel B. Nye, *George Bancroft: Brahmin Rebel*, p. 198.

2. On April 13, 1858, the New York *Tribune* filled five columns with comments about and quotations from the seventh volume of Bancroft's *History of the United States*, which was called "a panoramic view of the commencement of the Revolution." Dramatic episodes from the battles of Lexington, Concord, and Bunker Hill were quoted, as were Bancroft's memorable descriptions of Washington, Lafayette, Hamilton, Samuel Johnson, and John Wesley.

2564. *To Benson J. Lossing*

[Sunnyside, April 16, 1858]

I believe I am indebted to your kind attention for a copy of your biographical notice of Grandfather Knickerbocker,[1] which I received lately
by the mail; if so, I thank you most heartily for a world of curious and
amusing information which it has afforded me. I thought I knew all that
was known about the old gentleman, but I find that, in comparison with
you I was quite an ignoramus. I hope you may be equally successful in
your researches for your promised biography of General Schuyler.[2] . . .

PUBLISHED: *Sale of the Collection of the Late William F. Gable* (New York, 1923),
    part 3, item 437.

1. WI is probably referring to Lossing's article, "The Dutch in New Amsterdam,"
which appeared in the *National Magazine,* 12 (May, 1858), 443–48. In it Lossing
quotes from *Knickerbocker's History of New York* on pp. 445 and 447. A second
installment appeared in the June issue, pp. 494–501, with another quotation from
WI's book on p. 495.
    2. Lossing's *The Life and Times of Philip Schuyler* was not published until 1860.

2565. *To George Bancroft*

Sunnyside May 17th. 1858

My dear Bancroft
    I have delayed acknowledging the receipt of your volume[1] until I
should have read it through. I now thank you heartily for your kindness in
sending it to me. The interest with which I have devoured it, notwithstanding the staleness of the subject with me, is a proof that you have
told the story well.
    I was charmed with the opening of Your volume[2]—The political state of
England and France[3]—The decadence of the French Nobility[4]—The characters of the French Monarchs[5]—the beautiful sketch of Marie Antoinette[6]
—then the transition to sober earnest New England[7] the 'Meeting of the
Nine Committees." (p 35) "the lowly men accustomed to feed their own
cattle; to fold their own sheep; to guide their own plough; *all trained
to public life in the little democracies of their towns*"[8] &c &c How graphic
how suggestive—how true!
    I see you place Samuel Adams[9] in the Van of the Revolution and he
deserves the place. He was the apostle of popular liberty without a
thought of self interest or self glorification.

There is capital management through out all the chapters[10] treating of the New England states, wherein You go on building up the revolutionary pire, stick by stick, until at last you set it in a blaze.

You have a mode of *individualizing* if I may so use the word, which gives great spirit and a dramatic effect to your narration. You make brief citations from speeches, letters or conversations ↑which↓ stamp the characters, reveal the motives or express the actions of ⟨individual⟩ the persons concerned.—So also with regard to states, cities villages, communities—they are made to take a part in the drama by 'word of mouth' as it were—thus saving a world of detail and circumlocution.

In this way by turns you vocalize the whole Union and make the growing chimes of the revolution rise from every part of it. I hope you make out what I mean to say; for I consider, what I attempt to designate, a capital quality in your mode of narrating. I am delighted with the tribute you pay to the noble policy of chatham[11] and the cold charity which you dispense to Lord North. "Lord North was false only as he was weak and uncertain. He really wished to concede and conciliate, *but he had not force enough to come to a clear understanding with himself.*"[12] You have given me a hearty laugh at the expense of poor Lord North.

In a word, my dear Bancroft, I congratulate you upon the manner in which you have executed this volume[.] I have found it animated and spicy through out and take it as an earnest of the style in which you are to accomplish the history of a revolution "destined on every side to lead to the solution of the highest questions of state"

> With best regards to Mrs Bancroft / Yours, very faithfully
> Washington Irving

The Hon Geo. Bancroft

MANUSCRIPT: Cornell University Library. PUBLISHED: PMI, IV, 245–46.

1. WI refers to the seventh volume of Bancroft's *History of the United States,* which had just appeared. See WI to Bancroft, April 14, 1858.

2. Bancroft's volume begins with a review of affairs in England, France, and the New England colonies in 1774.

3. See George Bancroft, *History of the United States* (Boston, 1858), VII, 23–26.

4. See *ibid.,* p. 26.

5. *Ibid.,* p. 30.

6. *Ibid.,* pp. 31–32.

7. *Ibid.,* pp. 34–35.

8. Quoted from *ibid.,* p. 35.

9. Bancroft mentions Adams on pages 35, 37, and 47.

10. Bancroft, chaps. 4–5, pp. 56–75.

11. *Ibid.,* chap. 18, pp. 194–204. William Pitt, first earl of Chatham (1708–1778) had urged conciliation with the American colonies, with any settlement short of independence.

12. Quoted from *ibid.*, p. 285. Frederick North, second earl of Guilford and eighth Baron North (1732–1792), who was prime minister of England from 1770 to 1782 during the American Revolution, supported George III's policies.

2566.   To Francis Lieber

Sunnyside, June 3, 1858

My dear Sir:

* * * I am not aware of any authority for the fact stated, as you say, by Peschel[1] (whose work I have not seen), that Columbus "brooded over the prophesying song of the chorus in the Medea of Seneca."[2] I don't recollect that it is adverted to by Fernando Columbus, when furnishing the grounds of his father's belief of the existence of land in the West. Nor is there any mention of it by Columbus himself. The assertion of Peschel may have been made on what he considered a strong probability.

I am sorry Putnam could not have furnished an engraved likeness of Washington that would have matched more completely with the one you possess of William the Silent. Your idea of placing the likenesses of these illustrious men, so similar in character and virtue, side by side, is excellent; and the motto you have written round that of Washington, stamps his great merits at a blow.[3]

Ever, my dear sir, with high respect and regard, yours, very truly,

Washington Irving

Francis Lieber, LL. D., &c., &c., &c.

PUBLISHED: PMI, IV, 248.

1. Oskar Peschel (1826–1875) was a German geographer who published *Geschichte des Zeitalters der Endeckungen* in Stuttgart in 1858.

2. In his letter to WI, Lieber had quoted the following lines:

> "Venient annis saecula seris
> Quibus Oceanus vincula rerum
> Laxet, et ingens pateat tellus,
> Tethysque novos delegat orbes,
> Nec sit terris Ultima Thule."

> Distant the age, but surely it will come,
> When he—Oceanus—fettering all things,
> Yields, and the vast earth lieth before man,
> Tethys unveils that world, yet unknown,
> And no more than an Ultima Thule.

See PMI, IV, 247.

3. Writing in the third person, Lieber explained that he, "considering, as he does, William of Nassau and Washington akin in character, has hanging against the wall

JULY 3, 1858 661

of his entry a frame surrounding the portraits of the two great men, placed in close connection. Over them is the sign used by astronomers for a double star; under them is written, *Stella duplex.* Around the portrait of William is his own motto: *Saevis tranquillus in undis.* Around that of Washington, the owner had the words inscribed, *Justus et tenax,* Washington never having selected a motto for himself. It was aesthetically necessary to place a sentence corresponding in place to the beautiful one of William." See PMI, IV, 247–48.

2567. To Frederick Philips

Sunnyside June 3d. 1858

Dear Sir

Your note dated May 28th with its accompanyments,[1] through some delay in the post office has but just reached me[.] I regret very much my absence from home when you called last week,[2] but hope to be more fortunate when you make the second expedition to Sleepy Hollow, of which you talk.

My dining hour is three o'clock ⟨wh⟩ and if at any time you will take your chance for country fare I shall be happy to place it before you.

Yours very respectfully
Washington Irving

Frederick Philips Esqr.

Manuscript: University of California at Los Angeles Library.

1. This letter has not been located.
2. On May 26 WI had been in New York City to see off his niece Julia Grinnell, her husband, and their family on their departure for Europe. See PMI, IV, 248. Probably Philips called at Sunnyside during WI's absence.

2568. To James A. Dix

Sunnyside July 3d. 1858.

Dear Sir,

In reply to your inquiry I assure you that I did *not* write the words of 'Sweet home"[1]

I have always considered the late John Howard Payne[2] to be the author of that very popular song; and am still of that belief.

Yours very respectfully
Washington Irving

James A. Dix Esq / Editor of the / Boston Journal.

MANUSCRIPT: SHR.

1. "Home, Sweet Home" was a song from the first act of John Howard Payne's operetta, *Clari, the Maid of Milan*, which was first performed at Covent Garden in London on May 8, 1823. See Grace Overmyer, *America's First Hamlet* (New York, 1957), p. 211.

2. WI, who was a collaborator and an intimate of Payne's at the time the song was written, could speak with authority concerning the authorship of "Home, Sweet Home."

2569. To G. P. R. James

Sunnyside July 24t 1858

My dear James

I may seem tardy in thanking you for the copy of your last work[1] which you had directed Messr Childs ⟨a⟩ & Peterson[2] to send to me, but it laid for a long time in the hands of my publisher before he forwarded to me, so that I have but just finished reading it. I now thank You heartily for it[.] I have read it with great interest and pleasure and think it written in your best vein. I rejoice to see you retaining your powers and sensibilities and writing with youthful spirit, but my dear James you have that fountain of youth within you a kind good heart. May your feelings and fancies always remain fresh and green, and your heart never grow old.

I observe by the papers you have recieved an offer of an appointment[3] which I fear may lure you away from among us. I had hoped your consulate in Richmond would have anchored you; as, from my recollection of it and its people, (which to be sure are rather of ancient date [ )][4] are very agreeable. However, wherever you go God speed and prosper you.

Give my kindest remembrances to Mrs James and your family and believe me ever

Sincerely and cordially yours
Washington Irving

G. P. R. James Esq

MANUSCRIPT: NYPL—WI Papers.

George Payne Rainsford James, a popular English novelist and longtime acquaintance of WI, had visited Sunnyside in July, 1850. See WI to Sarah Storrow, July 18, 1850.

1. *Lord Montagu's Page: An Historical Romance of the Seventeenth Century.*
2. James's Philadelphia publishers. See WI to Childs and Peterson, August 23, 1855.

3. James accepted an appointment as British consul at Venice, where he remained until his death in 1860.

4. WI omitted the bracketed parenthesis.

2570.   *To Charles A. Davis*

Sunnyside Aug 16t. 1858

My dear Davis,

I feel truly and deeply sensible of the kindness and heartiness of your invitation[1] and regret that I have to steel myself against it; but the time is nearly elapsed that I had promised myself to be absent from home; a large supply of Congress water[2] has brought Saratoga to my door and I am in hourly expectation of the arrival of a friend who has notified me by letter that he is coming to pass some days with me. So I have unpacked my trunk and resigned all Watering place gayeties for the present season.

I am surprised to find by your letter that Lake Champlain and Montreal were visited by you ⟨for⟩ this year, for the first time; and I am still more surprised that you should turn back from Montreal without going on to Quebec, which is far more worth seeing, and is indeed one of the most interesting and historical places on this continent. You must take care to see it on your next visit to Canada

Give my kindest remembrances to Mrs Davis and daughter and believe me, my dear Davis,

Most sincerely and cordially / Yours,
Washington Irving

Ch. Aug. Davis Esq

ADDRESSED: Charles Aug. Davis Esq / U States Hotel / Saratoga   POSTMARKED [*handwritten*]: Irvington N Y / Aug 17
MANUSCRIPT: SHR.

1. This invitation has not been located. The context of WI's letter suggests that Davis had asked him to visit Saratoga Springs, as he had done in July and August, 1852.

2. A mineral water from the Congress Spring at Saratoga.

2571.   To George D. Canale

Sunnyside Aug. 21st. 1858

My dear Sir,
   I properly appreciate the kind feeling and favourable estimation which prompt your offer to dedicate to me your translation of my friend Hallecks beautiful poem on the death of Marco Botzaris[1] and gratefully accept it, suggesting however that the dedication be as simple as possible.

With great respect / Yours very truly
Washington Irving

Geo D Canale Esqr.

MANUSCRIPT: NYPL—WI Papers.

   1. WI misspelled the name of Marco Bozzaris, the Greek leader who was killed during a night attack on the Turkish camp at Lapsi on August 20, 1823. On April 19, 1859, WI acknowledged receipt of a copy of Canale's translation, which was published in Cambridge by Welch, Bigelow, and Company, Printers to the university. See Nelson F. Adkins, *Fitz-Greene Halleck: An Early Knickerbocker Wit and Poet* (New Haven, 1930), pp. 163, 378.

2572.   To Charles Lanman

Sunny Side August 24. 1858

My dear Mr. Lanman,
   I have no intention of being absent from home Early in September and will be most happy to receive a visit from you at Sunny Side.
   I will procure the information that you desire respecting my brother William[1] from his Son Pierre M. Irving, when he returns from an Excursion he is making.

Yours very truly
Washington Irving

Charles Lanman Esq. / ⟨Georgetown⟩ Norwich Conn.

MANUSCRIPT: NYPL—Hellman Collection (copy, not in WI's hand).

   1. Lanman was seeking biographical details for his *Dictionary of the United States Congress,* published in 1859. See WI to Lanman, March 28, 1859.

2573. To Julia I. Grinnell

Sunnyside, Sept. 2, 1858

My dear Julia:

                        * * * * *

By all your accounts, you have had uncommonly propitious weather throughout your tour in England, Scotland, and Ireland,[1] and have been able to bring off in your minds delightful pictures of scenery and places. Sightseeing is at times rather fatiguing and exhausting; but the fatigue is amply repaid by the stock of recollections hung up in one's mental picture gallery.

While the world is turning rapidly with you, who are continually on the move, with us who remain at home it seems to be almost standing still. * * * It is quite mournful to look at your deserted mansion,[2] with the flowering vines clambering about the columns, and no one at home to enjoy their beauty and fragrance.

We miss the evening gun of the yacht, as it returns from town.[3] The Fourth of July would have been a *triste* day, had there not been fireworks in the evening at Mr. ———'s. Archery is at an end; there is no more gathering on the lawn; the bows are unstrung, the arrows sleep in their quivers, and the green bodices of the fair archers are motheaten.

I do not know what would have become of us all, and whether we should not have sunk into the spell-bound oblivion of Sleepy Hollow, if we had not been suddenly roused from our apathy by the laying of the Atlantic Cable.[4] This has thrown the whole country into one of those paroxysms of excitement to which it is prone. Yesterday was the day set apart for everybody throughout the Union to go crazy on the subject. New York, you may be sure, was the craziest of cities on the occasion. I went down to town early in the morning, and found it already in a ferment, and boiling over, for all the country had poured into it. But I refer you to the newspapers, which you will undoubtedly see, for ample accounts of the civic rejoicings, which threw all former New York rejoicings in the shade.

I find my sheet is full, so I will conclude this scrawl, which can hardly be called anything more than an apology for a letter. Tell I——[5] I will answer his most acceptable letter on another occasion. Give my love to father, mother, and Fannie, and believe me, my dear, dear Julia, your affectionate uncle,

Washington Irving

PUBLISHED: PMI, IV, 251–52.

Julia Irving Grinnell was the daughter of Julia and Moses Grinnell.

1. The entire Grinnell family had left for a tour of Europe in late May. See PMI, IV, 248.

2. The Grinnell home adjoined Sunnyside.

3. Moses Grinnell had bought the yacht in 1855. See WI to Sarah Storrow, June 27, 1855.

4. An enthusiastic celebration honoring Cyrus Field (1819–1892) for the successful laying of the Atlantic cable was held in New York City on September 1, 1858. See New York *Times*, September 2, 1858.

5. Irving Grinnell, Julia's brother, to whom WI wrote on October 28, 1858.

2574.   To the Reverend Charles K. McHarg

Sunnyside Sept. 27t. 1858

My dear Sir

I return here with the pamphlet concerning Genl Lees Trial[1] which you have had the kindness to lend me and must apologize for having detained it so long. In fact I had forgotten all about it and it lay out of sight among my papers until Mr Henry B. Dawson[2] who is engaged on an important historical work enquired about it

With great respect / Your obliged friend & neighbor
Washington Irving

The Rev. Mr McHarg.

MANUSCRIPT: Va.–Barrett.

1. WI had discussed his treatment of General Charles Lee's trial in a letter to Charles C. Lee, July 31, 1857. The pamphlet has not been identified.

2. Henry B. Dawson (1821–1889), a British-born journalist, was preparing *Battles of the United States by Sea and Land*, which appeared in both serial and book form. His treatment of General Israel Putnam stirred up considerable controversy in Connecticut.

2575.   To Irving Grinnell

Sunnyside Octr. 28th. 1858.

My dear Irving

I will not apologize to you for leaving your letter of July 11th.[1] so long unanswered; You know my situation; how much my poor brain and pen are fagged and over tasked by regular literary labor and by the irregular and inevitable demands of the post office, and will make indulgent allowances for the tardiness of my reply.

Your letter was most acceptable and interesting giving such fresh animated accounts of your travels and expressing so naturally the feelings inspired by the objects around you. Speaking of Bothwell castle,[2] you say "when I am beholding any such magnificent or interesting spot I do not seem to be able to appreciate it enough. I take it in but do not realize it; and this is really a painful sensation, so different from what you would expect. I stand looking with all my eyes and senses open, and feel as though I were deficient in some ↑one↓ faculty which prevented me from really appreciating and enjoying all that I see"

My dear Irving this is all *honestly* expressed and describes a feeling which all hunters of the picturesque and historical ⟨must realize⟩ are apt to experience ↑in presence of the objects of their quest.↓ They in fact ↑do↓ *realize* the scene before them and the naked truth baulks the imagination. Those raptures and extacies ⟨in⟩ which writers of travels are so full of, at the ⟨sight⟩ sight of wonders in art and nature are generally the after coinage of the brain when they sit down in their stud⟨y⟩ies to detail what they have seen and to invent what they think they ought to have felt.

I reccollect how much I was vexed with my self in my young days, when in Italy, in reading the ⟨tour⟩ ↑work↓ of a French tourist, and finding how calmly I had contemplated Scenes and objects which had inspired him with the most exalted transports: it was a real consolation to learn afterwards that he had *never been in Italy* and that his whole book, ⟨had been⟩ with all its raptures, was a fabrication. I think true delight in these matters is apt to be quiet and contemplative.

I was very much interested by your account of your visit to Drum,[3] the old "Stamm haus", as the Germans express it, of the Irving family. I should have liked to have been of your party on that occasion having a strong curiosity about that old family nest, ever since the Scotch antiquarys have traced my origin to an egg hatched out of it in days of yore. We have all been kept well posted up as to the movements of your party by the letters of its different members to friends at home. You have all been diligent corespondents, and on your return you have only to collect your various letters to ⟨fr⟩ relatives and friends, to have a faithful and minute history of your travels. I have been delighted with some of your fathers letters from Switzerland to Susan Grinelle;[4] and to find him so completely open to fresh young enjoyment from the beauties of nature around him. What a cleaning out and freshening up of the mind after all the murky cares and botherings of Wall Street.

In going to town yesterday I had Phil Schuyler beside me in the rail road cars, and he gave me an account of letters just recieved from some of your party by which I found you were all safe in Paris, and in daily communion with the Hamiltons, Careys &c what a joyous meeting it must have been. What a relish of home it must have given you all. Phil I have no doubt keeps you well informed of every thing going on in the little world in which you and he mingled together. He is a worthy, manly fellow and I am glad you have an intimate friend of his stamp. I value him the more highly from the manner in which he conducted himself during his absence in Europe and the frank, simple, unspoiled manners he has brought home with him. and such I trust will be the case with you, my dear Irving. I have always valued in you what I considered to be an honorable nature—a conscientiousness in regard to duties—an open truthfulness—an absence of all low propensities and sensual indulgencies, a reverence for sacred things—a respect for others—a freedom from Selfishness and a prompt disposition to oblige. and with all these a gayety of spirit, flowing I believe from an uncorrupted heart, that gladdens every thing around you. I am not saying all this, my dear Irving to flatter you, but to let you know what precious qualities heaven has bestowed upon you which you are called upon to maintain in their original purity. You are mingling with the world at large at an extremely youthful age; fortunately you go surrounded by the sanctity of home in the company of your parents and sisters,—a moral halo, to protect you from the corruptions of the world. I am confident however that your own native good sense and good taste will protect you against the follies and vices and affectations in which "Young America" is too apt to indulge in Europe and that ⟨you will⟩ while you give free scope to your natural buoyancy of Spirit, you will maintain that frank, manly, modest simplicity of conduct that should characterize the American Gentleman.

I wish I could write you a more entertaining letter, but this, such as it is, is scrawled with some difficulty, for I am just recovered from a fit of illness and am little fitted for the exercise of the pen.

God bless you my dear Irving and bring you home to us with a mind stored with profitable and delightful reccollections, manners improved and refined by travel and a heart unspotted by the world.

Your affectionate uncle
Washington Irving

Irving Grinnell Esqr.

ADDRESSED: Irving Grinnell Esqr / Care Baring, Bros. & Co. / London. // Per Steamer / European   POSTMARKED: Irvington N Y Nov 1st [handwritten] // [unrecovered] / NO 19 / 58 / PAID   DOCKETED: "Recd Nov. 22nd. 1858. Nice" MANUSCRIPT: Helen Kingsford Preston.   PUBLISHED: PMI, IV, 257–59.

1. This letter has not been located.

2. The ruins of Bothwell castle are in the southern Scottish parish of Bothwell on the River Clyde, southeast of Glasgow. See New Century Book of Names, ed. Clarence R. Barnhart (New York, 1954), I, 594.

3. Drum, near Aberdeen, Scotland, was the ancestral home of the Irvings, conveyed to them in 1324 by Robert the Bruce. See PMI, I, 14–16; IV, 256; and WI to Sarah Storrow, October 27, 1856.

4. WI misspelled the surname, which should be "Grinnell."

2576. To Elizabeth Kennedy

Sunnyside, Octr 29t. 1858

My dear Mrs Kennedy,

I rejoice to learn that you are all once more safe on this side of the Atlantic, and regret that I did not know of your arrival on Wednesday,[1] when I was in town. I had intended to come to town this morning to welcome you home but was deterred by a shower of rain and the threat of a wet day, which I dared not encounter, having been much of an invalid of late.[2] However I trust I shall be able to come down tomorrow, and in the mean time, give you all my hearty congratulations.

Yours ever very affectionately
Washington Irving

MANUSCRIPT: Va.–Barrett.

1. October 27. The Kennedys had sailed for Europe in August, 1857. See WI to Sarah Storrow, August 4, 1857.

2. WI suffered from shortness of breath and catarrh. The newspapers of October 16 had noted that he was "dangerously ill." See PMI, IV, 254–55.

2577. To Lyman C. Draper

Sunnyside   Nov 22d 1858

Dear Sir,

I have to acknowledge the receipt of your circular announcing your intention to urge upon the attention of your legislature the adoption of a state system of supplying each town in Wisconsin with a school library of books selected with great care.[1]

The design you specify is admirable and ought to be adopted in every state throughout the Union. I hope and trust you will meet with entire success

With great respect / Your Obd Servt.
Washington Irving

Lyman C Draper Esqr.

MANUSCRIPT: State Historical Society of Wisconsin.

1. At this time Draper was state superintendent of instruction. In an effort to gain support for better library services in the public schools of Wisconsin he sent circulars to many writers, educators, and prominent citizens and asked for quotations in support of his plan. A copy of his circular is preserved in the Rare Book Collection of the State Historical Society of Wisconsin. See William B. Hesseltine, *Pioneer's Mission: The Story of Lyman Copeland Draper*, p. 176.

2578. To Wickham Hoffman

Sunnyside Nov 23d. 1858

Dear Sir.

I feel highly sensible of the Honor done me by the New York State Society of the Cincinnati,[1] in inviting me to the dinner to be given on thursday next; but regret extremely that the state of my health obliges me to excuse myself from accepting all invitations of the kind.

Very respectfully / Your obliged & hbl Servt
Washington Irving

Wickman Hoffman Esq / Secretary

MANUSCRIPT: SHR.

Wickham Hoffman (1821–1900), son of Murray Hoffman, was a New York attorney with an office at 64 Wall Street. He later served with distinction in the Civil War on the staff of Generals Sherman and Canby. After the war he filled various diplomatic posts in Europe until his retirement in 1888. See [Eugene A. Hoffman], *Genealogy of the Hoffman Family* (New York, 1899), pp. 367–70.

1. The Order of Cincinnati was a secret society founded in 1783 by officers in the American forces in the Revolutionary War to "promote and cherish national honor and union, but more particularly to keep the war memories green and afford mutual succor." Membership was hereditary. See Arthur Preuss, comp., *A Dictionary of Secret and Other Societies* (London, 1924), pp. 436–37; and *Encyclopedia of Associations*, vol. 1, *National Organizations of the U.S.*, 786.

2579. To Osmond Tiffany

Sunnyside Dec 22d. 1858

My dear Sir,

Accept my thanks for the Copy of your work[1] which you have had the kindness to send me. I recieved a copy of the work sometime since and perused it with much interest and satisfaction. I hope it has ⟨recieved⟩

↑met with↓ the success which it merits, ⟨that⟩ and that you will be encouraged to continue in a career for which it appears to me you have decided qualifications.

Excuse this scrawl written at a time when I am suffering from a troublesome indisposition[2]—and believe me

Yours very truly
Washington Irving

Osmond Tiffany Esq

MANUSCRIPT: Yale.

1. Tiffany's novel, *Brandon; or, A Hundred Years Ago. A Tale of the American Colonies*, had appeared in September, 1858.
2. At this time WI was having trouble with his breathing and suffered from "a sort of spasmodic affection of the stomach." See PMI, IV, 264–65.

2580. To Oliver Wendell Holmes

Sunnyside Jan 4. 1859

My dear Dr Holmes,

I thank you heartily for the the[1] bottle of Whitcombs prescription and the box of cigarettes[2] which you have had the kindness to send me. I have not yet made use of the former; as I am trying prescriptions furnished by my family physician,[3] but I have smoked several of the cigarettes and found much relief from them[.] I more especially thank you for the copy of your recent work;[4] which is ⟨especially⟩ ↑peculiarly↓ to my taste and which I shall keep by me to be resorted to whenever I require a tonic and a specific against low spirits

I do not know any thing that has gratified me more of late than your frank and cordial visit to Sunnyside[5] It was most opportune; for I was just then under the influence of your writings recently perused and longing to become personally acquainted with the author; but my disordered state of health had prevented my availing myself of the opportunity which presented itself at the dinner of the Century Club.[6]

I am still much of an invalid and in no vein to reply to your delightful letter[7] in a manner worthy of it; but I cannot delay assuring you how much I prize the friendship you have offered me and how happy I shall always feel to be grappled to you by the right hand of fellowship

Yours very truly
Washington Irving

O. W Holmes M D.

MANUSCRIPT: LC.

Oliver Wendell Holmes (1809–1894), essayist, poet, novelist, and physician, was professor of anatomy at Harvard from 1847 to 1882. Widely in demand as a speaker and occasional poet, he was acclaimed for his wit and humor.

1. WI repeated "the."

2. Holmes had given WI a bottle of Jonas Whitcomb's "Remedy for Asthma" and some medicated cigarettes for use in preventing coughing. The asthma remedy, of which a teaspoon was to be taken in a wineglass of water every four hours, was later prescribed by WI's regular physician. An ad for the medicine appears in NYEP, December 20, 1858, p. 2. See also PMI, IV, 272, 279.

3. Dr. John C. Peters of New York City.

4. WI refers to *The Autocrat of the Breakfast Table*, which had appeared in book form in 1858.

5. Holmes, in the company of Frederick S. Cozzens, had called on WI on December 20, 1858. See PMI, IV, 264.

6. The Century Club, which was organized in January, 1847, for the purpose of social enjoyment and cultivation of the arts, included men from all walks of life among its members. WI was one of the original members of the group. See Robert W. July, *The Essential New Yorker: Gulian Crommelin Verplanck* (Durham, N.C., 1951), pp. 251–52; and Albert H. Smyth, *Bayard Taylor* (Boston, 1896), p. 141.

7. This letter has not been located.

2581.   To Florence Jaffray

Sunnyside Jany 7th. 1859

My dear Florence,

You have made me very happy by the New Year present of your likeness and by the kind and ingeniously printed letter which accompanied it. You say you want me often to look at the likeness and think of you[.] I assure you I shall often look at it as a brightener and cheerer from the effect it has had in lightening up a very gloomy moment when I was suffering from indisposition

I send you as a reminder on my part, a volume in which my publisher has bound up the vignettes and illustrations of my works, with extracts from them and notices of their author, who I assure you treasures up the thoughts of you in a very tender corner of his heart.

Your affectionate friend
Washington Irving

Miss Florence Jaffray.

MANUSCRIPT: SHR.

On a separate covering sheet WI wrote: "To Miss Florence Jaffray / from her affectionate friend / Washington Irving / Jany 7th. 1859."

Florence Jaffray was the daughter of Edward S. Jaffray, a New York dry goods merchant and importer who bought the estate east of Sunnyside in 1854 and used it as a summer residence. See Scharf, *Westchester County*, II, 239.

On an earlier occasion when Jaffray was trying to divert the brook which flowed through WI's property for use in his own house WI sent her "The Lay of the Sunnyside Ducks," a poem in nine quatrains (draft and fair copies preserved at SHR). With the assistance of her father she responded in the meter of "The Song of Hiawatha" with "Florence's Reply to 'The Lay of the Sunnyside Ducks'" (also preserved at SHR). Both are printed in Scharf, *Westchester County*, II, 239–40.

2582. To S. Austin Allibone

Sunnyside Jany 12t 1859

My dear Sir

I have to thank you for a copy of ⟨your⟩ ↑the↓ first volume of ⟨the⟩ ↑your↓ Dictionary of Authors[1] which you have had the kindness to send me. It fully comes up to the high anticipations I had formed from the Specimens submitted to my inspection in 1855.[2]

Thus far you had fulfil[l]ed admirably the stupendous task undertaken by you and your work when completed will remain a monument of unsparing industry, indefatigable research, sound and impartial judgment, and critical acumen

It merits and cannot fail to have a wide circulation and to find a place in every library

With great regard / Yours very truly
Washington Irving

S. Austin Allibone Esqr

MANUSCRIPT: Huntington.

1. Allibone's *A Critical Dictionary of English Literature and British and American Authors, Living and Deceased*, which was published by Childs and Peterson of Philadelphia in 1858, is among the books in WI's library at Sunnyside.

2. For details, see WI to Childs and Peterson, August 23, 1855.

2583. To Charles A. Davis

Sunny side Jany. 12th. 1859

My dear Davis

I take pen in hand, although in a wretched mood for letter writing, merely to apologize to you for leaving your most kind and capital letters[1] so long unanswered, but I have been very much out of sorts for a long time past struggling with the remains of my asthmatic complaint, which has caused me sleepless nights and nerves very much deranged. I trust I am getting better, and as soon as I find myself in a tolerable vein for society and am in town I shall beat up your quarters in University place.

Your letter offering me such charming accommodations in your Box at the opera was deeply felt by me and had I been in a state for venturing upon evening amusements I should gladly have availed myself of your invitation. But I was in the doctors hands and absolutely good for nothing

Your account of your son in law was very interesting and satisfactory and I rejoice that the discreet princess has won the heart of *so* worthy a fellow. I trust you will all be happy together

Your last letter was a truly delightful one; written at the close of the year and in peace and good will with all the world. Your heart my than in your two last letters

Professor Holmes of whom you speak paid me a mornings visit at Sunnyside and I have since recieved a very pleasant and cordial letter from him with a copy of his work the Autocrat of the Breakfast table; a work which I had already read with great relish. I was very much pleased with him and I think you would be if you knew him[.] I trust you have read his work, which is very much to my humour

And now my dear Davis I will finish this scrawl, which, bad as it is has cost me an exertion to produce it Give my affectionate remembrances to your wife and the discreet princess and say a civil word to her husband for me, which I will say for myself when I meet him

With heart felt thanks my dear Davis for your kindness in persisting to write to me notwithstanding all my delinquencies

I remain / Yours ever most truly
Washington Irving

Ch A Davis Esqr

MANUSCRIPT: Va.–Barrett.

1. These letters have not been located.

2584.   To Thomas W. C. Moore

Sunnyside Jany 12t. 185⟨8⟩9

My dear Mr Moore

I am sorry ↑to say↓ that I cannot bring myself to comply with Mr Lawrences[1] wishes in regard to a photograph likeness. I have declined every thing of the kind for a long time past

The suggestion that it might be multiplied and sold about the U States in aid of the Mount Vernon fund,[2] does not mend the matter It would be deemed a great piece of vanity and presumption on my part to consent to such a thing

I am unwell this morning[3] which obliges me to be brief; but I wish to give you a definitive answer as soon as possible

With great regard and wishing you a happy New Year I remain yours truly

Washington Irving

T. W. C. Moore Esq

ADDRESSED: T. W. C Moore Esq / No 73 East 12th St / N York   POSTMARKED
    [*handwritten*]: Irvington N Y / Jan 13   DOCKETED: Recd. Jany 14. 1859 /
    Ansd–[*ditto*] 15 [*ditto*]
MANUSCRIPT: New York Society Library.

Thomas W. C. Moore, a friend of Fitz-Greene Halleck, was a patron of the arts in the New York area. For other details, see WI to Aaron Vail, May 11, 1841.

1. Probably Martin M. Lawrence, a daguerreotypist with a studio at 381 Broadway. See *Trow's New York City Directory for 1859*, p. 464.
2. The Mount Vernon Ladies' Association, which had collected money for the purchase of George Washington's home and two hundred acres surrounding it, acquired the property in 1859 for $200,000. Edward Everett contributed about $50,000 to the fund from proceeds of his oration on Washington. See Benson J. Lossing, *Mount Vernon and Its Associations* (Cincinnati, 1883), pp. 369–70.
3. WI was bothered by a return of nervousness. See PMI, IV, 267.

2585.   To William H. Prescott

Sunnyside Jany. 12t. 1859

My dear Mr Prescott

I cannot thank you enough for the third volume of your Philip[1] which you have had the kindness to send me. It came most opportunely to occupy and interest me when rather depressed by indisposition. I have read with great interest your account of the rebellion of the Mooriscoes[2] which took me among the Alpuxarra Mountains which I once traversed with great delight.[3] It is a sad story the trampling *down* and expulsion of that gallant race from the land they won so bravely and cultivated and adorned with such industry intelligence and good taste. You have done ample justice to your subject.

The battle of Lepanto[4] is the splendid picture of your work, and has never been so admirably handled.

I congratulate you on the achievement of this volume, which forms a fine variety from the other parts of your literary undertaking

Giving you my best wishes that you may go on and prosper I remain

My dear Mr Prescott / Yours very truly and heartily

Washington Irving

William H. Prescott Esq.

MANUSCRIPT: NYPL–Berg Collection.

1. The third and final volume of Prescott's *History of the Reign of Philip the Second* appeared late in 1858. The other two volumes were published in 1855.

2. In chapters 2 through 8 Prescott treated the rebellion, defeat, and expulsion from Spain of the Moorish population.

3. After visiting Granada, WI had traveled in these mountains from March 22 to 24, 1828, enroute to Malaga, Gibraltar, Cadiz, and Seville. See *Journal of 1828, and Miscellaneous Notes on Moorish Legend and History*, ed. Stanley T. Williams (New York, 1937), pp. 37f.

4. The four-hour battle of Lepanto between the Christian and Turkish fleets ended with the defeat of the Turks and the deaths of about 15,000 men. Prescott described the battle in chapter 10 of the third volume.

2586.   To John A. Stevens

Sunnyside Jany 15th. 1859.

My dear Sir,

My nephew Mr Pierre M. Irving informs me that he shewed you the letter of Mr Alfred Clarke,[1] stating that twelve or fourteen hundred dollars had been collected at Coopers town towards a monument to be erected over the remains of Mr James Fennimore Cooper at that place, and asking the transfer of the amount of the New York subscription in your hands, which he says can be of no possible use there, to enable them to complete in a suitable manner the monument at Coopers town. As I was placed at the head of the Committee of Arrangements for a suitable demonstration of respect to Mr Coopers memory,[2] I presume it is his wish that I should signify to you my sanction of the propriety of such transfer. The amount in your hands in trust is,

I understand 678 dollars; to which, I learn nothing has been added since the original contribution, at or about the time of Mr Bryants Discourse on his life character and genius in February 1852;[3] and as the plan then suggested contemplated a statue or other conspicuous monument in the city of New York, which would have probably involved an expense of 15000 dollars, there seems no likelihood now that that plan can be carried out. The sum therefore in your hands would seem to be useless for the object originally in view and could not well be claimed for a better object than the completion of the monument now projected in honor of Mr Cooper over the spot where his remains are deposited.[4] To appropriate it in this way would seem to be the nearest approximation to the fulfilment of the original object which the donors had in view in their contributions. I therefore hereby consent to the transfer of the $100 subscribed by me and the $21 handed in by me from persons whose names I cannot now recal[l];[5] and as chairman of the committee of arrangements I give it as my opinion that the 457 dollars collected as I understand on the evening of Mr Bryants Discourse—and which it would be impossible to trace to the individual donors, may fitly be applied by you in the way requested by Mr Clarke. For the residue of the sum in your hands, the hundred dollars subscribed by Mr Prescott the distinguished historian I presume Mr Clarke will get the express warrant of that gentleman, to whom I have advised him to apply—His consent obtained, Mr Clarke will probably lose no time in making application to you for the whole sum in your hands, which I presume, while you regret with me the failure of the original plan, you can have no hesitation in making over to him on receipt of a pledge and guarantee for its sacred application to the object for which it is solicited

With great regard / Yours my dear Sir very truly
Washington Irving

John A Stevens Esq

MANUSCRIPT: NYHS.

John A. Stevens, president of the Bank of Commerce in New York, acted as custodian of the funds raised for the Cooper memorial. For WI's other associations with Stevens, see WI to Catharine Irving, July 17, 1852; and to Mary Irving, July 21, 1852.

1. Clarke, the presumed nephew of Cooper, had written to WI about a Cooper memorial in late 1852. See WI to Clarke, December 21, 1852.

2. WI chaired a meeting on September 25, 1851, to plan a memorial observance for Cooper. See WI to Rufus W. Griswold, September 18, 1851; and to Lewis G. Clark, October 6, 1851; and Andrew B. Myers, *The Worlds of Washington Irving*, p. 109.

3. Bryant delivered his address at Tripler Hall on February 25, 1852. See NYEP, February 27, 1852.

4. The New York committee ultimately turned over its funds to the Cooperstown group, which used them to defray part of the expenses of the monument in Lakewood Cemetery near Cooperstown. See James Grossman, *James Fenimore Cooper* (New York, 1949), pp. 255–56; and Mary E. Phillips, *James Fenimore Cooper* (New York, 1912), pp. 355–56.

5. WI omitted the second "1."

2587. To Joseph Harrison

Sunnyside, Jany 17th 1859

Dear Sir

I have to acknowledge the receipt of the packet which you have had the kindness to forward to me on account of Mr James Nasmyth,[1] and shall write forthwith to that gentleman to express my thanks for the exquisite Fancy sketches which he has sent me. I never have received a more delicate and beautiful testimonial of regard, or one that touched my feelings more sensibly.

Accept my dear Sir my grateful thanks for the kind expressions of your letter and believe me, with great respect

Your truly obliged friend & servt
Washington Irving

Joseph Harrison Esqr

ADDRESSED: Joseph Harrison / Rittenhouse Square / Philadelphia   POSTMARKED
[*handwritten*]: Irvington N Y / Jan / 18
MANUSCRIPT: Miriam Lutcher Stark Library, University of Texas.

Joseph Harrison (1810–1874), an engineer who made a fortune designing and building locomotives, lived in Philadelphia and collected paintings and other works of art.

1. James Hall Nasmyth (1808–1890), a Scottish inventor who established a foundry for making tools near Manchester, sketched many English scenes before they were destroyed or had passed away.

2588. To [James W. Webb]

[January 17, 1859]

Mr W Irving regrets that the state of his health prevents his having the pleasure of accepting General Webbs invitation to dinner on Wednesday the 19t

Sunnyside Jany 17th. [1859]

Manuscript: SHR.

The date is determined by the perpetual calendar and WI's allusion to his health.

2589. To Henry W. Becher

Sunnyside Feb. 4th. 1859

My dear Sir,

It is with deep concern I have to inform you that I cannot lay my hands on the pamphlet concerning the Landfall of Columbus[1] which you have had the kindness to lend me. It has been missing for some time and I have searched for it repeatedly, and since the receipt of your last letter (Jany 26th)[2] have had the most scrupulous search ↑made↓ throughout my library and dwelling, but without Success. I fear somebody has taken it away.

This is extremely mortifying to me, but I trust you can provide yourself with another copy from England. In case the missing manuscript should turn up I will immediately forward it to you by express,[3] in the mean time I must entreat you to excuse this seeming but unavoidable negligence on my part

With great respect / Yours very truly
Washington Irving

Henry W Becher Esqr / &c &c &c

Manuscript: SHR.

Henry W. Becher is probably a relative of the author of the pamphlet mentioned in this letter.

1. *The Landfall of Columbus on His First Voyage to America* was written by Alexander B. Becher (1796–1876), an English naval officer, and published in London in 1856. (See Frederic Boase, *Modern English Biography,* 3 vols. and supplement [New York, 1965], I, 214–15.) A presentation copy from the author is among the books in WI's library at Sunnyside. Apparently the copy under discussion was a different one.

2. This letter has not been located.

3. During a spring housecleaning the missing pamphlet was found among the books in the bedroom of one of WI' s nieces. See WI to Becher, May 16, 1859.

2590. To Mary M. Hamilton

Sunnyside Feb 17th. 1859

My dear Miss Hamilton
I enclose a check for five hundred dollars in payment of my subscription to the Mount Vernon Fund Association[1]

Yours very truly
Washington Irving

Miss Mary M Hamilton

PUBLISHED: *Mt. Vernon Record*, 2 (extra issue, between November and December, 1859), 97 (holograph facsimile).

Miss Mary Morris Hamilton (later Mrs. George Lee Schuyler) was vice-regent of the Mount Vernon Ladies' Association for New York from 1858 until her resignation in 1866. See Elswyth Thane, *Mount Vernon: The Legacy* (Philadelphia, 1967), p. 230. For an account of her activities as vice-regent, see Grace King, *Mount Vernon on the Potomac* (New York, 1929), pp. 73–75. In a letter on January 7, 1859, to Ann Cunningham, regent of the Mount Vernon Ladies' Association, Miss Hamilton reported WI's donation: "Since I last wrote to you, we have recd a noble Contribution from Mr. Washington Irving—our much loved author, & neighbor, He asked me to put his name on my list for $500—This evinces his entire confidence & interest in our project, for he is not a man of wealth . . ." (letter in the library of the Mount Vernon Ladies' Association; our thanks to Ellen McAllister, librarian of the Mount Vernon Ladies' Association, letter of August 12, 1977).

1. WI did not use the official name of the organization. For details about it, see Benson J. Lossing, *Mount Vernon and Its Associations* pp. 370–71, 426–30. On December 25, 1859, Ann Cunningham wrote to Miss Hamilton: "I return you, with many thanks, the Autograph note of the lamented Irving. Feeling that you would have no objection & that every V Regent would like its facsimile—it has ↑been↓ lithographed for the No—just issued—" (letter in the library of the Mount Vernon Ladies' Association).

2591. To Charles A. Davis

Sunnyside Feb 22d. 1859

My dear Davis
I cannot sufficiently express my thankfulness for your most kind and enspiriting letters[1] and for the interest you take in my deranged state of health. A fortnight before the receipt of your last letter (dated Feb 16t) I had been taking the very remedy specified in it—Jonas Whitcomb—a bottle of which had been sent to me by Dr Holmes, The Autograt[2] of the Breakfast Table. I am happy to say I have experienced the most benefi-

cial effects from it and indeed find it the most effective remedy I have hitherto used. I still continue to take it and hope as spring opens to be a well man again.

I wish you had told me how long your friend (who I have some idea is Mr Sidney Brooks)[3] had taken the remedy and in what doses he took it, that, I may know if I am conducting right

I am merely writing to you as my medical advisor—to let you know how I am getting on. When I feel well enough to come to town I will call and state my case more fully to you. Give my kindest remembrances to Mrs Davis to the discreet princess and he[r] husband, and believe me my dear Davis,

Most gratefully and affectionately yours
Washington Irving

Ch. Aug Davis Esqr.

MANUSCRIPT: Va.–Barrett.

At the bottom of page 3 of the holograph is written "Mr Irving died in the / Autumn of '59."

1. These letters have not been located.
2. WI probably intended to write "Autocrat."
3. Brooks was Davis's business partner. See Scoville, *Old Merchants of NYC,* I, 84–87.

2592.   *To [George P. Putnam]*

[February, 1859?]

My dear Sir

I am suffering with a swelled face[1] which almost incapacitates me for doing any thing—

Yours truly / W   I.
Sunnyside, Tuesday

PS. I want revises of Pages ⟨268⟩ 267 & 268 as I may have to modify a sentence. It will not disturb the rest of the letter press. The other pages may be cast

MANUSCRIPT: NYHS.

From WI's reference in the postscript to pages 267 and 268 it is probable that he wrote this note to Putnam in February of 1859. According to PMI (IV, 274–75), WI was working on this section of the proofs at that time.

1. Throughout the winter of 1858–1859 WI was troubled with labored breathing, nervousness, neuralgia, and catarrhal symptoms. See PMI, IV, 263–75.

2593.   To Alfred Clarke

Sunnyside March 2d. 1859

My dear Sir,

The Otsego Lake trout which you had the kindness to send me arrived in good order and were perfectly delicious—For three days my family remained in conjecture and wonderment as to the good fairy who had bestowed this gift; Your letter,[1] received yesterday, dispelled the mystery; and on behalf of my house hold I return you my thanks, congratulating you that you have a lake in your neighbor hood affording such delicacies

With great respect / Yours very truly
Washington Irving

Alfred Clarke Esqr

ADDRESSED: Alfred Clarke Esqr / Springfield / Otsego   POSTMARKED [*handwritten*]:
Irvington N Y / March 3   DOCKETED: Washington Irving
MANUSCRIPT: New York State Historical Association.

WI had written to Clarke on December 21, 1852, about the Cooper memorial.

1. This letter has not been located.

2594.   To Benson J. Lossing

Sunnyside, March 25, 1859

I have completed the last volume of my work and it is going through the press to my great relief; for I have been so much troubled with a nervous indisposition lately arising from asthma that I am glad to have a holyday from the labor of the pen.

PUBLISHED: *Rare and Valuable Autograph Letters, Including a Consignment from Henry Chapman, of Philadelphia,* Anderson Galleries, December 6 and 7, 1915, item 211.

2595. *To Lydia M. Post*

Sunnyside, March 25, 1859

Dear Madam:

Your note of March 9th,[1] being directed to Tarrytown instead of Irvington, has been slow in reaching me. You have my full consent to the dedication of your forthcoming "Domestic Annals of the Revolution" to me,[2] if you think it would be of advantage to the work, or a gratification to yourself. I only request that the dedication be extremely simple, and void of compliment.[3]

With great respect, yours, very truly,
Washington Irving

PUBLISHED: PMI, IV, 277–78.

1. This letter has not been located.

2. The book appeared as *Personal Recollections of the American Revolution. A Private Journal. Prepared from Authentic Domestic Records. Together with Reminiscences of Washington and Lafayette,* ed. Sidney Barclay (1859). A second edition was published under the title of *Grace Barclay's Diary; or, Personal Recollections of the American Revolution.*

3. The following dedication appeared in both editions: "TO / WASHINGTON IRVING, ESQ. / THIS VOLUME / Is with permission inscribed, as a slight / Testimonial of Respect. / S. B."

2596. *To Charles Lanman*

Sunny Side March 28. 1859

My dear Mr Lanman,

Accept my thanks for the Copy of your Dictionary of Congress[1] which you have had the kindness to send me. Both the Conception and the Execution of the work do you great credit. It will remain a valuable book of reference.

With regard to my brother William I requested his son Pierre M Irving to send you some particulars concer[n]ing him—but I find he forgot to do so.[2] Your notice of him notwithstanding is quite satisfactory.

With great regard / Yours very truly
Washington Irving

Charles Lanman Esq / Georgetown D. C.

MANUSCRIPT: NYPL—Hellman Collection (copy).

This copy is not in WI's handwriting.

1. Lanman edited the *Dictionary of the United States Congress,* containing biographies of all persons who had served in Congress since 1774. A copy is among WI's books at Sunnyside.

2. In his letter of August 24, 1858, WI had promised that PMI would send information about William Irving, who had been a Democratic congressman from 1814 to 1819.

2597. To Charles A. Davis

Sunnyside April 4th 1859

My dear Davis

Your letter[1] brings up recolle[c]tion[2] of a time long past. When I was in Genoa in the Autumn of 1804 there was a famous robber Giuseppe Musso by name otherwise called The Great Devil of Genoa,[3] condemned to be shot—The day before his execution he was allowed according to a local custom to choose what dish he pleased for his last dinner. He chose ravioli. This called my attention to the dish. I tried it and found it one of the rarest tit bits I had ever tasted. I rejoice to find that you have a cook who can serve it up and I thank you for the receipt, which I have given to my women kind to study and profit by

I doubt however, even if ravioli were set before me just now I could relish it, my appetite is so completely prostrated. I am looking forward with anxious and hopeful eye to the coming of real Spring weather, that I may get ⟨apart?⟩ about in the open air without danger of taking cold and being thrown back in my convalescence as I already have been. I thank you for all your kind suggestions and offers, as to jaunting a little, and hope I may be sufficiently stout in body and stout hearted enough one of these days to undertake something of the kind. At present I am good for nothing and would prove a very stupid travelling companion

You hint at my working too hard but I must inform you that I gave up work sometime since having nearly knocked myself up in finishing my fifth volume of the life of Washington[4]—all the labor of revising the volume and getting it through the press, having been done by my nephew Pierre M Irving. So that I have given myself a complete holy day and now only take up my pen occasionally to scrawl a very good for nothing letter like the present.

I rejoice to learn from your letter that the French theatre[5] is succeeding. I was twice at it last year and was greatly pleased with the acting; and I hope to be well enough in the course of time to visit it again

Give my affectionate remembrance to Mrs Davis and the discreet princess and my hearty regards to your Son in law and believe me my dear Davis

Yours from the bottom of my heart
Washington Irving

Ch Aug Davis Esq

ADDRESSED: Charles A. Davis Esq / 1. University Place
MANUSCRIPT: Yale.

1. This letter has not been located.
2. WI omitted the second *c*.
3. Giuseppe Musso (1779?–1804) was executed on November 14, 1804. For WI's eyewitness account, see WI to William Irving, December 25, 1804; and *J&N*, I, 127–31.
4. On March 31, 1859, this volume was printed and awaiting only WI's preface. See the April 2, 1859, entry in PMI's unpublished journal (at NYPL).
5. A French theatrical company opened at the Olympic Theater, 585 Broadway on May 11, 1858, and played until early November. Apart from a few isolated performances, French plays were not offered again until March 8, 1859, following which there was a wide variety of productions until June 28, 1859. See Odell, *NY Stage*, VII, 67–71, 163–65.

2598.   To Henry B. Dawson

Sunnyside April 6th. 1859

My dear Sir

Accept my thanks for the Numbers of your historical work which you have had the kindness to send me.[1] I congratulate you on the admirable style in which the work is executed and the spirit with which it is carried on. It cannot fail to remain a most valuable and popular national work.

Yours very truly
Washington Irving

Henry B. Dawson Esqr.

MANUSCRIPT: SHR.

For details about Dawson, see WI to the Reverend Charles K. McHarg, September 27, 1858.

1. WI probably refers to sections of Dawson's *Battles of the United States, By Sea and Land*, which were issued in serial form in 1858. It is possible that Dawson sent WI an advance copy of *Sons of Liberty in New York*, which was published on May 3, 1859.

2599.   *To Rhoda E. White*

Sunnyside April 18th. [1859]

To / Rhoda E. White

Madam,

Your letter of March 16th.[1] came duly to hand, but arrived at a time when I was suffering under a nervous indisposition brought on by literary labor, ↑and↓ ⟨I⟩[2] was obliged to abstain as much as possible from the exercise of the pen. I was not in the vein therefore to ⟨furnish⟩ invent a letter for your collection of autographs nor had I any letters of friends that I could yield for such a purpose ↑without a breach of propriety↓[3]. In the deranged state of my health your letter with many others remained on my table unanswered. I am slowly recovering from my indisposition but still find it impossible to cope with the miscellaneous correspondence pressing upon me from all quarters and have to claim the indulgence of my friends and well-wishers to excuse me from literary tasks of the kind you propose

With great respect / Your Obdt Servant
Washington Irving

Manuscript: NYPL–Seligman Collection.

Apart from the correction in the first sentence, only the complimentary close and signature are in WI's handwriting.

Rhoda Elizabeth White brought out *Portraits of My Married Friends* (New York, 1858).

1. This letter has not been located.

2. The cancellation and insertion were made by WI in darker ink.

3. In his unpublished journal (at NYPL) under the date of April 16, 1859, PMI gives the background for WI's comment: "[WI was] Pestered with the necessity of replying to a Miss Rhoda E. White, of New York—who had written in March for his autograph to be inserted in a book of autographs which she was getting up for some charitable fair—where it was to be sold—requested not merely his own autograph—but the autographs of other distinguished personages with whom he had corresponded—Longfellow had sent her *ten*—He was too ill to reply to her first letter—& now the persevering saint sent him another—her object she thought no doubt, would excuse her officiousness—'Charity,' said he, 'covers a multitude of sins'—but it is sins against poor authors—Drafted a reply which he meant to get one of the girls to copy—& then merely append his signature—as he did not wish to have a letter of his paraded in an autograph book. . . ."

2600. To George D. Canale

Sunnyside April 19th. 1859

My dear Sir,
     Accept my thanks for the copies of your version of Mr Hallecks Ode
on the Death of Marco Botzaris which you have had the kindness to
send me, and my acknowledgements of the proof you have given me of
your favorable regard in honoring me by the dedication.[1]

I remain, Dear Sir / Yours very truly
Washington Irving

Geo. D. Canale Esqr

ADDRESSED: 70 / U. S. S. Tennessee / from [*unrecovered*] / G Canale LL. D.
MANUSCRIPT: Yale.

1. On August 21, 1858, WI had given Canale permission to dedicate to him the
translation of Fitz-Greene Halleck's "Marco Bozzaris" into modern Greek.

2601. To Evert A. Duyckinck

Sunnyside May 9t 1859.

My dear Mr Duyckinck
     I am infinitely obliged to you for you well timed letter[1] giving a cordial
cheer on the launching of my fifth volume,[2] while it is yet hardly afloat.
You are evidently aware how precious to an authors heart is an approv-
ing word uttered at such a moment of doubt and anxiety
     You congratulate me on the completion of my Life of Washington in
time for the unimpeded enjoyment of the opening season, and imagine
me enjoying the freedom of the fields with double alacrity now that my
task is no longer hanging over me. I assure you the receipt of your letter
has put me in the right mood for such enjoyment, and I shall take it out
into the fields with me and read it over again, amidst all the revelry
of Spring which the present genial weather has caused suddenly to burst
forth.
     Give my kind remembrances to your brother[3] and Mr Panton[4] and b[e]-
lieve me my dear Mr Duyckinck

Yours every very truly
Washington Irving

Evert A Duyckinck:

MANUSCRIPT: Huntington.

1. This letter has not been located.

2. In his unpublished journal (NYPL) under the date of April 30, 1859, PMI noted: "He ⌊WI⌋ receives this morning 6 ⟨volumes⟩ ↑copies↓ of the last volume of his Life of Washington, sent up yesterday by Mr Putnam—it is advertised for delivery May 10th—"

3. George L. Duyckinck.

4. Henry Panton, Evert Duyckinck's brother-in-law.

2602. To John P. Kennedy

Sunnyside May 11th. 1859

My dear Kennedy.

I have had to decline the very tempting invitation of Mr Prescott Smith on behalf of the Baltimore and Ohio Rail Road Company[1] In fact I am not in a condition to undertake the expedition proposed. I have been under the weather all winter suffering from an attack of asthma and a nervous indisposition brought on by overworking myself in endeavoring to bring my literary task to a conclusion—Thank heaven my fifth volume is launched and henceforth I give up all further tasking of the pen. I am slowly regaining health and strength and and[2] having my natural rest at night, for I suffered wretchedly from sleeplessness. Within the last two or three weeks I feel quite encouraged; but I still have to take great care of myself for Asthma is constantly dogging at my heels and watching every opportunity to get the mastery over me.

In my present precarious state of health I can make no engagements that would take me far from home and can therefore make you no promise of accompanying you to the mountains or even of visiting you at Ellicotts Mills.[3] In fact I have been but once to New York since last Christmas, and that was only a few days since;[4] and have not been able to jollify even at little parties in my immediate neighborhood.

Give my affectionate remembrances to Mrs Kennedy and Miss Grey and believe me, my dear Kennedy

Ever very truly yours
Washington Irving

John P Kennedy Esqr.

MANUSCRIPT: Peabody Library.   PUBLISHED: PMI, IV, 283.

1. William Prescott Smith (1822?–1872), master of transportation of the Baltimore & Ohio Railroad and chief aide of its president, John W. Garrett, had written *A History and Description of the Baltimore & Ohio Railroad* (Baltimore,

1853). See Edward Hungerford, *The Story of the Baltimore & Ohio Railroad, 1827–1927*, 2 vols. (New York, 1928), I, 335.

2. WI repeated "and."

3. Kennedy's country home, the former estate of his father-in-law, Edward Gray, was located about eight miles west of Baltimore and about one mile below Ellicott's Mills, on the Patapsco River.

4. WI, his brother Ebenezer, PMI, and Helen Irving had gone to the city on May 3. See PMI's unpublished journal (NYPL) for May 3, 1859.

2603. To William Prescott Smith

Sunnyside May 11t. 1859

William Prescott Smith Esqr / &c &c &c

Dear Sir

I feel deeply obliged by the invitation you give me on behalf of the Baltimore and Ohio Rail Road Company to form one of the party of guests in the trip of inspection about to be made to the Western extremity of the road. I grieve to say however that I am not in a condition to cope with such an expedition or to form one of the highly intellectual party that is to make it[.] I am slowly recovering from an indisposition that has harassed me for months past and been accompanied by nervous debility and dare not undertake any enterprise that calls for sustained energy and animal spirits

I beg you to present to the Company my sincere thanks for this second invitation with which they have honored me and my deep regret that I cannot avail myself of it

With great respect

Your friend & Servant
Washington Irving

MANUSCRIPT: Rabbi Howard A. Berman.

2604. To Henry W. Becher

Sunnyside May 16t. 1859

My dear Sir

The Landfall of Columbus inquest[1] of which my house, as I thought, had been completely ransacked, but in vain, was found this morning, accidentally, when no Search was made, lying perdue in the corner of a shelf of books in the bed room of one of my nieces.[2]

I now forward it to you by express, begging you to pardon its unintentional detention, which I assure you has caused me infinite chagrin and mortification.

With high respect / Yours, my dear Sir, very truly

Washington Irving

Henry W Becher Esqr / &c &c &c

MANUSCRIPT: SHR.

1. For WI's earlier reaction to the loss of this work, see WI to Becher, February 4, 1859.

2. Apparently the missing pamphlet was discovered during spring cleaning at Sunnyside. See PMI's unpublished journal (NYPL) for May 16, 1859.

2605. To Cornelius C. Felton

Sunnyside, May 17, 1859

My dear Sir,

I cannot sufficiently express to you how much I feel myself obliged by your very kind letter of the 12th instant, giving such a favorable notice of my last volume.[1] I have been very much out of health of late, with my nerves in a sad state, and with occasional depression of spirits; and, in this forlorn plight, had come to feel very dubious about the volume I had committed to the press. Your letter had a most salutary and cheering effect; and your assurance, that the last volume had been to you *of more absorbing interest than either of the others*, carried a ray of joy to my heart: for I was sadly afraid the interest might be considered as falling off.[2]

Excuse the brevity of this letter; for I am suffering to-day from the lingerings of a nervous complaint, from which I am slowly recovering: but I could not suffer another day to elapse without thanking you for correspondence which has a more balmy effect than any of my doctor's prescriptions.

With great regard, / I am, my dear Mr. Felton, / Yours very truly,

Washington Irving

Professor C. C. Felton.

PUBLISHED: Boston *Courier*, December 19, 1859; *Proceedings of the Massachusetts Historical Society*, 4 (December, 1859), 416; *Harper's Magazine*, 24 (February, 1862), 353.

Cornelius C. Felton (1807–1862), a graduate of Harvard in 1827, was professor of Greek there. He was to become president of Harvard in 1860.

1. This letter has not been located. According to PMI, WI was pleased with Felton's reaction to his *Life of Washington*. "He [WI] said it was particularly gratifying to get such testimonials from such men as he had found it impossible to repress great misgivings with regard to this last volume which he had never been able to look at since it was finished." See PMI's unpublished journal (NYPL), May 13, 1859.

2. Putnam had faith in the continuing interest of the reading public in the biography, for he had printed 5,000 copies of the 12mo edition and 500 copies of the octavo. See PMI's unpublished journal (NYPL), April 12, 1859. For the public reaction, see STW, II, 230–31, 297–98.

2606. To George Ticknor

Sunnyside May 30th. 1859

My dear Ticknor

I send you the only letters from Prescott[1] that have been found among my papers; should any others come to light they shall be forwarded to you. I will thank you to return them to me when you have done with them.[2] I ⟨ra⟩ am not in the habit of keeping copies of my own letters and have none of those I have written to Prescott. If you find any among his papers you are welcome to make such use of them as you may judge proper.

I am suffering under a slight return of the nervous malady which has harassed me during the past winter and which obliges me to excuse myself as much as possible from all exercise of the pen. I give this as an excuse for the brevity ⟨of⟩ and insufficiency of the present letter

Ever with affectionate regard / My dear Ticknor / Yours very truly
Washington Irving

George Ticknor Esq

MANUSCRIPT: Dartmouth College.

1. WI sent Ticknor six letters from Prescott after PMI had gone to New York City to get them from his office. See PMI's unpublished journal (NYPL), May 21, 31, 1859.

2. Ticknor used the letters in preparing his *Life of William Hickling Prescott*, published in 1864.

2607.   To Henry T. Tuckerman

Sunnyside, June 8th 1859

My dear Mr Tuckerman,

I have suffered a long time to elapse without acknowledging the receipt of your letter enclosing a printed notice of my fifth volume which
you had furnished to the press.[1] My only excuse is that since I have got
out of regular harness I find it exceedingly difficult to bring myself to
the slightest exercise of the pen.

I cannot sufficiently express to you my dear Mr Tuckerman how deeply
I I[2] have felt obliged by the kind interest you have manifested on
various occasions and in a variety of ways, in me and my literary concerns. It is truly gratifying to be able to inspire such interest in the
mind of a person of your stamp and intellectual character.

Your remarks on my last volume are especially inspiriting. Unnerved
as I was by a tedious indisposition I had come to regard that volume
with a dubious and almost desponding eye. Having nothing of the *drum
and trumpet* which gave bustle and animation to the earlier volumes
I feared it might be considered a falling off. Your letter has contributed
to put me in heart and and[3] I accept with gratitude your congratulation
on what you pronounce a "happy termination" of my undertaking.

Ever my dear Mr. Tuckerman, with great regard

Your truly obliged friend
Washington Irving

Henry T Tuckerman Esqr

Manuscript: NYPL–Seligman Collection.   Published: PMI, IV, 293.

1. Tuckerman's letter and review have not been located.
2. WI repeated "I."
3. WI repeated "and."

2608.   To John E. Cooke

Sunnyside June 24t. 1859

My dear Mr Cooke

I beg you to excuse my tardiness in replying to your very obliging
letter and acknowledging the receipt of the very entertaining volume[1]
which you have had the kindness to send me but in truth I have had a
temporary attack of my nervous complaint, which obliges me to forego
as much as possible the exercise of the pen.

I had already read your volume Some time since, when it first came out and had been greatly please[d][2] with the pictures it gave of Virginian life and Virginian characters both of the *leather stocking* and the *Silk* order. I delight in every thing that brings scenes before me of the Ancient Dominion; which to me is a region full of social and romantic associations, and I have re read your work with additional interest now that I have become personally acquainted with the Author

I look back with great pleasure to the visit of yourself and Mr Duyckinck[3] as giving me a most agreeable day of social chat, which is quite a god send to an invalid in the Country—and I shall be very happy if you will favor me with a treat of the kind whenever it may suit you[r][4] Convenience.

In the mean time believe me with great regard

Yours very truly
Washington Irving

John Esten Cooke Esq

MANUSCRIPT: LC.

John Esten Cooke (1830–1886) was a younger brother of the Virginia poet Philip Pendleton Cooke and of Henry Pendleton Cooke, who in 1855 had married Mary Kennedy, one of WI's favorite correspondents in 1853 and 1854. Cooke was the author of *The Virginia Comedians* (1854) and *Henry St. John, Gentleman* (1859), historical novels in the manner of Cooper. During the Civil War he served in the Confederate army.

1. Cooke's letter has not been located. The volume which Cooke sent may, as WI's comments in the next paragraph suggest, have been his *Leatherstocking and Silk, or Hunter John Myers and His Times, A Story of the Valley of Virginia* (1854), an imitation of WI's style and treatment in *The Sketch Book* and *Bracebridge Hall*.
2. WI omitted the bracketed letter.
3. Cooke and Evert Duyckinck called on WI on Saturday, June 11 and stayed to dinner. According to PMI, WI "was in excellent spirits (for him) and enjoyed the visit very much." See PMI's unpublished journal (NYPL), June 11, 1859.
4. WI omitted the bracketed letter.

2609. To George Ticknor

Sunnyside July 2d. 1859

My dear Ticknor

I should sooner have acknowledged the receipt of the letters of Prescott which you so punctually sent back to me[1]—but my nerves were unstrung by a perverse spell of bad weather and I had to await the turning of the weather cock before I could again take pen in hand.

The correspondence between Prescott and myself to which you allude, has, I fear, fallen into the hands of those worse than Egyptian plagues—autograph hunters—Should I however meet with any trace of it among my papers I will promptly put you in possession of it.

Ever my dear Ticknor

Yours with the warmest regard
Washington Irving

George Ticknor Esqr

MANUSCRIPT: Dartmouth College Library.

1. WI had sent six of Prescott's letters to Ticknor on May 30, 1859. Ticknor's letter accompanying them has not been located.

2610.   To Richard Henry Dana, Jr.

Sunnyside July 6th 1859

My dear Sir,

Accept my warmest thanks for the copy of your "Vacation Voyage["][1] which in its lively narrative and spirited and graphic picturings of Cuba and its people has rivalled the delight I had received from your "Two Years before the Mast"

Let me express at the same time how much I have been flattered and gratified by the expression of friendship and esteem[2] with which you have accompanied your gift

Believe me my dear Sir

with high respect and regard / Yours very truly
Washington Irving

Richard Henry Dana Jr Esqr

MANUSCRIPT: MHS.

Richard Henry Dana, Jr. (1815–1882), who related his experiences as a sailor in *Two Years Before the Mast* (1840), was a Harvard graduate and a Boston lawyer who often defended oppressed sailors.

1. WI omitted the bracketed quotation mark. *To Cuba and Back, A Vacation Voyage* was Dana's account of a trip to Cuba earlier in 1859.
2. Dana's letter has not been located.

2611. To Charles A. Davis

Sunnyside July 11th. 1859

My dear Davis

You are one of the most faithful and enduring of friends—otherwise you would not continue to favor me with your most entertaining and acceptable of letters notwithstanding my delinquency.[1] But you are aware that my abstinence from the pen is on account of my deranged state of health, and you not merely excuse it, but task yourself to cheer and animate me. Believe me my dear Davis I feel your kindness to my hearts Core.

The parcel which you sent to me a month since, and the receipt of which I fear I never acknowledged came safe to hand. The contents have proved excellent as far as Mr Geery's establishment[2] was concerned but I confess I have not made use of the bottle of cough mixture as I was following a different prescription which I find beneficial

In consequence of your caution I have nearly given up the use of Stramonium[3] and prefer the Nitre-paper. I have long been convinced of the soundness of your opinion that the organ most to be attended to in my case is the Stomach. Mine has been in a sad debilitated state, but is now recovering its tone slowly. Roasted potatoes are a standing dish on my table; Cayenne is properly appreciated—as to brandy I have long since learned what an invaluable tonic it is when the stomach and nerves are at fault. At present I am taking the "Peruvian Syrup, or Patented Solution of Protoxide of Iron Combined,"[4] and think it is doing me a great deal of good. It has been of vast service to my neighbor Col. James Hamilton, and to others of my acquaintance.

⟨In⟩ You ask me (in your month old letter) whether the Widow Custis had more than two children when she married General Washington[5]— I never heard or read of her having more than two—the son and daughter of whom I have made mention in my work.

Your tale of the Skeleton Apothecary appeared in the Home Journal of July 2d.[6] and I make no doubt has done more good throughout the country than any of the Apothecaries drugs. It is well told and highly graphic.

Your letter of the 7th. inst. gives a most gratifying account of Col Preston our present Minister at Madrid.[7] I am rejoiced that we are so well represented there. I have just received a letter from a lady at Madrid (wife of Mr O'Shea the Banker)[8] who says "the new American Minister and his lady[9] Seem very charming people He is quite a man of the world and both are agreeable."

I can make no promise ⟨or⟩ at present about going to Saratoga[10] or any where else—All must depend upon the state of my health, which has been very capricious—frequently put back by the tricky weather to which we have been subject, throughout the present year. However, I think I am gradually improving and hope soon to get free from the nervous attacks which at ⟨ha⟩ times have annoyed me.

With kindest remembrances to Mrs Davis I remain my dear Davis

Yours most gratefully and / Affectionately
Washington Irving

Ch. Aug. Davis Esqr

MANUSCRIPT: SHR.

At the end of the letter, below Davis's name, is written in another hand "*Grt Grt Uncle* / of / Elizabeth Bird Williams / on her grand Mother Bird's side."

1. This letter and the one mentioned in the sixth paragraph have not been located.

2. WI may be referring to the grocery store of Isaac and William Geery at 709 Broadway and 203 Canal Street. See *New York City Directory for 1859*, p. 299.

3. Stramonium, the dried leaf of the poisonous jimson weed, contains the alkaloids atropine, hyoscyamine, and scopolamine which are useful in the treatment of asthma.

4. According to PMI, WI started taking this medicine on June 30. On July 14 PMI bought another bottle of it in New York City. See PMI's unpublished journal (NYPL), June 30, July 14, 1859.

5. Martha Dandridge Custis (1732–1802), who married George Washington on January 6, 1759, had two children by her first marriage—Martha Parke Custis (d. 1773) and John Parke Custis (d. 1781).

6. This unsigned story of an apothecary who was a practical joker was printed on the front page of the *Home Journal*, July 2, 1859.

7. William Preston (1816–1887), a Kentuckian who was educated at Yale and Harvard, entered politics as a Whig and served in Congress from 1852 to 1856. After joining the Democrats and supporting Buchanan, he was appointed U.S. minister to Spain in 1858. He resigned at the outbreak of the Civil War, joined the Confederacy, and became Jefferson Davis's envoy to Mexico.

8. WI was on intimate terms with Henry O'Shea and his wife Sabina while he was minister to Spain. See WI to Sarah Storrow, January 18, 1845.

9. Preston was married in 1840 to Margaret Wickliffe, daughter of Robert Wickliffe of Lexington, Kentucky.

10. WI had been with Davis at Saratoga Springs in the summers of 1852 and 1853. See PMI, IV, 109, 156-57.

2612.   To Alfred L. Barbour

Sunnyside July 15th 1859

Dear Sir

It is with great interest and satisfaction that I have received the intelligence contained in your letter of the 7th inst.[1] of the prosperous condition of your Association and the zeal with which it pursues the highly intellectual objects for which it was instituted

I cannot but feel gratified and affected by the manifestations of favorable opinion and good will with which your Association has honored me on the first reunion of its officers and members, begging you will convey to it my warmest acknowledgements of its favors, I remain very respectfully

Your obliged friend & servt
Washington Irving

Alfred L. Barbour /Corresponding Secy of / the Irving Lit. Association

DOCKETED: Washington Irving / July 15 1859
MANUSCRIPT: Richard Maass.

1. This letter has not been located.

2613.   To Irving Paris

Sunnyside July 28t. 1859

My dear Irving

I find by your letter of the 25th.[1] that there is some chance of Sarah's[2] coming out with all her children to pass the Winter in America and that the only things likely to interfere with the accomplishment of the project are Susans lameness and the expense of the expedition—⟨Should⟩ I hope Susans foot may be sufficiently well in time ⟨and⟩ for the voyage and I will lighten the expense by paying for their passages both ways across the Atlantic. I wish if you are writing to Sarah, you would mention this—I would write to her myself on the subject, but writing is so very irksome to me just now that I should not get a letter ready in time

In great haste / Your affectionate Uncle
Washington Irving

Irving Paris Esq

ADDRESSED: Irving Paris Esq / No 15 Nassau St / N York   POSTMARKED: IRVING-
    TON NY / Jul / 28
MANUSCRIPT: SHR.

1. This letter has not been located.
2. Sarah Storrow, the sister of Irving Paris and WI's favorite niece, was still
living in Paris. Apparently she did not return to America before WI's death. See
STW, II, 239.

2614.   To the Reverend Francis Vinton

Sunnyside Aug 1t 1859

My dear Sir,
   It will give me great pleasure to recieve the visit which you propose
to make me on Wednesday next[1] and I shall be happy to make ⟨the⟩
acquaintance with your son.[2]

With great regard / Yours very truly
Washington Irving
The Rev Francis Vinton D. D.

P. S. Your note though dated July 29th[3] has but just reached me.

MANUSCRIPT: Huntington.

   Francis Vinton (1809–1872), who was in the military service from 1826 to 1836,
was ordained in the Protestant Episcopal Church in 1838. He served at St. Paul's
Chapel and Trinity Church before becoming a professor at General Theological
Seminary in New York.

   1. According to PMI, Vinton and his son were in the vicinity to attend a
meeting of county clergymen at Irvington. See PMI's unpublished journal (NYPL),
August 3, 1859.
   2. Since Vinton was the father of eight sons, it is not possible to determine
which one accompanied him on this visit.
   3. This letter has not been located.

2615.   To Charles A. Davis

Sunnyside Aug. 2d. 1859

My dear Davis
   I have been for days and days meditating a letter to you and vexing
myself because I could not achieve one, but, ever since I threw down
my pen as an author, I find it extremely difficult to take it up as an

Amateur ⟨and⟩ even to scrawl a letter to a friend. You still continue your attempts to lure me to Saratoga,[1] but, if I should cast myself loose from home,[2] I am engaged ⟨previously⟩ to visit some of my connexions before I go any where else; and truely I find this casting loose from home a formidable difficulty that ⟨I⟩ impedes every effort.

My health is much improved, and at times I feel quite in tune; but I am easily unstrung, ⟨as yet⟩ and as yet have not a ↑sufficient↓ stock of strength and spirits ↑⟨sufficient⟩↓ to stand the wear and tear of a watering place. Perhaps I have staid too much at home and (to use your words) have dropped into the *notion* of *inability.* a few days may make a great change in my feelings in this respect; I have grown very considerably younger within the last three weeks, and ↑the spirit of↓ enterprise begins to revive in me; but I have much to regain before I shall be my own man again.

History in Europe at present outruns romance, and Louis Napoleon[3] will furnish materials for some future Walter Scott to work upon. I am excessively interested by his career. Events are so striking and succeed each other so rapidly that they keep curiosity continually on the stretch.

I am scrawling this without the least mood for letter writing; as I am sure you will percieve; but you say ⟨you⟩ "it will gratify you much to hear from me if but to tell you how I am" and to that end I indite this epistle. So no more at present—but with kindest remembrances to Mrs Davis

Yours my dear Davis / Very truely and heartily
Washington Irving

Ch. Aug Davis Esqr

MANUSCRIPT: Newberry Library.

1. WI had received a letter from Davis at Saratoga on July 29. See PMI's unpublished journal (NYPL), July 29, 1859.

2. WI did not leave Sunnyside until August 31, when he visited Barrett Ames at Craigville, Orange County until September 5. See PMI's unpublished journal (NYPL), August 31 to September 5, 1859.

3. The forces of Napoleon III had campaigned against Austria in Lombardy in 1859. PMI noted that Davis had commented upon Napoleon's "abrupt termination of the war." (See PMI's unpublished journal [NYPL], July 29, 1859.) WI's third paragraph is a brief response to Davis's comment.

2616.   To Cyrus W. Field

Sunnyside Aug 3d. 1859

My dear Sir,

I feel greatly obliged to you for your kindness in forwarding to me the book entrusted to your care by your nephew Mr Fisk P Brewer.[1] I have this day written to Mr Brewer[2] acknowledging the receipt of it

With great respect / Yours very truly
Washington Irving

Cyrus W Field Esqr

MANUSCRIPT: SHR.

Cyrus W. Field (1819–1892) was a merchant and financier who promoted the successful laying of an Atlantic cable in 1858.

1. Fisk Parsons Brewer (1832–1890) was the son of Field's sister Emilia and Josiah Brewer, who had been a missionary to Turkey. The book sent by Field has not been identified.
2. WI's letter to Brewer has not been located.

2617.   To William C. Preston

Sunnyside Aug 9th. 1859

My dear Preston

I have suffered a long time to elapse without a reply to your most kind and welcome letter,[1] but the state of my health must plead my apology For many months I have been harassed by an attack of asthma accompanied by sleepless nights which deranged my whole nervous system. I have had to give up all literary occupation and to abstain as much as possible from the exercise of the pen, even in letter writing. I am slowly recovering but still have to be very careful of myself. Fortunately I have finished the life of Washington, about which you speak so kindly;[2] and now shall no more task myself with Authorship.

Your allusions to Jones of the Brinn and Loch Katrine[3] brought up a host of recollections of pleasant scenes and pleasant adventures which we enjoyed together in our in our[4] peregrinations in England and Scotland in our younger days. ⟨The⟩ I often recur in thought to those ramblings which furnish some of the most agreeable day dreams of past times; and if I dared to indulge my pen, could call up many an amusing incident in which you figured conspicuously. But this scribbling ⟨mus⟩ I must postpone to some future day, when I am less under the thraldom of nerves and the asthma. At present I merely scrawl these few lines to as[s]ure you of my constant and affectionate remembrance

I believe ⟨th⟩ our present Minister in Spain is a cousin of yours:[5] I am glad to hear he is likely to prove very popular there. A lady correspondent in Madrid[6] well acquainted with the Court Circle speaks in very favorable terms both of the Minister and his lady

Farewell my dear Preston. Believe me, though at present a very lame correspondent, Yet, as ever

Yours very faithfully
Washington Irving

William C Preston Esq

MANUSCRIPT: Virginia Historical Society.   PUBLISHED: PMI, IV, 287–88.

William C. Preston had traveled in England and Scotland with WI in 1817. For other details, see WI to Preston, July 13, 1852.

1. Preston's letter of May 11, 1859, was prompted by a news item in the *National Intelligencer* that WI had been ill. See PMI, IV, 286-87 for the complete text of Preston's letter.
2. Preston had written, "What a noble capital your Life of Washington makes to your literary column!" See PMI, IV, 287.
3. WI had commented on these same details in his letter of July 13, 1852.
4. WI wrote "in our" twice.
5. William Preston. See WI to Charles A. Davis, July 11, 1859.
6. Sabina O'Shea.

2618.   To Robert S. Oakley

Sunnyside Aug 22d. 1859

My dear Mr Oakley

I shall be happy to recieve the proposed visit of yourself and Mr Forrest[1] on any morning that you may find it convenient.[2] Since I had the pleasure of seeing you I have suffered severely from asthma; and am still troubled by sleepless nights and shortness of breathing which at times render me nervous and good for nothing. You must take your chance for finding me worth visiting; but, hoping your visit may happen on one of my good mornings when I am *in tune,*

I remain yours very cordially
Washington Irving

R. S. Oakley Esqr

MANUSCRIPT: Va.–Barrett.

Robert S. Oakley was cashier of the American Exchange Bank of New York. See *New York City Directory for 1859*, appendix, p. 9.

1. Probably Joseph Forrest, an engineer living at 25 Lewis Street, New York City. PMI had noted that Forrest was a mathematician. See *New York City Directory for 1859*, p. 280; and PMI's unpublished journal (NYPL), August 21, 1859.

2. Oakley and Forrest came to Sunnyside on August 31, the day that WI left on his visit to Barrett Ames. See PMI's unpublished journal, September 6, 1859.

2619. To Thomas W. Storrow, Sr.

Sunnyside Aug 25t. 1859

My dear Storrow

It is with deep regret we all learn that you are not coming to make us your promised visit, and that you are prevented by painful indisposition. For some time past my whole household had been daily looking out for your arrival.[1] A little consultation with my brother might have been of service to you. He is ⟨for⟩ several years your Senior, and has suffered much from rheumatism; especially about three or four years since; but has nearly cured himself by friction with "roll ↑brimstone"↓[2] and warm, or rather hot, baths. He is now very little troubled with rheumatic pains, which at one time were intense but he continues to take his bath at a very early hour every morning.

I have been harassed very much for many months past by asthma, accompanied by sleepless nights and disordered nerves; but flatter myself I am gradually getting better; though I am every now and then thrown back and almost made to despond. I have been so free from any painful malady during a long life and have in general enjoyed such active and cheerful health that I must not complain in my old age at undergoing a little of the bodily evils to which humanity is subject.

Thanking you for the kind good wishes so beautifully expressed in the end of your letter[3] and reciprocating them with all my heart I remain my dear Storrow

Ever affectionately yours
Washington Irving

Thomas W Storrow Esqr

MANUSCRIPT: Harvard.

Below the signature on manuscript page 3 is written, presumably in Storrow's hand: "(Died / Nov. 28 / 59)"

1. WI had received a letter from Storrow on August 6. See PMI's unpublished

journal (NYPL), August 6, 1859. PMI does not record the receipt of the letter to which WI is responding.

2. Sulfur melted down and cast into rolls and formerly used in the treatment of rheumatism. See W. A. Newman Dorland, *The American Illustrated Medical Dictionary* (Philadelphia, 1943), p. 1409; and *Stedman's Medical Dictionary*, 21st ed. (Baltimore, 1966), p. 1545.

3. This letter has not been located.

2620.   *To Irving Paris*

Sunnyside Sept 7t. 1859

My dear Irving

I am sadly disappointed at finding, by Sarahs last letter to you, that we must give up all hope of a visit from her and her children this autumn.

The protracted lameness of poor Susie must be a constant cause of anxiety to Sarah, but I am happy to learn that the Surgeons assure her of a perfect cure, "only requiring care and patience"

I return you Sarahs two letters.

Your affectionate Uncle
Washington Irving

Irving Paris Esqr

ADDRESSED: Irving Paris Esqr / No 15 Nassau St. / N York   POSTMARKED: [*unrecovered*] // U. S. MAIL / 4. P. M. / DELIVERY
MANUSCRIPT: SHR.

On the center fold of the verso of the letter sheet WI wrote "Irving Paris Esqr".

2620a.   *To Daniel W. Fiske*

Sunnyside Oct 6. 1859

My dear Mr Fiske,

I was far from considering your request[1] a bold one—but I had scruples about putting on record an opinion as to the comparative merits of the portraits of Washington which had been furnished by the proprietors or artists for the illustration of my work.[2]

I was suffering under an attack of nerves at the time of recieving your letter so that I could not immediately reply to it, and commissioned my nephew Mr Pierre M Irving to call on you and make an explanation

I regret extremely that we no longer have you at the Astor Library[3]

though, since my tedious indisposition, I am rarely there myself. I hope your new situation[4] is agreeable and advantageous to you.

Believe me with high esteem and regard

Yours very truly
Washington Irving

D. W Fiske Esqr.

MANUSCRIPT: Library of Century Association, New York City.

1. This letter has not been located.

2. In an appendix to his biography of Washington WI included H. T. Tuckerman's "Portraits of Washington," which describes various likenesses of the first president. See *Life of George Washington* (New York: G. P. Putnam, 1859), V, 325–353.

3. Fiske was assistant librarian at the Astor Library from 1852 to 1859. WI was trustee of the library during this time.

4. Fiske had taken the position of general secretary of the American Geographical Society, a post which he held for about a year.

2621.   To Charles A. Davis

Sunnyside Oct 18, 1859

My dear Davis

I hope you will excuse me for being in such a hurry and worry when I met you yesterday in the street.[1] I had just come to town, unexpectedly, for the first time since last I visited you in University Place,[2] and was fearful I had taken cold, having been chilled on my way down. I hope to be in town in the course of a few days when I will report myself at No 1. and have a long talk with you. Your recent letters[3] have been very interesting to me and I would have answered them promptly and amply but I was not in the vein for letter writing. I have had a *put back* since last I saw you, and for a time was good for nothing for all social purposes; but I am now under good head way and hope soon to make a good report of myself and to answer your kind letters by word of mouth[4]

The exercise of the pen at present is extremely irksome to me

Ever with affectionate regard / Yours very truly
Washington Irving

Ch. Aug Davis Esqr

MANUSCRIPT: SHR.

In the upper left corner of MS page 1 is written: *"Irvings last"*
On page 3, which WI had not used, Davis later wrote the following note:

"*Memo*—I met him (on my way to Grand Jury Duty) in Waverly Place—two days before date of this—say 16 Oct—he seem'd unwell but I could not join him & beg'd him to go to No. 1—University Place—this was the last time I met him. He came to town two weeks or so after—& took his lunch at our House ↑with my wife↓ & spent two hours there—but I was not at Home—he left warm regards for me—this was his last visit to town Vide P. M Irving's Letter to me 17 Decr 1859 He died on 28 Nov—just 40 days after Date of this letter & was buried *1 Decr* 1859"

1. WI had visited his dentist in the city on October 17. See PMI's unpublished journal (NYPL), October 17, 1859.

2. Davis resided at No. 1 University Place.

3. These have not been located.

4. WI visited the Davis home on November 5, although Davis was absent at the time. See Davis's memo above and PMI's unpublished journal (NYPL), November 3–8, 1859.

2622.   *To ——— Bellow*

[March 27, n.y.]

Mr W Irving regrets extremely that he will not be in town on Friday evening next to avail himself of Mr Bellow's obliging invitation.

Wednesday.
March 27th.

MANUSCRIPT: Yale.

2623.   *To Henry Brevoort, Jr.*

[1810–1811?]

Dr Brevoort,

I have just met in the Streets a virginian friend, Williams Carter Esqr.,[1] who was a great crony of mine at Paris—he leaves town on Saturday in the Steam boat in company with A Mr Roots of Virginia, on their way to Niagara. I wish you & Jim[2] would call on them at Mechanic Hall.[3] Carter is a hale, hearty, laughing fellow—whom you may reccollect I have mentioned as being so notorious for his marvellous performances in Palais Royal[4]—⟨[*unrecovered*]⟩ which place he could not approach within half a mile, without an insurrection of the members of the lower house.

Yours Ever
W. I.

P S. I shall be in town tomorrow afternoon to accompany them to the circus[5]—

MANUSCRIPT: Knox College Library.

The tentative date is established by the references to the Mechanics Hall and to the circus.

1. WI had dined with a Carter in Paris on June 7, 1805. Probably this is the same friend. See J&N, I, 426.

2. James Kirke Paulding.

3. Mechanics Hall, at the corner of Park Place and Broadway, was built in 1810. It became a leading hotel within a few years. Later it was known as the Park Place Hotel. See James Grant Wilson, *The Memorial History of New-York* (New York, 1893), III, 257.

4. Probably these performances occurred during the summer of 1805, when WI did not place entries in his notebook.

5. The Pepin and Breschard circus performed at Broadway and Anthony Street from June 21 to September 29, 1810, and from June 18 to September 28, 1811. It had also operated in 1808 and 1809. See Odell, *NY Stage*, II, 306, 325, 346–47, 375.

2624.   To Joseph G. Cogswell

[April 8, n.y.]

My dear Cogswell,

I will call on you tomorrow morning at ten oclock.

Yours very truly
Washington Irving

April 8th.

MANUSCRIPT: NYPL—Montague Collection.

2625.   To Joseph G. Cogswell

[Spring, 1842?]

My dear Cogswell,

Your letter of credit is not enclosed in this despatch, but will be delivered to you when you come to Washington.

Yours truly
Washington Irving

ADDRESSED: Joseph G. Cogswell Esqr.
MANUSCRIPT: Va.–Barrett.

This note may have been written in the spring of 1842, when Cogswell had been asked by WI to consider the post of secretary of the U.S. legation in Madrid.

2626. To Robert Donaldson

[March 17, n.y.]

My dear Sir,

I return you the designs which are beautiful. If I can find time and vein to communicate any thing for the periodical work proposed I will do it with pleasure: but I cannot promise. I am so fagged with the labor of the pen in my own pursuits; and so little master of my leisure, that I fear to make any engagements, which I may not be able to fulfil—

Very truly yours
Washington Irving

March 17th.

ADDRESSED: Robert Donaldson Esqr / State Street
MANUSCRIPT: Va.–Barrett.

2627. To William Frick

[March 23, n.y.]

Dear Sir:

I regret extremely that I cannot accept your kind invitation, as I expect to leave town tomorrow morning

Very truly yours
Washington Irving

Friday, March 22d.

ADDRESSED: Wm Frick Esqr
MANUSCRIPT: Peabody Library.

If Frick is from the Philadelphia area, the year may be 1839. WI had been in Philadelphia on March 22, 1839, for the wedding of Irving Van Wart and Sarah Ames. In a letter to Sarah Van Wart, written on March 26, 1839, WI said, "I have just returned" to New York.

2628.   *To Angelica Hamilton*

[n.d., n.y.]

My dear Miss Hamilton,

If Mr. Everett had never given any other proof of talent, this address would have been sufficient to give him a splendid & lasting reputation.

It is *magnificent!*

Yours ever
Washington Irving

Monday Morning

MANUSCRIPT: MHS.

At the top of the sheet is written "Copy of a note from Mr. Washington Irving to Miss Angelica Hamilton."

WI is probably alluding to the lecture on George Washington which Edward Everett delivered in New York on March 3, 1856, and again on March 18, 1857. (See WI to Edward Everett, February 6, 1856; and to Thomas W. Olcott et al., March 14, 1857.) It is not possible to determine which of these lectures WI is referring to or to ascertain the precise date of his note.

2629.   *To Angelica Hamilton*

[May 30, n.y.]

My dear Miss Angelica,

I have not forgotten my promise and shall be with you tomorrow at five

Yours very truly
Washington Irving

Sunnyside, May 30th

MANUSCRIPT: Boston Public Library.

2630.   *To William Harness*

[n.d., n.y.]

Dr Harness

The anecdotes to which I referred concerning the three worthies of Bermuda are scattered in *Stiths History of Virginia*,[1] which may be found in the British Museum. I have not the work at Hand, or would cull them out for you.

Yours truly

W I

MANUSCRIPT: Folger Shakespeare Library.

William Harness (1790–1869) was a liberal English clergyman, friend of Lord Byron, and editor of Elizabethan dramatists, including Shakespeare (8 vols., 1825), Philip Massinger (1830), and John Ford (1831).

It has not been determined if WI related the anecdotes to Harness personally or if Harness read them in "The Three Kings of Bermuda" in *Wolfert's Roost* (1855) or in the magazine version which appeared in *Knickerbocker's Magazine* for January, 1840. WI may have met Harness either during his secretaryship of the U.S. legation between 1829 and 1832 or on one of his visits to England from Spain between 1842 and 1846.

1. William Stith (1689–1755), a president of William and Mary College, wrote *The History of the First Discovery and Settlement of Virginia,* which was published in Williamsburg in 1746.

2631. To Pierre M. Irving

[n.d., n.y.]

Brotherhood is a holy alliance made by God and imprinted in our hearts, and we should adhere to it with religious faith. The more kindly and scrupulously we observe its dictates, the happier for us.

PUBLISHED: PMI, II, 14.

2632. To Pierre M. Irving

[n.d., n.y.]

My dear Pierre,

The state of the weather will prevent my coming to town to day. Perhaps I may to morrow—when I shall be happy to have a nest either at Mrs Lows or the Waverley

Yours affly

W I.

Thursday mrg

ADDRESSED: Pierre M. Irving
MANUSCRIPT: SHR.

2633. *To Edward W. Lorenz*

Sunnyside Aug 5t 18[*MS torn*]

Dear Sir,
One of the best rewards an author can derive from his labors is to
be assured that his writings have awakened such feelings towards him
as those expressed in your letter which lies before me
Be assured I should have considered the Salutation you say you were
tempted to offer me last Sunday as any thing ⟨but⟩ ↑rather than↓ an
officious obtrusion, and should have been most happy to take you
cordially by the hand
With great respect

Your truly obliged friend
Washington Irving

Edward W Lorenz Esqr

MANUSCRIPT: SHR.

2634. *To Catharine Paris?*

[n.d., n.y.]

Fare well my dear Sister. Let me hear from you soon; give my love
to all the households, and believe me your affectionate brother

Washington Irving

MANUSCRIPT: Va.–Barrett.

2635. *To Sarah Paris*

[Before March 31, 1841]

My dear Sarah
I regret to say that I cannot accept Mrs Jones kind invitation, being

engaged to dine today at Mr William Astors. I will call and see you after church.

Your affectionate uncle
W. Irving

Sunday Morning

ADDRESSED: Miss Paris
MANUSCRIPT: Yale.

WI wrote this note to Sarah Paris before her marriage to Thomas W. Storrow, Jr. on March 31, 1841.

2636. To George P. Putnam

[n.d., n.y.]

My dear Sir,
I have seen the portrait of Washington at Mr Wolfes. It is a mere copy of Stewarts.

Yours truly
W. I.

Thursday Morning.

MANUSCRIPT: Yale.

At the bottom of the page in another hand is written "Washington Irving."

2637. To George P. Putnam

[n.d., n.y.]

My Dear Sir
I leave the MS poem the Vision of Columbus; for the Author. I will thank you to write his name—(which I forget) on the parcel. I must decline giving any written opinion about it, but will give him my opinion ⟨whe⟩ of it when we meet.

Yours truly
W I

ADDRESSED: Geo. P Putnam Esq   DOCKETED: Washington / Irving / letter was in / his book "History / of New York."
MANUSCRIPT: Stanford University Library.

2638.   To Thomas Ramsay

Sunnyside June 7h. [n.y.]

My dear Sir

I feel much obliged to you for your offer of friendly services in England; but have no commission at present with which to tax your kindness. Hoping that your return there may be a happy one, but that you may carry with you cordial ties sufficiently strong to draw you back again to this country

I remain, my dear Sir,

Yours, with great regard
Washington Irving

Thomas Ramsay Esqr.

Manuscript: Yale.

2639.   To [Abraham?] Schermerhorn

[n.d., n.y.]

My dear Schermerhorn,

As I do not leave town tomorrow (Monday) I will come and dine with you if you will receive me. If so let me know your hour.

Yours very truly
Washington Irving

Sunday Evening.

Manuscript: SHR.

2640.   To Miss R. D. Smith

[February 28, n.y.]

Mr Washington Irving regrets that he cannot have the honor of availing himself of Miss R D Smiths polite invitation for this evening

Feb 28th. / 46. Twenty first St East

Addressed: Miss R D Smith / 691 Broadway
Manuscript: HSP.

2641. To Mrs. Smith

[December 11, n.y.]

Mr W Irving presents his compliments to Mrs Smith and regrets that absence from town will prevent his having the pleasure of waiting on her on Thursday Evening next.

Wednesday, Decr. 11th.

MANUSCRIPT: Connecticut State Library.

Although December 11 fell on Wednesday in 1805, 1811, 1816, 1822, 1833, 1839, 1844, and 1850, it is not possible to determine whether the date is 1811, 1833, 1839, or 1850. On the other dates he was in Europe.

2642. To Sarah Van Wart

[1837 or before]

I have no news to tell you, and indeed only write to draw a reply from you.

I send with this a letter from Mrs Storrow, who seems to entertain for you the friendship of an old intimate. I hope the boys [*rest of line cut away*]

* * * * * *

God bless you my dear Sister. Do not fail to write immediately, and do not let Mr Van Wart carry the letter for three or four days in his pocket. With my best love to all I am

Your affectionate Brother
Washington Irving

MANUSCRIPT: Cornell University Library.

This manuscript is a fragment of a letter with writing on both sides. The tentative date is ascertained by the allusion to Mrs. Thomas W. Storrow, who died in 1837.

2643. To Jonathan M. Wainwright

[1854 or before]

My dear Sir,

I am sorry to be so troublesome but if you have procured the volume of the Universal History & can let me have it by three O'clock you will greatly oblige me. I wish to put it in a parcel with my M. S. to be sent into the country prior to my leaving town for Boston.

Very truly yours
Washington Irving

Friday⎫ ½ past 11.
Morng⎭

ADDRESSED: Rev. J. M. Wainwright
MANUSCRIPT: Connecticut Historical Society.

Jonathan M. Wainwright (1793–1854) was an Episcopal clergyman long associated with Grace Church and Trinity Church in New York City. In 1852 he was consecrated as bishop of New York City.

2644.   To General ———

[n.d., n.y.]

My dear General,
I regret sincerely that I have to decline your most kind invitation being so much out of order with cold, catarrh and I hardly know what, that I am in no condition for society and only fit to keep at home and be nursed.

Yours very truly
Washington Irving

Sunnyside–Friday Morning

DOCKETED: Sunnyside / Washington Irving
MANUSCRIPT: NYPL–WI Papers.

The addressee may be George Pope Morris, who lived up the Hudson River beyond Tarrytown.

2645.   To ———

Sunnyside Feb. 26t. [n.y.]

My dear Sir,
We will all be very happy to join you and yours at tea, and I will be happy to accompany you to meet the Committee at ½ past 2.

Yours very truly
Washington Irving

MANUSCRIPT: SHR.

2646.   To ———

                                              [February 29, 1820 or 1848]

My dear Sir,
    It will give me great pleasure to dine with you tomorrow.

                                              very truly yours
                                              Washington Irving
Tuesday / Feb. 29h. [1820 or 1848]

MANUSCRIPT: Va.–Barrett.

According to the perpetual calendar, February 29 fell on Tuesday in 1820 and
1848 during WI's lifetime.

2647.   To ———

                                              [Friday, April 25, n.y.]

My dear Sir,
    I regret extremely that my engagements for this evening will not permit
me to avail myself of your kind invitation to the club.

                                              Very truly yours
                                              Washington Irving
Friday. April 25th.

MANUSCRIPT: Va.–Barrett.

April 25 fell on Friday in 1800, 1806, 1817, 1823, 1828, 1834, 1845, and 1851
during WI's adulthood. The exact year of this note cannot be determined from
the context.

2648.   To ———

                                              [May 7, n.y.]

My dear Sir,
    You had better call on me tomorrow when you are ready, and we will
take the nearest coach. ⟨If⟩ Two oclock will suit me perfectly well, & in-

deed I should like to be at the coach by that time, as I wish to enjoy a little of the country & to have time to do justice to Matthews cabinet of curiosities.

Yours truly
W Irving.

Tuesday. May 7th.

Manuscript: Middlebury College Library.

May 7 fell on Tuesday in 1805, 1811, 1816, 1822, 1833, 1839, 1844, and 1850. "Matthews" may refer to Cornelius Mathews (1817–1889), a New York writer and editor.

2649.   *To* ———

[June 26, n.y.]

My dear Sir,

I accept with great pleasure your invitation to dinner on Saturday next

Yours very truly
Washington Irving

Sunnyside / Tuesday June 26th

Manuscript: Andrew B. Myers.

During WI's residence at Sunnyside June 26 fell on Tuesday in 1838, 1849, and 1855. From the context of the note it has not been possible to determine the precise year.

2650.   *To* ———

[After 1836]

My dear Sir,

I accept Mr Corts conditions with great pleasure. We dine at four O clock.

Yours truly
Washington Irving

Sunnyside. Tuesday morng

Manuscript: Yale.

The letter is dated after 1836, the time when WI moved into Sunnyside.

2651. *To* ———

Sunnyside, Thursday Evg [1854?]

My dear Sir

I thank you for your kind enquiries. This is my well day and so far I have got on very well. To night I expect the fever and the doctor; the latter however has given me a supply of pills to battle off the former.

I am sorry to find the *Dear man* is to give way to such a man as myself who just now hold myself rather cheap.

Yours very truly
Washington Irving

MANUSCRIPT: Va.–Barrett.

The name of the village of Dearman was changed to Irvington in April, 1854, so this letter was written after that date, perhaps to the neighbor who had informed WI of the new name. See PMI, IV, 173.

2652. *To* ———

[n.d., n.y.]

I have at different times recieved Vols. 1. 3. 4. 5. 6. 7. & 9. of the Colonial documents of New York.[1] Vols. 2 and 8 are wanting to make the set so far complete. I have two copies of the 3d. volume.

very respectfully / Your obt Servt.
Washington Irving

MANUSCRIPT: Stanford University Library.

Since this small piece of paper contains only the last paragraph, complimentary close, and signature, it is probably part of a larger sheet. It may be written to Henry S. Randall, who had sent WI some of the volumes earlier on behalf of the Regents of the State of New York. See WI to Randall, January 3, 1854.

Probably the letter was written during or after 1855, the date of publication of volume 9.

1. *Documents Relative to the Colonial History of the State of New York* (Albany, 1853–1887).

2653. *To* ——

[n.d., n.y.]

My dear Sir,
     It will give me very great pleasure to dine with you on Saturday next—

Very truly yours
Washington Irving

MANUSCRIPT: British Library.

2654. *To Miss Rhinelander*

May 24 [n.y.]

     The young ladies from Mrs. O'Kill's school have just called to say that . . . they did not get their invitation for last evening until this morning. . . . They express great sorrow for the disappointment and so did my nieces, until, seeing so much tribulation it occurred to me that the whole matter might be remedied by . . . having the party this evening. This cleared up their countenances in an instant and the matter was arranged accordingly. Your company and that of your brother is alone wanting to put affairs on a right footing and make the happiness of all parties complete.

PUBLISHED: *The Collector*, 55 (June, 1947), 138, item A1032.

Possibly this letter was written in the early 1850's. WI mentions the Rhinelanders, who lived in the vicinity of Sunnyside, in a letter to Sarah Storrow on July 15, 1852.

2655. *To* ——

[Wednesday, 18, n.y.]

Worthy and dear Sir,
     As our intermittent mail has not arrived today, and there is danger of our getting behind hand in the history of the world, which turns round so fast, I will be much obliged to you for the loan of a newspaper when all your household have done with it.

Yours truly
Washington Irving

Sunnyside. Wednesday. 18th.

MANUSCRIPT: SHR.

This note may be addressed to Moses H. Grinnell, WI's neighbor at Sunnyside for many years. As Grinnell went regularly to Manhattan by railroad or steam yacht, he would presumably bring back with him a newspaper from the city.

2656. *To the director of the Phoenix Bank*

[n.d., n.y.]

Mr. W. Irving regrets that previous engagements prevent his having the honor of accepting the obliging invitation of the Director of the Phoenix Bank to dinner.

PUBLISHED: Kenneth Rendell Catalog, July, 1978.

APPENDIX I

Newly Located Letters

105a.   To Isaac Carow

Washington, Novr. 16th. 1812.

Dear Sir,

I received a letter[1] from you ⟨a few⟩ two or three days since, and should have answered it sooner had there been any thing particular to communicate. By this days mail we have received various letters and certificates from New York, and are promised more. These we will communicate tomorrow to the Committees,[2] and doubt not but they will be of importance in strengthening our statements.

Our business goes on slowly. The Committees of both houses have given us very full and candid hearings. the committees from Philadelphia and ⟨New Y⟩ Boston have likewise been heard before the Committee of the lower house this morning. Their statement agreed with ours, and after they had been heard ⟨over⟩ the amount of our testimony was read to them and they corroborated it entirely. They mention that our testimony has been written out at length and with great clearness and ability, so as to make a very plain, and eloquent appeal. There was a report yesterday that the committee of the lower house had determined to report in our favour, 4 to 3. If so they must have reconsidered the question for I fear that the committee stands divided, three being for a favourable report and three for referring it to Gallatin. One of the committee ⟨is⟩ (Mr Bibb)[3] is dangerously sick, should he be enabled to vote I am told it would be for referring it to Gallatin. There is not however, perfect confidence to be placed in these reports. I should not be surprised however, if the business is ultimately placed in Gallatin's hands; who, no doubt would be for making a bargain ⟨of⟩ out of us, perhaps obliging us to subscribe to the loan—this however is but conjecture, for on the whole I am satisfied Gallatin is favourable to us.

You will perceive ⟨upon the whole⟩ from what I have said that at present we are quite in a state of uncertainty, and though I look forward with steady hope to the ultimate result, yet I apprehend considerable trouble and anxiety before we extricate ourselves.

Mr Tiernan and other gentlemen[4] forming a committee from Baltimore have just arrived. The former appears to be a shrewd and active man and I anticipate ⟨great⟩ ↑considerable↓ assistance to our cause from him.

If the committee determine on reporting favourably I suppose the report will be made the day after tomorrow, or the day after. Should any thing occur in the mean time worthy of communicating you will hear from some one or other of us; in the mean time you may depend on our unremitting assiduity.

with great regard / Your friend & Servant
Washington Irving

Mr Isaac Carow.

ADDRESSED: Mr Isaac Carow / Merchant / New York.   POSTMARKED: [unre-
  covered] / NOV / 17   DOCKETED: Washington Irving / 16 Nover 1812
MANUSCRIPT: SHR.

Isaac Carow (1778–1850), a shipper and merchant who was born on St. Croix of Huguenot parents, was a member of the New York importing and merchandising firm of Kennet and Carow. He later was very active in the New York Chamber of Commerce.

1. This letter has not been located.
2. The House and Senate Committees on Ways and Means held numerous hearings on the subject of remitting or imposing forfeitures on the bonds on goods imported from Great Britain after the revocation of the British orders in council. The Treasury Department had seized these goods and had given bonds on their value. Albert Gallatin, the secretary of the treasury, refused to make the final decision in settling the case, and so it was referred to Congress for final disposition. See Henry Adams, *The Life of Albert Gallatin* (New York, 1943), pp. 472–73. The spokesmen for the New York merchants were WI, John G. Coster, and Abraham Lawrence. See *Annals of Congress,* 12th Cong., 2d sess., pp. 1250–63, 1268–74.
3. William W. Bibb (1780–1820) was a Congressman from Georgia.
4. Luke Tiernan, Philip E. Thomas, and Evan Thomas represented the Baltimore merchants. See *Annals of Congress,* 12th Cong., 2d sess., p. 1259.

105b.   To Isaac Carow

Washington, Novr. 21st. 1812.

Dear Sir,

I have just received your letter,[1] and though I have nothing particular to communicate, yet as I know you must be anxious to hear any thing from Washington, I will endeavour to scrawl a few lines. Our business is in much the same state as it has been for three or four days past. The Committees are occupied in deliberating upon it, and the Committee of ways and means in collecting every tag and rag of evidence they can lay their hands on. We were before them a few moments last evening and left the Philadelphia and Boston Committees with them, whom they finished examining last evening. Before we left them I took occasion (as we had before done after each examination) to mention explicitly that having produced abundance of testimony to refute any misrepresentations and dispel any prejudices that might exist as to the Merchants having put the amount of the bonds on their sales, we now reverted to what was our original and what we still considered as our strong and real ground of petition, the perfect innocency of our intention in shipping; which was grounded on a faith in the declarations of our Government, and the assurances of the diplomatic character then resident in England Indeed Mr Russel[2] in the morning had informed me that he had advised the Merchants to ship after the revocation of the orders in council; considering them as perfectly safe: And as the committee have requested his testimony before them I doubt not they have had ample satisfaction on that head.

Our examinations have been rather irksome, but I must say they have treated us with great respect and delicacy; and indeed have more than once taken occasion to pay the New York committee the handsomest compliments. Our statement will be laid before the house at full length. I am told Gallatin is to give them an opinion in writing.[3] I believe on the whole that he is favourable to us, but I rather think that he wants to get the business put in his hands; and if possible to induce ⟨from⟩ some compromising offers on our part. I have so full a conviction of the honesty of our cause, and am so satisfied that both as to motives of equity and policy the ⟨men⟩ houses of congress will find it necessary to listen to our petition, that I ⟨ha⟩ cannot suffer myself to dispond as to the ultimate event; though I look forward to much delay embarrassment and vexation in the struggle for our rights. As to the apprehended attack on our city; there has been a little talk of it hear. Admiral Warren[4] has sailed from Halifax; but it is now supposed he means to make a cruize and then go in to winter at Bermuda.

As to the chattering chap Whom you seem to consider as somewhat dangerous, he arrived here the other day in forty seven hours from New York by god sir—never takes more than fifty sir,—never sir,—means to sit down here for the winter—has tended congress for seven years sir, and means to tend it whenever he can sir—" But my dear Sir dont suffer yourself to think for a moment of such an arrant mountebank; at present he has affairs of his own to occupy his shallow head, and fears, ↑too much,↓ I have no doubt, the strength of our standing here, to meddle with us. If he should do so in the most trivial manner, I will make him such an object of ridic[ule] [MS torn] and scorn, that he shall raise a smile of merriment and contempt wherever he appears. But this is an unnecessary threat of which you need say nothing.

When any thing important occurs you shall hear from us. In the mean time let my Brothers know that I have nothing to inform them of and believe me with great respect

Your friend & Servt.
Washington Irving

Mr Isaac Carow.

ADDRESSED: Mr Isaac Carow / Pearl Street / New York.   POSTMARKED: [unre-covered] / NOV / 21   DOCKETED: W Irving 21st / Novem 1812
MANUSCRIPT: SHR.

1. This letter has not been located.
2. Probably John W. Russel, a New York merchant whose ships, the *Minerva* and the *Olive Branch,* were engaged in the Liverpool trade. See Scoville, *Old Merchants of NYC,* III, 112.
3. Albert Gallatin wrote to the Congressmen on November 18, 1812, outlining his position; on November 23 he reiterated it. After extensive debate the House, on December 23, approved, by a vote of 64 to 61, a Senate bill directing remission of forfeiture of the merchants' bonds and the payment of duties equivalent to those on regularly imported goods. See *Annals of Congress,* 12th Cong., 2d sess., pp. 214–350, 355–62, 366–91, 394–402, 403–4, 441–42; Henry Adams, *The Life of Albert Gallatin,* pp. 472–73.
4. Sir John Borlase Warren (1753–1822), who had participated in naval engagements during the American revolution and Britain's war with France, was promoted to the rank of admiral in 1810.

416a.   To Mrs. Gibbings

[March 10, 1824]

It would give me great pleasure my dear Madam to accept of Mrs Fairfax's[1] kind invitation but I have a nephew[2] ill at my lodgings with a virulent attack of the Smallpox whom I cannot quit—and indeed under such circumstances it would be improper for me to visit & run the risk of communicating contagion.

With kind compliments to Dr and Miss Gibbings

I am very faithfully / Your obliged
Washington Irving

Wednesday March 10. [1824]

MANUSCRIPT: Andrew B. Myers.

Mrs. Gibbings was a member of the English-speaking circle in which WI circulated in Paris. See *J&N*, III, 279, 282, and passim.

1. Mrs. Fairfax was another of WI's English-speaking acquaintances in Paris.

2. Irving Van Wart had become ill on March 2, with his ailment finally diagnosed as smallpox on March 9. He convalesced through the following week. See *J&N*, III, 298–304.

491a.   To Gulian Verplanck

Paris, July 20th. 1825.

My dear Verplanck,

Permit me to reccommend to your friendly offices Mr Berteau,[1] who is about departing for America, with the intention of teaching music and the French language. You have no doubt heard of him from your Brother, who has boarded for some months in his family. I feel great interest in the success of Mr Berteau, from a knowledge of his merit, and from the friendship I feel for his family, and I can reccommend him most confidently ⟨to the⟩ as a well educated, well bred and in every way a deserving Young man—I beg therefore, should his views lead him to New York, that You will do every thing in Your power to promote his Success.

With constant regard & esteem

Your friend
Washington Irving

MANUSCRIPT: Andrew B. Myers.

For details about Verplanck see WI's letter of November 6, 1830, to him.

1. Berteau was the son of a French couple with whom WI became acquainted in Paris through the Storrows. See *J&N*, III, 414, 429, 441, 443, 446, and passim.

680a.   To Lieutenant-Colonel Campbell

Seville, April 21st. 1829

My dear Colonel Campbell,

The bearer of this letter is Sebastian Becker[1] whom I have forwarded to Gibraltar according to the request of Col. Chapman,[2] to enter into his service as an Upper Servant. I can recommend him from my own experience for integrity, sobriety, cleanliness and an excellent disposition. He acquitted himself well in performing all the service of a mere

Bachelors establishment, which however, could be no test of his abilities in a service like that of Col Chapman, but I have learnt from other sources, that he has given great satisfaction to English families which he has served. Of his abilities Col. Chapman will soon be able to judge, and I hope and trust they will prove satisfactory His moral character is in every respect excellent[.] I have advanced ten dollars to him for his travelling expenses,[3] agreeably to the letter of Col. Chapman. The same can be repaid to Mr Henry[4] for me.

Present my kindest remembrances to Mrs Campbell and believe me ever, my dear Sir

Very faithfully your friend
Washington Irving.

ADDRESSED: Lieut Col. Campbell / Royal Artillery / Gibraltar   DOCKETED: Washington Irving
MANUSCRIPT: Andrew B. Myers.

1. Becker had been WI's servant in Puerto de Santa Maria. See WI to Thomas W. Storrow, October 22, 1828, and to ————, December 5, 1828.

2. Colonel Chapman was a British officer stationed at Gibraltar. For other comments about him see WI to Bernard Henry, May 13 and June 3, 1829.

3. WI refers to "60$ mentioned by Col Chapman" in his letter to Bernard Henry, June 3, 1829.

4. Bernard Henry was the American consul at Gibraltar.

748a. To Wilmington Fleming

[ca. December 10, 1829]

Sir,

On returning from the country recently[1] I found your note[2] and the copies of the Gentleman King[3] which you had the kindness to send me. I had intended to reply to your note as soon as I had perused the work; but from the hurry of various occupations in the present agitated times and in consequence of the indisposition of the Minister[4] I really have [not][5] had a moment to give to literary occupations. I feel very much obliged to you for the honor you have done me in sending ⟨my⟩ your work—and beg you will accept my sincere acknowledgement.

I have the honor to be

Your very obt. Servt
Washington Irving

Wilmington Fleming Esqr

ADDRESSED: Wilmington Fleming Esq / Castle St Long Acre   DOCKETED: Washington Irving
MANUSCRIPT: NYPL.

Wilmington Fleming had brought out *The Destroying Angel, A Fragment; The Captive Boy and Other Poems* in London in 1825. Other biographical details have not been found.

The approximate date can be determined by the reference to WI's return from the country (actually a visit to the Van Warts in Birmingham for several days in early December of 1829) and by WI's reference to the indisposition of the American minister, Louis McLane, who, after arriving in London on September 17, 1829, was bothered by a stomach disorder for several months. See WI to John Howard Payne, December 7, 1829; and John Munroe, *Louis McLane*, pp. 269–270.

1. WI had returned to London on December 7, 1829. See WI to John Howard Payne, December 7, 1829; and PMI, II, 422.

2. This note has not been located.

3. *The Gentleman King* is not listed in the *British Museum General Catalogue of Printed Books*, the *Library of Congress Catalog of Books*, or other registers of publication.

4. Louis McLane.

5. WI omitted the bracketed word.

780a. To Richard Cattermole

Argyll Street / April 16. 1830

Sir,

Absence from town[1] has prevented my replying at an earlier date to your note of the 5 inst.[2]

I cannot sufficiently express my deep & grateful sense of the very flattering mark of appreciation with which the Royal Society of Literature have thought proper to honor me;[3] and shall not fail to attend at the day and hour you have mentioned.[4]

I have the honor to be Sir

Very respectfully / Your obt humble Servt.
Washington Irving

Richard Cattermole Esqr
&c.   &c.   &c.

MANUSCRIPT: Library of the University of Exeter.

Richard Cattermole (1795?–1858) was a cleric who served as secretary of the Royal Society of Literature from its organization in 1823 until 1852.

1. The purpose and extent of WI's absence from London has not been determined. He may have visited the Van Warts in Birmingham at Easter, which occurred on April 11.

2. This letter is printed in PMI, II, 429.

3. The Royal Society of Literature awarded WI one of its fifty guinea gold medals. For other details see WI to William Sotheby, April 26, 1830.

4. The ceremony for presenting the medal was set for April 29, 1830 at 3 o'clock at the quarters of the Society on Parliament Street. See PMI, II, 429.

810a.   To T. P. Platt

8 Argyll Street / July 17th. 1830

Sir,

Having found the letters received by me relative to the translation of Mr Hodgson,[1] I hasten to give you a note of their purport. One is from Mr William Shaler,[2] who resided for many years at Algiers as American Consul, and published about three years since, a work called Sketches of Algiers.[3] He informs me that Mr Hodgson was several years employed in his consulate, in the study of the Oriental languages, during which time he availed himself of certain favorable circumstances to investigate the Berber or Ancient Libyan Language which is preserved among the mountains of North Africa in which he succeeded beyond Mr Shalers most Sanguine expectations. In the course of these investigations he found means to obtain a translation of the Gospels, and the book of Genesis into this language, "for the fidelity of which he can allege the strongest presumptive ⟨proof⟩ evidence," such indeed, adds Mr Shaler "as it appears to me must be satisfactory to all who are able to judge of the case."

Mr Hodgson speaking of the Translation ⟨says⟩ mentions his being in correspondence with you about the purchase of it, and says also, "The American Bible Society are now proposing to obtain this MS. and I of course shall dispose of it where I can obtain the best price. The value of the Manuscript may be inferred from the difficulties surmounted in procuring it.

1st. The acquisition of the Arabic as a medium

2d. To find a native Berber, qualified for the work This was a mere accident in my case,[4] and had it not been for the influence which the U.S Consulate enjoyed under Mr Shaler, perhaps from the jealousy of the Algerine Govt. I should not have been able to retain my *Taleb* or Teacher.

3d. There are few languages spoken by so immense a population which gives it important to the Bible Society.

4. The execution of the work by any individual would require a labor of 2 or 3 years."

Such Sir are the parts of the letters which bear upon the subject of

Mr Hodgsons translation. You will perceive they ⟨give me⟩ state no definite price for the MS. in question; and I profess my utter incompetency to judge what remuneration would meet his idea of the value of his labours, or would be warranted by the actual importance of the translation. It is a matter entirely out of my own walk of literature, and one in which you are much more competent to judge. I shall be happy to communicate to Mr Hogdson any offer that the British & Foreign Bible Society may be disposed to make,[5] and in the mean time remain

> Sir— / very respectfully / Your obdt. Hbl Servant
> Washington Irving

MANUSCRIPT: The British and Foreign Bible Society, London.

Thomas Pell Platt (1798–1852), B. A. (1820), M. A. (1823), Trinity College, Cambridge, began his association with the British and Foreign Bible Society while he was in college. A specialist in Ethiopic texts, he published a catalogue of Ethiopic Biblical manuscripts in the Bible Society and in the Royal Library of Paris, and he subsequently edited Ethiopic texts for the Society and prepared an edition of the Syriac Gospels, which was published in 1829.

Platt is established as recipient of this letter from a note in the minutes of the Editorial Sub-Committee of the Bible Society for July 22, 1830 which mentions "a letter . . . from Washington Irving Esq., addressed to T. P. Platt Esq. and dated the 17th inst." Information from Miss Kathleen Cann, Archivist, British and Foreign Bible Society, concerning details used in the notes for this letter.

1. William B. Hodgson (1800–1871), who returned to the United States after serving in the American consulate in Algiers, had written to Platt on June 15, 1829; November 26, 1829; and May 25, 1830 concerning his translation of St. Luke in Kabyle, the Berber language of Algeria. In the last letter he indicates that he is sending it through WI. WI's letter to Platt accompanied Hodgson's letter.

2. William Shaler (c. 1773–1833) was consul at Algiers from 1816 to 1828. From 1830 until his death from cholera he was consul at Havana.

3. *Sketches of Algiers, Political, Historical, and Civil* (Boston: Cummings, Hilliard and Company, 1826) was a careful, accurate description based on Shaler's observations.

4. Hodgson was assisted in his translation by Sidi Hamet, a Berber. See T. H. Darlow and H. F. Moule, *Historical Catalogue of the Printed Editions of Holy Scripture in the Library of the British and Foreign Bible Society* (London: Bible House, 1911), II, 855.

5. It is not known if the Society used WI as its agent, but his letter of December 17, 1830 indicates that Hodgson had received and accepted the Society's offer to purchase the manuscript for £150.

853a. To T. P. Platt

8 Argyll Street. Decr. 17th. 1830

Sir,

I have just received a letter from Mr William B Hodgson,[1] ↑(dated Washington Novr 5.th)↓ of which the following relates to the proposition of the British and Foreign Bible Society for the purchase of his Berber Mss.

"I am quite disposed to accept the offer of one hundred and fifty pounds Sterling, as this sum will cover the expense which I incurred in obtaining the Mss. My friends here had induced me to expect £200 for them; but as I have already intimated to Mr Platt, that the proposition of the Committee would be accepted, I shall be satisfied with that now made. The possession of the Berber Gospels, by the British and Foreign Bible Society[2] will be the fulfilment of wishes with which the Version was made."

"The manuscripts, which comprize the Gospels and the book of Genesis, are now in Philadelphia[.] I beg of your kindness to inform Mr Platt that they will be transmitted to the care of Mr Obadiah Rich, during this month."

I am Sir very respectfully

Your obt Servant
Washington Irving

P. S. The Residence of Mr O. Rich is No 12 Red Lion Square

T. P. Platt Esqr
&c.   &c.   &c.

Manuscript: The British and Foreign Bible Society, London.

1. This letter has not been located.

2. After its receipt "[t]he MS. was carefully examined and transcribed by John Hattersley, and in 1833 the B. F. B. S. published a small edition (250 copies) of Luke i-xii as an experiment. Copies were sent to N. Africa and to Malta for criticism but without satisfactory result, and the B. F. B. S. took no further steps to print the version," which appeared as *Extrait d'une traduction MS. en langue berbère de quelques parties de l'Écriture Sainte: contenant xii chapitres de S. Luc.* See T. H. Darlow and H. F. Moule, *Historical Catalogue of the Printed Editions of Holy Scripture in the Library of the British and Foreign Bible Society,* II, 855.

965 (complete letter).   To Catharine Paris

Sheffield, Octr. 14th. 1831

My dear Sister,

While Irving is making up his letters for the packet I will scrawl a hasty line. I arrived here two days since from Birmingham where I have been passing a few days delightfully and have left Brother Peter ↑there↓ in good health and good spirits. I am now snugly housed in Irvings little cottage which is as quiet and comfortable as heart could wish. It gives me the greatest delight to find him launched so prosperously in business and conducting himself so manfully. He is a most estimable lad; full of spirit, yet ⟨as⟩ amiable and gentle; with good sense, good principles and a right good heart. It is with the sincerest pleasure I have heard recently from our sister Sarah[1] of the engagement he has formed with his cousin Susan Irving.[2] It will no doubt be a happy one, and ⟨ser⟩ will serve to link the branches of the family more firmly together. I have always heard a most estimable character of Susan[.] I only reccollect her as a child, but my reccollection of her is very distinct. It is an additional cause of gratification to me that this match will unite a flourishing branch of the family with one that has not been so thriving; ⟨I feel⟩ and will promote the prosperity of one of the children of our dear brother William.

In looking over a letter of yours to Sister Sarah which Irving shewed to me last evening, I was pained to find, by a paragraph in it, that poor Dodge ⟨was⟩ and Helen[3] were in such straitened and dependent circumstances. I am surprized this has never been mentioned to me. I have written to them by this packet and ⟨shall⟩ will thank you to let me know from time to time of their situation and circumstances. Do not think because I am so far & so long away that I cease to feel the strongest interest in the welfare of all my relatives.

My friend Mr Newton[4] the painter, who sailed from London a few weeks since took with him a small portrait of me, for which I had sat at your request.[5] It is the most accurate likeness that has ever been taken of me & Mr Newton prizes [it] [*MS torn*] so much that he wishes to retain it, provided he can make a satisfactory copy for you, if not you will have the original.

I must conclude, for my letter is called for. God bless you my dear Sister. I trust to see you in the course of the coming year. Give my love to all your household

Your affectionate Brother
Washington Irving

ADDRESSED: Mrs Catharine Paris / Troy / State of N York

MANUSCRIPT: Star P. Myles.   PUBLISHED: PMI, II, 460 (in part).

1. This letter has not been located.

2. Susan Irving (1811–1836), the youngest daughter of Julia Paulding and William Irving, was married to Irving Van Wart in July, 1832.

3. Richard Dodge (1762–1832) had married WI's sister Ann Sarah (1770–1808) on February 14, 1788. Helen (1802-1885) was their youngest child.

4. Gilbert Stuart Newton visited the United States, married Sally Williams of Boston in August, 1832, and then returned to England, where he died of a mental disorder in 1835.

5. This portrait of WI was the second painted by Newton. See PMI, II, 460.

1003a.   To William I. Dodge

Washington June 13th. 1832

My dear Nephew,

I thank you for your very kind and affectionate letter[1]—It will give me great pleasure to visit you in the course of my Summers tour and to revisit the old Scenes of Johnstown.[2] I have had from time to time gratifying accounts of your Success in life, and of the creditable manner in which you have acquitted yourself in various public situations, especially from Mr Van Buren who appears to entertain a high respect for you. I shall leave this city in the course of a couple of days and, after stopping by the way at Baltimore & Philadelphia, ⟨hop⟩ expect to be in New York towards the end of the month—after which I shall think of visiting old friends and old haunts on the Hudson &c ⟨to the⟩

Give my love to your wife & family[3] and believe me ever

Your affectionate uncle
Washington Irving

ADDRESSED: William I Dodge Esq / Johnstown, Montgy Cy / State of New York   POSTMARKED: CITY of WASHINGTON / JUN / 13   FRANKED: Free Louis McLane   DOCKETED: Washington Irving / *1832*
MANUSCRIPT: Andrew B. Myers.

William Irving Dodge (1790–1873) was the son of Ann Sarah Irving and Richard Dodge.

1. This letter has not been located.

2. WI had visited his sister and her family before he had gone to Europe.

3. William I. Dodge had married Patricia Akin (1793–1879) in 1812. Their children included Ann Sarah (1816–1886), Julia Irving, Elizabeth Russell, William James, and Richard.

1052a.   To Theodore S. Fay

New York May 29th. 1833

My dear Sir,

I have been intending to call on you to apologize in person for having suffered so long a time to elapse without answering your note accompanying the essays of Mr. Cox.[1] That note was received when I was on the point of departure for Virginia, and remained unanswered through hurry and inadvertence I beg you will pardon this seeming inadvertence, and I am sure you would do so if you knew how little I am master at present of my time or thoughts

I need scarcely say that I feel flattered at being thought worthy the dedication[2] of any thing from the pen of Mr. Cox. For your own part, my dear Sir, I render you my thanks for the repeated proofs of good will received at your hands and which are the more grateful to me as proving that you inherit a portion of that cherished friendship which existed between your father[3] and myself

I remain, my dear Sir / very truly yours
Washington Irving

Theo. S. Fay Esq.

Manuscript: Yale—Stanley T. Williams Papers.

The text of this letter is taken from a transcript made by Stanley T. Williams. Theodore S. Fay (1807–1898) was an editorial assistant of George Pope Morris on the *New-York Mirror.*

1. William Cox (ca. 1805–1847) was the London correspondent of the *New-York Mirror.* Fay edited his *Crayon Sketches*, a two-volume collection of his contributions to the *Mirror.*
2. Fay's dedication, dated June 10, 1833, praised WI: "In early boyhood the charms of literature first broke upon me through the production of your pen; gratitude, therefore, as well as respect and admiration, includes me to dedicate to you the following compositions of one who also warmly appreciates the treasures which you have added to the English language."
3. Joseph Dewey Fay was a successful New York attorney who was interested in literature.

1073a.   To Edgar Irving

Washington Oct 28 1833

My dear Edgar,

I enclose your commission[1] which I have just received and about which there might have been considerable delay had I not fortunately come to Washington and been on the spot to attend to it personally

Col. Henderson is absent,[2] and will not be here for several days. The adjutant, Capt. Howell says the Col has an aid. He has a staff consisting of Paymaster, quarter master & adjutant—which situations are no doubt all supplied. You will of course be stationed for some time at one or other of the navy yards until you have been drilled into your new duties. The adjutant, who appears to be a worthy well-disposed man, will I have no doubt, do every thing in his power to make your situation agreeable. As I shall remain here some few days longer I may perhaps see Col Henderson before I depart, in which case I shall speak in your favor—If not, I shall leave a letter for him.

Drop me a line to the care of Mr. M'Lane[3] and let me know how you are all getting along at Baltimore. Remember me[5] kindly to the Calverts[4] and present my kind respects to Mr. Tennant[6] and the family

Your affectionate uncle
Washington Irving

P. S. Let me know what navy yard you would like to be stationed at—

MANUSCRIPT: Yale—Stanley T. Williams Papers.

The text of this letter is taken from a transcription made by Stanley T. Williams.

1. Edgar Irving's commission as a second lieutenant in the Marine Corps was dated October 1, 1833. See Navy Department to Edgar Irving, January 6, 1834 (NA, RG 45).
2. Colonel Archibald Henderson was commandant of the Marine Corps at this time.
3. Louis McLane was Secretary of State in Andrew Jackson's cabinet.
4. Probably George Calvert and his family.
5. The transcription has "be," which is probably an error for "me."
6. Colonel Thomas Tenant was the father of Edgar Irving's wife, Amanda (1814–1885).

1104a. To Colonel Thomas Aspinwall

New York Dec 29th 1834

My dear Aspinwall,

I send you, through the Legation, a pacquet containing a part of the ms. of a work which I wish to have put to press and published *immediately*. The residue of the Ms. somewhat *more than 100 pages* will come by the next packet, so that there need be no delay in the printing.[1] The work will form a volume about the size of a volume of the Sketch book, and be entitled "A TOUR ON THE PRAIRIES, By the

Author of the Sketch book—" There will be moreover a general title of "Miscellanies No. 1. By the Author of the Sketch Book—" for this is only the first of a series of volumes which I propose to publish from time to time and for which I have ample material in a forward state of preparation. According to the rate at which I sold my former works to Murray I ought to have 750 guineas for this volume—but I am willing to take five hundred.[2] In a word, make what bargain you can for it, so that it is put *instantly* to press—I do not wish the ms. to be submitted to the inspection of Booksellers and their "Elbow critics." They ought by this time to know enough of the general run of my writings to form a sufficient idea of any new thing I offer—as I have shewn that I do not throw things off[3] in a slovenly way, and for the mere love of filthy lucre. Besides in the present instance I am a little more cautious than usual, because I learn that my fellow traveller[4] Mr Latrobe[5] is about publishing his travels in the U. S. in which work he included this very excursion on the prairies, in which he accompanied me. The Bookseller[6] to whom my work was offered might have his in hand at the very time. Be on your guard, therefore, in this respect—but say nothing on the subject. I shall put the work to press here almost immediately—barely leaving time to give the publication in London a fair chance—So I entreat you not to procrastinate. If there is no other way to effect this promptness, have the work printed at my expense, and dispose of the edition. You can draw on Mr. Van Wart[7] for the necessary funds.

I reccommended[8] my friend Charles F. Hoffman[9] to send you the sheets of a new work he is putting through the press entitled "A Winter in the West" in hopes you might be able to make a bargain with some bookseller for the republication of it—Hoffman is a most particular friend in whose success I take great interest

We heard lately from my nieces at Cambridge,[10] who had just visited your family and found them all well; though William was still weak.

Yours ever
W. Irving

PS. My next volume[11] will relate to some scenes in England: and I think would particularly suit Murray.

Addressed: Col Thomas Aspinwall / American Consul / London / Caledonia L'pool

Manuscript: Yale—Stanley T. Williams Papers.

The text of this letter is taken from a transcription made by Stanley T. Williams.

1. On January 8, 1835 WI reported that he had "sent off the MS . . . to Colonel Aspinwall." See WI to Peter Irving, January 8, 1835.

2. Aspinwall negotiated the sale of the book to John Murray for four hundred pounds. See PMI, III, 66; WIHM, p. 216; and WI to Aspinwall, April 8, 1835.

3. The transcription has "of," but the sense suggests that W wrote "off."

4. The transcription has "traveler," but WI's customary spelling was "traveller."

5. Charles Joseph Latrobe (1801–1875) included an account of his trip to the Indian settlements in Oklahoma in *The Rambler in North America* (1835).

6. Carey, Lea, and Blanchard of Philadelphia published *A Tour on the Prairies*, and Harper and Brothers of New York issued Latrobe's book.

7. Henry Van Wart, Sr., WI's brother-in-law in Birmingham.

8. The transcription has "recommended," but WI's customary spelling was "reccommended."

9. Charles Fenno Hoffman (1806–1884) had written *A Winter in the West*, the account of his eight-month journey, mainly on horseback, between the Appalachians and the Mississippi River. His book was published in 1835 by Harper and Brothers in New York and by Richard Bentley in London.

10. Probably Matilda and Marianne Van Wart.

11. WI is alluding to *Abbotsford and Newstead Abbey*, which was published in Philadelphia on May 30, 1835 and in London on May 1, 1835. See Langfeld and Blackburn, *WI Bibliography*, pp. 33–34.

1119a.   To Francis Lieber

New York, April 22d. 1835

My dear Sir,

I feel much flattered that you should be so well pleased with my Tour on the Prairies[1] as to think it worthy of being abridged. I would observe, however, that the work is already so small in size and simple in matter as to be fitted for circulation among the majority of juvenile readers, and an abridgement, selecting its most striking features, could not but interfere with its circulation among that class, so important in the calculation of Booksellers. Now, however I might feel disposed to waive my own interests in this matter I have no right to compromise those of my publishers; to whom I have farmed out the work. Besides, were I to grant a privilege of the kind in one instance, it would be taken by others without asking, and, in this age of cheap abridgements and competition I might soon see my other works served up in portions, to the detriment of the literary property on which I depend for subsistence[.] I think, therefore, that upon reflection you will yourself perceive the impolicy as well as the impropriety of my acceeding to your suggestion though I must repeat, I cannot but feel gratified by the approbation which it implies of my my[2] humble production.

I am my dear Sir

Very respectfully Yours
Washington Irving

Dr Francis Lieber

ADDRESSED: Dr Francis Lieber / Philadelphia   POSTMARKED: NEW-YORK / APL /
    27   DOCKETED: Washington Irving / N. Y. April 22 (?) — / 1835. —
MANUSCRIPT: Leonard B. Stern.

Above the dateline on page 1 is written "W. Irving," probably by a previous owner of the letter.

1. This book had been published only a few days earlier.
2. WI repeated "my."

1122a.   To Samuel P. Walker

New York, May 11th, 1835.

Sir:

I have to apologize for having, in the press of various concerns, suffered your letter to remain so long unanswered. As its object was to obtain my autograph I presume this note will be sufficient for the purpose.

Respectfully / Your obedient servant,
Washington Irving.

Samuel P. Walker, **Esq.**

MANUSCRIPT: Yale—Stanley T. Williams Papers.

The text of this letter is taken from a transcription made by Stanley T. Williams.

1164a.   To William Howley

New York, March 16th. 1836

My Lord Archbishop,

It is with some diffidence that I take the liberty on the strength of the attention with which Your Grace honored me during my residence in London, to present to you the Rev. Dr Francis L Hawks[1] of this city; but I trust that the merit of this gentleman, and the interesting nature of his pursuits will be sufficient to plead my apology. Dr Hawks is one of the most distinguished and eloquent of our Episcopal clergy, and universally popular for the graces and virtues of his private character. He has gained a deserved reputation also in our literature and has just produced the first volume of a work of a high character and on a peculiar and interesting theme, The History of the Episcopal Church in the United States.[2] In the prosecution of his labours on the succeeding volumes he visits England principally for the purpose of examining certain papers in the Archiepiscopal palace at Lambeth.[3]

I feel assured that I have now said enough to satisfy Your Grace that in presenting Dr Hawks I am not intruding a commonplace personage upon your notice.

I have the Honor to remain / Your Graces very obt Servt.
Washington Irving

His Grace / The Lord Archbishop of Canterbury.

MANUSCRIPT: Lambeth Palace Library, London.

William Howley (1766–1848), who was Regius Professor of Divinity at Oxford before he became bishop of London in 1813, was elevated to archbishop of Canterbury in July, 1818. WI may have made his acquaintance through Charles Robert Leslie, who painted his portrait.

1. For details about Hawks, see WI to Robert Southey, March 21, 1836.

2. *Documentary History of the Protestant Episcopal Church in the United States of America: Protestant Episcopal Church in Virginia* (New York, 1836).

3. Lambeth Palace, the London residence of the archbishop of Canterbury, contains books, manuscripts, and church papers collected by various archbishops since 1610. For details, see Ann Cox-Johnson, "Lambeth Palace Library, 1610–1664," *Transactions of the Cambridge Bibliographical Society*, 2 (1955), 105–26; and M. R. James, "The History of Lambeth Palace Library," *Transactions of the Cambridge Bibliographical Society*, 3 (1959), 1–31.

1193a.   To Anthony Constant

Greenburg. Decr 20th. [1836?]

My dear Constant,

I understand you talk of coming up to eat your Christmas dinner with me, which would be acting the part of a most kind neighbor. I have accordingly ordered my purveyor Mr Lawrence to look out for a fat turkey ⟨for me⟩ for the occasion, and have put my cook in train for plum pudding and mince pies, so you must not disappoint me. I suppose it is in vain to ask Miss Constant to accompany you; that would indeed ensure a Merry Christmas. I shall eat my Christmas dinner on Monday, but as I shall have a dinner every preceding day you may come up as soon as you please. You know there is always a perch for you, and a hearty welcome, at the Roost.

Yours ever
Washington Irving

ADDRESSED: Anthony Constant Esq / at Mrs Pearsons / Vesey Street.
MANUSCRIPT: SHR.

The year 1836 is suggested for the following reasons. WI used the spelling "Greenburg," as he did in a letter to Sarah Paris on December 18, [1836]. Later he used the spelling "Greenburgh." In an earlier letter of December 10, 1836, to Sarah Paris, WI called his home the "Roost" and mentioned that Silas Lawrence had brought a pig to the cottage. Here, ten days later, WI referred to Lawrence as his "purveyor." Moreover, the fact that Constant brought Louis Napoleon on a visit to WI's home in the spring of 1837 would suggest that the two men were close acquaintances by that time.

The New York City directories during the 1830's did not list a Mrs. Pearson on Vesey Street.

For other details about Constant, see WI to Catharine Paris, March 22, 1838.

1200a. To Anthony Constant

[Greenburg, late 1836 or early 1837]

Worthy Neighbor,

Mrs Mary & Mrs George Jones & Miss Mason will pass the evening at the Cottage. If you and Mrs Constant feel disposed to favor us with your company we shall esteem it a great blessing.

Tea at 7 oclock precisely—A moon to go home with.

Yours truly
Washington Irving

Wolferts Roost.   Tuesday Morng.

MANUSCRIPT: SHR.

The date is conjectured as late 1836 or early 1837. At this time WI used the spelling "Greenburg," and he referred to the Jones family in letters of December 10 and 18, 1836, and January 11, 1837.

1211a. To Henry C. Carey

Tarrytown May 3d. 1837.

My dear Sir,

Your letter of the 25th ult[1] having touched at New York, on its way here, has but just reached me. As to the biography of Mr. Fulton,[2] I make no doubt an interesting work might be written on the subject, and one that would be very acceptable to the public, but, some how or other, I do not feel in the vein to undertake it; and unless a thing "jumps with my humor" I can make nothing of it. Besides I have work more than sufficient cut out to occupy all the moods of composition which I shall be able to command for some time to come. I wish however, you could suggest some profitable task to fill up intervals between such moods—the editing of any standard author or authors or any other of those tasks which require judgement taste and literary research, rather than fancy or invention. I need at this moment all the pecuniary aid that my pen can command: for my means, like those of most of my neighbors, are locked up in property not likely to yield any income for the present, and too much depreciated by the hard times to be brought to market, and in the meantime I am saddled with the expenses of house-keeping[3]—so throw any thing that you can in my way to help keep the pot boiling.

With kindest remembrances to Mrs. Carey I am, my dear Sir

Yours ever very truly,
Washington Irving

ADDRESSED: Henry C Carey Esq / care of Carey Lea & Blanchard / Philadelphia
MANUSCRIPT: Fruitlands Museum, Harvard, Massachusetts.

1. This letter has not been located.
2. Robert Fulton (1765–1815), an inventor and engineer who, after experimenting with submarines, built in 1807 a steamboat which successfully operated between New York City and Albany.
3. For other comments about his finances, see WI to Ebenezer Irving, January 10, 1837; to Colonel Thomas Aspinwall, March 29, 1837; and to Gouverneur Kemble, September 13, 1837.

1775a.   To John Miller

Paris, Sept. 24, 1844.

My dear Sir,

I wish you would ascertain whether there has really been published in London a translation of Weil's Mohammed.[1] I much doubt it; yet at the head of a review in Galignanis Observer it states Stuttgart & London. Perhaps it means that the German edition is published in both places.

I will thank you to send me, by return of post a copy of Punch, which contains the engraving of "The Royal Lady who lived in a Shoe."

Yours very truly
Washington Irving

MANUSCRIPT: Yale—Stanley T. Williams Collection (transcription).
PUBLISHED: Carroll A. Wilson, *Thirteen Author Collections of the Nineteenth Century and Five Centuries of Familiar Quotations*, ed. Jean C. S. Wilson and David A. Randall, I, 168.

1. Gustav Weil, *Mohammed der Prophet, sein Leben und sein Lehre* (Stuttgart, 1843). No London edition is listed in the National Union Catalog or the British Museum Catalogue. WI cites Weil twice in his study of Mohammed. See *Mahomet and His Successors*, ed. Henry A. Pochmann and E. F. Feltskog, The Complete Works of Washington Irving, vol. XVIII (Madison, 1970), pp. 33, 163.

APPENDIX II

Letters Sent by Washington Irving (Unlocated)

In *J&N*, I, WI's indication of the date on which he wrote a letter sometimes differs. He apparently jotted memoranda in his "Travelling Notes" and expanded them in his journal; e.g., his letters to Cathalin and Lee, given as September 14, 1804 in the journal (*J&N*, I, 93) and as September 15, 1804 in the "Travelling Notes" (*J&N*, I, 481). When there is a conflict in the dates in the two versions, the date given in the "Travelling Notes" will be used, since it was probably written earlier. The list will omit references to unlocated letters which are mentioned in WI's extant letters when these references duplicate those given in the notebooks and journals. When an unlocated letter is mentioned only in an extant letter, it is, of course, included in the list which follows.

LETTERS SENT BY WASHINGTON IRVING
(UNLOCATED)

July, 1804.   J. O. Hoffman. WI to A. Beebee, July 24, 1804. WI to E. Hicks, July 20, 1804.

September 14, 1804.   Dr. John Ellison. *J&N*, I, 93; WI to William Irving, September 20, 1804.

September 14, 1804.   William Lee. WI to William Irving, September 20, 1804; *J&N*, I, October 8, 1804, 102.

September 14, 1804.   Mr. Schwartz. *J&N*, I, 93, 481; WI to William Irving, September 20, 1804.

September 14, 1804.   Thomas Hall Storm. *J&N*, I, 93, 481; WI to A. Beebee, September 18, 1804. WI to William Irving, December 20, 1804.

September 15, 1804.   William Lee. *J&N*, I, September 15, 1804, 93, 481.

September 19, 1804.   Several letters to New York. *J&N*, I, 483.

September 21, 1804.   Mr. Schwartz. WI to William Irving, September 20, 1804.

September, 1804.   Thomas Hall Storm. WI to William Irving, December 20, 1804.

Early November, 1804.   To Andrew Quoz. WI to Andrew Quoz, January 1, 1805; WI to William Irving, November 30, 1804.

Late 1804.   Eliza Ogden. WI to Andrew Quoz. January 1, 1805.

Early October, 1805.   James Monroe. J&N, I, 453.

November, 1805.   William Irving (two letters). WI to William Irving, November?, 1805.

February, 1810.   J. O. Hoffman. WI to Mrs. J. O. Hoffman, February 12, 1810.

February, 1810.   Peter Kemble. WI to Mrs. J. O. Hoffman, February 12, 1810.

Late June, 1810.   Charles Nicholas. WI to Mrs. J. O. Hoffman, June 23, 1810.

Late December, 1810.   Mrs. J. O. Hoffman. WI to Mrs. J. O. Hoffman, January 6, 1811.

ca. February, 1811.   To his brothers. WI to Henry Brevoort, February 7, 1811.

February 9, 1811.   John Treat Irving. WI to William Irving, Jr., February 9, 1811.

February 26, 1811.   William P. Van Ness. Swann Auction Galleries, September, 1942 (68).

June 3, 1811.   William P. Van Ness. Goodspeed's, 1975.

June 3, 1811.   To ————. Charles Hamilton, Auction 63, item 191, December 7, 1972.

February, 1812.   Henry Brevoort. WI to Henry Brevoort, March 27, 1812.

March, 1812.   Henry Brevoort. WI to Henry Brevoort, March 27, 1812.

November 1, 1812.   Abram Lawrence. Stan V. Henkels, December 5, 1898 (156); Charles Hamilton, Auction 84, item 205, January 23, 1975.

December, 1812.   To ————. WI to James Renwick, December 18, 1812.

December, 1812.   Peter Irving. WI to Peter Irving, December 30, 1812.

June 20, 1814.   Commodore Bainbridge. Kennard Sale, Libbie's, April 26, 1904 (427); American Art Association, March 18, 1925.

June 29, 1814.   Moses Thomas. Clawson & Brown, Anderson Galleries, March 26, 1917 (199).

ca. July 5, 1815. Ebenezer Irving. WI to Ebenezer Irving, July 21, 1815.

May 25, 1816. Moses Thomas. Charles Hamilton, Auction 83, item 222, December 19, 1974; Charles Hamilton, Auction 90, item 215, September 4, 1975.

May–June, 1816. Eliza Bradish. WI to Henry Brevoort, July 16, 1816.

August 26, 1817. Francis Jeffrey. WI to Peter Irving, August 26, 1817.

Late August, 1817. Moses Thomas. WI to Peter Irving. September 20, 1817; WI to John Murray, October 16, 1817.

September, 1817. Peter Irving. September 20, 1817.

September 19, 1817. [Chauncey Hare?] Townshend. WI to Peter Irving, September 20, 1817.

January 28, 1818. Mrs. Henry Brevoort. WI to Henry Brevoort, January 28, 1818, and July 7, 1818.

January 28, 1818. Thomas Campbell. WI to Henry Brevoort, January 28, 1818.

Early February, 1818. William C. Preston. WI to Charles R. Leslie, February 8, 1818.

August 2, 1819. Ebenezer Irving. WI to Henry Brevoort, August 2, 1819.

Early September, 1819. William Coleman. WI to Henry Brevoort, September 9, 1819.

February 21, 1820. Thomas S. Norgate. Charles Hamilton, Auction 80, item 248, September 5, 1974.

Late March, 1820. Ebenezer Irving. WI to Henry Brevoort, March 27, 1820.

July, 1820. Henry Brevoort. WI to Henry Brevoort, August 15, 1820.

August 3, 1820. To ———. National Art Gallery, May 12, 1932, item 122.

September 22, 1820. William Irving. WI to Henry Brevoort, September 22, 1822.

December, 1820. Gilbert Stuart Newton. WI to Charles R. Leslie, November 30, 1820.

December, 1820. William Willes. WI to Charles R. Leslie, November 30, 1820.

Before March 10, 1821. William and Ebenezer Irving. WI to Henry Brevoort, March 10, 1821.

ca. April 5, 1821.   Ebenezer Irving. WI to Henry Brevoort,
                              April 5, 1821.
April 19, 1821, or   To Mrs. Holloway. WI to Colonel Fairman,
  shortly after.   April 19, 1821.
June?, 1821.   John E. Hall. WI to John E. Hall, June 30,
                             1822.
April 25, 1822.   Mr. & Mrs. John Murray II. *The Collector*, 68
                             (November–December, 1955), 118, no. 843a.
Early June, 1822.   Ebenezer Irving. WI to Henry Brevoort,
                             June 11, 1822.
June 6, 1822.   Charles Matthews. STW, I, 441; American-
                             Anderson Sale no. 4125, November 8, 1934.
Late June, 1822.   Ebenezer Irving. WI to Moses Thomas, June
                             29, 1822.
June, 1822.   Mrs. T. A. Cooper. WI to Henry Brevoort,
                             June 6, 1823.
June, 1822.   John Nicholson. WI to Henry Brevoort, June
                             11, 1822, and June 6, 1823.
July 6?, 1822.   Henry Van Wart. WI to Charles Williams,
                             July 6, 1822.
July 11, 1822.   Moses Thomas. Parke-Bernet Galleries, Oc-
                             tober 17–18, 1944 (121).
Mid-October, 1822.   Gilbert Stuart Newton. WI to Charles R. Les-
                             lie, December 2, 1822.
November, 1822.   Peter Irving. WI to Charles R. Leslie, Decem-
                             ber 2, 1822.
December 30, 1822.   Madame Williams. Swann Auction Galleries,
                             September 26, 1947 (192).
January 3, 1823.   To ———. (Several letters.) J&N, III, 105.
January 6, 1823.   Messrs. Duncker and Humblot. WI to Karl
                             A. Böttiger, January 6, 1823.
March 15, 1823.   Gilbert Stuart Newton. WI to Charles R. Les-
                             lie, March 15, 1823.
March 15, 1823.   To ———. (Several letters.) WI to Charles
                             R. Leslie, March 15, 1823.
March 25, 1823.   To ———. (Several letters.) J&N, III, 132.
April 1, 1823.   To ———. (Several letters.) J&N, III, 134.
Early May, 1823.   Prince Frederick of Saxony. WI to Amelia
                             Foster, May 4, 1823.
June 2, 1823.   Barham Livius. J&N, III, 170.
June 8, 1823.   Barham Livius. J&N, III, 171.
June 17–19, 1823.   Amelia Foster. J&N, III, 174.

August 5, 1823.	Sarah Van Wart. *J&N*, III, 206.
August 19, 1823.	Amelia Foster. *J&N*, III, 213.
August 20, 1823.	Robert Sullivan. *J&N*, III, 213.
August 21, 1823.	John Miller. *J&N*, III, 215.
August 28, 1823.	Peter Irving. *J&N*, III, 217.
August 30, 1823.	Ebenezer Irving. *J&N*, III, 217.
September 3, 1823.	Peter Irving. *J&N*, III, 218.
October 7, 1823.	Amelia Foster. *J&N*, III, 228.
October 7, 1823.	Sarah Van Wart. *J&N*, III, 228.
October 12, 1823.	William Irving. *J&N*, III, 230.
October 17, 1823.	Peter Irving. *J&N*, III, 231.
December 17, 1823.	Gilbert Stuart Newton. *J&N*, III, 258.
December 18, 1823.	Lady Susan Douglas. *J&N*, III, 259.
December 22, 1823.	Barham Livius. *J&N*, III, 261.
December 23, 1823.	Madame Duport. *J&N*, III, 261.
December 24, 1823.	Amelia Foster. *J&N*, III, 261.
December 26, 1823.	Thomas Grattan. *J&N*, III, 262.
December 27, 1823.	To ———— Reed. *J&N*, III, 262.
December 28–30, 1823.	Ebenezer Irving. *J&N*, III, 263.
1823?	Samuel Spiker. STW, I, 445.
January 7, 1824.	Amelia Foster. *J&N*, III, 266.
January 7, 1824.	Henry Van Wart. *J&N*, III, 266.
January 12, 1824.	Mrs. Speakeling. *J&N*, III, 270.
January 15, 1824.	Robert Sullivan. *J&N*, III, 271.
January 26, 1824.	Sarah Van Wart. *J&N*, III, 278.
January 27, 1824.	John Murray. American Art Association, February 14–15, 1895 (194).
January 27, 1824.	Robert Sullivan. *J&N*, III, 279.
January 28, 1824.	John Howard Payne. *J&N*, III, 279.
January 28, 1824.	Mrs. John Story. *J&N*, III, 279.
January 29, 1824.	Ebenezer Irving. *J&N*, III, 279.
January 29, 1824.	Barham Livius. *J&N*, III, 279.
January 29, 1824.	James K. Paulding. *J&N*, III, 279.
January 29–30, 1824.	Amelia Foster. *J&N*, III, 279, 280.
January 30, 1824.	Robert Sullivan. *J&N*, III, 280.
January 31, 1824.	Barham Livius. *J&N*, III, 280.
February 6, 1824.	Henry Van Wart, Jr. *J&N*, III, 285.
February 9, 1824.	Joshua Dodge. *J&N*, III, 286.
February 9, 1824.	Captain Holdridge. *J&N*, III, 286.
February 12, 1824.	Robert Cargill. *J&N*, III, 288.
February 15, 1824.	To ———— Appleton. *J&N*, III, 289.
February 15, 1824.	Sarah Van Wart. *J&N*, III, 289.

February 17, 1824.	Thomas Colley Grattan. *J&N*, III, 290.
February 22, 1824.	To ————. Kennard Sale, Libbie's, April 26, 1904 (1380).
February 27, 1824.	Lady Louisa Harvey. *J&N*, III, 296.
February 27, 1824.	Mrs. Samuel Welles. *J&N*, III, 298.
March 1, 1824.	J. W. Lake. *J&N*, III, 298.
March 13, 1824.	Amelia Foster. *J&N*, III, 303.
March 13, 1824.	Emily Foster. *J&N*, III, 303.
March 13, 1824.	Henry Van Wart. *J&N*, III, 303.
March 18, 1824.	Ebenezer Irving. *J&N*, III, 305.
March 18, 1824.	Robert Sullivan. *J&N*, III, 305.
March 20, 1824.	Barham Livius. *J&N*, III, 306.
April 3, 1824.	Amelia Foster. *J&N*, III, 313.
April 5, 1824.	John Miller. *J&N*, III, 315.
April 5, 1824.	Sarah Van Wart. *J&N*, III, 315.
April 12, 1824.	[John and William] Galignani. *J&N*, III, 319.
April 12, 1824.	Colonel Wheatley. *J&N*, III, 319.
April 15, 1824.	To ———— Lemoine. *J&N*, III, 320.
April 21, 1824.	David R. Morier. *J&N*, III, 322.
April 22, 1824.	Captain Cadogan. *J&N*, III, 322.
April 24, 1824.	Henry [Van Wart?]. *J&N*, III, 323.
May 16, 1824.	Sarah Van Wart. *J&N*, III, 333.
May 24, 1824.	Ebenezer Irving. (Two letters.) *J&N*, III, 334.
June 1, 1824.	Amelia Foster. *J&N*, III, 340.
June 1, 1824.	Sarah Van Wart. *J&N*, III, 340.
June 2, 1824.	John Liston. WI to J. H. Payne, June 2, 1824.
June 2, 1824.	Peter Irving. *J&N*, III, 340.
June 5, 1824.	David Morier. *J&N*, III, 342. (Cf. April 21, 1824.)
June 7, 1824.	Sarah Van Wart. *J&N*, III, 343.
June 10, 1824.	Ebenezer Irving. *J&N*, III, 345.
June 13, 1824.	Amelia Foster. *J&N*, III, 348.
June 22, 1824.	Ebenezer Irving. *J&N*, III, 353.
June 23, 1824.	Gilbert Stuart Newton. *J&N*, III, 353.
June 26, 1824.	Ebenezer Irving. *J&N*, III, 354.
June 29, 1824.	Marianne (housekeeper in Paris). *J&N*, III, 355.
June 29, 1824.	Thomas W. Storrow. *J&N*, III, 355.
July 1, 1824.	Amelia Foster. *J&N*, III, 355.
July 3, 1824.	Ebenezer Irving. (Two letters.) *J&N*, III, 356.

July 6, 1824.	[John and William] Galignani. *J&N*, III, 358.
July 6, 1824.	James K. Paulding. *J&N*, III, 358.
July 7, 1824.	Robert Sullivan. *J&N*, III, 358.
July 8, 1824.	Ebenezer Irving. *J&N*, III, 359.
July 8, 1824.	John Miller. *J&N*, III, 359.
July 8, 1824.	John Murray II. *J&N*, III, 359.
July 11, 1824.	John Murray II. *J&N*, III, 362.
July 13, 1824.	John Murray II. *J&N*, III, 363.
July 14, 1824.	Gilbert Stuart Newton, *J&N*, III, 364.
July 14, 1824.	John Howard Payne. *J&N*, III, 364.
July 14, 1824.	Sarah Van Wart. *J&N*, III, 364.
July 26, 1824.	Robert Sullivan. *J&N*, III, 374.
July 26, 1824.	Sarah Van Wart. *J&N*, III, 374.
July 30, 1824.	Sarah Van Wart. *J&N*, III, 375.
July 31, 1824.	John Miller. *J&N*, III, 375.
August 3, 1824.	Ebenezer Irving. *J&N*, III, 376.
August 14, 1824.	Amelia Foster. *J&N*, III, 382.
August 14, 1824.	John Miller. *J&N*, III, 382.
August 14, 1824.	Henry Van Wart. *J&N*, III, 382.
August 21, 1824.	Frank Mills. *J&N*, III, 384.
August 23, 1824.	Ebenezer Irving. *J&N*, III, 385.
September 1, 1824.	Peter Irving. *J&N*, III, 390.
September 1, 1824.	François Sieurac. *J&N*, III, 390.
September 3, 1824.	Thomas Aspinwall. *J&N*, III, 391.
September 6, 1824.	Frank Mills. *J&N*, III, 392.
September 6, 1824.	Lupton Rolfe. *J&N*, III, 392.
September 11, 1824.	Thomas Moore. *J&N*, III, 394.
September 11–12, 1824.	Ebenezer Irving. *J&N*, III, 394.
September 12, 1824.	Henry Van Wart. *J&N*, III, 394.
September 13, 1824.	Ebenezer Irving. *J&N*, III, 394.
September 13, 1824.	John Miller. *J&N*, III, 394.
September 13, 1824.	Henry Van Wart. *J&N*, III, 394.
September 16, 1824.	John A. Galignani. *J&N*, III, 396.
September 24, 1824.	Thomas Moore. *J&N*, III, 398.
September 29, 1824.	Ebenezer Irving. *J&N*, III, 399.
September 29, 1824.	Thomas W. Storrow. *J&N*, III, 400.
October 4, 1824.	Thomas Moore. *J&N*, III, 401.
October 5, 1824.	Duchess of Duras. *J&N*, III, 401.
October 6, 1824.	Catharine Paris. *J&N*, III, 401.
October 9, 1824.	Frank Mills. *J&N*, III, 402.
October 10, 1824.	John Miller. *J&N*, III, 402.
October 10, 1824.	Gilbert Stuart Newton. *J&N*, III, 402.
October 10, 1824.	Robert Sullivan. *J&N*, III, 402.

October 22, 1824.	Lady Susan Douglas. *J&N*, III, 413.
October 22, 1824.	John Miller. *J&N*, III, 413.
October 25, 1824.	John Miller. *J&N*, III, 415.
October 25, 1824.	Thomas Moore. *J&N*, III, 415.
November 3, 1824.	Ebenezer Irving. *J&N*, III, 418.
November 3, 1824.	Sarah Van Wart. *J&N*, III, 418.
November 4, 1824.	Amelia Foster. *J&N*, III, 420.
November 5, 1824.	Amelia Foster. *J&N*, III, 420.
November 5, 1824.	John Miller. *J&N*, III, 420.
November 5, 1824.	Gilbert Stuart Newton. *J&N*, III, 420.
November 5, 1824.	Sarah Van Wart. *J&N*, III, 420.
November 6, 1824.	Gilbert Stuart Newton. *J&N*, III, 421.
November 12, 1824.	Ebenezer Irving. *J&N*, III, 425.
November 13, 1824.	Frank Mills. *J&N*, III, 425.
November 14, 1824.	Henry and Irving Van Wart. *J&N*, III, 425.
December 5, 1824.	Julia Irving. *J&N*, III, 433.
December 9, 1824.	Robert Sullivan. *J&N*, III, 434.
December 11, 1824.	Luther Bradish. *J&N*, III, 435.
December 12, 1824.	Thomas Medwin. *J&N*, III, 435.
January 16, 1825.	James Brown. *J&N*, III, 446.
January 16, 1825.	John Howard Payne. *J&N*, III, 446.
January 16, 1825.	Baron de Stael. *J&N*, III, 446.
January 27, 1825.	Sarah Van Wart. *J&N*, III, 449.
February 14, 1825.	To ———. *J&N*, III, 455.
February 21, 1825.	Frank Mills. *J&N*, III, 458.
February 25, 1825.	Lady Granard. *J&N*, III, 459.
February 28, 1825.	Gilbert Stuart Newton. *J&N*, III, 460.
February 28, 1825.	Sarah Van Wart. *J&N*, III, 460.
March 3, 1825.	Editor of *European Gazette*. *J&N*, III, 461.
March 3, 182⁵.	John Murray. *J&N*, III, 461.
March 3, 1825.	Robert Sullivan. *J&N*, III, 461.
March 3, 1825.	To ———. Charles Hamilton, Auction 64, item 140, January 11, 1973.
March 4, 1825.	Editor of *Friendship's Offering* [Thomas K. Hervey]. *J&N*, III, 461.
March 21, 1825.	Frank Mills. *J&N*, III, 467.
March 28, 1825.	Ebenezer Irving. *J&N*, III, 470.
April 4, 1825.	Gilbert Stuart Newton. *J&N*, III, 472.
April 10, 1825.	Peter Irving. *J&N*, III, 474.
April 10, 1825.	Gilbert Stuart Newton. *J&N*, III, 474.
April 10, 1825.	Henry Van Wart. *J&N*, III, 474.
April 11, 1825.	Thomas Moore. *J&N*, III, 474.
April 11, 1825.	Sir Walter Scott. *J&N*, III, 474.

April 25, 1825.	Mrs. Thomas W. Storrow. *J&N*, III, 478.
May 1, 1825.	Peter Irving. *J&N*, III, 480.
May 1, 1825.	Gilbert Stuart Newton. *J&N*, III, 480.
May 2, 1825.	John Nicholson. *J&N*, III, 481.
ca. May 8, 1825.	Gilbert Stuart Newton. WI to Robert Sullivan, May 8, 1825.
May 12, 1825.	Mrs. Thomas Aspinwall. *J&N*, III, 483.
May 25, 1825.	William E. West. *J&N*, III, 486.
May 31, 1825.	Thomas Medwin. *J&N*, III, 487.
June 8, 1825.	Peter Irving. *J&N*, III, 490.
June 18, 1825.	Dominick Lynch. *J&N*, III, 498.
June 18, 1825.	Frank Mills. *J&N*, III, 498.
June 18, 1825.	Sarah Van Wart. *J&N*, III, 498.
July 13, 1825.	Amelia Foster. *J&N*, III, 501.
July 13, 1825.	Frank Mills. *J&N*, III, 501.
July 13, 1825.	Gilbert Stuart Newton. *J&N*, III, 501.
July 13, 1825.	James K. Paulding. *J&N*, III, 501.
July 20, 1825.	George Ticknor. Maggs Bros., Catalog 745, 1945.
July 20, 1825.	Gulian Verplanck. Charles Hamilton, Auction 76, item 214, March 28, 1974; Paul C. Richards, Autographs.
July 22, 1825.	Mrs. Reuben Beasley. *J&N*, III, 503.
July 22, 1825.	Sarah Van Wart. *J&N*, III, 503.
July 22, 1825.	William E. West. *J&N*, III, 503.
August 16, 1825.	To ——— Dewey. *J&N*, III, 509.
August 17, 1825.	Peter Irving. *J&N*, III, 510.
August 21, 1825.	Peter Irving. *J&N*, III, 511.
August 22, 1825.	Peter Irving. *J&N*, III, 511.
September 11, 1825.	Frank Mills. *J&N*, III, 517.
September 11, 1825.	Sarah Van Wart. *J&N*, III, 517.
September 15, 1825.	Frederick Gerald Byng. *J&N*, III, 517.
September 16, 1825.	Frank Mills. *J&N*, III, 518.
September 17, 1825.	Henry Van Wart. *J&N*, III, 518.
September 19, 1825.	Sir Walter Scott. *J&N*, III, 519.
October 17, 1825.	Stephen Price. *J&N*, III, 531.
November 3, 1825.	Frank Mills. *J&N*, III, 537.
November 8, 1825.	Samuel Welles. *J&N*, III, 541; Plaza Art Auction Galleries, January 19–20, 1939 (163).
November 16, 1825.	To ——— Jones. *J&N*, III, 543.
November 16, 1825.	Henry Van Wart. *J&N*, III, 543.
November 16, 1825.	Samuel Williams. *J&N*, III, 543.
November 24, 1825.	Ebenezer Irving. *J&N*, III, 546.

December 5, 1825.	James K. Paulding. *J&N*, III, 549.
December 5, 1825.	John Howard Payne. *J&N*, III, 549.
December 31, 1825.	C. B. Coles. *J&N*, III, 556.
December 31, 1825.	Stephen Price. *J&N*, III, 556.
1825.	Sir Egerton Brydges. Sotheby, May 16, 1972, item 494.
1825.	Sir Egerton Brydges. Maggs Bros., Catalog 417, Christmas, 1921.
1825.	Mrs. Sitwell. Maggs Bros., Catalog 355, Spring, 1917.
January 3, 1826.	Ebenezer Irving. *J&N*, III, 557.
January 7, 1826.	Ebenezer Irving. *J&N*, III, 558.
January 7, 1826.	Gilbert Stuart Newton. *J&N*, III, 558.
January 7, 1826.	Sarah Van Wart. *J&N*, III, 558.
January 10, 1826.	Alexander Everett. *J&N*, III, 559.
February 8, 1826.	Ebenezer Irving. WI to C. B. Coles, February 8, 1826.
February 8, 1826.	Frank Mills. *J&N*, III, 564.
February 25, 1826.	Ebenezer Irving. WI to Thomas W. Storrow, February 25, 1826.
February 27, 1826.	Nathaniel Johnston. *Journals of WI*, III, 11.
February 27, 1826.	John Howard Payne. *Journals of WI*, III, 11.
March 12, 1826.	Frank Mills. *Journals of WI*, III, 15.
March 12, 1826.	Charles R. Leslie. *Journals of WI*, III, 15.
March 13, 1826.	Robert Sullivan. *Journals of WI*, III, 15.
March 15, 1826.	Ebenezer Irving. *Journals of WI*, III, 15; Thomas W. Storrow, March 15, 1826.
March 15, 1826.	Charles R. Leslie. *Journals of WI*, III, 15.
March 27, 1826.	Timothy? Wiggins. *Journals of WI*, III, 18.
April 13, 1826.	Henry Van Wart. *Journals of WI*, III, 22.
April 20, 1826.	Frank Mills. *Journals of WI*, III, 22.
April 20, 1826.	Gilbert Stuart Newton. *Journals of WI*, III, 22.
May 9, 1826.	Mr. Henry. *Journals of WI*, III, 24.
May 18, 1826.	Nathaniel Johnston. *Journals of WI*, III, 25.
May 18, 1826.	Stephen Price. *Journals of WI*, III, 25; WI to J. H. Payne, May 25, 1826.
May 18, 1826.	Obadiah Rich. *Journals of WI*, III, 25.
May 18, 1826.	Marchioness of Wellesley. *Journals of WI*, III, 25.
June 1, 1826.	John Howard Payne. *Journals of WI*, III, 27.
June 1, 1826.	Sarah Van Wart. *Journals of WI*, III, 27.
June 8, 1826.	Obadiah Rich. *Journals of WI*, III, 28.

July 9, 1826.	Henry Van Wart. *Journals of WI*, III, 32; WI to Thomas W. Storrow, July 9, 1826.
July 20, 1826.	Stephen Price. *Journals of WI*, III, 33.
July 27, 1826.	Pierre M. Irving. *Journals of WI*, III, 34.
August 16, 1826.	Pierre M. Irving. *Journals of WI*, III, 37.
August 17, 1826.	Henry Van Wart. *Journals of WI*, III, 37.
August 31, 1826.	Ebenezer Irving. WI to Thomas W. Storrow, August 31, 1826. (Two letters.)
September 12, 1826.	F. Andrews. *Journals of WI*, III, 39.
October 20, 1826.	Henry Van Wart. *Journals of WI*, III, 43.
October 22, 1826.	To ———. WI to William Macready, October 22, 1826.
October 22, 1826.	To ———. WI to William Macready, October 22, 1826.
October 25, 1826.	Ebenezer Irving. *Journals of WI*, III, 43.
October 25, 1826.	Pierre M. Irving. WI to Thomas W. Storrow, October 26, 1826.
November 5, 1826.	Ebenezer Irving. *Journals of WI*, III, 44.
November 5, 1826.	Thomas W. Storrow. *Journals of WI*, III, 44.
November 22, 1826.	Henry Van Wart. *Journals of WI*, III, 46.
November 27, 1826.	Henry Van Wart. *Journals of WI*, III, 46.
Late 1826.	Ebenezer Irving. WI to Henry Brevoort, April 4, 1827.
January 3, 1827.	Lady Granard. *Journals of WI*, III, 49.
January 4, 1827.	Pierre M. Irving. *Journals of WI*, III, 50.
January 4, 1827.	Frank Mills. *Journals of WI*, III, 50.
February 22, 1827.	Henry Van Wart. *Journals of WI*, III, 55.
February 24, 1827.	Reuben Beasley. *Journals of WI*, III, 55.
February 24, 1827.	Ebenezer Irving. *Journals of WI*, III, 55.
April 23, 1827.	Pierre M. Irving. *Journals of WI*, III, 62.
April 27, 1827.	James Kenney. *Journals of WI*, III, 63.
April 27, 1827.	Alexander Slidell. *Journals of WI*, III, 63.
May 10, 1827.	Mrs. Thomas W. Storrow. *Journal 1827-1828*, p. 222.
May 14, 1827.	Pierre M. Irving and Henry Van Wart. *Journal 1827–1828*, p. 223.
May 14, 1827.	Frank Mills. *Journal 1827–1828*, p. 223.
May 14, 1827.	Mrs. John Storey. *Journal 1827–1828*, p. 223.
May, 1827.	Ebenezer Irving. WI to Thomas W. Storrow, July 9, 1827.
June 5, 1827.	Alexander Slidell. *Journal 1827–1828*, p. 300.
June 18, 1827.	Sarah Van Wart. *Journal 1827–1828*, p. 301.

June 22, 1827.   Henry Brevoort. *Journal 1827–1828*, p. 301.
June 22, 1827.   Henry Carey. *Journal 1827–1828*, p. 301.
June 22, 1827.   Ebenezer Irving. *Journal 1827–1828*, p. 301.
June 22, 1827.   To [Thomas W. White?]. *Journal 1827–1828*, p. 301.

July 2, 1827.   Daniel Strobel. *Journal 1827–1828*, p. 301.
July 9, 1827.   Anthony R. Brydges. *Journal 1827–1828*, p. 302.

July 23, 1827.   Ebenezer Irving. *Journal 1827–1828*, p. 303.
July 23, 1827.   Henry Van Wart. *Journal 1827–1828*, p. 303.
July 31, 1827.   Ebenezer Irving. *Journal 1827–1828*, p. 303.
July 31, 1827.   Thomas W. Storrow. *Journal 1827–1828*, p. 303.
August 15, 1827.   Colonel Thomas Aspinwall. American Art Association-Anderson Galleries, May 2–3, 1934 (late Reverend Dr. Roderick Terry), (135).

August 20, 1827.   Thomas W. Storrow. *Journal 1827–1828*, p. 305.

August 22, 1827.   James Brown. *Journal 1827–1828*, p. 305.
August 22, 1827.   Ebenezer Irving. *Journal 1827–1828*, p. 305.
August 22, 1827.   Thomas W. Storrow. *Journal 1827–1828*, p. 305.

August 30, 1827.   Karl Böttiger. *Journal 1827–1828*, p. 305; PMI, II, 267.

September 17, 1827.   Thomas Aspinwall. *Journal 1827–1828*, p. 306.
October 14, 1827.   Ebenezer Irving. *Journal 1827–1828*, p. 307.
October 15, 1827.   John Murray. *Journal 1827–1828*, p. 307.
November 26, 1827.   Thomas Moore. *Journal 1827–1828*, p. 409.
November 26, 1827.   Gilbert Stuart Newton. *Journal 1827–1828*, p. 409.

November 30, 1827.   James Brown. *Journal 1827–1828*, p. 409.
November 30, 1827.   Ebenezer Irving. *Journal 1827–1828*, p. 409.
November 30, 1827.   Alexander Slidell. *Journal 1827–1828*, p. 409.
November 30, 1827.   Mr. and Mrs. Thomas W. Storrow. *Journal 1827–1828*, p. 409.

December 6, 1827.   John Murray II. *Journal 1827–1828*, p. 410.
January 10, 1828.   Ebenezer Irving. *Journal 1827–1828*, p. 412.
January 22, 1828.   Theodore Irving. *Journal 1827–1828*, p. 413.
January 22, 1828.   Richard McCall. *Journal 1827–1828*, p. 413.
February 18, 1828.   John and William Galignani. *Journal 1827–1828*, p. 415.

February 20, 1828.   Gilbert Stuart Newton. *Journal 1827–1828*, p. 415.

February 24, 1828.   James Brown. *Journal 1827–1828*, p. 416.

February 24, 1828.	Ebenezer Irving. *Journal 1827–1828*, p. 416.
February 24, 1828.	Alexander Slidell. *Journal 1827–1828*, p. 416.
March 10, 1828.	Susan Storrow. WI to Thomas W. Storrow, March 10, 1828.
March 12, 1828.	Peter Irving. *Journal 1828*, p. 19.
March 12, 1828.	Susan Storrow. *Journal 1828*, p. 19.
March 15, 1828.	To ———— Arndt. *Journal 1828*, p. 22.
March 15, 1828.	Antoine? D'Oubril. *Journal 1828*, p. 22.
April 16, 1828.	Peter Irving. *Diary 1828–1829*, p. 10.
April 21, 1828.	Alexander Burton. *Diary 1828–1829*, p. 13.
April 23, 1828.	John Grigg. *Diary 1828–1829*, p. 14.
April 23, 1828.	To David ————. *Diary 1828–1829*, p. 14.
April 23, 1828.	Francis? Palgrave. *Diary 1828–1829*, p. 14.
April 29, 1828.	Alexander Burton. *Diary 1828–1829*, p. 18.
April 29, 1828.	Reverend Mr. ———— Grigg. *Diary 1828–1829*, p. 18.
April 29, 1828.	Ebenezer Irving. *Diary 1828–1829*, p. 18.
April 30, 1828.	Antoinette Bolviller. *Diary 1828–1829*, p. 18.
April 30, 1828.	Prince Dolgorouki. *Diary 1828–1829*, p. 18.
May 5, 1828.	To ———— Gessler. *Diary 1828–29*, p. 20.
May 6, 1828.	George G. Barrell. *Diary 1828–1829*, p. 20.
May 10, 1828.	To ———— Marsden. *Diary 1828–1829*, p. 21.
May 10, 1828.	Horatio Sprague. *Diary 1828–1829*, p. 21.
May 17, 1828.	Colonel Thomas Aspinwall. *Diary 1828–1829*, p. 26.
May 17, 1828.	Henry Van Wart. *Diary 1828–1829*, p. 26.
May 21, 1828.	To ———— Stoffregen. *Diary 1828–1829*, p. 29.
May 24, 1828.	Colonel Thomas Aspinwall. *Diary 1828–1829*, p. 30.
May 24, 1828.	Ebenezer Irving. *Diary 1828–1829*, p. 30.
May 24, 1828.	Henry Van Wart. *Diary 1828–1829*, p. 30.
May 28, 1828.	Pierre Irving. *Diary 1828–1829*, p. 31.
June 4, 1828.	Obadiah Rich. *Diary 1828–1829*, p. 33.
June 14, 1828.	To ———— Gessler. *Diary 1828–1829*, p. 35.
June 21, 1828.	Theodore Irving. *Diary 1828–1829*, p. 37.
June 24, 1828.	To ———— Gessler. *Diary 1828–1829*, p. 38.
June 28, 1828.	To ———— Duffield. *Diary 1828–1829*, p. 39.
June 28, 1828.	To ———— Marsden. *Diary 1828–1829*, p. 39.
June 28, 1828.	Richard McCall. *Diary 1828–1829*, p. 39.
June, 1828.	Theodore Irving. WI to Thomas W. Storrow, June 20, 1828.
July 12, 1828.	Alexander Burton. *Diary 1828–1829*, p. 43.

July 12, 1828.   Sarah Van Wart. *Diary 1828–1829*, p. 43.
July 19, 1828.   Alexander Burton. *Diary 1828–1829*, p. 45.
July 23, 1828.   David Wilkie. *Diary 1828–1829*, p. 45.
July 29, 1828.   Mrs. Alexander H. Everett. *Diary 1828–1829*, p. 46.

August 2, 1828.   Henry Van Wart. *Diary 1828–1829*, p. 47.
August 5, 1828.   Ebenezer Irving. *Diary 1828–1829*, p. 48.
August 25, 1828.   Johann Nikolaus Böhl von Faber. *Diary 1828–1829*, p. 62.

August 30, 1828.   Ebenezer Irving. *Diary 1828–1829*, p. 64.
September 2, 1828.   Ebenezer Irving. *Diary 1828–1829*, p. 65.
September 2, 1828.   Mrs. Stalker. *Diary 1828–1829*, p. 65.
September 2, 1828.   Julian Williams. *Diary 1828–1829*, p. 65.
September 6, 1828.   Ebenezer Irving. *Diary 1828–1829*, p. 66.
September 8, 1828.   Ebenezer Irving. *Diary 1828–1829*, p. 67.
September 16, 1828.   Miss Stalker. *Diary 1828–1829*, p. 69.
September 24, 1828.   Antoinette Bolviller. *Diary 1828–1829*, p. 70.
September 26, 1828.   Alexander Burton. *Diary 1828–1829*, p. 70.
September 26, 1828.   Miss Stalker. *Diary 1828–1829*, p. 70.
September 29, 1828.   Richard McCall. *Diary 1828–1829*, p. 71.
September 30, 1828.   Antoinette Bolviller. *Diary 1828–1829*, p. 71.
October 3, 1828.   Catherine D'Oubril. *Diary 1828–1829*, p. 71.
October 3, 1828.   Miss Stalker. *Diary 1828–1829*, p. 71.
October 17, 1828.   Michael Walsh. *Diary 1828–1829*, p. 74.
October 21, 1828.   Julian Williams. *Diary 1828–1829*, p. 74.
October 21, 1828.   George Barrell. *Diary 1828–1829*, p. 75.
October 21, 1828.   Julia Irving. *Diary 1828–1829*, p. 75.
October 21, 1828.   Messrs. Lopez, Roberts & Co. *Diary 1828–1829*, p. 75.

October 23, 1828.   John Treat Irving. *Diary 1828–1829*, p. 75.
October 23, 1828.   Peter Irving. *Diary 1828–1829*, p. 75.
October 23, 1828.   Henry Van Wart. *Diary 1828–1829*, p. 75.
October 24, 1828.   Alexander Slidell. *Diary 1828–1829*, p. 76.
October 24, 1828.   Horatio Swett. *Diary 1828–1829*, p. 76.
November 4, 1828.   John N. Hall. *Diary 1828–1829*, p. 78.
November 8, 1828.   John N. Hall. *Diary 1828–1829*, p. 79.
November 15, 1828.   Alexander Burton. *Diary 1828–1829*, p. 81.
November 15, 1828.   John N. Hall. *Diary 1828–1829*, p. 81.
November 22, 1828.   Peter Irving. *Diary 1828–1829*, p. 82.
November 29, 1828.   Johann Nikolaus Böhl von Faber. *Diary 1828–1829*, p. 84.

November 29, 1828.   Alexander Burton. *Diary 1828–1829*, p. 84.
November 29, 1828.   To ———— Gessler. *Diary 1828–1829*, p. 84.

December 18, 1828.	Alexander Burton. *Diary 1828–1829*, p. 86.
December 20, 1828.	Alexander Burton. *Diary 1828–1829*, p. 87.
December 20, 1828.	Midshipman Ferrand. *Diary 1828–1829*, p. 87.
December 20, 1828.	Dr. Greene. *Diary 1828–1829*, p. 87.
December 20, 1828.	Pierre M. Irving. *Diary 1828–1829*, p. 87.
December 23, 1828.	Alexander Burton. *Diary 1828–1829*, p. 88.
December 24, 1828.	Sarah Van Wart. *Diary 1828–1829*, p. 88.
December 27, 1828.	George Barrell. *Diary 1828–1829*, p. 89.
December 27, 1828.	Antoinette Bolviller. *Diary 1828–1829*, p. 89.
December 27, 1828.	Alexander Burton. *Diary 1828–1829*, p. 89.
December 27, 1828.	Ebenezer Irving. *Diary 1828–1829*, p. 89.
ca. 1828.	Alexander H. Everett. Sotheby Parke Bernet, June 11, 1974, item 468.
January 23, 1829.	To ———— Campos. *Diary 1828–1829*, p. 95.
February 7, 1829.	Sarah Van Wart. *Diary 1828–1829*, p. 98.
February 10, 1829.	Colonel Thomas Aspinwall. American-Anderson, Sale no. 4125, November 8, 1934.
February 10, 1829.	To ———— Gessler. *Diary 1828–1829*, p. 99.
March 25?, 1829.	Martín Fernández de Navarrete. WI to Alexander H. Everett, March 25, 1829.
April 15, 1829.	John Wetherell. Sotheby Parke Bernet, October 15, 1974, item 9 and October 29, 1975, item 197; Parke-Bernet Galleries, November 16–17, 1938 (120).
ca. April 25?, 1829.	David Wilkie. WI to David Wilkie, May 15, 1829.
Late April, 1829.	Sarah Van Wart. WI to Sara Van Wart, May 12, 1829.
April, 1829.	Alexander Burton. WI to Alexander Everett, May 16, 1829.
May 23, 1829.	Bernard Henry. Stan V. Henkels, November 12, 1920 (388); WI to Edgar Irving, May 26, 1829.
Late May, 1829.	Horatio Sprague. WI to Colonel Thomas Aspinwall, June 23, 1829.
July 27, 1829.	Alexander Burton. WI to Colonel Thomas Aspinwall, July 27, 1829.
July 27, 1829.	Michael Walsh. WI to Colonel Thomas Aspinwall, July 27, 1829.
August 21, 1829.	George W. Montgomery. *Journals of WI*, III, 96.
November 20, 1829.	Colonel Thomas Aspinwall. Libbie's, December 12, 1895 (923).

December 2, 1829.   Henry Sandham. American Art Association, April 29–30, 1937, item 262.

December 16, 1829.   William Godwin. WI to William Godwin, January 16, 1830.

1829.   To Legation of the United States. Chadbourne & Conover, C. F. Libbie & Co., December 11, 1926 (730).

January 27, 1830.   Thomas Moore. Parke-Bernet, October 26, 1965, item 169.

January 30, 1830.   Arthur Matthews. Charles Hamilton, Auction 95, item 128, March 4, 1976.

March, 1830.   Sir John Bowring. Sotheby, March 28, 1972, item 410.

April 6, 1830.   To "a few particular letters [of introduction] to my friends." WI to James Edward Alexander, April 6, 1830.

Late April, 1830.   Sir William Ouseley? WI to Sir Gore Ouseley, May 2, 1830.

May 20, 1830.   To ———. C. F. Libbie & Co., March 15, 1907 (173).

May, 1830.   John Wetherell (letters of introduction). WI to John Wetherell, May 13, 1830.

June 17, 1830.   To ———. C. F. Libbie & Co., March 15, 1907 (169).

June 27, 1830.   To Sir Robert Peel. Sotheby Parke-Bernet, December 12–13, 1977, item 343.

August 25, 1830.   Colonel Thomas Aspinwall. Charles Hamilton, Auction 17, item 62, February 1, 1967.

November 6, 1830.   Gulian C. Verplanck. Stan V. Henkels, May 8, 1918, item 152.

November, 1830.   Thomas Moore. STW, II, 332.

December 21, 1830.   Colonel Thomas Aspinwall. C. F. Libbie & Co., April 26, 1904, item 429.

1830.   J. J. Audubon. STW, II, 332.

January 2, 1831.   To ———. American Art Association, February 17–18, 1938, item 191.

March 21, 1831.   To ———. WI to John M. Niles, March 21, 1831.

April 2, 1831.   Colonel Thomas Aspinwall. Charles Hamilton, Catalog 9, item 142.

May 10, 1831.   William C. Rives. STW, II, 332.

May 14, 1831.   Reverend W. B. Sprague. ABC 1950, December 5, 1949.

May 31, 1831.	Reuben Beasley. WI to Nathaniel Niles, May 31, 1831.
May 31, 1831.	Miss Douglas. WI to Nathaniel Niles, May 31, 1831.
June 7, 1831.	Longman & Co. Sotheby, December 17, 1963, item 494.
June 21, 1831.	To ———. Tefft, C. F. Libbie & Co., December 3, 1906 (425).
June 28, 1831.	Colonel Thomas Aspinwall. C. F. Libbie & Co., April 26, 1904, item 428.
July 8, 1831.	To ———. Maggs Bros., Catalog 211, Summer 1911.
July 8, 1831.	To ———. American-Anderson, Sale no. 4154, February 15, 1935.
July 12, 1831.	To ———. C. F. Libbie & Co., December 3, 1906, item 427.
July 27, 1831.	Sergeant Pell. Charles Hamilton, Auction 12, item 74A, March 22, 1966.
July 28, 1831.	Ralph W. Fox. Sotheby, May 3, 1971, item 252.
July 29, 1831.	To ———. Parke-Bernet, February 2, 1971, item 236.
August 10, 1831.	To ———. Charles Hamilton, Auction 26, item 135, April 18, 1968.
September 27, 1831.	To ———. Carnegie Book Shop, Catalog 300, item 270 and Catalog 310, item 494.
September 28, 1831.	Colonel Thomas Aspinwall. Carnegie Book Shop, Catalog 292, item 265.
Early October, 1831.	Sarah Van Wart. WI to Catharine Paris, October 14, 1831.
October 13, 1831.	Martin Van Buren. Forest H. Sweet, List no. 125.
ca. October 14, 1831.	Richard Dodge. WI to Catharine Paris, October 14, 1831.
1831–1832.	To ——— (passport). Maggs Bros., Catalog 439, Summer, 1923, and Catalog 473, Spring, 1926, no. 296.
January 26?, 1832.	John Murray II. WI to William Cullen Bryant, January 26, 1832.
Late January, 1832.	Ebenezer Irving. WI to Pierre P. Irving, February 6, 1832.
January, 1832.	Alexander Slidell. WI to Pierre M. Irving, February 6, 1832.

February 8, 1832.	Captain W. H. Dillon. Swann Galleries, Sale no. 217, October 28, 1948, item 197.
March 31, 1832.	Henry Colburn & Richard Bentley. Sotheby, April 29, 1969, item 376.
April 3, 1832.	W. Ousley. Harry A. Levinson, June 5, 1951, item 28.
May 31, 1832.	To the Corporation of New York. Swann Auction Galleries, May 17, 1951 (64).
June 12, 1832.	J. Pennington. Stan V. Henkels, March 9, 1917 (105).
Early January, 1833.	To the Membership Committee of Washington Lyceum. WI to Jonah F. Polk, January 9, 1833.
May 29, 1833.	Martin Van Buren. STW, II, 344.
September 2, 1833.	Louis McLane. WI to Alexander Slidell, September 2, 1833.
September 5, 1833.	Edgar Irving. STW, II, 347.
September 24, 1833.	Colonel Thomas Aspinwall. C. F. Libbie & Co., April 26, 1904, item 429.
February 5, 1834.	George P. Morris. STW, II, 344.
April 3, 1834.	Robert H. Inglis. *The Collector*, No. 878 (1981), 7.
April 3, 1834.	J. Hamilton Spencer. Anderson Galleries, February 27, 1929 (Edward Wheelock Library), (226).
October 15, 1834.	Aaron Vail. Parke-Bernet, April 2, 1968, item 364.
November 4, 1834.	William Sullivan. Arnold, Anderson Auction Gallery, February 1, 1905 (445).
December 13, 1834.	William Dunlap. William Dunlap, *Diary* (New York, 1969), III, 846.
ca. December 15, 1834.	Louis Cass. WI to Martin Van Buren, December 15, 1834.
December 20, 1834.	To the Committee of the Union Society, N.Y. STW, II, 344.
December 20, 1834.	T. H. Wheeler. STW, II, 344.
January 4, 1835.	Messrs. Longman, Hurst, Rees & Brown. Swann Auction Galleries, May 13, 1948 (30).
January 23, 1835.	To a friend in Europe. American Art Association-Anderson Galleries, October 30, 1929.
February 24, 1835.	Colonel Thomas Aspinwall. Bangs & Co., Arnold Sale, May 7, 1901 (379).

February 24, 1835.	Colonel Thomas Aspinwall. Merwin-Clayton Sales Co., June 21, 1905, item 116.
April 11, 1835.	Colonel Thomas Aspinwall. Parke-Bernet, April 2, 1968, item 365.
April 23, 1835.	Colonel Thomas Aspinwall. STW, II, 349.
May 29, 1835.	T. S. Fay. Charles Hamilton, Auction 111, item 136, March 23, 1978.
May 31, 1835.	To Lord Vassal Holland. Swann Auction Galleries, September 26, 1947 (194).
June 10, 1835.	To ————. American-Anderson, Sale no. 4374, February 17–18, 1935.
October 19, 1835.	Miss Laura Andrews. Charles Hamilton, Auction 99, item 201, September 16, 1976.
December 17, 1835.	William Archer, Charles Hamilton, Auction 123, item 102, October 18, 1979.
1835.	Reverend Orville Dewey. Charles Hamilton, Auction 54, item 250, December 9, 1971.
March 15, 1836.	Peter Irving. Peter Irving to John Treat Irving, Jr. April 7, 1836.
March 17, 1836.	To the Society of the Friendly Sons of St. Patrick. Swann Auction Galleries, April 25, 1946 (33); *The Collector*, 58 (November, 1945), 195.
May 11, 1836.	Martin Van Buren. Doane, Anderson Auction Company and the Metropolitan Art Association, June 14, 1914 (203).
Mid-November, 1836.	John Jacob Astor. WI to Robert Gilmor, December 3, 1836.
December 31, 1836.	Pierre P. Irving. Hurst, Anderson Auction Company, March 20, 1905 (3441).
March 26, 1837.	Louis J. Cist. City Book Auction, New York City, September, 1941 (38).
May 3, 1837.	Henry C. Carey. American Art Association-Anderson Galleries, Inc., October 20, 1930.
September 12, 1837.	M. Woolson. *The Collector*, 58 (November, 1945), 195.
1837.	To ————. *The Collector*, 2 (December, 1888), 63.
March 24, 1838.	Colonel Thomas Aspinwall. STW, II, 357, n. 43.
April 10, 1838.	Henry R. Schoolcraft. Library of Congress-Schoolcraft Papers.

April 20, 1838.   Henry S. Randall. Stan V. Henkels, October 9, 1928 (David Newbold Collection, Phila.), (231).

May 3, 1838.   J. & J. Harper. WI to John Wiley and George P. Putnam, May 3, 1838.

December 4, 1838.   J. L. Chester. STW, II, 357.

January 12, 1839.   Samuel B. Ruggles. Huntington-Church, Anderson Galleries, March 29, 1916 (630).

February 10, 1839.   To ————. Brown, Merwin-Clayton Sales Co., May 13, 1912 (446).

February 24, 1839.   Colonel Thomas Aspinwall. WI to Henry R. Schoolcraft, February 24, 1839.

March 29, 1839.   Colonel Thomas Aspinwall. Chamberlain, Anderson Auction Company, February 16, 1909 (404).

April 8, 1839.   To A. J. Davis. STW, II, 357.

May 11, 1839.   To Governor William H. Seward. Stan V. Henkels, April 8, 1908 (131).

May 25, 1839.   To Messrs. Lea and Blanchard. American Art Association, January 21–22, 1926 (168).

November 6, 1839.   To Henry Whipple. Kenneth W. Rendell Catalog, April, 1970, p. 27, item 96.

September 28, 1840.   To ————. WI to Charles A. Bristed, September 28, 1840.

October 1, 1840.   To the Reverend William Harness. Maggs Bros., Catalog 329, 1914.

October 1, 1840.   To William Jerdan. WI to Charles A. Bristed, October 1, 1840.

October 1, 1840.   To Frank Mills. WI to Charles A. Bristed, October 1, 1840.

November 25, 1840.   To A. J. Downing. Charles Hamilton, Auction 42, item 187, June 4, 1970.

1840.   To ————. *The Collector*, 4 (October, 1890), 19.

March 13, 1841.   To Charles Dickens. WI to Sarah Storrow, May 25, 1841.

July 3, 1841.   To ————. Botta, C. F. Libbie & Co., November 17, 1904 (570).

August 9, 1841.   To Lewis Gaylord Clark. American Art Association-Anderson Galleries, January 12, 1932 (39).

August 9, 1841.	To Messrs. Lea & Blanchard. Parke-Bernet Galleries, March 11, 1946 (342); STW, II, 361, n. 114.
September, 1841.	To Francis Granger. WI to Francis Granger, September 15, 1841.
October 30, 1841.	To "My Dear Baron." Charles Hamilton, Auction 11, item 94, January 31, 1966.
January 8, 1842.	To Henry S. Randall. Charles Hamilton, Auction 95, item 129, March 4, 1976.
March 11, 1842.	To ————. Charles Hamilton, Auction 40, item 166, March 12, 1970.
March 23, 1842.	To Robert Gilmor. Parke-Bernet Galleries, October 26, 1965 (170).
March 27, 1842.	To J. W. Dwinelle. Wendell, Anderson Auction Company, May 19, 1905 (245).
April 30, 1842.	To ————. Carnegie Book Shop, Catalog 300, item 268.
May 18, 1842.	To James Kenney. Sotheby, March 4, 1969, item 409.
September?, 1842.	To Julia Grinnell. WI to Julia Grinnell, September 30, 1842.
ca. October 21, 1842.	To Catharine Paris. WI to Sarah Storrow, October 21, 1842.
January 19, 1843.	To John Wetherell. STW, I, 485, n. 60.
January, 1843.	To Miguel José Molina. WI to Sarah Storrow, January 5, 1843.
March 24, 1843.	To Thomas H. Newbold. New York *World-Telegram*, May 23, 1945.
March 25, 1843.	To Charles Leslie. Hamilton Autographs, May 31, 1966 (115), (possibly the same as March 28, 1843).
Early July, 1843.	Alexander Hamilton, Jr. (Two letters?) WI to Sarah Storrow, July 14, 1843.
ca. July 30, 1843.	Dr. Brewster. WI to Sarah Storrow, August 7, 1843.
Early August, 1843.	Alexander Hamilton, Jr. WI to Sarah Storrow, August 7, 1843.
August 13, 1843.	Madame Albuquerque. WI to Sarah Storrow, August 13, 1843.
August 20, 1843.	To ————. Parke-Bernet Galleries, April 29–30, 1958 (192).

August 22, 1843.	Sarah Storrow. WI to Sarah Storrow, August 23, 1843.
August 23, 1843.	Jasper H. Livingston. STW, II, 328.
February, 1844.	Sarah Storrow. WI to Sarah Storrow, March 8, 1844.
May, 1844.	Alexander Hamilton, Jr. (Three letters) WI to Sarah Storrow, June 2, 1844.
July 18, 1844.	Jasper Livingston. WI to Pierre M. Irving, July 18, 1844.
July 20, 1844.	Ramón María Narváez. Notation in letterbook of U.S. legation, Madrid, June 23, 1844–July 27, 1844, p. [32] (NYPL–Berg).
September 24, 1844.	To ———. STW, II.
November, 1844.	Pierre Caze. WI to Sarah Storrow, November 15, 1844.
January?, 1845.	William R. King. WI to Sarah Storrow, March 6, 1845.
August 16, 1845.	Mrs. Louis McLane. STW, II, 385.
September 8, 1845.	Antonio Caballero. STW, II, 385, n. 55.
Early September, 1845.	Pierre M. Irving. WI to Catharine Paris, November 1, 1845.
November 9, 1845.	To ———. *The Collector*, 57 (February–March, 1944), 78.
January?, 1846.	Pierre M. Irving. WI to Helen Dodge Irving, February 14, 1847.
March 29, 1846.	James Buchanan. WI to James Buchanan, April 8, 1846.
May?, 1846.	Mrs. de Wolff. WI to Sarah Storrow, June 23, 1846.
October 7, 1846.	Angel Calderón de la Barca. WI to James Buchanan, October 8, 1846.
February 4, 1847.	John G. Garrison. Parke-Bernet Galleries, March 11, 1946 (346).
February 5, 1847.	H. Grenville. Coggeshall, Anderson Galleries, April 25, 1916 (388).
February 14, 1847.	Henry O'Shea & Co. WI to Sabina O'Shea, February 14, 1847.
February 19, 1847.	Moses Grinnell. Chicago Book & Art Auction, February 18–19, 1937 (271).
July 20, 1847.	To ———. Joline, Anderson Galleries, February 23, 1915 (272).
November 27, 1847.	J. S. Lyon. *The Collector*, no. 854, p. 7.
January 22, 1848.	J. Hedges. STW, II, 389.

March 27, 1848. Messrs. Lea & Blanchard. Stan V. Henkels, June 7, 1907, item 1024.

March 28, 1848. Irving Society of College of St. James. STW, II, 389.

April 17, 1848. James Boorman. WI to James Boorman, April 17, 1848.

August 7, 1848. Gideon Nye. C. F. Libbie, May 2, 1899 (359).

September 24, 1848. To ———. Darley, Stan V. Henkels, April 9, 1908 (1034).

October 9, 1848. Maria Shelby. Chicago Book & Art Auction, April 27, 1932 (111).

1848. Charles A. Bristed. *The Collector*, 3 (March, 1890), 92.

1848. Margaret Oliver Lawrence. George S. Mac-Manus Co., Catalog 249 (1980), item 311.

1848. To ———. *The Collector*, 50 (February, 1936), 43, item 33219.

April 9, 1849. James T. Fields. Hamilton Autographs, September 30, 1965 (89).

May 8, 1849. Dorothea Astor Langdon. WI to Dorothea Astor Langdon, May 25, 1849.

September 19, 1849. Irving Van Wart. Swann Auction Galleries, January 12, 1950 (176).

October 30, 1849. To ———. Palmer, Merwin-Clayton Sales Co., February 13, 1906 (377).

1849. To ———. C. F. Libbie & Co., April 23, 1918 (559).

February 11, 1850. Charles A. Davis. STW, II, 391, n. 65.

April 8, 1850. To ———. City Book Auction, February, 1943, item 265.

October 7, 1850. To ——— Clark. Hamilton Autographs, Auction 38, December 11, 1969, item 182.

October, 1850. Miss Rivers. WI to Andrew Jackson, September 28, 1850.

ca. March, 1851. G. & C. Merriam. WI to James Beekman, June 25, 1851.

April 15, 1851. To ———. Merwin-Clayton Sales Co., December 15, 1911, item 177.

September 12, 1851. To Major C. A. Davis. J. C. Morgenthau & Co., December 11, 1933 (148).

September 20, 1851. Ebenezer Irving. Charles Hamilton, Auction 53, October 21, 1971, item 191.

October 31, 1851. To ———. Bangs, April 11, 1896 (59).

December 31, 1851. To ———. Thomas F. Madigan's *Autograph Album*, 1 (December, 1933), 71, item 152.

1851. To the Editor of New York *Tribune* [Horace Greeley]. Charles Hamilton Autographs, Catalog 37, item 167a.

February 23, 1852. Charles Lanman. Anderson Auction Co., May 26, 1909, item 144.

May 25, 1852. Charles R. Leslie. Leslie, *Autobiographical Recollections*, 348.

June 2, 1852. Major Charles A. Davis. J. C. Morgenthau & Co., December 11, 1933 (148).

June 16, 1852. To his nephews. WI to Henry Ogden, June 16, 1852.

June 16, 1852. Peter Skene Ogden. WI to Henry Ogden, June 16, 1852.

July, 1852. Mrs. de Wolff. WI to Sarah Storrow, July 15, 1852.

August 13, 1852. George P. Putnam. Parke-Bernet, November 25, 1962, item 184.

August 17, 1852. George P. Putnam. Parke-Bernet, November 27, 1962 (104).

September 20, 1852. Messrs. Camp & Perkins. Sotheby, November 12, 1963 (82).

October, 1852. To ———. City Book Auction, September 18, 1948 (82).

December 8, 1852. Samuel Rogers. WI to Henry T. Tuckerman, December 8, 1852.

December 8, 1852. Sir Robert Harry Inglis. STW, II, 390, n. 46.

1852. To ———.

January 10, 1853. To the Industrial Association of New York. Parke-Bernet Galleries, April 29, 1953.

April 20, 1853. George P. Putnam. Charles Hamilton, Auction 42, June 4, 1970, item 188.

April 26, 1853. W. W. T. Synge. Swann Galleries, October 28, 1948 (207).

May 27, 1853. Washington Lewis. WI to Mary E. Kennedy, May 27, 1853.

October 11, 1853. John Murray. Swann Galleries, Sale 1044, item 185, 1976.

October 27, 1853. Mrs. Grant Thorburn. Swann Galleries, Sale 1039, 1976, item 148.

November 11, 1853.	Andrew Kennedy. WI to Mary E. Kennedy, December 17, 1853.
January 25, 1854.	Reuben Beasley. WI to Sarah Storrow, January 25, 1854.
January 28, 1854.	To ———. Anderson Galleries, November 17, 1914 (74).
February, 1854.	Sarah Storrow. WI to Catharine Storrow, February 21, 1854.
April 6, 1854.	Helen Dodge Irving. G. S. MacManus Co., New York Antiquarian Book Fair, April, 1975.
November 17, 1854.	Sir Robert Harry Inglis. WI to W. C. Preston, November 17, 1854.
November 17, 1854.	John Murray. WI to W. C. Preston, November 17, 1854.
January 10, 1855.	John M. Hale. Charles Hamilton, Auction 40, March 12, 1970, item 167.
February 16, 1855.	To a little girl. Anderson Galleries, December 6, 1915 (207).
July 31, 1855.	Aaron B. Pratt. American Art Association-Anderson Galleries, Inc. (William Crannell-Littleton Tazewell Collection) (103).
October 19, 1855.	Louisa Andrews. Paul C. Richards Autographs.
1855.	Sarah J. Hale. Charles Hamilton, Auction 66, March 22, 1973, item 142.
1855.	George P. Morris. Tefft, Libbie & Co., December 3, 1906 (423).
ca. January 1856.	Sarah Storrow. WI to Sarah Storrow, April 24, 1856.
April 15, 1856.	Lewis Gaylord Clark. Merwin Sales Co., April 28, 1913, item 450.
August 6, 1856.	G. V. Lansing. Stan V. Henkels, April 27, 1900 (202).
August 6, 1856.	Geological Hall and Dudley Observatory Committee. Swann Auction Gallery, April 24, 1947 (153).
November 20, 1856.	Commodore Hiram Paulding. Charles Hamilton, Auction 86, item 168, April 3, 1975.
1856.	To ———. John Anderson, Jr., May 13, 1903, item 528.
January 3, 1857.	James H. Hackett. Charles Hamilton, Auction 23, item 134, December 12, 1967.

Mid-January 1857.   Henry T. Tuckerman. WI to Henry T. Tuck-
                             erman, January 26, 1857.
May 6, 1857.   Robert Donaldson. *The Collector*, 58 (July,
                             1950), 150, item D1363.
May 8, 1857.   Charles Carter Lee. Parke-Bernet, Sale no.
                             1556 (December 7, 1954), item 182.
July 10, 1857.   To ————. Anderson Auction Galleries, De-
                             cember 6–7, 1915, item 214.
July, 1857.   To James Maitland. New York *Times*, March
                             23, 1858.
September 10, 1857.   Mrs. North. American Art Association, Jan-
                             uary 30, 1929, item 51.
September 22, 1857.   Robert Balmanno. Stan V. Henkels, February
                             22, 1898 (503).
September 27, 1857.   Charles A. Davis. STW, II, 400, n. 25.
December 1, 1857.   Pierre M. Irving. Parke-Bernet, January 20,
                             1947 (400).
January 2, 1858.   To ————. Stan V. Henkels, March 21, 1918
                             (115).
March 6, 1858.   A. Bloomer Hart. Charles Hamilton, Auction
                             76, item 215, March 28, 1974.
May 18, 1858.   Joshua Bates. Parke-Bernet Galleries, Decem-
                             ber 7, 1954 (183).
May 20, 1858.   To ————. C. F. Libbie & Co., February 15,
                             1910 (857).
June 27, 1858.   To ————. Parke-Bernet Galleries, Novem-
                             ber 6, 1963 (111).
July 19, 1858.   Benjamin Silliman. Parke-Bernet Galleries,
                             October 7–8, 1958 (259).
September 2, 1858.   To ————.
September 28, 1858.   Mme. Octavia Le Vart. Parke-Bernet Galler-
                             ies, October 18–19, 1939.
October 5, 1858.   To ————. Swann Auction Galleries, May
                             13, 1948 (36).
November 12, 1858.   Lord Brown Houghton. E. J. Craig, Box 509,
                             Oyster Bay, L.I., item P4109.
December 24, 1858.   To ————. Hamilton Autographs, October
                             17, 1963 (134).
1858.   To ————. *The Collector*, 3 (March, 1890),
                             92.
January 8, 1859.   Henry T. Tuckerman. Stan V. Henkels, Feb-
                             ruary 17, 1911 (427).

January 17, 1859.	James Nasmyth. WI to Joseph Harrison, January 17, 1859.
March 25, 1859.	Benson J. Lossing. Anderson Galleries, December 6, 1915 (211).
April 5, 1859.	Augustus M. [Flythe?]. PMI, MS. journal (NYPL), p. 23.
April 6, 1859.	To ———. Stan V. Henkels, April 29, 1897, item 46.
May 20, 1859.	S. Austin Allibone. PMI, MS. journal (NYPL), May 29, 1859, p. 60.
May 20, 1859.	William C. Preston. PMI, MS. journal (NYPL), May 20, 1859. p. 51.
May 31, 1859.	To ——— Morten. PMI, MS. journal (NYPL), May 30, 1859. p. 61.
June 17, 1859.	Captain Warman. PMI, MS. journal (NYPL), June 17, 1859. p. 72.
August 3, 1859.	Fisk P. Brewer. WI to Cyrus W. Field, August 3, 1859.
1859.	Winthrop Sargent. Charles Hamilton, Auction 50, June 24, 1971, item 205.
January 4, n. y.	Mrs. Albuquerque. Charles Hamilton, Sale 101, December 9, 1976, item 212.
January 7, n. y.	Catharine Irving. *The Collector*, 61 (May, 1948), 115, item M924.
January 12, n. y.	Lady Ashburton. Parke-Bernet Galleries, April 29–30, 1958 (193).
January 13, n. y.	Mr. and Mrs. Brock. James Lowe Autographs, Catalog 7 (August, 1977), 8.
February 5, n. y.	Henry Carey. *The Collector*, 58 (July, 1950), 155, item D1364.
March 10, n. y.	Mr. Fairfax. Charles Hamilton, Auction 85, item 227, February 27, 1975.
Wednesday, March 11, n. y.	To ———. Merwin-Clayton Sales Co., May 13, 1912 (448).
March 26, n. y.	To ———. Maggs Bros., 1912, vol. 1, item 248.
April 2, n. y.	To ———. Maggs Bros., Catalog 266, Easter, 1911.
Sunday, April 5, n. y.	To ———. Carnegie Book Shop, Catalog 294, item 230.
August 22, n. y.	To ———. Parke-Bernet Galleries, November 1, 1950, item 597.

August 29, n. y.	To ———. Stan V. Henkels. May 25, 1906 (475).
October 10, n. y.	Andrew Jackson. Parke-Bernet Galleries, February 7–8, 1955, item 369.
October 15, n. y.	J. L. Martin. Swann Galleries, Inc., November 20, 1958 (110).
October 19, n. y.	To ———. American-Anderson, Sale no. 4125.
n.d.	Colonel Thomas Aspinwall. Kennard Sale, Libbie's, April 26, 1904 (429).
n.d.	H. Baldwin. American Art Auction, April 19–20, 1933, item 282.
n.d.	Marchioness of Donegal. *The Collector*, 51 (November, 1936), 10, item 216.
n.d.	Edward Everett. Carnegie Book Shop, Catalog 361 (September, 1977), 23.
n.d.	Pierre M. Irving. Parke-Bernet Galleries, March 11, 1946 (349).
n.d.	[Pierre M. Irving]. Merwin-Clayton Sales Co., 1906 (161).
n.d.	Alfred Jones. G. A. Baker & Co., March 10, 1939, item 132.
n.d.	James Kenney. Sotheby, March 4, 1969 (409).
n.d.	[George P. Putnam]. C. F. Libbie, April 10, 1912 (777).
n.d.	John Wetherell. Parke-Bernet Galleries, April 21, 1947.
n.d.	To ———. Sotheby, March 20, 1973, item 85.
n.d.	To ———. *The Collector*, 2 (December, 1888), 63.
n.d.	To ———. American Art Association-Anderson Galleries, November 10, 1932 (45).
n.d.	Fifty WI letters without name of recipient in entries in *American Book Prices Current*.

APPENDIX III

Letters Received by Washington Irving (Located)

May 28, 1804. Ebenezer Irving. John Granlund; copy at SHR.

May, 1804. William Irving, Jr. PMI, I, 62.

June 28, 1804. James K. Paulding. *Letters of J. K. Paulding*, pp. 25–26.

October 25, 1804. William Irving, Jr. SHR.

November 3, 1804. William Irving, Jr. PMI, I, 126–27.

1804. William Irving, Jr. PMI, I, 67–68.

1804. William Irving, Jr. PMI, I, 74.

July 8, 1805. William Irving, Jr. PMI, I, 139–40.

March 13, 1807. Mary Fairlie. NYPL–WI Papers.

March 30, 1807. A "female correspondent at Philadelphia." PMI, I, 183.

May 11, 1807. Mary Fairlie. PMI, I, 188.

July 9, 1807. Thomas A. Cooper. PMI, I, 203–4.

April 30, 1808. Peter Irving. PMI, I, 214.

August 19, 1808. Catharine Paris. PMI, I, 218–19.

March 9, 1809. Peter Irving. PMI, I, 22.

April, 1809. Peter Irving. PMI, I, 223.

May 29, 1809. Mrs. J. O. Hoffman. PMI, I, 228.

July 1, 1809. Gouverneur Kemble. Yale; copy at SHR.

May 31, 1810. Peter Irving. PMI, I, 257.

September 2, 1810. John Howard Payne. Union College.

1810. Peter Irving. PMI, I, 256.

1810. Peter Irving. PMI, I, 256–57.

January 19, 1811. Henry Brevoort. NYPL; LBI, I, 3–10.

February 14, 1811. Henry Brevoort. NYPL; LBI, I, 11–19.

June 26, 1811. Henry Brevoort. NYPL; LBI, I, 20–25.

June 28, 1811. Henry Brevoort. NYPL; LBI, I, 26–35.

July 14, 1811. Henry Brevoort. NYPL; LBI, I, 36–43.

July 29, 1811. Henry Brevoort. NYPL; LBI, I, 44–48.

April 14, 1812. Henry Brevoort. NYPL; LBI, I, 49–58.

May 12, 1812. Henry Brevoort. NYPL; LBI, I, 59–63.

September 5, 1812.   James K. Paulding. *Letters of J. K. Paulding*,
                           p. 32.
December   9, 1812.   Henry Brevoort. NYPL; LBI, I, 64–69; PMI,
                           I, 297–98.
1812.   Henry Brevoort. PMI, I, 282.
March 1, 1813.   Henry Brevoort. NYPL; LBI, I, 70–90; PMI,
                           I, 302–3.
June 24, 1813.   Henry Brevoort. NYPL; LBI, I, 91–100; PMI,
                           I, 300–2.
December 18, 1813.   Peter Irving. PMI, I, 303–5.
December 21, 1813.   Thomas Campbell. Yale.
September 28, 1814.   Daniel D. Tompkins. *Public Papers of Daniel
                           D. Tompkins* (New York, 1902), III, 551–52.
December 15, 1815.   James K. Paulding. *Letters of J. K. Paulding*,
                           pp. 43–44.
December 20, 1815.   Albert Gallatin. SHR.
April 15, 1817.   Washington Allston. PMI, I, 361.
May 6, 1817.   Thomas Campbell. University of Iowa; PMI,
                           I, 364.
May 9, 1817.   Washington Allston. PMI, I, 362–64; extracts
                           in Jared B. Flagg, *Life and Letters of Wash-
                           ington Allston* (New York, 1892), pp. 71–72;
                           and in Waldron, *WI & Cotemporaries*,
                           pp. 226–29.
July 22, 1817.   James Ogilvie. PMI, I, 369–70.
December 20, 1817.   Charles R. Leslie. Leslie, *Autobiographical
                           Recollections*, pp. 205–6.
December 22, 1817.   Charles R. Leslie (Fragment). Va.–Barrett.
February 5, 1818.   Charles R. Leslie. PMI, I, 399.
March 13, 1818.   Washington Allston. PMI, I, 397–99; extract
                           in Flagg, *Life and Letters of Washington
                           Allston*, pp. 72–74.
March 16, 1818.   William C. Preston. Virginia Historical So-
                           ciety.
April 5, 1818.   James K. Paulding. *Letters of J. K. Paulding*,
                           pp. 56–57.
May 11, 1818.   Thomas Campbell. Va.–Barrett.
July 24, 1818.   Washington Allston. PMI, I, 401–3.
October 2, 1818.   Henry Brevoort. NYPL; LBI, I, 101–8.
October 24, 1818.   William Irving, Jr. NYPL–Hellman; copy at
                           SHR; PMI, I, 408–9.
January 27, 1819.   John Howard Payne. Union College.
February, [1819?]   John Murray. Va.–Barrett; copy at SHR.

ca. Summer, 1819.	James Ogilvie. PMI, I, 423.
August 9, 1819.	Henry Brevoort. SHR.
After August 16, 1819.	Mrs. J. O. Hoffman. PMI, I, 431.
August, 1819.	Henry Brevoort. PMI, I, 446–47.
September 9, 1819.	Henry Brevoort. NYPL; LBI, I, 109–15; PMI, I, 426–27.
October 27, 1819.	John Murray. PMI, I, 437.
November 9, 1819.	Henry Brevoort. NYPL; LBI, I, 116–20.
November 17, 1819	Walter Scott. Yale; PMI, I, 439–40; *Letters of Sir Walter Scott*, ed. H. J. C. Grierson (New York, 1971), VI, 20–21.
December 4, 1819.	Walter Scott. Yale; PMI, I, 442–44; *Letters of Sir Walter Scott*, VI, 44–47.
1819.	Ebenezer Irving. PMI, I, 447.
January 20, 1820.	James K. Paulding. *Letters of J. K. Paulding*, pp. 60–62.
January 27, 1820.	John Howard Payne. Union College.
March 1, 1820.	Walter Scott. Yale; PMI, I, 450–51; *Letters of Sir Walter Scott*, VI, 142–43.
April, 1820.	Henry Brevoort. NYPL; LBI, I, 121–27.
September 15, 1820.	Charles R. Leslie. Leslie, *Autobiographical Recollections*, pp. 220–21.
October 18, 1820.	Charles R. Leslie. Leslie, *Autobiographical Recollections*, pp. 221–22.
October 20, 1820.	Richard Rush. PMI, II, 20.
October 26, 1820.	John Murray. PMI, II, 24–26.
October 26, 1820.	Peter Powell. PMI, II, 28.
November 24, 1820.	Henry Brevoort. NYPL; LBI, I, 128–31.
December 3, 1820.	Charles R. Leslie, Leslie, *Autobiographical Recollections*, pp. 226–28; PMI, II, 31.
December 3, 1820.	Peter Powell. PMI, II, 32.
After December 19, 1820.	Charles R. Leslie. PMI, II, 29.
December 24, 1820.	Charles R. Leslie. Leslie, *Autobiographical Recollections*, pp. 230–31; PMI, II, 32; *Home Journal*, July 28, 1860, p. 3.
ca. 1820.	Charles R. Leslie. PMI, I, 406.
January 8, 1821.	Henry Brevoort. NYPL; LBI, I, 132–36.
February 10, 1821.	Thomas Hope. PMI, II, 44.
February 10, 1821.	Charles R. Leslie. PMI, II, 44.
March, 1821.	Henry Brevoort. PMI, II, 38.
ca. April–June, 1821.	Thomas Moon. Va.–Barrett.
April 2, 1821.	Charles R. Leslie. Leslie, *Autobiographical Recollections*, pp. 232–33.

April 12, 1821.   William Harris. Columbia.
May 7, 1821.   Henry Brevoort. NYPL; LBI, I, 137–42.
May 8–15, 1821.   John Howard Payne. Columbia.
May 25, 1821.   Charles R. Leslie. Leslie, *Autobiographical Recollections*, pp. 234–35.

June 15, 1821.   John Murray. PMI, II, 48.
June 29, 1821.   John Murray. PMI, II, 48.
ca. June, 1821.   Thomas Moore. HSP.
September 15, 1821.   Gilbert Stuart Newton. PMI, II, 60–61.
October 9, 1821.   Henry Brevoort. NYPL; LBI, I, 147–51.
October 22, 1821.   Charles R. Leslie. Leslie, *Autobiographical Recollections*, pp. 237–38; PMI, II, 61; *Home Journal*, August 4, 1860, p. 3.

October 22, 1821.   Peter Powell. PMI, II, 62–63.
November 3, 1821.   Gilbert Stuart Newton. PMI, II, 67–68.
November 5, 1821.   Charles R. Leslie. Leslie, *Autobiographical Recollections*, p. 244; *Home Journal*, August 4, 1860, p. 3.

November 28, 1821.   Peter Irving. PMI, II, 66.
December 5, 1821.   Charles R. Leslie. Leslie, *Autobiographical Recollections*, pp. 245–46; *Home Journal*, August 4, 1860, p. 3.

ca. January, 1822.   Charles Wiley. PMI, II, 74.
ca. March–July, 1822.   Thomas Moore. Va.–Barrett.
March 30, 1822.   John Howard Payne. Columbia; *Scribner's*, 48 (October, 1910), 468–69.

ca. April, 1822.   Peter Irving. PMI, II, 78.
June 15, 1822.   Lady Spencer. Va.–Barrett.
June 30, 1822.   William Coleman. NYHS.
July 30, 1822.   James Fenimore Cooper. PMI, II, 74–75.
August 5, 1822.   Thomas Moore. PMI, II, 106–7.
October 5, 1823.   N. Willets. HSP.
November 7, 1823.   John Howard Payne. PMI, II, 170–71.
November 8, 1823.   John Murray. PMI, II, 177.
November 29, 1823.   Thomas Oxnard. Columbia.
Early December, 1823.   John Howard Payne. PMI, II, 171.
January 27, 1824.   John Howard Payne. PMI, II, 172.
March 20, 1824.   James K. Paulding. *Letters of J. K. Paulding*, pp. 68–70, 71 (two letters).

[September 5?] 1824.   Thomas Moore. Yale; PMI, II, 208–9; *Letters of Thomas Moore*, ed. Wilfred S. Dowden (Oxford, 1964), II, 527.

October 7, 1824.	Gilbert Stuart Newton. PMI, II, 212–13.
1824.	Gouverneur Kemble. PMI, I, 166–67.
1824.	Thomas Moore. PMI, II, 211.
1824.	Gilbert Stuart Newton. PMI, II, 211.
January 26, 1825.	John Howard Payne. East Hampton Free Library.
ca. January, 1825.	John Howard Payne. (Dedication of *Richelieu* to WI in the form of a letter.) *Scribner's*, 48 (November, 1910), 597.
February 28, 1825.	John Howard Payne. East Hampton Free Library.
April 4, 1825.	John Howard Payne. East Hampton Free Library.
Mid-May, 1825.	Thomas Medwin. *J&N*, III, 486.
Early June, 1825.	William E. West. *J&N*, III, 491.
June 10, 1825.	John Howard Payne. Columbia; *Scribner's*, 48 (November, 1910), 60.
August 16, 1825.	John Howard Payne. Huntington; *Romance of Mary Shelley, John Howard Payne and WI* (Boston, 1907), pp. 17–19.
August 31, 1825.	James K. Paulding. *Letters of J. K. Paulding*, pp. 81–82.
September 3, 1825.	James K. Paulding. *Letters of J. K. Paulding*, pp. 82–83.
ca. October, 1825.	Luther Bradish. NYHS.
ca. December, 1825.	"A literary friend." PMI, II, 174.
1825–1826[?].	Gilbert Stuart Newton. NYPL–Hellman.
January 4, 1826.	John Howard Payne. Columbia.
January 12, 1826.	Charles R. Leslie. Leslie, *Autobiographical Recollections*, pp. 265–66.
February 2, 1826.	John Howard Payne. Columbia; *Scribner's*, 48 (November, 1910), 605–7.
February 8, 1826.	John Howard Payne. Columbia; *Scribner's*, 48 (November, 1910), 609–11.
February 10, 1826.	John Howard Payne. *Scribner's*, 48 (November, 1910), 613–14.
February 16, 1826.	John Howard Payne. *Scribner's*, 48 (November, 1910), 613–14.
February 23, 1826.	Charles R. Leslie. Leslie, *Autobiographical Recollections*, pp. 268–69; PMI, II, 251.
May 31, 1826.	John Treat Irving, Sr. Columbia.
1826.	John Howard Payne. PMI, II, 174–75.

January 1, 1827.	Henry Brevoort. NYPL; LBI, I, 152–64.
January 4, 1827.	John Murray. Partially reprinted in WIHM, pp. 87–88.
March 15, 1827.	Ebenezer Irving. PMI, II, 175–76.
September 24, 1827.	Colonel Thomas Aspinwall. PMI, II, 268.
September 24, 1827.	Henry Wadsworth Longfellow. NYPL–Berg; *Bulletin NYPL,* 62 (September, 1958), 469–70.
October 8, 1827.	Gilbert Stuart Newton. NYPL–Hellman; PMI, II, 268–69.
ca. October 8, 1827.	Colonel Thomas Aspinwall. PMI, II, 268.
November 19, 1827.	Henry Brevoort. NYPL; LBI, II, 3–7.
December 19, 1827.	Henry Brevoort. NYPL; LBI, II, 8–17.
1827.	John Murray. PMI, II, 249.
ca. February, 1828.	Peter Irving. PMI, II, 279–80.
March 19, 1828.	Charles R. Leslie. Leslie, *Autobiographical Recollections,* pp. 279–80.
May 31, 1828.	Henry Brevoort. NYPL; LBI, II, 18–22.
Early November, 1828.	Peter Irving. PMI, II, 351–52.
ca. Early December, 1828.	John N. Hall. PMI, II, 360.
December 12, 1828.	Colonel Thomas Aspinwall. PMI, II, 362.
January 30, 1829.	Sir David Wilkie. NYPL–Hellman.
March 30, 1829.	Henry Brevoort. NYPL; LBI, II, 23–27.
ca. Spring, 1829.	Colonel Thomas Aspinwall. PMI, II, 379.
April 30, 1829.	Henry Brevoort. NYPL; LBI, II, 28–33.
May 31, 1829.	Henry Brevoort. NYPL; LBI, II, 34–40.
July 20, 1829.	Martin Van Buren. NA, RG 59.
July 28, 1829.	Alexander H. Everett. NYPL–Hellman.
September 21, 1829.	Martin Van Buren. NA, RG 59.
October 6, 1829.	————. University of Sussex, England.
October 7, 1829.	Colonel Thomas Aspinwall. NA, RG 84.
October 12, 1829.	William Godwin. C. Kegan Paul, *William Godwin: His Friends and Contemporaries* (London, 1876), II, 300–1.
October 23, 1829.	Johann Nikolaus Böhl von Faber. Count Osborne.
ca. October, 1829.	John Irving. PMI, II, 417.
November 6, 1829.	Henry Brevoort. NYPL; LBI, II, 41–45.
ca. October–November, 1829.	Thomas Moore. SHR.
ca. October–November, 1829.	Thomas Moore. Va.–Barrett.
November 9, 1829.	Thomas Moore. Va.–Barrett.

Fall, 1829.	Samuel Rogers. NYPL—WI Papers.
1829.	Ebenezer Irving. PMI, II, 417–18.
January 30, 1830.	James K. Paulding. *Letters of J. K. Paulding*, p. 110.
1830 (between January and August).	Thomas Moore. *Modern Language Notes*, 62 (April, 1947), 253.
March 12, 1830.	Martin Van Buren. NA, RG 59; Huntington (two letters).
March 23, 1830.	Henry Brevoort. NYPL; LBI, II, 46–49.
March 31, 1830.	L. M. Phillips. NA, RG 84.
April 2, 1830.	Colonel Thomas Aspinwall. George Arms.
April 5, 1830.	Richard Cattermole, PMI, II, 429.
April 20, 1830.	Charles Dickens. Huntington.
April 22, 1830.	S. Le Fevre. NA, RG 84.
May 19, 1830.	Arthur Matthews. PMI, II, 430.
May 19, 1830.	Martin Van Buren. NA, RG 59.
May 25, 1830.	Thomas Moore. Va.–Barrett.
June 3, [1830].	Arthur Matthews. Yale.
June 17, 1830.	Henry Brevoort. NYPL; LBI, II, 50–52.
July 6, 1830.	William Sotheby. Yale.
July 8, 1830.	Henry Brevoort. NYPL; LBI, II, 53–56.
July 30, 1830.	U.S. Department of State. NA, RG 59.
August 31, 1830.	B. R. Haydon. Yale.
ca. 1830–1831.	Thomas Moore. Va.–Barrett.
January 4, 1831.	Henry Brevoort. NYPL; LBI, II, 60–64.
January 31, 1831.	Thomas Moore. Va.–Barrett; PMI, II, 421.
March 1, 1831.	Sir Francis Freeling. NA, RG 84.
March 3, 1831.	Charles Leslie. NYPL—Hellman.
March 7, 1831.	Henry Brevoort. NYPL; LBI, II, 65–70.
March 11, 1831.	Thomas Moore. Va.–Barrett; PMI, II, 422.
April 1, 1831.	Martín Fernández de Navarette. NYPL—Hellman.
May 25, 1831.	Edward Livingston. NA, RG 59.
June 22, 1831.	Edward Livingston. NA, RG 84.
June 30, 1831.	Henry Brevoort. NYPL; LBI, II, 71–75.
June 30, 1831.	Robert R. Hunter. NA, RG 84.
July 8, 1831.	Colonel Thomas Aspinwall. NA, RG 84.
July 8, 1831.	Henry Brevoort. NYPL; LBI, II, 76–83.
July 9, 1831.	T. W. Fox. NA, RG 84.
August 3, 1831.	Colonel Thomas Aspinwall. NA, RG 84.
August 17, 1831.	Robert W. Fox. NA, RG 84.
August 17, 1831.	Lord Palmerston. SHR; NA, RG 84.
August 22, 1831.	John Randolph. Va.–Barrett.

August 24, 1831.	Lord Palmerston. Public Records Office, London.
August 24, 1831.	Gabriel Walker. NA, RG 84.
August 25, 1831.	Sir Robert Chester. NA, RG 84.
August 25, 1831.	Robert Grieve. NA, RG 84.
August 26, 1831.	Alex Thomson. NA, RG 84.
September 12, 1831.	Gabriel Walker. NA, RG, 84.
September 13, 1831.	Louis McLane. NYPL–Hellman, and Va.–Barrett.
September 13, 1831.	John Miller. NA, RG 59.
September 16, 1831.	Lord Palmerston. NA, RG 84.
October 19, 1831.	James K. Paulding. *Letters of J. K. Paulding*, pp. 118–19.
October 25, 1831.	John Murray II. John Murray.
November 4, 1831.	Louis McLane. Yale; copy at SHR.
December 29, 1831.	William Cullen Bryant. Pforzheimer Library; PMI, II, 472–73; Parke Godwin, *A Biography of William Cullen Bryant* (New York, 1883), I, 264–65.
December 31, 1831.	Gulian C. Verplanck. NYPL–Hellman; PMI, II, 473.
Early January, 1832.	Peter Irving. PMI, I, 167.
January 30, 1832.	John Murray II. Yale; PMI, II, 474.
February 2, 1832.	John Murray II. Godwin, *A Biography of William Cullen Bryant*, I, 271.
March 2, 1832.	James E. Alexander. SHR.
March 6, 1832.	Samuel Rogers. Yale; PMI, II, 477.
March 25, 1832.	Henry Brevoort. NYPL; LBI, II, 84–90.
April 17, 1832.	Prince Dolgorouki. NYPL–Hellman.
April 19, 1832.	Catharine Paris. Yale.
April 24, 1832.	William Cullen Bryant. Yale; PMI, II, 477–78; Godwin, *A Biography of William Cullen Bryant*, I, 273–74.
May 18, 1832.	Peter Irving. PMI, III, 23.
May 22, 1832.	William Cullen Bryant. Pforzheimer Library; PMI, II, 478–79; Godwin, *A Biography of William Cullen Bryant*, I, 274.
May 23, 1832.	James Renwick et al. NYPL; *New-York Mirror*, June 9, 1832; STW, II, 336.
ca. June–July, 1832.	Peter Irving. PMI, III, 23.
June 14, 1832.	Thomas Moore. HSP. *Letters of Thomas Moore*, II, 748–49.
July 28, 1832.	Henry Brevoort. NYPL; LBI, II, 91–98.

July, 1832.	Peter Irving. PMI, III, 14–15.
ca. July, 1832.	Peter Irving. PMI, III, 27–28.
August 16, 1832.	Levi Woodbury. LC.
August 19, 1832.	Peter Irving. PMI, III, 15–16.
ca. August, 1832.	Peter Irving. PMI, III, 16.
December 30, 1832.	James K. Paulding. *Letters of J. K. Paulding*, pp. 127–28.
January 7, 1833.	James K. Paulding. *Letters of J. K. Paulding*, pp. 128–29.
January 18, 1833.	Henry Brevoort. NYPL; LBI, II, 99–105.
February 2, 1833.	G. H. Stewart. Maryland Historical Society.
February 26, 1833.	Johann Nikolaus Böhl von Faber. Count Osborne.
March 7, 1833.	James K. Paulding. *Letters of J. K. Paulding*, pp. 129–30.
April 16, 1833.	J. Morton. Columbia.
April 24, 1833.	Thomas Moore. Va.–Barrett.
April 26, 1833.	Johann Nikolaus Böhl von Faber. Count Osborne.
June 13, 1833.	A. J. Donelson. NYEP, June 14, 1833.
October 23, 1833.	David Wilkie. Yale.
ca. 1833.	James Gardner. South Caroliniana Library, University of South Carolina.
February 28, 1834.	James K. Paulding. *Letters of J. K. Paulding*, p. 142.
March 6, 1834.	Martin Van Buren. *The Autobiography of Martin Van Buren*, II, 611.
June 27, 1834.	Henry Brevoort. NYPL; LBI, II, 106–9.
November, 1834.	Francis Lieber (dedication to WI). Francis Lieber, *Letters to a Gentleman in Germany* (Philadelphia, 1834).
December 29, 1834.	Charles R. Leslie. Leslie, *Autobiographical Recollections*, pp. 297–99.
March 5, 1835.	Colonel Thomas Aspinwall. PMI, III, 72.
May 6, 1835.	Henry R. Schoolcraft. LC.
May 8, 1835.	David Wilkie. Yale.
May 9, 1835.	Henry Clay. Brown University.
May 11, 1835.	Charles R. Leslie. Leslie, *Autobiographical Recollections*, pp. 300–301.
May 23, 1835.	Henry Carey. Carey & Lea letterbook (HSP).
July 8, 1835.	Charles R. Leslie. Leslie, *Autobiographical Recollections*, pp. 301–2.

July 14, 1835.   S. W. Newton (Mrs. Gilbert Stuart). Va.–
                            Barrett.
August 29, 1835.   Henry R. Schoolcraft. NYHS.
ca. 1835.   James Gadsden. *The Collector*, 65 (August–
                            September, 1952), 167 (R1448).
February 23, 1836.   James Renwick. *Astoria*, ed. Edgely W. Todd
                            (Norman, Okla., 1964), p. 518.
March 6, 1836.   Peter Irving. PMI, III, 113.
March 8, 1836.   Peter Irving. PMI, III, 86.
April 2, 1836.   William Cullen Bryant. Godwin, *A Biography
                            of William Cullen Bryant*, I, 313.
April, 1836.   L. A. Frankel. SHR.
June 7, 1836.   Edgar Allan Poe. Brown University.
September 24, 1836.   John Jacob Astor. SHR.
September, 1836.   Alexander J. Davis. NYPL; copy at SHR.
November 25, 1836.   John Jacob Astor. HSP.
[1836].   James K. Paulding. *Letters of J. K. Paulding*,
                            pp. 188–89.
February 20, 1837.   Samuel Rogers. Brown University.
May 13, 1837.   Richard Bentley. British Library.
August 27, 1837.   J. S. Knowles. University of Texas.
September 9, 1837.   D. Appleton & Co. Va.–Barrett.
October 28, 1837.   Catharine G. Wirt. NYPL–Hellman.
April 23, 1838.   Martin Van Buren. Richard Kemble; LC
                            (draft); PMI, III, 126–27.
July 30, 1838.   James K. Paulding. *Letters of J. K. Paulding*,
                            pp. 220–22.
September 10, 1838.   James K. Paulding. *Letters of J. K. Paulding*,
                            pp. 234–35.
December 24, 1838.   James K. Paulding. *Letters of J. K. Paulding*,
                            pp. 240–41.
December 31, 1838.   William H. Prescott. PMI, III, 134–37.
[1838?]   Edward Maturin. Haverford College.
January 24, 1839.   William H. Prescott. PMI, III, 140–43.
October 12, 1839.   Edgar Allan Poe. *Letters of Edgar Allan Poe*,
                            ed. John W. Ostrom (Cambridge, Mass.,
                            1948), pp. 688–90.
November 14, 1839.   Anthony J. Bleecker. Fenimore Cooper Fam-
                            ily Papers.
November 26, 1839.   James K. Paulding. *Letters of J. K. Paulding*,
                            p. 271.
December 24, 1839.   William H. Prescott. Yale; PMI, III, 151;
                            Ticknor, *Life of W. H. Prescott*, pp. 164–66;

	Papers of W. H. Prescott, ed. Harvey Gardiner, (Urbana, 1964), pp. 152–53.
Late 1830's.	Johann Nikolaus Böhl von Faber. Count Osborne.
March 3, 1840.	James K. Paulding. *Letters of J. K. Paulding*, p. 275.
June 2, 1840.	James K. Paulding. *Letters of J. K. Paulding*, p. 276.
September 17, 1840.	James K. Paulding. *Letters of J. K. Paulding*, p. 285.
November 10, 1840.	Henry Brevoort. NYPL; LBI, II, 110.
November 11, 1840.	James K. Paulding. *Letters of J. K. Paulding*, pp. 287–88.
Early 1841.	———— Van Bibber. PMI, III, 161–62.
January 4, 1841.	D. Henderson. NYPL–Seligman.
January 17, 1841.	G. P. R. James. PMI, III, 163.
March 2, 1841.	Lea & Blanchard. Earl L. Bradsher, *Mathew Carey* (New York, 1912), pp. 90–91.
March 16, 1841.	Daniel Webster. Newport (R.I.) Hist. Soc.
April 21, 1841.	Charles Dickens. PMI, III, 164–66; *Letters of Charles Dickens*, II, 267–69.
June 21, 1841.	Edgar Allan Poe. Va.–Barrett; *Letters of Edgar Allan Poe*, I, 161–63.
July 1, 1841.	Henry Brevoort. NYPL; LBI, II, 111–12.
August 30, 1841.	Henry Brevoort. NYPL; LBI, II, 113–19.
September 28, 1841.	Charles Dickens. *Letters of Charles Dickens*, II, 394–97.
October 18, 1841.	Henry Brevoort. NYPL; LBI, II, 120.
November 6, 1841.	James Edward Alexander. Va.–Barrett.
December 31, 1841.	Charles R. Leslie. Leslie, *Autobiographical Recollections*, pp. 322–23.
February 13, 1842.	George Ticknor. [Anna E. Ticknor], *The Life of Joseph Green Cogswell* (Cambridge, Mass., 1874), p. 227.
February 14, 1842.	Daniel Webster. PMI, III, 177–78.
February 16, 1842.	Daniel Webster. NYPL–Hellman; NA, RG 59.
February 17, 1842.	Charles A. Davis. NYPL–Hellman.
After February, 1842.	Hugh S. Legaré. PMI, III, 181–82.
March 3, 1842.	Lea & Blanchard. Bradsher, *Mathew Carey*, p. 91.
March 15, 1842.	Chandler Gibson. Yale.
March 17, 1842.	G. W. Bleecker. Yale.
March 17, 1842.	Ebenezer Irving. Va.–Barrett.

March 19, 1842.	Daniel Webster. NYPL–Hellman; NA, RG 59.
March 21, 1842.	Charles Dickens. Yale; PMI, III, 187.
March 21, 1842.	Benjamin Rush. Princeton (draft copy).
March 29, 1842.	Henry Clay. PMI, III, 188.
March 29, 1842.	Philip Hone et al. PMI, III, 189–90.
March 30, 1842.	George Ticknor. George Ticknor, *Letters to Pascual de Gayangos*, ed. Clara Louisa Penney (New York, 1927), pp. 32–33.
March 30, 1842.	Daniel Webster. NYPL–Hellman; NA, RG 59.
March 31, 1842.	George Ticknor. *Life, Letters, and Journals of George Ticknor*, II, 245–46.
April 1, 1842.	Philip Hone. *New-York Mirror*, 20 (April 16, 1842), 123; PMI, III, 189–90.
April 2, 1842.	Daniel Webster. NYPL–Hellman; NA, RG 59.
April 8, 1842.	William Cullen Bryant. Pforzheimer Library.
May 10, 1842.	William H. Prescott. NYPL–Seligman; *The Correspondence of W. H. Prescott*, ed. Roger Walcott, pp. 302–6.
May 22, 1842.	Aaron Vail. Va.–Barrett.
June 22, 1842.	Daniel Webster. NYPL–Hellman; NA, RG 59.
June 23, 1842.	Robert Howe Gould. NA, RG 84.
June 24, 1842.	T. M. Rodney. NA, RG 84.
June 25, 1842.	Charles Callaghan. NA, RG 84.
July 11, 1842.	Charles Callaghan. NA, RG 84.
July 15, 1842.	P. W. Gallaudet. SHR.
July 22, 1842.	Gurdon Bradley. NA, RG 84.
July 23, 1842.	F. Rudolph. NA, RG 84.
July 24, 1842.	Obadiah Rich. NA, RG 84.
July 26, 1842.	Gurdon Bradley. NA, RG 84.
July 27, 1842.	S. Lacuri. NA, RG 84.
July 27, 1842.	Aaron Vail. NA, RG 84.
July 30, 1842.	Daniel Webster. NYPL–Hellman; NA, RG 59.
July, 1842.	Horatio Sprague. NA, RG 84.
August 5, 1842.	Count Almodóvar. NA, RG 84.
August 18?, 1842.	Count Almodóvar. Archivo de Ministerio de Asuntes Exteriores, Madrid.
August 18, 1842.	John Miller. NA, RG 84.
August 20, 1842.	Pablo Anguera. NA, RG 84.
August 22, 1842.	Count Almodóvar. NA, RG 84.
August 22, 1842.	Alexander Burton. NA, RG 84.
August 28, 1842.	Count Almodóvar. (Two letters.) NA, RG 84.
August 29, 1842.	Daniel Webster. NYPL–Hellman; NA, RG 59.
August 30, 1842.	Count Almodóvar. NA, RG 84.

September 7, 1842.   Joseph? Smith. NA, RG 84.
September 8, 1842.   Fletcher Webster. NYPL—Hellman; NA, RG 59.

September 12, 1842.   Edwin Clark. NA, RG 84.
September 13, 1842.   P. Harmony. NA, RG 84.
September 13, 1842.   Fletcher Webster. NYPL—Hellman. NA, RG 59.

September 24, 1842.   Robert Howe Gould. NA, RG 84.
September 29, 1842.   Orlando S. Morse. NA, RG 84.
September 29, 1842.   Fletcher Webster. NYPL—Hellman; NA, RG 59.

September 30, 1842.   John Miller. NA, RG 84.
September, 1842.   Joseph? Smith. NA, RG 84.
October 7, 1842.   Obadiah Rich. NA, RG 84.
October 10, 1842.   Fletcher Webster. NYPL—Hellman; NA, RG 59.

October 15, 1842.   Obadiah Rich. NA, RG 84.
October 17, 1842.   Daniel Webster. NYPL—Hellman; NA, RG 59.
October 22, 1842.   Count Almodóvar. NA, RG 84.
October 24, 1842.   G. H. Stewart. NA, RG 84.
November 2, 1842.   R. B. Campbell. NA, RG 84.
November 2, 1842.   George Read. NA, RG 84.
November 5, 1842.   Paul Pon. NA, RG 84.
November 5, 1842.   George Read. NA, RG 84.
November 6, 1842.   ———— Bradford. NA, RG 84.
November 12, 1842.   Juan Costa y Gabriz?. NA, RG 84.
November 15, 1842.   Conde de Asalto. NA, RG 84.
November 15, 1842.   Alvano Somero. NA, RG 84.
November 18, 1842.   George Read. NA, RG 84.
November 22, 1842.   Edward Everett. NYPL—Hellman.
November 26, 1842.   R. B. Campbell. NA, RG 84.
November 30, 1842.   Count Almodóvar. NA, RG 84.
ca. November, 1842.   George Read. NA, RG 84.
December 4, 1842.   Count Almodóvar. NA, RG 84.
December 5, 1842.   R. B. Campbell. NA, RG 84.
December 6, 1842.   Maximo de Aguirre. NA, RG 84.
December 6, 1842.   George Read. NA, RG 84.
December 7, 1842.   Count Almodóvar. NA, RG 84.
December 14, 1842.   Count Almodóvar. NA, RG 84.
December 15, 1842.   P. Harmony. NA, RG 84.
December 15, 1842.   ————. NA, RG 84.
December 18, 1842.   George Read. NA, RG 84.
December 19, 1842.   James Miller. NA, RG 84.

December 24, 1842.	Count Almodóvar. NA, RG 59.
December 24, 1842.	A. F. de Gamboa. NA, RG 84.
December 26, 1842.	George Read. NA, RG 84.
December 28, 1842.	Henry Brevoort. NYPL; LBI, II, 121–29.
Sunday [1842?].	————. [signature page missing] Yale.
Late 1842–early 1843.	———— Blond. NA, RG 84.
January 4, 1843.	Conde de Asalto. NA, RG 84.
January 7, 1843.	A. F. de Gamboa. NA, RG 84.
January 7, 1843.	George Read. NA, RG 84.
January 12, 1843.	Joseph Cullen. NA, RG 84.
January 14, 1843.	Joaquín de Villaboa. NA, RG 84.
January 17, 1843.	Joseph Cullen. NA, RG 84.
January 17, 1843.	Daniel Webster. NYPL–Hellman; NA, RG 59.
January 18, 1843.	José Cabrera. NA, RG 84.
January 21, 1843.	Franco De Quero. NA, RG 84.
January 23, 1843.	George Read. NA, RG 84.
January 24, 1843.	Joaquín de Villaboa. NA, RG 84.
January 24, 1843.	Count Almodóvar. NA, RG 84.
January 25, 1843.	George Read. NA, RG 84.
January 28, 1843.	Joseph Cullen. NA, RG 84.
February 2, 1843.	Joseph Cullen. NA, RG 84.
February 6, 1843.	Joaquín de Villaboa. NA, RG 84.
February 9, 1843.	Pablo Anguera. NA, RG 84.
February 10, 1843.	George Read. NA, RG 84.
February 11, 1843.	Joseph Cullen. NA, RG 84.
February 21, 1843.	Daniel Webster. NYPL–Hellman; NA, RG 59.
February 23, 1843.	Juan Garcia Barzanallana. NA, RG 84.
February 25, 1843.	Juan Garcia Barzanallana. NA, RG 84.
February 25, 1843.	Joseph Cullen. NA, RG 84.
February, 1843.	Madame de Viar. NA, RG 84.
March 2, 1843.	Paul Pon. NA, RG 84.
March 9, 1843.	Count Almodóvar. NA, RG 84.
March 12, 1843.	José Cabrera. NA, RG 84.
March 13, 1843.	George Read. NA, RG 84.
March 14, 1843.	Ramón Calabrava. NA, RG 84.
March 14, 1843.	Daniel Webster. NYPL–Hellman; *Writings and Speeches of Daniel Webster*, XIV, 404.
March 17, 1843.	Ramón Calabrava. NA, RG 84.
March 17, 1843.	George Read. NA, RG 84.
March 18, 1843.	Count Almodóvar. NA, RG 84.
March 18, 1843.	Daniel Webster. NYPL–Hellman; NA, RG 59.
March 20, 1843.	George Read. NA, RG 84.
March 22, 1843.	H. P. Sturgis. NA, RG 84.

March 25, 1843.	Count Almodóvar. NA, RG 84.
March 27, 1843.	George Read. NA, RG 84.
March 29, 1843.	George Read. (Two letters.) NA, RG 84.
March 30, 1843.	Daniel Webster. NYPL–Hellman; NA, RG 59.
March 31, 1843.	Count Almodóvar. NA, RG 84.
March 31, 1843.	George Read. NA, RG 84.
April 2, 1843.	Count Almodóvar. NA, RG 84.
April 3, 1843.	Count Almodóvar. NA, RG 84.
April 3, 1843.	Conde de Asalto. NA, RG 84.
April 3, 1843.	Arthur MacCulloch. NA, RG 84.
April 3, 1843.	George Read. NA, RG 84.
April 4, 1843.	Alvaro Somero. NA, RG 84.
April 5, 1843.	Horatio Sprague. NA, RG 84.
April 6, 1843.	Count Almodóvar. NA, RG 84.
April 10, 1843.	George Read. NA, RG 84.
April 12, 1843.	George Read. NA, RG 84.
April 18, 1843.	Alexander Burton. NA, RG 84.
April 20, 1843.	Daniel Webster. NYPL–Hellman; NA, RG 59.
April 27, 1843.	Alexander Burton. NA, RG 84.
April 27, 1843.	Paul Pon. NA, RG 84.
April 27, 1843.	Daniel Webster. Dartmouth.
May 1, 1843.	Count Almodóvar. NA, RG 84.
May 1, 1843.	Alexander Burton. (Two letters.) NA, RG 84.
May 4, 1843.	Alexander Burton. NA, RG 84.
May 6, 1843.	Count Almodóvar. NA, RG 84.
May 7, 1843.	Arthur MacCulloch. NA, RG 59; NA, RG 84.
May 8, 1843.	Alexander Burton. NA, RG 84.
May 9, 1843.	H. S. Legaré. NYPL–Hellman; NA, RG 59.
May 10, 1843.	Joaquín de Frías. NA, RG 84.
May 10, 1843.	George Read. NA, RG 84.
May 12, 1843.	Joaquín de Frías. NA, RG 84.
May 16, 1843.	Juan Garcia Barzanallana. NA, RG 84.
May 18, 1843.	Obadiah Rich. NA, RG 84.
May 20, 1843.	Conde de Asalto. NA, RG 84.
May 21, 1843.	Olegario de los Cuetos. NA, RG 84.
May 26, 1843.	George Read. NA, RG 84.
June 2, 1843.	Charles Morris. (Two letters.) NA, RG 84.
June 2, 1843.	Obadiah Rich. NA, RG 84.
June 3, 1843.	Juan Mendizábel. NA, RG 84.
June 5, 1843.	George Read. NA, RG 84.
June 7, 1843.	George Read. NA, RG 84.
ca. June 8, 1843.	Olegario de los Cuetos. NA, RG 84.
June 8, 1843.	Paul Pon. (Two letters.) NA, RG 84.

June 9, 1843.	George Read. NA, RG 84.
June 12, 1843.	Gurdon Bradley. NA, RG 84.
June 12, 1843.	Paul Pon. NA, RG 84.
June 12, 1843.	George Read. NA, RG 84.
June 17, 1843.	Thomas Carey. NA, RG 84.
June 20, 1843.	Olegario de los Cuetos. NA, RG 84.
June 23, 1843.	W. S. Derrick. NYPL—Hellman. NA, RG 59.
June 24, 1843.	John Hartmann. NA, RG 84.
June 24, 1843.	A. P. Upshur. NYPL—Hellman; NA, RG 59.
June 27, 1843.	Alexander Burton. NA, RG 84.
June 28, 1843.	George Read. NA, RG 84.
July 4, 1843.	Maximo de Aguirre. NA, RG 84.
July 5, 1843.	Maximo de Aguirre. NA, RG 84.
July 5, 1843.	Matthew C. Perry. NA, RG 84.
July 6, 1843.	George Read. (Two letters.) NA, RG 84.
July 7, 1843.	Alexander Burton. NA, RG 84.
July 11, 1843.	Alexander Burton. NA, RG 84.
July 13, 1843.	Paul Pon. NA, RG 84.
July 14, 1843.	Olegario de los Cuetos. NA, RG 84.
July 15, 1843.	Paul Pon. NA, RG 84.
July 16, 1843.	Olegario de los Cuetos. NA, RG 84.
July 17, 1843.	George Read. NA, RG 84.
July 18, 1843.	Maximo de Aguirre. NA, RG 84.
July 19, 1843.	George Read. NA, RG 84.
July 24, 1843.	Alexander Burton. NA, RG 84.
July 24, 1843.	Joaquín de Frías. NA, RG 84.
July 27, 1843.	Alexander Burton. NA, RG 84.
July 30, 1843.	Agustín Nogueras. NA, RG 84.
August 6, 1843.	———— Breson. NA, RG 84.
August 7, 1843.	George Read. NA, RG 84.
August 7, 1843.	A. P. Upshur. NYPL—Hellman; NA, RG 59.
[August 8, 1843].	Duke of Bailén. NA, RG 84.
August 9, 1843.	George Read. NA, RG 84.
August 15, 1843.	John Miller. NA, RG 84.
August 16, 1843.	Joaquín de Frías. NA, RG 84.
August 17, 1843.	Paul Pon. NA, RG 84.
August 19, 1843.	Paul Pon. NA, RG 84.
August 24, 1843.	Paul Pon. NA, RG 84.
August 28, 1843.	Alexander Burton. NA, RG 84.
August 28, 1843.	George Read. NA, RG 84.
August 29, 1843.	Joaquín de Frías. NA, RG 84.
August 31, 1843.	Joseph Cullen. NA, RG 84.
September 1, 1843.	George Read. NA, RG 84.

September 2, 1843.   Paul Pon. NA, RG 84.
September 4, 1843.   Paul Pon. NA, RG 84.
September 6, 1843.   Joseph Cullen. NA, RG 84.
September 13, 1843.   Paul Pon. NA, RG 84.
September 13, 1843.   George Read. NA, RG 84.
September 21, 1843.   W. P. Hall. NA, RG 84.
October 6, 1843.   Alexander Burton. NA, RG 84.
October 8, 1843.   Count de Alsalto. NA, RG 84.
October 10, 1843.   A. P. Upshur. NYPL—Hellman; NA, RG 59.
October 13, 1843.   A. P. Upshur. NYPL—Hellman; NA, RG 59.
October 16, 1843.   Count de Asalto. NA, RG 84.
October 17, 1843.   Duke de Rivas. NA, RG 84.
October 18, 1843.   Henry Brevoort. NYPL; LBI, II, 130–40.
October 20, 1843.   Alexander Burton. NA, RG 84.
November 6, 1843.   George Read. NA, RG 84.
November 9, 1843.   Count de Asalto. NA, RG 84.
November 11, 1843.   Alexander Burton. NA, RG 84.
November 11, 1843.   Joaquín de Frías. NA, RG 84.
November 15, 1843.   Juana de Viar Keefe. NA, RG 84.
November 16, 1843.   Alexander Burton. NA, RG 84.
November 19, 1843.   Maximo de Aguirre. NA, RG 84.
November 21, 1843.   Salustiano de Olózaga. NA, RG 84.
November 25, 1843.   Joseph Cullen. NA, RG 84.
November 30, 1843.   Edward Everett. NA, RG 84.
November 30, 1843.   Paul Pon. NA, RG 84.
December 10, 1843.   Luis González Bravo. NA, RG 84.
December 12, 1843.   G. Bratish. NA, RG 84.
December 14, 1843.   Luis González Bravo. (Two letters.) NA, RG
                          84.

January 5, 1844.   John Hartmann, NA, RG 84.
January 5, 1844.   George Read. NA, RG 84.
January 8, 1844.   A. P. Upshur. NYPL—Hellman; NA, RG 59.
January 9, 1844.   A. P. Upshur. NYPL—Hellman; NA, RG 59.
January 15, 1844.   A. P. Upshur. NYPL—Hellman; NA, RG 59.
January 17, 1844.   A. P. Upshur. NYPL—Hellman; NA, RG 59.
January 29, 1844.   Luis González Bravo. NA, RG 84.
February 1, 1844.   Luis González Bravo. NA, RG 84.
February 3, 1844.   Arthur MacCulloch. NA, RG 84.
February 6, 1844.   Luis González Bravo. NA, RG 84.
February 16, 1844.   Luis González Bravo. NA, RG 84.
February 29, 1844.   John Nelson. NYPL—Hellman; NA, RG 59.
March 5, 1844.   John Nelson. NYPL—Hellman; NA, RG 59.
March 8, 1844.   Maximo de Aguirre. NA, RG 84.

March 13, 1844.	John Nelson. NYPL–Hellman; NA, RG 59.
March 21, 1844.	Maximo de Aguirre. NA, RG 84.
March 30, 1844.	Alejandro Mon. NA, RG 84.
April 1, 1844.	John C. Calhoun. NYPL–Hellman; NA, RG 59.
April 6, 1844.	Joseph Cullen. NA, RG 84.
April 8, 1844.	George Read. NA, RG 84.
April 9, 1844.	Luis González Bravo. NA, RG 84.
April 10, 1844.	John C. Calhoun. NYPL–Hellman; NA, RG 59.
April 20, 1844.	Joaquín de Frías. Archivo de Ministerio de Asuntes Exteriores, Madrid.
April 23, 1844.	Franklin Gage. NA, RG 84.
April 24, 1844.	John C. Calhoun. NYPL–Hellman; NA, RG 59.
April 27, 1844.	Luttrell Jewett. NA, RG 84.
April 30, 1844.	John C. Calhoun. NYPL–Hellman; NA, RG 59.
April 30, 1844.	Luttrell Jewett. NA, RG 84.
May 1, 1844.	George Evans. NA, RG 84.
May 3, 1844.	Alejandro Mon. NA, RG 84.
May 6, 1844.	George Evans. NA, RG 84.
May 8, 1844.	Alejandro Mon. NA, RG 84.
May 9, 1844.	Joseph Cullen. NA, RG 84.
May 29, 1844.	John C. Calhoun. NYPL–Hellman; NA, RG 59.
May 30, 1844.	—— Gorman. NA, RG 84.
May 30, 1844.	A. MacLure. NA, RG 84.
May 31, 1844.	Alejandro Mon. NA, RG 84.
June 6, 1844.	The Marquis of Viluma. NA, RG 84.
June 7, 1844.	Alejandro Mon. NA, RG 84.
July 1, 1844.	The Marquis of Viluma. NA, RG 84.
July 2, 1844.	Ramón María Narváez. (Two letters.) NA, RG 84.
July 8, 1844.	George Read. NA, RG 84.
July 10, 1844.	George Read. NA, RG 84.
July 11, 1844.	Joseph Cullen. NA, RG 84.
July 19, 1844.	Pedro Saban. NA, RG 84.
July 26, 1844.	Ramón María Narváez. (Two letters.) NA, RG 84.
July 28, 1844.	Ramón María Narváez. NA, RG 84.
August 6, 1844.	Con ONeal Bryson. NA, RG 84.

August 23, 1844.	John C. Calhoun. NYPL—Hellman; NA, RG 59.
August 26, 1844.	George Read. NA, RG 84.
August 27, 1844.	John C. Calhoun. NYPL—Hellman; NA, RG 59.
September 10, 1844.	John C. Calhoun. NYPL—Hellman; NA, RG 59.
September 12, 1844.	John C. Calhoun. NYPL—Hellman; NA, RG 59.
September 16, 1844.	Francisco Martínez de la Rosa. NA, RG 84.
September 19, 1844.	Paul Pon. NA, RG 84.
September 26, 1844.	George Read. NA, RG 84.
September 28, 1844.	Paul Pon. NA, RG 84.
October 2, 1844.	Joseph Cullen. NA, RG 84.
October 5, 1844.	Francisco Martínez de la Rosa. NA, RG 84.
October 13, 1844.	Maximo de Aguirre. NA, RG 84.
October 21, 1844.	Francisco Martínez de la Rosa. NA, RG 84.
October 25, 1844.	R. K. Cralle. NYPL—Hellman; NA, RG 59.
November 2, 1844.	Francisco Martínez de la Rosa. NA, RG 84.
November 9, 1844.	Francisco Martínez de la Rosa. NA, RG 84.
November 11, 1844.	John C. Calhoun. NYPL—Hellman; NA, RG 59.
November 26, 1844.	John C. Calhoun. NYPL—Hellman; NA, RG 59.
December 6, 1844.	Francisco Martínez de la Rosa. NA, RG 84.
December 16, 1844.	Lombard & Whitmore. NA, RG 84.
December 29, 1844.	Francisco Martínez de la Rosa. NA, RG 84.
January 1, 1845.	Arthur MacCulloch. NA, RG 84.
January 10, 1845.	George Read. NA, RG 84.
January 20, 1845.	Joseph Cullen. NA, RG 84.
January 20, 1845.	Pedro J. Pidal. NA, RG 84.
January 21, 1845.	Paul Pon. (Two letters.) NA, RG 84.
January 30, 1845.	William Kilham. NA, RG 84.
February 4, 1845.	Francisco Martínez de la Rosa. NA, RG 84.
February 17, 1845.	Alexander Burton. NA, RG 84.
February 17, 1845.	Luis Mayan. NA, RG 84.
February 19, 1845.	Pedro J. Pidal. NA, RG 84.
February 19, 1845.	George Read. NA, RG 84.
February 20, 1845.	Alexander Burton. NA, RG 84.
February 21, 1845.	Francisco Martínez de la Rosa. NA, RG 84.
February 22, 1845.	John C. Calhoun. NYPL—Hellman; NA, RG 59.
February 26, 1845.	Francisco Martínez de la Rosa. NA, RG 84.

March 2, 1845.	Francisco Martínez de la Rosa. NA, RG 84.
March 4, 1845.	Francisco Martínez de la Rosa. NA, RG 84.
March 7, 1845.	Francisco Martínez de la Rosa. NA, RG 84.
March 8, 1845.	Javier de Quinto. NA, RG 84.
March 10, 1845.	James Buchanan. NYPL–Hellman; NA, RG 59.
March 18, 1845.	Joseph Smith. NA, RG 84.
March 19, 1845.	Ramón María Narváez. NYPL–Hellman; NA, RG 59.
March 24, 1845.	Ramón María Narváez. NA, RG 84.
March 31, 1845.	Francisco Martínez de la Rosa. NA, RG 84.
April 5, 1845.	Fitch Bros. & Co. NA, RG 84.
April 6, 1845.	Francisco Martínez de la Rosa. NA, RG 84.
April 7, 1845.	Francisco Martínez de la Rosa. NA, RG 84.
April 8, 1845.	Francisco Martínez de la Rosa. NA, RG 84.
April 9, 1845.	Francisco Martínez de la Rosa. NA, RG 84.
April 24, 1845.	George Read. NA, RG 84.
April 24, 1845.	Francisco Martínez de la Rosa. NA, RG 84.
April 29, 1845.	Francisco Martínez de la Rosa. NYPL–Hellman.
April 30, 1845.	R. G. Beasley. NA, RG 84.
April 30, 1845.	Francisco Martínez de la Rosa. NA, RG 84.
May 5, 1845.	Francisco Martínez de la Rosa. NYPL–Hellman; NA, RG 84.
May 5, 1845.	Paul Pon. NA, RG 84.
May 7, 1845.	James Buchanan. NYPL–Hellman; NA, RG 59.
May 9, 1845.	Francisco Martínez de la Rosa. NA, RG 84.
May 9, 1845.	James Buchanan. NYPL–Hellman; NA, RG 59; *Works of James Buchanan*, ed. J. B. Moore (New York, 1960), VI, 155–56.
May 10, 1845.	Francisco Martínez de la Rosa. NA, RG 84.
May 14, 1845.	James Buchanan. NYPL–Hellman; NA, RG 59.
May 17, 1845.	Francisco Martínez de la Rosa. NA, RG 84.
May 18, 1845.	Francisco Martínez de la Rosa. NYPL–Hellman; NA, RG 84.
May 28, 1845.	James Buchanan. NYPL–Hellman; NA, RG 59.
June 5, 1845.	Fitch Bros. & Co. NA, RG 84.
June 12, 1845.	Arthur MacCulloch. NA, RG 84.
June 23, 1845.	James Buchanan. NYPL–Hellman; NA, RG 59.

July 2, 1845.	Alexander Burton. NA, RG 84.
July 8, 1845.	James Buchanan. NYPL—Hellman; NA, RG 84.
July 10, 1845.	Francisco Martínez de la Rosa. NA, RG 84.
July 14, 1845.	Francisco Martínez de la Rosa. NA, RG 84.
July 19, 1845.	James Buchanan. NYPL—Hellman; NA, RG 59.
July 21, 1845.	George Read. NA, RG 84.
July 25, 1845.	James Buchanan. NYPL—Hellman; NA, RG 59.
July 31, 1845.	Charles Callaghan. NA, RG 84.
August 13, 1845.	A. M. NA, RG 84.
September 23, 1845.	James Buchanan. NYPL—Hellman; NA, RG 84.
October 4, 1845.	Horatio Sprague. NA, RG 84.
October 6, 1845.	Maximo de Aguirre. NA, RG 84.
October 17, 1845.	Bernard de Marigny. NA, RG 84.
October 17, 1845.	A. Morales de Marigny (Mrs. Bernard). NA, RG 84.
October 24, 1845.	Horatio Sprague. NA, RG 84.
November 20, 1845.	S. M. Johnson. NA, RG 84.
November 21, 1845.	Thomas B. Abrams. NA, RG 84.
November 24, 1845.	Thomas B. Abrams. NA, RG 84.
November 29, 1845.	Maximo de Aguirre. NA, RG 84.
December 5, 1845.	John W. Holding. NA, RG 84.
December 8, 1845.	Thomas B. Abrams. NA, RG 84.
December 8, 1845.	George Read. (Two letters.) NA, RG 84.
December 15, 1845.	William H. Prescott. *Correspondence of W. H. Prescott*, pp. 564–65.
January 1, 1846.	Alexander Burton. NA, RG 84.
January 5, 1846.	George Read. NA, RG 84.
January 20, 1846.	Benjamin H. Wright. NA, RG 84.
January 22, 1846.	Henry G. Hubbard. NA, RG 84.
January 30, 1846.	Benjamin H. Wright, NA, RG 84.
January 31, 1846.	George Read. NA, RG 84.
February 5, 1846.	Paul Pon. NA, RG 84.
March 3, 1846.	Marques of Miraflores. NA, RG 84.
March 13, 1846.	Marques of Miraflores. NA, RG 84.
March 17, 1846.	Duke of Valencia. NA, RG 84.
March 18, 1846.	Duke of Valencia. NA, RG 84.
March 21, 1846.	Duke of Valencia. NA, RG 84.
March 26, 1846.	Junius Boyle. NA, RG 84.
March 30, 1846.	Duke of Valencia. NA, RG 84.

April 5, 1846.	Francisco de Istúriz. NA, RG 84.
April 7, 1846.	Francisco de Istúriz. NA, RG 84.
April 7, 1846.	Henry Santos. NA, RG 84.
April 17, 1846.	Henry Santos. NA, RG 84.
April 20, 1846.	Francisco de Istúriz. NA, RG 84.
April 22, 1846.	Francisco de Istúriz. NA, RG 84.
April 23, 1846.	Francisco de Istúriz. NA, RG 84.
April 25, 1846.	James Buchanan. NYPL–Hellman; NA, RG 59; *Works of James Buchanan*, VI, 465–66.
April 28, 1846.	Francisco de Istúriz. NA, RG 84.
April 29, 1846.	Francisco de Istúriz. NA, RG 84.
May 1, 1846.	George Read. NA, RG 84.
May 4, 1846.	George Read. NA, RG 84.
May 5, 1846.	Joseph Cullen. NA, RG 84.
May 9, 1846.	Francisco de Istúriz. NA, RG 84.
May 11, 1846.	Francisco de Istúriz. NA, RG 84.
May 12, 1846.	Fitch Bros. & Co. NA, RG 84.
May 12, 1846.	Francisco de Istúriz. NA, RG 84.
May 13, 1846.	Francisco de Istúriz. NA, RG 84.
May 14, 1846.	James Buchanan. (Two letters.) NYPL–Hellman; NA, RG 59; *Works of James Buchanan*, VI, 489.
May 16, 1846.	Francisco de Istúriz. NA, RG 84.
May 16, 1846.	Arthur MacCulloch. (Two letters.) NA, RG 84.
May 30, 1846.	N. B. Boyle. NA, RG 84.
June 10, 1846.	George Read. NA, RG 84.
June 12, 1846.	Arthur MacCulloch. NA, RG 84.
June 16, 1846.	Francisco de Istúriz. NA, RG 84.
June 27, 1846.	Francisco de Istúriz. NA, RG 84.
June 28, 1846.	Francisco de Istúriz. NA, RG 84.
June 29, 1846.	Francisco de Istúriz. NA, RG 84.
June 30, 1846.	Francisco de Istúriz. NA, RG 84.
July 2, 1846.	George Read. NA, RG 84.
July 7, 1846.	Alexander Burton. NA, RG 84.
July 7, 1846.	Francisco de Istúriz. NA, RG 84.
July 8, 1846.	Francisco de Istúriz. NA, RG 84.
July 9, 1846.	Francisco de Istúriz. Archivo de Ministerio de Asuntes Exteriores, Madrid.
July 11, 1846.	Maria Cullen. NA, RG 84.
July 11, 1846.	Charles LeBrun. NA, RG 84.
July 26, 1846.	Francisco de Istúriz. NA, RG 84.
July 27, 1846.	Alexander Burton. NA, RG 84.

July 28, 1846.	Francisco de Istúriz. NA, RG 84.
August 17, 1846.	William Jerdan. University of Kansas Library.
March 5, 1847.	Henry Van Wart. PMI, IV, 20.
April, 1847.	Pierre M. Irving. PMI, IV, 16.
May 26, 1847.	John Fallon. SHR.
May 31, 1847.	Charles R. Leslie. Leslie, *Autobiographical Recollections*, p. 336.
April 4, 1848.	"A committee buying land for a railroad." PMI, IV, 37–38.
November 22, 1848.	Charles R. Leslie. Leslie, *Autobiographical Recollections*, p. 341.
December 8, 1848.	Leslie Combs. University of Chicago.
July, 1849.	George Ripley. PMI, IV, 54–56.
September 6, 1849.	George Ripley. NYPL–Hellman.
August 1, 1850.	Sir William Sterling. NYHS.
September 1, 1850.	J. F. Reigart. SHR.
November 4, 1850.	George Bancroft. NYPL–Hellman.
December 26, 1850.	G. P. R. James. Location unknown.
January 27, 1851.	William H. Bogart. SHR.
June 3, 1851.	Richard Bentley. British Library.
June 17, 1851.	Herman Knickerbocker. NYPL–Hellman.
June 19, 1851.	James W. Beekman. Va.–Barrett.
September 19, 1851.	John Murray III. PMI, IV, 89–90.
October 3, 1851.	Mrs. Laurence. SHR.
October 4, 1851.	Henry R. Schoolcraft. LC.
October 13, 1851.	Irving Paris. Va.–Barrett.
December 14, 1851.	Daniel Webster. Harvard.
December 19, 1851.	Richard Bentley. British Library.
December 20, 1851.	Edward Everett. NYPL–Hellman.
January 18, 1852.	Charles R. Leslie. Leslie, *Autobiographical Recollections*, p. 347.
March 31, 1852.	William C. Preston. NYPL–Hellman.
March, 1852.	J. H. Perkins. SHR.
July 16, 1852.	Nathaniel Hawthorne. Yale.
August 29, 1852.	Charles R. Leslie. Leslie, *Autobiographical Recollections*, pp. 348–49.
October 14, 1852.	Donald G. Mitchell. Brown University.
November 26, 1852.	"Fellow Citizen." SHR.
December 6, 1852.	Henry Tuckerman. PMI, IV, 91.
February 5, 1853.	Helen Dodge Irving. Yale.
Late March, 1853.	Robert C. Winthrop. PMI, IV, 141.
April 4, 1853.	Mary E. Kennedy. *American Literature*, 6 (March, 1934), 45–46.

April 21, 1853.	Alfred Pell. SHR.
June 13, 1853.	Donald G. Mitchell. NYPL–Hellman.
July 6, 1853.	Pierre M. Irving. PMI, IV, 153.
September 19, 1853.	John P. Kennedy. Peabody Library; SHR (copy).
September 22, 1853.	John P. Kennedy. Tuckerman, *Life of J. P. Kennedy*, pp. 381–84.
November 11, 1853.	John P. Kennedy. Peabody Library; SHR (copy).
December 15, 1853.	John P. Kennedy. Peabody Library; SHR (copy).
January 17, 1854.	William H. Prescott. Columbia.
April, 1854.	An unknown neighbor. PMI, IV, 173.
May 13, 1854.	Charles R. Leslie. Leslie, *Autobiographical Recollections*, pp. 350–51.
June 19, 1854.	John P. Kennedy. Peabody Library; Tuckerman, *Life of J. P. Kennedy*, pp. 384–86.
August 8, 1854.	John P. Kennedy. Tuckerman, *Life of J. P. Kennedy*, pp. 387–88.
November 2, 1854.	Frank W. Ballard. *Irvingiana*, p. xli.
January 2, 1855.	George Bancroft. Redwood Library and Athenaeum (Newport, R. I.).
January 9, 1855.	Nathaniel P. Willis. Yale.
January 11, 1855.	George P. Putnam. PMI, IV, 189.
March 31, 1855.	Edwin Forrest. SHR.
May 15, 1855.	George R. Gilmer. SHR.
Mid-May, 1855.	John Murray III. PMI, IV, 193.
May 21, 1855.	Elisha Bartlett. SHR.
May 22, 1855.	George Bancroft. NYHS.
May 30, 1855.	George Bancroft. Va.–Barrett; PMI, IV, 194.
August 2, 1855.	George W. Childs and Robert Peterson. Yale.
October 24, 1855.	John P. Kennedy. Peabody Library; *Sewanee Review*, 25 (January, 1917), 18.
December 16, 1855.	James K. Paulding. *Letters of J. K. Paulding*, p. 558.
January 3, 1856.	William H. Prescott. NYPL–Hellman; PMI, IV, 203–5.
January 5, 1856.	Henry T. Tuckerman. Va.–Barrett.
January 8, 1856.	George Sumner. NYEP, January 10, 1856.
January 22, 1856.	C. L. Brace. PMI, IV, 207–8.
March 21, 1856.	John P. Kennedy. NYPL–Hellman.
April 21, 1856.	Alfred Pell. SHR.
April 23, 1856.	John C. Schaad. SHR.

May 25, 1856.	Emily Foster Fuller. PMI, IV, 217–18.
July 5, 1856.	Charles Dickens. PMI, IV, 220–22.
August 3, 1856.	William H. Prescott. NYPL—Hellman.
August 27, 1856.	Charles Lanman. Yale.
November 4, 1856.	J. Earl Williams. SHR.
December 16, 1856.	Daniel Curtin. SHR.
December 30, 1856.	Daniel Curtin. SHR.
February, 1857.	John S. Williams. Va.–Barrett.
Mid-May, 1857.	George Bancroft. PMI, IV, 230.
August 7, 1857.	John Lothrop Motley. PMI, IV, 233–35.
August 7, 1857.	William H. Prescott. PMI, IV, 232–33.
September 12, 1857.	S. Austin Allibone. Va.–Barrett.
October 28, 1857.	S. Austin Allibone. PMI, IV, 236.
November 24, 1857.	Nathaniel P. Willis. NYHS.
December 31, 1857.	Pierre M. Irving. PMI, IV, 238.
Early January, 1858.	Pierre M. Irving. PMI, IV, 238.
ca. January, 1858.	An unknown boy. PMI, III, 53.
April 3, 1858.	John Thomas Williams. SHR.
May 22, 1858.	George Bancroft. NYHS.
May, 1858.	Francis Lieber. PMI, IV, 247.
December 28, 1858.	W. H. Prescott. PMI, IV, 266.
January 11, 1859.	Joseph Harrison. NYPL—WI Papers.
May 7, 1859.	George Bancroft. PMI, IV, 281–82.
May 11, 1859.	Joseph Harrison. NYPL—WI Papers.
May 11, 1859.	William C. Preston. PMI, IV, 286–87.
May 20, 1859.	Henry T. Tuckerman. PMI, IV, 291–92.
June 8, 1859.	General V. P. Van Antwerp and Colonel John T. Heard, PMI, MS journal (NYPL), June 13, 1859.
June 24, 1859.	————. PMI, IV, 297–99.
October 23, 1859.	John P. Kennedy. NYPL—Hellman.
"long years after" 1822.	A daughter of Mrs. Foster. PMI, II, 127–28.
February 26, n. y.	Lady Lansdowne. Va.–Barrett; SHR (copy).
March 6, n. y.	Mrs. Brooks. SHR.
March 10, n. y.	Sir Howard and Lady Douglas. Va.–Barrett; SHR (copy).
March 23, n. y.	Duke of Devonshire. Va.–Barrett; SHR (copy).
March 31, n. y.	William C. Preston. NYPL—Seligman.
April 20, n. y.	Lord and Lady Stafford. Va.–Barrett; SHR (copy).
April 28, n. y.	Duchess of Northumberland. Va.–Barrett; SHR (copy).
May 9, n. y.	Lord and Lady Stanhope. SHR.

May 14, n. y.	Lord and Lady Darnley. SHR.
June 5, n. y.	Cornelius Mathews. Yale.
July 16, n. y.	Lord Lansdowne. SHR.
Sunday the 14th.	Mrs. Charles Kemble. Va.–Barrett; SHR (copy).
Tuesday evening.	J. H. Payne. Huntington.
Friday.	Thomas Moore. SHR.

APPENDIX IV

Letters Received by Washington Irving
(Unlocated)

The dates of many of the unlocated letters which WI received are approximations based on the estimated time required for the letter to reach him. In general, letters from England addressed to WI in Paris are dated five or six days before their receipt, and letters from other directions follow the patterns of known examples. In other instances, where the pattern of mail deliveries is unknown, the date is listed as the approximate month or time of the month. It should be emphasized that the dates are approximations unless WI refers to a specific date or unless documentary details clearly establish them. Even with these limitations, the list will suggest the range and scope of the unlocated letters which WI received.

The list will omit references to unlocated letters in WI's extant letters when these duplicate information given in the notebooks and journals. When an unlocated letter is mentioned only in an extant letter, it is, of course, included in the list which follows.

June 30, 1804.	William Irving, Jr. WI to William Irving, Jr., August 1, 1804.
June, 1804.	Alexander Beebee. WI to Alexander Beebee, July 22, 1804.
June, 1804.	George Dibblie. WI to Alexander Beebee, August 24, 1804.
June, 1804.	Elias Hicks. (Two letters.) WI to Elias Hicks, July 24, 1804.
June?, 1804.	John Treat Irving. WI to William Irving, Jr., September 20, 1804.
June, 1804.	James K. Paulding. WI to William Irving, Jr., August 1, 1804.
June, 1804.	Andrew Quoz. WI to Andrew Quoz, July 20, 1804.
June, 1804.	Samuel Swartwout? WI to William Irving, Jr., July 20, 1804.

July 7, 1804.   John Furman. WI to John Furman, October 24, 1804.

July 7–8, 1804.   William Irving, Jr. WI to William Irving, Jr., September 20, 1804.

July, 1804.   Alexander Beebee. WI to Alexander Beebee, July 22, 1804.

July, 1804.   Cadwallader Colden. WI to Elias Hicks, July 24, 1804.

July, 1804.   George Dibblie ("Diddler"). WI to Alexander Beebee, September 18, 1804.

July, 1804.   Elias Hicks. WI to Elias Hicks, July 24, 1804.

July, 1804.   John Treat Irving. WI to William Irving, Jr., September 20, 1804.

ca. July–August, 1804.   John Nicholson? WI to John Furman, October 24, 1804.

August, 1804.   Cadwallader Colden. WI to William Irving, Jr., December 20, 1804.

September 20, 1804.   Dr. Henory. J&N, I, 484.

ca. September 20, 1804.   ———— Schwartz. J&N, I, 483.

September 23, 1804.   Dr. Henory. J&N, I, 485.

September 23?, 1804.   Thomas Hall Storm. J&N, I, 485.

September 24?, 1804.   Stephen Cathalan. J&N, I, 485.

Late September, 1804.   William Lee. J&N, I, 488.

October, 1804.   Thomas Hall Storm. J&N, I, 489.

October, 1804.   Dr. John G. Ellison. J&N, I, 489.

October, 1804.   Robert L. Livingston. J&N, I, 489.

October, 1804.   Robert L. Livingston. J&N, I, 490.

Late 1804.   Alexander Beebee. WI to William Irving, Jr., April 4, 1805.

Late 1804.   John Treat Irving. WI to William Irving, Jr., April 4, 1805.

1804.   William Irving, Jr. (Nine letters through November 30, 1804.) WI to William Irving, Jr., April 4, 1805.

ca. January, 1805.   ———— [from America]. J&N, I, 225.

January–February, 1805.   Thomas Hall Storm. (Several letters.) J&N, I, 224, 526.

January?–March?, 1805.   William Irving, Jr. (Four letters.) WI to William Irving, Jr., May 31, 1805.

May 24, 1806.   Gouverneur Kemble. WI to Gouverneur Kemble, May 26, 1806.

March 13, 1807.   Mary Fairlie. WI to Mary Fairlie, March 17, 1807.

April 30, 1807.	Mary Fairlie. WI to Mary Fairlie, May 13, 1807.
Late May, 1807.	Mrs. J. O. Hoffman. WI to Mrs. J .O. Hoffman, June 4, 1807.
June 5, 1807.	Mary Fairlie. American Art Association, William F. Gabler Sale, January 8–9, 1925; pt. 6, vol. 2, item 389.
November, 1807.	Ann Hoffman. WI to Ann Hoffman, November 17, 1807.
Late May, 1808.	Mrs. J. O. Hoffman. WI to Mrs. J. O. Hoffman, June 2, 1808.
May, 1808.	Henry Brevoort. WI to Henry Brevoort, June 11, 1808.
Early May, 1809.	Mrs. J. O. Hoffman. (Two letters.) WI to Mrs. J. O. Hoffman, May 19, 1809.
Mid-May, 1809.	Sarah Irving. WI to Sarah Irving, May 20, 1809.
Mid-May, 1809.	Daniel Paris. WI to Sarah Irving, May 20, 1809.
May, 1809.	Peter Kemble. WI to Henry Brevoort, May 20, 1809.
June, 1809.	William P. Van Ness. WI to William P. Van Ness, June 24, 1809.
ca. June, 1809.	Mrs. J. O. Hoffman. WI to Mrs. J. O. Hoffman, [June, 1809].
October, 1809.	John Howard Payne. WI to John Howard Payne, November 2, 1809.
December, 1809.	William P. Van Ness. WI to William P. Van Ness, December 18, 1809.
June, 1810.	Mrs. J. O. Hoffman. WI to Mrs. J. O. Hoffman, June 23, 1810.
1810.	John E. Hall. (Several letters.) WI to John E. Hall, September 26, 1810.
January, 1811.	Henry Brevoort. WI to Henry Brevoort, January 13, 1811.
January, 1811.	Mrs. J. O. Hoffman. WI to Henry Brevoort, January 13, 1811.
February 5, 1811.	William Irving, Jr. WI to William Irving, Jr., February 9, 1811.
February, 1811.	Peter Kemble. WI to Henry Brevoort, March 5, 1811.
March, 1811.	Henry Brevoort. WI to Henry Brevoort, March 16, 1811.

Late March, 1811.   Henry Brevoort. WI to Henry Brevoort,
                            April 11, 1811.

May 18, 1811.   John Irwin. WI to Henry Brevoort, May
                            15, 1811.

November, 1812.   James Renwick. WI to James Renwick, No-
                            vember 24, 1812.

December, 1812.   James Renwick. (Two letters.) WI to James
                            Renwick, December 18, 1812.

March, 1814.   William Bainbridge. WI to William Bain-
                            bridge, March 24, 1814.

Late March, 1814.   Charles Prentiss. WI to Charles Prentiss,
                            April 4, 1814.

July 15, 1814.   Moses Thomas. WI to Moses Thomas, July
                            15, 1814.

August, 1814.   Joseph Delaplaine. WI to Joseph Delaplaine,
                            August 10, 1814.

ca. August, 1814.   Commodore and Mrs. Stephen Decatur. WI
                            to Henry Brevoort, [August?, 1814?].

September?–October,   Moses Thomas. (Several letters.) WI to Moses
  1814.   Thomas, October 21, 1814.

October, 1814.   Peter Irving. WI to Henry Brevoort, October
                            16, 1814.

January 17, 1815.   Gulian C. Verplanck. WI to Gulian C. Ver-
                            planck, January 21, 1815.

January, 1815.   Mrs. S. B. Ryckman. WI to Mrs. S. B. Ryck-
                            man, February 13, 1815.

Late May, 1815.   Henry Lee. WI to Henry Brevoort, May 25,
                            1815.

June, 1815.   Cadwallader Colden. WI to Cadwallader Col-
                            den, July 29, 1815.

July 7, 1815.   John Nicholson. WI to Henry Brevoort, Au-
                            gust 19, 1815.

July, 1815.   Henry Brevoort. (Two letters.) WI to Henry
                            Brevoort, August 19, 1815; August 23, 1815.

July, 1815.   James Renwick. (Several letters.) WI to Jean
                            Renwick, July 27, 1815.

August, 1815.   Henry Brevoort. WI to Henry Brevoort, Sep-
                            tember 26, 1815.

September, 1815.   Henry Brevoort. WI to Henry Brevoort, No-
                            vember 2, 1815.

October, 1815.   Peter Irving. WI to Henry Brevoort, October
                            17, 1815.

November, 1815.	Jean Renwick. WI to Henry Brevoort, December 28, 1815.
Late 1815–early 1816.	John Nicholson. (Several letters.) WI to Henry Brevoort, March 15, 1816.
January 1, 1816.	Henry Brevoort. WI to Henry Brevoort, March 15, 1816.
February 10, 1816.	Henry Brevoort. WI to Henry Brevoort, March 15, 1816.
February, 1816.	Samuel Swartwout. WI to Henry Brevoort, March 15, 1816.
March, 1816.	Alexander B. Johnson. WI to Henry Brevoort, March 15, 1816.
May 18, 1816.	Henry Brevoort. WI to Henry Brevoort, July 16, 1816.
June?, 1816.	John Nicholson. WI to Henry Brevoort, July 16, 1816.
July, 1816.	Peter Irving. WI to Henry Brevoort, November 6, 1816.
July, 1816.	Sarah Irving. WI to Sarah Irving, August 31, 1816.
September 8, 1816.	Henry Brevoort. WI to Henry Brevoort, November 6, 1816.
September, 1816.	Catharine Paris. WI to Sarah Irving, October 18, 1816.
October 16, 1816.	Henry Brevoort. WI to Henry Brevoort, December 9, 1816.
November 21, 1816.	Henry Brevoort. WI to Henry Brevoort, January 29, 1817.
1816–1817.	Mrs. J. O. Hoffman. WI to Mrs. J. O. Hoffman, November 23, 1817.
March, 1817.	Henry Brevoort. WI to Henry Brevoort, May 26, 1817.
April 30, 1817.	Henry Brevoort. WI to Henry Brevoort, June 7, 1817.
May?, 1817.	John Nicholson. WI to Henry Brevoort, June 7, 1817.
June 11, 1817.	Henry Brevoort. WI to Henry Brevoort, July 11, 1817.
July 2, 1817.	Henry Brevoort. WI to Henry Brevoort, August 28, 1817.
Mid-July, 1817.	Henry Brevoort. WI to Peter Irving, August 19, 1817.

July, 1817.	Mrs. Bradish. WI to Peter Irving, August 19, 1817.
July, 1817.	Mathew Carey. WI to Henry Brevoort, August 28, 1817.
Late July–early August, 1817.	"a letter from N York." WI to Peter Irving, September 6, 1817.
August 17, 1817.	Peter Irving. WI to Peter Irving, August 19, 1817.
August 20, 1817.	Henry Brevoort. WI to Henry Brevoort, October 10, 1817.
ca. August 22, 1817.	Peter Irving. WI to Peter Irving, August 26, 1817.
Late August, 1817.	Andrew Hamilton. WI to Peter Irving, September 6, 1817.
Late August, 1817.	Peter Irving. WI to Peter Irving, September 6, 1817.
Late August, 1817.	———— Woolley. WI to Peter Irving, September 6, 1817.
September 6, 1817.	Peter Irving. WI to Peter Irving, September 20, 1817.
September, 1817.	Francis Jeffrey. WI to Peter Irving, September 20, 1817.
September, 1817.	Chauncey Townshend. WI to Peter Irving, September 20, 1817.
October, 1817.	William C. Preston. WI to Charles R. Leslie, February 8, 1818.
December 4, 1817.	Henry Brevoort. WI to Henry Brevoort, January 28, 1818.
December?, 1817.	Laura Carson Brevoort. WI to Henry Brevoort, January 28, 1818.
1817?	Francis Jeffrey. WI to John? Bolton, [June 18, 1818].
1817?	Walter Scott. WI to John? Bolton, [June 18, 1818].
January, 1818.	William C. Preston. WI to Charles R. Leslie, February 9, 1818.
February, 1818.	Henry Brevoort. WI to Henry Brevoort, March 22, 1818.
March 8, 1818.	Henry Brevoort. WI to Henry Brevoort, April 30, 1818.
April, 1818.	Henry Brevoort. WI to Henry Brevoort, April 30, 1818.

Mid-May, 1818.	Thomas Campbell. WI to Henry Brevoort, May 19, 1818.
Before July, 1818.	Gouverneur Kemble. WI to Henry Brevoort, July 7, 1818.
July 2, 1818.	Henry Brevoort. WI to Henry Brevoort, September 27, 1818.
Mid-July, 1818.	Silas Richards. WI to Silas Richards, July 17, 1818.
July 21, 1818.	Henry Brevoort. WI to Henry Brevoort, September 27, 1818.
ca. July 24, 1818.	Charles R. Leslie. WI to Charles R. Leslie, July 29, 1818.
September 23, 1818.	———— Cape. WI to George Bartley, September 24, 1818.
November, 1818.	William Irving, Jr. WI to Ebenezer Irving, late November, 1818.
Early January, 1819.	Samuel Rogers. WI to Samuel Rogers, January 12, 1819.
February 2, 1819.	Henry Brevoort. WI to Henry Brevoort, March 3, 1819.
May 2, 1819.	Henry Brevoort. WI to Henry Brevoort, July 10, 1819.
May 8, 1819.	Henry Brevoort. WI to Henry Brevoort, July 10, 1819.
June 9, 1819.	Henry Brevoort. WI to Henry Brevoort, July 10, 1819.
July 9, 1819.	Henry Brevoort. WI to Henry Brevoort, August 12, 1819.
July, 1819.	Ebenezer Irving. WI to Henry Brevoort, August 12, 1819.
August, 1819.	Henry Brevoort. WI to Henry Brevoort, September 9, 1819.
September?, 1819.	Henry Van Wart. WI to Henry Van Wart, [September?, 1819].
November, 1819.	Ebenezer Irving. WI to Ebenezer Irving, December 29, 1819.
February 23, 1820.	John Howard Payne. WI to John Howard Payne, February 23, 1820.
March, 1820.	Henry Brevoort. WI to Henry Brevoort, March 27, 1820.
July?, 1820.	Henry Carey. WI to Henry Brevoort, August 15, 1820.

August, 1820.   William S. Cardell. WI to William S. Cardell, August 14, 1820.

October, 1820.   James Eastburn. WI to John Murray, October 31, 1820.

October, 1820.   William Willes. WI to Charles R. Leslie, October 31, 1820.

November?, 1820.   Gilbert Stuart Newton. WI to Charles R. Leslie, November 30, 1820.

November, 1820.   Richard Rush. WI to Richard Rush, December 6, 1820.

December, 1820.   Ebenezer Irving. WI to Henry Brevoort, March 10, 1821; April 14, 1821.

December?, 1820.   William Irving, Jr. WI to Henry Brevoort, March 10, 1821.

December, 1820.   David B. Warden. WI to David B. Warden, [December 30, 1820].

March?, 1821.   Gilbert Stuart Newton. WI to Charles R. Leslie, [March or spring, 1821].

April, 1821.   Colonel Gideon Fairman. WI to Colonel Gideon Fairman, April 19, 1821.

Early May, 1821.   Mrs. John Story. WI to Mrs. John Story, May 4, 1821.

May?, 1821.   John E. Hall. WI to John E. Hall, June 30, 1821.

Summer, 1821.   Minny and Susan Storrow. WI to Mrs. Thomas W. Storrow, December 10, 1821.

Summer, 1821.   Mrs. Thomas W. Storrow. WI to Mrs. Thomas W. Storrow, December 10, 1821.

July 16, 1821.   John Howard Payne. WI to John Howard Payne, August 1, 1821.

August 12, 1821.   John Howard Payne. WI to John Howard Payne, August 23, 1821.

August, 1821.   Peter Irving. WI to Peter Irving, September 6, 1821.

August, 1821.   John Miller. WI to John Howard Payne, August 23, 1821.

September 15, 1821. Gilbert Stuart Newton. WI to Charles R. Leslie, October 7, 1821.

October 8, 1821.   Ebenezer Irving. WI to Ebenezer Irving, November 1, 1821.

October 16, 1821. William S. Cardell. J&N, III, 249.

December 7, 1821. Charles R. Leslie. WI to Charles R. Leslie, December 8, 1821.

January 24, 1822.   John Howard Payne. WI to Henry Colburn, February 12, 1822.

January?, 1822.   Thomas W. Storrow. WI to Thomas W. Storrow, February 1, 1822.

February?, 1822.   Charles Wiley. WI to Charles Wiley, March 6, 1822.

Early April, 1822.   Rebecca Bond. WI to Rebecca Bond, April 6, 1822.

May 10?, 1822.   ————. WI to ————, May 11, 1822.

May 13, 1822.   Catharine Paris. WI to Catharine Paris, June 21, 1822.

May, 1822.   Moses Thomas. WI to Moses Thomas, June 29, 1822.

June 2?, 1822.   Lady Holland. WI to Lady Holland, June 3, 1822.

Early June, 1822.   Richard Rush. WI to Richard Rush, June 5, 1822.

June 7, 1822.   Richard Rush. WI to Richard Rush, June 8, 1822.

Early August, 1822.   Mr. & Mrs. Henry Van Wart. WI to Sarah Van Wart, August 19, 1822.

September 1, 1822.   Sarah Van Wart. WI to Sarah Van Wart, October 27, 1822.

September 21, 1822.   Sarah Van Wart. WI to Sarah Van Wart, October 27, 1822.

October 7, 1822.   Sarah Van Wart. WI to Sarah Van Wart, October 27, 1822.

October 14, 1822.   Thomas W. Storrow. WI to Thomas W. Storrow, November 16, 1822.

October, 1822.   Louisa Storrow. WI to Louisa Storrow, November 10, 1822.

October, 1822.   Susan Storrow. WI to Susan Storrow, November 10, 1822.

November, 1822.   Peter Irving. WI to Charles R. Leslie, December 2, 1822.

December, 1822.   Henry Van Wart. WI to Thomas W. Storrow, December 22, 1822.

February, 1823.   Gilbert Stuart Newton. WI to Charles R. Leslie, March 15, 1823.

May 4, 1823.   Amelia Foster. J&N, III, 147.
May 25, 1823.   Amelia Foster. J&N, III, 169.
May 28, 1823.   Amelia Foster. J&N, III, 170.
May 30, 1823.   Amelia Foster. J&N, III, 170.

June 5, 1823.	Amelia Foster. *J&N*, III, 171.
June 5, 1823.	Barham Livius. *J&N*, III, 171.
June 10, 1823.	Amelia Foster. WI to Amelia Foster, June 13, 1823.
June 12, 1823.	Amelia Foster. *J&N*, III, 173.
June 15, 1823.	Amelia Foster. *J&N*, III, 174.
June 16, 1823.	Amelia Foster. *J&N*, III, 174.
June 22, 1823.	Amelia Foster, *J&N*, III, 176.
June, 1823.	Charles R. Leslie, *J&N*, III, 177.
June, 1823.	Gilbert Stuart Newton. *J&N*, III, 177.
July, 1823.	Henry Brevoort. *J&N*, III, 217.
August 7, 1823.	Peter Irving. *J&N*, III, 208.
August 8, 1823.	Sarah Van Wart. *J&N*, III, 212.
August 9, 1823.	James Kenney. *J&N*, III, 209.
August 11, 1823.	Madame Bonet. *J&N*, III, 210.
August 14?, 1823.	Messrs. Plummer London. *J&N*, III, 213.
August 14?, 1823.	Gilbert Stuart Newton. *J&N*, III, 213.
August 15?, 1823.	Amelia Foster. *J&N*, III, 214.
August 17, 1823.	Pierre F. Guestier. *J&N*, III, 213.
August 17, 1823.	——— Villamil. *J&N*, III, 213.
August 19?, 1823.	Amelia Foster. *J&N*, III, 215.
August 23, 1823.	Madame Bonet. *J&N*, III, 215.
August 25?, 1823.	Peter Irving, *J&N*, III, 216.
August 25?, 1823.	Charles R. Leslie. *J&N*, III, 217.
August, 1823.	John Nicholson. *J&N*, III, 217.
Early September, 1823.	Dr. Antonio Montucci. *J&N*, III, 220.
September 7?, 1823.	Peter Irving. *J&N*, III, 219.
September 8?, 1823.	Robert Sullivan. *J&N*, III, 220.
September 9?, 1823.	John Miller. *J&N*, III, 220.
September 9?, 1823.	Gilbert Stuart Newton. *J&N*, III, 220.
September 10?, 1823.	Amelia Foster. *J&N*, III, 220.
September 25?, 1823.	John Howard Payne. WI to John Howard Payne, September 27, 1823.
Late September, 1823.	William Irving, Jr. *J&N*, III, 228.
September?, 1823.	Charles Nicholas. *J&N*, III, 236.
October 1?, 1823.	Sarah Van Wart. *J&N*, III, 228.
October 5, 1823.	——— Willet. WI to ——— Willet, October 12, 1823.
October 6?, 1823.	Peter Irving. *J&N*, III, 229.
October 7, 1823.	Madame Bonet. *J&N*, III, 228.
October 7?, 1823.	Peter Irving. *J&N*, III, 229.
October 10, 1823.	Thomas W. Storrow. *J&N*, III, 230.
October 10?, 1823.	Barham Livius. *J&N*, III, 231.

October 16?, 1823.   Peter Irving. *J&N*, III, 232.
October 18?, 1823.   Amelia Foster. *J&N*, III, 234.
October 18?, 1823.   Sarah Van Wart. *J&N*, III, 234.
October 19?, 1823.   ———— Ritchie. *J&N*, III, 234.
October 20?, 1823.   Peter Irving. *J&N*, III, 233.
October 21?, 1823.   Peter Irving. *J&N*, III, 234.
October 25?, 1823.   Sarah and Matilda Van Wart. *J&N*, III, 237.
October 27?, 1823.   Peter Irving. *J&N*, III, 236.
Late October, 1823.   Madame Bonet. *J&N*, III, 237.
Late October, 1823.   William Irving, Jr. *J&N*, III, 237.
Late October, 1823.   John Howard Payne. WI to John Howard
                          Payne, November 5, 1823.
October, 1823.   ———— Raguet. *J&N*, III, 232.
November 9?, 1823.   Sarah & Henry Van Wart. *J&N*, III, 243.
November 10, 1823.   William Irving, Jr. *J&N*, III, 243.
November 11?, 1823.   Amelia Foster. *J&N*, III, 244.
November 11?, 1823.   John Foster. *J&N*, III, 244.
November 13, 1823.   Gilbert Stuart Newton. *J&N*, III, 296.
November 14, 1823.   John Howard Payne. *J&N*, III, 245.
November 16, 1823.   Lord John Russell. *J&N*, III, 243.
November 17, 1823.   William Irving, Jr. *J&N*, III, 244.
November 17?, 1823.   ———— Ker. *J&N*, III, 246.
November 18, 1823.   John Howard Payne. *J&N*, III, 245.
November 18?, 1823.   ———— Willet. *J&N*, III, 246.
November 19, 1823.   Lord William & Lady Elizabeth Thomond.
                          J&N, III, 244.
November 20?, 1823.   Captain Holdridge. *J&N*, III, 247.
November 21?, 1823.   John Howard Payne. *J&N*, III, 247.
November 21, 1823.   Captain Sotheby. *J&N*, III, 245.
November 21, 1823.   Mrs. Samuel Welles. *J&N*, III, 245.
November 27, 1823.   Mr. & Mrs. Croley. *J&N*, III, 247.
November 27, 1823.   Lady Louisa Harvey. *J&N*, III, 247.
November, 1823.   ———— Artiguenave. *J&N*, III, 240.
November, 1823.   ———— Drury. *J&N*, III, 242.
November, 1823.   John Miller. *J&N*, III, 242.
Late November, 1823.   Henry Brevoort. *J&N*, III, 263.
Late November, 1823.   Ebenezer Irving. *J&N*, III, 262.
November, 1823.   Barham Livius. *J&N*, III, 249.
November, 1823.   Gilbert Stuart Newton. WI to John Howard
                          Payne, March 19, 1824.
November, 1823.   Postmaster in England. *J&N*, III, 245.
December 6, 1823.   Amelia Foster. *J&N*, III, 257.
December 6, 1823.   John P. Morier. *J&N*, III, 254.

December 8, 1823.	Lord William & Lady Elizabeth Thomond. *J&N*, III, 254.
December 9, 1823.	Mrs. Forster. *J&N*, III, 254.
December 10, 1823.	Madame Bonet. *J&N*, III, 255.
December 10, 1823.	Lady Susan Douglas. *J&N*, III, 255.
December 12, 1823.	John Howard Payne. *J&N*, III, 258.
December 12, 1823.	——— Philips. *J&N*, III, 256.
December 13, 1823.	——— Philips. *J&N*, III, 257.
December 14, 1823.	Mrs. Pierre F. Guestier. *J&N*, III, 257.
Mid-December, 1823.	——— Douglas. *J&N*, III, 259.
Mid-December, 1823.	Barham Livius. *J&N*, III, 259.
Mid-December, 1823.	John Murray II. WI to John Murray II, December 22, 1823.
Mid-December, 1823.	Peter Powell. *J&N*, III, 262.
December 17, 1823.	——— Douglas. *J&N*, III, 259.
December 20?, 1823.	Gilbert Stuart Newton. *J&N*, III, 262.
December 22?, 1823.	Henry Van Wart. *J&N*, III, 263.
December 23, 1823.	——— Douglas. *J&N*, III, 261.
December 23, 1823.	John Howard Payne. *J&N*, III, 262.
December 23, 1823.	Samuel Welles. *J&N*, III, 261.
December 23, 1823.	Mrs. Samuel Welles. *J&N*, III, 261.
December 24, 1823.	John Howard Payne. *J&N*, III, 262.
December 25, 1823.	——— Bonet. *J&N*, III, 262.
December 27, 1823.	Lady Louisa Harvey. *J&N*, III, 262.
December 27, 1823.	——— Reed. *J&N*, III, 262.
December 31, 1823.	Count Franz G. Bray. *J&N*, III, 264.
December 31, 1823.	General Carl von Kniaziewicz. *J&N*, III, 264.
December 31, 1823.	Daniel Sheldon. *J&N*, III, 264.
Late December, 1823.	General George Airey. *J&N*, III, 262.
Late December, 1823.	——— Douglas. *J&N*, III, 262.
Late December, 1823.	Sir John Eardley-Wilmot. *J&N*, III, 262.
December, 1823.	John Treat Irving. *J&N*, III, 279.
December, 1823.	Julia Irving. *J&N*, III, 279.
December, 1823.	Mary Colin Robertson. *J&N*, III, 278.
Early January, 1824.	Amelia Foster. *J&N*, III, 270.
Early January, 1824.	Barham Livius. *J&N*, III, 270.
January 14, 1824.	Miss Barton. *J&N*, III, 271.
Mid-January, 1824.	Amelia Foster. *J&N*, III, 278.
Mid-January, 1824.	John Howard Payne. WI to John Howard Payne, January 17, 1824.
Mid-January, 1824.	Sarah Van Wart. *J&N*, III, 278.
January 20, 1824.	General George Airey. *J&N*, III, 274.
January 23, 1824.	John Howard Payne. *J&N*, III, 278.

January 24, 1824.   Mrs. John Storey. *J&N*, III, 277.
January 25?, 1824.   John Howard Payne. *J&N*, III, 280.
Early February, 1824.   Captain Holdridge. *J&N*, III, 286.
February 2, 1824.   James Kenney. *J&N*, III, 282.
February 11?, 1824.   Amelia & Emily Foster. *J&N*, III, 290.
Mid-February, 1824.   Joshua Dodge. *J&N*, III, 294.
Mid-February, 1824.   Samuel H. Spiker. *J&N*, III, 292.
February 16?, 1824.   Barham Livius. *J&N*, III, 291.
February 20?, 1824.   Mrs. John Story. *J&N*, III, 293.
February 23, 1824.   Captain Holdridge. *J&N*, III, 296.
February 29, 1824.   J. W. Lake. *J&N*, III, 298.
Late February, 1824.   Henry Carey. *J&N*, III, 307.
Late February, 1824.   ———— Dewey. *J&N*, III, 310.
Late February, 1824.   Ebenezer Irving. *J&N*, III, 309.
Late February, 1824.   J. W. Lake. *J&N*, III, 298.
Late February, 1824.   "letters . . . from New York." *J&N*, III, 307.
Early March, 1824.   Charles R. Leslie. *J&N*, III, 299.
Early March, 1824.   Robert Sullivan. *J&N*, III, 299.
March 1?, 1824.   John Miller. *J&N*, III, 300.
March 7, 1824.   Barham Livius. *J&N*, III, 303.
March 18, 1824.   John Murray II. *J&N*, III, 307.
March 21?, 1824.   Amelia Foster. *J&N*, III, 310.
March 21?, 1824.   Sarah Van Wart. *J&N*, III, 310.
Late March, 1824.   Amelia Foster. *J&N*, III, 314.
March, 1824.   John Miller. *J&N*, III, 307.
Early April, 1824.   Pierre P. Irving. *J&N*, III, 325.
Early April, 1824.   James K. Paulding. *J&N*, III, 325.
April 7?, 1824.   John Howard Payne. *J&N*, III, 319.
April 9?, 1824.   Sir Henry Mildmay. *J&N*, III, 318.
April 11?, 1824.   John Howard Payne. *J&N*, III, 320.
April 16?, 1824.   General Carlo Andrea Pózzo di Bórgo. *J&N*, III, 320.
April 17?, 1824.   Sarah & Henry Van Wart. *J&N*, III, 323.
April 20, 1824.   Duchess of Duras. *J&N*, III, 322.
Early May, 1824.   Benjamin U. Coles. WI to John Howard Payne, May 8, 1824; WI to Benjamin U. Coles, May 13, 1824.
May 6, 1824.   John Howard Payne. WI to Benjamin U. Coles, May 13, 1824.
May 11?, 1824.   Peter Irving. *J&N*, III, 330.
May 13?, 1824.   John Howard Payne. *J&N*, III, 333.
May 14, 1824.   Frank Mills. *J&N*, III, 332.
May 15, 1824.   Frank Mills. *J&N*, III, 333.

Mid-May, 1824.	Charles W. Storrow. WI to Mrs. Thomas W. Storrow, May 24, 1824.
May 19, 1824.	Frank Mills. *J&N*, III, 334.
June 3?, 1824.	Amelia Foster. *J&N*, III, 341.
June 9, 1824.	John Howard Payne. *J&N*, III, 345.
June 17?, 1824.	Marianne (housekeeper in Paris). *J&N*, III, 353.
June 21?, 1824.	Peter Irving. *J&N*, III, 354.
June 24?, 1824.	Robert Sullivan. *J&N*, III, 354.
June 25?, 1824.	Amelia Foster. *J&N*, III, 354.
Early July, 1824.	——— Ewing. *J&N*, III, 375.
July 3?, 1824.	Amelia Foster. *J&N*, III, 357.
July 5?, 1824.	——— Jones. *J&N*, III, 357.
July 7?, 1824.	Marianne (housekeeper in Paris). *J&N*, III, 364.
July 8?, 1824.	John Howard Payne. *J&N*, III, 360.
July 9, 1824.	John Murray II. *J&N*, III, 361.
July 10, 1824.	John Murray II. *J&N*, III, 362.
July 13, 1824.	John Murray II. *J&N*, III, 364.
July 13?, 1824.	John Howard Payne. *J&N*, III, 364.
July 14?, 1824.	Peter Irving. *J&N*, III, 368.
July 18?, 1824.	Sarah Van Wart. *J&N*, III, 368.
July 19?, 1824.	Peter Irving. *J&N*, III, 373.
July 25?, 1824.	Mr. & Mrs. Thomas W. Storrow. *J&N*, III, 375.
July 25?, 1824.	Henry Van Wart. *J&N*, III, 374.
July 29?, 1824.	Sarah Van Wart. *J&N*, III, 375.
Late July, 1824.	Gulian C. Verplanck. *J&N*, III, 384.
August 1, 1824.	——— Edgill. *J&N*, III, 376.
August 1, 1824.	J. M. Jones. *J&N*, III, 376.
August 1, 1824.	——— Sebright. *J&N*, III, 376.
August 3, 1824.	Amelia Foster. *J&N*, III, 377.
August 4, 1824.	John Murray II. *J&N*, III, 377.
August 4, 1824.	Henry Van Wart. *J&N*, III, 377.
Mid-August, 1824.	——— Coleman. *J&N*, III, 394.
Late August, 1824.	Ruxton Dine. *J&N*, III, 390.
Late August, 1824.	Frank Mills. *J&N*, III, 392.
Late August, 1824.	John Howard Payne. *J&N*, III, 391.
August, 1824.	Catharine Paris. WI to Catharine Paris, September 20, 1824.
Early September, 1824.	General Devereux. *J&N*, III, 392.
Early September, 1824.	Ebenezer Irving. *J&N*, III, 399.
Early September, 1824.	James K. Paulding. *J&N*, III, 399.

September 3, 1824.   Peter Irving. *J&N*, III, 392.
September 4?, 1824.   Colonel Thomas Aspinwall. *J&N*, III, 392.
September 4?, 1824.   Henry Van Wart. *J&N*, III, 394.
September 5?, 1824.   Amelia Foster. *J&N*, III, 393.
September 19?, 1824.   John Miller. *J&N*, III, 398.
September 29, 1824.   Frank Mills. *J&N*, III, 401.
September 29, 1824.   Thomas W. Storrow. *J&N*, III, 400.
Early October, 1824.   Henry Van Wart. *J&N*, III, 402.
October 5, 1824.   Ebenezer Irving. *J&N*, III, 418.
October 8, 1824.   Duchess of Duras. *J&N*, III, 402.
October 15, 1824.   John Howard Payne. *J&N*, III, 413.
October 25?, 1824.   Sarah Van Wart. *J&N*, III, 418.
October 31, 1824.   Duchess of Duras. *J&N*, III, 418.
Late October, 1824.   Gilbert Stuart Newton. *J&N*, III, 421.
Early November, 1824.   Dr. Clark. *J&N*, III, 431.
November 2?, 1824.   John Miller. *J&N*, III, 422.
November 2?, 1824.   Frank Mills. *J&N*, III, 422.
November 5?, 1824.   Henry & Irving Van Wart. *J&N*, III, 425.
November 8?, 1824.   John Miller. *J&N*, III, 426.
November 8?, 1824.   Gilbert Stuart Newton. *J&N*, III, 426.
November 10, 1824.   ———— Bremner. *J&N*, III, 424.
November 10, 1824.   Dominick Lynch. *J&N*, III, 424.
November 10, 1824.   ———— Prince. *J&N*, III, 424.
Mid-November, 1824.   Luther Bradish. *J&N*, III, 429.
Mid-November, 1824.   "a friend" in New York. *J&N*, III, 436.
November 24, 1824.   James Brown. *J&N*, III, 429.
December 7?, 1824.   Captain Thomas Medwin. *J&N*, III, 434.
December 15, 1824.   John Howard Payne. *J&N*, III, 438.
Late December, 1824.   Charles R. Leslie. *J&N*, III, 443.
January 5, 1825.   Frank Mills. *J&N*, III, 443.
January 7?, 1825.   John Howard Payne. *J&N*, III, 445.
January 10?, 1825.   John Howard Payne, *J&N*, III, 446.
January 14?, 1825.   A Frenchman. *J&N*, III, 445.
January 15?, 1825.   Sarah Van Wart. *J&N*, III, 447.
January 17?, 1825.   John Murray II. *J&N*, III, 447.
January 17?, 1825.   Robert Sullivan. *J&N*, III, 447.
January 29, 1825.   Amelia Foster. *J&N*, III, 449.
January, 1825.   Captain John B. Nicholson. *J&N*, III, 454.
February 5?, 1825.   Henry & Irving Van Wart. *J&N*, III, 455.
February 13?, 1825.   Frank Mills. *J&N*, III, 457.
February 14?, 1825.   Proprietor of *European Magazine*. *J&N*, III, 457.
February 21?, 1825.   Frank Mills. *J&N*, III, 460.

February 26?, 1825.   Sarah Van Wart. *J&N*, III, 460.
February 28, 1825.   John Howard Payne. *J&N*, III, 461.
Late February, 1825.   Ebenezer Irving. *J&N*, III, 469.
Late February, 1825.   Pierre P. Irving. *J&N*, III, 469.
Late February, 1825.   Frank Mills. *J&N*, III, 462.
Late February, 1825.   Charles Rhind. *J&N*, III, 469.
Late February, 1825.   Mrs. John Story. *J&N*, III, 462.
March 2, 1825.   Charles W. Storrow. *J&N*, III, 461.
March 5?, 1825.   Sarah Van Wart. *J&N*, III, 463.
March 8, 1825.   Samuel Welles. *J&N*, III, 463.
March 9?, 1825.   Peter Irving. *J&N*, III, 464.
March 13?, 1825.   Peter Irving. *J&N*, III, 466.
March 13?, 1825.   Frank Mills. *J&N*, III, 466.
March 27?, 1825.   Peter Irving. *J&N*, III, 471.
Late March, 1825.   James K. Paulding. *J&N*, III, 476.
Early April?, 1825.   Ebenezer Irving. *J&N*, III, 479.
April 14?, 1825.   Gilbert Stuart Newton. *J&N*, III, 476.
April 23?, 1825.   ———— Reid. WI to ———— Reid, April 24,
                        1825.

May 3?, 1825.   Robert Sullivan. *J&N*, III, 482.
May 8?, 1825.   Peter Irving. *J&N*, III, 483.
May 14?, 1825.   Peter Irving. *J&N*, III, 485.
May 18?, 1825.   Peter Irving. *J&N*, III, 485.
May 19?, 1825.   Captain Thomas Medwin. *J&N*, III, 486.
May 21?, 1825.   Robert Sullivan. *J&N*, III, 486.
Early June, 1825.   Baron Carl August von Lützerode, *J&N*, III,
                        491.

June 1, 1825.   Peter Irving. *J&N*, III, 489.
June 6?, 1825.   William E. West. *J&N*, III, 491.
June 9?, 1825.   Frank Mills. *J&N*, III, 495.
June 19?, 1825.   Peter Irving. *J&N*, III, 496.
June 20?, 1825.   Dominick Lynch. *J&N*, III, 496.
June 20?, 1825.   Thomas W. Storrow. *J&N*, III, 496.
June 22?, 1825.   Thomas K. Hervey. *J&N*, III, 497.
Late June, 1825.   Captain John B. Nicholson. *J&N*, III, 500.
Early July, 1825.   Julia Irving. *J&N*, III, 506.
Early July, 1825.   Frank Mills. *J&N*, III, 500.
Early July, 1825.   Gilbert Stuart Newton. *J&N*, III, 500.
July 4?, 1825.   Thomas W. Storrow. *J&N*, III, 499.
July 15?, 1825.   John Murray II. *J&N*, III, 503.
July 23?, 1825.   John Howard Payne. *J&N*, III, 505.
July 25?, 1825.   Archibald Constable. *J&N*, III, 506.
July 25?, 1825.   Thomas K. Hervey. *J&N*, III, 506.

July 26?, 1825.   William E. West. *J&N*, III, 506.
July 31, 1825.   John Howard Payne. *J&N*, III, 507.
July, 1825.   ———— Dewey? *J&N*, III, 506.
August 9?, 1825.   Emily Foster. *J&N*, III, 509.
August 12, 1825.   Mrs. Thomas W. Storrow. WI to Mrs. Thomas
                         W. Storrow, August 12, 1825.
August 14?, 1825.   Frank Mills. *J&N*, III, 510.
August 16?, 1825.   Peter Irving. *J&N*, III, 510.
August 19?, 1825.   Alexander H. Everett. *J&N*, III, 511.
August 21?, 1825.   Peter Irving. *J&N*, III, 511.
August 24?, 1825.   Peter Irving. *J&N*, III, 512.
Late August, 1825.   Peter Irving. *J&N*, III, 513.
Early September, 1825.   Ebenezer Irving. *J&N*, III, 529.
September 4?, 1825.   Sarah Van Wart. *J&N*, III, 516.
September 13?, 1825.   The Fosters. *J&N*, III, 519.
Early October, 1825.   Sarah Van Wart. *J&N*, III, 531.
October 7?, 1825.   Reuben Beasley. *J&N*, III, 529.
October 9, 1825.   John Howard Payne. *J&N*, III, 531.
October 13?, 1825.   Thomas W. Storrow. *J&N*, III, 531.
October 17?, 1825.   John Howard Payne. *J&N*, III, 534.
October 23?, 1825.   John Howard Payne. *J&N*, III, 535.
October 25, 1825.   Frank Mills. *J&N*, III, 537.
Late October, 1825.   "a letter from England." *J&N*, III, 540.
Early November, 1825.   ———— Jones. *J&N*, III, 543.
Early November, 1825.   John Howard Payne. *J&N*, III, 540.
November 5?, 1825.   Thomas W. Storrow. *J&N*, III, 540.
November 7?, 1825.   Henry Van Wart. *J&N*, III, 543.
November 7?, 1825.   Samuel Williams. *J&N*, III, 543.
December 4?, 1825.   Mrs. Thomas W. Storrow. *J&N*, III, 551.
December 11?, 1825.   Amelia Foster. *J&N*, III, 553.
December 11?, 1825.   John Howard Payne. *J&N*, III, 553.
December 12?, 1825.   Thomas W. Storrow. *J&N*, III, 553.
December 15?, 1825.   C. B. Coles. *J&N*, III, 556.
December 18?, 1825.   Henry Van Wart. WI to Thomas W. Storrow,
                         December 25, 1825.
December 22, 1825.   Stephen Price. *J&N*, III, 556.
December 30?, 1825.   John Howard Payne. *J&N*, III, 557.
Late December, 1825.   John Murray II. WI to John Murray II, Jan-
                         uary 3, 1826.
December, 1825.   Alexander H. Everett. *J&N*, III, 558.
December, 1825.   Amelia Foster. WI to Amelia Foster, January
                         9, 1826.
December, 1825.   Edward St. Aubyn. *J&N*, III, 558.

December, 1825.	Thomas W. White. *J&N*, III, 558.
Early January?, 1826.	Henry C. Carey. *J&N*, III, 562.
Early January?, 1826.	Gilbert Stuart Newton. WI to Charles R. Leslie, February 3, 1826.
Early January, 1826.	Captain John B. Nicholson. *J&N*, III, 559.
January 3?, 1826.	Thomas W. Storrow. *J&N*, III, 558.
January 5?, 1826.	John Howard Payne. *J&N*, III, 559.
January 11?, 1826.	C. B. Coles. *J&N*, III, 560.
January 16?, 1826.	Frank Mills. *J&N*, III, 561.
January 22?, 1826.	John Howard Payne. *J&N*, III, 562.
January 26?, 1826.	Alexander H. Everett. *J&N*, III, 563.
Early February?, 1826.	Ebenezer Irving. *Journals of WI*, III, 13.
Early February?, 1826.	Frank Mills. *Journals of WI*, III, 9.
Early February?, 1826.	Daniel Strobel. *Journals of WI*, III, 9.
February 8, 1826.	John Howard Payne. *Journals of WI*, III, 11.
February 8, 1826.	Thomas W. Storrow. *Journals of WI*, III, 9.
Mid-February, 1826.	Frank Mills. *Journals of WI*, III, 13.
Mid-February, 1826.	John Howard Payne. *Journals of WI*, III, 11.
February 19?, 1826.	General Martín Iriarti. *Journals of WI*, III, 9.
Late February, 1826.	John Howard Payne. *Journals of WI*, III, 13.
February, 1826.	Captain Thomas Medwin. *Journals of WI*, III, 13.
Early March, 1826.	Robert Sullivan. *Journals of WI*, III, 15.
March 9?, 1826.	Daniel Strobel. *Journals of WI*, III, 15.
March 16?, 1826.	Mrs. Nathaniel Johnston. *Journals of WI*, III, 16.
March 16?, 1826.	John Howard Payne. *Journals of WI*, III, 18.
March 17?, 1826.	Henry Van Wart. *Journals of WI*, III, 18.
March 20, 1826.	Thomas W. Storrow. WI to Thomas W. Storrow, April 14, 1826.
March 23?, 1826.	Bernard Henry. *Journals of WI*, III, 18.
March 23, 1826.	Thomas W. Storrow. WI to Thomas W. Storrow, April 14, 1826.
March 28, 1826.	John Wiseman. *Journals of WI*, III, 19.
Mid-April, 1826.	Thomas W. Storrow. *Journals of WI*, III, 23.
April 29, 1826.	Nathaniel Johnston. *Journals of WI*, III, 25.
Early May, 1826.	Pierre M. Irving. *Journals of WI*, III, 24.
May 10, 1826.	John Howard Payne. *Journals of WI*, III, 25.
Mid-May, 1826.	Bernard Henry. *Journals of WI*, III, 26.
Mid-May, 1826.	Obadiah Rich. *Journals of WI*, III, 26.
Mid-May, 1826.	Henry Van Wart. *Journals of WI*, III, 26.
Late May, 1826.	Reuben Beasley. *Journals of WI*, III, 27.
Late May, 1826.	The Storrows. *Journals of WI*, III, 27.

Early June, 1826.	Countess Granard. *Journals of WI*, III, 28.
Early June, 1826.	Stephen Price. *Journals of WI*, III, 29.
Mid-June, 1826.	Frank Mills. *Journals of WI*, III, 29.
Mid-June, 1826.	———— Okell. *Journals of WI*, III, 29.
Late June, 1826.	Henry Van Wart? WI to Thomas W. Storrow, July 9, 1826.
Early July, 1826.	Sarah & Henry Van Wart. *Journals of WI*, III, 32.
July 10?, 1826.	Obadiah Rich. *Journals of WI*, III, 33.
Mid-July, 1826.	Gilbert Stuart Newton. *Journals of WI*, III, 35.
Late July, 1826.	Pierre M. Irving. *Journals of WI*, III, 35.
August 4, 1826.	Thomas W. Storrow. *Journals of WI*, III, 37.
ca. August 20, 1826.	Pierre M. Irving. *Journals of WI*, III, 39.
August 26, 1826.	Henry Carey. *Journals of WI*, III, 54.
Late August, 1826.	F. Andrews. *Journals of WI*, III, 39.
ca. September 8, 1826.	Henry Van Wart. *Journals of WI*, III, 40.
Mid-September, 1826.	Pierre M. Irving. *Journals of WI*, III, 40.
Mid-September, 1826.	Mr. & Mrs. Thomas W. Storrow. *Journals of WI*, III, 40.
Early October, 1826.	Henry Van Wart. *Journals of WI*, III, 43.
Early October, 1826.	Sarah Van Wart. (Three letters.) *Journals of WI*, III, 43.
Mid-October, 1826.	Pierre M. Irving. *Journals of WI*, III, 43.
Mid-October, 1826.	Gilbert Stuart Newton. *Journals of WI*, III, 43.
Mid-October, 1826.	Minny Storrow. *Journals of WI*, III, 43.
Mid-October, 1826.	Susan Storrow. *Journals of WI*, III, 43.
November 14, 1826.	Ebenezer Irving. *Journals of WI*, III, 48.
Mid-November, 1826.	Thomas W. Storrow. *Journals of WI*, III, 46.
Early December, 1826.	Thomas W. Storrow. WI to Thomas W. Storrow, January 3, 1827.
December 15, 1826.	Thomas W. Storrow. WI to Thomas W. Storrow, January 3, 1827.
January 6, 1827.	Pierre M. Irving. *Journals of WI*, III, 51.
Mid-January, 1827.	James Kenney. *Journals of WI*, III, 52.
Mid-January, 1827.	Secretary of the Athenaeum. *Journals of WI*, III, 52.
Mid-January, 1827.	Mrs. John Story. *Journals of WI*, III, 52.
ca. January 20, 1827.	Sarah & Henry Van Wart. *Journals of WI*, III, 53.
January 21?, 1827.	Frank Mills. *Journals of WI*, III, 53.
January 25?, 1827.	Sarah Van Wart. *Journals of WI*, III, 53.

January, 1827.	Henry Carey. *Journals of WI*, III, 54.
January, 1827.	Ebenezer Irving. *Journals of WI*, III, 54.
Early February, 1827.	Lady Granard. *Journals of WI*, III, 54.
February 7?, 1827.	Reuben Beasley. *Journals of WI*, III, 54.
February 8?, 1827.	Henry Van Wart. *Journals of WI*, III, 55.
Late February, 1827.	Pierre M. Irving. *Journals of WI*, III, 56.
Late February, 1827.	Minny Storrow. WI to Thomas W. Storrow, March 20, 1827.
Late February, 1827.	Susan Sorrow. WI to Thomas W. Storrow, March 20, 1827.
Late February, 1827.	Thomas W. Storrow. *Journals of WI*, III, 56.
Early March, 1827.	Pierre M. Irving. *Journals of WI*, III, 57.
March 8, 1827.	Thomas W. Storrow. *Journals of WI*, III, 58.
Late March, 1827.	Pierre M. Irving. *Journals of WI*, III, 60.
April 12?, 1827.	Pierre M. Irving. *Journals of WI*, III, 62.
Mid-April, 1827.	Alexander Slidell. (Two letters.) *Journals of WI*, III, 62, 63.
Mid-April, 1827.	"Spaniard in America occupied on grammar." *Journals of WI*, III, 63.
April 24, 1827.	Pierre M. Irving & Henry Van Wart. (One letter.) *Journal 1827–1828*, p. 223.
Late April, 1827.	Ebenezer Irving. *Journal 1827–1828*, p. 223.
Mid-May, 1827.	Alexander Slidell. *Journal 1827–1828*, p. 300.
Late May, 1827.	Sir Egerton Brydges. *Journal 1827–1828*, p. 300.
May, 1827.	Ebenezer Irving. *Journal 1827–1828*, p. 300.
June 30?, 1827.	Daniel Strobel. *Journal 1827–1828*, p. 301.
Early July?, 1827.	Alexander Slidell. *Journal 1827–1828*, p. 302.
Early July, 1827.	Henry Van Wart. *Journal 1827–1828*, p. 303.
Mid-July, 1827.	Frank Mills. *Journal 1827–1828*, p. 303.
July 16?, 1827.	Daniel Strobel. *Journal 1827–1828*, p. 303.
July 19?, 1827.	Chevalier de Verneuil. *Journal 1827–1828*, p. 303.
Early August?, 1827.	Ebenezer Irving. *Journal 1827–1828*, p. 305.
Mid-August, 1827.	Thomas W. Storrow. *Journal 1827–1828*, p. 305.
Mid-August, 1827.	Sarah & Henry Van Wart. *Journal 1827–1828*, p. 305.
Late August?, 1827.	Pierre M. Irving. *Journal 1827–1828*, p. 306.
Early September?, 1827.	Colonel Thomas Aspinwall. (Two letters.) *Journal 1827–1828*, p. 306.
Early September?, 1827.	Thomas W. Storrow. *Journal 1827–1828*, p. 306.
September 3, 1827.	Catharine Paris. WI to Catharine Paris, February 17, 1828.

September 24, 1827.   Colonel Thomas Aspinwall. *Journal 1827–1828*, p. 307.

September 24, 1827.   Henry W. Longfellow. *Journal 1827–1828*, p. 307.

October 23, 1827.   Ebenezer Irving. *Journal 1827–1828*, p. 409.

October 30, 1827.   Messrs. Baring & Co. *Journal 1827–1828*, p. 408.

November 10, 1827.   Mr. & Mrs. Thomas W. Storrow. *Journal 1827–1828*, p. 409.

Mid-November?, 1827.   Ebenezer Irving. *Journal 1827–1828*, p. 410.

November, 1827.   Sarah Van Wart. WI to Mrs. Thomas W. Storrow, December 1, 1827.

December 11, 1827.   Colonel Thomas Aspinwall. *Journal 1827–1828*, p. 411.

December 15, 1827.   Alexander H. Everett. *Journal 1827–1828*, p. 410.

December 16, 1827.   Alexander H. Everett. *Journal 1827–1828*, p. 410.

December 24?, 1827.   Charles R. Leslie. *Journal 1827–1828*, p. 412.

December 24?, 1827.   Gilbert Stuart Newton. *Journal 1827–1828*, p. 412.

December 31, 1827.   Ebenezer Irving. *Journal 1827–1828*, p. 414.

December, 1827.   Ebenezer Irving. (Three letters.) *Journal 1827–1828*, pp. 412–13.

December, 1827.   Julia Irving. *Journal 1827–1828*, p. 413.

Early January, 1828.   Colonel Thomas Aspinwall. *Journal 1827–1828*, p. 413.

Early January, 1828.   W. B. Lawrence. *Journal 1827–1828*, p. 412.

Mid-January, 1828.   Prince Dolgorouki. *Journal 1827–1828*, p. 413.

Mid-January, 1828.   Thomas W. Storrow and daughters. *Journal 1827–1828*, p. 414.

Mid-January, 1828.   Timothy Wiggins. *Journal 1827–1828*, p. 414.

January 21?, 1828.   Theodore Irving. *Journal 1827–1828*, p. 413.

Late January, 1828.   Prince Dolgorouki. *Journal 1827–1828*, p. 414.

Late January, 1828.   Sarah Van Wart. *Journal 1827–1828*, p. 414.

Early February, 1828.   Reuben Beasley. *Journal 1827–1828*, p. 415.

Early February, 1828.   Richard McCall. *Journal 1827–1828*, p. 415.

Mid-February, 1828.   Obadiah Rich. *Journal 1827–1828*, p. 416.

Mid-February, 1828.   Sarah Van Wart. *Journal 1827–1828*, p. 416.

February 19?, 1828.   Prince Dolgorouki. WI to Prince Dolgorouki, February 19, 1828.

March 5, 1828.   Prince Dolgorouki. WI to Prince Dolgorouki, March 29, 1828.

March 8, 1828.   Prince Dolgorouki. WI to Prince Dolgorouki,
                              March 29, 1828.
March 21, 1828.   Prince Dolgorouki. WI to Prince Dolgorouki,
                              March 29, 1828.
March 31, 1828.   Ebenezer Irving. *Diary 1828–1829*, p. 21.
Late March, 1828.   Colonel Thomas Aspinwall. *Diary 1828–1829*,
                              p. 3.
Late March, 1828.   Peter Irving. *Diary 1828–1829*, p. 3.
Late March, 1828.   Charles R. Leslie. *Diary 1828–1829*, p. 10.
Late March, 1828.   Sir James Mackintosh. WI to Alexander Ever-
                              ett, April 23, 1828.
Late March, 1828.   Gilbert Stuart Newton. *Diary 1828–1829*, p. 3.
March, 1828.   Antoinette Bolviller. WI to Antoinette Bolvil-
                              ler, April 2, 1828.
Early April, 1828.   Colonel Thomas Aspinwall. *Diary 1828–1829*,
                              p. 10.
Early April, 1828.   Peter Irving. (Two letters.) *Diary 1828–1829*,
                              pp. 10, 12.
Early April?, 1828.   Obadiah Rich. *Diary 1828–1829*, p. 10.
April 11, 1828.   Alexander H. Everett. *Diary 1828–1829*, p. 18.
Mid-April, 1828.   Catharine D'Oubril. WI to Catharine D'Ou-
                              bril, April 19, 1828.
Mid-April, 1828.   Prince Dolgorouki. WI to Peter Irving, April
                              15, 1828.
Mid-April, 1828.   Obadiah Rich. *Diary 1828–1829*, p. 12.
April 25?, 1828.   George B. Barrell. *Diary 1828–1829*, p. 18.
April 27–30, 1828.   Prince Dolgorouki. WI to Prince Dolgorouki,
                              May 18, 1828.
Late April, 1828.   Alexander H. Everett. *Diary 1828–1829*, p. 19.
Late April, 1828.   ——— Gessler. *Diary 1828–1829*, p. 19.
Late April, 1828.   George W. Montgomery. *Diary 1828–1829*,
                              p. 19.
Early May, 1828.   Peter Irving, *Diary 1828–1829*, p. 26.
Early May, 1828.   Theodore Irving. *Diary 1828–1829*, p. 26.
Early May, 1828.   ——— Stoffregen. *Diary 1828–1829*, p. 21.
Early May, 1828.   Henry Van Wart. *Diary 1828–1829*, p. 26.
May 1?, 1828.   Alexander Burton. *Diary 1828–1829*, p. 19.
May 6?, 1828.   George G. Barrell. *Diary 1828–1829*, p. 21.
May 7?, 1828.   Antoinette Bolviller. *Diary 1828–1829*, p. 21.
Mid-May, 1828.   John Treat Irving. *Diary 1828–1829*, p. 35.
Mid-May, 1828.   ——— Stoffregen. *Diary 1828–1829*, p. 29.
Mid-May, 1828.   Peter Irving. *Diary 1828–1829*, p. 30.
May 17?, 1828.   Horatio Sprague. *Diary 1828–1829*, p. 29.

May 18?, 1828.   Alexander Burton. *Diary 1828–1829*, p. 29.
May 18?, 1828.   ———— Roberts. *Diary 1828–1829*, p. 29.
May 24?, 1828.   George G. Barrell. *Diary 1828–1829*, p. 31.
Late May, 1828.   Obadiah Rich. *Diary 1828–1829*, p. 33.
Early June, 1828.   Peter Irving. *Diary 1828–1829*, p. 36.
June 8?, 1828.   John O'Shea. *Diary 1828–1829*, p. 35.
June 10?, 1828.   Antoinette Bolviller. *Diary 1828–1829*, p. 35.
June 10?, 1828.   Prince Dolgorouki. *Diary 1828–1829*, p. 35.
Mid-June, 1828.   Colonel Thomas Aspinwall. *Diary 1828–1829*, p. 29.

Mid-June, 1828.   ———— Gessler. *Diary 1828–1829*, p. 36.
Mid-June, 1828.   Peter Irving. *Diary 1828–1829*, p. 39.
June 16?, 1828.   Alexander Burton. *Diary 1828–1829*, p. 37.
June 20?, 1828.   ———— Gessler. *Diary 1828–1829*, p. 38.
Late June, 1828.   Obadiah Rich. *Diary 1828–1829*, pp. 41–42.
June, 1828.   Henry Brevoort. *Diary 1828–1829*, p. 43.
June?, 1828.   Henry Carey. WI to Henry Carey, August 31, 1828.
June?, 1828.   Alexander Slidell. *Diary 1828–1829*, p. 43.
Early July, 1828.   Johann Nikolaus Böhl von Faber. *Diary 1828–1829*, p. 42.
Early July, 1828.   Peter Irving. *Diary 1828–1829*, p. 43.
July 8, 1828.   Alexander H. Everett. *Diary 1828–1829*, p. 44.
July 8, 1828.   Michael Walsh. *Diary 1828–1829*, p. 42.
Mid-July, 1828.   ———— Duffield. *Diary 1828–1829*, p. 44.
Mid-July, 1828.   ———— Stirling. *Diary 1828–1829*, p. 45.
July 23?, 1828.   Alexander Burton. *Diary 1828–1829*, p. 46.
July 25?, 1828.   Alexander Burton. *Diary 1828–1829*, p. 46.
Late July, 1828.   Alexander H. Everett. *Diary 1828–1829*, p. 47.
Late July, 1828.   Peter Irving. *Diary 1828–1829*, p. 48.
Late July?, 1828.   Alexander Slidell. *Diary 1828–1829*, p. 61.
Late July, 1828.   Thomas W. Storrow. *Diary 1828–1829*, p. 47.
Early August, 1828.   Colonel Thomas Aspinwall. *Diary 1828–1829*, pp. 59–60.
Early August, 1828.   Antoinette Bolviller. *Diary 1828–1829*, p. 48.
Early August, 1828.   Ebenezer Irving. *Diary 1828–1829*, p. 66.
Early August, 1828.   Theodore Irving. *Diary 1828–1829*, p. 60.
Early August, 1828.   Sarah & Henry Van Wart. *Diary 1828–1829*, p. 62.
August 1?, 1828.   Alexander Burton. *Diary 1828–1829*, p. 47.
August 12, 1828.   Alexander H. Everett. *Diary 1828–1829*, p. 59.
Mid-August, 1828.   ———— Gessler. (Two letters.) *Diary 1828–1829*, pp. 60, 61.

August 20?, 1828.   Peter Irving. *Diary 1828–1829*, p. 64.

August 21?, 1828.   Alexander Burton. *Diary 1828–1829*, p. 61.

Late August, 1828.   Prince Dolgorouki. *Diary 1828–1829*, p. 66.

Early September, 1828.   Peter Irving. *Diary 1828–1829*, p. 68.

Early September, 1828.   John Murray II. *Diary 1828–1829*, p. 69.

Early September, 1828.   Thomas W. Storrow. *Diary 1828–1829*, p. 68.

Early September, 1828.   Henry Van Wart. *Diary 1828–1829*, p. 68.

September 1, 1828.   David Wilkie. *Diary 1828–1829*, p. 70.

September 4?, 1828.   Miss Stalker. *Diary 1828–1829*, p. 66.

September 10?, 1828.   ———— Eviton. *Diary 1828–1829*, p. 70.

September 12?, 1828.   Antoinette Bolviller. *Diary 1828–1829*, p. 69.

September 12?, 1828.   Alexander Burton. *Diary 1828–1829*, p. 68.

September 12?, 1828.   Catharine D'Oubril. *Diary 1828–1829*, p. 69.

September 15?, 1828.   Alexander Burton. *Diary 1828–1829*, p. 69.

Mid-September, 1828.   Colonel Thomas Aspinwall. *Diary 1828–1829*, p. 69.

Mid-September, 1828.   ———— Sterling. *Diary 1828–1829*, p. 70.

September 17?, 1828.   Prince Dolgorouki. *Diary 1828–1829*, p. 69.

September 24?, 1828.   Miss Stalker. *Diary 1828–1829*, p. 71.

September 24, 1828.   John Murray II. *Diary 1828–1829*, p. 73.

September 27, 1828.   Colonel Thomas Aspinwall. *Diary 1828–1829*, p. 73.

September 28?, 1828.   Miss Stalker. *Diary 1828–1829*, p. 71.

Early October, 1828.   Peter Irving. *Diary 1828–1829*, p. 73.

October 8?, 1828.   Miss Stalker. *Diary 1828–1829*, p. 73.

October 9?, 1828.   George B. Barrell. *Diary 1828–1829*, p. 73.

Mid-October, 1828.   Miss Gore. *Diary 1828–1829*, p. 77.

Mid-October, 1828.   Peter Irving. *Diary 1828–1829*, p. 77.

Mid-October, 1828.   The Storrows. *Diary 1828–1829*, p. 77.

Mid-October, 1828.   Michael Walsh. *Diary 1828–1829*, p. 75.

October 24?, 1828.   Prince Dolgorouki. *Diary 1828–1829*, p. 76.

Late October, 1828.   Lopez, Roberts & Co. *Diary 1828–1829*, p. 78.

Early November, 1828.   Alexander Burton. *Diary 1828–1829*, p. 79.

Early November, 1828.   Alexander H. Everett. *Diary 1828–1829*, p. 79.

Early November, 1828.   John Murray II. *Diary 1828–1829*, p. 81.

Early November, 1828.   Gilbert Stuart Newton. *Diary 1828–1829*, p. 81.

Early November, 1828.   Horatio Swett. *Diary 1828–1829*, p. 77.

November 7?, 1828.   John N. Hall. *Diary 1828–1829*, p. 79.

November 9?, 1828.   Antoinette Bolviller. *Diary 1828–1829*, p. 80.

November 11, 1828.   Colonel Thomas Aspinwall. *Diary 1828–1829*, p. 94.

November 11?, 1828.   John N. Hall. *Diary 1828–1829*, p. 80.

November 14?, 1828.   Alexander Burton. *Diary 1828–1829*, p. 81.

November 19?, 1828.   George G. Barrell. *Diary 1828–1829*, p. 82.
November 22?, 1828.   George G. Barrell. *Diary 1828–1829*, p. 83.
November 24?, 1828.   Johann Nikolaus Böhl von Faber. *Diary 1828–1829*, p. 84.
November 24?, 1828.   Alexander Burton. *Diary 1828–1829*, p. 84.
November 24?, 1828.   ———— Gessler. *Diary 1828–1829*, p. 84.
Late November, 1828.   Allan Cunningham. *Diary 1828–1829*, p. 85.
Early December, 1828. Alexander H. Everett. *Diary 1828–1829*, p. 85.
Early December, 1828. Count ————. *Diary 1828–1829*, p. 85.
December 1?, 1828.   Alexander Burton. *Diary 1828–1829*, p. 84.
December 2, 1828.   Colonel Thomas Aspinwall. *Diary 1828–1829*, p. 87.
December 2, 1828.   Johann Nikolaus Böhl von Faber. *Diary 1828–1829*, p. 84.
December 5, 1828.   Colonel Thomas Aspinwall. *Diary 1828–1829*, p. 87.
December 5?, 1828.   Alexander Burton. *Diary 1828–1829*, p. 85.
December 10?, 1828.   Alexander Burton. *Diary 1828–1829*, p. 85.
December 13?, 1828.   Alexander Burton. *Diary 1828–1829*, p. 86.
December 13, 1828.   Diego Clemencín. *Diary 1828–1829*, p. 91.
Mid-December, 1828.   Colonel Thomas Aspinwall. *Diary 1828–1829*, p. 88.
Mid-December, 1828.   Peter Irving. *Diary 1828–1829*, p. 89.
Mid-December, 1828.   John Murray II. *Diary 1828–1829*, p. 88.
December 17?, 1828.   Alexander Burton. *Diary 1828–1829*, p. 86.
Late December, 1828.   Prince Dolgorouki. *Diary 1828–1829*, p. 91.
December, 1828.   Ebenezer Irving. *Diary 1828–1829*, p. 93.
December, 1828.   Peter Irving. *Diary 1828–1829*, p. 91.
December?, 1828.   Colonel Chapman. WI to Bernard Henry, May 13, 1829.
1828.   Lord Mahon. WI to David Wilkie, May 15, 1829.
Early January?, 1829. Henry Carey. *Diary 1828–1829*, p. 100.
Early January, 1829.   Miss Gore. *Diary 1828–1829*, p. 93.
Early January, 1829.   Peter Irving, *Diary 1828–1829*, p. 93.
Early January, 1829.   Thomas W. Storrow. *Diary 1828–1829*, p. 93.
January 6?, 1829.   George G. Barrell. *Diary 1828–1829*, p. 93.
January 13, 1829.   Alexander Burton. *Diary 1828–1829*, p. 94.
Mid-January, 1829.   Colonel Thomas Aspinwall. *Diary 1828–1829*, p. 96.
Mid-January, 1829.   Peter Irving. *Diary 1828–1829*, p. 97.
Mid-January, 1829.   Lord Mahon. *Diary 1828–1829*, p. 96.
January 15?, 1829.   ———— Gessler. *Diary 1828–1829*, p. 94.

January 22?, 1829.	Prince Dolgorouki. *Diary 1828–1829*, p. 96.
January 22?, 1829.	Sarah & Henry Van Wart. *Diary 1828–1829*, p. 98.
January 23?, 1829.	Johann Nikolaus Böhl von Faber. *Diary 1828–1829*, p. 96.
January 26, 1829.	Alexander Burton. *Diary 1828–1829*, p. 97.
Late January, 1829.	Alexander Burton. *Diary 1828–1829*, p. 97.
Late January, 1829.	Peter Irving. *Diary 1828–1829*, p. 98.
Late January?, 1829.	Henry Van Wart. *Diary 1828–1829*, p. 100.
January?, 1829.	Theodore Irving. *Diary 1828–1829*, p. 98.
Early February, 1829.	Peter Irving. *Diary 1828–1829*, p. 100.
February 6?, 1829.	Alexander H. Burton. *Diary 1828–1829*, p. 99.
February 15?, 1829.	Peter Irving. *Diary, 1828–1829*, p. 104.
February 17?, 1829.	George G. Barrell. *Diary 1828–1829*, p. 102.
February 24, 1829.	Peter Irving. WI to Peter Irving, March 11, 1829.
February?, 1829.	——— Donnel. *Diary 1828–1829*, p. 102.
Early March, 1829.	Antoinette Bolviller. WI to Prince Dolgorouki, March 11, 1829.
March 7?, 1829.	Prince Dolgorouki. WI to Prince Dolgorouki, March 11, 1829.
Mid-March, 1829.	Alexander Burton. WI to Alexander H. Everett, March 25, 1829.
Mid-March, 1829.	Peter Irving. WI to Colonel Thomas Aspinwall, April 4, 1829.
March 17, 1829.	Colonel Thomas Aspinwall. WI to Colonel Thomas Aspinwall, April 4, 1829.
March 17, 1829.	Prince Dolgorouki. WI to Prince Dolgorouki, March 21, 1829.
March 20, 1829.	Colonel Thomas Aspinwall. WI to Colonel Thomas Aspinwall, April 4, 1829.
March 20?, 1829.	Mlle. Constance. WI to Prince Dolgorouki, March 25, 1829.
March 21?, 1829.	Prince Dolgorouki. WI to Prince Dolgorouki, March 25, 1829.
April 9?, 1829.	J. M. Brackenbury. WI to J. M. Brackenbury, April 11, 1829.
April 10?, 1829.	Catharine D'Oubril. WI to Catharine D'Oubril, April 21, 1829.
April 10?, 1829.	Madame Pierre D'Oubril. WI to Madame Pierre D'Oubril, April 17, 1829.
April 10?, 1829.	Alexander H. Everett. WI to Alexander H. Everett, April 15, 1829.

April 10?, 1829.	Nathalie Richter. WI to Nathalie Richter, April 22, 1829.
Mid-April, 1829.	Colonel Thomas Aspinwall. WI to Colonel Thomas Aspinwall, April 29, 1829.
April 17, 1829.	John K. Kane. WI to John K. Kane, September 27, 1830.
April 20, 1829.	Peter Irving. WI to Peter Irving, May 9, 1829.
May 1, 1829.	Colonel Thomas Aspinwall. WI to Colonel Thomas Aspinwall, May 27, 1829.
May 19, 1829.	Colonel Thomas Aspinwall. WI to Colonel Thomas Aspinwall, June 23, 1829.
May 19?, 1829.	Prince Dolgorouki. WI to Prince Dolgorouki, May 23, 1829.
May 20, 1829.	Miss Stalker. WI to Prince Dolgorouki, May 23, 1829.
May 24, 1829.	Edgar Irving. WI to Edgar Irving, May 26, 1829.
May 28, 1829.	Bernard Henry. WI to Bernard Henry, June 3, 1829.
May 29, 1829.	Colonel Thomas Aspinwall. WI to Colonel Thomas Aspinwall, June 23, 1829.
Late May?, 1829.	Antoinette Bolviller. WI to Prince Dolgorouki, June 15, 1829.
Early June, 1829.	Prince Dolgorouki. WI to Prince Dolgorouki, June 15, 1829.
Early June, 1829.	Alexander H. Everett. WI to Alexander H. Everett, July 22, 1829.
Early June, 1829.	Ebenezer Irving. WI to Peter Irving, July 18, 1829.
Early June, 1829.	James K. Paulding. WI to Peter Irving, July 22, 1829.
Early June, 1829.	Horatio Sprague. WI to Colonel Thomas Aspinwall, June 23, 1829.
June 19, 1829.	Colonel Thomas Aspinwall. WI to Colonel Thomas Aspinwall, July 4, 1829.
June, 1829.	Edward Livingston. WI to Peter Irving, July 28, 1829.
June, 1829.	Martin Van Buren. WI to Peter Irving, July 28, 1829.
Early July, 1829.	Reuben Beasley. WI to Peter Irving, July 22, 1829.
July 1, 1829.	Peter Irving. WI to Peter Irving, July 18, 1829.
July 5, 1829.	Peter Irving. WI to Peter Irving, July 18, 1829.

July 6, 1829.	Peter Irving. WI to Peter Irving, July 22, 1829.
July 9, 1829.	Peter Irving. WI to Peter Irving, July 25, 1829.
July 12, 1829.	Peter Irving. WI to Peter Irving, July 25, 1829.
Mid-July, 1829.	Peter Irving. WI to Peter Irving, July 28, 1829.
Late July, 1829.	John Wetherell. WI to Alexander H. Everett, July 27, 1829.
July, 1829.	Henry Brevoort. WI to Henry Brevoort, August 10, 1829.
Late September, 1829.	Sarah Van Wart. WI to Henry Van Wart, October 1, 1829.
Early October, 1829.	Francis B. Ogden. WI to Francis B. Ogden, October 6, 1829.
October?, 1829.	Major William B. Lewis. WI to Major William B. Lewis, November 20, 1829.
November, 1829.	Mrs. John Murray II. WI to Mrs. John Murray II, [November 29?, 1829].
November, 1829.	John Howard Payne. WI to John Howard Payne, December 7, 1829.
November?, 1829.	Miss Stalker. WI to Prince Dolgorouki, January 18, 1830.
Early December, 1829.	John Howard Payne. WI to John Howard Payne, December 7, 1829.
December 24, 1829.	Ebenezer Irving. WI to Thomas Moore, January 27, 1830.
December 31, 1829.	Ebenezer Irving. WI to William Godwin, January 30, 1830.
Late December, 1829.	Antoinette Bolviller. WI to Prince Dolgorouki, January 18, 1830.
Late December, 1829.	Peter Irving. WI to Thomas Moore, January 30, 1830.
December, 1829.	Prince Dolgorouki. WI to Prince Dolgorouki, January 18, 1830.
December, 1829.	Gouverneur Kemble. WI to Gouverneur Kemble, January 18, 1830.
December, 1829.	Miguel (in Granada). WI to Prince Dolgorouki, January 18, 1830.
December, 1829.	Lord & Lady Sidmouth. WI to Lord & Lady Sidmouth, December 21, 1829.
December, 1829.	————. WI to ————, December 2, 1829.
Early January, 1830.	Prince Dolgorouki. WI to Prince Dolgorouki, January 22, 1830.
January 29, 1830.	Thomas Moore. WI to Thomas Moore, January 30, 1830.

January 30, 1830.   I. K. Tefft. WI to I. K. Tefft, March 13, 1830.

January, 1830–July,   John Backhouse. WI to John Backhouse,
  1831.   January, 1830–July, 1831.

Early February, 1830.   Samuel Rogers. WI to Samuel Rogers, February 3, 1830.

February 7?, 1830.   Lord Mahon. WI to Lord Mahon, February 8, 1830.

March 12?, 1830.   Mr. & Mrs. John Backhouse. WI to Mr. & Mrs. John Backhouse, March 12, 1830.

March 20?, 1830.   Mr. & Mrs. Biggs. WI to Mr. & Mrs. Biggs, March 20, 1830.

March 21?, 1830.   Joseph Snow. WI to Joseph Snow, March 21, 1830.

April 17, 1830.   John K. Kane. WI to John K. Kane, September 27, 1830.

April, 1830.   William Sotheby. WI to William Sotheby, April 26, 1830.

Late May?, 1830.   Captain John Nicholson. WI to Captain John Nicholson, June 18, 1830.

Late May?, 1830.   Mary Shelley. WI to Mary Shelley, May 28, 1830.

Late May?, 1830.   Mrs. Roget. WI to Mrs. Roget, June 3, 1830.

May, 1830.   Dionysius Lardner. WI to Dionysius Lardner, May 13, 1830.

May, 1830.   Sir Gore Ouseley. WI to Sir Gore Ouseley, May 25, 1830.

May, 1830.   ————. WI to ————, May 27, 1830.

June, 1830.   Colonel Thomas Aspinwall. WI to Colonel Thomas Aspinwall, June 8, 1830.

ca. June, 1830.   William B. Hodgson and William Shaler. WI to T. W. Platt, July 17, 1830.

July, 1830.   John G. Lockhart. WI to Peter Irving, August 3, 1830.

August 2?, 1830.   John Murray II. WI to John Murray II, August 3, 1830.

August 3?, 1830.   John Murray II. WI to John Murray II, August 3, 1830.

August 10?, 1830.   William C. Rives. WI to William C. Rives, August 10, 1830.

Late August?, 1830.   Alexander H. Everett. WI to Alexander H. Everett, October 2, 1830.

Early October?, 1830.   Maria Hipkins. WI to Maria Hipkins, October 21, 1830.

October 5?, 1830.   John Backhouse. WI to John Backhouse, October 5, 1830.

October 7, 1830.   Ebenezer Irving. WI to John Murray II, November 4, 1830.

October 17, 1830.   Peter Irving. WI to Peter Irving, October 22, 1830.

October 26?, 1830.   Mrs. John G. Lockhart. WI to Mrs. John G. Lockhart, October 26, 1830.

November 5, 1830.   William B. Hodgson. WI to T. P. Platt, December 17, 1830.

Late November?, 1830.   Ebenezer Irving. WI to John Treat Irving, December 22, 1830.

Late November, 1830.   John Wetherell. WI to John Wetherell, December 7, 1830.

Early December, 1830.   Pierre P. Irving. WI to Pierre P. Irving, December 30, 1830.

Early December, 1830.   John Wetherell. WI to John Wetherell, December 17, 1830.

December 20?, 1830.   John Howard Payne. WI to John Howard Payne, December 20, 1830.

December, 1830.   ————. WI to Colonel Thomas Aspinwall, January 28, 1831.

Late 1830?   John F. Watson. WI to John F. Watson, March 30, 1831.

1830?   James Bandinel. WI to James Bandinel, 1830?
January 4, 1831.   ————. WI to ————, January 4, 1831.
Mid-January?, 1831.   ————. WI to Colonel Thomas Aspinwall, January 28, 1831.

January 17, 1831.   Mrs. Baring. WI to Mrs. Baring, January 19, 1831.

January 27, 1831.   The Reverend George Miller. WI to the Reverend George Miller, January 27, 1831.

January, 1831.   Ebenezer Irving. WI to Peter Irving, February 3, 1831.

January, 1831.   Gulian C. Verplanck. WI to Peter Irving, February 3, 1831.

Late February, 1831.   James Kenney. WI to Peter Irving, March 1, 1831.

February, 1831.   Committee of the Theatrical Fund. WI to Daniel Egerton, March 3, 1831.

February, 1831.   Ebenezer Irving. WI to Peter Irving, March 1, 1831.

February?, 1831.   Captain John Nicholson. WI to Henry Brevoort, March 1, 1831.

April, 1831.   John Murray II. WI to John Murray II, April, 1831.

Before June 7, 1831.   James Renwick. WI to John Murray II, July 5, 1831.

June 8, 1831.   Ebenezer Irving. WI to Thomas Moore, July 9, 1831.

June, 1831.   Lady Ashburton. WI to Lady Ashburton, [June 12, 1831].

July 9, 1831.   Mrs. John Story. WI to Mrs. John Story, [July 9, 1831].

July 25?, 1831.   The Reverend. C. H. Reaston Rodes. WI to the Reverend C. H. Reaston Rodes, July 27, 1831.

July 31, 1831.   Louis McLane. WI to Louis McLane, August 30, 1831.

July, 1831.   John Backhouse. WI to Henry Wheaton, [July 16, 1831].

July, 1831.   "the Brokers." WI to John Backhouse, July 5, 1831.

July, 1831.   Royal Asiatic Society. WI to William Huttman, [before July 16, 1831].

August 22?, 1831.   Madame ———. WI to Madame ———, August 22, 1831.

August 26, 1831.   Gabriel Walker. WI to Gabriel Walker, September 26, 1831.

August 27, 1831.   Gabriel Walker. WI to Gabriel Walker, September 1, 1831.

September 24?, 1831.   Colonel Thomas Aspinwall. WI to Colonel Thomas Aspinwall, September 24, 1831.

September 29?, 1831.   Colonel Thomas Aspinwall. WI to Colonel Thomas Aspinwall, September 29, 1831.

Early October, 1831.   Sarah Van Wart. WI to Catharine Paris, October 14, 1831.

October 11, 1831.   Colonel Thomas Aspinwall. WI to Colonel Thomas Aspinwall, October 14, 1831.

October 21, 1831.   Colonel Thomas Aspinwall. WI to John Murray II, October 22, 1831.

Late December?, 1831.   Peter Irving. WI to Peter Irving, January 20, 1832.

December?, 1831.   Robert Montgomery. WI to Robert Montgomery, April 3, 1832.

February 27, 1832.   Peter Irving. WI to Peter Irving, March 6, 1832.

Late March, 1832.   Robert Montgomery. WI to Robert Montgomery, April 3, 1832.

May, 1832.   Dr. David Hosack. WI to Dr. David Hosack, May 29, 1832.

June 2, 1832.   James Watson Webb. WI to James Watson Webb, June 20, 1832.

June 8?, 1832.   Peter S. Duponceau et al. WI to Peter S. Duponceau, June 9, 1832.

June 8?, 1832.   Levi Woodbury. WI to Levi Woodbury, June 8, 1832.

June?, 1832.   Rebecca McLane. WI to Rebecca McLane, August 1, 1832.

Early July, 1832.   ——— [of Boston]. WI to Martin Van Buren, July 12, 1832.

July, 1832.   Rebecca McLane. WI to Rebecca McLane, August 1, 1832.

Early August, 1832.   Martin Van Buren. WI to Levi Woodbury, August 9, 1832.

August 20, 1832.   Charles Tousley & David Malin. WI to Charles Tousley & David Malin, December 20, 1832.

August 30, 1832.   Ebenezer Irving. WI to Catharine Paris, September 13, 1832.

August?, 1832.   Peter Irving. WI to Catharine Paris, September 13, 1832.

August, 1832.   Louis McLane. WI to Catharine Paris, September 13, 1832.

August, 1832.   Aaron Vail. WI to Catharine Paris, September 13, 1832.

Early September, 1832.   Catharine Paris. WI to Catharine Paris, November 16, 1832.

November 5, 1832.   Josiah Quincy. WI to Josiah Quincy, April 3, 1833.

November 17?, 1832.   Citizens of Vicksburg. WI to Citizens of Vicksburg, November 17, 1832.

December, 1832.   Catharine Paris. WI to Catharine Paris, January 23, 1833.

December?, 1832.   Samuel Swartwout. WI to Gouverneur Kemble, January 4, 1833.

Early January, 1833.   "the Lyceum." WI to Jonah F. Polk, January 9, 1833.

January 4, 1833. D. W. Buckley & C. Anderson. WI to D. W. Buckley & C. Anderson, January 18, 1833.

January 7, 1833. Richard Rush. WI to Richard Rush, January 4, 1833.

January 9?, 1833. Jonah F. Polk. WI to Jonah F. Polk, January 9, 1833.

Mid-January, 1833. Martin Van Buren. WI to Gouverneur Kemble, January 25, 1833.

January 20?, 1833. Martin Van Buren. WI to Gouverneur Kemble, January 25, 1833.

January, 1833. Peter Kemble. WI to Catharine Paris, February 27, 1833.

January, 1833. Pierre M. Irving. WI to Catharine Paris, January 23, 1833.

February?, 1833. John P. Kennedy. WI to John P. Kennedy, February 24, 1833.

February, 1833. ——— [of New Orleans]. WI to Catharine Paris, February 27, 1833.

April, 1833. John A. Dix. WI to John A. Dix, April 23, 1833.

May 4, 1833. Mrs. Bache. WI to Mrs. Bache, May 29, 1833.

May 9?, 1833. Benjamin F. Minor et al. WI to Benjamin F. Minor et al., May 9, 1833.

May 13, 1833. Mathew Carey & Alexander D. Bache. WI to Mathew Carey & Alexander D. Bache, May 25, 1833.

Early June, 1833. John A. Dix. WI to John A. Dix, June 12, 1833.

July 3, 1833. Harrison Hall. WI to Harrison Hall, July 11, 1833.

July, 1833. Richard Rush. WI to Richard Rush, August 1, 1833.

September 10, 1833. William M. Blackford. WI to William M. Blackford, October 27, 1833.

September 21, 1833. C. C. Felton. WI to C. C. Felton, October 18, 1833.

September?, 1833. Peter Irving. (Several letters.) WI to Peter Irving, October 28, 1833.

Early October, 1833. Alexander Slidell. WI to Alexander Slidell, October 7, 1833.

Early October, 1833. Levi Woodbury. WI to Levi Woodbury, [mid-October, 1833].

October 2, 1833. Martin Van Buren. WI to Martin Van Buren, October 5, 1833.

Mid-October, 1833.   Levi Woodbury. WI to Levi Woodbury, [mid-
                             October, 1833].
October?, 1833.   Peter Irving. WI to Peter Irving, November
                             8, 1833.
December 27, 1833.   William Dunlap. William Dunlap, *Diary*, III,
                             766.
Late December, 1833.   Mrs. Martha? Stuyvesant. WI to Mrs. Martha?
                             Stuyvesant, December 31?, 1833.
January, 1834.   James Watson Webb. WI to James Watson
                             Webb, January 29, 1834.
Early February, 1834.   George P. Morris. WI to George P. Morris,
                             February 5, 1834.
February 3, 1834.   William Dunlap. William Dunlap, *Diary*, III,
                             772.
March 14, 1834.   William Dunlap. William Dunlap, *Diary*, III,
                             776.
March, 1834.   William Irving. WI to William Irving, April
                             3, 1834.
Late April, 1834.   Ann L. Clark. WI to Ann L. Clark, May 2,
                             1834.
Early May, 1834.   Thomas W. White. WI to Thomas W. White,
                             May 10, 1834.
June, 1834.   Ann L. Clark. WI to Ann L. Clark, June 26,
                             1834.
June, 1834.   Catherine McLane. WI to Catherine McLane,
                             June 26, 1834.
August 20, 1834.   William Dunlap. William Dunlap, *Diary*, III,
                             816.
September 15, 1834.   William Dunlap. William Dunlap, *Diary*, III,
                             822.
October 5, 1834.   Pierre M. Irving. WI to Pierre M. Irving, Oc-
                             tober 29, 1834.
October, 1834.   Peter Irving. WI to Peter Irving, October,
                             1834.
December, 1834.   Students of Hamilton College. WI to Fred-
                             erick R. Spencer, December 20, 1834.
December, 1834.   Martin Van Buren. WI to Martin Van Buren,
                             December 15, 1834.
Late March?, 1835.   Colonel Thomas Aspinwall. WI to Colonel
                             Thomas Aspinwall, April 28, 1835.
March?, 1835.   Edward Bulwer-Lytton. WI to Edward Bul-
                             wer-Lytton, May 2, 1835.

March, 1835.	"letters from London." WI to Henry Carey, April 8, 1835.
April 14, 1835.	Colonel Thomas Aspinwall. WI to Peter Irving, May 25, 1835.
April 24, 1835.	Peter Irving. WI to Peter Irving, June 10, 1835.
April?, 1835.	George Ticknor. WI to George Ticknor, May 11, 1835.
Late May?, 1835.	John P. Kennedy. WI to John P. Kennedy, June 5, 1835.
June 17, 1835.	John W. Burruss. WI to John W. Burruss, June 24, 1835.
August?, 1835.	Thomas Cole. WI to Thomas Cole, September 15, 1835.
December 24, 1835.	John Murray III. WI to Peter Irving, February 16, 1836; WI to John Murray III, February 24, 1836.
December, 1835.	John P. Kennedy. WI to John P. Kennedy, December 25, 1835.
December?, 1835.	David Wilkie. WI to David Wilkie, February 4, 1836.
1835?	The Reverend James M. Mathews. WI to the Reverend James M. Mathews, 1835?
Late January, 1836.	Edgar Irving. WI to Martin Van Buren, February 1, 1836.
January, 1836.	Peter Irving. WI to Peter Irving, February 16, 1836.
March 23?, 1836.	Captain Benjamin L. E. Bonneville. WI to Major James H. Hook, March 27, 1836.
April 12?, 1836.	John McVickar. WI to John McVickar, April 12, 1836.
April 12, 1836.	David Wilkie. WI to David Wilkie, June 1, 1836.
April 13, 1836.	Virgil David. WI to Virgil David, April 23, 1836.
May 2, 1836.	Orange Ferriss. WI to Orange Ferriss, May 22, 1836.
September 19, 1836.	Gouverneur Kemble. WI to Gouverneur Kemble, September 28, 1836.
September 26, 1836.	E. R. Billings. WI to E. R. Billings, October 3, 1836.
October, 1836.	James Mead et al. WI to James Mead et al., October 26, 1836.

November 6, 1836.	Pierre M. Irving. WI to Pierre M. Irving, December 12, 1836.
Mid-November, 1836.	Robert Gilmor. WI to Robert Gilmor, December 3, 1836.
December 9?, 1836.	Sarah Paris. WI to Sarah Paris, December 10, 1836.
December 28, 1836.	George W. Welker et al. WI to George W. Welker, January 5, 1837.
Late December?, 1836.	James H. Hackett. WI to James H. Hackett, January 3, 1837.
December, 1836.	William C. Preston. WI to William C. Preston, February 22, 1837.
Early January?, 1837.	Colonel Thomas Aspinwall. WI to Colonel Thomas Aspinwall, February 9, 1837.
Early January?, 1837.	Richard Bentley. WI to Colonel Thomas Aspinwall, February 9, 1837.
January?, 1837.	Pierre M. Irving. WI to Pierre M. Irving, [January?, 1837].
January, 1837.	Elkanah Watson. WI to Elkanah Watson, July 8, 1837.
February 10, 1837.	John Treat Irving, Jr. WI to John Treat Irving, Jr., April 2, 1837.
February, 1837.	William C. Preston. WI to William C. Preston, February 22, 1837.
Mid-March, 1837.	Gouverneur Kemble. WI to Gouverneur Kemble, March 17, 1837.
Late May, 1837.	Colonel Thomas Aspinwall. WI to Colonel Thomas Aspinwall, June 20, 1837.
May, 1837.	Richard Bentley. WI to Colonel Thomas Aspinwall, June 20, 1837.
June 24, 1837.	Edward Everett. WI to Edward Everett, July 12, 1837.
Summer, 1837.	George Harvey. WI to George Harvey, August, 1837.
July 6?, 1837.	Elkanah Watson. WI to Elkanah Watson. July 8, 1837.
Early October, 1837.	Samuel G. Drake. WI to Samuel G. Drake, October 10, 1837.
October, 1837.	Harry Chester. WI to Harry Chester, October 10, 1837.
December 6, 1837.	Richard Penn Smith. WI to Richard Penn Smith, December 15, 1837.

January 3, 1838.	Gouverneur Kemble. WI to Gouverneur Kemble, January 10, 1838.
February 3, 1838.	Mrs. William Astor. WI to Mrs. William Astor, February 10?, 1838.
March 4, 1838.	Gouverneur Kemble. WI to Gouverneur Kemble, March 13, 1838.
Late May?, 1838.	Washington McCartney. WI to Washington McCartney, June 2, 1838.
June 13, 1838.	George F. Houghton. WI to George F. Houghton, June 24, 1838.
June, 1838.	James Hamilton. WI to James Hamilton, June 8, 1838.
Summer?, 1838.	———— Van Wart (WI's niece). WI to Sarah Van Wart, October 24, 1838.
August 8, 1838.	Sarah Van Wart. WI to Sarah Van Wart, September 22, 1838.
September 15?, 1838.	Gouverneur Kemble. WI to Gouverneur Kemble, September 16, 1838.
September 17, 1838.	A. Wickham. WI to A. Wickham, September 22, 1838.
October 20?, 1838.	David M. Bowen. WI to David M. Bowen, October 24, 1838.
November, 1838.	Samuel H. Rives. WI to Samuel H. Rives, November 17, 1838.
November, 1838.	Sarah Van Wart. WI to Sarah Van Wart, December 1, 1838.
Early January, 1839.	William H. Prescott. WI to William H. Prescott, January 18, 1839.
January 28, 1839.	Messrs. Lea & Blanchard. WI to Messrs. Lea & Blanchard, January 25, 1839.
January?, 1839.	The Reverend Robert Bolton. WI to the Reverend Robert Bolton, May 27, 1839.
February 14, 1839.	Messrs. Lea & Blanchard, WI to Messrs. Lea & Blanchard, February 13, 1839.
February 21?, 1839.	Charles Elliott & J. W. Royer. WI to Charles Elliott & J. W. Royer, February 24, 1839.
Early March, 1839.	Horatio Woodman. WI to Horatio Woodman, March 11, 1839.
March 15, 1839.	Messrs. March, Capen, Lyon & Webb. WI to Messrs. March, Capen, Lyon & Webb, April 15, 1839.
Early May?, 1839.	The Reverend Robert Bolton. WI to the Reverend Robert Bolton, May 27, 1839.

June 21, 1839.   Joseph L. Chester. WI to Joseph L. Chester, June 26, 1839.

July 9, 1839.   I. K. Tefft. WI to I. K. Tefft, July 21, 1839.

July?, 1839.   David Hoffman. WI to David Hoffman, August 22, 1839.

October 7, 1839.   John S. Littell. WI to John S. Littell, October 13, 1839.

December 15, 1839.   Lewis Gaylord Clark. WI to Lewis Gaylord Clark, December 21, 1839.

December, 1839.   Eliza Leslie. WI to Eliza Leslie, December 20, 1839.

Late January?, 1840.   Gouverneur Kemble. WI to Gouverneur Kemble, February 4, 1840.

February 26?, 1840.   John K. Mitchell. WI to John K. Mitchell, February 28, 1840.

February, 1840.   Jared Sparks. WI to Jared Sparks, June 29, 1840.

Early March, 1840.   I. Benson Boyd. WI to I. Benson Boyd, March 5, 1840.

Early March, 1840.   John Harris, Jr. WI to John Harris, Jr., March 5, 1840.

March 10?, 1840.   Lewis Gaylord Clark. WI to Lewis Gaylord Clark, March 17, 1840.

March 28, 1840.   ————. WI to ————, April 11, 1840.

Late March?, 1840.   Gulian C. Verplanck. WI to Gulian C. Verplanck, April 7, 1840.

Spring, 1840.   Conego Januário da Cunha Barbosa. WI to Conego Januário da Barbosa, June 29, 1840.

April 11, 1840.   Sarah Van Wart. WI to Sarah Van Wart, May 4, 1840.

May?, 1840.   Alexander Valteman. WI to Alexander Valteman, May 7, 1840.

October 30, 1840.   Gouverneur Kemble. WI to Gouverneur Kemble, October 31, 1840.

October?, 1840.   Charles Storrow. WI to Charles Storrow, November 8, 1840.

November 6?, 1840.   William L. Stone. WI to William L. Stone, November 8, 1840.

Late November?, 1840.   Sarah Van Wart. WI to Sarah Van Wart, December 26, 1840.

December 23, 1840.   Sarah Van Wart. WI to Sarah Van Wart, January 19, 1841.

December 26, 1840.	George Roberts, WI to George Roberts, January 14, 1841.
January, 1841.	Thomas W. Storrow. WI to Sarah Paris, January 25, 1841.
January?, 1841.	Sarah Van Wart. WI to Sarah Van Wart, February 26, 1841.
Late February?, 1841.	John S. Popkin. WI to John S. Popkin, March 6, 1841.
March 29, 1841.	Messrs. Lea & Blanchard. WI to Messrs. Lea & Blanchard, March 14, 1841.
May, 1841.	Sarah Storrow. WI to Sarah Storrow, June 13, 1841.
May?, 1841.	Thomas E. Van Bibber. WI to Sarah Storrow, May 25, 1841.
Early June, 1841.	William W. Waldron. WI to William W. Waldron, June 14, 1841.
June 18, 1841.	Lewis Gaylord Clark. WI to Lewis Gaylord Clark, July 8, 1841.
Late June?, 1841.	Sarah Van Wart. WI to Sarah Van Wart, August 1, 1841.
June, 1841.	Sarah Storrow. WI to Sarah Storrow, July 18, 1841.
July 17, 1841.	Isaac Lea. WI to Messrs. Lea & Blanchard, July 21, 1841.
July, 1841.	Sarah Storrow. WI to Sarah Storrow, September 1, 1841.
October, 1841.	Sarah Storrow. WI to Sarah Storrow, November 19, 1841.
November 4, 1841.	William C. Rives. WI to William C. Rives, December 8, 1841.
November, 1841.	Sarah Storrow. WI to Sarah Storrow, December 1, 1841.
Early December? 1841.	James M. Tower. WI to James M. Tower, December 8, 1841.
Mid-December, 1841.	Cornelius Mathews. WI to Cornelius Mathews, December 18, 1841.
January 31, 1842.	George Ticknor. WI to George Ticknor, February 16, 1842.
Late January, 1842.	S. B. Grant et al. WI to S. B. Grant et al., February 1, 1842.
Early February, 1842.	Lewis Gaylord Clark. WI to Lewis Gaylord Clark, February 9, 1842.

February 13, 1842.	George Ticknor. WI to George Ticknor, February 16, 1842.
February 19?, 1842.	Samuel Ward. WI to T. L. Ogden, February 20, 1842.
February 20?, 1842.	Lucius D. Baldwin. WI to Lucius D. Baldwin, February 22, 1842.
February 22, 1842.	George Ticknor. WI to George Ticknor, March 7, 1842.
Late February, 1842.	J. Bayard Taylor. WI to J. Bayard Taylor, February 28, 1842.
March 13, 1842.	C. W. Richardson. Ebenezer Irving to WI, March 17, 1842.
Mid-March, 1842.	Two letters from Cambridge, Mass. requesting autographs. Ebenezer Irving to WI, March 17, 1842.
March 30, 1842.	Daniel Webster. WI to Daniel Webster, April 2, 1842.
March, 1842.	Gouverneur Kemble. WI to Gouverneur Kemble, April 5, 1842.
Early April, 1842.	John G. Chapman. WI to John G. Chapman, April 4, 1842.
Early April?, 1842.	Francis Markoe, Jr. WI to Francis Markoe, Jr., April 4, 1842.
April 25, 1842.	Sarah Irving. WI to Sarah Irving, May 29, 1842.
Late April?, 1842.	Sarah Storrow. WI to Sarah Storrow, May 10, 1842.
April, 1842.	William H. Freeman. WI to Aaron Vail, May 18, 1842.
Early May, 1842.	James Kenney. WI to James Kenney, May 18, 1842.
May 2, 1842.	Thomas Todd. WI to Thomas Todd, May 5, 1842.
May 3, 1842.	Edward Everett. WI to Edward Everett, May 3, 1842.
May 5, 1842.	D. M. Corkendale. WI to D. M. Corkendale, May 11, 1842.
May 7?, 1842.	Walter Buchanan. WI to Walter Buchanan, May 8, 1842.
May 8?, 1842.	Charles Bristed. WI to Charles Bristed, May 10, 1842.
May 21, 1842.	Messrs. Peters & Co. WI to Messrs. Peters & Co., August 5, 1842.

May 26, 1842.	Catharine Paris. WI to Catharine Paris, July 25, 1842.
May 29, 1842.	Ebenezer Irving. WI to Ebenezer Irving, July 25, 1842.
May 31, 1842.	Helen Dodge Irving. WI to Helen Dodge Irving, June 26, 1842.
May 31, 1842.	Pierre M. Irving. WI to Pierre M. Irving, PMI, III, 211.
May, 1842.	G. S. Gibson. WI to G. S. Gibson, May 18, 1842.
Early June?, 1842.	Henry Brevoort. WI to Henry Brevoort, July 1, 1842.
June 1, 1842.	James C. Calhoun. WI to James C. Calhoun, August 27, 1842.
June 1, 1842.	Catharine Paris. WI to Catharine Paris, July 7, 1842.
June 3, 1842.	Sarah Van Wart. WI to Sarah Van Wart, June 8, 1842.
June 23, 1842.	Catharine Paris. WI to Catharine Paris, August 3, 1842.
June 25, 1842.	George Ticknor. WI to George Ticknor, January 11, 1843.
June 29, 1842.	Ebenezer Irving. WI to Catharine Paris, July 30, 1842.
Early July, 1842.	Mary Irving. WI to Mary Irving, August 3, 1842.
July 8, 1842.	Catharine Irving. WI to Catharine Irving, August 15, 1842.
July 19, 1842.	Catharine Paris. WI to Catharine Paris, September 2, 1842.
July 20, 1842.	Sarah Storrow. WI to Sarah Storrow, July 30, 1842.
July 27, 1842.	Sarah Storrow. WI to Sarah Storrow, August 4, 1842.
July 28, 1842.	Charlotte Irving. WI to Charlotte Irving, September 16, 1842.
July 29, 1842.	Catharine Paris. WI to Sarah Storrow, September 17, 1842.
July 31, 1842.	Sarah Irving. WI to Sarah Irving, September 28, 1842.
July, 1842.	Sarah Storrow. WI to Sarah Storrow, August 12, 1842.

Early August, 1842.   Sarah Storrow. WI to Sarah Storrow, August
                               12, 1842.

August 4, 1842.   Ebenezer Irving. WI to Sarah Storrow, Sep-
                               tember 10, 1842.

August 7, 1842.   Sarah Irving. WI to Sarah Irving, September
                               28, 1842.

August 18, 1842.   Gurdon Bradley. WI to Gurdon Bradley, April
                               10, 1843.

August 24, 1842.   Sarah Storrow. WI to Sarah Storrow, Septem-
                               ber 26, 1842.

August 25, 1842.   Julia Grinnell. WI to Julia Grinnell, Septem-
                               ber 30, 1842.

August 29, 1842.   Daniel Webster. WI to Daniel Webster, No-
                               vember 26, 1842.

August, 1842.   Eliza Irving. WI to Sarah Irving, September
                               28, 1842.

August, 1842.   Helen Dodge Irving. WI to Julia Grinnell,
                               September 9, 1842.

August, 1842.   Catharine Paris. WI to Sarah Irving, Sep-
                               tember 28, 1842.

August?, 1842.   Richard de la Saussaye. WI to Sarah Storrow,
                               November 5, 1842.

Early September, 1842.   Mary Irving. WI to Sarah Irving, October
                               28, 1842.

September 1, 1842.   Sarah Storrow. WI to Sarah Storrow, Septem-
                               ber 10, 1842.

September 4, 1842.   Sarah Storrow. WI to Sarah Storrow, Septem-
                               ber 11, 1842.

September 7, 1842.   Ebenezer Irving. WI to Sarah Storrow, Oc-
                               tober 28, 1842.

September 8, 1842.   Sarah Storrow. WI to Sarah Storrow, October
                               8, 1842.

September 10, 1842.   Edward Everett. WI to Edward Everett, Oc-
                               tober 7, 1842.

September 12, 1842.   Sarah Storrow. WI to Sarah Storrow, Septem-
                               ber 26, 1842.

September 12, 1842.   Daniel Webster. WI to Daniel Webster, Oc-
                               tober 8, 1842.

September 15, 1842.   Catharine Paris. WI to Sarah Storrow, No-
                               vember 5, 1842.

September 19, 1842.   Sarah Storrow. WI to Sarah Storrow, Septem-
                               ber 26, 1842.

September 27–29, 1842.	Sarah Storrow. WI to Sarah Storrow, October 8, 1842.
September 29, 1842.	Catharine Paris. WI to Sarah Storrow, November 5, 1842.
September 29, 1842.	Daniel Webster. WI to Daniel Webster, November 11, 1842.
September, 1842.	Prince Dolgorouki. WI to Prince Dolgorouki, October 18, 1842.
October 1, 1842.	Catharine Ann Irving. WI to Sarah Storrow, November 12, 1842; WI to Catharine Ann Irving, November 15, 1842.
October 3–4, 1842.	Sarah Storrow. WI to Sarah Storrow, October 10, 1842.
October 5, 1842.	Helen Dodge Irving. WI to Helen Dodge Irving, November 12, 1842.
October 6, 1842.	Pierre M. Irving. WI to Pierre M. Irving, November 12, 1842.
October 15, 1842.	Alexander Hamilton, Jr. WI to Catharine Paris, October 18, 1842.
October 15, 1842.	Obadiah Rich. WI to Obadiah Rich, November 14, 1842; NA, RG 84.
October 15, 1842.	Sarah Storrow. WI to Sarah Storrow, November 21, 1842.
October 15?, 1842.	John Wetherell. WI to John Wetherell, October 18, 1842.
October 21, 1842.	Sarah Storrow. WI to Sarah Storrow, October 28, 1842.
October 24, 1842.	Irving Paris. WI to Irving Paris, January 10, 1843.
October 27, 1842.	Catharine Paris. WI to Catharine Paris, December 10, 1842.
October 27?, 1842.	Sarah Storrow. WI to Sarah Storrow, November 5, 1842.
October 28, 1842.	Daniel Webster. WI to Daniel Webster, November 5, 1842.
October 29, 1842.	George Ticknor. WI to George Ticknor, January 11, 1843.
October 31, 1842.	Alexander Hamilton, Jr. WI to Sarah Storrow, November 5, 1842.
October 31, 1842.	Pierre M. Irving. WI to Catharine Paris, November 20, 1842.
Late October, 1842.	Sarah Storrow. WI to Sarah Storrow, November 5, 1842.

October, 1842.	Alexander Burton. WI to Alexander Burton, April 24, 1843.
October, 1842.	Alexander Hamilton, Jr. & friends. WI to Sarah Storrow, October 28, 1842.
October, 1842.	Sarah Storrow. WI to Sarah Storrow, October 21, 1842.
October, 1842.	Sarah Van Wart. WI to Sarah Storrow, November 5, 1842.
November 2, 1842.	Sarah Storrow. WI to Sarah Storrow, November 12, 1842.
November 6, 1842.	Ebenezer Irving. WI to Sarah Storrow, December 12, 1842.
November 18, 1842.	Sarah Storrow. WI to Sarah Storrow, November 26, 1842.
November 22, 1842.	Catharine Paris. WI to Catharine Paris, December 24, 1842.
November?, 1842.	T. W. C. Moore. WI to T. W. C. Moore, January 10, 1843.
Early December, 1842.	Sarah Storrow. WI to Sarah Storrow, December 10, 1842.
December 6, 1842.	Sarah Storrow. WI to Sarah Storrow, December 12, 1842.
December 13, 1842.	Catharine Paris. WI to Catharine Paris, January 12, 1843.
Late December, 1842.	Sarah Storrow. WI to Sarah Storrow, January 5, 1843.
December, 1842.	Sarah Irving. WI to Sarah Irving, January 13, 1843.
December, 1842.	Eliza McCloud. WI to Eliza McCloud, February 25, 1843.
December, 1842.	Miguel José Molina. WI to Sarah Storrow, January 5, 1843.
December, 1842.	William H. Prescott. WI to George Ticknor, January 11, 1843; WI to William H. Prescott, October 15, 1844.
December, 1842.	Daniel Webster. WI to Daniel Webster, February 11, 1843.
December, 1842.	Mateo Ximenez. WI to Sarah Storrow, January 5, 1843.
January 1–7, 1843.	Sarah Storrow. WI to Sarah Storrow, January 15, 1843.
January 31, 1843.	Sarah Storrow. WI to Sarah Storrow, February 11, 1843.

January, 1843.	Catharine Paris. WI to Catharine Paris, February 6, 1843.
February 10?, 1843.	Sarah Storrow. WI to Sarah Storrow, February 24, 1843.
February 17, 1843.	Sarah Storrow. WI to Sarah Storrow, February 24, 1843.
Late February, 1843.	Eliza Romeyn Irving. WI to Catharine Paris, March 25, 1843.
Late February, 1843.	Helen Dodge Irving. WI to Catharine Paris, March 25, 1843.
Late February, 1843.	Mary Irving. WI to Catharine Paris, March 25, 1843.
Late February, 1843.	Pierre M. Irving. WI to Catharine Paris, March 25, 1843.
February, 1843.	David Davidson. WI to Catharine Paris, March 4, 1843.
February, 1843.	Mary Irving. WI to Catharine Paris, March 4, 1843.
February?, 1843.	John Merino. WI to Eliza McCloud, February 25, 1843.
February?, 1843.	Catharine Paris. WI to Sarah Storrow, April 13, 1843.
February, 1843.	Daniel Webster. WI to Daniel Webster, March 10, 1843.
March 8, 1843.	Ebenezer Irving. WI to Sarah Storrow, April 22, 1843.
March 22, 1843.	Catharine Paris. WI to Sarah Storrow, April 29, 1843; WI to Catharine Paris, May 6, 1843.
March, 1843.	Sarah Storrow. WI to Sarah Storrow, March 25, 1843.
March, 1843.	Henry Van Wart. WI to Sarah Storrow, April 13, 1843.
Early April?, 1843.	Thomas Storrow, Jr. WI to Sarah Storrow, April 13, 1843.
April 5, 1843.	Sarah Storrow. WI to Sarah Storrow, April 13, 1843.
April 10?, 1843.	Sarah Storrow. WI to Sarah Storrow, April 22, 1843.
April 20?, 1843.	Sarah Storrow. WI to Sarah Storrow, April 29, 1843.
May 9, 1843.	Hugh S. Legaré. WI to Hugh S. Legaré, July 9, 1843.

May, 1843.	Sarah Irving. WI to Catharine Paris, June 21, 1843.
May, 1843.	Catharine Paris. WI to Sarah Storrow, June 17, 1843; WI to Catharine Paris, June 21, 1843.
May, 1843.	Eliza Romeyn. WI to Catharine Paris, June 21, 1843.
May, 1843.	Sarah Storrow. (Several letters.) WI to Sarah Storrow, May 25, 1843.
June 10?, 1843.	Sarah Storrow. WI to Sarah Storrow, June 17, 1843.
June 15, 1843.	Sarah Storrow. WI to Sarah Storrow, June 24, 1843.
June 18, 1843.	I. K. Tefft. WI to I. K. Tefft, May 17, 1844.
June 24, 1843.	A. P. Upshur. WI to A. P. Upshur, September 6, 1843.
July 4, 1843.	Olegario de los Cuetos. WI to Olegario de los Cuetos, July 10, 1843.
July 8, 1843.	Sarah Storrow. WI to Sarah Storrow, July 14, 1843.
July 11, 1843.	I. K. Tefft. WI to I. K. Tefft, May 17, 1844.
Mid-July, 1843.	Alexander Hamilton, Jr. WI to Sarah Storrow, July 18, 1843.
July 22?, 1843.	Sarah Storrow. WI to Sarah Storrow, August 7, 1843.
July 19–20, 1843.	Catharine Paris. WI to Catharine Paris, August 25, 1843.
July 29, 1843.	Madame Albuquerque. WI to Sarah Storrow, July 29, 1843.
Early August, 1843.	Alexander Hamilton, Jr. WI to Sarah Storrow, August 7, 1843.
August 3–6, 1843.	Catharine Paris. WI to Catharine Paris, September 18, 1843.
August 4, 1843.	Julia Grinnell. WI to Julia Grinnell, December 29, 1843.
August 11, 1843.	Jasper Livingston. WI to Sarah Storrow, August 23, 1843.
August 14–16, 1843.	Sarah Storrow. WI to Sarah Storrow, August 23, 1843.
September 19?, 1843.	J. Carson Brevoort. WI to J. Carson Brevoort, September 19, 1843.
September, 1843.	Ebenezer Irving. WI to Catharine Paris, October 12, 1843.

Early October, 1843. Marianne Van Wart. WI to Catharine Paris, October 12, 1843.

Mid-November, 1843. Catharine Paris. WI to Catharine Paris, December 10, 1843.

November 25, 1843. Sarah Irving. WI to Sarah Irving, January 19, 1844.

Late November, 1843. Sarah Storrow. WI to Sarah Storrow, December 20, 1843.

November–December, 1843. Sarah Storrow. (Several letters.) WI to Sarah Storrow, December 20, 1843.

December 1, 1843. Luis González Bravo. (Two letters.) WI to Luis González Bravo, December 4, 1843.

December 19, 1843. J. S. Buckingham. WI to J. S. Buckingham, February 9, 1844.

December 22–29, 1843. Catharine Paris. WI to Catharine Paris, February 9, 1844.

Late December, 1843. Sarah Storrow. WI to Sarah Storrow, January 7, 1844.

Early 1844. Lord Morpeth. WI to William H. Prescott, October 15, 1844.

Early 1844. William H. Prescott. WI to William H. Prescott, October 15, 1844.

January 9, 1844. Sarah Storrow. WI to Sarah Storrow, January 21, 1844.

January 29, 1844. Catharine Paris. WI to Sarah Storrow, February 29, 1844.

February 3, 1844. Sarah Storrow. WI to Sarah Storrow, February 10, 1844.

February 19, 1844. Sarah Storrow. WI to Sarah Storrow, February 29, 1844.

February 25–29, 1844. Catharine Paris. WI to Catharine Paris, March 23, 1844.

February 29, 1844. Pierre M. Irving. WI to Catharine Paris, March 23, 1844; WI to Pierre M. Irving, March 24, 1844.

Late February, 1844. Julia Grinnell. WI to Sarah Storrow, March 30, 1844.

March 2, 1844. Sarah Storrow. WI to Sarah Storrow, March 8, 1844.

March 9?, 1844. Sarah Storrow. WI to Sarah Storrow, March 16, 1844.

March 30?, 1844. Sarah Storrow. WI to Sarah Storrow, April 6, 1844.

March, 1844.	Madame Albuquerque. WI to Sarah Storrow, March 16, 1844.
March, 1844.	Pierre M. Irving. WI to Sarah Storrow, April 27, 1844.
March, 1844.	Catharine Paris. WI to Sarah Storrow, April 27, 1844.
April 1, 1844.	John C. Calhoun. WI to John C. Calhoun, June 8, 1844.
April 6, 1844.	Sarah Storrow. WI to Sarah Storrow, April 13, 1844.
April 13?, 1844.	Sarah Storrow. WI to Sarah Storrow, April 20, 1844.
May 4, 1844.	Sarah Storrow. WI to Sarah Storrow, May 10, 1844.
May 9, 1844.	Alejandro Mon. WI to Alejandro Mon, May 10, 1844.
May 18?, 1844.	Sarah Storrow. WI to Sarah Storrow, June 3, 1844.
Mid-May, 1844.	Alexander Hamilton, Jr. WI to Sarah Storrow, May 24, 1844.
May 18?, 1844.	Sarah Storrow. WI to Sarah Storrow, June 3, 1844.
May 27, 1844.	Sarah Storrow. WI to Sarah Storrow, June 2, 1844.
May, 1844.	O'Neal Bryson. WI to O'Neal Bryson, June 24, 1844.
May, 1844.	Alexander Hamilton, Jr. WI to Sarah Storrow, June 3, 1844.
May, 1844.	Pierre M. Irving. WI to Sarah Storrow, June 9, 1844.
May, 1844.	Jasper Livingston. WI to Sarah Storrow, June 1, 1844.
Late May?, 1844.	Moses H. Grinnell. WI to Sarah Storrow, June 1, 1844.
May?, 1844.	Catharine Paris. WI to Catharine Paris, June 15, 1844.
June 13, 1844.	Sarah Storrow. WI to Sarah Storrow, June 25, 1844.
June 21, 1844.	Sarah Storrow. WI to Sarah Storrow, July 7, 1844.
June 26, 1844.	Sarah Storrow. WI to Sarah Storrow, July 7, 1844.

Late June?, 1844.   Alexander Hamilton, Jr. WI to Catharine
                         Paris, July 28, 1844.

June, 1844.   Helen & Pierre M. Irving. WI to Pierre M.
                         Irving, July 18, 1844.

Early July?, 1844.   Thomas Storrow, Jr. WI to Catharine Paris,
                         July 28, 1844.

July 23, 1844.   Ebenezer Irving. WI to Catharine Paris, Sep-
                         tember 15, 1844.

July 23, 1844.   Eliza Romeyn. WI to Catharine Paris, Sep-
                         tember 15, 1844.

August 1, 1844.   Catharine Paris. WI to Catharine Paris, Au-
                         gust 30, 1844.

August, 1844.   Jasper Livingston. (Several letters.) WI to
                         Catharine Paris, August 30, 1844.

September 11, 1844.   Jasper Livingston. WI to Jasper Livingston,
                         September 25, 1844.

September 14, 1844.   Jasper Livingston. WI to Jasper Livingston,
                         September 25, 1844.

September 19, 1844.   Jasper Livingston. WI to Jasper Livingston,
                         September 25, 1844.

October 26?, 1844.   Lady Rancliffe. WI to Lady Rancliffe, Octo-
                         ber 26, 1844.

October 28–29, 1844.   Catharine Paris. WI to Catharine Paris, No-
                         vember 29, 1844.

Early November, 1844.   Pierre M. Irving. WI to Sarah Storrow, De-
                         cember 6, 1844.

November 16?, 1844.   Sarah Storrow. WI to Sarah Storrow, Novem-
                         ber 23, 1844.

November 23, 1844.   Sarah Storrow. WI to Sarah Storrow, Novem-
                         ber 30, 1844.

November 28, 1844.   Catharine Irving. WI to Catharine Irving,
                         January 11, 1845.

November 30?, 1844.   Sarah Storrow. WI to Sarah Storrow, Decem-
                         ber 6, 1844

November, 1844.   Pierre M. Irving. WI to Sarah Storrow, De-
                         cember 29, 1844.

November?, 1844.   Catharine Paris. WI to Sarah Storrow, De-
                         cember 29, 1844.

December 14, 1844.   Sarah Storrow. WI to Sarah Storrow, Decem-
                         ber 20, 1844.

December 28, 1844.   Sarah Storrow. WI to Sarah Storrow, Jan-
                         uary 2, 1845.

December, 1844.	Alexander Hamilton, Jr. WI to Sarah Storrow, January 25, 1845.
December, 1844.	Catharine Paris. WI to Sarah Storrow, January 25, 1845.
January 4, 1845.	Irving Paris. WI to Irving Paris, April 19, 1845.
January 11?, 1845.	Sarah Storrow. WI to Sarah Storrow, January 18, 1845.
January 18?, 1845.	Sarah Storrow. WI to Sarah Storrow, January 25, 1845.
January 25?, 1845.	Sarah Storrow. WI to Sarah Storrow, January 31, 1845.
January, 1845.	Pierre M. Irving. WI to Sarah Storrow, February 14, 1845.
January, 1845.	Catharine Paris. WI to Sarah Storrow, February 21, 1845.
February 1, 1845.	Sarah Storrow. WI to Sarah Storrow, February 5–7, 1845.
February 7, 1845.	Sarah Storrow. WI to Sarah Storrow, February 14, 1845.
February 14, 1845.	Sarah Storrow. WI to Sarah Storrow, February 21, 1845.
February 22, 1845.	Sarah Storrow. WI to Sarah Storrow, February 27, 1845.
February 25–27, 1845.	Catharine Paris. WI to Sarah Storrow, March 27, 1845.
Late February?, 1845.	Julia Irving (Mrs. Sanders). WI to Sarah Storrow, March 27, 1845.
Late February?, 1845.	Pierre M. Irving. WI to Sarah Storrow, March 27, 1845.
February, 1845.	Ebenezer Irving. WI to Sarah Storrow, March 18, 1845.
February, 1845.	Helen Dodge Irving. WI to Sarah Storrow, March 6, 1845.
March 1, 1845.	George P. Putnam. WI to George P. Putnam, August 13, 1845; WI to George P. Putnam, April 3, 1845.
March 3, 1845.	Sarah Storrow. WI to Sarah Storrow, March 12, 1845.
March 10, 1845.	James Buchanan. WI to James Buchanan, May 25, 1845.
March 11, 1845.	Sarah Storrow. WI to Sarah Storrow, March 18, 1845.

March 15, 1845.   Sarah Storrow. WI to Sarah Storrow, March 18, 1845.

March 21, 1845.   Sarah Storrow. WI to Sarah Storrow, March 27, 1845.

March 29, 1845.   Sarah Storrow. WI to Sarah Storrow, April 3, 1845.

Late March, 1845.   Catharine Paris. WI to Sarah Storrow, April 23, 1845.

March, 1845.   Reuben Beasley. WI to Sarah Storrow, April 3, 1845.

March, 1845.   Alexander Hamilton, Jr. WI to Sarah Storrow, April 3, 1845.

March, 1845.   Ebenezer Irving. WI to Sarah Storrow, April 23, 1845.

March, 1845.   William R. King. WI to Sarah Storrow, April 3, 1845.

April 4, 1845.   Sarah Storrow. WI to Sarah Storrow, April 11, 1845.

April 10, 1845.   William R. King. WI to Sarah Storrow, April 23, 1845.

April 14, 1845.   Francisco Martínez de la Rosa. WI to Martínez de la Rosa, April 18, 1845.

April 15, 1845.   Ebenezer Irving. WI to Catharine Irving, June 26, 1845.

Mid-April, 1845.   Sarah Storrow. WI to Sarah Storrow, April 23, 1845.

April 19?, 1845.   Sarah Storrow. WI to Sarah Storrow, April 23, 1845.

April 20, 1845.   Francisco Martínez de la Rosa. WI to Martínez de la Rosa, May 3, 1845.

April 21, 1845.   Catharine Irving. WI to Catharine Irving, June 26, 1845.

April 25, 1845.   Sarah Storrow. WI to Sarah Storrow, May 2, 1845.

April 29, 1845.   Francisco Martínez de la Rosa. WI to James Buchanan, May 4, 1845.

April, 1845.   Brantz Mayer. WI to Brantz Mayer, May 24, 1845.

April, 1845.   Catharine Paris. WI to Sarah Storrow, May 24, 1845.

April, 1845.   John Schell. WI to Sarah Storrow, May 10, 1845.

May 1–3, 1845.	Sarah Storrow. WI to Sarah Storrow, May 10, 1845.
May 10, 1845.	Sarah Storrow. WI to Sarah Storrow, May 16, 1845.
Mid-May, 1845.	Francisco Martínez de la Rosa. WI to Martínez de la Rosa, May 19, 1845.
Mid-May, 1845.	Sarah Storrow. WI to Sarah Storrow, May 24, 1845.
May 16, 1845.	Arthur MacCulloch. WI to Arthur MacCulloch, May 22, 1845.
May 20, 1845.	Francisco Martínez de la Rosa. WI to Martínez de la Rosa, August 4, 1845.
May 20, 1845.	Sarah Storrow. WI to Sarah Storrow, June 5, 1845.
May 30, 1845.	Sarah Storrow. WI to Sarah Storrow, June 5, 1845.
Late May, 1845.	Reuben Beasley. WI to Sarah Storrow, June 5, 1845.
May?, 1845.	Ebenezer Irving. WI to Catharine Paris, August 9, 1845.
May, 1845.	Pierre M. Irving. WI to Sarah Storrow, June 13, 1845.
June 7, 1845.	Sabina O'Shea. WI to Sabina O'Shea, June 15, 1845.
June 7?, 1845.	Sarah Storrow. WI to Sarah Storrow, June 13, 1845.
June 14, 1845.	Sarah Storrow. WI to Sarah Storrow, June 20, 1845.
Mid-June, 1845.	Madame Albuquerque. WI to Sarah Storrow, June 20, 1845.
June 21, 1845.	Sarah Storrow. WI to Sarah Storrow, June 29, 1845.
June 23, 1845.	Irving Paris. WI to Sarah Storrow, August 2, 1845.
June 24, 1845.	Horatio Sprague. WI to Horatio Sprague, July 12, 1845.
Late June?, 1845.	A "letter ... from London." WI to Sarah Storrow, July 10, 1845.
June?, 1845.	Moses H. Grinnell. WI to Sarah Storrow, August 14, 1845.
June?, 1845.	Ebenezer Irving. WI to Catharine Paris, August 9, 1845.

July 5, 1845.   Sarah Storrow. WI to Sarah Storrow, August 2, 1845.

July 7, 1845.   George P. Putnam. WI to George P. Putnam, August 13, 1845.

July 18, 1845.   Sarah Storrow. WI to Sarah Storrow, August 2, 1845.

July 20, 1845.   Marques de Viluma. WI to Martínez de la Rosa, August 12, 1845.

July 31, 1845.   Sarah Storrow. WI to Sarah Storrow, August 14, 1845.

Late July?, 1845.   Francisco Martínez de la Rosa. WI to Martínez de la Rosa, August 2, 1845.

July, 1845.   Charles A. Davis. WI to Sarah Storrow, August 14, 1845.

July, 1845.   Samuel I. Hunt. WI to Sarah Storrow, August 14, 1845.

July, 1845.   Helen Dodge Irving. WI to Sarah Storrow, August 9, 1845.

August 7, 1845.   Sarah Storrow. WI to Sarah Storrow, August 14, 1845.

August 19, 1845.   Sarah Storrow. WI to Sarah Storrow, August 29, 1845.

August 29, 1845.   Sarah Storrow. WI to Sarah Storrow, September 6, 1845.

August, 1845.   Charles A. Davis. WI to Sarah Storrow, August 14, 1845.

October 30, 1845.   ———. WI to ———, December 16, 1845.
October, 1845.   Charlotte Irving. WI to Catharine Paris, November 1, 1845.

October, 1845.   Pierre M. Irving. WI to Catharine Paris, November 1, 1845.

October, 1845.   Irving Paris. WI to Catharine Paris, November 1, 1845.

Early November, 1845.   Jasper Livingston. WI to Sabina O'Shea, November 15, 1845.

November 13, 1845.   Sabina O'Shea. WI to Sabina O'Shea, November 13, 1845.

November, 1845.   Louis McLane. WI to Catharine Paris, November 30, 1845.

December 12, 1845.   Sabina O'Shea. WI to Sabina O'Shea, December 13, 1845.

December 15, 1845.   Benjamin Perley Poore. WI to Benjamin Perley Poore, December 20, 1845.

December?, 1845.   Georgiana Bonnet. WI to Georgiana Bonnet,
                                February 10, 1846.

January 7?, 1846.   Sarah Storrow. WI to Sarah Storrow, Jan-
                                uary 15, 1846.

January 13, 1846.   Sarah Storrow. WI to Sarah Storrow, Jan-
                                uary 17, 1846.

January 20, 1846.   Sabina O'Shea. WI to Sabina O'Shea, Feb-
                                ruary 5, 1846.

Late January, 1846.   Sarah Storrow. WI to Sarah Storrow, Feb-
                                ruary 2, 1846.

January, 1846.   Flora Foster Dawson. WI to Flora Foster
                                Dawson, February 5, 1846.

January, 1846.   Ebenezer Irving. WI to Sarah Storrow, Jan-
                                uary 17, 1846.

January, 1846.   Sarah Storrow. WI to Sarah Storrow, Jan-
                                uary 15, 1846.

Early February, 1846.   Catharine Irving. WI to Sarah Storrow, March
                                14, 1846.

Early February, 1846.   Sarah Storrow. WI to Sabina O'Shea, Feb-
                                ruary 5, 1846.

February 6?, 1846.   Sabina O'Shea. WI to Henry O'Shea, Jr., Feb-
                                ruary 10, 1846.

February 10, 1846.   John Murray III. WI to Rosa Van Wart, Feb-
                                ruary 10, 1846.

February 27, 1846.   Pierre M. Irving. WI to Sarah Storrow, April
                                7, 1846.

March 6?, 1846.   Sarah Storrow. WI to Sarah Storrow, March
                                14, 1846.

Mid-March, 1846.   Ramón María Narváez. WI to Ramón María
                                Narváez, March 19, 1846.

Mid-March, 1846.   Sabina O'Shea. WI to Sabina O'Shea, March
                                28, 1846.

March 27?, 1846.   Sarah Storrow. WI to Sarah Storrow, April
                                5, 1846.

March 27–30, 1846.   Catharine Paris. WI to Catharine Paris, April
                                25, 1846.

Late March, 1846.   Sabina O'Shea. WI to Sabina O'Shea, April
                                5, 1846.

March, 1846.   Mrs. Brigstocke. WI to Sarah Storrow, April
                                5, 1846.

Late March, 1846.   Sabina O'Shea. WI to Sabina O'Shea, April
                                5, 1846.

April 10?, 1846.   Sabina O'Shea. WI to Sabina O'Shea, April 18, 1846.

April 17, 1846.   Sabina O'Shea. WI to Sabina O'Shea, April 25, 1846.

April 23?, 1846.   Xavier Istúriz. WI to George Read, April 26, 1846.

April, 1846.   Sarah & Henry Van Wart. WI to Catharine Paris, April 25, 1846.

May 2, 1846.   Sabina O'Shea. WI to Sabina O'Shea, June 4, 1846.

May 14, 1846.   James Buchanan. WI to James Buchanan, July 18, 1846.

May 28, 1846.   Sarah Storrow. WI to Sarah Storrow, June 23, 1846.

May, 1846.   Dion Acebal. WI to Dion Acebal, June 6, 1846.

May, 1846.   Thomas Storrow, Jr. WI to Sarah Storrow, June 23, 1846.

June 9, 1846.   Sabina O'Shea. WI to Sabina O'Shea, June 24, 1846.

June 16, 1846.   Xavier Istúriz. WI to Bernard de Marigny, June 18, 1846.

June 20, 1846.   Thomas Storrow, Jr. WI to Sarah Storrow, June 23, 1846; WI to Thomas Storrow, Jr., July 12, 1846.

June 28, 1846.   Catharine Paris. WI to Catharine Paris, July 25, 1846.

June?, 1846.   Emilia Renshaw de Wolff. WI to Sarah Storrow, June 23, 1846.

July 8, 1846.   Xavier Istúriz. WI to Alexander Burton, July 10, 1846.

July 29, 1846.   Sarah Storrow. WI to Sarah Storrow, August 18, 1846.

September 26, 1846.   Madame Albuquerque. WI to Sabina O'Shea, November 8, 1846.

September, 1846.   Curtis Guild, Jr. WI to Curtis Guild, Jr., September 30, 1846.

Early October, 1846.   Angel Calderón de la Barca. WI to James Buchanan, October 8, 1846.

December 20?, 1846.   The Reverend Robert Bolton. WI to the Reverend Robert Bolton, December 24, 1846.

January 21, 1847.   Messrs. Wiley & Putnam. WI to Messrs. Wiley & Putnam, January 30, 1847.

January 23, 1847.	Sabina O'Shea. WI to Sabina O'Shea, September 18, 1847.
January?, 1847.	L. Howard Newman. WI to L. Howard Newman, February 20, 1847.
February 10?, 1847.	Helen Dodge Irving. WI to Helen Dodge Irving, February 14, 1847.
February, 1847.	Sarah Storrow. WI to Catharine Paris, March 12, 1847.
March 5, 1847.	George A. Ward. WI to George A. Ward, March 23, 1847.
March?, 1847.	Henry O'Shea. WI to Sabina O'Shea, September 18, 1847.
March, 1847.	Sarah Storrow. WI to Catharine Paris, April 4, 1847.
April 15, 1847.	Pierre M. Irving. WI to Pierre M. Irving, April 15, 1847.
May 15, 1847.	Sarah Storrow. WI to Sarah Storrow, June 6, 1847.
July, 1847.	Gouverneur Kemble. WI to Gouverneur Kemble, July 8, 1847.
July, 1847.	Sabina O'Shea. WI to Sabina O'Shea, September 18, 1847; WI to Sarah Storrow, August 23, 1847.
July, 1847.	Sarah Storrow. WI to Sarah Storrow, August 23, 1847.
September 10, 1847.	Charles Lanman. WI to Charles Lanman, October 15, 1847.
October?, 1847.	George R. Graham. WI to George R. Graham, October 15, 1847.
1847?	Miss Moore. WI to Catharine, Sarah, & Mary Irving, February 4, 1853.
Mid-January, 1848.	J. Hedges. WI to J. Hedges, January 22, 1848.
January?, 1848.	James H. Hackett. WI to James H. Hackett, April 17, 1848.
February 24, 1848.	Irving Literary Society. WI to Irving Literary Society, March 1, 1848.
Early March, 1848.	Charles A. Bristed. WI to Charles A. Bristed, [March 6, 1848?].
Early April, 1848.	Gouverneur Kemble. WI to Aaron Ward, April 7, 1848.
April 1, 1848.	John F. Watson. WI to John F. Watson, April 6, 1848.

April 12, 1848.	Sarah Storrow. WI to Sarah Storrow, May 5, 1848.
April 17, 1848.	The Reverend I. Prince. WI to the Reverend I. Prince, April 24, 1848.
April ?, 1848.	Catharine Irving. WI to Catharine Irving, April 10, 1848.
Mid-1848.	James Wynne. WI to James Wynne, October 23, 1848.
Early October, 1848.	Matthew Clarkson. WI to Matthew Clarkson, October 10, 1848.
November 23, 1848.	Irving Literary Society. WI to Irving Literary Society, December 11, 1848.
December, 1848.	Maunsell B. Field. WI to Maunsell B. Field, December 19, 1848.
January 2, 1849.	John A. Dix. WI to John A. Dix, January 10, 1849.
Early March, 1849.	Ephraim George Squier. WI to Ephraim George Squier, March 6, 1849.
May 22, 1849.	Dorothea Astor Langdon. WI to Dorothea Astor Langdon, May 25, 1849.
May?, 1849.	Thomas Picton. WI to Thomas Picton, June 10, 1849.
Early June, 1849.	Lewis Gaylord Clark. WI to Lewis Gaylord Clark, June 5, 1849.
June 12, 1849.	Charles Dexter. WI to Charles Dexter, July 14, 1849.
Fall, 1849.	David Thomas. WI to David Thomas, June 4, 1849.
October, 1849.	————. WI to ————, October 22, 1849.
December?, 1849.	George Ticknor. WI to George Ticknor, February 15, 1850.
1849?	Sabina O'Shea. WI to Sabina O'Shea, February 22, 1850.
January?, 1850.	Gouverneur Kemble. WI to Gouverneur Kemble, February 7, 1850.
Early February, 1850.	Charles A. Davis. WI to Charles A. Davis, February 11, 1850.
April, 1850.	Robert Balmanno. WI to Robert Balmanno, April 15, 1850.
Mid-May, 1850.	John V. Hall. WI to John V. Hall, May 19, 1850.
Early June, 1850.	————. WI to ————, June 7, 1850.

June, 1850.	Sarah Storrow. WI to Sarah Storrow, July 18, 1850.
Late July, 1850.	John Murray III. WI to John Murray III, August 19, 1850.
July, 1850.	John Murray III. WI to John Murray III, August 8, 1850.
Early August, 1850.	Gouverneur Kemble. WI to Gouverneur Kemble, August 7, 1850.
August 9, 1850.	John Murray III. WI to John Murray III, September 22, 1850.
August 11, 1850.	George H. Throop. WI to George H. Throop, September 17, 1850.
August 26?, 1850.	Joseph G. Cogswell. WI to Joseph G. Cogswell, August 27, 1850.
August 27, 1850.	The Reverend Frederick G. Clark. WI to the Reverend Frederick G. Clark, October 4, 1850.
August, 1850.	George Harvey. WI to George Harvey, August, 1850.
Early September, 1850.	Benson J. Lossing. WI to Benson J. Lossing, September 17, 1850.
Early November, 1850.	Helen Dodge Irving. WI to Helen Dodge Irving, November 17, 1850.
Early December, 1850.	Henry Lee, Jr. WI to Henry Lee, Jr., December 18, 1850.
December, 1850.	Mrs. Betts. WI to Mrs. Betts, December 24, 1850.
1850?	Donald G. Mitchell. WI to Sarah Storrow, May 6, 1851.
Mid-January, 1851.	Benson J. Lossing. WI to Benson J. Lossing, January 17, 1851.
January 22, 1851.	Robert F. Adair. WI to Robert F. Adair, February 6, 1851.
January 27, 1851.	William H. Bogart. WI to William H. Bogart, February 22, 1851.
January 31, 1851.	Pliny Miles. WI to Pliny Miles, February 21, 1851.
January, 1851.	Jesse Merwin. WI to Jesse Merwin, February 12, 1851.
Early February, 1851.	———. WI to ———, February 8, 1851.
February, 1851.	Caleb Lyon. WI to Caleb Lyon, February 28, 1851.
March 5, 1851.	Sarah Storrow. WI to Sarah Storrow, May 6, 1851.

April 13?, 1851.	William W. Waldron. WI to William W. Waldron, April 15, 1851.
April 25, 1851.	John P. Kennedy. WI to John P. Kennedy, April 27, 1851.
April 25?, 1851.	————. WI to ————, April 25, 1851.
April, 1851.	John R. Brodhead. WI to Pierre M. Irving, April 12, 1851.
Early May, 1851.	Henry R. Schoolcraft. WI to Henry R. Schoolcraft, May 5, 1851.
May 5, 1851.	Irving Literary Society. WI to Irving Literary Society, May 15, 1851.
May 19?, 1851.	Moses H. Grinnell. WI to Moses H. Grinnell, May 20, 1851.
June 3, 1851.	Richard Bentley. WI to Richard Bentley, July 7, 1851.
June 4, 1851.	Richard Bentley. WI to Richard Bentley, July 7, 1851.
July?, 1851.	Sarah Storrow. WI to Sarah Storrow, October 21, 1851.
August?, 1851.	Sarah Storrow. WI to Sarah Storrow, October 21, 1851.
Early September, 1851.	Charles A. Davis. WI to Charles A. Davis, September 12, 1851.
September 10, 1851.	Henry R. Schoolcraft. WI to Henry R. Schoolcraft, September 20, 1851.
September 17?, 1851.	Rufus W. Griswold. WI to Rufus W. Griswold, September 18, 1851.
September 29, 1851.	Sarah Storrow. WI to Sarah Storrow, October 21, 1851.
September 30, 1851.	Edward B. Turney. WI to Edward B. Turney, October 8, 1851.
October 13?, 1851.	Rufus W. Griswold. WI to Rufus W. Griswold, October 15, 1851.
October 14?, 1851.	Chester P. Dewey. WI to Chester P. Dewey, October 16, 1851.
October 25, 1851.	John Barney. WI to John Barney, October 30, 1851.
Late October, 1851.	Joseph E. Bloomfield. WI to Joseph E. Bloomfield, October 28, 1851.
October, 1851.	Thomas W. Storrow. WI to Thomas W. Storrow, October 27, 1851.
Early November, 1851.	William C. Bryant. WI to William C. Bryant, November 1, 1851.

December 12?, 1851.   ———. WI to Rufus W. Griswold, December 15, 1851.

Late December, 1851.   Donald G. Mitchell. WI to Donald G. Mitchell, December 31, 1851.

Late December, 1851.   ———. WI to ———, January 4, 1852.

December, 1851.   Pierre M. Irving. WI to Mary Irving, December 5, 1851.

December?, 1851.   Frederick Saunders. WI to Frederick Saunders, January 14, 1852.

December, 1851.   Sarah Storrow. WI to Sarah Storrow, January 13, 1852.

January 8?, 1852.   David Davidson. WI to David Davidson, January 10, 1852.

Mid-January, 1852.   Charles Lanman. WI to Charles Lanman, January 23, 1852.

Late January, 1852.   James Nack. WI to James Nack, January 29, 1852.

January, 1852.   Nathaniel Hawthorne. WI to Nathaniel Hawthorne, January 29, 1852.

January, 1852.   James L. Whitney. WI to James L. Whitney, February 2, 1852.

Early February, 1852.   Gouverneur Kemble. WI to Gouverneur Kemble, February 5, 1852.

February, 1852.   M. D. Phillips. WI to M. D. Phillips, February 17, 1852.

February, 1852.   ———. WI to ———, February 5, 1852.
March, 1852.   James Parton. WI to George L. Duyckinck, March 15, 1852.

April 19, 1852.   Robert Balmanno. WI to Robert Balmanno, April 21, 1852.

April 21?, 1852.   William W. Waldron. WI to William W. Waldron, April 22, 1852.

April, 1852.   Lewis Gaylord Clark. WI to Lewis Gaylord Clark, April 10, 1852.

April, 1852.   Franklin B. Hough. WI to Franklin B. Hough, April 21, 1852.

Early May?, 1852.   Sarah Storrow. WI to Sarah Storrow, May 29, 1852.

May, 1852.   Henry R. Schoolcraft. WI to Henry R. Schoolcraft, May 27, 1852.

June, 1852.   Catharine Storrow. WI to Catharine Storrow, July 15, 1852.

June, 1852.   Sarah Storrow. WI to Sarah Storrow, July 15, 1852.

June, 1852.   Thomas W. Storrow, Sr. WI to Thomas W. Storrow, Sr., July 7, 1852.

Early July, 1852.   William J. Lewis. WI to William J. Lewis, July 5, 1852.

July 21, 1852.   Irving Literary Union. WI to Richard C. McCormick, August 9, 1852.

July 24, 1852.   Catharine Irving. WI to Catharine Irving, July 25, 1852.

July 24, 1852.   George Sumner. WI to George Sumner, August 9, 1852.

July 25, 1852.   Catharine Irving. WI to Catharine Irving, July 28, 1852.

July?, 1852.   Emilia Renshaw de Wolff. WI to Sarah Storrow, July 15, 1852.

July, 1852.   Edward Everett. WI to Edward Everett, July 14, 1852.

July, 1852.   William J. Lewis. WI to William J. Lewis, July 5, 1852.

July, 1852.   Catharine Storrow. WI to Catharine Storrow, July 15, 1852.

July, 1852.   Sarah Storrow. WI to Sarah Storrow, July 15, 1852.

Early August, 1852.   Charles A. Davis. WI to Charles A. Davis, August 10, 1852.

Early August, 1852.   Helen Dodge Irving. WI to Catharine Irving, August 5, 1852.

October, 1852.   Philip J. Forbes. WI to Philip J. Forbes, October 25, 1852.

October, 1852.   Sarah Storrow. WI to Sarah Storrow, November 10, 1852.

October, 1852.   William W. Waldron. WI to William W. Waldron, January 10, 1853.

November 11, 1852.   Alfred Clarke. WI to Alfred Clarke, December 21, 1852.

Mid-November, 1852.   Henry Ogden. WI to Henry Ogden, November 23, 1852.

December 23?, 1852.   George P. Putnam. WI to George P. Putnam, December 27, 1852.

December 30, 1852.   Sarah Irving. WI to Sarah Irving, January 22, 1853.

December, 1852.	John P. Kennedy. WI to John P. Kennedy, December 31, 1852.
December, 1852.	Charles Lanman. WI to Charles Lanman, December 22, 1852.
December, 1852.	Thomas W. Storrow, Sr. WI to Thomas W. Storrow, Sr., December 14, 1852.
December, 1852.	Mrs. Tiffany. WI to Mary Irving, January 18, 1853.
December, 1852.	———. WI to ———, December 11, 1852.
December, 1852.	———. WI to ———, December 27, 1852.
1852?	Sir William Stirling-Maxwell. WI to Thomas W. Storrow, Sr., April 17, 1853.
January 1, 1853.	George P. Morris. WI to George P. Morris, January 3, 1853.
January 4?, 1853.	George P. Morris. WI to George P. Morris, January 6, 1853.
January 20, 1853.	Sarah Irving. WI to Sarah Irving, January 22, 1853.
January 20?, 1853.	Charles Lanman. WI to Charles Lanman, January 23, 1853.
January 21, 1853.	Henry R. Schoolcraft. WI to Henry R. Schoolcraft, January 28, 1853.
January 22?, 1853.	Helen Dodge Irving. WI to Helen Dodge Irving, February 10, 1853.
January, 1853.	Catharine, Mary, & Sarah Irving. WI to Catharine, Mary, & Sarah Irving, February 4, 1853.
January, 1853.	Pierre M. Irving. (Two letters.) WI to Sarah Irving, January 22, 1853; WI to Helen Dodge Irving, February 10, 1853.
January, 1853.	Benson J. Lossing. WI to Sarah Storrow, January 25, 1853.
January?, 1853.	Sarah Storrow. WI to Sarah Storrow, January 25, 1853; February 28, 1853.
February 1?, 1853.	Susan de Forest Lord. WI to Daniel Lord, February 3, 1853.
February 4?, 1853.	Catharine Storrow. WI to Sarah Irving, February 6, 1853.
February 10, 1853.	Sarah Irving. WI to Sarah Irving, February 16, 1853.
February 18?, 1853.	Helen Dodge Irving. WI to Catharine Irving, February 21, 1853.

February 24, 1853.	Sarah Irving. WI to Sarah Irving, February 25, 1853.
Late February, 1853.	Pierre M. Irving. WI to Helen Dodge Irving, February 28, 1853.
February, 1853.	Sarah Storrow. WI to Sarah Storrow, March 28, 1853.
Late March, 1853.	Elizabeth Kennedy. WI to Elizabeth Kennedy, April 2, 1853.
March, 1853.	Mary E. Kennedy. WI to Mary E. Kennedy, March 19, 1853.
March?, 1853.	Thomas W. Storrow, Sr. WI to Thomas W. Storrow, Sr., April 17, 1853.
Early April, 1853.	Mary E. Kennedy. WI to Mary E. Kennedy, April 10, 1853.
April, 1853.	Frederick S. Cozzens. WI to Frederick S. Cozzens, May 5, 1853.
April, 1853.	Edward Gray. WI to Edward Gray, April 24, 1853.
April, 1853.	Julia Irving. WI to Julia Irving, May 26, 1853.
April, 1853.	Elizabeth Kennedy. WI to Elizabeth Kennedy, April 24, 1853.
April, 1853.	Donald G. Mitchell. WI to Donald G. Mitchell, April 21, 1853.
April, 1853.	William W. Waldron. WI to William W. Waldron, April 29, 1853.
April, 1853.	Francis C. Wemyss. WI to Francis C. Wemyss, April 8, 1853.
May, 1853.	Robert Balmanno. WI to Robert Balmanno, May 29, 1853.
May, 1853.	Mary E. Kennedy. WI to Mary E. Kennedy, May 27, 1853.
May, 1853.	Robert Winthrop. WI to Robert Winthrop, May 23, 1853.
Early June, 1853.	Mary E. Kennedy. WI to Mary E. Kennedy, June 10, 1853.
June 19, 1853.	Pierre M. Irving. WI to Pierre M. Irving, June 25, 1853.
June 22, 1853.	Helen Dodge Irving. WI to Helen Dodge Irving, June 26, 1853.
June 26–27, 1853.	Catharine Irving. WI to Catharine Irving, July 1, 1853.
June, 1853.	Emilia Renshaw de Wolff. WI to Sarah Storrow, September 19, 1853.

June, 1853.	Washington Lewis. WI to Mary E. Kennedy, June 10, 1853.
June, 1853.	Catharine Storrow. WI to Sarah Storrow, July 29, 1853.
June, 1853.	Sarah Storrow. WI to Sarah Storrow, July 29, 1853.
June, 1853.	William W. Waldron. WI to William W. Waldron, June 10, 1853.
July 1, 1853.	Sarah Irving. WI to Pierre M. Irving, July 8, 1853.
July, 1853.	John P. Kennedy. WI to Mary E. Kennedy, July 19, 1853.
Early August, 1853.	Sarah Irving. WI to Sarah Irving, August 6, 1853.
Early August, 1853.	Frederick Saunders. WI to Frederick Saunders, September 8, 1853.
August 4, 1853.	Mary E. Kennedy. WI to Mary E. Kennedy, September 8, 1853.
August, 1853.	John P. Kennedy. WI to John P. Kennedy, August 28, 1853.
August, 1853.	Sarah Storrow. WI to Sarah Storrow, September 19, 1853.
September, 1853	Miss Alderson. WI to Sarah Storrow, September 19, 1853.
October 4, 1853.	Sarah Irving. WI to Sarah Irving, October 6, 1853.
October 6, 1853.	Helen Dodge Irving. WI to Helen Dodge Irving, October 11, 1853.
October 9, 1853.	Catharine Irving. WI to Helen Dodge Irving, October 11, 1853.
October 14, 1853.	Sarah Irving. WI to Sarah Irving, October 21, 1853.
October, 1853.	Henry R. Schoolcraft. WI to Henry R. Schoolcraft, October 27, 1853.
Early November, 1853.	Andrew Kennedy. WI to Alexander R. Boteler, November 11, 1853.
Early November, 1853.	Elizabeth Kennedy. WI to Elizabeth Kennedy, November 11, 1853.
November, 1853.	Henry S. Randall. WI to Henry S. Randall, November 26, 1853.
Late December, 1853.	Henry S. Randall. WI to Henry S. Randall, January 3, 1854.

Late December?, 1853.	Sarah Storrow. WI to Sarah Storrow, January 25, 1854.
December, 1853.	John P. Kennedy. WI to John P. Kennedy, December 20, 1853.
December, 1853.	Benjamin Silliman. WI to Benjamin Silliman, December 13, 1853.
Early 1854.	James Boardman. WI to James Boardman, June 30, 1854.
Early January, 1854.	Henry Fox. WI to Henry Fox, January 17, 1854.
January 12, 1854.	Mary E. Kennedy. WI to Elizabeth Kennedy, February 21, 1854; WI to Mary E. Kennedy, February 21, 1854.
Mid-January, 1854.	J. Narine et al. WI to J. Narine et al., January 16, 1854.
January, 1854.	Henry R. Schoolcraft. WI to Henry R. Schoolcraft, February 21, 1854.
January, 1854.	Catharine Storrow. WI to Catharine Storrow, February 21, 1854.
January?, 1854.	William W. Waldron. WI to William W. Waldron, February 13, 1854.
February, 1854.	Elizabeth Kennedy. WI to Elizabeth Kennedy, February 21, 1854.
February, 1854.	Osmond Tiffany. WI to Osmond Tiffany, March 19, 1854.
February, 1854.	————. WI to ————, February 6, 1854.
March, 1854.	Lyman C. Draper. WI to Lyman C. Draper, March 17, 1854.
March, 1854.	Julia Irving. WI to Julia Irving, April 3, 1854.
Early April, 1854.	————. WI to ————, April 8, 1854.
Late April, 1854.	Sabina O'Shea. WI to Sabina O'Shea, May 4, 1854.
April, 1854.	William W. Waldron. WI to William W. Waldron, April 13, 1854.
April, 1854.	Robert C. Winthrop. WI to Robert C. Winthrop, April 23, 1854.
May, 1854.	Mary E. Kennedy. WI to Mary E. Kennedy, May 30, 1854.
May, 1854.	Robert C. Winthrop. WI to Robert C. Winthrop, May 22, 1854.
June, 1854.	James Boardman. WI to James Boardman, June 30, 1854.

Mid-July, 1854.   William Creighton. WI to William Creighton, July 18, 1854.

Late July, 1854.   Andrew Kennedy. WI to Mary E. Kennedy, July 30, 1854.

July, 1854.   Sarah Storrow. WI to Sarah Storrow, August 7, 1854.

August 18, 1854.   Mary E. Kennedy. WI to Mary E. Kennedy, September 1, 1854.

August, 1854.   Elizabeth Kennedy. WI to Elizabeth Kennedy, August 31, 1854.

August, 1854.   Buckingham Smith. WI to Joseph Henry, August 26, 1854.

Late September, 1854.   Bayard Taylor. WI to Bayard Taylor, October 1, 1854.

September, 1854.   John P. Kennedy. WI to John P. Kennedy, October 5, 1854.

September, 1854.   Bayard Taylor. WI to Bayard Taylor, September 12, 1854.

October 20, 1854.   Evert A. Duyckinck. WI to Evert A. Duyckinck, November 23, 1854.

October, 1854.   George Bancroft. WI to George Bancroft, October 27, 1854.

Late October?, 1854.   Sarah Storrow. WI to Sarah Storrow, November 23, 1854.

October, 1854.   George M. Moore. WI to George M. Moore, October 26, 1854.

Early November, 1854.   Francis P. Corben. WI to Francis P. Corben, November 3, 1854.

November, 1854.   H. H. Brigham et al. WI to H. H. Brigham et al., November 23, 1854.

November, 1854.   John P. Kennedy. WI to John P. Kennedy, November 22, 1854.

November, 1854.   James Lenox. WI to James Lenox, December 4, 1854.

November, 1854.   William C. Preston. WI to William C. Preston, November 17, 1854.

Late December, 1854.   Catharine Irving. WI to Helen Dodge Irving, January 4, 1855.

Late December, 1854.   Mary E. Kennedy. WI to Mary E. Kennedy, December 26, 1854.

December, 1854.   Thomas W. Storrow, Sr. WI to Thomas W. Storrow, Sr., December 9, 1854.

January 2, 1855.	Helen Dodge Irving. WI to Helen Dodge Irving, January 4, 1855.
January 15, 1855.	Nathaniel Scarse. WI to Nathaniel Scarse, January 31, 1855.
Late January, 1855.	George Lunt. WI to George Lunt, February 3, 1855.
January, 1855.	Elizabeth Kennedy. WI to Elizabeth Kennedy, February 8, 1855.
January, 1855.	Charles G. Leland. WI to Charles G. Leland, January 10, 1855.
February 12, 1855.	W. C. Schermerhorn. WI to Julia Grinnell, February 16, 1855.
Mid-February, 1855.	Julia Grinnell. WI to Julia Grinnell, February 16, 1855.
February, 1855.	Henry W. Bellows. WI to Julia Grinnell, February 16, 1855.
March 5, 1855.	Charles M. Watson. WI to Charles M. Watson, March 12, 1855.
Mid-March, 1855.	S. C. Foster. WI to S. C. Foster, March 23, 1855.
April 5, 1855.	John Murray III. WI to John Murray III, April 27, 1855.
Mid-April, 1855.	James Watson Webb. WI to James Watson Webb, April 21, 1855.
April, 1855.	John P. Kennedy. WI to John P. Kennedy, April 23, 1855.
Early May, 1855.	William Irving Dodge. WI to William Irving Dodge, May 6, 1855.
Early May, 1855.	Evert A. Duyckinck. WI to Evert A. Duyckinck, May 4, 1855.
Mid-May, 1855.	William W. Waldron. WI to William W. Waldron, May 16, 1855.
May, 1855.	Elisha Bartlett. WI to Elisha Bartlett, May 28, 1855.
Mid-June, 1855.	Lewis Gaylord Clark. WI to Lewis Gaylord Clark, June 14, 1855.
June, 1855.	The Reverend Sylvanus Read. WI to George P. Putnam, June 24, 1855.
June, 1855.	Sarah Storrow. WI to Sarah Storrow, June 27, 1855.
July 27, 1855.	Robert C. Winthrop. WI to Robert C. Winthrop, July 31, 1855.

July, 1855.	Alexander Jones. WI to Alexander Jones, July 19, 1855.
July, 1855.	Elizabeth Kennedy. WI to Elizabeth Kennedy, August 24, 1855.
July, 1855.	Henry A. Smythe. WI to Henry A. Smythe, July 19, 1855.
July, 1855.	Robert Torrey, Jr. WI to Robert Torrey, Jr., July 20, 1855.
August 20, 1855.	R. Shelton Mackenzie. WI to R. Shelton Mackenzie, September 4, 1855.
August, 1855.	George W. Childs & Robert E. Peterson. WI to George W. Childs & Robert E. Peterson, August 23, 1855.
August, 1855.	Charles Lanman. WI to Charles Lanman, August 24, 1855.
August, 1855.	John H. B. Latrobe. WI to John H. B. Latrobe, September 10, 1855.
August, 1855.	Charles R. Terry. WI to Charles R. Terry, August 23, 1855.
Early September, 1855.	George P. Morris. WI to George P. Morris, September 6, 1855.
Early September, 1855.	Martin Van Buren. WI to Martin Van Buren, September 4, 1855.
September 8, 1855.	Gustav W. Lurman. WI to Gustav W. Lurman, September 25, 1855.
Late September, 1855.	Joseph E. Worcester. WI to Joseph E. Worcester, October 3, 1855.
September, 1855.	Thomas S. Hastings. WI to Thomas S. Hastings, October 5, 1855.
September, 1855.	George H. Moore. WI to George H. Moore, September 25, 1855.
September, 1855.	Henry Onderdonk, Jr. WI to Henry Onderdonk, Jr., September 30, 1855.
September, 1855.	Stephen J. W. Tabor. WI to Stephen J. W. Tabor, September 25, 1855.
October, 1855.	Charles Gould. WI to Charles Gould, November 13, 1855.
October, 1855.	Thomas S. Hastings. WI to Thomas S. Hastings, October 15, 1855.
October, 1855.	Benjamin Silliman. WI to Benjamin Silliman, October 18, 1855.
November 19, 1855.	Osmond Tiffany. WI to Osmond Tiffany, December 15, 1855.

November 24, 1855.	T. Addison Richards. WI to T. Addison Richards, December 15, 1855.
November, 1855.	Alvah Beebe. WI to Alvah Beebe, December 7, 1855.
November, 1855.	Duncan F. Curry. WI to Duncan F. Curry, November 24, 1855.
November, 1855.	William A. Duer. WI to William A. Duer, December 5, 1855.
November, 1855.	Eugene H. Munday. WI to Eugene H. Munday, December 5, 1855.
December, 1855.	Robert Forsyth. WI to Robert Forsyth, December 18, 1855.
December, 1855.	H. A. Smythe. WI to H. A. Smythe, December 26, 1855.
December, 1855.	Moses Thomas. WI to Moses Thomas, December 14, 1855.
December, 1855.	Abiel S. Thurston. WI to Abiel S. Thurston, December 11, 1855.
Early January, 1856.	Lewis Gaylord Clark. WI to Lewis Gaylord Clark, January 10, 1856.
January, 1856.	George Bancroft. WI to George Bancroft, January 30, 1856.
January, 1856.	Gouverneur Kemble. WI to Gouverneur Kemble, January 21, 1856.
January, 1856.	Jacob Snider, Jr. WI to Jacob Snider, Jr., January 30, 1856.
January?, 1856.	Isaac W. Stuart. WI to Isaac W. Stuart, February 16, 1856.
January, 1856.	The Reverend Joseph F. Tuttle. WI to the Reverend Joseph F. Tuttle, February 2, 1856.
February, 1856.	George Bancroft. WI to George Bancroft, February 6, 1856.
February, 1856.	Edward Everett. WI to Mercantile Library Association, February 6, 1856.
March, 1856.	Benson J. Lossing. WI to Benson J. Lossing, March 15, 1856.
March, 1856.	John Murray III. WI to John Murray III, March 12, 1856.
April 4, 1856.	Charles Boner. WI to Charles Boner, June 18, 1856.
April 7, 1856.	Sarah Storrow. WI to Sarah Storrow, April 24, 1856.

May, 1856.	William Duane. WI to William Duane, June 3, 1856.
May, 1856.	Charles Godfrey Leland. WI to Charles Godfrey Leland, May 31, 1856.
June, 1856.	Benjamin Silliman. WI to Benjamin Silliman, July 15, 1856.
June, 1856.	Sarah Storrow. WI to Sarah Storrow, October 27, 1856.
June, 1856.	James Watson Webb. WI to George D. Morgan, July 4, 1856.
July 17?, 1856.	Benjamin Silliman. WI to Benjamin Silliman, July 19, 1856.
July, 1856.	Samuel Mordecai. WI to Samuel Mordecai, July 6, 1856.
July, 1856.	The Reverend J. B. Wakeley. WI to the Reverend J. B. Wakeley, August 6, 1856.
Mid-August, 1856.	Lewis Gaylord Clark. WI to Lewis Gaylord Clark, August 15, 1856.
August, 1856.	Thomas W. Storrow, Sr. WI to Thomas W. Storrow, Sr., August 6, 1856.
September, 1856.	Mary Kennedy Cooke. WI to Mary Kennedy Cooke, October 9, 1856.
September, 1856.	Elizabeth Kennedy. WI to Mary Kennedy Cooke, October 9, 1856.
September, 1856.	The Reverend Charles K. McHarg. WI to the Reverend Charles K. McHarg, September 26, 1856.
September, 1856.	Sarah Storrow. WI to Sarah Storrow, October 27, 1856.
October, 1856.	Thomas I. McGrath. WI to Thomas I. McGrath, October 24, 1856.
October, 1856.	Townsend Ward. WI to Townsend Ward, October 27, 1856.
October, 1856.	————. WI to ————, October 16, 1856.
Early November, 1856.	Andrew P. Peabody. WI to Andrew P. Peabody, November 3, 1856.
November, 1856.	George William Curtis. WI to George William Curtis, November 20, 1856.
November, 1856.	Hiram Paulding. WI to Hiram Paulding, November, 11, 1856.
November, 1856.	T. Addison Richards. WI to T. Addison Richards, November 20, 1856.

December, 1856.	George Bancroft. WI to George Bancroft, December 24, 1856.
Late 1856.	Charles Lanman. WI to Charles Lanman, March 2, 1857.
1856?	Elisha Kane. WI to George W. Childs & Robert E. Peterson, April 9, 1857.
January?, 1857.	George W. Childs & Robert E. Peterson. WI to George W. Childs & Robert E. Peterson, April 9, 1857.
January?, 1857.	Charles C. Lee. WI to Charles C. Lee, May 6, 1857.
January, 1857.	Henry C. Wetmore. WI to Henry C. Wetmore, May 20, 1857.
Early February, 1857.	Anna K. Hiener. WI to Anna K. Hiener, February 7, 1857.
February 15, 1857.	F. C. Yarnell. WI to F. C. Yarnell, May 12, 1857.
February 17, 1857.	Daniel Appleton. WI to Daniel Appleton, May 14, 1857.
February?, 1857.	Charles Lanman. WI to Charles Lanman, March 2, 1857.
February, 1857.	John S. Williams. WI to John S. Williams, March 4, 1857.
March 21?, 1857.	Pierre M. Irving. WI to Pierre M. Irving, March 22, 1857.
March 24, 1857.	Charles Lanman. WI to Charles Lanman, May 9, 1857.
March, 1857.	William Fox. WI to William Fox, March 5, 1857.
March, 1857.	Thomas W. Olcott et al. WI to Thomas Olcott et al., March 14, 1857.
Early April, 1857.	George W. Childs & Robert E. Peterson. WI to George W. Childs & Robert E. Peterson, April 9, 1857.
April 6, 1857.	Frederick Saunders. WI to Frederick Saunders, May 9, 1857.
Late April, 1857.	George W. Childs & Robert E. Peterson. WI to George W. Childs & Robert E. Peterson, May 6, 1857.
Late April?, 1857.	Charles C. Lee. WI to Charles C. Lee, May 6, 1857.
Early May?, 1857.	Charles C. Lee. WI to Charles C. Lee, May 6, 1857.

May, 1857.	Frederick S. Cozzens. WI to Frederick S. Cozzens, May 22, 1857.
May, 1857.	Charles A. Davis. WI to Charles A. Davis, June 2, 1857.
May, 1857.	Lyman C. Draper. WI to Lyman C. Draper, June 1, 1857.
May, 1857.	W. Alfred Jones. WI to W. Alfred Jones, May 10, 1857.
May, 1857.	W. F. Smith. WI to W. F. Smith, May 12, 1857.
May, 1857.	G. Washington Warren. WI to G. Washington Warren, May 29, 1857.
June, 1857.	S. Austin Allibone. WI to S. Austin Allibone, June 29, 1857.
June, 1857.	George Bancroft. WI to George Bancroft, June 24, 1857.
June, 1857.	The Reverend Lucius King. WI to the Reverend Lucius King, June 17, 1857.
June, 1857.	Francis Lieber. WI to Francis Lieber, June 10, 1857.
July 24, 1857.	Charles C. Lee. WI to Charles C. Lee, July 31, 1857.
July, 1857.	Joseph G. Cogswell. WI to John L. Motley, July 17, 1857.
July, 1857.	John L. Motley. WI to John L. Motley, July 17, 1857.
July, 1857.	Irving Paris. WI to Sarah Storrow, August 4, 1857.
July, 1857.	Sarah Storrow. WI to Sarah Storrow, August 4, 1857.
July, 1857.	Henry Van Wart, Jr. WI to Henry Van Wart, Jr., July 31, 1857.
July, 1857.	———. WI to ———, July 22, 1857.
September, 1857.	Charles J. Everett. WI to Charles J. Everett, September 19, 1857.
September, 1857.	Hannah E. North. WI to Hannah E. North, September 16, 1857.
October, 1857.	Jane Major. WI to Jane Major, November 26, 1857.
October, 1857.	Jesse B. Turley. WI to Jesse B. Turley, November 9, 1857.
October, 1857.	S. B. Woolworth. WI to S. B. Woolworth, November 6, 1857.

December 10?, 1857.	Robert Bolton. WI to Robert Bolton, December 11, 1857.
December?, 1857.	D. Appleton & Co. WI to D. Appleton & Co., January 6, 1858.
December, 1857.	H. W. Muzzey et al. WI to H. W. Muzzey et al., December 27, 1857.
December?, 1857.	Edgar Irving. WI to Edgar Irving, January 25, 1858.
December, 1857.	————. WI to ————, December 28, 1857.
1857?	G. P. R. James. WI to G. P. R. James, July 24, 1858.
1857.	A literary gentleman of Paris. New York *Times*, January 27, 1860.
1857.	Lydia H. Sigourney. WI to Lydia H. Sigourney, 1857.
January 9, 1858.	Sarah Storrow. WI to Sarah Storrow, February 15, 1858.
Mid-January, 1858.	John E. Williams. WI to John E. Williams, January 19, 1858.
January 18, 1858.	A. L. Huntt et al. WI to A. L. Huntt et al., January 22, 1858.
January, 1858.	Samuel L. Waldo. WI to Samuel L. Waldo, February 5, 1858.
Early February, 1858.	William A. Whitehead. WI to William A. Whitehead, February 5, 1858.
February, 1858.	Harriet Backus. WI to Harriet Backus, March 6, 1858.
February, 1858.	James Watson Webb. WI to James Watson Webb, February 13, 1858.
February, 1858.	————. WI to ————, February 5, 1858.
March, 1858.	George Bancroft. WI to George Bancroft, April 16, 1858.
March, 1858.	George Jones. WI to George Jones, April 8, 1858.
March, 1858.	H. A. Smythe. WI to H. A. Smythe, March 30, 1858.
April, 1858.	Benson J. Lossing. WI to Benson J. Lossing, April 16, 1858.
May 28, 1858.	Frederick Phillips. WI to Frederick Phillips, June 3, 1858.
Late June?, 1858.	James A. Dix. WI to James A. Dix, July 3, 1858.

July 11, 1858.	Irving Grinnell. WI to Irving Grinnell, October 28, 1858.
August, 1858.	George D. Canale. WI to George D. Canale, August 21, 1858.
August, 1858.	Charles A. Davis. WI to Charles A. Davis, August 16, 1858.
August, 1858.	Julia Grinnell. WI to Julia Grinnell, September 2, 1858.
August, 1858.	Charles Lanman. WI to Charles Lanman, August 24, 1858.
August, 1858.	————. WI to Charles A. Davis, August 16, 1858.
October, 1858.	Elizabeth Kennedy. WI to Elizabeth Kennedy, October 29, 1858.
November, 1858.	Lyman C. Draper. WI to Lyman C. Draper, November 22, 1858.
November, 1858.	Wickham Hoffman. WI to Wickham Hoffman, November 23, 1858.
December, 1858.	Charles A. Davis. (Two letters?) WI to Charles A. Davis, January 12, 1859.
December, 1858.	Oliver Wendell Holmes. WI to Oliver Wendell Holmes, January 4, 1859.
December, 1858.	Osmond Tiffany. WI to Osmond Tiffany, December 22, 1858.
January 26, 1859.	Henry W. Becher. WI to Henry W. Becher, February 4, 1859.
January, 1859.	S. Austin Allibone. WI to S. Austin Allibone, January 12, 1859.
January, 1859.	Florence Jaffray. WI to Florence Jaffray, January 7, 1859.
January, 1859.	Thomas W. C. Moore. WI to Thomas W. C. Moore, January 12, 1859.
January, 1859.	James Watson Webb. WI to James Watson Webb, January 17, 1859.
February 16, 1859.	Charles A. Davis. WI to Charles A. Davis, February 22, 1859.
Late February, 1859.	Alfred Clarke. WI to Alfred Clarke, March 2, 1859.
March 9, 1859.	Lydia Minturn Post. WI to Lydia Minturn Post, March 25, 1859.
March 16, 1859.	Rhoda E. White. WI to Rhoda E. White, April 18, 1859.

Late March, 1859.	Augustus M. Flythe? PMI, MS. journal (NYPL), April 2, 1859.
March, 1859.	Charles Lanman. WI to Charles Lanman, March 28, 1859.
Early April, 1859.	Charles A. Davis. WI to Charles A. Davis, April 4, 1859.
Early April, 1859.	Henry B. Dawson. WI to Henry B. Dawson, April 6, 1859.
April 12?, 1859.	Young autograph collector. PMI, MS. journal (NYPL), April 14, 1859.
April, 1859.	George D. Canale. WI to George D. Canale, April 19, 1859.
May 7?, 1859.	Evert A. Duyckinck. WI to Evert A. Duyckinck, May 9, 1859.
May 8?, 1859.	John P. Kennedy. WI to John P. Kennedy, May 11, 1859.
May 12, 1859.	C. C. Felton. WI to C. C. Felton, May 17, 1859.
Mid-May, 1859.	William C. Preston. PMI, MS. journal (NYPL), May 17, 1859.
May 19?, 1859.	Evert A. Duyckinck. PMI, MS. journal (NYPL), May 20, 1859.
May 19?, 1859.	Henry T. Tuckerman. PMI, MS. journal (NYPL), May 20, 1859.
May 26, 1859.	Pierre M. Irving. PMI, MS. journal (NYPL), May 27, 1859.
Late May, 1859.	George Ticknor. WI to George Ticknor, May 30, 1859.
May, 1859.	S. Austin Allibone. PMI, MS. journal (NYPL), May 29, 1859.
May, 1859.	John Esten Cooke. WI to John Esten Cooke, June 24, 1859.
May, 1859.	William P. Smith. WI to John P. Kennedy, May 11, 1859.
Early June, 1859.	Edward Everett. PMI, MS. journal (NYPL), June 7, 1859.
June 13?, 1859.	Joshua J. Cohen. PMI, MS. journal (NYPL), June 15, 1859.
June 17, 1859.	Charles D. Cleveland. PMI, MS. journal (NYPL), June 20, 1859.
June 21, 1859.	Frederick S. Cozzens. PMI, MS. journal (NYPL), June 22, 1859.

June 27, 1859.	H. A. Smythe. PMI, MS. journal (NYPL), June 27, 1859.
June, 1859.	James [Brown?]. PMI, MS. journal (NYPL), June 22, 1859.
June, 1859.	Charles A. Davis. WI to Charles A. Davis, July 11, 1859.
June, 1859.	Sarah Storrow. PMI, MS. journal (NYPL), July 6, 1859.
June, 1859.	George Ticknor. WI to George Ticknor, July 2, 1859.
Early July, 1859.	Richard Henry Dana, Jr. WI to Richard Henry Dana, Jr., July 6, 1859.
Early July, 1859.	Sabina O'Shea. WI to Charles A. Davis, July 11, 1859.
July 7, 1859.	Alfred A. Barbour. WI to Alfred A. Barbour, July 15, 1859.
July 7, 1859.	Charles A. Davis. WI to Charles A. Davis, July 11, 1859.
July 15, 1859.	Charles A. Davis. PMI, MS. journal (NYPL), July 16, 1859.
July 25, 1859.	Irving Paris. WI to Irving Paris, July 28, 1859.
July 29, 1859.	Charles A. Davis. WI to Charles A. Davis, August 2, 1859.
July 29, 1859.	The Reverend Francis Vinton. WI to the Reverend Francis Vinton, August 1, 1859.
July?, 1859.	William C. Preston. PMI, MS. journal (NYPL), August 9, 1859.
August 4?, 1859.	Thomas W. Storrow, Sr. PMI, MS. journal (NYPL), August 6, 1859.
August 18, 1859.	J. J. Flournoy. PMI, MS. journal (NYPL), August 25, 1859.
August 21?, 1859.	Barrett Ames. PMI, MS. journal (NYPL), August 22, 1859.
August, 1859.	Robert S. Oakley. WI to Robert S. Oakley, August 22, 1859.
August, 1859.	Thomas W. Storrow, Sr. WI to Thomas W. Storrow, Sr., August 25, 1859.
Late Summer, 1859.	Daniel W. Fiske. WI to Daniel W. Fiske, October 6, 1859.
September & October, 1859.	Charles A. Davis. (Several letters.) WI to Charles A. Davis, October 18, 1859.
October 11?, 1859.	—————— Balch. PMI, MS. journal (NYPL), October 12, 1859.

October 13, 1859.   Eliza F. Ellet. PMI, MS. journal (NYPL),
                           October 14, 1859.

October, 1859.   ———— Erwin. PMI, MS. journal (NYPL),
                           October 13, 1859.

November 12?, 1859.   ———— (concerning subscription for Ply-
                           mouth monument). PMI, MS. journal (NYPL),
                           November 14, 1859.

February, 1820 or 1848.   ————. WI to ————, [February, 1820 or
                           1848].

After 1836.   ————. WI to ————, [after 1836].

Before March 31, 1841.   Mrs. Jones or Sarah Paris. WI to Sarah Paris,
                           [before March, 1841].

1854?   ————. WI to ————, [1854?].

February, n.y.   Miss R. D. Smith. WI to Miss R. D. Smith,
                           February 28, n.y.

March, n.y.   William Frick. WI to William Frick, March
                           23, n.y.

March, n.y.   ———— Bellow. WI to ———— Bellow,
                           March, n.y.

April, n.y.   ————. WI to ————, April 25, n.y.

May, n.y.   Thomas Ramsay. WI to Thomas Ramsay,
                           June 7, n.y.

June, n.y.   ————. WI to ————, June 26, n.y.

August, n.y.   Edward W. Lorenz. WI to Edward W. Lorenz,
                           August 5, n.y.

n.d.   General ————. WI to General ————, n.d.

n.d.   ————. WI to ————, n.d.

APPENDIX V

Spurious Irving Letters

SPURIOUS IRVING LETTERS

The following letters, which James Walter in *Memorials of Washington and of Mary, His Mother, and Martha, His Wife, from Letters and Papers of Robert Carey and James Sharples* (New York, 1887), pages 16–19, prints as being written by WI, are probably spurious, the fabrications of Mr. Walter himself. A number of reasons can be advanced for questioning their authenticity. In the letter of April 13, 1854, WI notes that the shape of the mouth in the Sharples portrait differed from that in the Stuart portrait, probably because of badly fitting teeth. These remarks are similar to those made by the Reverend Dr. Van Pelt at the meeting of the New-York Historical Society on April 4, 1854, as reported in the New York *Times* of April 5, 1854. Although Walter quotes a letter from Dr. Van Pelt (probably counterfeit) describing his childhood meeting with Washington, that letter says nothing about the shape of the mouth. It is probable that Walter picked up Dr. Van Pelt's observation about the mouth from the newspaper account and incorporated it into WI's letter.

In the purported letter to Cadwallader Colden WI first suggests that Mr. Astor is willing to be security for the purchase of the Sharples paintings; then he shifts ground and indicates that Astor's wishes are not expressed directly but through the agency of James K. Armstrong. The ambiguity is heightened by the fact that WI does not give Astor's first name. Consequently it is not clear whether John Jacob Astor, who died in 1848, or William Astor, his son, is intended. A reader in 1887, recalling that WI had written *Astoria* in 1836, might conclude that the elder, more famous Astor was the potential benefactor when in reality he had been dead for six years. The confusion and vagueness are not typical of WI; rather, they suggest that Walter was ignorant of the facts when he was creating the letters.

There is still more confusion to be noted in the letter addressed to Cadwallader Colden, who had died in 1834. His son, David C. Colden, was interested in the arts in New York City; but WI's undated letter, as printed by Walter, is addressed to his father, who had been dead for twenty years.

When the Sharples paintings were exhibited again in the United States in 1882, their authenticity was questioned, with the result that the Massachusetts Historical Society appointed a committee headed by Francis Parkman to investigate. The committee also examined the letters offered by Walter in support of his claims and concluded on the basis of stylistic similarities between Walter's writing and the letters from well-known figures that these letters were not genuine. (See Francis Parkman, "Report on the Historical Portraits Exhibited by Major Walter," *Massachusetts Historical Society Proceedings*, 2d ser., 3 [1886–1887], 179–87, 215–16). Other details concerning the problem are set forth in Katherine McCook Knox, *The Sharples* (New York, 1972), pp. 63–64.

Nowhere does James Walter indicate how the letters of WI and other prominent figures came into his possession. For him to collect these letters would have involved correspondence with several families, and in the course of that correspondence he should have become aware of some of the inconsistencies which the printed letters display.

In view of the problems and questions discussed above, it is doubtful that the following letters belong to the Irving canon. They have, therefore, been relegated to this appendix.

To ———

Sunnyside, April 13, 1854

I have seen the portrait of Washington by Sharples. There is much more of life and animation than in that by Stuart, but the latter has more calm dignity. I should think it was taken several years previously, probably during the war, when Washington was leading a life of personal activity and mental excitement.

The mouth is different from that by Stuart, and approaches more to the natural shape of that taken of him when he was forty years of age, by Peale. A set of artificial teeth, which I believe he did not wear until after the revolutionary war, altered the shape of his mouth, drew it down at the corners, and lengthened the upper lip.

The Sharples portrait gives a better idea of the innate energy of his character; which, after he laid by the sword and assumed the toga, may have been somewhat veiled by the sober decorums and restraint of official station.

I think the portrait a very valuable one, and should like very much to have the privilege of having it engraved for the Life of Washington, should I ever complete and publish that work, which the booksellers have so often announced without my authority, and even before the plan of it had been turned in my mind.

I am, my dear sir, with high respect,

Your obliged and humble servant,
Washington Irving

To Prosper M. Wetmore

Sunnyside, April 13, 1854.

Dear Mr. Wetmore:

I wish you would convey to the members of the Historical Society that Mr. Bryant and myself are equally anxious with them and others that these portraits and the Stuyvesant picture should not again leave the country. What, however, is there to do that has not been done?

Mr. Astor unavailingly stood forward as money sponsor, so that any idea of lack of funds being a difficulty is utterly erroneous. The owning family are described by Dr. Beale as "English gentlefolks;" and we can only hope that when the time comes for any disposal of the pictures, the spirit of that class may be evidenced.

I coveted having the portraits engraved for my purposed Life, but see clearly no such permission could be given.

Respectfully, your humble servant,

Washington Irving.

P. M. Wetmore, Esq.

To Cadwallader Colden

[April?, 1854]

My dear Colden:

It is indeed a matter for national regret that the Sharples Washington portrait cannot be allowed to rest in America. The Historical Society took it up in a very earnest way, and Dr. Beale, President of St. George's Society, helped all he could; but as explained to Mr. Astor and Mr. Wetmore, the pictures cannot be sold for many years.

Mr. Astor generously offered to be security in a large sum for the three portraits and the Stuyvesant Army Procession, or to deposit a sum to accumulate until a sale could be made; but Mr. Astor's counsel advised that unless a price could *now* be agreed upon, any such course would be increasing the difficulty when the occasion may arise for the portrait's return to America.

James K. Armstrong, on behalf of Mr. Astor, has done his utmost. Bryant, too, and Mr. Charles Leupp and myself concur that the owning family have done all in their power to meet our wishes for the pictures to be owned on this side. All that we can hope for is that at some distant day this yearning of all patriots may be realized.

My dear Colden, with high respect,

> Your faithful, humble servant,
> Washington Irving

Cadwallader Colden, Esq., / President, Cambrian Society.

APPENDIX VI
Irving Family Genealogy

Compiled by
Alice R. Aderman

Since the records for the various lines of the Irving family are scattered, disorganized, and incomplete, the compiler has not been able to find complete dates and names for some of the persons listed. Although the specific sources have not been documented here, the compiler has collected evidence from letters, family Bibles, obituaries, tombstones, public records, and other genealogies to support her facts.

1. **WILLIAM IRVING**   and   **SARAH SANDERS**

> *born* September 11, 1731   *born* April 25, 1738
> *died* October 25, 1807   *died* April 9, 1817

married May 18, 1761

2. William Irving   b. December 24, 1762
                                  d. December 24, 1762

3. William Irving   b. February 22, 1764
                                  d. August 22, 1765

4. William Irving, Jr.   b. August 15, 1766
                                  d. November 9, 1821

5. John Irving   b. August 8, 1768
                                  d. September 30, 1769

6. Ann Sarah Irving   b. February 14, 1770
                                  d. May 10, 1808

7. Peter Irving   b. October 30, 1772
                                  d. June 27, 1838

8. Catharine Rodgers Irving   b. January 1, 1774
                                  d. December 25, 1849

9. Ebenezer Irving   b. January 27, 1776
                                       d. August 22, 1868

10. John Treat Irving   b. May 26, 1778
                                       d. March 15, 1838

11. Sarah Sanders Irving   b. June 30, 1780
                                       d. November 19, 1848

12. Washington Irving   b. April 3, 1783
                                       d. November 28, 1859

4. *WILLIAM IRVING, JR.* (1766–1821)   *married* November 7, 1793

        to Julia Paulding,   *born* August 10, 1768
                             died January 24, 1823

13. Lewis Graham Irving   b. September 17, 1795
                                       d. June 26, 1879

14. William Sanders Irving   b. July 17, 1797
                                       d. November 15, 1823

15. Oscar Irving   b. May 17, 1800
                                       d. April 1, 1865

16. Pierre Munro Irving   b. April 3, 1802
                                       d. February 25, 1876

17. Julia Irving   b. November 21, 1803
                                       d. February 22, 1872

18. Edwin Irving   b. October 23, 1805
                                       d. October 23, 1805

19. Henry Ogden Irving   b. March 16, 1807
                                       d. March 18, 1869

20. Euphemia Irving   b. November 17, 1808
                                       d. March 28, 1830

21. Susan Anne Irving   b. May 26, 1811
                                       d. March 19, 1836

6. *ANN SARAH IRVING* (1770–1808)   *married* February 14, 1788

        to Richard Dodge,   *born* December 31, 1762
                            died September 20, 1832

22. William Irving Dodge   b. July 10, 1790
                                    d. January 30, 1873

23. James Richard Dodge   b. October 27, 1795
                                    d. February 24, 1880

24. Samuel Dodge   b.   1798
                                    d.

25. Jane Ann Dodge   b. January 18, 1799
                                    d. July 28, 1875

26. Eliza Dodge   b. June 14, 1801
                                    d. January 5, 1887

27. Helen Dodge   b. September 17, 1802
                                    d. March 5, 1885

8. *CATHARINE RODGERS IRVING* (1774–1849)
                                            married October 1, 1796

        to John Daniel Paris,   *born* February 20, 1773
                                died April 4, 1851

28. Child Paris   b.
                                    d.   1820

29. Isaac Paris   b. April 19, 1799
                                    d. May 23, 1824

30. William Sanders Paris   b. December 24, 1800
                                    d. February 5, 1812

31. Pierre Irving Paris   b. August 5, 1802
                                    d. October 26, 1812

32. Margaret Paris   b. September 3, 1804
                                    d. September 30, 1821

33. Catharine Paris   b. December 20, 1807
                                    d.   1828

34. Ann Mary Paris   b. December 26, 1810
                                    d. July 25, 1821

35. Sarah Sanders Paris   b. May 3, 1813
                                    d. August 8, 1885

36. Irving Paris   b. September 18, 1816
                                    d. October 30, 1879

9. *EBENEZER IRVING* (1776–1868) *married* November 14, 1805

    to Elizabeth Kip, *born* March 18, 1784
                   died April 18, 1827

37.	Pierre Paris Irving	b.	September 24, 1806
		d.	September 10, 1878
38.	Edgar Irving	b.	February 8, 1808
		d.	January 31, 1873
39.	Theodore Irving	b.	May 9, 1809
		d.	December 20, 1880
40.	William Irving	b.	February 16, 1811
		d.	July 28, 1854
41.	Sanders Irving	b.	February 19, 1813
		d.	March 23, 1884
42.	Eliza Irving	b.	May 27, 1814
		d.	January 20, 1819
43.	Catharine Ann Irving	b.	May 6, 1816
		d.	October 2, 1911
44.	Sarah Irving	b.	June 20, 1817
		d.	March 13, 1900
45.	Jane Irving	b.	September 26, 1818
		d.	June 2, 1827
46.	Julia Tunis Irving	b.	September 26, 1818
		d.	July 22, 1861
47.	Mary Elizabeth Irving	b.	May 23, 1820
		d.	March 17, 1868
48.	Washington Ebenezer Irving	b.	March 14, 1822
		d.	July 7, 1894
49.	Charlotte Van Wart Irving	b.	September 3, 1824
		d.	March 16, 1911

10. *JOHN TREAT IRVING* (1778–1838) *married* April 27, 1806

    to Abigail Spicer Furman, *born* September 29, 1779
                           died November 7, 1864

50. Gabriel Furman Irving   b.   February 24, 1807
                                      d.   May 18, 1845

51. William Furman Irving   b.   January 29, 1809
                                      d.   November 4, 1832

52. Sarah Sanders Irving   b.   January 21, 1811
                                      d.   April 22, 1836

53. John Treat Irving, Jr.   b.   December 2, 1812
                                      d.   February 27, 1906

54. Washington Irving   b.   December 20, 1814
                                      d.   July 6, 1894

55. George Irving   b.   December 13, 1818
                                      d.   August 18, 1820

56. Mary Irving   b.   January 14, 1821
                                      d.   August 3, 1822

57. Abbey Irving   b.   September 23, 1822
                                      d.   1906

58. George Irving   b.   January 24, 1824
                                      d.   October 5, 1908

11. *SARAH SANDERS IRVING* (1780–1848)
                              married January 8, 1806

        to Henry Van Wart, *born* September 25, 1783
                            died February 15, 1873

59. Henry Van Wart   b.   1806
                                     d.   July 4, 1878

60. Irving Van Wart   b.   March 7, 1808
                                     d.   February 19, 1896

61. William Van Wart   b.   1814
                                     d.   May 14, 1868

62. Matilda Van Wart   b.
                                     d.

63. Marianne Van Wart   b.
                                     d.   August 20, 1887

64. George Van Wart   b. May 9, 1818
                                  d. September 29, 1903

65. Washington Irving Van Wart   b. January   1819
                                  d. May 10, 1823

13. *LEWIS GRAHAM IRVING* (1795–1879) *married* June 16, 1823

          to Maria Carleton Hale,   *born* April 10, 1797
                                    died December 12, 1869

66. William Hale Irving   b. April 12, 1824
                                  d. September 14, 1824

67. Lewis Irving   b. July 1, 1825
                                  d. May 14, 1861

68. Charles Irving   b. October 12, 1826
                                  d. April 18, 1895

69. Paulding Irving   b. March 26, 1832
                                  d. May 29, 1851

70. Henry Irving   b. March 28, 1834
                                  d. August 24, 1834

71. Ellen Irving   b. October 23, 1835
                                  d. January 1, 1871

72. Julia Irving   b. July 8, 1837
                                  d. July 26, 1922

73. Edward Irving   b. August 28, 1838
                                  d. September 24, 1839

15. *OSCAR IRVING* (1800–1865)   *married* (1) September 6, 1825

          to Catherine E. C. Dayton, *born* April 28, 1800
                                      died March 2, 1842

                                                married (2) April 3, 1845

          to Eliza Dodge Romeyn   *born* June 14, 1801
                                   died January 5, 1887

          by (1) Catherine E. C. Dayton

74. Nathaniel Paulding Irving   b. September 9 or 10, 1826
                                  d. November 8, 1869

75. William Irving   b.   1827
                                           d.   July 30, 1859

16. *PIERRE MUNRO IRVING* (1802–1876)
                                  married (1) September 19, 1829

         to Margaret Ann Berdan,   *born* November 26, 1808
                                   died October 4, 1832

                                  married (2) October 10, 1836

         to Helen Dodge,   *born* September 17, 1802
                           died March 5, 1885

17. *JULIA IRVING* (1803–1872)   *married* June 30, 1836

         to Moses Hicks Grinnell,   *born* March 3, 1803
                                    died November 24, 1877

76. Julia Irving Grinnell   b.   March 16, 1837
                                           d.   February 16, 1915

77. [William] Irving Grinnell   b.   August 9, 1839
                                           d.   May 11, 1921

78. Fanny Leslie Grinnell   b.   September 23, 1842
                                           d.   May 14, 1887

21. *SUSAN ANNE IRVING* (1811–1836)   *married* July   1832

         to Irving Van Wart,   *born* March 7, 1808
                               died February 19, 1896

         (*SEE* Number 60, Irving Van Wart, for child)

22. *WILLIAM IRVING DODGE* (1790–1873)
                                  married January 23, 1812

         to Patience Akin,   *born*   1793
                             died May 14, 1879

79. Ann Sarah Dodge   b.   September 28, 1816
                                            d.   December 20, 1886

80. Julia Irving Dodge   b.
                                            d.

81.   William James Dodge   b.   May 30, 1822
                                        d.   August 19, 1879

82.   Elizabeth Russell Dodge   b.   December 24, 1826
                                        d.

83.   Richard Dodge   b.
                                        d.

83a. Washington Irving Dodge   b.   October 18, 1831
                                        d.

23.   *JAMES RICHARD DODGE* (1795–1880)   *married* May 24, 1826

        to first wife   *born*
                        died

        to Susan Williams,   *born*
                             died

84.   Richard Irving Dodge   b.   May 19, 1827
                                        d.   June 1, 1895

85.   Susan Taylor Dodge   b.   April 20, 1829
                                        d.

86.   Ann Sarah Dodge   b.   May 31, 1831
                                        d.

87.   Mary Helen Dodge   b.   March 15, 1835
                                        d.

25.   *JANE ANN DODGE* (1799–1875)   *married* December 23, 1816

        to John Frost Frothingham,   *born* February 19, 1789
                                            died February 1, 1868

88.   Thomas Frothingham   b.   September 27, 1818
                                        d.   1887

89.   Richard Dodge Frothingham   b.   January 31, 1820
                                        d.   January 29, 1880

90.   Washington Frothingham   b.   February 28, 1822
                                        d.   October 21, 1914

91.   Augustus Frothingham   b.   July 30, 1825
                                        d.   December 8, 1874

92. John Frothingham
    b. September 9, 1827
    d. March 26, 1869

93. William Frothingham
    b. May 12, 1830
    d. November 19, 1885

94. Catharine Paris Frothingham
    b. July 4, 1832
    d. May 29, 1914

95. James Frothingham
    b. September 21, 1834
    d. December 7, 1921

96. Anna Frothingham
    b. December, 1836
    d. October 13, 1839

97. Edward Frothingham
    b.   1841
    d. January 23, 1870

26. *ELIZA DODGE* (1801–1887) *married* (1) August 6, 1828

    to Theodore F. H. Romeyn *born*
                                    died June 1833

                      married (2) April 3, 1845

    to Oscar Irving,   *born* May 7, 1800
                  died April 1, 1865

  (*SEE* also Number 15, Oscar Irving, children by first wife)

27. *HELEN DODGE* (1802–1885) *married* October 10, 1836

    to Pierre Munro Irving, *born* April 3, 1802
                         died February 25, 1876

    (*SEE* also Number 16, Pierre Munro Irving)

35. *SARAH SANDERS PARIS* (1813–1885) *married* March 31, 1841

    to Thomas Wentworth Storrow, Jr., *born* July 20, 1805
                                    died September 25, 1861

98. Catharine Paris Storrow
    b. March 12, 1842
    d. February 24, 1917

99. Susan Van Wart Storrow
    b. July 26, 1844
    d. December 25, 1865

100. Julia Grinnell Storrow   b. June or July, 1847
                                       d. July 12, 1920

36. *IRVING PARIS* (1816–1879)   *married* November 1, 1848

       to Nancy Gracie Ulshoeffer,   *born* October 17, 1823
                                      died February 18, 1884

101. Mary Ulshoeffer Paris   b. August 17, 1849
                                      d. July 21, 1931

102. Catharine Irving Paris   b. September 26, 1853
                                      d. May 19, 1937

103. Irving Paris   b. January 17, 1855
                                      d. April 8, 1938

104. Margaret Paris   b. September 27, 1857
                                      d. October 19, 1952

105. Francis Ulshoeffer Paris   b. July 4, 1864
                                      d. September 11, 1954

37. *PIERRE PARIS IRVING* (1806–1878)   *married* November 1, 1826

       to Anna Henrietta Duer,   *born* July 21, 1807
                                     died August 21, 1874

106. Pierre Leslie Irving   b. July 25, 1828
                                     d. April 12, 1891

107. Anna Duer Irving   b. August 28, 1830
                                     d. August 16, 1884

108. John Duer Irving   b. January 29, 1832
                                     d. April 19, 1836

109. Elizabeth Irving   b. April 15, 1834
                                     d. March 25, 1908

110. Harriet Robinson Irving   b. September 17, 1835
                                     d. December 23, 1906

111. Grace Irving   b. May 8, 1838
                                     d. August 25, 1839

112. Ellen J. Irving   b. August 21, 1840
                                     d. April 4, 1895

113. Alexander Duer Irving   b. December 28, 1842
                                         d. June 12, 1910

114. Francis Sutherland Irving   b. March 20, 1845
                                         d. April 24, 1846

115. Roland Duer Irving   b. April 27, 1847
                                         d. May 30, 1888

 38. *EDGAR IRVING* (1808–1873) *married* July 29, 1834

          to Amanda Tenant, *born* February 7, 1814
                             died June 6, 1885

116. Washington Irving   b. April 19, 1835
                                         d. January 9, 1910

117. Tenant Irving   b. August 1, 1843
                                         d. May 17, 1857 (1858?)

118. Mary Tenant Irving   b. July 19, 1849
                                         d. February 2, 1932

 39. *THEODORE IRVING* (1809–1880) *married* (1) August 28, 1838

          to Jane Westerlow Sutherland,   *born*
                                          died March 18, 1853

                                  married (2) June 24, 1857

          to Louisa Ketching,   *born*
                                died

                                  married (3)

          to Maria L.   *born*
                               died

          by (1) Jane Westerlow Sutherland

119. Fanny Irving   b.   1839
                                         d.

120. Elizabeth Kip Irving   b.   1842
                                         d.   1876

121. Mary Sutherland Irving   b.
                                         d.

122. Cornelia Irving   b.
                                        d. July 1, 1922

123. Sutherland Irving   b.
                                        d.

      by (2) Louisa Ketching

124. Grace Irving   b.
                                        d.

40. *WILLIAM IRVING* (1811–1854) *married* June 27, 1844

         to Sarah Mann,   *born* March 24, 1824
                          died November 20, 1913

125. Katrina Van Tassel Irving   b. April 20, 1845
                                       d. June 15, 1915

126. William Irving   b. December 8, 1847
                                       d. August   , 1893

127. Francis Wallace Irving   b. June 8, 1852
                                       d. December 25, 1888

41. *SANDERS IRVING* (1813–1884) *married* September 15, 1840

         to Julia A. Granger,   *born* June 2, 1822
                               died November 18, 1897

48. *WASHINGTON EBENEZER IRVING* (1822–1894) *married* 1866

         to Guadaloupe Gomez,   *born*
                               died

49. *CHARLOTTE VAN WART IRVING* (1824–1911)
                                        married June 8, 1847

         to William Russell Grinnell,   *born* March 10, 1819
                                       died October 11, 1888

128. Edwin Morgan Grinnell   b. March 18, 1849
                                       d. July 1, 1935

129. Lawrence Leslie Grinnell   b. September 18, 1851
    d. August 20, 1881

130. William Irving Grinnell   b. May 3, 1855
    d.

50. *GABRIEL FURMAN IRVING* (1807–1845) *married* April 9, 1831

    to Eliza Eckford,   *born*   1813
                      died July 22, 1866

131. Henrietta Eckford Irving   b. February 1, 1832
    d. April 12, 1921

132. Elizabeth Eckford Irving   b.
    d. April 23, 1883

52. *SARAH SANDERS IRVING* (1811–1836) *married* April 9, 1832

    to Edwin Clark,   *born* February 18, 1802
                      died January 23, 1878

133. Sarah Irving Clark   b. February 1, 1833
    d.

134. William Irving Clark   b. September 10, 1834
    d. June 5, 1925

53. *JOHN TREAT IRVING, JR.* (1812–1906) *married* June 5, 1838

    to Helen Schermerhorn,   *born* July 22, 1820
                            died December 18, 1893

135. John Treat Irving III   b. December 25, 1841
    d. June 24, 1936

136. Cortlandt Irving   b. October 8, 1843
    d. August 8, 1913

137. Helen Cordelia Irving   b. March 17, 1846
    d. September 30, 1929

138. Henry Irving   b. December 25, 1847
    d. June 28, 1906

139. Frances Rogers Irving   b. July 31, 1849
    d. December 18, 1912

140. Frederick Irving   b. July 28, 1852
                                       d. August 10, 1852

141. Edward Irving   b. December 1, 1853
                                       d. April 21, 1880

142. Eugene Irving   b. January 2, 1856
                                       d. January 4, 1856

143. Walter Irving   b. February 11, 1857
                                       d. December 30, 1915

144. Marian Harwood Irving   b. February 15, 1860
                                       d. May 22, 1877

54. *WASHINGTON IRVING* (1814–1894) *married*

    to Amelia Ardell,   *born*
                     died April 29, 1910

145. Child Irving   b.
                                      d.

146. Child Irving   b.
                                      d.

57. *ABBEY IRVING* (1822–1906) *married* September 23, 1845

    to Henry Van Wart,   *born*   1806
                     died July 4, 1878

    (*SEE* Number 59, Henry Van Wart, for children)

58. *GEORGE IRVING* (1824–1908) *married* (1) December 9, 1845

    to Robertine Blackwell,   *born*
                      died March 3, 1858

                      married (2) December 30, 1872

    to Louisa Maria Putnam,   *born*
                      died December 12, 1913

    by (1) Robertine Blackwell

147. George Irving   b.   1849
                                      d.   1850 (1880?)

148. Alice Irving   b.   1850
                                            d. September 27, 1855

149. Emily Irving   b. January   1853
                                            d. October 15, 1853

150. Laura Irving   b. October   1857
                                            d. March 6, 1858

59. *HENRY VAN WART* (1806–1878) *married* (1) August 18, 1830

        to Susan Clark Storrow,   *born*   1807
                                  died September 1843

                            married (2) September 23, 1845

        to Abbey Irving,   *born* September 23, 1822
                           died   1906

        by (2) Abbey Irving

151. Sarah Irving Van Wart   b.   1847
                                          d.   March 18, 1919

152. Helen Irving Van Wart   b.
                                          d.

153. Marion Irving Van Wart   b.   1854
                                          d.   September 22, 1874

154. Henry Irving Van Wart   b.   1855
                                          d.   1867

155. Edwin Clark Van Wart   b.
                                          d.

156. Washington Irving Van Wart   b.   1860
                                          d.   1930

60. *IRVING VAN WART* (1808–1896) *married* (1) July 1832

        to Susan Anne Irving,   *born* May 26, 1811
                                died March 19, 1836

                                married (2) March 26, 1839

        to Sarah Craig Ames,   *born*   1821
                               died April 20, 1873

by (1) Susan Anne Irving

157. Child Van Wart   b.
                                        d. infancy

by (2) Sarah Craig Ames

158. [Henry] Irving Van Wart   b. January 20, 1841
                                        d. June 4, 1876

159. Avery Ames Van Wart   b. January 20, 1841
                                        d.   1926

61. *WILLIAM VAN WART* (1814–1868) *married* (1)

to Rosalinda Bond, *born*
                    died

married (2)

to Emma Mason, *born*
                died December 31, 1888

by (1) Rosalinda Bond

160. Washington Irving Van Wart   b. January 23, 1836
                                        d. August 16, 1844

161. Wilfred Van Wart   b.   1837
                                        d.   1906

162. Harry Van Wart   b.   1840
                                        d. June 30, 1874

163. Oscar Irving Van Wart   b.
                                        d.

164. Alyce Claude Van Wart   b.   1842
                                        d. June 26, 1891

165. Frank Van Wart   b.   1844
                                        d. July 19, 1876

166. Katherine Van Wart   b.   1845
                                        d. January 8, 1928

167. Albert Van Wart   b.
                                        d.

by (2) Emma Mason

168. Margaret Irving Van Wart   b.
                                        d.

 62. *MATILDA VAN WART* (   ) *married* June, 1840

        to Charles Aylett Kell,   *born*
                                  died May 12, 1861

169. Rosalind Kell   b.   1843
                                        d. January 13, 1924

170. Robert Henry Van Wart Kell   b.
                                        d. May 6, 1876

171. Sarah Matilda Kell   b. June 2, 1847
                                        d.   1919

172. Charles Van Wart Kell   b.
                                        d. August 20, 1930

173. Harry Kell   b.
                                        d.

174. Lucy Irving Kell   b.   1850?
                                        d.

175. Washington Van Wart Kell   b.   1851
                                        d. December 26, 1927

INDEX

Note: This index includes items from the four volumes arranged in a single alphabetical sequence, except for those under "Washington Irving," where they are arranged chronologically for each volume at the point of first reference.

776, 1018; letters to, III, 262, 266, 274, 291, 296, 297, 333, 344, 368, 381, 386, 418 (2), 423, 426, 476, 489, 492, 499, 509, 516, 518

Alonso, José, III, 508

Alpujarras Mountains, II, 279, 287, 288, 289, 291, 292, 294, 298; IV, 676

Alta Cañada, Marchioness of (mother of Narváez), III, 888–89

Altdorf, I, 186, 189, 204

Althorp, Lord, II, 633n

Alsace, I, 186, 189

Alva, Countess of, III, 883

Alvarez, General, III, 538n

Ambois, Chateau of, II, 81n

Amelia Augusta (wife of Prince Johann of Saxony), I, 729n

Amelia of Saxony (wife of Ferdinand VII), III, 888, 891n

America, The (yacht), III, 514n

American Academy of Language and Belles Lettres, I, 587, 589n; II, 24

American Art Union, II, 867n

American Bible Society, IV, 728

American Exchange Bank (New York), IV, 702n

American Express Company, IV, 534n

American Fur Company, II, 724n

American Geographical and Statistical Society, IV, 586n, 615n, 704n

American Hotel (New York City), III, 172n

American Lyceum in Paris, the, III, 21n

American Monthly Magazine, II, 816; IV, 497n

American Museum, the, III, 122

American Philosophical Society, II, 551

American Quarterly Review, II, 362, 366, 368n, 606, 615

Ames, Barrett, II, 944n; III, 12, 13n, 63, 68, 78, 79n, 222n; IV, 211, 214n, 236, 238n, 492, 699n, 702n

Ames, Hector, III, 13n, 220, 222n, 225, 229, 233, 242, 244, 247–48, 250, 254, 258, 268, 276, 322, 339, 341, 355, 358, 360, 362, 364, 370, 371, 394, 399, 405, 488, 497, 498, 513, 530, 531, 535, 549, 550, 555, 728n, 922; IV, 236, 238n

Ames, Sarah (*see also* Mrs. Irving Van Wart), II, 943, 944n

Amistad (U. S. ship), III, 420–21, 422, 423n, 424, 457n, 685

"Amphibious Warriors of Marblehead," IV, 621

Amsterdam, I, 180, 193

Anacreon, IV, 550n

Analectic Magazine (*see also Select Reviews*), I, 437, 439n; II, 600n; III, 15n, 73n

Anamoosing River, II, 712

Ancient, True and Admirable History of Patient Grissel..., *The*, I, 471, 472

Ancona, I, 119, 122, 176, 179, 189

Andalusia, Spain, II, 318, 352, 367, 377, 388, 393, 404, 418, 422, 451, 499, 521, 529; III, 354, 355, 358; IV, 42, 45

Andersen, Hans Christian: *Danish Story Book*, IV, 588; *The Nightingale, and Other Stories*, IV, 588n; *Dream of Little Tuk*, IV, 588n

Anderson, C.: letter to, II, 747

Anderson, Charles, II, 748n

Anderson, Henry J., II, 866, 867n

André, Major John, II, 463, 467; III, 128n, 143; IV, 456, 620n, 629, 630n

Andrew, John A., IV, 145n

Andrews, John, I, xlii, 669, 670, 671n; II, 661n, 688n, 691, 694

Andrews, Louisa (*see also* Mrs. Sam Early), IV, 355, 356n, 358, 360, 362, 365, 366, 381, 397, 411, 412, 424, 431, 432, 441, 442, 443, 452, 453n, 463, 502, 526, 532, 533n, 547

Andrews, William E., II, 660

Andujar, II, 281, 285n, 286, 300, 422, 427

Angelina (Italian peasant girl), I, 131

Angeline (housemaid at Sunnyside), IV, 278, 350, 369, 372–73, 404, 425

Angera, I, 183, 187n

Angleterre, Hotel d' (Paris), I, 194n

Augoulême, Duke of (Louis Antoine), III, 317n

Angoulême, France, III, 247, 249n, 252

Anguera, Pablo, III, 300, 302n, 791, 807, 938, 951; letters to, III, 419, 484

Anguera, Mrs. Pablo, III, 791, 792, 807

Anguera children, III, 807

Angulo (Spanish minister in 1843), III, 492n

PLAYS AND BALLETS ATTENDED BY WI:
Pierre Gardel, *Psyche*, I, 79, 87n; Jean
François de La Harpe, *Philoctete*, I,
30n, 37n; Charles Macklin, *The Man
of the World*, I, 212, 214n; Thomas
Otway, *Venice Preserved*, I, 211, 212,
213; Nicholas Rowe, *The Fair Peni-
tent*, I, 213, 214n; William Shakespeare, *Othello*, I, 211, 212; Richard
Brinsley Sheridan, *Pizarro*, I, 211,
213n; Voltaire, *Oedipe*, I, 30, 37n;
Edward Young, *The Revenge*, I, 211

AUTHORS, BOOKS, PLAYS, AND
   POEMS MENTIONED:
Joseph Addison, III, 106; Aesop, III,
937; *The Arabian Nights*, I, 327,
332n; II, 12, 13; III, 937; Bible: Dan-
iel, I, 280; III, 804; Deuteronomy, IV,
113n, 413, 414n; Exodus, I, 436;
Genesis, I, 316, 731, 733n; II, 881,
883n; III, 929; IV, 255; Job, II, 280;
Jonah, II, 281; 1 Kings, III, 363; IV,
152, 365; 2 Kings, IV, 403, 405n;
Luke, II, 203; IV, 353; 2 Samuel, I,
327; Andrew Barnaby, *Travels
Through the Middle Settlements in
North America*, III, 205; John R.
Broadhead, *The History of New York*,
III, 247n; Patrick Brydone, *Tour
Through Sicily and Italy*, I, 150;
John Bunyan's dream, I, 329; *The
Pilgrim's Progress*, III, 79, 953, 956n;
Robert Burns, "The Twa Dogs," I,
230; Miguel de Cervantes, *Don Quix-
ote*, I, 365, 440; II, 350, 458, 462;
III, 105; IV, 125, 261, 313; Adel-
bert von Chamisso, *Peter Schlemihl*,
II, 280–81, 285n; Geoffrey Chaucer,
I, 356; "The Pardoner's Tale," I,
224, 227n; Giuseppe Buonfiglio Con-
stanzo, *Historia Siciliana*, I, 151;
James Fenimore Cooper, *The Path-
finder*, III, 51; William Cowper, "The
Diverting History of John Gilpin,"
III, 105, 107n; George Crabbe, *The
Parish Register*, II, 68; *Tales of the
Hall*, II, 68; Dante, II, 288; Charles
Dickens, III, 100, 103n; *Dombey and
Son*, IV, 233; *Nicholas Nickleby*, III,

106; *The Old Curiosity Shop*, III, 105,
106, 218; *The Pickwick Papers*, III,
105; Charles Dibden, *The Great Devil*,
I, 135; John Dryden, I, 227; Alexandre
Dumas, IV, 233; Pierce Egan, *Life
in London*, II, 425, 427n; Henry
Fielding, *Tom Thumb, A Tragedy*, I,
107, 218; Thomas Fuller, *The History
of the Worthies of England*, I, 30n;
Giles Gingerbread, IV, 169; Oliver
Goldsmith, *The Citizen of the World*,
I, 38, 53; "The Traveller," I, 53; *The
Vicar of Wakefield*, I, 255, 256; Greek
mythology, IV, 236, 315–16; Padre
Joseph Gumilla, *Historia Natural . . .* ,
III, 153, 156n; Nathaniel Hawthorne,
The Scarlet Letter, IV, 237, 238n;
John Heywood, *A Woman Killed With
Kindness*, IV, 361, 362; Homer, *The
Odyssey*, I, 150, 154; Washington Irv-
ing, *Knickerbocker's History*, IV, 242;
"Rip Van Winkle," II, 709; Theodore
Irving, *The Conquest of Florida*, III,
92; G. P. R. James, III, 100; *Richard
Coeur de Leon*, III, 108; Alain Renée
LeSage, *Gil Blas*, I, 435; III, 359,
378; IV, 235, 313, 314n; William Lith-
gow, *The Totall Discourse*, I, 47, 51n;
James B. Longacre and James Her-
ring, *National Portrait Gallery*, III,
174; John Lyly, *Euphues*, III, 460;
The Maid and the Magpie, III, 168,
171n; John Marshall, *The Life of
George Washington*, III, 174; Cor-
nelius Mathews, *The Career of Puffer
Hopkins*, III, 174; "Wakondah," III,
174, 176n; Donald G. Mitchell, *Reveries of a Bachelor*, IV, 252; John
Milton, *Paradise Lost*, I, 216; verse,
I, 516; George Washington Montgomery, . . . *Journey to Guatemala*, III, 82;
Thomas Moore, "The Last Rose of
Summer," III, 364, 365n; Ovid, *Meta-
morphoses*, I, 152; James K. Paulding,
A Life of Washington, III, 174; Lucas
Fernández de Piedrahita, *Historia
General . . .* , III, 153; François Rabelais, *Gargantua and Pantagruel*, I,
311; II, 592; III, 154; IV, 365; Samuel Richardson, *Sir Charles Grandi-*